FREQUENTLY USED SYMBOLS AND ABBREVIATIONS (CONTINUED)

N	• Number of Days Payment Can Be Delayed by Giving up the Cash Discount	
	• Number of Shares of Common Stock Obtainable with One Warrant	
N_d	Net Proceeds from the Sale of Debt (Bond)	
N_n	Net Proceeds from the Sale of New Common Stock	
N_p	Net Proceeds from the Sale of the Preferred Stock	
NAFTA	North American Free Trade Agreement	
NCAI	Net Current Asset Investment	
NFAI	Net Fixed Asset Investment	
NOPAT	Net operating profits after taxes	
NPV	Net Present Value	
O	Order Cost Per Order	
OC	Operating Cycle	
OCF	Operating Cash Flow	
P	Price (value) of asset	
P_0	Value of Common Stock	
$PBDT_t$	Profits Before Depreciation and Taxes in year t	
PD	Preferred Stock Dividend	
P/E	Price/Earnings Ratio	
PMT	Amount of Payment	
Pr	Probability	
PV	Present Value	
PVA_n	Present Value of an n-Year Annuity	
$PVIF_{i,n}$	Present Value Interest Factor for a Single Amount Discounted at i Percent for n Periods	
$PVIFA_{i,n}$	Present Value Interest Factor for an Annuity When Interest is Discounted Annually at i Percent for n Periods	
Q	• Order Quantity in Units	
	• Sales Quantity in Units	
r	• Actual, Expected ($\bar{r}$), or Required Rate of Return	
	• Cost of Capital	
r^*	Real Rate of Interest	
r_a	Weighted Average Cost of Capital	
r_d	Required Return on Bond	

r_i	After-Tax Cost of Debt
r_j	Required Return on Asset j
r_m	Market Return; Return on the Market Portfolio of Assets
r_p	• Cost of Preferred Stock
	• Portfolio Return
r_r	Cost of Retained Earnings
r_s	Required Return on Common Stock
R_F	Risk-Free Rate of Interest
RADR	Risk-Adjusted Discount Rate
RE	Ratio of Exchange
ROA	Return on Total Assets
ROE	Return on Common Equity
S	Usage in Units per Period
SML	Security Market Line
t	Time
T	Firm's Marginal Tax Rate
TVW	Theoretical Value of a Warrant
V	• Value of an Asset or Firm
	• Venture Capital
V_C	Value of Entire Company
V_D	Value of All Debt
V_P	Value of Preferred Stock
V_S	Value of Common Stock
VC	Variable Operating Cost per Unit
w_j	• Proportion of the Portfolio's Total Dollar Value Represented by Asset j
	• Proportion of a Specific Source of Financing j in the Firm's Capital Structure
WACC	Weighted Average Cost of Capital
WMCC	Weighted Marginal Cost of Captial
WTO	World Trade Organization
YTM	Yield to Maturity
ZBA	Zero Balance Account
σ	Standard Deviation
Σ	Summation Sign

PRINCIPLES OF
MANAGERIAL
FINANCE

The Prentice Hall Series in Finance

Alexander/Sharpe/Bailey
Fundamentals of Investments

Andersen
Global Derivatives: A Strategic Risk Management Perspective

Bear/Moldonado-Bear
Free Markets, Finance, Ethics, and Law

Berk/DeMarzo
*Corporate Finance**
*Corporate Finance: The Core**

Bierman/Smidt
The Capital Budgeting Decision: Economic Analysis of Investment Projects

Bodie/Merton/Cleeton
Financial Economics

Click/Coval
The Theory and Practice of International Financial Management

Copeland/Weston/Shastri
Financial Theory and Corporate Policy

Cornwall/Vang/Hartman
Entrepreneurial Financial Management

Cox/Rubinstein
Options Markets

Dorfman
Introduction to Risk Management and Insurance

Dietrich
Financial Services and Financial Institutions: Value Creation in Theory and Practice

Dufey/Giddy
Cases in International Finance

Eakins
Finance in .learn

Eiteman/Stonehill/Moffett
Multinational Business Finance

Emery/Finnerty/Stowe
Corporate Financial Management

Fabozzi
Bond Markets: Analysis and Strategies

Fabozzi/Modigliani
Capital Markets: Institutions and Instruments

Fabozzi/Modigliani/Jones/Ferri
Foundations of Financial Markets and Institutions

Finkler
Financial Management for Public, Health, and Not-for-Profit Organizations

Francis/Ibbotson
Investments: A Global Perspective

Fraser/Ormiston
Understanding Financial Statements

Geisst
Investment Banking in the Financial System

Gitman
*Principles of Managerial Finance**
*Principles of Managerial Finance—Brief Edition**

Gitman/Joehnk
*Fundamentals of Investing**

Gitman/Madura
Introduction to Finance

Guthrie/Lemon
Mathematics of Interest Rates and Finance

Haugen
The Inefficient Stock Market: What Pays Off and Why
Modern Investment Theory
The New Finance: Overreaction, Complexity, and Uniqueness

Holden
Excel Modeling and Estimation in the Fundamentals of Corporate Finance
Excel Modeling and Estimation in the Fundamentals of Investments
Excel Modeling and Estimation in Investments
Excel Modeling and Estimation in Corporate Finance

Hughes/MacDonald
International Banking: Text and Cases

Hull
Fundamentals of Futures and Options Markets
Options, Futures, and Other Derivatives
Risk Management and Financial Institutions

Keown
Personal Finance: Turning Money into Wealth

Keown/Martin/Petty/Scott
Financial Management: Principles and Applications
Foundations of Finance: The Logic and Practice of Financial Management

Kim/Nofsinger
Corporate Governance

Levy/Post
Investments

May/May/Andrew
Effective Writing: A Handbook for Finance People

Madura
Personal Finance

Marthinsen
Risk Takers: Uses and Abuses of Financial Derivations

McDonald
Derivatives Markets
Fundamentals of Derivatives Markets

Megginson
Corporate Finance Theory

Melvin
International Money and Finance

Mishkin/Eakins
Financial Markets and Institutions

Moffett
Cases in International Finance

Moffett/Stonehill/Eiteman
Fundamentals of Multinational Finance

Nofsinger
Psychology of Investing

Ogden/Jen/O'Connor
Advanced Corporate Finance

Pennacchi
Theory of Asset Pricing

Rejda
Principles of Risk Management and Insurance

Schoenebeck
Interpreting and Analyzing Financial Statements

Scott/ Martin/ Petty/Keown/Thatcher
Cases in Finance

Seiler
Performing Financial Studies: A Methodological Cookbook

Shapiro
Capital Budgeting and Investment Analysis

Sharpe/Alexander/Bailey
Investments

Solnik/McLeavey
Global Investments

Stretcher/Michael
Cases in Financial Management

Titman/Martin
Valuation: The Art and Science of Corporate Investment Decisions

Trivoli
Personal Portfolio Management: Fundamentals and Strategies

Van Horne
Financial Management and Policy
Financial Market Rates and Flows

Van Horne/Wachowicz
Fundamentals of Financial Management

Vaughn
Financial Planning for the Entrepreneur

Weston/Mitchel/Mulherin
Takeovers, Restructuring, and Corporate Governance

Winger/Frasca
Personal Finance

PRINCIPLES OF
MANAGERIAL
FINANCE

TWELFTH EDITION

LAWRENCE J. GITMAN
SAN DIEGO STATE UNIVERSITY

Boston San Francisco New York
London Toronto Sydney Tokyo Singapore Madrid
Mexico City Munich Paris Cape Town Hong Kong Montreal

Editor-in-Chief: Denise Clinton
Executive Editor: Donna Battista
Development Editor: Ann Torbert
Project Manager/EA: Mina Kim
Editorial Assistant: Kerri McQueen
Managing Editor: Nancy Fenton
Senior Marketing Manager: Jodi Bassett
Senior Media Producer: Bethany Tidd
Supplements Editor: Heather McNally
Permissions Editor: Dana Weightman
Project Coordination, Text Design, Art Studio,
    and Electronic Page Makeup: Thompson Steele, Inc.
Design Manager: Joyce Wells
Cover Photograph: George Hammerstein/Solus Photography/Veer
Senior Manufacturing Buyer: Carol Melville

Credits: 55: Data from Dun & Bradstreet, "Industry Norms and Ratios, 2006"; 341: From *The Wall Street Journal*, 3/28/07; 339: © 2007 MetroPCS Wireless, Inc. All Rights Reserved; 563: © 2006 by Risk Management Association; 816: From David K. Eiteman, Arthur I. Stonehill, and Michael H. Moffett, *Multinational Business Finance*, 11th ed. (Boston, MA: Pearson Education, 2007), pp. 336–342. © 2007 Pearson Education. Reprinted with permission; 816: From David K. Eiteman, Arthur I. Stonehill, and Michael H. Moffett, *Multinational Business Finance*, 11th ed. (Boston, MA: Pearson Education, 2007), p. 341. © 2007 Pearson Education. Reprinted with permission; 823: From Rita M. Rodriguez and E. Eugene Carter, *International Financial Management*, 3rd ed. (Englewood Cliffs, NJ: Prentice-Hall), p. 512. Reprinted with permission.

Library of Congress Cataloging-in-Publication Data

Gitman, Lawrence J.
  Principles of managerial finance / Lawrence J. Gitman. — 12th ed.
      p. cm. — (The Prentice Hall series in finance)
  Includes bibliographical references and index.
  ISBN 978-0-321-52413-3 (alk. paper)
  1. Corporations—Finance. 2. Business enterprises—Finance.   I. Title.
  HG4011.G5 2009
  658.15—dc22

                                        2007046000

For information on obtaining permission for the use of material from this work, please submit a written request to Pearson Education, Inc., Rights and Contracts Department, 75 Arlington Street, Suite 300, Boston, MA 02116 or fax your request to (617) 848-7047. Printed in the United States.

ISBN 978-0-321-52413-3
ISBN 0-321-52413-6

2 3 4 5 6 7 8 9 10—CRK—11 10 09

*Dedicated to the memory
of my mother, Dr. Edith Gitman,
who instilled in me the importance
of education and hard work*

The Key to Your Success in Three Easy Steps!

① Take a Sample Test
to assess your knowledge.

② Review your personalized
Study Plan to see where you
need more work.

③ Use the Study Plan exercises
and step-by-step tutorials to get
practice–and individualized
feedback–where you need it.

If your Instructor assigns homework and tests using MyFinanceLab...

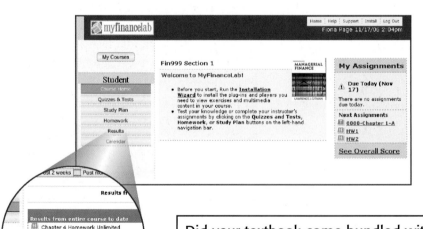

The MyFinanceLab Course
Home page makes it easy
for you to stay on track
by displaying class
announcements and
automatic reminders
of upcoming assignments.

Did your textbook come bundled with a MyFinanceLab access
code? If so, simply go to www.myfinancelab.com to register
using the code. If not, you can purchase access to MyFinanceLab
online at www.myfinancelab.com.

Gitman's
Proven Teaching/Learning System

Users of *Principles of Managerial Finance* have praised the effectiveness of the book's teaching/learning system, which they hail as one of its hallmarks. The system, driven by a set of carefully developed learning goals, has been retained and polished in this twelfth edition. The "walkthrough" on the pages that follow illustrates and describes the key elements of the teaching/learning system. We encourage both students and instructors to acquaint themselves at the start of the semester with the many useful features the book offers.

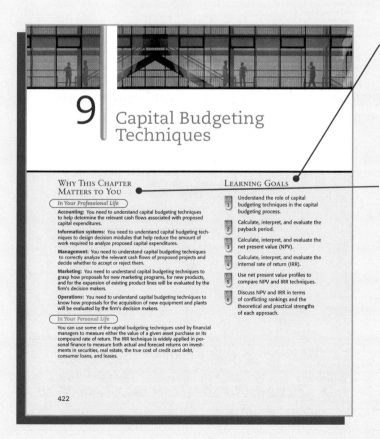

Six **Learning Goals** at the start of the chapter anchor the most important concepts and techniques in the chapter. The learning goal icons reappear next to related text sections and again in the chapter-end summary, end-of-chapter homework materials, and supplements such as the Study Guide, Test Bank, and MyFinanceLab.

Every chapter opens with a feature, titled **Why This Chapter Matters to You**, that helps motivate student interest.

Its first part, **In Your Professional Life**, discusses the intersection of the finance topics covered in the chapter with the concerns of other major business disciplines. It encourages students majoring in accounting, information systems, management, marketing, and operations to appreciate the numerous cross-disciplinary interactions that routinely occur in business.

The second part, **In Your Personal Life**, identifies topics in the chapter that will have particular application to personal finance.

Each chapter opens with a short **vignette** that describes a recent real-company event related to the chapter topic. These stories raise interest in the chapter by demonstrating its relevance in the business world.

A *critical thinking question* at the end of each vignette encourages readers to give additional thought to the story and its application to the chapter topic.

Apple, Inc.

The iPhone Is Revealed

On January 17, 2007, **Apple, Inc.** introduced the iPhone, which combines a mobile phone, an iPod, and an Internet communications device. The phone's Internet connection allows users to surf the Web over Wi-Fi, access email, watch TV shows and videos, and use Google maps. A new interface allows the user to communicate by touching the screen with a finger. Another feature is that the screen will shift from portrait to landscape view when you simply rotate the device in your hand.

Apple managed to keep the details of the project secret both from the public and its partner **Cingular Wireless**, now the wireless unit of **AT&T.** Several small teams within Cingular worked on the project, but each handled its own specific task without knowing what the other teams were up to. Cingular technical personnel tested the device to make sure that it would work on the carrier's network, but were not allowed to handle or see the actual phone. When it hit the market in mid-2007, the iPhone was sold exclusively by Apple and by AT&T.

Before developing the new phone, Apple had to ensure the project's economic viability. This involved estimating the cost of developing, manufacturing, and marketing the iPhone, as well as estimating the potential revenue. Apple expects to sell 10 million iPhones through 2008, with price tags of $499 and $599 for two different models. This estimate gives the firm's finance personnel some dollar figures, but there is no guarantee that the sales estimates are accurate.

Estimating development and marketing expenses is more difficult. There is virtually no way to precisely predict the worker-hours that will be sunk into the project. The iPhone development team mushroomed into hundreds of people and involved all levels of the company. One method of estimating development costs is to make reasonable estimates based on similar past projects. In Apple's case, it most likely used information from its development of the iPod several years earlier.

However it develops its estimates of a project's future revenues and expenses, once it has those estimates, a company can use one of several techniques to determine whether a project is acceptable. These capital budgeting techniques are the subject of Chapter 9.

> In addition to the revenues directly provided by the sale of the new iPhone, what other benefits to Apple might be relevant to evaluating the iPhone project?

Learning goal icons, which appear next to first-level text headings, tie chapter content to the learning goals.

 15.2 | **Unsecured Sources of Short-Term Loans**

Businesses obtain unsecured short-term loans from two major sources, banks and sales of commercial paper. Unlike the spontaneous sources of unsecured short-term financing, bank loans and commercial paper are negotiated and result from actions taken by the firm's financial manager. Bank loans are more popular, because they are available to firms of all sizes; commercial paper tends to be available only to large firms. In addition, firms can use international loans to finance international transactions.

For help in study and review, **key terms** are printed in boldface type, and their definitions appear in the margin where they are first introduced. These terms are also boldfaced in the book's index and appear in the end-of-book glossary.

annual percentage yield (APY)
The *effective annual rate* of interest that must be disclosed to consumers by banks on their savings products as a result of "truth-in-savings laws."

"Truth-in-savings laws," on the other hand, require banks to quote the **annual percentage yield (APY)** on their savings products. The APY is the *effective annual rate* a savings product pays. For example, a savings account that pays 0.5 percent per month would have an APY of 6.17 percent $[(1.005)^{12} - 1]$.

Quoting loan interest rates at their lower nominal annual rate (the APR) and savings interest rates at the higher effective annual rate (the APY) offers two advantages: It tends to standardize disclosure to consumers, and it enables financial institutions to quote the most attractive interest rates: low loan rates and high savings rates.

Examples are an important component of the book's learning system. Clearly set off from the text, they provide an immediate and concrete demonstration of how to apply financial concepts, tools, and techniques.

Examples in certain chapters demonstrate time value of money techniques. These examples show the use of time lines, financial calculators, spreadsheets (with cell formulas), and factor tables.

New! **Personal Finance Examples** demonstrate how students can apply managerial finance concepts, tools, and techniques to their personal financial decisions.

Key equations are printed in blue throughout the text to help readers identify the most important mathematical relationships. The variables used in these equations are, for convenience, printed on the *front endpapers* of the book.

Marginal hints add useful ideas, comments, and pieces of information to enrich the text discussion and boost student learning.

Review Questions appear at the end of each major text section. These questions challenge readers to stop and test their understanding of key concepts, tools, techniques, and practices before moving on to the next section.

In Practice boxes offer insights into important topics in managerial finance through the experiences of real companies, both large and small. There are three categories of In Practice boxes:

Focus on Ethics boxes in every chapter help readers understand and appreciate important ethical issues and problems related to managerial finance.

Focus on Practice boxes take a corporate focus that relates a business event or situation to a specific financial concept or technique.

Global Focus boxes look specifically at the managerial finance experiences of international companies.

All three types of In Practice boxes end with a *critical thinking question* to help readers broaden the lesson from the content of the box. Guideline answers to these questions can be found at the book's Companion Website.

Focus on Ethics How Fair Is "Check Into Cash"?

IN PRACTICE

In 1993, the first **Check Into Cash** location opened in Cleveland, Tennessee. Today there are 1,250 Check Into Cash centers among an estimated 22,000 payday-advance lenders in the United States. There is no doubt about the demand for such organizations, but the debate continues on the "fairness" of payday-advance loans.

aggravating to opponents of the payday-advance industry. A typical fee is $15 for every $100 borrowed. Payday advance companies that belong to the Community Financial Services Association of America (CFSA), an organization dedicated to promoting responsible regulation of the industry, limit their member companies to a maximum of

protection is $26.90, a credit card late fee on $100 is $37, and the late/disconnect fee on a $100 utility bill is $46.16. Bankrate.com reports that non-sufficient funds (NSF) fees average $26.90 per occurrence.

A payday advance could be useful, for example, if you have six outstanding checks at the time you are notified that the

---

Focus on Practice New Century Brings Trouble for Subprime Mortgages

IN PRACTICE

As the housing market began to boom at the end of the twentieth century and into the early twenty-first, the market share of subprime mortgages climbed from near 0 percent in 1997 to about 20 percent of mortgage originations in 2006. Several factors combined to fuel the rapid growth of lending to borrowers with tarnished credit, including

ARMs were reset to higher rates. In 2007, that figure will triple. The rise in interest rates will push monthly payments beyond what some homeowners can afford. For those who cannot make their payments, foreclosure and repossession by the lender may be the only way out.

Foreclosure on a nonproductive mortgage is particularly

its reorganization. One of the largest providers of subprime mortgages, New Century made $51.6 billion in subprime loans in 2006.

Problems with subprime loans were not limited to New Century. The Mortgage Bankers Association estimates that subprime loans were used to finance about 17 percent of home pur-

---

Global Focus An International Flavor to Risk Reduction

IN PRACTICE

What do Friskies cat food, Kit Kat candy bars, aspirin, and DirecTV have in common? They are all products of non-U.S. corporations. Friskies cat food and Kit Kat bars are products of **Nestle S.A.** (Switzerland); **Bayer AG,** a German company, produces Bayer aspirin; and DirecTV is part of **News Corporation,** an Australian company. Just as we use many products of foreign companies, many U.S. corporations seek to have their products used internationally. The result is a more globally integrated economy.

One way to reduce investment risk is through diversification. Allocating a portion of one's portfolio to non-U.S. equities has historically provided better risk-adjusted returns than a portfolio consisting solely of U.S. assets. The benefit of diversification between two assets increases if the two asset classes are not well correlated, and the ben-

efit is largest when two asset classes are perfectly negatively correlated.

From the mid-1990s through 2000 when the tech-bubble burst, international and U.S. markets moved more closely together than usual. The increased correlation between the U.S. assets and international asset classes caused some to question the wisdom of international diversification. Although investors were willing to accept less risk in the form of less volatility of their portfolios, it was not easy to recognize the benefits of diversification when the diversified portfolio lagged a pure U.S. equity portfolio.

In the early part of this decade, however, the U.S. markets suffered some significant declines, leading investors to once again search for alternatives outside the U.S. markets. Adding some international diversification would have paid off handsomely

in 2006, if an investor had been lucky enough to be in one of the top ten international stock markets. Returns ranged from 37 percent in Sweden and 47 percent in Spain, to 60 percent in Indonesia, and a whopping 159 percent in Cyprus.

In terms of pure risk-adjusted reward, diversification does work. It is safe to say that international markets and U.S. markets will never be entirely correlated. The easiest way to diversify a portfolio is to include an international or global mutual fund in an investment portfolio. The professional portfolio managers have more experience in navigating the international markets than does the average investor.

■ *International mutual funds do not include any domestic assets whereas global mutual funds include both foreign and domestic assets. How might this difference affect their correlation with U.S. equity mutual funds?*

The end-of-chapter **Summary** consists of two sections. The first section, **Focus on Value,** explains how the chapter's content relates to the firm's goal of maximizing owner wealth. The feature helps reinforce understanding of the link between the financial manager's actions and share value.

The second part of the Summary, the **Review of Learning Goals,** restates each learning goal and summarizes the key material that was presented to support mastery of that goal.

Summary

Focus on Value

Financial managers review and analyze the firm's financial statements periodically, both to uncover developing problems and to assess the firm's progress toward achieving its goals. These actions are aimed at **preserving and creating value for the firm's owners.** Financial ratios enable financial managers to monitor the pulse of the firm and its progress toward its strategic goals. Although financial statements and financial ratios rely on accrual concepts, they can provide useful insights into important aspects of risk and return (cash flow) that affect share price.

Review of Learning Goals

LG 1 **Understand tax depreciation procedures and the effect of depreciation on the firm's cash flows.** Depreciation is an important factor affecting a firm's cash flow. An asset's depreciable value and depreciable life are determined by using the MACRS standards in the federal tax code. MACRS groups assets (excluding real estate) into six property classes based on length of recovery period.

Self-Test Problems (Solutions in Appendix B)

 ST2–1 Ratio formulas and interpretations Without referring to the text, indicate for each of the following ratios the formula for calculating it and the kinds of problems, if any, the firm is likely to have if that ratio is too high relative to the industry average. What if the ratio is too low relative to the industry average? Create a table similar to the one that follows and fill in the empty blocks.

Ratio	Too high	Too low
Current ratio =		
Inventory turnover =	⨯	⨯
Times interest earned =	⨯	⨯
Gross profit margin =	⨯	⨯
Return on total assets =	⨯	⨯

Warm-Up Exercises

A blue box (■) indicates exercises available in 🔷myfinancelab.

 E4–1 Assume a firm makes a $2,500 deposit into its money market account. If this account is currently paying 0.7%, (yes, that's right, less than 1%!), what will the account balance be after 1 year?

 E4–2 If Bob and Judy combine their savings of $1,260 and $975, respectively, and deposit this amount into an account that pays 2% annual interest, compounded monthly, what will the account balance be after 4 years?

Problems

A blue box (■) indicates problems available in 🔷myfinancelab.

 P4–1 Using a time line The financial manager at Starbuck Industries is considering an investment that requires an initial outlay of $25,000 and is expected to result in cash inflows of $3,000 at the end of year 1, $6,000 at the end of years 2 and 3, $10,000 at the end of year 4, $8,000 at the end of year 5, and $7,000 at the end of year 6.
  a. Draw and label a time line depicting the cash flows associated with Starbuck Industries' proposed investment.
  b. Use arrows to demonstrate, on the time line in part **a**, how compounding to find future value can be used to measure all cash flows at the end of year 6.
  c. Use arrows to demonstrate, on the time line in part **b**, how discounting to find present value can be used to measure all cash flows at time zero.
  d. Which of the approaches—*future value* or *present value*—do financial managers rely on most often for decision making? Why?

PERSONAL FINANCE PROBLEM

 P4–53 Choosing the best annuity Raina Herzig wishes to choose the best of four immediate-retirement annuities available to her. In each case, in exchange for paying a single premium today, she will receive equal, annual, end-of-year cash benefits for a specified number of years. She considers the annuities to be equally risky and is not concerned about their differing lives. Her decision will be based solely on the rate of return she will earn on each annuity. The key terms of the four annuities are shown in the following table.

Annuity	Premium paid today	Annual benefit	Life (years)
A	$30,000	$3,100	20
B	25,000	3,900	10
C	40,000	4,200	15
D	35,000	4,000	12

  a. Calculate to the nearest 1% the rate of return on each of the four annuities Raina is considering.
  b. Given Raina's stated decision criterion, which annuity would you recommend?

 P3–20 Integrative—Pro forma statements Provincial Imports, Inc., has assembled past (2009) financial statements (income statement below and balance sheet on page 150) and financial projections for use in preparing financial plans for the coming year (2010).

 P4–60 ETHICS PROBLEM A manager at a "check into cash" business (see *Focus on Ethics* box on page 192) defends his business practice as simply "charging what the market will bear." "After all," says the manager, "we don't force people to come in the door." How would you respond to this ethical defense of the payday-advance business?

Self-Test Problems, keyed to the learning goals, give readers an opportunity to strengthen their understanding of topics by doing a sample problem. For reinforcement, solutions to the Self-Test Problems appear in Appendix B at the back of the book.

Warm-Up Exercises follow the Self-Test Problems. These short, numerical exercises give students practice in applying tools and techniques presented in the chapter.

A blue box indicates the **Exercises and Problems available in MyFinanceLab.**

Comprehensive **Problems**, keyed to the learning goals, are longer and more complex than the Warm-Up Exercises. In this section, instructors will find multiple problems that address the important concepts, tools, and techniques in the chapter.

New! **Personal Finance Problems** specifically relate to personal finance situations and examples in each chapter. These new problems will help students see how they can apply the tools and techniques of managerial finance in managing their own finances.

A short descriptor identifies the essential concept or technique of the problem. Problems labeled as **Integrative** tie together related topics. Guideline answers to selected end-of-chapter problems appear in Appendix C.

The last item in the chapter Problems is an **Ethics Problem**. The ethics problem gives students another opportunity to think about and apply ethics principles to managerial financial situations.

Chapter Cases call for application of concepts and techniques to a more complex, realistic situation than in the regular Problems. These cases help strengthen practical application of financial tools and techniques.

Chapter 2 Case

Assessing Martin Manufacturing's Current Financial Position

Terri Spiro, an experienced budget analyst at Martin Manufacturing Company, has been charged with assessing the firm's financial performance during 2009 and its financial position at year-end 2009. To complete this assignment, she gathered the firm's 2009 financial statements (below and on page 99). In addition, Terri obtained the firm's ratio values for 2007 and 2008, along with the 2009 industry average ratios (also applicable to 2007 and 2008). These are presented in the table on page 100.

Every chapter includes a **Spreadsheet Exercise**. This exercise gives students an opportunity to use Excel® software to create one or more spreadsheets with which to analyze a financial problem. The spreadsheet to be created often is modeled on a table in the chapter or a spreadsheet template that can be viewed at the book's Companion Website.

Spreadsheet Exercise

The income statement and balance sheet are the basic reports that a firm constructs for use by management and for distribution to stockholders, regulatory bodies, and the general public. They are the primary sources of historical financial information about the firm. Dayton Products, Inc., is a moderate-sized manufacturer. The company's management has asked you to perform a detailed financial statement analysis of the firm.

The income statement data for the years ending December 31, 2009 and 2008, respectively, is presented in the table at the top of page 101. (*Note:* Purchases of inventory during 2009 amounted to $109,865.)

Every chapter offers a **Group Exercise** in which students work together in the context of an ongoing company. Each group will create a company and follow it through the various managerial finance topics and business activities presented in the textbook.

Group Exercise

"Cash is king." Donald Trump made this statement at the end of the 1980s, referring to the climate for real estate investment. Most people would agree that in life, cash is, indeed, king. The management and proper valuation of cash flows is the most important factor in the survival of a business. Almost all businesses receive cash payments in spurts but must make cash payments at regular intervals. Many businesses have failed not for a lack of sales success, but rather for a lack of *timely* cash. Therefore, the timing of cash flows and implied time value are of utmost importance.

Now available online at the book's Companion Website, a **Web Exercise** for every chapter links the chapter topic to a related site on the Internet and asks students to use information found there to answer questions. These exercises capture student interest while showing sources of finance information online.

Web Exercise

Go to the book's companion website at www.prenhall.com/gitman to find the Web Exercise for this chapter.

> Remember to check the book's website at www.prenhall.com/gitman to find additional resources, including Web Exercises and a Web Case.

An **Integrative Case** at the end of each part of the book challenges students to use what they have learned over the course of several chapters.

Integrative Case 1

Track Software, Inc.

Seven years ago, after 15 years in public accounting, Stanley Booker, CPA, resigned his position as Manager of Cost Systems for Davis, Cohen, and O'Brien Public Accountants and started Track Software, Inc. In the 2 years preceding his departure from Davis, Cohen, and O'Brien, Stanley had spent nights and weekends developing a sophisticated cost-accounting software program that became Track's initial product offering. As the firm grew, Stanley planned to develop and expand the software product offerings—all of which would be related to streamlining the accounting processes of medium- to large-sized manufacturers.

Although Track experienced losses during its first 2 years of operation—2003 and 2004—its profit has increased steadily from 2005 to the present (2009). The firm's profit history, including dividend payments and contributions to retained earnings, is summarized in Table 1.

Brief Contents

Contents

Part One | Introduction to Managerial Finance   1

Chapter 1
**The Role
and Environment
of Managerial
Finance**
page 2

Starbucks—A Taste for Growth
page 3

Chapter 2
Financial Statements and Analysis
page 42

Netflix, Inc.—The Red Tide Is Coming
page 43

Part Two | Important Financial Concepts   159

Chapter 7
Stock Valuation
page 328

Crocs, Inc.—Initial Public Offering page 329

Part Three | Long-Term Investment Decisions   377

Part Four | Long-Term Financial Decisions   501

Chapter 11
The Cost
of Capital
page 502

United Airlines—Taking Off Again
page 503

Chapter 12
Leverage
and Capital
Structure
page 544

CVS/Caremark Corporation—
Optimizing Its Capital Structure
page 545

Part Five | Short-Term Financial Decisions 635

Part Six | Special Topics in Managerial Finance 719

Preface

The desire to write *Principles of Managerial Finance* came out of my experience teaching the introductory managerial finance course early in my career. I was not very far removed from my own undergraduate studies and therefore could appreciate the difficulties some of my students were having with the textbook we used. They wanted a book that spoke to them in plain English. They wanted a book that tied concepts to reality. And they wanted not just description, but demonstration of concepts, tools, and techniques. Recognizing that, I decided to write an introductory finance text that would effectively resolve these concerns.

Courses and students have changed since that initial book, but the goals of the text have not changed. The conversational tone and wide use of examples set off in the text still characterize *Principles of Managerial Finance*. Building on those strengths, over 11 editions, numerous translations, and well over half a million U.S. users, I've continued to listen carefully to feedback from both instructors and students, from adopters, nonadopters, and practitioners.

The Twelfth Edition

Like the first edition, the twelfth edition still uses plain English, ties concepts to reality, and demonstrates concepts, tools, and techniques. It incorporates a proven learning system, which integrates pedagogy with concepts and practical applications. It concentrates on the knowledge that is needed to make keen financial decisions in an increasingly competitive business environment. The strong pedagogy and generous use of examples—including, new in this edition, personal finance examples—make the text an easily accessible resource for long-distance learning, online courses, and self-study programs. The book also has been well received in the core MBA course and in management development and executive training programs.

Organization

The text's organization, described in detail in the following pages, conceptually links the firm's actions and its value as determined in the securities market. Each major decision area is presented in terms of both risk and return factors and their potential impact on owners' wealth. A *Focus on Value* element at the end of each chapter helps reinforce the student's understanding of the link between the financial manager's actions and the firm's share value.

In organizing each chapter, I have adhered to a managerial decision-making perspective, relating decisions to the firm's overall goal of wealth maximization. Once a particular concept has been developed, its application is illustrated by an example—a hallmark feature of this book. These examples demonstrate, and solidify in the student's thought, financial decision-making considerations and their consequences. As described next, this edition expands this feature with the addition of examples related to personal finance.

International Considerations

We live in a world where international considerations cannot be divorced from the study of business in general and finance in particular. As in prior editions, discussions of international dimensions of chapter topics are integrated throughout the book. A marginal icon of a globe highlights these discussions, and international material is integrated into learning goals and end-of-chapter materials. In addition, for those who want to spend more time addressing the topic, a separate chapter on international managerial finance concludes the book.

Personal Finance Linkages

The twelfth edition has responded to reviewers' requests for more personal finance linkages and to calls for educators to help improve the financial literacy of young people. At the start of each chapter, the feature titled *Why This Chapter Matters to You* helps motivate student interest by discussing how the topic of the chapter relates to the concerns of other major business disciplines and to personal finance. Within the chapter, *Personal Finance Examples* explicitly link the concepts, tools, and techniques of each chapter to personal finance applications. In the homework material, the book has more than 75 personal finance problems. The purpose of these personal finance materials is to demonstrate to students the usefulness of managerial finance knowledge in both business and personal financial dealings.

Ethical Issues

The need for ethics in business remains as important as ever. Students need to understand the ethical issues that financial managers face as they attempt to maximize shareholder value and to solve business problems. Thus, every chapter includes an In Practice box that focuses on ethical issues. Half of these ethics boxes are new in this edition, and those that are not new have been updated.

Homework Opportunities

Of course, practice is essential for students' learning of managerial finance concepts, tools, and techniques. To meet that need, the book offers a rich and varied menu of homework assignments: short, numerical Warm-Up Exercises; a comprehensive set of Problems, including more than one problem for each important concept or technique and now also including personal finance problems; an Ethics Problem for each chapter; a Chapter Case; a Spreadsheet Exercise; a Group Exercise; an online Web Exercise; and at the end of each part of the book, an Integrative Case. In addition, most of the end-of-chapter problems are available in algorithmic form in myfinancelab. These materials (see pages xi through xii for detailed descriptions) offer students solid learning opportunities, and they offer instructors opportunities to expand and enrich the classroom environment.

From classroom to boardroom, the twelfth edition of *Principles of Managerial Finance* can help users get to where they want to be. I believe that it is the best edition yet—more relevant, more accurate, and more effective than ever. I hope you agree that *Principles of Managerial Finance*, Twelfth Edition, is the most effective introductory managerial finance text for your students.

Lawrence J. Gitman
La Jolla, California

Revised Content

As we made plans to publish the twelfth edition, we carefully assessed market feedback about content changes that would better meet the needs of instructors teaching the course.

The chapter sequence remains the same as in the prior edition. Although the text content is sequential, instructors can assign almost any chapter as a self-contained unit, enabling instructors to customize the text to various teaching strategies and course lengths. For those instructors who want to assign an entire chapter on financial institutions and markets as a foundational chapter in the managerial finance course, a complete chapter on institutions and markets is available online at the book's Companion Website, www.prenhall.com/gitman.

A number of new topics have been added at appropriate places, and existing discussions have been updated and/or smoothed. In Chapter 5 and beyond, we have changed the notation for returns from "k" to "r" to improve familiarity with notational use in other courses. In addition, as the detailed list shows, the chapter-opening vignettes and boxes have been heavily revised: For example, three-quarters of the chapter-opening vignettes are new, focusing on companies such as Google, Apple, and Crocs that have student appeal, and half of the Focus on Ethics boxes are new.

The following list details the chapter-by-chapter content changes in the twelfth edition.

Chapter 1 The Role and Environment of Managerial Finance
- Revised opening vignette (Starbucks' growth)
- Revised discussion of the role of business ethics
- Significantly revised and restructured presentation of "Securities Exchanges," now labeled "Broker Markets and Dealer Markets"
- Added one new Personal Finance Example
- Revised Focus on Ethics box (ethics at Hewlett-Packard)
- Revised Focus on Practice box (Warren Buffett's leadership at Berkshire Hathaway)
- Added one new Personal Finance Problem

Chapter 2 Financial Statements and Analysis
- New opening vignette (financial results, Netflix)
- Added three new Personal Finance Examples
- Revised Focus on Ethics box (courses on business ethics)
- New Focus on Practice box evaluating the effects of the Sarbanes-Oxley Act
- Added three new Personal Finance Problems

Chapter 3 Cash Flow and Financial Planning
- New opening vignette (use of cash by Google)
- Added two new Personal Finance Examples
- New Focus on Practice box (free cash flow at eBay)

- New Focus on Ethics box (Bob Nardelli at Home Depot)
- Added one new Personal Finance Problem
- Revised Spreadsheet Exercise and Group Exercise
- Added to Companion Website detailed discussion of developing the statement of cash flows

Chapter 4 Time Value of Money

- Revised opening vignette (research and development costs at Eli Lilly)
- Shifted computational emphasis to calculator and spreadsheet use, de-emphasizing the use of financial tables
- Re-labeled 22 existing Examples as Personal Finance Examples
- Revised Focus on Practice box (subprime mortgages)
- Revised Focus on Ethics box (payday loans)
- Re-labeled 32 existing Problems as Personal Finance Problems

Chapter 5 Risk and Return

- New opening vignette (venture capital)
- Changed notation for returns from "k" to "r" beginning in this chapter and throughout entire text to improve familiarity
- Switched emphasis from "Sensitivity Analysis" to "Scenario Analysis"
- Updated discussion of country risk in Venezuela
- Added one new Personal Finance Example
- Revised Global Focus box (international diversification)
- Revised Focus on Ethics box (moral risk)
- Added one new Personal Finance Problem

Chapter 6 Interest Rates and Bond Valuation

- Revised opening vignette (U.S. Treasury, public debt)
- Revised discussion of bond yields and bond prices
- Added footnotes on bond duration and bond yield to call
- Re-labeled five existing Examples as Personal Finance Examples
- Revised Focus on Practice box (adjustable-rate I-bonds)
- Revised Focus on Ethics box (new legislation affecting the credit-rating agencies)
- Re-labeled four Problems as Personal Finance Problems

Chapter 7 Stock Valuation

- New opening vignette (Crocs Inc. IPO)
- Revised discussion of American depositary receipts and American depositary shares
- Revised discussion of interpreting stock quotations consistent with latest format of stock quotations
- Re-labeled three existing Examples as Personal Finance Examples
- New Focus on Practice box (behavioral finance)
- New Focus on Ethics box (additional costs of pre-earnings guidance)
- Re-labeled six Problems as Personal Finance Problems

Chapter 8   Capital Budgeting Cash Flows
- New opening vignette (project costs at ExxonMobil)
- Added two new Personal Finance Examples
- New Global Focus box (foreign direct investment in China)
- Revised Focus on Ethics box (accuracy of cash flow estimates)
- Added three new Personal Finance Problems

Chapter 9   Capital Budgeting Techniques
- New opening vignette (Apple's iPhone)
- Clarified tabular explanation of project preferences with extreme discount rates and dissimilar cash inflow patterns
- Added two new Personal Finance Examples
- Revised Focus on Practice box (limits of payback analysis)
- Revised Focus on Ethics box (nonfinancial considerations in project selection)
- Added three new Personal Finance Problems

Chapter 10   Risk and Refinements in Capital Budgeting
- New opening vignette (State Farm Insurance claims associated with Hurricane Katrina)
- Changed terminology and clarified discussion relating to scenario analysis
- Added two new Personal Finance Examples
- Revised Focus on Practice box (Monte Carlo simulation)
- New Focus on Ethics box (environmental compliance costs)
- Added three new Personal Finance Problems
- Added new Ethics Problem

Chapter 11   The Cost of Capital
- New opening vignette (capital needs of United Airlines)
- Moved text coverage of EVA® to Companion Website
- Added two new Personal Finance Examples
- Revised Focus on Practice box (EVA®)
- New Focus on Ethics box (legal liabilities for asbestos claims)
- Added three new Personal Finance Problems
- Added new Ethics Problem

Chapter 12   Leverage and Capital Structure
- New opening vignette (capital structure of CVS/Caremark)
- Added three new Personal Finance Examples
- Revised Focus on Practice box (Adobe's operating leverage)
- Revised Focus on Ethics box (private-equity buyouts)
- Added three new Personal Finance Problems

Chapter 13   Dividend Policy
- Revised opening vignette (Microsoft's dividend payouts)
- Added two new Personal Finance Examples

- Revised Focus on Practice box (update on capital gains and dividend tax treatment)
- New Focus on Ethics box (motives for stock buybacks)
- Added one new Personal Finance Problem and re-labeled three existing Problems as Personal Finance Problems
- Added new Ethics Problem

Chapter 14   Working Capital and Current Assets Management

- Revised opening vignette (AT&T's outsourcing of phone cards)
- Added new footnote demonstrating the derivation of the simple EOQ model
- Added two new Personal Finance Examples
- Revised Focus on Practice box (RFID)
- New Focus on Ethics box (stretching accounts payable)
- Added two new Personal Finance Problems
- Added new Ethics Problem

Chapter 15   Current Liabilities Management

- New opening vignette (reducing accounts payable expenses at Memorial Sloan-Kettering)
- Added two new Personal Finance Examples
- Revised Focus on Practice box (commercial paper)
- New Focus on Ethics box (loan fraud)
- Added two new Personal Finance Problems

Chapter 16   Hybrid and Derivative Securities

- New opening vignette (Boeing's 787 Dreamliner)
- Added one new Personal Finance Problem
- New Focus on Practice box (leveraged leases at Disney)
- New Focus on Ethics box (options backdating)
- Re-labeled three existing Problems as Personal Finance Problems

Chapter 17   Mergers, LBOs, Divestitures, and Business Failure

- New opening vignette (Sprint Nextel merger)
- Added two new Personal Finance Examples
- New Global Focus box (News Corp acquisitions)
- Revised Focus on Ethics box (ethics of bankruptcy)
- Added two new Personal Finance Problems

Chapter 18   International Managerial Finance

- Significantly revised and updated the entire chapter to describe today's global financial marketplace and include the latest data
- Revised opening vignette (GE's business in China)
- Added new section on subsidiary characterization and functional currency in financial statements, including a short section on the temporal method
- Added two new Personal Finance Examples
- Revised Global Focus box (overseas assignments)
- New Focus on Ethics box (antibribery laws)
- Added two new Personal Finance Problems

Supplements to the Twelfth Edition

The *PMF* Teaching/Learning System includes a variety of useful supplements for teachers and for students.

Teaching Tools for Instructors

The key teaching tools available to instructors are the *Instructor's Manual*, testing materials, and *PowerPoint Lecture Presentations*.

Instructor's Manual *Revised by Thomas Krueger, University of Wisconsin at La Crosse.* This comprehensive resource pulls together the teaching tools so that instructors can use the textbook easily and effectively in the classroom. Each chapter provides an overview of key topics and detailed answers and solutions to all review questions, Warm-Up Exercises, end-of-chapter problems, and chapter cases, plus suggested answers to all critical thinking questions in chapter openers and boxes, Ethics Problems, Group Exercises, and Web Exercises. At the end of the manual are practice quizzes and solutions. The complete Instructor's Manual, including Spreadsheet Exercises, is available online at the Instructor's Resource Center (http://www.prenhall.com/irc) and on the Instructor's Resource CD-ROM.

Test Bank *Created by Daniel J. Borgia, Florida Gulf Coast University.* Thoroughly revised to accommodate changes in the text, the Test Bank consists of a mix of true/false, multiple-choice, and essay questions. Each test question includes identifiers for type of question, skill tested by learning goal, and key topic tested plus, where appropriate, the formula(s) or equation(s) used in deriving the answer. The Test Bank is available in both printed and electronic formats, including Windows or Macintosh *TestGen* files and Microsoft Word files. The Test Bank and TestGen are available online at the Instructor's Resource Center (http://www.prenhall.com/irc) and on the Instructor's Resource CD-ROM.

Instructors can download the *TestGen* version of the Test Bank into *QuizMaster,* an online testing program for Windows and Macintosh that enables users to conduct timed or untimed exams at computer workstations. After completing tests, students can see their scores and view or print a diagnostic report of those topics or objectives requiring more attention. When installed on a local area network, *QuizMaster* allows instructors to save the scores on disk, print study diagnoses, and monitor progress of students individually or by class section and by all sections of the course.

PowerPoint Lecture Presentation *Created by Daniel J. Borgia, Florida Gulf Coast University.* This presentation combines lecture notes with all of the art from the textbook. The PowerPoint Lecture Presentation is available online at the

Instructor's Resource Center (http://www.prenhall.com/irc) and on the Instructor's Resource CD-ROM.

Instructor's Resource CD-ROM   Electronic files of the *Instructor's Manual, Test Bank, Computerized Test Bank,* and *PowerPoint Lecture Presentations* are available on one convenient CD-ROM, compatible with both Windows and Macintosh computers. The electronic versions allow instructors to customize the support materials to their individual classroom needs. All the resources on the Instructor's Resource CD-ROM are also available online at the Instructor's Resource Center (http://www.prenhall.com/irc).

Learning Tools for Students

Beyond the book itself, students have access to several resources for success in this course: MyFinanceLab, *Study Guide,* and the *Principles of Managerial Finance,* Twelfth Edition Companion Website.

MyFinanceLab   Packaged with new copies of this text, the Student Access Kit for MyFinanceLab opens the door to a powerful Web-based diagnostic testing and tutorial system designed specifically for the Gitman, *Principles of Managerial Finance* textbooks. With MyFinanceLab, instructors can create, edit, and assign online homework, and test and track all student work in the online gradebook. MyFinanceLab allows students to take practice tests correlated to the textbook and receive a customized study plan based on the test results. Most end-of-chapter problems are available in MyFinanceLab, and because the problems have algorithmically generated values, no student will have the same homework as another, and there is an unlimited opportunity for practice and testing. Students get the help they need, when they need it, from the robust tutorial options, including "View an Example" and "Help Me Solve This," which breaks the problem into its steps and links to the relevant textbook page.

Students can use MyFinanceLab with no instructor intervention. However, to take advantage of the full capabilities of MyFinanceLab, including assigning homework and tracking student progress in the automated gradebook, instructors will want to set up their class. To view a demo of MyFinanceLab or to request instructor access go to www.myfinancelab.com.

Study Guide   *Updated by Thomas Kreuger, University of Wisconsin at La Crosse.* The *Study Guide* is an integral component of the *PMF* Learning System. It offers many tools for studying finance. Each chapter contains the following features: chapter summary enumerated by learning goals; topical chapter outline, also broken down by learning goals for quick review; sample problem solutions; study tips and a full sample exam with the answers at the end of the chapter. A financial dictionary of key terms is located at the end of the Study Guide, along with an appendix with tips on using financial calculators.

Principles of Managerial Finance, Twelfth Edition Website   The website to accompany this textbook, located at www.prenhall.com/gitman, contains many additional resources. For each chapter on the website you will find

- Web Cases, which ask students to use the Web to find information and solve finance problems

- Web Exercises
- Self-Assessment Quizzes
- Case Studies in Finance, *updated by Michael Seiler of Hawaii Pacific University*

In addition to the chapter resources, you will find

- A Web chapter, "Financial Markets and Institutions," from the text *Introduction to Finance* by Lawrence J. Gitman and Jeff Madura
- An online glossary, both as review flashcards and as a quick-reference document
- Spreadsheet examples from the textbook
- A Financial Calculator Guide
- Our Online Career Center

In addition to the Companion Website, the course content is available in Blackboard and WebCT. Please contact your local sales representative for more information on obtaining course content in these various formats.

Acknowledgments

To My Colleagues, Friends, and Family

No textbook can consistently meet market needs without continual feedback from colleagues, students, practitioners, and members of the publishing team. Once again, I invite colleagues to relate their classroom experiences using this book and its package to me in care of the Acquisitions Editor in Finance, Prentice Hall Publishing Company, 75 Arlington Street, Suite 300, Boston, Massachusetts 02116. Your constructive criticism will help me to continue to improve the textbook and its Teaching/Learning System still further.

Prentice Hall and former publisher HarperCollins sought the advice of a great many excellent reviewers, all of whom strongly influenced various aspects of this book. The following individuals provided extremely thoughtful and useful comments for the preparation of the twelfth edition:

Omar Benkato, *Ball State University*
Boyd D. Collier, *Tarleton State University*
Michael Giuliano, *University of Maryland–Asia Division*
John E. Harper, *Texas A&M at Commerce*
Raj K. Kohli, *Indiana University–South Bend*
Inayat Mangla, *Western Michigan University*
Bala Maniam, *Sam Houston State University*
Brian Maris, *Northern Arizona University*
Lee McClain, *Western Washington University*
Mukunthan Santhanakrishnan, *Idaho State University*
Tom Schmidt, *Simpson College*
Sandeep Singh, *SUNY Brockport*
Gordon M. Stringer, *University of Colorado–Colorado Springs*
Faye (Hefei) Wang, *University of Illinois–Chicago*

My special thanks go to the following individuals who analyzed the manuscript in previous editions:

Saul W. Adelman	Scott Besley	Omer Carey
M. Fall Ainina	Douglas S. Bible	Patrick A. Casabona
Gary A. Anderson	Charles W. Blackwell	Robert Chatfield
Ronald F. Anderson	Russell L. Block	K. C. Chen
James M. Andre	Calvin M. Boardman	Roger G. Clarke
Gene L. Andrusco	Paul Bolster	Terrence M. Clauretie
Antonio Apap	Robert J. Bondi	Mark Cockalingam
David A. Arbeit	Jeffrey A. Born	Thomas Cook
Allen Arkins	Jerry D. Boswell	Maurice P. Corrigan
Saul H. Auslander	Denis O. Boudreaux	Mike Cudd
Peter W. Bacon	Kenneth J. Boudreaux	Donnie L. Daniel
Richard E. Ball	Wayne Boyet	Prabir Datta
Thomas Bankston	Ron Braswell	Joel J. Dauten
Alexander Barges	Christopher Brown	Lee E. Davis
Charles Barngrover	William Brunsen	Irv DeGraw
Michael Becker	Samuel B. Bulmash	Richard F. DeMong
Omar Benkato	Francis E. Canda	Peter A. DeVito

James P. D'Mello
R. Gordon Dippel
Carleton Donchess
Thomas W. Donohue
Shannon Donovan
Vincent R. Driscoll
Betty A. Driver
Lorna Dotts
David R. Durst
Dwayne O. Eberhardt
Ronald L. Ehresman
Ted Ellis
F. Barney English
Greg Filbeck
Ross A. Flaherty
Rich Fortin
Timothy J. Gallagher
George W. Gallinger
Sharon Garrison
Gerald D. Gay
Deborah Giarusso
R. H. Gilmer
Anthony J. Giovino
Philip W. Glasgo
Jeffrey W. Glazer
Joel Gold
Ron B. Goldfarb
Dennis W. Goodwin
David A. Gordon
J. Charles Granicz
C. Ramon Griffin
Reynolds Griffith
Arthur Guarino
Lewell F. Gunter
Melvin W. Harju
Phil Harrington
George F. Harris
George T. Harris
John D. Harris
Mary Hartman
R. Stevenson Hawkey
Roger G. Hehman
Harvey Heinowitz
Glenn Henderson
Russell H. Hereth
Kathleen T. Hevert
J. Lawrence Hexter
Douglas A. Hibbert
Roger P. Hill
Linda C. Hittle
James Hoban
Hugh A. Hobson
Keith Howe
Kenneth M. Huggins

Jerry G. Hunt
Mahmood Islam
James F. Jackson
Stanley Jacobs
Dale W. Janowsky
Jeannette R. Jesinger
Nalina Jeypalan
Timothy E. Johnson
Roger Juchau
Ashok K. Kapoor
Daniel J. Kaufman, Jr.
Joseph K. Kiely
Terrance E. Kingston
Thomas M. Krueger
Lawrence Kryzanowski
Harry R. Kuniansky
Richard E. La Near
William R. Lane
James Larsen
Rick LeCompte
B. E. Lee
Scott Lee
Michael A. Lenarcic
A. Joseph Lerro
Thomas J. Liesz
Alan Lines
Christopher K. Ma
James C. Ma
Dilip B. Madan
Judy Maese
James Mallet
Timothy A. Manuel
Brian Maris
Daniel S. Marrone
William H. Marsh
John F. Marshall
Linda J. Martin
Stanley A. Martin
Charles E. Maxwell
Timothy Hoyt McCaughey
Jay Meiselman
Vincent A. Mercurio
Joseph Messina
John B. Mitchell
Daniel F. Mohan
Charles Mohundro
Gene P. Morris
Edward A. Moses
Tarun K. Mukherjee
William T. Murphy
Randy Myers
Lance Nail
Donald A. Nast
Vivian F. Nazar

G. Newbould
Charles Ngassam
Gary Noreiko
Dennis T. Officer
Kathleen J. Oldfather
Kathleen F. Oppenheimer
Richard M. Osborne
Jerome S. Osteryoung
Prasad Padmanabahn
Roger R. Palmer
Don B. Panton
John Park
Ronda S. Paul
Bruce C. Payne
Gerald W. Perritt
Gladys E. Perry
Stanley Piascik
Gregory Pierce
Mary L. Piotrowski
D. Anthony Plath
Jerry B. Poe
Gerald A. Pogue
Suzanne Polley
Ronald S. Pretekin
Fran Quinn
Rich Ravichandran
David Rayone
Walter J. Reinhart
Jack H. Reubens
Benedicte Reyes
William B. Riley, Jr.
Ron Rizzuto
Gayle A. Russell
Patricia A. Ryan
Murray Sabrin
Kanwal S. Sachedeva
R. Daniel Sadlier
Hadi Salavitabar
Gary Sanger
William L. Sartoris
Michael Schinski
Carl J. Schwendiman
Carl Schweser
Jim Scott
John W. Settle
Richard A. Shick
A. M. Sibley
Surendra S. Singhvi
Stacy Sirmans
Barry D. Smith
Gerald Smolen
Ira Smolowitz
Jean Snavely
Joseph V. Stanford

John A. Stocker
Lester B. Strickler
Elizabeth Strock
Donald H. Stuhlman
Sankar Sundarrajan
Philip R. Swensen
S. Tabriztchi
John C. Talbott
Gary Tallman
Harry Tamule
Richard W. Taylor
Rolf K. Tedefalk
Richard Teweles
Kenneth J. Thygerson
Robert D. Tollen
Emery A. Trahan
Pieter A. Vandenberg
Nikhil P. Varaiya
Oscar Varela
Kenneth J. Venuto
James A. Verbrugge
Ronald P. Volpe
John M. Wachowicz, Jr.
William H. Weber III
Herbert Weinraub
Jonathan B. Welch
Grant J. Wells
Larry R. White
Peter Wichert
C. Don Wiggins
Howard A. Williams
Richard E. Williams
Glenn A. Wilt, Jr.
Bernard J. Winger
Tony R. Wingler
I. R. Woods
John C. Woods
Robert J. Wright
Richard H. Yanow
Seung J. Yoon
Charles W. Young
Philip J. Young
Joe W. Zeman
J. Kenton Zumwalt
John T. Zeitlow
Tom Zwirlein

My special thanks go to all members of my book team whose vision, creativity, and ongoing support helped me to engineer all elements of the Teaching/Learning System: to Michael J. Woodworth of Purdue University for the chapter-opening vignettes and the *In Practice:* Focus on Practice, Ethics, and Global Focus boxes; to Mehdi Salehizadeh of San Diego State University for help in revising the chapter on International Finance; to Steven Lifland of High Point University for the new personal finance problems, and for updating the in-chapter spreadsheet examples, Spreadsheet Exercises, Warm-Up Exercises, Group Exercises, and Web Exercises; to Daniel J. Borgia of Florida Gulf Coast University for revising the Test Banks and the PowerPoint Lecture Presentations; to Thomas Kreuger of the University of Wisconsin at La Crosse for updating the *Instructor's Manual* and *Study Guide;* to Michael Seiler of Hawaii Pacific University for updating the Case Studies in Finance on the book's website; and to Nikhil Varaiya of San Diego State University for assistance in obtaining data. I'm pleased by and proud of all their efforts.

A hearty round of applause also goes to the publishing team assembled by Prentice Hall—including Donna Battista, Mina Kim, Nancy Fenton, Bethany Tidd, Dana Weightman, Heather McNally, Jodi Bassett, and others who worked on the book—for the inspiration and the perspiration that define teamwork. Nancy Freihofer and all the people at Thompson Steele, Inc. deserve an equally resounding ovation. A standing ovation is due Ann Torbert, whose development expertise and hard work have contributed to the book's standard of excellence. Also, special thanks to the formidable Prentice Hall sales force in finance, whose ongoing efforts keep the business fun!

Finally, and most important, many thanks to my wife, Robin, and to our children, Zachary and Jessica, for patiently providing support, understanding, and good humor throughout the revision process. To them, I will be forever grateful.

Lawrence J. Gitman
La Jolla, California

To the Student

Because you have a good many options for getting your assigned reading materials, I appreciate your choosing this textbook as the best means for learning in your managerial finance course. You should not be disappointed. I was not far removed from my own undergraduate studies when I wrote the first edition of this book, and so I set out to write a book that would meet the needs of students. In every edition, I have been mindful of students and careful to maintain a student focus.

The learning system in this book has been used by many of your predecessors in the course and proven effective. It integrates various learning tools with the concepts, tools, techniques, and practical applications you will need to learn about managerial finance. I have worked hard to present in a clear and interesting way the information you will need. This book is loaded with features designed to motivate your study of finance and to help you learn the course material. Go to pages vii-xii ("Gitman's Proven Learning/Teaching System") for an overview and walkthrough of those features. Notice that the book includes Personal Finance Examples (and related end-of-chapter problems) that show how to apply managerial finance concepts and tools to your personal financial life.

About some of the specific features: First, pay attention to the Learning Goals, which will help you focus on what material you need to learn, where you can find it in the chapter, and whether you've mastered it by the end of the chapter.

Second, avoid the temptation to rush past the Review Questions at the end of each major text section. Pausing briefly to test your understanding of the section content will help you cement your understanding of it. Give yourself an honest assessment. If some details are fuzzy, go back (even briefly) and review anything that still seems unclear.

Third, look for (or make) opportunities to talk with classmates or friends about what you are reading and learning in the course. Talking about the concepts and techniques of finance demonstrates how much you've learned, uncovers things you haven't yet understood fully, and gives you valuable practice for class and (eventually) the business world. While you're talking, don't neglect to discuss the issues raised in the *Focus on Ethics* boxes, which look at some of the opportunities to do right (or not) that business people face.

Packaged with new copies of the book, the Student Access Kit for MyFinanceLab opens the door to a powerful Web-based diagnostic testing and tutorial system designed for this text. MyFinanceLab allows you to take practice exams correlated to the textbook and receive a customized study plan based on your results. The assignment Problems in MyFinanceLab, based on the even-numbered end-of-chapter Problems in the book, have algorithmically generated values. Thus, the numbers in your homework will differ from those of your classmates, and there is an unlimited opportunity for practice and testing. You can get the help you need, when you need it, from the robust tutorial options, including

"View an Example" and "Help Me Solve This," which breaks the problem into steps and links to the relevant textbook page.

Given today's rapidly changing technology, who knows what might be available next? Prentice Hall and I are striving to keep pace with your needs and interests, and would like to hear your ideas for improving the teaching and learning of finance. Please feel free to share your ideas with us by e-mailing finance@prenhall.com.

I wish you all the best in this course, and in your academic and professional careers.

Lawrence J. Gitman
La Jolla, California

Part One

Introduction to Managerial Finance

Chapters in This Part

1 **The Role and Environment of Managerial Finance**

2 **Financial Statements and Analysis**

3 **Cash Flow and Financial Planning**

INTEGRATIVE CASE 1: **Track Software, Inc.**

1

The Role and Environment of Managerial Finance

WHY THIS CHAPTER MATTERS TO YOU

In Your Professional Life

Accounting: You need to understand the relationships between the firm's accounting and finance functions; how the financial statements you prepare will be used; business ethics; agency costs and why the firm must bear them; and how to calculate the tax effects of proposed transactions.

Information systems: You need to understand the organization of the firm; why finance personnel require both historical and projected data; and what data are necessary for determining the firm's tax liability.

Management: You need to understand the legal forms of business organization; the tasks that will be performed by finance personnel; the goal of the firm; management compensation; ethics in the firm; the agency problem; and the role of financial institutions and markets.

Marketing: You need to understand how the activities you pursue will be affected by the finance function, such as the firm's cash and credit management policies; ethical behaviors; and the role of financial markets in raising capital.

Operations: You need to understand the organization of the firm and of the finance function in particular; why maximizing profit is not the main goal of the firm; the role of financial institutions and markets in financing; and ethics and the agency problem.

In Your Personal Life

Many of the principles of managerial finance apply to your personal life: to making purchase and sale transactions, borrowing money, and saving and investing to achieve financial goals. These actions require you to interact with financial institutions and markets. You also need to consider the impact of taxes on your financial plans. Learning the basics of managerial finance can help you manage your personal finances effectively.

LEARNING GOALS

LG 1 Define *finance*, its major areas and opportunities, and the legal forms of business organization.

LG 2 Describe the managerial finance function and its relationship to economics and accounting.

LG 3 Identify the primary activities of the financial manager.

LG 4 Explain the goal of the firm, corporate governance, the role of ethics, and the agency issue.

LG 5 Understand financial institutions and markets, and the role they play in managerial finance.

LG 6 Discuss business taxes and their importance in financial decisions.

Starbucks

A Taste for Growth

Sometimes it seems that there's a **Starbucks** on every corner—and now in supermarkets and hospitals too. The company that revolutionized the way we think about coffee now has more than 13,000 retail locations worldwide. Expansion in the international market is a key element in the company's long-term goal of reaching 40,000 (20,000 U.S. and 20,000 international) retail outlets. By early 2007, Starbucks had retail outlets in 39 countries and plans to open its first stores in Russia and China.

The chain's success is tied to somewhat unusual business strategies. Its mission statement emphasizes, first, creating a better work environment for employees. (Starbucks was one of the first companies to offer part-time employees health benefits.) Next in the mission statement are the goals of satisfying customers and promoting good corporate citizenship within its communities. Profits are among the last of the company's stated guiding principles.

Starbucks' bond with employees and customers has translated into sales and earnings as strong as its coffee. Sales growth for the 5-year period 2002 to 2006 averaged more than 24 percent compounded per year, and growth in earnings averaged more than 25 percent per year. A share of Starbucks' stock purchased at the start of 1997 increased in value by 25.7 percent per year over the next 10 years, easily beating the S&P 500 return of 6.7 percent per year.

Accomplishing its business objectives while building shareholder value requires that Starbucks practices sound financial management—raising funds to open new stores and build more roasting plants, deciding when and where to put them, managing cash collections, reducing purchasing costs, and dealing with the fluctuations in the value of foreign currency and other risks as it buys coffee beans and expands overseas.

> One potential drawback to a growth strategy is market saturation and slower same-store sales growth. How might Starbucks combat these potential problems?

Like Starbucks, every company must deal with many different issues to keep its financial condition solid. Chapter 1 introduces managerial finance and its key role in helping an organization meet its financial and business objectives.

1.1 | Finance and Business

The field of finance is broad and dynamic. It directly affects the life of every person and of every organization. There are many areas and career opportunities in the field of finance. Basic principles of finance, such as those you will learn in this textbook, can be universally applied in business organizations of different types. In addition, many of these principles are applicable to your personal financial life.

What Is Finance?

finance
The art and science of managing money.

Finance can be defined as the art and science of managing money. Virtually all individuals and organizations earn or raise money and spend or invest money. Finance is concerned with the process, institutions, markets, and instruments involved in the transfer of money among individuals, businesses, and governments. Most adults will benefit from an understanding of finance, which will enable them to make better personal financial decisions. Those who work in nonfinancial jobs will benefit by being able to interact effectively with the firm's financial personnel, processes, and procedures.

Major Areas and Opportunities in Finance

The major areas of finance can be summarized by reviewing the career opportunities in finance. These opportunities can, for convenience, be divided into two broad areas: financial services and managerial finance.

Financial Services

financial services
The area of finance concerned with the design and delivery of advice and financial products to individuals, business, and government.

Financial services is the area of finance concerned with the design and delivery of advice and financial products to individuals, business, and government. It involves a variety of interesting career opportunities within the areas of banking and related institutions, personal financial planning, investments, real estate, and insurance. Career opportunities available in each of these areas are described at this textbook's website.

Managerial Finance

managerial finance
Concerns the duties of the *financial manager* in the business firm.

financial manager
Actively manages the financial affairs of any type of business, whether financial or nonfinancial, private or public, large or small, profit-seeking or not-for-profit.

Managerial finance is concerned with the duties of the *financial manager* in the business firm. **Financial managers** actively manage the financial affairs of any type of businesses—financial and nonfinancial, private and public, large and small, profit-seeking and not-for-profit. They perform such varied financial tasks as planning, extending credit to customers, evaluating proposed large expenditures, and raising money to fund the firm's operations. In recent years, changing economic, competitive, and regulatory environments have increased the importance and complexity of the financial manager's duties. Today's financial manager is more actively involved in developing and implementing corporate strategies aimed at "growing the firm" and improving its competitive position. As a result, many top executives have come from the finance area.

Another ongoing trend has been the globalization of business activity. U.S. corporations have dramatically increased their sales, purchases, investments, and fund raising in other countries, and foreign corporations have likewise increased their corresponding activities in the United States. These changes have increased the need for financial managers who can manage cash flows in different currencies and protect against the risks that naturally arise from international transactions. Although these changes make the managerial finance function more complex, they can lead to a more rewarding and fulfilling career.

Legal Forms of Business Organization

The three most common legal forms of business organization are the *sole proprietorship*, the *partnership*, and the *corporation*. Other specialized forms of business organization also exist. Sole proprietorships are the most numerous. However, corporations are overwhelmingly dominant with respect to business receipts and net profits. Corporations are given primary emphasis in this textbook.

Sole Proprietorships

sole proprietorship
A business owned by one person and operated for his or her own profit.

A **sole proprietorship** is a business owned by one person who operates it for his or her own profit. About 75 percent of all business firms are sole proprietorships. The typical sole proprietorship is a small business, such as a bike shop, personal trainer, or plumber. The majority of sole proprietorships are found in the wholesale, retail, service, and construction industries.

unlimited liability
The condition of a sole proprietorship (or general partnership) allowing the owner's total wealth to be taken to satisfy creditors.

Typically, the proprietor, along with a few employees, operates the proprietorship. He or she normally raises capital from personal resources or by borrowing and is responsible for all business decisions. The sole proprietor has **unlimited liability;** his or her total wealth—not merely the amount originally invested—can be taken to satisfy creditors. The key strengths and weaknesses of sole proprietorships are summarized in Table 1.1 (see page 6).

Partnerships

partnership
A business owned by two or more people and operated for profit.

A **partnership** consists of two or more owners doing business together for profit. Partnerships account for about 10 percent of all businesses, and they are typically larger than sole proprietorships. Finance, insurance, and real estate firms are the most common types of partnership. Public accounting and stock brokerage partnerships often have large numbers of partners.

articles of partnership
The written contract used to formally establish a business partnership.

Most partnerships are established by a written contract known as **articles of partnership.** In a *general* (or *regular*) *partnership*, all partners have unlimited liability, and each partner is legally liable for *all* of the debts of the partnership. Strengths and weaknesses of partnerships are summarized in Table 1.1.

corporation
An artificial being created by law (often called a "legal entity").

Corporations

A **corporation** is an artificial being created by law. Often called a "legal entity," a corporation has the powers of an individual in that it can sue and be sued, make and be party to contracts, and acquire property in its own name. Although only about 15 percent of all businesses are incorporated, the corporation is the dominant form of business organization in terms of receipts and profits. It accounts for nearly 90 percent of business receipts and 80 percent of net profits. Although corporations are involved in all types of businesses, manufacturing corporations

Hint Many small corporations, as well as small proprietorships and partnerships, have no access to financial markets. In addition, whenever the owners take out a loan, they usually must personally cosign the loan.

TABLE 1.1	Strengths and Weaknesses of the Common Legal Forms of Business Organization		
	Sole proprietorship	Partnership	Corporation
Strengths	• Owner receives all profits (and sustains all losses) • Low organizational costs • Income included and taxed on proprietor's personal tax return • Independence • Secrecy • Ease of dissolution	• Can raise more funds than sole proprietorships • Borrowing power enhanced by more owners • More available brain power and managerial skill • Income included and taxed on partner's personal tax return	• Owners have *limited liability,* which guarantees that they cannot lose more than they invested • Can achieve large size via sale of ownership (stock) • Ownership (stock) is readily transferable • Long life of firm • Can hire professional managers • Has better access to financing • Can offer attractive retirement plans
Weaknesses	• Owner has *unlimited liability*— total wealth can be taken to satisfy debts • Limited fund-raising power tends to inhibit growth • Proprietor must be jack-of-all-trades • Difficult to give employees long-run career opportunities • Lacks continuity when proprietor dies	• Owners have *unlimited liability* and may have to cover debts of other partners • Partnership is dissolved when a partner dies • Difficult to liquidate or transfer partnership	• Taxes generally higher, because corporate income is taxed, and dividends paid to owners are also taxed at a maximum 15% rate • More expensive to organize than other business forms • Subject to greater government regulation • Lacks secrecy, because stockholders must receive financial reports

stockholders
The owners of a corporation, whose ownership, or *equity,* is evidenced by either common stock or preferred stock.

common stock
The purest and most basic form of corporate ownership.

dividends
Periodic distributions of earnings to the stockholders of a firm.

board of directors
Group elected by the firm's stockholders and typically responsible for developing strategic goals and plans, setting general policy, guiding corporate affairs, approving major expenditures, and hiring/firing, compensating, and monitoring key officers and executives.

account for the largest portion of corporate business receipts and net profits. The key strengths and weaknesses of large corporations are summarized in Table 1.1.

The owners of a corporation are its **stockholders,** whose ownership, or *equity,* is evidenced by either common stock or preferred stock.[1] These forms of ownership are discussed in detail in Chapter 7; at this point it is enough to say that **common stock** is the purest and most basic form of corporate ownership. Stockholders expect to earn a return by receiving **dividends**—periodic distributions of earnings—or by realizing gains through increases in share price.

As noted in the upper portion of Figure 1.1, control of the corporation is structured as a democracy. The stockholders (owners) vote periodically to elect members of the *board of directors* and to decide other issues such as amending the corporate charter. The **board of directors** is typically responsible for developing strategic goals and plans, setting general policy, guiding corporate affairs, approving major expenditures, and hiring/firing, compensating, and monitoring key officers and executives. The directors typically include both "inside directors," such as key corporate executives, and "outside directors," such as executives from other companies, major shareholders, and national or community leaders. Outside directors for major corporations are generally paid an annual fee of $15,000 to

_____

1. Some corporations do not have stockholders but rather have "members" who often have rights similar to those of stockholders—that is, they are entitled to vote and receive dividends. Examples include mutual savings banks, credit unions, mutual insurance companies, and a whole host of charitable organizations.

Corporate Organization
The general organization
of a corporation and the
finance function (which is
shown in yellow)

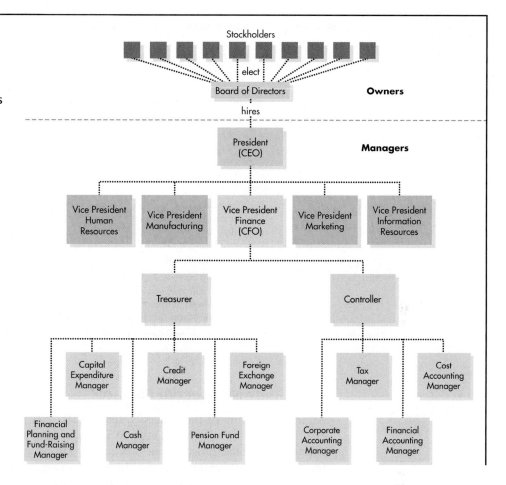

$25,000 or more. Also, they are frequently granted options to buy a specified number of shares of the firm's stock at a stated—and often attractive—price.

The **president or chief executive officer (CEO)** is responsible for managing day-to-day operations and carrying out the policies established by the board of directors. The CEO is required to report periodically to the firm's directors.

It is important to note the division between owners and managers in a large corporation, as shown by the dashed horizontal line in Figure 1.1. This separation and some of the issues surrounding it will be addressed in the discussion of *the agency issue* later in this chapter.

president or chief executive officer (CEO)
Corporate official responsible for managing the firm's day-to-day operations and carrying out the policies established by the board of directors.

Other Limited Liability Organizations

A number of other organizational forms provide owners with limited liability. The most popular are **limited partnerships (LPs)**, **S corporations (S corps)**, **limited liability corporations (LLCs)**, and **limited liability partnerships (LLPs)**. Each represents a specialized form or blending of the characteristics of the organizational forms described previously. What they have in common is that their owners enjoy limited liability, and they typically have fewer than 100 owners. Each of these limited liability organizations is briefly described in Table 1.2 (see page 8).

limited partnership (LP)
S corporation (S corp)
limited liability corporation (LLC)
limited liability partnership (LLP)
See Table 1.2.

TABLE 1.2	Other Limited Liability Organizations
Organization	Description
Limited partnership (LP)	A partnership in which one or more partners have limited liability as long as at least *one* partner (the general partner) has unlimited liability. The *limited partners* cannot take an active role in the firm's management; they are passive investors.
S corporation (S corp)	A tax-reporting entity that (under Subchapter S of the Internal Revenue Code) allows certain corporations with 100 or fewer stockholders to choose to be taxed as partnerships. Its stockholders receive the organizational benefits of a corporation and the tax advantages of a partnership. But S corps lose certain tax advantages related to pension plans.
Limited liability corporation (LLC)	Permitted in most states, the LLC gives its owners, like those of S corps, limited liability and taxation as a partnership. But unlike an S corp, the LLC can own more than 80% of another corporation, and corporations, partnerships, or non-U.S. residents can own LLC shares. LLCs work well for corporate joint ventures or projects developed through a subsidiary.
Limited liability partnership (LLP)	A partnership permitted in many states; governing statutes vary by state. All LLP partners have limited liability. They are liable for their own acts of malpractice, but not for those of other partners. The LLP is taxed as a partnership. LLPs are frequently used by legal and accounting professionals.

Why Study Managerial Finance?

An understanding of the concepts, techniques, and practices presented throughout this text will fully acquaint you with the financial manager's activities and decisions. Because most business decisions are measured in financial terms, the financial manager plays a key role in the operation of the firm. People in all areas of responsibility—accounting, information systems, management, marketing, operations, and so forth—need a basic understanding of the managerial finance function.

Okay, so you're not planning to major in finance! You still will need to understand the activities of the financial manager to improve your chance of success in your chosen business career. All managers in the firm, regardless of their job descriptions, work with financial personnel to justify labor requirements, negotiate operating budgets, deal with financial performance appraisals, and sell proposals at least partly on the basis of their financial merits. Clearly, those managers who understand the financial decision-making process will be better able to address financial concerns and will therefore more often get the resources they need to attain their own goals. The "Why This Chapter Matters to You" section that appears on each chapter-opening page should help you understand the importance of each chapter in both your professional and personal life.

As you study this text, you will learn about the career opportunities in managerial finance, which are briefly described in Table 1.3. Although this text focuses on publicly held profit-seeking firms, the principles presented here are equally applicable to private and not-for-profit organizations. The decision-making principles developed in this text can also be applied to personal financial decisions. I hope that this first exposure to the exciting field of finance will provide the foundation and initiative for further study and possibly even a future career.

TABLE 1.3	Career Opportunities in Managerial Finance
Position	Description
Financial analyst	Primarily prepares the firm's financial plans and budgets. Other duties include financial forecasting, performing financial comparisons, and working closely with accounting.
Capital expenditures manager	Evaluates and recommends proposed long-term investments. May be involved in the financial aspects of implementing approved investments.
Project finance manager	In large firms, arranges financing for approved long-term investments. Coordinates consultants, investment bankers, and legal counsel.
Cash manager	Maintains and controls the firm's daily cash balances. Frequently manages the firm's cash collection and disbursement activities and short-term investments; coordinates short-term borrowing and banking relationships.
Credit analyst/manager	Administers the firm's credit policy by evaluating credit applications, extending credit, and monitoring and collecting accounts receivable.
Pension fund manager	In large companies, oversees or manages the assets and liabilities of the employees' pension fund.
Foreign exchange manager	Manages specific foreign operations and the firm's exposure to fluctuations in exchange rates.

REVIEW QUESTIONS

1–1 What is *finance?* Explain how this field affects the life of everyone and of every organization.

1–2 What is the *financial services* area of finance? Describe the field of *managerial finance.*

1–3 Which legal form of business organization is most common? Which form is dominant in terms of business receipts and net profits?

1–4 Describe the roles and the basic relationship among the major parties in a corporation—stockholders, board of directors, and president. How are corporate owners compensated?

1–5 Briefly name and describe some organizational forms other than corporations that provide owners with limited liability.

1–6 Why is the study of managerial finance important to your professional life regardless of the specific area of responsibility you may have within the business firm? Why is it important to your personal life?

1.2 | The Managerial Finance Function

People in all areas of responsibility within the firm must interact with finance personnel and procedures to get their jobs done. For financial personnel to make useful forecasts and decisions, they must be willing and able to talk to individuals in other areas of the firm. For example, when considering a new product, the financial manager needs to obtain sales forecasts, pricing guidelines, and advertising and promotion budget estimates from marketing personnel. The managerial finance function can be broadly described by considering its role within the organization, its relationship to economics and accounting, and the primary activities of the financial manager.

Organization of the Finance Function

treasurer
The firm's chief financial manager, who is responsible for the firm's financial activities, such as financial planning and fund raising, making capital expenditure decisions, and managing cash, credit, the pension fund, and foreign exchange.

controller
The firm's chief accountant, who is responsible for the firm's accounting activities, such as corporate accounting, tax management, financial accounting, and cost accounting.

Hint A *controller* is sometimes referred to as a *comptroller.* Not-for-profit and governmental organizations frequently use the title of comptroller.

The size and importance of the managerial finance function depend on the size of the firm. In small firms, the finance function is generally performed by the accounting department. As a firm grows, the finance function typically evolves into a separate department linked directly to the company president or CEO through the chief financial officer (CFO). The lower portion of the organizational chart in Figure 1.1 (on page 7) shows the structure of the finance function in a typical medium-to-large-size firm.

Reporting to the CFO are the treasurer and the controller. The **treasurer** (the chief financial manager) is commonly responsible for handling financial activities, such as financial planning and fund raising, making capital expenditure decisions, managing cash, managing credit activities, managing the pension fund, and managing foreign exchange. The **controller** (the chief accountant) typically handles the accounting activities, such as corporate accounting, tax management, financial accounting, and cost accounting. The treasurer's focus tends to be more external, the controller's focus more internal. *The activities of the treasurer, or financial manager, are the primary concern of this text.*

If international sales or purchases are important to a firm, it may well employ one or more finance professionals whose job is to monitor and manage the firm's exposure to loss from currency fluctuations. A trained financial manager can "hedge," or protect against such a loss, at reasonable cost by using a variety of financial instruments. These **foreign exchange managers** typically report to the firm's treasurer.

Relationship to Economics

foreign exchange manager
The manager responsible for monitoring and managing the firm's exposure to loss from currency fluctuations.

marginal cost–benefit analysis
Economic principle that states that financial decisions should be made and actions taken only when the added benefits exceed the added costs.

The field of finance is closely related to economics. Financial managers must understand the economic framework and be alert to the consequences of varying levels of economic activity and changes in economic policy. They must also be able to use economic theories as guidelines for efficient business operation. Examples include supply-and-demand analysis, profit-maximizing strategies, and price theory. The primary economic principle used in managerial finance is **marginal cost–benefit analysis,** the principle that financial decisions should be made and actions taken only when the added benefits exceed the added costs. Nearly all financial decisions ultimately come down to an assessment of their marginal benefits and marginal costs.

Example Jamie Teng is a financial manager for Nord Department Stores, a large chain of upscale department stores operating primarily in the western United States. She is currently trying to decide whether to replace one of the firm's online computers with a new, more sophisticated one that would both speed processing and handle a larger volume of transactions. The new computer would require a cash outlay of $80,000, and the old computer could be sold to net $28,000. The total benefits from the new computer (measured in today's dollars) would be $100,000. The benefits over a similar time period from the old computer (measured in today's dollars) would be $35,000. Applying marginal cost–benefit analysis, Jamie organizes the data as follows:

Benefits with new computer	$100,000	
Less: Benefits with old computer	35,000	
(1) Marginal (added) benefits		$65,000
Cost of new computer	$ 80,000	
Less: Proceeds from sale of old computer	28,000	
(2) Marginal (added) costs		52,000
Net benefit [(1) − (2)]		$13,000

Because the marginal (added) benefits of $65,000 exceed the marginal (added) costs of $52,000, Jamie recommends that the firm purchase the new computer to replace the old one. The firm will experience a net benefit of $13,000 as a result of this action.

Relationship to Accounting

The firm's finance (treasurer) and accounting (controller) activities are closely related and generally overlap. Indeed, managerial finance and accounting are often not easily distinguishable. In small firms the controller often carries out the finance function, and in large firms many accountants are closely involved in various finance activities. However, there are two basic differences between finance and accounting; one is related to the emphasis on cash flows and the other to decision making.

Emphasis on Cash Flows

accrual basis
In preparation of financial statements, recognizes revenue at the time of sale and recognizes expenses when they are incurred.

The accountant's primary function is to develop and report data for measuring the performance of the firm, assess its financial position, comply with and file reports required by securities regulators, and file and pay taxes. Using certain standardized and generally accepted principles, the accountant prepares financial statements that recognize revenue at the time of sale (whether payment has been received or not) and recognize expenses when they are incurred. This approach is referred to as the **accrual basis.**

cash basis
Recognizes revenues and expenses only with respect to actual inflows and outflows of cash.

The financial manager, on the other hand, places primary emphasis on *cash flows,* the intake and outgo of cash. He or she maintains the firm's solvency by planning the cash flows necessary to satisfy its obligations and to acquire assets needed to achieve the firm's goals. The financial manager uses this **cash basis** to recognize the revenues and expenses only with respect to actual inflows and outflows of cash. Regardless of its profit or loss, *a firm must have a sufficient flow of cash to meet its obligations as they come due.*

Example

Nassau Corporation, a small yacht dealer, sold one yacht for $100,000 in the calendar year just ended. The yacht was purchased during the year at a total cost of $80,000. Although the firm paid in full for the yacht during the year, at year-end it has yet to collect the $100,000 from the customer. The accounting view and the financial view of the firm's performance during the year are given by the following income and cash flow statements, respectively.

Accounting view (accrual basis)			Financial view (cash basis)		
Nassau Corporation income statement for the year ended 12/31			Nassau Corporation cash flow statement for the year ended 12/31		
Sales revenue		$100,000	Cash inflow		$ 0
Less: Costs		80,000	Less: Cash outflow		80,000
Net profit		$ 20,000	Net cash flow		($80,000)

In an accounting sense Nassau Corporation is profitable, but in terms of actual cash flow it is a financial failure. Its lack of cash flow resulted from the uncollected account receivable of $100,000. Without adequate cash inflows to meet its obligations, the firm will not survive, regardless of its level of profits.

Hint The primary emphasis of accounting is on accrual methods; the primary emphasis of financial management is on cash flow methods.

As the example shows, accrual accounting data do not fully describe the circumstances of a firm. Thus the financial manager must look beyond financial statements to obtain insight into existing or developing problems. Of course, accountants are well aware of the importance of cash flows, and financial managers use and understand accrual-based financial statements. Nevertheless, the financial manager, by concentrating on cash flows, should be able to avoid insolvency and achieve the firm's financial goals.

Personal Finance Example Individuals do not use accrual concepts. Rather, they rely solely on cash flows to measure their financial outcomes. Generally, individuals plan, monitor, and assess their financial activities using cash flows over a given period, typically a month or a year. Ann Bach projects her cash flows during October 2009 as follows:

	Amount	
Item	Inflow	Outflow
Net pay received	$4,400	
Rent		$1,200
Car payment		450
Utilities		300
Groceries		800
Clothes		750
Dining out		650
Gasoline		260
Interest received	220	
Misc. expense		425
Totals	$4,620	$4,835

Ann subtracts her total outflows of $4,835 from her total inflows of $4,620, and finds that her *net cash flow* for October will be −$215. To cover the $215 shortfall, Ann would have to either borrow $215 (putting it on a credit card is a form of borrowing), or withdraw $215 from her savings. Or she could decide to reduce her outflows in areas of discretionary spending—e.g., clothing purchases, dining out, or areas that make up the $425 of miscellaneous expense.

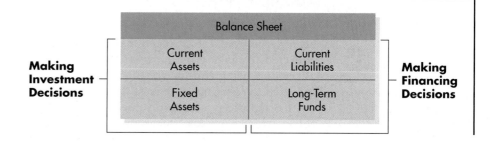

FIGURE 1.2

Financial Activities
Primary activities of the financial manager

Decision Making

The second major difference between finance and accounting has to do with decision making. Accountants devote most of their attention to the *collection and presentation of financial data.* Financial managers evaluate the accounting statements, develop additional data, and *make decisions* on the basis of their assessment of the associated returns and risks. Of course, this does not mean that accountants never make decisions or that financial managers never gather data. Rather, the primary focuses of accounting and finance are distinctly different.

Primary Activities of the Financial Manager

 Hint Technically, financial managers make recommendations with regard to decisions that are ultimately made by the CEO and/or corporate board of directors.

In addition to ongoing involvement in financial analysis and planning, the financial manager's primary activities are making investment decisions and making financing decisions. Investment decisions determine both the mix and the type of assets held by the firm. Financing decisions determine both the mix and the type of financing used by the firm. These sorts of decisions can be conveniently viewed in terms of the firm's balance sheet, as shown in Figure 1.2. However, the decisions are actually made on the basis of their cash flow effects on the overall value of the firm.

REVIEW QUESTIONS

1–7 What financial activities is the treasurer, or financial manager, responsible for handling in the mature firm?

1–8 What is the primary economic principle used in managerial finance?

1–9 What are the major differences between accounting and finance with respect to emphasis on cash flows and decision making?

1–10 What are the two primary activities of the financial manager that are related to the firm's balance sheet?

LG 4   1.3 | Goal of the Firm

As noted earlier, the owners of a corporation are normally distinct from its managers. Actions of the financial manager should be taken to achieve the objectives of the firm's owners, its stockholders. In most cases, if financial managers are successful in this endeavor, they will also achieve their own financial and professional objectives. Thus financial managers need to know what the objectives of the firm's owners are.

Maximize Profit?

earnings per share (EPS)
The amount earned during the period on behalf of each outstanding share of common stock, calculated by dividing the period's total earnings available for the firm's common stockholders by the number of shares of common stock outstanding.

Some people believe that the firm's objective is always to maximize profit. To achieve this goal, the financial manager would take only those actions that were expected to make a major contribution to the firm's overall profits. For each alternative being considered, the financial manager would select the one that is expected to result in the highest monetary return.

Corporations commonly measure profits in terms of **earnings per share (EPS)**, which represent the amount earned during the period on behalf of each outstanding share of common stock. EPS are calculated by dividing the period's total earnings available for the firm's common stockholders by the number of shares of common stock outstanding.

Example

Nick Dukakis, the financial manager of Neptune Manufacturing, a producer of marine engine components, is choosing between two investments, Rotor and Valve. The following table shows the EPS that each investment is expected to have over its 3-year life.

	Earnings per share (EPS)			
Investment	Year 1	Year 2	Year 3	Total for years 1, 2, and 3
Rotor	$1.40	$1.00	$0.40	$2.80
Valve	0.60	1.00	1.40	3.00

In terms of the profit maximization goal, Valve would be preferred over Rotor, because it results in higher total earnings per share over the 3-year period ($3.00 EPS compared with $2.80 EPS).

But is profit maximization a reasonable goal? No. It fails for a number of reasons: It ignores (1) the timing of returns, (2) cash flows available to stockholders, and (3) risk.[2]

Timing

Because the firm can earn a return on funds it receives, *the receipt of funds sooner rather than later is preferred*. In our example, in spite of the fact that the total earnings from Rotor are smaller than those from Valve, Rotor provides much greater earnings per share in the first year. The larger returns in year 1 could be reinvested to provide greater future earnings.

Cash Flows

Profits do *not* necessarily result in cash flows available to the stockholders. Owners receive cash flow in the form of either cash dividends paid them or the proceeds from selling their shares for a higher price than initially paid. Greater EPS do not necessarily mean that a firm's board of directors will vote to increase dividend payments.

---

2. Another criticism of profit maximization is the potential for profit manipulation through the creative use of elective accounting practices. This issue has received close scrutiny from securities regulators during recent years.

Furthermore, higher EPS do not necessarily translate into a higher stock price. Firms sometimes experience earnings increases without any correspondingly favorable change in stock price. Only when earnings increases are accompanied by increased future cash flows would a higher stock price be expected. For example, a firm with a high-quality product sold in a very competitive market could increase its earnings by significantly reducing its equipment maintenance expenditures. As a result the firm's expenses would be reduced, thereby increasing its profits. But because the reduced maintenance will result in lower product quality, the firm would impair its competitive position and its stock price would drop as many well-informed investors sell the stock in recognition of lower future cash flows. In this case, the earnings increase was accompanied by lower future cash flows and therefore a lower stock price.

Risk

risk
The chance that actual outcomes may differ from those expected.

Profit maximization also disregards **risk**—the chance that actual outcomes may differ from those expected. A basic premise in managerial finance is that a tradeoff exists between return (cash flow) and risk. *Return and risk are, in fact, the key determinants of share price, which represents the wealth of the owners in the firm.*

Hint The relationship between risk and return is one of the most important concepts in the book. Investors who seek to avoid risk will *always* require a bigger return for taking bigger risks.

Cash flow and risk affect share price differently: Higher cash flow is generally associated with a higher share price. Higher risk tends to result in a lower share price because the stockholder must be compensated for the greater risk. For example, if a firm's highly successful CEO dies suddenly and a suitable successor is not available, its share price typically will drop immediately. This occurs not because of any near-term cash flow reduction but in response to the firm's increased risk—there's a chance that the firm's lack of near-term leadership could result in reduced future cash flows. Simply put, the increased risk reduces the firm's share price. In general, stockholders are **risk-averse**—that is, they want to avoid risk. When risk is involved, stockholders expect to earn higher rates of return on investments of higher risk and lower rates on lower-risk investments. The key point, which will be fully developed in Chapter 5, is that differences in risk can significantly affect the value of an investment.

risk-averse
Seeking to avoid risk.

Because profit maximization does not achieve the objectives of the firm's owners, it should *not* be the primary goal of the financial manager.

Maximize Shareholder Wealth

The goal of the firm, and therefore of all managers and employees, is *to maximize the wealth of the owners for whom it is being operated.* The wealth of corporate owners is measured by the share price of the stock, which in turn is based on the timing of returns (cash flows), their magnitude, and their risk.

When considering each financial decision alternative or possible action in terms of its effect on the share price of the firm's stock, *financial managers should accept only those actions that are expected to increase share price.* Figure 1.3 (see page 16) depicts this process. Because share price represents the owners' wealth in the firm, maximizing share price will maximize owner wealth. Note that *return (cash flows) and risk are the key decision variables in maximizing owner wealth.*

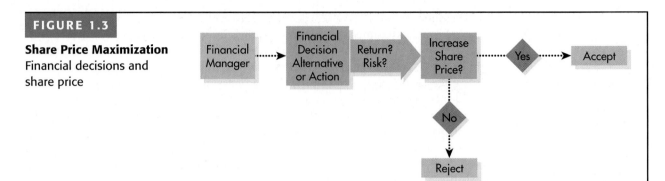

FIGURE 1.3

Share Price Maximization
Financial decisions and
share price

It is important to recognize that earnings per share, because they are viewed as an indicator of the firm's future returns (cash flows), often appear to affect share price.

What About Stakeholders?

stakeholders
Groups such as employees, customers, suppliers, creditors, owners, and others who have a direct economic link to the firm.

Although maximization of shareholder wealth is the primary goal, many firms broaden their focus to include the interests of *stakeholders* as well as shareholders. **Stakeholders** are groups such as employees, customers, suppliers, creditors, owners, and others who have a direct economic link to the firm. A firm with a *stakeholder focus* consciously avoids actions that would prove detrimental to stakeholders. The goal is not to maximize stakeholder well-being but to preserve it.

The stakeholder view does not alter the goal of maximizing shareholder wealth. Such a view is often considered part of the firm's "social responsibility." It is expected to provide long-run benefit to shareholders by maintaining positive stakeholder relationships. Such relationships should minimize stakeholder turnover, conflicts, and litigation. Clearly, the firm can better achieve its goal of shareholder wealth maximization by fostering cooperation with its other stakeholders, rather than conflict with them.

Corporate Governance

corporate governance
The system used to direct and control a corporation. Defines the rights and responsibilities of key corporate participants, decision-making procedures, and the way in which the firm will set, achieve, and monitor its objectives.

The system used to direct and control a corporation is referred to as **corporate governance**. It defines the rights and responsibilities of the key corporate participants such as the shareholders, board of directors, officers and managers, and other stakeholders, and the rules and procedures for making corporate decisions. It also typically specifies the structure through which the company sets objectives, develops plans for achieving them, and establishes procedures for monitoring performance.

Figure 1.1 on page 7 depicts the typical corporate governance structure, in which the stockholders (owners) elect a board of directors (their representatives), who in turn hire officers and managers (professional managers) to operate the firm in a manner consistent with the goals, plans, and policies established and monitored by the board on behalf of the shareholders. Typically, the board's policies specify ethical practices and provide for the protection of stakeholder interests.

Individual versus Institutional Investors

individual investors
Investors who buy relatively small quantities of shares so as to meet personal investment goals.

Clearly, the corporate board's first responsibility is to the shareholders. To better understand this responsibility it is helpful to differentiate between the two broad classes of owners—individuals and institutions. **Individual investors** are investors who buy relatively small quantities of shares so as to earn a return on idle funds, build a source of retirement income, or provide financial security. **Institutional investors** are investment professionals that are paid to manage other people's money. They hold and trade large quantities of securities for individuals, businesses, and governments. Institutional investors include banks, insurance companies, mutual funds, and pension funds, which invest large sums of money to earn competitive returns for their clients/plan participants.

institutional investors
Investment professionals, such as banks, insurance companies, mutual funds, and pension funds, that are paid to manage other people's money and that hold and trade large quantities of securities.

Because they hold and trade large blocks of stock, institutional investors tend to have a much greater influence on corporate governance than do individual investors. Simply stated, because they own large amounts of common stock and have the resources to buy and sell large blocks of shares, institutional investors are able to maintain management's attention. If a large institutional investor sells or buys a sizable block of shares, the share price will likely be driven down or up, respectively. Clearly, these large investors speak in a much louder voice than does the individual investor.

The Sarbanes-Oxley Act of 2002

Beginning in 2000, numerous corporate misdeeds were uncovered and disclosed by various regulatory bodies. The misdeeds derived from two main types of issues: (1) false disclosures in financial reporting and other information releases, and (2) undisclosed conflicts of interest between corporations and their analysts, auditors, and attorneys and between corporate directors, officers, and shareholders. In response to these fraudulent disclosures and conflicts of interest, in July 2002 Congress passed the **Sarbanes-Oxley Act of 2002** (commonly called **SOX**).

Sarbanes-Oxley Act of 2002 (SOX)
An act aimed at eliminating corporate disclosure and conflict of interest problems. Contains provisions about corporate financial disclosures and the relationships among corporations, analysts, auditors, attorneys, directors, officers, and shareholders.

Sarbanes-Oxley focused on eliminating the many disclosure and conflict of interest problems that had surfaced. It did the following: established an oversight board to monitor the accounting industry; tightened audit regulations and controls; toughened penalties against executives who commit corporate fraud; strengthened accounting disclosure requirements and ethical guidelines for corporate officers; established corporate board structure and membership guidelines; established guidelines with regard to analyst conflicts of interest; mandated instant disclosure of stock sales by corporate executives; and increased securities regulation authority and budgets for auditors and investigators.

Although most commentators believe SOX is effective in reducing fraudulent disclosures and conflicts of interest in corporations, its implementation has placed a huge financial burden on the corporations that must comply with its requirements. Regulators and corporations continue to discuss how to simplify compliance with SOX. As a result, future modifications aimed at simplifying SOX are widely anticipated.

The Role of Business Ethics

business ethics
Standards of conduct or moral judgment that apply to persons engaged in commerce.

Business ethics are the standards of conduct or moral judgment that apply to persons engaged in commerce. Violations of these standards in finance involve a variety of actions: "creative accounting," earnings management, misleading financial forecasts, insider trading, fraud, excessive executive compensation, options backdating, bribery, and kickbacks. The financial press has reported many such violations in recent years, involving such well-known companies as **Apple, Boeing, Enron,** and **Tyco.** As a result, the business community in general and the financial community in particular are developing and enforcing ethical standards. The goal of these ethical standards is to motivate business and market participants to adhere to both the letter and the spirit of laws and regulations concerned with business and professional practice. Most business leaders believe businesses actually strengthen their competitive positions by maintaining high ethical standards.

Considering Ethics

Robert A. Cooke, a noted ethicist, suggests that the following questions be used to assess the ethical viability of a proposed action.[3]

1. Is the action arbitrary or capricious? Does it unfairly single out an individual or group?
2. Does the action violate the moral or legal rights of any individual or group?
3. Does the action conform to accepted moral standards?
4. Are there alternative courses of action that are less likely to cause actual or potential harm?

Clearly, considering such questions before taking an action can help to ensure its ethical viability.

Today, an increasing number of firms are directly addressing the issue of ethics by establishing corporate ethics policies and requiring employee compliance with them. The *Focus on Ethics* box on the facing page, for example, describes ethics concerns at Hewlett-Packard. A major impetus toward the development of corporate ethics policies has been the *Sarbanes-Oxley Act of 2002* described earlier. Frequently, employees are required to sign a formal pledge to uphold the firm's ethics policies. Such policies typically apply to employee actions in dealing with all corporate stakeholders, including the public. Many companies also require employees to participate in ethics seminars and training programs.

To provide further insight into the ethical dilemmas and issues sometimes facing the financial manager, one of the two *In Practice* boxes in each chapter focuses on ethics.

Ethics and Share Price

An effective ethics program is believed to enhance corporate value. An ethics program can produce a number of positive benefits. It can reduce potential litigation and judgment costs; maintain a positive corporate image; build shareholder confidence; and gain the loyalty, commitment, and respect of the firm's stakeholders. Such actions, by maintaining and enhancing cash flow and reducing perceived risk, can positively affect the firm's share price. *Ethical behavior is therefore viewed as necessary for achieving the firm's goal of owner wealth maximization.*[4]

---

3. Robert A. Cooke, "Business Ethics: A Perspective," in *Arthur Andersen Cases on Business Ethics* (Chicago: Arthur Andersen, September 1991), pp. 2 and 5.

4. For an excellent discussion of this and related issues by a number of finance academics and practitioners who have given a lot of thought to financial ethics, see James S. Ang, "On Financial Ethics," *Financial Management* (Autumn 1993), pp. 32–59.

Focus on Ethics   Ethics at HP

Like many U.S. corporations, **Hewlett-Packard Company** (NYSE: HPQ) maintains a set of rules that guides the daily actions of its employees. In his "CEO's Message" at the beginning of the "Standards of Business Conduct" section of the annual report, Mark Hurd, HP's CEO, president, and chairman, states (p. 3): "Unethical or illegal business conduct on the part of HP is simply unacceptable and will not be tolerated." HP's standards include a warning that all HP employees are subject to the standards. Hurd's predecessor, CEO Carley Fiorina, had issued a similar message in her letter 2 years earlier.

Such a stance puts the company under the microscope. When HP began its publicity blitz to gain stockholder acceptance of its eventual merger with Compaq, Walter Hewitt, a member of the board, filed suit alleging misstatement of financial facts and improper pressure of shareholder Deutsche Bank by the HP management team. Although a Delaware judge dis-

missed the lawsuit, its mere existence underscored the fact that a company's ethics constantly face the scrutiny of the public and investors.

In 2006, HP received more negative publicity when an internal investigation to find the source of news leaks within the company apparently involved a subcontractor who used questionable means of obtaining information, called "pretexting," in which people pose as someone else to gain access to personal records. The ensuing scandal forced the resignation of Board Chair Patricia Dunn.

As part of its FY06 Global Citizenship Report, HP addressed the situation: "Unfortunately, the recent events connected with HP's investigation into the leaks of confidential information from the Board of Directors have tarnished HP's reputation in this area. We are embarrassed by our actions and deeply regret our failure to meet our own high expectations for corporate behavior, as well as the expectations of our employees, cus-

tomers, and stockholders. Our well-publicized misstep has led HP to renew its commitment to the areas of governance, ethics, and compliance. HP is engaged in a broad review of its policies, practices, and procedures to ensure that they are best-in-class." As part of those efforts, HP agreed to set up a $13.5 million Privacy and Piracy Fund to help California state prosecutors investigate and prosecute consumer privacy and information-piracy violations. The company also agreed to implement a series of corporate governance changes.

American business professionals have tended to operate from within a strong moral foundation, based on early childhood moral development that takes place in families and religious institutions. This ethos does not prevent every critical lapse, of course, as shown by the events at Hewlett-Packard.

■ *List three or four basic ethics "lessons" that might be said to form the basis of your ethical foundation.*

The Agency Issue

We have seen that the goal of the financial manager should be to maximize the wealth of the firm's owners. Thus managers can be viewed as *agents* of the owners who have hired them and given them decision-making authority to manage the firm. Technically, any manager who owns less than 100 percent of the firm is to some degree an agent of the other owners. This separation of owners and managers is shown by the dashed horizontal line in Figure 1.1 on page 7.

In theory, most financial managers would agree with the goal of owner wealth maximization. In practice, however, managers are also concerned with their personal wealth, job security, and fringe benefits. Such concerns may make

Hint A stockbroker
confronts the same issue. If she
gets you to buy and sell more
stock, it's good for *her,* but it
may *not* be good for you.

managers reluctant or unwilling to take more than moderate risk if they perceive that taking too much risk might jeopardize their jobs or reduce their personal wealth. The result is a less-than-maximum return and a potential loss of wealth for the owners.

The Agency Problem

agency problem
The likelihood that managers may place personal goals ahead of corporate goals.

From this conflict of owner and personal goals arises what has been called the **agency problem,** the likelihood that managers may place personal goals ahead of corporate goals.[5] Two factors—market forces and *agency costs*—serve to prevent or minimize agency problems.

Market Forces   One market force is major shareholders, particularly large *institutional investors* such as life insurance companies, mutual funds, and pension funds. These holders of large blocks of a firm's stock exert pressure on management to perform, by communicating their concerns to the firm's board. They often threaten to exercise their voting rights or liquidate their holdings if the board does not respond positively to their concerns.

Another market force is the *threat of takeover* by another firm that believes it can enhance the target firm's value by restructuring its management, operations, and financing.[6] The constant threat of a takeover tends to motivate management to act in the best interests of the firm's owners.

agency costs
The costs borne by stockholders to maintain a *corporate governance structure* that minimizes agency problems and contributes to the maximization of owner wealth.

Agency Costs   To minimize agency problems and contribute to the maximization of owners' wealth, stockholders incur **agency costs.** These are the costs of maintaining a *corporate governance structure* that monitors management behavior, ensures against dishonest acts of management, and gives managers the financial incentive to maximize share price.

The most popular, powerful, and expensive approach is to *structure management compensation* to correspond with share price maximization. The objective is to give managers incentives to act in the best interests of the owners. In addition, the resulting compensation packages allow firms to compete for and hire the best managers available. The two key types of compensation plans are incentive plans and performance plans.

incentive plans
Management compensation plans that tend to tie management compensation to share price; the most popular incentive plan involves the grant of *stock options.*

Incentive plans tend to tie management compensation to share price. The most popular incentive plan is the granting of **stock options** to management. These options allow managers to purchase stock at the market price set at the time of the grant. If the market price rises, managers will be rewarded by being able to resell the shares at the higher market price.

stock options
An incentive allowing managers to purchase stock at the market price set at the time of the grant.

Many firms also offer **performance plans,** which tie management compensation to measures such as earnings per share (EPS), growth in EPS, and other ratios of return. **Performance shares,** shares of stock given to management as a result of meeting the stated performance goals, are often used in these plans.

performance plans
Plans that tie management compensation to measures such as EPS, growth in EPS, and other ratios of return. *Performance shares* and/or *cash bonuses* are used as compensation under these plans.

performance shares
Shares of stock given to management for meeting stated performance goals.

5. The agency problem and related issues were first addressed by Michael C. Jensen and William H. Meckling, "Theory of the Firm: Managerial Behavior, Agency Costs and Ownership Structure," *Journal of Financial Economics* 3 (October 1976), pp. 305–306. For an excellent discussion of Jensen and Meckling and subsequent research on the agency problem, see William L. Megginson, *Corporate Finance Theory* (Boston, MA: Addison Wesley, 1997), Chapter 2.

6. Detailed discussion of the important aspects of corporate takeovers is included in Chapter 17, "Mergers, LBOs, Divestitures, and Business Failure."

cash bonuses
Cash paid to management for achieving certain performance goals.

Another form of performance-based compensation is **cash bonuses,** cash payments tied to the achievement of certain performance goals.

The Current View of Management Compensation

The execution of many compensation plans has been closely scrutinized in recent years. Both individuals and institutional stockholders, as well as the Securities and Exchange Commission (SEC), continue to publicly question the appropriateness of the multimillion-dollar compensation packages that many corporate executives receive. For example, the three highest-paid CEOs in 2006 were (1) Steven P. Jobs of Apple Inc., who earned $646.60 million; (2) Ray R. Irani of Occidental Petroleum, who earned $321.64 million; and (3) Barry Diller of IAC/InterActiveCorp, who earned $295.14 million. Tenth on the same list was Henry C. Duques of First Data, who earned $98.21 million. During 2006, the average compensation of the CEOs of America's 500 biggest companies surveyed by *Forbes*.com using data from a variety of sources was $15.20 million, up 38 percent from 2005. The average compensation of the top 20 highest-paid CEOs was $144.66 million.

Recent studies have failed to find a strong relationship between CEO compensation and share price. During the past few years, publicity surrounding these large compensation packages (without corresponding share price performance) has driven down executive compensation. Contributing to this publicity is the SEC requirement that publicly traded companies disclose to shareholders and others the amount of compensation to their CEO, CFO, three other highest-paid executives, and directors, the method used to determine it and a narrative discussion regarding the underlying compensation policies. At the same time, new compensation plans that better link managers' performance with regard to shareholder wealth to their compensation are being developed and implemented.

Unconstrained, managers may have other goals in addition to share price maximization, but much of the evidence suggests that share price maximization—the focus of this book—is the primary goal of most firms.

REVIEW QUESTIONS

1–11 For what three basic reasons is profit maximization inconsistent with wealth maximization?

1–12 What is *risk?* Why must risk as well as return be considered by the financial manager who is evaluating a decision alternative or action?

1–13 What is the goal of the firm and, therefore, of all managers and employees? Discuss how one measures achievement of this goal.

1–14 What is *corporate governance?* How has the Sarbanes-Oxley Act of 2002 affected it? Explain.

1–15 Describe the role of corporate ethics policies and guidelines, and discuss the relationship that is believed to exist between ethics and share price.

1–16 How do market forces—both shareholder activism and the threat of takeover—act to prevent or minimize the *agency problem?* What role do *institutional investors* play in shareholder activism?

1–17 Define *agency costs,* and explain their relationship to a firm's *corporate governance structure.* How can the firm *structure management compensation* to minimize agency problems? What is the current view with regard to the execution of many compensation plans?

1.4 | Financial Institutions and Markets

Most successful firms have ongoing needs for funds. They can obtain funds from external sources in three ways. The first source is through a *financial institution* that accepts savings and transfers them to those that need funds. A second source is through *financial markets,* organized forums in which the suppliers and demanders of various types of funds can make transactions. A third source is through *private placement.* Because of the unstructured nature of private placements, here we focus primarily on the role of financial institutions and financial markets in facilitating business financing.

For an in-depth, chapter-length discussion of financial institutions and financial markets, see the online chapter at WWW the book's website.

Financial Institutions

financial institution
An intermediary that channels the savings of individuals, businesses, and governments into loans or investments.

Financial institutions serve as intermediaries by channeling the savings of individuals, businesses, and governments into loans or investments. Many financial institutions directly or indirectly pay savers interest on deposited funds; others provide services for a fee (for example, checking accounts for which customers pay service charges). Some financial institutions accept customers' savings deposits and lend this money to other customers or to firms; others invest customers' savings in earning assets such as real estate or stocks and bonds; and some do both. Financial institutions are required by the government to operate within established regulatory guidelines.

Hint Think about how inefficient it would be if each individual saver had to negotiate with each potential user of savings. Institutions make the process very efficient by becoming intermediaries between savers and users.

Key Customers of Financial Institutions

For financial institutions, the key suppliers of funds and the key demanders of funds are individuals, businesses, and governments. The savings that individual consumers place in financial institutions provide these institutions with a large portion of their funds. Individuals not only supply funds to financial institutions but also demand funds from them in the form of loans. However, individuals as a group are the *net suppliers* for financial institutions: They save more money than they borrow.

Business firms also deposit some of their funds in financial institutions, primarily in checking accounts with various commercial banks. Like individuals, firms borrow funds from these institutions, but firms are *net demanders* of funds: They borrow more money than they save.

Governments maintain deposits of temporarily idle funds, certain tax payments, and Social Security payments in commercial banks. They do not borrow funds *directly* from financial institutions, although by selling their debt securities to various institutions, governments indirectly borrow from them. The government, like business firms, is typically a *net demander* of funds: It typically borrows more than it saves. We've all heard about the federal budget deficit.

Major Financial Institutions

The major financial institutions in the U.S. economy are commercial banks, savings and loans, credit unions, savings banks, insurance companies, mutual funds, and pension funds. These institutions attract funds from individuals, businesses, and governments, combine them, and make loans available to individuals and businesses. Descriptions of the major financial institutions are found at the textbook's website.

Financial Markets

financial markets
Forums in which suppliers of funds and demanders of funds can transact business directly.

Financial markets are forums in which suppliers of funds and demanders of funds can transact business directly. Whereas the loans and investments of institutions are made without the direct knowledge of the suppliers of funds (savers), suppliers in the financial markets know where their funds are being lent or invested. The two key financial markets are the money market and the capital market. Transactions in short-term debt instruments, or marketable securities, take place in the *money market*. Long-term securities—bonds and stocks—are traded in the *capital market*.

private placement
The sale of a new security issue, typically bonds or preferred stock, directly to an investor or group of investors.

public offering
The nonexclusive sale of either bonds or stocks to the general public.

To raise money, firms can use either private placements or public offerings. **Private placement** involves the sale of a new security issue, typically bonds or preferred stock, directly to an investor or group of investors, such as an insurance company or pension fund. Most firms, however, raise money through a **public offering** of securities, which is the nonexclusive sale of either bonds or stocks to the general public.

primary market
Financial market in which securities are initially issued; the only market in which the issuer is directly involved in the transaction.

All securities are initially issued in the **primary market.** This is the only market in which the corporate or government issuer is directly involved in the transaction and receives direct benefit from the issue. That is, the company actually receives the proceeds from the sale of securities. Once the securities begin to trade between savers and investors, they become part of the **secondary market.** The primary market is the one in which "new" securities are sold. The secondary market can be viewed as a "preowned" securities market.

secondary market
Financial market in which preowned securities (those that are not new issues) are traded.

The Relationship between Institutions and Markets

Financial institutions actively participate in the financial markets as both suppliers and demanders of funds. Figure 1.4 (see page 24) depicts the general flow of funds through and between financial institutions and financial markets; private placement transactions are also shown. The individuals, businesses, and governments that supply and demand funds may be domestic or foreign. We next briefly discuss the money market, including its international equivalent—the *Eurocurrency market*. We then end this section with a discussion of the capital market, which is of key importance to the firm.

The Money Market

money market
A financial relationship created between suppliers and demanders of *short-term funds.*

The **money market** is created by a financial relationship between suppliers and demanders of *short-term funds* (funds with maturities of one year or less). The money market exists because some individuals, businesses, governments, and financial institutions have temporarily idle funds that they wish to put to some interest-earning use. At the same time, other individuals, businesses, governments, and financial institutions find themselves in need of seasonal or temporary

FIGURE 1.4

Flow of Funds
Flow of funds for financial institutions and markets

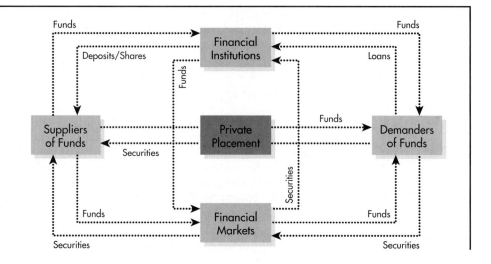

---

marketable securities
Short-term debt instruments, such as U.S. Treasury bills, commercial paper, and negotiable certificates of deposit issued by government, business, and financial institutions, respectively.

financing. The money market brings together these suppliers and demanders of short-term funds.

Most money market transactions are made in **marketable securities**—short-term debt instruments, such as U.S. Treasury bills, commercial paper, and negotiable certificates of deposit issued by government, business, and financial institutions, respectively. (Marketable securities are described in Chapter 14.)

The Eurocurrency Market

Eurocurrency market
International equivalent of the domestic money market.

The international equivalent of the domestic money market is called the **Eurocurrency market.** This is a market for short-term bank deposits denominated in U.S. dollars or other easily convertible currencies. Eurocurrency deposits arise when a corporation or individual makes a bank deposit in a currency other than the local currency of the country where the bank is located. If, for example, a multinational corporation were to deposit U.S. dollars in a London bank, this would create a Eurodollar deposit (a dollar deposit at a bank in Europe). Nearly all Eurodollar deposits are *time deposits*. This means that the bank would promise to repay the deposit, with interest, at a fixed date in the future—say, in 6 months. During the interim, the bank is free to lend this dollar deposit to creditworthy corporate or government borrowers. If the bank cannot find a borrower on its own, it may lend the deposit to another international bank.

Hint Remember that the *money market* is for short-term fund raising and is represented by current liabilities on the balance sheet. The *capital market* is for long-term fund raising and is reflected by long-term debt and equity on the balance sheet.

The Capital Market

capital market
A market that enables suppliers and demanders of *long-term funds* to make transactions.

The **capital market** is a market that enables suppliers and demanders of *long-term funds* to make transactions. Included are securities issues of business and government. The backbone of the capital market is formed by the broker and dealer markets that provide a forum for bond and stock transactions. International capital markets also exist.

Key Securities Traded: Bonds and Stocks

The key capital market securities are *bonds* (long-term debt) and both *common stock* and *preferred stock* (equity, or ownership).

bond
Long-term debt instrument used by business and government to raise large sums of money, generally from a diverse group of lenders.

Bonds are long-term debt instruments used by business and government to raise large sums of money, generally from a diverse group of lenders. *Corporate bonds* typically pay interest *semiannually* (every 6 months) at a stated *coupon interest rate*. They have an initial *maturity* of from 10 to 30 years, and a *par,* or *face, value* of $1,000 that must be repaid at maturity. Bonds are described in detail in Chapter 6.

Example

Lakeview Industries, a major microprocessor manufacturer, has issued a 9 percent coupon interest rate, 20-year bond with a $1,000 par value that pays interest semiannually. Investors who buy this bond receive the contractual right to $90 annual interest (9% coupon interest rate $\times$ $1,000 par value) distributed as $45 at the end of each 6 months (1/2 $\times$ $90) for 20 years, plus the $1,000 par value at the end of year 20.

---

preferred stock
A special form of ownership having a fixed periodic dividend that must be paid prior to payment of any dividends to common stockholders.

broker market
The securities exchanges on which the two sides of a transaction, the buyer and seller, are brought together to trade securities.

securities exchanges
Organizations that provide the marketplace in which firms can raise funds through the sale of new securities and purchasers can resell securities.

dealer market
The market in which the buyer and seller are not brought together directly but instead have their orders executed by securities dealers that "make markets" in the given security.

market makers
Securities dealers who "make markets" by offering to buy or sell certain securities at stated prices.

Nasdaq market
An all-electronic trading platform used to execute securities trades.

over-the-counter (OTC) market
Market where smaller, unlisted securities are traded.

As noted earlier, shares of *common stock* are units of ownership, or equity, in a corporation. Common stockholders earn a return by receiving dividends—periodic distributions of earnings—or by realizing increases in share price. **Preferred stock** is a special form of ownership that has features of both a bond and common stock. Preferred stockholders are promised a fixed periodic dividend that must be paid prior to payment of any dividends to common stockholders. In other words, preferred stock has "preference" over common stock. Preferred and common stock are described in detail in Chapter 7.

Broker Markets and Dealer Markets

By far, the vast majority of trades made by individual investors take place in the secondary market. When you look at the secondary market *on the basis of how securities are traded,* you will find you can essentially divide the market into two segments: broker markets and dealer markets.

The key difference between broker and dealer markets is a technical point dealing with the way trades are executed. That is, when a trade occurs in a **broker market,** the two sides to the transaction, the buyer and the seller, are brought together and the trade takes place at that point: Party A sells his or her securities directly to the buyer, Party B. In a sense, with the help of a *broker,* the securities effectively change hands on the floor of the exchange. The broker market consists of national and regional **securities exchanges,** which are organizations that provide a marketplace in which firms can raise funds through the sale of new securities and purchasers can resell securities.

In contrast, when trades are made in a **dealer market,** the buyer and the seller are never brought together directly. Instead, **market makers** execute the buy/sell orders. Market makers are *securities dealers* who "make markets" by offering to buy or sell certain securities at stated prices. Essentially, two separate trades are made: Party A sells his or her securities (in, say, Dell) to a dealer, and Party B buys his or her securities (in Dell) from another, or possibly even the same, dealer. Thus, there is always a dealer (*market maker*) on one side of a dealer-market transaction. The dealer market is made up of both the **Nasdaq market,** an all-electronic trading platform used to execute securities trades, and the **over-the-counter (OTC) market,** where smaller, unlisted securities are traded.

Broker Markets   If you are like most individual investors, when you think of the "stock market" the first name to come to mind is the New York Stock

Exchange (NYSE). In point of fact, the NYSE is the dominant broker market. Also included in this market are the American Stock Exchange (AMEX), which is another *national exchange,* and several so-called *regional exchanges.* These exchanges account for about 60 percent of *the total dollar volume* of all shares traded in the U.S. stock market. In broker markets all the trading takes place on centralized trading floors.

Most exchanges are modeled after the New York Stock Exchange. For a firm's securities to be listed for trading on a stock exchange, a firm must file an application for listing and meet a number of requirements. For example, to be eligible for listing on the NYSE, a firm must have at least 2,200 stockholders owning 100 or more shares; a minimum of 1.1 million shares of publicly held stock outstanding; pretax earnings of at least $10 million over the previous 3 years, with no loss in the previous 2 years; and a minimum market value of public shares of $100 million. Clearly, only large, widely held firms are candidates for NYSE listing.

Once placed, an order to buy or sell on the NYSE can be executed in minutes, thanks to sophisticated telecommunication devices. New Internet-based brokerage systems enable investors to place their buy and sell orders electronically. Information on publicly traded securities is reported in various media, both print, such as the *Wall Street Journal,* and electronic, such as MSN Money (**www.moneycentral.msn.com**).

Dealer Markets   One of the key features of the *dealer market* is that it has no centralized trading floors. Instead, it is made up of a large number of *market makers* who are linked together via a mass-telecommunications network.

Each market maker is actually a securities dealer who makes a market in one or more securities by offering to buy or sell them at stated bid/ask prices. The **bid price** and **ask price** represent, respectively, the highest price offered to purchase a given security and the lowest price at which the security is offered for sale. In effect, an investor pays the ask price when buying securities and receives the bid price when selling them.

As described earlier, the dealer market is made up of both the *Nasdaq market* and the *over-the-counter (OTC) market,* which together account for about 40 percent of all shares traded in the U.S. market—with the Nasdaq accounting for the overwhelming majority of those trades. (As an aside, the *primary market* is also a dealer market, because all new issues are sold to the investing public by securities dealers, acting on behalf of the investment banker.)

The largest dealer market consists of a select group of stocks that are listed and traded on the *National Association of Securities Dealers Automated Quotation System,* typically referred to as *Nasdaq.* Founded in 1971, Nasdaq had its origins in the OTC market, but is today considered *a totally separate entity that's no longer a part of the OTC market.* In fact, in 2006 the Nasdaq was formally recognized by the SEC as a "listed exchange," essentially giving it the same stature and prestige as the NYSE.

International Capital Markets

Although U.S. capital markets are by far the world's largest, there are important debt and equity markets outside the United States. In the **Eurobond market**, corporations and governments typically issue bonds denominated in dollars and sell

bid price
The highest price offered to purchase a security.

ask price
The lowest price at which a security is offered for sale.

Eurobond market
The market in which corporations and governments typically issue bonds denominated in dollars and sell them to investors located outside the United States.

them to investors located outside the United States. A U.S. corporation might, for example, issue dollar-denominated bonds that would be purchased by investors in Belgium, Germany, or Switzerland. Through the Eurobond market, issuing firms and governments can tap a much larger pool of investors than would be generally available in the local market.

foreign bond
Bond that is issued by a foreign corporation or government and is denominated in the investor's home currency and sold in the investor's home market.

The *foreign bond market* is another international market for long-term debt securities. A **foreign bond** is a bond issued by a foreign corporation or government that is denominated in the investor's home currency and sold in the investor's home market. A bond issued by a U.S. company that is denominated in Swiss francs and sold in Switzerland is an example of a foreign bond. Although the foreign bond market is much smaller than the Eurobond market, many issuers have found it to be an attractive way of tapping debt markets in Germany, Japan, Switzerland, and the United States.

international equity market
A market that allows corporations to sell blocks of shares to investors in a number of different countries simultaneously.

Finally, the **international equity market** allows corporations to sell blocks of shares to investors in a number of different countries simultaneously. This market enables corporations to raise far larger amounts of capital than they could raise in any single national market. International equity sales have also proven to be indispensable to governments that have sold state-owned companies to private investors during recent years.

The Role of Capital Markets

efficient market
A market that allocates funds to their most productive uses as a result of competition among wealth-maximizing investors that determines and publicizes prices that are believed to be close to their true value.

The capital market creates continuous liquid markets in which firms can obtain needed financing. It also creates **efficient markets** that allocate funds to their most productive uses. This is especially true for securities that are actively traded in broker or dealer markets, where the competition among wealth-maximizing investors determines and publicizes prices that are believed to be close to their true value. See *Focus on Practice* box on page 28 for the story of one legendary stock price, and the equally legendary man who brought it about.

The price of an individual security is determined by the demand for and supply of the security. Figure 1.5 depicts the interaction of the forces of demand (represented by line D_0) and supply (represented by line S) for a given security currently selling at an equilibrium price P_0. At that price, Q_0 shares of the stock are traded.

FIGURE 1.5

Supply and Demand
Supply and demand for a security

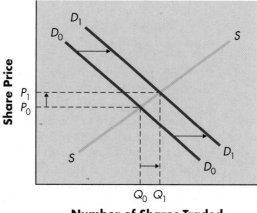

Number of Shares Traded

Focus on Practice   Berkshire Hathaway—Can Buffett Be Replaced?

In early 1980, investors could buy one share of **Berkshire Hathaway** Class A common stock (stock symbol: BRKA) for $285. That may have seemed expensive at the time, but by mid-2007 the price of just one share had climbed to $111,000. The wizard behind such phenomenal growth in shareholder value is the chairman of Berkshire Hathaway, Warren Buffett, nicknamed the Oracle of Omaha.

With his partner, Vice-Chairman Charlie Munger, Buffett runs a large conglomerate of 73 businesses with 217,000 employees and nearly $100 billion in annual revenues. He makes it look easy. In his words, "I've taken the easy route, just sitting back and working through great managers who run their own shows. My only tasks are to cheer them on, sculpt and harden our corporate culture, and make major capital-allocation decisions. Our managers have returned this trust by working hard and effectively."

Buffett's style of corporate leadership seems rather laid back, but behind that "aw-shucks" manner lies one of the best analytical minds in business. He believes in aligning managerial incentives with performance. Berkshire employs many different incentive arrangements, with their terms depending on such elements as the economic potential or capital intensity of a CEO's business. Whatever the compensation arrangement, Buffett tries to keep it both simple and fair. Buffett himself receives an annual salary of $100,000—not much in this age of super-sized CEO compensation packages. However, with nearly 31 percent ownership in Berkshire Hathaway, valued at nearly $44 billion, Buffett is doing fine financially, even after announcing recently his plans to donate $40 billion to philanthropic causes.

Berkshire's annual report is a must-read for many investors due to the popularity of Buffett's annual letter to shareholders with his homespun take on such topics as investing, corporate governance, and corporate leadership. Shareholder meetings in Omaha, Nebraska, have turned into cult-like gatherings, with thousands traveling to listen to Buffett answer questions from shareholders. One question that has been firmly answered is the question of Mr. Buffett's ability to create shareholder value.

The next question that needs to be answered is whether Berkshire Hathaway can successfully replace Buffett (age 77), Munger (age 83), and the board of directors (average age of 70). Time will tell. Given its track record, the company is likely to be successful in finding a new generation of leadership that takes action based on the best interests of employees, customers, and shareholders, as long as Warren Buffett is able to impart his special wisdom to the process.

■ *The share price of BRKA has never been split. Why might the company refuse to split its shares to make them more affordable to average investors?*

Changing evaluations of a firm's prospects cause changes in the demand for and supply of its securities and ultimately result in a new price for the securities. Suppose, for example, that the firm shown in Figure 1.5 announces a favorable discovery. Investors expect rewarding results from the discovery, so they increase their valuations of the firm's shares. The changing evaluation results in a shift in demand from D_0 to D_1. At that new level of demand, Q_1 shares will be traded, and a new, higher equilibrium price of P_1 will result. The competitive market created by the major securities exchanges provides a forum in which share prices are continuously adjusted to changing demand and supply.

REVIEW QUESTIONS

1–18 Who are the key participants in the transactions of financial institutions? Who are *net suppliers* and who are *net demanders?*

1–19 What role do *financial markets* play in our economy? What are *primary* and *secondary* markets? What relationship exists between financial institutions and financial markets?

1–20 What is the *money market?* What is the *Eurocurrency market?*

1–21 What is the *capital market?* What are the primary securities traded in it?

1–22 What are *broker markets?* What are *dealer markets?* How do they differ?

1–23 Briefly describe the international capital markets, particularly the *Eurobond market* and the *international equity market.*

1–24 What are *efficient markets?* What determines the price of an individual security in such a market?

1.5 | Business Taxes

Taxes are a fact of life, and businesses, like individuals, must pay taxes on income. The income of sole proprietorships and partnerships is taxed as the income of the individual owners; corporate income is subject to corporate taxes.

Regardless of their legal form, all businesses can earn two types of income: ordinary and capital gains. Under current law, these two types of income are treated differently in the taxation of individuals; they are not treated differently for entities subject to corporate taxes. Frequent amendments are made to the tax code.

Ordinary Income

ordinary income
Income earned through the sale of a firm's goods or services.

The **ordinary income** of a corporation is income earned through the sale of goods or services. Ordinary income in 2007 was taxed subject to the rates depicted in the corporate tax rate schedule in Table 1.4.

TABLE 1.4	**Corporate Tax Rate Schedule**		
		Tax calculation	
Range of taxable income	**Base tax**	**+**	**(Marginal rate × amount over base bracket)**
$ 0 to $ 50,000	$ 0	+	(15% × amount over $ 0)
50,000 to 75,000	7,500	+	(25 × amount over 50,000)
75,000 to 100,000	13,750	+	(34 × amount over 75,000)
100,000 to 335,000	22,250	+	(39 × amount over 100,000)
335,000 to 10,000,000	113,900	+	(34 × amount over 335,000)
10,000,000 to 15,000,000	3,400,000	+	(35 × amount over 10,000,000)
15,000,000 to 18,333,333	5,150,000	+	(38 × amount over 15,000,000)
Over 18,333,333	6,416,667	+	(35 × amount over 18,333,333)

Example

Webster Manufacturing, Inc., a small manufacturer of kitchen knives, has before-tax earnings of $250,000. The tax on these earnings can be found by using the tax rate schedule in Table 1.4:

$$\text{Total taxes due} = \$22{,}250 + [0.39 \times (\$250{,}000 - \$100{,}000)]$$
$$= \$22{,}250 + (0.39 \times \$150{,}000)$$
$$= \$22{,}250 + \$58{,}500 = \underline{\underline{\$80{,}750}}$$

From a financial point of view, it is important to understand the difference between average and marginal tax rates, the treatment of interest and dividend income, and the effects of tax deductibility.

Average versus Marginal Tax Rates

average tax rate
A firm's taxes divided by its taxable income.

The **average tax rate** paid on the firm's ordinary income can be calculated by dividing its taxes by its taxable income. For firms with taxable income of $10 million or less, the average tax rate ranges from 15 to 34 percent, reaching 34 percent when taxable income equals or exceeds $335,000. For firms with taxable income in excess of $10 million, the average tax rate ranges between 34 and 35 percent. The average tax rate paid by Webster Manufacturing, Inc., in the preceding example was 32.3 percent ($80,750 ÷ $250,000). As a corporation's taxable income increases, its average tax rate approaches and finally reaches 34 percent. It remains at that level up to $10 million of taxable income, beyond which it rises toward and reaches 35 percent at $18,333,333.

marginal tax rate
The rate at which *additional income* is taxed.

The **marginal tax rate** represents the rate at which *additional income* is taxed. In the current corporate tax structure, the marginal tax rate on income up to $50,000 is 15 percent; from $50,000 to $75,000 it is 25 percent; and so on, as shown in Table 1.4. Webster Manufacturing's marginal tax rate is currently 39 percent because its next dollar of taxable income (bringing its before-tax earnings to $250,001) would be taxed at that rate.

To simplify calculations in the text, we assume *a fixed 40 percent tax rate to be applicable to ordinary corporate income.* Given our focus on financial decision making, this rate is assumed to represent the firm's *marginal tax rate.*

Interest and Dividend Income

double taxation
Occurs when the already once-taxed earnings of a corporation are distributed as cash dividends to stockholders, who must pay taxes of up to a maximum rate of 15 percent on them.

In the process of determining taxable income, any *interest received* by the corporation is included as ordinary income. Dividends, on the other hand, are treated differently. This different treatment moderates the effect of **double taxation,** which occurs when the already once-taxed earnings of a corporation are distributed as cash dividends to stockholders, who must pay taxes of up to a maximum rate of 15 percent on them. Therefore, dividends that the firm receives on common and preferred stock held in other corporations, and representing less than 20 percent ownership in them, are subject to a 70 percent exclusion for tax purposes.[7] The dividend exclusion in effect eliminates most of the potential tax liability from the dividends received by the second and any subsequent corporations.

---

7. The exclusion is 80% if the corporation owns between 20% and 80% of the stock in the corporation paying it dividends; 100% of the dividends received are excluded if it owns more than 80% of the corporation paying it dividends. For convenience, we are assuming here that the ownership interest in the dividend-paying corporation is less than 20%.

Tax-Deductible Expenses

In calculating their taxes, corporations are allowed to deduct operating expenses, as well as interest expense. The tax deductibility of these expenses reduces their after-tax cost. The following example illustrates the benefit of tax deductibility.

Example

Two companies, Debt Co. and No-Debt Co., both expect in the coming year to have earnings before interest and taxes of $200,000. Debt Co. during the year will have to pay $30,000 in interest. No-Debt Co. has no debt and therefore will have no interest expense. Calculation of the earnings after taxes for these two firms is as follows:

	Debt Co.	No-Debt Co.
Earnings before interest and taxes	$200,000	$200,000
Less: Interest expense	30,000	0
Earnings before taxes	$170,000	$200,000
Less: Taxes (40%)	68,000	80,000
Earnings after taxes	$102,000	$120,000
Difference in earnings after taxes		$18,000

Debt Co. had $30,000 more interest expense than No-Debt Co., but Debt Co.'s earnings after taxes are only $18,000 less than those of No-Debt Co. This difference is attributable to the fact that Debt Co.'s $30,000 interest expense deduction provided a tax savings of $12,000 ($68,000 for Debt Co. versus $80,000 for No-Debt Co.). This amount can be calculated directly by multiplying the tax rate by the amount of interest expense ($0.40 \times \$30,000 = \$12,000$). Similarly, the $18,000 *after-tax cost* of the interest expense can be calculated directly by multiplying one minus the tax rate by the amount of interest expense [$(1 - 0.40) \times \$30,000 = \$18,000$].

For discussion of another corporate tax provision—a tax loss carryback—see the book's website.

The tax deductibility of certain expenses reduces their actual (after-tax) cost to the profitable firm. Note that both for accounting and tax purposes *interest is a tax-deductible expense, whereas dividends are not.* Because dividends are not tax deductible, their after-tax cost is equal to the amount of the dividend. Thus a $30,000 cash dividend has an after-tax cost of $30,000.

Capital Gains

capital gain
The amount by which the sale price of an asset exceeds the asset's initial purchase price.

If a firm sells a capital asset (such as stock held as an investment) for more than its initial purchase price, the difference between the sale price and the purchase price is called a **capital gain.** For corporations, capital gains are added to ordinary corporate income and taxed at the regular corporate rates, with a maximum marginal tax rate of 39 percent. To simplify the computations presented in the text, as for ordinary income, *a fixed 40 percent tax rate is assumed to be applicable to corporate capital gains.*

Example

Ross Company, a manufacturer of pharmaceuticals, has pretax operating earnings of $500,000 and has just sold for $150,000 an asset that was purchased 2 years ago for $125,000. Because the asset was sold for more than its initial purchase price, there is a capital gain of $25,000 ($150,000 sale price − $125,000 initial purchase price). The corporation's taxable income will total $525,000 ($500,000 ordinary income plus $25,000 capital gain). Because this total exceeds $335,000, the capital gain will be taxed at the 34% rate (see Table 1.4), resulting in a tax of $8,500 (0.34 × $25,000).

Hint If you have not done so already, look at the "To the Student" letter on p. xliii. It describes organization of this book and how you can make best use of its various features.

REVIEW QUESTIONS

1–25 Describe the tax treatment of *ordinary income* and that of *capital gains*. What is the difference between the *average tax rate* and the *marginal tax rate?*

1–26 How does the tax treatment of dividend income by the corporation moderate the effects of *double taxation?*

1–27 What benefit results from the tax deductibility of certain corporate expenses?

Summary

Focus on Value

Chapter 1 established the primary goal of the firm—**to maximize the wealth of the owners for whom the firm is being operated.** For public companies, value at any time is reflected in the stock price. Therefore, management should act only on those opportunities that are expected to create value for owners by increasing the stock price. Doing this requires management to consider the returns (magnitude and timing of cash flows), the risk of each proposed action, and their combined effect on value.

Review of Learning Goals

LG 1 Define *finance,* **its major areas and opportunities, and the legal forms of business organization.** Finance is the art and science of managing money. It affects the life of every person and of every organization. Major opportunities in financial services exist within banking and related institutions, personal financial planning, investments, real estate, and insurance. Managerial finance is concerned with the duties of the financial manager in the business firm. The recent trend toward globalization of business activity has created new demands and opportunities in managerial finance.

The legal forms of business organization are the sole proprietorship, the partnership, and the corporation. The corporation is dominant in terms of business receipts and profits, and its owners are its common and preferred stockholders. Stockholders expect to earn a return by receiving dividends or by realizing gains through increases in share price.

LG 2 **Describe the managerial finance function and its relationship to economics and accounting.** All areas of responsibility within a firm interact with finance personnel and procedures. The financial manager must understand the economic environment and relies heavily on the economic principle of marginal cost–benefit analysis to make financial decisions. Financial managers use accounting but concentrate on cash flows and decision making.

LG 3 **Identify the primary activities of the financial manager.** The primary activities of the financial manager, in addition to ongoing involvement in financial analysis and planning, are making investment decisions and making financing decisions.

LG 4 **Explain the goal of the firm, corporate governance, the role of ethics, and the agency issue.** The goal of the financial manager is to maximize the owners' wealth, as evidenced by stock price. The financial manager who is evaluating decision alternatives must assess both return and risk. The wealth-maximizing actions of financial managers should also reflect the interests of stakeholders.

The corporate governance structure is used to direct and control the corporation by defining the rights and responsibilities of the key corporate participants. Both individual and institutional investors hold the stock of most companies, but institutional investors tend to have much greater influence on corporate governance. The Sarbanes-Oxley Act of 2002 (SOX) was passed to eliminate fraudulent financial disclosure and conflict of interest problems. Positive ethical practices help a firm and its managers to achieve the firm's goal of owner wealth maximization. SOX has provided impetus toward such practices.

An agency problem results when managers, as agents for owners, place personal goals ahead of corporate goals. Market forces, in the form of shareholder activism and the threat of takeover, tend to prevent or minimize agency problems. Firms incur agency costs to maintain a corporate governance structure that monitors managers' actions and provides incentives for them to act in the best interests of owners. Stock options and performance plans are examples of such agency costs.

LG 5 **Understand financial institutions and markets, and the role they play in managerial finance.** Financial institutions serve as intermediaries by channeling into loans or investments the savings of individuals, businesses, and governments. The financial markets are forums in which suppliers and demanders of funds can transact business directly. Financial institutions actively participate in the financial markets as both suppliers and demanders of funds.

In the money market, suppliers and demanders of short-term funds trade marketable securities (short-term debt instruments). The Eurocurrency market is the international equivalent of the domestic money market.

In the capital market, investors make transactions in long-term debt (bonds) and equity (common and preferred stock). Broker markets and dealer markets provide secondary markets for securities. The broker market consists of national and regional securities exchanges, which bring together buyers and sellers. Dealer markets, which include the Nasdaq and over-the-counter (OTC) markets, have orders executed by dealers who "make markets" in given securities. The primary market is a dealer market. Important international debt and equity markets are the Eurobond market and the international equity market. The capital market creates continuous liquid markets for needed financing and allocates funds to their most productive uses.

LG 6 **Discuss business taxes and their importance in financial decisions.** Corporate income is subject to corporate taxes. Corporate tax rates apply to both ordinary income (after deduction of allowable expenses) and capital gains. The average tax rate paid by a corporation ranges from 15 to 35 percent. Corporate taxpayers can reduce their taxes through certain provisions in the tax code: dividend income exclusions and tax-deductible expenses. A capital gain occurs when an asset is sold for more than its initial purchase price; they are added to ordinary corporate income and taxed at regular corporate tax rates. (For convenience, we assume a 40 percent marginal tax rate in this book.)

Self-Test Problem (Solution in Appendix B)

 ST1–1 **Corporate taxes** Montgomery Enterprises, Inc., had operating earnings of $280,000 for the year just ended. During the year the firm sold stock that it held in another company for $180,000, which was $30,000 above its original purchase price of $150,000, paid 1 year earlier.

a. What is the amount, if any, of capital gains realized during the year?
b. How much total taxable income did the firm earn during the year?
c. Use the corporate tax rate schedule given in Table 1.4 to calculate the firm's total taxes due.
d. Calculate both the *average tax rate* and the *marginal tax rate* on the basis of your findings.

Warm-Up Exercises   A blue box (■) indicates exercises available in .

 E1–1 Ann and Jack have been partners for several years. Their firm, A & J Tax Preparation, has been very successful, as the pair agree on most business-related questions. One disagreement, however, concerns the legal form of their business. Ann has tried for the past 2 years to get Jack to agree to incorporate. She believes that there is no downside to incorporating and sees only benefits. Jack strongly disagrees; he thinks that the business should remain a partnership forever.

First, take Ann's side and explain the positive side to incorporating the business. Next, take Jack's side and state the advantages to remaining a partnership. Lastly, what information would you want if you were asked to make the decision for Ann and Jack?

 E1–2 You have been made treasurer for a day at AIMCO, Inc. AIMCO develops technology for video conferencing. A manager of the satellite division has asked you to authorize a capital expenditure in the amount of $10,000. The manager states that this expenditure is necessary to continue a long-running project designed to use satellites to allow video conferencing anywhere on the planet. The manager admits that the satellite concept has been surpassed by recent technological advances in telephony, but he feels that AIMCO should continue the project. His reasoning is based on the fact that $2.5 million has already been spent over the past 15 years on this project. Although the project has little chance to be viable, the manager believes it would be a shame to waste the money and time already spent.

Use *marginal cost–benefit analysis* to make your decision regarding whether you should authorize the $10,000 expenditure to continue the project.

 E1–3 The end-of-year parties at Yearling, Inc., are known for their extravagance. Management provides the best food and entertainment to thank the employees for their hard work. During the planning for this year's bash, a disagreement broke out between the treasurer's staff and the controller's staff. The treasurer's staff contended that the firm was running low on cash and might have trouble paying its bills over the coming months; they requested that cuts be made to the budget for the party. The controller's staff felt that any cuts were unwarranted as the firm continued to be very profitable.

Can both sides be right? Explain your answer.

 E1–4 Recently, some branches of Donut Shop, Inc., have dropped the practice of allowing employees to accept tips. Customers who once said, "Keep the change," now have to get used to waiting for their nickels. Management even instituted a policy of requiring that the change be thrown out if a customer drives off without it. As a frequent customer who gets coffee and doughnuts for the office, you notice that the lines are longer and that more mistakes are being made in your order.

Explain why tips could be viewed as similar to stock options and why the delays and incorrect orders could represent a case of *agency costs*. If tips are gone forever, how could Donut Shop reduce these agency costs?

 E1–5 Reston, Inc., has asked your corporation, Pruro, Inc., for financial assistance. As a long-time customer of Reston, your firm has decided to give that assistance. The question you are debating is whether Pruro should take Reston stock with a 5% annual dividend or a promissory note paying 5% annual interest.

Assuming payment is guaranteed and the dollar amounts for annual interest and dividend income are identical, which option will result in greater after-tax income for the first year?

Problems

A blue box (■) indicates problems available in .

 P1–1 **Liability comparisons**   Merideth Harper has invested $25,000 in Southwest Development Company. The firm has recently declared bankruptcy and has $60,000 in unpaid debts. Explain the nature of payments, if any, by Ms. Harper in each of the following situations.
  a. Southwest Development Company is a *sole proprietorship* owned by Ms. Harper.
  b. Southwest Development Company is a 50–50 *partnership* of Ms. Harper and Christopher Black.
  c. Southwest Development Company is a *corporation*.

P1–2 Marginal cost–benefit analysis and the goal of the firm   Ken Allen, capital budgeting analyst for Bally Gears, Inc., has been asked to evaluate a proposal. The manager of the automotive division believes that replacing the robotics used on the heavy truck gear line will produce total benefits of $560,000 (in today's dollars) over the next 5 years. The existing robotics would produce benefits of $400,000 (also in today's dollars) over that same time period. An initial cash investment of $220,000 would be required to install the new equipment. The manager estimates that the existing robotics can be sold for $70,000. Show how Ken will apply *marginal cost–benefit analysis* techniques to determine the following:

a. The marginal (added) benefits of the proposed new robotics.
b. The marginal (added) cost of the proposed new robotics.
c. The net benefit of the proposed new robotics.
d. What should Ken Allen recommend that the company do? Why?
e. What factors besides the costs and benefits should be considered before the final decision is made?

 P1–3 Accrual income versus cash flow for a period   Thomas Book Sales, Inc., supplies textbooks to college and university bookstores. The books are shipped with a proviso that they must be paid for within 30 days but can be returned for a full refund credit within 90 days. In 2009, Thomas shipped and billed book titles totaling $760,000. Collections, net of return credits, during the year totaled $690,000. The company spent $300,000 acquiring the books that it shipped.

a. Using accrual accounting and the preceding values, show the firm's net profit for the past year.
b. Using cash accounting and the preceding values, show the firm's net cash flow for the past year.
c. Which of these statements is more useful to the financial manager? Why?

PERSONAL FINANCE PROBLEM

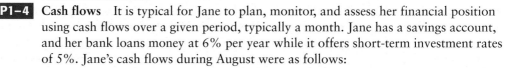 **P1–4 Cash flows**   It is typical for Jane to plan, monitor, and assess her financial position using cash flows over a given period, typically a month. Jane has a savings account, and her bank loans money at 6% per year while it offers short-term investment rates of 5%. Jane's cash flows during August were as follows:

Item	Cash inflow	Cash outflow
Clothes		$1,000
Interest received	$ 450	
Dining out		500
Groceries		800
Salary	4,500	
Auto payment		355
Utilities		280
Mortgage		1,200
Gas		222

a. Determine Jane's total cash inflows and cash outflows.
b. Determine the *net cash flow* for the month of August.
c. If there is a shortage, what are a few options open to Jane?
d. If there is a surplus, what would be a prudent strategy for her to follow?

P1–5   **Identifying agency problems, costs, and resolutions**   Explain why each of the following situations is an agency problem and what costs to the firm might result from it. Suggest how the problem might be dealt with short of firing the individual(s) involved.

a. The front desk receptionist routinely takes an extra 20 minutes of lunch to run personal errands.

b. Division managers are padding cost estimates so as to show short-term efficiency gains when the costs come in lower than the estimates.

c. The firm's chief executive officer has secret talks with a competitor about the possibility of a merger in which (s)he would become the CEO of the combined firms.

d. A branch manager lays off experienced full-time employees and staffs customer service positions with part-time or temporary workers to lower employment costs and raise this year's branch profit. The manager's bonus is based on profitability.

 P1–6   **Corporate taxes**   Tantor Supply, Inc., is a small corporation acting as the exclusive distributor of a major line of sporting goods. During 2009 the firm earned $92,500 before taxes.

a. Calculate the firm's tax liability using the corporate tax rate schedule given in Table 1.4.

b. How much are Tantor Supply's 2009 after-tax earnings?

c. What was the firm's *average tax rate*, based on your findings in part **a**?

d. What is the firm's *marginal tax rate*, based on your findings in part **a**?

 P1–7   **Average corporate tax rates**   Using the corporate tax rate schedule given in Table 1.4, perform the following:

a. Calculate the tax liability, after-tax earnings, and average tax rates for the following levels of corporate earnings before taxes: $10,000; $80,000; $300,000; $500,000; $1.5 million; $10 million; and $20 million.

b. Plot the *average tax rates* (measured on the y axis) against the pretax income levels (measured on the x axis). What generalization can be made concerning the relationship between these variables?

 P1–8   **Marginal corporate tax rates**   Using the corporate tax rate schedule given in Table 1.4, perform the following:

a. Find the marginal tax rate for the following levels of corporate earnings before taxes: $15,000; $60,000; $90,000; $200,000; $400,000; $1 million; and $20 million.

b. Plot the *marginal tax rates* (measured on the y axis) against the pretax income levels (measured on the x axis). Explain the relationship between these variables.

 P1–9   **Interest versus dividend income**   During the year just ended, Shering Distributors, Inc., had pretax earnings from operations of $490,000. In addition, during the year it received $20,000 in income from interest on bonds it held in Zig Manufacturing and received $20,000 in income from dividends on its 5% common stock holding in Tank Industries, Inc. Shering is in the 40% tax bracket and is eligible for a 70% dividend exclusion on its Tank Industries stock.

a. Calculate the firm's tax on its operating earnings only.

b. Find the tax and the after-tax amount attributable to the interest income from Zig Manufacturing bonds.

c. Find the tax and the after-tax amount attributable to the dividend income from the Tank Industries, Inc., common stock.

d. Compare, contrast, and discuss the after-tax amounts resulting from the interest income and dividend income calculated in parts **b** and **c**.

e. What is the firm's total tax liability for the year?

 P1–10 **Interest versus dividend expense**   Michaels Corporation expects earnings before interest and taxes to be $40,000 for this period. Assuming an ordinary tax rate of 40%, compute the firm's earnings after taxes and earnings available for common stockholders (earnings after taxes and preferred stock dividends, if any) under the following conditions:

a. The firm pays $10,000 in interest.

b. The firm pays $10,000 in preferred stock dividends.

 P1–11 **Capital gains taxes**   Perkins Manufacturing is considering the sale of two nondepreciable assets, X and Y. Asset X was purchased for $2,000 and will be sold today for $2,250. Asset Y was purchased for $30,000 and will be sold today for $35,000. The firm is subject to a 40% tax rate on capital gains.

a. Calculate the amount of capital gain, if any, realized on each of the assets.

b. Calculate the tax on the sale of each asset.

 P1–12 **Capital gains taxes**   The following table contains purchase and sale prices for the nondepreciable capital assets of a major corporation. The firm paid taxes of 40% on capital gains.

Asset	Purchase price	Sale price
A	$ 3,000	$ 3,400
B	12,000	12,000
C	62,000	80,000
D	41,000	45,000
E	16,500	18,000

a. Determine the amount of capital gain realized on each of the five assets.

b. Calculate the amount of tax paid on each of the assets.

 P1–13 **ETHICS PROBLEM**   What does it mean to say that managers should maximize shareholder wealth "subject to ethical constraints"? What ethical considerations might enter into decisions that result in cash flow and stock price effects that are less than they might otherwise have been?

Chapter 1 Case

Assessing the Goal of Sports Products, Inc.

Loren Seguara and Dale Johnson both work for Sports Products, Inc., a major producer of boating equipment and accessories. Loren works as a clerical assistant in the Accounting Department, and Dale works as a packager in the Shipping Department.

During their lunch break one day, they began talking about the company. Dale complained that he had always worked hard trying not to waste packing materials and efficiently and cost-effectively performing his job. In spite of his efforts and those of his co-workers in the department, the firm's stock price had declined nearly $2 per share over the past 9 months. Loren indicated that she shared Dale's frustration, particularly because the firm's profits had been rising. Neither could understand why the firm's stock price was falling as profits rose.

Loren indicated that she had seen documents describing the firm's profit-sharing plan under which all managers were partially compensated on the basis of the firm's profits. She suggested that maybe it was profit that was important to management, because it directly affected their pay. Dale said, "That doesn't make sense, because the stockholders own the firm. Shouldn't management do what's best for stockholders? Something's wrong!" Loren responded, "Well, maybe that explains why the company hasn't concerned itself with the stock price. Look, the only profits that stockholders receive are in the form of cash dividends, and this firm has never paid dividends during its 20-year history. We as stockholders therefore don't directly benefit from profits. The only way we benefit is for the stock price to rise." Dale chimed in, "That probably explains why the firm is being sued by state and federal environmental officials for dumping pollutants in the adjacent stream. Why spend money for pollution control? It increases costs, lowers profits, and therefore lowers management's earnings!"

Loren and Dale realized that the lunch break had ended and they must quickly return to work. Before leaving, they decided to meet the next day to continue their discussion.

To Do

a. What should the management of Sports Products, Inc., pursue as its overriding goal? Why?
b. Does the firm appear to have an *agency problem?* Explain.
c. Evaluate the firm's approach to pollution control. Does it seem to be *ethical?* Why might incurring the expense to control pollution be in the best interests of the firm's owners despite its negative effect on profits?
d. Does the firm appear to have an effective *corporate governance structure?* Explain any shortcomings.
e. On the basis of the information provided, what specific recommendations would you offer the firm?

Spreadsheet Exercise

Assume that Monsanto Corporation is considering the renovation and/or replacement of some of its older and outdated carpet-manufacturing equipment. Its objective is to improve the efficiency of operations in terms of both speed and reduction in the number of defects. The company's finance department has compiled pertinent data that will allow it to conduct a *marginal cost–benefit analysis* for the proposed equipment replacement.

The cash outlay for new equipment would be approximately $600,000. The net book value of the old equipment and its potential net selling price is $250,000. The total benefits from the new equipment (measured in today's dollars) would be $900,000. The benefits of the old equipment over a similar period of time (measured in today's dollars) would be $300,000.

To Do

Create a spreadsheet to conduct a *marginal cost–benefit analysis* for Monsanto Corporation and determine the following:

a. The marginal (added) benefits of the proposed new equipment.
b. The marginal (added) cost of the proposed new equipment.
c. The net benefit of the proposed new equipment.
d. What would you recommend that the firm do? Why?

Group Exercise

You may not recall it, but in kindergarten one yardstick of your development was summarized as "plays well with others." As you moved through your school years, this explicit characteristic was deleted, and you were graded based on your attainment of more concrete learning goals such as addition, spelling, and, eventually, logical thinking. Of course, playing well—getting along with others—is not a skill that disappears along with our baby teeth. Humans are social animals, and as such we spend much of our day in close proximity to other people. This is particularly true in the workplace. Most jobs include at least some component of teamwork. Working well within groups is necessary for success in most firms.

With this fact in mind, in each chapter you will be asked to complete a group assignment linked to the learning goals of each chapter. The size of the groups is flexible, although groups of 3 to 5 students are probably most appropriate. These assignments will be continuous in the sense that the groups will be establishing a firm and, in each chapter, will attempt to simulate decisions made by corporations in their normal course of financial management. The group assignments begin with this chapter, and each subsequent chapter will build on your previous work.

Your group must first form a fictitious partnership. Assume that this partnership has existed for several years and is in the process of going public. This "firm-group" will continue throughout the semester. You will also follow a real, publicly traded firm throughout the semester, which should be related in some way to your fictitious business.

To Do

a. Name your firm, describe the business it is in, and state what advantages you (as management) see in going public.
b. Discuss the necessary managerial roles of your fictitious firm, and explain the responsibilities for each within the firm. (Although individual roles could be assigned here, the *group* is responsible for all parts of all assignments.)
c. Choose a publicly traded corporation to act as a "shadow firm."
   (1) Go to www.smartmoney.com, the site run by the *Wall Street Journal*, and look up the most recent annual financial statements for your shadow firm.

(2) Find the exchange on which your firm's stock trades, and find the industry classification within which your firm operates.

(3) Check the profitability by looking solely at recent movements in *earnings per share (EPS)* and by finding the expected future earnings growth rate.

(4) Note any taxation issues that are apparent in the annual report.

Web Exercise

The World Wide Web (a part of the larger Internet) has become such a powerful force in every aspect of our society that to ignore its potential would lessen your learning experience. As a source of timely information, the Web is unrivaled. Anyone in the world now has the ability to do in-depth research into almost any topic with just a few mouse clicks. The Web exercise in each chapter of this book will continue the work done within the chapter, applying real-world and real-time data to the subjects taught therein. A relatively brief "deliverable" is attached with the assigned searches. These documents are meant to serve as verification of your time spent online. Often the exercises will build on past exercises and match closely the work done in the group exercises; this correspondence is created purposefully. The chapter, its examples and problems, and the group and Web exercises should all be seen as continuous tools whereby overlap reinforces the key elements of the material.

Go to the book's companion website at **www.prenhall.com/gitman** to find the Web Exercise for this chapter.

> Remember to check the book's website at **www.prenhall.com/gitman** to find additional resources, including Web Exercises and a Web Case.

2 Financial Statements and Analysis

WHY THIS CHAPTER MATTERS TO YOU

In Your Professional Life

Accounting: You need to understand the stockholders' report and preparation of the four key financial statements; how firms consolidate international financial statements; and how to calculate and interpret financial ratios for decision making.

Information systems: You need to understand what data are included in the firm's financial statements to design systems that will supply such data to those who prepare the statements and to those in the firm who use the data for ratio calculations.

Management: You need to understand what parties are interested in the stockholders' report and why; how the financial statements will be analyzed by those both inside and outside the firm to assess various aspects of performance; the caution that should be exercised in using financial ratio analysis; and how the financial statements affect the value of the firm.

Marketing: You need to understand the effects your decisions will have on the financial statements, particularly the income statement and the statement of cash flows, and how analysis of ratios, especially those involving sales figures, will affect the firm's decisions about levels of inventory, credit policies, and pricing decisions.

Operations: You need to understand how the costs of operations are reflected in the firm's financial statements and how analysis of ratios, particularly those involving assets, cost of goods sold, or inventory, may affect requests for new equipment or facilities.

In Your Personal Life

A routine step in personal financial planning is to prepare and analyze personal financial statements, so that you can monitor progress toward your financial goals. Also, you need to understand and analyze corporate financial statements to build and monitor your investment portfolio.

LEARNING GOALS

LG 1 Review the contents of the stockholders' report and the procedures for consolidating international financial statements.

LG 2 Understand who uses financial ratios, and how.

LG 3 Use ratios to analyze a firm's liquidity and activity.

LG 4 Discuss the relationship between debt and financial leverage and the ratios used to analyze a firm's debt.

LG 5 Use ratios to analyze a firm's profitability and its market value.

LG 6 Use a summary of financial ratios and the DuPont system of analysis to perform a complete ratio analysis.

Netflix, Inc.

The Red Tide Is Coming

You have probably seen them in the mail: Those little red envelopes with Netflix movies inside are becoming ever more prevalent. The world's largest online subscription service, **Netflix,** helps subscribers rent movies from more than 75,000 DVD titles, with no shipping fees, no due dates, and no late fees. Since Netflix was launched in 1999, its subscriber base has grown at a 7-year compound annual growth rate (CAGR) of 79 percent, and revenues have increased at a CAGR of 113 percent. With 5.66 million sub-scribers at the end of 2006, Netflix hopes to grow to 20 million subscribers within the next 5 years.

Anyone looking for reasons to be bullish on Netflix stock received good news in October 2006. Netflix rival Blockbuster said that it would stop offering a service that lets customers rent two videos per month at $5.99, the same price as a competing service from Netflix.

Netflix has had virtually zero long-term debt after its May 2002 initial public offering. Its current ratio of 2.21 indicates that it can easily pay off any short-term liabilities. Net income increased from $6.51 million in 2003 to $21.6 million in 2004, $42.03 million in 2005, and $49.09 million in 2006. During the same 3-year period, total equity grew from $112 million to $414 million. Based on this growth, Netflix was ranked 18 on *Fortune* Magazine's 100 fastest-growing companies in 2006.

One area of concern has been "churn"—a term that describes the loss of customers who are subsequently replaced by new customers. Netflix measures churn through a ratio of quarterly cancella-tions divided by the sum of beginning subscribers and gross subscriber additions. A lower churn rate indicates better customer retention. In the fourth quarter of 2006, Netflix calculated its churn at 3.6 per-cent, down from 6 percent 4 years earlier. Based on this informa-tion, investors pushed the stock nearly 30 percent higher by the end of 2006.

> What are the benefits of having no long-term debt? Are there any negatives to having no long-term debt?

In this chapter you will learn how to calculate financial ratios and how to use those ratios to analyze a company's financial statements.

2.1 | The Stockholders' Report

generally accepted accounting principles (GAAP)
The practice and procedure guidelines used to prepare and maintain financial records and reports; authorized by the *Financial Accounting Standards Board (FASB)*.

Financial Accounting Standards Board (FASB)
The accounting profession's rule-setting body, which authorizes *generally accepted accounting principles (GAAP)*.

Public Company Accounting Oversight Board (PCAOB)
A not-for-profit corporation established by the *Sarbanes-Oxley Act of 2002* to protect the interests of investors and further the public interest in the preparation of informative, fair, and independent audit reports.

Securities and Exchange Commission (SEC)
The federal regulatory body that governs the sale and listing of securities.

stockholders' report
Annual report that publicly owned corporations must provide to stockholders; it summarizes and documents the firm's financial activities during the past year.

letter to stockholders
Typically, the first element of the annual stockholders' report and the primary communication from management.

Every corporation has many and varied uses for the standardized records and reports of its financial activities. Periodically, reports must be prepared for regulators, creditors (lenders), owners, and management. The guidelines used to prepare and maintain financial records and reports are known as **generally accepted accounting principles (GAAP)**. These accounting practices and procedures are authorized by the accounting profession's rule-setting body, the **Financial Accounting Standards Board (FASB)**.

In addition, the *Sarbanes-Oxley Act of 2002*, enacted in an effort to eliminate the many disclosure and conflict of interest problems of corporations, established the **Public Company Accounting Oversight Board (PCAOB)**, a not-for-profit corporation that oversees auditors of public corporations. The PCAOB is charged with protecting the interests of investors and furthering the public interest in the preparation of informative, fair, and independent audit reports. The expectation is that it will instill confidence in investors with regard to the accuracy of the audited financial statements of public companies.

Publicly owned corporations with more than $5 million in assets and 500 or more stockholders[1] are required by the **Securities and Exchange Commission (SEC)**—the federal regulatory body that governs the sale and listing of securities—to provide their stockholders with an annual **stockholders' report**. The stockholders' report summarizes and documents the firm's financial activities during the past year. It begins with a letter to the stockholders from the firm's president and/or chairman of the board.

The Letter to Stockholders

The **letter to stockholders** is the primary communication from management. It describes the events that are considered to have had the greatest effect on the firm during the year. It also generally discusses management philosophy, corporate governance issues, strategies, and actions, as well as plans for the coming year. Links at this book's website (**www.prenhall.com/gitman**) will take you to some representative letters to stockholders.

The Four Key Financial Statements

The four key financial statements required by the SEC for reporting to shareholders are (1) the income statement, (2) the balance sheet, (3) the statement of stockholders' equity, and (4) the statement of cash flows.[2] The financial statements from the 2009 stockholders' report of Bartlett Company, a manufacturer of metal fasteners, are presented and briefly discussed. Most likely, you have

---

1. Although the Securities and Exchange Commission (SEC) does not have an official definition of *publicly owned*, these financial measures mark the cutoff point it uses to require informational reporting, regardless of whether the firm publicly sells its securities. Firms that do not meet these requirements are commonly called "closely owned" firms.

2. Whereas these statement titles are consistently used throughout this text, it is important to recognize that in practice, companies frequently use different titles. For example, General Electric uses "Statement of Earnings" rather than "Income Statement" and "Statement of Financial Position" rather than "Balance Sheet." Both Sprint Nextel and Qualcomm use "Statement of Operations" rather than "Income Statement."

Focus on Ethics   Back to School on Ethics

Academics who have toiled thanklessly in the field of business ethics now marvel at their recent popularity on campus. "It's been unbelievable," says Timothy Fort, a professor at George Washington University. "When I started teaching an ethics class in 1994, the first third of the class was spent convincing students that it was worth taking. Now the class size has quadrupled." Part of the appetite for ethics courses has grown because of a mandate from the Association to Advance Collegiate Schools of Business. In 2004, the AACSB issued a report that acknowledged the embarrassment felt throughout the business school community following the exposure of accounting frauds at **Enron, Tyco, WorldCom**, and elsewhere. The report urged business schools to do more to teach ethics in the classroom.

While the Enron and WorldCom scandals are old news, the topic of ethical corporate cultures has taken on a life of its own. If you are a student at Rutgers University, you may have taken the new course "Cooking the Books," which focuses entirely on financial fraud. If you study business at Seton Hall University (ex-Tyco CEO Dennis Kozlowski's alma mater), you may enroll in a class showing how accounting numbers can be altered by manipulation. Courses such as these may help deter future accounting fiascos. According to Professors Richard McKenzie of the University of California at Irvine and Tibor Machan of Chapman University, knowing which accounting and finance practices are proper is key to keeping companies honest, as is the personal integrity of accounting and financial managers.

One issue under debate is whether ethics should be integrated into the curriculum or covered in a dedicated ethics course. One view is that learning ethics theory requires at least one dedicated course *in addition to* the integration of ethics into traditional business courses. Doing so would allow students to apply the concepts they learn in the dedicated ethics course.

Investors were cheered by the passage in 2002 of the Sarbanes-Oxley Act (SOX), whose subtitle is the "Public Company Accounting Reform and Investor Protection Act." Included in SOX are criminal penalties for altering documents and requirements for a code of ethics for senior financial officers. Investors should likewise be cheered by the increased emphasis on ethics in our business schools. More accurate and truthful information will reduce the uncertainty of the information flow that investors use in valuing a stock.

■ *What are some innovative approaches that can be used to teach ethics at the university level?*

studied these four financial statements in an accounting course, so the purpose of looking at them here is to refresh your memory of the basics, rather than provide an exhaustive review. While you are thinking of other college courses, take a look at the nearby *Focus on Ethics* box, which discusses courses on business ethics.

Income Statement

income statement
Provides a financial summary of the firm's operating results during a specified period.

The **income statement** provides a financial summary of the firm's operating results during a specified period. Most common are income statements covering a 1-year period ending at a specified date, ordinarily December 31 of the calendar year. Many large firms, however, operate on a 12-month financial cycle, or *fiscal year*, that ends at a time other than December 31. In addition, monthly income statements are typically prepared for use by management, and quarterly statements must be made available to the stockholders of publicly owned corporations.

Table 2.1 (see page 46) presents Bartlett Company's income statements for the years ended December 31, 2009 and 2008. The 2009 statement begins with *sales*

TABLE 2.1	Bartlett Company Income Statements ($000)

	For the years ended December 31	
	2009	2008
Sales revenue	$3,074	$2,567
Less: Cost of goods sold	2,088	1,711
Gross profits	$ 986	$ 856
Less: Operating expenses		
Selling expense	$ 100	$ 108
General and administrative expenses	194	187
Lease expense[a]	35	35
Depreciation expense	239	223
Total operating expense	$ 568	$ 553
Operating profits	$ 418	$ 303
Less: Interest expense	93	91
Net profits before taxes	$ 325	$ 212
Less: Taxes (rate = 29%)[b]	94	64
Net profits after taxes	$ 231	$ 148
Less: Preferred stock dividends	10	10
Earnings available for common stockholders	$ 221	$ 138
Earnings per share (EPS)[c]	$2.90	$1.81
Dividend per share (DPS)[d]	$1.29	$0.75

[a]Lease expense is shown here as a separate item rather than being included as part of interest expense, as specified by the FASB for financial reporting purposes. The approach used here is consistent with tax reporting rather than financial reporting procedures.

[b]The 29% tax rate for 2009 results because the firm has certain special tax write-offs that do not show up directly on its income statement.

[c]Calculated by dividing the earnings available for common stockholders by the number of shares of common stock outstanding—76,262 in 2009 and 76,244 in 2008. Earnings per share in 2009: $221,000 ÷ 76,262 = $2.90; in 2008: $138,000 ÷ 76,244 = $1.81.

[d]Calculated by dividing the dollar amount of dividends paid to common stockholders by the number of shares of common stock outstanding. Dividends per share in 2009: $98,000 ÷ 76,262 = $1.29; in 2008: $57,183 ÷ 76,244 = $0.75.

Hint Some firms, such as retailers and agricultural firms, end their fiscal year at the end of their operating cycle rather than at the end of the calendar year—for example, retailers at the end of January and agricultural firms at the end of September.

revenue—the total dollar amount of sales during the period—from which the *cost of goods sold* is deducted. The resulting *gross profits* of $986,000 represent the amount remaining to satisfy operating, financial, and tax costs. Next, *operating expenses,* which include selling expense, general and administrative expense, lease expense, and depreciation expense, are deducted from gross profits.[3] The resulting *operating profits* of $418,000 represent the profits earned from producing and selling products; this amount does not consider financial and tax costs. (Operating profit is often called *earnings before interest and taxes,* or *EBIT.*) Next, the financial cost—*interest expense*—is subtracted from operating

3. Depreciation expense can be, and frequently is, included in manufacturing costs—cost of goods sold—to calculate gross profits. Depreciation is shown as an expense in this text to isolate its effect on cash flows.

profits to find *net profits* (or *earnings*) *before taxes.* After subtracting $93,000 in 2009 interest, Bartlett Company had $325,000 of net profits before taxes.

Next, taxes are calculated at the appropriate tax rates and deducted to determine *net profits* (or *earnings*) *after taxes.* Bartlett Company's net profits after taxes for 2009 were $231,000. Any preferred stock dividends must be subtracted from net profits after taxes to arrive at *earnings available for common stockholders.* This is the amount earned by the firm on behalf of the common stockholders during the period.

Dividing earnings available for common stockholders by the number of shares of common stock outstanding results in *earnings per share (EPS).* EPS represent the number of dollars earned during the period on behalf of each outstanding share of common stock. In 2009, Bartlett Company earned $221,000 for its common stockholders, which represents $2.90 for each outstanding share. The actual cash **dividend per share (DPS),** which is the dollar amount of cash distributed during the period on behalf of each outstanding share of common stock, paid in 2009 was $1.29.

dividend per share (DPS)
The dollar amount of cash distributed during the period on behalf of each outstanding share of common stock.

Personal Finance Example   Jan and Jon Smith, a mid-30s married couple with no children, prepared a personal income and expense statement, which is similar to a corporate income statement. A condensed version of their income and expense statement appears below. A more detailed version appears at the book's website.

Jan and Jon Smith Income and Expense Statement for the year ended December 31, 2009	
Income	
Salaries (incl. sales commissions)	$72,725
Interest received	195
Dividends received	120
(1) Total income	$73,040
Expenses	
Mortgage payments	$16,864
Auto loan payments	2,520
Utilities (incl. cable)	2,470
Home repairs & maintenance	1,050
Food (incl. dining out)	5,825
Car expense	2,265
Health care and insurance	1,505
Clothes, shoes, accessories	1,700
Insurance (homeowners, auto, & life)	1,380
Taxes (income, Soc. Security, prop.)	16,430
Appliance and furniture payments	1,250
Recreation and entertainment	4,630
Tuition and books for Jan	1,400
Personal care & other items	2,415
(2) Total expenses	$61,704
(3) Cash surplus (or deficit) [(1) − (2)]	$11,336

During the year, the Smiths had total income of $73,040 and total expenses of $61,704, which left them with a cash surplus of $11,336. They can use the surplus to increase their savings and investments.

Balance Sheet

balance sheet
Summary statement of the firm's financial position at a given point in time.

The **balance sheet** presents a summary statement of the firm's financial position at a given point in time. The statement balances the firm's *assets* (what it owns) against its financing, which can be either *debt* (what it owes) or *equity* (what was provided by owners). Bartlett Company's balance sheets as of December 31 of 2009 and 2008 are presented in Table 2.2. They show a variety of asset, liability (debt), and equity accounts.

current assets
Short-term assets, expected to be converted into cash within 1 year or less.

current liabilities
Short-term liabilities, expected to be paid within 1 year or less.

An important distinction is made between short-term and long-term assets and liabilities. The **current assets** and **current liabilities** are *short-term* assets and liabilities. This means that they are expected to be converted into cash (current assets) or paid (current liabilities) within 1 year or less. All other assets and liabilities, along with stockholders' equity, which is assumed to have an infinite life, are considered *long-term*, or *fixed*, because they are expected to remain on the firm's books for more than 1 year.

As is customary, the assets are listed from the most liquid—*cash*—down to the least liquid. *Marketable securities* are very liquid short-term investments, such as U.S. Treasury bills or certificates of deposit, held by the firm. Because they are highly liquid, marketable securities are viewed as a form of cash ("near cash"). *Accounts receivable* represent the total monies owed the firm by its customers on credit sales made to them. *Inventories* include raw materials, work in process (partially finished goods), and finished goods held by the firm. The entry for *gross fixed assets* is the original cost of all fixed (long-term) assets owned by the firm.[4] *Net fixed assets* represent the difference between gross fixed assets and *accumulated depreciation*—the total expense recorded for the depreciation of fixed assets. (The net value of fixed assets is called their *book value*.)

Hint Another interpretation of the balance sheet is that on one side are the assets that have been purchased to be used to increase the profit of the firm. The other side indicates how these assets were acquired, either by borrowing or by investing the owners' money.

Like assets, the liabilities and equity accounts are listed from short-term to long-term. Current liabilities include *accounts payable,* amounts owed for credit purchases by the firm; *notes payable,* outstanding short-term loans, typically from commercial banks; and *accruals,* amounts owed for services for which a bill may not or will not be received. (Examples of accruals include taxes due the government and wages due employees.) **Long-term debt** represents debt for which payment is not due in the current year. *Stockholders' equity* represents the owners' claims on the firm. The *preferred stock* entry shows the historical proceeds from the sale of preferred stock ($200,000 for Bartlett Company).

long-term debt
Debts for which payment is not due in the current year.

paid-in capital in excess of par
The amount of proceeds in excess of the par value received from the original sale of common stock.

Next, the amount paid by the original purchasers of common stock is shown by two entries: common stock and paid-in capital in excess of par on common stock. The *common stock* entry is the *par value* of common stock. **Paid-in capital in excess of par** represents the amount of proceeds in excess of the par value received from the original sale of common stock. The sum of the common stock and paid-in capital accounts divided by the number of shares outstanding represents the original price per share received by the firm on a single issue of common

---

4. For convenience the term *fixed assets* is used throughout this text to refer to what, in a strict accounting sense, is captioned "property, plant, and equipment." This simplification of terminology permits certain financial concepts to be more easily developed.

Hint The key components of the balance sheet can be shown as:

Current assets	Current liabilities
	Long-term debt
Fixed assets	Stockholders' equity

or

Total assets	=	Total liabilities and stockholders' equity

TABLE 2.2	**Bartlett Company Balance Sheets ($000)**

	December 31	
Assets	2009	2008
Current assets		
Cash	$ 363	$ 288
Marketable securities	68	51
Accounts receivable	503	365
Inventories	289	300
Total current assets	$1,223	$1,004
Gross fixed assets (at cost)[a]		
Land and buildings	$2,072	$1,903
Machinery and equipment	1,866	1,693
Furniture and fixtures	358	316
Vehicles	275	314
Other (includes financial leases)	98	96
Total gross fixed assets (at cost)	$4,669	$4,322
Less: Accumulated depreciation	2,295	2,056
Net fixed assets	$2,374	$2,266
Total assets	$3,597	$3,270

Liabilities and Stockholders' Equity		
Current liabilities		
Accounts payable	$ 382	$ 270
Notes payable	79	99
Accruals	159	114
Total current liabilities	$ 620	$ 483
Long-term debt (includes financial leases)[b]	$1,023	$ 967
Total liabilities	$1,643	$1,450
Stockholders' equity		
Preferred stock—cumulative 5%, $100 par, 2,000 shares authorized and issued[c]	$ 200	$ 200
Common stock—$2.50 par, 100,000 shares authorized, shares issued and outstanding in 2009: 76,262; in 2008: 76,244	191	190
Paid-in capital in excess of par on common stock	428	418
Retained earnings	1,135	1,012
Total stockholders' equity	$1,954	$1,820
Total liabilities and stockholders' equity	$3,597	$3,270

[a]In 2009, the firm has a 6-year financial lease requiring annual beginning-of-year payments of $35,000. Four years of the lease have yet to run.

[b]Annual principal repayments on a portion of the firm's total outstanding debt amount to $71,000.

[c]The annual preferred stock dividend would be $5 per share (5% × $100 par), or a total of $10,000 annually ($5 per share × 2,000 shares).

stock. Bartlett Company therefore received about $8.12 per share [($191,000 par + $428,000 paid-in capital in excess of par) ÷ 76,262 shares] from the sale of its common stock.

retained earnings
The cumulative total of all earnings, net of dividends, that have been retained and reinvested in the firm since its inception.

Finally, **retained earnings** represent the cumulative total of all earnings, net of dividends, that have been retained and reinvested in the firm since its inception. It is important to recognize that retained earnings *are not cash* but rather have been utilized to finance the firm's assets.

Bartlett Company's balance sheets in Table 2.2 show that the firm's total assets increased from $3,270,000 in 2008 to $3,597,000 in 2009. The $327,000 increase was due primarily to the $219,000 increase in current assets. The asset increase, in turn, appears to have been financed primarily by an increase of $193,000 in total liabilities. Better insight into these changes can be derived from the statement of cash flows, which we will discuss shortly.

Personal Finance Example   The following personal balance sheet for Jan and Jon Smith—the couple introduced earlier, who are married, in their mid-30s, and have no children—is similar to a corporate balance sheet. Again, a more detailed version appears at the book's website.

WWW

Jan and Jon Smith
Balance Sheet
December 31, 2009

Assets		Liabilities and Net Worth	
Cash on hand	$ 90	Credit card balances	$ 665
Checking accounts	575	Utility bills	120
Savings accounts	760	Medical bills	75
Money market funds	800	Other current liab.	45
Total liquid assets	$ 2,225	Total cur. liab.	$ 905
Stocks & bonds	$ 2,250	Real estate mortg.	$ 92,000
Mutual funds	1,500	Auto loans	4,250
Retirement funds, IRA	2,000	Education loan	3,800
Total investments	$ 5,750	Personal loan	4,000
Real estate	$120,000	Furniture loan	800
Cars	14,000	Tot. L-T liab.	$104,850
Household furnishings	3,700	Tot. liab.	$105,755
Jewelry & artwork	1,500	Net worth (N/W)	$ 41,420
Total personal prop.	$139,200	Tot. liab.	
Total assets	$147,175	& N/W	$147,175

The Smiths have total assets of $147,175 and total liabilities of $105,755. Personal net worth (N/W) is a "plug figure"—the difference between total assets and total liabilities—which in the case of Jan and Jon Smith is $41,420.

TABLE 2.3	Bartlett Company Statement of Retained Earnings ($000) for the Year Ended December 31, 2009	
Retained earnings balance (January 1, 2009)		$1,012
Plus: Net profits after taxes (for 2009)		231
Less: Cash dividends (paid during 2009)		
Preferred stock	$10	
Common stock	98	
Total dividends paid		108
Retained earnings balance (December 31, 2009)		$1,135

Statement of Retained Earnings

statement of stockholders' equity
Shows all equity account transactions that occurred during a given year.

statement of retained earnings
Reconciles the net income earned during a given year, and any cash dividends paid, with the change in retained earnings between the start and the end of that year. An abbreviated form of the *statement of stockholders' equity.*

The *statement of retained earnings* is an abbreviated form of the statement of stockholders' equity. Unlike the **statement of stockholders' equity,** which shows all equity account transactions that occurred during a given year, the **statement of retained earnings** reconciles the net income earned during a given year, and any cash dividends paid, with the change in retained earnings between the start and the end of that year. Table 2.3 presents this statement for Bartlett Company for the year ended December 31, 2009. The statement shows that the company began the year with $1,012,000 in retained earnings and had net profits after taxes of $231,000, from which it paid a total of $108,000 in dividends, resulting in year-end retained earnings of $1,135,000. Thus the net increase for Bartlett Company was $123,000 ($231,000 net profits after taxes minus $108,000 in dividends) during 2009.

Statement of Cash Flows

statement of cash flows
Provides a summary of the firm's operating, investment, and financing cash flows and reconciles them with changes in its cash and marketable securities during the period.

The **statement of cash flows** is a summary of the cash flows over the period of concern. The statement provides insight into the firm's operating, investment, and financing cash flows and reconciles them with changes in its cash and marketable securities during the period. Bartlett Company's statement of cash flows for the year ended December 31, 2009, is presented in Table 2.4 (see page 52). Further insight into this statement is included in the discussion of cash flow in Chapter 3.

Notes to the Financial Statements

notes to the financial statements
Explanatory notes keyed to relevant accounts in the statements; they provide detailed information on the accounting policies, procedures, calculations, and transactions underlying entries in the financial statements.

Included with published financial statements are explanatory notes keyed to the relevant accounts in the statements. These **notes to the financial statements** provide detailed information on the accounting policies, procedures, calculations, and transactions underlying entries in the financial statements. Common issues addressed by these notes include revenue recognition, income taxes, breakdowns of fixed asset accounts, debt and lease terms, and contingencies. Since passage of Sarbanes-Oxley, notes to the financial statements have also included some details about compliance with that law. The *Focus on Practice* box on page 53 discusses issues relating to SOX compliance. Professional securities analysts use the data in the statements and notes to develop estimates of the value of securities that the firm issues, and these estimates influence the actions of investors and therefore the firm's share value.

TABLE 2.4	Bartlett Company Statement of Cash Flows ($000) for the Year Ended December 31, 2009	
Cash Flow from Operating Activities		
Net profits after taxes	$231	
Depreciation	239	
Increase in accounts receivable	(138)[a]	
Decrease in inventories	11	
Increase in accounts payable	112	
Increase in accruals	45	
Cash provided by operating activities		$500
Cash Flow from Investment Activities		
Increase in gross fixed assets	($347)	
Change in equity investments in other firms	0	
Cash provided by investment activities		(347)
Cash Flow from Financing Activities		
Decrease in notes payable	($ 20)	
Increase in long-term debts	56	
Changes in stockholders' equity[b]	11	
Dividends paid	(108)	
Cash provided by financing activities		(61)
Net increase in cash and marketable securities		$ 92

[a]As is customary, parentheses are used to denote a negative number, which in this case is a cash outflow.

[b]Retained earnings are excluded here, because their change is actually reflected in the combination of the "net profits after taxes" and "dividends paid" entries.

Financial Accounting Standards Board (FASB) Standard No. 52
Mandates that U.S.-based companies translate their foreign-currency-denominated assets and liabilities into dollars, for consolidation with the parent company's financial statements. This is done by using the *current rate (translation) method.*

current rate (translation) method
Technique used by U.S.-based companies to translate their foreign-currency-denominated assets and liabilities into dollars, for consolidation with the parent company's financial statements, using the year-end (current) exchange rate.

Consolidating International Financial Statements

So far, we've discussed financial statements involving only one currency, the U.S. dollar. The issue of how to consolidate a company's foreign and domestic financial statements has bedeviled the accounting profession for many years. The current policy is described in **Financial Accounting Standards Board (FASB) Standard No. 52,** which mandates that U.S.-based companies translate their foreign-currency-denominated assets and liabilities into dollars, for consolidation with the parent company's financial statements. This is done by using a technique called the **current rate (translation) method,** under which all of a U.S. parent company's foreign-currency-denominated assets and liabilities are converted into dollar values using the exchange rate prevailing at the fiscal year ending date (the current rate). Income statement items are treated similarly. Equity accounts, on the other hand, are translated into dollars by using the exchange rate that prevailed when the parent's equity investment was made (the historical rate). Retained earnings are adjusted to reflect each year's operating profits or losses. For an example that demonstrates consolidation of international financial statements, go to the book's website.

Focus on Practice   Is It Time to Change SOX?

IN PRACTICE

In 2000 and 2001, accounting irregularities at a number of large corporations forced Congress to take action, passing the Sarbanes-Oxley Act of 2002 (SOX). However, not everyone is pleased with the law. Many companies complain that compliance with the Sarbanes-Oxley corporate reporting regulations require them to spend much time and money. Large corporations, for example, spent an average of $3.8 million in 2005 to comply with the law. The most onerous aspect of SOX appears to be Section 404, which requires companies to first review their own systems for ensuring accurate financial reports and then have them tested by outside auditors.

Several high-ranking government officials have weighed in on the debate. In a speech to the Economic Club in November 2006, U.S. Treasury Secretary Henry Paulson acknowledged the impact of the accounting provi-

sions, especially on small businesses. Rather than passing a new law to amend the act, he said, Section 404 should be implemented in a more efficient and cost-effective manner. Also, Securities and Exchange Commission (SEC) Chairman Christopher Cox wrote a letter to the Public Company Accounting Oversight Board (the auditing industry's overseer) urging that the rule be adapted to companies based on company size.

Supporters of SOX claim that the law and related reforms have produced more reliable corporate financial statements, which investors rely on when deciding whether to buy or sell shares. According to Duncan W. Richardson, chief equity investment officer at Eaton Vance Management and overseer of $80 billion in stock holdings, even the act's much-disparaged requirements for testing internal financial controls could drive gains in corporate productivity

and profits. Thompson Financial's Earnings Purity Index, which tracks earnings adjusted for unusual charges and write-offs—techniques used to make earnings look better—reports that improvements have been shown in each of the past 4 years.

The jury is still out on whether Sarbanes-Oxley will be changed to alleviate the burden on U.S. corporations. However, consider this: On the day SOX was signed into law, the market value of the Wilshire 5000, a proxy for all public companies in the United States, stood at $10.5 trillion. By April 2007, the value of the Wilshire 5000 was $14.5 trillion. While the markets factor in many events, the passage of SOX has not had a significantly negative impact, as some might argue.

■ *In addition to investors, who else might be benefiting directly from the implementation of the Sarbanes-Oxley Act?*

REVIEW QUESTIONS

2–1   What roles do GAAP, the FASB, and the PCAOB play in the financial reporting activities of public companies?

2–2   Describe the purpose of each of the four major financial statements.

2–3   Why are the notes to the financial statements important to professional securities analysts?

2–4   How is the *current rate (translation) method* used to consolidate a firm's foreign and domestic financial statements?

2.2 | Using Financial Ratios

The information contained in the four basic financial statements is of major significance to a variety of interested parties who regularly need to have relative measures of the company's performance. *Relative* is the key word here, because

ratio analysis
Involves methods of calculating and interpreting financial ratios to analyze and monitor the firm's performance.

the analysis of financial statements is based on the use of *ratios* or *relative values*. **Ratio analysis** involves methods of calculating and interpreting financial ratios to analyze and monitor the firm's performance. The basic inputs to ratio analysis are the firm's income statement and balance sheet.

Interested Parties

Hint Management should be the most interested party of this group. Managers not only have to worry about the financial situation of the firm, but they are also critically interested in what the other parties think about the firm.

Ratio analysis of a firm's financial statements is of interest to shareholders, creditors, and the firm's own management. Both current and prospective shareholders are interested in the firm's current and future level of risk and return, which directly affect share price. The firm's creditors are interested primarily in the short-term liquidity of the company and its ability to make interest and principal payments. A secondary concern of creditors is the firm's profitability; they want assurance that the business is healthy. Management, like stockholders, is concerned with all aspects of the firm's financial situation, and it attempts to produce financial ratios that will be considered favorable by both owners and creditors. In addition, management uses ratios to monitor the firm's performance from period to period.

Types of Ratio Comparisons

Ratio analysis is not merely the calculation of a given ratio. More important is the *interpretation* of the ratio value. A meaningful basis for comparison is needed to answer such questions as "Is it too high or too low?" and "Is it good or bad?" Two types of ratio comparisons can be made: cross-sectional and time-series.

Cross-Sectional Analysis

cross-sectional analysis
Comparison of different firms' financial ratios at the same point in time; involves comparing the firm's ratios to those of other firms in its industry or to industry averages.

benchmarking
A type of *cross-sectional analysis* in which the firm's ratio values are compared to those of a key competitor or group of competitors that it wishes to emulate.

Cross-sectional analysis involves the comparison of different firms' financial ratios at the same point in time. Analysts are often interested in how well a firm has performed in relation to other firms in its industry. Frequently, a firm will compare its ratio values to those of a key competitor or group of competitors that it wishes to emulate. This type of cross-sectional analysis, called **benchmarking**, has become very popular.

Comparison to industry averages is also popular. These figures can be found in the *Almanac of Business and Industrial Financial Ratios, Dun & Bradstreet's Industry Norms and Key Business Ratios, RMA Annual Statement Studies, Value Line,* and industry sources.[5] A sample from one available source of industry averages is given in Table 2.5.

Hint Industry averages are not particularly useful for analyzing firms with multiproduct lines. In the case of multiproduct firms, it is difficult to select the appropriate benchmark industry.

Many people mistakenly believe that as long as the firm being analyzed has a value "better than" the industry average, it can be viewed favorably. However, this "better than average" viewpoint can be misleading. Quite often a ratio value that is far better than the norm can indicate problems that, on more careful analysis, may be more severe than had the ratio been worse than the industry average. It is therefore important to investigate significant deviations *to either side* of the industry standard.

---

5. Cross-sectional comparisons of firms operating in several lines of business are difficult to perform. Weighted-average industry average ratios based on the firm's product-line mix can be used or, if data are available, analysis of the firm on a product-line basis can be performed to evaluate a multiproduct firm.

TABLE 2.5	Industry Average Ratios for Selected Lines of Business[a]								
Line of business (number of concerns reporting)[b]	Current ratio (X)	Quick ratio (X)	Sales to inventory (X)	Collection period (days)	Total assets to sales (%)	Total liabilities to net worth (%)	Return on sales (%)	Return on total assets (%)	Return on net worth (%)
Department	4.9	1.4	6.6	1.8	32.0	25.1	2.8	6.8	16.2
stores	2.6	0.6	4.6	6.1	43.8	76.6	1.0	2.3	4.5
(143)	1.6	0.2	3.5	21.2	64.9	176.9	0.1	0.1	0.2
Electronic	2.3	1.5	31.6	27.4	24.6	54.3	3.4	7.3	20.6
computers	1.6	0.9	11.3	40.9	58.9	114.3	0.5	1.3	4.6
(76)	1.2	0.7	6.8	68.5	104.1	238.3	(9.7)	(10.4)	(20.6)
Grocery	2.6	1.0	29.6	1.1	15.3	48.5	2.2	9.4	24.8
stores	1.6	0.5	19.6	2.9	21.3	105.2	1.0	4.4	10.0
(455)	1.1	0.2	13.9	6.9	31.2	277.3	0.3	1.4	3.5
Motor	2.9	1.1	11.4	16.1	27.8	56.4	4.2	10.3	26.9
vehicles	1.7	0.7	8.3	24.1	37.4	150.8	1.5	4.1	9.6
(42)	1.2	0.5	5.5	40.5	47.3	357.2	0.2	0.8	1.2

[a]These values are given for each ratio for each line of business. The center value is the median, and the values immediately above and below it are the upper and lower quartiles, respectively.

[b]Standard Industrial Classification (SIC) codes for the lines of business shown are, respectively: SIC #5311, SIC #3571, SIC #5411, SIC #3711.

Source: "Industry Norms and Key Business Ratios," Dun & Bradstreet, Inc. Reprinted with permission.

Example

In early 2010, Mary Boyle, the chief financial analyst at Caldwell Manufacturing, a producer of heat exchangers, gathered data on the firm's financial performance during 2009, the year just ended. She calculated a variety of ratios and obtained industry averages. She was especially interested in inventory turnover, which reflects the speed with which the firm moves its inventory from raw materials through production into finished goods and to the customer as a completed sale. Generally, higher values of this ratio are preferred, because they indicate a quicker turnover of inventory. Caldwell Manufacturing's calculated inventory turnover for 2009 and the industry average inventory turnover were as follows:

	Inventory turnover, 2009
Caldwell Manufacturing	14.8
Industry average	9.7

Mary's initial reaction to these data was that the firm had managed its inventory significantly *better than* the average firm in the industry. The turnover was nearly 53% faster than the industry average. Upon reflection, however, she realized that a very high inventory turnover could also mean very low levels of inventory. The consequence of low inventory could be excessive stockouts (insufficient inventory). Discussions with people in the manufacturing and marketing departments did, in fact, uncover such a problem: Inventories during the year were extremely low, the result of numerous production delays that hindered the firm's ability to meet demand and resulted in lost sales. A ratio that initially appeared to reflect extremely efficient inventory management was actually the symptom of a major problem.

Time-Series Analysis

time-series analysis
Evaluation of the firm's financial performance over time using financial ratio analysis.

Time-series analysis evaluates performance over time. Comparison of current to past performance, using ratios, enables analysts to assess the firm's progress. Developing trends can be seen by using multiyear comparisons. Any significant year-to-year changes may be symptomatic of a major problem.

Combined Analysis

The most informative approach to ratio analysis combines cross-sectional and time-series analyses. A combined view makes it possible to assess the trend in the behavior of the ratio in relation to the trend for the industry. Figure 2.1 depicts this type of approach using the average collection period ratio of Bartlett Company, over the years 2006–2009. This ratio reflects the average amount of time (in days) it takes the firm to collect bills, and lower values of this ratio generally are preferred. The figure quickly discloses that (1) Bartlett's effectiveness in collecting its receivables is poor in comparison to the industry, and (2) Bartlett's trend is toward longer collection periods. Clearly, Bartlett needs to shorten its collection period.

Cautions about Using Ratio Analysis

Before discussing specific ratios, we should consider the following cautions about their use:

1. Ratios that reveal large deviations from the norm merely indicate *symptoms* of a problem. Additional analysis is typically needed to isolate the *causes* of the problem.

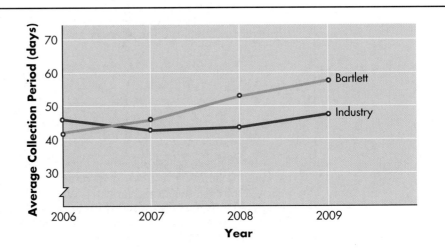

FIGURE 2.1

Combined Analysis
Combined cross-sectional and time-series view of Bartlett Company's average collection period, 2006–2009

2. A single ratio does not generally provide sufficient information from which to judge the *overall* performance of the firm. However, if an analysis is concerned only with certain *specific* aspects of a firm's financial position, one or two ratios may suffice.

3. The ratios being compared should be calculated using financial statements dated at the same point in time during the year. If they are not, the effects of *seasonality* may produce erroneous conclusions and decisions.

4. It is preferable to use *audited financial statements* for ratio analysis. If they have not been audited, the data in them may not reflect the firm's true financial condition.

5. The financial data being compared should have been developed in the same way. The use of differing accounting treatments—especially relative to inventory and depreciation—can distort the results of ratio comparisons, regardless of whether cross-sectional or time-series analysis is used.

6. Results can be distorted by *inflation,* which can cause the book values of inventory and depreciable assets to differ greatly from their replacement values. Additionally, inventory costs and depreciation write-offs can differ from their true values, thereby distorting profits. Without adjustment, inflation tends to cause older firms (older assets) to appear more efficient and profitable than newer firms (newer assets). Clearly, in using ratios, you must be careful when comparing older to newer firms or a firm to itself over a long period of time.

Categories of Financial Ratios

Financial ratios can be divided for convenience into five basic categories: liquidity, activity, debt, profitability, and market ratios. Liquidity, activity, and debt ratios primarily measure risk. Profitability ratios measure return. Market ratios capture both risk and return.

As a rule, the inputs necessary for an effective financial analysis include, at a minimum, the income statement and the balance sheet. We will use the 2009 and 2008 income statements and balance sheets for Bartlett Company, presented earlier in Tables 2.1 and 2.2, to demonstrate ratio calculations. Note, however, that the ratios presented in the remainder of this chapter can be applied to almost any company. Of course, many companies in different industries use ratios that focus on aspects peculiar to their industry.

REVIEW QUESTIONS

2–5   With regard to financial ratio analysis, how do the viewpoints held by the firm's present and prospective shareholders, creditors, and management differ?

2–6   What is the difference between *cross-sectional* and *time-series* ratio analysis? What is *benchmarking?*

2–7   What types of deviations from the norm should the analyst pay primary attention to when performing cross-sectional ratio analysis? Why?

2–8   Why is it preferable to compare ratios calculated using financial statements that are dated at the same point in time during the year?

2.3 | Liquidity Ratios

liquidity
A firm's ability to satisfy its short-term obligations *as they come due.*

The **liquidity** of a firm is measured by its ability to satisfy its short-term obligations *as they come due.* Liquidity refers to the solvency of the firm's *overall* financial position—the ease with which it can pay its bills. Because a common precursor to financial distress and bankruptcy is low or declining liquidity, these ratios can provide early signs of cash flow problems and impending business failure. The two basic measures of liquidity are the current ratio and the quick (acid-test) ratio.

Current Ratio

current ratio
A measure of liquidity calculated by dividing the firm's current assets by its current liabilities.

The **current ratio,** one of the most commonly cited financial ratios, measures the firm's ability to meet its short-term obligations. It is expressed as follows:

$$\text{Current ratio} = \frac{\text{Current assets}}{\text{Current liabilities}}$$

The current ratio for Bartlett Company in 2009 is

$$\frac{\$1,223,000}{\$620,000} = 1.97$$

Generally, the higher the current ratio, the more liquid the firm is considered to be. A current ratio of 2.0 is occasionally cited as acceptable, but a value's acceptability depends on the industry in which the firm operates. For example, a current ratio of 1.0 would be considered acceptable for a public utility but might be unacceptable for a manufacturing firm. The more predictable a firm's cash flows, the lower the acceptable current ratio. Because Bartlett Company is in a business with a relatively predictable annual cash flow, its current ratio of 1.97 should be quite acceptable.

Personal Finance Example   Individuals, like corporations, can use financial ratios to analyze and monitor their performance. Typically personal finance ratios are calculated using the personal income and expense statement and personal balance sheet for the period of concern. Here we use these statements, presented in the preceding personal finance examples, to demonstrate calculation of Jan and Jon Smith's liquidity ratio for calendar year 2009.

The personal *liquidity ratio* is calculated by dividing total liquid assets by total current debt. It indicates the percent of annual debt obligations that an individual can meet using current liquid assets. The Smiths' total liquid assets were $2,225. Their total current debts are $21,539 (total current liabilities of $905 + mortgage payments of $16,864 + auto loan payments of $2,520 + appliance and furniture payments of $1,250). Substituting these values into the ratio formula, we get:

$$\text{Liquidity ratio} = \frac{\text{Total liquid assets}}{\text{Total current debts}} = \frac{\$2,225}{\$21,539} = 0.1033, \text{ or } 10.3\%$$

That ratio indicates that the Smiths can cover only about 10 percent of their existing 1-year debt obligations with their current liquid assets. Clearly, the Smiths plan to meet these debt obligations from their income, but this ratio suggests that their liquid funds do not provide a large cushion. One of their goals should probably be to build up a larger fund of liquid assets to meet unexpected expenses.

Quick (Acid-Test) Ratio

quick (acid-test) ratio
A measure of liquidity calculated by dividing the firm's current assets minus inventory by its current liabilities.

The **quick (acid-test) ratio** is similar to the current ratio except that it excludes inventory, which is generally the least liquid current asset. The generally low liquidity of inventory results from two primary factors: (1) many types of inventory cannot be easily sold because they are partially completed items, special-purpose items, and the like; and (2) inventory is typically sold on credit, which means that it becomes an account receivable before being converted into cash. The quick ratio is calculated as follows:[6]

$$\text{Quick ratio} = \frac{\text{Current assets} - \text{Inventory}}{\text{Current liabilities}}$$

The quick ratio for Bartlett Company in 2009 is

$$\frac{\$1,223,000 - \$289,000}{\$620,000} = \frac{\$934,000}{\$620,000} = 1.51$$

A quick ratio of 1.0 or greater is occasionally recommended, but as with the current ratio, what value is acceptable depends largely on the industry. The quick ratio provides a better measure of overall liquidity only when a firm's inventory cannot be easily converted into cash. If inventory is liquid, the current ratio is a preferred measure of overall liquidity.

REVIEW QUESTION

2–9 Under what circumstances would the current ratio be the preferred measure of overall firm liquidity? Under what circumstances would the quick ratio be preferred?

2.4 | Activity Ratios

activity ratios
Measure the speed with which various accounts are converted into sales or cash—inflows or outflows.

Activity ratios measure the speed with which various accounts are converted into sales or cash—inflows or outflows. With regard to current accounts, measures of liquidity are generally inadequate because differences in the *composition* of a firm's current assets and current liabilities can significantly affect its "true" liquidity. It is therefore important to look beyond measures of overall liquidity and to assess the activity (liquidity) of specific current accounts. A number of

---

6. Sometimes the quick ratio is defined as (cash + marketable securities + accounts receivable) ÷ current liabilities. If a firm were to show as current assets items other than cash, marketable securities, accounts receivable, and inventories, its quick ratio might vary, depending on the method of calculation.

ratios are available for measuring the activity of the most important current accounts, which include inventory, accounts receivable, and accounts payable.[7] The efficiency with which total assets are used can also be assessed.

Inventory Turnover

inventory turnover
Measures the activity, or liquidity, of a firm's inventory.

Inventory turnover commonly measures the activity, or liquidity, of a firm's inventory. It is calculated as follows:

$$\text{Inventory turnover} = \frac{\text{Cost of goods sold}}{\text{Inventory}}$$

Applying this relationship to Bartlett Company in 2009 yields

$$\text{Inventory turnover} = \frac{\$2,088,000}{\$289,000} = 7.2$$

The resulting turnover is meaningful only when it is compared with that of other firms in the same industry or to the firm's past inventory turnover. An inventory turnover of 20.0 would not be unusual for a grocery store, whereas a common inventory turnover for an aircraft manufacturer is 4.0.

average age of inventory
Average number of days' sales in inventory.

Inventory turnover can be easily converted into an **average age of inventory** by dividing it into 365—the assumed number of days in a year.[8] For Bartlett Company, the average age of inventory in 2009 is 50.7 days ($365 \div 7.2$). This value can also be viewed as the average number of days' sales in inventory.

Average Collection Period

average collection period
The average amount of time needed to collect accounts receivable.

The **average collection period,** or average age of accounts receivable, is useful in evaluating credit and collection policies.[9] It is arrived at by dividing the average daily sales[10] into the accounts receivable balance:

$$\text{Average collection period} = \frac{\text{Accounts receivable}}{\text{Average sales per day}}$$
$$= \frac{\text{Accounts receivable}}{\frac{\text{Annual sales}}{365}}$$

7. For convenience, the activity ratios involving these current accounts assume that their end-of-period values are good approximations of the average account balance during the period—typically 1 year. Technically, when the month-end balances of inventory, accounts receivable, or accounts payable vary during the year, the average balance, calculated by summing the 12 month-end account balances and dividing the total by 12, should be used instead of the year-end value. If month-end balances are unavailable, the average can be approximated by dividing the sum of the beginning-of-year and end-of-year balances by 2. These approaches ensure a ratio that on the average better reflects the firm's circumstances. Because the data needed to find averages are generally unavailable to the external analyst, year-end values are frequently used to calculate activity ratios for current accounts.

8. Unless otherwise specified, a 365-day year is used throughout this textbook. This assumption makes the calculations more realistic than would use of a 360-day year consisting of twelve 30-day months.

9. The average collection period is sometimes called the *days' sales outstanding (DSO)*. A discussion of the evaluation and establishment of credit and collection policies is presented in Chapter 14.

10. The formula as presented assumes, for simplicity, that all sales are made on a credit basis. If this is not the case, *average credit sales per day* should be substituted for average sales per day.

The average collection period for Bartlett Company in 2009 is

$$\frac{\$503,000}{\frac{\$3,074,000}{365}} = \frac{\$503,000}{\$8,422} = 59.7 \text{ days}$$

On the average, it takes the firm 59.7 days to collect an account receivable.

The average collection period is meaningful only in relation to the firm's credit terms. If Bartlett Company extends 30-day credit terms to customers, an average collection period of 59.7 days may indicate a poorly managed credit or collection department, or both. It is also possible that the lengthened collection period resulted from an intentional relaxation of credit-term enforcement in response to competitive pressures. If the firm had extended 60-day credit terms, the 59.7-day average collection period would be quite acceptable. Clearly, additional information is needed to evaluate the effectiveness of the firm's credit and collection policies.

Average Payment Period

average payment period
The average amount of time needed to pay accounts payable.

The **average payment period,** or average age of accounts payable, is calculated in the same manner as the average collection period:

$$\text{Average payment period} = \frac{\text{Accounts payable}}{\text{Average purchases per day}}$$
$$= \frac{\text{Accounts payable}}{\frac{\text{Annual purchases}}{365}}$$

The difficulty in calculating this ratio stems from the need to find annual purchases,[11] a value not available in published financial statements. Ordinarily, purchases are estimated as a given percentage of cost of goods sold. If we assume that Bartlett Company's purchases equaled 70 percent of its cost of goods sold in 2009, its average payment period is

$$\frac{\$382,000}{\frac{0.70 \times \$2,088,000}{365}} = \frac{\$382,000}{\$4,004} = 95.4 \text{ days}$$

This figure is meaningful only in relation to the average credit terms extended to the firm. If Bartlett Company's suppliers have extended, on average, 30-day credit terms, an analyst would give Bartlett a low credit rating. Prospective lenders and suppliers of trade credit are most interested in the average payment period because it provides insight into the firm's bill-paying patterns.

---

11. Technically, annual *credit* purchases—rather than annual purchases—should be used in calculating this ratio. For simplicity, this refinement is ignored here.

Total Asset Turnover

total asset turnover
Indicates the efficiency with which the firm uses its assets to generate sales.

The **total asset turnover** indicates the efficiency with which the firm uses its assets to generate sales. Total asset turnover is calculated as follows:

$$\text{Total asset turnover} = \frac{\text{Sales}}{\text{Total assets}}$$

The value of Bartlett Company's total asset turnover in 2009 is

$$\frac{\$3,074,000}{\$3,597,000} = 0.85$$

Hint The higher the cost of the new assets, the larger the denominator and thus the smaller the ratio. Therefore, because of inflation and the use of historical costs, firms with newer assets will tend to have lower turnovers than those with older assets.

This means the company turns over its assets 0.85 times per year.

Generally, the higher a firm's total asset turnover, the more efficiently its assets have been used. This measure is probably of greatest interest to management, because it indicates whether the firm's operations have been financially efficient.

REVIEW QUESTION

2–10 To assess the firm's average collection period and average payment period ratios, what additional information is needed, and why?

2.5 | Debt Ratios

The *debt position* of a firm indicates the amount of other people's money being used to generate profits. In general, the financial analyst is most concerned with long-term debts, because these commit the firm to a stream of contractual payments over the long run. The more debt a firm has, the greater its risk of being unable to meet its contractual debt payments. Because creditors' claims must be satisfied before the earnings can be distributed to shareholders, current and prospective shareholders pay close attention to the firm's ability to repay debts. Lenders are also concerned about the firm's indebtedness.

financial leverage
The magnification of risk and return through the use of fixed-cost financing, such as debt and preferred stock.

In general, the more debt a firm uses in relation to its total assets, the greater its *financial leverage*. **Financial leverage** is the magnification of risk and return through the use of fixed-cost financing, such as debt and preferred stock. The more fixed-cost debt a firm uses, the greater will be its expected risk and return.

Example

Patty Akers is in the process of incorporating her new business. After much analysis she determined that an initial investment of $50,000—$20,000 in current assets and $30,000 in fixed assets—is necessary. These funds can be obtained in either of two ways. The first is the *no-debt plan,* under which she would invest the full $50,000 without borrowing. The other alternative, the *debt plan,* involves investing $25,000 and borrowing the balance of $25,000 at 12% annual interest.

Regardless of which alternative she chooses, Patty expects sales to average $30,000, costs and operating expenses to average $18,000, and earnings to be taxed at a 40% rate. Projected balance sheets and income statements associated with the two plans are summarized in Table 2.6. The no-debt plan results in after-

TABLE 2.6	Financial Statements Associated with Patty's Alternatives		
		No-debt plan	Debt plan
Balance Sheets			
Current assets		$20,000	$20,000
Fixed assets		30,000	30,000
Total assets		$50,000	$50,000
Debt (12% interest)		$ 0	$25,000
(1) Equity		50,000	25,000
Total liabilities and equity		$50,000	$50,000
Income Statements			
Sales		$30,000	$30,000
Less: Costs and operating expenses		18,000	18,000
Operating profits		$12,000	$12,000
Less: Interest expense		0	$0.12 \times \$25,000 =$ 3,000
Net profits before taxes		$12,000	$ 9,000
Less: Taxes (rate = 40%)		4,800	3,600
(2) Net profits after taxes		$ 7,200	$ 5,400
Return on equity [(2) ÷ (1)]		$\frac{\$7,200}{\$50,000} = 14.4\%$	$\frac{\$5,400}{\$25,000} = 21.6\%$

tax profits of $7,200, which represent a 14.4% rate of return on Patty's $50,000 investment. The debt plan results in $5,400 of after-tax profits, which represent a 21.6% rate of return on Patty's investment of $25,000. The debt plan provides Patty with a higher rate of return, but the risk of this plan is also greater, because the annual $3,000 of interest must be paid before receipt of earnings.

The example demonstrates that *with increased debt comes greater risk as well as higher potential return.* Therefore, the greater the financial leverage, the greater the potential risk and return. A detailed discussion of the impact of debt on the firm's risk, return, and value is included in Chapter 12. Here, we emphasize the use of financial debt ratios to assess externally a firm's debt position.

There are two general types of debt measures: measures of the degree of indebtedness and measures of the ability to service debts. The **degree of indebtedness** measures the amount of debt relative to other significant balance sheet amounts. A popular measure of the degree of indebtedness is the debt ratio.

The second type of debt measure, the **ability to service debts,** reflects a firm's ability to make the payments required on a scheduled basis over the life of a debt.[12] The firm's ability to pay certain fixed charges is measured using **coverage ratios.** Typically, higher coverage ratios are preferred, but too high a ratio (above industry norms) may result in unnecessarily low risk and return. In general, the

degree of indebtedness
Measures the amount of debt relative to other significant balance sheet amounts.

ability to service debts
The ability of a firm to make the payments required on a scheduled basis over the life of a debt.

coverage ratios
Ratios that measure the firm's ability to pay certain fixed charges.

12. The term *service* refers to the payment of interest and repayment of principal associated with a firm's debt obligations. When a firm services its debts, it pays—or fulfills—these obligations.

lower the firm's coverage ratios, the less certain it is to be able to pay fixed obligations. If a firm is unable to pay these obligations, its creditors may seek immediate repayment, which in most instances would force a firm into bankruptcy. Two popular coverage ratios are the times interest earned ratio and the fixed-payment coverage ratio.[13]

Debt Ratio

debt ratio
Measures the proportion of total assets financed by the firm's creditors.

The **debt ratio** measures the proportion of total assets financed by the firm's creditors. The higher this ratio, the greater the amount of other people's money being used to generate profits. The ratio is calculated as follows:

$$\text{Debt ratio} = \frac{\text{Total liabilities}}{\text{Total assets}}$$

The debt ratio for Bartlett Company in 2009 is

$$\frac{\$1,643,000}{\$3,597,000} = 0.457 = 45.7\%$$

This value indicates that the company has financed close to half of its assets with debt. The higher this ratio, the greater the firm's degree of indebtedness and the more financial leverage it has.

Times Interest Earned Ratio

times interest earned ratio
Measures the firm's ability to make contractual interest payments; sometimes called the *interest coverage ratio.*

The **times interest earned ratio,** sometimes called the *interest coverage ratio,* measures the firm's ability to make contractual interest payments. The higher its value, the better able the firm is to fulfill its interest obligations. The times interest earned ratio is calculated as follows:

$$\text{Times interest earned ratio} = \frac{\text{Earnings before interest and taxes}}{\text{Interest}}$$

The figure for *earnings before interest and taxes* is the same as that for *operating profits* shown in the income statement. Applying this ratio to Bartlett Company yields the following 2009 value:

$$\text{Times interest earned ratio} = \frac{\$418,000}{\$93,000} = 4.5$$

The times interest earned ratio for Bartlett Company seems acceptable. A value of at least 3.0—and preferably closer to 5.0—is often suggested. The firm's earnings before interest and taxes could shrink by as much as 78 percent [$(4.5 - 1.0) \div 4.5$], and the firm would still be able to pay the $93,000 in interest it owes. Thus it has a good margin of safety.

---

13. Coverage ratios use data that are derived on an *accrual basis* (discussed in Chapter 1) to measure what in a strict sense should be measured on a *cash basis.* This occurs because debts are serviced by using cash flows, not the accounting values shown on the firm's financial statements. But because it is difficult to determine cash flows available for debt service from the firm's financial statements, the calculation of coverage ratios as presented here is quite common thanks to the ready availability of financial statement data.

Fixed-Payment Coverage Ratio

fixed-payment coverage ratio
Measures the firm's ability to meet all fixed-payment obligations.

The **fixed-payment coverage ratio** measures the firm's ability to meet all fixed-payment obligations, such as loan interest and principal, lease payments, and preferred stock dividends.[14] As is true of the times interest earned ratio, the higher this value, the better. The formula for the fixed-payment coverage ratio is

$$\text{Fixed-payment coverage ratio} = \frac{\text{Earnings before interest and taxes} + \text{Lease payments}}{\text{Interest} + \text{Lease payments} + \{(\text{Principal payments} + \text{Preferred stock dividends}) \times [1/(1-T)]\}}$$

where T is the corporate tax rate applicable to the firm's income. The term $1/(1-T)$ is included to adjust the after-tax principal and preferred stock dividend payments back to a before-tax equivalent that is consistent with the before-tax values of all other terms. Applying the formula to Bartlett Company's 2009 data yields

$$\text{Fixed-payment coverage ratio} = \frac{\$418,000 + \$35,000}{\$93,000 + \$35,000 + \{(\$71,000 + \$10,000) \times [1/(1-0.29)]\}}$$

$$= \frac{\$453,000}{\$242,000} = 1.9$$

Because the earnings available are nearly twice as large as its fixed-payment obligations, the firm appears safely able to meet the latter.

Like the times interest earned ratio, the fixed-payment coverage ratio measures risk. The lower the ratio, the greater the risk to both lenders and owners; the greater the ratio, the lower the risk. This ratio allows interested parties to assess the firm's ability to meet additional fixed-payment obligations without being driven into bankruptcy.

REVIEW QUESTIONS

2–11 What is *financial leverage?*
2–12 What ratio measures the firm's *degree of indebtedness*? What ratios assess the firm's *ability to service debts?*

2.6 | Profitability Ratios

There are many measures of profitability. As a group, these measures enable analysts to evaluate the firm's profits with respect to a given level of sales, a certain level of assets, or the owners' investment. Without profits, a firm could not attract outside capital. Owners, creditors, and management pay close attention to boosting profits because of the great importance the market places on earnings.

14. Although preferred stock dividends, which are stated at the time of issue, can be "passed" (not paid) at the option of the firm's directors, it is generally believed that the payment of such dividends is necessary. *This text therefore treats the preferred stock dividend as a contractual obligation, to be paid as a fixed amount, as scheduled.*

Common-Size Income Statements

common-size income statement
An income statement in which each item is expressed as a percentage of sales.

A popular tool for evaluating profitability in relation to sales is the **common-size income statement.**[15] Each item on this statement is expressed as a percentage of sales. Common-size income statements are especially useful in comparing performance across years. Three frequently cited ratios of profitability that can be read directly from the common-size income statement are (1) the gross profit margin, (2) the operating profit margin, and (3) the net profit margin.

Common-size income statements for 2009 and 2008 for Bartlett Company are presented and evaluated in Table 2.7. These statements reveal that the firm's cost of goods sold increased from 66.7 percent of sales in 2008 to 67.9 percent in 2009, resulting in a worsening gross profit margin. However, thanks to a decrease in total operating expenses, the firm's net profit margin rose from 5.4 percent of sales in 2008 to 7.2 percent in 2009. The decrease in expenses more than com-

TABLE 2.7   Bartlett Company Common-Size Income Statements

	For the years ended December 31		Evaluation[a]
	2009	2008	2008–2009
Sales revenue	100.0%	100.0%	same
Less: Cost of goods sold	67.9	66.7	worse
(1) Gross profit margin	32.1%	33.3%	worse
Less: Operating expenses			
Selling expense	3.3%	4.2%	better
General and administrative expenses	6.8	6.7	better
Lease expense	1.1	1.3	better
Depreciation expense	7.3	9.3	better
Total operating expense	18.5%	21.5%	better
(2) Operating profit margin	13.6%	11.8%	better
Less: Interest expense	3.0	3.5	better
Net profits before taxes	10.6%	8.3%	better
Less: Taxes	3.1	2.5	worse[b]
Net profits after taxes	7.5%	5.8%	better
Less: Preferred stock dividends	0.3	0.4	better
(3) Net profit margin	7.2%	5.4%	better

[a]Subjective assessments based on data provided.

[b]Taxes as a percentage of sales increased noticeably between 2008 and 2009 because of differing costs and expenses, whereas the average tax rates (taxes ÷ net profits before taxes) for 2008 and 2009 remained about the same—30% and 29%, respectively.

15. This statement is sometimes called a *percent income statement*. The same treatment is often applied to the firm's balance sheet to make it easier to evaluate changes in the asset and financial structures of the firm. In addition to measuring profitability, these statements in effect can be used as an alternative or supplement to liquidity, activity, and debt-ratio analysis.

pensated for the increase in the cost of goods sold. A decrease in the firm's 2009 interest expense (3.0 percent of sales versus 3.5 percent in 2008) added to the increase in 2009 profits.

Gross Profit Margin

gross profit margin
Measures the percentage of each sales dollar remaining after the firm has paid for its goods.

The **gross profit margin** measures the percentage of each sales dollar remaining after the firm has paid for its goods. The higher the gross profit margin, the better (that is, the lower the relative cost of merchandise sold). The gross profit margin is calculated as follows:

$$\text{Gross profit margin} = \frac{\text{Sales} - \text{Cost of goods sold}}{\text{Sales}} = \frac{\text{Gross profits}}{\text{Sales}}$$

Hint This is a very significant ratio for small retailers, especially during times of inflationary prices. If the owner of the firm does not raise prices when the cost of sales is rising, the gross profit margin will erode.

Bartlett Company's gross profit margin for 2009 is

$$\frac{\$3,074,000 - \$2,088,000}{\$3,074,000} = \frac{\$986,000}{\$3,074,000} = 32.1\%$$

This value is labeled (1) on the common-size income statement in Table 2.7.

Operating Profit Margin

operating profit margin
Measures the percentage of each sales dollar remaining after all costs and expenses *other than* interest, taxes, and preferred stock dividends are deducted; the "pure profits" earned on each sales dollar.

The **operating profit margin** measures the percentage of each sales dollar remaining after all costs and expenses *other than* interest, taxes, and preferred stock dividends are deducted. It represents the "pure profits" earned on each sales dollar. Operating profits are "pure" because they measure only the profits earned on operations and ignore interest, taxes, and preferred stock dividends. A high operating profit margin is preferred. The operating profit margin is calculated as follows:

$$\text{Operating profit margin} = \frac{\text{Operating profits}}{\text{Sales}}$$

Bartlett Company's operating profit margin for 2009 is

$$\frac{\$418,000}{\$3,074,000} = 13.6\%$$

This value is labeled (2) on the common-size income statement in Table 2.7.

Net Profit Margin

net profit margin
Measures the percentage of each sales dollar remaining after all costs and expenses, *including* interest, taxes, and preferred stock dividends, have been deducted.

The **net profit margin** measures the percentage of each sales dollar remaining after all costs and expenses, *including* interest, taxes, and preferred stock dividends, have been deducted. The higher the firm's net profit margin, the better. The net profit margin is calculated as follows:

$$\text{Net profit margin} = \frac{\text{Earnings available for common stockholders}}{\text{Sales}}$$

Bartlett Company's net profit margin for 2009 is

$$\frac{\$221,000}{\$3,074,000} = 7.2\%$$

Hint The net profit margin is sometimes defined as net profits after taxes divided by sales. The formula used here places greater emphasis on the common stockholders.

This value is labeled (3) on the common-size income statement in Table 2.7.

The net profit margin is a commonly cited measure of the firm's success with respect to earnings on sales. "Good" net profit margins differ considerably across industries. A net profit margin of 1 percent or less would not be unusual for a grocery store, whereas a net profit margin of 10 percent would be low for a retail jewelry store.

Earnings per Share (EPS)

Hint EPS represents the dollar amount earned *on behalf of* each outstanding share of common stock—not the amount of earnings *actually distributed* to shareholders.

The firm's *earnings per share (EPS)* is generally of interest to present or prospective stockholders and management. As we noted earlier, EPS represents the number of dollars earned during the period on behalf of each outstanding share of common stock. Earnings per share is calculated as follows:

$$\text{Earnings per share} = \frac{\text{Earnings available for common stockholders}}{\text{Number of shares of common stock outstanding}}$$

Bartlett Company's earnings per share in 2009 is

$$\frac{\$221,000}{76,262} = \$2.90$$

This figure represents the dollar amount earned *on behalf of* each outstanding share of common stock. The dollar amount of cash *actually distributed* to each shareholder is the *dividend per share (DPS)*, which, as noted in Bartlett Company's income statement (Table 2.1), rose to $1.29 in 2009 from $0.75 in 2008. EPS is closely watched by the investing public and is considered an important indicator of corporate success.

Return on Total Assets (ROA)

return on total assets (ROA) Measures the overall effectiveness of management in generating profits with its available assets; also called the *return on investment (ROI)*.

The **return on total assets (ROA)**, often called the *return on investment (ROI)*, measures the overall effectiveness of management in generating profits with its available assets. The higher the firm's return on total assets, the better. The return on total assets is calculated as follows:

$$\text{Return on total assets} = \frac{\text{Earnings available for common stockholders}}{\text{Total assets}}$$

Hint Some firms use this measure as a simple decision technique for evaluating proposed fixed-asset investments.

Bartlett Company's return on total assets in 2009 is

$$\frac{\$221,000}{\$3,597,000} = 6.1\%$$

This value indicates that the company earned 6.1 cents on each dollar of asset investment.

Return on Common Equity (ROE)

return on common equity (ROE)
Measures the return earned on the common stockholders' investment in the firm.

The **return on common equity (ROE)** measures the return earned on the common stockholders' investment in the firm. Generally, the higher this return, the better off are the owners. Return on common equity is calculated as follows:

$$\text{Return on common equity} = \frac{\text{Earnings available for common stockholders}}{\text{Common stock equity}}$$

This ratio for Bartlett Company in 2009 is

$$\frac{\$221,000}{\$1,754,000} = 12.6\%$$

Note that the value for common stock equity ($1,754,000) was found by subtracting the $200,000 of preferred stock equity from the total stockholders' equity of $1,954,000 (see Bartlett Company's 2009 balance sheet in Table 2.2). The calculated ROE of 12.6 percent indicates that during 2009 Bartlett earned 12.6 cents on each dollar of common stock equity.

REVIEW QUESTIONS

2–13 What three ratios of profitability are found on a *common-size income statement?*

2–14 What would explain a firm's having a high gross profit margin and a low net profit margin?

2–15 Which measure of profitability is probably of greatest interest to the investing public? Why?

2.7 | Market Ratios

market ratios
Relate a firm's market value, as measured by its current share price, to certain accounting values.

Market ratios relate the firm's market value, as measured by its current share price, to certain accounting values. These ratios give insight into how well investors in the marketplace feel the firm is doing in terms of risk and return. They tend to reflect, on a relative basis, the common stockholders' assessment of all aspects of the firm's past and expected future performance. Here we consider two popular market ratios, one that focuses on earnings and another that considers book value.

Price/Earnings (P/E) Ratio

price/earnings (P/E) ratio
Measures the amount that investors are willing to pay for each dollar of a firm's earnings; the higher the P/E ratio, the greater the investor confidence.

The **price/earnings (P/E) ratio** is commonly used to assess the owners' appraisal of share value.[16] The P/E ratio measures the amount that investors are willing to pay for each dollar of a firm's earnings. The level of this ratio indicates the degree of

---

16. Use of the price/earnings ratio to estimate the value of the firm is part of the discussion of "Other approaches to common stock valuation" in Chapter 7.

confidence that investors have in the firm's future performance. The higher the P/E ratio, the greater the investor confidence. The P/E ratio is calculated as follows:

$$\text{Price/earnings (P/E) ratio} = \frac{\text{Market price per share of common stock}}{\text{Earnings per share}}$$

If Bartlett Company's common stock at the end of 2009 was selling at $32.25, using the EPS of $2.90, the P/E ratio at year-end 2009 is

$$\frac{\$32.25}{\$2.90} = 11.1$$

This figure indicates that investors were paying $11.10 for each $1.00 of earnings. The P/E ratio is most informative when applied in cross-sectional analysis using an industry average P/E ratio or the P/E ratio of a benchmark firm.

Market/Book (M/B) Ratio

market/book (M/B) ratio
Provides an assessment of how investors view the firm's performance. Firms expected to earn high returns relative to their risk typically sell at higher M/B multiples.

The **market/book (M/B) ratio** provides an assessment of how investors view the firm's performance. It relates the market value of the firm's shares to their book—strict accounting—value. To calculate the firm's M/B ratio, we first need to find the *book value per share of common stock:*

$$\frac{\text{Book value per share}}{\text{of common stock}} = \frac{\text{Common stock equity}}{\text{Number of shares of common stock outstanding}}$$

Substituting the appropriate values for Bartlett Company from its 2009 balance sheet, we get

$$\frac{\text{Book value per share}}{\text{of common stock}} = \frac{\$1,754,000}{76,262} = \$23.00$$

The formula for the market/book ratio is

$$\text{Market/book (M/B) ratio} = \frac{\text{Market price per share of common stock}}{\text{Book value per share of common stock}}$$

Substituting Bartlett Company's end of 2009 common stock price of $32.25 and its $23.00 book value per share of common stock (calculated above) into the M/B ratio formula, we get

$$\text{Market/book (M/B) ratio} = \frac{\$32.25}{\$23.00} = 1.40$$

This M/B ratio means that investors are currently paying $1.40 for each $1.00 of book value of Bartlett Company's stock.

The stocks of firms that are expected to perform well—improve profits, increase their market share, or launch successful products—typically sell at higher M/B ratios than the stocks of firms with less attractive outlooks. Simply stated, firms expected to earn high returns relative to their risk typically sell at higher M/B multiples. Clearly, Bartlett's future prospects are being viewed favorably by investors, who are willing to pay more than its book value for the firm's shares. Like P/E ratios, M/B ratios are typically assessed cross-sectionally, to get a feel for the firm's return and risk compared to peer firms.

REVIEW QUESTION

2–16 How do the *price/earnings (P/E) ratio* and the *market/book (M/B) ratio* provide a feel for the firm's return and risk?

 ## 2.8 | A Complete Ratio Analysis

Analysts frequently wish to take an overall look at the firm's financial performance and status. Here we consider two popular approaches to a complete ratio analysis: (1) summarizing all ratios and (2) the DuPont system of analysis. The summary analysis approach tends to view *all aspects* of the firm's financial activities to isolate key areas of responsibility. The DuPont system acts as a search technique aimed at finding the *key areas* responsible for the firm's financial condition.

Summarizing All Ratios

We can use Bartlett Company's ratios to perform a complete ratio analysis using both cross-sectional and time-series analysis approaches. The 2009 ratio values calculated earlier and the ratio values calculated for 2007 and 2008 for Bartlett Company, along with the industry average ratios for 2009, are summarized in Table 2.8 (see pages 72 and 73), which also shows the formula used to calculate each ratio. Using these data, we can discuss the five key aspects of Bartlett's performance—liquidity, activity, debt, profitability, and market.

Liquidity

The overall liquidity of the firm seems to exhibit a reasonably stable trend, having been maintained at a level that is relatively consistent with the industry average in 2009. The firm's liquidity seems to be good.

Activity

Bartlett Company's inventory appears to be in good shape. Its inventory management seems to have improved, and in 2009 it performed at a level above that of the industry. The firm may be experiencing some problems with accounts receivable. The average collection period seems to have crept up above that of the industry. Bartlett also appears to be slow in paying its bills; it pays nearly 30 days slower than the industry average. This could adversely affect the firm's credit standing. Although overall liquidity appears to be good, the management of receivables and payables should be examined. Bartlett's total asset turnover reflects a decline in the efficiency of total asset utilization between 2007 and 2008. Although in 2009 it rose to a level considerably above the industry average, it appears that the pre-2008 level of efficiency has not yet been achieved.

TABLE 2.8   Summary of Bartlett Company Ratios (2007–2009, Including 2009 Industry Averages)

Ratio	Formula	Year 2007[a]	Year 2008[b]	Year 2009[b]	Industry average 2009[c]	Cross-sectional 2009	Time-series 2007–2009	Overall
Liquidity								
Current ratio	$\dfrac{\text{Current assets}}{\text{Current liabilities}}$	2.04	2.08	1.97	2.05	OK	OK	OK
Quick (acid-test) ratio	$\dfrac{\text{Current assets} - \text{Inventory}}{\text{Current liabilities}}$	1.32	1.46	1.51	1.43	OK	good	good
Activity								
Inventory turnover	$\dfrac{\text{Cost of goods sold}}{\text{Inventory}}$	5.1	5.7	7.2	6.6	good	good	good
Average collection period	$\dfrac{\text{Accounts receivable}}{\text{Average sales per day}}$	43.9 days	51.2 days	59.7 days	44.3 days	poor	poor	poor
Average payment period	$\dfrac{\text{Accounts payable}}{\text{Average purchases per day}}$	75.8 days	81.2 days	95.4 days	66.5 days	poor	poor	poor
Total asset turnover	$\dfrac{\text{Sales}}{\text{Total assets}}$	0.94	0.79	0.85	0.75	OK	OK	OK
Debt								
Debt ratio	$\dfrac{\text{Total liabilities}}{\text{Total assets}}$	36.8%	44.3%	45.7%	40.0%	OK	OK	OK
Times interest earned ratio	$\dfrac{\text{Earnings before interest and taxes}}{\text{Interest}}$	5.6	3.3	4.5	4.3	good	OK	OK
Fixed-payment coverage ratio	$\dfrac{\text{Earnings before interest and taxes} + \text{Lease payments}}{\text{Int.} + \text{Lease pay.} + \{(\text{Prin.} + \text{Pref. div.}) \times [1/(1-T)]\}}$	2.4	1.4	1.9	1.5	good	OK	good

Ratio	Formula	Year 2007[a]	Year 2008[b]	Year 2009[b]	Industry average 2009[c]	Evaluation[d] Cross-sectional 2009	Evaluation[d] Time-series 2007–2009	Evaluation[d] Overall
Profitability								
Gross profit margin	$\dfrac{\text{Gross profits}}{\text{Sales}}$	31.4%	33.3%	32.1%	30.0%	OK	OK	OK
Operating profit margin	$\dfrac{\text{Operating profits}}{\text{Sales}}$	14.6%	11.8%	13.6%	11.0%	good	OK	good
Net profit margin	$\dfrac{\text{Earnings available for common stockholders}}{\text{Sales}}$	8.2%	5.4%	7.2%	6.2%	good	OK	good
Earnings per share (EPS)	$\dfrac{\text{Earnings available for common stockholders}}{\text{Number of shares of common stock outstanding}}$	$3.26	$1.81	$2.90	$2.26	good	OK	good
Return on total assets (ROA)	$\dfrac{\text{Earnings available for common stockholders}}{\text{Total assets}}$	7.8%	4.2%	6.1%	4.6%	good	OK	good
Return on common equity (ROE)	$\dfrac{\text{Earnings available for common stockholders}}{\text{Common stock equity}}$	13.7%	8.5%	12.6%	8.5%	good	OK	good
Market								
Price/earnings (P/E) ratio	$\dfrac{\text{Market price per share of common stock}}{\text{Earnings per share}}$	10.5	10.0[e]	11.1	12.5	OK	OK	OK
Market/book (M/B) ratio	$\dfrac{\text{Market price per share of common stock}}{\text{Book value per share of common stock}}$	1.25	0.85[e]	1.40	1.30	OK	OK	OK

[a]Calculated from data not included in the chapter.
[b]Calculated by using the financial statements presented in Tables 2.1 and 2.2.
[c]Obtained from sources not included in this chapter.
[d]Subjective assessments based on data provided.
[e]The market price per share at the end of 2008 was $18.06.

Debt

Bartlett Company's indebtedness increased over the 2007–2009 period and is currently above the industry average. Although this increase in the debt ratio could be cause for alarm, the firm's ability to meet interest and fixed-payment obligations improved, from 2008 to 2009, to a level that outperforms the industry. The firm's increased indebtedness in 2008 apparently caused a deterioration in its ability to pay debt adequately. However, Bartlett has evidently improved its income in 2009 so that it is able to meet its interest and fixed-payment obligations at a level consistent with the average in the industry. In summary, it appears that although 2008 was an off year, the company's improved ability to pay debts in 2009 compensates for its increased degree of indebtedness.

Profitability

Bartlett's profitability relative to sales in 2009 was better than the average company in the industry, although it did not match the firm's 2007 performance. Although the *gross* profit margin was better in 2008 and 2009 than in 2007, higher levels of operating and interest expenses in 2008 and 2009 appear to have caused the 2009 *net* profit margin to fall below that of 2007. However, Bartlett Company's 2009 net profit margin is quite favorable when compared to the industry average.

The firm's earnings per share, return on total assets, and return on common equity behaved much as its net profit margin did over the 2007–2009 period. Bartlett appears to have experienced either a sizable drop in sales between 2007 and 2008 or a rapid expansion in assets during that period. The exceptionally high 2009 level of return on common equity suggests that the firm is performing quite well. The firm's above-average returns—net profit margin, EPS, ROA, and ROE—may be attributable to the fact that it is more risky than average. A look at market ratios is helpful in assessing risk.

Market

Investors have greater confidence in the firm in 2009 than in the prior two years, as reflected in the price/earnings (P/E) ratio of 11.1. However, this ratio is below the industry average. The P/E ratio suggests that the firm's risk has declined but remains above that of the average firm in its industry. The firm's market/book (M/B) ratio has increased over the 2007–2009 period, and in 2009 it exceeds the industry average. This implies that investors are optimistic about the firm's future performance. The P/E and M/B ratios reflect the firm's increased profitability over the 2007–2009 period: Investors expect to earn high future returns as compensation for the firm's above-average risk.

In summary, the firm appears to be growing and has recently undergone an expansion in assets, financed primarily through the use of debt. The 2008–2009 period seems to reflect a phase of adjustment and recovery from the rapid growth in assets. Bartlett's sales, profits, and other performance factors seem to be growing with the increase in the size of the operation. In addition, the market response to these accomplishments appears to have been positive. In short, the firm seems to have done well in 2009.

DuPont System of Analysis

DuPont system of analysis
System used to dissect the firm's financial statements and to assess its financial condition.

The **DuPont system of analysis** is used to dissect the firm's financial statements and to assess its financial condition. It merges the income statement and balance sheet into two summary measures of profitability: return on total assets (ROA) and return on common equity (ROE). Figure 2.2 (see page 76) depicts the basic DuPont system with Bartlett Company's 2009 monetary and ratio values. The upper portion of the chart summarizes the income statement activities; the lower portion summarizes the balance sheet activities.

DuPont Formula

DuPont formula
Multiplies the firm's *net profit margin* by its *total asset turnover* to calculate the firm's *return on total assets (ROA)*.

The DuPont system first brings together the *net profit margin*, which measures the firm's profitability on sales, with its *total asset turnover*, which indicates how efficiently the firm has used its assets to generate sales. In the **DuPont formula**, the product of these two ratios results in the *return on total assets (ROA)*:

$$ROA = \text{Net profit margin} \times \text{Total asset turnover}$$

Substituting the appropriate formulas into the equation and simplifying results in the formula given earlier,

$$ROA = \frac{\text{Earnings available for common stockholders}}{\text{Sales}} \times \frac{\text{Sales}}{\text{Total assets}} = \frac{\text{Earnings available for common stockholders}}{\text{Total assets}}$$

When the 2009 values of the net profit margin and total asset turnover for Bartlett Company, calculated earlier, are substituted into the DuPont formula, the result is

$$ROA = 7.2\% \times 0.85 = 6.1\%$$

This value is the same as that calculated directly in an earlier section (page 68). The DuPont formula enables the firm to break down its return into profit-on-sales and efficiency-of-asset-use components. Typically, a firm with a low net profit margin has a high total asset turnover, which results in a reasonably good return on total assets. Often, the opposite situation exists.

Modified DuPont Formula

modified DuPont formula
Relates the firm's *return on total assets (ROA)* to its *return on common equity (ROE)* using the *financial leverage multiplier (FLM)*.

financial leverage multiplier (FLM)
The ratio of the firm's total assets to its common stock equity.

The second step in the DuPont system employs the **modified DuPont formula**. This formula relates the firm's *return on total assets (ROA)* to its *return on common equity (ROE)*. The latter is calculated by multiplying the return on total assets (ROA) by the **financial leverage multiplier (FLM)**, which is the ratio of total assets to common stock equity:

$$ROE = ROA \times FLM$$

Substituting the appropriate formulas into the equation and simplifying results in the formula given earlier,

$$ROE = \frac{\text{Earnings available for common stockholders}}{\text{Total assets}} \times \frac{\text{Total assets}}{\text{Common stock equity}} = \frac{\text{Earnings available for common stockholders}}{\text{Common stock equity}}$$

FIGURE 2.2 DuPont System of Analysis

The DuPont system of analysis with application to Bartlett Company (2009)

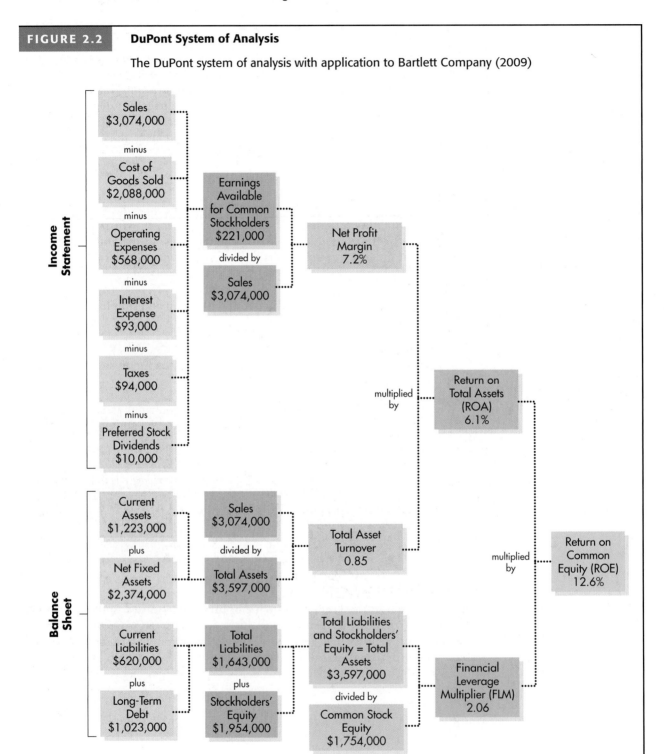

Use of the financial leverage multiplier (FLM) to convert the ROA into the ROE reflects the impact of financial leverage on owners' return. Substituting the values for Bartlett Company's ROA of 6.1 percent, calculated earlier, and Bartlett's FLM of 2.06 ($3,597,000 total assets ÷ $1,754,000 common stock equity) into the modified DuPont formula yields

$$ROE = 6.1\% \times 2.06 = 12.6\%$$

The 12.6 percent ROE calculated by using the modified DuPont formula is the same as that calculated directly (page 69).

Applying the DuPont System

The advantage of the DuPont system is that it allows the firm to break its return on equity into a profit-on-sales component (net profit margin), an efficiency-of-asset-use component (total asset turnover), and a use-of-financial-leverage component (financial leverage multiplier). The total return to owners therefore can be analyzed in these important dimensions.

The use of the DuPont system of analysis as a diagnostic tool is best explained using Figure 2.2. Beginning with the rightmost value—the ROE—the financial analyst moves to the left, dissecting and analyzing the inputs to the formula to isolate the probable cause of the resulting above-average (or below-average) value.

Example

For the sake of demonstration, let's ignore all industry average data in Table 2.8 and assume that Bartlett's ROE of 12.6 % is actually below the industry average. Moving to the left in Figure 2.2, we would examine the inputs to the ROE—the ROA and the FLM—relative to the industry averages. Let's assume that the FLM is in line with the industry average, but the ROA is below the industry average. Moving farther to the left, we examine the two inputs to the ROA—the net profit margin and total asset turnover. Assume that the net profit margin is in line with the industry average, but the total asset turnover is below the industry average. Moving still farther to the left, we find that whereas the firm's sales are consistent with the industry value, Bartlett's total assets have grown significantly during the past year. Looking farther to the left, we would review the firm's activity ratios for current assets. Let's say that whereas the firm's inventory turnover is in line with the industry average, its average collection period is well above the industry average.

We can readily trace the possible problem back to its cause: Bartlett's low ROE is primarily the consequence of slow collections of accounts receivable, which resulted in high levels of receivables and therefore high levels of total assets. The high total assets slowed Bartlett's total asset turnover, driving down its ROA, which then drove down its ROE. By using the DuPont system of analysis to dissect Bartlett's overall returns as measured by its ROE, we found that slow collections of receivables caused the below-industry-average ROE. Clearly, the firm needs to better manage its credit operations.

REVIEW QUESTIONS

2–17 Financial ratio analysis is often divided into five areas: *liquidity, activity, debt, profitability,* and *market* ratios. Differentiate each of these areas of analysis from the others. Which is of the greatest concern to creditors?

2–18 Describe how you would use a large number of ratios to perform a complete ratio analysis of the firm.

2–19 What three areas of analysis are combined in the *modified DuPont formula?* Explain how the *DuPont system of analysis* is used to dissect the firm's results and isolate their causes.

Summary

Focus on Value

Financial managers review and analyze the firm's financial statements periodically, both to uncover developing problems and to assess the firm's progress toward achieving its goals. These actions are aimed at **preserving and creating value for the firm's owners.** Financial ratios enable financial managers to monitor the pulse of the firm and its progress toward its strategic goals. Although financial statements and financial ratios rely on accrual concepts, they can provide useful insights into important aspects of risk and return (cash flow) that affect share price.

Review of Learning Goals

LG 1   **Review the contents of the stockholders' report and the procedures for consolidating international financial statements.** The annual stockholders' report, which publicly owned corporations must provide to stockholders, documents the firm's financial activities of the past year. It includes the letter to stockholders and various subjective and factual information. It also contains four key financial statements: the income statement, the balance sheet, the statement of stockholders' equity (or its abbreviated form, the statement of retained earnings), and the statement of cash flows. Notes describing the technical aspects of the financial statements follow. Financial statements of companies that have operations whose cash flows are denominated in one or more foreign currencies must be translated into dollars in accordance with *FASB Standard No. 52.*

LG 2   **Understand who uses financial ratios, and how.** Ratio analysis enables stockholders, lenders, and the firm's managers to evaluate the firm's financial performance. It can be performed on a cross-sectional or a time-series basis. Benchmarking is a popular type of cross-sectional analysis. Users of ratios should understand the cautions that apply to their use.

LG 3   **Use ratios to analyze a firm's liquidity and activity.** Liquidity, or the ability of the firm to pay its bills as they come due, can be measured by the current ratio and the quick (acid-test) ratio. Activity ratios measure the speed with which accounts are converted into sales or cash—inflows or outflows. The activity of inventory can be measured by its turnover; that of accounts receivable by the average collection period; and that of accounts payable by the average payment period. Total asset turnover measures the efficiency with which the firm uses its assets to generate sales.

LG 4 **Discuss the relationship between debt and financial leverage and the ratios used to analyze a firm's debt.** The more debt a firm uses, the greater its financial leverage, which magnifies both risk and return. Financial debt ratios measure both the degree of indebtedness and the ability to service debts. A common measure of indebtedness is the debt ratio. The ability to pay fixed charges can be measured by times interest earned and fixed-payment coverage ratios.

LG 5 **Use ratios to analyze a firm's profitability and its market value.** The common-size income statement, which shows all items as a percentage of sales, can be used to determine gross profit margin, operating profit margin, and net profit margin. Other measures of profitability include earnings per share, return on total assets, and return on common equity. Market ratios include the price/earnings ratio and the market/book ratio.

LG 6 **Use a summary of financial ratios and the DuPont system of analysis to perform a complete ratio analysis.** A summary of all ratios can be used to perform a complete ratio analysis using cross-sectional and time-series analysis. The DuPont system of analysis is a diagnostic tool used to find the key areas responsible for the firm's financial performance. It enables the firm to break the return on common equity into three components: profit on sales, efficiency of asset use, and use of financial leverage.

Self-Test Problems (Solutions in Appendix B)

   ST2–1 **Ratio formulas and interpretations**   Without referring to the text, indicate for each of the following ratios the formula for calculating it and the kinds of problems, if any, the firm is likely to have if that ratio is too high relative to the industry average. What if the ratio is too low relative to the industry average? Create a table similar to the one that follows and fill in the empty blocks.

Ratio	Too high	Too low
Current ratio =		
Inventory turnover =		
Times interest earned =	✕	
Gross profit margin =		
Return on total assets =	✕	
Price/earnings (P/E) ratio =		

ST2–2 Balance sheet completion using ratios   Complete the 2009 balance sheet for O'Keefe Industries using the information that follows it.

O'Keefe Industries Balance Sheet December 31, 2009			
Assets		**Liabilities and Stockholders' Equity**	
Cash	$32,720	Accounts payable	$120,000
Marketable securities	25,000	Notes payable	_____
Accounts receivable	_____	Accruals	20,000
Inventories	_____	Total current liabilities	_____
Total current assets	_____	Long-term debt	_____
Net fixed assets	_____	Stockholders' equity	$600,000
Total assets	$ _____	Total liabilities and stockholders' equity	$ _____

The following financial data for 2009 are also available:
(1) Sales totaled $1,800,000.
(2) The gross profit margin was 25%.
(3) Inventory turnover was 6.0.
(4) There are 365 days in the year.
(5) The average collection period was 40 days.
(6) The current ratio was 1.60.
(7) The total asset turnover ratio was 1.20.
(8) The debt ratio was 60%.

Warm-Up Exercises

A blue box (■) indicates exercises available in .

 E2–1 You are a summer intern at the office of a local tax-preparer. To test your basic knowledge of financial statements, your manager, who graduated from your alma mater 2 years ago, gives you the following list of accounts and asks you to prepare a simple income statement using those accounts.

Accounts	($000,000)
Depreciation	25
General and administrative expenses	22
Sales	345
Sales expenses	18
Cost of goods sold	255
Lease expense	4
Interest expense	3

a. Arrange the accounts into a well-labeled income statement. Make sure you label and solve for gross profit, operating profit, and net profit before taxes.

b. Using a 35% tax rate, calculate taxes paid and net profit after taxes.

c. Assuming a dividend of $1.10 per share with 4.25 million shares outstanding, calculate EPS and additions to retained earnings.

E2–2 Explain why the income statement can also be called a "profit and loss statement." What exactly does the word "balance" mean in the title of the balance sheet? Why do we balance the two halves?

E2–3 Cooper Industries, Inc., began 2009 with retained earnings of $25.32 million. During the year it paid four quarterly dividends of $0.35 per share to 2.75 million common stockholders. Preferred stockholders, holding 500,000 shares, were paid two semiannual dividends of $0.75 per share. The firm had a net profit after taxes of $5.15 million. Prepare the statement of retained earnings for the year ended December 31, 2009.

E2–4 Bluestone Metals, Inc., is a metal fabrication firm which manufactures prefabricated metal parts for customers in a variety of industries. The firm's motto is "If you need it, we can make it." The CEO of Bluestone recently held a board meeting during which he extolled the virtues of the corporation. The company, he stated confidently, had the capability to build any product and could do so using a lean manufacturing model. The firm would soon be profitable, claimed the CEO, because the company used state-of-the-art technology to build a variety of products while keeping inventory levels low. As a business press reporter, you have calculated some ratios to analyze the financial health of the firm. Bluestone's current ratios and quick ratios for the past 6 years are shown in the table below:

	2004	2005	2006	2007	2008	2009
Current ratio	1.2	1.4	1.3	1.6	1.8	2.2
Quick ratio	1.1	1.3	1.2	0.8	0.6	0.4

What do you think of the CEO's claim that the firm is lean and soon to be profitable? (*Hint:* Is there a possible warning sign in the relationship between the two ratios?)

E2–5 If we know that a firm has a net profit margin of 4.5%, total asset turnover of 0.72, and a financial leverage multiplier of 1.43, what is its ROE? What is the advantage to using the DuPont system to calculate ROE over the direct calculation of earnings available for common stockholders divided by common stock equity?

Problems

A blue box (■) indicates problems available in .

P2–1 **Reviewing basic financial statements**   The income statement for the year ended December 31, 2009, the balance sheets for December 31, 2009 and 2008, and the statement of retained earnings for the year ended December 31, 2009, for Technica, Inc., are given on pages 82 and 83. Briefly discuss the form and informational content of each of these statements.

Technica, Inc.
Income Statement
for the Year Ended December 31, 2009

Sales revenue		$600,000
Less: Cost of goods sold		460,000
Gross profits		$140,000
Less: Operating expenses		
General and administrative expenses	$30,000	
Depreciation expense	30,000	
Total operating expense		60,000
Operating profits		$ 80,000
Less: Interest expense		10,000
Net profits before taxes		$ 70,000
Less: Taxes		27,100
Earnings available for common stockholders		$ 42,900
Earnings per share (EPS)		$2.15

Technica, Inc.
Balance Sheets

	December 31	
Assets	2009	2008
Cash	$ 15,000	$ 16,000
Marketable securities	7,200	8,000
Accounts receivable	34,100	42,200
Inventories	82,000	50,000
Total current assets	$138,300	$116,200
Land and buildings	$150,000	$150,000
Machinery and equipment	200,000	190,000
Furniture and fixtures	54,000	50,000
Other	11,000	10,000
Total gross fixed assets	$415,000	$400,000
Less: Accumulated depreciation	145,000	115,000
Net fixed assets	$270,000	$285,000
Total assets	$408,300	$401,200

Liabilities and Stockholders' Equity		
Accounts payable	$ 57,000	$ 49,000
Notes payable	13,000	16,000
Accruals	5,000	6,000
Total current liabilities	$ 75,000	$ 71,000
Long-term debt	$150,000	$160,000
Stockholders' equity		
Common stock equity (shares outstanding: 19,500 in 2009 and 20,000 in 2008)	$110,200	$120,000
Retained earnings	73,100	50,200
Total stockholders' equity	$183,300	$170,200
Total liabilities and stockholders' equity	$408,300	$401,200

Technica, Inc. Statement of Retained Earnings for the Year Ended December 31, 2009	
Retained earnings balance (January 1, 2009)	$50,200
Plus: Net profits after taxes (for 2009)	42,900
Less: Cash dividends (paid during 2009)	20,000
Retained earnings balance (December 31, 2009)	$73,100

P2–2 Financial statement account identification   Mark each of the accounts listed in the following table as follows:

a. In column (1), indicate in which statement—income statement (IS) or balance sheet (BS)—the account belongs.

b. In column (2), indicate whether the account is a current asset (CA), current liability (CL), expense (E), fixed asset (FA), long-term debt (LTD), revenue (R), or stockholders' equity (SE).

Account name	(1) Statement	(2) Type of account
Accounts payable	_____	_____
Accounts receivable	_____	_____
Accruals	_____	_____
Accumulated depreciation	_____	_____
Administrative expense	_____	_____
Buildings	_____	_____
Cash	_____	_____
Common stock (at par)	_____	_____
Cost of goods sold	_____	_____
Depreciation	_____	_____
Equipment	_____	_____
General expense	_____	_____
Interest expense	_____	_____
Inventories	_____	_____
Land	_____	_____
Long-term debts	_____	_____
Machinery	_____	_____
Marketable securities	_____	_____
Notes payable	_____	_____
Operating expense	_____	_____
Paid-in capital in excess of par	_____	_____
Preferred stock	_____	_____
Preferred stock dividends	_____	_____
Retained earnings	_____	_____
Sales revenue	_____	_____
Selling expense	_____	_____
Taxes	_____	_____
Vehicles	_____	_____

P2–3   Income statement preparation   On December 31, 2009, Cathy Chen, a self-employed certified public accountant (CPA), completed her first full year in business. During the year, she billed $360,000 for her accounting services. She had two employees: a bookkeeper and a clerical assistant. In addition to her *monthly* salary of $8,000, Ms. Chen paid *annual* salaries of $48,000 and $36,000 to the bookkeeper and the clerical assistant, respectively. Employment taxes and benefit costs for Ms. Chen and her employees totaled $34,600 for the year. Expenses for office supplies, including postage, totaled $10,400 for the year. In addition, Ms. Chen spent $17,000 during the year on tax-deductible travel and entertainment associated with client visits and new business development. Lease payments for the office space rented (a tax-deductible expense) were $2,700 *per month*. Depreciation expense on the office furniture and fixtures was $15,600 for the year. During the year, Ms. Chen paid interest of $15,000 on the $120,000 borrowed to start the business. She paid an average tax rate of 30% during 2009.

a. Prepare an income statement for Cathy Chen, CPA, for the year ended December 31, 2009.
b. Evaluate her 2009 financial performance.

PERSONAL FINANCE PROBLEM

P2–4   Income statement preparation   Adam and Arin Adams have collected their personal income and expense information and have asked you to put together an income and expense statement for the year ended December 31, 2009. The following information is received from the Adams family.

Adam's salary	$45,000	Utilities	$ 3,200
Arin's salary	30,000	Groceries	2,200
Interest received	500	Medical	1,500
Dividends received	150	Property taxes	1,659
Auto insurance	600	Income tax, soc. security	13,000
Home insurance	750	Clothes & accessories	2,000
Auto loan payment	3,300	Gas and auto repair	2,100
Mortgage payment	14,000	Entertainment	2,000

a. Create a personal *income and expense statement* for the period ended December 31, 2009. It should be similar to a corporate income statement.
b. Did the Adams family have a cash surplus or cash deficit?
c. If the result is a surplus, how can the Adams family use that surplus?

P2–5   Calculation of EPS and retained earnings   Philagem, Inc., ended 2009 with a net profit *before* taxes of $218,000. The company is subject to a 40% tax rate and must pay $32,000 in preferred stock dividends before distributing any earnings on the 85,000 shares of common stock currently outstanding.

a. Calculate Philagem's 2009 earnings per share (EPS).
b. If the firm paid common stock dividends of $0.80 per share, how many dollars would go to retained earnings?

P2–6 **Balance sheet preparation**   Use the *appropriate items* from the following list to prepare in good form Owen Davis Company's balance sheet at December 31, 2009.

Item	Value ($000) at December 31, 2009	Item	Value ($000) at December 31, 2009
Accounts payable	$ 220	Inventories	$ 375
Accounts receivable	450	Land	100
Accruals	55	Long-term debts	420
Accumulated depreciation	265	Machinery	420
Buildings	225	Marketable securities	75
Cash	215	Notes payable	475
Common stock (at par)	90	Paid-in capital in excess	
Cost of goods sold	2,500	of par	360
Depreciation expense	45	Preferred stock	100
Equipment	140	Retained earnings	210
Furniture and fixtures	170	Sales revenue	3,600
General expense	320	Vehicles	25

PERSONAL FINANCE PROBLEM

P2–7 **Balance sheet preparation**   Adam and Arin Adams have collected their personal asset and liability information and have asked you to put together a balance sheet as of December 31, 2009. The following information is received from the Adams family.

Cash	$ 300	Retirement funds, IRA	$ 2,000
Checking	3,000	2008 Sebring	15,000
Savings	1,200	2007 Jeep	8,000
IBM stock	2,000	Money market funds	1,200
Auto loan	8,000	Jewelry & artwork	3,000
Mortgage	100,000	Net worth	76,500
Medical bills payable	250	Household furnishings	4,200
Utility bills payable	150	Credit card balance	2,000
Real estate	150,000	Personal loan	3,000

a. Create a personal balance sheet as of December 31, 2009. It should be similar to a corporate balance sheet.
b. What must the total assets of the Adams family be equal to by December 31, 2009?
c. What was their *net working capital (NWC)* for the year? (*Hint:* NWC is the difference between total liquid assets and total current liabilities.)

P2–8 **Impact of net income on a firm's balance sheet**   Conrad Air, Inc., reported net income of $1,365,000 for the year ended December 31, 2009. Show the effect of these funds on the firm's balance sheet for the previous year (top of page 86) in each of the scenarios following the balance sheet.

Conrad Air, Inc. Balance Sheet as of December 31, 2009			
Assets		**Liabilities and Stockholders' Equity**	
Cash	$ 120,000	Accounts payable	$ 70,000
Marketable securities	35,000	Short-term notes	55,000
Accounts receivable	45,000	Current liabilities	$ 125,000
Inventories	130,000	Long-term debt	$2,700,000
Current assets	$ 330,000	Total liabilities	$2,825,000
Equipment	$2,970,000	Common stock	$ 500,000
Buildings	1,600,000	Retained earnings	1,575,000
Fixed assets	$4,570,000	Stockholders' equity	$2,075,000
Total assets	$4,900,000	Total liabilities and equity	$4,900,000

a. Conrad paid no dividends during the year and invested the funds in marketable securities.

b. Conrad paid dividends totaling $500,000 and used the balance of the net income to retire (pay off) long-term debt.

c. Conrad paid dividends totaling $500,000 and invested the balance of the net income in building a new hangar.

d. Conrad paid out all $1,365,000 as dividends to its stockholders.

P2–9 Initial sale price of common stock   Beck Corporation has one issue of preferred stock and one issue of common stock outstanding. Given Beck's stockholders' equity account that follows, determine the original price per share at which the firm sold its single issue of common stock.

Stockholders' equity ($000)	
Preferred stock	$ 125
Common stock ($0.75 par, 300,000 shares outstanding)	225
Paid-in capital in excess of par on common stock	2,625
Retained earnings	900
Total stockholders' equity	$3,875

P2–10 Statement of retained earnings   Hayes Enterprises began 2009 with a retained earnings balance of $928,000. During 2009, the firm earned $377,000 after taxes. From this amount, preferred stockholders were paid $47,000 in dividends. At year-end 2009, the firm's retained earnings totaled $1,048,000. The firm had 140,000 shares of common stock outstanding during 2009.

a. Prepare a statement of retained earnings for the year ended December 31, 2009, for Hayes Enterprises. (*Note:* Be sure to calculate and include the amount of cash dividends paid in 2009.)

b. Calculate the firm's 2009 earnings per share (EPS).

c. How large a per-share cash dividend did the firm pay on common stock during 2009?

P2–11   **Changes in stockholders' equity**   Listed are the equity sections of balance sheets for years 2008 and 2009 as reported by Mountain Air Ski Resorts, Inc. The overall value of stockholders' equity has risen from $2,000,000 to $7,500,000. Use the statements to discover how and why this happened.

Mountain Air Ski Resorts, Inc. Balance Sheets (partial)		
Stockholders' equity	2008	2009
Common stock ($1.00 par)		
Authorized—5,000,000 shares		
Outstanding—1,500,000 shares 2009		$1,500,000
— 500,000 shares 2008	$ 500,000	
Paid-in capital in excess of par	500,000	4,500,000
Retained earnings	1,000,000	1,500,000
Total stockholders' equity	$2,000,000	$7,500,000

The company paid total dividends of $200,000 during fiscal 2009.

a. What was Mountain Air's net income for fiscal 2009?

b. How many new shares did the corporation issue and sell during the year?

c. At what average price per share did the new stock sold during 2009 sell?

d. At what price per share did Mountain Air's original 500,000 shares sell?

        P2–12   **Ratio comparisons**   Robert Arias recently inherited a stock portfolio from his uncle. Wishing to learn more about the companies in which he is now invested, Robert performs a ratio analysis on each one and decides to compare them to each other. Some of his ratios are listed below.

Ratio	Island Electric Utility	Burger Heaven	Fink Software	Roland Motors
Current ratio	1.10	1.3	6.8	4.5
Quick ratio	0.90	0.82	5.2	3.7
Debt ratio	0.68	0.46	0	0.35
Net profit margin	6.2%	14.3%	28.5%	8.4%

Assuming that his uncle was a wise investor who assembled the portfolio with care, Robert finds the wide differences in these ratios confusing. Help him out.

a. What problems might Robert encounter in comparing these companies to one another on the basis of their ratios?

b. Why might the current and quick ratios for the electric utility and the fast-food stock be so much lower than the same ratios for the other companies?

c. Why might it be all right for the electric utility to carry a large amount of debt, but not the software company?

d. Why wouldn't investors invest all of their money in software companies instead of in less profitable companies? (Focus on risk and return.)

P2–13 **Liquidity management**   Bauman Company's total current assets, total current liabilities, and inventory for each of the past 4 years follow:

Item	2006	2007	2008	2009
Total current assets	$16,950	$21,900	$22,500	$27,000
Total current liabilities	9,000	12,600	12,600	17,400
Inventory	6,000	6,900	6,900	7,200

a. Calculate the firm's current and quick ratios for each year. Compare the resulting time series for these measures of liquidity.
b. Comment on the firm's liquidity over the 2006–2009 period.
c. If you were told that Bauman Company's inventory turnover for each year in the 2006–2009 period and the industry averages were as follows, would this information support or conflict with your evaluation in part **b?** Why?

Inventory turnover	2006	2007	2008	2009
Bauman Company	6.3	6.8	7.0	6.4
Industry average	10.6	11.2	10.8	11.0

PERSONAL FINANCE PROBLEM

P2–14 **Liquidity ratio**   Josh Smith has compiled some of his personal financial data in order to determine his liquidity position. The data are as follows.

Account	Amount
Cash	$3,200
Marketable securities	1,000
Checking account	800
Credit card payables	1,200
Short-term notes payable	900

a. Calculate Josh's *liquidity ratio.*
b. Several of Josh's friends have told him that they have liquidity ratios of about 1.8. How would you analyze Josh's liquidity relative to his friends?

P2–15 **Inventory management**   Wilkins Manufacturing has annual sales of $4 million and a gross profit margin of 40%. Its *end-of-quarter inventories* are

Quarter	Inventory
1	$ 400,000
2	800,000
3	1,200,000
4	200,000

a. Find the average quarterly inventory and use it to calculate the firm's inventory turnover and the average age of inventory.
b. Assuming that the company is in an industry with an average inventory turnover of 2.0, how would you evaluate the activity of Wilkins' inventory?

P2–16 **Accounts receivable management** An evaluation of the books of Blair Supply, which follows, gives the end-of-year accounts receivable balance, which is believed to consist of amounts originating in the months indicated. The company had annual sales of $2.4 million. The firm extends 30-day credit terms.

Month of origin	Amounts receivable
July	$ 3,875
August	2,000
September	34,025
October	15,100
November	52,000
December	193,000
Year-end accounts receivable	$300,000

a. Use the year-end total to evaluate the firm's collection system.
b. If 70% of the firm's sales occur between July and December, would this affect the validity of your conclusion in part **a**? Explain.

P2–17 **Interpreting liquidity and activity ratios** The new owners of Bluegrass Natural Foods, Inc., have hired you to help them diagnose and cure problems that the company has had in maintaining adequate liquidity. As a first step, you perform a liquidity analysis. You then do an analysis of the company's short-term activity ratios. Your calculations and appropriate industry norms are listed.

Ratio	Bluegrass	Industry norm
Current ratio	4.5	4.0
Quick ratio	2.0	3.1
Inventory turnover	6.0	10.4
Average collection period	73 days	52 days
Average payment period	31 days	40 days

a. What recommendations relative to the amount and the handling of inventory could you make to the new owners?
b. What recommendations relative to the amount and the handling of accounts receivable could you make to the new owners?
c. What recommendations relative to the amount and the handling of accounts payable could you make to the new owners?
d. What results, overall, would you hope your recommendations would achieve? Why might your recommendations not be effective?

P2–18 **Debt analysis** Springfield Bank is evaluating Creek Enterprises, which has requested a $4,000,000 loan, to assess the firm's financial leverage and financial risk. On the basis of the debt ratios for Creek, along with the industry averages (see top of page 91) and Creek's recent financial statements (below), evaluate and recommend appropriate action on the loan request.

Creek Enterprises Income Statement for the Year Ended December 31, 2009		
Sales revenue		$30,000,000
Less: Cost of goods sold		21,000,000
Gross profits		$ 9,000,000
Less: Operating expenses		
Selling expense	$3,000,000	
General and administrative expenses	1,800,000	
Lease expense	200,000	
Depreciation expense	1,000,000	
Total operating expense		6,000,000
Operating profits		$ 3,000,000
Less: Interest expense		1,000,000
Net profits before taxes		$ 2,000,000
Less: Taxes (rate = 40%)		800,000
Net profits after taxes		$ 1,200,000
Less: Preferred stock dividends		100,000
Earnings available for common stockholders		$ 1,100,000

Creek Enterprises Balance Sheet December 31, 2009				
Assets		**Liabilities and Stockholders' Equity**		
Current assets		Current liabilities		
Cash	$ 1,000,000	Accounts payable		$ 8,000,000
Marketable securities	3,000,000	Notes payable		8,000,000
Accounts receivable	12,000,000	Accruals		500,000
Inventories	7,500,000	Total current liabilities		$16,500,000
Total current assets	$23,500,000	Long-term debt (includes financial leases)[b]		$20,000,000
Gross fixed assets (at cost)[a]		Stockholders' equity		
Land and buildings	$11,000,000	Preferred stock (25,000 shares,		
Machinery and equipment	20,500,000	$4 dividend)		$ 2,500,000
Furniture and fixtures	8,000,000	Common stock (1 million shares at $5 par)		5,000,000
Gross fixed assets	$39,500,000	Paid-in capital in excess of par value		4,000,000
Less: Accumulated depreciation	13,000,000	Retained earnings		2,000,000
Net fixed assets	$26,500,000	Total stockholders' equity		$13,500,000
Total assets	$50,000,000	Total liabilities and stockholders' equity		$50,000,000

[a]The firm has a 4-year financial lease requiring annual beginning-of-year payments of $200,000. Three years of the lease have yet to run.
[b]Required annual principal payments are $800,000.

Industry averages	
Debt ratio	0.51
Times interest earned ratio	7.30
Fixed-payment coverage ratio	1.85

P2–19 **Common-size statement analysis**   A common-size income statement for Creek Enterprises' 2008 operations follows. Using the firm's 2009 income statement presented in Problem 2–18, develop the 2009 common-size income statement and compare it to the 2008 statement. Which areas require further analysis and investigation?

Creek Enterprises Common-Size Income Statement for the Year Ended December 31, 2008		
Sales revenue ($35,000,000)		100.0%
Less: Cost of goods sold		65.9
Gross profits		34.1%
Less: Operating expenses		
Selling expense	12.7%	
General and administrative expenses	6.3	
Lease expense	0.6	
Depreciation expense	3.6	
Total operating expense		23.2
Operating profits		10.9%
Less: Interest expense		1.5
Net profits before taxes		9.4%
Less: Taxes (rate = 40%)		3.8
Net profits after taxes		5.6%
Less: Preferred stock dividends		0.1
Earnings available for common stockholders		5.5%

P2–20 **The relationship between financial leverage and profitability**   Pelican Paper, Inc., and Timberland Forest, Inc., are rivals in the manufacture of craft papers. Some financial statement values for each company follow. Use them in a ratio analysis that compares the firms' financial leverage and profitability.

Item	Pelican Paper, Inc.	Timberland Forest, Inc.
Total assets	$10,000,000	$10,000,000
Total equity (all common)	9,000,000	5,000,000
Total debt	1,000,000	5,000,000
Annual interest	100,000	500,000
Total sales	$25,000,000	$25,000,000
EBIT	6,250,000	6,250,000
Earnings available for common stockholders	3,690,000	3,450,00

a. Calculate the following debt and coverage ratios for the two companies. Discuss their financial risk and ability to cover the costs in relation to each other.
   (1) Debt ratio
   (2) Times interest earned ratio
b. Calculate the following profitability ratios for the two companies. Discuss their profitability relative to each other.
   (1) Operating profit margin
   (2) Net profit margin
   (3) Return on total assets
   (4) Return on common equity
c. In what way has the larger debt of Timberland Forest made it more profitable than Pelican Paper? What are the risks that Timberland's investors undertake when they choose to purchase its stock instead of Pelican's?

P2–21 **Ratio proficiency**   McDougal Printing, Inc., had sales totaling $40,000,000 in fiscal year 2009. Some ratios for the company are listed below. Use this information to determine the dollar values of various income statement and balance sheet accounts as requested.

McDougal Printing, Inc. Year Ended December 31, 2009	
Sales	$40,000,000
Gross profit margin	80%
Operating profit margin	35%
Net profit margin	8%
Return on total assets	16%
Return on common equity	20%
Total asset turnover	2
Average collection period	62.2 days

Calculate values for the following:
a. Gross profits
b. Cost of goods sold
c. Operating profits
d. Operating expenses
e. Earnings available for common stockholders
f. Total assets
g. Total common stock equity
h. Accounts receivable

P2–22 **Cross-sectional ratio analysis**   Use the financial statements on page 93 for Fox Manufacturing Company for the year ended December 31, 2009, along with the industry average ratios at the top of page 94, to:
a. Prepare and interpret a complete ratio analysis of the firm's 2009 operations.
b. Summarize your findings and make recommendations.

Fox Manufacturing Company
Income Statement
for the Year Ended December 31, 2009

Sales revenue		$600,000
Less: Cost of goods sold		460,000
Gross profits		$140,000
Less: Operating expenses		
General and administrative expenses	$30,000	
Depreciation expense	30,000	
Total operating expense		60,000
Operating profits		$ 80,000
Less: Interest expense		10,000
Net profits before taxes		$ 70,000
Less: Taxes		27,100
Net profits after taxes (earnings available for common stockholders)		$ 42,900
Earnings per share (EPS)		$2.15

Fox Manufacturing Company
Balance Sheet
December 31, 2009

Assets

Cash	$ 15,000
Marketable securities	7,200
Accounts receivable	34,100
Inventories	82,000
Total current assets	$138,300
Net fixed assets	$270,000
Total assets	$408,300

Liabilities and Stockholders' Equity

Accounts payable	$ 57,000
Notes payable	13,000
Accruals	5,000
Total current liabilities	$ 75,000
Long-term debt	$150,000
Stockholders' equity	
Common stock equity (20,000 shares outstanding)	$110,200
Retained earnings	73,100
Total stockholders' equity	$183,300
Total liabilities and stockholders' equity	$408,300

Ratio	Industry average, 2009
Current ratio	2.35
Quick ratio	0.87
Inventory turnover[a]	4.55
Average collection period[a]	35.8 days
Total asset turnover	1.09
Debt ratio	0.300
Times interest earned ratio	12.3
Gross profit margin	0.202
Operating profit margin	0.135
Net profit margin	0.091
Return on total assets (ROA)	0.099
Return on common equity (ROE)	0.167
Earnings per share (EPS)	$3.10

[a]Based on a 365-day year and on end-of-year figures.

P2–23 **Financial statement analysis**   The financial statements of Zach Industries for the year ended December 31, 2009, follow.

Zach Industries Income Statement for the Year Ended December 31, 2009	
Sales revenue	$160,000
Less: Cost of goods sold	106,000
Gross profits	$ 54,000
Less: Operating expenses	
Selling expense	$ 16,000
General and administrative expenses	10,000
Lease expense	1,000
Depreciation expense	10,000
Total operating expense	$ 37,000
Operating profits	$ 17,000
Less: Interest expense	6,100
Net profits before taxes	$ 10,900
Less: Taxes	4,360
Net profits after taxes	$ 6,540

Zach Industries Balance Sheet December 31, 2009	
Assets	
Cash	$ 500
Marketable securities	1,000
Accounts receivable	25,000
Inventories	45,500
Total current assets	$ 72,000
Land	$ 26,000
Buildings and equipment	90,000
Less: Accumulated depreciation	38,000
Net fixed assets	$ 78,000
Total assets	$150,000
Liabilities and Stockholders' Equity	
Accounts payable	$ 22,000
Notes payable	47,000
Total current liabilities	$ 69,000
Long-term debt	$ 22,950
Common stock[a]	$ 31,500
Retained earnings	$ 26,550
Total liabilities and stockholders' equity	$150,000

[a]The firm's 3,000 outstanding shares of common stock closed 2009 at a price of $25 per share.

a. Use the preceding financial statements to complete the following table. Assume the industry averages given in the table are applicable for both 2008 and 2009.

Ratio	Industry average	Actual 2008	Actual 2009
Current ratio	1.80	1.84	_____
Quick ratio	0.70	0.78	_____
Inventory turnover[a]	2.50	2.59	_____
Average collection period[a]	37.5 days	36.5 days	_____
Debt ratio	65%	67%	_____
Times interest earned ratio	3.8	4.0	_____
Gross profit margin	38%	40%	_____
Net profit margin	3.5%	3.6%	_____
Return on total assets	4.0%	4.0%	_____
Return on common equity	9.5%	8.0%	_____
Market/book ratio	1.1	1.2	_____

[a]Based on a 365-day year and on end-of-year figures.

b. Analyze Zach Industries' financial condition as it is related to (1) liquidity, (2) activity, (3) debt, (4) profitability, and (5) market. Summarize the company's overall financial condition.

P2–24   Integrative—Complete ratio analysis   Given the following financial statements (below and on page 96), historical ratios, and industry averages, calculate Sterling Company's financial ratios for the most recent year. (Assume a 365-day year.) Analyze its overall financial situation from both a cross-sectional and a time-series viewpoint. Break your analysis into evaluations of the firm's liquidity, activity, debt, profitability, and market.

Sterling Company Income Statement for the Year Ended December 31, 2009		
Sales revenue		$10,000,000
Less: Cost of goods sold		7,500,000
Gross profits		$ 2,500,000
Less: Operating expenses		
Selling expense	$300,000	
General and administrative expenses	650,000	
Lease expense	50,000	
Depreciation expense	200,000	
Total operating expense		1,200,000
Operating profits		$ 1,300,000
Less: Interest expense		200,000
Net profits before taxes		$ 1,100,000
Less: Taxes (rate = 40%)		440,000
Net profits after taxes		$ 660,000
Less: Preferred stock dividends		50,000
Earnings available for common stockholders		$ 610,000
Earnings per share (EPS)		$3.05

Sterling Company Balance Sheet December 31, 2009				
Assets			**Liabilities and Stockholders' Equity**	
Current assets			Current liabilities	
Cash	$ 200,000		Accounts payable[b]	$ 900,000
Marketable securities	50,000		Notes payable	200,000
Accounts receivable	800,000		Accruals	100,000
Inventories	950,000		Total current liabilities	$ 1,200,000
Total current assets	$ 2,000,000		Long-term debt (includes financial leases)[c]	$ 3,000,000
Gross fixed assets (at cost)[a]	$12,000,000		Stockholders' equity	
Less: Accumulated depreciation	3,000,000		Preferred stock (25,000 shares, $2 dividend)	$ 1,000,000
Net fixed assets		$ 9,000,000	Common stock (200,000 shares at $3 par)[d]	600,000
Other assets		$ 1,000,000	Paid-in capital in excess of par value	5,200,000
Total assets		$12,000,000	Retained earnings	1,000,000
			Total stockholders' equity	$ 7,800,000
			Total liabilities and stockholders' equity	$12,000,000

[a]The firm has an 8-year financial lease requiring annual beginning-of-year payments of $50,000. Five years of the lease have yet to run.
[b]Annual credit purchases of $6,200,000 were made during the year.
[c]The annual principal payment on the long-term debt is $100,000.
[d]On December 31, 2009, the firm's common stock closed at $39.50 per share.

Historical and Industry Average Ratios for Sterling Company			
Ratio	Actual 2007	Actual 2008	Industry average, 2009
Current ratio	1.40	1.55	1.85
Quick ratio	1.00	0.92	1.05
Inventory turnover	9.52	9.21	8.60
Average collection period	45.6 days	36.9 days	35.5 days
Average payment period	59.3 days	61.6 days	46.4 days
Total asset turnover	0.74	0.80	0.74
Debt ratio	0.20	0.20	0.30
Times interest earned ratio	8.2	7.3	8.0
Fixed-payment coverage ratio	4.5	4.2	4.2
Gross profit margin	0.30	0.27	0.25
Operating profit margin	0.12	0.12	0.10
Net profit margin	0.062	0.062	0.053
Return on total assets (ROA)	0.045	0.050	0.040
Return on common equity (ROE)	0.061	0.067	0.066
Earnings per share (EPS)	$1.75	$2.20	$1.50
Price/earnings (P/E) ratio	12.0	10.5	11.2
Market/book (M/B) ratio	1.20	1.05	1.10

P2–25 **DuPont system of analysis**   Use the following ratio information for Johnson International and the industry averages for Johnson's line of business to:
  a. Construct the DuPont system of analysis for both Johnson and the industry.
  b. Evaluate Johnson (and the industry) over the 3-year period.
  c. Indicate in which areas Johnson requires further analysis. Why?

Johnson	2007	2008	2009
Financial leverage multiplier	1.75	1.75	1.85
Net profit margin	0.059	0.058	0.049
Total asset turnover	2.11	2.18	2.34
Industry Averages			
Financial leverage multiplier	1.67	1.69	1.64
Net profit margin	0.054	0.047	0.041
Total asset turnover	2.05	2.13	2.15

P2–26 **Complete ratio analysis, recognizing significant differences**   Home Health, Inc., has come to Jane Ross for a yearly financial checkup. As a first step, Jane has prepared a complete set of ratios for fiscal years 2008 and 2009. She will use them to look for significant changes in the company's situation from one year to the next.

Home Health, Inc. Financial Ratios		
Ratio	2008	2009
Current ratio	3.25	3.00
Quick ratio	2.50	2.20
Inventory turnover	12.80	10.30
Average collection period	42.6 days	31.4 days
Total asset turnover	1.40	2.00
Debt ratio	0.45	0.62
Times interest earned ratio	4.00	3.85
Gross profit margin	68%	65%
Operating profit margin	14%	16%
Net profit margin	8.3%	8.1%
Return on total assets	11.6%	16.2%
Return on common equity	21.1%	42.6%
Price/earnings ratio	10.7	9.8
Market/book ratio	1.40	1.25

  a. To focus on the degree of change, calculate the year-to-year proportional change by subtracting the year 2008 ratio from the year 2009 ratio, then dividing the difference by the year 2008 ratio. Multiply the result by 100. Preserve the positive or negative sign. The result is the percentage change in the ratio from 2008 to 2009. Calculate the proportional change for the ratios shown here.

b. For any ratio that shows a year-to-year difference of 10% or more, state whether the difference is in the company's favor or not.

c. For the most significant changes (25% or more), look at the other ratios and cite at least one other change that may have contributed to the change in the ratio that you are discussing.

P2–27   ETHICS PROBLEM   Do some reading in periodicals and/or on the Internet to find out more about the Sarbanes-Oxley Act's provisions for companies. Select one of those provisions, and indicate why you think financial statements will be more trustworthy if company financial executives implement this provision of SOX.

Chapter 2 Case

Assessing Martin Manufacturing's Current Financial Position

Terri Spiro, an experienced budget analyst at Martin Manufacturing Company, has been charged with assessing the firm's financial performance during 2009 and its financial position at year-end 2009. To complete this assignment, she gathered the firm's 2009 financial statements (below and on page 99). In addition, Terri obtained the firm's ratio values for 2007 and 2008, along with the 2009 industry average ratios (also applicable to 2007 and 2008). These are presented in the table on page 100.

Martin Manufacturing Company Income Statement for the Year Ended December 31, 2009		
Sales revenue		$5,075,000
Less: Cost of goods sold		3,704,000
Gross profits		$1,371,000
Less: Operating expenses		
Selling expense	$650,000	
General and administrative expenses	416,000	
Depreciation expense	152,000	
Total operating expense		1,218,000
Operating profits		$ 153,000
Less: Interest expense		93,000
Net profits before taxes		$ 60,000
Less: Taxes (rate = 40%)		24,000
Net profits after taxes		$ 36,000
Less: Preferred stock dividends		3,000
Earnings available for common stockholders		$ 33,000
Earnings per share (EPS)		$0.33

Martin Manufacturing Company Balance Sheets		
	December 31	
Assets	2009	2008
Current assets		
Cash	$ 25,000	$ 24,100
Accounts receivable	805,556	763,900
Inventories	700,625	763,445
Total current assets	$1,531,181	$1,551,445
Gross fixed assets (at cost)	$2,093,819	$1,691,707
Less: Accumulated depreciation	500,000	348,000
Net fixed assets	$1,593,819	$1,343,707
Total assets	$3,125,000	$2,895,152
Liabilities and Stockholders' Equity		
Current liabilities		
Accounts payable	$ 230,000	$ 400,500
Notes payable	311,000	370,000
Accruals	75,000	100,902
Total current liabilities	$ 616,000	$ 871,402
Long-term debt	$1,165,250	$ 700,000
Total liabilities	$1,781,250	$1,571,402
Stockholders' equity		
Preferred stock (2,500 shares, $1.20 dividend)	$ 50,000	$ 50,000
Common stock (100,000 shares at $4 par)[a]	400,000	400,000
Paid-in capital in excess of par value	593,750	593,750
Retained earnings	300,000	280,000
Total stockholders' equity	$1,343,750	$1,323,750
Total liabilities and stockholders' equity	$3,125,000	$2,895,152

[a]The firm's 100,000 outstanding shares of common stock closed 2009 at a price of $11.38 per share.

		Martin Manufacturing Company Historical and Industry Average Ratios		
Ratio	Actual 2007	Actual 2008	Actual 2009	Industry average 2009
Current ratio	1.7	1.8	_____	1.5
Quick ratio	1.0	0.9	_____	1.2
Inventory turnover (times)	5.2	5.0	_____	10.2
Average collection period	50.7 days	55.8 days	_____	46 days
Total asset turnover (times)	1.5	1.5	_____	2.0
Debt ratio	45.8%	54.3%	_____	24.5%
Times interest earned ratio	2.2	1.9	_____	2.5
Gross profit margin	27.5%	28.0%	_____	26.0%
Net profit margin	1.1%	1.0%	_____	1.2%
Return on total assets (ROA)	1.7%	1.5%	_____	2.4%
Return on common equity (ROE)	3.1%	3.3%	_____	3.2%
Price/earnings (P/E) ratio	33.5	38.7	_____	43.4
Market/book (M/B) ratio	1.0	1.1	_____	1.2

To Do

a. Calculate the firm's 2009 financial ratios, and then fill in the preceding table. (Assume a 365-day year.)
b. Analyze the firm's current financial position from both a cross-sectional and a time-series viewpoint. Break your analysis into evaluations of the firm's liquidity, activity, debt, profitability, and market.
c. Summarize the firm's overall financial position on the basis of your findings in part **b**.

Spreadsheet Exercise

The income statement and balance sheet are the basic reports that a firm constructs for use by management and for distribution to stockholders, regulatory bodies, and the general public. They are the primary sources of historical financial information about the firm. Dayton Products, Inc., is a moderate-sized manufacturer. The company's management has asked you to perform a detailed financial statement analysis of the firm.

The income statement data for the years ending December 31, 2009 and 2008, respectively, is presented in the table at the top of page 101. (*Note:* Purchases of inventory during 2009 amounted to $109,865.)

Annual Income Statement (Values in millions)		
	For the year ended	
	December 31, 2009	December 31, 2008
Sales	$178,909.00	$187,510.00
Cost of goods sold	?	111,631.00
Selling, general, and administrative expenses	12,356.00	12,900.00
Other tax expense	33,572.00	33,377.00
Depreciation and amortization	12,103.00	7,944.00
Other income (add to EBIT to arrive at EBT)	3,147.00	3,323.00
Interest expense	398	293
Income tax rate (average)	35.324%	37.945%
Dividends paid per share	$1.47	$0.91
Basic EPS from total operations	$1.71	$2.25

You also have the following balance sheet information as of December 31, 2009 and 2008, respectively.

Annual Balance Sheet (Values in millions)		
	December 31, 2009	December, 31, 2008
Cash and equivalents	$ 7,229.00	$ 6,547.00
Receivables	21,163.00	19,549.00
Inventories	8,068.00	7,904.00
Other current assets	1,831.00	1,681.00
Property, plant, and equipment, gross	204,960.00	187,519.00
Accumulated depreciation and depletion	110,020.00	97,917.00
Other noncurrent assets	19,413.00	17,891.00
Accounts payable	$ 13,792.00	$ 22,862.00
Short-term debt payable	4,093.00	3,703.00
Other current liabilities	15,290.00	3,549.00
Long-term debt payable	6,655.00	7,099.00
Deferred income taxes	16,484.00	16,359.00
Other noncurrent liabilities	21,733.00	16,441.00
Retained earnings	$ 74,597.00	$ 73,161.00
Total common shares outstanding	6.7 billion	6.8 billion

To Do

a. Create a spreadsheet similar to the spreadsheet in Table 2.1 (which can be viewed at **www.prenhall.com/gitman**) to model the following:

    (1) A multiple-step comparative income statement for Dayton, Inc., for the periods ending December 31, 2009 and 2008. You must calculate the cost of goods sold for the year 2009.

    (2) A common-size income statement for Dayton, Inc., covering the years 2009 and 2008.

b. Create a spreadsheet similar to the spreadsheet in Table 2.2 (which can be viewed at **www.prenhall.com/gitman**) to model the following:

    (1) A detailed, comparative balance sheet for Dayton, Inc., for the years ended December 31, 2009 and 2008.

    (2) A common-size balance sheet for Dayton, Inc., covering the years 2009 and 2008.

c. Create a spreadsheet similar to the spreadsheet in Table 2.8 (which can be viewed at **www.prenhall.com/gitman**) to perform the following analysis:

    (1) Create a table that reflects both 2009 and 2008 operating ratios for Dayton, Inc., segmented into (a) liquidity, (b) activity, (c) debt, (d) profitability, and (e) market. Assume that the current market price for the stock is $90.

    (2) Compare the 2009 ratios to the 2008 ratios. Indicate whether the results "outperformed the prior year" or "underperformed relative to the prior year."

Group Exercise

This assignment will focus on your group's shadow corporation. The group will be asked to utilize the latest SEC 10-K filing.

To Do

a. Go to the SEC's website (**www.sec.gov**) and access the latest 10-K filing. Describe the content of the letter to stockholders.

b. Calculate the basic ratios as done in the text. Sort the ratios into the five categories found in Table 2.8 (pages 72 and 73).

c. State what use each ratio has in analyzing the health of your corporation.

d. Analyze these ratios through time by calculating them over the most recent years. For any ratios that have changed, give possible explanations as to why these changes may have occurred.

e. Conclude with a financial summary of the ratios using the *DuPont system of analysis*.

Web Exercise

Go to the book's companion website at **www.prenhall.com/gitman** to find the Web Exercise for this chapter.

Remember to check the book's website at **www.prenhall.com/gitman** to find additional resources, including Web Exercises and a Web Case.

3 Cash Flow and Financial Planning

WHY THIS CHAPTER MATTERS TO YOU

In Your Professional Life

Accounting: You need to understand how depreciation is used for both tax and financial reporting purposes; how to develop the statement of cash flows; the primary focus on cash flows, rather than accruals, in financial decision making; and how pro forma financial statements are used within the firm.

Information systems: You need to understand the data that must be kept to record depreciation for tax and financial reporting; the information needs for strategic and operating plans; and what data are needed as inputs for preparing cash plans and profit plans.

Management: You need to understand the difference between strategic and operating plans, and the role of each; the importance of focusing on the firm's cash flows; and how use of pro forma statements can head off trouble for the firm.

Marketing: You need to understand the central role that marketing plays in formulating the firm's long-term, strategic plans, and the importance of the sales forecast as the key input for both cash planning and profit planning.

Operations: You need to understand how depreciation affects the value of the firm's plant assets; how the results of operations are captured in the statement of cash flows; that operations provide key inputs into the firm's short-term financial plans; and the distinction between fixed and variable operating costs.

In Your Personal Life

Individuals, like corporations, should focus on cash flow when planning and monitoring finances. You should establish short- and long-term financial goals (destinations) and develop personal financial plans (road maps) that will guide their achievement. Cash flows and financial plans are as important for individuals as for corporations.

LEARNING GOALS

LG 1 Understand tax depreciation procedures and the effect of depreciation on the firm's cash flows.

LG 2 Discuss the firm's statement of cash flows, operating cash flow, and free cash flow.

LG 3 Understand the financial planning process, including long-term (strategic) financial plans and short-term (operating) financial plans.

LG 4 Discuss the cash-planning process and the preparation, evaluation, and use of the cash budget.

LG 5 Explain the simplified procedures used to prepare and evaluate the pro forma income statement and the pro forma balance sheet.

LG 6 Evaluate the simplified approaches to pro forma financial statement preparation and the common uses of pro forma statements.

Google, Inc.

Searching for a Use for Its Cash

If you google the Web to find a company with lots of cash, you might just find **Google, Inc.** In less than nine years from its founding, Google has become a cash machine, generating $3.58 billion in operating cash flow in 2006 on revenues of $10.6 billion. With more than $11 billion in cash and short-term marketable securities, Google is in a position to take advantage of any compelling acquisitions that may appear.

What should the company's management do with this $11 billion "war chest"? Common uses for cash are to pursue new opportunities (including acquisitions), pay dividends, buy back stock, and reduce debt. Google has virtually no long-term debt. Google also has no history of paying dividends. In its 2006 annual report, Google stated that it had "never declared or paid any cash dividend on our capital stock. We currently intend to retain any future earnings and do not expect to pay any dividends in the foreseeable future." Will Google use its cash to buy back its stock? With a price/earnings ratio of around 47, the stock is not inexpensive. Therefore the company is not likely to buy back its stock.

Since its incorporation, Google has pursued a growth policy fueled by its acquisition of high-tech companies that enhance its dominance in automated search technology and online advertising. It currently has 87 subsidiaries, including **YouTube,** the video-sharing website, which it bought for $1.65 billion in late 2006. With its stock trading at over $400 per share, Google didn't even have to spend cash for YouTube. It simply issued stock for the purchase. Google continued its aggressive acquisition binge in 2007, when it announced it would purchase **DoubleClick,** the online advertising company, for $3.1 billion in cash.

If Google continues to amass additional cash, some shareholders may demand that the company issue dividends. In the near term, Google's shareholders can be comforted by the knowledge that the company is clearly able to generate profits, unlike many of the dot-com stocks that crashed and burned in the early part of this decade.

What are some possible negatives that could arise from a company hoarding large amounts of cash?

Like Google, companies must make strategic plans and implement those plans. As you will see in this chapter, part of that decision-making process involves what to do when cash inflows routinely exceed cash outflows.

3.1 | Analyzing the Firm's Cash Flow

Cash flow, the lifeblood of the firm, is the primary focus of the financial manager both in managing day-to-day finances and in planning and making strategic decisions focused on creating shareholder value. We therefore place major emphasis on estimating and analyzing the cash flows associated with the major financial decisions discussed and demonstrated throughout this book.

An important factor affecting a firm's cash flow is depreciation (and any other noncash charges). From an accounting perspective, a firm's cash flows can be summarized in the statement of cash flows, which was described in Chapter 2. From a strict financial perspective, firms often focus on both *operating cash flow*, which is used in managerial decision making, and *free cash flow*, which is closely watched by participants in the capital market. We begin our analysis of cash flow by considering the key aspects of depreciation, which is closely related to the firm's cash flow.

Depreciation

depreciation
The systematic charging of a portion of the costs of fixed assets against annual revenues over time.

Business firms are permitted for tax and financial reporting purposes to charge a portion of the costs of fixed assets systematically against annual revenues. This allocation of historical cost over time is called **depreciation.** For tax purposes, the depreciation of business assets is regulated by the Internal Revenue Code. Because the objectives of financial reporting sometimes differ from those of tax legislation, firms often use different depreciation methods for financial reporting than those required for tax purposes. Keeping two different sets of records for these two different purposes is legal.

modified accelerated cost recovery system (MACRS)
System used to determine the depreciation of assets for tax purposes.

Depreciation for tax purposes is determined by using the **modified accelerated cost recovery system** (**MACRS**); a variety of depreciation methods are available for financial reporting purposes. Before we discuss the methods of depreciating an asset, you must understand the depreciable value of an asset and the depreciable life of an asset.

Depreciable Value of an Asset

Under the basic MACRS procedures, the depreciable value of an asset (the amount to be depreciated) is its *full* cost, including outlays for installation.[1] No adjustment is required for expected salvage value.

Example   Baker Corporation acquired a new machine at a cost of $38,000, with installation costs of $2,000. Regardless of its expected salvage value, the depreciable value of the machine is $40,000: $38,000 cost + $2,000 installation cost.

Depreciable Life of an Asset

depreciable life
Time period over which an asset is depreciated.

The time period over which an asset is depreciated—its **depreciable life**—can significantly affect the pattern of cash flows. The shorter the depreciable life, the

---

1. Land values are *not* depreciable. Therefore, to determine the depreciable value of real estate, the value of the land is subtracted from the cost of real estate. In other words, only buildings and other improvements are depreciable.

TABLE 3.1	First Four Property Classes under MACRS
Property class (recovery period)	**Definition**
3 years	Research equipment and certain special tools
5 years	Computers, typewriters, copiers, duplicating equipment, cars, light-duty trucks, qualified technological equipment, and similar assets
7 years	Office furniture, fixtures, most manufacturing equipment, railroad track, and single-purpose agricultural and horticultural structures
10 years	Equipment used in petroleum refining or in the manufacture of tobacco products and certain food products

recovery period
The appropriate depreciable life of a particular asset as determined by MACRS.

more quickly the cash flow created by the depreciation write-off will be received. Given the financial manager's preference for faster receipt of cash flows, a shorter depreciable life is preferred to a longer one. However, the firm must abide by certain Internal Revenue Service (IRS) requirements for determining depreciable life. These MACRS standards, which apply to both new and used assets, require the taxpayer to use as an asset's depreciable life the appropriate MACRS **recovery period**.[2] There are six MACRS recovery periods—3, 5, 7, 10, 15, and 20 years—excluding real estate. It is customary to refer to the property classes as 3-, 5-, 7-, 10-, 15-, and 20-year property. The first four property classes—those routinely used by business—are defined in Table 3.1.

Depreciation Methods

For *financial reporting purposes,* companies can use a variety of depreciation methods (straight-line, double-declining balance, and sum-of-the-years'-digits[3]). For *tax purposes,* assets in the first four MACRS property classes are depreciated by the double-declining balance (200%) method, using the half-year convention and switching to straight-line when advantageous. The *approximate percentages* (rounded to the nearest whole percent) written off each year for the first four property classes are shown in Table 3.2 (see page 108). Rather than using the percentages in the table, the firm can either use straight-line depreciation over the asset's recovery period with the half-year convention or use the alternative depreciation system. For purposes of this text, we will use the MACRS depreciation percentages, because they generally provide for the fastest write-off and therefore the best cash flow effects for the profitable firm.

Because MACRS requires use of the half-year convention, assets are assumed to be acquired in the middle of the year; therefore only one-half of the first year's depreciation is recovered in the first year. As a result, the final half-year of depreciation is recovered in the year immediately following the asset's stated recovery period. In Table 3.2, the depreciation percentages for an *n*-year class asset

2. An exception occurs in the case of assets depreciated under the *alternative depreciation system.* For convenience, in this text we ignore the depreciation of assets under this system.

3. For a review of these depreciation methods as well as other aspects of financial reporting, see any recently published financial accounting text.

| TABLE 3.2 | Rounded Depreciation Percentages by Recovery Year Using MACRS for First Four Property Classes |

	Percentage by recovery year[a]			
Recovery year	3 years	5 years	7 years	10 years
1	33%	20%	14%	10%
2	45	32	25	18
3	15	19	18	14
4	7	12	12	12
5		12	9	9
6		5	9	8
7			9	7
8			4	6
9				6
10				6
11				4
Totals	100%	100%	100%	100%

[a]These percentages have been rounded to the nearest whole percent to simplify calculations while retaining realism. To calculate the *actual* depreciation for tax purposes, be sure to apply the actual unrounded percentages or directly apply double-declining balance (200%) depreciation using the half-year convention.

are given for $n + 1$ years. For example, a 5-year asset is depreciated over 6 recovery years. The application of the tax depreciation percentages given in Table 3.2 can be demonstrated by a simple example.

Example

Baker Corporation acquired, for an installed cost of $40,000, a machine having a recovery period of 5 years. Using the applicable percentages from Table 3.2, Baker calculates the depreciation in each year as follows:

Year	Cost (1)	Percentages (from Table 3.2) (2)	Depreciation [(1) × (2)] (3)
1	$40,000	20%	$ 8,000
2	40,000	32	12,800
3	40,000	19	7,600
4	40,000	12	4,800
5	40,000	12	4,800
6	40,000	5	2,000
Totals		100%	$40,000

Column 3 shows that the full cost of the asset is written off over 6 recovery years.

Because financial managers focus primarily on cash flows, *only tax depreciation methods will be utilized throughout this textbook.*

Developing the Statement of Cash Flows

The *statement of cash flows,* introduced in Chapter 2, summarizes the firm's cash flow over a given period of time. Before discussing the statement and its interpretation, we will review the cash flow through the firm and the classification of inflows and outflows of cash.

Hint In finance, cash is king. Income statement profits are good, but they don't pay the bills, nor do asset owners accept them in place of cash.

The Firm's Cash Flows

Figure 3.1 illustrates the firm's cash flows. Note that marketable securities are considered the same as cash because of their highly liquid nature. Both cash and

---

FIGURE 3.1   Cash Flows

The firm's cash flows

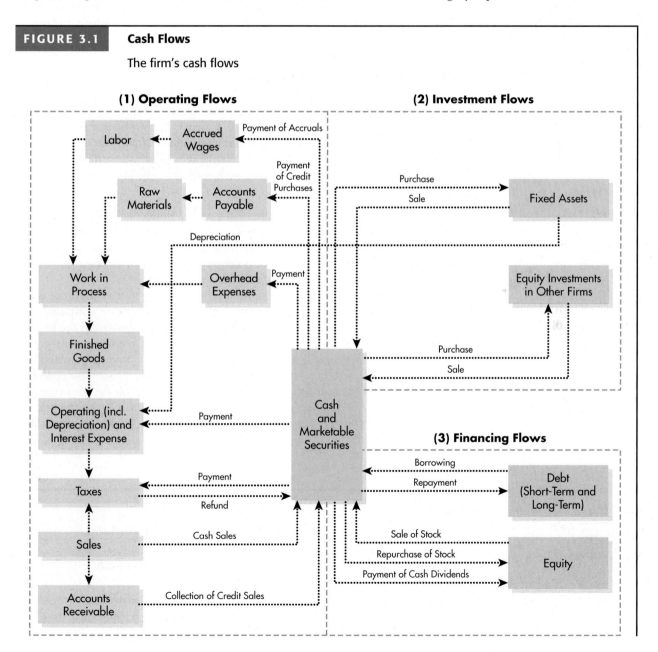

operating flows
Cash flows directly related to sale and production of the firm's products and services.

investment flows
Cash flows associated with purchase and sale of both fixed assets and equity investments in other firms.

financing flows
Cash flows that result from debt and equity financing transactions; include incurrence and repayment of debt, cash inflow from the sale of stock, and cash outflows to repurchase stock or pay cash dividends.

marketable securities represent a reservoir of liquidity that is *increased by cash inflows* and *decreased by cash outflows.*

Also note that the firm's cash flows can be divided into (1) operating flows, (2) investment flows, and (3) financing flows. The **operating flows** are cash inflows and outflows directly related to the sale and production of the firm's products and services. **Investment flows** are cash flows associated with the purchase and sale of both fixed assets and equity investments in other firms. Clearly, purchase transactions would result in cash outflows, whereas sales transactions would generate cash inflows. The **financing flows** result from debt and equity financing transactions. Incurring either short-term or long-term debt would result in a corresponding cash inflow; repaying debt would result in an outflow. Similarly, the sale of the company's stock would result in a cash inflow; the repurchase of stock or payment of cash dividends would result in an outflow.

Classifying Inflows and Outflows of Cash

The statement of cash flows, in effect, summarizes the inflows and outflows of cash during a given period. Table 3.3 classifies the basic inflows (sources) and outflows (uses) of cash. For example, if a firm's accounts payable balance increased by $1,000 during the year, the change would be an *inflow of cash.* If the firm's inventory increased by $2,500, the change would be an *outflow of cash.*

A few additional points can be made with respect to the classification scheme in Table 3.3:

1. A *decrease* in an asset, such as the firm's cash balance, is an *inflow of cash.* Why? Because cash that has been tied up in the asset is released and can be used for some other purpose, such as repaying a loan. On the other hand, an *increase* in the firm's cash balance is an *outflow of cash,* because additional cash is being tied up in the firm's cash balance.

   The classification of decreases and increases in a firm's cash balance is difficult for many to grasp. To clarify, imagine that you store all your cash in a bucket. Your cash balance is represented by the amount of cash in the bucket. When you need cash, you withdraw it from the bucket, which *decreases your cash balance and provides an inflow* of cash to you. Conversely, when you have excess cash, you deposit it in the bucket, which *increases your cash balance and represents an outflow* of cash from you. Focus on the movement of funds *in and out of your pocket*: Clearly, a decrease in cash (from the bucket) is an inflow (to your pocket); an increase in cash (in the bucket) is an outflow (from your pocket).

TABLE 3.3	Inflows and Outflows of Cash
Inflows (sources)	**Outflows (uses)**
Decrease in any asset	Increase in any asset
Increase in any liability	Decrease in any liability
Net profits after taxes	Net loss
Depreciation and other noncash charges	Dividends paid
Sale of stock	Repurchase or retirement of stock

noncash charge
An expense that is deducted on the income statement but does not involve the actual outlay of cash during the period; includes depreciation, amortization, and depletion.

2. Depreciation (like amortization and depletion) is a **noncash charge**—an expense that is deducted on the income statement but does not involve the actual outlay of cash during the period. Because it shields the firm from taxes by lowering taxable income, the noncash charge is considered a cash inflow. From a strict accounting perspective, adding depreciation back to the firm's net profits after taxes provides an estimate of cash flow from operations:[4]

$$\text{Cash flow from operations} = $$
$$\text{Net profits after taxes} + \text{Depreciation and other noncash charges} \quad \text{(3.1)}$$

Note that a firm can have a *net loss* (negative net profits after taxes) and still have positive cash flow from operations when depreciation (and other noncash charges) during the period is greater than the net loss. In the statement of cash flows, net profits after taxes (or net losses) and depreciation (and other noncash charges) are therefore treated as separate entries.

3. We will refine Equation 3.1 in the next section and apply the revised equation (Equation 3.4) in Chapter 8 to estimate the relevant operating cash inflows associated with a firm's present and proposed fixed-asset investments.

4. Because depreciation is treated as a separate cash inflow, only *gross* rather than *net* changes in fixed assets appear on the statement of cash flows. This treatment avoids the potential double counting of depreciation.

5. Direct entries of changes in retained earnings are not included on the statement of cash flows. Instead, entries for items that affect retained earnings appear as net profits or losses after taxes and dividends paid.

Preparing the Statement of Cash Flows

The statement of cash flows for a given period is developed using the income statement for the period, along with the beginning- and end-of-period balance sheets. The income statement for the year ended December 31, 2009, and the December 31 balance sheets for 2008 and 2009 for Baker Corporation are given in Tables 3.4 (see page 112) and 3.5 (see page 113), respectively. The statement of cash flows for the year ended December 31, 2009, for Baker Corporation is presented in Table 3.6 (see page 114). Note that all cash inflows as well as net profits after taxes and depreciation are treated as positive values. All cash outflows, any losses, and dividends paid are treated as negative values. The items in each category—operating, investment, and financing—are totaled, and the three totals are added to get the "Net increase (decrease) in cash and marketable securities" for the period. As a check, this value should reconcile with the actual change in cash and marketable securities for the year, which is obtained from the beginning- and end-of-period balance sheets. A detailed description of the procedures used to prepare Baker Corporation's statement of cash flows is posted on this book's website.

Interpreting the Statement

The statement of cash flows allows the financial manager and other interested parties to analyze the firm's cash flow. The manager should pay special attention

---

4. This equation is merely an estimate because it is based on the assumption that the firm's accounts receivable, inventory, accounts payable, and accruals remain unchanged during the period. Generally, these account balances will change over the period.

TABLE 3.4	Baker Corporation Income Statement ($000) for the Year Ended December 31, 2009
Sales revenue	$1,700
Less: Cost of goods sold	1,000
Gross profits	$ 700
Less: Operating expenses	
Selling expense	$ 70
General and administrative expenses	120
Lease expense[a]	40
Depreciation expense	100
Total operating expense	$ 330
Earnings before interest and taxes (EBIT)	$ 370
Less: Interest expense	70
Net profits before taxes	$ 300
Less: Taxes (rate = 40%)	120
Net profits after taxes	$ 180
Less: Preferred stock dividends	10
Earnings available for common stockholders	$ 170
Earnings per share (EPS)[b]	$1.70

[a]Lease expense is shown here as a separate item rather than included as interest expense as specified by the FASB for financial reporting purposes. The approach used here is consistent with tax reporting rather than financial reporting procedures.

[b]Calculated by dividing the earnings available for common stockholders by the number of shares of common stock outstanding ($170,000 ÷ 100,000 shares = $1.70 per share).

both to the major categories of cash flow and to the individual items of cash inflow and outflow, to assess whether any developments have occurred that are contrary to the company's financial policies. In addition, the statement can be used to evaluate progress toward projected goals or to isolate inefficiencies. The financial manager also can prepare a statement of cash flows developed from projected financial statements to determine whether planned actions are desirable in view of the resulting cash flows.

Operating Cash Flow

operating cash flow (OCF)
The cash flow a firm generates from its normal operations; calculated as *net operating profits after taxes (NOPAT)* plus depreciation.

A firm's **operating cash flow (OCF)** is the cash flow it generates from its normal operations—producing and selling its output of goods or services. A variety of definitions of OCF can be found in the financial literature. Equation 3.1 introduced the simple accounting definition of cash flow from operations. Here we refine this definition to estimate cash flows more accurately. Unlike the earlier definition, this one excludes interest and taxes to enable us to focus on the true cash flow resulting from operations without regard to interest expense and taxes.

TABLE 3.5	Baker Corporation Balance Sheets ($000)		
		December 31	
Assets		2009	2008
Current assets			
Cash		$ 400	$ 300
Marketable securities		600	200
Accounts receivable		400	500
Inventories		600	900
Total current assets		$2,000	$1,900
Gross fixed assets (at cost)			
Land and buildings		$1,200	$1,050
Machinery and equipment		850	800
Furniture and fixtures		300	220
Vehicles		100	80
Other (includes certain leases)		50	50
Total gross fixed assets (at cost)		$2,500	$2,200
Less: Accumulated depreciation		1,300	1,200
Net fixed assets		$1,200	$1,000
Total assets		$3,200	$2,900
Liabilities and Stockholders' Equity			
Current liabilities			
Accounts payable		$ 700	$ 500
Notes payable		600	700
Accruals		100	200
Total current liabilities		$1,400	$1,400
Long-term debt		$ 600	$ 400
Total liabilities		$2,000	$1,800
Stockholders' equity			
Preferred stock		$ 100	$ 100
Common stock—$1.20 par, 100,000 shares outstanding in 2009 and 2008		120	120
Paid-in capital in excess of par on common stock		380	380
Retained earnings		600	500
Total stockholders' equity		$1,200	$1,100
Total liabilities and stockholders' equity		$3,200	$2,900

net operating profits after taxes (NOPAT)
A firm's earnings before interest and after taxes, $EBIT \times (1 - T)$.

The first step is to calculate **net operating profits after taxes (NOPAT),** which represent the firm's earnings before interest and after taxes. Letting T equal the applicable corporate tax rate, NOPAT is calculated as follows:

$$NOPAT = EBIT \times (1 - T) \tag{3.2}$$

To convert NOPAT to operating cash flow (OCF), we merely add back depreciation:

$$OCF = NOPAT + Depreciation \tag{3.3}$$

TABLE 3.6	Baker Corporation Statement of Cash Flows ($000) for the Year Ended December 31, 2009		
Cash Flow from Operating Activities			
Net profits after taxes		$180	
Depreciation		100	
Decrease in accounts receivable		100	
Decrease in inventories		300	
Increase in accounts payable		200	
Decrease in accruals		(100)*a*	
Cash provided by operating activities			$780
Cash Flow from Investment Activities			
Increase in gross fixed assets		($300)	
Changes in equity investments in other firms		0	
Cash provided by investment activities			(300)
Cash Flow from Financing Activities			
Decrease in notes payable		($100)	
Increase in long-term debts		200	
Changes in stockholders' equity*b*		0	
Dividends paid		(80)	
Cash provided by financing activities			20
Net increase in cash and marketable securities			$500

*a*As is customary, parentheses are used to denote a negative number, which in this case is a cash outflow.

*b*Retained earnings are excluded here, because their change is actually reflected in the combination of the "Net profits after taxes" and "Dividends paid" entries.

We can substitute the expression for NOPAT from Equation 3.2 into Equation 3.3 to get a single equation for OCF:

$$OCF = [EBIT \times (1 - T)] + \text{Depreciation} \tag{3.4}$$

Example

Substituting the values for Baker Corporation from its income statement (Table 3.4) into Equation 3.4, we get

$$OCF = [\$370 \times (1.00 - 0.40)] + \$100 = \$222 + \$100 = \$322$$

During 2009, Baker Corporation generated $322,000 of cash flow from producing and selling its output. Therefore, we can conclude that Baker's operations are generating positive cash flows.

Comparing Equations 3.1 and 3.4 reveals the key difference between the accounting and finance definitions of operating cash flow: The finance definition excludes interest—a financing cost—as an operating cash flow, whereas the accounting definition includes it as an operating flow. In the unlikely case that a firm has no interest expense, the accounting definition (Equation 3.1) and the finance definition (Equation 3.4) of operating cash flow would be the same.

Free Cash Flow

free cash flow (FCF)
The amount of cash flow available to investors (creditors and owners) after the firm has met all operating needs and paid for investments in net fixed assets and net current assets.

The firm's **free cash flow** (FCF) represents the amount of cash flow available to investors—the providers of debt (creditors) and equity (owners)—after the firm has met all operating needs and paid for investments in net fixed assets and net current assets. It represents the summation of the net amount of cash flow available to creditors and owners during the period. Free cash flow can be defined as follows:

$$FCF = OCF - \text{Net fixed asset investment (NFAI)}$$
$$- \text{Net current asset investment (NCAI)} \quad (3.5)$$

The *net fixed asset investment* (NFAI) can be calculated as shown here:

$$NFAI = \text{Change in net fixed assets} + \text{Depreciation} \quad (3.6)$$

Example

Using the Baker Corporation's balance sheets in Table 3.5, we see that its change in net fixed assets between 2008 and 2009 was +$200 ($1,200 in 2009 − $1,000 in 2008). Substituting this value and the $100 of depreciation for 2009 into Equation 3.6, we get Baker's net fixed asset investment (NFAI) for 2009:

$$NFAI = \$200 + \$100 = \$300$$

Baker Corporation therefore invested a net $300,000 in fixed assets during 2009. This amount would, of course, represent a net cash outflow to acquire fixed assets during 2009.

Looking at Equation 3.6, we can see that if the depreciation during a year is less than the *decrease* during that year in net fixed assets, the NFAI would be negative. A negative NFAI represents a net cash *inflow* attributable to the fact that the firm sold more assets than it acquired during the year.

The *net current asset investment (NCAI)* represents the net investment made by the firm in its current (operating) assets. "Net" refers to the difference between current assets and the sum of accounts payable and accruals. Notes payable are not included in the NCAI calculation because they represent a negotiated creditor claim on the firm's free cash flow. Equation 3.7 shows the NCAI calculation.

$$NCAI = \text{Change in current assets} -$$
$$\text{Change in (accounts payable + accruals)} \quad (3.7)$$

Example

Looking at the Baker Corporation's balance sheets for 2008 and 2009 in Table 3.5, we see that the change in current assets between 2008 and 2009 is +$100 ($2,000 in 2009 − $1,900 in 2008). The difference between Baker's accounts payable plus accruals of $800 in 2009 ($700 in accounts payable + $100 in accruals) and of $700 in 2008 ($500 in accounts payable + $200 in accruals) is +$100 ($800 in 2009 − $700 in 2008). Substituting into Equation 3.7 the change in current assets and the change in the sum of accounts payable plus accruals for Baker Corporation, we get its 2009 NCAI:

$$NCAI = \$100 - \$100 = \$0$$

Focus on Practice   Free Cash Flow at eBay

Free cash flow is the lifeblood of any company and is the only true way to measure how much cash a company is generating. Free cash flow is, broadly, operating cash flow minus investments in net fixed assets and net current assets. It represents the net amount of cash flow available to creditors and owners. Free cash flow is an ideal way to measure a company's health and cash-generating growth.

Take **eBay,** for example. The company which brings together millions of people every day in its online marketplace produced $1.73 billion in free cash flow for the year ending December 31, 2006. Net cash provided by operating activities was $2.24 billion, and the company invested $0.51 billion in property, equipment, and net current assets during 2006, leaving $1.73 billion in free cash flow, a 10.09 percent increase over the previous year.

However, despite the increase in free cash flow, eBay faces some challenges. Users

of eBay generated a total of 610 million listings in the fourth quarter of 2006, a 12 percent increase over the fourth quarter of 2005. But the company is spending more and more, mostly paying Google, a chief competitor, to draw traffic to the site. When expenses start to increase more than free cash flow, it suggests that a company's competitive edge is under attack.

Having free cash flows is one thing; what a company does with it is quite another. According to the Motley Fool (www.fool.com), as an investor you are much better served by companies that use free cash flow to buy back their stock (if the stock is undervalued) or, better yet, use it toward a regular cash dividend. The investor then has the option to reinvest the dividend back into the company or use the dividend to pursue a different opportunity.

In 2006, eBay chose to use its excess cash to buy back stock. Since announcing a share buy-back program in July 2006, the

company repurchased approximately 50 million shares of its common stock at a total cost of nearly $1.7 billion. In addition, the company has the capacity to buy back an additional $300 million of stock under the initial plan, and the company's board of directors has authorized an expansion of the stock repurchase program to provide for the repurchase of up to an additional $2 billion of the company's common stock within the next 2 years. For the time being, stockholders expecting the start of a dividend stream can put those expectations on hold. The company's intentions are clearly not to begin paying dividends for the foreseeable future.

■ *Free cash flow is often considered a more reliable measure of a company's income than reported earnings. What are some possible ways that corporate accountants might be able to change their earnings to portray a more favorable earnings statement?*

This means that during 2009 Baker Corporation made no investment ($0) in its current assets net of accounts payable and accruals.

Now we can substitute Baker Corporation's 2009 operating cash flow (OCF) of $322, its net fixed asset investment (NFAI) of $300, and its net current asset investment (NCAI) of $0 into Equation 3.5 to find its free cash flow (FCF):

$$FCF = \$322 - \$300 - \$0 = \$22$$

We can see that during 2009 Baker generated $22,000 of free cash flow, which it can use to pay its investors—creditors (payment of interest) and owners (payment of dividends). Thus, the firm generated adequate cash flow to cover all of its operating costs and investments and had free cash flow available to pay investors.

Clearly, cash flow is the lifeblood of the firm. The *Focus on Practice* box at the top of this page discusses eBay's free cash flow.

In the next section, we consider various aspects of financial planning for cash flow and profit.

REVIEW QUESTIONS

3–1 Briefly describe the first four *modified accelerated cost recovery system (MACRS)* property classes and recovery periods. Explain how the depreciation percentages are determined by using the MACRS recovery periods.

3–2 Describe the overall cash flow through the firm in terms of operating flows, investments flows, and financing flows.

3–3 Explain why a decrease in cash is classified as a *cash inflow (source)* and why an increase in cash is classified as a *cash outflow (use)* in preparing the statement of cash flows.

3–4 Why is depreciation (as well as amortization and depletion) considered a *noncash charge?* How do accountants estimate *cash flow from operations?*

3–5 Describe the general format of the statement of cash flows. How are cash inflows differentiated from cash outflows on this statement?

3–6 What is the difference between the accounting and finance definitions of *operating cash flow?* Under what circumstances are they the same?

3–7 From a strict financial perspective, define and differentiate between a firm's *operating cash flow (OCF)* and its *free cash flow (FCF).*

3.2 | The Financial Planning Process

Financial planning is an important aspect of the firm's operations because it provides road maps for guiding, coordinating, and controlling the firm's actions to achieve its objectives. Two key aspects of the financial planning process are *cash planning* and *profit planning.* Cash planning involves preparation of the firm's cash budget. Profit planning involves preparation of pro forma statements. Both the cash budget and the pro forma statements are useful for internal financial planning; they also are routinely required by existing and prospective lenders.

The **financial planning process** begins with long-term, or *strategic,* financial plans. These, in turn, guide the formulation of short-term, or *operating,* plans and budgets. Generally, the short-term plans and budgets implement the firm's long-term strategic objectives. Although the remainder of this chapter places primary emphasis on short-term financial plans and budgets, a few preliminary comments on long-term financial plans are in order.

financial planning process
Planning that begins with long-term, or *strategic,* financial plans that in turn guide the formulation of short-term, or *operating,* plans and budgets.

Long-Term (Strategic) Financial Plans

Long-term (strategic) financial plans lay out a company's planned financial actions and the anticipated impact of those actions over periods ranging from 2 to 10 years. Five-year strategic plans, which are revised as significant new information becomes available, are common. Generally, firms that are subject to high degrees of operating uncertainty, relatively short production cycles, or both, tend to use shorter planning horizons.

long-term (strategic) financial plans
Lay out a company's planned financial actions and the anticipated impact of those actions over periods ranging from 2 to 10 years.

> ## (Focus on Ethics)   How Much Is a CEO Worth?

When Jack Welch retired as chairman and CEO of **General Electric** in 2000, Robert L. Nardelli was part of a lengthy and well-publicized succession planning saga; he eventually lost the job to Jeff Immelt. Nardelli was quickly hired by **Home Depot,** one of several companies competing for his services, who offered generous incentives for him to come on board.

Using the "Six Sigma" management strategy from GE, Nardelli dramatically overhauled Home Depot and replaced its freewheeling entrepreneurial culture. He changed the decentralized management structure by eliminating and consolidating division executives. He also installed processes and streamlined operations, most notably implementing a computerized automated inventory system and centralizing supply orders at the Atlanta headquarters. Nardelli was credited with doubling the

sales of the chain and improving its competitive position. Revenue increased from $45.7 billion in 2000 to $81.5 billion in 2005, while profit rose from $2.6 billion to $5.8 billion.

However, the company's stagnating share price, his results-driven management style, which turned off both employees and customers, and his compensation package eventually earned the ire of investors. Despite having received the solid support of Home Depot's board of directors, Nardelli abruptly resigned on January 3, 2007. He was not destined for poverty, as his severance package had been negotiated years earlier when he joined Home Depot. The total severance package amounted to $210 million, including $55.3 million of life insurance coverage, reimbursement of $1.3 million of Nardelli's personal taxes related to the life insurance, $50,000 to cover his legal fees, $33.8 mil-

lion in cash due July 3, 2007, an additional $18 million over 4 years for abiding by the terms of the deal, and the balance of the package from accelerated vesting of stock options. In addition, Nardelli and his family would receive health-care benefits from the company for the next 3 years.

The mammoth pay-off for Nardelli's departure caused uproar among many shareholder activists because Home Depot's stock fell 8 percent during his 6-year tenure. Clearly, the mantra of shareholder activists today is, "Ask not what you can do for your company, ask what your company can do for shareholders." The spotlight will no longer be on only what a CEO does, but also on how much the CEO is paid.

■ *What are some possible activities that Nardelli must avoid in order to reap the additional $18 million over 4 years?*

Long-term financial plans are part of an integrated strategy that, along with production and marketing plans, guides the firm toward strategic goals. Those long-term plans consider proposed outlays for fixed assets, research and development activities, marketing and product development actions, capital structure, and major sources of financing. Also included would be termination of existing projects, product lines, or lines of business; repayment or retirement of outstanding debts; and any planned acquisitions. Such plans tend to be supported by a series of annual budgets. The *Focus on Ethics* box above shows how one CEO dramatically reshaped his company's operating structure, although it later cost him his job.

Hint Preparation of the annual budget is an important part of the firm's planning process that involves all managers. It represents a tedious but important management activity.

Short-Term (Operating) Financial Plans

short-term (operating) financial plans
Specify short-term financial actions and the anticipated impact of those actions.

Short-term (operating) financial plans specify short-term financial actions and the anticipated impact of those actions. These plans most often cover a 1- to 2-year period. Key inputs include the sales forecast and various forms of operating and

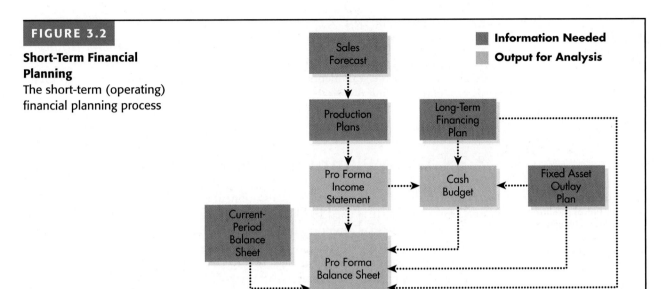

FIGURE 3.2

Short-Term Financial Planning
The short-term (operating) financial planning process

financial data. Key outputs include a number of operating budgets, the cash budget, and pro forma financial statements. The entire short-term financial planning process is outlined in Figure 3.2. Here we focus solely on cash and profit planning from the financial manager's perspective.

Short-term financial planning begins with the sales forecast. From it, companies develop production plans that take into account lead (preparation) times and include estimates of the required raw materials. Using the production plans, the firm can estimate direct labor requirements, factory overhead outlays, and operating expenses. Once these estimates have been made, the firm can prepare a pro forma income statement and cash budget. With these basic inputs, the firm can finally develop a pro forma balance sheet.

Hint Excel spreadsheets are widely used to streamline the process of preparing and evaluating these short-term financial planning statements.

Personal Finance Example   The first step in personal financial planning requires you to define your goals. Whereas in a corporation, the goal is to maximize owner wealth (i.e., share price), individuals typically have a number of major goals.

Generally personal goals can be short-term (1 year), intermediate-term (2–5 years), or long-term (6+ years). The short- and intermediate-term goals support the long-term goals. Clearly, types of long-term personal goals depend on the individual's or family's age, and goals will continue to change with one's life situation.

You should set your personal financial goals carefully and realistically. Each goal should be clearly defined and have a priority, time frame, and cost estimate. For example, a college senior's intermediate-term goal in 2009 might include earning a master's degree at a cost of $40,000 by 2012, and his or her long-term goal might be to buy a condominium at a cost of $125,000 by 2016.

Throughout the remainder of this chapter, we will concentrate on the key outputs of the short-term financial planning process: the cash budget, the pro forma income statement, and the pro forma balance sheet.

REVIEW QUESTIONS

3–8 What is the *financial planning process?* Contrast *long-term (strategic) financial plans* and *short-term (operating) financial plans.*

3–9 Which three statements result as part of the short-term (operating) financial planning process?

 3.3 | Cash Planning: Cash Budgets

cash budget (cash forecast)
A statement of the firm's planned inflows and outflows of cash that is used to estimate its short-term cash requirements.

The **cash budget,** or **cash forecast,** is a statement of the firm's planned inflows and outflows of cash. It is used by the firm to estimate its short-term cash requirements, with particular attention being paid to planning for surplus cash and for cash shortages.

Typically, the cash budget is designed to cover a 1-year period, divided into smaller time intervals. The number and type of intervals depend on the nature of the business. The more seasonal and uncertain a firm's cash flows, the greater the number of intervals. Because many firms are confronted with a seasonal cash flow pattern, the cash budget is quite often presented on a *monthly basis.* Firms with stable patterns of cash flow may use quarterly or annual time intervals.

The Sales Forecast

sales forecast
The prediction of the firm's sales over a given period, based on external and/or internal data; used as the key input to the short-term financial planning process.

The key input to the short-term financial planning process is the firm's **sales forecast.** This prediction of the firm's sales over a given period is ordinarily prepared by the marketing department. On the basis of the sales forecast, the financial manager estimates the monthly cash flows that will result from projected sales and from outlays related to production, inventory, and sales. The manager also determines the level of fixed assets required and the amount of financing, if any, needed to support the forecast level of sales and production. In practice, obtaining good data is the most difficult aspect of forecasting.[5] The sales forecast may be based on an analysis of external data, internal data, or a combination of the two.

external forecast
A sales forecast based on the relationships observed between the firm's sales and certain key external economic indicators.

An **external forecast** is based on the relationships observed between the firm's sales and certain key external economic indicators such as the gross domestic product (GDP), new housing starts, consumer confidence, and disposable personal income. Forecasts containing these indicators are readily available.

internal forecast
A sales forecast based on a buildup, or consensus, of sales forecasts through the firm's own sales channels.

Internal forecasts are based on a consensus of sales forecasts through the firm's own sales channels. Typically, the firm's salespeople in the field are asked to estimate how many units of each type of product they expect to sell in the coming year. These forecasts are collected and totaled by the sales manager, who may adjust the figures using knowledge of specific markets or of the salesperson's forecasting ability. Finally, adjustments may be made for additional internal factors, such as production capabilities.

---

5. Calculation of the various forecasting techniques, such as regression, moving averages, and exponential smoothing, is not included in this text. For a description of the technical side of forecasting, refer to a basic statistics, econometrics, or management science text.

TABLE 3.7	The General Format of the Cash Budget					
	Jan.	Feb.	. . .	Nov.	Dec.
Cash receipts	$XXX	$XXG		$XXM	$XXT
Less: Cash disbursements	XXA	XXH	. . .	XXN	XXU
Net cash flow	$XXB	$XXI		$XXO	$XXV
Add: Beginning cash	XXC	XXD	XXJ	XXP	XXQ
Ending cash	$XXD	$XXJ		$XXQ	$XXW
Less: Minimum cash balance	XXE	XXK	. . .	XXR	XXY
Required total financing		$XXL		$XXS	
Excess cash balance	$XXF				$XXZ

Firms generally use a combination of external and internal forecast data to make the final sales forecast. The internal data provide insight into sales expectations, and the external data provide a means of adjusting these expectations to take into account general economic factors. The nature of the firm's product also often affects the mix and types of forecasting methods used.

Preparing the Cash Budget

The general format of the cash budget is presented in Table 3.7. We will discuss each of its components individually.

Cash Receipts

cash receipts
All of a firm's inflows of cash during a given financial period.

Cash receipts include all of a firm's inflows of cash during a given financial period. The most common components of cash receipts are cash sales, collections of accounts receivable, and other cash receipts.

Example

Coulson Industries, a defense contractor, is developing a cash budget for October, November, and December. Coulson's sales in August and September were $100,000 and $200,000, respectively. Sales of $400,000, $300,000, and $200,000 have been forecast for October, November, and December, respectively. Historically, 20% of the firm's sales have been for cash, 50% have generated accounts receivable collected after 1 month, and the remaining 30% have generated accounts receivable collected after 2 months. Bad-debt expenses (uncollectible accounts) have been negligible.[6] In December, the firm will receive a $30,000 dividend from stock in a subsidiary. The schedule of expected cash receipts for the company is presented in Table 3.8. It contains the following items:

Forecast sales This initial entry is *merely informational*. It is provided as an aid in calculating other sales-related items.

Cash sales The cash sales shown for each month represent 20% of the total sales forecast for that month.

6. Normally, it would be expected that the collection percentages would total slightly less than 100%, because some of the accounts receivable would be uncollectible. In this example, the sum of the collection percentages is 100% (20% + 50% + 30%), which reflects the fact that all sales are assumed to be collected.

TABLE 3.8	A Schedule of Projected Cash Receipts for Coulson Industries ($000)				
Forecast sales	Aug. $100	Sept. $200	Oct. $400	Nov. $300	Dec. $200
Cash sales (0.20)	$20	$40	$ 80	$ 60	$ 40
Collections of A/R:					
Lagged 1 month (0.50)		50	100	200	150
Lagged 2 months (0.30)			30	60	120
Other cash receipts					30
Total cash receipts			$210	$320	$340

Collections of A/R   These entries represent the collection of accounts receivable (A/R) resulting from sales in earlier months.

Lagged 1 month   These figures represent sales made in the preceding month that generated accounts receivable collected in the current month. Because 50% of the current month's sales are collected 1 month later, the collections of A/R with a 1-month lag shown for September represent 50% of the sales in August, collections for October represent 50% of September sales, and so on.

Lagged 2 months   These figures represent sales made 2 months earlier that generated accounts receivable collected in the current month. Because 30% of sales are collected 2 months later, the collections with a 2-month lag shown for October represent 30% of the sales in August, and so on.

Other cash receipts   These are cash receipts expected from sources other than sales. Interest received, dividends received, proceeds from the sale of equipment, stock and bond sale proceeds, and lease receipts may show up here. For Coulson Industries, the only other cash receipt is the $30,000 dividend due in December.

Total cash receipts   This figure represents the total of all the cash receipts listed for each month. For Coulson Industries, we are concerned only with October, November, and December, as shown in Table 3.8.

Cash Disbursements

cash disbursements
All outlays of cash by the firm during a given financial period.

Cash disbursements include all outlays of cash by the firm during a given financial period. The most common cash disbursements are

Cash purchases	Fixed-asset outlays
Payments of accounts payable	Interest payments
Rent (and lease) payments	Cash dividend payments
Wages and salaries	Principal payments (loans)
Tax payments	Repurchases or retirements of stock

It is important to recognize that *depreciation and other noncash charges are NOT included in the cash budget,* because they merely represent a scheduled write-off of an earlier cash outflow. The impact of depreciation, as we noted earlier, is reflected in the reduced cash outflow for tax payments.

Example

Coulson Industries has gathered the following data needed for the preparation of a cash disbursements schedule for October, November, and December.

Purchases   The firm's purchases represent 70% of sales. Of this amount, 10% is paid in cash, 70% is paid in the month immediately following the month of purchase, and the remaining 20% is paid 2 months following the month of purchase.[7]

Rent payments   Rent of $5,000 will be paid each month.

Wages and salaries   Fixed salary cost for the year is $96,000, or $8,000 per month. In addition, wages are estimated as 10% of monthly sales.

Tax payments   Taxes of $25,000 must be paid in December.

Fixed-asset outlays   New machinery costing $130,000 will be purchased and paid for in November.

Interest payments   An interest payment of $10,000 is due in December.

Cash dividend payments   Cash dividends of $20,000 will be paid in October.

Principal payments (loans)   A $20,000 principal payment is due in December.

Repurchases or retirements of stock   No repurchase or retirement of stock is expected between October and December.

The firm's cash disbursements schedule, using the preceding data, is shown in Table 3.9. Some items in the table are explained in greater detail below.

Purchases   This entry is *merely informational*. The figures represent 70% of the forecast sales for each month. They have been included to facilitate calculation of the cash purchases and related payments.

TABLE 3.9	A Schedule of Projected Cash Disbursements for Coulson Industries ($000)				
	Aug.	Sept.	Oct.	Nov.	Dec.
Purchases (0.70 × sales)	$70	$140	$280	$210	$140
Cash purchases (0.10)	$7	$14	$ 28	$ 21	$ 14
Payments of A/P:					
Lagged 1 month (0.70)		49	98	196	147
Lagged 2 months (0.20)			14	28	56
Rent payments			5	5	5
Wages and salaries			48	38	28
Tax payments					25
Fixed-asset outlays				130	
Interest payments					10
Cash dividend payments			20		
Principal payments					20
Total cash disbursements			$213	$418	$305

---

7. Unlike the collection percentages for sales, the total of the payment percentages should equal 100%, because it is expected that the firm will pay off all of its accounts payable.

Cash purchases   The cash purchases for each month represent 10% of the month's purchases.

Payments of A/P   These entries represent the payment of accounts payable (A/P) resulting from purchases in earlier months.

Lagged 1 month   These figures represent purchases made in the preceding month that are paid for in the current month. Because 70% of the firm's purchases are paid for 1 month later, the payments with a 1-month lag shown for September represent 70% of the August purchases, payments for October represent 70% of September purchases, and so on.

Lagged 2 months   These figures represent purchases made 2 months earlier that are paid for in the current month. Because 20% of the firm's purchases are paid for 2 months later, the payments with a 2-month lag for October represent 20% of the August purchases, and so on.

Wages and salaries   These amounts were obtained by adding $8,000 to 10% of the *sales* in each month. The $8,000 represents the salary component; the rest represents wages.

The remaining items on the cash disbursements schedule are self-explanatory.

net cash flow
The mathematical difference between the firm's cash receipts and its cash disbursements in each period.

ending cash
The sum of the firm's beginning cash and its net cash flow for the period.

required total financing
Amount of funds needed by the firm if the ending cash for the period is less than the desired minimum cash balance; typically represented by notes payable.

excess cash balance
The (excess) amount available for investment by the firm if the period's ending cash is greater than the desired minimum cash balance; assumed to be invested in marketable securities.

Net Cash Flow, Ending Cash, Financing, and Excess Cash

Look back at the general-format cash budget in Table 3.7. We have inputs for the first two entries, and we now continue calculating the firm's cash needs. The firm's **net cash flow** is found by subtracting the cash disbursements from cash receipts in each period. Then we add beginning cash to the firm's net cash flow to determine the **ending cash** for each period.

Finally, we subtract the desired minimum cash balance from ending cash to find the **required total financing** or the **excess cash balance**. If the ending cash is less than the minimum cash balance, *financing* is required. Such financing is typically viewed as short-term and is therefore represented by notes payable. If the ending cash is greater than the minimum cash balance, *excess cash* exists. Any excess cash is assumed to be invested in a liquid, short-term, interest-paying vehicle—that is, in marketable securities.

Example

Table 3.10 (see page 125) presents Coulson Industries' cash budget, based on the data already developed. At the end of September, Coulson's cash balance was $50,000, and its notes payable and marketable securities equaled $0.[8] The company wishes to maintain, as a reserve for unexpected needs, a minimum cash balance of $25,000.

For Coulson Industries to maintain its required $25,000 ending cash balance, it will need total borrowing of $76,000 in November and $41,000 in December.

---

8. If Coulson either had outstanding notes payable or held marketable securities at the end of September, its "beginning cash" value would be misleading. It could be either overstated or understated, depending on whether the firm had notes payable or marketable securities on its books at that time. For simplicity, the cash budget discussions and problems presented in this chapter assume that the firm's notes payable and marketable securities equal $0 at the beginning of the period of concern.

TABLE 3.10	A Cash Budget for Coulson Industries ($000)		
	Oct.	Nov.	Dec.
Total cash receipts[a]	$210	$320	$340
Less: Total cash disbursements[b]	213	418	305
Net cash flow	($ 3)	($ 98)	$ 35
Add: Beginning cash	50	47	(51)
Ending cash	$ 47	($ 51)	($ 16)
Less: Minimum cash balance	25	25	25
Required total financing (notes payable)[c]	—	$ 76	$ 41
Excess cash balance (marketable securities)[d]	$ 22	—	—

[a]From Table 3.8.

[b]From Table 3.9.

[c]Values are placed in this line when the ending cash is less than the desired minimum cash balance. These amounts are typically financed short-term and therefore are represented by notes payable.

[d]Values are placed in this line when the ending cash is greater than the desired minimum cash balance. These amounts are typically assumed to be invested short-term and therefore are represented by marketable securities.

In October the firm will have an excess cash balance of $22,000, which can be held in an interest-earning marketable security. The required total financing figures in the cash budget refer to *how much will be owed at the end of the month;* they do *not* represent the monthly changes in borrowing.

The monthly changes in borrowing and in excess cash can be found by further analyzing the cash budget. In October the $50,000 beginning cash, which becomes $47,000 after the $3,000 net cash outflow, results in a $22,000 excess cash balance once the $25,000 minimum cash is deducted. In November the $76,000 of required total financing resulted from the $98,000 net cash outflow less the $22,000 of excess cash from October. The $41,000 of required total financing in December resulted from reducing November's $76,000 of required total financing by the $35,000 of net cash inflow during December. Summarizing, the *financial activities for each month* would be as follows:

October: **Invest the $22,000** excess cash balance in marketable securities.

November: Liquidate the $22,000 of marketable securities and **borrow $76,000** (notes payable).

December: **Repay $35,000** of notes payable to leave $41,000 of outstanding required total financing.

Hint Not only is the cash budget a great tool to let management know when it has cash shortages or excesses, but it may be a document required by potential creditors. It communicates to them what the money will be used for, and how and when their loans will be repaid.

Evaluating the Cash Budget

The cash budget indicates whether a cash shortage or surplus is expected in each of the months covered by the forecast. Each month's figure is based on the internally imposed requirement of a minimum cash balance and *represents the total balance at the end of the month.*

At the end of each of the 3 months, Coulson expects the following balances in cash, marketable securities, and notes payable:

| | End-of-month balance ($000) | | |
Account	Oct.	Nov.	Dec.
Cash	$25	$25	$25
Marketable securities	22	0	0
Notes payable	0	76	41

Hint Because of the uncertainty of the ending cash values, the financial manager will usually seek to borrow more than the maximum financing indicated in the cash budget.

Note that the firm is assumed first to liquidate its marketable securities to meet deficits and then to borrow with notes payable if additional financing is needed. As a result, it will not have marketable securities and notes payable on its books at the same time. Because it may be necessary to borrow up to $76,000 for the 3-month period, the financial manager should be certain that some arrangement is made to ensure the availability of these funds.

Personal Finance Example

Because individuals receive only a finite amount of income (cash inflow) during a given period, they need to prepare budgets in order to make sure they can cover their expenses (cash outflows) during the period. The *personal budget* is a short-term financial planning report that helps an individual or family achieve its short-term financial goals. Personal budgets typically cover a 1-year period, broken into months.

A condensed version of a personal budget for the first quarter (3 months) is shown below. You can see a more detailed version (with breakouts of expenses) at the book's companion website.

	Jan.	Feb.	Mar.
Income			
Take-home pay	$4,775	$4,775	$4,775
Investment income			90
(1) Total income	$4,775	$4,775	$4,865
Expenses			
(2) Total expenses	$4,026	$5,291	7,396
Cash surplus or deficit [(1) − (2)]	$ 749	($ 516)	($2,531)
Cumulative cash surplus or deficit	$ 749	$ 233	($2,298)

The personal budget shows a cash surplus of $749 in January followed by monthly deficits in February and March of $516 and $2,531, resulting in a cumulative deficit of $2,298 through March. Clearly, to cover the deficit, some action—such as increasing income, reducing expenses, drawing down savings, or borrowing—will be necessary to bring the budget into balance. Borrowing by using credit can offset a deficit in the short term but can lead to financial trouble if done repeatedly.

Coping with Uncertainty in the Cash Budget

Aside from careful estimation of cash budget inputs, there are two ways of coping with uncertainty in the cash budget.[9] One is to prepare several cash budgets—based on pessimistic, most likely, and optimistic forecasts. From this range of cash flows, the financial manager can determine the amount of financing necessary to cover the most adverse situation. The use of several cash budgets, based on differing scenarios, also should give the financial manager a sense of the riskiness of the various alternatives. This *scenario analysis,* or "what if" approach, is often used to analyze cash flows under a variety of circumstances. Clearly, the use of electronic spreadsheets simplifies the process of performing scenario analysis.

Example

Table 3.11 presents the summary of Coulson Industries' cash budget prepared for each month of concern using pessimistic, most likely, and optimistic estimates of total cash receipts and disbursements. The most likely estimate is based on the expected outcomes presented earlier.

During October, Coulson will, at worst, need a maximum of $15,000 of financing and, at best, will have a $62,000 excess cash balance. During November, its financing requirement will be between $0 and $185,000, or it could experience an excess cash balance of $5,000. The December projections show maximum borrowing of $190,000 with a possible excess cash balance of $107,000. By considering the extreme values in the pessimistic and optimistic outcomes, Coulson Industries should be better able to plan its cash requirements. For the 3-month period, the peak borrowing requirement under the worst circumstances would be $190,000, which happens to be considerably greater than the most likely estimate of $76,000 for this period.

TABLE 3.11   A Scenario Analysis of Coulson Industries' Cash Budget ($000)

	October			November			December		
	Pessi-mistic	Most likely	Opti-mistic	Pessi-mistic	Most likely	Opti-mistic	Pessi-mistic	Most likely	Opti-mistic
Total cash receipts	$160	$210	$285	$210	$320	$410	$275	$340	$422
Less: Total cash disbursements	200	213	248	380	418	467	280	305	320
Net cash flow	($ 40)	($ 3)	$ 37	($170)	($ 98)	($ 57)	($ 5)	$ 35	$102
Add: Beginning cash	50	50	50	10	47	87	(160)	(51)	30
Ending cash	$ 10	$ 47	$ 87	($160)	($ 51)	$ 30	($165)	($ 16)	$132
Less: Minimum cash balance	25	25	25	25	25	25	25	25	25
Required total financing	$ 15	—	—	$185	$ 76	—	$190	$ 41	—
Excess cash balance	—	$ 22	$ 62	—	—	$ 5	—	—	$107

9. The term *uncertainty* is used here to refer to the variability of the cash flow outcomes that may actually occur.

A second and much more sophisticated way of coping with uncertainty in the cash budget is *simulation* (discussed in Chapter 10). By simulating the occurrence of sales and other uncertain events, the firm can develop a probability distribution of its ending cash flows for each month. The financial decision maker can then use the probability distribution to determine the amount of financing needed to protect the firm adequately against a cash shortage.

Cash Flow within the Month

Because the cash budget shows cash flows only on a total monthly basis, the information provided by the cash budget is not necessarily adequate for ensuring solvency. A firm must look more closely at its pattern of daily cash receipts and cash disbursements to ensure that adequate cash is available for paying bills as they come due. For an example related to this topic, see the book's website.

The synchronization of cash flows in the cash budget at month-end does not ensure that the firm will be able to meet its daily cash requirements. Because a firm's cash flows are generally quite variable when viewed on a daily basis, effective cash planning requires a look *beyond* the cash budget. The financial manager must therefore plan and monitor cash flow more frequently than on a monthly basis. The greater the variability of cash flows from day to day, the greater the amount of attention required.

REVIEW QUESTIONS

3–10 What is the purpose of the *cash budget?* What role does the sales forecast play in its preparation?

3–11 Briefly describe the basic format of the cash budget.

3–12 How can the two "bottom lines" of the cash budget be used to determine the firm's short-term borrowing and investment requirements?

3–13 What is the cause of uncertainty in the cash budget, and what two techniques can be used to cope with this uncertainty?

3.4 | Profit Planning: Pro Forma Statements

pro forma statements
Projected, or forecast, income statements and balance sheets.

Hint A key point in understanding pro forma statements is that they reflect the goals and objectives of the firm for the planning period. For these goals and objectives to be achieved, operational plans will have to be developed. Financial plans can be realized only if the correct actions are implemented.

Whereas cash planning focuses on forecasting cash flows, *profit planning* relies on accrual concepts to project the firm's profit and overall financial position. Shareholders, creditors, and the firm's management pay close attention to the **pro forma statements,** which are projected, or forecast, income statements and balance sheets. The basic steps in the short-term financial planning process were shown in the flow diagram of Figure 3.2. The approaches for estimating the pro forma statements are all based on the belief that the financial relationships reflected in the firm's past financial statements will not change in the coming period. The commonly used simplified approaches are presented in subsequent discussions.

Two inputs are required for preparing pro forma statements: (1) financial statements for the preceding year and (2) the sales forecast for the coming year. A variety of assumptions must also be made. The company that we will use to illustrate the simplified approaches to pro forma preparation is Vectra Manufacturing, which manufactures and sells one product. It has two basic product models—X and Y—which are produced by the same process but require different amounts of raw material and labor.

Preceding Year's Financial Statements

The income statement for the firm's 2009 operations is given in Table 3.12. It indicates that Vectra had sales of $100,000, total cost of goods sold of $80,000, net profits before taxes of $9,000, and net profits after taxes of $7,650. The firm paid $4,000 in cash dividends, leaving $3,650 to be transferred to retained earnings. The firm's balance sheet for 2009 is given in Table 3.13 (see page 130).

Sales Forecast

Just as for the cash budget, the key input for pro forma statements is the sales forecast. Vectra Manufacturing's sales forecast for the coming year (2010), based on both external and internal data, is presented in Table 3.14 (see page 130). The unit sale prices of the products reflect an increase from $20 to $25 for model X and from $40 to $50 for model Y. These increases are necessary to cover anticipated increases in costs.

REVIEW QUESTION

3–14 What is the purpose of *pro forma statements*? What inputs are required for preparing them using the simplified approaches?

TABLE 3.12	Vectra Manufacturing's Income Statement for the Year Ended December 31, 2009		
Sales revenue			
Model X (1,000 units at $20/unit)		$20,000	
Model Y (2,000 units at $40/unit)		80,000	
Total sales			$100,000
Less: Cost of goods sold			
Labor		$28,500	
Material A		8,000	
Material B		5,500	
Overhead		38,000	
Total cost of goods sold			80,000
Gross profits			$ 20,000
Less: Operating expenses			10,000
Operating profits			$ 10,000
Less: Interest expense			1,000
Net profits before taxes			$ 9,000
Less: Taxes (0.15 × $9,000)			1,350
Net profits after taxes			$ 7,650
Less: Common stock dividends			4,000
To retained earnings			$ 3,650

TABLE 3.13	Vectra Manufacturing's Balance Sheet, December 31, 2009		
Assets		**Liabilities and Stockholders' Equity**	
Cash	$ 6,000	Accounts payable	$ 7,000
Marketable securities	4,000	Taxes payable	300
Accounts receivable	13,000	Notes payable	8,300
Inventories	16,000	Other current liabilities	3,400
Total current assets	$39,000	Total current liabilities	$19,000
Net fixed assets	$51,000	Long-term debt	$18,000
Total assets	$90,000	Stockholders' equity	
		Common stock	$30,000
		Retained earnings	$23,000
		Total liabilities and stockholders' equity	$90,000

TABLE 3.14	2010 Sales Forecast for Vectra Manufacturing
Unit sales	
Model X	1,500
Model Y	1,950
Dollar sales	
Model X ($25/unit)	$ 37,500
Model Y ($50/unit)	97,500
Total	$135,000

3.5 | Preparing the Pro Forma Income Statement

percent-of-sales method
A simple method for developing the pro forma income statement; it forecasts sales and then expresses the various income statement items as percentages of projected sales.

A simple method for developing a pro forma income statement is the **percent-of-sales method**. It forecasts sales and then expresses the various income statement items as percentages of projected sales. The percentages used are likely to be the percentages of sales for those items in the previous year. By using dollar values taken from Vectra's 2009 income statement (Table 3.12), we find that these percentages are

$$\frac{\text{Cost of goods sold}}{\text{Sales}} = \frac{\$80,000}{\$100,000} = 80.0\%$$

$$\frac{\text{Operating expenses}}{\text{Sales}} = \frac{\$10,000}{\$100,000} = 10.0\%$$

$$\frac{\text{Interest expense}}{\text{Sales}} = \frac{\$1,000}{\$100,000} = 1.0\%$$

Applying these percentages to the firm's forecast sales of $135,000 (developed in Table 3.14), we get the 2010 pro forma income statement shown in Table 3.15.

TABLE 3.15	A Pro Forma Income Statement, Using the Percent-of-Sales Method, for Vectra Manufacturing for the Year Ended December 31, 2010
Sales revenue	$135,000
Less: Cost of goods sold (0.80)	108,000
Gross profits	$ 27,000
Less: Operating expenses (0.10)	13,500
Operating profits	$ 13,500
Less: Interest expense (0.01)	1,350
Net profits before taxes	$ 12,150
Less: Taxes (0.15 × $12,150)	1,823
Net profits after taxes	$ 10,327
Less: Common stock dividends	4,000
To retained earnings	$ 6,327

We have assumed that Vectra will pay $4,000 in common stock dividends, so the expected contribution to retained earnings is $6,327. This represents a considerable increase over $3,650 in the preceding year (see Table 3.12).

Considering Types of Costs and Expenses

The technique that is used to prepare the pro forma income statement in Table 3.15 assumes that all the firm's costs and expenses are *variable*. That is, for a given percentage increase in sales, the same percentage increase in cost of goods sold, operating expenses, and interest expense would result. For example, as Vectra's sales increased by 35 percent, we assumed that its costs of goods sold also increased by 35 percent. On the basis of this assumption, the firm's net profits before taxes also increased by 35 percent.

This approach implies that the firm will not receive the benefits that result from fixed costs when sales are increasing.[10] Clearly, though, if the firm has fixed costs, these costs do not change when sales increase; the result is increased profits. But by remaining unchanged when sales decline, these costs tend to lower profits. Therefore, the use of past cost and expense ratios generally *tends to understate profits when sales are increasing.* (Likewise, it *tends to overstate profits when sales are decreasing.*) The best way to adjust for the presence of fixed costs when preparing a pro forma income statement is to break the firm's historical costs and expenses into *fixed* and *variable* components.[11]

10. The potential returns as well as risks resulting from use of fixed (operating and financial) costs to create "leverage" are discussed in Chapter 12. The key point to recognize here is that when the firm's revenue is *increasing*, fixed costs can magnify returns.

11. The application of *regression analysis*—a statistically based technique for measuring the relationship between variables—to past cost data as they relate to past sales could be used to develop equations that recognize the fixed and variable nature of each cost. Such equations could be employed when preparing the pro forma income statement from the sales forecast. The use of the regression approach in pro forma income statement preparation is widespread, and many computer software packages for use in pro forma preparation rely on this technique. Expanded discussions of the application of this technique can be found in most second-level managerial finance texts.

Example

Vectra Manufacturing's 2009 actual and 2010 pro forma income statements, broken into fixed and variable cost and expense components, follow:

Vectra Manufacturing Income Statements	2009 Actual	2010 Pro forma
Sales revenue	$100,000	$135,000
Less: Cost of good sold		
Fixed cost	40,000	40,000
Variable cost (0.40 × sales)	40,000	54,000
Gross profits	$ 20,000	$ 41,000
Less: Operating expenses		
Fixed expense	5,000	5,000
Variable expense (0.05 × sales)	5,000	6,750
Operating profits	$ 10,000	$ 29,250
Less: Interest expense (all fixed)	1,000	1,000
Net profits before taxes	$ 9,000	$ 28,250
Less: Taxes (0.15 × net profits before taxes)	1,350	4,238
Net profits after taxes	$ 7,650	$ 24,012

Breaking Vectra's costs and expenses into fixed and variable components provides a more accurate projection of its pro forma profit. By assuming that *all* costs are variable (as shown in Table 3.15), we find that projected net profits before taxes would continue to equal 9% of sales (in 2009, $9,000 net profits before taxes ÷ $100,000 sales). Therefore, the 2010 net profits before taxes would have been $12,150 (0.09 × $135,000 projected sales) instead of the $28,250 obtained by using the firm's fixed-cost–variable-cost breakdown.

Clearly, when using a simplified approach to prepare a pro forma income statement, we should break down costs and expenses into fixed and variable components.

REVIEW QUESTIONS

3–15 How is the *percent-of-sales method* used to prepare pro forma income statements?

3–16 Why does the presence of fixed costs cause the percent-of-sales method of pro forma income statement preparation to fail? What is a better method?

3.6 | Preparing the Pro Forma Balance Sheet

A number of simplified approaches are available for preparing the pro forma balance sheet. One involves estimating all balance sheet accounts as a strict percentage of sales. A better and more popular approach is the **judgmental**

judgmental approach
A simplified approach for preparing the pro forma balance sheet under which the firm estimates the values of certain balance sheet accounts and uses its external financing as a balancing, or "plug," figure.

Hint Forty-five days expressed fractionally is about one-eighth of a year: $45/365 \approx 1/8$.

approach,[12] under which the firm estimates the values of certain balance sheet accounts and uses its external financing as a balancing, or "plug," figure.

To apply the judgmental approach to prepare Vectra Manufacturing's 2010 pro forma balance sheet, a number of assumptions must be made about levels of various balance sheet accounts:

1. A minimum cash balance of $6,000 is desired.
2. Marketable securities will remain unchanged from their current level of $4,000.
3. Accounts receivable on average represent about 45 days of sales. Because Vectra's annual sales are projected to be $135,000, accounts receivable should average $16,875 ($1/8 \times \$135,000$).
4. The ending inventory should remain at a level of about $16,000, of which 25 percent (approximately $4,000) should be raw materials and the remaining 75 percent (approximately $12,000) should consist of finished goods.
5. A new machine costing $20,000 will be purchased. Total depreciation for the year is $8,000. Adding the $20,000 acquisition to the existing net fixed assets of $51,000 and subtracting the depreciation of $8,000 yields net fixed assets of $63,000.
6. Purchases will represent approximately 30 percent of annual sales, which in this case is approximately $40,500 ($0.30 \times \$135,000$). The firm estimates that it can take 73 days on average to satisfy its accounts payable. Thus accounts payable should equal one-fifth (73 days ÷ 365 days) of the firm's purchases, or $8,100 ($1/5 \times \$40,500$).
7. Taxes payable will equal one-fourth of the current year's tax liability, which equals $455 (one-fourth of the tax liability of $1,823 shown in the pro forma income statement in Table 3.15).
8. Notes payable will remain unchanged from their current level of $8,300.
9. No change in other current liabilities is expected. They remain at the level of the previous year: $3,400.
10. The firm's long-term debt and its common stock will remain unchanged at $18,000 and $30,000, respectively; no issues, retirements, or repurchases of bonds or stocks are planned.
11. Retained earnings will increase from the beginning level of $23,000 (from the balance sheet dated December 31, 2009, in Table 3.13) to $29,327. The increase of $6,327 represents the amount of retained earnings calculated in the year-end 2010 pro forma income statement in Table 3.15.

external financing required ("plug" figure)
Under the judgmental approach for developing a pro forma balance sheet, the amount of external financing needed to bring the statement into balance. It can be either a positive or a negative value.

A 2010 pro forma balance sheet for Vectra Manufacturing based on these assumptions is presented in Table 3.16 (see page 134). A **"plug" figure**—called the **external financing required**—of $8,293 is needed to bring the statement into balance. This means that the firm will have to obtain about $8,300 of additional external financing to support the increased sales level of $135,000 for 2010.

A *positive* value for "external financing required," like that shown in Table 3.16, means that, based on its plans, the firm will not generate enough internal financing to support its forecast growth in assets. To support the forecast level of operation, the firm must raise funds externally by using debt and/or equity financing or by reducing dividends. Once the form of financing is determined, the

12. The judgmental approach represents an improved version of the *percent-of-sales approach* to pro forma balance sheet preparation. Because the judgmental approach requires only slightly more information and should yield better estimates than the somewhat naive percent-of-sales approach, it is presented here.

TABLE 3.16	A Pro Forma Balance Sheet, Using the Judgmental Approach, for Vectra Manufacturing (December 31, 2010)

Assets			Liabilities and Stockholders' Equity	
Cash		$ 6,000	Accounts payable	$ 8,100
Marketable securities		4,000	Taxes payable	455
Accounts receivable		16,875	Notes payable	8,300
Inventories			Other current liabilities	3,400
Raw materials	$ 4,000		Total current liabilities	$ 20,255
Finished goods	12,000		Long-term debt	$ 18,000
Total inventory		16,000	Stockholders' equity	
Total current assets		$ 42,875	Common stock	$ 30,000
Net fixed assets		$ 63,000	Retained earnings	$ 29,327
Total assets		$105,875	Total	$ 97,582
			External financing required[a]	$ 8,293
			Total liabilities and stockholders' equity	$105,875

[a]The amount of external financing needed to force the firm's balance sheet to balance. Because of the nature of the judgmental approach, the balance sheet is not expected to balance without some type of adjustment.

pro forma balance sheet is modified to replace "external financing required" with the planned increases in the debt and/or equity accounts.

A *negative* value for "external financing required" indicates that, based on its plans, the firm will generate more financing internally than it needs to support its forecast growth in assets. In this case, funds are available for use in repaying debt, repurchasing stock, or increasing dividends. Once the specific actions are determined, "external financing required" is replaced in the pro forma balance sheet with the planned reductions in the debt and/or equity accounts. Obviously, besides being used to prepare the pro forma balance sheet, the judgmental approach is frequently used specifically to estimate the firm's financing requirements.

REVIEW QUESTIONS

3–17 Describe the *judgmental approach* for simplified preparation of the pro forma balance sheet.

3–18 What is the significance of the "plug" figure, *external financing required?* Differentiate between strategies associated with positive values and with negative values for external financing required.

3.7 | Evaluation of Pro Forma Statements

It is difficult to forecast the many variables involved in preparing pro forma statements. As a result, investors, lenders, and managers frequently use the techniques presented in this chapter to make rough estimates of pro forma financial statements. Yet, it is important to recognize the basic weaknesses of these simplified approaches. The weaknesses lie in two assumptions: (1) that the firm's past financial condition is an accurate indicator of its future, and (2) that certain variables (such as cash, accounts receivable, and inventories) can be forced to take on certain "desired" values. These assumptions cannot be justified solely on the basis of their ability to simplify the calculations involved. However, despite their weaknesses, the simplified approaches to pro forma statement preparation are likely to remain popular because of their relative simplicity. The widespread use of spreadsheets certainly helps to streamline the financial planning process.

However pro forma statements are prepared, analysts must understand how to use them to make financial decisions. Both financial managers and lenders can use pro forma statements to analyze the firm's inflows and outflows of cash, as well as its liquidity, activity, debt, profitability, and market value. Various ratios can be calculated from the pro forma income statement and balance sheet to evaluate performance. Cash inflows and outflows can be evaluated by preparing a pro forma statement of cash flows. After analyzing the pro forma statements, the financial manager can take steps to adjust planned operations to achieve short-term financial goals. For example, if projected profits on the pro forma income statement are too low, a variety of pricing and/or cost-cutting actions might be initiated. If the projected level of accounts receivable on the pro forma balance sheet is too high, changes in credit or collection policy may be called for. Pro forma statements are therefore of great importance in solidifying the firm's financial plans for the coming year.

REVIEW QUESTIONS

3–19 What are the two basic weaknesses of the simplified approaches to preparing pro forma statements?

3–20 What is the financial manager's objective in evaluating pro forma statements?

Summary

Focus on Value

Cash flow, the lifeblood of the firm, is a key determinant of the value of the firm. The financial manager must plan and manage the firm's cash flow. The goal is to ensure the firm's solvency and to generate positive cash flow for the firm's owners. Both the magnitude and the risk of the cash flows generated on behalf of the owners determine the firm's value.

To carry out the responsibility **to create value for owners,** the financial manager uses tools such as cash budgets and pro forma financial statements as part of the process of generating positive cash flow. Good financial plans should result in large free cash flows. Clearly, the financial manager must deliberately and carefully plan and manage the firm's cash flows to achieve the firm's goal of maximizing share price.

Review of Learning Goals

LG 1 **Understand tax depreciation procedures and the effect of depreciation on the firm's cash flows.** Depreciation is an important factor affecting a firm's cash flow. An asset's depreciable value and depreciable life are determined by using the MACRS standards in the federal tax code. MACRS groups assets (excluding real estate) into six property classes based on length of recovery period.

LG 2 **Discuss the firm's statement of cash flows, operating cash flow, and free cash flow.** The statement of cash flows is divided into operating, investment, and financing flows. It reconciles changes in the firm's cash flows with changes in cash and marketable securities for the period. Interpreting the statement of cash flows involves both the major categories of cash flow and the individual items of cash inflow and outflow. From a strict financial point of view, a firm's operating cash flow is defined to exclude interest; the simpler accounting view does not make this exclusion. Of greater importance is a firm's free cash flow, which is the amount of cash flow available to creditors and owners.

LG 3 **Understand the financial planning process, including long-term (strategic) financial plans and short-term (operating) financial plans.** The two key aspects of the financial planning process are cash planning and profit planning. Cash planning involves the cash budget or cash forecast. Profit planning relies on the pro forma income statement and balance sheet. Long-term (strategic) financial plans act as a guide for preparing short-term (operating) financial plans. Long-term plans tend to cover periods ranging from 2 to 10 years; short-term plans most often cover a 1- to 2-year period.

LG 4 **Discuss the cash-planning process and the preparation, evaluation, and use of the cash budget.** The cash-planning process uses the cash budget, based on a sales forecast, to estimate short-term cash surpluses and shortages. The cash budget is typically prepared for a 1-year period divided into months. It nets cash receipts and disbursements for each period to calculate net cash flow. Ending cash is estimated by adding beginning cash to the net cash flow. By subtracting the desired minimum cash balance from the ending cash, the firm can determine required total financing or the excess cash balance. To cope with uncertainty in the cash budget, scenario analysis or simulation can be used. A firm must also consider its pattern of daily cash receipts and cash disbursements.

LG 5 **Explain the simplified procedures used to prepare and evaluate the pro forma income statement and the pro forma balance sheet.** A pro forma income statement can be developed by calculating past percentage relationships between certain cost and expense items and the firm's sales and then applying these percentages to forecasts. Because this approach implies that all costs and expenses are variable, it tends to understate profits when sales are increasing and to overstate profits when sales are decreasing. This problem can be avoided by breaking down costs and expenses into fixed and variable components. In this case, the fixed components remain unchanged from the most recent year, and the variable costs and expenses are forecast on a percent-of-sales basis.

Under the judgmental approach, the values of certain balance sheet accounts are estimated and the firm's external financing is used as a balancing, or "plug," figure. A positive value for "external financing required" means that the firm will not generate enough internal financing to support its forecast growth in assets and will have to raise funds externally or reduce dividends. A negative value for "external financing required" indicates that the firm will generate more financing internally than it needs to support its forecast growth in assets and funds will be available for use in repaying debt, repurchasing stock, or increasing dividends.

LG 6 **Evaluate the simplified approaches to pro forma financial statement preparation and the common uses of pro forma statements.** Simplified approaches for preparing pro forma statements assume that the firm's past financial condition is an accurate indicator of the future. Pro forma statements are commonly used to forecast and analyze the firm's level of profitability and overall financial performance so that adjustments can be made to planned operations to achieve short-term financial goals.

Self-Test Problems (Solutions in Appendix B)

ST3–1 **Depreciation and cash flow**   A firm expects to have earnings before interest and taxes (EBIT) of $160,000 in each of the next 6 years. It pays annual interest of $15,000. The firm is considering the purchase of an asset that costs $140,000, requires $10,000 in installation cost, and has a recovery period of 5 years. It will be the firm's only asset, and the asset's depreciation is already reflected in its EBIT estimates.

    a. Calculate the annual depreciation for the asset purchase using the MACRS depreciation percentages in Table 3.2 on page 108.

    b. Calculate the annual operating cash flows for each of the 6 years, using both the accounting and the finance definitions of *operating cash flow.* Assume that the firm is subject to a 40% ordinary tax rate.

    c. Suppose the firm's net fixed assets, current assets, accounts payable, and accruals had the following values at the start and end of the final year (year 6). Calculate the firm's free cash flow (FCF) for that year.

Account	Year 6 start	Year 6 end
Net fixed assets	$ 7,500	$ 0
Current assets	90,000	110,000
Accounts payable	40,000	45,000
Accruals	8,000	7,000

    d. Compare and discuss the significance of each value calculated in parts **b** and **c.**

ST3–2 Cash budget and pro forma balance sheet inputs   Jane McDonald, a financial analyst for Carroll Company, has prepared the following sales and cash disbursement estimates for the period February–June of the current year.

Month	Sales	Cash disbursements
February	$500	$400
March	600	300
April	400	600
May	200	500
June	200	200

McDonald notes that historically, 30% of sales have been for cash. Of *credit sales,* 70% are collected 1 month after the sale, and the remaining 30% are collected 2 months after the sale. The firm wishes to maintain a minimum ending balance in its cash account of $25. Balances above this amount would be invested in short-term government securities (marketable securities), whereas any deficits would be financed through short-term bank borrowing (notes payable). The beginning cash balance at April 1 is $115.

a. Prepare a cash budget for April, May, and June.
b. How much financing, if any, at a maximum would Carroll Company require to meet its obligations during this 3-month period?
c. A pro forma balance sheet dated at the end of June is to be prepared from the information presented. Give the size of each of the following: cash, notes payable, marketable securities, and accounts receivable.

 ST3–3 Pro forma income statement   Euro Designs, Inc., expects sales during 2010 to rise from the 2009 level of $3.5 million to $3.9 million. Because of a scheduled large loan payment, the interest expense in 2010 is expected to drop to $325,000. The firm plans to increase its cash dividend payments during 2010 to $320,000. The company's year-end 2009 income statement is below.

Euro Designs, Inc. Income Statement for the Year Ended December 31, 2009	
Sales revenue	$3,500,000
Less: Cost of goods sold	1,925,000
Gross profits	$1,575,000
Less: Operating expenses	420,000
Operating profits	$1,155,000
Less: Interest expense	400,000
Net profits before taxes	$ 755,000
Less: Taxes (rate = 40%)	302,000
Net profits after taxes	$ 453,000
Less: Cash dividends	250,000
To retained earnings	$ 203,000

a. Use the *percent-of-sales method* to prepare a 2010 pro forma income statement for Euro Designs, Inc.
b. Explain why the statement may underestimate the company's actual 2010 pro forma income.

Warm-Up Exercises

A blue box (■) indicates exercises available in .

E3–1 The installed cost of a new computerized controller was $65,000. Calculate the depreciation schedule by year assuming a recovery period of 5 years and using the appropriate MACRS depreciation percentages given in Table 3.2 on page 108.

E3–2 Classify the following changes in each of the accounts as either an *inflow* or an *outflow* of cash. During the year (a) marketable securities increased, (b) land and buildings decreased, (c) accounts payable increased, (d) vehicles decreased, (e) accounts receivable increased, and (f) dividends were paid.

E3–3 Determine the *operating cash flow (OCF)* for Kleczka, Inc., based on the following data. (All values are in thousands of dollars.) During the year the firm had sales of $2,500, cost of goods sold totaled $1,800, operating expenses totaled $300, and depreciation expenses were $200. The firm is in the 35% tax bracket.

E3–4 During the year, Xero, Inc., experienced an increase in net fixed assets of $300,000 and had depreciation of $200,000. It also experienced an increase in current assets of $150,000 and an increase in accounts payable and accruals of $75,000. If operating cash flow (OCF) for the year was $700,000, calculate the firm's *free cash flow (FCF)* for the year.

E3–5 Rimier Corp. forecasts sales of $650,000 for 2010. Assume the firm has fixed costs of $250,000 and variable costs amounting to 35% of sales. Operating expenses are estimated to include fixed costs of $28,000 and a variable portion equal to 7.5% of sales. Interest expenses for the coming year are estimated to be $20,000. Estimate Rimier's net profits before taxes for 2010.

Problems

A blue box (■) indicates problems available in .

P3–1 **Depreciation**   On March 20, 2009, Norton Systems acquired two new assets. Asset A was research equipment costing $17,000 and having a 3-year recovery period. Asset B was duplicating equipment having an installed cost of $45,000 and a 5-year recovery period. Using the MACRS depreciation percentages in Table 3.2 on page 108, prepare a depreciation schedule for each of these assets.

P3–2 **Accounting cash flow**   A firm had earnings after taxes of $50,000 in 2009. Depreciation charges were $28,000, and a $2,000 charge for amortization of a bond discount was incurred. What was the firm's accounting *cash flow from operations* (see Equation 3.1) during 2009?

P3–3 **MACRS depreciation expense and accounting cash flow**   Pavlovich Instruments, Inc., a maker of precision telescopes, expects to report pre-tax income of $430,000 this year. The company's financial manager is considering the timing of a purchase of new computerized lens grinders. The grinders will have an installed cost of $80,000 and a cost recovery period of 5 years. They will be depreciated using the MACRS schedule.

a. If the firm purchases the grinders before year end, what depreciation expense will it be able to claim this year? (Use Table 3.2 on page 108.)

b. If the firm reduces its reported income by the amount of the depreciation expense calculated in part **a,** what tax savings will result?

c. Assuming that Pavlovich does purchase the grinders this year and that they are its only depreciable asset, use the accounting definition given in Equation 3.1 to find the firm's *cash flow from operations* for the year.

  P3–4 **Depreciation and accounting cash flow**   A firm in the third year of depreciating its only asset, which originally cost $180,000 and has a 5-year MACRS recovery period, has gathered the following data relative to the current year's operations.

Accruals	$ 15,000
Current assets	120,000
Interest expense	15,000
Sales revenue	400,000
Inventory	70,000
Total costs before depreciation, interest, and taxes	290,000
Tax rate on ordinary income	40%

a. Use the *relevant data* to determine the accounting *cash flow from operations* (see Equation 3.1) for the current year.

b. Explain the impact that depreciation, as well as any other noncash charges, has on a firm's cash flows.

  P3–5 **Classifying inflows and outflows of cash**   Classify each of the following items as an inflow (I) or an outflow (O) of cash, or as neither (N).

Item	Change ($)	Item	Change ($)
Cash	+100	Accounts receivable	−700
Accounts payable	−1,000	Net profits	+600
Notes payable	+500	Depreciation	+100
Long-term debt	−2,000	Repurchase of stock	+600
Inventory	+200	Cash dividends	+800
Fixed assets	+400	Sale of stock	+1,000

 P3–6 **Finding operating and free cash flows**   Consider the balance sheets and selected data from the income statement of Keith Corporation that follow on page 141.

a. Calculate the firm's accounting *cash flow from operations* for the year ended December 31, 2009, using Equation 3.1.

b. Calculate the firm's *net operating profit after taxes (NOPAT)* for the year ended December 31, 2009, using Equation 3.2.

Keith Corporation Balance Sheets		
	December 31	
Assets	2009	2008
Cash	$ 1,500	$ 1,000
Marketable securities	1,800	1,200
Accounts receivable	2,000	1,800
Inventories	2,900	2,800
Total current assets	$ 8,200	$ 6,800
Gross fixed assets	$29,500	$28,100
Less: Accumulated depreciation	14,700	13,100
Net fixed assets	$14,800	$15,000
Total assets	$23,000	$21,800
Liabilities and Stockholders' Equity		
Accounts payable	$ 1,600	$ 1,500
Notes payable	2,800	2,200
Accruals	200	300
Total current liabilities	$ 4,600	$ 4,000
Long-term debt	$ 5,000	$ 5,000
Common stock	$10,000	$10,000
Retained earnings	3,400	2,800
Total stockholders' equity	$13,400	$12,800
Total liabilities and stockholders' equity	$23,000	$21,800
Income Statement Data (2009)		
Depreciation expense	$1,600	
Earnings before interest and taxes (EBIT)	2,700	
Interest expense	367	
Net profits after taxes	1,400	
Tax rate	40%	

c. Calculate the firm's *operating cash flow* (OCF) for the year ended December 31, 2009, using Equation 3.3.

d. Calculate the firm's *free cash flow* (FCF) for the year ended December 31, 2009, using Equation 3.5.

e. Interpret, compare, and contrast your cash flow estimates in parts **a, c,** and **d.**

 P3–7 **Cash receipts**   A firm has actual sales of $65,000 in April and $60,000 in May. It expects sales of $70,000 in June and $100,000 in July and in August. Assuming that sales are the only source of cash inflows and that half of them are for cash and the remainder are collected evenly over the following 2 months, what are the firm's expected cash receipts for June, July, and August?

 P3–8 **Cash disbursements schedule**   Maris Brothers, Inc., needs a cash disbursement schedule for the months of April, May, and June. Use the format of Table 3.9 (on page 123) and the following information in its preparation.

Sales: February = $500,000; March = $500,000; April = $560,000; May = $610,000; June = $650,000; July = $650,000

Purchases: Purchases are calculated as 60% of the next month's sales, 10% of purchases are made in cash, 50% of purchases are paid for 1 month after purchase, and the remaining 40% of purchases are paid for 2 months after purchase.

Rent: The firm pays rent of $8,000 per month.

Wages and salaries: Base wage and salary costs are fixed at $6,000 per month plus a variable cost of 7% of the current month's sales.

Taxes: A tax payment of $54,500 is due in June.

Fixed asset outlays: New equipment costing $75,000 will be bought and paid for in April.

Interest payments: An interest payment of $30,000 is due in June.

Cash dividends: Dividends of $12,500 will be paid in April.

Principal repayments and retirements: No principal repayments or retirements are due during these months.

P3–9   **Cash budget—Basic**   Grenoble Enterprises had sales of $50,000 in March and $60,000 in April. Forecast sales for May, June, and July are $70,000, $80,000, and $100,000, respectively. The firm has a cash balance of $5,000 on May 1 and wishes to maintain a minimum cash balance of $5,000. Given the following data, prepare and interpret a cash budget for the months of May, June, and July.
(1) The firm makes 20% of sales for cash, 60% are collected in the next month, and the remaining 20% are collected in the second month following sale.
(2) The firm receives other income of $2,000 per month.
(3) The firm's actual or expected purchases, all made for cash, are $50,000, $70,000, and $80,000 for the months of May through July, respectively.
(4) Rent is $3,000 per month.
(5) Wages and salaries are 10% of the previous month's sales.
(6) Cash dividends of $3,000 will be paid in June.
(7) Payment of principal and interest of $4,000 is due in June.
(8) A cash purchase of equipment costing $6,000 is scheduled in July.
(9) Taxes of $6,000 are due in June.

PERSONAL FINANCE EXAMPLE

P3–10   **Preparation of cash budget**   Sam and Suzy Sizeman need to prepare a cash budget for the last quarter of 2010 in order to make sure they can cover their expenditures during the period. Sam and Suzy have been preparing budgets for the past several years and have been able to establish specific percentages for most of their cash out-flows. These percentages are based on their take-home pay (i.e., monthly utilities normally run 5% of monthly take-home pay). The information on the next page can be used to create their fourth-quarter budget for 2010.
a. Prepare a quarterly cash budget for Sam and Suzy covering the months October through December 2010.
b. Are there are individual months that incur a deficit?
c. What is the cumulative cash surplus or deficit by the end of December 2010?

Income	
Monthly take-home pay	$4,900
Expenses	
Housing	30%
Utilities	5%
Food	10%
Transportation	7%
Medical/dental	.5%
Clothing for Oct. & Nov.	3%
Clothing for Dec.	$440
Property taxes (Nov. only)	11.5%
Appliances	1%
Personal care	2%
Entertainment for Oct. & Nov.	6%
Entertainment for Dec.	$1,500
Savings	7.5%
Other	5%
Excess cash	4.5%

P3–11 **Cash budget—Advanced**   The actual sales and purchases for Xenocore, Inc., for September and October 2009, along with its forecast sales and purchases for the period November 2009 through April 2010, follow.

Year	Month	Sales	Purchases
2009	September	$210,000	$120,000
2009	October	250,000	150,000
2009	November	170,000	140,000
2009	December	160,000	100,000
2010	January	140,000	80,000
2010	February	180,000	110,000
2010	March	200,000	100,000
2010	April	250,000	90,000

The firm makes 20% of all sales for cash and collects on 40% of its sales in each of the 2 months following the sale. Other cash inflows are expected to be $12,000 in September and April, $15,000 in January and March, and $27,000 in February. The firm pays cash for 10% of its purchases. It pays for 50% of its purchases in the following month and for 40% of its purchases 2 months later.

Wages and salaries amount to 20% of the preceding month's sales. Rent of $20,000 per month must be paid. Interest payments of $10,000 are due in January and April. A principal payment of $30,000 is also due in April. The firm expects to pay cash dividends of $20,000 in January and April. Taxes of $80,000 are due in April. The firm also intends to make a $25,000 cash purchase of fixed assets in December.

a. Assuming that the firm has a cash balance of $22,000 at the beginning of November, determine the end-of-month cash balances for each month, November through April.

    b. Assuming that the firm wishes to maintain a $15,000 minimum cash balance, determine the required total financing or excess cash balance for each month, November through April.

    c. If the firm were requesting a line of credit to cover needed financing for the period November to April, how large would this line have to be? Explain your answer.

P3–12 **Cash flow concepts** The following represent financial transactions that Johnsfield & Co. will be undertaking in the next planning period. For each transaction, check the statement or statements that will be affected immediately.

| Transaction | Statement | | |
	Cash budget	Pro forma income statement	Pro forma balance sheet
Cash sale			
Credit sale			
Accounts receivable are collected			
Asset with 5-year life is purchased			
Depreciation is taken			
Amortization of goodwill is taken			
Sale of common stock			
Retirement of outstanding bonds			
Fire insurance premium is paid for the next 3 years			

P3–13 **Cash budget—Scenario analysis** Trotter Enterprises, Inc., has gathered the following data to plan for its cash requirements and short-term investment opportunities for October, November, and December. All amounts are shown in thousands of dollars.

| | October | | | November | | | December | | |
	Pessi-mistic	Most likely	Opti-mistic	Pessi-mistic	Most likely	Opti-mistic	Pessi-mistic	Most likely	Opti-mistic
Total cash receipts	$260	$342	$462	$200	$287	$366	$191	$294	$353
Total cash disbursements	285	326	421	203	261	313	287	332	315

    a. Prepare a *scenario analysis* of Trotter's cash budget using −$20,000 as the beginning cash balance for October and a minimum required cash balance of $18,000.

b. Use the analysis prepared in part **a** to predict Trotter's financing needs and investment opportunities over the months of October, November, and December. Discuss how knowledge of the timing and amounts involved can aid the planning process.

P3–14   **Multiple cash budgets—Scenario analysis**   Brownstein, Inc., expects sales of $100,000 during each of the next 3 months. It will make monthly purchases of $60,000 during this time. Wages and salaries are $10,000 per month plus 5% of sales. Brownstein expects to make a tax payment of $20,000 in the next month and a $15,000 purchase of fixed assets in the second month and to receive $8,000 in cash from the sale of an asset in the third month. All sales and purchases are for cash. Beginning cash and the minimum cash balance are assumed to be zero.

a. Construct a cash budget for the next 3 months.
b. Brownstein is unsure of the sales levels, but all other figures are certain. If the most pessimistic sales figure is $80,000 per month and the most optimistic is $120,000 per month, what are the monthly minimum and maximum ending cash balances that the firm can expect for each of the 1-month periods?
c. Briefly discuss how the financial manager can use the data in parts **a** and **b** to plan for financing needs.

P3–15   **Pro forma income statement**   The marketing department of Metroline Manufacturing estimates that its sales in 2010 will be $1.5 million. Interest expense is expected to remain unchanged at $35,000, and the firm plans to pay $70,000 in cash dividends during 2010. Metroline Manufacturing's income statement for the year ended December 31, 2009, is given below, along with a breakdown of the firm's cost of goods sold and operating expenses into their fixed and variable components.

Metroline Manufacturing Income Statement for the Year Ended December 31, 2009	
Sales revenue	$1,400,000
Less: Cost of goods sold	910,000
Gross profits	$ 490,000
Less: Operating expenses	120,000
Operating profits	$ 370,000
Less: Interest expense	35,000
Net profits before taxes	$ 335,000
Less: Taxes (rate = 40%)	134,000
Net profits after taxes	$ 201,000
Less: Cash dividends	66,000
To retained earnings	$ 135,000

Metroline Manufacturing Breakdown of Costs and Expenses into Fixed and Variable Components for the Year Ended December 31, 2009	
Cost of goods sold	
Fixed cost	$210,000
Variable cost	700,000
Total cost	$910,000
Operating expenses	
Fixed expenses	$ 36,000
Variable expenses	84,000
Total expenses	$120,000

a. Use the *percent-of-sales method* to prepare a pro forma income statement for the year ended December 31, 2010.
b. Use *fixed and variable cost data* to develop a pro forma income statement for the year ended December 31, 2010.
c. Compare and contrast the statements developed in parts **a** and **b**. Which statement probably provides the better estimate of 2010 income? Explain why.

P3–16 **Pro forma income statement—Scenario analysis**   Allen Products, Inc., wants to do a *scenario analysis* for the coming year. The pessimistic prediction for sales is $900,000; the most likely amount of sales is $1,125,000; and the optimistic prediction is $1,280,000. Allen's income statement for the most recent year follows.

Allen Products, Inc. Income Statement for the Year Ended December 31, 2009	
Sales revenue	$937,500
Less: Cost of goods sold	421,875
Gross profits	$515,625
Less: Operating expenses	234,375
Operating profits	$281,250
Less: Interest expense	30,000
Net profits before taxes	$251,250
Less: Taxes (rate = 25%)	62,813
Net profits after taxes	$188,437

a. Use the *percent-of-sales method*, the income statement for December 31, 2009, and the sales revenue estimates to develop pessimistic, most likely, and optimistic pro forma income statements for the coming year.

b. Explain how the percent-of-sales method could result in an overstatement of profits for the pessimistic case and an understatement of profits for the most likely and optimistic cases.

c. Restate the pro forma income statements prepared in part **a** to incorporate the following assumptions about the 2009 costs:

   $250,000 of the cost of goods sold is fixed; the rest is variable.

   $180,000 of the operating expenses is fixed; the rest is variable.

   All of the interest expense is fixed.

d. Compare your findings in part **c** to your findings in part **a**. Do your observations confirm your explanation in part **b**?

P3–17 **Pro forma balance sheet—Basic**   Leonard Industries wishes to prepare a pro forma balance sheet for December 31, 2010. The firm expects 2010 sales to total $3,000,000. The following information has been gathered.

(1) A minimum cash balance of $50,000 is desired.

(2) Marketable securities are expected to remain unchanged.

(3) Accounts receivable represent 10% of sales.

(4) Inventories represent 12% of sales.

(5) A new machine costing $90,000 will be acquired during 2010. Total depreciation for the year will be $32,000.

(6) Accounts payable represent 14% of sales.

(7) Accruals, other current liabilities, long-term debt, and common stock are expected to remain unchanged.

(8) The firm's net profit margin is 4%, and it expects to pay out $70,000 in cash dividends during 2010.

(9) The December 31, 2009, balance sheet follows.

Leonard Industries Balance Sheet December 31, 2009			
Assets		**Liabilities and Stockholders' Equity**	
Cash	$ 45,000	Accounts payable	$ 395,000
Marketable securities	15,000	Accruals	60,000
Accounts receivable	255,000	Other current liabilities	30,000
Inventories	340,000	Total current liabilities	$ 485,000
Total current assets	$ 655,000	Long-term debt	$ 350,000
Net fixed assets	$ 600,000	Common stock	$ 200,000
Total assets	$1,255,000	Retained earnings	$ 220,000
		Total liabilities and stockholders' equity	$1,255,000

a. Use the *judgmental approach* to prepare a pro forma balance sheet dated December 31, 2010, for Leonard Industries.
b. How much, if any, additional financing will Leonard Industries require in 2010? Discuss.
c. Could Leonard Industries adjust its planned 2010 dividend to avoid the situation described in part **b**? Explain how.

P3–18 **Pro forma balance sheet**   Peabody & Peabody has 2009 sales of $10 million. It wishes to analyze expected performance and financing needs for 2011—2 years ahead. Given the following information, respond to parts **a** and **b**.
  (1) The percents of sales for items that vary directly with sales are as follows:
       Accounts receivable, 12%
       Inventory, 18%
       Accounts payable, 14%
       Net profit margin, 3%
  (2) Marketable securities and other current liabilities are expected to remain unchanged.
  (3) A minimum cash balance of $480,000 is desired.
  (4) A new machine costing $650,000 will be acquired in 2010, and equipment costing $850,000 will be purchased in 2011. Total depreciation in 2010 is forecast as $290,000, and in 2011 $390,000 of depreciation will be taken.
  (5) Accruals are expected to rise to $500,000 by the end of 2011.
  (6) No sale or retirement of long-term debt is expected.
  (7) No sale or repurchase of common stock is expected.
  (8) The dividend payout of 50% of net profits is expected to continue.
  (9) Sales are expected to be $11 million in 2010 and $12 million in 2011.
 (10) The December 31, 2009, balance sheet is on page 148.
a. Prepare a pro forma balance sheet dated December 31, 2011.
b. Discuss the financing changes suggested by the statement prepared in part **a**.

Peabody & Peabody Balance Sheet December 31, 2009 ($000)			
Assets		**Liabilities and Stockholders' Equity**	
Cash	$ 400	Accounts payable	$1,400
Marketable securities	200	Accruals	400
Accounts receivable	1,200	Other current liabilities	80
Inventories	1,800	Total current liabilities	$1,880
Total current assets	$3,600	Long-term debt	$2,000
Net fixed assets	$4,000	Common equity	$3,720
Total assets	$7,600	Total liabilities and stockholders' equity	$7,600

 P3–19 Integrative—Pro forma statements   Red Queen Restaurants wishes to prepare financial plans. Use the financial statements and the other information provided in what follows and on page 149 to prepare the financial plans.

Red Queen Restaurants Income Statement for the Year Ended December 31, 2009	
Sales revenue	$800,000
Less: Cost of goods sold	600,000
Gross profits	$200,000
Less: Operating expenses	100,000
Net profits before taxes	$100,000
Less: Taxes (rate = 40%)	40,000
Net profits after taxes	$ 60,000
Less: Cash dividends	20,000
To retained earnings	$ 40,000

Red Queen Restaurants Balance Sheet December 31, 2009			
Assets		**Liabilities and Stockholders' Equity**	
Cash	$ 32,000	Accounts payable	$100,000
Marketable securities	18,000	Taxes payable	20,000
Accounts receivable	150,000	Other current liabilities	5,000
Inventories	100,000	Total current liabilities	$125,000
Total current assets	$300,000	Long-term debt	$200,000
Net fixed assets	$350,000	Common stock	$150,000
Total assets	$650,000	Retained earnings	$175,000
		Total liabilities and stockholders' equity	$650,000

The following financial data are also available:
  (1) The firm has estimated that its sales for 2010 will be $900,000.
  (2) The firm expects to pay $35,000 in cash dividends in 2010.
  (3) The firm wishes to maintain a minimum cash balance of $30,000.
  (4) Accounts receivable represent approximately 18% of annual sales.
  (5) The firm's ending inventory will change directly with changes in sales in 2010.
  (6) A new machine costing $42,000 will be purchased in 2010. Total depreciation for 2010 will be $17,000.
  (7) Accounts payable will change directly in response to changes in sales in 2010.
  (8) Taxes payable will equal one-fourth of the tax liability on the pro forma income statement.
  (9) Marketable securities, other current liabilities, long-term debt, and common stock will remain unchanged.
  a. Prepare a pro forma income statement for the year ended December 31, 2010, using the *percent-of-sales method.*
  b. Prepare a pro forma balance sheet dated December 31, 2010, using the *judgmental approach.*
  c. Analyze these statements, and discuss the resulting *external financing required.*

 P3–20 Integrative—Pro forma statements Provincial Imports, Inc., has assembled past (2009) financial statements (income statement below and balance sheet on page 150) and financial projections for use in preparing financial plans for the coming year (2010).

Provincial Imports, Inc. Income Statement for the Year Ended December 31, 2009	
Sales revenue	$5,000,000
Less: Cost of goods sold	2,750,000
Gross profits	$2,250,000
Less: Operating expenses	850,000
Operating profits	$1,400,000
Less: Interest expense	200,000
Net profits before taxes	$1,200,000
Less: Taxes (rate = 40%)	480,000
Net profits after taxes	$ 720,000
Less: Cash dividends	288,000
To retained earnings	$ 432,000

Information related to financial projections for the year 2010:
  (1) Projected sales are $6,000,000.
  (2) Cost of goods sold in 2009 includes $1,000,000 in fixed costs.
  (3) Operating expense in 2009 includes $250,000 in fixed costs.
  (4) Interest expense will remain unchanged.
  (5) The firm will pay cash dividends amounting to 40% of net profits after taxes.
  (6) Cash and inventories will double.

Provincial Imports, Inc.
Balance Sheet
December 31, 2009

Assets		Liabilities and Stockholders' Equity	
Cash	$ 200,000	Accounts payable	$ 700,000
Marketable securities	275,000	Taxes payable	95,000
Accounts receivable	625,000	Notes payable	200,000
Inventories	500,000	Other current liabilities	5,000
Total current assets	$1,600,000	Total current liabilities	$1,000,000
Net fixed assets	$1,400,000	Long-term debt	$ 500,000
Total assets	$3,000,000	Common stock	$ 75,000
		Retained earnings	$1,375,000
		Total liabilities and equity	$3,000,000

(7) Marketable securities, notes payable, long-term debt, and common stock will remain unchanged.

(8) Accounts receivable, accounts payable, and other current liabilities will change in direct response to the change in sales.

(9) A new computer system costing $356,000 will be purchased during the year. Total depreciation expense for the year will be $110,000.

(10) The tax rate will remain at 40%.

a. Prepare a pro forma income statement for the year ended December 31, 2010, using the *fixed cost data* given to improve the accuracy of the *percent-of-sales method*.

b. Prepare a pro forma balance sheet as of December 31, 2010, using the information given and the *judgmental approach*. Include a reconciliation of the retained earnings account.

c. Analyze these statements, and discuss the resulting *external financing required*.

P3–21 ETHICS PROBLEM The SEC is trying to get companies to notify the investment community more quickly when a "material change" will affect their forthcoming financial results. In what sense might a financial manager be seen as "more ethical" if he or she follows this directive and issues a press release indicating that sales will not be as high as previously anticipated?

Chapter 3 Case

Preparing Martin Manufacturing's 2010 Pro Forma Financial Statements

To improve its competitive position, Martin Manufacturing is planning to implement a major equipment modernization program. Included will be replacement and modernization of key manufacturing equipment at a cost of $400,000 in 2010. The planned program is expected to lower the variable cost per unit of finished product. Terri Spiro, an experienced budget analyst, has been charged with preparing a forecast of the firm's 2010 financial position, assuming replacement and modernization of manufacturing equipment. She plans to use the 2009 financial statements presented on pages 98 and 99, along with the key projected financial data summarized in the following table.

Martin Manufacturing Company Key Projected Financial Data (2010)	
Data item	Value
Sales revenue	$6,500,000
Minimum cash balance	$25,000
Inventory turnover (times)	7.0
Average collection period	50 days
Fixed-asset purchases	$400,000
Total dividend payments (preferred and common)	$20,000
Depreciation expense	$185,000
Interest expense	$97,000
Accounts payable increase	20%
Accruals and long-term debt	Unchanged
Notes payable, preferred and common stock	Unchanged

To Do

a. Use the historical and projected financial data provided to prepare a pro forma income statement for the year ended December 31, 2010. (*Hint:* Use the *percent-of-sales method* to estimate all values *except* depreciation expense and interest expense, which have been estimated by management and included in the table.)

b. Use the projected financial data along with relevant data from the pro forma income statement prepared in part **a** to prepare the pro forma balance sheet at December 31, 2010. (*Hint:* Use the *judgmental approach*.)

c. Will Martin Manufacturing Company need to obtain *external financing* to fund the proposed equipment modernization program? Explain.

Spreadsheet Exercise

You have been assigned the task of putting together a statement for the ACME Company that shows its expected inflows and outflows of cash over the months of July 2010 through December 2010.

You have been given the following data for ACME Company:

1. Expected gross sales for May through December, respectively, are $300,000, $290,000, $425,000, $500,000, $600,000, $625,000, $650,000, and $700,000.

2. 12% of the sales in any given month are collected during that month. However, the firm has a credit policy of 3/10 net 30, so factor a 3% discount into the current month's sales collection.

3. 75% of the sales in any given month are collected during the following month after the sale.

4. 13% of the sales in any given month are collected during the second month following the sale.

5. The expected purchases of raw materials in any given month are based on 60% of the expected sales during the following month.

6. The firm pays 100% of its current month's raw materials purchases in the following month.

7. Wages and salaries are paid on a monthly basis and are based on 6% of the current month's expected sales.

8. Monthly lease payments are 2% of the current month's expected sales.

9. The monthly advertising expense amounts to 3% of sales.

10. R&D expenditures are expected to be allocated to August, September, and October at the rate of 12% of sales in those months.

11. During December a prepayment of insurance for the following year will be made in the amount of $24,000.

12. During the months of July through December, the firm expects to have miscellaneous expenditures of $15,000, $20,000, $25,000, $30,000, $35,000, and $40,000, respectively.

13. Taxes will be paid in September in the amount of $40,000 and in December in the amount of $45,000.

14. The beginning cash balance in July is $15,000.

15. The target cash balance is $15,000.

16. The firm can invest its surplus cash to earn a 6% annual return.

To Do

a. Prepare a cash budget for July 2010 through December 2010 by creating a combined spreadsheet that incorporates spreadsheets similar to those in Tables 3.8, 3.9, and 3.10. Divide your spreadsheet into three sections:
   (1) Collections from sales and payments to purchase inventory
   (2) Operating expenditures over the time period
   (3) Cash budget covering the period of July through December

   The cash budget should reflect the following:
   (1) Beginning and ending monthly cash balances
   (2) The month(s) in which there will be a cash deficit
   (3) The month(s) which there will be a cash surplus
   (4) The cumulative cash deficit and/or cash surplus

b. Based on your analysis, briefly describe the outlook for this company over the next 6 months. Discuss its specific obligations and the funds available to meet them. What could the firm do in the case of a cash deficit? (Where could it get the money?) What should the firm do if it has a cash surplus?

Group Exercise

Depreciation is an intricate topic, complicated greatly by the tax law. This exercise is designed to extend the description in the text to the real world of compliance under IRS regulations. Financial planning analysis and statement preparation will follow, as you will be asked to continue analyzing your shadow firm's financial reports and prepare projected statements.

To Do

a. Visit the IRS's website at www.irs.gov/. Click on the "Business" tab located on the top-left side of the IRS home page. Next, on your left, click on the link for *forms and publications*. Under "Download Forms and Publications by," choose "topical index." Go to this link. Highlight "D" for depreciation. Now scroll down to Depreciation/Publication and highlight "946 pdf." Using the explanations provided, give several examples of property that your fictitious firm is depreciating.

b. Return to the 10-K filing for your shadow firm.
   (1) Using a time-series approach, describe changes in your shadow firm's statement of cash flows.
   (2) As you did with the ratio analysis in Chapter 2, provide possible explanations for the changes you have noted.
   (3) Extend this analysis to your own firm by using these possible explanations within the context of your fictitious firm.

c. Begin the financial planning analysis of your shadow firm by viewing the strategy section of the annual report. Make a note of short- and long-term planning. Now apply these real details to your fictitious firm.

d. Develop a cash budget for your fictitious firm for the following year. Pay close attention to inflow and outflow assumptions.

e. Take the most recent corporate filings and develop pro forma statements for your shadow corporation. Keep it simple here. Likewise, keep evaluations of these pro forma statements simple.

Web Exercise

Go to the book's companion website at www.prenhall.com/gitman to find the Web Exercise for this chapter.

> Remember to check the book's website at www.prenhall.com/gitman to find additional resources, including Web Exercises and a Web Case.

Integrative Case 1

Track Software, Inc.

Seven years ago, after 15 years in public accounting, Stanley Booker, CPA, resigned his position as Manager of Cost Systems for Davis, Cohen, and O'Brien Public Accountants and started Track Software, Inc. In the 2 years preceding his departure from Davis, Cohen, and O'Brien, Stanley had spent nights and weekends developing a sophisticated cost-accounting software program that became Track's initial product offering. As the firm grew, Stanley planned to develop and expand the software product offerings—all of which would be related to streamlining the accounting processes of medium- to large-sized manufacturers.

Although Track experienced losses during its first 2 years of operation—2003 and 2004—its profit has increased steadily from 2005 to the present (2009). The firm's profit history, including dividend payments and contributions to retained earnings, is summarized in Table 1.

Stanley started the firm with a $100,000 investment—his savings of $50,000 as equity and a $50,000 long-term loan from the bank. He had hoped to maintain his initial 100 percent ownership in the corporation, but after experiencing a $50,000 loss during the first year of operation (2003), he sold 60 percent of the stock to a group of investors to obtain needed funds. Since then, no other stock transactions have taken place. Although he owns only 40 percent of the firm, Stanley actively manages all aspects of its activities; the other stockholders are not active in management of the firm. The firm's stock was valued at $4.50 per share in 2008 and at $5.28 per share in 2009.

Stanley has just prepared the firm's 2009 income statement, balance sheet, and statement of retained earnings, shown in Tables 2 (on page 155), 3, and 4 (on page 156), along with the 2008 balance sheet. In addition, he has compiled the

TABLE 1

Track Software, Inc.
Profit, Dividends, and Retained Earnings, 2003–2009

Year	Net profits after taxes (1)	Dividends paid (2)	Contribution to retained earnings [(1) − (2)] (3)
2003	($50,000)	$ 0	($50,000)
2004	(20,000)	0	(20,000)
2005	15,000	0	15,000
2006	35,000	0	35,000
2007	40,000	1,000	39,000
2008	43,000	3,000	40,000
2009	48,000	5,000	43,000

2008 ratio values and industry average ratio values for 2009, which are applicable to both 2008 and 2009 and are summarized in Table 5 (on page 157). He is quite pleased to have achieved record earnings of $48,000 in 2009, but he is concerned about the firm's cash flows. Specifically, he is finding it more and more difficult to pay the firm's bills in a timely manner and generate cash flows to investors—both creditors and owners. To gain insight into these cash flow problems, Stanley is planning to determine the firm's 2009 operating cash flow (OCF) and free cash flow (FCF).

Stanley is further frustrated by the firm's inability to afford to hire a software developer to complete development of a cost estimation package that is believed to have "blockbuster" sales potential. Stanley began development of this package 2 years ago, but the firm's growing complexity has forced him to devote more of his time to administrative duties, thereby halting the development of this product. Stanley's reluctance to fill this position stems from his concern that the added $80,000 per year in salary and benefits for the position would certainly lower the firm's earnings per share (EPS) over the next couple of years. Although the project's success is in no way guaranteed, Stanley believes that if the money were spent to hire the software developer, the firm's sales and earnings would significantly rise once the 2- to 3-year development, production, and marketing process was completed.

With all of these concerns in mind, Stanley set out to review the various data to develop strategies that would help to ensure a bright future for Track Software. Stanley believed that as part of this process, a thorough ratio analysis of the firm's 2009 results would provide important additional insights.

TABLE 2

Track Software, Inc.
Income Statement ($000)
for the Year Ended December 31, 2009

Sales revenue		$1,550
Less: Cost of goods sold		1,030
Gross profits		$ 520
Less: Operating expenses		
Selling expense	$150	
General and administrative expenses	270	
Depreciation expense	11	
Total operating expense		431
Operating profits (EBIT)		$ 89
Less: Interest expense		29
Net profits before taxes		$ 60
Less: Taxes (20%)		12
Net profits after taxes		$ 48

TABLE 3

Track Software, Inc.
Balance Sheet ($000)

	December 31	
Assets	2009	2008
Current assets		
Cash	$ 12	$ 31
Marketable securities	66	82
Accounts receivable	152	104
Inventories	191	145
Total current assets	$421	$362
Gross fixed assets	$195	$180
Less: Accumulated depreciation	63	52
Net fixed assets	$132	$128
Total assets	$553	$490
Liabilities and Stockholders' Equity		
Current liabilities		
Accounts payable	$136	$126
Notes payable	200	190
Accruals	27	25
Total current liabilities	$363	$341
Long-term debt	$ 38	$ 40
Total liabilities	$401	$381
Stockholders' equity		
Common stock (50,000 shares outstanding at $0.40 par value)	$ 20	$ 20
Paid-in capital in excess of par	30	30
Retained earnings	102	59
Total stockholders' equity	$152	$109
Total liabilities and stockholders' equity	$553	$490

TABLE 4

Track Software, Inc.
Statement of Retained Earnings ($000)
for the Year Ended December 31, 2009

Retained earnings balance (January 1, 2009)	$ 59
Plus: Net profits after taxes (for 2009)	48
Less: Cash dividends on common stock (paid during 2009)	5
Retained earnings balance (December 31, 2009)	$102

TABLE 5

Ratio	Actual 2008	Industry average 2009
Current ratio	1.06	1.82
Quick ratio	0.63	1.10
Inventory turnover	10.40	12.45
Average collection period	29.6 days	20.2 days
Total asset turnover	2.66	3.92
Debt ratio	0.78	0.55
Times interest earned ratio	3.0	5.6
Gross profit margin	32.1%	42.3%
Operating profit margin	5.5%	12.4%
Net profit margin	3.0%	4.0%
Return on total assets (ROA)	8.0%	15.6%
Return on common equity (ROE)	36.4%	34.7%
Price/earnings (P/E) ratio	5.2	7.1
Market/book (M/B) ratio	2.1	2.2

To Do

a. (1) Upon what financial goal does Stanley seem to be focusing? Is it the correct goal? Why or why not?

   (2) Could a potential *agency problem* exist in this firm? Explain.

b. Calculate the firm's earnings per share (EPS) for each year, recognizing that the number of shares of common stock outstanding has remained *unchanged* since the firm's inception. Comment on the EPS performance in view of your response in part **a.**

c. Use the financial data presented to determine Track's *operating cash flow (OCF)* and *free cash flow (FCF)* in 2009. Evaluate your findings in light of Track's current cash flow difficulties.

d. Analyze the firm's financial condition in 2009 as it relates to (1) liquidity, (2) activity, (3) debt, (4) profitability, and (5) market, using the financial statements provided in Tables 2 and 3 and the ratio data included in Table 5. Be sure to *evaluate* the firm on both a cross-sectional and a time-series basis.

e. What recommendation would you make to Stanley regarding hiring a new software developer? Relate your recommendation here to your responses in part **a.**

Part Two
Important Financial Concepts

Chapters in This Part

4 Time Value of Money

WHY THIS CHAPTER MATTERS TO YOU

In Your Professional Life

Accounting: You need to understand time-value-of-money calculations to account for certain transactions such as loan amortization, lease payments, and bond interest rates.

Information systems: You need to understand time-value-of-money calculations to design systems that accurately measure and value the firm's cash flows.

Management: You need to understand time-value-of-money calculations so that you can manage cash receipts and disbursements in a way that will enable the firm to receive the greatest value from its cash flows.

Marketing: You need to understand time value of money because funding for new programs and products must be justified financially using time-value-of-money techniques.

Operations: You need to understand time value of money because the value of investments in new equipment, in new processes, and in inventory will be affected by the time value of money.

In Your Personal Life

Time value of money techniques are widely used in personal financial planning. You can use them to calculate the value of savings at given future dates and to estimate the amount you need now to accumulate a given amount at a future date. You also can apply them to value lump-sum amounts or streams of periodic cash flows and to the interest rate or amount of time needed to achieve a given financial goal.

LEARNING GOALS

LG 1 Discuss the role of time value in finance, the use of computational tools, and the basic patterns of cash flow.

LG 2 Understand the concepts of future value and present value, their calculation for single amounts, and the relationship between them.

LG 3 Find the future value and the present value of both an ordinary annuity and an annuity due, and find the present value of a perpetuity.

LG 4 Calculate both the future value and the present value of a mixed stream of cash flows.

LG 5 Understand the effect that compounding interest more frequently than annually has on future value and on the effective annual rate of interest.

LG 6 Describe the procedures involved in (1) determining deposits needed to accumulate a future sum, (2) loan amortization, (3) finding interest or growth rates, and (4) finding an unknown number of periods.

Eli Lilly and Company

Riding the Pipeline

Before a company will approve a project or venture, it must be sure that the capital expenditures will be repaid by future revenue. For pharmaceutical companies, this calculation is complicated by the lengthy process of research and development that they hope ends with the approval of the Food and Drug Administration (FDA).

For **Eli Lilly and Company,** the average length of time from the discovery of a new drug until delivery to a patient is 10 to 15 years. After the drug-discovery process produces a promising lead, a drug is still a long way from being ready for testing in human subjects. The researchers must probe further to determine what dosage will be required and at what level it might be toxic to the patient. They also must explore practical issues like whether Lilly will be able to manufacture the compound on a large scale. The clinical trials themselves can take years.

To help recoup its investment, a drug manufacturer can get a 20-year patent that grants the company exclusive rights to the new drug. However, with the research and approval process lasting from 10 to 15 years, the useful patent life after approval is often less than 10 years. Once patent protection expires, generic drug manufacturers can flood the market with low-priced alternatives to the name-brand drug. The generic drug manufacturers' share of the prescription market has grown from 19 percent of the volume in 1984 to 53 percent in 2006 and is expected to continue to rise as some key blockbuster brand-name drug patents expire during the next 3 years.

> From your knowledge of the cost of name-brand and generic drugs, how do you believe the market share of generics compares with the market share of name-brand prescription drugs in *dollar* terms?

For Eli Lilly, the cost of bringing a new drug to market runs from $800 million to $1.2 billion. To keep its drug pipeline full, Eli Lilly plows some 20 percent of sales back into the R&D programs on which its future depends. With large cash expenditures occurring years before any cash return, the time value of money is an important factor in calculating the economic viability of a new drug. In this chapter, you will learn how to determine the present value of future cash flows and other time-value-of-money calculations.

4.1 | The Role of Time Value in Finance

Financial managers and investors are always confronted with opportunities to earn positive rates of return on their funds, whether through investment in attractive projects or in interest-bearing securities or deposits. Therefore, the timing of cash outflows and inflows has important economic consequences, which financial managers explicitly recognize as the *time value of money*. Time value is based on the belief that a dollar today is worth more than a dollar that will be received at some future date. We begin our study of time value in finance by considering the two views of time value—future value and present value, the computational tools used to streamline time value calculations, and the basic patterns of cash flow.

Future Value versus Present Value

Financial values and decisions can be assessed by using either future value or present value techniques. Although these techniques will result in the same decisions, they view the decision differently. Future value techniques typically measure cash flows at the *end* of a project's life. Present value techniques measure cash flows at the *start* of a project's life (time zero). *Future value* is cash you will receive at a given future date, and *present value* is just like cash in hand today.

time line
A horizontal line on which time zero appears at the leftmost end and future periods are marked from left to right; can be used to depict investment cash flows.

A **time line** can be used to depict the cash flows associated with a given investment. It is a horizontal line on which time zero appears at the leftmost end and future periods are marked from left to right. A time line covering five periods (in this case, years) is given in Figure 4.1. The cash flows occurring at time zero and at the end of each year are shown above the line; the negative values represent *cash outflows* ($10,000 at time zero) and the positive values represent *cash inflows* ($3,000 inflow at the end of year 1, $5,000 inflow at the end of year 2, and so on).

Because money has a time value, all of the cash flows associated with an investment, such as those in Figure 4.1, must be measured at the same point in time. Typically, that point is either the end or the beginning of the investment's life. The future value technique uses *compounding* to find the *future value* of each cash flow at the end of the investment's life and then sums these values to find the investment's future value. This approach is depicted above the time line in Figure 4.2. The figure shows that the future value of each cash flow is measured at the end of the investment's 5-year life. Alternatively, the present value technique uses *discounting* to find the *present value* of each cash flow at time zero and then sums these values to find the investment's value today. Application of this approach is depicted below the time line in Figure 4.2.

FIGURE 4.1

Time Line
Time line depicting an investment's cash flows

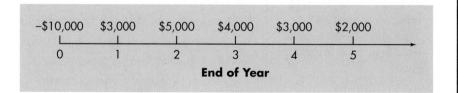

FIGURE 4.2

Compounding and Discounting
Time line showing compounding to find future value and discounting to find present value

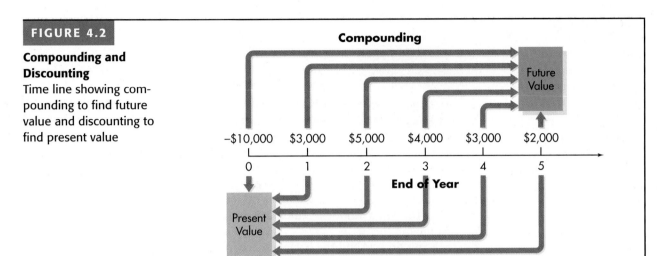

The meaning and mechanics of compounding to find future value and of discounting to find present value are covered in this chapter. Although future value and present value result in the same decisions, *financial managers—because they make decisions at time zero—tend to rely primarily on present value techniques.*

Computational Tools

Time-consuming calculations are often involved in finding future and present values. Although you should understand the concepts and mathematics underlying these calculations, the application of time value techniques can be streamlined. We focus on the use of hand-held financial calculators, electronic spreadsheets, and financial tables as aids in computation.

Financial Calculators

Financial calculators can be used to simplify time value computations. Generally, *financial calculators* include numerous preprogrammed financial routines. This chapter and those that follow show the keystrokes for calculating interest factors and making other financial computations. For convenience, we use the important financial keys, labeled in a fashion consistent with most major financial calculators.

We focus primarily on the keys pictured and defined in Figure 4.3 (see page 164). We typically use four of the first five keys shown in the left column, along with the compute (**CPT**) key. One of the four keys represents the unknown value being calculated. (Occasionally, all five of the keys are used, with one representing the unknown value.) The keystrokes on some of the more sophisticated calculators are menu-driven: After you select the appropriate routine, the calculator prompts you to input each value; on these calculators, a compute key is not needed to obtain a solution. Regardless, any calculator with the basic future and present value functions can be used to simplify time value calculations. See Appendix A for keystrokes for some of the more popular calculators. The

FIGURE 4.3

Calculator Keys
Important financial keys
on the typical calculator

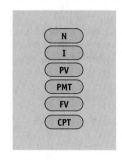

N — Number of periods
I — Interest rate per period
PV — Present value
PMT — Amount of payment (used only for annuities)
FV — Future value
CPT — Compute key used to initiate financial calculation once all values are input

keystrokes for other financial calculators are explained in the reference guides that accompany them.

Once you understand the basic underlying concepts, you probably will want to use a calculator to streamline routine financial calculations. With a little practice, you can increase both the speed and the accuracy of your financial computations. Remember that *conceptual understanding of the material is the objective.* An ability to solve problems with the aid of a calculator does not necessarily reflect such an understanding, so don't just settle for answers. Work with the material until you are sure you also understand the concepts.

Electronic Spreadsheets

Hint Anyone familiar with an electronic spreadsheet, such as Excel, realizes that most of the time-value-of-money calculations can be performed expeditiously by using the special functions contained in the spreadsheet.

Like financial calculators, electronic spreadsheets have built-in routines that simplify time value calculations. We provide in the text a number of spreadsheet solutions that identify the cell entries for calculating time values. The value for each variable is entered in a cell in the spreadsheet, and the calculation is programmed using an equation that links the individual cells. If values of the variables are changed, the solution automatically changes as a result of the equation linking the cells. In the spreadsheet solutions in this book, the equation that determines the calculation is shown at the bottom of the spreadsheet.

The ability to use electronic spreadsheets has become a prime skill for today's managers. As the saying goes, "Get aboard the bandwagon, or get run over." The spreadsheet solutions we present in this book will help you climb up onto that bandwagon!

Financial Tables

Financial tables include various future and present value interest factors that simplify time value calculations. The values shown in these tables are easily developed from formulas, with various degrees of rounding. As a result, slight differences are likely to exist between table-based calculations and the more precise values obtained using a financial calculator or spreadsheet.

The financial tables are typically indexed by the interest rate (in columns) and the number of periods (in rows). Figure 4.4 shows this general layout. The interest factor at a 20 percent interest rate for 10 years would be found at the intersection of the 20% column and the 10-period row, as shown by the dark blue box. A full set of the four basic financial tables is included in Appendix A at the end of the book. These tables are described more fully later in the chapter.

FIGURE 4.4

Financial Tables
Layout and use of
a financial table

Period		Interest Rate ↓						
	1%	2%	⋯	10%	⋯	**20%**	⋯	50%
1			⋯		⋯	⋮	⋯	
2			⋯		⋯	⋮	⋯	
3			⋯		⋯	⋮	⋯	
⋮	⋮	⋮	⋯	⋮	⋯	⋮	⋯	⋮
→ 10	⋯	⋯	⋯	⋯	⋯	**X.XXX**	⋯	⋯
⋮	⋮	⋮	⋯	⋮	⋯	⋮	⋯	⋮
20			⋯		⋯		⋯	
⋮	⋮	⋮	⋯	⋮	⋯	⋮	⋯	⋮
50			⋯		⋯		⋯	

Basic Patterns of Cash Flow

The cash flow—both inflows and outflows—of a firm can be described by its general pattern. It can be defined as a single amount, an annuity, or a mixed stream.

Single amount: A lump-sum amount either currently held or expected at some future date. Examples include $1,000 today and $650 to be received at the end of 10 years.

Annuity: A level periodic stream of cash flow. For our purposes, we'll work primarily with *annual* cash flows. Examples include either paying out or receiving $800 at the end of each of the next 7 years.

Mixed stream: A stream of cash flow that is *not* an annuity; a stream of unequal periodic cash flows that reflect no particular pattern. Examples include the following two cash flow streams A and B.

	Mixed cash flow stream	
End of year	A	B
1	$ 100	− $ 50
2	800	100
3	1,200	80
4	1,200	− 60
5	1,400	
6	300	

Note that neither cash flow stream has equal, periodic cash flows and that A is a 6-year mixed stream and B is a 4-year mixed stream.

In the next three sections of this chapter, we develop the concepts and techniques for finding future and present values of single amounts, annuities, and mixed streams, respectively. Detailed demonstrations of these cash flow patterns are included.

REVIEW QUESTIONS

4–1 What is the difference between *future value* and *present value*? Which approach is generally preferred by financial managers? Why?

4–2 Define and differentiate among the three basic patterns of cash flow: (1) a single amount, (2) an annuity, and (3) a mixed stream.

4.2 | Single Amounts

Imagine that at age 25 you began making annual purchases of $2,000 of an investment that earns a guaranteed 5 percent annually. At the end of 40 years, at age 65, you would have invested a total of $80,000 (40 years × $2,000 per year). Assuming that all funds remain invested, how much would you have accumulated at the end of the fortieth year? $100,000? $150,000? $200,000? No, your $80,000 would have grown to $242,000! Why? Because the time value of money allowed your investments to generate returns that built on each other over the 40 years.

Future Value of a Single Amount

The most basic future value and present value concepts and computations concern single amounts, either present or future amounts. We begin by considering the future value of present amounts. Then we will use the underlying concepts to determine the present value of future amounts. You will see that although future value is more intuitively appealing, present value is more useful in financial decision making.

future value
The value at a given future date of a present amount placed on deposit today and earning interest at a specified rate. Found by applying *compound interest* over a specified period of time.

We often need to find the value at some future date of a given amount of money placed on deposit today. For example, if you deposit $500 today into an account that pays 5 percent annual interest, how much would you have in the account at the end of exactly 10 years? **Future value** is the value at a given future date of a present amount placed on deposit today and earning interest at a specified rate. It depends on the rate of interest earned and the length of time a given amount is left on deposit. Here we explore the future value of a single amount.

The Concept of Future Value

compound interest
Interest that is earned on a given deposit and has become part of the *principal* at the end of a specified period.

principal
The amount of money on which interest is paid.

We speak of **compound interest** to indicate that the amount of interest earned on a given deposit has become part of the *principal* at the end of a specified period. The term **principal** refers to the amount of money on which the interest is paid. Annual compounding is the most common type.

The *future value* of a present amount is found by applying *compound interest* over a specified period of time. Savings institutions advertise compound interest returns at a rate of *x* percent, or *x* percent interest, compounded annually, semiannually, quarterly, monthly, weekly, daily, or even continuously. The concept of future value with annual compounding can be illustrated by a simple example.

Personal Finance Example   If Fred Moreno places $100 in a savings account paying 8% interest compounded annually, at the end of 1 year he will have $108 in the account—the initial principal of $100 plus 8% ($8) in interest. The future value at the end of the first year is calculated by using Equation 4.1:

$$\text{Future value at end of year 1} = \$100 \times (1 + 0.08) = \$108 \tag{4.1}$$

If Fred were to leave this money in the account for another year, he would be paid interest at the rate of 8% on the new principal of $108. At the end of this second year there would be $116.64 in the account. This amount would represent the principal at the beginning of year 2 ($108) plus 8% of the $108 ($8.64) in interest. The future value at the end of the second year is calculated by using Equation 4.2:

$$\text{Future value at end of year 2} = \$108 \times (1 + 0.08) \tag{4.2}$$
$$= \$116.64$$

Substituting the expression between the equals signs in Equation 4.1 for the $108 figure in Equation 4.2 gives us Equation 4.3:

$$\text{Future value at end of year 2} = \$100 \times (1 + 0.08) \times (1 + 0.08) \tag{4.3}$$
$$= \$100 \times (1 + 0.08)^2$$
$$= \$116.64$$

The equations in the preceding example lead to a more general formula for calculating future value.

The Equation for Future Value

The basic relationship in Equation 4.3 can be generalized to find the future value after any number of periods. We use the following notation for the various inputs:

FV_n = future value at the end of period n

PV = initial principal, or present value

i = annual rate of interest paid. (*Note:* On financial calculators, **I** is typically used to represent this rate.)

n = number of periods (typically years) that the money is left on deposit

The general equation for the future value at the end of period n is

$$FV_n = PV \times (1 + i)^n \tag{4.4}$$

A simple example will illustrate how to apply Equation 4.4.

Personal Finance Example   Jane Farber places $800 in a savings account paying 6% interest compounded annually. She wants to know how much money will be in the account at the end of 5 years. Substituting $PV = \$800$, $i = 0.06$, and $n = 5$ into Equation 4.4 gives the amount at the end of year 5.

$$FV_5 = \$800 \times (1 + 0.06)^5 = \$800 \times (1.338) = \$1,070.40$$

Time line for future value of a single amount ($800 initial principal, earning 6%, at the end of 5 years)

This analysis can be depicted on a time line as follows:

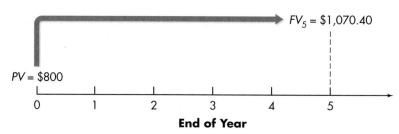

Using Computational Tools to Find Future Value

Solving the equation in the preceding example involves raising 1.06 to the fifth power. Using a financial calculator, an electronic spreadsheet, or a future value interest table greatly simplifies the calculation. A table that provides values for $(1 + i)^n$ in Equation 4.4 is included near the back of the book in Appendix Table A–1. The value in each cell of the table is called the **future value interest factor**. This factor is the multiplier used to calculate, at a specified interest rate, the future value of a present amount as of a given time. The future value interest factor for an initial principal of $1 compounded at i percent for n periods is referred to as $FVIF_{i,n}$.

future value interest factor
The multiplier used to calculate, at a specified interest rate, the future value of a present amount as of a given time.

$$\text{Future value interest factor} = FVIF_{i,n} = (1 + i)^n \tag{4.5}$$

By finding the intersection of the annual interest rate, i, and the appropriate periods, n, you will find the future value interest factor that is relevant to a particular problem.[1] Using $FVIF_{i,n}$ as the appropriate factor, we can rewrite the general equation for future value (Equation 4.4) as follows:

$$FV_n = PV \times (FVIF_{i,n}) \tag{4.6}$$

This expression indicates that to find the future value at the end of period n of an initial deposit, we have merely to multiply the initial deposit, PV, by the appropriate future value interest factor.[2]

Personal Finance Example   In the preceding example, Jane Farber placed $800 in her savings account at 6% interest compounded annually and wishes to find out how much will be in the account at the end of 5 years.

Calculator Use[3]   The financial calculator can be used to calculate the future value directly.[4] First punch in $800 and depress **PV**; next punch in 5 and depress

---

1. Although we commonly deal with years rather than periods, financial tables are frequently presented in terms of periods to provide maximum flexibility.

2. Occasionally, you may want to estimate roughly how long a given sum must earn at a given annual rate to double the amount. The *Rule of 72* is used to make this estimate; dividing the annual rate of interest into 72 results in the approximate number of periods it will take to double one's money at the given rate. For example, to double one's money at a 10% annual rate of interest will take about 7.2 years (72 ÷ 10 = 7.2). Looking at Table A–1, we can see that the future value interest factor for 10% and 7 years is slightly less than 2 (1.949); this approximation therefore appears to be reasonably accurate.

3. Many calculators allow the user to set the number of payments per year. Most of these calculators are preset for monthly payments—12 payments per year. Because we work primarily with annual payments—one payment per year—it is important to *be sure that your calculator is set for one payment per year*. And although most calculators are preset to recognize that all payments occur at the end of the period, it is important to *make sure that your calculator is correctly set on the END mode*. Consult the reference guide that accompanies your calculator for instructions for setting these values.

4. To avoid including previous data in current calculations, *always clear all registers of your calculator before inputting values and making each computation*.

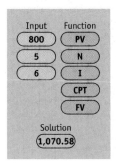

Input   Function
800   PV
5   N
6   I
CPT
FV

Solution
1,070.58

N; then punch in 6 and depress **I** (which is equivalent to "*i*" in our notation)[5]; finally, to calculate the future value, depress **CPT** and then **FV.** The future value of $1,070.58 should appear on the calculator display as shown at the left. On many calculators, this value will be preceded by a minus sign (−1,070.58). *If a minus sign appears on your calculator, ignore it here as well as in all other "Calculator Use" illustrations in this text.*[6] (*Note:* In future examples of calculator use, we will use only a display similar to that shown on this page. If you need a reminder of the procedures involved, go back and review this paragraph.)

Spreadsheet Use   The future value of the single amount also can be calculated as shown on the following Excel spreadsheet.

	A	B
1	FUTURE VALUE OF A SINGLE AMOUNT	
2	Present value	$800
3	Interest rate, pct per year compounded annually	6%
4	Number of years	5
5	Future value	$1,070.58
	Entry in Cell B5 is =FV(B3,B4,0,−B2,0) The minus sign appears before B2 because the present value is an outflow (i.e., a deposit made by Jane Farber).	

Table Use   The future value interest factor for an initial principal of $1 on deposit for 5 years at 6% interest compounded annually, $FVIF_{6\%, \, 5yrs}$, found in Table A–1, is 1.338. Using Equation 4.6, $800 × 1.338 = $1,070.40. Therefore, the future value of Jane's deposit at the end of year 5 will be $1,070.40.

Because both the calculator and the spreadsheet are more accurate than the future value factors, which have been rounded to the nearest 0.001, a slight difference—in this case, $0.18—will frequently exist between the values found by these alternative methods. Clearly, the improved accuracy and ease of calculation tend to favor the use of the calculator.

A Graphical View of Future Value

Remember that we measure future value at the *end* of the given period. Figure 4.5 (see page 170) illustrates the relationship among various interest rates, the number of periods interest is earned, and the future value of one dollar. The figure shows that (1) the higher the interest rate, the higher the future value, and (2) the longer the period of time, the higher the future value. Note that for an interest rate of 0 percent, the future value always equals the present value ($1.00). But for any interest rate greater than zero, the future value is greater than the present value of $1.00.

---

5. The known values *can be punched into the calculator in any order;* the order specified in this as well as other demonstrations of calculator use included in this text merely reflects convenience and personal preference.

6. The calculator differentiates inflows from outflows by preceding the outflows with a negative sign. For example, in the problem just demonstrated, the $800 present value (PV), because it was keyed as a positive number (800), is considered an inflow or deposit. Therefore, the calculated future value (FV) of −1,070.58 is preceded by a minus sign to show that it is the resulting outflow or withdrawal. Had the $800 present value been keyed in as a negative number (−800), the future value of $1,070.58 would have been displayed as a positive number (1,070.58). Simply stated, *the cash flows—present value* (PV) *and future value* (FV)*—will have opposite signs.*

Future Value Relationship
Interest rates, time periods, and future value of one dollar

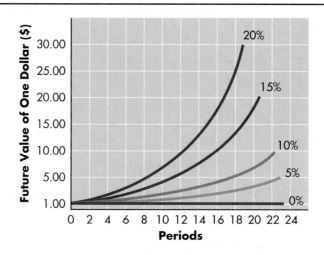

Present Value of a Single Amount

present value
The current dollar value of a future amount—the amount of money that would have to be invested today at a given interest rate over a specified period to equal the future amount.

It is often useful to determine the value today of a future amount of money. For example, how much would I have to deposit today into an account paying 7 percent annual interest to accumulate $3,000 at the end of 5 years? **Present value** is the current dollar value of a future amount—the amount of money that would have to be invested today at a given interest rate over a specified period to equal the future amount. Present value depends largely on the investment opportunities and the point in time at which the amount is to be received. This section explores the present value of a single amount.

The Concept of Present Value

discounting cash flows
The process of finding present values; the inverse of compounding interest.

The process of finding present values is often referred to as **discounting cash flows.** It is concerned with answering the following question: If I can earn i percent on my money, what is the most I would be willing to pay now for an opportunity to receive FV_n dollars n periods from today?

This process is actually the inverse of compounding interest. Instead of finding the future value of present dollars invested at a given rate, discounting determines the present value of a future amount, assuming an opportunity to earn a certain return on the money. This annual rate of return is variously referred to as the *discount rate, required return, cost of capital,* and *opportunity cost.*[7] These terms will be used interchangeably in this text.

Personal Finance Example   Paul Shorter has an opportunity to receive $300 one year from now. If he can earn 6% on his investments in the normal course of events, what is the most he should pay now for this opportunity? To answer this question, Paul must determine how many dollars he would have to invest at 6% today to have $300 one year from now. Letting *PV* equal this unknown amount and using the same notation as in the future value discussion, we have

$$PV \times (1 + 0.06) = \$300 \tag{4.7}$$

7. The theoretical underpinning of this "required return" is introduced in Chapter 5 and further refined in subsequent chapters.

Solving Equation 4.7 for *PV* gives us Equation 4.8:

$$PV = \frac{\$300}{(1 + 0.06)} \qquad \text{(4.8)}$$
$$= \$283.02$$

The value today ("present value") of $300 received one year from today, given an opportunity cost of 6%, is $283.02. That is, investing $283.02 today at the 6% opportunity cost would result in $300 at the end of one year.

The Equation for Present Value

The present value of a future amount can be found mathematically by solving Equation 4.4 for *PV*. In other words, the present value, *PV*, of some future amount, FV^n, to be received *n* periods from now, assuming an opportunity cost of *i*, is calculated as follows:

$$PV = \frac{FV_n}{(1 + i)^n} = FV_n \times \left[\frac{1}{(1 + i)^n} \right] \qquad \text{(4.9)}$$

Note the similarity between this general equation for present value and the equation in the preceding example (Equation 4.8). Let's use this equation in an example.

Personal Finance Example   Pam Valenti wishes to find the present value of $1,700 that will be received 8 years from now. Pam's opportunity cost is 8%. Substituting $FV_8 = \$1{,}700$, $n = 8$, and $i = 0.08$ into Equation 4.9 yields Equation 4.10:

$$PV = \frac{\$1{,}700}{(1 + 0.08)^8} = \frac{\$1{,}700}{1.851} = \$918.42 \qquad \text{(4.10)}$$

The following time line shows this analysis.

Time line for present value of a single amount ($1,700 future amount, discounted at 8%, from the end of 8 years)

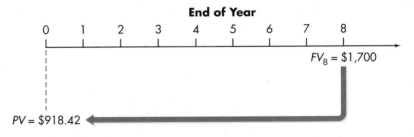

Using Computational Tools to Find Present Value

present value interest factor
The multiplier used to calculate, at a specified discount rate, the present value of an amount to be received in a future period.

The present value calculation can be simplified by using a **present value interest factor**. This factor is the multiplier used to calculate, at a specified discount rate, the present value of an amount to be received in a future period. The present value interest factor for the present value of $1 discounted at *i* percent for *n* periods is referred to as $PVIF_{i,n}$.

$$\text{Present value interest factor} = PVIF_{i,n} = \frac{1}{(1 + i)^n} \qquad \text{(4.11)}$$

Appendix Table A–2 presents present value interest factors for $1. By letting $PVIF_{i,n}$ represent the appropriate factor, we can rewrite the general equation for present value (Equation 4.9) as follows:

$$PV = FV_n \times (PVIF_{i,n}) \tag{4.12}$$

This expression indicates that to find the present value of an amount to be received in a future period, n, we have merely to multiply the future amount, FV_n, by the appropriate present value interest factor.

Personal Finance Example   As noted, Pam Valenti wishes to find the present value of $1,700 to be received 8 years from now, assuming an 8% opportunity cost.

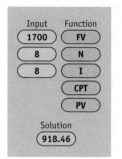

Input	Function
1700	FV
8	N
8	I
	CPT
	PV

Solution
918.46

Calculator Use   Using the calculator's financial functions and the inputs shown at the left, you should find the present value to be $918.46. The value obtained with the calculator is more accurate than the values found using the equation or the table (shown below), although for the purposes of this text, these differences are insignificant.

Spreadsheet Use   The present value of the single future amount also can be calculated as shown on the following Excel spreadsheet.

	A	B
1	PRESENT VALUE OF A SINGLE AMOUNT	
2	Future value	$1,700
3	Interest rate, pct per year compounded annually	8%
4	Number of years	8
5	Present value	$918.46
	Entry in Cell B5 is =–PV(B3,B4,0,B2) The minus sign appears before PV to change the present value to a positive amount.	

Table Use   The present value interest factor for 8% and 8 years, $PVIF_{8\%,8\ yrs}$, found in Table A–2, is 0.540. Using Equation 4.12, $1,700 \times 0.540 = 918. The present value of the $1,700 Pam expects to receive in 8 years is $918.

A Graphical View of Present Value

Remember that present value calculations assume that the future values are measured at the *end* of the given period. The relationships among the factors in a present value calculation are illustrated in Figure 4.6. The figure clearly shows that, everything else being equal, (1) the higher the discount rate, the lower the present value, and (2) the longer the period of time, the lower the present value. Also note that given a discount rate of 0 percent, the present value always equals the future value ($1.00). But for any discount rate greater than zero, the present value is less than the future value of $1.00.

Comparing Present Value and Future Value

We will close this section with some important observations about present values. One is that the expression for the present value interest factor for i percent and n periods, $1/(1 + i)^n$, is the *inverse* of the future value interest factor for i percent and

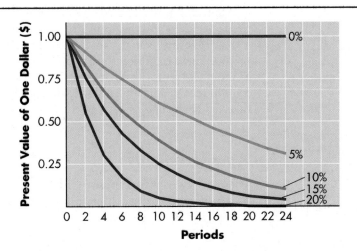

FIGURE 4.6

Present Value Relationship

Discount rates, time periods, and present value of one dollar

n periods, $(1 + i)^n$. You can confirm this very simply: Divide a present value interest factor for i percent and n periods, $PVIF_{i,n}$, given in Table A–2, into 1.0, and compare the resulting value to the future value interest factor given in Table A–1 for i percent and n periods, $FVIF_{i,n}$. The two values should be equivalent.

Second, because of the relationship between present value interest factors and future value interest factors, we can find the present value interest factors given a table of future value interest factors, and vice versa. For example, the future value interest factor (from Table A–1) for 10 percent and 5 periods is 1.611. Dividing this value into 1.0 yields 0.621, which is the present value interest factor (given in Table A–2) for 10 percent and 5 periods.

REVIEW QUESTIONS

4–3 How is the *compounding process* related to the payment of interest on savings? What is the general equation for future value?

4–4 What effect would a *decrease* in the interest rate have on the future value of a deposit? What effect would an *increase* in the holding period have on future value?

4–5 What is meant by "the present value of a future amount"? What is the general equation for present value?

4–6 What effect does *increasing* the required return have on the present value of a future amount? Why?

4–7 How are present value and future value calculations related?

4.3 | Annuities

How much would you pay today, given that you can earn 7 percent on low-risk investments, to receive a guaranteed $3,000 at the end of *each* of the next 20 years? How much will you have at the end of 5 years if your employer withholds and invests $1,000 of your year-end bonus at the end of *each* of the next 5 years,

annuity
A stream of equal periodic cash flows, over a specified time period. These cash flows can be *inflows* of returns earned on investments or *outflows* of funds invested to earn future returns.

ordinary annuity
An annuity for which the cash flow occurs at the *end* of each period.

annuity due
An annuity for which the cash flow occurs at the *beginning* of each period.

guaranteeing you a 9 percent annual rate of return? To answer these questions, you need to understand the application of the time value of money to *annuities.*

An **annuity** is a stream of equal periodic cash flows, over a specified time period. These cash flows are usually annual but can occur at other intervals, such as monthly (rent, car payments). The cash flows in an annuity can be *inflows* (the $3,000 received at the end of each of the next 20 years) or *outflows* (the $1,000 invested at the end of each of the next 5 years).

Types of Annuities

There are two basic types of annuities. For an **ordinary annuity,** the cash flow occurs at the *end* of each period. For an **annuity due,** the cash flow occurs at the *beginning* of each period.

Personal Finance Example   Fran Abrams is choosing which of two annuities to receive. Both are 5-year, $1,000 annuities; annuity A is an ordinary annuity, and annuity B is an annuity due. To better understand the difference between these annuities, she has listed their cash flows in Table 4.1. Note that the amount of each annuity totals $5,000. The two annuities differ in the timing of their cash flows: The cash flows are received sooner with the annuity due than with the ordinary annuity.

Although the cash flows of both annuities in Table 4.1 total $5,000, the annuity due would have a higher future value than the ordinary annuity, because each of its five annual cash flows can earn interest for one year more than each of the ordinary annuity's cash flows. In general, as will be demonstrated later in this chapter, *both the future value and the present value of an annuity due are always greater than the future value and the present value, respectively, of an otherwise identical ordinary annuity.*

Because ordinary annuities are more frequently used in finance, *unless otherwise specified, the term* annuity *is intended throughout this book to refer to ordinary annuities.*

TABLE 4.1	Comparison of Ordinary Annuity and Annuity Due Cash Flows ($1,000, 5 Years)	
	Annual cash flows	
End of year[a]	Annuity A (*ordinary*)	Annuity B (*annuity due*)
0	$ 0	$1,000
1	1,000	1,000
2	1,000	1,000
3	1,000	1,000
4	1,000	1,000
5	1,000	0
Totals	$5,000	$5,000

[a]The ends of years 0, 1, 2, 3, and 4 are equivalent to the beginnings of years 1, 2, 3, 4, and 5, respectively.

Finding the Future Value of an Ordinary Annuity

The calculations required to find the future value of an ordinary annuity are illustrated in the following example.

Personal Finance Example   Fran Abrams wishes to determine how much money she will have at the end of 5 years if she chooses annuity A, the ordinary annuity. It represents deposits of $1,000 annually, at the *end of each* of the next 5 years, into a savings account paying 7% annual interest. This situation is depicted on the following time line:

Time line for future value of an ordinary annuity ($1,000 end-of-year deposit, earning 7%, at the end of 5 years)

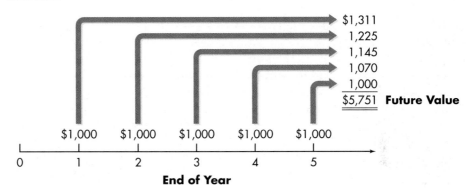

As the figure shows, at the end of year 5, Fran will have $5,751 in her account. Note that because the deposits are made at the end of the year, the first deposit will earn interest for 4 years, the second for 3 years, and so on.

Using Computational Tools to Find the Future Value of an Ordinary Annuity

Annuity calculations can be simplified by using a financial calculator, an electronic spreadsheet, or an interest table. A table for the future value of a $1 *ordinary annuity* is given in Appendix Table A–3. The factors in the table are derived by summing the future value interest factors for the appropriate number of years. For example, the factor for the annuity in the preceding example is the sum of the factors for the five years (years 4 through 0): $1.311 + 1.225 + 1.145 + 1.070 + 1.000 = 5.751$. Because the deposits occur at the end of each year, they will earn interest from the end of the year in which each occurs to the end of year 5. Therefore, the first deposit earns interest for 4 years (end of year 1 through end of year 5), and the last deposit earns interest for zero years. The future value interest factor for zero years at any interest rate i, $FVIF_{i,0}$, is 1.000, as we have noted. The formula for the **future value interest factor for an ordinary annuity** when interest is compounded annually at i percent for n periods, $FVIFA_{i,n}$, is[8]

future value interest factor for an ordinary annuity The multiplier used to calculate the future value of an *ordinary annuity* at a specified interest rate over a given period of time.

$$FVIFA_{i,n} = \sum_{t=1}^{n} (1+i)^{t-1} \qquad (4.13)$$

---

8. A mathematical expression that can be applied to calculate the future value interest factor for an ordinary annuity more efficiently is

$$FVIFA_{i,n} = \frac{1}{i} \times [(1+i)^n - 1] \qquad (4.13a)$$

The use of this expression is especially attractive in the absence of any financial calculator, electronic spreadsheet, or the appropriate financial tables.

This factor is the multiplier used to calculate the future value of an *ordinary annuity* at a specified interest rate over a given period of time.

Using FVA_n for the future value of an *n*-year annuity, *PMT* for the amount to be deposited annually at the *end* of each year, and $FVIFA_{i,n}$ for the appropriate *future value interest factor for a one-dollar ordinary annuity compounded at i percent for n years*, we can express the relationship among these variables as

$$FVA_n = PMT \times (FVIFA_{i,n})$$ (4.14)

The following example illustrates this calculation using a calculator, a spreadsheet, and a table.

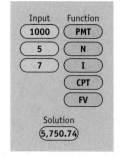

Input   Function
1000   PMT
5   N
7   I
         CPT
         FV

Solution
5,750.74

Personal Finance Example   As noted earlier, Fran Abrams wishes to find the future value (FVA_n) at the end of 5 years (*n*) of an annual *end-of-year deposit* of $1,000 (*PMT*) into an account paying 7% annual interest (*i*) during the next 5 years.

Calculator Use   Using the calculator inputs shown at the left, you will find the future value of the ordinary annuity to be $5,750.74, a slightly more precise answer than that found using the table (shown below).

Spreadsheet Use   The future value of the ordinary annuity also can be calculated as shown on the following Excel spreadsheet.

	A	B
1	FUTURE VALUE OF AN ORDINARY ANNUITY	
2	Annual payment	$1,000
3	Annual rate of interest, compounded annually	7%
4	Number of years	5
5	Future value of an ordinary annuity	$5,750.74

Entry in Cell B5 is =FV(B3,B4,−B2)
The minus sign appears before B2 because
the annual payment is a cash outflow.

Table Use   The future value interest factor for an ordinary 5-year annuity at 7% ($FVIFA_{7\%, 5yrs}$), found in Table A–3, is 5.751. Using Equation 4.14, the $1,000 deposit × 5.751 results in a future value for the annuity of $5,751.

Finding the Present Value of an Ordinary Annuity

Quite often in finance, there is a need to find the present value of a *stream* of cash flows to be received in future periods. An annuity is, of course, a stream of equal periodic cash flows. (We'll explore the case of mixed streams of cash flows in a later section.) The method for finding the present value of an ordinary annuity is similar to the method just discussed. There are long and short methods for making this calculation.

Example   Braden Company, a small producer of plastic toys, wants to determine the most it should pay to purchase a particular ordinary annuity. The annuity consists of cash flows of $700 at the end of each year for 5 years. The firm requires the annuity to provide a minimum return of 8%. This situation is depicted on the following time line:

Time line for present value of an ordinary annuity ($700 end-of-year cash flows, discounted at 8%, over 5 years)

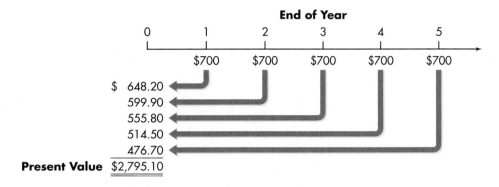

Table 4.2 (see page 178) shows the long method for finding the present value of the annuity. This method involves finding the present value of each payment and summing them. This procedure yields a present value of $2,795.10.

Using Computational Tools to Find the Present Value of an Ordinary Annuity

present value interest factor for an ordinary annuity
The multiplier used to calculate the present value of an *ordinary annuity* at a specified discount rate over a given period of time.

Annuity calculations can be simplified by using a financial calculator, an electronic spreadsheet, or an interest table for the present value of an annuity. The values for the present value of a $1 ordinary annuity are given in Appendix Table A–4. The factors in the table are derived by summing the present value interest factors (in Table A–2) for the appropriate number of years at the given discount rate. The formula for the **present value interest factor for an ordinary annuity** with cash flows that are discounted at i percent for n periods, $PVIFA_{i,n}$, is[9]

$$PVIFA_{i,n} = \sum_{t=1}^{n} \frac{1}{(1 + i)^t} \qquad (4.15)$$

This factor is the multiplier used to calculate the present value of an *ordinary annuity* at a specified discount rate over a given period of time.

By letting PVA_n equal the present value of an *n*-year *ordinary annuity*, letting PMT equal the amount to be received annually at the *end* of each year, and letting $PVIFA_{i,n}$ represent the appropriate *present value interest factor for a one-dollar ordinary annuity discounted at* i *percent for* n *years,* we can express the relationship among these variables as

$$PVA_n = PMT \times (PVIFA_{i,n}) \qquad (4.16)$$

The following example illustrates this calculation using a calculator, a spreadsheet, and a table.

---

9. A mathematical expression that can be applied to calculate the present value interest factor for an ordinary annuity more efficiently is

$$PVIFA_{i,n} = \frac{1}{i} \times \left[1 - \frac{1}{(1 + i)^n} \right] \qquad (4.15a)$$

The use of this expression is especially attractive in the absence of any financial calculator, electronic spreadsheet, or the appropriate financial tables.

TABLE 4.2	Long Method for Finding the Present Value of an Ordinary Annuity		
Year (n)	Cash flow (1)	$PVIF_{8\%,n}{}^{a}$ (2)	Present value [(1) × (2)] (3)
1	$700	0.926	$ 648.20
2	700	0.857	599.90
3	700	0.794	555.80
4	700	0.735	514.50
5	700	0.681	476.70
		Present value of annuity	$2,795.10

^{a}Present value interest factors at 8% are from Table A–2.

Example

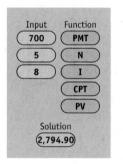

Input   Function
700   PMT
5   N
8   I
         CPT
         PV

Solution
2,794.90

Braden Company, as we have noted, wants to find the present value of a 5-year ordinary annuity of $700, assuming an 8% opportunity cost.

Calculator Use   Using the calculator's inputs shown at the left, you will find the present value of the ordinary annuity to be $2,794.90. The value obtained with the calculator is more accurate than those found using the equation or the table (shown below).

Spreadsheet Use   The present value of the ordinary annuity also can be calculated as shown on the following Excel spreadsheet.

	A	B
1	PRESENT VALUE OF AN ORDINARY ANNUITY	
2	Annual payment	$700
3	Annual rate of interest, compounded annually	8%
4	Number of years	5
5	Present value of an ordinary annuity	$2,794.90
	Entry in Cell B5 is =PV(B3,B4,−B2) The minus sign appears before B2 because the annual payment is a cash outflow.	

Table Use   The present value interest factor for an ordinary annuity at 8% for 5 years ($PVIFA_{8\%,5yrs}$), found in Table A–4, is 3.993. If we use Equation 4.16, $700 annuity × 3.993 results in a present value of $2,795.10.

Finding the Future Value of an Annuity Due

We now turn our attention to annuities due. Remember that the cash flows of an annuity due occur at the *start of the period*. A simple conversion is applied to use the future value interest factors for an ordinary annuity (in Table A–3) with annuities due. Equation 4.17 presents this conversion:

$$FVIFA_{i,n}(\text{annuity due}) = FVIFA_{i,n} \times (1 + i) \tag{4.17}$$

This equation says that the future value interest factor for an annuity due can be found merely by multiplying the future value interest factor for an ordinary annuity at the same percent and number of periods by $(1 + i)$. Why is this adjustment necessary? Because each cash flow of an annuity due earns interest for one year more than an ordinary annuity (from the start to the end of the year). Multiplying $FVIFA_{i,n}$ by $(1 + i)$ simply adds an additional year's interest to *each* annuity cash flow. The following example demonstrates how to find the future value of an annuity due.

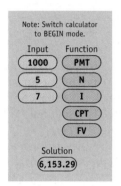

Note: Switch calculator to BEGIN mode.

Input	Function
1000	PMT
5	N
7	I
	CPT
	FV

Solution
6,153.29

Personal Finance Example   Recall from an earlier example that Fran Abrams wanted to choose between an ordinary annuity and an annuity due, both offering similar terms except for the timing of cash flows. We calculated the future value of the ordinary annuity in the example on page 175. We now will calculate the future value of the annuity due, using the cash flows represented by annuity B in Table 4.1 (page 174).

Calculator Use   Before using your calculator to find the future value of an annuity due, depending on the specific calculator, you must either switch it to BEGIN mode or use the DUE key. Then, using the inputs shown at the left, you will find the future value of the annuity due to be $6,153.29. (*Note:* Because we nearly always assume end-of-period cash flows, *be sure to switch your calculator back to END mode when you have completed your annuity-due calculations.*)

Spreadsheet Use   The future value of the annuity due also can be calculated as shown on the following Excel spreadsheet.

	A	B
1	FUTURE VALUE OF AN ANNUITY DUE	
2	Annual payment	$1,000
3	Annual rate of interest, compounded annually	7%
4	Number of years	5
5	Future value of an annuity due	$6,153.29
	Entry in Cell B5 is =FV(B3,B4,−B2,0,1) The minus sign appears before B2 because the annual payment is a cash outflow.	

Table Use   Substituting $i = 7\%$ and $n = 5$ years into Equation 4.17, with the aid of the appropriate interest factor from Table A–3, we get

$$FVIFA_{7\%,5\text{yrs}}(\text{annuity due}) = FVIFA_{7\%,5\text{yrs}} \times (1 + 0.07)$$
$$= 5.751 \times 1.07 = 6.154$$

Then, substituting $PMT = \$1,000$ and $FVIFA_{7\%,5\text{ yrs}}$ (annuity due) = 6.154 into Equation 4.14, we get a future value for the annuity due:

$$FVA_5 = \$1,000 \times 6.154 = \$6,154$$

Comparison of an Annuity Due with an Ordinary Annuity Future Value

The future value of an annuity due is *always greater* than the future value of an otherwise identical ordinary annuity. We can see this by comparing the future values at the end of year 5 of Fran Abrams's two annuities:

Ordinary annuity = $5,750.74   Annuity due = $6,153.29

Because the cash flow of the annuity due occurs at the beginning of the period rather than at the end, its future value is greater. In the example, Fran would earn about $400 more with the annuity due.

Finding the Present Value of an Annuity Due

We can also find the present value of an annuity due. This calculation can be easily performed by adjusting the ordinary annuity calculation. Because the cash flows of an annuity due occur at the beginning rather than the end of the period, to find their present value, each annuity due cash flow is discounted back one less year than for an ordinary annuity. A simple conversion can be applied to use the present value interest factors for an ordinary annuity (in Table A–4) with annuities due.

$$PVIFA_{i,n}(\text{annuity due}) = PVIFA_{i,n} \times (1 + i) \qquad \textbf{(4.18)}$$

The equation indicates that the present value interest factor for an annuity due can be obtained by multiplying the present value interest factor for an ordinary annuity at the same percent and number of periods by $(1 + i)$. This conversion adjusts for the fact that each cash flow of an annuity due is discounted back one less year than a comparable ordinary annuity. Multiplying $PVIFA_{i,n}$ by $(1 + i)$ effectively adds back one year of interest to *each* annuity cash flow. Adding back one year of interest to each cash flow in effect reduces by 1 the number of years *each* annuity cash flow is discounted.

Example

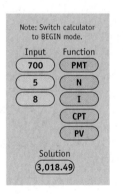

Note: Switch calculator to BEGIN mode.

Input	Function
700	PMT
5	N
8	I
	CPT
	PV

Solution
3,018.49

In the earlier example of Braden Company on page 178, we found the present value of Braden's $700, 5-year ordinary annuity discounted at 8% to be about $2,795. If we now assume that Braden's $700 annual cash flow occurs at the *start* of each year and is thereby an annuity due, we can calculate its present value using a calculator, a spreadsheet, or a table.

Calculator Use   Before using your calculator to find the present value of an annuity due, depending on the specifics of your calculator, you must either switch it to BEGIN mode or use the DUE key. Then, using the inputs shown at the left, you will find the present value of the annuity due to be $3,018.49 (*Note: Because we nearly always assume end-of-period cash flows, be sure to switch your calculator back to END mode when you have completed your annuity-due calculations.*)

Spreadsheet Use   The present value of the annuity due also can be calculated as shown on the following Excel spreadsheet.

	A	B
1	PRESENT VALUE OF AN ANNUITY DUE	
2	Annual payment	$700
3	Annual rate of interest, compounded annually	8%
4	Number of years	5
5	Present value of an annuity due	$3,018.49
	Entry in Cell B5 is =PV(B3,B4,−B2,0,1) The minus sign appears before B2 because the annual payment is a cash outflow.	

Table Use   Substituting $i = 8\%$ and $n = 5$ years into Equation 4.18, with the aid of the appropriate interest factor from Table A–4, we get

$$PVIFA_{8\%,5yrs}(\text{annuity due}) = PVIFA_{8\%,5yrs} \times (1 + 0.08)$$
$$= 3.993 \times 1.08 = 4.312$$

Then, substituting $PMT = \$700$ and $PVIFA_{8\%,5yrs}(\text{annuity due}) = 4.312$ into Equation 4.16, we get a present value for the annuity due:

$$PVA_5 = \$700 \times 4.312 = \$3,018.40$$

Comparison of an Annuity Due with an Ordinary Annuity Present Value

The present value of an annuity due is always greater than the present value of an otherwise identical ordinary annuity. We can see this by comparing the present values of the Braden Company's two annuities:

$$\text{Ordinary annuity} = \$2,794.90 \qquad \text{Annuity due} = \$3,018.49$$

Because the cash flow of the annuity due occurs at the beginning of the period rather than at the end, its present value is greater. In the example, Braden Company would realize about $200 more in present value with the annuity due.

Finding the Present Value of a Perpetuity

perpetuity
An annuity with an infinite life, providing continual annual cash flow.

A **perpetuity** is an annuity with an infinite life—in other words, an annuity that never stops providing its holder with a cash flow at the end of each year (for example, the right to receive $500 at the end of each year forever).

It is sometimes necessary to find the present value of a perpetuity. The present value interest factor for a perpetuity discounted at the rate i is

$$PVIFA_{i,\infty} = \frac{1}{i} \tag{4.19}$$

As the equation shows, the appropriate factor, $PVIFA_{i,\infty}$, is found simply by dividing the discount rate, i (stated as a decimal), into 1. The validity of this method can be seen by looking at the factors in Table A–4 for 8, 10, 20, and 40 percent: As the number of periods (typically years) approaches 50, these factors approach the values calculated using Equation 4.19: $1 \div 0.08 = 12.50$; $1 \div 0.10 = 10.00$; $1 \div 0.20 = 5.00$; and $1 \div 0.40 = 2.50$.

Personal Finance Example   Ross Clark wishes to endow a chair in finance at his alma mater. The university indicated that it requires $200,000 per year to support the chair, and the endowment would earn 10% per year. To determine the amount Ross must give the university to fund the chair, we must determine the present value of a $200,000 perpetuity discounted at 10%. The appropriate present value interest factor can be found by dividing 1 by 0.10, as noted in Equation 4.19. Substituting the resulting factor, $PVIFA_{10\%,\infty} = 10$, and the amount of the perpetuity, $PMT = \$200,000$, into Equation 4.16 results in a present value of $2,000,000 for the perpetuity. In other words, to generate $200,000 every year for an indefinite period requires $2,000,000 today if Ross Clark's alma mater can earn 10% on its investments. If the university earns 10% interest annually on the $2,000,000, it can withdraw $200,000 per year indefinitely without touching the initial $2,000,000, which would never be drawn upon.

REVIEW QUESTIONS

4–8   What is the difference between an *ordinary annuity* and an *annuity due?* Which always has greater future value and present value for identical annuities and interest rates? Why?

4–9   What are the most efficient ways to calculate the present value of an ordinary annuity? What is the relationship between the *PVIF* and *PVIFA* interest factors given in Tables A–2 and A–4, respectively?

4–10   How can the future value interest factors for an ordinary annuity be modified to find the future value of an annuity due?

4–11   How can the present value interest factors for an ordinary annuity be modified to find the present value of an annuity due?

4–12   What is a *perpetuity?* How can the present value interest factor for such a stream of cash flows be determined?

4.4 | Mixed Streams

mixed stream
A stream of unequal periodic cash flows that reflect no particular pattern.

Two basic types of cash flow streams are possible: the annuity and the mixed stream. Whereas an *annuity* is a pattern of equal periodic cash flows, a **mixed stream** is a stream of unequal periodic cash flows that reflect no particular pattern. Financial managers frequently need to evaluate opportunities that are expected to provide mixed streams of cash flows. Here we consider both the future value and the present value of mixed streams.

Future Value of a Mixed Stream

Determining the future value of a mixed stream of cash flows is straightforward. We determine the future value of each cash flow at the specified future date and then add all the individual future values to find the total future value.

Example   Shrell Industries, a cabinet manufacturer, expects to receive the following mixed stream of cash flows over the next 5 years from one of its small customers.

End of year	Cash flow
1	$11,500
2	14,000
3	12,900
4	16,000
5	18,000

If Shrell expects to earn 8% on its investments, how much will it accumulate by the end of year 5 if it immediately invests these cash flows when they are received? This situation is depicted on the following time line:

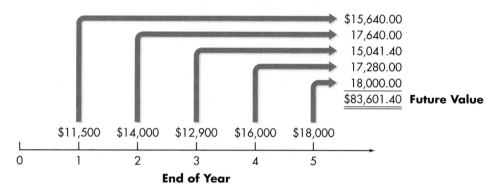

Time line for future value of a mixed stream (end-of-year cash flows, compounded at 8% to the end of year 5)

$15,640.00
17,640.00
15,041.40
17,280.00
18,000.00
$83,601.40 **Future Value**

$11,500 $14,000 $12,900 $16,000 $18,000

0   1   2   3   4   5

End of Year

Calculator Use   You can use your calculator to find the future value of each individual cash flow, as demonstrated earlier (pages 168 and 169), and then sum the future values, to get the future value of the stream. Unfortunately, unless you can program your calculator, most calculators lack a function that would allow you to input *all of the cash flows,* specify the interest rate, and directly calculate the future value of the entire cash flow stream. Had you used your calculator to find the individual cash flow future values and then summed them, the future value of Shrell Industries' cash flow stream at the end of year 5 would have been $83,608.15.

Spreadsheet Use   The future value of the mixed stream also can be calculated as shown on the following Excel spreadsheet.

	A	B
1	FUTURE VALUE OF A MIXED STREAM	
2	Interest rate, pct/year	8%
3	Year	Year-End Cash Flow
4	1	$11,500
5	2	$14,000
6	3	$12,900
7	4	$16,000
8	5	$18,000
9	Future value	$83,608.15
	Entry in Cell B9 is =−FV(B2,A8,0,NPV(B2,B4:B8)). The minus sign appears before FV to convert the future value to a positive amount.	

Table Use   To solve this problem, we determine the future value of each cash flow compounded at 8% for the appropriate number of years. Note that the first cash flow of $11,500, received at the end of year 1, will earn interest for 4 years (end of year 1 through end of year 5); the second cash flow of $14,000, received

TABLE 4.3 **Future Value of a Mixed Stream of Cash Flows**

Year	Cash flow (1)	Number of years earning interest (n) (2)	$FVIF_{8\%,n}{}^a$ (3)	Future value [(1) × (3)] (4)
1	$11,500	5 − 1 = 4	1.360	$15,640.00
2	14,000	5 − 2 = 3	1.260	17,640.00
3	12,900	5 − 3 = 2	1.166	15,041.40
4	16,000	5 − 4 = 1	1.080	17,280.00
5	18,000	5 − 5 = 0	1.000^b	18,000.00
			Future value of mixed stream	$83,601.40

^{a}Future value interest factors at 8% are from Table A–1.

^{b}The future value of the end-of-year-5 deposit at the end of year 5 is its present value because it earns interest for zero years and $(1 + 0.08)^0 = 1.000$.

at the end of year 2, will earn interest for 3 years (end of year 2 through end of year 5); and so on. The sum of the individual end-of-year-5 future values is the future value of the mixed cash flow stream. The future value interest factors required are those shown in Table A–1. Table 4.3 presents the calculations needed to find the future value of the cash flow stream, which turns out to be $83,601.40. This value is less precise than the value obtained using a calculator or spreadsheet.

If Shrell Industries invests at 8% interest the cash flows received from its customer over the next 5 years, the company will accumulate about $83,600 by the end of year 5.

Present Value of a Mixed Stream

Finding the present value of a mixed stream of cash flows is similar to finding the future value of a mixed stream. We determine the present value of each future amount and then add all the individual present values together to find the total present value.

Example

Frey Company, a shoe manufacturer, has been offered an opportunity to receive the following mixed stream of cash flows over the next 5 years:

End of year	Cash flow
1	$400
2	800
3	500
4	400
5	300

If the firm must earn at least 9% on its investments, what is the most it should pay for this opportunity? This situation is depicted on the following time line:

Time line for present value of a mixed stream (end-of-year cash flows, discounted at 9% over the corresponding number of years)

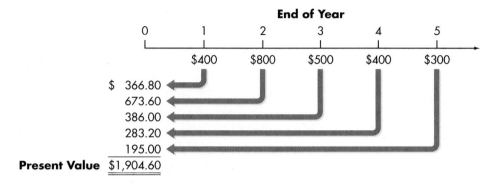

Calculator Use   You can use a calculator to find the present value of each individual cash flow, as demonstrated earlier (page 172), and then sum the present values, to get the present value of the stream. However, most financial calculators have a function that allows you to punch in *all cash flows*, specify the discount rate, and then directly calculate the present value of the entire cash flow stream. Because calculators provide solutions more precise than those based on rounded table factors, the present value of Frey Company's cash flow stream found using a calculator is $1,904.76.

Spreadsheet Use   The present value of the mixed stream of future cash flows also can be calculated as shown on the following Excel spreadsheet.

	A	B
1	PRESENT VALUE OF A MIXED STREAM OF CASH FLOWS	
2	Interest rate, pct/year	9%
3	Year	Year-End Cash Flow
4	1	$400
5	2	$800
6	3	$500
7	4	$400
8	5	$300
9	Present value	$1,904.76
	Entry in Cell B9 is =NPV(B2,B4:B8).	

Table Use   To solve this problem, determine the present value of each cash flow discounted at 9% for the appropriate number of years. The sum of these individual values is the present value of the total stream. The present value interest factors required are those shown in Table A–2. Table 4.4 (see page 186) presents the calculations needed to find the present value of the cash flow stream, which turns out to be $1,904.60. This value is close to the more precise value of $1,904.76 found by using a calculator or spreadsheet.

Paying about $1,905 would provide exactly a 9% return. Frey should pay no more than that amount for the opportunity to receive these cash flows.

	Cash flow	$PVIF_{9\%,n}{}^a$	Present value [(1) × (2)]
Year (n)	(1)	(2)	(3)
1	$400	0.917	$ 366.80
2	800	0.842	673.60
3	500	0.772	386.00
4	400	0.708	283.20
5	300	0.650	195.00
		Present value of mixed stream	$1,904.60

TABLE 4.4   Present Value of a Mixed Stream of Cash Flows

^{a}Present value interest factors at 9% are from Table A–2.

REVIEW QUESTION

4–13 How is the future value of a mixed stream of cash flows calculated? How is the present value of a mixed stream of cash flows calculated?

4.5 | Compounding Interest More Frequently Than Annually

Interest is often compounded more frequently than once a year. Savings institutions compound interest semiannually, quarterly, monthly, weekly, daily, or even continuously. This section discusses various issues and techniques related to these more frequent compounding intervals.

Semiannual Compounding

semiannual compounding
Compounding of interest over two periods within the year.

Semiannual compounding of interest involves two compounding periods within the year. Instead of the stated interest rate being paid once a year, one-half of the stated interest rate is paid twice a year.

Personal Finance Example Fred Moreno has decided to invest $100 in a savings account paying 8% interest *compounded semiannually.* If he leaves his money in the account for 24 months (2 years), he will be paid 4% interest compounded over four periods, each of which is 6 months long. Table 4.5 uses interest factors to show that at the end of 12 months (1 year) with 8% semiannual compounding, Fred will have $108.16; at the end of 24 months (2 years), he will have $116.99.

Quarterly Compounding

quarterly compounding
Compounding of interest over four periods within the year.

Quarterly compounding of interest involves four compounding periods within the year. One-fourth of the stated interest rate is paid four times a year.

TABLE 4.5	Future Value from Investing $100 at 8% Interest Compounded Semiannually over 24 Months (2 Years)		
Period	Beginning principal (1)	Future value interest factor (2)	Future value at end of period [(1) × (2)] (3)
6 months	$100.00	1.04	$104.00
12 months	104.00	1.04	108.16
18 months	108.16	1.04	112.49
24 months	112.49	1.04	116.99

Personal Finance Example   Fred Moreno has found an institution that will pay him 8% interest *compounded quarterly.* If he leaves his money in this account for 24 months (2 years), he will be paid 2% interest compounded over eight periods, each of which is 3 months long. Table 4.6 uses interest factors to show the amount Fred will have at the end of each period. At the end of 12 months (1 year), with 8% quarterly compounding, Fred will have $108.24; at the end of 24 months (2 years), he will have $117.17.

Table 4.7 (see page 188) compares values for Fred Moreno's $100 at the end of years 1 and 2 given annual, semiannual, and quarterly compounding periods at the 8 percent rate. As shown, *the more frequently interest is compounded, the greater the amount of money accumulated.* This is true for *any interest rate* for *any period of time.*

A General Equation for Compounding More Frequently Than Annually

The interest-factor formula for annual compounding (Equation 4.5) can be rewritten for use when compounding takes place more frequently. If *m* equals the

TABLE 4.6	Future Value from Investing $100 at 8% Interest Compounded Quarterly over 24 Months (2 Years)		
Period	Beginning principal (1)	Future value interest factor (2)	Future value at end of period [(1) × (2)] (3)
3 months	$100.00	1.02	$102.00
6 months	102.00	1.02	104.04
9 months	104.04	1.02	106.12
12 months	106.12	1.02	108.24
15 months	108.24	1.02	110.41
18 months	110.40	1.02	112.62
21 months	112.61	1.02	114.87
24 months	114.86	1.02	117.17

TABLE 4.7	Future Value at the End of Years 1 and 2 from Investing $100 at 8% Interest, Given Various Compounding Periods		

	Compounding period		
End of year	Annual	Semiannual	Quarterly
1	$108.00	$108.16	$108.24
2	116.64	116.99	117.17

number of times per year interest is compounded, the interest-factor formula for annual compounding can be rewritten as

$$FVIF_{i,n} = \left(1 + \frac{i}{m}\right)^{m \times n}$$ (4.20)

The basic equation for future value (Equation 4.4) can now be rewritten as

$$FV_n = PV \times \left(1 + \frac{i}{m}\right)^{m \times n}$$ (4.21)

If $m = 1$, Equation 4.21 reduces to Equation 4.4. Thus, if interest is compounded annually (once a year), Equation 4.21 will provide the same result as Equation 4.4. The general use of Equation 4.21 can be illustrated with a simple example.

Personal Finance Example   The preceding examples calculated the amount that Fred Moreno would have at the end of 2 years if he deposited $100 at 8% interest compounded semiannually and compounded quarterly. For semiannual compounding, m would equal 2 in Equation 4.21; for quarterly compounding, m would equal 4. Substituting the appropriate values for semiannual and quarterly compounding into Equation 4.21, we find that

1. *For semiannual compounding:*

$$FV_2 = \$100 \times \left(1 + \frac{0.08}{2}\right)^{2 \times 2} = \$100 \times (1 + 0.04)^4 = \$116.99$$

2. *For quarterly compounding:*

$$FV_2 = \$100 \times \left(1 + \frac{0.08}{4}\right)^{4 \times 2} = \$100 \times (1 + 0.02)^8 = \$117.17$$

These results agree with the values for FV_2 in Tables 4.5 and 4.6.

If the interest were compounded monthly, weekly, or daily, m would equal 12, 52, or 365, respectively.

Using Computational Tools for Compounding More Frequently Than Annually

We can use the future value interest factors for one dollar, given in Table A–1, when interest is compounded m times each year. Instead of indexing the table for i percent and n years, as we do when interest is compounded annually, we index it for $(i \div m)$ percent and $(m \times n)$ periods. However, the table is less useful, because it includes only selected rates for a limited number of periods. Instead, a financial calculator or an electronic spreadsheet is typically required.

Personal Finance Example   Fred Moreno wished to find the future value of $100 invested at 8% interest compounded both semiannually and quarterly for 2 years. The number of compounding periods m, the interest rate $(i \div m)$, and the number of periods $(m \times n)$ used, along with the future value interest factor, are as follows:

Compounding period	m	Interest rate $(i \div m)$	Periods $(m \times n)$	Future value interest factor from Table A–1
Semiannual	2	$8\% \div 2 = 4\%$	$2 \times 2 = 4$	1.170
Quarterly	4	$8\% \div 4 = 2\%$	$4 \times 2 = 8$	1.172

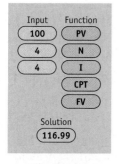

Calculator Use   If the calculator were used for the semiannual compounding calculation, the number of periods would be 4 and the interest rate would be 4%. The future value of $116.99 will appear on the calculator display as shown at the top left.

For the quarterly compounding case, the number of periods would be 8 and the interest rate would be 2%. The future value of $117.17 will appear on the calculator display as shown in the second display at the left.

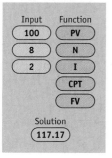

Spreadsheet Use   The future value of the single amount with semiannual and quarterly compounding also can be calculated as shown on the following Excel spreadsheet.

	A	B
1	FUTURE VALUE OF A SINGLE AMOUNT WITH SEMIANNUAL AND QUARTERLY COMPOUNDING	
2	Present value	$100
3	Interest rate, pct per year compounded semiannually	8%
4	Number of years	2
5	Future value with semiannual compounding	$116.99
6	Present value	$100
7	Interest rate, pct per year compounded quarterly	8%
8	Number of years	2
9	Future value with quarterly compounding	$117.17

Entry in Cell B5 is =FV(B3/2,B4*2,0,–B2,0).
Entry in Cell B9 is =FV(B7/4,B8*4,0,–B2,0).
The minus sign appears before B2 because the present value
is a cash outflow (i.e., a deposit made by Fred Moreno).

Table Use   Multiplying each of the future value interest factors by the initial $100 deposit results in a value of $117.00 ($1.170 \times \$100$) for semiannual compounding and a value of $117.20 ($1.172 \times \$100$) for quarterly compounding.

Comparing the calculator, spreadsheet, and table values, we can see that the calculator and spreadsheet values agree with the values in Table 4.7 but are more precise because the table factors have been rounded.

Continuous Compounding

continuous compounding
Compounding of interest an infinite number of times per year at intervals of microseconds.

In the extreme case, interest can be compounded continuously. **Continuous compounding** involves compounding over every microsecond—the smallest time period imaginable. In this case, m in Equation 4.20 would approach infinity. Through the use of calculus, we know that as m approaches infinity, the interest-factor equation becomes

$$FVIF_{i,n} \text{ (continuous compounding)} = e^{i \times n} \qquad (4.22)$$

where e is the exponential function,[10] which has a value of 2.7183. The future value for continuous compounding is therefore

$$FV_n \text{ (continuous compounding)} = PV \times (e^{i \times n}) \qquad (4.23)$$

Personal Finance Example   To find the value at the end of 2 years ($n = 2$) of Fred Moreno's $100 deposit ($PV = \$100$) in an account paying 8% annual interest ($i = 0.08$) compounded continuously, we can substitute into Equation 4.23:

$$
\begin{aligned}
FV_2 \text{ (continuous compounding)} &= \$100 \times e^{0.08 \times 2} \\
&= \$100 \times 2.7183^{0.16} \\
&= \$100 \times 1.1735 = \$117.35
\end{aligned}
$$

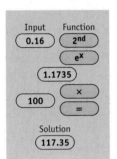

Calculator Use   To find this value using the calculator, you need first to find the value of $e^{0.16}$ by punching in 0.16 and then pressing **2nd** and then e^{x} to get 1.1735. Next multiply this value by $100 to get the future value of $117.35 as shown at the left. (*Note:* On some calculators, you may not have to press **2nd** before pressing e^{x}.)

Spreadsheet Use   The future value of the single amount with continuous compounding of Fred's deposit also can be calculated as shown on the following Excel spreadsheet.

	A	B
1	FUTURE VALUE OF A SINGLE AMOUNT WITH CONTINUOUS COMPOUNDING	
2	Present value	$100
3	Annual rate of interest, compounded continuously	8%
4	Number of years	2
5	Future value with continuous compounding	$117.35
	Entry in Cell B5 is =B2*EXP(B3*B4).	

The future value with continuous compounding therefore equals $117.35. As expected, the continuously compounded value is larger than the future value of interest compounded semiannually ($116.99) or quarterly ($117.17). Contin-

---

10. Most calculators have the exponential function, typically noted by e^{x}, built into them. The use of this key is especially helpful in calculating future value when interest is compounded continuously.

uous compounding results in the largest future value that would result from compounding interest more frequently than annually at a given rate over a stated period of time.

Nominal and Effective Annual Rates of Interest

nominal (stated) annual rate
Contractual annual rate of interest charged by a lender or promised by a borrower.

effective (true) annual rate (EAR)
The annual rate of interest actually paid or earned.

Both businesses and investors need to make objective comparisons of loan costs or investment returns over different compounding periods. To put interest rates on a common basis, so as to allow comparison, we distinguish between nominal and effective annual rates. The **nominal**, or **stated, annual rate** is the contractual annual rate of interest charged by a lender or promised by a borrower. The **effective**, or **true, annual rate (EAR)** is the annual rate of interest actually paid or earned. The effective annual rate reflects the effects of compounding frequency, whereas the nominal annual rate does not.

Using the notation introduced earlier, we can calculate the effective annual rate, EAR, by substituting values for the nominal annual rate, i, and the compounding frequency, m, into Equation 4.24:

$$EAR = \left(1 + \frac{i}{m}\right)^m - 1 \qquad (4.24)$$

We can apply this equation using data from preceding examples.

Personal Finance Example Fred Moreno wishes to find the effective annual rate associated with an 8% nominal annual rate ($i = 0.08$) when interest is compounded (1) annually ($m = 1$); (2) semiannually ($m = 2$); and (3) quarterly ($m = 4$). Substituting these values into Equation 4.24, we get

1. *For annual compounding:*

$$EAR = \left(1 + \frac{0.08}{1}\right)^1 - 1 = (1 + 0.08)^1 - 1 = 1 + 0.08 - 1 = 0.08 = 8\%$$

2. *For semiannual compounding:*

$$EAR = \left(1 + \frac{0.08}{2}\right)^2 - 1 = (1 + 0.04)^2 - 1 = 1.0816 - 1 = 0.0816 = 8.16\%$$

3. *For quarterly compounding:*

$$EAR = \left(1 + \frac{0.08}{4}\right)^4 - 1 = (1 + 0.02)^4 - 1 = 1.0824 - 1 = 0.0824 = 8.24\%$$

These values demonstrate two important points: The first is that nominal and effective annual rates are equivalent for annual compounding. The second is that the effective annual rate increases with increasing compounding frequency, up to a limit that occurs with *continuous compounding*.[11]

---

11. The effective annual rate for this extreme case can be found by using the following equation:

$$EAR \text{ (continuous compounding)} = e^i - 1 \qquad (4.24a)$$

For the 8% nominal annual rate ($i = 0.08$), substitution into Equation 4.24a results in an effective annual rate of

$$e^{0.08} - 1 = 1.0833 - 1 = 0.0833 = 8.33\%$$

in the case of continuous compounding. This is the highest effective annual rate attainable with an 8% nominal rate.

Focus on Ethics   How Fair Is "Check Into Cash"?

IN PRACTICE

In 1993, the first **Check Into Cash** location opened in Cleveland, Tennessee. Today there are 1,250 Check Into Cash centers among an estimated 22,000 payday-advance lenders in the United States. There is no doubt about the demand for such organizations, but the debate continues on the "fairness" of payday-advance loans.

A payday loan is a small, unsecured, short-term loan ranging from $100 to $1,000 (depending upon the state) offered by a payday lender such as Check Into Cash. A payday loan can solve temporary cash-flow problems without bouncing a check or incurring late-payment penalties. To receive a payday advance, borrowers simply write a personal post-dated check for the amount they wish to borrow, plus the payday loan fee. Check Into Cash holds their checks until payday when the loans are either paid off in person or the check is presented to the borrowers' banks for payment.

Although payday-advance borrowers usually pay a flat fee in lieu of interest, it is the size of the fee in relation to the amount borrowed that is particularly aggravating to opponents of the payday-advance industry. A typical fee is $15 for every $100 borrowed. Payday advance companies that belong to the Community Financial Services Association of America (CFSA), an organization dedicated to promoting responsible regulation of the industry, limit their member companies to a maximum of four rollovers of the original amount borrowed. Thus, a borrower who rolled over an initial $100 loan for the maximum of four times would accumulate a total of $75 in fees all within a 10-week period. On an annualized basis, the fees would amount to a whopping 391%.

An annual rate of 391% is a huge cost in relation to interest charged on home equity loans, personal loans, and even credit cards. However, advocates of the payday-advance industry make the following arguments: Most payday loan recipients do so either because funds are unavailable through conventional loans or because the payday loan averts a penalty or bank fee which is, in itself, onerous. According to Check Into Cash, the cost for $100 of overdraft protection is $26.90, a credit card late fee on $100 is $37, and the late/disconnect fee on a $100 utility bill is $46.16. Bankrate.com reports that non-sufficient funds (NSF) fees average $26.90 per occurrence.

A payday advance could be useful, for example, if you have six outstanding checks at the time you are notified that the first check has been returned for insufficient funds and you have been charged an NSF fee of $26. A payday advance could potentially avert subsequent charges of $26 per check for each of the remaining five checks and allow you time to rearrange your finances. When used judiciously, a payday advance can be a viable option to meet a short-term cash flow problem despite its high cost. Used unwisely, or by someone who continuously relies on a payday loan to try to make ends meet, payday advances can seriously harm one's personal finances.

■ *The 391% mentioned above is an annual nominal rate [15% × (365/14)]. Should the 2-week rate (15%) be compounded to calculate the effective annual interest rate?*

annual percentage rate (APR)
The *nominal annual rate* of interest, found by multiplying the periodic rate by the number of periods in one year, that must be disclosed to consumers on credit cards and loans as a result of "truth-in-lending laws."

For an EAR example related to the "payday loan" business, with discussion of the ethical issues involved, see the *Focus on Ethics* box above.

At the consumer level, "truth-in-lending laws" require disclosure on credit card and loan agreements of the **annual percentage rate (APR)**. The APR is the *nominal annual rate* found by multiplying the periodic rate by the number of periods in one year. For example, a bank credit card that charges 1¹/₂ percent per month (the periodic rate) would have an APR of 18 percent (1.5% per month × 12 months per year).

annual percentage yield (APY)
The *effective annual rate* of interest that must be disclosed to consumers by banks on their savings products as a result of "truth-in-savings laws."

"Truth-in-savings laws," on the other hand, require banks to quote the **annual percentage yield (APY)** on their savings products. The APY is the *effective annual rate* a savings product pays. For example, a savings account that pays 0.5 percent per month would have an APY of 6.17 percent $[(1.005)^{12} - 1]$.

Quoting loan interest rates at their lower nominal annual rate (the APR) and savings interest rates at the higher effective annual rate (the APY) offers two advantages: It tends to standardize disclosure to consumers, and it enables financial institutions to quote the most attractive interest rates: low loan rates and high savings rates.

REVIEW QUESTIONS

4–14 What effect does compounding interest more frequently than annually have on (**a**) future value and (**b**) the *effective annual rate (EAR)?* Why?

4–15 How does the future value of a deposit subject to continuous compounding compare to the value obtained by annual compounding?

4–16 Differentiate between a *nominal annual rate* and an *effective annual rate (EAR)*. Define *annual percentage rate (APR)* and *annual percentage yield (APY)*.

 ## 4.6 | **Special Applications of Time Value**

Future value and present value techniques have a number of important applications in finance. We'll study four of them in this section: (1) determining deposits needed to accumulate a future sum, (2) loan amortization, (3) finding interest or growth rates, and (4) finding an unknown number of periods.

Determining Deposits Needed to Accumulate a Future Sum

Suppose you want to buy a house 5 years from now, and you estimate that an initial down payment of $30,000 will be required at that time. To accumulate the $30,000, you will wish to make equal annual end-of-year deposits into an account paying annual interest of 6 percent. The solution to this problem is closely related to the process of finding the future value of an annuity. You must determine what size annuity will result in a single amount equal to $30,000 at the end of year 5.

Earlier in the chapter we found the future value of an *n*-year ordinary annuity, FVA_n, by multiplying the annual deposit, *PMT*, by the appropriate interest factor, $FVIFA_{i,n}$. The relationship of the three variables was defined by Equation 4.14, which is repeated here as Equation 4.25:

$$FVA_n = PMT \times (FVIFA_{i,n}) \qquad \textbf{(4.25)}$$

We can find the annual deposit required to accumulate FVA_n dollars by solving Equation 4.25 for *PMT*. Isolating *PMT* on the left side of the equation gives us

$$PMT = \frac{FVA_n}{FVIFA_{i,n}} \qquad \textbf{(4.26)}$$

Once this is done, we have only to substitute the known values of FVA_n and $FVIFA_{i,n}$ into the right side of the equation to find the annual deposit required.

Personal Finance Example   As just stated, you want to determine the equal annual end-of-year deposits required to accumulate $30,000 at the end of 5 years, given an interest rate of 6%.

Input	Function
30000	FV
5	N
6	I
	CPT
	PMT

Solution
5,321.89

Calculator Use   Using the calculator inputs shown at the left, you will find the annual deposit amount to be $5,321.89. Thus, if $5,321.89 is deposited at the end of each year for 5 years at 6% interest, there will be $30,000 in the account at the end of 5 years.

Spreadsheet Use   The annual deposit needed to accumulate the future sum also can be calculated as shown on the following Excel spreadsheet.

	A	B
1	ANNUAL DEPOSITS NEEDED TO ACCUMULATE A FUTURE SUM	
2	Future value	$30,000
3	Number of years	5
4	Annual rate of interest	6%
5	Annual deposit	$5,321.89
Entry in Cell B5 is =−PMT(B4,B3,0,B2). The minus sign appears before PMT because the annual deposits are cash outflows.		

Table Use   Table A–3 indicates that the future value interest factor for an ordinary annuity at 6% for 5 years ($FVIFA_{6\%,5yrs}$) is 5.637. Substituting $FVA_5 =$ $30,000 and $FVIFA_{6\%,5yrs} = 5.637$ into Equation 4.26 yields an annual required deposit, *PMT*, of $5,321.98. Note that this value, except for a slight rounding difference, agrees with the value found using a calculator and spreadsheet.

Loan Amortization

loan amortization
The determination of the equal periodic loan payments necessary to provide a lender with a specified interest return and to repay the loan principal over a specified period.

loan amortization schedule
A schedule of equal payments to repay a loan. It shows the allocation of each loan payment to interest and principal.

The term **loan amortization** refers to the determination of equal periodic loan payments. These payments provide a lender with a specified interest return and repay the loan principal over a specified period. The loan amortization process involves finding the future payments, over the term of the loan, whose present value at the loan interest rate equals the amount of initial principal borrowed. Lenders use a **loan amortization schedule** to determine these payment amounts and the allocation of each payment to interest and principal. In the case of home mortgages, these tables are used to find the equal *monthly* payments necessary to *amortize*, or pay off, the mortgage at a specified interest rate over a 15- to 30-year period.

Amortizing a loan actually involves creating an annuity out of a present amount. For example, say you borrow $6,000 at 10 percent and agree to make equal annual end-of-year payments over 4 years. To find the size of the payments, the lender determines the amount of a 4-year annuity discounted at 10 percent that has a present value of $6,000. This process is actually the inverse of finding the present value of an annuity.

Earlier in the chapter, we found the present value, PVA_n, of an n-year ordinary annuity by multiplying the annual amount, PMT, by the present value interest factor for an annuity, $PVIFA_{i,n}$. This relationship, which was originally expressed as Equation 4.16, is repeated here as Equation 4.27:

$$PVA_n = PMT \times (PVIFA_{i,n})$$ **(4.27)**

To find the equal annual payment required to pay off, or amortize, the loan, PVA_n, over a certain number of years at a specified interest rate, we need to solve Equation 4.27 for PMT. Isolating PMT on the left side of the equation gives us

$$PMT = \frac{PVA_n}{PVIFA_{i,n}}$$ **(4.28)**

Once this is done, we have only to substitute the known values into the righthand side of the equation to find the annual payment required.

Personal Finance Example As just stated, you want to determine the equal annual end-of-year payments necessary to amortize fully a $6,000, 10% loan over 4 years.

Calculator Use Using the calculator inputs shown at the left, you will find the annual payment amount to be $1,892.82. Thus, to repay the interest and principal on a $6,000, 10%, 4-year loan, equal annual end-of-year payments of $1,892.82 are necessary.

The allocation of each loan payment (based on table use, a payment of $1,892.74) to interest and principal can be seen in columns 3 and 4 of the *loan amortization schedule* in Table 4.8. The portion of each payment that represents interest (column 3) declines over the repayment period, and the portion going to principal repayment (column 4) increases. This pattern is typical of amortized loans; as the principal is reduced, the interest component declines, leaving a larger portion of each subsequent loan payment to repay principal.

Spreadsheet Use The annual payment to repay the loan also can be calculated as shown on the first Excel spreadsheet shown on page 196. The amortization

Input	Function
6000	PV
4	N
10	I
	CPT
	PMT

Solution
1,892.82

TABLE 4.8	**Loan Amortization Schedule ($6,000 Principal, 10% Interest, 4-Year Repayment Period)**				
End of year (1)	Beginning-of-year principal (1)	Loan payment[a] (2)	Interest [0.10 × (1)] (3)	Principal [(2) − (3)] (4)	End-of-year principal [(1) − (4)] (5)
1	$6,000.00	$1,892.74	$600.00	$1,292.74	$4,707.26
2	4,707.26	1,892.74	470.73	1,422.01	3,285.25
3	3,285.25	1,892.74	328.53	1,564.21	1,721.04
4	1,721.04	1,892.74	172.10	1,720.64	—[b]

[a]Based on the use of tables.

[b]Because of rounding, a slight difference ($0.40) exists between the beginning-of-year-4 principal (in column 1) and the year-4 principal payment (in column 4).

schedule allocating each loan payment to interest and principal can be calculated precisely as shown on the second spreadsheet.

	A	B
1	ANNUAL PAYMENT TO REPAY A LOAN	
2	Loan principal (present value)	$6,000
3	Annual rate of interest	10%
4	Number of years	4
5	Annual payment	$1,892.82

Entry in Cell B5 is =–PMT(B3,B4,B2).
The minus sign appears before PMT because
the annual payments are cash outflows.

	A	B	C	D	E
1		LOAN AMORTIZATION SCHEDULE			
2		Data: Loan principal		$6,000	
3		Annual rate of interest		10%	
4		Number of years		4	
5		Annual Payments			
6	Year	Total	To Interest	To Principal	Year-End Principal
7	0				$6,000.00
8	1	$1,892.82	$600.00	$1,292.82	4,707.18
9	2	$1,892.82	$470.72	$1,422.11	3,285.07
10	3	$1,892.82	$328.51	$1,564.32	1,720.75
11	4	$1,892.82	$172.07	$1,720.75	0.00

Key Cell Entries
Cell B8: =–PMT(D3,D4,D2), copy to B9:B11
Cell C8: =–CUMIPMT(D3,D4,D2,A8,A8,0), copy to C9:C11
Cell D8: =–CUMPRINC(D3,D4,D2,A8,A8,0), copy to D9:D11
Cell E8: =E7–D8, copy to E9:E11
The minus signs appear before the entries in Cells B8, C8, and D8
because these are cash outflows.

Table Use   Table A–4 indicates that the present value interest factor for an ordinary annuity corresponding to 10% and 4 years ($PVIFA_{10\%,4yrs}$) is 3.170. Substituting $PVA_4 = \$6,000$ and $PVIFA_{10\%,4yrs} = 3.170$ into Equation 4.28 and solving for PMT yield an annual loan payment of $1,892.74. Except for a slight rounding difference, this agrees with the calculator and spreadsheet value.

To attract buyers who could not immediately afford 15- to 30-year mortgages of equal annual payments, lenders offered mortgages whose interest rates adjusted at certain points. The *Focus on Practice* box on page 197 discusses how such mortgages have worked out for some "subprime" borrowers.

Finding Interest or Growth Rates

It is often necessary to calculate the compound annual interest or *growth rate* (that is, the annual rate of change in values) of a series of cash flows. Examples include finding the interest rate on a loan, the rate of growth in sales, and the rate of growth in earnings. In doing this, we can use either future value or present value interest factors. The use of present value interest factors is described in this

Focus on Practice   New Century Brings Trouble for Subprime Mortgages

As the housing market began to boom at the end of the twentieth century and into the early twenty-first, the market share of subprime mortgages climbed from near 0 percent in 1997 to about 20 percent of mortgage originations in 2006. Several factors combined to fuel the rapid growth of lending to borrowers with tarnished credit, including a low interest rate environment, loose underwriting standards, and innovations in mortgage financing such as "affordability programs" to increase rates of homeownership among lower-income borrowers.

Particularly attractive to new homebuyers was the hybrid adjustable rate mortgage (ARM), which featured a low introductory interest rate that reset upward after a preset period of time. Interest rates began a steady upward trend beginning in late 2004. In 2006, some $300 billion worth of adjustable

ARMs were reset to higher rates. In 2007, that figure will triple. The rise in interest rates will push monthly payments beyond what some homeowners can afford. For those who cannot make their payments, foreclosure and repossession by the lender may be the only way out.

Foreclosure on a nonproductive mortgage is particularly unwelcome and unrewarding for subprime mortgages. With very small equity margins in the original purchase, any drop in housing prices, as is currently happening in some overheated housing markets, exposes the lender to losses. They simply cannot sell the repossessed home for more than the outstanding loan. Typical of such lenders is **New Century Financial Corp.** The company, based in Irvine, California, entered Chapter 11 bankruptcy in April 2007, cutting 3,200 of its 7,200 employees as part of

its reorganization. One of the largest providers of subprime mortgages, New Century made $51.6 billion in subprime loans in 2006.

Problems with subprime loans were not limited to New Century. The Mortgage Bankers Association estimates that subprime loans were used to finance about 17 percent of home purchases in 2006. The mortgage bankers group reported in March 2007 that 13 percent of all subprime loans were in delinquency, more than five times the delinquency rate for home loans to borrowers with the best credit ratings. Like most bubbles, excesses will lead to corrections and the financial fallout from the subprime delinquencies will eventually run its course.

■ *As a reaction to problems in the subprime area, lenders are already tightening lending standards. What effect will this have on the housing market?*

section. The simplest situation is one in which a person wishes to find the rate of interest or growth in a *series of cash flows*.[12]

Personal Finance Example   Ray Noble wishes to find the rate of interest or growth reflected in the stream of cash flows he received from a real estate investment over the period 2005 through 2009. The following table lists those cash flows:

Year	Cash flow	
2009	$1,520	4
2008	1,440	3
2007	1,370	2
2006	1,300	1
2005	1,250	

---

12. Because the calculations required for finding interest rates and growth rates, given the series of cash flows, are the same, this section refers to the calculations as those required to find interest *or* growth rates.

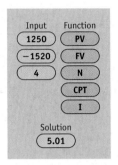

Input	Function
1250	PV
−1520	FV
4	N
	CPT
	I

Solution
5.01

By using the first year (2005) as a base year, we see that interest has been earned (or growth experienced) for 4 years.

Calculator Use   Using the calculator to find the interest or growth rate, we treat the earliest value as a present value, PV, and the latest value as a future value, FV_n. (*Note:* Most calculators require *either* the PV or the FV value to be input as a negative number to calculate an unknown interest or growth rate. That approach is used here.) Using the inputs shown at the left, you will find the interest or growth rate to be 5.01%.

Spreadsheet Use   The interest or growth rate for the series of cash flows also can be calculated as shown on the following Excel spreadsheet.

	A	B
1	INTEREST OR GROWTH RATE– SERIES OF CASH FLOWS	
2	Year	Cash Flow
3	2009	$1,520
4	2008	$1,440
5	2007	$1,370
6	2006	$1,300
7	2005	$1,250
8	Annual growth rate	5.01%

Entry in Cell B8 is =RATE((A3–A7),0,B7,–B3,0). The expression A3–A7 in the entry calculates the number of years of growth. The minus sign appears before B3 because the investment in 2009 is treated as a cash outflow.

Table Use   The first step is to divide the amount received in the earliest year (PV) by the amount received in the latest year (FV_n). Looking back at Equation 4.12, we see that this results in the present value interest factor for a *single amount* for 4 years, $PVIF_{i,4yrs}$, which is 0.822 ($1,250 ÷ $1,520). The interest rate in Table A–2 associated with the factor closest to 0.822 for 4 years is the interest or growth rate of Ray's cash flows. In the row for year 4 in Table A–2, the factor for 5 percent is 0.823—almost exactly the 0.822 value. Therefore, the interest or growth rate of the given cash flows is approximately (to the nearest whole percent) 5%, which is consistent with the value found using a calculator or spreadsheet.[13]

Another type of interest-rate problem involves finding the interest rate associated with an *annuity*, or equal-payment loan.

Personal Finance Example   Jan Jacobs can borrow $2,000 to be repaid in equal annual end-of-year amounts of $514.14 for the next 5 years. She wants to find the interest rate on this loan.

Calculator Use   (*Note:* Most calculators require *either* the PMT or the PV value to be input as a negative number to calculate an unknown interest rate on an

---

13. To obtain more precise estimates of interest or growth rates, *interpolation*—a mathematical technique for estimating unknown intermediate values—can be applied. For information on how to interpolate a more precise answer in this example, see the book's home page at **www.prenhall.com/gitman**.

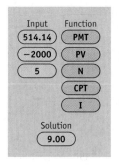

Input	Function
514.14	PMT
−2000	PV
5	N
	CPT
	I

Solution
9.00

equal-payment loan. That approach is used here.) Using the inputs shown at the left, you will find the interest rate to be 9.00%.

Spreadsheet Use   The interest or growth rate for the annuity also can be calculated as shown on the following Excel spreadsheet.

	A	B
1	INTEREST OR GROWTH RATE– ANNUITY	
2	Present value (loan principal)	$2,000
3	Number of years	5
4	Annual payments	$514.14
5	Annual interest rate	9.00%

Entry in Cell B5 is =RATE(B3,B4,−B2).
The minus sign appears before B2 because
the loan principal is treated as a cash outflow.

Table Use   Substituting $PVA_5 = \$2,000$ and $PMT = \$514.14$ into Equation 4.27 and rearranging the equation to solve for $PVIFA_{i,5\text{yrs}}$, we get

$$PVIFA_{i,5\text{yrs}} = \frac{PVA_5}{PMT} = \frac{\$2,000}{\$514.14} = 3.890 \qquad \textbf{(4.29)}$$

The interest rate for 5 years associated with the annuity factor closest to 3.890 in Table A–4 is 9%. Therefore, the interest rate on the loan is approximately (to the nearest whole percent) 9%, which is consistent with the value found using a calculator or spreadsheet.

Finding an Unknown Number of Periods

Sometimes it is necessary to calculate the number of time periods needed to generate a given amount of cash flow from an initial amount. Here we briefly consider this calculation for both single amounts and annuities. This simplest case is when a person wishes to determine the number of periods, n, it will take for an initial deposit, PV, to grow to a specified future amount, FV_n, given a stated interest rate, i.

Personal Finance Example   Ann Bates wishes to determine the number of years it will take for her initial $1,000 deposit, earning 8% annual interest, to grow to equal $2,500. Simply stated, at an 8% annual rate of interest, how many years, n, will it take for Ann's $1,000, PV, to grow to $2,500, FV_n?

Input	Function
1000	PV
−2500	FV
8	I
	CPT
	N

Solution
11.91

Calculator Use   Using the calculator, we treat the initial value as the present value, PV, and the latest value as the future value, FV_n. (*Note:* Most calculators require *either* the PV or the FV value to be input as a negative number to calculate an unknown number of periods. That approach is used here.) Using the inputs shown at the left, we find the number of periods to be 11.91 years.

Spreadsheet Use   The number of years for the present value to grow to a specified future value also can be calculated as shown on the following Excel spreadsheet.

	A	B
1	YEARS FOR A PRESENT VALUE TO GROW TO A SPECIFIED FUTURE VALUE	
2	Present value (deposit)	$1,000
3	Annual rate of interest, compounded annually	8%
4	Future value	$2,500
5	Number of years	11.91

Entry in Cell B5 is =NPER(B3,0,B2,−B4).
The minus sign appears before B4 because
the future value is treated as a cash outflow.

Table Use In a manner similar to our approach for finding an unknown interest or growth rate in a series of cash flows, we begin by dividing the amount deposited in the earliest year by the amount received in the latest year. This results in the present value interest factor for 8% and n years, $PVIF_{8\%,n}$, which is 0.400 ($1,000 ÷ $2,500). The number of years (periods) in Table A–2 associated with the factor closest to 0.400 for an 8% interest rate is the number of years required for $1,000 to grow to $2,500 at 8%. In the 8% column of Table A–2, the factor for 12 years is 0.397—almost exactly the 0.400 value. Therefore, the number of years necessary for the $1,000 to grow to a future value of $2,500 at 8% is approximately (to the nearest year) 12. This number is consistent with, but not as precise as, the value found using a calculator or spreadsheet.

Another type of number-of-periods problem involves finding the number of periods associated with an *annuity*. Occasionally we wish to find the unknown life, n, of an annuity, PMT, that is intended to achieve a specific objective, such as repaying a loan of a given amount, PVA_n, with a stated interest rate, i.

Personal Finance Example Bill Smart can borrow $25,000 at an 11% annual interest rate; equal, annual, end-of-year payments of $4,800 are required. He wishes to determine how long it will take to fully repay the loan. In other words, he wishes to determine how many years, n, it will take to repay the $25,000, 11% loan, PVA_n, if the payments of $4,800, PMT, are made at the end of each year.

Input	Function
−4800	PMT
25000	PV
11	I
	CPT
	N

Solution
8.15

Calculator Use (*Note:* Most calculators require *either* the PV or the PMT value to be input as a negative number to calculate an unknown number of periods. That approach is used here.) Using the inputs shown at the left, you will find the number of periods to be 8.15 years.

Spreadsheet Use The number of years to pay off the loan also can be calculated as shown on the following Excel spreadsheet.

	A	B
1	YEARS TO PAY OFF A LOAN	
2	Annual payment	$4,800
3	Annual rate of interest, compounded annually	11%
4	Present value (loan principal)	$25,000
5	Number of years to pay off the loan	8.15

Entry in Cell B5 is =NPER(B3,−B2,B4).
The minus sign appears before B2 because
the payments are treated as cash outflows.

Table Use Substituting $PVA_n = \$25{,}000$ and $PMT = \$4{,}800$ into Equation 4.27 and rearranging the equation to solve $PVIFA_{11\%,n}$, we get

$$PVIFA_{11\%,n} = \frac{PVA_n}{PMT} = \frac{\$25{,}000}{\$4{,}800} = 5.208 \qquad \text{(4.30)}$$

The number of periods for an 11% interest rate associated with the annuity factor closest to 5.208 in Table A–4 is 8 years. Therefore, the number of periods necessary to repay the loan fully is approximately (to the nearest year) 8 years. This value is consistent with the number of periods found using a calculator or spreadsheet.

REVIEW QUESTIONS

4–17 How can you determine the size of the equal, annual, end-of-period deposits necessary to accumulate a certain future sum at the end of a specified future period at a given annual interest rate?

4–18 Describe the procedure used to amortize a loan into a series of equal periodic payments.

4–19 Which present value interest factors would be used to find (a) the growth rate associated with a series of cash flows and (b) the interest rate associated with an equal-payment loan?

4–20 How can you determine the unknown number of periods when you know the present and future values—single amount or annuity—and the applicable rate of interest?

Summary

Focus on Value

Time value of money is an important tool that financial managers and other market participants use to assess the effects of proposed actions. Because firms have long lives and some decisions affect their long-term cash flows, the effective application of time-value-of-money techniques is extremely important. These techniques enable financial managers to evaluate cash flows occurring at different times so as to combine, compare, and evaluate them and link them to the firm's **overall goal of share price maximization.** It will become clear in Chapters 6 and 7 that the application of time value techniques is a key part of the value determination process needed to make intelligent value-creating decisions.

Review of Learning Goals

Key definitions, formulas, and equations for this chapter are summarized in Table 4.9.

LG 1 **Discuss the role of time value in finance, the use of computational tools, and the basic patterns of cash flow.** Financial managers and investors use time-value-of-money techniques when assessing the value of expected cash flow streams. Alternatives can be assessed by either compounding to find future value or discounting to find present value. Financial managers rely primarily on present value techniques. Financial calculators, electronic spreadsheets, and financial tables can streamline the application of time value techniques. The cash flow of a firm can be described by its pattern—single amount, annuity, or mixed stream.

LG 2 **Understand the concepts of future value and present value, their calculation for single amounts, and the relationship between them.** Future value (FV) relies on compound interest to measure future amounts: The initial principal or deposit in one period, along with the interest earned on it, becomes the beginning principal of the following period.

The present value (PV) of a future amount is the amount of money today that is equivalent to the given future amount, considering the return that can be earned. Present value is the inverse of future value.

LG 3 **Find the future value and the present value of both an ordinary annuity and an annuity due, and find the present value of a perpetuity.** An annuity is a pattern of equal periodic cash flows. For an ordinary annuity, the cash flows occur at the end of the period. For an annuity due, cash flows occur at the beginning of the period.

The future value of an ordinary annuity can be found by using the future value interest factor for an annuity. The present value of an ordinary annuity can be found by using the present value interest factor for an annuity. A simple conversion can be applied to use the FV and PV interest factors for an ordinary annuity to find, respectively, the future value and the present value of an annuity due. The present value of a perpetuity—an infinite-lived annuity—is found using 1 divided by the discount rate to represent the present value interest factor.

LG 4 **Calculate both the future value and the present value of a mixed stream of cash flows.** A mixed stream of cash flows is a stream of unequal periodic cash flows that reflect no particular pattern. The future value of a mixed stream of cash flows is the sum of the future values of each individual cash flow. Similarly, the present value of a mixed stream of cash flows is the sum of the present values of the individual cash flows.

LG 5 **Understand the effect that compounding interest more frequently than annually has on future value and on the effective annual rate of interest.** Interest can be compounded at intervals ranging from annually to daily, and even continuously. The more often interest is compounded, the larger the future amount that will be accumulated, and the higher the effective, or true, annual rate (EAR).

TABLE 4.9	**Summary of Key Definitions, Formulas, and Equations for Time Value of Money**

Definitions of variables

e = exponential function = 2.7183

EAR = effective annual rate

FV_n = future value or amount at the end of period n

FVA_n = future value of an n-year annuity

i = annual rate of interest

m = number of times per year interest is compounded

n = number of periods—typically years—over which money earns a return

PMT = amount deposited or received annually at the end of each year

PV = initial principal or present value

PVA_n = present value of an n-year annuity

t = period number index

Interest factor formulas

Future value of a single amount with annual compounding:

$$FVIF_{i,n} = (1 + i)^n \qquad \text{[Equation 4.5; factors in Table A–1]}$$

Present value of a single amount:

$$PVIF_{i,n} = \frac{1}{(1 + i)^n} \qquad \text{[Equation 4.11; factors in Table A–2]}$$

Future value of an ordinary annuity:

$$FVIFA_{i,n} = \sum_{t=1}^{n} (1 + i)^{t-1} \qquad \text{[Equation 4.13; factors in Table A–3]}$$

Present value of an ordinary annuity:

$$PVIFA_{i,n} = \sum_{t=1}^{n} \frac{1}{(1 + i)^t} \qquad \text{[Equation 4.15; factors in Table A–4]}$$

Future value of an annuity due:

$$FVIFA_{i,n} \text{ (annuity due)} = FVIFA_{i,n} \times (1 + i) \qquad \text{[Equation 4.17]}$$

Present value of an annuity due:

$$PVIFA_{i,n} \text{ (annuity due)} = PVIFA_{i,n} \times (1 + i) \qquad \text{[Equation 4.18]}$$

Present value of a perpetuity:

$$PVIFA_{i,\infty} = \frac{1}{i} \qquad \text{[Equation 4.19]}$$

Future value with compounding more frequently than annually:

$$FVIF_{i,n} = \left(1 + \frac{i}{m}\right)^{m \times n} \qquad \text{[Equation 4.20]}$$

For continuous compounding, $m = \infty$:

$$FVIF_{i,n} \text{ (continuous compounding)} = e^{i \times n} \qquad \text{[Equation 4.22]}$$

To find the effective annual rate:

$$EAR = \left(1 + \frac{i}{m}\right)^m - 1 \qquad \text{[Equation 4.24]}$$

Basic equations

Future value (single amount):	$FV_n = PV \times (FVIF_{i,n})$	[Equation 4.6]
Present value (single amount):	$PV = FV_n \times (PVIF_{i,n})$	[Equation 4.12]
Future value (annuity):	$FVA_n = PMT \times (FVIFA_{i,n})$	[Equation 4.14]
Present value (annuity):	$PVA_n = PMT \times (PVIFA_{i,n})$	[Equation 4.16]

The annual percentage rate (APR)—a nominal annual rate—is quoted on credit cards and loans. The annual percentage yield (APY)—an effective annual rate—is quoted on savings products.

 Describe the procedures involved in (1) determining deposits needed to accumulate a future sum, (2) loan amortization, (3) finding interest or growth rates, and (4) finding an unknown number of periods. (1) The periodic deposit to accumulate a given future sum can be found by solving the equation for the future value of an annuity for the annual payment. (2) A loan can be amortized into equal periodic payments by solving the equation for the present value of an annuity for the periodic payment. (3) Interest or growth rates can be estimated by finding the unknown interest rate in the equation for the present value of a single amount or an annuity. (4) An unknown number of periods can be estimated by finding the unknown number of periods in the equation for the present value of a single amount or an annuity.

Self-Test Problems (Solutions in Appendix B)

  ST4–1 **Future values for various compounding frequencies**   Delia Martin has $10,000 that she can deposit in any of three savings accounts for a 3-year period. Bank A compounds interest on an annual basis, bank B compounds interest twice each year, and bank C compounds interest each quarter. All three banks have a stated annual interest rate of 4%.

   a. What amount would Ms. Martin have at the end of the third year, leaving all interest paid on deposit, in each bank?
   b. What *effective annual rate* (*EAR*) would she earn in each of the banks?
   c. On the basis of your findings in parts **a** and **b,** which bank should Ms. Martin deal with? Why?
   d. If a fourth bank (bank D), also with a 4% stated interest rate, compounds interest continuously, how much would Ms. Martin have at the end of the third year? Does this alternative change your recommendation in part **c?** Explain why or why not.

 ST4–2 **Future values of annuities**   Ramesh Abdul wishes to choose the better of two equally costly cash flow streams: annuity X and annuity Y. X is an *annuity due* with a cash inflow of $9,000 for each of 6 years. Y is an *ordinary annuity* with a cash inflow of $10,000 for each of 6 years. Assume that Ramesh can earn 15% on his investments.

   a. On a purely subjective basis, which annuity do you think is more attractive? Why?
   b. Find the future value at the end of year 6, FVA_6, for both annuity X and annuity Y.
   c. Use your finding in part **b** to indicate which annuity is more attractive. Why? Compare your finding to your subjective response in part **a.**

    ST4–3 **Present values of single amounts and streams**   You have a choice of accepting either of two 5-year cash flow streams or single amounts. One cash flow stream is an ordinary annuity, and the other is a mixed stream. You may accept alternative A or B—either as a cash flow stream or as a single amount. Given the cash flow stream and single amounts associated with each (see the following table), and assuming a

9% opportunity cost, which alternative (A or B) and in which form (cash flow stream or single amount) would you prefer?

| | Cash flow stream | |
End of year	Alternative A	Alternative B
1	$700	$1,100
2	700	900
3	700	700
4	700	500
5	700	300
	Single amount	
At time zero	$2,825	$2,800

ST4–4 **Deposits needed to accumulate a future sum** Judi Janson wishes to accumulate $8,000 by the end of 5 years by making equal, annual, end-of-year deposits over the next 5 years. If Judi can earn 7% on her investments, how much must she deposit at the *end of each year* to meet this goal?

Warm-Up Exercises   A blue box (■) indicates exercises available in .

E4–1 Assume a firm makes a $2,500 deposit into its money market account. If this account is currently paying 0.7%, (yes, that's right, less than 1%!), what will the account balance be after 1 year?

E4–2 If Bob and Judy combine their savings of $1,260 and $975, respectively, and deposit this amount into an account that pays 2% annual interest, compounded monthly, what will the account balance be after 4 years?

E4–3 Gabrielle just won $2.5 million in the state lottery. She is given the option of receiving a total of $1.3 million now or she can elect to be paid $100,000 at the end of each of the next 25 years. If Gabrielle can earn 5% annually on her investments, from a strict economic point of view which option should she take?

E4–4 Your firm has the option of making an investment in new software that will cost $130,000 today and is estimated to provide the savings shown in the following table over its 5-year life:

Year	Savings estimate
1	$35,000
2	50,000
3	45,000
4	25,000
5	15,000

Should the firm make this investment if it requires a minimum annual return of 9% on all investments?

E4–5 Joseph is a friend of yours. He has plenty of money but little financial sense. He received a gift of $12,000 for his recent graduation and is looking for a bank in which to deposit the funds. Partners' Savings Bank offers an account with an annual interest rate of 3% compounded semiannually, while Selwyn's offers an account with a 2.75% annual interest rate compounded continuously. Calculate the value of the two accounts at the end of one year and recommend to Joseph which account he should choose.

 E4–6 Jack and Jill have just had their first child. If college is expected to cost $150,000 per year in 18 years, how much should the couple begin depositing annually at the end of each year to accumulate enough funds to pay the first year's tuition at the beginning of the 19th year? Assume that they can earn a 6% annual rate of return on their investment.

 Go to the book's companion website at **www.prenhall.com/gitman** to find a series of Personal Finance Warm-Up Exercises.

Problems   A blue box (■) indicates problems available in [myfinancelab].

 P4–1 **Using a time line**   The financial manager at Starbuck Industries is considering an investment that requires an initial outlay of $25,000 and is expected to result in cash inflows of $3,000 at the end of year 1, $6,000 at the end of years 2 and 3, $10,000 at the end of year 4, $8,000 at the end of year 5, and $7,000 at the end of year 6.
a. Draw and label a time line depicting the cash flows associated with Starbuck Industries' proposed investment.
b. Use arrows to demonstrate, on the time line in part **a**, how compounding to find future value can be used to measure all cash flows at the end of year 6.
c. Use arrows to demonstrate, on the time line in part **b**, how discounting to find present value can be used to measure all cash flows at time zero.
d. Which of the approaches—*future value* or *present value*—do financial managers rely on most often for decision making? Why?

 P4–2 **Future value calculation**   *Without referring to the preprogrammed function on your financial calculator or to tables,* use the basic formula for future value along with the given interest rate, *i*, and the number of periods, *n*, to calculate the future value interest factor in each of the cases shown in the following table. Compare the calculated value to the value in Appendix Table A–1.

Case	Interest rate, *i*	Number of periods, *n*
A	12%	2
B	6	3
C	9	2
D	3	4

P4–3 **Future value tables**   Use the future value interest factors in Appendix Table A–1 in each of the cases shown in the following table to estimate, to the nearest year, how long it would take an initial deposit, assuming no withdrawals,
a. To double.
b. To quadruple.

Case	Interest rate
A	7%
B	40
C	20
D	10

P4–4 **Future values**   For each of the cases shown in the following table, calculate the future value of the single cash flow deposited today that will be available at the end of the deposit period if the interest is compounded annually at the rate specified over the given period.

Case	Single cash flow	Interest rate	Deposit period (years)
A	$ 200	5%	20
B	4,500	8	7
C	10,000	9	10
D	25,000	10	12
E	37,000	11	5
F	40,000	12	9

PERSONAL FINANCE PROBLEM

P4–5 **Time value**   You have $1,500 to invest today at 7% interest compounded annually.
a. Find how much you will have accumulated in the account at the end of
   (1) 3 years, (2) 6 years, and (3) 9 years.
b. Use your findings in part **a** to calculate the amount of interest earned in
   (1) the first 3 years (years 1 to 3), (2) the second 3 years (years 4 to 6),
   and (3) the third 3 years (years 7 to 9).
c. Compare and contrast your findings in part **b**. Explain why the amount of
   interest earned increases in each succeeding 3-year period.

PERSONAL FINANCE PROBLEM

P4–6 **Time value**   As part of your financial planning, you wish to purchase a new car exactly 5 years from today. The car you wish to purchase costs $14,000 today, and your research indicates that its price will increase by 2% to 4% per year over the next 5 years.
a. Estimate the price of the car at the end of 5 years if inflation is (1) 2% per year
   and (2) 4% per year.
b. How much more expensive will the car be if the rate of inflation is 4% rather
   than 2%?

PERSONAL FINANCE PROBLEM

P4–7   **Time value**   You can deposit $10,000 into an account paying 9% annual interest either today or exactly 10 years from today. How much better off will you be at the end of 40 years if you decide to make the initial deposit today rather than 10 years from today?

PERSONAL FINANCE PROBLEM

P4–8   **Time value**   Misty needs to have $15,000 at the end of 5 years to fulfill her goal of purchasing a small sailboat. She is willing to invest the funds as a single amount today but wonders what sort of investment return she will need to earn. Use your calculator or the time value tables to figure out the approximate annually compounded rate of return needed in each of these cases:

   a.   Misty can invest $10,200 today.
   b.   Misty can invest $8,150 today.
   c.   Misty can invest $7,150 today.

PERSONAL FINANCE PROBLEM

P4–9   **Single-payment loan repayment**   A person borrows $200 to be repaid in 8 years with 14% annually compounded interest. The loan may be repaid at the end of any earlier year with no prepayment penalty.

   a.   What amount will be due if the loan is repaid at the end of year 1?
   b.   What is the repayment at the end of year 4?
   c.   What amount is due at the end of the eighth year?

P4–10   **Present value calculation**   *Without referring to the preprogrammed function on your financial calculator or to tables,* use the basic formula for present value, along with the given opportunity cost, i, and the number of periods, n, to calculate the present value interest factor in each of the cases shown in the following table. Compare the calculated value to the table value.

Case	Opportunity cost, i	Number of periods, n
A	2%	4
B	10	2
C	5	3
D	13	2

P4–11   **Present values**   For each of the cases shown in the following table, calculate the present value of the cash flow, discounting at the rate given and assuming that the cash flow is received at the end of the period noted.

Case	Single cash flow	Discount rate	End of period (years)
A	$ 7,000	12%	4
B	28,000	8	20
C	10,000	14	12
D	150,000	11	6
E	45,000	20	8

P4–12 **Present value concept**   Answer each of the following questions.

a. What single investment made today, earning 12% annual interest, will be worth $6,000 at the end of 6 years?

b. What is the present value of $6,000 to be received at the end of 6 years if the discount rate is 12%?

c. What is the most you would pay today for a promise to repay you $6,000 at the end of 6 years if your opportunity cost is 12%?

d. Compare, contrast, and discuss your findings in parts **a** through **c**.

PERSONAL FINANCE PROBLEM

 P4–13 **Time value**   Jim Nance has been offered a future payment of $500 three years from today. If his opportunity cost is 7% compounded annually, what value should he place on this opportunity today? What is the most he should pay to purchase this payment today?

 P4–14 **Time value**   An Iowa state savings bond can be converted to $100 at maturity 6 years from purchase. If the state bonds are to be competitive with U.S. savings bonds, which pay 8% annual interest (compounded annually), at what price must the state sell its bonds? Assume no cash payments on savings bonds prior to redemption.

PERSONAL FINANCE PROBLEM

 P4–15 **Time value and discount rates**   You just won a lottery that promises to pay you $1,000,000 exactly 10 years from today. Because the $1,000,000 payment is guaranteed by the state in which you live, opportunities exist to sell the claim today for an immediate single cash payment.

a. What is the least you will sell your claim for if you can earn the following rates of return on similar-risk investments during the 10-year period?

(1) 6%

(2) 9%

(3) 12%

b. Rework part **a** under the assumption that the $1,000,000 payment will be received in 15 rather than 10 years.

c. On the basis of your findings in parts **a** and **b**, discuss the effect of both the size of the rate of return and the time until receipt of payment on the present value of a future sum.

PERSONAL FINANCE PROBLEM

 P4–16 **Time value comparisons of single amounts**   In exchange for a $20,000 payment today, a well-known company will allow you to choose *one* of the alternatives shown in the following table. Your opportunity cost is 11%.

Alternative	Single amount
A	$28,500 at end of 3 years
B	$54,000 at end of 9 years
C	$160,000 at end of 20 years

a. Find the value today of each alternative.

b. Are all the alternatives acceptable—that is, worth $20,000 today?

c. Which alternative, if any, will you take?

PERSONAL FINANCE PROBLEM

P4–17   **Cash flow investment decision**   Tom Alexander has an opportunity to purchase any of the investments shown in the following table. The purchase price, the amount of the single cash inflow, and its year of receipt are given for each investment. Which purchase recommendations would you make, assuming that Tom can earn 10% on his investments?

Investment	Price	Single cash inflow	Year of receipt
A	$18,000	$30,000	5
B	600	3,000	20
C	3,500	10,000	10
D	1,000	15,000	40

P4–18   **Future value of an annuity**   For each case in the accompanying table, answer the questions that follow.

Case	Amount of annuity	Interest rate	Deposit period (years)
A	$ 2,500	8%	10
B	500	12	6
C	30,000	20	5
D	11,500	9	8
E	6,000	14	30

a. Calculate the future value of the annuity assuming that it is
   (1) An ordinary annuity.
   (2) An annuity due.
b. Compare your findings in parts **a**(1) and **a**(2). All else being identical, which type of annuity—ordinary or annuity due—is preferable? Explain why.

P4–19   **Present value of an annuity**   Consider the following cases.

Case	Amount of annuity	Interest rate	Period (years)
A	$ 12,000	7%	3
B	55,000	12	15
C	700	20	9
D	140,000	5	7
E	22,500	10	5

a. Calculate the present value of the annuity assuming that it is
   (1) An ordinary annuity.
   (2) An annuity due.
b. Compare your findings in parts **a**(1) and **a**(2). All else being identical, which type of annuity—ordinary or annuity due—is preferable? Explain why.

PERSONAL FINANCE PROBLEM

P4–20 **Time value—Annuities**   Marian Kirk wishes to select the better of two 10-year annuities, C and D. Annuity C is an *ordinary annuity* of $2,500 per year for 10 years. Annuity D is an *annuity due* of $2,200 per year for 10 years.

    a. Find the *future value* of both annuities at the end of year 10, assuming that Marian can earn (1) 10% annual interest and (2) 20% annual interest.

    b. Use your findings in part **a** to indicate which annuity has the greater future value at the end of year 10 for both the (1) 10% and (2) 20% interest rates.

    c. Find the *present value* of both annuities, assuming that Marian can earn (1) 10% annual interest and (2) 20% annual interest.

    d. Use your findings in part **c** to indicate which annuity has the greater present value for both (1) 10% and (2) 20% interest rates.

    e. Briefly compare, contrast, and explain any differences between your findings using the 10% and 20% interest rates in parts **b** and **d**.

PERSONAL FINANCE PROBLEM

P4–21 **Retirement planning**   Hal Thomas, a 25-year-old college graduate, wishes to retire at age 65. To supplement other sources of retirement income, he can deposit $2,000 each year into a tax-deferred individual retirement arrangement (IRA). The IRA will be invested to earn an annual return of 10%, which is assumed to be attainable over the next 40 years.

    a. If Hal makes annual end-of-year $2,000 deposits into the IRA, how much will he have accumulated by the end of his sixty-fifth year?

    b. If Hal decides to wait until age 35 to begin making annual end-of-year $2,000 deposits into the IRA, how much will he have accumulated by the end of his sixty-fifth year?

    c. Using your findings in parts **a** and **b**, discuss the impact of delaying making deposits into the IRA for 10 years (age 25 to age 35) on the amount accumulated by the end of Hal's sixty-fifth year.

    d. Rework parts **a**, **b**, and **c**, assuming that Hal makes all deposits at the beginning, rather than the end, of each year. Discuss the effect of beginning-of-year deposits on the future value accumulated by the end of Hal's sixty-fifth year.

PERSONAL FINANCE PROBLEM

P4–22 **Value of a retirement annuity**   An insurance agent is trying to sell you an immediate-retirement annuity, which for a single amount paid today will provide you with $12,000 at the end of each year for the next 25 years. You currently earn 9% on low-risk investments comparable to the retirement annuity. Ignoring taxes, what is the most you would pay for this annuity?

PERSONAL FINANCE PROBLEM

P4–23 **Funding your retirement**   You plan to retire in exactly 20 years. Your goal is to create a fund that will allow you to receive $20,000 at the end of each year for the 30 years between retirement and death (a psychic told you would die exactly 30 years after you retire). You know that you will be able to earn 11% per year during the 30-year retirement period.

    a. How large a fund will you need *when you retire* in 20 years to provide the 30-year, $20,000 retirement annuity?

b. How much will you need *today* as a single amount to provide the fund calculated in part **a** if you earn only 9% per year during the 20 years preceding retirement?

c. What effect would an increase in the rate you can earn both during and prior to retirement have on the values found in parts **a** and **b**? Explain.

PERSONAL FINANCE PROBLEM

   Value of an annuity versus a single amount   Assume that you just won the state lottery. Your prize can be taken either in the form of $40,000 at the end of each of the next 25 years (i.e., $1,000,000 over 25 years) or as a single amount of $500,000 paid immediately.

a. If you expect to be able to earn 5% annually on your investments over the next 25 years, ignoring taxes and other considerations, which alternative should you take? Why?

b. Would your decision in part **a** change if you could earn 7% rather than 5% on your investments over the next 25 years? Why?

c. On a strictly economic basis, at approximately what earnings rate would you be indifferent between the two plans?

  Perpetuities   Consider the data in the following table.

Perpetuity	Annual amount	Discount rate
A	$ 20,000	8%
B	100,000	10
C	3,000	6
D	60,000	5

Determine, for each of the perpetuities:

a. The appropriate present value interest factor.

b. The present value.

PERSONAL FINANCE PROBLEM

 Creating an endowment   Upon completion of her introductory finance course, Marla Lee was so pleased with the amount of useful and interesting knowledge she gained that she convinced her parents, who were wealthy alumni of the university she was attending, to create an endowment. The endowment is to allow three needy students to take the introductory finance course each year in perpetuity. The guaranteed annual cost of tuition and books for the course is $600 per student. The endowment will be created by making a single payment to the university. The university expects to earn exactly 6% per year on these funds.

a. How large an initial single payment must Marla's parents make to the university to fund the endowment?

b. What amount would be needed to fund the endowment if the university could earn 9% rather than 6% per year on the funds?

Value of a mixed stream   For each of the mixed streams of cash flows shown in the following table, determine the future value at the end of the final year if deposits are made into an account paying annual interest of 12%, assuming that no withdrawals are made during the period and that the deposits are made:

a. At the *end* of each year.
b. At the *beginning* of each year.

| | Cash flow stream | | |
Year	A	B	C
1	$ 900	$30,000	$1,200
2	1,000	25,000	1,200
3	1,200	20,000	1,000
4		10,000	1,900
5		5,000	

PERSONAL FINANCE PROBLEM

P4–28 **Value of a single amount versus a mixed stream**   Gina Vitale has just contracted to sell a small parcel of land that she inherited a few years ago. The buyer is willing to pay $24,000 at the closing of the transaction or will pay the amounts shown in the following table at the *beginning* of each of the next 5 years. Because Gina doesn't really need the money today, she plans to let it accumulate in an account that earns 7% annual interest. Given her desire to buy a house at the end of 5 years after closing on the sale of the lot, she decides to choose the payment alternative— $24,000 single amount or the mixed stream of payments in the following table— that provides the higher future value at the end of 5 years. Which alternative will she choose?

| Mixed stream | |
Beginning of year	Cash flow
1	$ 2,000
2	4,000
3	6,000
4	8,000
5	10,000

P4–29 **Value of mixed streams**   Find the present value of the streams of cash flows shown in the following table. Assume that the firm's opportunity cost is 12%.

| A | | B | | C | |
Year	Cash flow	Year	Cash flow	Year	Cash flow
1	−$2,000	1	$10,000	1–5	$10,000/yr
2	3,000	2–5	5,000/yr	6–10	8,000/yr
3	4,000	6	7,000		
4	6,000				
5	8,000				

P4–30 **Present value—Mixed streams** Consider the mixed streams of cash flows shown in the following table.

| | Cash flow stream | |
Year	A	B
1	$ 50,000	$ 10,000
2	40,000	20,000
3	30,000	30,000
4	20,000	40,000
5	10,000	50,000
Totals	$150,000	$150,000

a. Find the present value of each stream using a 15% discount rate.
b. Compare the calculated present values and discuss them in light of the fact that the undiscounted cash flows total $150,000 in each case.

P4–31 **Value of a mixed stream** Harte Systems, Inc., a maker of electronic surveillance equipment, is considering selling to a well-known hardware chain the rights to market its home security system. The proposed deal calls for the hardware chain to pay Harte $30,000 and $25,000 at the end of years 1 and 2 and to make annual year-end payments of $15,000 in years 3 through 9. A final payment to Harte of $10,000 would be due at the end of year 10.
a. Lay out the cash flows involved in the offer on a time line.
b. If Harte applies a required rate of return of 12% to them, what is the present value of this series of payments?
c. A second company has offered Harte an immediate one-time payment of $100,000 for the rights to market the home security system. Which offer should Harte accept?

PERSONAL FINANCE PROBLEM

P4–32 **Funding budget shortfalls** As part of your personal budgeting process, you have determined that in each of the next 5 years you will have budget shortfalls. In other words, you will need the amounts shown in the following table at the end of the given year to balance your budget—that is, to make inflows equal outflows. You expect to be able to earn 8% on your investments during the next 5 years and wish to fund the budget shortfalls over the next 5 years with a single amount.

End of year	Budget shortfall
1	$ 5,000
2	4,000
3	6,000
4	10,000
5	3,000

a. How large must the single deposit today into an account paying 8% annual interest be to provide for full coverage of the anticipated budget shortfalls?

b. What effect would an increase in your earnings rate have on the amount calculated in part **a**? Explain.

P4–33 Relationship between future value and present value—Mixed stream   Using *only* the information in the accompanying table, answer the questions that follow.

Year (*t*)	Cash flow	Future value interest factor at 5% ($FVIF_{5\%,n}$)
1	$ 800	1.050
2	900	1.102
3	1,000	1.158
4	1,500	1.216
5	2,000	1.276

a. Determine the *present value* of the mixed stream of cash flows using a 5% discount rate.

b. How much would you be willing to pay for an opportunity to buy this stream, assuming that you can at best earn 5% on your investments?

c. What effect, if any, would a 7% rather than a 5% opportunity cost have on your analysis? (Explain verbally.)

P4–34 Changing compounding frequency   Using annual, semiannual, and quarterly compounding periods, for each of the following, (1) calculate the future value if $5,000 is deposited initially, and (2) determine the *effective annual rate (EAR)*.

a. At 12% annual interest for 5 years.

b. At 16% annual interest for 6 years.

c. At 20% annual interest for 10 years.

P4–35 Compounding frequency, time value, and effective annual rates   For each of the cases in the following table:

a. Calculate the future value at the end of the specified deposit period.

b. Determine the *effective annual rate, EAR.*

c. Compare the nominal annual rate, *i*, to the effective annual rate, EAR. What relationship exists between compounding frequency and the nominal and effective annual rates?

Case	Amount of initial deposit	Nominal annual rate, *i*	Compounding frequency, *m* (times/year)	Deposit period (years)
A	$ 2,500	6%	2	5
B	50,000	12	6	3
C	1,000	5	1	10
D	20,000	16	4	6

P4–36 Continuous compounding   For each of the cases in the following table, find the future value at the end of the deposit period, assuming that interest is compounded continuously at the given nominal annual rate.

Case	Amount of initial deposit	Nominal annual rate, i	Deposit period (years), n
A	$1,000	9%	2
B	600	10	10
C	4,000	8	7
D	2,500	12	4

PERSONAL FINANCE PROBLEM

P4–37 Compounding frequency and time value   You plan to invest $2,000 in an individual retirement arrangement (IRA) today at a *nominal annual rate* of 8%, which is expected to apply to all future years.
a. How much will you have in the account at the end of 10 years if interest is compounded (1) annually, (2) semiannually, (3) daily (assume a 365-day year), and (4) continuously?
b. What is the *effective annual rate, EAR*, for each compounding period in part **a?**
c. How much greater will your IRA balance be at the end of 10 years if interest is compounded continuously rather than annually?
d. How does the compounding frequency affect the future value and effective annual rate for a given deposit? Explain in terms of your findings in parts **a** through **c.**

PERSONAL FINANCE PROBLEM

P4–38 Comparing compounding periods   René Levin wishes to determine the future value at the end of 2 years of a $15,000 deposit made today into an account paying a nominal annual rate of 12%.
a. Find the future value of René's deposit, assuming that interest is compounded (1) annually, (2) quarterly, (3) monthly, and (4) continuously.
b. Compare your findings in part **a,** and use them to demonstrate the relationship between compounding frequency and future value.
c. What is the maximum future value obtainable given the $15,000 deposit, the 2-year time period, and the 12% nominal annual rate? Use your findings in part **a** to explain.

PERSONAL FINANCE PROBLEM

P4–39 Annuities and compounding   Janet Boyle intends to deposit $300 per year in a credit union for the next 10 years, and the credit union pays an annual interest rate of 8%.
a. Determine the future value that Janet will have at the end of 10 years, given that end-of-period deposits are made and no interest is withdrawn, if
    (1) $300 is deposited annually and the credit union pays interest annually.
    (2) $150 is deposited semiannually and the credit union pays interest semiannually.
    (3) $75 is deposited quarterly and the credit union pays interest quarterly.
b. Use your finding in part **a** to discuss the effect of more frequent deposits and compounding of interest on the future value of an annuity.

P4–40 **Deposits to accumulate future sums**   For each of the cases shown in the following table, determine the amount of the equal, annual, end-of-year deposits necessary to accumulate the given sum at the end of the specified period, assuming the stated annual interest rate.

Case	Sum to be accumulated	Accumulation period (years)	Interest rate
A	$ 5,000	3	12%
B	100,000	20	7
C	30,000	8	10
D	15,000	12	8

PERSONAL FINANCE PROBLEM

P4–41 **Creating a retirement fund**   To supplement your planned retirement in exactly 42 years, you estimate that you need to accumulate $220,000 by the end of 42 years from today. You plan to make equal, annual, end-of-year deposits into an account paying 8% annual interest.
  a. How large must the annual deposits be to create the $220,000 fund by the end of 42 years?
  b. If you can afford to deposit only $600 per year into the account, how much will you have accumulated by the end of the forty-second year?

PERSONAL FINANCE PROBLEM

P4–42 **Accumulating a growing future sum**   A retirement home at Deer Trail Estates now costs $185,000. Inflation is expected to cause this price to increase at 6% per year over the 20 years before C. L. Donovan retires. How large an equal, annual, end-of-year deposit must be made each year into an account paying an annual interest rate of 10% for Donovan to have the cash needed to purchase a home at retirement?

PERSONAL FINANCE PROBLEM

P4–43 **Deposits to create a perpetuity**   You have decided to endow your favorite university with a scholarship. It is expected to cost $6,000 per year to attend the university into perpetuity. You expect to give the university the endowment in 10 years and will accumulate it by making equal annual (end-of-year) deposits into an account. The rate of interest is expected to be 10% for all future time periods.
  a. How large must the endowment be?
  b. How much must you deposit at the end of each of the next 10 years to accumulate the required amount?

PERSONAL FINANCE PROBLEM

P4–44 **Inflation, time value, and annual deposits**   While vacationing in Florida, John Kelley saw the vacation home of his dreams. It was listed with a sale price of $200,000. The only catch is that John is 40 years old and plans to continue working until he is 65. Still, he believes that prices generally increase at the overall rate of inflation. John believes that he can earn 9% annually after taxes on his investments. He is willing to invest a fixed amount at the end of each of the next 25 years to fund the cash purchase of such a house (one that can be purchased today for $200,000) when he retires.

a. Inflation is expected to average 5% per year for the next 25 years. What will John's dream house cost when he retires?
b. How much must John invest at the *end* of each of the next 25 years to have the cash purchase price of the house when he retires?
c. If John invests at the *beginning* instead of at the end of each of the next 25 years, how much must he invest each year?

 P4–45 Loan payment Determine the equal, annual, end-of-year payment required each year over the life of the loans shown in the following table to repay them fully during the stated term of the loan.

Loan	Principal	Interest rate	Term of loan (years)
A	$12,000	8%	3
B	60,000	12	10
C	75,000	10	30
D	4,000	15	5

PERSONAL FINANCE PROBLEM

 P4–46 Loan amortization schedule Joan Messineo borrowed $15,000 at a 14% annual rate of interest to be repaid over 3 years. The loan is amortized into three equal, annual, end-of-year payments.
a. Calculate the annual, end-of-year loan payment.
b. Prepare a loan amortization schedule showing the interest and principal breakdown of each of the three loan payments.
c. Explain why the interest portion of each payment declines with the passage of time.

 P4–47 Loan interest deductions Liz Rogers just closed a $10,000 business loan that is to be repaid in three equal, annual, end-of-year payments. The interest rate on the loan is 13%. As part of her firm's detailed financial planning, Liz wishes to determine the annual interest deduction attributable to the loan. (Because it is a business loan, the interest portion of each loan payment is tax-deductible to the business.)
a. Determine the firm's annual loan payment.
b. Prepare an amortization schedule for the loan.
c. How much interest expense will Liz's firm have in *each* of the next 3 years as a result of this loan?

PERSONAL FINANCE PROBLEM

 P4–48 Monthly loan payments Tim Smith is shopping for a used car. He has found one priced at $4,500. The dealer has told Tim that if he can come up with a down payment of $500, the dealer will finance the balance of the price at a 12% annual rate over 2 years (24 months).
a. Assuming that Tim accepts the dealer's offer, what will his *monthly* (end-of-month) payment amount be?
b. Use a financial calculator or Equation 4.15a (found in footnote 9) to help you figure out what Tim's *monthly* payment would be if the dealer were willing to finance the balance of the car price at a 9% annual rate.

P4–49 **Growth rates** You are given the series of cash flows shown in the following table.

	Cash flows		
Year	A	B	C
1	$500	$1,500	$2,500
2	560	1,550	2,600
3	640	1,610	2,650
4	720	1,680	2,650
5	800	1,760	2,800
6		1,850	2,850
7		1,950	2,900
8		2,060	
9		2,170	
10		2,280	

    a. Calculate the compound annual growth rate associated with each cash flow stream.

    b. If year-1 values represent initial deposits in a savings account paying annual interest, what is the annual rate of interest earned on each account?

    c. Compare and discuss the growth rate and interest rate found in parts **a** and **b**, respectively.

PERSONAL FINANCE PROBLEM

P4–50 **Rate of return** Rishi Singh has $1,500 to invest. His investment counselor suggests an investment that pays no stated interest but will return $2,000 at the end of 3 years.

    a. What annual rate of return will Rishi earn with this investment?

    b. Rishi is considering another investment, of equal risk, that earns an annual return of 8%. Which investment should he make, and why?

PERSONAL FINANCE PROBLEM

P4–51 **Rate of return and investment choice** Clare Jaccard has $5,000 to invest. Because she is only 25 years old, she is not concerned about the length of the investment's life. What she is sensitive to is the rate of return she will earn on the investment. With the help of her financial advisor, Clare has isolated four equally risky investments, each providing a single amount at the end of its life, as shown in the following table. All of the investments require an initial $5,000 payment.

Investment	Single amount	Investment life (years)
A	$ 8,400	6
B	15,900	15
C	7,600	4
D	13,000	10

    a. Calculate, to the nearest 1%, the rate of return on each of the four investments available to Clare.

    b. Which investment would you recommend to Clare, given her goal of maximizing the rate of return?

P4–52 **Rate of return—Annuity**   What is the rate of return on an investment of $10,606 if the company will receive $2,000 each year for the next 10 years?

PERSONAL FINANCE PROBLEM

P4–53 **Choosing the best annuity**   Raina Herzig wishes to choose the best of four immediate-retirement annuities available to her. In each case, in exchange for paying a single premium today, she will receive equal, annual, end-of-year cash benefits for a specified number of years. She considers the annuities to be equally risky and is not concerned about their differing lives. Her decision will be based solely on the rate of return she will earn on each annuity. The key terms of the four annuities are shown in the following table.

Annuity	Premium paid today	Annual benefit	Life (years)
A	$30,000	$3,100	20
B	25,000	3,900	10
C	40,000	4,200	15
D	35,000	4,000	12

a. Calculate to the nearest 1% the rate of return on each of the four annuities Raina is considering.
b. Given Raina's stated decision criterion, which annuity would you recommend?

PERSONAL FINANCE PROBLEM

P4–54 **Interest rate for an annuity**   Anna Waldheim was seriously injured in an industrial accident. She sued the responsible parties and was awarded a judgment of $2,000,000. Today, she and her attorney are attending a settlement conference with the defendants. The defendants have made an initial offer of $156,000 per year for 25 years. Anna plans to counteroffer at $255,000 per year for 25 years. Both the offer and the counteroffer have a present value of $2,000,000, the amount of the judgment. Both assume payments at the end of each year.
a. What interest rate assumption have the defendants used in their offer (rounded to the nearest whole percent)?
b. What interest rate assumption have Anna and her lawyer used in their counteroffer (rounded to the nearest whole percent)?
c. Anna is willing to settle for an annuity that carries an interest rate assumption of 9%. What annual payment would be acceptable to her?

PERSONAL FINANCE PROBLEM

P4–55 **Loan rates of interest**   John Flemming has been shopping for a loan to finance the purchase of a used car. He has found three possibilities that seem attractive and wishes to select the one with the lowest interest rate. The information available with respect to each of the three $5,000 loans is shown in the following table.

Loan	Principal	Annual payment	Term (years)
A	$5,000	$1,352.81	5
B	5,000	1,543.21	4
C	5,000	2,010.45	3

a. Determine the interest rate associated with each of the loans.
b. Which loan should John take?

P4–56 **Number of years to equal future amount**   For each of the following cases, determine the number of years it will take for the initial deposit to grow to equal the future amount at the given interest rate.

Case	Initial deposit	Future amount	Interest rate
A	$ 300	$ 1,000	7%
B	12,000	15,000	5
C	9,000	20,000	10
D	100	500	9
E	7,500	30,000	15

PERSONAL FINANCE PROBLEM

P4–57 **Time to accumulate a given sum**   Manuel Rios wishes to determine how long it will take an initial deposit of $10,000 to double.
a. If Manuel earns 10% annual interest on the deposit, how long will it take for him to double his money?
b. How long will it take if he earns only 7% annual interest?
c. How long will it take if he can earn 12% annual interest?
d. Reviewing your findings in parts **a, b,** and **c,** indicate what relationship exists between the interest rate and the amount of time it will take Manuel to double his money.

P4–58 **Number of years to provide a given return**   In each of the following cases, determine the number of years that the given annual *end-of-year* cash flow must continue to provide the given rate of return on the given initial amount.

Case	Initial amount	Annual cash flow	Rate of return
A	$ 1,000	$ 250	11%
B	150,000	30,000	15
C	80,000	10,000	10
D	600	275	9
E	17,000	3,500	6

PERSONAL FINANCE PROBLEM

P4–59 **Time to repay installment loan**   Mia Salto wishes to determine how long it will take to repay a loan with initial proceeds of $14,000 where annual *end-of-year* installment payments of $2,450 are required.
a. If Mia can borrow at a 12% annual rate of interest, how long will it take for her to repay the loan fully?
b. How long will it take if she can borrow at a 9% annual rate?
c. How long will it take if she has to pay 15% annual interest?
d. Reviewing your answers in parts **a, b,** and **c,** describe the general relationship between the interest rate and the amount of time it will take Mia to repay the loan fully.

P4–60   ETHICS PROBLEM   A manager at a "check into cash" business (see *Focus on Ethics* box on page 192) defends his business practice as simply "charging what the market will bear." "After all," says the manager, "we don't force people to come in the door." How would you respond to this ethical defense of the payday-advance business?

Chapter 4 Case

Funding Jill Moran's Retirement Annuity

Sunrise Industries wishes to accumulate funds to provide a retirement annuity for its vice president of research, Jill Moran. Ms. Moran, by contract, will retire at the end of exactly 12 years. Upon retirement, she is entitled to receive an annual end-of-year payment of $42,000 for exactly 20 years. If she dies prior to the end of the 20-year period, the annual payments will pass to her heirs. During the 12-year "accumulation period," Sunrise wishes to fund the annuity by making equal, annual, end-of-year deposits into an account earning 9% interest. Once the 20-year "distribution period" begins, Sunrise plans to move the accumulated monies into an account earning a guaranteed 12% per year. At the end of the distribution period, the account balance will equal zero. Note that the first deposit will be made at the end of year 1 and that the first distribution payment will be received at the end of year 13.

To Do

a. Draw a time line depicting all of the cash flows associated with Sunrise's view of the retirement annuity.
b. How large a sum must Sunrise accumulate by the end of year 12 to provide the 20-year, $42,000 annuity?
c. How large must Sunrise's equal, annual, end-of-year deposits into the account be over the 12-year accumulation period to fund fully Ms. Moran's retirement annuity?
d. How much would Sunrise have to deposit annually during the accumulation period if it could earn 10% rather than 9% during the accumulation period?
e. How much would Sunrise have to deposit annually during the accumulation period if Ms. Moran's retirement annuity were a perpetuity and all other terms were the same as initially described?

Spreadsheet Exercise

At the end of 2009, Uma Corporation was considering undertaking a major long-term project in an effort to remain competitive in its industry. The production and sales departments determined the potential annual cash flow savings that could accrue to the firm if it acts soon. Specifically, they estimate that a mixed stream of future cash flow savings will occur at the end of the years 2010 through 2015. The years 2016 through 2020 will see consecutive and equal cash flow savings at the end of each year. The firm estimates that its discount rate over the first 6 years will be 7%. The expected discount rate over the years 2016 through 2020 will be 11%.

The project managers will find the project acceptable if it results in present cash flow savings of at least $860,000. The following cash flow savings data are supplied to the finance department for analysis:

End of Year	Cash Flow Savings
2010	$110,000
2011	120,000
2012	130,000
2013	150,000
2014	160,000
2015	150,000
2016	90,000
2017	90,000
2018	90,000
2019	90,000
2020	90,000

To Do

Create spreadsheets similar to Tables 4.2 and 4.4 (which can be viewed at www.prenhall.com/gitman), and then answer the following questions:

a. Determine the value (at the beginning of 2010) of the future cash flow savings expected to be generated by this project.
b. Based solely on the one criterion set by management, should the firm undertake this specific project? Explain.
c. What is the "interest rate risk," and how might it influence the recommendation made in part **b**? Explain.

Group Exercise

"Cash is king." Donald Trump made this statement at the end of the 1980s, referring to the climate for real estate investment. Most people would agree that in life, cash is, indeed, king. The management and proper valuation of cash flows is the most important factor in the survival of a business. Almost all businesses receive cash payments in spurts but must make cash payments at regular intervals. Many businesses have failed not for a lack of sales success, but rather for a lack of *timely* cash. Therefore, the timing of cash flows and implied time value are of utmost importance.

To Do

In this assignment, you will evaluate scenarios involving your group's fictitious firm.

a. Your firm has a single copy machine for the tenth floor, and it has broken down yet again. Your firm must decide how to proceed in replacing the copier. So far, you have received two competing offers for comparable machines. Both offers are 3-year leases.

> *Option A* requires an up-front payment of $1,700 with additional annual payments of $1,200 at the beginning of years 2 and 3. The firm is also charged one-half of 1 cent, ($0.005), for each sheet printed, payable at the end of each year.

> *Option B* has no up-front cost. Its lease payment is $1,300, payable at the beginning of the year, and the per-sheet charge is 1 cent ($0.01), payable at the end of each year.

You estimate that monthly use of the copy machine will amount to 1,500 copies. Determine an appropriate discount rate and discount the cash flows for each lease. Choose the best lease based on which lease costs less in present value terms. Be prepared to defend your choice.

b. A second option is to purchase the machine outright. In fact, after the lease expires, you are considering buying your firm's next copier.

(1) You need to obtain a minimum of two offers before buying a copy machine. Your needs include a multifunction machine capable of copying, faxing, and printing, with networking capability because all workers on the tenth floor will be sharing it. The purchase price should approximate the present value calculations from part a. In your search, you must consider not only the purchase price of the machine, but also the cost of any warranty/service agreement. In addition, you must adjust the current price for expected inflation. Take the price for the machine today and find out what the price will be in 3 years given a 3% compound annual inflation rate. Alternatively, you could calculate what the price would be given a 5% annual rate of decrease, as that is the observed trend over recent years.

(2) Because you want to save for this expenditure (rather than take out a loan for it), you need information about savings rates at a local bank. (Here "bank" refers to any depository institution, including those that are strictly online operations.) After getting a rate for a savings account, calculate what amount you would have to deposit today to have the dollar value of the machine you wish to buy at the end of 3 years. If, instead, you wanted to make annual deposits at the end of each of the next 3 years, how much should you deposit? What if those three equal deposits were made at the beginning of each year?

c. Your firm plans to upgrade its computer systems. The computers will be financed with a 5-year bank loan totaling $25,000. Your firm can obtain a loan at the prime rate and you are asked to provide this information to your firm's management. Obtain this information from a local bank and use that interest rate to prepare an amortization schedule for the loan.

d. A recent court ruling concluded that a competitor had violated one of your patents without properly paying for its use. The court-ordered settlement provides the following annual payments to your firm:

Year	Payment
1	$150,000
2	125,000
3	100,000
4	75,000
5	50,000

Find the present value of these cash flows using a 6% discount rate.

Web Exercise

Go to the book's companion website at **www.prenhall.com/gitman** to find the Web Exercise for this chapter.

> Remember to check the book's website at **www.prenhall.com/gitman** to find additional resources, including Web Exercises and a Web Case.

5 | Risk and Return

WHY THIS CHAPTER MATTERS TO YOU

(**In Your Professional Life**)

Accounting: You need to understand the relationship between risk and return because of the effect that riskier projects will have on the firm's annual net income and on your efforts to stabilize reported net income.

Information systems: You need to understand how to do scenario and correlation analyses to build decision packages that help management analyze the risk and return of various business opportunities.

Management: You need to understand the relationship between risk and return, and how to measure that relationship to evaluate data that come from finance personnel and translate those data into decisions that increase the value of the firm.

Marketing: You need to understand that although higher-risk projects may produce higher returns, they may not be the best choice for the firm if they produce an erratic earnings pattern and fail to optimize the value of the firm.

Operations: You need to understand why investments in plant, equipment, and systems need to be evaluated in light of their impact on the firm's risk and return, which together will affect the firm's value.

(**In Your Personal Life**)

The tradeoff between risk and return enters into numerous personal financial decisions. You will use risk and return concepts when you select savings vehicles, buy real estate, finance major purchases, purchase insurance, invest in securities, and implement retirement plans. Although risk and return are difficult to measure precisely, you can get a feel for them and make decisions based upon the tradeoffs between risk and return in light of your personal disposition toward risk.

LEARNING GOALS

LG 1 Understand the meaning and fundamentals of risk, return, and risk preferences.

LG 2 Describe procedures for assessing and measuring the risk of a single asset.

LG 3 Discuss the measurement of return and standard deviation for a portfolio and the concept of correlation.

LG 4 Understand the risk and return characteristics of a portfolio in terms of correlation and diversification, and the impact of international assets on a portfolio.

LG 5 Review the two types of risk and the derivation and role of beta in measuring the relevant risk of both a security and a portfolio.

LG 6 Explain the capital asset pricing model (CAPM), its relationship to the security market line (SML), and the major forces causing shifts in the SML.

Venture Capitalists

Finding the Right Startup Can Lead to Big Gains

When the tech-stock bubble burst in the early part of this decade, venture capitalists felt the sting and pulled back. Today, venture capitalists are becoming more active. Mega-deals such as **YouTube's** recent sale to **Google** for $1.65 billion and **Skype's** sale in 2006 to **eBay** for $2.6 billion are giving venture investors new confidence in their ability to cash out.

The venture capital sector has long offered rollercoaster returns. Its investors take hefty risks, typically backing unproven companies with unproven products or services, and they often end up losing money. Many companies backed by venture capital fail, but when they win, they win big. Firms such as **Google, Genentech,** and **Apple** were originally venture-funded.

Venture capital often comes from wealthy investors seeking exceptional returns, albeit at increased risk of their capital. Peter Kash, chairman of the New York–based Two Rivers holding group, estimates that worldwide there are 70,000 people with at least $30 million in assets each, including 950 billionaires with a total of more than $3.5 trillion in assets. The riskiness of venture deals demand generous returns on capital. According to David Mathias, a managing partner at the Washington, D.C.–based Carlyle Group, "If the capital markets return 8 percent on average, then venture capital has to earn a substantial premium over that. So you will need to have expected returns of 20 percent to 25 percent and actual returns of 17 percent to 18 percent."

Where are investors seeking these kinds of return today? The Internet still gets some interest, but "clean tech," which represents a host of technologies propelled by public concern over carbon emissions and global warming, is beginning to attract attention. Established companies are seeking ways to reduce the impact of pollution produced by their factories, and startups are offering environmentally friendly solutions. Other environmental problems also create investment opportunities. Freshwater shortages in some parts of the world have already led countries to turn to desalinization, and private firms will have a role in its delivery. In the developed world, health care and medical research remain attractive fields for venture investors.

Like all investors, venture capitalists seek a return that compensates them for risking their capital. In this chapter, you will learn how risk is measured and what methods are used to minimize risk in a portfolio.

> Venture capital is a form of private equity in which capital is raised in private markets as opposed to the public markets. How can the venture capitalists eventually capitalize on their investments?

227

5.1 | Risk and Return Fundamentals

To maximize share price, the financial manager must learn to assess two key determinants: risk and return.[1] Each financial decision presents certain risk and return characteristics, and the unique combination of these characteristics has an impact on share price. Risk can be viewed as it is related either to a single asset or to a **portfolio**—a collection, or group, of assets. We will look at both, beginning with the risk of a single asset. First, though, it is important to introduce some fundamental ideas about risk, return, and risk preferences.

portfolio
A collection, or group, of assets.

Risk Defined

risk
The chance of financial loss or, more formally, the *variability of returns associated with a given asset.*

In the most basic sense, **risk** is the chance of financial loss. Assets having greater chances of loss are viewed as more risky than those with lesser chances of loss. More formally, the term *risk* is used interchangeably with *uncertainty* to refer to the *variability of returns associated with a given asset.* A $1,000 government bond that guarantees its holder $5 interest after 30 days has no risk, because there is no variability associated with the return. A $1,000 investment in a firm's common stock, which over the same 30 days may earn anywhere from $0 to $10, is very risky because of the high variability of its return. The more nearly certain the return from an asset, the less variability and therefore the less risk.

Some risks directly affect both financial managers and shareholders. Table 5.1 briefly describes the common sources of risk that affect both firms and their shareholders. As you can see, business risk and financial risk are more firm-specific and therefore are of greatest interest to financial managers. Interest rate, liquidity, and market risks are more shareholder-specific and therefore are of greatest interest to stockholders. Event, exchange rate, purchasing-power, and tax risk directly affect both firms and shareholders. The *Focus on Ethics* box on page 230 addresses another risk that affects both firms and shareholders—moral risk. A number of these risks are discussed in more detail later in this text. Clearly, both financial managers and shareholders must assess these and other risks as they make investment decisions.

Return Defined

return
The total gain or loss experienced on an investment over a given period of time; calculated by dividing the asset's cash distributions during the period, plus change in value, by its beginning-of-period investment value.

Obviously, if we are going to assess risk on the basis of variability of return, we need to be certain we know what *return* is and how to measure it. The **return** is the total gain or loss experienced on an investment over a given period of time. It is commonly measured as cash distributions during the period plus the change in value, expressed as a percentage of the beginning-of-period investment value. The expression for calculating the rate of return earned on any asset over period t, r_t, is commonly defined as

$$r_t = \frac{C_t + P_t - P_{t-1}}{P_{t-1}}$$

(5.1)

---

1. Two important points should be recognized here: (1) Although for convenience the publicly traded corporation is being discussed, the risk and return concepts presented apply to all firms; and (2) concern centers only on the wealth of common stockholders, because they are the "residual owners" whose returns are in no way specified in advance.

TABLE 5.1	**Popular Sources of Risk Affecting Financial Managers and Shareholders**
Source of risk	Description
Firm-Specific Risks	
Business risk	The chance that the firm will be unable to cover its operating costs. Level is driven by the firm's revenue stability and the structure of its operating costs (fixed versus variable).
Financial risk	The chance that the firm will be unable to cover its financial obligations. Level is driven by the predictability of the firm's operating cash flows and its fixed-cost financial obligations.
Shareholder-Specific Risks	
Interest rate risk	The chance that changes in interest rates will adversely affect the value of an investment. Most investments lose value when the interest rate rises and increase in value when it falls.
Liquidity risk	The chance that an investment cannot be easily liquidated at a reasonable price. Liquidity is significantly affected by the size and depth of the market in which an investment is customarily traded.
Market risk	The chance that the value of an investment will decline because of market factors that are independent of the investment (such as economic, political, and social events). In general, the more a given investment's value responds to the market, the greater its risk; the less it responds, the smaller its risk.
Firm and Shareholder Risks	
Event risk	The chance that a totally unexpected event will have a significant effect on the value of the firm or a specific investment. These infrequent events, such as government-mandated withdrawal of a popular prescription drug, typically affect only a small group of firms or investments.
Exchange rate risk	The exposure of future expected cash flows to fluctuations in the currency exchange rate. The greater the chance of undesirable exchange rate fluctuations, the greater the risk of the cash flows and therefore the lower the value of the firm or investment.
Purchasing-power risk	The chance that changing price levels caused by inflation or deflation in the economy will adversely affect the firm's or investment's cash flows and value. Typically, firms or investments with cash flows that move with general price levels have a low purchasing-power risk, and those with cash flows that do not move with general price levels have a high purchasing-power risk.
Tax risk	The chance that unfavorable changes in tax laws will occur. Firms and investments with values that are sensitive to tax law changes are more risky.

where

r_t = actual, expected, or required rate of return[2] during period t

C_t = cash (flow) received from the asset investment in the time period $t - 1$ to t

P_t = price (value) of asset at time t

P_{t-1} = price (value) of asset at time $t - 1$

---

2. The terms *expected return* and *required return* are used interchangeably throughout this text, because in an efficient market (discussed later) they would be expected to be equal. The actual return is an *ex post* value, whereas expected and required returns are *ex ante* values. Therefore, the actual return may be greater than, equal to, or less than the expected/required return.

IN PRACTICE

Focus on Ethics — What about Moral Risk?

The poster boy for "moral risk," exemplifying the devastating effects of unethical behavior for a company's investors, has to be Nick Leeson. As a futures trader, Leeson violated his bank's investing rules while secretly placing huge bets on the direction of the Japanese stock market. When those bets proved wrong, the $1.24 billion losses resulted in the 1995 demise of the centuries-old Barings Bank. More than any other single episode in world financial history, Leeson's misdeeds proved the importance of character in the financial industry.

Problems with ethics can be found throughout the business world. In a survey conducted by *CFO* magazine, 41 percent of surveyed chief financial officers admitted ethical problems in their organizations, and 48 percent of surveyed employees admitted engaging in unethical practices such as cheating on expense accounts or forging signatures. In the 2004 survey, 47 percent of CFOs said that they felt pressure from CEOs to use aggressive accounting to "make the numbers work." One

of the main reasons cited for accounting fraud uncovered in recent years was the pressure to "hit the numbers" expected by some Wall Street security analysts. The good news was that the same survey found CFOs standing up to CEO pressure and improving ethical standards in their departments, thanks to the 2002 Sarbanes-Oxley Act.

What can be done to minimize moral risk? A first step is to build awareness through a code of ethics. Almost all *Fortune* 500 companies and about half of all companies have an ethics code that spells out general principles of right and wrong conduct. Because ethical codes are often faulted for being vague and abstract, companies such as **Texas Instruments** have written detailed standards of conduct. Organizations also reveal their ethical commitment in other ways. Some administer honesty tests prior to hiring new workers; others require ethics training of mid-level managers. Additional methods of strengthening corporate ethics include providing whistle-blower protection for employees with ethics-related

concerns, establishing an *ethics director*, and evaluating managers' ethics in performance reviews.

The trend may be toward higher ethical standards, according to a study conducted by five Baylor University professors. They surveyed 10,000 U.S. business professionals three times over a 20-year period, asking the respondents to judge acceptable responses to 16 common business situations with questionable ethical dimensions. The responses, compiled into a single "ethics index" for each survey year, show an upward trend, according to the study published in 2006. Debate continues, however, over whether there is a gap between attitudes and actual actions. People who otherwise might do the right thing can be pressured to do something wrong.

■ *Is "hitting the numbers" an appropriate goal, given the Chapter 1 contrast of profit and shareholder wealth maximization? If not, why do executives emphasize it?*

The return, r_t, reflects the combined effect of cash flow, C_t, and changes in value, $P_t - P_{t-1}$, over period t.[3]

Equation 5.1 is used to determine the rate of return over a time period as short as 1 day or as long as 10 years or more. However, in most cases, t is 1 year, and r therefore represents an annual rate of return.

---

3. The beginning-of-period value, P_{t-1}, and the end-of-period value, P_t, are not necessarily *realized values*. They are often *unrealized*, which means that although the asset was *not* actually purchased at time $t-1$ and sold at time t, values P_{t-1} and P_t *could* have been realized had those transactions been made.

Example

Robin's Gameroom, a high-traffic video arcade, wishes to determine the return on two of its video machines, Conqueror and Demolition. Conqueror was purchased 1 year ago for $20,000 and currently has a market value of $21,500. During the year, it generated $800 of after-tax cash receipts. Demolition was purchased 4 years ago; its value in the year just completed declined from $12,000 to $11,800. During the year, it generated $1,700 of after-tax cash receipts. Substituting into Equation 5.1, we can calculate the annual rate of return, r, for each video machine.

Conqueror (C):

$$r_C = \frac{\$800 + \$21,500 - \$20,000}{\$20,000} = \frac{\$2,300}{\$20,000} = \underline{\underline{11.5\%}}$$

Demolition (D):

$$r_D = \frac{\$1,700 + \$11,800 - \$12,000}{\$12,000} = \frac{\$1,500}{\$12,000} = \underline{\underline{12.5\%}}$$

Although the market value of Demolition declined during the year, its cash flow caused it to earn a higher rate of return than Conqueror earned during the same period. Clearly, the combined impact of cash flow and changes in value, as measured by the rate of return, is important.

Historical Returns

Investment returns vary both over time and between different types of investments. By averaging historical returns over a long period of time, it becomes possible to eliminate the impact of market and other types of risk. This enables the financial decision maker to focus on the differences in return that are attributable primarily to the types of investment. Table 5.2 shows the average annual rates of return for a number of popular security investments (and inflation) over the 81-year period January 1, 1926, through December 31, 2006. Each rate represents the average annual rate of return an investor would have realized had he or she purchased the investment on January 1, 1926, and sold it on December 31,

TABLE 5.2	Historical Returns for Selected Security Investments (1926–2006)
Investment	**Average annual return**
Large-company stocks	12.3%
Small-company stocks	17.4
Long-term corporate bonds	6.2
Long-term government bonds	5.8
U.S. Treasury bills	3.8
Inflation	3.1%

Source: Stocks, Bonds, Bills, and Inflation, 2007 Yearbook (Chicago: Ibbotson Associates, Inc., 2007).

2006. You can see that significant differences exist between the average annual rates of return realized on the various types of stocks, bonds, and bills shown. Later in this chapter, we will see how these differences in return can be linked to differences in the risk of each of these investments.

Risk Preferences

Feelings about risk differ among managers (and firms).[4] Thus it is important to specify a generally acceptable level of risk. The three basic risk preference behaviors—risk-averse, risk-indifferent, and risk-seeking—are depicted graphically in Figure 5.1.

risk-indifferent
The attitude toward risk in which no change in return would be required for an increase in risk.

risk-averse
The attitude toward risk in which an increased return would be required for an increase in risk.

risk-seeking
The attitude toward risk in which a decreased return would be accepted for an increase in risk.

Hint Remember that most *shareholders* are risk-averse. Like risk-averse managers, for a given increase in risk, they require an increase in return on their investment in that firm.

- For the **risk-indifferent** manager, the required return does not change as risk goes from x_1 to x_2. In essence, no change in return would be required for the increase in risk. Clearly, this attitude is nonsensical in almost any business context.

- For the **risk-averse** manager, the required return increases for an increase in risk. Because they shy away from risk, these managers require higher expected returns to compensate them for taking greater risk.

- For the **risk-seeking** manager, the required return decreases for an increase in risk. Theoretically, because they enjoy risk, these managers are willing to give up some return to take more risk. However, such behavior would not be likely to benefit the firm.

Most managers are risk-averse; for a given increase in risk, they require an increase in return. They generally tend to be conservative rather than aggressive when accepting risk for their firm. Accordingly, a *risk-averse financial manager requiring higher returns for greater risk is assumed throughout this text.*

FIGURE 5.1

Risk Preferences
Risk preference behaviors

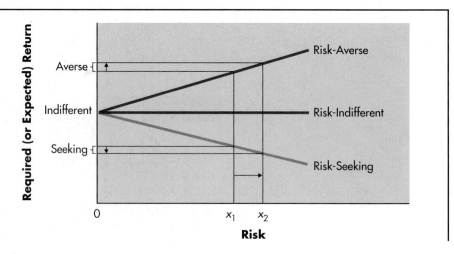

4. The risk preferences of the managers should, in theory, be consistent with the risk preferences of the firm. Although the *agency problem* suggests that, in practice, managers may not behave in a manner consistent with the firm's risk preferences, it is assumed here that they do. Therefore, the managers' risk preferences and those of the firm are assumed to be identical.

REVIEW QUESTIONS

5–1 What is *risk* in the context of financial decision making?

5–2 Define *return*, and describe how to find the rate of return on an investment.

5–3 Compare the following risk preferences: (**a**) risk-averse, (**b**) risk-indifferent, and (**c**) risk-seeking. Which is most common among financial managers?

5.2 | Risk of a Single Asset

The concept of risk can be developed by first considering a single asset held in isolation. We can look at expected-return behaviors to assess risk, and use statistics to measure it.

Risk Assessment

scenario analysis
An approach for assessing risk that uses several possible alternative outcomes (scenarios) to obtain a sense of the variability among returns.

Scenario analysis and probability distributions can be used to assess the general level of risk embodied in a given asset.

Scenario Analysis

Scenario analysis uses several possible alternative outcomes (scenarios) to obtain a sense of the variability among returns.[5] One common method involves considering pessimistic (worst), most likely (expected), and optimistic (best) outcomes and the returns associated with them for a given asset. In this case, the asset's risk can be measured by the range of returns. The **range** is found by subtracting the return associated with the pessimistic outcome from the return associated with the optimistic outcome. The greater the range, the more variability, or risk, the asset is said to have.

range
A measure of an asset's risk, which is found by subtracting the return associated with the pessimistic (worst) outcome from the return associated with the optimistic (best) outcome.

Example

Norman Company, a custom golf equipment manufacturer, wants to choose the better of two investments, A and B. Each requires an initial outlay of $10,000, and each has a *most likely* annual rate of return of 15%. Management has estimated returns associated with each investment's *pessimistic* and *optimistic* outcomes. The three estimates for each asset, along with its range, are given in Table 5.3 (see page 234). Asset A appears to be less risky than asset B; its range of 4% (17% − 13%) is less than the range of 16% (23% − 7%) for asset B. The risk-averse decision maker would prefer asset A over asset B, because A offers the same most likely return as B (15%) with lower risk (smaller range).

Although the use of scenario analysis and the range is rather crude, it does give the decision maker a feel for the behavior of returns, which can be used to estimate the risk involved.

---

5. The term *scenario analysis* is intentionally used in a general rather than a technically correct fashion here to simplify this discussion. A more technical and precise definition and discussion of this technique and of "sensitivity analysis" are presented in Chapter 10.

TABLE 5.3	Assets A and B	
	Asset A	Asset B
Initial investment	$10,000	$10,000
Annual rate of return		
Pessimistic	13%	7%
Most likely	15%	15%
Optimistic	17%	23%
Range	4%	16%

probability
The *chance* that a given outcome will occur.

probability distribution
A model that relates probabilities to the associated outcomes.

Probability Distributions

Probability distributions provide a more quantitative insight into an asset's risk. The **probability** of a given outcome is its *chance* of occurring. An outcome with an 80 percent probability of occurrence would be expected to occur 8 out of 10 times. An outcome with a probability of 100 percent is certain to occur. Outcomes with a probability of zero will never occur.

Example

Norman Company's past estimates indicate that the probabilities of the pessimistic, most likely, and optimistic outcomes are 25%, 50%, and 25%, respectively. Note that the sum of these probabilities must equal 100%; that is, they must be based on all the alternatives considered.

---

bar chart
The simplest type of probability distribution; shows only a limited number of outcomes and associated probabilities for a given event.

continuous probability distribution
A probability distribution showing all the possible outcomes and associated probabilities for a given event.

A **probability distribution** is a model that relates probabilities to the associated outcomes. The simplest type of probability distribution is the **bar chart,** which shows only a limited number of outcome–probability coordinates. The bar charts for Norman Company's assets A and B are shown in Figure 5.2. Although both assets have the same most likely return, the range of return is much greater, or more dispersed, for asset B than for asset A—16 percent versus 4 percent.

If we knew all the possible outcomes and associated probabilities, we could develop a **continuous probability distribution.** This type of distribution can be thought of as a bar chart for a very large number of outcomes.[6] Figure 5.3 presents

---

FIGURE 5.2

Bar Charts
Bar charts for asset A's and asset B's returns

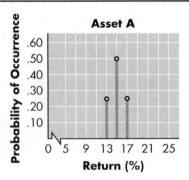

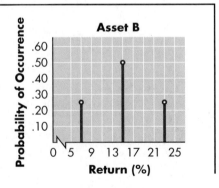

---

6. To develop a continuous probability distribution, one must have data on a large number of historical occurrences for a given event. Then, by developing a frequency distribution indicating how many times each outcome has occurred over the given time horizon, one can convert these data into a probability distribution. Probability distributions for risky events can also be developed by using *simulation*—a process discussed briefly in Chapter 10.

FIGURE 5.3

Continuous Probability Distributions
Continuous probability distributions for asset A's and asset B's returns

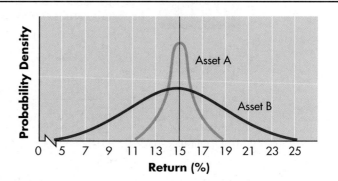

continuous probability distributions for assets A and B.[7] Note that although assets A and B have the same most likely return (15 percent), the distribution of returns for asset B has much greater *dispersion* than the distribution for asset A. Clearly, asset B is more risky than asset A.

Risk Measurement

In addition to considering its *range,* the risk of an asset can be measured quantitatively by using statistics. Here we consider two statistics—the standard deviation and the coefficient of variation—that can be used to measure the variability of asset returns.

Standard Deviation

standard deviation (σ_r)
The most common statistical indicator of an asset's risk; it measures the dispersion around the *expected value.*

expected value of a return ($\bar{r}$)
The most likely return on a given asset.

The most common statistical indicator of an asset's risk is the **standard deviation, σ_r,** which measures the dispersion around the *expected value.*[8] The **expected value of a return, $\bar{r}$,** is the most likely return on an asset. It is calculated as follows:[9]

$$\bar{r} = \sum_{j=1}^{n} r_j \times Pr_j \tag{5.2}$$

where

r_j = return for the *j*th outcome

Pr_j = probability of occurrence of the *j*th outcome

n = number of outcomes considered

---

7. The continuous distribution's probabilities change because of the large number of additional outcomes considered. The area under each of the curves is equal to 1, which means that 100% of the outcomes, or all the possible outcomes, are considered.

8. Although risk is typically viewed as determined by the dispersion of outcomes around an expected value, many people believe that risk exists only when outcomes are below the expected value, because only returns below the expected value are considered bad. Nevertheless, the common approach is to view risk as determined by the variability on either side of the expected value, because the greater this variability, the less confident one can be of the outcomes associated with an investment.

9. The formula for finding the expected value of return, $\bar{r}$, when all of the outcomes, r_j, are known *and* their related probabilities are assumed to be equal, is a simple arithmetic average:

$$\bar{r} = \frac{\sum_{j=1}^{n} r_j}{n} \tag{5.2a}$$

where *n* is the number of observations. Equation 5.2 is emphasized in this chapter because returns and related probabilities are often available.

TABLE 5.4   Expected Values of Returns for Assets A and B

Possible outcomes	Probability (1)	Returns (2)	Weighted value [(1) × (2)] (3)
Asset A			
Pessimistic	.25	13%	3.25%
Most likely	.50	15	7.50
Optimistic	.25	17	4.25
Total	1.00	Expected return	15.00%
Asset B			
Pessimistic	.25	7%	1.75%
Most likely	.50	15	7.50
Optimistic	.25	23	5.75
Total	1.00	Expected return	15.00%

Example

The expected values of returns for Norman Company's assets A and B are presented in Table 5.4. Column 1 gives the Pr_j's and column 2 gives the r_j's. In each case n equals 3. The expected value for each asset's return is 15%.

The expression for the *standard deviation of returns*, σ_r, is[10]

$$\sigma_r = \sqrt{\sum_{j=1}^{n} (r_j - \bar{r})^2 \times Pr_j}$$ (5.3)

In general, the higher the standard deviation, the greater the risk.

Example

Table 5.5 presents the standard deviations for Norman Company's assets A and B, based on the earlier data. The standard deviation for asset A is 1.41%, and the standard deviation for asset B is 5.66%. The higher risk of asset B is clearly reflected in its higher standard deviation.

Historical Returns and Risk[11]   We can now use the standard deviation as a measure of risk to assess the historical (1926–2006) investment return data in Table 5.2. Table 5.6 repeats the historical returns in column 1 and shows the

10. The formula that is commonly used to find the standard deviation of returns, σ_r, in a situation in which *all* outcomes are known *and* their related probabilities are assumed equal, is

$$\sigma_r = \sqrt{\frac{\sum_{j=1}^{n} (r_j - \bar{r})^2}{n - 1}}$$ (5.3a)

where n is the number of observations. Equation 5.3 is emphasized in this chapter because returns and related probabilities are often available.

11. In a fashion similar to returns, analysts can use the standard deviation to measure risk on an *ex post* basis using historical or actual returns or on an *ex ante* basis using expected or required returns. Therefore, the actual risk may be greater than, equal to, or less than the expected risk.

TABLE 5.5	The Calculation of the Standard Deviation of the Returns for Assets A and B[a]

j	r_j	$\bar{r}$	$r_j - \bar{r}$	$(r_j - \bar{r})^2$	Pr_j	$(r_j - \bar{r})^2 \times Pr_j$
			Asset A			
1	13%	15%	−2%	4%	.25	1%
2	15	15	0	0	.50	0
3	17	15	2	4	.25	1

$$\sum_{j=1}^{3}(r_j - \bar{r})^2 \times Pr_j = 2\%$$

$$\sigma_{r_A} = \sqrt{\sum_{j=1}^{3}(r_j - \bar{r})^2 \times Pr_j} = \sqrt{2\%} = \underline{\underline{1.41\%}}$$

j	r_j	$\bar{r}$	$r_j - \bar{r}$	$(r_j - \bar{r})^2$	Pr_j	$(r_j - \bar{r})^2 \times Pr_j$
			Asset B			
1	7%	15%	−8%	64%	.25	16%
2	15	15	0	0	.50	0
3	23	15	8	64	.25	16

$$\sum_{j=1}^{3}(r_j - \bar{r})^2 \times Pr_j = 32\%$$

$$\sigma_{r_B} = \sqrt{\sum_{j=1}^{3}(r_j - \bar{r})^2 \times Pr_j} = \sqrt{32\%} = \underline{\underline{5.66\%}}$$

[a]Calculations in this table are made in percentage form rather than decimal form—e.g., 13% rather than 0.13. As a result, some of the intermediate computations may appear to be inconsistent with those that would result from using decimal form. Regardless, the resulting standard deviations are correct and identical to those that would result from using decimal rather than percentage form.

TABLE 5.6	Historical Returns, Standard Deviations, and Coefficients of Variation for Selected Security Investments (1926–2006)

Investment	Average annual return (1)	Standard deviation (2)	Coefficient of variation[a] (3)
Large-company stocks	12.3%	20.1%	1.63
Small-company stocks	17.4	32.7	1.88
Long-term corporate bonds	6.2	8.5	1.37
Long-term government bonds	5.8	9.2	1.59
U.S. Treasury bills	3.8	3.1	0.82
Inflation	3.1%	4.3%	1.39

[a]Calculated by dividing the standard deviation in column 2 by the average annual return in column 1.

Source: Stocks, Bonds, Bills, and Inflation, 2007 Yearbook (Chicago: Ibbotson Associates, Inc., 2007).

FIGURE 5.4

Bell-Shaped Curve
Normal probability
distribution, with ranges

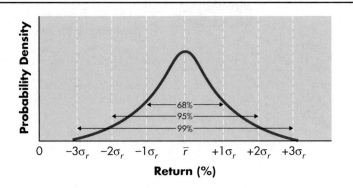

standard deviations associated with each of them in column 2. A close relationship can be seen between the investment returns and the standard deviations: Investments with higher returns have higher standard deviations. Because higher standard deviations are associated with greater risk, the historical data confirm the existence of a positive relationship between risk and return. That relationship reflects *risk aversion* by market participants, who require higher returns as compensation for greater risk. The historical data in columns 1 and 2 of Table 5.6 clearly show that during the 1926–2006 period, investors were rewarded with higher returns on higher-risk investments.

**normal probability
distribution**
A symmetrical probability
distribution whose shape
resembles a "bell-shaped"
curve.

Normal Distribution   A **normal probability distribution,** depicted in Figure 5.4, always resembles a "bell-shaped" curve. It is symmetrical: From the peak of the graph, the curve's extensions are mirror images (reflections) of each other. The symmetry of the curve means that half the probability is associated with the values to the left of the peak and half with the values to the right. As noted on the figure, for normal probability distributions, 68 percent of the possible outcomes will lie between ±1 standard deviation from the expected value, 95 percent of all outcomes will lie between ±2 standard deviations from the expected value, and 99 percent of all outcomes will lie between ±3 standard deviations from the expected value.[12]

Example

If we assume that the probability distribution of returns for the Norman Company is normal, 68% of the possible outcomes would have a return ranging between 13.59% and 16.41% for asset A and between 9.34% and 20.66% for asset B; 95% of the possible return outcomes would range between 12.18% and 17.82% for asset A and between 3.68% and 26.32% for asset B; and 99% of the possible return outcomes would range between 10.77% and 19.23% for asset A and between −1.98% and 31.98% for asset B. The greater risk of asset B is clearly reflected in its much wider range of possible returns for each level of confidence (68%, 95%, and so on).

---

12. Tables of values indicating the probabilities associated with various deviations from the expected value of a normal distribution can be found in any basic statistics text. These values can be used to establish confidence limits and make inferences about possible outcomes. Such applications can be found in most basic statistics and upper-level managerial finance textbooks.

Coefficient of Variation

coefficient of variation (CV)
A measure of relative dispersion that is useful in comparing the risks of assets with differing expected returns.

The **coefficient of variation, CV,** is a measure of relative dispersion that is useful in comparing the risks of assets with differing expected returns. Equation 5.4 gives the expression for the coefficient of variation:

$$CV = \frac{\sigma_r}{\bar{r}} \tag{5.4}$$

The higher the coefficient of variation, the greater the risk and therefore the higher the expected return. This relationship can be seen by comparing the coefficients of variation in column 3 of Table 5.6, which shows historical 1926–2006 investment data, with the average annual returns in column 1. As with the standard deviations in column 2, higher returns are associated with higher coefficients of variation.

Example

When the standard deviations (from Table 5.5) and the expected returns (from Table 5.4) for assets A and B are substituted into Equation 5.4, the coefficients of variation for A and B are 0.094 (1.41% ÷ 15%) and 0.377 (5.66% ÷ 15%), respectively. Asset B has the higher coefficient of variation and is therefore more risky than asset A—which we already know from the standard deviation. (Because both assets have the same expected return, the coefficient of variation has not provided any new information.)

The real utility of the coefficient of variation comes in comparing the risks of assets that have *different* expected returns.

Example

A firm wants to select the less risky of two alternative assets—C and D. The expected return, standard deviation, and coefficient of variation for each of these assets' returns are

Statistics	Asset C	Asset D
(1) Expected return	12%	20%
(2) Standard deviation	9%[a]	10%
(3) Coefficient of variation [(2) ÷ (1)]	0.75	0.50[a]

[a]Preferred asset using the given risk measure.

Judging solely on the basis of their standard deviations, the firm would prefer asset C, which has a lower standard deviation than asset D (9% versus 10%). However, management would be making a serious error in choosing asset C over asset D, because the dispersion—the risk—of the asset, as reflected in the coefficient of variation, is lower for D (0.50) than for C (0.75). Clearly, using the coefficient of variation to compare asset risk is effective because it also considers the relative size, or expected return, of the assets.

Personal Finance Example   Marilyn Ansbro is reviewing stocks for inclusion in her investment portfolio. The stock she wishes to analyze is Danhaus Industries, Inc. (DII), a diversified manufacturer of pet products. One of her key concerns is risk; as a rule she will invest only in stocks with a coefficient of variation of returns below 0.75. She has gathered price and dividend data shown below for DII over the past 3 years, 2007–2009, and assumes that each year's return is equally probable.

Year	Stock Price Beginning	End	Dividend paid
2007	$35.00	$36.50	$3.50
2008	36.50	34.50	3.50
2009	34.50	35.00	4.00

Substituting the price and dividend data for each year into Equation 5.1, we get:

Year	Returns
2007	[$3.50 + ($36.50 − $35.00)]/$35.00 = $5.00 / $35.00 = 14.3%
2008	[$3.50 + ($34.50 − $36.50)]/$36.50 = $1.50 / $36.50 = 4.1%
2009	[$4.00 + ($35.00 − $34.50)]/$34.50 = $4.50 / $34.50 = 13.0%

Substituting into Equation 5.2a, given that the returns are equally probable, we get the average return, $\bar{r}_{2007-2009}$:

$$\bar{r}_{2007-2009} = (14.3\% + 4.1\% + 13.0\%)/3 = \mathbf{10.5\%}$$

Substituting the average return and annual returns into Equation 5.3a, we get the standard deviation, $\sigma_{r2007-2009}$:

$$\sigma_{r2007-2009} = \sqrt{[(14.3\% - 10.5\%)^2 + (4.1\% - 10.5\%)^2 + (13.0\% - 10.5\%)^2]/(3-1)}$$
$$= \sqrt{(14.44\% + 40.96\% + 6.25\%)/2} = \sqrt{30.825\%} = 5.6\%$$

Finally, substituting the standard deviation of returns and the average return into Equation 5.4, we get the coefficient of variation, CV:

$$CV = 5.6\%/10.5\% = \mathbf{0.53}$$

Because the coefficient of variation of returns on the DII stock over the 2007–2009 period of 0.53 is well below Marilyn's maximum coefficient of variation of 0.75, she concludes that the DII stock would be an acceptable investment.

REVIEW QUESTIONS

5–4   Explain how the *range* is used in scenario analysis.
5–5   What does a plot of the *probability distribution* of outcomes show a decision maker about an asset's risk?
5–6   What relationship exists between the size of the *standard deviation* and the degree of asset risk?
5–7   When is the *coefficient of variation* preferred over the standard deviation for comparing asset risk?

5.3 | Risk of a Portfolio

In real-world situations, the risk of any single investment would not be viewed independently of other assets. (We did so for teaching purposes.) New investments must be considered in light of their impact on the risk and return of the *portfolio* of assets.[13] The financial manager's goal is to create an **efficient portfolio**, one that maximizes return for a given level of risk or minimizes risk for a given level of return. We therefore need a way to measure the return and the standard deviation of a portfolio of assets. Once we can do that, we will look at the statistical concept of *correlation*, which underlies the process of diversification that is used to develop an efficient portfolio.

efficient portfolio
A portfolio that maximizes return for a given level of risk or minimizes risk for a given level of return.

Portfolio Return and Standard Deviation

The *return on a portfolio* is a weighted average of the returns on the individual assets from which it is formed. We can use Equation 5.5 to find the portfolio return, r_p:

$$r_p = (w_1 \times r_1) + (w_2 \times r_2) + \cdots + (w_n \times r_n) = \sum_{j=1}^{n} w_j \times r_j \qquad (5.5)$$

where

w_j = proportion of the portfolio's total dollar value represented by asset j

r_j = return on asset j

Of course, $\sum_{j=1}^{n} w_j = 1$, which means that 100 percent of the portfolio's assets must be included in this computation.

The *standard deviation of a portfolio's returns* is found by applying the formula for the standard deviation of a single asset. Specifically, Equation 5.3 is used when the probabilities of the returns are known, and Equation 5.3a (from footnote 10) is applied when the outcomes are known and their related probabilities of occurrence are assumed to be equal.

Example   Assume that we wish to determine the expected value and standard deviation of returns for portfolio XY, created by combining equal portions (50%) of assets X and Y. The forecasted returns of assets X and Y for each of the next 5 years (2010–2014) are given in columns 1 and 2, respectively, in part A of Table 5.7 (page 242). In column 3, the weights of 50% for both assets X and Y along with their respective returns from columns 1 and 2 are substituted into Equation 5.5. Column 4 shows the results of the calculation—an expected portfolio return of 12% for each year, 2010 to 2014.

Furthermore, as shown in part B of Table 5.7, the expected value of these portfolio returns over the 5-year period is also 12% (calculated by using Equation 5.2a, in footnote 9). In part C of Table 5.7, portfolio XY's standard

---

13. The portfolio of a firm, which would consist of its total assets, is not differentiated from the portfolio of an owner, which would probably contain a variety of different investment vehicles (i.e., assets). The differing characteristics of these two types of portfolios should become clear upon completion of Chapter 10.

TABLE 5.7	Expected Return, Expected Value, and Standard Deviation of Returns for Portfolio XY

A. Expected portfolio returns

Year	Forecasted return Asset X (1)	Forecasted return Asset Y (2)	Portfolio return calculation[a] (3)	Expected portfolio return, r_p (4)
2010	8%	16%	$(.50 \times 8\%) + (.50 \times 16\%) =$	12%
2011	10	14	$(.50 \times 10\%) + (.50 \times 14\%) =$	12
2012	12	12	$(.50 \times 12\%) + (.50 \times 12\%) =$	12
2013	14	10	$(.50 \times 14\%) + (.50 \times 10\%) =$	12
2014	16	8	$(.50 \times 16\%) + (.50 \times 8\%) =$	12

B. Expected value of portfolio returns, 2010–2014[b]

$$\bar{r}_p = \frac{12\% + 12\% + 12\% + 12\% + 12\%}{5} = \frac{60\%}{5} = \underline{\underline{12\%}}$$

C. Standard deviation of expected portfolio returns[c]

$$\sigma_{r_p} = \sqrt{\frac{(12\% - 12\%)^2 + (12\% - 12\%)^2 + (12\% - 12\%)^2 + (12\% - 12\%)^2 + (12\% - 12\%)^2}{5 - 1}}$$

$$= \sqrt{\frac{0\% + 0\% + 0\% + 0\% + 0\%}{4}}$$

$$= \sqrt{\frac{0\%}{4}} = \underline{\underline{0\%}}$$

[a]Using Equation 5.5.
[b]Using Equation 5.2a found in footnote 9.
[c]Using Equation 5.3a found in footnote 10.

correlation
A statistical measure of the relationship between any two series of numbers representing data of any kind.

positively correlated
Describes two series that move in the same direction.

negatively correlated
Describes two series that move in opposite directions.

deviation is calculated to be 0% (using Equation 5.3a, in footnote 10). This value should not be surprising because the expected return each year is the same—12%. No variability is exhibited in the expected returns from year to year.

Correlation

Correlation is a statistical measure of the relationship between any two series of numbers. The numbers may represent data of any kind, from returns to test scores. If two series move in the same direction, they are **positively correlated**. If the series move in opposite directions, they are **negatively correlated**.[14]

---

14. The general *long-term trends* of two series could be the same (both increasing or both decreasing) or different (one increasing, the other decreasing), and the correlation of their *short-term (point-to-point) movements* in both situations could be either positive or negative. In other words, the pattern of movement around the trends could be correlated independent of the actual relationship between the trends. Further clarification of this seemingly inconsistent behavior can be found in most basic statistics texts.

FIGURE 5.5

Correlations
The correlation between
series M and series N

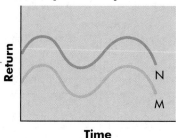

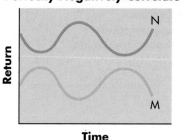

correlation coefficient
A measure of the degree
of correlation between two
series.

**perfectly positively
correlated**
Describes two *positively
correlated* series that have a
correlation coefficient of +1.

**perfectly negatively
correlated**
Describes two *negatively
correlated* series that have a
correlation coefficient of −1.

uncorrelated
Describes two series that lack
any interaction and therefore
have a *correlation coefficient*
close to zero.

The degree of correlation is measured by the **correlation coefficient,** which ranges from +1 for **perfectly positively correlated** series to −1 for **perfectly negatively correlated** series. These two extremes are depicted for series M and N in Figure 5.5. The perfectly positively correlated series move exactly together; the perfectly negatively correlated series move in exactly opposite directions.

Diversification

The concept of correlation is essential to developing an efficient portfolio. To reduce overall risk, it is best to *diversify* by combining, or adding to the portfolio, assets that have a negative (or a low positive) correlation. Combining negatively correlated assets can reduce the overall variability of returns. Figure 5.6 (see page 244) shows that a portfolio containing the negatively correlated assets F and G, both of which have the same expected return, $\bar{r}$, also has that same return $\bar{r}$ but has less risk (variability) than either of the individual assets. Even if assets are not negatively correlated, the lower the positive correlation between them, the lower the resulting risk.

Some assets are **uncorrelated**—that is, there is no interaction between their returns. Combining uncorrelated assets can reduce risk, not so effectively as combining negatively correlated assets, but more effectively than combining positively correlated assets. The *correlation coefficient for uncorrelated assets is close to zero* and acts as the midpoint between perfect positive and perfect negative correlation.

The creation of a portfolio that combines two assets with perfectly positively correlated returns results in overall portfolio risk that at minimum equals that of the least risky asset and at maximum equals that of the most risky asset. However, a portfolio combining two assets with less than perfectly positive correlation *can* reduce total risk to a level below that of either of the components, which in certain situations may be zero. For example, assume that you manufacture machine tools. The business is very *cyclical,* with high sales when the economy is expanding and low sales during a recession. If you acquired another machine-tool company, with sales positively correlated with those of your firm, the combined sales would still be cyclical and risk would remain the same. Alternatively, however, you could acquire a sewing machine manufacturer, whose sales are *countercyclical.* It typically has low sales during economic expansion and high sales during recession (when consumers are more likely to make their own clothes). Combination with the sewing machine manufacturer, which has negatively correlated sales, should reduce risk.

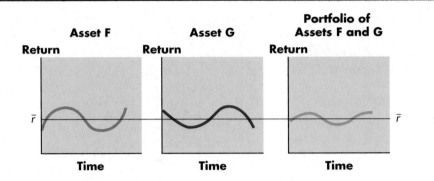

FIGURE 5.6

Diversification
Combining negatively correlated assets to reduce, or diversify, risk

---

Example

Table 5.8 presents the forecasted returns from three different assets—X, Y, and Z—over the next 5 years, along with their expected values and standard deviations. Each of the assets has an expected value of return of 12% and a standard deviation of 3.16%. The assets therefore have equal return and equal risk. The return patterns of assets X and Y are perfectly negatively correlated. They move in exactly opposite directions over time. The returns of assets X and Z are perfectly positively correlated. They move in precisely the same direction. (*Note:* The returns for X and Z are identical.)[15]

Portfolio XY   Portfolio XY (shown in Table 5.8) is created by combining equal portions of assets X and Y, the perfectly negatively correlated assets.[16] (Calculation of portfolio XY's annual expected returns, the expected value of portfolio returns, and the standard deviation of expected portfolio returns was demonstrated in Table 5.7 on page 242.) The risk in this portfolio, as reflected by its standard deviation, is reduced to 0%, whereas the expected return remains at 12%. Thus the combination results in the complete elimination of risk. Whenever assets are perfectly negatively correlated, an optimal combination (similar to the 50–50 mix in the case of assets X and Y) exists for which the resulting standard deviation will equal 0.

Portfolio XZ   Portfolio XZ (shown in Table 5.8) is created by combining equal portions of assets X and Z, the perfectly positively correlated assets. The risk in this portfolio, as reflected by its standard deviation, is unaffected by this combination. Risk remains at 3.16%, and the expected return value remains at 12%. Because assets X and Z have the same standard deviation, the minimum and maximum standard deviations are the same (3.16%).

Hint Remember, low correlation between two series of numbers is less positive and more negative—indicating greater dissimilarity of behavior of the two series.

Correlation, Diversification, Risk, and Return

In general, the lower the correlation between asset returns, the greater the potential diversification of risk. (This should be clear from the behaviors illustrated in Table 5.8.) For each pair of assets, there is a combination that will result in the

---

15. Identical return streams are used in this example to permit clear illustration of the concepts, but it is *not* necessary for return streams to be identical for them to be perfectly positively correlated. Any return streams that move (i.e., vary) exactly together—regardless of the relative magnitude of the returns—are perfectly positively correlated.

16. For illustrative purposes it has been assumed that each of the assets—X, Y, and Z—can be divided up and combined with other assets to create portfolios. This assumption is made only to permit clear illustration of the concepts. The assets are not actually divisible.

	Assets			Portfolios	
Year	X	Y	Z	XY[a] (50% X + 50% Y)	XZ[b] (50% X + 50% Z)
2010	8%	16%	8%	12%	8%
2011	10	14	10	12	10
2012	12	12	12	12	12
2013	14	10	14	12	14
2014	16	8	16	12	16
Statistics:[c]					
Expected value	12%	12%	12%	12%	12%
Standard deviation[d]	3.16%	3.16%	3.16%	0%	3.16%

TABLE 5.8   Forecasted Returns, Expected Values, and Standard Deviations for Assets X, Y, and Z and Portfolios XY and XZ

[a]Portfolio XY, which consists of 50% of asset X and 50% of asset Y, illustrates *perfect negative correlation* because these two return streams behave in completely opposite fashion over the 5-year period. Its return values shown here were calculated in part A of Table 5.7.

[b]Portfolio XZ, which consists of 50% of asset X and 50% of asset Z, illustrates *perfect positive correlation* because these two return streams behave identically over the 5-year period. Its return values were calculated by using the same method demonstrated for portfolio XY in part A of Table 5.7.

[c]Because the probabilities associated with the returns are not given, the general equations, Equation 5.2a in footnote 9 and Equation 5.3a in footnote 10, were used to calculate expected values and standard deviations, respectively. Calculation of the expected value and standard deviation for portfolio XY is demonstrated in parts B and C, respectively, of Table 5.7.

[d]The portfolio standard deviations can be directly calculated from the standard deviations of the component assets with the following formula:

$$\sigma_{r_p} = \sqrt{w_1^2\sigma_1^2 + w_2^2\sigma_2^2 + 2w_1w_2c_{1,2}\sigma_1\sigma_2}$$

where w_1 and w_2 are the proportions of component assets 1 and 2, σ_1 and σ_2 are the standard deviations of component assets 1 and 2, and $c_{1,2}$ is the correlation coefficient between the returns of component assets 1 and 2.

lowest risk (standard deviation) possible. The amount that risk can be reduced by this combination depends on the degree of correlation. Many potential combinations (assuming divisibility) could be made, but only one combination of the infinite number of possibilities will minimize risk.

Three possible correlations—perfect positive, uncorrelated, and perfect negative—illustrate the effect of correlation on the diversification of risk and return. Table 5.9 (see page 246) summarizes the impact of correlation on the range of return and risk for various two-asset portfolio combinations. The table shows that as we move from perfect positive correlation to uncorrelated assets to perfect negative correlation, the ability to reduce risk is improved. Note that in no case will a portfolio of assets be riskier than the riskiest asset included in the portfolio.

Example

A firm has calculated the expected return and the risk for each of two assets—P and Q.

Asset	Expected return, $\bar{r}$	Risk (standard deviation), σ
P	6%	3%
Q	8	8

Clearly, asset P is a lower-return, lower-risk asset than asset Q.

TABLE 5.9	Correlation, Return, and Risk for Various Two-Asset Portfolio Combinations		
Correlation coefficient	Ranges of return	Ranges of risk	
+1 (perfect positive)	Between returns of two assets held in isolation	Between risk of two assets held in isolation	
0 (uncorrelated)	Between returns of two assets held in isolation	Between risk of most risky asset and an amount less than risk of least risky asset but greater than 0	
−1 (perfect negative)	Between returns of two assets held in isolation	Between risk of most risky asset and 0	

To evaluate possible combinations, the firm considered three possible correlations—perfect positive, uncorrelated, and perfect negative. The results of the analysis are shown in Figure 5.7, using the ranges of return and risk noted above. In all cases, the return will range between the 6% return of P and the 8% return of Q. The risk, on the other hand, ranges between the individual risks of P and Q (from 3% to 8%) in the case of perfect positive correlation, from below 3% (the risk of P) and greater than 0% to 8% (the risk of Q) in the uncorrelated case, and between 0% and 8% (the risk of Q) in the perfectly negatively correlated case.

Note that *only in the case of perfect negative correlation can the risk be reduced to 0.* Also note that as the correlation becomes less positive and more negative (moving from the top of the "Ranges of Risk" figure down), the ability to reduce risk improves. The amount of risk reduction achieved depends on the proportions in which the assets are combined. Although determining the risk-minimizing combination is beyond the scope of this discussion, it is an important issue in developing portfolios of assets.

FIGURE 5.7

Possible Correlations
Range of portfolio return ($\bar{r}_p$) and risk (σ_{r_p}) for combinations of assets P and Q for various correlation coefficients

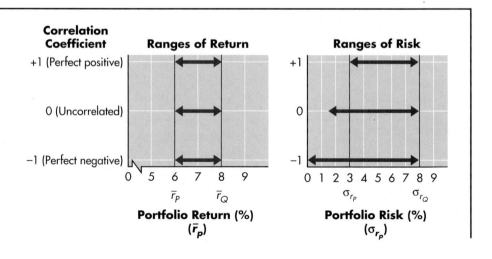

International Diversification

The ultimate example of portfolio diversification involves including foreign assets in a portfolio. The inclusion of assets from countries with business cycles that are not highly correlated with the U.S. business cycle reduces the portfolio's responsiveness to market movements and to foreign currency fluctuations.

Returns from International Diversification

Over long periods, returns from internationally diversified portfolios tend to be superior to those of purely domestic ones. This is particularly so if the U.S. economy is performing relatively poorly and the dollar is depreciating in value against most foreign currencies. At such times, the dollar returns to U.S. investors on a portfolio of foreign assets can be very attractive. However, over any single short or intermediate period, international diversification can yield subpar returns, particularly when the dollar is appreciating in value relative to other currencies. When the U.S. currency gains in value, the dollar value of a foreign-currency-denominated portfolio of assets declines. Even if this portfolio yields a satisfactory return in local currency, the return to U.S. investors will be reduced when translated into dollars. Subpar local currency portfolio returns, coupled with an appreciating dollar, can yield truly dismal dollar returns to U.S. investors.

Overall, though, the logic of international portfolio diversification assumes that these fluctuations in currency values and relative performance will average out over long periods. Compared to similar, purely domestic portfolios, an internationally diversified portfolio will tend to yield a comparable return at a lower level of risk.

Risks of International Diversification

political risk
Risk that arises from the possibility that a host government will take actions harmful to foreign investors or that political turmoil will endanger investments.

In addition to the risk induced by currency fluctuations, several other financial risks are unique to international investing. Most important is **political risk,** which arises from the possibility that a host government will take actions harmful to foreign investors or that political turmoil will endanger investments. Political risks are particularly acute in developing countries, where unstable or ideologically motivated governments may attempt to block return of profits by foreign investors or even seize (nationalize) their assets in the host country. For example, reflecting President Chavez's desire to broaden the country's socialist revolution, Venezuela issued a list of priority goods for import that excluded a large percentage of the necessary inputs to the automobile production process. As a result, Toyota halted auto production in Venezuela, and three other auto manufacturers temporarily closed or deeply cut their production there. Chavez also has forced most foreign energy firms to reduce their stakes and give up control of oil projects in Venezuela.

Even where governments do not impose exchange controls or seize assets, international investors may suffer if a shortage of hard currency prevents payment of dividends or interest to foreigners. When governments are forced to allocate scarce foreign exchange, they rarely give top priority to the interests of foreign investors. Instead, hard-currency reserves are typically used to pay for necessary imports such as food, medicine, and industrial materials and to pay interest on the

IN PRACTICE

Global Focus   An International Flavor to Risk Reduction

What do Friskies cat food, Kit Kat candy bars, aspirin, and DirecTV have in common? They are all products of non-U.S. corporations. Friskies cat food and Kit Kat bars are products of **Nestle S.A.** (Switzerland); **Bayer AG,** a German company, produces Bayer aspirin; and DirecTV is part of **News Corporation,** an Australian company. Just as we use many products of foreign companies, many U.S. corporations seek to have their products used internationally. The result is a more globally integrated economy.

One way to reduce investment risk is through diversification. Allocating a portion of one's portfolio to non-U.S. equities has historically provided better risk-adjusted returns than a portfolio consisting solely of U.S. assets. The benefit of diversification between two assets increases if the two asset classes are not well correlated, and the ben-

efit is largest when two asset classes are perfectly negatively correlated.

From the mid-1990s through 2000 when the tech-bubble burst, international and U.S. markets moved more closely together than usual. The increased correlation between the U.S. assets and international asset classes caused some to question the wisdom of international diversification. Although investors were willing to accept less risk in the form of less volatility of their portfolios, it was not easy to recognize the benefits of diversification when the diversified portfolio lagged a pure U.S. equity portfolio.

In the early part of this decade, however, the U.S. markets suffered some significant declines, leading investors to once again search for alternatives outside the U.S. markets. Adding some international diversification would have paid off handsomely

in 2006, if an investor had been lucky enough to be in one of the top ten international stock markets. Returns ranged from 37 percent in Sweden and 47 percent in Spain, to 60 percent in Indonesia, and a whopping 159 percent in Cyprus.

In terms of pure risk-adjusted reward, diversification does work. It is safe to say that international markets and U.S. markets will never be entirely correlated. The easiest way to diversify a portfolio is to include an international or global mutual fund in an investment portfolio. The professional portfolio managers have more experience in navigating the international markets than does the average investor.

■ *International mutual funds do not include any domestic assets whereas global mutual funds include both foreign and domestic assets. How might this difference affect their correlation with U.S. equity mutual funds?*

government's debt. Because most of the debt of developing countries is held by banks rather than individuals, foreign investors are often badly harmed when a country experiences political or economic problems.

For more discussion of reducing risk through international diversification, see the *Global Focus* box above.

REVIEW QUESTIONS

5–8   What is an *efficient portfolio?* How can the return and standard deviation of a portfolio be determined?

5–9   Why is the *correlation* between asset returns important? How does diversification allow risky assets to be combined so that the risk of the portfolio is less than the risk of the individual assets in it?

5–10   How does international diversification enhance risk reduction? When might international diversification result in subpar returns? What are *political risks*, and how do they affect international diversification?

5.4 | Risk and Return: The Capital Asset Pricing Model (CAPM)

The most important aspect of risk is the *overall risk* of the firm as viewed by investors in the marketplace. Overall risk significantly affects investment opportunities and—even more important—the owners' wealth. The basic theory that links risk and return for all assets is the **capital asset pricing model (CAPM)**.[17] We will use CAPM to understand the basic risk–return tradeoffs involved in all types of financial decisions.

capital asset pricing model (CAPM)
The basic theory that links risk and return for all assets.

Types of Risk

To understand the basic types of risk, consider what happens to the risk of a portfolio consisting of a single security (asset), to which we add securities randomly selected from, say, the population of all actively traded securities. Using the standard deviation of return, σ_{r_p}, to measure the total portfolio risk, Figure 5.8 depicts the behavior of the total portfolio risk (*y* axis) as more securities are added (*x* axis). With the addition of securities, the total portfolio risk declines, as a result of the effects of diversification, and tends to approach a lower limit. Research has shown that, on average, most of the risk-reduction benefits of diversification can be gained by forming portfolios containing 15 to 20 randomly selected securities.[18]

FIGURE 5.8

Risk Reduction
Portfolio risk and diversification

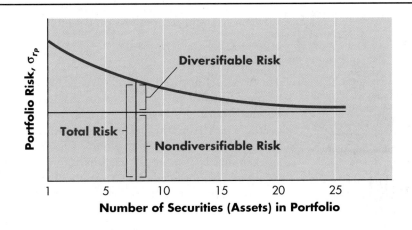

17. The initial development of this theory is generally attributed to William F. Sharpe, "Capital Asset Prices: A Theory of Market Equilibrium Under Conditions of Risk," *Journal of Finance* 19 (September 1964), pp. 425–442, and John Lintner, "The Valuation of Risk Assets and the Selection of Risky Investments in Stock Portfolios and Capital Budgets," *Review of Economics and Statistics* 47 (February 1965), pp. 13–37. A number of authors subsequently advanced, refined, and tested this now widely accepted theory.

18. See, for example, W. H. Wagner and S. C. Lau, "The Effect of Diversification on Risk," *Financial Analysts Journal* 26 (November–December 1971), pp. 48–53, and Jack Evans and Stephen H. Archer, "Diversification and the Reduction of Dispersion: An Empirical Analysis," *Journal of Finance* 23 (December 1968), pp. 761–767. A more recent study, Gerald D. Newbould and Percy S. Poon, "The Minimum Number of Stocks Needed for Diversification," *Financial Practice and Education* (Fall 1993), pp. 85–87, shows that because an investor holds but one of a large number of possible *x*-security portfolios, it is unlikely that he or she will experience the average outcome. As a consequence, the study suggests that a minimum of 40 stocks is needed to diversify a portfolio fully. This study tends to support the widespread popularity of mutual fund investments.

total risk
The combination of a security's *nondiversifiable risk* and *diversifiable risk*.

diversifiable risk
The portion of an asset's risk that is attributable to firm-specific, random causes; can be eliminated through diversification. Also called *unsystematic risk*.

nondiversifiable risk
The relevant portion of an asset's risk attributable to market factors that affect all firms; cannot be eliminated through diversification. Also called *systematic risk*.

The **total risk** of a security can be viewed as consisting of two parts:

$$\text{Total security risk} = \text{Nondiversifiable risk} + \text{Diversifiable risk} \qquad (5.6)$$

Diversifiable risk (sometimes called *unsystematic risk*) represents the portion of an asset's risk that is associated with random causes that can be eliminated through diversification. It is attributable to firm-specific events, such as strikes, lawsuits, regulatory actions, and loss of a key account. **Nondiversifiable risk** (also called *systematic risk*) is attributable to market factors that affect all firms; it cannot be eliminated through diversification. (It is the shareholder-specific *market risk* described in Table 5.1.) Factors such as war, inflation, international incidents, and political events account for nondiversifiable risk.

Because any investor can create a portfolio of assets that will eliminate virtually all diversifiable risk, *the only relevant risk is nondiversifiable risk.* Any investor or firm therefore must be concerned solely with nondiversifiable risk. The measurement of nondiversifiable risk is thus of primary importance in selecting assets with the most desired risk–return characteristics.

The Model: CAPM

The capital asset pricing model (CAPM) links nondiversifiable risk and return for all assets. We will discuss the model in five sections. The first deals with the beta coefficient, which is a measure of nondiversifiable risk. The second section presents an equation of the model itself, and the third graphically describes the relationship between risk and return. The fourth section discusses the effects of changes in inflationary expectations and risk aversion on the relationship between risk and return. The final section offers some comments on the CAPM.

Beta Coefficient

beta coefficient (b)
A relative measure of non-diversifiable risk. An *index* of the degree of movement of an asset's return in response to a change in the *market return*.

market return
The return on the market portfolio of all traded securities.

The **beta coefficient**, *b*, is a relative measure of nondiversifiable risk. It is an *index* of the degree of movement of an asset's return in response to a change in the *market return*. An asset's historical returns are used in finding the asset's beta coefficient. The **market return** is the return on the market portfolio of all traded securities. The *Standard & Poor's 500 Stock Composite Index* or some similar stock index is commonly used as the market return. Betas for actively traded stocks can be obtained from a variety of sources, but you should understand how they are derived and interpreted and how they are applied to portfolios.

Deriving Beta from Return Data   An asset's historical returns are used in finding the asset's beta coefficient. Figure 5.9 plots the relationship between the returns of two assets—R and S—and the market return. Note that the horizontal (*x*) axis measures the historical market returns and that the vertical (*y*) axis measures the individual asset's historical returns. The first step in deriving beta involves plotting the coordinates for the market return and asset returns from various points in time. Such annual "market return–asset return" coordinates are shown *for asset S only* for the years 2002 through 2009. For example, in 2009, asset S's return was 20 percent when the market return was 10 percent. By use of statistical techniques, the "characteristic line" that best explains the relationship between the asset return and the market return coordinates is fit to the data

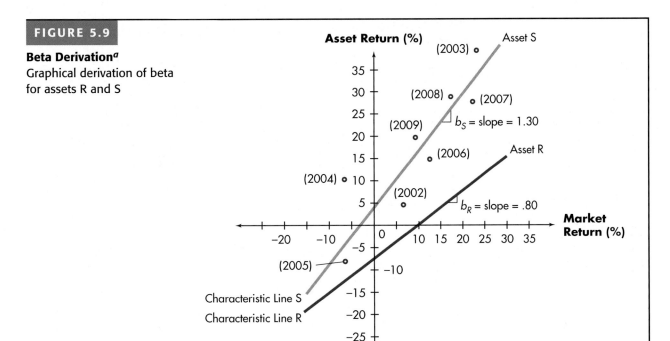

FIGURE 5.9

Beta Derivation^a
Graphical derivation of beta for assets R and S

^{a} All data points shown are associated with asset S. No data points are shown for asset R.

points.[19] The slope of this line is *beta*. The beta for asset R is about .80 and that for asset S is about 1.30. Asset S's higher beta (steeper characteristic line slope) indicates that its return is more responsive to changing market returns. *Therefore asset S is more risky than asset R.*[20]

---

19. The empirical measurement of beta is approached by using *least-squares regression analysis* to find the regression coefficient (b_j) in the equation for the "characteristic line":

$$r_j = a_j + b_j r_m + e_j$$

where

r_j = return on asset j

a_j = intercept

b_j = beta coefficient, which equals $\dfrac{Cov\ (r_j, r_m)}{\sigma_m^2}$

where

$Cov\ (r_j, r_m)$ = covariance of the return on asset j, r_j, and the return on the market portfolio, r_m

σ_m^2 = variance of the return on the market portfolio

r_m = required rate of return on the market portfolio of securities

e_j = random error term, which reflects the diversifiable, or unsystematic, risk of asset j

The calculations involved in finding betas are somewhat rigorous. If you want to know more about these calculations, consult an advanced managerial finance or investments text.

20. The values of beta also depend on the time interval used for return calculations and on the number of returns used in the regression analysis. In other words, betas calculated using monthly returns would not necessarily be comparable to those calculated using a similar number of daily returns.

TABLE 5.10   Selected Beta Coefficients and Their Interpretations

Beta	Comment	Interpretation
2.0	Move in same direction as market	Twice as responsive as the market
1.0		Same response as the market
.5		Only half as responsive as the market
0		Unaffected by market movement
−.5	Move in opposite direction to market	Only half as responsive as the market
−1.0		Same response as the market
−2.0		Twice as responsive as the market

Hint Remember that published betas are calculated using historical data. When investors use beta for decision making, they should recognize that past performance relative to the market average may not accurately predict future performance.

Interpreting Betas   The beta coefficient for the market is considered to be equal to 1.0. All other betas are viewed in relation to this value. Asset betas may be positive or negative, but positive betas are the norm. The majority of beta coefficients fall between .5 and 2.0. The return of a stock that is half as responsive as the market ($b = .5$) is expected to change by .5 percent for each 1 percent change in the return of the market portfolio. A stock that is twice as responsive as the market ($b = 2.0$) is expected to experience a 2 percent change in its return for each 1 percent change in the return of the market portfolio. Table 5.10 provides various beta values and their interpretations. Beta coefficients for actively traded stocks can be obtained from published sources such as *Value Line Investment Survey*, via the Internet, or through brokerage firms. Betas for some selected stocks are given in Table 5.11.

Portfolio Betas   The beta of a portfolio can be easily estimated by using the betas of the individual assets it includes. Letting w_j represent the proportion of

TABLE 5.11   Beta Coefficients for Selected Stocks (July 10, 2007)

Stock	Beta	Stock	Beta
Amazon.com	1.20	JP Morgan Chase & Co.	1.40
Anheuser-Busch	.65	Merrill Lynch & Co.	1.35
DaimlerChrysler AG	1.30	Microsoft	.95
Disney	1.30	Nike, Inc.	.85
eBay	1.10	PepsiCo, Inc.	.75
ExxonMobil Corp.	.90	Qualcomm	1.00
Gap (The), Inc.	.95	Sempra Energy	1.05
General Electric	1.10	Wal-Mart Stores	.75
Intel	1.15	Xerox	1.40
Int'l Business Machines	1.05	Yahoo! Inc.	1.40

Source: Value Line Investment Survey (New York: Value Line Publishing, July 20, 2007).

the portfolio's total dollar value represented by asset j, and letting b_j equal the beta of asset j, we can use Equation 5.7 to find the portfolio beta, b_p:

$$b_p = (w_1 \times b_1) + (w_2 \times b_2) + \cdots + (w_n \times b_n) = \sum_{j=1}^{n} w_j \times b_j \qquad (5.7)$$

Of course, $\sum_{j=1}^{n} w_j = 1$, which means that 100 percent of the portfolio's assets must be included in this computation.

Hint Mutual fund managers are key users of the portfolio beta and return concepts. They are continually evaluating what would happen to the fund's beta and return if the securities of a particular firm were added to or deleted from the fund's portfolio.

Portfolio betas are interpreted in the same way as the betas of individual assets. They indicate the degree of responsiveness of the *portfolio's* return to changes in the market return. For example, when the market return increases by 10 percent, a portfolio with a beta of .75 will experience a 7.5 percent increase in its return (.75 × 10%); a portfolio with a beta of 1.25 will experience a 12.5 percent increase in its return (1.25 × 10%). Clearly, a portfolio containing mostly low-beta assets will have a low beta, and one containing mostly high-beta assets will have a high beta.

Personal Finance Example   Mario Austino, an individual investor, wishes to assess the risk of two small portfolios he is considering—V and W. Both portfolios contain five assets, with the proportions and betas shown in Table 5.12. The betas for the two portfolios, b_v and b_w, can be calculated by substituting data from the table into Equation 5.7:

$$b_v = (.10 \times 1.65) + (.30 \times 1.00) + (.20 \times 1.30) + (.20 \times 1.10) + (.20 \times 1.25)$$
$$= .165 + .300 + .260 + .220 + .250 = 1.195 \approx \underline{1.20}$$

$$b_w = (.10 \times .80) + (.10 \times 1.00) + (.20 \times .65) + (.10 \times .75) + (.50 \times 1.05)$$
$$= .080 + .100 + .130 + .075 + .525 = \underline{.91}$$

Portfolio V's beta is about 1.20, and portfolio W's is .91. These values make sense, because portfolio V contains relatively high-beta assets, and portfolio W contains relatively low-beta assets. Mario's calculations show that portfolio V's returns are more responsive to changes in market returns and are therefore more risky than portfolio W's. He must now decide which, if either, portfolio he feels comfortable adding to his existing investments.

	Portfolio V		**Portfolio W**	
Asset	Proportion	Beta	Proportion	Beta
1	.10	1.65	.10	.80
2	.30	1.00	.10	1.00
3	.20	1.30	.20	.65
4	.20	1.10	.10	.75
5	.20	1.25	.50	1.05
Totals	1.00		1.00	

TABLE 5.12   Mario Austino's Portfolios V and W

The Equation

Using the beta coefficient to measure nondiversifiable risk, the *capital asset pricing model (CAPM)* is given in Equation 5.8:

$$r_j = R_F + [b_j \times (r_m - R_F)] \tag{5.8}$$

where

r_j = required return on asset j

R_F = risk-free rate of return, commonly measured by the return on a U.S. Treasury bill

b_j = beta coefficient or index of nondiversifiable risk for asset j

r_m = market return; return on the market portfolio of assets

risk-free rate of return, (R_F)
The required return on a *risk-free asset,* typically a 3-month *U.S. Treasury bill.*

U.S. Treasury bills (T-bills)
Short-term IOUs issued by the U.S. Treasury; considered the *risk-free asset.*

The CAPM can be divided into two parts: (1) the **risk-free rate of return, R_F,** which is the required return on a *risk-free asset,* typically a 3-month **U.S. Treasury bill (T-bill),** a short-term IOU issued by the U.S. Treasury, and (2) the *risk premium.* These are, respectively, the two elements on either side of the plus sign in Equation 5.8. The $(r_m - R_F)$ portion of the risk premium is called the *market risk premium,* because it represents the premium the investor must receive for taking the average amount of risk associated with holding the market portfolio of assets.[21]

Historical Risk Premiums   Using the historical return data for selected security investments for the 1926–2006 period shown in Table 5.2, we can calculate the risk premiums for each investment category. The calculation (consistent with Equation 5.8) involves merely subtracting the historical U.S. Treasury bill's average return from the historical average return for a given investment:

Investment	Risk premium[a]		
Large-company stocks	12.3%	− 3.8% =	8.5%
Small company stocks	17.4	− 3.8 =	13.6
Long-term corporate bonds	6.2	− 3.8 =	2.4
Long-term government bonds	5.8	− 3.8 =	2.0
U.S. Treasury bills	3.8	− 3.8 =	0.0

[a]Return values obtained from Table 5.2.

Reviewing the risk premiums calculated above, we can see that the risk premium is highest for small-company stocks, followed by large-company stocks, long-term corporate bonds, and long-term government bonds. This outcome makes sense intuitively because small-company stocks are riskier than large-company stocks, which are riskier than long-term corporate bonds (equity is riskier than debt investment). Long-term corporate bonds are riskier than long-term government bonds (because the government is less likely to renege on debt). And of

---

21. Although CAPM has been widely accepted, a broader theory, *arbitrage pricing theory (APT),* first described by Stephen A. Ross, "The Arbitrage Theory of Capital Asset Pricing," *Journal of Economic Theory* (December 1976), pp. 341–360, has received a great deal of attention in the financial literature. The theory suggests that the risk premium on securities may be better explained by a number of factors underlying and in place of the market return used in CAPM. The CAPM in effect can be viewed as being derived from APT. Although testing of APT confirms the importance of the market return, it has thus far failed to identify other risk factors clearly. As a result of this failure, as well as APT's lack of practical acceptance and usage, we concentrate our attention here on CAPM.

course, U.S. Treasury bills, because of their lack of default risk and their very short maturity, are virtually risk-free, as indicated by their lack of any risk premium.

Example

Benjamin Corporation, a growing computer software developer, wishes to determine the required return on an asset Z, which has a beta of 1.5. The risk-free rate of return is 7%; the return on the market portfolio of assets is 11%. Substituting $b_Z = 1.5$, $R_F = 7\%$, and $r_m = 11\%$ into the capital asset pricing model given in Equation 5.8 yields a required return of

$$r_Z = 7\% + [1.5 \times (11\% - 7\%)] = 7\% + 6\% = \underline{\underline{13\%}}$$

The market risk premium of 4% (11% − 7%), when adjusted for the asset's index of risk (beta) of 1.5, results in a risk premium of 6% (1.5 × 4%). That risk premium, when added to the 7% risk-free rate, results in a 13% required return.

Other things being equal, *the higher the beta, the higher the required return, and the lower the beta, the lower the required return.*

The Graph: The Security Market Line (SML)

security market line (SML)
The depiction of the *capital asset pricing model (CAPM)* as a graph that reflects the required return in the marketplace for each level of nondiversifiable risk (beta).

When the capital asset pricing model (Equation 5.8) is depicted graphically, it is called the **security market line (SML)**. The SML will, in fact, be a straight line. It reflects the required return in the marketplace for each level of nondiversifiable risk (beta). In the graph, risk as measured by beta, b, is plotted on the x axis, and required returns, r, are plotted on the y axis. The risk–return tradeoff is clearly represented by the SML.

Example

In the preceding example for Benjamin Corporation, the risk-free rate, R_F, was 7%, and the market return, r_m, was 11%. The SML can be plotted by using the two sets of coordinates for the betas associated with R_F and r_m, b_{R_F} and b_m (that is, $b_{R_F} = 0$,[22] $R_F = 7\%$; and $b_m = 1.0$, $r_m = 11\%$). Figure 5.10 (on page 256) presents the resulting security market line. As traditionally shown, the security market line in Figure 5.10 presents the required return associated with all positive betas. The market risk premium of 4% (r_m of 11% − R_F of 7%) has been highlighted. For a beta for asset Z, b_Z, of 1.5, its corresponding required return, r_Z, is 13%. Also shown in the figure is asset Z's risk premium of 6% (r_Z of 13% − R_F of 7%). It should be clear that for assets with betas greater than 1, the risk premium is greater than that for the market; for assets with betas less than 1, the risk premium is less than that for the market.

Shifts in the Security Market Line

The security market line is not stable over time, and shifts in the security market line can result in a change in required return. The position and slope of the SML are affected by two major forces—inflationary expectations and risk aversion—which are analyzed next.[23]

---

22. Because R_F is the rate of return on a risk-free asset, the beta associated with the risk-free asset, b_{R_F}, would equal 0. The zero beta on the risk-free asset reflects not only its absence of risk but also that the asset's return is unaffected by movements in the market return.

23. A firm's beta can change over time as a result of changes in the firm's asset mix, in its financing mix, or in external factors not within management's control, such as earthquakes, toxic spills, and so on. The impacts of changes in beta on value are discussed in Chapter 7.

FIGURE 5.10

Security Market Line
Security market line (SML) with Benjamin Corporation's asset Z data shown

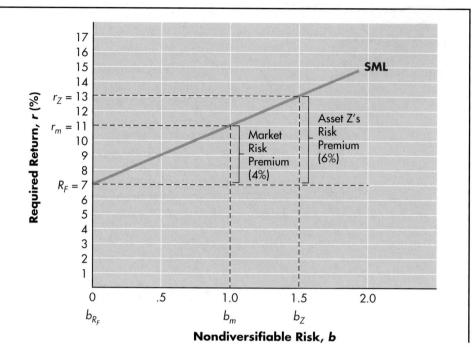

Changes in Inflationary Expectations   Changes in inflationary expectations affect the risk-free rate of return, R_F. The equation for the risk-free rate of return is

$$R_F = r^* + IP \qquad (5.9)$$

This equation shows that, assuming a constant real rate of interest, r^*, changes in inflationary expectations, reflected in an inflation premium, IP, will result in corresponding changes in the risk-free rate. Therefore, a change in inflationary expectations that results from events such as international trade embargoes or major changes in Federal Reserve policy will result in a shift in the SML. Because the risk-free rate is a basic component of all rates of return, any change in R_F will be reflected in *all* required rates of return.

Changes in inflationary expectations result in parallel shifts in the SML in direct response to the magnitude and direction of the change. This effect can best be illustrated by an example.

Example

In the preceding example, using CAPM, the required return for asset Z, r_Z, was found to be 13%. Assuming that the risk-free rate of 7% includes a 2% real rate of interest, r^*, and a 5% inflation premium, IP, then Equation 5.9 confirms that

$$R_F = 2\% + 5\% = 7\%$$

Now assume that recent economic events have resulted in an *increase of 3% in inflationary expectations, raising the inflation premium to 8% (IP_1).* As a result, all returns likewise rise by 3%. In this case, the new returns (noted by subscript 1) are

$$R_{F_1} = 10\% \text{ (rises from 7\% to 10\%)}$$
$$r_{m_1} = 14\% \text{ (rises from 11\% to 14\%)}$$

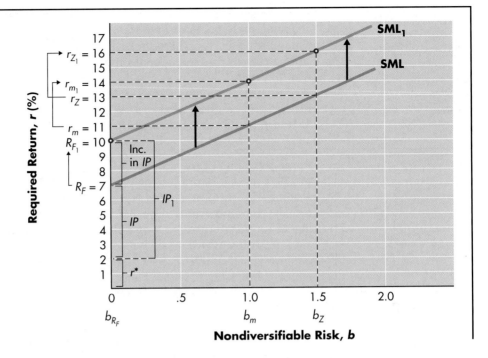

FIGURE 5.11

Inflation Shifts SML
Impact of increased
inflationary expectations
on the SML

Substituting these values, along with asset Z's beta (b_Z) of 1.5, into the CAPM (Equation 5.8), we find that asset Z's new required return (r_{Z_1}) can be calculated:

$$r_{Z_1} = 10\% + [1.5 \times (14\% - 10\%)] = 10\% + 6\% = \underline{\underline{16\%}}$$

Comparing r_{Z_1} of 16% to r_Z of 13%, we see that the change of 3% in asset Z's required return exactly equals the change in the inflation premium. The same 3% increase results for all assets.

Figure 5.11 depicts the situation just described. It shows that the 3% increase in inflationary expectations results in a parallel shift upward of 3% in the SML. Clearly, the required returns on all assets rise by 3%. Note that the rise in the inflation premium from 5% to 8% (IP to IP_1) causes the risk-free rate to rise from 7% to 10% (R_F to R_{F_1}) and the market return to increase from 11% to 14% (r_m to r_{m_1}). The security market line therefore shifts upward by 3% (SML to SML₁), causing the required return on all risky assets, such as asset Z, to rise by 3%. It should now be clear that *a given change in inflationary expectations will be fully reflected in a corresponding change in the returns of all assets, as reflected graphically in a parallel shift of the SML.*

Changes in Risk Aversion   The slope of the security market line reflects the general risk preferences of investors in the marketplace. As discussed earlier and shown in Figure 5.1, most investors are *risk-averse*—they require increased returns for increased risk. This positive relationship between risk and return is graphically represented by the SML, which depicts the relationship between nondiversifiable risk as measured by beta (*x* axis) and the required return (*y* axis). The slope of the SML reflects the degree of risk aversion: *the steeper its slope, the greater the degree of risk aversion,* because a higher level of return will be required for each level of risk as measured by beta. In other words, *risk premiums increase with increasing risk avoidance.*

Changes in risk aversion, and therefore shifts in the SML, result from changing preferences of investors, which generally result from economic, political, and social events. Examples of events that *increase* risk aversion include a stock market crash, assassination of a key political leader, and the outbreak of war. In general, widely accepted expectations of hard times ahead tend to cause investors to become more risk-averse, requiring higher returns as compensation for accepting a given level of risk. The impact of increased risk aversion on the SML can best be demonstrated by an example.

Example

In the preceding examples, the SML in Figure 5.10 reflected a risk-free rate (R_F) of 7%, a market return (r_m) of 11%, a market risk premium $(r_m - R_F)$ of 4%, and a required return on asset Z (r_Z) of 13% with a beta (b_Z) of 1.5. Assume that recent economic events have made investors more risk-averse, causing a new higher market return (r_{m_1}) of 14%. Graphically, this change would cause the SML to shift upward as shown in Figure 5.12, causing a new market risk premium $(r_{m_1} - R_F)$ of 7%. As a result, the required return on all risky assets will increase. For asset Z, with a beta of 1.5, the new required return (r_{Z_1}) can be calculated by using CAPM (Equation 5.8):

$$r_{Z_1} = 7\% + [1.5 \times (14\% - 7\%)] = 7\% + 10.5\% = \underline{\underline{17.5\%}}$$

This value can be seen on the new security market line (SML_1) in Figure 5.12. Note that although asset Z's risk, as measured by beta, did not change, its required return has increased because of the increased risk aversion reflected in

FIGURE 5.12

Risk Aversion Shifts SML
Impact of increased risk aversion on the SML

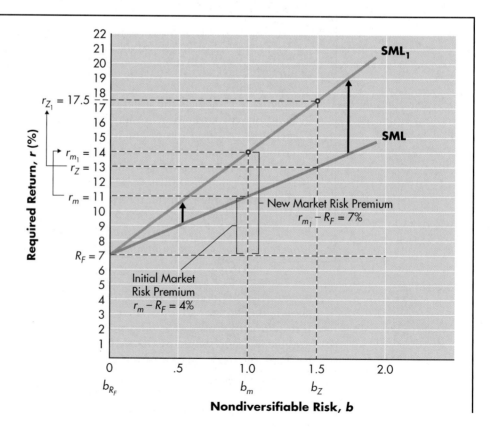

the market risk premium. It should now be clear that *greater risk aversion results in higher required returns for each level of risk. Similarly, a reduction in risk aversion causes the required return for each level of risk to decline.*

Some Comments on CAPM

The capital asset pricing model generally relies on historical data. The betas may or may not actually reflect the *future* variability of returns. Therefore, the required returns specified by the model can be viewed only as rough approximations. Users of betas commonly make subjective adjustments to the historically determined betas to reflect their expectations of the future.

The CAPM was developed to explain the behavior of security prices and provide a mechanism whereby investors could assess the impact of a proposed security investment on their portfolio's overall risk and return. It is based on an assumed **efficient market** with the following characteristics: many small investors, all having the same information and expectations with respect to securities; no restrictions on investment, no taxes, and no transaction costs; and rational investors, who view securities similarly and are risk-averse, preferring higher returns and lower risk.

Although the perfect world of the efficient market appears to be unrealistic, studies have provided support for the existence of the expectational relationship described by CAPM in active markets such as the New York Stock Exchange.[24] In the case of real corporate assets, such as plant and equipment, research thus far has failed to prove the general applicability of CAPM because of indivisibility, relatively large size, limited number of transactions, and absence of an efficient market for such assets.

Despite the limitations of CAPM, it provides a useful conceptual framework for evaluating and linking risk and return. An awareness of this tradeoff and an attempt to consider risk as well as return in financial decision making should help financial managers achieve their goals.

efficient market
A market with the following characteristics: many small investors, all having the same information and expectations with respect to securities; no restrictions on investment, no taxes, and no transaction costs; and rational investors, who view securities similarly and are risk-averse, preferring higher returns and lower risk.

REVIEW QUESTIONS

5–11 How are total risk, nondiversifiable risk, and diversifiable risk related? Why is nondiversifiable risk the *only relevant risk?*

5–12 What risk does *beta* measure? How can you find the beta of a portfolio?

5–13 Explain the meaning of each variable in the *capital asset pricing model (CAPM)* equation. What is the *security market line (SML)?*

5–14 What impact would the following changes have on the security market line and therefore on the required return for a given level of risk? (**a**) An *increase* in inflationary expectations. (**b**) Investors become *less* risk-averse.

5–15 Why do financial managers have some difficulty applying CAPM in financial decision making? Generally, what benefit does CAPM provide them?

---

24. A study by Eugene F. Fama and Kenneth R. French, "The Cross-Section of Expected Stock Returns," *Journal of Finance* 47 (June 1992), pp. 427–465, raised serious questions about the validity of CAPM. The study failed to find a significant relationship between the *historical* betas and *historical* returns on over 2,000 stocks during 1963–1990. In other words, it found that the magnitude of a stock's *historical* beta had no relationship to the level of its *historical* return. Although Fama and French's study continues to receive attention, CAPM has not been abandoned because its rejection as a *historical* model fails to discredit its validity as an *expectational* model. Therefore, in spite of this challenge, CAPM continues to be viewed as a logical and useful framework—both conceptually and operationally—for linking *expected* nondiversifiable risk and return.

Summary

Focus on Value

A firm's risk and expected return directly affect its share price. As we shall see in Chapter 7, risk and return are the two key determinants of the firm's value. It is therefore the financial manager's responsibility to assess carefully the risk and return of all major decisions so as to ensure that the expected returns justify the level of risk being introduced.

The financial manager can expect to achieve **the firm's goal of increasing its share price** (and thereby benefiting its owners) by taking only those actions that earn returns at least commensurate with their risk. Clearly, financial managers need to recognize, measure, and evaluate risk–return tradeoffs to ensure that their decisions contribute to the creation of value for owners.

Review of Learning Goals

Key definitions and formulas for this chapter are summarized in Table 5.13.

LG 1 **Understand the meaning and fundamentals of risk, return, and risk preferences.** Risk is the chance of loss or, more formally, the variability of returns. A number of sources of firm-specific and shareholder-specific risks exist. Return is any cash distributions plus the change in value over a given period of time expressed as a percentage of the initial value. Investment returns vary both over time and between different types of investments. Managers may be risk-averse, risk-indifferent, or risk-seeking. Most financial decision makers are risk-averse. They generally prefer less-risky alternatives, and they require higher expected returns in exchange for greater risk.

LG 2 **Describe procedures for assessing and measuring the risk of a single asset.** The risk of a single asset is measured in much the same way as the risk of a portfolio of assets. Scenario analysis and probability distributions can be used to assess risk. The range, the standard deviation, and the coefficient of variation can be used to measure risk quantitatively.

LG 3 **Discuss the measurement of return and standard deviation for a portfolio and the concept of correlation.** The return of a portfolio is calculated as the weighted average of returns on the individual assets from which it is formed. The portfolio standard deviation is found by using the formula for the standard deviation of a single asset.

Correlation—the statistical relationship between any two series of numbers—can be positive, negative, or uncorrelated. At the extremes, the series can be perfectly positively correlated or perfectly negatively correlated.

LG 4 **Understand the risk and return characteristics of a portfolio in terms of correlation and diversification, and the impact of international assets on a portfolio.** Diversification involves combining assets with low correlation to reduce the risk of the portfolio. The range of risk in a two-asset portfolio depends on the correlation between the two assets. If they are perfectly

TABLE 5.13   Summary of Key Definitions and Formulas for Risk and Return

Definitions of variables

b_j = beta coefficient or index of nondiversifiable risk for asset j

b_p = portfolio beta

C_t = cash received from the asset investment in the time period $t-1$ to t

CV = coefficient of variation

$\bar{r}$ = expected value of a return

r_j = return for the jth outcome; return on asset j; required return on asset j

r_m = market return; the return on the market portfolio of assets

r_p = portfolio return

r_t = actual, expected, or required rate of return during period t

n = number of outcomes considered

P_t = price (value) of asset at time t

P_{t-1} = price (value) of asset at time $t-1$

Pr_j = probability of occurrence of the jth outcome

R_F = risk-free rate of return

σ_r = standard deviation of returns

w_j = proportion of total portfolio dollar value represented by asset j

Risk and return formulas

Rate of return during period t:

$$r_t = \frac{C_t + P_t - P_{t-1}}{P_{t-1}}$$ [Equation 5.1]

Expected value of a return:

For probabilistic data:

$$\bar{r} = \sum_{j=1}^{n} r_j \times Pr_j$$ [Equation 5.2]

General formula:

$$\bar{r} = \frac{\sum_{j=1}^{n} r_j}{n}$$ [Equation 5.2a]

Standard deviation of return:

For probabilistic data:

$$\sigma_r = \sqrt{\sum_{j=1}^{n} (r_j - \bar{r})^2 \times Pr_j}$$ [Equation 5.3]

General formula:

$$\sigma_r = \sqrt{\frac{\sum_{j=1}^{n} (r_j - \bar{r})^2}{n-1}}$$ [Equation 5.3a]

Coefficient of variation:

$$CV = \frac{\sigma_r}{\bar{r}}$$ [Equation 5.4]

Portfolio return:

$$r_p = \sum_{j=1}^{n} w_j \times r_j$$ [Equation 5.5]

Total security risk = Nondiversifiable risk + Diversifiable risk [Equation 5.6]

Portfolio beta:

$$b_p = \sum_{j=1}^{n} w_j \times b_j$$ [Equation 5.7]

Capital asset pricing model (CAPM):

$$r_j = R_F + [b_j \times (r_m - R_F)]$$ [Equation 5.8]

positively correlated, the portfolio's risk will be between the individual assets' risks. If they are uncorrelated, the portfolio's risk will be between the risk of the more risky asset and an amount less than the risk of the less risky asset but greater than zero. If they are perfectly negatively correlated, the portfolio's risk will be between the risk of the more risky asset and zero.

International diversification can further reduce a portfolio's risk. Foreign assets have the risk of currency fluctuation and political risks.

LG 5 **Review the two types of risk and the derivation and role of beta in measuring the relevant risk of both a security and a portfolio.** The total risk of a security consists of nondiversifiable and diversifiable risk. Diversifiable risk can be eliminated through diversification. Nondiversifiable risk is the only relevant risk. Nondiversifiable risk is measured by the beta coefficient, which is a relative measure of the relationship between an asset's return and the market return. Beta is derived by finding the slope of the "characteristic line" that best explains the historical relationship between the asset's return and the market return. The beta of a portfolio is a weighted average of the betas of the individual assets that it includes.

LG 6 **Explain the capital asset pricing model (CAPM), its relationship to the security market line (SML), and the major forces causing shifts in the SML.** The capital asset pricing model (CAPM) uses beta to relate an asset's risk relative to the market to the asset's required return. The graphical depiction of CAPM is the security market line (SML), which shifts over time in response to changing inflationary expectations and/or changes in investor risk aversion. Changes in inflationary expectations result in parallel shifts in the SML. Increasing risk aversion results in a steepening in the slope of the SML. Decreasing risk aversion reduces the slope of the SML. Although it has some shortcomings, CAPM provides a useful conceptual framework for evaluating and linking risk and return.

Self-Test Problems (Solutions in Appendix B)

  ST5–1 **Portfolio analysis** You have been asked for your advice in selecting a portfolio of assets and have been given the following data:

	Expected return		
Year	Asset A	Asset B	Asset C
2010	12%	16%	12%
2011	14	14	14
2012	16	12	16

No probabilities have been supplied. You have been told that you can create two portfolios—one consisting of assets A and B and the other consisting of assets A and C—by investing equal proportions (50%) in each of the two component assets.

a. What is the expected return for each asset over the 3-year period?

b. What is the standard deviation for each asset's return?

   c. What is the expected return for each of the two portfolios?

   d. How would you characterize the correlations of returns of the two assets making up each of the two portfolios identified in part **c**?

   e. What is the standard deviation for each portfolio?

   f. Which portfolio do you recommend? Why?

ST5–2 Beta and CAPM   Currently under consideration is a project with a beta, b, of 1.50. At this time, the risk-free rate of return, R_F, is 7%, and the return on the market portfolio of assets, r_m, is 10%. The project is actually *expected* to earn an annual rate of return of 11%.

   a. If the return on the market portfolio were to increase by 10%, what would you expect to happen to the project's *required return*? What if the market return were to decline by 10%?

   b. Use the capital asset pricing model (CAPM) to find the *required return* on this investment.

   c. On the basis of your calculation in part **b**, would you recommend this investment? Why or why not?

   d. Assume that as a result of investors becoming less risk-averse, the market return drops by 1% to 9%. What impact would this change have on your responses in parts **b** and **c**?

Warm-Up Exercises

A blue box (■) indicates exercises available in .

E5–1   An analyst predicted last year that the stock of Logistics, Inc., would offer a total return of at least 10% in the coming year. At the beginning of the year, the firm had a stock market value of $10 million. At the end of the year, it had a market value of $12 million even though it experienced a loss, or negative net income, of $2.5 million. Did the analyst's prediction prove correct? Explain using the values for total annual return.

E5–2   Four analysts cover the stock of Fluorine Chemical. One forecasts a 5% return for the coming year. A second expects the return to be negative 5%. A third predicts a 10% return. A fourth expects a 3% return in the coming year. You are relatively confident that the return will be positive but not large, so you arbitrarily assign probabilities of being correct of 35%, 5%, 20%, and 40%, respectively, to the analysts' forecasts. Given these probabilities, what is Fluorine Chemical's *expected return* for the coming year?

E5–3   The expected annual returns are 15% for investment 1 and 12% for investment 2. The standard deviation of the first investment's return is 10%; the second investment's return has a standard deviation of 5%. Which investment is less risky based solely on *standard deviation*? Which investment is less risky based on *coefficient of variation*? Which is a better measure given that the expected returns of the two investments are not the same?

E5–4   Your portfolio has three asset classes. U.S. government T-bills account for 45% of the portfolio, large-company stocks constitute another 40%, and small-company stocks make up the remaining 15%. If the expected returns are 3.8% for the T-bills, 12.3% for the large-company stocks, and 17.4% for the small-company stocks, what is the expected return of the portfolio?

E5–5 You wish to calculate the risk level of your portfolio based on its beta. The five stocks in the portfolio with their respective weights and betas are shown below. Calculate the beta of your portfolio.

Stock	Portfolio weight	Beta
Alpha	20%	1.15
Centauri	10	.85
Zen	15	1.6
Wren	20	1.35
Yukos	35	1.85

E5–6 a. Calculate the required rate of return for an asset that has a beta of 1.8, given a risk-free rate of 5% and a market return of 10%.
  b. If investors have become more risk-averse due to recent geopolitical events, and the market return rises to 13%, what is the required rate of return for the same asset?
  c. Use your findings in part **a** to graph the initial *security market line (SML)*, and then use your findings in part **b** to graph (on the same set of axes) the shift in the SML.

Problems

A blue box (■) indicates problems available in myfinancelab.

P5–1 Rate of return   Douglas Keel, a financial analyst for Orange Industries, wishes to estimate the rate of return for two similar-risk investments, X and Y. Douglas's research indicates that the immediate past returns will serve as reasonable estimates of future returns. A year earlier, investment X had a market value of $20,000; investment Y had a market value of $55,000. During the year, investment X generated cash flow of $1,500 and investment Y generated cash flow of $6,800. The current market values of investments X and Y are $21,000 and $55,000, respectively.
  a. Calculate the expected rate of return on investments X and Y using the most recent year's data.
  b. Assuming that the two investments are equally risky, which one should Douglas recommend? Why?

P5–2 Return calculations   For each of the investments shown in the following table, calculate the rate of return earned over the unspecified time period.

Investment	Cash flow during period	Beginning-of-period value	End-of-period value
A	− $ 100	$ 800	$ 1,100
B	15,000	120,000	118,000
C	7,000	45,000	48,000
D	80	600	500
E	1,500	12,500	12,400

P5–3 **Risk preferences**   Sharon Smith, the financial manager for Barnett Corporation, wishes to evaluate three prospective investments: X, Y, and Z. Currently, the firm earns 12% on its investments, which have a risk index of 6%. The expected return and expected risk of the investments are as follows:

Investment	Expected return	Expected risk index
X	14%	7%
Y	12	8
Z	10	9

a. If Sharon were *risk-indifferent,* which investments would she select? Explain why.
b. If she were *risk-averse,* which investments would she select? Why?
c. If she were *risk-seeking,* which investments would she select? Why?
d. Given the traditional risk preference behavior exhibited by financial managers, which investment would be preferred? Why?

P5–4 **Risk analysis**   Solar Designs is considering an investment in an expanded product line. Two possible types of expansion are being considered. After investigating the possible outcomes, the company made the estimates shown in the following table:

	Expansion A	Expansion B
Initial investment	$12,000	$12,000
Annual rate of return		
Pessimistic	16%	10%
Most likely	20%	20%
Optimistic	24%	30%

a. Determine the *range* of the rates of return for each of the two projects.
b. Which project is less risky? Why?
c. If you were making the investment decision, which one would you choose? Why? What does this imply about your feelings toward risk?
d. Assume that expansion B's most likely outcome is 21% per year and that all other facts remain the same. Does this change your answer to part **c**? Why?

P5–5 **Risk and probability**   Micro-Pub, Inc., is considering the purchase of one of two microfilm cameras, R and S. Both should provide benefits over a 10-year period, and each requires an initial investment of $4,000. Management has constructed the table (on page 266) of estimates of rates of return and probabilities for pessimistic, most likely, and optimistic results.
a. Determine the *range* for the rate of return for each of the two cameras.
b. Determine the *expected value* of return for each camera.
c. Purchase of which camera is riskier? Why?

	Camera R		Camera S	
	Amount	Probability	Amount	Probability
Initial investment	$4,000	1.00	$4,000	1.00
Annual rate of return				
Pessimistic	20%	.25	15%	.20
Most likely	25%	.50	25%	.55
Optimistic	30%	.25	35%	.25

P5–6 Bar charts and risk   Swan's Sportswear is considering bringing out a line of designer jeans. Currently, it is negotiating with two different well-known designers. Because of the highly competitive nature of the industry, the two lines of jeans have been given code names. After market research, the firm has established the expectations shown in the following table about the annual rates of return:

		Annual rate of return	
Market acceptance	Probability	Line J	Line K
Very poor	.05	.0075	.010
Poor	.15	.0125	.025
Average	.60	.0850	.080
Good	.15	.1475	.135
Excellent	.05	.1625	.150

Use the table to:
a. Construct a bar chart for each line's annual rate of return.
b. Calculate the *expected value* of return for each line.
c. Evaluate the relative riskiness for each jean line's rate of return using the bar charts.

P5–7 Coefficient of variation   Metal Manufacturing has isolated four alternatives for meeting its need for increased production capacity. The following table summarizes data gathered relative to each of these alternatives.

Alternative	Expected return	Standard deviation of return
A	20%	7.0%
B	22	9.5
C	19	6.0
D	16	5.5

a. Calculate the *coefficient of variation* for each alternative.
b. If the firm wishes to minimize risk, which alternative do you recommend? Why?

P5–8 Standard deviation versus coefficient of variation as measures of risk   Greengage, Inc., a successful nursery, is considering several expansion projects. All of the alternatives promise to produce an acceptable return. The owners are extremely risk-averse; therefore, they will choose the least risky of the alternatives. Data on four possible projects follow.

Project	Expected return	Range	Standard deviation
A	12.0%	4.0%	2.9%
B	12.5	5.0	3.2
C	13.0	6.0	3.5
D	12.8	4.5	3.0

a. Which project is least risky, judging on the basis of *range?*
b. Which project has the lowest *standard deviation?* Explain why standard deviation is not an appropriate measure of risk for purposes of this comparison.
c. Calculate the *coefficient of variation* for each project. Which project will Greengage's owners choose? Explain why this may be the best measure of risk for comparing this set of opportunities.

PERSONAL FINANCE PROBLEM

P5–9   Rate of return, standard deviation, coefficient of variation   Mike is searching for a stock to include in his current stock portfolio. He is interested in Apple Inc.; he has been impressed with the company's computer products and believes Apple is an innovative market player. However, Mike realizes that any time you consider a so-called high-tech stock, risk is a major concern. The rule he follows is to include only securities with a coefficient of variation of returns below 0.90.

Mike has obtained the following price information for the period 2006 through 2009. Apple stock, being growth-oriented, did not pay any dividends during these 4 years.

Year	Stock price	
	Beginning	End
2006	$14.36	$21.55
2007	21.55	64.78
2008	64.78	72.38
2009	72.38	91.80

a. Calculate the *rate of return* for each year, 2006 through 2009, for Apple stock.
b. Assume that each year's return is equally probable and calculate the *average return* over this time period.
c. Calculate the *standard deviation* of returns over the past 4 years. (*Hint:* Treat this data as a sample.)
d. Based on **b** and **c** determine the *coefficient of variation* of returns for the security.
e. Given the calculation in **d** what should be Mike's decision regarding the inclusion of Apple stock in his portfolio?

P5–10   Assessing return and risk   Swift Manufacturing must choose between two asset purchases. The annual rate of return and the related probabilities given in the following table (on page 268) summarize the firm's analysis to this point.

Project 257		Project 432	
Rate of return	Probability	Rate of return	Probability
−10%	.01	10%	.05
10	.04	15	.10
20	.05	20	.10
30	.10	25	.15
40	.15	30	.20
45	.30	35	.15
50	.15	40	.10
60	.10	45	.10
70	.05	50	.05
80	.04		
100	.01		

a. For each project, compute:
  (1) The range of possible rates of return.
  (2) The expected value of return.
  (3) The standard deviation of the returns.
  (4) The coefficient of variation of the returns.
b. Construct a bar chart of each distribution of rates of return.
c. Which project would you consider less risky? Why?

P5–11 **Integrative—Expected return, standard deviation, and coefficient of variation**
Three assets—F, G, and H—are currently being considered by Perth Industries.
The probability distributions of expected returns for these assets are shown in the
following table:

j	Asset F		Asset G		Asset H	
	Pr_j	Return, r_j	Pr_j	Return, r_j	Pr_j	Return, r_j
1	.10	40%	.40	35%	.10	40%
2	.20	10	.30	10	.20	20
3	.40	0	.30	−20	.40	10
4	.20	− 5			.20	0
5	.10	−10			.10	−20

a. Calculate the expected value of return, $\bar{r}$, for each of the three assets.
    Which provides the largest expected return?
b. Calculate the standard deviation, σ_r, for each of the three assets' returns.
    Which appears to have the greatest risk?
c. Calculate the coefficient of variation, CV, for each of the three assets' returns.
    Which appears to have the greatest *relative* risk?

P5–12 **Normal probability distribution**   Assuming that the rates of return associated
with a given asset investment are normally distributed and that the expected
return, $\bar{r}$, is 18.9% and the coefficient of variation, CV, is .75, answer the following
questions:

a. Find the standard deviation of returns, σ_r.
b. Calculate the range of expected return outcomes associated with the following probabilities of occurrence: (1) 68%, (2) 95%, (3) 99%.
c. Draw the probability distribution associated with your findings in parts **a** and **b**.

PERSONAL FINANCE PROBLEM

P5–13   **Portfolio return and standard deviation**   Jamie Wong is considering building an investment portfolio containing two stocks, L and M. Stock L will represent 40% of the dollar value of the portfolio, and stock M will account for the other 60%. The expected returns over the next 6 years, 2010–2015, for each of these stocks are shown in the following table:

	Expected return	
Year	Stock L	Stock M
2010	14%	20%
2011	14	18
2012	16	16
2013	17	14
2014	17	12
2015	19	10

a. Calculate the expected portfolio return, r_p, for *each* of the 6 years.
b. Calculate the expected value of portfolio returns, $\bar{r}_p$, over the 6-year period.
c. Calculate the standard deviation of expected portfolio returns, σ_{r_p}, over the 6-year period.
d. How would you characterize the correlation of returns of the two stocks L and M?
e. Discuss any benefits of diversification achieved by Jamie through creation of the portfolio.

P5–14   **Portfolio analysis**   You have been given the expected return data shown in the first table on three assets—F, G, and H—over the period 2010–2013.

	Expected return		
Year	Asset F	Asset G	Asset H
2010	16%	17%	14%
2011	17	16	15
2012	18	15	16
2013	19	14	17

Using these assets, you have isolated the three investment alternatives shown in the following table:

Alternative	Investment
1	100% of asset F
2	50% of asset F and 50% of asset G
3	50% of asset F and 50% of asset H

a. Calculate the expected return over the 4-year period for each of the three alternatives.

b. Calculate the standard deviation of returns over the 4-year period for each of the three alternatives.

c. Use your findings in parts **a** and **b** to calculate the coefficient of variation for each of the three alternatives.

d. On the basis of your findings, which of the three investment alternatives do you recommend? Why?

 P5–15 **Correlation, risk, and return**   Matt Peters wishes to evaluate the risk and return behaviors associated with various combinations of assets V and W under three assumed degrees of correlation: perfect positive, uncorrelated, and perfect negative. The expected return and risk values calculated for each of the assets are shown in the following table.

Asset	Expected return, $\bar{r}$	Risk (standard deviation), σ_r
V	8%	5%
W	13	10

a. If the returns of assets V and W are *perfectly positively correlated* (correlation coefficient $= +1$), describe the *range* of (1) expected return and (2) risk associated with all possible portfolio combinations.

b. If the returns of assets V and W are *uncorrelated* (correlation coefficient $= 0$), describe the *approximate range* of (1) expected return and (2) risk associated with all possible portfolio combinations.

c. If the returns of assets V and W are *perfectly negatively correlated* (correlation coefficient $= -1$), describe the *range* of (1) expected return and (2) risk associated with all possible portfolio combinations.

PERSONAL FINANCE PROBLEM

  P5–16 **International investment returns**   Joe Martinez, a U.S. citizen living in Brownsville, Texas, invested in the common stock of Telmex, a Mexican corporation. He purchased 1,000 shares at 20.50 pesos per share. Twelve months later, he sold them at 24.75 pesos per share. He received no dividends during that time.

a. What was Joe's investment return (in percentage terms) for the year, on the basis of the peso value of the shares?

b. The exchange rate for pesos was 9.21 pesos per US$1.00 at the time of the purchase. At the time of the sale, the exchange rate was 9.85 pesos per US$1.00. Translate the purchase and sale prices into US$.

c. Calculate Joe's investment return on the basis of the US$ value of the shares.

d. Explain why the two returns are different. Which one is more important to Joe? Why?

 P5–17 **Total, nondiversifiable, and diversifiable risk**   David Talbot randomly selected securities from all those listed on the New York Stock Exchange for his portfolio. He began with a single security and added securities one by one until a total of 20 securities were held in the portfolio. After each security was added, David calculated the portfolio standard deviation, σ_{r_p}. The calculated values are shown in the following table.

Number of securities	Portfolio risk, σ_{r_p}	Number of securities	Portfolio risk, σ_{r_p}
1	14.50%	11	7.00%
2	13.30	12	6.80
3	12.20	13	6.70
4	11.20	14	6.65
5	10.30	15	6.60
6	9.50	16	6.56
7	8.80	17	6.52
8	8.20	18	6.50
9	7.70	19	6.48
10	7.30	20	6.47

a. On a set of "number of securities in portfolio (*x* axis)–portfolio risk (*y* axis)" axes, plot the portfolio risk data given in the preceding table.
b. Divide the total portfolio risk in the graph into its *nondiversifiable* and *diversifiable* risk components and label each of these on the graph.
c. Describe which of the two risk components is the *relevant risk*, and explain why it is relevant. How much of this risk exists in David Talbot's portfolio?

P5–18 Graphical derivation of beta A firm wishes to estimate graphically the betas for two assets, A and B. It has gathered the return data shown in the following table for the market portfolio and for both assets over the last 10 years, 2000–2009.

Year	Actual return Market portfolio	Asset A	Asset B
2000	6%	11%	16%
2001	2	8	11
2002	−13	− 4	−10
2003	− 4	3	3
2004	− 8	0	− 3
2005	16	19	30
2006	10	14	22
2007	15	18	29
2008	8	12	19
2009	13	17	26

a. On a set of "market return (*x* axis)–asset return (*y* axis)" axes, use the data given to draw the characteristic line for asset A and for asset B.
b. Use the characteristic lines from part **a** to estimate the betas for assets A and B.
c. Use the betas found in part **b** to comment on the relative risks of assets A and B.

P5–19 Interpreting beta A firm wishes to assess the impact of changes in the market return on an asset that has a beta of 1.20.
a. If the market return increased by 15%, what impact would this change be expected to have on the asset's return?
b. If the market return decreased by 8%, what impact would this change be expected to have on the asset's return?

   c. If the market return did not change, what impact, if any, would be expected on the asset's return?
   d. Would this asset be considered more or less risky than the market? Explain.

P5–20 Betas   Answer the questions below for assets A to D shown in the following table.

Asset	Beta
A	.50
B	1.60
C	− .20
D	.90

   a. What impact would a *10% increase* in the market return be expected to have on each asset's return?
   b. What impact would a *10% decrease* in the market return be expected to have on each asset's return?
   c. If you were certain that the market return would *increase* in the near future, which asset would you prefer? Why?
   d. If you were certain that the market return would *decrease* in the near future, which asset would you prefer? Why?

PERSONAL FINANCE PROBLEM

P5–21 Betas and risk rankings   You are considering three stocks—A, B, and C—for possible inclusion in your investment portfolio. Stock A has a beta of .80, stock B has a beta of 1.40, and stock C has a beta of − .30.
   a. Rank these stocks from the most risky to the least risky.
   b. If the return on the market portfolio increased by 12%, what change would you expect in the return for each of the stocks?
   c. If the return on the market portfolio decreased by 5%, what change would you expect in the return for each of the stocks?
   d. If you felt that the stock market was getting ready to experience a significant decline, which stock would you probably add to your portfolio? Why?
   e. If you anticipated a major stock market rally, which stock would you add to your portfolio? Why?

PERSONAL FINANCE PROBLEM

P5–22 Portfolio betas   Rose Berry is attempting to evaluate two possible portfolios, which consist of the same five assets held in different proportions. She is particularly interested in using beta to compare the risks of the portfolios, so she has gathered the data shown in the following table.

		Portfolio weights	
Asset	Asset beta	Portfolio A	Portfolio B
1	1.30	10%	30%
2	.70	30	10
3	1.25	10	20
4	1.10	10	20
5	.90	40	20
Totals		100%	100%

a. Calculate the betas for portfolios A and B.
b. Compare the risks of these portfolios to the market as well as to each other. Which portfolio is more risky?

 P5–23 **Capital asset pricing model (CAPM)**   For each of the cases shown in the following table, use the capital asset pricing model to find the required return.

Case	Risk-free rate, R_F	Market return, r_m	Beta, b
A	5%	8%	1.30
B	8	13	.90
C	9	12	− .20
D	10	15	1.00
E	6	10	.60

PERSONAL FINANCE PROBLEM

  P5–24 **Beta coefficients and the capital asset pricing model**   Katherine Wilson is wondering how much risk she must undertake to generate an acceptable return on her portfolio. The risk-free return currently is 5%. The return on the average stock (market return) is 16%. Use the CAPM to calculate the beta coefficient associated with each of the following portfolio returns.
a. 10%
b. 15%
c. 18%
d. 20%
e. Katherine is risk-averse. What is the highest return she can expect if she is unwilling to take more than an average risk?

 P5–25 **Manipulating CAPM**   Use the basic equation for the capital asset pricing model (CAPM) to work each of the following problems.
a. Find the *required return* for an asset with a beta of .90 when the risk-free rate and market return are 8% and 12%, respectively.
b. Find the *risk-free rate* for a firm with a required return of 15% and a beta of 1.25 when the market return is 14%.
c. Find the *market return* for an asset with a required return of 16% and a beta of 1.10 when the risk-free rate is 9%.
d. Find the *beta* for an asset with a required return of 15% when the risk-free rate and market return are 10% and 12.5%, respectively.

PERSONAL FINANCE PROBLEM

    P5–26 **Portfolio return and beta**   Jamie Peters invested $100,000 to set up the following portfolio one year ago:

Asset	Cost	Beta at purchase	Yearly income	Value today
A	$20,000	.80	$1,600	$20,000
B	35,000	.95	1,400	36,000
C	30,000	1.50	—	34,500
D	15,000	1.25	375	16,500

a. Calculate the portfolio beta on the basis of the original cost figures.
b. Calculate the percentage return of each asset in the portfolio for the year.
c. Calculate the percentage return of the portfolio on the basis of original cost, using income and gains during the year.
d. At the time Jamie made his investments, investors were estimating that the market return for the coming year would be 10%. The estimate of the risk-free rate of return averaged 4% for the coming year. Calculate an expected rate of return for each stock on the basis of its beta and the expectations of market and risk-free returns.
e. On the basis of the actual results, explain how each stock in the portfolio performed relative to those CAPM-generated expectations of performance. What factors could explain these differences?

P5–27 **Security market line (SML)**   Assume that the risk-free rate, R_F, is currently 9% and that the market return, r_m, is currently 13%.
a. Draw the security market line (SML) on a set of "nondiversifiable risk (x axis)–required return (y axis)" axes.
b. Calculate and label the *market risk premium* on the axes in part **a.**
c. Given the previous data, calculate the required return on asset A having a beta of .80 and asset B having a beta of 1.30.
d. Draw in the betas and required returns from part **c** for assets A and B on the axes in part **a.** Label the *risk premium* associated with each of these assets, and discuss them.

P5–28 **Shifts in the security market line**   Assume that the risk-free rate, R_F, is currently 8%, the market return, r_m, is 12%, and asset A has a beta, b_A, of 1.10.
a. Draw the security market line (SML) on a set of "nondiversifiable risk (x axis)–required return (y axis)" axes.
b. Use CAPM to calculate the required return, r_A, on asset A, and depict asset A's beta and required return on the SML drawn in part **a.**
c. Assume that as a result of recent economic events, inflationary expectations have declined by 2%, lowering R_F and r_m to 6% and 10%, respectively. Draw the new SML on the axes in part **a,** and calculate and show the new required return for asset A.
d. Assume that as a result of recent events, investors have become more risk-averse, causing the market return to rise by 1%, to 13%. Ignoring the shift in part **c,** draw the new SML on the same set of axes that you used before, and calculate and show the new required return for asset A.
e. From the previous changes, what conclusions can be drawn about the impact of (1) decreased inflationary expectations and (2) increased risk aversion on the required returns of risky assets?

P5–29 **Integrative—Risk, return, and CAPM**   Wolff Enterprises must consider several investment projects, A through E, using the capital asset pricing model (CAPM) and its graphical representation, the security market line (SML). Relevant information is presented in the following table.

Item	Rate of return	Beta, b
Risk-free asset	9%	0
Market portfolio	14	1.00
Project A	—	1.50
Project B	—	.75
Project C	—	2.00
Project D	—	0
Project E	—	– .5

a. Calculate (1) the required rate of return and (2) the risk premium for each project, given its level of nondiversifiable risk.

b. Use your findings in part **a** to draw the security market line (required return relative to nondiversifiable risk).

c. Discuss the relative nondiversifiable risk of projects A through E.

d. Assume that recent economic events have caused investors to become less risk-averse, causing the market return to decline by 2%, to 12%. Calculate the new required returns for assets A through E, and draw the new security market line on the same set of axes that you used in part **b**.

e. Compare your findings in parts **a** and **b** with those in part **d**. What conclusion can you draw about the impact of a decline in investor risk aversion on the required returns of risky assets?

 P5–30   ETHICS PROBLEM   Integrity, especially honesty, is trait number one for being hired as a CFO in corporate America today. How might you assess a job candidate's honesty if you were interviewing a potential CFO candidate?

Chapter 5 Case

Analyzing Risk and Return on Chargers Products' Investments

Junior Sayou, a financial analyst for Chargers Products, a manufacturer of stadium benches, must evaluate the risk and return of two assets, X and Y. The firm is considering adding these assets to its diversified asset portfolio. To assess the return and risk of each asset, Junior gathered data on the annual cash flow and beginning- and end-of-year values of each asset over the immediately preceding 10 years, 2000–2009. These data are summarized in the following table (see page 276). Junior's investigation suggests that both assets, on average, will tend to perform in the future just as they have during the past 10 years. He therefore believes that the expected annual return can be estimated by finding the average annual return for each asset over the past 10 years.

	Return Data for Assets X and Y, 2000–2009					
	Asset X			Asset Y		
		Value			Value	
Year	Cash flow	Beginning	Ending	Cash flow	Beginning	Ending
2000	$1,000	$20,000	$22,000	$1,500	$20,000	$20,000
2001	1,500	22,000	21,000	1,600	20,000	20,000
2002	1,400	21,000	24,000	1,700	20,000	21,000
2003	1,700	24,000	22,000	1,800	21,000	21,000
2004	1,900	22,000	23,000	1,900	21,000	22,000
2005	1,600	23,000	26,000	2,000	22,000	23,000
2006	1,700	26,000	25,000	2,100	23,000	23,000
2007	2,000	25,000	24,000	2,200	23,000	24,000
2008	2,100	24,000	27,000	2,300	24,000	25,000
2009	2,200	27,000	30,000	2,400	25,000	25,000

Junior believes that each asset's risk can be assessed in two ways: in isolation and as part of the firm's diversified portfolio of assets. The risk of the assets in isolation can be found by using the standard deviation and coefficient of variation of returns over the past 10 years. The capital asset pricing model (CAPM) can be used to assess the asset's risk as part of the firm's portfolio of assets. Applying some sophisticated quantitative techniques, Junior estimated betas for assets X and Y of 1.60 and 1.10, respectively. In addition, he found that the risk-free rate is currently 7% and that the market return is 10%.

To Do

a. Calculate the annual rate of return for each asset in *each* of the 10 preceding years, and use those values to find the average annual return for each asset over the 10-year period.
b. Use the returns calculated in part **a** to find (1) the standard deviation and (2) the coefficient of variation of the returns for each asset over the 10-year period 2000–2009.
c. Use your findings in parts **a** and **b** to evaluate and discuss the return and risk associated with each asset. Which asset appears to be preferable? Explain.
d. Use the CAPM to find the required return for each asset. Compare this value with the average annual returns calculated in part **a**.
e. Compare and contrast your findings in parts **c** and **d**. What recommendations would you give Junior with regard to investing in either of the two assets? Explain to Junior why he is better off using beta rather than the standard deviation and coefficient of variation to assess the risk of each asset.
f. Rework parts **d** and **e** under each of the following circumstances:
   (1) A rise of 1% in inflationary expectations causes the risk-free rate to rise to 8% and the market return to rise to 11%.
   (2) As a result of favorable political events, investors suddenly become less risk-averse, causing the market return to drop by 1%, to 9%.

Spreadsheet Exercise

Jane is considering investing in three different stocks or creating three distinct two-stock portfolios. Jane considers herself to be a rather conservative investor. She is able to obtain forecasted returns for the three securities for the years 2010 through 2016. The data are as follows:

Year	Stock A	Stock B	Stock C
2010	10%	10%	12%
2011	13	11	14
2012	15	8	10
2013	14	12	11
2014	16	10	9
2015	14	15	9
2016	12	15	10

In any of the possible two-stock portfolios, the weight of each stock in the portfolio will be 50%. The three possible portfolio combinations are AB, AC, and BC.

To Do

Create a spreadsheet similar to Tables 5.7 and 5.8 (which can be viewed at www .prenhall.com/gitman) to answer the following:

a. Calculate the expected return for each individual stock.
b. Calculate the standard deviation for each individual stock.
c. Calculate the expected returns for portfolio AB, AC, and BC.
d. Calculate the standard deviations for portfolios AB, AC, and BC.
e. Would you recommend that Jane invest in the single stock A or the portfolio consisting of stocks A and B? Explain your answer from a risk–return viewpoint.
f. Would you recommend that Jane invest in the single stock B or the portfolio consisting of stocks B and C? Explain your answer from a risk–return viewpoint.

Group Exercise

This chapter begins the book's exploration of the important topics of risk and return. This assignment will bring the group back to an analysis of your real-world firm. Many websites provide the necessary type of market information, such as historical price data, returns, and betas. You should always be careful, as with any research, about the source of information; it is safest to stick to the more well-known or government-sponsored sites. One small part of this exercise will be to compare different sources of information and the information contained therein.

To Do

a. Obtain financial information for both broad market indices and your shadow firm. Begin by checking several websites, which will serve as a good way to compare these sites. At each site, look up your shadow firm and investigate what information each website has available. It should include current, historical, and market index information. As there are many quality sites with publicly available, free information, the following is merely a short list of suggestions. You will use some of these data in the other parts of this assignment.

   Point your browser to the Nasdaq home page, www.nasdaq.com/. Begin by asking for financial data on your shadow firm. To do so, use the stock symbol for your firm. Ask for a "summary quote," which will give you basic financial information along with options for other data and charts. Next, look up information on broader indices. Now, direct your browser to the home page of the NYSE, www.nyse.com/. Repeat the steps from the Nasdaq site. A very useful site is Yahoo's finance site http://finance.yahoo.com/. Next, go to Bloomberg's Web page, www.bloomberg.com/index.html, and repeat the steps. MSN's site, at www.moneycentral.msn.com/home.asp, is also useful. You may also use www.bigcharts.com to find historical stock prices and graphs. Lastly, you could visit Reuters' website at www.reuters.com/.

b. Using the site of your choice, find the price of your shadow corporation's stock one year earlier. Calculate its 1-year return based solely on the change in the price of a share of stock. Compare this return to the return for a market benchmark—for example, the Dow Jones Industrial Average, the S&P 500, or a Nasdaq-based metric such as the Nasdaq 100. Next, calculate the return for your stock over the past 5 years. How does the return over 5 years compare to the recent 1-year return? Now compare the 5-year return on your benchmark to your corporation's stock.

c. Using the same data as part **b**, calculate the annual return for each of the past 5 years for your stock. Use these data to compute the expected return and the standard deviation of the returns.

d. You can graphically check for correlation by eyeballing a 5-year chart that contains the past history of your stock and the benchmark you have chosen. Discuss the degree of correlation and any changes you notice over the period.

e. Use recent data to calculate the required return on your corporation. You will need to get the rate on 3-month T-bills to be used as the risk-free rate. You can use the beta reported by a site of your choice and use the historical return for your benchmark as the market return.

f. Using your answers from part **c**, graph the SML.

Web Exercise

 Go to the book's companion website at **www.prenhall.com/gitman** to find the Web Exercise for this chapter.

Remember to check the book's website at **www.prenhall.com/gitman** to find additional resources, including Web Exercises and a Web Case.

6 Interest Rates and Bond Valuation

Why This Chapter Matters to You

In Your Professional Life

Accounting: You need to understand interest rates and the various types of bonds to be able to account properly for amortization of bond premiums and discounts and for bond purchases and retirements.

Information systems: You need to understand the data that you will need to track in bond amortization schedules and bond valuation.

Management: You need to understand the behavior of interest rates and how they will affect the types of funds the firm can raise and the timing and cost of bond issues and retirements.

Marketing: You need to understand how the interest rate level and the firm's ability to issue bonds may affect the availability of financing for marketing research projects and new-product development.

Operations: You need to understand how the interest rate level may affect the firm's ability to raise funds to maintain and grow the firm's production capacity.

In Your Personal Life

Interest rates have a direct impact on personal financial planning. Movements in interest rates occur frequently and affect the returns from and values of savings and investments. The rate of interest you are charged on credit cards and loans can have a profound effect on your personal finances. Understanding the basics of interest rates is important to your personal financial plans.

Learning Goals

LG 1 Describe interest rate fundamentals, the term structure of interest rates, and risk premiums.

LG 2 Review the legal aspects of bond financing and bond cost.

LG 3 Discuss the general features, yields, prices, ratings, popular types, and international issues of corporate bonds.

LG 4 Understand the key inputs and basic model used in the valuation process.

LG 5 Apply the basic valuation model to bonds and describe the impact of required return and time to maturity on bond values.

LG 6 Explain yield to maturity (YTM), its calculation, and the procedure used to value bonds that pay interest semiannually.

The Federal Debt

A Huge Appetite for Money

Who is the largest debtor in the United States? The federal government, of course. As of May 12, 2007, the national debt was $8,819,278,857,652, with almost $5 trillion of the debt held by the public and around $3.8 trillion of debt held by intragovernmental holdings. With annual deficits of $423 billion in 2006 and a Congressional Budget Office deficits projection of as much as $1.76 trillion over the next decade, the federal government has a huge need for outside financing, which dwarfs any corporate bond issue.

To feed this huge demand, the **U.S Treasury Department** can issue T-bills, debt securities that mature in less than 1 year, Treasury notes that mature in 1 to 10 years, Treasury bonds that mature in more than 10 years, and savings bonds. Treasury securities can be purchased at banks (EE- and I-series savings bonds), at public auctions, and through TreasuryDirect, a Web-based system that allows investors to establish accounts to conduct transactions in Treasury securities online.

The Treasury Department did not offer a 30-year bond between August 2001 and February 2006. Falling interest rates in 2001 encouraged the U.S. Treasury to move toward the short-term end of the investment spectrum. But by February 2006, rising interest rates again made the 30-year bond attractive and the Treasury Department reintroduced the 30-year bond into the lineup. By doing so, the Treasury will diversify its funding options, expand its investor base, and stabilize the average maturity of the public debt. The 30-year bond has long been a favorite of fixed-income market participants seeking to match assets to future liabilities, and it serves as an important benchmark by which to measure other long-term fixed-income securities.

In fiscal year 2003, the U.S. government spent $405 billion on interest payments to holders of the national debt. As the national debt continues to rise, interest expense will continue to increase. Individuals can directly attack this interest expense by making payments to the Treasury

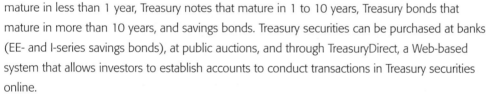

How might the issuance of large amounts of public debt affect the corporate debt market?

for the express purpose of reducing our national debt. In 2006 the Treasury received $1,646,209 from citizens wishing to reduce the federal debt. With the debt increasing at the pace of more than $1.39 billion per day, the contributions stopped the growth of the federal debt for just under two minutes.

6.1 | Interest Rates and Required Returns

As noted in Chapter 1, financial institutions and markets create the mechanism through which funds flow between savers (funds suppliers) and investors (funds demanders). The level of funds flow between suppliers and demanders can significantly affect economic growth. The interest rate level acts as a regulating device that controls the flow of funds between suppliers and demanders. The *Board of Governors of the Federal Reserve System* regularly assesses economic conditions and, when necessary, initiates actions to raise or lower interest rates to control inflation and economic growth. Generally, the lower the interest rate, the greater the funds flow and therefore the greater the economic growth; the higher the interest rate, the lower the funds flow and economic growth.

Interest Rate Fundamentals

interest rate
The compensation paid by the borrower of funds to the lender; from the borrower's point of view, the cost of borrowing funds.

required return
The cost of funds obtained by selling an ownership interest; it reflects the funds supplier's level of expected return.

liquidity preferences
General preferences of investors for shorter-term securities.

real rate of interest
The rate that creates an equilibrium between the supply of savings and the demand for investment funds in a perfect world, without inflation, where funds suppliers and demanders are indifferent to the term of loans or investments because they have no *liquidity preference,* and where all outcomes are certain.

The *interest rate* or *required return* represents the cost of money. It is the compensation that a demander of funds must pay a supplier. When funds are lent, the cost of borrowing the funds is the **interest rate**. When funds are obtained by selling an ownership interest—as in the sale of stock—the cost to the issuer (demander) is commonly called the **required return,** which reflects the funds supplier's level of expected return. In both cases the supplier is compensated for providing funds. Ignoring risk factors, the cost of funds results from the *real rate of interest* adjusted for inflationary expectations and **liquidity preferences**—general preferences of investors for shorter-term securities.

The Real Rate of Interest

Assume a *perfect world* in which there is no inflation and in which funds suppliers and demanders are indifferent to the term of loans or investments because they have no *liquidity preference* and all outcomes are certain.[1] At any given point in time in that perfect world, there would be one cost of money—the **real rate of interest.** The real rate of interest creates an equilibrium between the supply of savings and the demand for investment funds. It represents the most basic cost of money. The real rate of interest in the United States is assumed to be stable and equal to around 1 percent.[2] This supply–demand relationship is shown in Figure 6.1 by the supply function (labeled S_0) and the demand function (labeled D). An equilibrium between the supply of funds and the demand for funds ($S_0 = D$) occurs at a rate of interest r_0^*, the real rate of interest.

Clearly, the real rate of interest changes with changing economic conditions, tastes, and preferences. A trade surplus could result in an increased supply of funds, causing the supply function in Figure 6.1 to shift to, say, S_1. This could result in a lower real rate of interest, r_1^*, at equilibrium ($S_1 = D$). Likewise, a

---

1. These assumptions are made to describe the most basic interest rate, the *real rate of interest.* Subsequent discussions relax these assumptions to develop the broader concept of the interest rate and required return.

2. Data in *Stocks, Bonds, Bills, and Inflation, 2007 Yearbook* (Chicago: Ibbotson Associates, Inc., 2007), show that over the period 1926–2006, U.S. Treasury bills provided an average annual real rate of return of about 0.70 percent. Because of certain major economic events that occurred during the 1926–2006 period, many economists believe that the real rate of interest during recent years has been about 1 percent.

FIGURE 6.1

Supply–Demand Relationship
Supply of savings and demand for investment funds

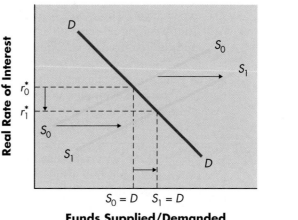

change in tax laws or other factors could affect the demand for funds, causing the real rate of interest to rise or fall to a new equilibrium level.

Nominal or Actual Rate of Interest (Return)

nominal rate of interest
The actual rate of interest charged by the supplier of funds and paid by the demander.

The **nominal rate of interest** is the actual rate of interest charged by the supplier of funds and paid by the demander. *Throughout this book, interest rates and required rates of return are nominal rates unless otherwise noted.* The nominal rate of interest differs from the real rate of interest, r^*, as a result of two factors: (1) inflationary expectations reflected in an inflation premium (*IP*), and (2) issuer and issue characteristics, such as default risk and contractual provisions, reflected in a risk premium (*RP*). When this notation is adopted, the nominal rate of interest for security 1, r_1, is given in Equation 6.1:

$$r_1 = \underbrace{r^* + IP}_{\substack{\text{risk-free} \\ \text{rate, } R_F}} + \underbrace{RP_1}_{\substack{\text{risk} \\ \text{premium}}} \qquad \text{(6.1)}$$

As the horizontal braces below the equation indicate, the nominal rate, r_1, can be viewed as having two basic components: a risk-free rate of return, R_F, and a risk premium, RP_1:

$$r_1 = R_F + RP_1 \qquad \text{(6.2)}$$

To simplify the discussion, we will assume that the risk premium, RP_1, is equal to zero. By drawing from Equation 6.1,[3] the risk-free rate can (as earlier noted in Equation 5.9) be represented as

$$R_F = r^* + IP \qquad \text{(6.3)}$$

Thus we concern ourselves only with the *risk-free rate of return, R_F,* which was defined in Chapter 5 as the required return on a risk-free asset.[4] The risk-free rate

---

3. This equation is commonly called the *Fisher equation,* named for the renowned economist Irving Fisher, who first presented this approximate relationship between nominal interest and the rate of inflation. See Irving Fisher, *The Theory of Interest* (New York: Macmillan, 1930).

4. The risk premium and its effect on the nominal rate of interest are discussed and illustrated in a later part of this section.

(as shown in Equation 6.3) embodies the real rate of interest plus the inflationary expectation. Three-month *U.S. Treasury bills* (*T-bills*), which are (as noted in Chapter 5) short-term IOUs issued by the U.S. Treasury, are commonly considered the risk-free asset. *The real rate of interest can be estimated by subtracting the inflation premium from the nominal rate of interest.* For the risk-free asset in Equation 6.3, the real rate of interest, r^*, would equal $R_F - IP$. A simple personal finance example can demonstrate the practical distinction between nominal and real rates of interest.

Personal Finance Example   Marilyn Carbo has $10 that she can spend on candy costing $0.25 per piece. She could buy 40 pieces of candy ($10.00/$0.25) today. The nominal rate of interest on a 1-year deposit is currently 7%, and the expected rate of inflation over the coming year is 4%. Instead of buying the 40 pieces of candy today, Marilyn could invest the $10 in a 1-year deposit account now. At the end of 1 year she would have $10.70 because she would have earned 7% interest—an additional $0.70 ($0.07 \times $10.00)—on her $10 deposit. The 4% inflation rate would over the 1-year period increase the cost of the candy by 4%—an additional $0.01 ($0.04 \times $0.25)—to $0.26 per piece. As a result, at the end of the 1-year period Marilyn would be able to buy about 41.2 pieces of candy ($10.70/$0.26), or roughly 3% more (41.2/40.0 = 1.03). The increase in the amount of money available to Marilyn at the end of 1 year is merely her nominal rate of return (7%), which must be reduced by the rate of inflation (4%) during the period to determine her real rate of return of 3%. Marilyn's increased buying power therefore equals her 3% real rate of return.

The premium for *inflationary expectations* in Equation 6.3 represents the average rate of *inflation* expected over the life of a loan or investment. It is *not* the rate of inflation experienced over the immediate past; rather, it reflects the forecasted rate. Take, for example, the risk-free asset. During the week ended March 18, 2007, 3-month T-bills earned a 4.95 percent rate of return. Assuming an approximate 0.70 percent real rate of interest, funds suppliers were forecasting a 4.25 percent (annual) rate of inflation (4.95% − 0.70%) over the next 3 months. This expectation was in striking contrast to the expected rate of inflation 26 years earlier in the week ending May 22, 1981. At that time the 3-month T-bill rate was 16.60 percent, which meant an expected (annual) inflation rate of 15.90 percent (16.60% − 0.70%). The inflationary expectation premium changes over time in response to many factors, including recent rates, government policies, and international events. For discussion of a U.S. debt security whose interest rate is adjusted for inflation, see the nearby *Focus on Practice* box.

Figure 6.2 (see page 286) illustrates the annual movement of the rate of inflation and the risk-free rate of return during the period 1978–2007. During this period the two rates tended to move in a similar fashion. Between 1978 and the early 1980s, inflation and interest rates were quite high, peaking at over 13 percent in 1980–1981. Since 1981 these rates have declined to levels generally below those in 1978. Note that between 2002 and 2005 the annual rate of inflation actually exceeded the average 3-month Treasury bill rate. The data in Figure 6.2 clearly illustrate the significant impact of inflation on the nominal rate of interest for the risk-free asset.

IN PRACTICE

Focus on Practice   I-Bonds Adjust for Inflation

One of the negatives of debt instruments when compared with equity assets is that once issued, fixed-rate debt instruments cannot adjust for inflation. In fact, rising inflation generally increases the risk-free rate of return, and new bond issues command a higher coupon rate than previously issued bonds. From your study of the time value of money in Chapter 4, you may have discovered that when interest rates rise, the market value of previously issued bonds falls.

The **U.S. Treasury Department** now offers the I-bond, which is an inflation-adjusted savings bond. A Series-I bond earns interest through the application of a *composite rate*. The composite rate consists of a *fixed rate* that remains the same for the life of the bond and an *inflation rate* that is subject to change twice a year. Interest accrues monthly and compounds semiannually. Interest earnings are payable only upon redemption. Like all federal debt instruments, interest earnings are exempt from state and local income taxes. I-bonds are issued at face value in denominations of $50, $75, $100, $200, $500, $1,000, $5,000, and $10,000. Individuals can purchase up to $30,000 per year of paper I-bonds and an additional $30,000 of I-bonds electronically.

To adjust the inflation portion of the I-bond's interest rate, the Treasury uses the Consumer Price Index for All Urban Consumers (CPI-U) as the inflation rate. The CPI-U rate is announced semiannually in May and November. The May and November figures are applicable for a 6-month period for any bonds issued before the next composite rate announcement. The I-bond's composite rate will be *higher* than its fixed rate if the semiannual inflation rate reflects any *inflation*. Likewise, an I-bond's composite rate will be *lower* than its fixed rate if the semiannual inflation rate reflects any *deflation*. However, even if deflation becomes so great that it would reduce the composite rate below zero, the Treasury will not allow the value of the bond to decrease from its most recent redemption value.

The I-bond is not without its deficiencies. First, any redemption within the first 5 years results in a 3-month interest penalty. Also, you should redeem an I-bond only at the first of the month because none of the interest earned during a month is included in the redemption value until the first day of the following month. Nevertheless, if inflation ever comes back as aggressively as it did in the late 1970s, I-bond holders will enjoy the benefits of its inflation-protection feature.

■ *What effect do you think the inflation-adjusted interest rate has on the cost of an I-bond in comparison with similar bonds with no allowance for inflation?*

Term Structure of Interest Rates

term structure of interest rates
The relationship between the interest rate or rate of return and the time to maturity.

For any class of similar-risk securities, the **term structure of interest rates** relates the interest rate or rate of return to the time to maturity. For convenience we will use Treasury securities as an example, but other classes could include securities that have similar overall quality or risk. The riskless nature of Treasury securities also provides a laboratory in which to develop the term structure.

Yield Curves

yield to maturity
Compound annual rate of return earned on a debt security purchased on a given day and held to maturity.

A debt security's **yield to maturity** (discussed later in this chapter) represents the compound annual rate of return earned on it assuming it is purchased on a given day and held to maturity. At any point in time, the relationship between the debt's remaining time to maturity and its yield to maturity is represented by the

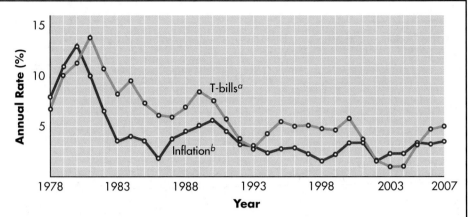

FIGURE 6.2

Impact of Inflation
Relationship between annual rate of inflation and 3-month U.S. Treasury bill average annual returns, 1978–2007

a Average annual rate of return on 3-month U.S. Treasury bills.
b Annual pecentage change in the consumer price index.

Sources: Data from selected *Federal Reserve Bulletins* and *U.S. Department of Labor Bureau of Labor Statistics.*

yield curve
A graph of the relationship between the debt's remaining time to maturity (*x* axis) and its yield to maturity (*y* axis); it shows the yield to maturity for debts of equal quality and different maturities. Graphically depicts the *term structure of interest rates.*

inverted yield curve
A *downward-sloping* yield curve that indicates generally cheaper long-term borrowing costs than short-term borrowing costs.

normal yield curve
An *upward-sloping* yield curve that indicates generally cheaper short-term borrowing costs than long-term borrowing costs.

flat yield curve
A yield curve that reflects relatively similar borrowing costs for both short- and longer-term loans.

expectations theory
The theory that the yield curve reflects investor expectations about future interest rates and inflation; an increasing inflation expectation results in an upward-sloping yield curve, and a decreasing inflation expectation results in a downward-sloping yield curve.

yield curve. The yield curve shows the yield to maturity for debts of equal quality and different maturities; it is a graphical depiction of the *term structure of interest rates.* Figure 6.3 shows three yield curves for all U.S. Treasury securities: one at May 22, 1981, a second at September 29, 1989, and a third at May 17, 2004. (Note that we purposefully kept the yield curve for 2004 because it better shows some key lessons than do more current yield curves, which are relatively flat.)

Observe that both the position and the shape of the yield curves change over time. The yield curve of May 22, 1981, indicates that short-term interest rates at that time were above longer-term rates. This curve is described as *downward-sloping,* reflecting long-term borrowing costs generally cheaper than short-term borrowing costs. Historically, the downward-sloping yield curve, which is often called an **inverted yield curve,** has been the exception. More frequently, yield curves similar to that of May 17, 2004, have existed. These *upward-sloping* or **normal yield curves** indicate that short-term borrowing costs are below long-term borrowing costs. Sometimes, a **flat yield curve,** similar to that of September 29, 1989, exists. It reflects relatively similar borrowing costs for both short- and longer-term loans. In mid-March 2007, the yield curve (not shown) was flat with yields over the 30 years ranging between 4.46 and 5.07 percent.

The shape of the yield curve may affect the firm's financing decisions. A financial manager who faces a downward-sloping yield curve is likely to rely more heavily on cheaper, long-term financing; when the yield curve is upward-sloping, the manager is more likely to use cheaper, short-term financing. Although a variety of other factors influence the choice of loan maturity, the shape of the yield curve provides useful insights into future interest rate expectations.

Theories of Term Structure

Three theories are frequently cited to explain the general shape of the yield curve: the expectations theory, the liquidity preference theory, and the market segmentation theory.

Expectations Theory   One theory of the term structure of interest rates, the **expectations theory,** suggests that the yield curve reflects investor expectations

FIGURE 6.3 **Treasury Yield Curves** Yield curves for U.S. Treasury securities: May 22, 1981; September 29, 1989; and May 17, 2004	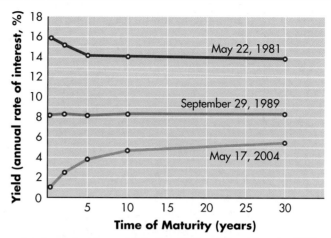

Sources: Data from *Federal Reserve Bulletins* (June 1981), p. A25 and (December 1989), p. A24; and U.S. Department of Treasury Office of Debt Management, www.ustreas.gov/offices/domestic-finance/debt-management/interest-rate/yield.html

about future interest rates and inflation. Higher future rates of expected inflation will result in higher long-term interest rates; the opposite occurs with lower future rates. This widely accepted explanation of the term structure can be applied to the securities of any issuer.

For example, take the case of U.S. Treasury securities. Thus far, we have concerned ourselves solely with the 3-month Treasury bill. In fact, all Treasury securities are *riskless* in terms of (1) the chance that the Treasury will default on the issue and (2) the ease with which they can be liquidated for cash without losing value. Because it is believed to be easier to forecast inflation over shorter periods of time, the shorter-term 3-month U.S. Treasury bill is considered the risk-free asset. Of course, differing inflation expectations associated with different maturities will cause nominal interest rates to vary. With the addition of a maturity subscript, *t*, Equation 6.3 can be rewritten as

$$R_{F_t} = r^* + IP_t \tag{6.4}$$

In other words, for U.S. Treasury securities the nominal, or risk-free, rate for a given maturity varies with the inflation expectation over the term of the security.[5]

Example | The nominal interest rate, R_F, for four maturities of U.S. Treasury securities on May 17, 2004, is given in column 1 of the table on page 288. Assuming that the real rate of interest is 0.70%, as noted in column 2, the inflation expectation for each maturity in column 3 is found by solving Equation 6.4 for IP_t. Although a 0.36% rate of inflation was expected over the 3-month period beginning May 17, 2004, a 1.81% average rate of inflation was expected over the 2-year period, and so on. An analysis of the inflation expectations in column 3 for May 17, 2004, suggests that at that time a general expectation of increasing inflation existed. Simply stated, the May 17, 2004, yield curve for U.S. Treasury securities shown

---

5. Although U.S. Treasury securities have no risk of default or illiquidity, they do suffer from "maturity, or interest rate, risk"—the risk that interest rates will change in the future and thereby affect longer maturities more than shorter maturities. Therefore, the longer the maturity of a Treasury (or any other) security, the greater its interest rate risk. The impact of interest rate changes on bond values is discussed later in this chapter; here we ignore this effect.

in Figure 6.3 was upward-sloping as a result of the expectation that the rate of inflation would increase in the future.[6]

Maturity, t	Nominal interest rate, R_{F_t} (1)	Real interest rate, r^* (2)	Inflation expectation, IP_t [(1) − (2)] (3)
3 months	1.06%	0.70%	0.36%
2 years	2.51	0.70	1.81
5 years	3.83	0.70	3.13
30 years	5.49	0.70	4.79

Generally, under the expectations theory, an increasing inflation expectation results in an upward-sloping yield curve; a decreasing inflation expectation results in a downward-sloping yield curve; and a stable inflation expectation results in a flat yield curve. Although, as we'll see, other theories exist, the observed strong relationship between inflation and interest rates (see Figure 6.2) supports this widely accepted theory.

Liquidity Preference Theory   The tendency for yield curves to be upward-sloping can be further explained by the **liquidity preference theory.** This theory holds that for a given issuer, such as the U.S. Treasury, long-term rates tend to be higher than short-term rates. This belief is based on two behavioral facts:

1. Investors perceive less risk in short-term securities than in longer-term securities and are therefore willing to accept lower yields on them. The reason is that shorter-term securities are more liquid and less responsive to general interest rate movements.[7]
2. Borrowers are generally willing to pay a higher rate for long-term than for short-term financing. By locking in funds for a longer period of time, they can eliminate the potential adverse consequences of having to roll over short-term debt at unknown costs to obtain long-term financing.

Investors (lenders) tend to require a premium for tying up funds for longer periods, whereas borrowers are generally willing to pay a premium to obtain longer-term financing. These preferences of lenders and borrowers cause the yield curve to tend to be upward-sloping. Simply stated, longer maturities tend to have higher interest rates than shorter maturities.

Market Segmentation Theory   The **market segmentation theory** suggests that the market for loans is segmented on the basis of maturity and that the supply of and demand for loans within each segment determine its prevailing interest rate. In other words, the equilibrium between suppliers and demanders of short-term funds, such as seasonal business loans, would determine prevailing short-

liquidity preference theory
Theory suggesting that for any given issuer, long-term interest rates tend to be higher than short-term rates because (1) lower liquidity and higher responsiveness to general interest rate movements of longer-term securities exists and (2) borrower willingness to pay a higher rate for long-term financing cause the yield curve to be upward-sloping.

market segmentation theory
Theory suggesting that the market for loans is segmented on the basis of maturity and that the supply of and demand for loans within each segment determine its prevailing interest rate; the slope of the yield curve is determined by the general relationship between the prevailing rates in each market segment.

6. It is interesting to note (in Figure 6.3) that the expectations reflected by the September 29, 1989, yield curve were not fully borne out by actual events. By May 2004, interest rates had fallen for all maturities, and the yield curve at that time had shifted downward and become upward-sloping, reflecting an expectation of increasing future interest rates and inflation rates.

7. Later in this chapter we demonstrate that debt instruments with longer maturities are more sensitive to changing market interest rates. For a given change in market rates, the price or value of longer-term debts will be more significantly changed (up or down) than the price or value of debts with shorter maturities.

term interest rates, and the equilibrium between suppliers and demanders of long-term funds, such as real estate loans, would determine prevailing long-term interest rates. The slope of the yield curve would be determined by the general relationship between the prevailing rates in each market segment. Simply stated, low rates in the short-term segment and high rates in the long-term segment cause the yield curve to be upward-sloping. The opposite occurs for high short-term rates and low long-term rates.

All three theories of term structure have merit. From them we can conclude that at any time, the slope of the yield curve is affected by (1) inflationary expectations, (2) liquidity preferences, and (3) the comparative equilibrium of supply and demand in the short- and long-term market segments. Upward-sloping yield curves result from higher future inflation expectations, lender preferences for shorter-maturity loans, and greater supply of short-term loans than of long-term loans relative to demand. The opposite behaviors would result in a downward-sloping yield curve. At any time, the interaction of these three forces determines the prevailing slope of the yield curve.

Risk Premiums: Issuer and Issue Characteristics

So far we have considered only risk-free U.S. Treasury securities. We now reintroduce the risk premium and assess it in view of risky non-Treasury issues. Recall Equation 6.1:

$$r_1 = \underbrace{r^* + IP}_{\substack{\text{risk-free} \\ \text{rate, } R_F}} + \underbrace{RP_1}_{\substack{\text{risk} \\ \text{premium}}}$$

In words, the nominal rate of interest for security 1 (r_1) is equal to the risk-free rate, consisting of the real rate of interest (r^*) plus the inflation expectation premium (IP), plus the risk premium (RP_1). The *risk premium* varies with specific issuer and issue characteristics[8]; it causes similar-maturity securities to have differing nominal rates of interest.

Example

The nominal interest rates on a number of classes of long-term securities on May 17, 2004, were as follows:[9]

Security	Nominal interest rate
U.S. Treasury bonds (average)	5.44%
Corporate bonds (by ratings):	
High quality (Aaa–Aa)	6.04
Medium quality (A–Baa)	6.82
Speculative (Ba–C)	11.32
Utility bonds (average rating)	6.61

8. To provide for the same risk-free rate of interest, $r^* + IP$, it is necessary to assume equal maturities. When we do so, the inflationary expectations premium, IP, and therefore R_F, will be held constant, and the issuer and issue characteristics premium, RP, becomes the key factor differentiating the nominal rates of interest on various securities.

9. These yields were obtained from yields and spreads from Reuters as posted on the Bondsonline website, www.bondsonline.com, on May 17, 2004. Note that bond ratings are explained later in this chapter, beginning on page 295.

Because the U.S. Treasury bond would represent the risk-free, long-term security, we can calculate the risk premium of the other securities by subtracting the risk-free rate, 5.44%, from each nominal rate (yield):

Security	Risk premium
Corporate bonds (by ratings):	
High quality (Aaa–Aa)	$6.04\% - 5.44\% = 0.60\%$
Medium quality (A–Baa)	$6.82 \quad - 5.44 \quad = 1.38$
Speculative (Ba–C)	$11.32 \quad - 5.44 \quad = 5.88$
Utility bonds (average rating)	$6.61 \quad - 5.44 \quad = 1.17$

These risk premiums reflect differing issuer and issue risks. The lower-rated corporate issues (speculative) have a far higher risk premium than that of the higher-rated corporates (high quality and medium quality), and the utility issue has a risk premium near that of the medium-quality corporates.

The risk premium consists of a number of issuer- and issue-related components, including business risk, financial risk, interest rate risk, liquidity risk, and tax risk, which were defined in Table 5.1 on page 229, and the purely debt-specific risks—default risk, maturity risk, and contractual provision risk, briefly defined in Table 6.1. In general, the highest risk premiums and therefore the highest returns result from securities issued by firms with a high risk of default and from long-term maturities that have unfavorable contractual provisions.

TABLE 6.1	Debt-Specific Issuer- and Issue-Related Risk Premium Components
Component	**Description**
Default risk	The possibility that the issuer of debt will not pay the contractual interest or principal as scheduled. The greater the uncertainty as to the borrower's ability to meet these payments, the greater the risk premium. High bond ratings reflect low default risk, and low bond ratings reflect high default risk.
Maturity risk	The fact that the longer the maturity, the more the value of a security will change in response to a given change in interest rates. If interest rates on otherwise similar-risk securities suddenly rise as a result of a change in the money supply, the prices of long-term bonds will decline by more than the prices of short-term bonds, and vice versa.[a]
Contractual provision risk	Conditions that are often included in a debt agreement or a stock issue. Some of these reduce risk, whereas others may increase risk. For example, a provision allowing a bond issuer to retire its bonds prior to their maturity under favorable terms increases the bond's risk.

[a]A detailed discussion of the effects of interest rates on the price or value of bonds and other fixed-income securities is presented later in this chapter.

REVIEW QUESTIONS

6–1   What is the *real rate of interest?* Differentiate it from the *nominal rate of interest* for the risk-free asset, a 3-month U.S. Treasury bill.

6–2   What is the *term structure of interest rates,* and how is it related to the *yield curve?*

6–3   For a given class of similar-risk securities, what does each of the following yield curves reflect about interest rates: **(a)** downward-sloping; **(b)** upward-sloping; and **(c)** flat? Which form has been historically dominant?

6–4   Briefly describe the following theories of the general shape of the yield curve: **(a)** expectations theory; **(b)** liquidity preference theory; and **(c)** market segmentation theory.

6–5   List and briefly describe the potential issuer- and issue-related risk components that are embodied in the risk premium. Which are the purely debt-specific risks?

6.2 | Corporate Bonds

corporate bond
A long-term debt instrument indicating that a corporation has borrowed a certain amount of money and promises to repay it in the future under clearly defined terms.

coupon interest rate
The percentage of a bond's par value that will be paid annually, typically in two equal semiannual payments, as interest.

A **corporate bond** is a long-term debt instrument indicating that a corporation has borrowed a certain amount of money and promises to repay it in the future under clearly defined terms. Most bonds are issued with maturities of 10 to 30 years and with a par value, or face value, of $1,000. The **coupon interest rate** on a bond represents the percentage of the bond's par value that will be paid annually, typically in two equal semiannual payments, as interest. The bondholders, who are the lenders, are promised the semiannual interest payments and, at maturity, repayment of the principal amount.

Legal Aspects of Corporate Bonds

Certain legal arrangements are required to protect purchasers of bonds. Bondholders are protected primarily through the indenture and the trustee.

Bond Indenture

bond indenture
A legal document that specifies both the rights of the bondholders and the duties of the issuing corporation.

A **bond indenture** is a legal document that specifies both the rights of the bondholders and the duties of the issuing corporation. Included in the indenture are descriptions of the amount and timing of all interest and principal payments, various standard and restrictive provisions, and, frequently, sinking-fund requirements and security interest provisions.

standard debt provisions
Provisions in a *bond indenture* specifying certain record-keeping and general business practices that the bond issuer must follow; normally, they do not place a burden on a financially sound business.

Standard Provisions   The **standard debt provisions** in the bond indenture specify certain record-keeping and general business practices that the bond issuer must follow. Standard debt provisions do not normally place a burden on a financially sound business.

The borrower commonly must (1) *maintain satisfactory accounting records* in accordance with generally accepted accounting principles (GAAP); (2) periodically *supply audited financial statements;* (3) *pay taxes and other liabilities when due;* and (4) *maintain all facilities in good working order.*

Restrictive Provisions   Bond indentures also normally include certain **restrictive covenants,** which place operating and financial constraints on the borrower. These provisions help protect the bondholder against increases in borrower risk. Without them, the borrower could increase the firm's risk but not have to pay increased interest to compensate for the increased risk.

The most common restrictive covenants do the following:

1. Require a *minimum level of liquidity,* to ensure against loan default.
2. *Prohibit the sale of accounts receivable* to generate cash. Selling receivables could cause a long-run cash shortage if proceeds were used to meet current obligations.
3. Impose *fixed-asset restrictions.* The borrower must maintain a specified level of fixed assets to guarantee its ability to repay the bonds.
4. *Constrain subsequent borrowing.* Additional long-term debt may be prohibited, or additional borrowing may be *subordinated* to the original loan. **Subordination** means that subsequent creditors agree to wait until all claims of the *senior debt* are satisfied.
5. *Limit the firm's annual cash dividend payments* to a specified percentage or amount.

Other restrictive covenants are sometimes included in bond indentures.

The violation of any standard or restrictive provision by the borrower gives the bondholders the right to demand immediate repayment of the debt. Generally, bondholders evaluate any violation to determine whether it jeopardizes the loan. They may then decide to demand immediate repayment, continue the loan, or alter the terms of the bond indenture.

Sinking-Fund Requirements   Another common restrictive provision is a **sinking-fund requirement.** Its objective is to provide for the systematic retirement of bonds prior to their maturity. To carry out this requirement, the corporation makes semiannual or annual payments that are used to retire bonds by purchasing them in the marketplace.

Security Interest   The bond indenture identifies any collateral pledged against the bond and specifies how it is to be maintained. The protection of bond collateral is crucial to guarantee the safety of a bond issue.

Trustee

A **trustee** is a third party to a *bond indenture.* The trustee can be an individual, a corporation, or (most often) a commercial bank trust department. The trustee is paid to act as a "watchdog" on behalf of the bondholders and can take specified actions on behalf of the bondholders if the terms of the indenture are violated.

Cost of Bonds to the Issuer

The cost of bond financing is generally greater than the issuer would have to pay for short-term borrowing. The major factors that affect the cost, which is the rate of interest paid by the bond issuer, are the bond's maturity, the size of the offering, the issuer's risk, and the basic cost of money.

Impact of Bond Maturity

Generally, as we noted earlier, long-term debt pays higher interest rates than short-term debt. In a practical sense, the longer the maturity of a bond, the less accuracy there is in predicting future interest rates, and therefore the greater the bondholders' risk of giving up an opportunity to lend money at a higher rate. In addition, the longer the term, the greater the chance that the issuer might default.

Impact of Offering Size

The size of the bond offering also affects the interest cost of borrowing, but in an inverse manner: Bond flotation and administration costs per dollar borrowed are likely to decrease with increasing offering size. On the other hand, the risk to the bondholders may increase, because larger offerings result in greater risk of default.

Impact of Issuer's Risk

The greater the issuer's *default risk,* the higher the interest rate. Some of this risk can be reduced through inclusion of appropriate restrictive provisions in the bond indenture. Clearly, bondholders must be compensated with higher returns for taking greater risk. Frequently, bond buyers rely on bond ratings (discussed later) to determine the issuer's overall risk.

Impact of the Cost of Money

The cost of money in the capital market is the basis for determining a bond's coupon interest rate. Generally, the rate on U.S. Treasury securities of equal maturity is used as the lowest-risk cost of money. To that basic rate is added a *risk premium* (as described earlier in this chapter) that reflects the factors mentioned above (maturity, offering size, and issuer's risk).

General Features of a Bond Issue

Three features sometimes included in a corporate bond issue are a conversion feature, a call feature, and stock purchase warrants. These features provide the issuer or the purchaser with certain opportunities for replacing or retiring the bond or supplementing it with some type of equity issue.

Convertible bonds offer a **conversion feature** that allows bondholders to change each bond into a stated number of shares of common stock. Bondholders convert their bonds into stock only when the market price of the stock is such that conversion will provide a profit for the bondholder. Inclusion of the conversion feature by the issuer lowers the interest cost and provides for automatic conversion of the bonds to stock if future stock prices appreciate noticeably.

The **call feature** is included in nearly all corporate bond issues. It gives the issuer the opportunity to repurchase bonds prior to maturity. The **call price** is the stated price at which bonds may be repurchased prior to maturity. Sometimes the call feature can be exercised only during a certain period. As a rule, the call price exceeds the par value of a bond by an amount equal to 1 year's interest. For example, a $1,000 bond with a 10 percent coupon interest rate would be callable for around $1,100 [$1,000 + (10% × $1,000)]. The amount by which the call

conversion feature
A feature of *convertible bonds* that allows bondholders to change each bond into a stated number of shares of common stock.

call feature
A feature included in nearly all corporate bond issues that gives the issuer the opportunity to repurchase bonds at a stated *call price* prior to maturity.

call price
The stated price at which a bond may be repurchased, by use of a *call feature,* prior to maturity.

call premium
The amount by which a bond's *call price* exceeds its par value.

price exceeds the bond's par value is commonly referred to as the **call premium.** This premium compensates bondholders for having the bond called away from them; to the issuer, it is the cost of calling the bonds.

The call feature enables an issuer to call an outstanding bond when interest rates fall and issue a new bond at a lower interest rate. When interest rates rise, the call privilege will not be exercised, except possibly to meet *sinking-fund requirements*. Of course, to sell a callable bond in the first place, the issuer must pay a higher interest rate than on noncallable bonds of equal risk, to compensate bondholders for the risk of having the bonds called away from them.

stock purchase warrants
Instruments that give their holders the right to purchase a certain number of shares of the issuer's common stock at a specified price over a certain period of time. Occasionally attached to bonds as "sweeteners."

Bonds occasionally have stock purchase warrants attached as "sweeteners" to make them more attractive to prospective buyers. **Stock purchase warrants** are instruments that give their holders the right to purchase a certain number of shares of the issuer's common stock at a specified price over a certain period of time. Their inclusion typically enables the issuer to pay a slightly lower coupon interest rate than would otherwise be required.

Bond Yields

The *yield*, or rate of return, on a bond is frequently used to assess a bond's performance over a given period of time, typically 1 year. Because there are a number of ways to measure a bond's yield, it is important to understand popular yield measures. The three most widely cited bond yields are (1) *current yield*, (2) *yield to maturity (YTM)*, and (3) *yield to call (YTC)*. Each of these yields provides a unique measure of the return on a bond.

current yield
A measure of a bond's cash return for the year; calculated by dividing the bond's annual interest payment by its current price.

The simplest yield measure is the **current yield,** the annual interest payment divided by the current price. For example, a $1,000 par value bond with an 8% coupon interest rate that currently sells for $970 would have a current yield of 8.25% [(0.08 × $1,000)/$970]. This measure indicates the cash return for the year from the bond. However, because current yield ignores any change in bond value, it does not measure the total return. As we'll see later in this chapter, both the yield to maturity and the yield to call measure the total return.

Bond Prices

Because most corporate bonds are purchased and held by institutional investors, such as banks, insurance companies, and mutual funds, rather than individual investors, bond trading and price data are not readily available to individuals. Table 6.2 includes some assumed current data on the bonds of five companies, noted A through E. Looking at the data for Company C's bond, which is highlighted in the table, we see that the bond has a coupon interest rate of 7.200% and a maturity date of January 15, 2014. These data identify a specific bond issued by Company C. (The company could have more than a single bond issue outstanding.) The price represents the final price at which the bond traded on the current day.

Although most corporate bonds are issued with a *par*, or *face*, *value* of $1,000, *all bonds are quoted as a percentage of par*. A $1,000-par-value bond quoted at 94.007 is priced at $940.07 (94.007% × $1,000). Corporate bonds are quoted in dollars and cents. Thus, Company C's price of 103.143 for the day was $1,031.43—that is, 103.143% × $1,000.

TABLE 6.2	Data on Selected Bonds			
Company	Coupon	Maturity	Price	Yield (YTM)
Company A	6.125%	Nov. 15, 2011	105.336	4.788%
Company B	6.000	Oct. 31, 2036	94.007	6.454
Company C	7.200	Jan. 15, 2014	103.143	6.606
Company D	5.150	Jan. 15, 2017	95.140	5.814
Company E	5.850	Jan. 14, 2012	100.876	5.631

The final column of Table 6.2 represents the bond's *yield to maturity (YTM)*, which is the compound annual rate of return that would be earned on the bond if it were purchased on the given day and held to maturity. (YTM is discussed in detail later in this chapter.)

Bond Ratings

Independent agencies such as Moody's and Standard & Poor's assess the riskiness of publicly traded bond issues. These agencies derive their ratings by using financial ratio and cash flow analyses to assess the likely payment of bond interest and principal. Table 6.3 summarizes these ratings. For discussion of ethical issues related to the bond-rating agencies, see the *Focus on Ethics* box on page 296.

Normally an inverse relationship exists between the quality of a bond and the rate of return that it must provide bondholders: High-quality (high-rated) bonds provide lower returns than lower-quality (low-rated) bonds. This reflects the lender's risk–return tradeoff. When considering bond financing, the financial

Hint Note that Moody's has 9 major ratings; Standard & Poor's has 10.

TABLE 6.3	Moody's and Standard & Poor's Bond Ratings[a]			
Moody's	Interpretation	Standard & Poor's	Interpretation
---	---	---	---
Aaa	Prime quality	AAA	Bank investment quality
Aa	High grade	AA	
A	Upper medium grade	A	
Baa	Medium grade	BBB	
Ba	Lower medium grade	BB	Speculative
	or speculative	B	
B	Speculative		
Caa	From very speculative	CCC	
Ca	to near or in default	CC	
C	Lowest grade	C	Income bond
		D	In default

[a]Some ratings may be modified to show relative standing within a major rating category; for example, Moody's uses numerical modifiers (1, 2, 3), whereas Standard & Poor's uses plus (+) and minus (−) signs.
Sources: Moody's Investors Service, Inc. and Standard & Poor's Corporation.

Focus on Ethics   Can We Trust the Bond Raters?

IN PRACTICE

Assessing default risk requires an evaluation of creditworthiness. Most investors have neither the time nor the expertise to do their own credit appraisals for potential bond investments, so they rely on credit-rating agencies for this service. But how reliable are their ratings?

"The dominant rating agencies failed millions of investors by neglecting to lower their ratings on Enron, WorldCom, and other companies heading for bankruptcy," said Alabama Senator Richard Shelby, past-chair of the Senate Banking Committee and sponsor of legislation to hold rating agencies more accountable. "The absence of timely downgrades in these cases was a product of an industry that was beset with conflicts of interest and a lack of competition. Ultimately, this compromised the integrity of the market and investors paid the price," he concluded.

On September 29, 2006, President Bush signed the *Credit*

Rating Agency Reform Act of 2006, which abolished the SEC's authority to designate credit-rating agencies as "nationally recognized rating agencies (NRSROs)." Instead, a credit-rating company with 3 years of experience that meets certain standards would be allowed to register with the SEC as a "statistical ratings organization."

The new law is designed to curb alleged abusive practices cited by members of Congress and corporate trade groups, including the practice of sending a company unsolicited ratings with a bill; *notching*, which occurs when a firm lowers ratings on asset-backed securities unless the firm rates a substantial portion of the underlying assets; and tying ratings to the purchase of additional services.

"Importantly, the new law gives the SEC the tools necessary to hold recognized rating agencies accountable if they fail to produce credible and reliable ratings," declared Jim Kaitz, presi-

dent of the Association for Financial Professionals (AFP), in a statement. AFP represents 15,000 members working in corporate treasury and financial management functions.

One credit-rating agency, S&P, voiced its objection to the original House bill, saying that ratings agencies are members of the financial press and that the proposed legislation represented an unconstitutional infringement of the company's free speech. Despite their objection, the legislation is now law.

Performing risk–return analysis in the bond markets depends on having accurate and timely information. The increased scrutiny from the SEC along with increased competition should add to the value of the ratings received by the investing public.

■ *What effect will the new legislation likely have on the market share of the largest rating agencies? How will the new legislation affect the process of finding ratings information for investors?*

manager must be concerned with the expected ratings of the bond issue, because these ratings affect salability and cost.

debentures
subordinated debentures
income bonds
mortgage bonds
collateral trust bonds
equipment trust certificates
See Table 6.4.

zero- (or low-) coupon bonds
junk bonds
floating-rate bonds
extendible notes
putable bonds
See Table 6.5 on page 298.

Popular Types of Bonds

Bonds can be classified in a variety of ways. Here we break them into traditional bonds (the basic types that have been around for years) and contemporary bonds (newer, more innovative types). The traditional types of bonds are summarized in terms of their key characteristics and priority of lender's claim in Table 6.4. Note that the first three types—**debentures, subordinated debentures,** and **income bonds**—are unsecured, whereas the last three—**mortgage bonds, collateral trust bonds,** and **equipment trust certificates**—are secured.

Table 6.5 (see page 298) describes the key characteristics of five contemporary types of bonds: **zero- (or low-) coupon bonds, junk bonds, floating-rate bonds, extendible notes,** and **putable bonds.** These bonds can be either unsecured

TABLE 6.4	Characteristics and Priority of Lender's Claim of Traditional Types of Bonds	
Bond type	Characteristics	Priority of lender's claim
Unsecured Bonds		
Debentures	Unsecured bonds that only creditworthy firms can issue. Convertible bonds are normally debentures.	Claims are the same as those of any general creditor. May have other unsecured bonds subordinated to them.
Subordinated debentures	Claims are not satisfied until those of the creditors holding certain (senior) debts have been fully satisfied.	Claim is that of a general creditor but not as good as a senior debt claim.
Income bonds	Payment of interest is required only when earnings are available. Commonly issued in reorganization of a failing firm.	Claim is that of a general creditor. Are not in default when interest payments are missed, because they are contingent only on earnings being available.
Secured Bonds		
Mortgage bonds	Secured by real estate or buildings.	Claim is on proceeds from sale of mortgaged assets; if not fully satisfied, the lender becomes a general creditor. The *first-mortgage* claim must be fully satisfied before distribution of proceeds to *second-mortgage* holders, and so on. A number of mortgages can be issued against the same collateral.
Collateral trust bonds	Secured by stock and (or) bonds that are owned by the issuer. Collateral value is generally 25% to 35% greater than bond value.	Claim is on proceeds from stock and (or) bond collateral; if not fully satisfied, the lender becomes a general creditor.
Equipment trust certificates	Used to finance "rolling stock"—airplanes, trucks, boats, railroad cars. A trustee buys the asset with funds raised through the sale of trust certificates and then leases it to the firm; after making the final scheduled lease payment, the firm receives title to the asset. A type of leasing.	Claim is on proceeds from the sale of the asset; if proceeds do not satisfy outstanding debt, trust certificate lenders become general creditors.

or secured. Changing capital market conditions and investor preferences have spurred further innovations in bond financing in recent years and will probably continue to do so.

International Bond Issues

Companies and governments borrow internationally by issuing bonds in two principal financial markets: the Eurobond market and the foreign bond market. Both give borrowers the opportunity to obtain large amounts of long-term debt financing quickly, in the currency of their choice and with flexible repayment terms.

A **Eurobond** is issued by an international borrower and sold to investors in countries with currencies other than the currency in which the bond is denominated. An example is a dollar-denominated bond issued by a U.S. corporation and sold to Belgian investors. From the founding of the Eurobond market in the 1960s until the mid-1980s, "blue chip" U.S. corporations were the largest single class of Eurobond issuers. Some of these companies were able to borrow in this

Eurobond
A bond issued by an international borrower and sold to investors in countries with currencies other than the currency in which the bond is denominated.

TABLE 6.5	Characteristics of Contemporary Types of Bonds

Bond type	Characteristics[a]
Zero- (or low-) coupon bonds	Issued with no (zero) or a very low coupon (stated interest) rate and sold at a large discount from par. A significant portion (or all) of the investor's return comes from gain in value (i.e., par value minus purchase price). Generally callable at par value. Because the issuer can annually deduct the current year's interest accrual without having to pay the interest until the bond matures (or is called), its cash flow each year is increased by the amount of the tax shield provided by the interest deduction.
Junk bonds	Debt rated Ba or lower by Moody's or BB or lower by Standard & Poor's. Commonly used by rapidly growing firms to obtain growth capital, most often as a way to finance mergers and takeovers. High-risk bonds with high yields—often yielding 2% to 3% more than the best-quality corporate debt.
Floating-rate bonds	Stated interest rate is adjusted periodically within stated limits in response to changes in specified money market or capital market rates. Popular when future inflation and interest rates are uncertain. Tend to sell at close to par because of the automatic adjustment to changing market conditions. Some issues provide for annual redemption at par at the option of the bondholder.
Extendible notes	Short maturities, typically 1 to 5 years, that can be renewed for a similar period at the option of holders. Similar to a floating-rate bond. An issue might be a series of 3-year renewable notes over a period of 15 years; every 3 years, the notes could be extended for another 3 years, at a new rate competitive with market interest rates at the time of renewal.
Putable bonds	Bonds that can be redeemed at par (typically, $1,000) at the option of their holder either at specific dates after the date of issue and every 1 to 5 years thereafter or when and if the firm takes specified actions, such as being acquired, acquiring another company, or issuing a large amount of additional debt. In return for its conferring the right to "put the bond" at specified times or when the firm takes certain actions, the bond's yield is lower than that of a nonputable bond.

[a]The claims of lenders (i.e., bondholders) against issuers of each of these types of bonds vary, depending on the bonds' other features. Each of these bonds can be unsecured or secured.

market at interest rates below those the U.S. government paid on Treasury bonds. As the market matured, issuers became able to choose the currency in which they borrowed, and European and Japanese borrowers rose to prominence. In more recent years, the Eurobond market has become much more balanced in terms of the mix of borrowers, total issue volume, and currency of denomination.

foreign bond
A bond issued in a host country's financial market, in the host country's currency, by a foreign borrower.

In contrast, a **foreign bond** is issued in a host country's financial market, in the host country's currency, by a foreign borrower. A Swiss-franc–denominated bond issued in Switzerland by a U.S. company is an example of a foreign bond. The three largest foreign-bond markets are Japan, Switzerland, and the United States.

REVIEW QUESTIONS

6–6   What are typical maturities, denominations, and interest payments of a corporate bond? What mechanisms protect bondholders?

6–7   Differentiate between *standard debt provisions* and *restrictive covenants* included in a bond indenture. What are the consequences of violation of them by the bond issuer?

6–8   How is the cost of bond financing typically related to the cost of short-term borrowing? In addition to a bond's maturity, what other major factors affect its cost to the issuer?

6–9   What is a *conversion feature?* A *call feature?* Stock purchase warrants?

6–10   What is the *current yield* for a bond? How are bond prices quoted? How are bonds rated, and why?

6–11   Compare the basic characteristics of *Eurobonds* and *foreign bonds*.

6.3 | Valuation Fundamentals

valuation
The process that links risk and return to determine the worth of an asset.

Valuation is the process that links risk and return to determine the worth of an asset. It is a relatively simple process that can be applied to *expected* streams of benefits from bonds, stocks, income properties, oil wells, and so on. To determine an asset's worth at a given point in time, a financial manager uses the time-value-of-money techniques presented in Chapter 4 and the concepts of risk and return developed in Chapter 5.

Key Inputs

There are three key inputs to the valuation process: (1) cash flows (returns), (2) timing, and (3) a measure of risk, which determines the required return. Each is described below.

Cash Flows (Returns)

The value of any asset depends on the cash flow(s) it is *expected* to provide over the ownership period. To have value, an asset does not have to provide an annual cash flow; it can provide an intermittent cash flow or even a single cash flow over the period.

Personal Finance Example   Celia Sargent wishes to estimate the value of three assets she is considering investing in: common stock in Michaels Enterprises, an interest in an oil well, and an original painting by a well-known artist. Her cash flow estimates for each are as follows:

Stock in Michaels Enterprises   *Expect* to receive cash dividends of $300 per year indefinitely.

Oil well   *Expect* to receive cash flow of $2,000 at the end of year 1, $4,000 at the end of year 2, and $10,000 at the end of year 4, when the well is to be sold.

Original painting   *Expect* to be able to sell the painting in 5 years for $85,000.

With these cash flow estimates, Celia has taken the first step toward placing a value on each of the assets.

Timing

In addition to making cash flow estimates, we must know the timing of the cash flows.[10] For example, Celia expects the cash flows of $2,000, $4,000, and $10,000 for the oil well to occur at the ends of years 1, 2, and 4, respectively. The combination of the cash flow and its timing fully defines the return expected from the asset.

---

10. Although cash flows can occur at any time during a year, for computational convenience as well as custom, we will assume they occur at the *end of the year* unless otherwise noted.

Hint The required rate of return is the result of investors being risk-averse. For the risk-averse investor to purchase a given asset, the investor *must expect* at least enough return to compensate for the asset's perceived risk.

Risk and Required Return

The level of risk associated with a given cash flow can significantly affect its value. In general, the greater the risk of (or the less certain) a cash flow, the lower its value. Greater risk can be incorporated into a valuation analysis by using a higher required return or discount rate. As in the previous chapter, the higher the risk, the greater the required return, and the lower the risk, the less the required return.

Personal Finance Example   Let's return to Celia Sargent's task of placing a value on the original painting and consider two scenarios.

Scenario 1—Certainty   A major art gallery has contracted to buy the painting for $85,000 at the end of 5 years. Because this is considered a certain situation, Celia views this asset as "money in the bank." She thus would use the prevailing risk-free rate of 9% as the required return when calculating the value of the painting.

Scenario 2—High Risk   The values of original paintings by this artist have fluctuated widely over the past 10 years. Although Celia expects to be able to sell the painting for $85,000, she realizes that its sale price in 5 years could range between $30,000 and $140,000. Because of the high uncertainty surrounding the painting's value, Celia believes that a 15% required return is appropriate.

These two estimates of the appropriate required return illustrate how this rate captures risk. The often subjective nature of such estimates is also clear.

Basic Valuation Model

Simply stated, the value of any asset is *the present value of all future cash flows it is expected to provide over the relevant time period.* The time period can be any length, even infinity. The value of an asset is therefore determined by discounting the expected cash flows back to their present value, using the required return commensurate with the asset's risk as the appropriate discount rate. Utilizing the present value techniques explained in Chapter 4, we can express the value of any asset at time zero, V_0, as

$$V_0 = \frac{CF_1}{(1+r)^1} + \frac{CF_2}{(1+r)^2} + \cdots + \frac{CF_n}{(1+r)^n} \tag{6.5}$$

where

V_0 = value of the asset at time zero
CF_t = cash flow *expected* at the end of year t
r = appropriate required return (discount rate)
n = relevant time period

Using present value interest factor notation, $PVIF_{r,n}$ from Chapter 4, Equation 6.5 can be rewritten as

$$V_0 = [CF_1 \times (PVIF_{r,1})] + [CF_2 \times (PVIF_{r,2})] + \cdots + [CF_n \times (PVIF_{r,n})] \tag{6.6}$$

We can use Equation 6.6 to determine the value of any asset.

TABLE 6.6	Valuation of Assets by Celia Sargent

Asset	Cash flow, CF	Appropriate required return	Valuation[a]
Michaels Enterprises stock[b]	$300/year indefinitely	12%	$V_0 = \$300 \times (PVIFA_{12\%,\infty})$ $= \$300 \times \dfrac{1}{0.12} = \underline{\underline{\$2,500}}$
Oil well[c]	Year (t) CF_t 1 $2,000 2 4,000 3 0 4 10,000	20%	$V_0 = [\$2,000 \times (PVIF_{20\%,1})]$ $+ [\$4,000 \times (PVIF_{20\%,2})] + [\$0 \times (PVIF_{20\%,3})]$ $+ [\$10,000 \times (PVIF_{20\%,4})]$ $= [\$2,000 \times (0.833)]$ $+ [\$4,000 \times (0.694)] + [\$0 \times (0.579)]$ $+ [\$10,000 \times (0.482)]$ $= \$1,666 + \$2,776 + \$0 + \$4,820$ $= \underline{\underline{\$9,262}}$
Original painting[d]	$85,000 at end of year 5	15%	$V_0 = \$85,000 \times (PVIF_{15\%,5})$ $= \$85,000 \times (0.497)$ $= \underline{\underline{\$42,245}}$

[a]Based on *PVIF* interest factors from Table A–2. If calculated using a calculator, the values of the oil well and original painting would have been $9,266.98 and $42,260.03, respectively.

[b]This is a perpetuity (infinite-lived annuity), and therefore the present value interest factor given in Equation 4.19 is applied.

[c]This is a mixed stream of cash flows and therefore requires a number of *PVIF*s, as noted.

[d]This is a single-amount cash flow and therefore requires a single *PVIF*.

Personal Finance Example   Celia Sargent used Equation 6.6 to calculate the value of each asset (using present value interest factors from Table A–2), as shown in Table 6.6. Michaels Enterprises stock has a value of $2,500, the oil well's value is $9,262, and the original painting has a value of $42,245. Note that regardless of the pattern of the expected cash flow from an asset, the basic valuation equation can be used to determine its value.

REVIEW QUESTIONS

6–12 Why is it important for financial managers to understand the valuation process?

6–13 What are the three key inputs to the valuation process?

6–14 Does the valuation process apply only to assets that provide an annual cash flow? Explain.

6–15 Define and specify the general equation for the value of any asset, V_0.

6.4 | Bond Valuation

The basic valuation equation can be customized for use in valuing specific securities: bonds, common stock, and preferred stock. We describe bond valuation in this chapter, and valuation of common stock and preferred stock in Chapter 7.

Bond Fundamentals

As noted earlier in this chapter, *bonds* are long-term debt instruments used by business and government to raise large sums of money, typically from a diverse group of lenders. Most corporate bonds pay interest *semiannually* (every 6 months) at a stated *coupon interest rate,* have an initial *maturity* of 10 to 30 years, and have a *par value,* or *face value,* of $1,000 that must be repaid at maturity.[11]

Example

Mills Company, a large defense contractor, on January 1, 2010, issued a 10% coupon interest rate, 10-year bond with a $1,000 par value that pays interest semiannually. Investors who buy this bond receive the contractual right to two cash flows: (1) $100 annual interest (10% coupon interest rate × $1,000 par value) distributed as $50 (1/2 × $100) at the end of each 6 months, and (2) the $1,000 par value at the end of the tenth year.

We will use data for Mills's bond issue to look at basic bond valuation.

Basic Bond Valuation

The value of a bond is the present value of the payments its issuer is contractually obligated to make, from the current time until it matures. The basic model for the value, B_0, of a bond is given by Equation 6.7:

$$B_0 = I \times \left[\sum_{t=1}^{n} \frac{1}{(1 + r_d)^t} \right] + M \times \left[\frac{1}{(1 + r_d)^n} \right] \tag{6.7}$$

$$= I \times (PVIFA_{r_d,n}) + M \times (PVIF_{r_d,n}) \tag{6.7a}$$

where

B_0 = value of the bond at time zero

I = *annual* interest paid in dollars[12]

n = number of years to maturity

M = par value in dollars

r_d = required return on a bond

We can calculate bond value by using Equation 6.7a and a financial calculator or by using a spreadsheet or financial tables (Tables A–2 and A–4).

Personal Finance Example   Tim Sanchez wishes to determine the current value of the Mills Company bond. *Assuming that interest on the Mills Company bond issue is paid annually* and that the required return is equal to the bond's coupon interest rate, $I = \$100$, $r_d = 10\%$, $M = \$1,000$, and $n = 10$ years.

---

11. Bonds often have features that allow them to be retired by the issuer prior to maturity; these *conversion* and *call* features were presented earlier in this chapter. For the purpose of the current discussion, these features are ignored.

12. The payment of annual rather than semiannual bond interest is assumed throughout the following discussion. This assumption simplifies the calculations involved, while maintaining the conceptual accuracy of the valuation procedures presented.

The computations involved in finding the bond value are depicted graphically on the following time line.

Time line for bond valuation (Mills Company's 10% coupon interest rate, 10-year maturity, $1,000 par, January 1, 2010, issue paying annual interest; required return = 10%)

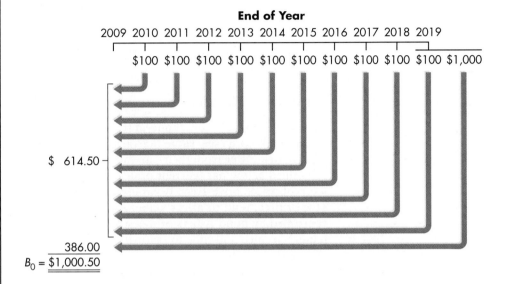

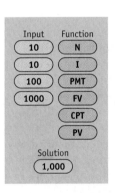

Calculator Use   Using the Mills Company's inputs shown at the left, you should find the bond value to be exactly $1,000. Note that *the calculated bond value is equal to its par value; this will always be the case when the required return is equal to the coupon interest rate.*[13]

Spreadsheet Use   The value of the Mills Company bond also can be calculated as shown in the following Excel spreadsheet.

	A	B
1	BOND VALUE, ANNUAL INTEREST, REQUIRED RETURN = COUPON INTEREST RATE	
2	Annual interest payment	$100
3	Coupon interest rate	10%
4	Number of years to maturity	10
5	Par value	$1,000
6	Bond value	$1,000.00

Entry in Cell B6 is
(B2*(1-(1/(1+B3)^B4)))/B3 + (B6*(1/(1+B3)^B4))

The expression 1-(1/(1+B3)^B4))/B3 calculates the Present Value Interest Factor for an Annuity.
The expression 1/(1+B3)^B4 calculates the Present Value Interest Factor for a Single Amount.

---

13. Note that because bonds pay interest in arrears, the prices at which they are quoted and traded reflect their value *plus* any accrued interest. For example, a $1,000 par value, 10% coupon bond paying interest semiannually and having a calculated value of $900 would pay interest of $50 at the end of each 6-month period. If it is now 3 months since the beginning of the interest period, three-sixths of the $50 interest, or $25 (i.e., 3/6 × $50), would be accrued. The bond would therefore be quoted at $925—its $900 value plus the $25 in accrued interest. For convenience, *throughout this book, bond values will always be assumed to be calculated at the beginning of the interest period,* thereby avoiding the need to consider accrued interest.

Table Use   Substituting the appropriate values into Equation 6.7a yields

$$B_0 = \$100 \times (PVIFA_{10\%,10\text{yrs}}) + \$1,000 \times (PVIF_{10\%,10\text{yrs}})$$
$$= \$100 \times (6.145) + \$1,000 \times (0.386)$$
$$= \$614.50 + \$386.00 = \underline{\$1,000.50}$$

The bond therefore has a value of approximately $1,000.[14]

Bond Value Behavior

In practice, the value of a bond in the marketplace is rarely equal to its par value. In the bond data (see Table 6.2 on page 295), it can be seen that the prices of bonds often differ from their par values of 100 (100 percent of par). Some bonds are valued below par (current price below 100), and others are valued above par (current price above 100). A variety of forces in the economy, as well as the passage of time, tend to affect value. Although these external forces are in no way controlled by bond issuers or investors, it is useful to understand the impact that required return and time to maturity have on bond value.

Required Returns and Bond Values

Whenever the required return on a bond differs from the bond's coupon interest rate, the bond's value will differ from its par value. The required return is likely to differ from the coupon interest rate because either (1) economic conditions have changed, causing a shift in the basic cost of long-term funds, or (2) the firm's risk has changed. Increases in the basic cost of long-term funds or in risk will raise the required return; decreases in the cost of funds or in risk will lower the required return.

Regardless of the exact cause, what is important is the relationship between the required return and the coupon interest rate: When the required return is greater than the coupon interest rate, the bond value, B_0, will be less than its par value, M. In this case, the bond is said to sell at a **discount**, which will equal $M - B_0$. When the required return falls below the coupon interest rate, the bond value will be greater than par. In this situation, the bond is said to sell at a **premium**, which will equal $B_0 - M$.

discount
The amount by which a bond sells at a value that is less than its par value.

premium
The amount by which a bond sells at a value that is greater than its par value.

Example

The preceding example showed that when the required return equaled the coupon interest rate, the bond's value equaled its $1,000 par value. If for the same bond the required return were to rise to 12% or fall to 8%, its value in each case would be found as follows (using Equation 6.7a):

Calculator Use   Using the inputs shown at the left and on the next page for the two different required returns, you will find the value of the bond to be below or above par. At a 12% required return, the bond would sell at a *discount* of $113.00 ($1,000 par value − $887.00 value). At the 8% required return, the bond would sell for a *premium* of about $134.00 ($1,134.00 value − $1,000 par

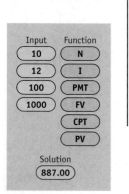

---

14. Note that a slight rounding error ($0.50) results here from the use of the table factors, which are rounded to the nearest thousandth.

TABLE 6.7	Bond Values for Various Required Returns (Mills Company's 10% Coupon Interest Rate, 10-Year Maturity, $1,000 Par, January 1, 2010, Issue Paying Annual Interest)		
Required return, r_d		Bond value, B_0	Status
12%		$ 887.00	Discount
10		1,000.00	Par value
8		1,134.20	Premium

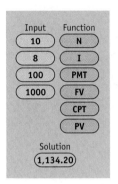

Input	Function
10	N
8	I
100	PMT
1000	FV
	CPT
	PV

Solution
1,134.20

value). The results of this and the following calculations for Mills Company's bond values are summarized in Table 6.7 and graphically depicted in Figure 6.4 (see page 306). The inverse relationship between bond value and required return is clearly shown in the figure.

Spreadsheet Use   The values for the Mills Company bond at required returns of 12% and 8% also can be calculated as shown in the following Excel spreadsheet. (See the book's website, **www.prenhall.com/gitman**, Chapter 6, for another spreadsheet model that computes the values of the Mills Company bond at a discount and a premium.)

WWW

	A	B	C
1	BOND VALUE, ANNUAL INTEREST, REQUIRED RETURN NOT EQUAL TO COUPON INTEREST RATE		
2	Annual interest payment	$100	$100
3	Coupon interest rate	10%	10%
4	Required return	12%	8%
5	Number of years to maturity	10	10
6	Par value	$1,000	$1,000
7	Bond value	$887.00	$1,134.20

Entry in Cell B7, a **bond discount**, is
(B2*(1-(1/(1+B4)^B5))/B4) + (B6*(1/(1+B4)^B5))
The expression 1-(1/(1+B4)^B5))/B4 calculates the Present Value Interest Factor for an Annuity.
The expression 1/(1+B4)^B5 calculates the Present Value Interest Factor for a Single Amount.

Entry in Cell C7, a **bond premium**, is
(C2*(1-(1/(1+C4)^C5))/C4) + (C6*(1/(1+C4)^C5))
The expression 1-(1/(1+C4)^C5))/C4 calculates the Present Value Interest Factor for an Annuity.
The expression 1/(1+C4)^C5 calculates the Present Value Interest Factor for a Single Amount.

Table Use

Required Return = 12%

$$B_0 = \$100 \times (PVIFA_{12\%,10yrs}) + \$1,000 \times (PVIF_{12\%,10yrs})$$

$$= \$887.00$$

Required Return = 8%

$$B_0 = \$100 \times (PVIFA_{8\%,10yrs}) + \$1,000 \times (PVIF_{8\%,10yrs})$$

$$= \$1,134.00$$

FIGURE 6.4

Bond Values and Required Returns
Bond values and required returns (Mills Company's 10% coupon interest rate, 10-year maturity, $1,000 par, January 1, 2010, issue paying annual interest)

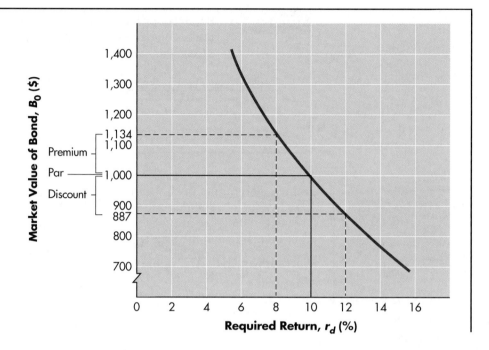

Time to Maturity and Bond Values

Whenever the required return is different from the coupon interest rate, the amount of time to maturity affects bond value. An additional factor is whether required returns are constant or change over the life of the bond.

Constant Required Returns   When the required return is different from the coupon interest rate and is assumed to be *constant until maturity,* the value of the bond will approach its par value as the passage of time moves the bond's value closer to maturity. (Of course, when the required return *equals* the coupon interest rate, the bond's value will remain at par until it matures.)

| Example |

Figure 6.5 depicts the behavior of the bond values calculated earlier and presented in Table 6.7 for Mills Company's 10% coupon interest rate bond paying annual interest and having 10 years to maturity. Each of the three required returns—12%, 10%, and 8%—is assumed to remain constant over the 10 years to the bond's maturity. The bond's value at both 12% and 8% approaches and ultimately equals the bond's $1,000 par value at its maturity, as the discount (at 12%) or premium (at 8%) declines with the passage of time.

interest rate risk
The chance that interest rates will change and thereby change the required return and bond value. Rising rates, which result in decreasing bond values, are of greatest concern.

Changing Required Returns   The chance that interest rates will change and thereby change the required return and bond value is called **interest rate risk**.[15]

---

15. A more robust measure of a bond's response to interest rate changes is *duration.* Duration measures the volatility (sensitivity of bond value) to changing interest rates. It incorporates both the interest rate (coupon rate) and the time to maturity into a single statistic. Duration is simply a weighted average of the maturity of the present values of all the contractual cash flows yet to be paid by the bond. Duration is stated in years, so a bond with a 5-year duration will decrease in value by 5% if interest rates rise by 1%, or will increase in value by 5% if interest rates fall by 1%. For more on duration, see any recent investments text, such as Lawrence J. Gitman and Michael D. Joehnk, *Fundamentals of Investing,* 10th Edition (Boston: Addison Wesley, 2008), pp. 464–471.

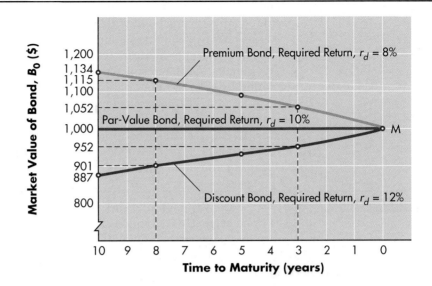

FIGURE 6.5

Time to Maturity and Bond Values

Relationship among time to maturity, required returns, and bond values (Mills Company's 10% coupon interest rate, 10-year maturity, $1,000 par, January 1, 2010, issue paying annual interest)

(This was described as a shareholder-specific risk in Chapter 5, Table 5.1.) Bondholders are typically more concerned with rising interest rates because a rise in interest rates, and therefore in the required return, causes a decrease in bond value. The shorter the amount of time until a bond's maturity, the less responsive its market value to a given change in the required return. In other words, *short maturities have less interest rate risk than long maturities when all other features (coupon interest rate, par value, and interest payment frequency) are the same.* This is because of the mathematics of time value; the present values of short-term cash flows change far less than the present values of longer-term cash flows in response to a given change in the discount rate (required return).

Example

The effect of changing required returns on bonds with differing maturities can be illustrated by using Mills Company's bond and Figure 6.5. If the required return rises from 10% to 12% when the bond has 8 years to maturity (see the dashed line at 8 years), the bond's value decreases from $1,000 to $901—a 9.9% decrease. If the same change in required return had occurred with only 3 years to maturity (see the dashed line at 3 years), the bond's value would have dropped to just $952—only a 4.8% decrease. Similar types of responses can be seen for the change in bond value associated with decreases in required returns. The shorter the time to maturity, the less the impact on bond value caused by a given change in the required return.

yield to maturity (YTM)
The rate of return that investors earn if they buy a bond at a specific price and hold it until maturity. (Assumes that the issuer makes all scheduled interest and principal payments as promised.)

Yield to Maturity (YTM)

When investors evaluate bonds, they commonly consider **yield to maturity (YTM)**. This is the rate of return that investors earn if they buy the bond at a specific price and hold it until maturity. (The measure assumes, of course, that the issuer makes all scheduled interest and principal payments as promised.)[16] The yield to maturity on a bond with a current price equal to its par value (that is, $B_0 = M$) will always equal the coupon interest rate. When the bond value differs from par, the yield to maturity will differ from the coupon interest rate.

Assuming that interest is paid annually, the yield to maturity on a bond can be found by solving Equation 6.7 for r_d. In other words, the current value, the annual interest, the par value, and the number of years to maturity are known, and the required return must be found. The required return is the bond's yield to maturity. The YTM can be found by using a financial calculator, by using an Excel spreadsheet, or by trial and error. The calculator provides accurate YTM values with minimum effort.

Personal Finance Example   Earl Washington wishes to find the YTM on the Mills Company bond. The bond currently sells for $1,080, has a 10% coupon interest rate and $1,000 par value, pays interest annually, and has 10 years to maturity. Because $B_0 = \$1,080$, $I = \$100$ $(0.10 \times \$1,000)$, $M = \$1,000$, and $n = 10$ years, substituting into Equation 6.7a yields

$$\$1,080 = \$100 \times (PVIFA_{r_d,10\text{yrs}}) + \$1,000 \times (PVIF_{r_d,10\text{yrs}})$$

Earl's objective is to solve the equation for r_d, the YTM.

Calculator Use   [*Note:* Most calculators require *either* the present value (B_0 in this case) or the future values (I and M in this case) to be input as negative numbers to calculate yield to maturity. That approach is employed here.] Using the inputs shown at the left, you should find the YTM to be 8.766%.

Spreadsheet Use   The yield to maturity of the 10% coupon rate Mills Company bond also can be calculated as shown in the following Excel spreadsheet.

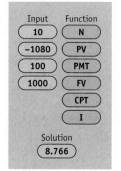

Input	Function
10	N
−1080	PV
100	PMT
1000	FV
	CPT
	I

Solution
8.766

	A	B
1	YIELD TO MATURITY, ANNUAL INTEREST	
2	Annual interest payment	$100
3	Coupon interest rate	10%
4	Number of years to maturity	10
5	Par value	$1,000
6	Current bond price	$1,080
7	Yield to maturity	8.77%
8	Trial and error method:	
9	Choose various required rates and place them in Cell A14	
10	The spreadsheet will recalculate each time. Continue the process	
11	until the value ofthe bond equals the currentprice of the bond	
12	(in this example, it is $1,080).	
13		
14	8.77%	
15	Payments PVIFA PVIF	PV
16	$ 100 6.4831	$ 648.31
17	1,000 0.4314	431.40
18	Bond Value	≈ $1,080.00

16. Many bonds have a *call feature*, which means they may not reach maturity if the issuer, after a specified time period, calls them back. Because the call feature typically cannot be exercised until a specific future date, investors often calculate the *yield to call (YTC)*. The yield to call represents the rate of return that investors earn if they buy a callable bond at a specific price and hold it until it is called back and they receive the *call price*, which would be set above the bond's par value. Here our focus is solely on the more general measure of yield to maturity.

Trial and Error   Because we know that a required return, r_d, of 10% (which equals the bond's 10% coupon interest rate) would result in a value of $1,000, the discount rate that would result in $1,080 must be less than 10%. (Remember that the lower the discount rate, the higher the present value, and the higher the discount rate, the lower the present value.) Trying 9%, we get

$$\$100 \times (PVIFA_{9\%,10\text{yrs}}) + \$1,000 \times (PVIF_{9\%,10\text{yrs}})$$
$$= \$100 \times (6.418) + \$1,000 \times (0.422)$$
$$= \$641.80 + \$422.00$$
$$= \$1,063.80$$

Because the 9% rate is not quite low enough to bring the value up to $1,080, we next try 8% and get

$$\$100 \times (PVIFA_{8\%,10\text{yrs}}) + \$1,000 \times (PVIF_{8\%,10\text{yrs}})$$
$$= \$100 \times (6.710) + \$1,000 \times (0.463)$$
$$= \$671.00 + \$463.00$$
$$= \$1,134.00$$

Because the value at the 8% rate is higher than $1,080 and the value at the 9% rate is lower than $1,080, the bond's yield to maturity must be between 8% and 9%. Because the $1,063.80 is closer to $1,080, the YTM to the nearest whole percent is 9%. (By using *interpolation*, we could eventually find the more precise YTM value to be 8.77%.)[17]

Semiannual Interest and Bond Values

The procedure used to value bonds paying interest semiannually is similar to that shown in Chapter 4 for compounding interest more frequently than annually, except that here we need to find present value instead of future value. It involves

1. Converting annual interest, I, to semiannual interest by dividing I by 2.
2. Converting the number of years to maturity, n, to the number of 6-month periods to maturity by multiplying n by 2.
3. Converting the required stated (rather than effective)[18] annual return for similar-risk bonds that also pay semiannual interest from an annual rate, r_d, to a semiannual rate by dividing r_d by 2.

17. For information on how to interpolate to get a more precise answer, see the book's website at www.prenhall.com/gitman.

18. As we noted in Chapter 4, the effective annual rate of interest, EAR, for stated interest rate i, when interest is paid semiannually ($m = 2$), can be found by using Equation 4.24:

$$EAR = \left(1 + \frac{i}{2}\right)^2 - 1$$

For example, a bond with a 12% required stated annual return, r_d, that pays semiannual interest would have an effective annual rate of

$$EAR = \left(1 + \frac{0.12}{2}\right)^2 - 1 = (1.06)^2 - 1 = 1.1236 - 1 = 0.1236 = \underline{\underline{12.36\%}}$$

Because most bonds pay semiannual interest at semiannual rates equal to 50% of the stated annual rate, their effective annual rates are generally higher than their stated annual rates.

Substituting these three changes into Equation 6.7 yields

$$B_0 = \frac{I}{2} \times \left[\sum_{t=1}^{2n} \frac{1}{\left(1 + \frac{r_d}{2}\right)^t} \right] + M \times \left[\frac{1}{\left(1 + \frac{r_d}{2}\right)^{2n}} \right] \qquad \text{(6.8)[19]}$$

$$= \frac{I}{2} \times (PVIFA_{r_d/2, 2n}) + M \times (PVIF_{r_d/2, 2n}) \qquad \text{(6.8a)}$$

Example

Assuming that the Mills Company bond pays interest semiannually and that the required stated annual return, r_d, is 12% for similar-risk bonds that also pay semiannual interest, substituting these values into Equation 6.8a yields

$$B_0 = \frac{\$100}{2} \times (PVIFA_{12\%/2, 2 \times 10\text{yrs}}) + \$1,000 \times (PVIF_{12\%/2, 2 \times 10\text{yrs}})$$

Input	Function
20	N
6	I
50	PMT
1000	FV
	CPT
	PV

Solution
885.30

Calculator Use In using a calculator to find bond value when interest is paid semiannually, we must double the number of periods and divide both the required stated annual return and the annual interest by 2. For the Mills Company bond, we would use 20 periods (2×10 years), a required return of 6% ($12\% \div 2$), and an interest payment of $50 ($\$100 \div 2$). Using these inputs, you should find the bond value with semiannual interest to be $885.30, as shown at the left.

Spreadsheet Use The value of the Mills Company bond paying semiannual interest at a required return of 12% also can be calculated as shown in the following Excel spreadsheet.

	A	B
1	BOND VALUE, SEMIANNUAL INTEREST	
2	Annual interest payment	$100
3	Stated annual return	12%
4	Number of years to maturity	10
5	Par value	$1,000
6	Bond value	$885.30

Entry in Cell B6 is
(B2/2*(1-(1/(1+B3/2)^(2*B4)))/(B3/2) + (B5*(1/(1+B3/2)^(2*B4)))
The expression 1-(1/(1+B3/2)^(2*B4)))/(B3/2) calculates the Present Value Interest Factor for an Annuity (semiannual interest).
The expression 1/(1+B3/2)^(2*B4) calculates the Present Value Interest Factor for a Single Amount (semiannual interest).

---

19. Although it may appear inappropriate to use the semiannual discounting procedure on the maturity value, M, this technique is necessary to find the correct bond value. One way to confirm the accuracy of this approach is to calculate the bond value for the case where the required stated annual return and coupon interest rate are equal; for B_0 to equal M, as would be expected in such a case, the maturity value must be discounted on a semiannual basis.

Table Use

$$B_0 = \$50 \times (PVIFA_{6\%,20\text{periods}}) + \$1,000 \times (PVIF_{6\%,20\text{periods}})$$
$$= \$50 \times (11.470) + \$1,000 \times (0.312) = \underline{\$885.50}$$

Note that this value is not as precise as that found using a financial calculator or spreadsheet.

Comparing this result with the $887.00 value found earlier for annual compounding (see Table 6.7 on page 305), we can see that the bond's value is lower when semiannual interest is paid. *This will always occur when the bond sells at a discount.* For bonds selling at a premium, the opposite will occur: The value with semiannual interest will be greater than with annual interest.

REVIEW QUESTIONS

6–16 What basic procedure is used to value a bond that pays annual interest? Semiannual interest?

6–17 What relationship between the required return and the coupon interest rate will cause a bond to sell at a *discount?* At a *premium?* At its *par value?*

6–18 If the required return on a bond differs from its coupon interest rate, describe the behavior of the bond value over time as the bond moves toward maturity.

6–19 As a risk-averse investor, would you prefer bonds with short or long periods until maturity? Why?

6–20 What is a bond's *yield to maturity (YTM)?* Briefly describe the use of a financial calculator, the use of an Excel spreadsheet, and the trial-and-error approach for finding YTM.

Summary

Focus on Value

Interest rates and required returns embody the real cost of money, inflationary expectations, and issuer and issue risk. They reflect the level of return required by market participants as compensation for the risk perceived in a specific security or asset investment. Because these returns are affected by economic expectations, they vary as a function of time, typically rising for longer-term maturities. The yield curve reflects such market expectations at any point in time.

The value of an asset can be found by calculating the present value of its expected cash flows, using the required return as the discount rate. Bonds are the easiest financial assets to value; both the amounts and the timing of their cash flows are contractual and therefore known with certainty. The financial manager needs to understand how to apply valuation techniques to bonds, stocks, and tangible assets (as we will demonstrate in the following chapters) to make decisions that are consistent with the firm's **share price maximization goal.**

Review of Learning Goals

Key definitions and formulas for this chapter are summarized in Table 6.8.

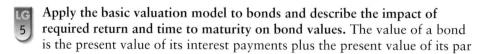 **Describe interest rate fundamentals, the term structure of interest rates, and risk premiums.** The flow of funds between savers and investors is regulated by the interest rate or required return. In a perfect, inflation-free, certain world there would be one cost of money—the real rate of interest. The nominal or actual interest rate is the sum of the risk-free rate and a risk premium reflecting issuer and issue characteristics. The risk-free rate is the real rate of interest plus an inflation premium.

For any class of similar-risk securities, the term structure of interest rates reflects the relationship between the interest rate or rate of return and the time to maturity. Yield curves can be downward-sloping (inverted), upward-sloping (normal), or flat. The expectations theory, liquidity preference theory, and market segmentation theory are cited to explain the shape of the yield curve. Risk premiums for non-Treasury debt issues result from business risk, financial risk, interest rate risk, liquidity risk, tax risk, default risk, maturity risk, and contractual provision risk.

Review the legal aspects of bond financing and bond cost. Corporate bonds are long-term debt instruments indicating that a corporation has borrowed an amount that it promises to repay in the future under clearly defined terms. Most bonds are issued with maturities of 10 to 30 years and a par value of $1,000. The bond indenture, enforced by a trustee, states all conditions of the bond issue. It contains both standard debt provisions and restrictive covenants, which may include a sinking-fund requirement and/or a security interest. The cost of a bond to an issuer depends on its maturity, offering size, and issuer risk and on the basic cost of money.

Discuss the general features, yields, prices, ratings, popular types, and international issues of corporate bonds. A bond issue may include a conversion feature, a call feature, or stock purchase warrants. The yield, or rate of return, on a bond can be measured by its current yield, yield to maturity (YTM), or yield to call (YTC). Bond prices are typically reported along with their coupon, maturity date, and yield to maturity (YTM). Bond ratings by independent agencies indicate the risk of a bond issue. Various types of traditional and contemporary bonds are available. Eurobonds and foreign bonds enable established creditworthy companies and governments to borrow large amounts internationally.

Understand the key inputs and basic model used in the valuation process. Key inputs to the valuation process include cash flows (returns), timing, and risk and the required return. The value of any asset is equal to the present value of all future cash flows it is *expected* to provide over the relevant time period.

Apply the basic valuation model to bonds and describe the impact of required return and time to maturity on bond values. The value of a bond is the present value of its interest payments plus the present value of its par

TABLE 6.8	Summary of Key Valuation Definitions and Formulas for Any Asset and for Bonds

Definitions of variables

B_0 = bond value

CF_t = cash flow *expected* at the end of year t

I = annual interest on a bond

r = appropriate required return (discount rate)

r_d = required return on a bond

M = par, or face, value of a bond

n = relevant time period, or number of years to maturity

V_0 = value of the asset at time zero

Valuation formulas

Value of any asset:

$$V_0 = \frac{CF_1}{(1+r)^1} + \frac{CF_2}{(1+r)^2} + \cdots + \frac{CF_n}{(1+r)^n} \qquad \text{[Equation 6.5]}$$

$$= [CF_1 \times (PVIF_{r,1})] + [CF_2 \times (PVIF_{r,2})] + \cdots + [CF_n \times (PVIF_{r,n})] \qquad \text{[Equation 6.6]}$$

Bond value:

$$B_0 = I \times \left[\sum_{t=1}^{n} \frac{1}{(1+r_d)^t} \right] + M \times \left[\frac{1}{(1+r_d)^n} \right] \qquad \text{[Equation 6.7]}$$

$$= I \times (PVIFA_{r_d,n}) + M \times (PVIF_{r_d,n}) \qquad \text{[Equation 6.7a]}$$

value. The discount rate used to determine bond value is the required return, which may differ from the bond's coupon interest rate. A bond can sell at a discount, at par, or at a premium, depending on whether the required return is greater than, equal to, or less than its coupon interest rate. The amount of time to maturity affects bond values. The value of a bond will approach its par value as the bond moves closer to maturity. The chance that interest rates will change and thereby change the required return and bond value is called interest rate risk. The shorter the amount of time until a bond's maturity, the less responsive is its market value to a given change in the required return.

LG 6 **Explain yield to maturity (YTM), its calculation, and the procedure used to value bonds that pay interest semiannually.** Yield to maturity is the rate of return investors earn if they buy a bond at a specific price and hold it until maturity. YTM can be calculated by using a financial calculator, by using an Excel spreadsheet, or by trial and error. Bonds that pay interest semiannually are valued by using the same procedure used to value bonds paying annual interest, except that the interest payments are one-half of the annual interest payments, the number of periods is twice the number of years to maturity, and the required return is one-half of the stated annual required return on similar-risk bonds.

Self-Test Problems (Solutions in Appendix B)

  ST6–1 **Bond valuation** Lahey Industries has outstanding a $1,000 par-value bond with an 8% coupon interest rate. The bond has 12 years remaining to its maturity date.

    a. If interest is paid *annually*, find the value of the bond when the required return is (1) 7%, (2) 8%, and (3) 10%.

    b. Indicate for each case in part **a** whether the bond is selling at a discount, at a premium, or at its par value.

    c. Using the 10% required return, find the bond's value when interest is paid *semiannually*.

  ST6–2 **Bond yields** Elliot Enterprises' bonds currently sell for $1,150, have an 11% coupon interest rate and a $1,000 par value, pay interest *annually*, and have 18 years to maturity.

    a. Calculate the bonds' *current yield*.

    b. Calculate the bonds' *yield to maturity (YTM)*.

    c. Compare the YTM calculated in part **b** to the bonds' coupon interest rate and current yield (calculated in part **a**). Use a comparison of the bonds' current price and par value to explain these differences.

Warm-Up Exercises

A blue box (■) indicates exercises available in .

 E6–1 The risk-free rate on T-bills recently was 1.23%. If the real rate of interest is estimated to be 0.80%, what was the expected level of inflation?

 E6–2 The yields for Treasuries with differing maturities on a recent day were as shown in the following table:

Maturity	Yield
3 months	1.41%
6 months	1.71
2 years	2.68
3 years	3.01
5 years	3.70
10 years	4.51
30 years	5.25

Use the information above to construct a *yield curve* for this date.

E6-3 The yields for Treasuries with differing maturities, including an estimate of the real rate of interest, on a recent day were as shown in the following table:

Maturity	Yield	Real rate of interest
3 months	1.41%	0.80%
6 months	1.71	0.80
2 years	2.68	0.80
3 years	3.01	0.80
5 years	3.70	0.80
10 years	4.51	0.80
30 years	5.25	0.80

Use the information above to calculate the *inflation expectation* for each maturity.

 E6-4 Recently, the annual inflation rate measured by the Consumer Price Index (CPI) was forecast to be 3.3%. How could a T-bill have had a negative real rate of return over the same period? How could it have had a zero real rate of return? What minimum rate of return must the T-bill have earned to meet your requirement of a 2% real rate of return?

 E6-5 Calculate the *risk premium* for each of the following rating classes of long-term securities, assuming that the yield to maturity (YTM) for comparable Treasuries is 4.51%.

Rating class	Nominal interest rate
AAA	5.12%
BBB	5.78
B	7.82

 E6-6 You have two assets and must calculate their values today based on their different payment streams and appropriate required returns. Asset 1 has a required return of 15% and will produce a stream of $500 at the end of each year indefinitely. Asset 2 has a required return of 10% and will produce an end-of-year cash flow of $1,200 in the first year, $1,500 in the second year, and $850 in its third and final year.

 E6-7 A bond with 5 years to maturity and a coupon rate of 6% has a par, or face, value of $20,000. Interest is paid annually. If you required a return of 8% on this bond, what is the value of this bond to you?

 E6-8 Assume a 5-year Treasury bond has a coupon rate of 4.5%.
  a. Give examples of required rates of return that would make the bond sell at a discount, at a premium, and at par.
  b. If this bond's par value is $10,000, calculate the differing values for this bond given the required rates you chose in part **a.**

Problems

A blue box (■) indicates problems available in myfinancelab.

P6–1   Interest rate fundamentals: The real rate of return   Carl Foster, a trainee at an investment banking firm, is trying to get an idea of what real rate of return investors are expecting in today's marketplace. He has looked up the rate paid on 3-month U.S. Treasury bills and found it to be 5.5%. He has decided to use the rate of change in the Consumer Price Index as a proxy for the inflationary expectations of investors. That annualized rate now stands at 3%. On the basis of the information that Carl has collected, what estimate can he make of the *real rate of return?*

P6–2   Real rate of interest   To estimate the real rate of interest, the economics division of Mountain Banks—a major bank holding company—has gathered the data summarized in the following table. Because there is a high likelihood that new tax legislation will be passed in the near future, current data as well as data reflecting the probable impact of passage of the legislation on the demand for funds are also included in the table. (*Note:* The proposed legislation will not affect the supply schedule of funds. Assume a perfect world in which inflation is expected to be zero, funds suppliers and demanders have no liquidity preference, and all outcomes are certain.)

Amount of funds supplied/demanded ($ billion)	Currently		With passage of tax legislation
	Interest rate required by funds suppliers	Interest rate required by funds demanders	Interest rate required by funds demanders
$ 1	2%	7%	9%
5	3	6	8
10	4	4	7
20	6	3	6
50	7	2	4
100	9	1	3

a. Draw the supply curve and the demand curve for funds using the current data. (*Note:* Unlike the functions in Figure 6.1 on page 283, the functions here will not appear as straight lines.)

b. Using your graph, label and note the *real rate of interest* using the current data.

c. Add to the graph drawn in part **a** the new demand curve expected in the event that the proposed tax legislation is passed.

d. What is the new real rate of interest? Compare and analyze this finding in light of your analysis in part **b**.

PERSONAL FINANCE PROBLEM

P6–3   Real and nominal rates interest   Zane Perelli currently has $100 that he can spend today on polo shirts costing $25 each. Alternatively, he could invest the $100 in a risk-free U.S. Treasury security that is expected to earn a 9% nominal rate of interest. The consensus forecast of leading economists is a 5% rate of inflation over the coming year.

a. How many polo shirts can Zane purchase today?

b. How much money will Zane have at the end of 1 year if he forgoes purchasing the polo shirts today?

c. How much would you expect the polo shirts to cost at the end of 1 year in light of the expected inflation?

d. Use your findings in parts **b** and **c** to determine how many polo shirts (fractions are okay) Zane can purchase at the end of 1 year. In percentage terms, how many more or fewer polo shirts can Zane buy at the end of 1 year?

e. What is Zane's *real rate of return* over the year? How is it related to the percentage change in Zane's buying power found in part **d**? Explain.

 P6–4 **Yield curve**   A firm wishing to evaluate interest rate behavior has gathered yield data on five U.S. Treasury securities, each having a different maturity and all measured at the same point in time. The summarized data follow.

U.S. Treasury security	Time to maturity	Yield
A	1 year	12.6%
B	10 years	11.2
C	6 months	13.0
D	20 years	11.0
E	5 years	11.4

a. Draw the yield curve associated with these data.

b. Describe the resulting yield curve in part **a**, and explain the general expectations embodied in it.

 P6–5 **Nominal interest rates and yield curves**   A recent study of inflationary expectations has revealed that the consensus among economic forecasters yields the following average annual rates of inflation expected over the periods noted. (*Note:* Assume that the risk that future interest rate movements will affect longer maturities more than shorter maturities is zero; that is, there is no *maturity risk*.)

Period	Average annual rate of inflation
3 months	5%
2 years	6
5 years	8
10 years	8.5
20 years	9

a. If the real rate of interest is currently 2.5%, find the *nominal rate of interest* on each of the following U.S. Treasury issues: 20-year bond, 3-month bill, 2-year note, and 5-year bond.

b. If the real rate of interest suddenly dropped to 2% without any change in inflationary expectations, what effect, if any, would this have on your answers in part **a**? Explain.

c. Using your findings in part **a,** draw a yield curve for U.S. Treasury securities. Describe the general shape and expectations reflected by the curve.

d. What would a follower of the *liquidity preference theory* say about how the preferences of lenders and borrowers tend to affect the shape of the yield curve drawn in part **c?** Illustrate that effect by placing on your graph a dotted line that approximates the yield curve without the effect of liquidity preference.

e. What would a follower of the *market segmentation theory* say about the supply and demand for long-term loans versus the supply and demand for short-term loans given the yield curve constructed for part **c** of this problem?

P6–6   Nominal and real rates and yield curves   A firm wishing to evaluate interest rate behavior has gathered data on the nominal rate of interest and on inflationary expectations for five U.S. Treasury securities, each having a different maturity and each measured at a different point in time during the year just ended. (*Note:* Assume that the risk that future interest rate movements will affect longer maturities more than shorter maturities is zero; that is, there is no *maturity risk.*) These data are summarized in the following table.

U.S. Treasury security	Point in time	Maturity	Nominal rate of interest	Inflationary expectation
A	Jan. 7	2 years	12.6%	9.5%
B	Mar. 12	10 years	11.2	8.2
C	May 30	6 months	13.0	10.0
D	Aug. 15	20 years	11.0	8.1
E	Dec. 30	5 years	11.4	8.3

a. Using the preceding data, find the *real rate of interest* at each point in time.

b. Describe the behavior of the real rate of interest over the year. What forces might be responsible for such behavior?

c. Draw the yield curve associated with these data, assuming that the nominal rates were measured at the same point in time.

d. Describe the resulting yield curve in part **c,** and explain the general expectations embodied in it.

P6–7   Term structure of interest rates   The following yield data for a number of highest-quality corporate bonds existed at each of the three points in time noted.

| Time to maturity (years) | Yield | | |
	5 years ago	2 years ago	Today
1	9.1%	14.6%	9.3%
3	9.2	12.8	9.8
5	9.3	12.2	10.9
10	9.5	10.9	12.6
15	9.4	10.7	12.7
20	9.3	10.5	12.9
30	9.4	10.5	13.5

a. On the same set of axes, draw the yield curve at each of the three given times.
b. Label each curve in part **a** with its general shape (downward-sloping, upward-sloping, flat).
c. Describe the general inflationary and interest rate expectation existing at each of the three times.

P6–8 **Risk-free rate and risk premiums**   The real rate of interest is currently 3%; the inflation expectation and risk premiums for a number of securities follow.

Security	Inflation expectation premium	Risk premium
A	6%	3%
B	9	2
C	8	2
D	5	4
E	11	1

a. Find the *risk-free rate of interest*, R_F, that is applicable to each security.
b. Although not noted, what factor must be the cause of the differing risk-free rates found in part **a**?
c. Find the *nominal rate of interest* for each security.

P6–9 **Risk premiums**   Eleanor Burns is attempting to find the nominal rate of interest for each of two securities—A and B—issued by different firms at the same point in time. She has gathered the following data:

Characteristic	Security A	Security B
Time to maturity	3 years	15 years
Inflation expectation premium	9.0%	7.0%
Risk premium for:		
Liquidity risk	1.0%	1.0%
Default risk	1.0%	2.0%
Maturity risk	0.5%	1.5%
Other risk	0.5%	1.5%

a. If the real rate of interest is currently 2%, find the *risk-free rate of interest* applicable to each security.
b. Find the total risk premium attributable to each security's issuer and issue characteristics.
c. Calculate the *nominal rate of interest* for each security. Compare and discuss your findings.

P6–10 **Bond interest payments before and after taxes**   Charter Corp. has issued 2,500 debentures with a total principal value of $2,500,000. The bonds have a coupon interest rate of 7%.
a. What dollar amount of interest per bond can an investor expect to receive each year from Charter?
b. What is Charter's total interest expense per year associated with this bond issue?

c. Assuming that Charter is in a 35% corporate tax bracket, what is the company's net after-tax interest cost associated with this bond issue?

P6–11 **Bond prices and yields**   Assume that the Financial Management Corporation's $1,000-par-value bond had a 5.700% coupon, matured on May 15, 2017, had a current price quote of 97.708, and had a yield to maturity (YTM) of 6.034%. Given this information, answer the following questions.
a. What was the dollar price of the bond?
b. What is the bond's *current yield?*
c. Is the bond selling at par, at a discount, or at a premium? Why?
d. Compare the bond's current yield calculated in part **b** to its YTM and explain why they differ.

PERSONAL FINANCE PROBLEM

P6–12 **Valuation fundamentals**   Imagine that you are trying to evaluate the economics of purchasing an automobile. You expect the car to provide annual after-tax cash benefits of $1,200 at the end of each year, and assume that you can sell the car for after-tax proceeds of $5,000 at the end of the planned 5-year ownership period. All funds for purchasing the car will be drawn from your savings, which are currently earning 6% after taxes.
a. Identify the cash flows, their timing, and the required return applicable to valuing the car.
b. What is the maximum price you would be willing to pay to acquire the car? Explain.

P6–13 **Valuation of assets**   Using the information provided in the following table, find the value of each asset.

Asset	End of year	Amount	Appropriate required return
	Cash flow		
A	1	$ 5,000	18%
	2	5,000	
	3	5,000	
B	1 through ∞	$ 300	15%
C	1	$ 0	16%
	2	0	
	3	0	
	4	0	
	5	35,000	
D	1 through 5	$ 1,500	12%
	6	8,500	
E	1	$ 2,000	14%
	2	3,000	
	3	5,000	
	4	7,000	
	5	4,000	
	6	1,000	

PERSONAL FINANCE PROBLEM

P6–14   **Asset valuation and risk**   Laura Drake wishes to estimate the value of an asset expected to provide cash inflows of $3,000 per year at the end of years 1 through 4 and $15,000 at the end of year 5. Her research indicates that she must earn 10% on low-risk assets, 15% on average-risk assets, and 22% on high-risk assets.

a. Determine what is the most Laura should pay for the asset if it is classified as (1) low-risk, (2) average-risk, and (3) high-risk.

b. Suppose Laura is unable to assess the risk of the asset and wants to be certain she's making a good deal. On the basis of your findings in part **a**, what is the most she should pay? Why?

c. All else being the same, what effect does increasing risk have on the value of an asset? Explain in light of your findings in part **a**.

P6–15   **Basic bond valuation**   Complex Systems has an outstanding issue of $1,000-par-value bonds with a 12% coupon interest rate. The issue pays interest *annually* and has 16 years remaining to its maturity date.

a. If bonds of similar risk are currently earning a 10% rate of return, how much should the Complex Systems bond sell for today?

b. Describe the *two* possible reasons why the rate on similar-risk bonds is below the coupon interest rate on the Complex Systems bond.

c. If the required return were at 12% instead of 10%, what would the current value of Complex Systems' bond be? Contrast this finding with your findings in part **a** and discuss.

P6–16   **Bond valuation—Annual interest**   Calculate the value of each of the bonds shown in the following table, all of which pay interest *annually*.

Bond	Par value	Coupon interest rate	Years to maturity	Required return
A	$1,000	14%	20	12%
B	1,000	8	16	8
C	100	10	8	13
D	500	16	13	18
E	1,000	12	10	10

P6–17   **Bond value and changing required returns**   Midland Utilities has outstanding a bond issue that will mature to its $1,000 par value in 12 years. The bond has a coupon interest rate of 11% and pays interest *annually*.

a. Find the value of the bond if the required return is (1) 11%, (2) 15%, and (3) 8%.

b. Plot your findings in part **a** on a set of "required return (*x* axis)–market value of bond (*y* axis)" axes.

c. Use your findings in parts **a** and **b** to discuss the relationship between the coupon interest rate on a bond and the required return and the market value of the bond relative to its par value.

d. What *two* possible reasons could cause the required return to differ from the coupon interest rate?

P6–18 **Bond value and time—Constant required returns**   Pecos Manufacturing has just issued a 15-year, 12% coupon interest rate, $1,000-par bond that pays interest *annually*. The required return is currently 14%, and the company is certain it will remain at 14% until the bond matures in 15 years.

a. Assuming that the required return does remain at 14% until maturity, find the value of the bond with (1) 15 years, (2) 12 years, (3) 9 years, (4) 6 years, (5) 3 years, and (6) 1 year to maturity.

b. Plot your findings on a set of "time to maturity (*x* axis)–market value of bond (*y* axis)" axes constructed similarly to Figure 6.5 on page 307.

c. All else remaining the same, when the required return differs from the coupon interest rate and is assumed to be constant to maturity, what happens to the bond value as time moves toward maturity? Explain in light of the graph in part **b.**

PERSONAL FINANCE PROBLEM

P6–19 **Bond value and time—Changing required returns**   Lynn Parsons is considering investing in either of two outstanding bonds. The bonds both have $1,000 par values and 11% coupon interest rates and pay *annual* interest. Bond A has exactly 5 years to maturity, and bond B has 15 years to maturity.

a. Calculate the value of bond A if the required return is (1) 8%, (2) 11%, and (3) 14%.

b. Calculate the value of bond B if the required return is (1) 8%, (2) 11%, and (3) 14%.

c. From your findings in parts **a** and **b,** complete the following table, and discuss the relationship between time to maturity and changing required returns.

Required return	Value of bond A	Value of bond B
8%	?	?
11	?	?
14	?	?

d. If Lynn wanted to minimize *interest rate risk,* which bond should she purchase? Why?

P6–20 **Yield to maturity**   The relationship between a bond's yield to maturity and coupon interest rate can be used to predict its pricing level. For each of the bonds listed, state whether the price of the bond will be at a premium to par, at par, or at a discount to par.

Bond	Coupon interest rate	Yield to maturity	Price
A	6%	10%	_____
B	8	8	_____
C	9	7	_____
D	7	9	_____
E	12	10	_____

P6–21 **Yield to maturity** The Salem Company bond currently sells for $955, has a 12% coupon interest rate and a $1,000 par value, pays interest *annually,* and has 15 years to maturity.
a. Calculate the *yield to maturity* (*YTM*) on this bond.
b. Explain the relationship that exists between the coupon interest rate and yield to maturity and the par value and market value of a bond.

P6–22 **Yield to maturity** Each of the bonds shown in the following table pays interest *annually.*

Bond	Par value	Coupon interest rate	Years to maturity	Current value
A	$1,000	9%	8	$ 820
B	1,000	12	16	1,000
C	500	12	12	560
D	1,000	15	10	1,120
E	1,000	5	3	900

a. Calculate the *yield to maturity* (*YTM*) for each bond.
b. What relationship exists between the coupon interest rate and yield to maturity and the par value and market value of a bond? Explain.

PERSONAL FINANCE PROBLEM

P6–23 **Bond valuation and yield to maturity** Mark Goldsmith's broker has shown him two bonds. Each has a maturity of 5 years, a par value of $1,000, and a yield to maturity of 12%. Bond A has a coupon interest rate of 6% paid annually. Bond B has a coupon interest rate of 14% paid annually.
a. Calculate the selling price for each of the bonds.
b. Mark has $20,000 to invest. Judging on the basis of the price of the bonds, how many of either one could Mark purchase if he were to choose it over the other? (Mark cannot really purchase a fraction of a bond, but for purposes of this question, pretend that he can.)
c. Calculate the yearly interest income of each bond on the basis of its coupon rate and the number of bonds that Mark could buy with his $20,000.
d. Assume that Mark will reinvest the interest payments as they are paid (at the end of each year) and that his rate of return on the reinvestment is only 10%. For each bond, calculate the value of the principal payment plus the value of Mark's reinvestment account at the end of the 5 years.
e. Why are the two values calculated in part **d** different? If Mark were worried that he would earn less than the 12% yield to maturity on the reinvested interest payments, which of these two bonds would be a better choice?

P6–24 **Bond valuation—Semiannual interest** Find the value of a bond maturing in 6 years, with a $1,000 par value and a coupon interest rate of 10% (5% paid semiannually) if the required return on similar-risk bonds is 14% annual interest (7% paid semiannually).

P6–25 **Bond valuation—Semiannual interest**   Calculate the value of each of the bonds shown in the following table, all of which pay interest *semiannually*.

Bond	Par value	Coupon interest rate	Years to maturity	Required stated annual return
A	$1,000	10%	12	8%
B	1,000	12	20	12
C	500	12	5	14
D	1,000	14	10	10
E	100	6	4	14

P6–26 **Bond valuation—Quarterly interest**   Calculate the value of a $5,000-par-value bond paying quarterly interest at an annual coupon interest rate of 10% and having 10 years until maturity if the required return on similar-risk bonds is currently a 12% annual rate paid *quarterly*.

P6–27 **ETHICS PROBLEM**   Bond rating agencies have invested significant sums of money in an effort to determine which quantitative and nonquantitative factors best predict bond defaults. Furthermore, some of the raters invest time and money to meet privately with corporate personnel to get nonpublic information that is used in assigning the issue's bond rating. In order to recoup those costs, some bond rating agencies have tied their ratings to the purchase of additional services. Do you believe that this is an acceptable practice? Defend your position.

Chapter 6 Case

Evaluating Annie Hegg's Proposed Investment in Atilier Industries Bonds

Annie Hegg has been considering investing in the bonds of Atilier Industries. The bonds were issued 5 years ago at their $1,000 par value and have exactly 25 years remaining until they mature. They have an 8% coupon interest rate, are convertible into 50 shares of common stock, and can be called any time at $1,080. The bond is rated Aa by Moody's. Atilier Industries, a manufacturer of sporting goods, recently acquired a small athletic-wear company that was in financial distress. As a result of the acquisition, Moody's and other rating agencies are considering a rating change for Atilier bonds. Recent economic data suggest that expected inflation, currently at 5% annually, is likely to increase to a 6% annual rate.

Annie remains interested in the Atilier bond but is concerned about inflation, a potential rating change, and maturity risk. To get a feel for the potential impact of these factors on the bond value, she decided to apply the valuation techniques she learned in her finance course.

To Do

a. If the price of the common stock into which the bond is convertible rises to $30 per share after 5 years and the issuer calls the bonds at $1,080, should Annie let the bond be called away from her or should she convert it into common stock?

b. For each of the following required returns, calculate the bond's value, assuming annual interest. Indicate whether the bond will sell at a discount, at a premium, or at par value.
   (1) Required return is 6%.
   (2) Required return is 8%.
   (3) Required return is 10%.

c. Repeat the calculations in part **b,** assuming that interest is paid *semiannually* and that the semiannual required returns are one-half of those shown. Compare and discuss differences between the bond values for each required return calculated here and in part **b** under the annual versus semiannual payment assumptions.

d. If Annie strongly believes that expected inflation will rise by 1% during the next few months, what is the most she should pay for the bond, assuming annual interest?

e. If the Atilier bonds are downrated by Moody's from Aa to A, and if such a rating change will result in an increase in the required return from 8% to 8.75%, what impact will this have on the bond value, assuming annual interest?

f. If Annie buys the bond today at its $1,000 par value and holds it for exactly 3 years, at which time the required return is 7%, how much of a gain or loss will she experience in the value of the bond (ignoring interest already received and assuming annual interest)?

g. Rework part **f,** assuming that Annie holds the bond for 10 years and sells it when the required return is 7%. Compare your finding to that in part **f,** and comment on the bond's *maturity risk.*

h. Assume that Annie buys the bond at its current price of 98.380 and holds it until maturity. What will her *current yield* and *yield to maturity* (*YTM*) be, assuming annual interest?

i. After evaluating all of the issues raised above, what recommendation would you give Annie with regard to her proposed investment in the Atilier Industries bonds?

Spreadsheet Exercise

CSM Corporation has a bond issue outstanding at the end of 2009. The bond has 15 years remaining to maturity and carries a coupon interest rate of 6%. Interest on the bond is compounded on a semiannual basis. The par value of the CSM bond is $1,000 and it is currently selling for $874.42.

To Do

Create a spreadsheet similar to the spreadsheets for yield to maturity and semiannual interest that can be viewed at www.prenhall.com/gitman, to model the following:

a. Using the trial and error method, determine the *annual* required rate of return (r_d). Find one interest rate that results in a bond value greater than the current bond price, and then find another rate that results in a bond value lower than the current bond price.
b. What is the time to maturity (n)?
c. What is the semiannual coupon payment (pmt)?
d. What is the semiannual required rate of return ($r_d/2$)?

Group Exercise

This chapter continued our discussion of valuation using the concept of risk. You will again use your shadow firm to investigate the issue of credit ratings.

To Do

a. Retrieve current information on the most recent debt issuance by your shadow firm. Several sites are available, including Standard & Poor's home page. Although you can use this site free of charge, you are required to register. Alternatively, you can use the bond screener tool at Yahoo! Finance (bonds.yahoo.com/).
b. Conduct a search for ratings on your corporation. Most likely you will find several ratings if your firm has issued multiple debt instruments. Note not only the rating but also the interest rate and yield to maturity of the most recently issued debt.
c. Using the current rating on your shadow company's most recent debt and a current quote on comparable Treasuries, estimate the risk premium inherent in the difference between the rates on the most recently issued debt and the risk-free Treasury.
d. Let's use the debt rating on your shadow firm to borrow money for your fictitious firm. Beyond determining the rate, your group must decide on an appropriate use for the funds. In other words, you must design an investment project that makes sense in the context of your fictitious firm. What is the purpose of the investment? What are the returns expected from the investment? Essentially, you should design and defend this investment. Show how this bond's valuation will change given differing assumptions on required return. In other words, what is likely to happen to the bond's valuation if market rates rise (or fall) following the issuance of this debt?

Web Exercise

Go to the book's companion website at **www.prenhall.com/gitman** to find the Web Exercise for this chapter.

Remember to check the book's website at **www.prenhall.com/gitman** to find additional resources, including Web Exercises and a Web Case.

7 | Stock Valuation

WHY THIS CHAPTER MATTERS TO YOU

In Your Professional Life

Accounting: You need to understand the difference between debt and equity in terms of tax treatment; the ownership claims of capital providers, including venture capitalists and stockholders; and why book value per share is not a sophisticated basis for common stock valuation.

Information systems: You need to understand the procedures used to issue common stock; the information needed to value stock; and how proposed actions affect the share price.

Management: You need to understand the difference between debt and equity capital; the rights and claims of stockholders; the process of issuing common stock; and the stock valuation models used to value the firm's common stock.

Marketing: You need to understand that the firm's ideas for products and services will greatly affect its ability to raise capital and that a perceived increase in risk from new projects may negatively affect the firm's stock value.

Operations: You need to understand that the amount of capital the firm has to invest in plant assets and inventory will depend on the evaluations of venture capitalists and would-be investors; the better the prospects look for growth, the more money the firm will have for operations.

In Your Personal Life

At some point, you are likely to hold stocks as an asset in your retirement program. You may want to estimate a stock's value. If the stock is selling below its estimated value, you may buy the stock; if its market price is above its value, you may sell it. Some individuals rely on financial advisors to make such buy or sell recommendations. Regardless of how you approach investment decisions, it will be helpful for you to understand how stocks are valued.

LEARNING GOALS

LG 1 Differentiate between debt and equity capital.

LG 2 Discuss the rights, characteristics, and features of both common and preferred stock.

LG 3 Describe the process of issuing common stock, including venture capital, going public, and the investment banker, and interpreting stock quotations.

LG 4 Understand the concept of market efficiency and basic common stock valuation using zero-growth, constant-growth, and variable-growth models.

LG 5 Discuss the free cash flow valuation model and the book value, liquidation value, and price/earnings (P/E) multiple approaches.

LG 6 Explain the relationships among financial decisions, return, risk, and the firm's value.

Crocs, Inc.

Initial Public Offering

One of the hottest initial public offerings (IPOs) in 2006 was shoemaker **Crocs, Inc.**. Initially priced at $13 to $15 per share, strong demand for the stock allowed the underwriters, Piper Jaffray and Thomas Weisel Partners, to revise the price range to $19 to $20. On February 7, 2006, the company went public at $21 per share, with 9.9 million shares issued in the IPO.

Crocs designs, manufactures, and markets a specialty line of footwear. Its brightly colored plastic shoes are made with a proprietary "closed-cell resin material" to create pliable, lightweight, nonmarking, and odor-resistant shoes that mold to fit the wearer's feet. Originally intended as a boating/outdoor shoe, Crocs became a fashion phenomenon, selling for $30 to $60 a pair. Crocs, Inc., sells its products through its own website, traditional footwear outlets, and various specialty shops.

At the time of the IPO, many were skeptical of Crocs' ability to grow over the long haul; the fear was that the shoes would become a passing fad or that competitors would flood the market with cheap imitations. Typical of most IPOs, a portion of the IPO allowed insiders to cash in on their investments. Nearly half of the shares offered for public sale came from insiders; the company would receive nothing from the sale of those 4.5 million shares. Crocs planned to use the remainder of the offering—funds from the sale of about 5.4 million shares—to repay debt, expand manufacturing capacity, and upgrade the company's computer systems.

Since its IPO, short interest (the percentage of public Crocs shares that has been sold short) has ranged from 27 percent to 40 percent. Clearly, many investors doubt the ability of the company to continue its growth. However, it would have been unrewarding to bet against this stock. On the day Crocs went public, its share price jumped from $21 to close at $28.55, a 1-day increase of nearly 36 percent. For those unable to buy the stock at its initial offering, the secondary market has offered an opportunity to participate in further gains. As of mid-May 2007, the stock had risen to more than $75 per share, and the company announced a 2-for-1 stock split on May 31, 2007.

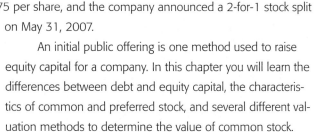

How might the current owners of a closely held company react to an IPO that immediately rises significantly above its initial offering price?

An initial public offering is one method used to raise equity capital for a company. In this chapter you will learn the differences between debt and equity capital, the characteristics of common and preferred stock, and several different valuation methods to determine the value of common stock.

7.1 | Differences between Debt and Equity Capital

capital
The long-term funds of a firm; all items on the right-hand side of the firm's balance sheet, *excluding current liabilities.*

debt capital
All long-term borrowing incurred by a firm, including bonds.

equity capital
The long-term funds provided by the firm's owners, the stockholders.

The term **capital** denotes the long-term funds of a firm. All items on the right-hand side of the firm's balance sheet, *excluding current liabilities,* are sources of capital. **Debt capital** includes all long-term borrowing incurred by a firm, including bonds, which were discussed in Chapter 6. **Equity capital** consists of long-term funds provided by the firm's owners, the stockholders. A firm can obtain equity capital either *internally,* by retaining earnings rather than paying them out as dividends to its stockholders, or *externally,* by selling common or preferred stock. The key differences between debt and equity capital are summarized in Table 7.1 and discussed below.

Voice in Management

Unlike creditors (lenders), holders of equity capital (common and preferred stockholders) are owners of the firm. Holders of common stock have voting rights that permit them to select the firm's directors and to vote on special issues. In contrast, debtholders and preferred stockholders may receive voting privileges only when the firm has violated its stated contractual obligations to them.

Claims on Income and Assets

Holders of equity have claims on both income and assets that are secondary to the claims of creditors. Their *claims on income* cannot be paid until the claims of all creditors (including both interest and scheduled principal payments) have been satisfied. After satisfying these claims, the firm's board of directors decides whether to distribute dividends to the owners.

The equity holders' *claims on assets* also are secondary to the claims of creditors. If the firm fails, its assets are sold, and the proceeds are distributed in this order: employees and customers, the government, creditors, and (finally) equity holders. Because equity holders are the last to receive any distribution of assets, they expect greater returns from dividends and/or increases in stock price.

	Type of capital	
TABLE 7.1 Key Differences between Debt and Equity Capital		
Characteristic	Debt	Equity
Voice in management[a]	No	Yes
Claims on income and assets	Senior to equity	Subordinate to debt
Maturity	Stated	None
Tax treatment	Interest deduction	No deduction

[a]In the event that the issuer violates its stated contractual obligations to them, debtholders and preferred stockholders *may* receive a voice in management; otherwise, only common stockholders have voting rights.

The costs of equity financing are generally higher than debt costs. One reason is that the suppliers of equity capital take more risks because of their subordinate claims on income and assets. Despite being more costly, equity capital is necessary for a firm to grow. All corporations must initially be financed with some common stock equity.

Maturity

Unlike debt, equity capital is a *permanent form* of financing for the firm. It does not "mature" so repayment is not required. Because equity is liquidated only during bankruptcy proceedings, stockholders must recognize that although a ready market may exist for their shares, the price that can be realized may fluctuate. This fluctuation of the market price of equity makes the overall returns to a firm's stockholders even more risky.

Tax Treatment

Interest payments to debtholders are treated as tax-deductible expenses by the issuing firm, whereas dividend payments to a firm's common and preferred stockholders are not tax-deductible. The tax deductibility of interest lowers the corporation's cost of debt financing, further causing it to be lower than the cost of equity financing.

REVIEW QUESTION

7–1   What are the key differences between *debt capital* and *equity capital?*

7.2 | Common and Preferred Stock

A firm can obtain equity capital by selling either common or preferred stock. All corporations initially issue common stock to raise equity capital. Some of these firms later issue either additional common stock or preferred stock to raise more equity capital. Although both common and preferred stock are forms of equity capital, preferred stock has some similarities to debt capital that significantly differentiate it from common stock. Here we first consider the features of both common and preferred stock and then describe the process of issuing common stock, including the use of venture capital.

Common Stock

The true owners of business firms are the common stockholders. Common stockholders are sometimes referred to as *residual owners* because they receive what is left—the residual—after all other claims on the firm's income and assets have been satisfied. They are assured of only one thing: that they cannot lose any more than they have invested in the firm. As a result of this generally uncertain position, common stockholders expect to be compensated with adequate dividends and, ultimately, capital gains.

privately owned (stock)
All common stock of a firm owned by a single individual.

closely owned (stock)
All common stock of a firm owned by a small group of investors (such as a family).

publicly owned (stock)
Common stock of a firm owned by a broad group of unrelated individual or institutional investors.

par value (stock)
A relatively useless value for a stock established for legal purposes in the firm's corporate charter.

preemptive right
Allows common stockholders to maintain their *proportionate* ownership in the corporation when new shares are issued.

dilution of ownership
Occurs when a new stock issue results in each present shareholder having a claim on a *smaller* part of the firm's earnings than previously.

rights
Financial instruments that allow stockholders to purchase additional shares at a price below the market price, in direct proportion to their number of owned shares.

authorized shares
The number of shares of common stock that a firm's corporate charter allows it to issue.

outstanding shares
The number of shares of common stock held by the public.

treasury stock
The number of shares of outstanding stock that have been repurchased by the firm.

issued shares
The number of shares of common stock that have been put into circulation; the sum of *outstanding shares* and *treasury stock*.

Ownership

The common stock of a firm can be **privately owned** by a single individual, **closely owned** by a small group of investors (such as a family), or **publicly owned** by a broad group of unrelated individual or institutional investors. Typically, small corporations are privately or closely owned; if their shares are traded, this trading occurs infrequently and in small amounts. Large corporations, which are emphasized in the following discussions, are publicly owned, and their shares are generally actively traded in the broker or dealer markets described in Chapter 1.

Par Value

Unlike bonds, which always have a par value, common stock may be sold with or without a par value. The **par value** of a common stock is a relatively useless value established for legal purposes in the firm's corporate charter. It is generally quite low, about $1.

Firms often issue stock with no par value, in which case they may assign the stock a value or record it on the books at the price at which it is sold. A low par value may be advantageous in states where certain corporate taxes are based on the par value of stock; if a stock has no par value, the tax may be based on an arbitrarily determined per-share figure.

Preemptive Rights

The **preemptive right** allows common stockholders to maintain their *proportionate* ownership in the corporation when new shares are issued. It allows existing shareholders to maintain voting control and protects them against the dilution of their ownership. **Dilution of ownership** usually results in the dilution of earnings, because each present shareholder has a claim on a *smaller* part of the firm's earnings than previously.

In a *rights offering*, the firm grants **rights** to its shareholders. These financial instruments allow stockholders to purchase additional shares at a price below the market price, in direct proportion to their number of owned shares. Rights are used primarily by smaller corporations whose shares are either *closely owned* or *publicly owned* and not actively traded. In these situations, rights are an important financing tool without which shareholders would run the risk of losing their proportionate control of the corporation. From the firm's viewpoint, the use of rights offerings to raise new equity capital may be less costly and may generate more interest than a public offering of stock.

Authorized, Outstanding, and Issued Shares

A firm's corporate charter indicates how many **authorized shares** it can issue. The firm cannot sell more shares than the charter authorizes without obtaining approval through a shareholder vote. To avoid later having to amend the charter, firms generally attempt to authorize more shares than they initially plan to issue.

Authorized shares become **outstanding shares** when they are held by the public. If the *firm* repurchases any of its outstanding shares, these shares are recorded as **treasury stock** and are no longer considered to be outstanding shares. **Issued shares** are the shares of common stock that have been put into circulation; they represent the sum of *outstanding shares* and *treasury stock*.

> *Example*

Golden Enterprises, a producer of medical pumps, has the following stockholders' equity account on December 31:

Stockholders' Equity

Common stock—$0.80 par value:	
Authorized 35,000,000 shares; issued 15,000,000 shares	$ 12,000,000
Paid-in capital in excess of par	63,000,000
Retained earnings	31,000,000
	$106,000,000
Less: Cost of treasury stock (1,000,000 shares)	4,000,000
Total stockholders' equity	$102,000,000

How many shares of additional common stock can Golden sell without gaining approval from its shareholders? The firm has 35 million authorized shares, 15 million issued shares, and 1 million shares of treasury stock. Thus 14 million shares are outstanding (15 million issued shares − 1 million shares of treasury stock), and Golden can issue 21 million additional shares (35 million authorized shares − 14 million outstanding shares) without seeking shareholder approval. This total includes the treasury shares currently held, which the firm can reissue to the public without obtaining shareholder approval.

Voting Rights

Generally, each share of common stock entitles its holder to one vote in the election of directors and on special issues. Votes are generally assignable and may be cast at the annual stockholders' meeting.

In recent years, many firms have issued two or more classes of common stock; they differ mainly in having unequal voting rights. A firm can use different classes of stock as a defense against a *hostile takeover* in which an outside group, without management support, tries to gain voting control of the firm by buying its shares in the marketplace. **Supervoting shares** of stock give each owner multiple votes. Supervoting shares allow "insiders" to maintain control against an outside group whose shares have only one vote each. At other times, a class of **nonvoting common stock** is issued when the firm wishes to raise capital through the sale of common stock but does not want to give up its voting control.

When different classes of common stock are issued on the basis of unequal voting rights, class A common is typically—but not universally—designated as nonvoting, and class B common has voting rights. Generally, higher classes of shares (class A, for example) are given preference in the distribution of earnings (dividends) and assets; lower-class shares, in exchange, receive voting rights. Treasury stock, which is held within the corporation, generally *does not* have voting rights, *does not* earn dividends, and *does not* have a claim on assets in liquidation.

Because most small stockholders do not attend the annual meeting to vote, they may sign a **proxy statement** transferring their votes to another party. The solicitation of proxies from shareholders is closely controlled by the Securities and Exchange Commission to ensure that proxies are not being solicited on the

supervoting shares
Stock that carries with it multiple votes per share rather than the single vote per share typically given on regular shares of common stock.

nonvoting common stock
Common stock that carries no voting rights; issued when the firm wishes to raise capital through the sale of common stock but does not want to give up its voting control.

proxy statement
A statement transferring the votes of a stockholder to another party.

proxy battle
The attempt by a non-management group to gain control of the management of a firm by soliciting a sufficient number of proxy votes.

basis of false or misleading information. Existing management generally receives the stockholders' proxies, because it is able to solicit them at company expense.

Occasionally, when the firm is widely owned, outsiders may wage a **proxy battle** to unseat the existing management and gain control. To win a corporate election, votes from a majority of the shares voted are required. However, the odds of a nonmanagement group winning a proxy battle are generally slim.

Dividends

The payment of dividends to the firm's shareholders is at the discretion of the corporation's board of directors. Most corporations pay dividends quarterly. Dividends may be paid in cash, stock, or merchandise. Cash dividends are the most common, merchandise dividends the least.

Common stockholders are not promised a dividend, but they come to expect certain payments on the basis of the historical dividend pattern of the firm. Before dividends are paid to common stockholders, the claims of the government, all creditors, and preferred stockholders must be satisfied. Since passage of the *Jobs and Growth Tax Relief Reconciliation Act of 2003,* many firms now pay larger dividends to shareholders, who are subject to a maximum tax rate of 15 percent on dividends rather than the maximum tax rate of 39 percent in effect prior to passage of the act. Because of the importance of the dividend decision to the growth and valuation of the firm, dividends are discussed in greater detail in Chapter 13.

International Stock Issues

Although the international market for common stock is not as large as the international market for bonds, cross-border issuance and trading of common stock have increased dramatically in the past 30 years.

Some corporations *issue stock in foreign markets.* For example, the stock of General Electric trades in Frankfurt, London, Paris, and Tokyo; the stocks of Time Warner and Microsoft trade in Frankfurt and London; and the stock of McDonalds trades in Frankfurt, London, and Paris. The Frankfurt, London, and Tokyo markets are the most popular. Issuing stock internationally broadens the ownership base and helps a company to integrate itself into the local business scene. A listing on a foreign stock exchange both increases local business press coverage and serves as effective corporate advertising. Having locally traded stock can also facilitate corporate acquisitions, because shares can be used as an acceptable method of payment.

Foreign corporations have also discovered the benefits of trading their stock in the United States. The disclosure and reporting requirements mandated by the U.S. Securities and Exchange Commission have historically discouraged all but the largest foreign firms from directly listing their shares on the New York Stock Exchange or the American Stock Exchange. For example, in 1993, Daimler-Benz (now DaimlerChrysler) became the first large German company to be listed on the NYSE.

American depositary receipts (ADRs)
Dollar-denominated receipts for the stocks of foreign companies that are held in the vaults of banks in the companies' home countries.

American depositary shares (ADSs)
Securities, backed by *American depositary receipts (ADRs)*, that permit U.S. investors to hold shares of non-U.S. companies and trade them in U.S. markets.

As an alternative, most foreign companies choose to tap the U.S. market through **American depositary receipts (ADRs).** These are dollar-denominated receipts for the stocks of foreign companies that are held in the vaults of banks in the companies' home countries. They serve as backing for **American depositary shares (ADSs)**, which are securities that permit U.S. investors to hold shares of non-U.S. companies and trade them in U.S. markets. Because ADSs are issued, in dollars, to U.S. investors, they are subject to U.S. securities laws. At the same time, they give investors the opportunity to diversify their portfolios internationally.

Preferred Stock

par-value preferred stock
Preferred stock with a stated face value that is used with the specified dividend percentage to determine the annual dollar dividend.

no-par preferred stock
Preferred stock with no stated face value but with a stated annual dollar dividend.

Preferred stock gives its holders certain privileges that make them senior to common stockholders. Preferred stockholders are promised a fixed periodic dividend, which is stated either as a percentage or as a dollar amount. How the dividend is specified depends on whether the preferred stock has a *par value*. **Par-value preferred stock** has a stated face value, and its annual dividend is specified as a percentage of this value. **No-par preferred stock** has no stated face value, but its annual dividend is stated in dollars. Preferred stock is most often issued by public utilities, by acquiring firms in merger transactions, and by firms that are experiencing losses and need additional financing.

Basic Rights of Preferred Stockholders

The basic rights of preferred stockholders are somewhat more favorable than the rights of common stockholders. Preferred stock is often considered *quasi-debt* because, much like interest on debt, it specifies a fixed periodic payment (dividend). Of course, as ownership, preferred stock is unlike debt in that it has no maturity date. Because they have a fixed claim on the firm's income that takes precedence over the claim of common stockholders, preferred stockholders are exposed to less risk. They are consequently *not normally given a voting right*.

Preferred stockholders have *preference over common stockholders in the distribution of earnings*. If the stated preferred stock dividend is "passed" (not paid) by the board of directors, the payment of dividends to common stockholders is prohibited. It is this preference in dividend distribution that makes common stockholders the true risk takers.

Preferred stockholders are also usually given *preference over common stockholders in the liquidation of assets* in a legally bankrupt firm, although they must "stand in line" behind creditors. The amount of the claim of preferred stockholders in liquidation is normally equal to the par or stated value of the preferred stock.

Features of Preferred Stock

A preferred stock issue generally includes a number of features, which, along with the stock's par value, the amount of dividend payments, the dividend payment dates, and any restrictive covenants, are specified in an agreement similar to a *bond indenture*.

Restrictive Covenants   The restrictive covenants in a preferred stock issue focus on ensuring the firm's continued existence and regular payment of the dividend. These covenants include provisions about passing dividends, the sale of senior securities, mergers, sales of assets, minimum liquidity requirements, and repurchases of common stock. The violation of preferred stock covenants usually permits preferred stockholders either to obtain representation on the firm's board of directors or to force the retirement of their stock at or above its par or stated value.

cumulative (preferred stock)
Preferred stock for which all passed (unpaid) dividends in arrears, along with the current dividend, must be paid before dividends can be paid to common stockholders.

noncumulative (preferred stock)
Preferred stock for which passed (unpaid) dividends do not accumulate.

conversion feature (preferred stock)
A feature of *convertible preferred stock* that allows holders to change each share into a stated number of shares of common stock.

Cumulation   Most preferred stock is **cumulative** with respect to any dividends passed. That is, all dividends in arrears, along with the current dividend, must be paid before dividends can be paid to common stockholders. If preferred stock is **noncumulative,** passed (unpaid) dividends do not accumulate. In this case, only the current dividend must be paid before dividends can be paid to common stockholders. Because the common stockholders can receive dividends only after the dividend claims of preferred stockholders have been satisfied, it is in the firm's best interest to pay preferred dividends when they are due.[1]

Other Features   Preferred stock is generally *callable*—the issuer can retire outstanding stock within a certain period of time at a specified price. The call option generally cannot be exercised until after a specified date. The call price is normally set above the initial issuance price, but it may decrease as time passes. Making preferred stock callable provides the issuer with a way to bring the fixed-payment commitment of the preferred issue to an end if conditions in the financial markets make it desirable to do so.

Preferred stock quite often contains a **conversion feature** that allows *holders of convertible preferred stock* to change each share into a stated number of shares of common stock. Sometimes the number of shares of common stock that the preferred stock can be exchanged for changes according to a prespecified formula.

Issuing Common Stock

Because of the high risk associated with a business startup, a firm's initial financing typically comes from its founders in the form of a common stock investment. Until the founders have made an equity investment, it is highly unlikely that others will contribute either equity or debt capital. Early-stage investors in the firm's equity, as well as lenders who provide debt capital, want to be assured that they are taking no more risk than the founding owner(s). In addition, they want confirmation that the founders are confident enough in their vision for the firm that they are willing to risk their own money.

The initial nonfounder financing for business startups with attractive growth prospects comes from private equity investors. Then, as the firm establishes the viability of its product or service offering and begins to generate revenues, cash flow, and profits, it will often "go public" by issuing shares of common stock to a much broader group of investors.

Before we consider the initial *public* sales of equity, let's review some of the key aspects of early-stage equity financing in firms that have attractive growth prospects.

venture capital
Privately raised external equity capital used to fund early-stage firms with attractive growth prospects.

Venture Capital

The initial external equity financing privately raised by firms, typically early-stage firms with attractive growth prospects, is called **venture capital.** Those who pro-

---

1. Most preferred stock is cumulative, because it is difficult to sell noncumulative stock. Common stockholders obviously prefer issuance of noncumulative preferred stock, because it does not place them in quite so risky a position. But it is often in the best interest of the firm to sell cumulative preferred stock because of its lower cost.

Most preferred stock has a fixed dividend, but some firms issue *adjustable-rate (floating-rate) preferred stock (ARPS)* whose dividend rate is tied to interest rates on specific government securities. Rate adjustments are commonly made quarterly. ARPS offers investors protection against sharp rises in interest rates, which means that the issue can be sold at an initially lower dividend rate.

venture capitalists (VCs)
Providers of venture capital; typically, formal businesses that maintain strong oversight over the firms they invest in and that have clearly defined exit strategies.

angel capitalists (angels)
Wealthy individual investors who do not operate as a business but invest in promising early-stage companies in exchange for a portion of the firm's equity.

vide venture capital are known as **venture capitalists** (VCs). They typically are formal business entities that maintain strong oversight over the firms they invest in and that have clearly defined exit strategies. Less visible early-stage investors called **angel capitalists** (or **angels**) tend to be investors who do not actually operate as a business; they are often wealthy individual investors who are willing to invest in promising early-stage companies in exchange for a portion of the firm's equity. Although angels play a major role in early-stage equity financing, we will focus on VCs because of their more formal structure and greater public visibility.

Organization and Investment Stages   Institutional venture capital investors tend to be organized in one of four basic ways, as described in Table 7.2. The *VC limited partnership* is by far the dominant structure. These funds have as their sole objective to earn high returns, rather than to obtain access to the companies in order to sell or buy other products or services.

VCs can invest in early-stage companies, later-stage companies, or buyouts and acquisitions. Generally, about 40 to 50 percent of VC investments are devoted to early-stage companies (for startup funding and expansion) and a similar percentage to later-stage companies (for marketing, production expansion, and preparation for public offering); the remaining 5 to 10 percent are devoted to the buyout or acquisition of other companies. Generally, VCs look for compound annual rates of return ranging from 20 to 50 percent or more, depending on both the development stage and the attributes of each company. Earlier-stage investments tend to demand higher returns than later-stage investments because of the higher risk associated with the earlier stages of a firm's growth.

Deal Structure and Pricing   Regardless of the development stage, venture capital investments are made under a legal contract that clearly allocates responsibilities and ownership interests between existing owners (founders) and the VC fund or limited partnership. The terms of the agreement will depend on numerous factors related to the founders; the business structure, stage of development, and outlook; and other market and timing issues. The specific financial terms will, of

TABLE 7.2	Organization of Institutional Venture Capital Investors
Organization	**Description**
Small business investment companies (SBICs)	Corporations chartered by the federal government that can borrow at attractive rates from the U.S. Treasury and use the funds to make venture capital investments in private companies.
Financial VC funds	Subsidiaries of financial institutions, particularly banks, set up to help young firms grow and, it is hoped, become major customers of the institution.
Corporate VC funds	Firms, sometimes subsidiaries, established by nonfinancial firms, typically to gain access to new technologies that the corporation can access to further its own growth.
VC limited partnerships	Limited partnerships organized by professional VC firms, which serve as the general partner and organize, invest, and manage the partnership using the limited partners' funds; the professional VCs ultimately liquidate the partnership and distribute the proceeds to all partners.

course, depend on the value of the enterprise, the amount of funding, and the perceived risk. To control the VC's risk, various covenants are included in the agreement, and the actual funding may be pegged to the achievement of *measurable milestones*. The VC will negotiate numerous other provisions into the contract, both to ensure the firm's success and to control its risk exposure. The contract will have an explicit exit strategy for the VC that may be tied both to measurable milestones and to time.

The amount of equity to which the VC is entitled will, of course, depend on the value of the firm, the terms of the contract, the exit terms, and the minimum compound annual rate of return required by the VC on its investment. Although each VC investment is unique and no standard contract exists, the transaction will be structured to provide the VC with a high rate of return that is consistent with the typically high risk of such transactions. The exit strategy of most VC investments is to take the firm public through an initial public offering.

Going Public

When a firm wishes to sell its stock in the primary market, it has three alternatives. It can make (1) a *public offering*, in which it offers its shares for sale to the general public; (2) a *rights offering*, in which new shares are sold to existing stockholders; or (3) a *private placement*, in which the firm sells new securities directly to an investor or group of investors. Here we focus on public offerings, particularly the **initial public offering (IPO)**, which is the first public sale of a firm's stock. IPOs are typically made by small, rapidly growing companies that either require additional capital to continue expanding or have met a milestone for going public that was established in a contract signed earlier in order to obtain VC funding.

initial public offering (IPO)
The first public sale of a firm's stock.

To go public, the firm must first obtain the approval of its current shareholders, the investors who own its privately issued stock. Next, the company's auditors and lawyers must certify that all documents for the company are legitimate. The company then finds an investment bank willing to *underwrite* the offering. This underwriter is responsible for promoting the stock and facilitating the sale of the company's IPO shares. The underwriter often brings in other investment banking firms as participants. We'll discuss the role of the investment banker in more detail in the next section.

prospectus
A portion of a security registration statement that describes the key aspects of the issue, the issuer, and its management and financial position.

The company files a registration statement with the SEC. One portion of the registration statement is called the **prospectus**. It describes the key aspects of the issue, the issuer, and its management and financial position. During the waiting period between the statement's filing and its approval, prospective investors can receive a preliminary prospectus. This preliminary version is called a **red herring**, because a notice printed in red on the front cover indicates the tentative nature of the offer. The cover of the preliminary prospectus describing the 2007 stock issue of Metro PCS Communications, Inc., is shown in Figure 7.1. Note the red herring printed vertically on its left edge.

red herring
A preliminary prospectus made available to prospective investors during the waiting period between the registration statement's filing with the SEC and its approval.

After the SEC approves the registration statement, the investment community can begin analyzing the company's prospects. However, from the time it files until at least one month after the IPO is complete, the company must observe a *quiet period*, during which there are restrictions on what company officials may say about the company. The purpose of the quiet period is to make sure that all potential investors have access to the same information about the company—the

FIGURE 7.1

Cover of a Preliminary Prospectus for a Stock Issue
Some of the key factors related to the 2007 common stock issue by Metro PCS Communications, Inc., are summarized on the cover of the prospectus. The type printed vertically on the left edge is normally red, which explains its name "red herring." (*Source:* Metro PCS Communications, Inc., April 3, 2007, p. 1.)

The information in this prospectus is not complete and may be changed. We may not sell these securities until the registration statement filed with the Securities and Exchange Commission is effective. This prospectus is not an offer to sell these securities and it is not soliciting an offer to buy these securities in any jurisdiction where the offer or sale is not permitted.

SUBJECT TO COMPLETION, DATED APRIL 3, 2007

PROSPECTUS

50,000,000 Shares

MetroPCS Communications, Inc.
Common Stock

This is our initial public offering. We are offering 37,500,000 shares of our common stock and the selling stockholders identified in this prospectus are offering an additional 12,500,000 shares of our common stock. We will not receive any proceeds from the sale of our common stock by the selling stockholders. We currently expect the initial public offering price for our stock will be between $19.00 and $21.00 per share.

Unless otherwise indicated, all share numbers and per share prices in this prospectus give effect to a 3 for 1 stock split effected by means of a stock dividend of two shares of common stock for each share of common stock issued and outstanding at the close of business on March 14, 2007.

Prior to this offering, there has been no public market for our common stock. We have applied to list our common stock on the New York Stock Exchange under the symbol "PCS".

Investing in our common stock involves risks. See "Risk Factors" beginning on page 12.

	Per Share	Total
Public offering price	$	$
Underwriting discounts	$	$
Proceeds, before expenses, to us	$	$
Proceeds to the selling stockholders	$	$

Neither the Securities and Exchange Commission nor any state securities commission has approved or disapproved of these securities or passed upon the adequacy or accuracy of this prospectus. Any representation to the contrary is a criminal offense.

The underwriters expect to deliver the shares against payment in New York, New York on or about   , 2007.

The underwriters have a 30-day option to purchase up to 7,500,000 additional shares of common stock from the selling stockholders to cover over-allotments, if any. We will not receive any proceeds from the exercise of the over-allotment option.

Bear, Stearns & Co. Inc.
Banc of America Securities LLC
Merrill Lynch & Co.
Morgan Stanley

UBS Investment Bank
Thomas Weisel Partners LLC
Wachovia Securities
Raymond James

The date of this prospectus is   , 2007.

information presented in the preliminary prospectus—and not to any unpublished data that might give them an unfair advantage.

The investment bankers and company executives promote the company's stock offering through a *road show*, a series of presentations to potential investors around the country and sometimes overseas. In addition to providing investors with information about the new issue, road show sessions help the investment bankers gauge the demand for the offering and set an expected pricing range. After the underwriter sets terms and prices the issue, the SEC must approve the offering.

The Investment Banker's Role

investment banker
Financial intermediary that specializes in selling new security issues and advising firms with regard to major financial transactions.

underwriting
The role of the *investment banker* in bearing the risk of reselling, at a profit, the securities purchased from an issuing corporation at an agreed-on price.

underwriting syndicate
A group of other bankers formed by an investment banker to share the financial risk associated with *underwriting* new securities.

selling group
A large number of brokerage firms that join the originating investment banker(s); each accepts responsibility for selling a certain portion of a new security issue on a commission basis.

Most public offerings are made with the assistance of an **investment banker.** The investment banker is a financial intermediary (such as Morgan Stanley or Goldman, Sachs) that specializes in selling new security issues and advising firms with regard to major financial transactions. The main activity of the investment banker is **underwriting.** This process involves purchasing the security issue from the issuing corporation at an agreed-on price and bearing the risk of reselling it to the public at a profit. The investment banker also provides the issuer with advice about pricing and other important aspects of the issue.

In the case of very large security issues, the investment banker brings in other bankers as partners to form an **underwriting syndicate.** The syndicate shares the financial risk associated with buying the entire issue from the issuer and reselling the new securities to the public. The originating investment banker and the syndicate members put together a **selling group,** normally made up of themselves and a large number of brokerage firms. Each member of the selling group accepts the responsibility for selling a certain portion of the issue and is paid a commission on the securities it sells. The selling process for a large security issue is depicted in Figure 7.2.

Compensation for underwriting and selling services typically comes in the form of a discount on the sale price of the securities. For example, an investment banker may pay the issuing firm $24 per share for stock that will be sold for $26 per share. The investment banker may then sell the shares to members of the selling group for $25.25 per share. In this case, the original investment banker earns $1.25 per share ($25.25 sale price − $24 purchase price). The members of the selling group earn 75 cents for each share they sell ($26 sale price − $25.25

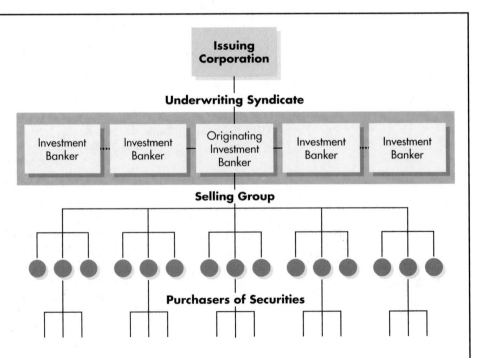

FIGURE 7.2

The Selling Process for a Large Security Issue
The investment banker hired by the issuing corporation may form an underwriting syndicate. The underwriting syndicate buys the entire security issue from the issuing corporation at an agreed-on price. The underwriters then have the opportunity (and bear the risk) of reselling the issue to the public at a profit. Both the originating investment banker and the other syndicate members put together a selling group to sell the issue on a commission basis to investors.

purchase price). Although some primary security offerings are directly placed by the issuer, the majority of new issues are sold through public offering via the mechanism just described.

Interpreting Stock Quotations

The financial manager needs to stay abreast of the market values of the firm's outstanding stock, whether it is traded domestically or in international markets. Similarly, existing and prospective stockholders need to monitor the prices of the securities they own because these prices represent the current value of their investments. Price *quotations,* which include current price data along with statistics on recent price behavior, are readily available for actively traded stocks. The most up-to-date "quotes" can be obtained electronically, via a personal computer. Price information is available from stockbrokers and is widely published in news media. Popular sources of daily security price quotations include financial newspapers, such as the *Wall Street Journal* and *Investor's Business Daily,* and the business sections of daily general newspapers.

Figure 7.3 includes an excerpt from the NYSE quotations, reported in the *Wall Street Journal* on March 28, 2007, for transactions through the close of trading on Tuesday, March 27, 2007. We'll look at the quotation for the common stock of McDonald's, highlighted in the figure. The quotations show that stock prices are quoted in dollars and cents. Listed to the right of the company's name is its *stock symbol;* McDonald's goes by "MCD." The next column, labeled "CLOSE," contains the closing (last) price at which the stock sold on the given day. The value for McDonald's was $45.04. The final column, "NET CHG," indicates the change in the closing price from that on the prior trading day. McDonald's closed down $0.08 from March 26, 2007, which means the closing price on that day was $45.12.

Hint Preferred stock quotations typically are not listed in the financial press, but can be obtained online or through a stockbroker.

FIGURE 7.3

Stock Quotations
Selected stock quotations for March 27, 2007

STOCK	SYM	CLOSE	NET CHG
Masco	MAS	27.80	–0.15
Masisa ADS	MYS	11.24	–0.03
MasseyEngy	MEE	24.20	–0.64
MasterCard	MA	107.25	–1.23
MatsuElec	MC	20.74	–0.22
Mattel	MAT	28.26	–0.47
McAfee	MFE	29.82	–0.07
McClatchy A	MNI	37.61	–0.37
McCrmkCo	MKC	38.68	–0.43
McDermInt	MDR	49.82	–0.64
McDonalds	MCD	45.04	–0.08
McGrawH	MHP	63.33	–0.26
McKesson	MCK	58.50	0.58
MeadWVaco	MWV	30.66	–0.03
Mechel OAO	MTL	31.75	–0.31
MedcoHlthSol	MHS	71.80	–0.57
Medtronic	MDT	48.68	–1.15
MellonFnl	MEL	43.11	–0.47
MensWearhs	MW	48.26	–0.05

Source: Wall Street Journal, March 28, 2007, p. C13.

Similar quotations systems are used for stocks that trade in other markets such as the Nasdaq market. Also note that when a stock issue is not traded on a given day, it generally is not quoted in the financial and business press.

REVIEW QUESTIONS

7–2 What risks do common stockholders take that other suppliers of long-term capital do not?

7–3 How does a *rights offering* protect a firm's stockholders against the *dilution of ownership*?

7–4 Explain the relationships among authorized shares, outstanding shares, treasury stock, and issued shares.

7–5 What are the advantages to both U.S.-based and foreign corporations of issuing stock outside their home markets? What are *American depositary receipts (ADRs)*? What are *American depositary shares (ADSs)*?

7–6 What claims do preferred stockholders have with respect to distribution of earnings (dividends) and assets?

7–7 Explain the *cumulative feature* of preferred stock. What is the purpose of a *call feature* in a preferred stock issue?

7–8 What is the difference between a *venture capitalist (VC)* and an *angel capitalist (angel)*?

7–9 Into what bodies are institutional VCs most commonly organized? How are their deals structured and priced?

7–10 What general procedures must a private firm follow to go public via an *initial public offering (IPO)*?

7–11 What role does an *investment banker* play in a public offering? Explain the sequence of events in the issuing of stock.

7–12 What are the key sources of *stock quotations*? Describe the items of information included in a published stock quotation.

7.3 | Common Stock Valuation

Common stockholders expect to be rewarded through periodic cash dividends and an increasing—or at least nondeclining—share value. Like current owners, prospective owners and security analysts frequently estimate the firm's value. Investors purchase the stock when they believe that it is *undervalued*—when its true value is greater than its market price. They sell the stock when they feel that it is *overvalued*—when its market price is greater than its true value.

In this section, we will describe specific stock valuation techniques. First, though, we will look at the concept of an efficient market, which questions whether the prices of actively traded stocks can differ from their true values.

Market Efficiency

Economically rational buyers and sellers use their assessment of an asset's risk and return to determine its value. To a buyer, the asset's value represents the maximum price that he or she would pay to acquire it; a seller views the asset's value as a minimum sale price. In competitive markets with many active participants, such as the New York Stock Exchange, the interactions of many buyers and sellers result in an equilibrium price—the *market value*—for each security. This price reflects the collective actions that buyers and sellers take on the basis of all available information. Buyers and sellers are assumed to digest new information immediately as it becomes available and, through their purchase and sale activities, to create a new market equilibrium price quickly. This general concept is known as *market efficiency*.[2]

Market Adjustment to New Information

The process of market adjustment to new information can be viewed in terms of rates of return. From Chapter 5, we know that for a given level of risk, investors require a specified periodic return—the *required return, r*—which can be estimated by using beta and CAPM. At each point in time, investors estimate the **expected return, $\hat{r}$**—the return that is expected to be earned on a given asset each period over an infinite time horizon. The expected return can be estimated by using a simplified form of Equation 5.1:

expected return, $\hat{r}$
The return that is expected to be earned on a given asset each period over an infinite time horizon.

$$\hat{r} = \frac{\text{Expected benefit during each period}}{\text{Current price of asset}} \qquad \textbf{(7.1)}$$

Whenever investors find that the expected return is not equal to the required return ($\hat{r} \neq r$), a market price adjustment occurs. If the expected return is less than the required return ($\hat{r} < r$), investors sell the asset, because they do not expect it to earn a return commensurate with its risk. Such action drives the asset's price down, which (assuming no change in expected benefits) causes its expected return to rise to the level of its required return. If the expected return were above the required return ($\hat{r} > r$), investors would buy the asset, driving its price up and its expected return down to the point where it equals the required return.

Example

The common stock of Alton Industries (AI) is currently selling for $50 per share, and market participants expect it to generate benefits of $6.50 per share during each coming period. In addition, the risk-free rate, R_F, is currently 7%; the market return, r_m, is 12%; and the stock's beta, b_{AI}, is 1.20. When the appropriate values are substituted into Equation 7.1, the firm's current expected return, $\hat{r}_0$, is

$$\hat{r}_0 = \frac{\$6.50}{\$50.00} = \underline{\underline{13\%}}$$

When the appropriate values are substituted into the CAPM (Equation 5.8), the current required return, r_0, is

$$r_0 = 7\% + [1.20 \times (12\% - 7\%)] = 7\% + 6\% = \underline{\underline{13\%}}$$

Because $\hat{r}_0 = r_0$, the market is currently in equilibrium, and the stock is fairly priced at $50 per share.

---

2. A great deal of theoretical and empirical research has been performed in the area of market efficiency. For purposes of this discussion, generally accepted beliefs about market efficiency are described, rather than the technical aspects of the various forms of market efficiency and their theoretical implications. For a good discussion of the theory and evidence relative to market efficiency, see Scott B. Smart, William L. Megginson, and Lawrence J. Gitman, *Corporate Finance*, 2nd Edition (Mason, OH: South-Western, 2007), Chapter 10.

Assume that a press release announces that a major product liability suit has been filed against Alton Industries. As a result, investors immediately adjust their risk assessment upward, raising the firm's beta from 1.20 to 1.40. The new required return, r_1, becomes

$$r_1 = 7\% + [1.40 \times (12\% - 7\%)] = 7\% + 7\% = \underline{\underline{14\%}}$$

Because the expected return of 13% is now below the required return of 14%, many investors sell the stock—driving its price down to about \$46.43—the price that will result in a 14% expected return, $\hat{r}_1$.

$$\hat{r}_1 = \frac{\$6.50}{\$46.43} = \underline{\underline{14\%}}$$

The new price of \$46.43 brings the market back into equilibrium, because the expected return now equals the required return.

The Efficient-Market Hypothesis

efficient-market hypothesis (EMH)
Theory describing the behavior of an assumed "perfect" market in which (1) securities are typically in equilibrium, (2) security prices fully reflect all public information available and react swiftly to new information, and, (3) because stocks are fully and fairly priced, investors need not waste time looking for mispriced securities.

As noted in Chapter 1, active broker and dealer markets, such as the New York Stock Exchange and the Nasdaq market, are *efficient*—they are made up of many rational investors who react quickly and objectively to new information. The **efficient-market hypothesis (EMH)**, which is the basic theory describing the behavior of such a "perfect" market, specifically states that

1. Securities are typically in equilibrium, which means that they are fairly priced and that their expected returns equal their required returns.
2. At any point in time, security prices fully reflect all public information available about the firm and its securities,[3] and these prices react swiftly to new information.
3. Because stocks are fully and fairly priced, investors need not waste their time trying to find mispriced (undervalued or overvalued) securities.

Not all market participants are believers in the efficient-market hypothesis. Some feel that it is worthwhile to search for undervalued or overvalued securities and to trade them to profit from market inefficiencies. Others argue that it is mere luck that would allow market participants to anticipate new information correctly and as a result earn *excess returns*—that is, actual returns greater than required returns. They believe it is unlikely that market participants can *over the long run* earn excess returns. Contrary to this belief, some well-known investors such as Warren Buffett and Peter Lynch *have* over the long run consistently earned excess returns on their portfolios. It is unclear whether their success is the

---

3. Those market participants who have nonpublic—*inside*—information may have an unfair advantage that enables them to earn an excess return. Since the mid-1980s disclosure of the insider-trading activities of a number of well-known financiers and investors, major national attention has been focused on the "problem" of insider trading and its resolution. Clearly, those who trade securities on the basis of inside information have an unfair and illegal advantage. Empirical research has confirmed that those with inside information do indeed have an opportunity to earn an excess return. Here we ignore this possibility, given its illegality and the fact that enhanced surveillance and enforcement by the securities industry and the government have in recent years (it appears) significantly reduced insider trading. We, in effect, assume that all relevant information is public and that therefore the market is efficient.

result of their superior ability to anticipate new information or of some form of market inefficiency.

The Behavioral Finance Challenge

Although considerable evidence supports the concept of market efficiency, a growing body of academic evidence has begun to cast doubt on the validity of this notion. The research documents various *anomalies*—deviations from accepted beliefs—in stock returns. A number of academics and practitioners have also recognized that emotions and other subjective factors play a role in investment decisions.

This focus on investor behavior has resulted in a significant body of research, collectively referred to as **behavioral finance.** Advocates of behavioral finance are commonly referred to as "behaviorists." Daniel Kahneman was awarded the 2002 Nobel Prize in economics for his work in behavioral finance, specifically for integrating insights from psychology and economics. Ongoing research into the psychological factors that can affect investor behavior and the resulting effects on stock prices will likely result in growing acceptance of behavioral finance. The *Focus on Practice* box on page 346 further explains some of the findings of behavioral finance.

> *Throughout this text we ignore both disbelievers and behaviorists and continue to assume market efficiency.* This means that *the terms "expected return" and "required return" are used interchangeably,* because they should be equal in an efficient market. This also means that stock prices accurately reflect true value based on risk and return. In other words, we will operate under the assumption that a stock's market price at any point in time is the best estimate of its value. We're now ready to look closely at the mechanics of common stock valuation.

behavioral finance
A growing body of research that focuses on investor behavior and its impact on investment decisions and stock prices. Advocates are commonly referred to as "behaviorists."

Basic Common Stock Valuation Equation

Like the value of a bond, which we discussed in Chapter 6, *the value of a share of common stock is equal to the present value of all future cash flows (dividends) that it is expected to provide over an infinite time horizon.*[4] Although a stockholder can earn capital gains by selling stock at a price above that originally paid, what is really sold is the right to all future dividends. What about stocks that are not expected to pay dividends in the foreseeable future? Such stocks have a value attributable to a distant dividend expected to result from sale of the company or liquidation of its assets. Therefore, *from a valuation viewpoint, only dividends are relevant.*

By redefining terms, the basic valuation model in Equation 6.5 can be specified for common stock, as given in Equation 7.2:

$$P_0 = \frac{D_1}{(1 + r_s)^1} + \frac{D_2}{(1 + r_s)^2} + \cdots + \frac{D_\infty}{(1 + r_s)^\infty} \tag{7.2}$$

---

4. The need to consider an infinite time horizon is not critical, because a sufficiently long period—say, 50 years—will result in about the same present value as an infinite period for moderate-sized required returns. For example, at 15%, a dollar to be received 50 years from now, $PVIF_{15\%, 50yrs}$, is worth only about $0.001 today.

Focus on Practice

Understanding Human Behavior Helps Us Understand Investor Behavior

Market anomalies are not always explained by the efficient market hypothesis. Behavioral finance has a number of theories to help explain how human emotions influence people in their investment decision-making processes.

Regret theory deals with the emotional reaction people experience after realizing they have made an error in judgment. Faced with the prospect of selling a stock, investors become emotionally affected by the price at which they purchased the stock. A sale at a loss would confirm that the investor miscalculated the value of the stock when it was purchased. The correct approach when considering whether to sell a stock is, "Would I buy this stock today if it were already liquidated?" If the answer is "no," it is time to sell. Regret theory also holds true for investors who passed up buying a stock that now is selling at a much higher price. Again, the correct approach is to value the stock today without regard to its prior value.

Herding is another market behavior affecting investor decisions. Some investors rationalize their decision to buy certain stocks with "everyone else is doing it." Investors may feel less embarrassment about losing money on a popular stock than about losing money on an unknown or unpopular stock.

People have a tendency to place particular events into *mental compartments*, and the difference between these compartments sometimes impacts behavior more than the events themselves. Researchers have asked people the following question: "Would you purchase a $20 ticket at the local theater if you realize after you get there that you have lost a $20 bill?" Roughly 88 percent of people would do so. Under another scenario, people were asked whether they would buy a second $20 ticket if they arrived at the theater and realized that they had left at home a ticket purchased in advance for $20. Only 40 percent of respondents would buy another. In both scenarios the person is out $40, but mental accounting leads to a different outcome. In investing, compartmentalization is best illustrated by the hesitation to sell an investment that once had monstrous gains and now has a modest gain. During bull markets, people get accustomed to paper gains. When a market correction deflates investors' net worth, they are hesitant to sell, causing them to wait for the return of that gain.

Other investor behaviors are prospect theory and anchoring. According to *prospect theory*, people express a different degree of emotion toward gains than losses. Individuals are stressed more by prospective losses than they are buoyed by the prospect of equal gains. *Anchoring* is the tendency of investors to place more value on recent information. People tend to give too much credence to recent market opinions and events and mistakenly extrapolate recent trends that differ from historical, long-term averages and probabilities. Anchoring is a partial explanation for the longevity of some bull markets.

Most stock-valuation techniques require that all relevant information be available to properly determine a stock's value and potential for future gain. Behavioral finance may explain the connection between valuation and an investor's actions based on that valuation.

■ *Theories of behavioral finance can apply to other areas of human behavior in addition to investing. Think of a situation in which you may have demonstrated one of these behaviors. Share your situation with a classmate.*

where

P_0 = value of common stock

D_t = per-share dividend *expected* at the end of year t

r_s = required return on common stock

The equation can be simplified somewhat by redefining each year's dividend, D_t, in terms of anticipated growth. We will consider three models here: zero-growth, constant-growth, and variable-growth.

Zero-Growth Model

zero-growth model
An approach to dividend
valuation that assumes
a constant, nongrowing
dividend stream.

The simplest approach to dividend valuation, the **zero-growth model**, assumes a constant, nongrowing dividend stream. In terms of the notation already introduced,

$$D_1 = D_2 = \cdots = D_\infty$$

When we let D_1 represent the amount of the annual dividend, Equation 7.2 under zero growth reduces to

$$P_0 = D_1 \times \sum_{t=1}^{\infty} \frac{1}{(1+r_s)^t} = D_1 \times (PVIFA_{r_s,\infty}) = D_1 \times \frac{1}{r_s} = \frac{D_1}{r_s} \qquad (7.3)$$

The equation shows that with zero growth, the value of a share of stock would equal the present value of a perpetuity of D_1 dollars discounted at a rate r_s. (Perpetuities were introduced in Chapter 4; see Equation 4.19 and the related discussion.)

Personal Finance Example   Chuck Swimmer estimates that the dividend of Denham Company, an established textile producer, is expected to remain constant at $3 per share indefinitely. If his required return on its stock is 15%, the stock's value is $20 ($3 ÷ 0.15) per share.

Preferred Stock Valuation   Because preferred stock typically provides its holders with a fixed annual dividend over its assumed infinite life, *Equation 7.3 can be used to find the value of preferred stock.* The value of preferred stock can be estimated by substituting the stated dividend on the preferred stock for D_1 and the required return for r_s in Equation 7.3. For example, a preferred stock paying a $5 stated annual dividend and having a required return of 13 percent would have a value of $38.46 ($5 ÷ 0.13) per share.

Constant-Growth Model

constant-growth model
A widely cited dividend
valuation approach that
assumes that dividends will
grow at a constant rate, but
a rate that is less than the
required return.

The most widely cited dividend valuation approach, the **constant-growth model**, assumes that dividends will grow at a constant rate, but a rate that is less than the required return. (The assumption that the constant rate of growth, g, is less than the required return, r_s, is a necessary mathematical condition for deriving this model.[5]) By letting D_0 represent the most recent dividend, we can rewrite Equation 7.2 as follows:

$$P_0 = \frac{D_0 \times (1+g)^1}{(1+r_s)^1} + \frac{D_0 \times (1+g)^2}{(1+r_s)^2} + \cdots + \frac{D_0 \times (1+g)^\infty}{(1+r_s)^\infty} \qquad (7.4)$$

---

5. Another assumption of the constant-growth model as presented is that earnings and dividends grow at the same rate. This assumption is true only in cases in which a firm pays out a fixed percentage of its earnings each year (has a fixed payout ratio). In the case of a declining industry, a negative growth rate ($g < 0\%$) might exist. In such a case, the constant-growth model, as well as the variable-growth model presented in the next section, remains fully applicable to the valuation process.

If we simplify Equation 7.4, it can be rewritten as[6]

$$P_0 = \frac{D_1}{r_s - g} \tag{7.5}$$

Gordon model
A common name for the *constant-growth model* that is widely cited in dividend valuation.

The constant-growth model in Equation 7.5 is commonly called the **Gordon model.** An example will show how it works.

Example

Lamar Company, a small cosmetics company, from 2004 through 2009 paid the following per-share dividends:

Year	Dividend per share
2009	$1.40
2008	1.29
2007	1.20
2006	1.12
2005	1.05
2004	1.00

We assume that the historical compound annual growth rate of dividends is an accurate estimate of the future constant annual rate of dividend growth, *g*. Using a financial calculator, a spreadsheet, or Appendix Table A–2, we find that the historical compound annual growth rate of Lamar Company dividends equals 7%.[7]

---

6. For the interested reader, the calculations necessary to derive Equation 7.5 from Equation 7.4 follow. The first step is to multiply each side of Equation 7.4 by $(1 + r_s)/(1 + g)$ and subtract Equation 7.4 from the resulting expression. This yields

$$\frac{P_0 \times (1 + r_s)}{1 + g} - P_0 = D_0 - \frac{D_0 \times (1 + g)^\infty}{(1 + r_s)^\infty} \tag{1}$$

Because r_s is assumed to be greater than *g*, the second term on the right side of Equation 1 should be zero. Thus

$$P_0 \times \left(\frac{1 + r_s}{1 + g} - 1\right) = D_0 \tag{2}$$

Equation 2 is simplified as follows:

$$P_0 \times \left[\frac{(1 + r_s) - (1 + g)}{1 + g}\right] = D_0 \tag{3}$$

$$P_0 \times (r_s - g) = D_0 \times (1 + g) \tag{4}$$

$$P_0 = \frac{D_1}{r_s - g} \tag{5}$$

Equation 5 equals Equation 7.5.

7. The technique involves solving the following equation for *g*:

$$D_{2009} = D_{2004} \times (1 + g)^5$$

$$\frac{D_{2004}}{D_{2009}} = \frac{1}{(1 + g)^5} = PVIF_{g,5}$$

Input	Function
1.00	PV
−1.40	FV
5	N
	CPT
	I
Solution	
6.96	

To do so, we can use a financial calculator, a spreadsheet, or financial tables.

A financial calculator can be used. (*Note:* Most calculators require *either* the *PV* or *FV* value to be input as a negative number to calculate an unknown interest or growth rate. That approach is used here.) Using the inputs shown at the left, you should find the growth rate to be 6.96%, which we round to 7%.

An electronic spreadsheet could also be used to make this computation. Given space considerations, we have forgone that computational aid here.

We could also use a financial table. Two basic steps can be followed using the present value table. First, dividing the earliest dividend ($D_{2004} = \$1.00$) by the most recent dividend ($D_{2009} = \$1.40$) yields a factor for the present value of one dollar, *PVIF*, of 0.714 ($1.00 ÷ $1.40). Although six dividends are shown, *they reflect only 5 years of growth.* (The number of years of growth can also be found by subtracting the earliest year from the most recent year—that is, $2009 - 2004 = 5$ *years of growth*.) By looking across the Appendix Table A–2 at the *PVIF* for 5 years, we find that the factor closest to 0.714 occurs at 7% (0.713). Therefore, the growth rate of the dividends, rounded to the nearest whole percent, is 7%.

CHAPTER 7   Stock Valuation

349

The company estimates that its dividend in 2010, D_1, will equal \$1.50. The required return, r_s, is assumed to be 15%. By substituting these values into Equation 7.5, we find the value of the stock to be

$$P_0 = \frac{\$1.50}{0.15 - 0.07} = \frac{\$1.50}{0.08} = \$18.75 \text{ per share}$$

Assuming that the values of D_1, r_s, and g are accurately estimated, Lamar Company's stock value is \$18.75 per share.

Variable-Growth Model

variable-growth model
A dividend valuation approach that allows for a change in the dividend growth rate.

The zero- and constant-growth common stock models do not allow for any shift in expected growth rates. Because future growth rates might shift up or down because of changing expectations, it is useful to consider a **variable-growth model** that allows for a change in the dividend growth rate.[8] We will assume that a single shift in growth rates occurs at the end of year N, and we will use g_1 to represent the initial growth rate and g_2 for the growth rate after the shift. To determine the value of a share of stock in the case of variable growth, we use a four-step procedure.

Step 1   Find the value of the cash dividends at the end of *each year, D_t*, during the initial growth period, years 1 through N. This step may require adjusting the most recent dividend, D_0, using the initial growth rate, g_1, to calculate the dividend amount for each year. Therefore, for the first N years,

$$D_t = D_0 \times (1 + g_1)^t = D_0 \times FVIF_{g_1,t}$$

Step 2   Find the present value of the dividends expected during the initial growth period. Using the notation presented earlier, we can give this value as

$$\sum_{t=1}^{N} \frac{D_0 \times (1 + g_1)^t}{(1 + r_s)^t} = \sum_{t=1}^{N} \frac{D_t}{(1 + r_s)^t} = \sum_{t=1}^{N} (D_t \times PVIF_{r_s,t})$$

Step 3   Find the value of the stock *at the end of the initial growth period*, $P_N = (D_{N+1})/(r_s - g_2)$, which is the present value of all dividends expected from year $N+1$ to infinity, assuming a constant dividend growth rate, g_2. This value is found by applying the constant-growth model (Equation 7.5) to the dividends expected from year $N+1$ to infinity. The present value of P_N would represent the value *today* of all dividends that are expected to be received from year $N+1$ to infinity. This value can be represented by

$$\frac{1}{(1 + r_s)^N} \times \frac{D_{N+1}}{r_s - g_2} = PVIF_{r_s,N} \times P_N$$

8. More than one change in the growth rate can be incorporated into the model, but to simplify the discussion we will consider only a single growth-rate change. The number of variable-growth valuation models is technically unlimited, but concern over all possible shifts in growth is unlikely to yield much more accuracy than a simpler model.

Step 4   Add the present value components found in Steps 2 and 3 to find the value of the stock, P_0, given in Equation 7.6:

$$P_0 = \underbrace{\sum_{t=1}^{N} \frac{D_0 \times (1 + g_1)^t}{(1 + r_s)^t}}_{\substack{\textit{Present value of} \\ \textit{dividends} \\ \textit{during initial} \\ \textit{growth period}}} + \underbrace{\left[\frac{1}{(1 + r_s)^N} \times \frac{D_{N+1}}{r_s - g_2} \right]}_{\substack{\textit{Present value of} \\ \textit{price of stock} \\ \textit{at end of initial} \\ \textit{growth period}}}$$ (7.6)

The following example illustrates the application of these steps to a variable-growth situation with only one change in growth rate.

Personal Finance Example   Victoria Robb is considering purchasing the common stock of Warren Industries, a rapidly growing boat manufacturer. She finds that the firm's most recent (2009) annual dividend payment was $1.50 per share. Victoria estimates that these dividends will increase at a 10% annual rate, g_1, over the next 3 years (2010, 2011, and 2012) because of the introduction of a hot new boat. At the end of the 3 years (the end of 2012), she expects the firm's mature product line to result in a slowing of the dividend growth rate to 5% per year, g_2, for the foreseeable future. Victoria's required return, r_s, is 15%. To estimate the current (end-of-2009) value of Warren's common stock, $P_0 = P_{2009}$, she applies the four-step procedure to these data.

Step 1   The value of the cash dividends in each of the next 3 years is calculated in columns 1, 2, and 3 of Table 7.3. The 2010, 2011, and 2012 dividends are $1.65, $1.82, and $2.00, respectively.

Step 2   The present value of the three dividends expected during the 2010–2012 initial growth period is calculated in columns 3, 4, and 5 of Table 7.3. The sum of the present values of the three dividends is $4.14.

Step 3   The value of the stock at the end of the initial growth period ($N = 2012$) can be found by first calculating $D_{N+1} = D_{2013}$:

$$D_{2013} = D_{2012} \times (1 + 0.05) = \$2.00 \times (1.05) = \$2.10$$

					Present value of dividends
	End of	$D_0 = D_{2009}$	$FVIF_{10\%,t}$	D_t $[(1) \times (2)]$	$PVIF_{15\%,t}$	$[(3) \times (4)]$
t	year	(1)	(2)	(3)	(4)	(5)
1	2010	$1.50	1.100	$1.65	0.870	$1.44
2	2011	1.50	1.210	1.82	0.756	1.38
3	2012	1.50	1.331	2.00	0.658	<u>1.32</u>

TABLE 7.3   Calculation of Present Value of Warren Industries Dividends (2010–2012)

$$\text{Sum of present value of dividends} = \sum_{t=1}^{3} \frac{D_0 \times (1 + g_1)^t}{(1 + r_s)^t} = \underline{\underline{\$4.14}}$$

By using $D_{2013} = \$2.10$, a 15% required return, and a 5% dividend growth rate, the value of the stock at the end of 2012 is calculated as follows:

$$P_{2012} = \frac{D_{2013}}{r_s - g_2} = \frac{\$2.10}{0.15 - 0.05} = \frac{\$2.10}{0.10} = \$21.00$$

Finally, in Step 3, the share value of $21 at the end of 2012 must be converted into a present (end-of-2009) value. Using the 15% required return, we get

$$PVIF_{r_s,N} \times P_N = PVIF_{15\%,3} \times P_{2012} = 0.658 \times \$21.00 = \$13.82$$

Step 4 Adding the present value of the initial dividend stream (found in Step 2) to the present value of the stock at the end of the initial growth period (found in Step 3) as specified in Equation 7.6, the current (end-of-2009) value of Warren Industries stock is:

$$P_{2009} = \$4.14 + \$13.82 = \underline{\$17.96} \text{ per share}$$

Victoria's calculations indicate that the stock is currently worth $17.96 per share. Her calculation of this value is depicted graphically on the following time line.

Time line for finding Warren Industries current (end-of-2009) common stock value with variable growth

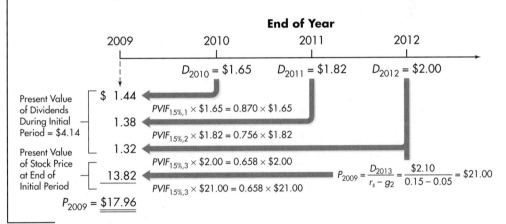

The zero-, constant-, and variable-growth valuation models provide useful frameworks for estimating stock value. Clearly, the estimates produced cannot be very precise, given that the forecasts of future growth and discount rates are themselves necessarily approximate. Furthermore, a great deal of measurement error can be introduced into the stock price estimate as a result of the imprecise and rounded growth and discount rate estimates used as inputs. When applying valuation models, it is therefore advisable to estimate these rates carefully and round them conservatively, probably to the nearest tenth of a percent.

Free Cash Flow Valuation Model

As an alternative to the dividend valuation models presented above, a firm's value can be estimated by using its projected *free cash flows (FCFs)*. This approach is appealing when one is valuing firms that have no dividend history or are startups or when one is valuing an operating unit or division of a larger public company.

free cash flow valuation model
A model that determines the value of an entire company as the present value of its expected *free cash flows* discounted at the firm's *weighted average cost of capital,* which is its expected average future cost of funds over the long run.

Although dividend valuation models are widely used and accepted, in these situations it is preferable to use a more general free cash flow valuation model.

The **free cash flow valuation model** is based on the same basic premise as dividend valuation models: The value of a share of common stock is the present value of all future cash flows it is expected to provide over an infinite time horizon. However, in the free cash flow valuation model, instead of valuing the firm's expected dividends, we value the firm's expected *free cash flows,* defined in Equation 3.5 (on page 115). They represent the amount of cash flow available to investors—the providers of debt (creditors) and equity (owners)—after all other obligations have been met.

The free cash flow valuation model estimates the value of the entire company by finding the present value of its expected free cash flows discounted at its *weighted average cost of capital,* which is its expected average future cost of funds over the long run (see Chapter 11), as specified in Equation 7.7.

$$V_C = \frac{FCF_1}{(1 + r_a)^1} + \frac{FCF_2}{(1 + r_a)^2} + \cdots + \frac{FCF_\infty}{(1 + r_a)^\infty} \tag{7.7}$$

where

V_C = value of the entire company

FCF_t = free cash flow *expected* at the end of year t

r_a = the firm's weighted average cost of capital

Note the similarity between Equations 7.7 and 7.2, the general stock valuation equation.

Because the value of the entire company, V_C, is the market value of the entire enterprise (that is, of all assets), to find common stock value, V_S, we must subtract the market value of all of the firm's debt, V_D, and the market value of preferred stock, V_P, from V_C.

$$V_S = V_C - V_D - V_P \tag{7.8}$$

Because it is difficult to forecast a firm's free cash flow, specific annual cash flows are typically forecast for only about 5 years, beyond which a constant growth rate is assumed. Here we assume that the first 5 years of free cash flows are explicitly forecast and that a constant rate of free cash flow growth occurs beyond the end of year 5 to infinity.[9] This model is methodologically similar to the variable-growth model presented earlier. Its application is best demonstrated with an example.

Example

Dewhurst, Inc., wishes to determine the value of its stock by using the free cash flow valuation model. To apply the model, the firm's CFO developed the data given in Table 7.4. Application of the model can be performed in four steps.

Step 1 Calculate the present value of the free cash flow occurring from the end of 2015 to infinity, measured at the beginning of 2015 (that is, at the end of 2014). Because a constant rate of growth in FCF is forecast beyond 2014,

9. The approach demonstrated here is consistent with that found in Alfred Rappaport, *Creating Shareholder Value* (New York: The Free Press, 1998). A somewhat similar approach to value can be found in G. Bennett Stewart III, *The Quest for Value* (New York: HarperCollins, 1999).

TABLE 7.4	Dewhurst, Inc.'s Data for the Free Cash Flow Valuation Model	

	Free cash flow	
Year (t)	$(FCF_t)^a$	Other data
2010	$400,000	Growth rate of FCF, beyond 2014 to infinity, $g_{FCF} = 3\%$
2011	450,000	Weighted average cost of capital, $r_a = 9\%$
2012	520,000	Market value of all debt, $V_D = \$3,100,000$
2013	560,000	Market value of preferred stock, $V_P = \$800,000$
2014	600,000	Number of shares of common stock outstanding $= 300,000$

^{a}Developed using Equations 3.4 and 3.5 (on pages 114 and 115).

we can use the constant-growth dividend valuation model (Equation 7.5) to calculate the value of the free cash flows from the end of 2015 to infinity.

$$\text{Value of } FCF_{2015 \to \infty} = \frac{FCF_{2015}}{r_a - g_{FCF}}$$

$$= \frac{\$600,000 \times (1 + 0.03)}{0.09 - 0.03}$$

$$= \frac{\$618,000}{0.06} = \underline{\underline{\$10,300,000}}$$

Note that to calculate the FCF in 2015, we had to increase the 2014 FCF value of $600,000 by the 3% FCF growth rate, g_{FCF}.

Step 2 Add the present value of the FCF from 2015 to infinity, which is measured at the end of 2014, to the 2014 FCF value to get the total FCF in 2014.

Total $FCF_{2014} = \$600,000 + \$10,300,000 = \$10,900,000$

Step 3 Find the sum of the present values of the FCFs for 2010 through 2014 to determine the value of the entire company, V_C. This calculation is shown in Table 7.5 (see page 354), using present value interest factors, *PVIFs*, from Appendix Table A–2.

Step 4 Calculate the value of the common stock using Equation 7.8. Substituting into Equation 7.8 the value of the entire company, V_C, calculated in Step 3, and the market values of debt, V_D, and preferred stock, V_P, given in Table 7.4, yields the value of the common stock, V_S:

$V_S = \$8,628,620 - \$3,100,000 - \$800,000 = \underline{\underline{\$4,728,620}}$

The value of Dewhurst's common stock is therefore estimated to be $4,728,620. By dividing this total by the 300,000 shares of common stock that the firm has outstanding, we get a common stock value of *$15.76 per share* ($4,728,620 ÷ 300,000).

It should now be clear that the free cash flow valuation model is consistent with the dividend valuation models presented earlier. The appeal of this approach

TABLE 7.5 Calculation of the Value of the Entire Company for Dewhurst, Inc.

Year (t)	FCF_t (1)	$PVIF_{9\%,t}$ (2)	Present value of FCF_t [(1) × (2)] (3)
2010	$ 400,000	0.917	$ 366,800
2011	450,000	0.842	378,900
2012	520,000	0.772	401,440
2013	560,000	0.708	396,480
2014	10,900,000[a]	0.650	7,085,000
		Value of entire company, $V_C =$	$8,628,620

[a]This amount is the sum of the FCF_{2014} of $600,000 from Table 7.4 and the $10,300,000 value of the $FCF_{2015 \to \infty}$ calculated in Step 1.

is its focus on the free cash flow estimates rather than on forecast dividends, which are far more difficult to estimate, given that they are paid at the discretion of the firm's board. The more general nature of the free cash flow model is responsible for its growing popularity, particularly with CFOs and other financial managers.

Other Approaches to Common Stock Valuation

Many other approaches to common stock valuation exist. The more popular approaches include book value, liquidation value, and some type of price/earnings multiple.

book value per share
The amount per share of common stock that would be received if all of the firm's assets were *sold for their exact book (accounting) value* and the proceeds remaining after paying all liabilities (including preferred stock) were divided among the common stockholders.

Book Value

Book value per share is simply the amount per share of common stock that would be received if all of the firm's assets were *sold for their exact book (accounting) value* and the proceeds remaining after paying all liabilities (including preferred stock) were divided among the common stockholders. This method lacks sophistication and can be criticized on the basis of its reliance on historical balance sheet data. It ignores the firm's expected earnings potential and generally lacks any true relationship to the firm's value in the marketplace. Let us look at an example.

Example

At year-end 2009, Lamar Company's balance sheet shows total assets of $6 million, total liabilities (including preferred stock) of $4.5 million, and 100,000 shares of common stock outstanding. Its book value per share therefore would be

$$\frac{\$6,000,000 - \$4,500,000}{100,000 \text{ shares}} = \underline{\$15} \text{ per share}$$

Because this value assumes that assets could be sold for their book value, it may not represent the minimum price at which shares are valued in the marketplace. As a matter of fact, although most stocks sell above book value, it is not unusual to find stocks selling below book value when investors believe either that assets are overvalued or that the firm's liabilities are understated.

liquidation value per share
The *actual amount* per share of common stock that would be received if all of the firm's assets were *sold for their market value,* liabilities (including preferred stock) were paid, and any remaining money were divided among the common stockholders.

Liquidation Value

Liquidation value per share is the *actual amount* per share of common stock that would be received if all of the firm's assets were *sold for their market value,* liabilities (including preferred stock) were paid, and any remaining money were divided among the common stockholders.[10] This measure is more realistic than book value—because it is based on the current market value of the firm's assets—but it still fails to consider the earning power of those assets. An example will illustrate.

Example

Lamar Company found upon investigation that it could obtain only $5.25 million if it sold its assets today. The firm's liquidation value per share therefore would be

$$\frac{\$5,250,000 - \$4,500,000}{100,000 \text{ shares}} = \underline{\$7.50} \text{ per share}$$

Ignoring liquidation expenses, this amount would be the firm's minimum value.

Price/Earnings (P/E) Multiples

The *price/earnings (P/E) ratio,* introduced in Chapter 2, reflects the amount investors are willing to pay for each dollar of earnings. The average P/E ratio in a particular industry can be used as the guide to a firm's value—if it is assumed that investors value the earnings of that firm in the same way they do the "average" firm in the industry. The **price/earnings multiple approach** is a popular technique used to estimate the firm's share value; it is calculated by multiplying the firm's expected earnings per share (EPS) by the average price/earnings (P/E) ratio for the industry. The average P/E ratio for the industry can be obtained from a source such as *Standard & Poor's Industrial Ratios.*

price/earnings multiple approach
A popular technique used to estimate the firm's share value; calculated by multiplying the firm's expected earnings per share (EPS) by the average price/earnings (P/E) ratio for the industry.

The P/E ratio valuation technique is a simple method of determining a stock's value and can be quickly calculated after firms make earnings announcements, which accounts for its popularity. Naturally, this has increased the demand for more frequent announcements or "guidance" regarding future earnings. Some firms feel that pre-earnings guidance creates additional costs and can lead to ethical issues, as discussed in the *Focus on Ethics* box on page 356.

The use of P/E multiples is especially helpful in valuing firms that are not publicly traded, whereas market price quotations can be used to value publicly traded firms.[11] In any case, the price/earnings multiple approach is considered superior to the use of book or liquidation values because it considers *expected* earnings.[12] An example will demonstrate the use of price/earnings multiples.

---

10. In the event of liquidation, creditors' claims must be satisfied first, then those of the preferred stockholders. Anything left goes to common stockholders. A more detailed discussion of liquidation procedures is presented in Chapter 17.

11. Generally, when the P/E ratio is used to value *privately owned* or *closely owned* corporations, a premium is added to adjust for the issue of control. This adjustment is necessary because the P/E ratio implicitly reflects minority interests of noncontrolling investors in *publicly owned* companies—a condition that does not exist in privately or closely owned corporations.

12. The price/earnings multiple approach to valuation does have a theoretical explanation. If we view 1 divided by the price/earnings ratio, or the *earnings/price ratio,* as the rate at which investors discount the firm's earnings, and if we assume that the projected earnings per share will be earned indefinitely (i.e., no growth in earnings per share), the price/earnings multiple approach can be looked on as a method of finding the present value of a perpetuity of projected earnings per share at a rate equal to the earnings/price ratio. This method is, in effect, a form of the zero-growth model presented in Equation 7.3 on page 347.

Focus on Ethics

Psst—Have You Heard Any Good Quarterly Earnings Forecasts Lately?

Corporate managers have long complained about the pressure to focus on the short term, and now business groups are coming to their defense. "The focus on the short term is a huge problem," says William Donaldson, former chairman of the Securities and Exchange Commission. "With all of the attention paid to quarterly performance, managers are taking their eyes off long-term strategic goals."

Donaldson, the U.S. Chamber of Commerce, and others believe that the best way to focus companies toward long-term goals is to do away with the practice of giving quarterly earnings guidance. In March 2007 the CFA Centre for Financial Market Integrity and the Business Roundtable Institute for Corporate Ethics proposed a template for quarterly earnings reports that would, in their view, obviate the need for earnings guidance.

Meanwhile, many companies are hesitant to give up issuing quarterly guidance. The practice of issuing earnings forecasts began in the early 1980s, a few years after the SEC's decision to allow companies to include forward-looking projections, provided they were accompanied by appropriate cautionary language. The result was what former SEC chairman Arthur Levitt once called a "game of winks and nods." Companies used earnings guidance to lower analysts' estimates; when the actual numbers came in higher, their stock prices jumped. The practice reached a fever pitch during the late 1990s when companies that missed the consensus earnings estimate, even by just a penny, saw their stock prices tumble.

One of the first companies to stop issuing earnings guidance was **Gillette,** in 2001. Others that abandoned quarterly guidance were **Coca-Cola, Intel,** and **McDonald's.** It became a trend. By 2005, just 61 percent of companies were offering quarterly projections to the public; according to the National Investor Relations Institute, the number declined to 52 percent in 2006.

Not everyone agrees with eliminating quarterly guidance. A survey conducted by New York University's Stern School of Business finance professor Baruch Lev, along with University of Florida professors Joel Houston and Jennifer Tucker, showed that companies that ended quarterly guidance reaped almost no benefit from doing so. Their study found no evidence that guidance-stoppers increased capital investments or research and development. So when should companies give up earnings guidance? According to Lev, they should do so only when they are not very good at predicting their earnings. "If you are not better than others at forecasting, then don't bother," he says.

■ *What are some of the real costs a company must face in preparing quarterly earnings guidance?*

Personal Finance Example

Ann Perrier plans to use the price/earnings multiple approach to estimate the value of Lamar Company's stock, which she currently holds in her retirement account. She estimates that Lamar Company will earn $2.60 per share next year (2010). This expectation is based on an analysis of the firm's historical earnings trend and of expected economic and industry conditions. She finds the price/earnings (P/E) ratio for firms in the same industry to average 7. Multiplying Lamar's expected earnings per share (EPS) of $2.60 by this ratio gives her a value for the firm's shares of $18.20, assuming that investors will continue to value the average firm at 7 times its earnings.

So how much is Lamar Company's stock really worth? That's a trick question, because there's no one right answer. It is important to recognize that the answer depends on the assumptions made and the techniques used. Professional securities analysts typically use a variety of models and techniques to value stocks. For example, an analyst might use the constant-growth model, liquidation value, and a price/earnings (P/E) multiple to estimate the worth of a given stock. If the analyst feels comfortable with his or her estimates, the stock would be valued at no more than the largest estimate. Of course, should the firm's estimated liquidation value per share exceed its "going concern" value per share, estimated by using one of the valuation models (zero-, constant-, or variable-growth or free cash flow) or the P/E multiple approach, the firm would be viewed as being "worth more dead than alive." In such an event, the firm would lack sufficient earning power to justify its existence and should probably be liquidated.

Hint From an investor's perspective, the stock in this situation would be an attractive investment only if it could be purchased at a price below its liquidation value—which in an efficient market could never occur.

REVIEW QUESTIONS

7–13 Describe the events that occur in an *efficient market* in response to new information that causes the expected return to exceed the required return. What happens to the market value?

7–14 What does the *efficient-market hypothesis (EMH)* say about (a) securities prices, (b) their reaction to new information, and (c) investor opportunities to profit? What is the *behavioral finance* challenge to this hypothesis?

7–15 Describe, compare, and contrast the following common stock dividend valuation models: (a) zero-growth, (b) constant-growth, and (c) variable-growth.

7–16 Describe the *free cash flow valuation model* and explain how it differs from the dividend valuation models. What is the appeal of this model?

7–17 Explain each of the three other approaches to common stock valuation: (a) book value, (b) liquidation value, and (c) price/earnings (P/E) multiples. Which of these is considered the best?

7.4 | Decision Making and Common Stock Value

Valuation equations measure the stock value at a point in time based on expected return and risk. Any decisions of the financial manager that affect these variables can cause the value of the firm to change. Figure 7.4 depicts the relationship among financial decisions, return, risk, and stock value.

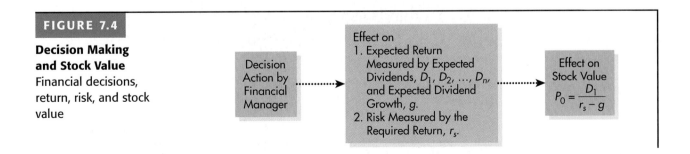

FIGURE 7.4

Decision Making and Stock Value
Financial decisions, return, risk, and stock value

Changes in Expected Return

Assuming that economic conditions remain stable, any management action that would cause current and prospective stockholders to raise their dividend expectations should increase the firm's value. In Equation 7.5,[13] we can see that P_0 will increase for any increase in D_1 or g. Any action of the financial manager that will increase the level of expected returns without changing risk (the required return) should be undertaken, because it will positively affect owners' wealth.

> **Example**
>
> Using the constant-growth model in an earlier example (on pages 348 and 349), we found Lamar Company to have a share value of $18.75. On the following day, the firm announced a major technological breakthrough that would revolutionize its industry. Current and prospective stockholders would not be expected to adjust their required return of 15%, but they would expect that future dividends will increase. Specifically, they expect that although the dividend next year, D_1, will remain at $1.50, the expected rate of growth thereafter will increase from 7% to 9%. If we substitute $D_1 = \$1.50$, $r_s = 0.15$, and $g = 0.09$ into Equation 7.5, the resulting share value is $25 [$1.50 ÷ (0.15 − 0.09)]. The increased value therefore resulted from the higher expected future dividends reflected in the increase in the growth rate.

Changes in Risk

Although r_s is defined as the required return, we know from Chapter 5 that it is directly related to the nondiversifiable risk, which can be measured by beta. The *capital asset pricing model (CAPM)* given in Equation 5.8 is restated here as Equation 7.9:

$$r_s = R_F + [b \times (r_m - R_F)] \qquad \text{(7.9)}$$

With the risk-free rate, R_F, and the market return, r_m, held constant, the required return, r_s, depends directly on beta. Any action taken by the financial manager that increases risk (beta) will also increase the required return. In Equation 7.5, we can see that with everything else constant, an increase in the required return, r_s, will reduce share value, P_0. Likewise, a decrease in the required return will increase share value. Thus any action of the financial manager that increases risk contributes to a reduction in value, and any action that decreases risk contributes to an increase in value.

> **Example**
>
> Assume that Lamar Company's 15% required return resulted from a risk-free rate of 9%, a market return of 13%, and a beta of 1.50. Substituting into the capital asset pricing model, Equation 7.9, we get a required return, r_s, of 15%:
>
> $$r_s = 9\% + [1.50 \times (13\% - 9\%)] = \underline{\underline{15\%}}$$
>
> With this return, the firm's share value was calculated in an earlier example (on pages 348 and 349) to be $18.75.

---

13. To convey the interrelationship among financial decisions, return, risk, and stock value, the constant-growth model is used. Other models—zero-growth, variable-growth, or free cash flow—could be used, but the simplicity of exposition using the constant-growth model justifies its use here.

Now imagine that the financial manager makes a decision that, without changing expected dividends, causes the firm's beta to increase to 1.75. Assuming that R_F and r_m remain at 9% and 13%, respectively, the required return will increase to 16% ($9\% + [1.75 \times (13\% - 9\%)]$) to compensate stockholders for the increased risk. Substituting $D_1 = \$1.50$, $r_s = 0.16$, and $g = 0.07$ into the valuation equation, Equation 7.5, results in a share value of $16.67 [$1.50 \div (0.16 - 0.07)$]. As expected, raising the required return, without any corresponding increase in expected return, causes the firm's stock value to decline. Clearly, the financial manager's action was not in the owners' best interest.

Combined Effect

A financial decision rarely affects return and risk independently; most decisions affect both factors. In terms of the measures presented, with an increase in risk (b), one would expect an increase in return (D_1 or g, or both), assuming that R_F and r_m remain unchanged. The net effect on value depends on the size of the changes in these variables.

Example

If we assume that the two changes illustrated for Lamar Company in the preceding examples occur simultaneously, key variable values would be $D_1 = \$1.50$, $r_s = 0.16$, and $g = 0.09$. Substituting into the valuation model, we obtain a share price of $21.43 [$1.50 \div (0.16 - 0.09)$]. The net result of the decision, which increased return (g, from 7% to 9%) as well as risk (b, from 1.50 to 1.75 and therefore r_s from 15% to 16%), is positive: The share price increased from $18.75 to $21.43. The decision appears to be in the best interest of the firm's owners, because it increases their wealth.

REVIEW QUESTIONS

7–18 Explain the linkages among financial decisions, return, risk, and stock value.

7–19 Assuming that all other variables remain unchanged, what impact would *each* of the following have on stock price? (a) The firm's beta increases. (b) The firm's required return decreases. (c) The dividend expected next year decreases. (d) The rate of growth in dividends is expected to increase.

Summary

Focus on Value

The price of each share of a firm's common stock is the value of each ownership interest. Although common stockholders typically have voting rights, which indirectly give them a say in management, their only significant right is their claim on the residual cash flows of the firm. This claim is subordinate to those of vendors, employees, customers, lenders, the government (for taxes), and preferred stockholders. The value of the common stockholders' claim is embodied in the cash flows they are entitled to receive from now to infinity. The present value of those expected cash flows is the firm's share value.

To determine this present value, forecast cash flows are discounted at a rate that reflects their risk. Riskier cash flows are discounted at higher rates, resulting in lower present values than less risky expected cash flows, which are discounted at lower rates. The value of the firm's common stock is therefore driven by its expected cash flows (returns) and risk (certainty of the expected cash flows).

In pursuing the firm's goal of **maximizing the stock price,** the financial manager must carefully consider the balance of return and risk associated with each proposal and must undertake only those actions that create value for owners. By focusing on value creation and by managing and monitoring the firm's cash flows and risk, the financial manager should be able to achieve the firm's goal of share price maximization.

Review of Learning Goals

Key definitions and formulas for this chapter are summarized in Table 7.6.

LG 1 Differentiate between debt and equity capital. Holders of equity capital (common and preferred stock) are owners of the firm. Typically, only common stockholders have a voice in management. Equity holders' claims on income and assets are secondary to creditors' claims, there is no maturity date, and dividends paid to stockholders are not tax-deductible.

LG 2 Discuss the rights, characteristics, and features of both common and preferred stock. The common stock of a firm can be privately owned, closely owned, or publicly owned. It can be sold with or without a par value. Preemptive rights allow common stockholders to avoid dilution of ownership when new shares are issued. Not all shares authorized in the corporate charter are outstanding. If a firm has treasury stock, it will have issued more shares than are outstanding. Some firms have two or more classes of common stock that differ mainly in having unequal voting rights. Proxies transfer voting rights from one party to another. The decision to pay dividends to common stockholders is made by the firm's board of directors. Firms can issue stock in foreign markets. The stock of many foreign corporations is traded in U.S. markets in the form of American depositary shares (ADSs), which are backed by American depositary receipts (ADRs).

Preferred stockholders have preference over common stockholders with respect to the distribution of earnings and assets. They do not normally have voting privileges. Preferred stock issues may have certain restrictive covenants, cumulative dividends, a call feature, and a conversion feature.

LG 3 Describe the process of issuing common stock, including venture capital, going public, and the investment banker, and interpreting stock quotations. The initial nonfounder financing for business startups with attractive growth prospects typically comes from private equity investors. These investors can be either angel capitalists or venture capitalists (VCs). VCs usually invest in both early-stage and later-stage companies that they hope to take public so as to cash out their investments.

TABLE 7.6	Summary of Key Valuation Definitions and Formulas for Common Stock

Definitions of variables

D_t = per-share dividend *expected* at the end of year t

FCF_t = free cash flow *expected* at the end of year t

g = constant rate of growth in dividends

g_1 = initial dividend growth rate (in variable-growth model)

g_2 = subsequent dividend growth rate (in variable-growth model)

r_a = weighted average cost of capital

r_s = required return on common stock

N = last year of initial growth period (in variable-growth model)

P_0 = value of common stock

V_C = value of the entire company

V_D = market value of all the firm's debt

V_P = market value of preferred stock

V_S = value of common stock

Valuation formulas

Basic stock value:

$$P_0 = \frac{D_1}{(1+r_s)^1} + \frac{D_2}{(1+r_s)^2} + \cdots + \frac{D_\infty}{(1+r_s)^\infty} \qquad \text{[Equation 7.2]}$$

Common stock value:

Zero-growth:

$$P_0 = \frac{D_1}{r_s} \ (\text{also used to value preferred stock}) \qquad \text{[Equation 7.3]}$$

Constant-growth:

$$P_0 = \frac{D_1}{r_s - g} \qquad \text{[Equation 7.5]}$$

Variable-growth:

$$P_0 = \sum_{t=1}^{N} \frac{D_0 \times (1+g_1)^t}{(1+r_s)^t} + \left[\frac{1}{(1+r_s)^N} \times \frac{D_{N+1}}{r_s - g_2} \right] \qquad \text{[Equation 7.6]}$$

FCF value of entire company:

$$V_C = \frac{FCF_1}{(1+r_a)^1} + \frac{FCF_2}{(1+r_a)^2} + \cdots + \frac{FCF_\infty}{(1+r_a)^\infty} \qquad \text{[Equation 7.7]}$$

FCF common stock value:

$$V_S = V_C - V_D - V_P \qquad \text{[Equation 7.8]}$$

The first public issue of a firm's stock is called an initial public offering (IPO). The company selects an investment banker to advise it and to sell the securities. The lead investment banker may form a selling syndicate with other investment bankers. The IPO process includes getting SEC approval, promoting the offering to investors, and pricing the issue.

Stock quotations provide information on the closing (last) price at which the stock sold on the given day and the net price change from the prior trading day.

Understand the concept of market efficiency and basic common stock valuation using zero-growth, constant-growth, and variable-growth models. Market efficiency assumes that the quick reactions of rational investors to new information cause the market value of common stock to adjust upward or downward quickly. The efficient-market hypothesis (EMH) suggests that securities are fairly priced, that they reflect fully all publicly available information, and that investors should therefore not waste time trying to find and capitalize on mispriced securities. Behavioral finance advocates challenge this hypothesis by arguing that emotion and other factors play a role in investment decisions.

The value of a share of common stock is the present value of all future dividends it is expected to provide over an infinite time horizon. Three dividend growth models—zero-growth, constant-growth, and variable-growth—can be considered in common stock valuation. The most widely cited model is the constant-growth model.

Discuss the free cash flow valuation model and the book value, liquidation value, and price/earnings (P/E) multiple approaches. The free cash flow valuation model values firms that have no dividend history, startups, or an operating unit or division of a larger public company. The model finds the value of the entire company by discounting the firm's expected free cash flow at its weighted average cost of capital. The common stock value is found by subtracting the market values of the firm's debt and preferred stock from the value of the entire company.

Book value per share is the amount per share of common stock that would be received if all of the firm's assets were *sold for their exact book (accounting) value* and the proceeds remaining after paying all liabilities (including preferred stock) were divided among the common stockholders. Liquidation value per share is the *actual amount* per share of common stock that would be received if all of the firm's assets were *sold for their market value*, liabilities (including preferred stock) were paid, and the remaining money were divided among the common stockholders. The price/earnings (P/E) multiple approach estimates stock value by multiplying the firm's expected earnings per share (EPS) by the average price/earnings (P/E) ratio for the industry.

Explain the relationships among financial decisions, return, risk, and the firm's value. In a stable economy, any action of the financial manager that increases the level of expected return without changing risk should increase share value; any action that reduces the level of expected return without changing risk should reduce share value. Similarly, any action that increases risk (required return) will reduce share value; any action that reduces risk will increase share value. An assessment of the combined effect of return and risk on stock value must be part of the financial decision-making process.

Self-Test Problems (Solutions in Appendix B)

 ST7–1 **Common stock valuation**   Perry Motors' common stock currently pays an annual dividend of $1.80 per share. The required return on the common stock is 12%. Estimate the value of the common stock under each of the following assumptions about the dividend.
a. Dividends are expected to grow at an annual rate of 0% to infinity.
b. Dividends are expected to grow at a constant annual rate of 5% to infinity.
c. Dividends are expected to grow at an annual rate of 5% for each of the next 3 years, followed by a constant annual growth rate of 4% in years 4 to infinity.

 ST7–2 **Free cash flow valuation**   Erwin Footwear wishes to assess the value of its Active Shoe Division. This division has debt with a market value of $12,500,000 and no preferred stock. Its weighted average cost of capital is 10%. The Active Shoe Division's estimated free cash flow each year from 2010 through 2013 is given in the following table. Beyond 2013 to infinity, the firm expects its free cash flow to grow at 4% annually.

Year (t)	Free cash flow (FCF_t)
2010	$ 800,000
2011	1,200,000
2012	1,400,000
2013	1,500,000

a. Use the *free cash flow valuation model* to estimate the value of Erwin's entire Active Shoe Division.
b. Use your finding in part **a** along with the data provided above to find this division's common stock value.
c. If the Active Shoe Division as a public company will have 500,000 shares outstanding, use your finding in part **b** to calculate its value per share.

Warm-Up Exercises   A blue box (■) indicates exercises available in .

 E7–1 A balance sheet balances assets with their sources of debt and equity financing. If a corporation has assets equal to $5.2 million and a debt ratio of 75.0%, how much debt does the corporation have on its books?

 E7–2 Angina, Inc., has 5 million shares outstanding. The firm is considering issuing an additional 1 million shares. After selling these shares at their $20 per share offering price and netting 95% of the sale proceeds, the firm is obligated by an earlier agreement to sell an additional 250,000 shares at 90% of the offering price. In total, how much cash will the firm net from these stock sales?

E7–3 Figurate Industries has 750,000 shares of cumulative preferred stock outstanding. It has passed the last three quarterly dividends of $2.50 per share and now (at the end of the current quarter) wishes to distribute a total of $12 million to its shareholders. If Figurate has 3 million shares of common stock outstanding, how large a per-share common stock dividend will it be able to pay?

E7–4 Today the common stock of Gresham Technology closed at $24.60 per share, down $0.35 from yesterday. If the company has 4.6 million shares outstanding and annual earnings of $11.2 million, what is its P/E ratio today? What was its P/E ratio yesterday?

E7–5 Stacker Weight Loss currently pays an annual year-end dividend of $1.20 per share. It plans to increase this dividend by 5% next year and maintain it at the new level for the foreseeable future. If the required return on this firm's stock is 8%, what is the value of Stacker's stock?

E7–6 Brash Corporation initiated a new corporate strategy that fixes its annual dividend at $2.25 per share forever. Currently the risk-free rate is 4.5%, and Brash has a beta of 1.8. If the market return is 10.5%, what is the value of Brash's stock?

Problems

A blue box (■) indicates problems available in myfinancelab.

P7–1 **Authorized and available shares** Aspin Corporation's charter authorizes issuance of 2,000,000 shares of common stock. Currently, 1,400,000 shares are outstanding and 100,000 shares are being held as treasury stock. The firm wishes to raise $48,000,000 for a plant expansion. Discussions with its investment bankers indicate that the sale of new common stock will net the firm $60 per share.
a. What is the maximum number of new shares of common stock that the firm can sell without receiving further authorization from shareholders?
b. Judging on the basis of the data given and your finding in part **a**, will the firm be able to raise the needed funds without receiving further authorization?
c. What must the firm do to obtain authorization to issue more than the number of shares found in part **a**?

P7–2 **Preferred dividends** Slater Lamp Manufacturing has an outstanding issue of preferred stock with an $80 par value and an 11% annual dividend.
a. What is the annual dollar dividend? If it is paid quarterly, how much will be paid each quarter?
b. If the preferred stock is *noncumulative* and the board of directors has passed the preferred dividend for the last 3 quarters, how much must be paid to preferred stockholders in the current quarter before dividends are paid to common stockholders?
c. If the preferred stock is *cumulative* and the board of directors has passed the preferred dividend for the last 3 quarters, how much must be paid to preferred stockholders in the current quarter before dividends are paid to common stockholders?

P7–3 **Preferred dividends**   In each case in the following table, how many dollars of pre-ferred dividends per share must be paid to preferred stockholders in the current period before common stock dividends are paid?

Case	Type	Par value	Dividend per share per period	Periods of dividends passed
A	Cumulative	$ 80	$ 5	2
B	Noncumulative	110	8%	3
C	Noncumulative	100	$11	1
D	Cumulative	60	8.5%	4
E	Cumulative	90	9%	0

P7–4 **Convertible preferred stock**   Valerian Corp. convertible preferred stock has a fixed conversion ratio of 5 common shares per 1 share of preferred stock. The preferred stock pays a dividend of $10.00 per share per year. The common stock currently sells for $20.00 per share and pays a dividend of $1.00 per share per year.

a. Judging on the basis of the conversion ratio and the price of the common shares, what is the current conversion value of each preferred share?

b. If the preferred shares are selling at $96.00 each, should an investor convert the preferred shares to common shares?

c. What factors might cause an investor not to convert from preferred to common stock?

PERSONAL FINANCE PROBLEM

P7–5 **Stock quotation**   Assume that the following quote for the Advanced Business Machines stock (traded on the NYSE) was found in the Thursday, December 14, issue of the *Wall Street Journal*.

AdvBusMach   ABM   81.75   1.63

Given this information, answer the following questions:

a. On what day did the trading activity occur?

b. At what price did the stock sell at the end of the day on Wednesday, December 13?

c. What is the last price at which the stock traded on the day quoted?

d. How much, if any, of a change in stock price took place between the day quoted and the day before? At what price did the stock close on the day before?

P7–6 **Common stock valuation—Zero growth**   Scotto Manufacturing is a mature firm in the machine tool component industry. The firm's most recent common stock dividend was $2.40 per share. Because of its maturity as well as its stable sales and earn-ings, the firm's management feels that dividends will remain at the current level for the foreseeable future.

a. If the required return is 12%, what will be the value of Scotto's common stock?

b. If the firm's risk as perceived by market participants suddenly increases, causing the required return to rise to 20%, what will be the common stock value?

c. Judging on the basis of your findings in parts **a** and **b**, what impact does risk have on value? Explain.

P7–7 **Common stock value—Zero growth**   Kelsey Drums, Inc., is a well-established supplier of fine percussion instruments to orchestras all over the United States. The company's class A common stock has paid a dividend of $5.00 per share per year for the last 15 years. Management expects to continue to pay at that amount for the foreseeable future. Sally Talbot purchased 100 shares of Kelsey class A common 10 years ago at a time when the required rate of return for the stock was 16%. She wants to sell her shares today. The current required rate of return for the stock is 12%. How much capital gain or loss will Sally have on her shares?

P7–8 **Preferred stock valuation**   Jones Design wishes to estimate the value of its outstanding preferred stock. The preferred issue has an $80 par value and pays an annual dividend of $6.40 per share. Similar-risk preferred stocks are currently earning a 9.3% annual rate of return.
a. What is the market value of the outstanding preferred stock?
b. If an investor purchases the preferred stock at the value calculated in part **a**, how much does she gain or lose per share if she sells the stock when the required return on similar-risk preferreds has risen to 10.5%? Explain.

P7–9 **Common stock value—Constant growth**   Use the constant-growth model (Gordon model) to find the value of each firm shown in the following table.

Firm	Dividend expected next year	Dividend growth rate	Required return
A	$1.20	8%	13%
B	4.00	5	15
C	0.65	10	14
D	6.00	8	9
E	2.25	8	20

P7–10 **Common stock value—Constant growth**   McCracken Roofing, Inc., common stock paid a dividend of $1.20 per share last year. The company expects earnings and dividends to grow at a rate of 5% per year for the foreseeable future.
a. What required rate of return for this stock would result in a price per share of $28?
b. If McCracken expects both earnings and dividends to grow at an annual rate of 10%, what required rate of return would result in a price per share of $28?

P7–11 **Common stock value—Constant growth**   Elk County Telephone has paid the dividends shown in the following table over the past 6 years.

Year	Dividend per share
2009	$2.87
2008	2.76
2007	2.60
2006	2.46
2005	2.37
2004	2.25

The firm's dividend per share next year is expected to be $3.02.

a. If you can earn 13% on similar-risk investments, what is the most you would be willing to pay per share?

b. If you can earn only 10% on similar-risk investments, what is the most you would be willing to pay per share?

c. Compare and contrast your findings in parts **a** and **b,** and discuss the impact of changing risk on share value.

P7–12   Common stock value—Variable growth   Newman Manufacturing is considering a cash purchase of the stock of Grips Tool. During the year just completed, Grips earned $4.25 per share and paid cash dividends of $2.55 per share ($D_0 = \$2.55$). Grips' earnings and dividends are expected to grow at 25% per year for the next 3 years, after which they are expected to grow at 10% per year to infinity. What is the maximum price per share that Newman should pay for Grips if it has a required return of 15% on investments with risk characteristics similar to those of Grips?

PERSONAL FINANCE PROBLEM

P7–13   Common stock value—Variable growth   Home Place Hotels, Inc., is entering into a 3-year remodeling and expansion project. The construction will have a limiting effect on earnings during that time, but when it is complete, it should allow the company to enjoy much improved growth in earnings and dividends. Last year, the company paid a dividend of $3.40. It expects zero growth in the next year. In years 2 and 3, 5% growth is expected, and in year 4, 15% growth. In year 5 and thereafter, growth should be a constant 10% per year. What is the maximum price per share that an investor who requires a return of 14% should pay for Home Place Hotels common stock?

P7–14   Common stock value—Variable growth   Lawrence Industries' most recent annual dividend was $1.80 per share ($D_0 = \$1.80$), and the firm's required return is 11%. Find the market value of Lawrence's shares when:

a. Dividends are expected to grow at 8% annually for 3 years, followed by a 5% constant annual growth rate in years 4 to infinity.

b. Dividends are expected to grow at 8% annually for 3 years, followed by a 0% constant annual growth rate in years 4 to infinity.

c. Dividends are expected to grow at 8% annually for 3 years, followed by a 10% constant annual growth rate in years 4 to infinity.

PERSONAL FINANCE PROBLEM

P7–15   Common stock value—All growth models   You are evaluating the potential purchase of a small business currently generating $42,500 of after-tax cash flow ($D_0 = \$42,500$). On the basis of a review of similar-risk investment opportunities, you must earn an 18% rate of return on the proposed purchase. Because you are relatively uncertain about future cash flows, you decide to estimate the firm's value using several possible assumptions about the growth rate of cash flows.

a. What is the firm's value if cash flows are expected to grow at an annual rate of 0% from now to infinity?

b. What is the firm's value if cash flows are expected to grow at a constant annual rate of 7% from now to infinity?

c. What is the firm's value if cash flows are expected to grow at an annual rate of 12% for the first 2 years, followed by a constant annual rate of 7% from year 3 to infinity?

P7–16 **Free cash flow valuation**   Nabor Industries is considering going public but is unsure of a fair offering price for the company. Before hiring an investment banker to assist in making the public offering, managers at Nabor have decided to make their own estimate of the firm's common stock value. The firm's CFO has gathered data for performing the valuation using the free cash flow valuation model.

The firm's weighted average cost of capital is 11%, and it has $1,500,000 of debt at market value and $400,000 of preferred stock at its assumed market value. The estimated free cash flows over the next 5 years, 2010 through 2014, are given below. Beyond 2014 to infinity, the firm expects its free cash flow to grow by 3% annually.

Year (t)	Free cash flow (FCF_t)
2010	$200,000
2011	250,000
2012	310,000
2013	350,000
2014	390,000

a. Estimate the value of Nabor Industries' entire company by using the *free cash flow valuation model.*

b. Use your finding in part **a,** along with the data provided above, to find Nabor Industries' common stock value.

c. If the firm plans to issue 200,000 shares of common sock, what is its estimated value per share?

PERSONAL FINANCE PROBLEM

P7–17 **Using the free cash flow valuation model to price an IPO**   Assume that you have an opportunity to buy the stock of CoolTech, Inc., an IPO being offered for $12.50 per share. Although you are very much interested in owning the company, you are concerned about whether it is fairly priced. To determine the value of the shares, you have decided to apply the free cash flow valuation model to the firm's financial data that you've developed from a variety of data sources. The key values you have compiled are summarized in the following table.

Year (t)	Free cash flow FCF_t	Other data
2010	$ 700,000	Growth rate of FCF, beyond 2013 to infinity = 2%
2011	800,000	Weighted average cost of capital = 8%
2012	950,000	Market value of all debt = $2,700,000
2013	1,100,000	Market value of preferred stock = $1,000,000
		Number of shares of common stock outstanding = 1,100,000

a. Use the *free cash flow valuation model* to estimate CoolTech's common stock value per share.

b. Judging on the basis of your finding in part **a** and the stock's offering price, should you buy the stock?

c. Upon further analysis, you find that the growth rate in FCF beyond 2013 will be 3% rather than 2%. What effect would this finding have on your responses in parts **a** and **b**?

P7–18 **Book and liquidation value**   The balance sheet for Gallinas Industries is as follows.

Gallinas Industries Balance Sheet December 31			
Assets		**Liabilities and Stockholders' Equity**	
Cash	$ 40,000	Accounts payable	$100,000
Marketable securities	60,000	Notes payable	30,000
Accounts receivable	120,000	Accrued wages	30,000
Inventories	160,000	Total current liabilities	$160,000
Total current assets	$380,000	Long-term debt	$180,000
Land and buildings (net)	$150,000	Preferred stock	$ 80,000
Machinery and equipment	250,000	Common stock (10,000 shares)	260,000
Total fixed assets (net)	$400,000	Retained earnings	100,000
Total assets	$780,000	Total liabilities and stockholders' equity	$780,000

Additional information with respect to the firm is available:
(1) Preferred stock can be liquidated at book value.
(2) Accounts receivable and inventories can be liquidated at 90% of book value.
(3) The firm has 10,000 shares of common stock outstanding.
(4) All interest and dividends are currently paid up.
(5) Land and buildings can be liquidated at 130% of book value.
(6) Machinery and equipment can be liquidated at 70% of book value.
(7) Cash and marketable securities can be liquidated at book value.

Given this information, answer the following:
a. What is Gallinas Industries' *book value per share?*
b. What is its *liquidation value per share?*
c. Compare, contrast, and discuss the values found in parts **a** and **b**.

P7–19 **Valuation with price/earnings multiples**   For each of the firms shown in the following table, use the data given to estimate its common stock value employing price/earnings (P/E) multiples.

Firm	Expected EPS	Price/earnings multiple
A	$3.00	6.2
B	4.50	10.0
C	1.80	12.6
D	2.40	8.9
E	5.10	15.0

P7–20 **Management action and stock value**   REH Corporation's most recent dividend was $3 per share, its expected annual rate of dividend growth is 5%, and the required return is now 15%. A variety of proposals are being considered by management to redirect the firm's activities. Determine the impact on share price for each of the following proposed actions, and indicate the best alternative.

a. Do nothing, which will leave the key financial variables unchanged.

b. Invest in a new machine that will increase the dividend growth rate to 6% and lower the required return to 14%.

c. Eliminate an unprofitable product line, which will increase the dividend growth rate to 7% and raise the required return to 17%.

d. Merge with another firm, which will reduce the growth rate to 4% and raise the required return to 16%.

e. Acquire a subsidiary operation from another manufacturer. The acquisition should increase the dividend growth rate to 8% and increase the required return to 17%.

P7–21 **Integrative—Valuation and CAPM formulas**   Given the following information for the stock of Foster Company, calculate its beta.

Current price per share of common	$50.00
Expected dividend per share next year	$ 3.00
Constant annual dividend growth rate	9%
Risk-free rate of return	7%
Return on market portfolio	10%

P7–22 **Integrative—Risk and valuation**   Giant Enterprises has a beta of 1.20, the risk-free rate of return is currently 10%, and the market return is 14%. The company, which plans to pay a dividend of $2.60 per share in the coming year, anticipates that its future dividends will increase at an annual rate consistent with that experienced over the 2003–2009 period, when the following dividends were paid:

Year	Dividend per share
2009	$2.45
2008	2.28
2007	2.10
2006	1.95
2005	1.82
2004	1.80
2003	1.73

a. Use the capital asset pricing model (CAPM) to determine the required return on Giant's stock.

b. Using the constant-growth model and your finding in part **a**, estimate the value of Giant's stock.

c. Explain what effect, if any, a decrease in beta would have on the value of Giant's stock.

P7–23 **Integrative—Valuation and CAPM**   Hamlin Steel Company wishes to determine the value of Craft Foundry, a firm that it is considering acquiring for cash. Hamlin wishes to use the capital asset pricing model (CAPM) to determine the applicable discount rate to use as an input to the constant-growth valuation model. Craft's stock is not publicly traded. After studying the betas of firms similar to Craft that are publicly traded, Hamlin believes that an appropriate beta for Craft's stock would be 1.25. The risk-free rate is currently 9%, and the market return is 13%. Craft's dividend per share for each of the past 6 years is shown in the following table.

Year	Dividend per share
2009	$3.44
2008	3.28
2007	3.15
2006	2.90
2005	2.75
2004	2.45

  a. Given that Craft is expected to pay a dividend of $3.68 next year, determine the maximum cash price that Hamlin should pay for each share of Craft.

  b. Discuss the use of the CAPM for estimating the value of common stock, and describe the effect on the resulting value of Craft of:

    (1) A decrease in its dividend growth rate of 2% from that exhibited over the 2004–2009 period.

    (2) A decrease in its beta to 1.

P7–24 **ETHICS PROBLEM** Melissa is trying to value Generic Utility, Inc.'s stock, which is clearly not growing at all. Generic declared and paid a $5 dividend last year. The required rate of return for utility stocks is 11%, but Melissa is unsure about the financial reporting integrity of Generic's finance team. She decides to add an extra 1% "credibility" risk premium to the required return as part of her valuation analysis.

  a. What is the value of Generic's stock, assuming that the financials are trustworthy?

  b. What is the value of Generic's stock, assuming that Melissa includes the extra 1% "credibility" risk premium?

  c. What is the difference between the values found in parts **a** and **b**, and how might one interpret that difference?

Chapter 7 Case

Assessing the Impact of Suarez Manufacturing's Proposed Risky Investment on Its Stock Value

Early in 2010, Inez Marcus, the chief financial officer for Suarez Manufacturing, was given the task of assessing the impact of a proposed risky investment on the firm's stock value. To perform the necessary analysis, Inez gathered the following information on the firm's stock.

During the immediate past 5 years (2005–2009), the annual dividends paid on the firm's common stock were as follows:

Year	Dividend per share
2009	$1.90
2008	1.70
2007	1.55
2006	1.40
2005	1.30

The firm expects that without the proposed investment, the dividend in 2010 will be $2.09 per share and the historical annual rate of growth (rounded to the nearest whole percent) will continue in the future. Currently, the required return on the common stock is 14%. Inez's research indicates that if the proposed investment is undertaken, the 2010 dividend will rise to $2.15 per share and the annual rate of dividend growth will increase to 13%. She feels that in the *best case,* the dividend would continue to grow at this rate each year into the future and that in the *worst case,* the 13% annual rate of growth in dividends would continue only through 2012, and then, at the beginning of 2013, would return to the rate that was experienced between 2005 and 2009. As a result of the increased risk associated with the proposed risky investment, the required return on the common stock is expected to increase by 2% to an annual rate of 16%, regardless of which dividend growth outcome occurs.

Armed with the preceding information, Inez must now assess the impact of the proposed risky investment on the market value of Suarez's stock. To simplify her calculations, she plans to round the historical growth rate in common stock dividends to the nearest whole percent.

To Do

a. Find the *current* value per share of Suarez Manufacturing's common stock.
b. Find the value of Suarez's common stock in the event that it *undertakes the proposed risky investment* and assuming that the dividend growth rate stays at 13% forever. Compare this value to that found in part **a.** What effect would the proposed investment have on the firm's stockholders? Explain.
c. On the basis of your findings in part **b,** do the stockholders win or lose as a result of undertaking the proposed risky investment? Should the firm do it? Why?
d. Rework parts **b** and **c** assuming that at the beginning of 2013 the annual dividend growth rate returns to the rate experienced between 2005 and 2009.

Spreadsheet Exercise

You are interested in purchasing the common stock of Azure Corporation. The firm recently paid a dividend of $3 per share. It expects its earnings—and hence its dividends—to grow at a rate of 7% for the foreseeable future. Currently, similar-risk stocks have required returns of 10%.

To Do

a. Given the data above, calculate the present value of this security. Use the constant-growth model (Equation 7.5) to find the stock value.

b. One year later, your broker offers to sell you additional shares of Azure at $73. The most recent dividend paid was $3.21, and the expected growth rate for earnings remains at 7%. To determine the required rate of return, you decide to use the capital asset pricing model (CAPM). The risk-free rate, R_F, is currently 5.25%; the market return, r_m, is 11.55%; and the stock's beta, b_{Azure}, is 1.07. Substitute the appropriate values into the CAPM (Equation 5.8) to determine the firm's current required return, r_{Azure}.

c. Applying Equation 7.5, determine the value of the stock using the new dividend and required return from part **b.**

d. Given your calculation in part **c,** would you buy the additional shares from your broker at $73 per share? Explain.

e. Given your calculation in part **c,** would you sell your old shares for $73? Explain.

Group Exercise

This chapter discussed the basics of equity financing, including the specifics of the IPO process. We began this semester with your fictitious firm going public; here, we will revisit that process. We will also consider some recent real-world IPOs, and will look at recent quotes for your shadow firm.

To Do

a. Your first task is to develop a preliminary prospectus for your firm following closely the sample prospectus in Figure 7.1 on page 339 of the text. Specify the number of shares issued and the price per share at issuance.

b. Look up recent IPO activity. Familiarize yourself with a particular offering, and summarize its details. A Google search will provide you with several Web sites that can be used for this task.

c. Look up the current quotation and recent market information on your shadow firm. Several websites have up-to-date information; one suggestion is the website **moneycentral.msn.com/investor/home.asp**. Report all the market numbers and concentrate on the recent news and analyses regarding your firm. The information should include ratings for your shadow firm.

Web Exercise

Go to the book's companion website at **www.prenhall.com/gitman** to find the Web Exercise for this chapter.

> Remember to check the book's website at **www.prenhall.com/gitman** to find additional resources, including Web Exercises and a Web Case.

Integrative Case 2

Encore International

In the world of trendsetting fashion, instinct and marketing savvy are prerequisites to success. Jordan Ellis had both. During 2009, his international casual-wear company, Encore, rocketed to $300 million in sales after 10 years in business. His fashion line covered the young woman from head to toe with hats, sweaters, dresses, blouses, skirts, pants, sweatshirts, socks, and shoes. In Manhattan, there was an Encore shop every five or six blocks, each featuring a different color. Some shops showed the entire line in mauve, and others featured it in canary yellow.

Encore had made it. The company's historical growth was so spectacular that no one could have predicted it. However, securities analysts speculated that Encore could not keep up the pace. They warned that competition is fierce in the fashion industry and that the firm might encounter little or no growth in the future. They estimated that stockholders also should expect no growth in future dividends.

Contrary to the conservative securities analysts, Jordan Ellis felt that the company could maintain a constant annual growth rate in dividends per share of 6% in the future, or possibly 8% for the next 2 years and 6% thereafter. Ellis based his estimates on an established long-term expansion plan into European and Latin American markets. Venturing into these markets was expected to cause the risk of the firm, as measured by beta, to increase immediately from 1.10 to 1.25.

In preparing the long-term financial plan, Encore's chief financial officer has assigned a junior financial analyst, Marc Scott, to evaluate the firm's current stock price. He has asked Marc to consider the conservative predictions of the securities analysts and the aggressive predictions of the company founder, Jordan Ellis.

Marc has compiled these 2009 financial data to aid his analysis:

Data item	2009 value
Earnings per share (EPS)	$6.25
Price per share of common stock	$40.00
Book value of common stock equity	$60,000,000
Total common shares outstanding	2,500,000
Common stock dividend per share	$4.00

To Do

a. What is the firm's current book value per share?

b. What is the firm's current P/E ratio?

c. (1) What are the required return and risk premium for Encore stock using the capital asset pricing model, assuming a beta of 1.10? (*Hint:* Use the security market line—with data points noted—given in Figure 1 to find the market return.)

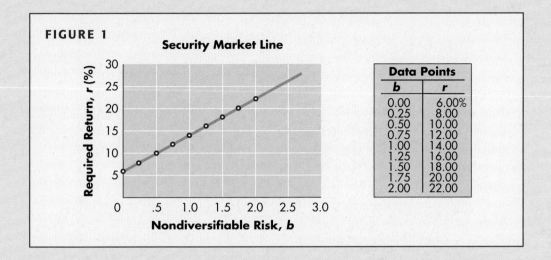

FIGURE 1

Security Market Line

Required Return, r (%)

Nondiversifiable Risk, b

Data Points	
b	**r**
0.00	6.00%
0.25	8.00
0.50	10.00
0.75	12.00
1.00	14.00
1.25	16.00
1.50	18.00
1.75	20.00
2.00	22.00

   (2) What are the required return and risk premium for Encore stock using the capital asset pricing model, assuming a beta of 1.25?

   (3) What will be the effect on the required return if the beta rises as expected?

d. If the securities analysts are correct and there is no growth in future dividends, what will be the value per share of the Encore stock? (*Note:* Beta = 1.25.)

e. (1) If Jordan Ellis's predictions are correct, what will be the value per share of Encore stock if the firm maintains a constant annual 6% growth rate in future dividends? (*Note:* Beta = 1.25.)

   (2) If Jordan Ellis's predictions are correct, what will be the value per share of Encore stock if the firm maintains a constant annual 8% growth rate in dividends per share over the next 2 years and 6% thereafter? (*Note:* Beta = 1.25.)

f. Compare the current (2009) price of the stock and the stock values found in parts **a, d,** and **e.** Discuss why these values may differ. Which valuation method do you believe most clearly represents the true value of the Encore stock?

Part Three
Long-Term Investment Decisions

Chapters in This Part

8 Capital Budgeting Cash Flows

WHY THIS CHAPTER MATTERS TO YOU

In Your Professional Life

Accounting: You need to understand capital budgeting cash flows to provide revenue, cost, depreciation, and tax data for use both in monitoring existing projects and in developing cash flows for proposed projects.

Information systems: You need to understand capital budgeting cash flows to maintain and facilitate the retrieval of cash flow data for both completed and existing projects.

Management: You need to understand capital budgeting cash flows so that you will understand which cash flows are relevant in making decisions about proposals for acquiring additional production facilities, for new marketing programs, for new products, and for the expansion of existing product lines.

Marketing: You need to understand capital budgeting cash flows so that you can make revenue and cost estimates for proposals for new marketing programs, for new products, and for the expansion of existing product lines.

Operations: You need to understand capital budgeting cash flows so that you can make revenue and cost estimates for proposals for the acquisition of new equipment and production facilities.

In Your Personal Life

You are not mandated to provide financial statements prepared using GAAP, so you naturally focus on cash flows. When considering a major outflow of funds (e.g., purchase of a house, funding of a college education), you can project the associated cash flows and use these estimates to assess the value and affordability of the assets and any associated future outlays.

LEARNING GOALS

LG 1 Understand the key motives for capital expenditure and the steps in the capital budgeting process.

LG 2 Define basic capital budgeting terminology.

LG 3 Discuss relevant cash flows, expansion versus replacement decisions, sunk costs and opportunity costs, and international capital budgeting.

LG 4 Calculate the initial investment associated with a proposed capital expenditure.

LG 5 Find the relevant operating cash inflows associated with a proposed capital expenditure.

LG 6 Determine the terminal cash flow associated with a proposed capital expenditure.

ExxonMobil

Maintaining Its Project Inventory

As the largest publicly traded oil company in the world, **ExxonMobil** has reaped the benefit of higher gas prices. Its annual net income for 2006 reached $39.5 billion, up 9 percent from $36.1 billion in 2005. This gush of profits comes at a time when geopolitical events and rampant instability in many of the world's oil-producing nations create increasing risks for oil companies.

In order to maintain its petroleum reserves, ExxonMobil must continually add to its inventory of discovered oil and gas resources. It holds exploration rights to 109 million undeveloped acres in 37 countries. Each year, the company initiates a number of mega-projects that add to its exploration rights, locate and "prove" additional reserves, or increase the productivity of currently producing wells.

Total capital and exploration expenditures in 2006 amounted to nearly $20 billion. As of May 2007, ExxonMobil had more than 110 major new development projects with potential net investment of more than $120 billion. Among these were deepwater projects in West Africa and the Gulf of Mexico and a liquefied gas project in Qatar. Many of these projects are undertaken in some of the world's most remote regions and under extreme conditions—in deep seas, arctic ice, deserts, and topical rainforests.

While Exxon was able to bring in many projects on or under budget in the past, increasing costs could cause some future development projects to go over budget. Drilling and exploration costs are expected to rise. Recent high oil prices have led to a surge in demand for exploration and the cost of drilling equipment and workers has jumped at least 15 percent a year during the last several years. Further complicating oil production efforts in the future will be an increase in the use of less-than-suitable oil sources, such as shale oil and tar sands.

Like ExxonMobil, every firm must evaluate the costs and returns of projects for expansion, asset replacement or renewal, research and development, advertising, and other areas that require long-term commitment of funds in expectation of future returns. Chapter 8 introduces this process, called *capital budgeting,* and explains how to identify the relevant cash outflows and inflows that must be considered in making capital budgeting decisions.

> **Where might financial managers find the type of information they need in order to evaluate the cost-effectiveness of a new project?**

8.1 | Capital Budgeting Decision Process

Long-term investments represent sizable outlays of funds that commit a firm to some course of action. Consequently, the firm needs procedures to analyze and properly select its long-term investments. It must be able to measure cash flows and apply appropriate decision techniques. As time passes, fixed assets may become obsolete or may require an overhaul; at these points, too, financial decisions may be required. **Capital budgeting** is the process of evaluating and selecting long-term investments that are consistent with the firm's goal of maximizing owner wealth. Firms typically make a variety of long-term investments, but the most common for the manufacturing firm is in *fixed assets,* which include property (land), plant, and equipment. These assets, often referred to as *earning assets,* generally provide the basis for the firm's earning power and value.

Because firms treat capital budgeting (investment) and financing decisions *separately,* Chapters 8 through 10 concentrate on fixed-asset acquisition without regard to the specific method of financing used. We begin by discussing the motives for capital expenditure.

capital budgeting
The process of evaluating and selecting long-term investments that are consistent with the firm's goal of maximizing owner wealth.

Motives for Capital Expenditure

A **capital expenditure** is an outlay of funds by the firm that is expected to produce benefits over a period of time *greater than* 1 year. An **operating expenditure** is an outlay resulting in benefits received *within* 1 year. Fixed-asset outlays are capital expenditures, but not all capital expenditures are classified as fixed assets. A $60,000 outlay for a new machine with a usable life of 15 years is a capital expenditure that would appear as a fixed asset on the firm's balance sheet. A $60,000 outlay for an advertising campaign that is expected to produce benefits over a long period is also a capital expenditure, but would rarely be shown as a fixed asset.[1]

Companies make capital expenditures for many reasons. The basic motives for capital expenditures are to expand operations, replace or renew fixed assets, or to obtain some other, less tangible benefit over a long period. Table 8.1 briefly describes the key motives for making capital expenditures.

capital expenditure
An outlay of funds by the firm that is expected to produce benefits over a period of time *greater than* 1 year.

operating expenditure
An outlay of funds by the firm resulting in benefits received *within* 1 year.

Steps in the Process

The **capital budgeting process** consists of five distinct but interrelated steps.

1. *Proposal generation.* Proposals are made at all levels within a business organization and are reviewed by finance personnel. Proposals that require large outlays are more carefully scrutinized than less costly ones.
2. *Review and analysis.* Formal review and analysis is performed to assess the appropriateness of proposals and evaluate their economic viability. Once the analysis is complete, a summary report is submitted to decision makers.

capital budgeting process
Five distinct but interrelated steps: *proposal generation, review and analysis, decision making, implementation,* and *follow-up.*

---

1. Some firms do, in effect, capitalize advertising outlays if there is reason to believe that the benefit of the outlay will be received at some future date. The capitalized advertising may appear as a deferred charge such as "deferred advertising expense," which is then amortized over the future. Expenses of this type are often deferred for reporting purposes to increase reported earnings, whereas for tax purposes, the entire amount is expensed to reduce tax liability.

TABLE 8.1	Key Motives for Making Capital Expenditures
Motive	Description
Expansion	The most common motive for a capital expenditure is to expand the level of operations—usually through acquisition of fixed assets. A growing firm often needs to acquire new fixed assets rapidly, as in the purchase of property and plant facilities.
Replacement or renewal	As a firm's growth slows and it reaches maturity, most capital expenditures will be made to increase efficiency by replacing or renewing obsolete or worn-out assets. Renewal may involve rebuilding, overhauling, or retrofitting an existing fixed asset. Each time a machine requires a major repair, the outlay for the repair should be compared to the outlay to replace the machine and the benefits of replacement.
Other purposes	Some capital expenditures do not result in the acquisition or transformation of tangible fixed assets. Instead, they involve a long-term commitment of funds in expectation of a future return. These expenditures include outlays for advertising campaigns, research and development, management consulting, and new products.

3. *Decision making.* Firms typically delegate capital expenditure decision making on the basis of dollar limits. Generally, the board of directors must authorize expenditures beyond a certain amount. Often plant managers are given authority to make decisions necessary to keep the production line moving.
4. *Implementation.* Following approval, expenditures are made and projects implemented. Expenditures for a large project often occur in phases.
5. *Follow-up.* Results are monitored, and actual costs and benefits are compared with those that were expected. Action may be required if actual outcomes differ from projected ones.

Each step in the process is important. Review and analysis and decision making (Steps 2 and 3) consume the majority of time and effort, however. Follow-up (Step 5) is an important but often ignored step aimed at allowing the firm to improve the accuracy of its cash flow estimates continuously. Because of their fundamental importance, this and the following chapters give primary consideration to review and analysis and to decision making.

Personal Finance Example   Individuals can approach the acquisition of major assets much as do corporations. Using the five-step process:

1. A personal financial plan or a special situation initiates the proposed asset purchase. For example, your personal financial plan specifies a new car purchase in 2010.
2. Review and analyze the proposed asset purchase to isolate attractive alternatives in terms of features and costs. For the car purchase, you would shop for cars with the desired features and costs that are consistent with the budgeted amount.
3. Compare the features and costs of the alternative assets and choose the preferred alternative. That is, you would decide which car you are going to buy.
4. Make the purchase. This would involve arranging financing/payment for the car, possibly negotiating a trade-in price, closing the transaction, and taking delivery of the new car.

5. Compare the actual asset performance to its expected performance. You would assess how well the new car meets your expectations. If the actual performance fails to meet expectations, you might consider new alternatives (e.g., trade in the car).

Basic Terminology

Before we develop the concepts, techniques, and practices related to the capital budgeting process, we need to explain some basic terminology. In addition, we will present some key assumptions that are used to simplify the discussion in the remainder of this chapter and in Chapters 9 and 10.

Independent versus Mutually Exclusive Projects

independent projects
Projects whose cash flows are unrelated or independent of one another; the acceptance of one *does not eliminate* the others from further consideration.

mutually exclusive projects
Projects that compete with one another, so that the acceptance of one *eliminates* from further consideration all other projects that serve a similar function.

The two most common types of projects are (1) independent projects and (2) mutually exclusive projects. **Independent projects** are those whose cash flows are unrelated or independent of one another; the acceptance of one *does not eliminate* the others from further consideration. **Mutually exclusive projects** are those that have the same function and therefore compete with one another. The acceptance of one *eliminates* from further consideration all other projects that serve a similar function. For example, a firm in need of increased production capacity could obtain it by (1) expanding its plant, (2) acquiring another company, or (3) contracting with another company for production. Clearly, accepting any one option eliminates the need for either of the others.

Unlimited Funds versus Capital Rationing

unlimited funds
The financial situation in which a firm is able to accept all independent projects that provide an acceptable return.

capital rationing
The financial situation in which a firm has only a fixed number of dollars available for capital expenditures, and numerous projects compete for these dollars.

The availability of funds for capital expenditures affects the firm's decisions. If a firm has **unlimited funds** for investment, making capital budgeting decisions is quite simple: All independent projects that will provide an acceptable return can be accepted. Typically, though, firms operate under **capital rationing** instead. This means that they have only a fixed number of dollars available for capital expenditures and that numerous projects will compete for these dollars. Procedures for dealing with capital rationing are presented in Chapter 10. The discussions that follow here and in the following chapter assume unlimited funds.

Accept–Reject versus Ranking Approaches

accept–reject approach
The evaluation of capital expenditure proposals to determine whether they meet the firm's minimum acceptance criterion.

ranking approach
The ranking of capital expenditure projects on the basis of some predetermined measure, such as the rate of return.

Two basic approaches to capital budgeting decisions are available. The **accept–reject approach** involves evaluating capital expenditure proposals to determine whether they meet the firm's minimum acceptance criterion. This approach can be used when the firm has unlimited funds, as a preliminary step when evaluating mutually exclusive projects, or in a situation in which capital must be rationed. In these cases, only acceptable projects should be considered.

The second method, the **ranking approach**, involves ranking projects on the basis of some predetermined measure, such as the rate of return. The project with the highest return is ranked first, and the project with the lowest return is ranked last. Only acceptable projects should be ranked. Ranking is useful in selecting the "best" of a group of mutually exclusive projects and in evaluating projects with a view to capital rationing.

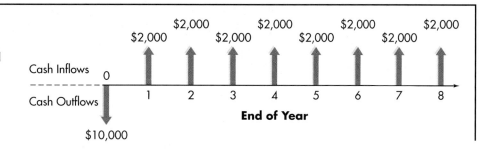

FIGURE 8.1

Conventional Cash Flow
Time line for a conventional
cash flow pattern

Conventional versus Nonconventional Cash Flow Patterns

**conventional cash
flow pattern**
An initial outflow followed
only by a series of inflows.

**nonconventional cash
flow pattern**
An initial outflow followed
by a series of inflows *and*
outflows.

Cash flow patterns associated with capital investment projects can be classified as *conventional* or *nonconventional*. A **conventional cash flow pattern** consists of an initial outflow followed only by a series of inflows. For example, a firm may spend $10,000 today and as a result expect to receive equal annual cash inflows (an annuity) of $2,000 each year for the next 8 years, as depicted on the timeline in Figure 8.1.[2] A conventional cash flow pattern that provides a mixed stream of cash inflows is depicted in Figure 8.3 on page 385.

A **nonconventional cash flow pattern** is one in which an initial outflow is followed by a series of inflows *and* outflows. For example, the purchase of a machine may require an initial cash outflow of $20,000 and may generate cash inflows of $5,000 each year for 4 years. In the fifth year after purchase, an outflow of $8,000 may be required to overhaul the machine, after which it generates inflows of $5,000 each year for 5 more years. This nonconventional pattern is illustrated on the time line in Figure 8.2.

Difficulties often arise in evaluating projects with nonconventional patterns of cash flow. *The discussions in the remainder of this chapter and in Chapters 9 and 10 are therefore limited to the evaluation of conventional cash flow patterns.*

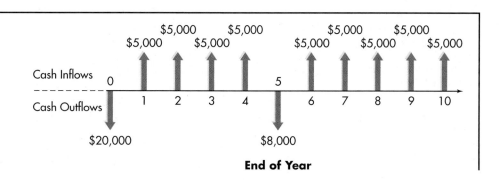

FIGURE 8.2

**Nonconventional
Cash Flow**
Time line for a
nonconventional
cash flow pattern

REVIEW QUESTIONS

8–1 What is *capital budgeting?* Do all capital expenditures involve fixed assets? Explain.

8–2 What are the key motives for making capital expenditures? Discuss, compare, and contrast them.

8–3 What are the five steps involved in the capital budgeting process?

8–4 Differentiate between the members of each of the following pairs of capital budgeting terms: (**a**) independent versus mutually exclusive projects; (**b**) unlimited funds versus capital rationing; (**c**) accept–reject versus ranking approaches; and (**d**) conventional versus nonconventional cash flow patterns.

8.2 | Relevant Cash Flows

relevant cash flows
The *incremental cash outflow (investment) and resulting subsequent inflows* associated with a proposed capital expenditure.

incremental cash flows
The *additional* cash flows—outflows or inflows—expected to result from a proposed capital expenditure.

To evaluate capital expenditure alternatives, the firm must determine the **relevant cash flows.** These are the *incremental cash outflow (investment) and resulting subsequent inflows.* The **incremental cash flows** represent the *additional* cash flows—outflows or inflows—expected to result from a proposed capital expenditure. As noted in Chapter 3, cash flows rather than accounting figures are used, because cash flows directly affect the firm's ability to pay bills and purchase assets. The nearby *Focus on Ethics* box discusses the accuracy of cash flow estimates and cites one reason that even well-estimated deals may not work out as planned.

The remainder of this chapter is devoted to the procedures for measuring the relevant cash flows associated with proposed capital expenditures.

Major Cash Flow Components

initial investment
The relevant cash outflow for a proposed project at time zero.

operating cash inflows
The incremental after-tax cash inflows resulting from implementation of a project during its life.

terminal cash flow
The after-tax nonoperating cash flow occurring in the final year of a project. It is usually attributable to liquidation of the project.

The cash flows of any project having the *conventional pattern* can include three basic components: (1) an initial investment, (2) operating cash inflows, and (3) terminal cash flow. All projects—whether for expansion, replacement or renewal, or some other purpose—have the first two components. Some, however, lack the final component, terminal cash flow.

Figure 8.3 depicts on a time line the cash flows for a project. The **initial investment** for the proposed project is $50,000. This is the relevant cash outflow at time zero. The **operating cash inflows,** which are the incremental after-tax cash inflows resulting from implementation of the project during its life, gradually increase from $4,000 in its first year to $10,000 in its tenth and final year. The **terminal cash flow** is the after-tax nonoperating cash flow occurring in the final year of the project. It is usually attributable to liquidation of the project. In this case it is $25,000, received at the end of the project's 10-year life. Note that the terminal cash flow does *not* include the $10,000 operating cash inflow for year 10.

Expansion versus Replacement Decisions

Developing relevant cash flow estimates is most straightforward in the case of *expansion decisions.* In this case, the initial investment, operating cash inflows, and terminal cash flow are merely the after-tax cash outflow and inflows associated with the proposed capital expenditure.

Focus on Ethics   A Question of Value

IN PRACTICE

The process of capital budgeting based on calculating various decision measures from projected cash flows has been a part of the investment decision process for more than 40 years. This procedure for evaluating investment opportunities works well when cash flows can be estimated with certainty, but in real-world corporate practice, many investment decisions involve a high degree of uncertainty. The decision is even more complicated when the project under consideration is the acquisition of another company or part of another company.

Because estimates of the cash flows from an investment project involve making assumptions about the future, they may be subject to considerable error. The problem becomes more complicated as the period of time under consideration becomes longer and when the project is unique in nature with no comparables. Other complications may arise involving

accounting for additional (extraordinary) cash flows—for example, the cost of litigation, compliance with tougher environmental standards, or the costs of disposal or recycling of an asset at the completion of the project.

All too often, the initial champagne celebration gives way once the final cost of a deal is tallied. In fact, taken as a whole, mergers and acquisitions in recent years have produced a disheartening *negative* 12 percent return on investment. While acquirers have found the financial data to create good models ever more readily available, which result in the increased reliability of discounted cash flow estimates, more attention is being paid to the accuracy of the numbers. Inspired in part by post-Enron focus on governance and the threat of shareholder lawsuits, board members have been pushing corporate managers to make a stronger case for the deals they propose.

Says Glenn Gurtcheff, managing director and co-head of middle market M&A for Piper Jaffray & Co., "They're not just taking the company's audited and unaudited financial statements at face value; they are really diving into the numbers and trying to understand not just their accuracy, but what they mean in terms of trends."

If valuation has improved so much, why do analyses show that companies often overpay? The answer lies in the imperial CEO. Improvements in valuation techniques can be negated when the process deteriorates into a game of tweaking the numbers to justify a deal the CEO wants to do, regardless of price. Value is one thing, price is quite another.

■ *What would your options be when faced with the demands of an imperial CEO who expects you to "make it work"? Brainstorm several options.*

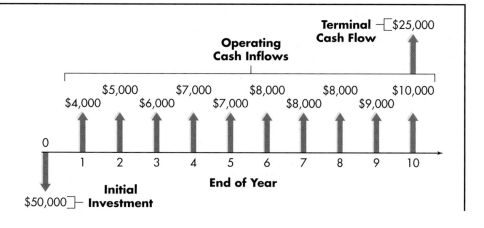

FIGURE 8.3

Cash Flow Components
Time line for major cash flow components

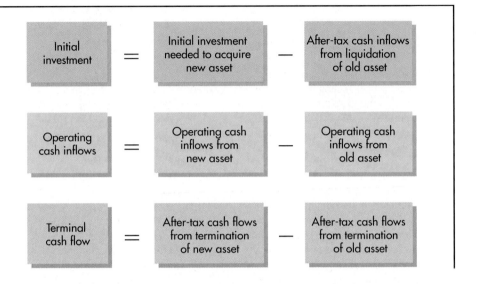

FIGURE 8.4

Relevant Cash Flows for Replacement Decisions
Calculation of the three components of relevant cash flow for a replacement decision

Identifying relevant cash flows for *replacement decisions* is more complicated, because the firm must identify the *incremental* cash outflow and inflows that would result from the proposed replacement. The initial investment in the case of replacement is the difference between the initial investment needed to acquire the new asset and any after-tax cash inflows expected from liquidation of the old asset. The operating cash inflows are the difference between the operating cash inflows from the new asset and those from the old asset. The terminal cash flow is the difference between the after-tax cash flows expected upon termination of the new and the old assets. These relationships are shown in Figure 8.4.

Actually, all capital budgeting decisions can be viewed as replacement decisions. *Expansion decisions are merely replacement decisions in which all cash flows from the old asset are zero.* In light of this fact, this chapter focuses primarily on replacement decisions.

Sunk Costs and Opportunity Costs

When estimating the relevant cash flows associated with a proposed capital expenditure, the firm must recognize any sunk costs and opportunity costs. These costs are easy to mishandle or ignore, particularly when determining a project's incremental cash flows. **Sunk costs** are cash outlays that have already been made (past outlays) and therefore have no effect on the cash flows relevant to the current decision. As a result, *sunk costs should not be included in a project's incremental cash flows.*

Opportunity costs are cash flows that could be realized from the best alternative use of an owned asset. They therefore represent cash flows that *will not be realized* as a result of employing that asset in the proposed project. Because of this, any *opportunity costs should be included as cash outflows when one is determining a project's incremental cash flows.*

sunk costs
Cash outlays that have already been made (past outlays) and therefore have no effect on the cash flows relevant to a current decision.

opportunity costs
Cash flows that could be realized from the best alternative use of an owned asset.

Example

Jankow Equipment is considering renewing its drill press X12, which it purchased 3 years earlier for $237,000, by retrofitting it with the computerized control system from an obsolete piece of equipment it owns. The obsolete equipment could be sold today for a high bid of $42,000, but without its computerized control system, it would be worth nothing. Jankow is in the process of estimating the labor and materials costs of retrofitting the system to drill press X12 and the benefits expected from the retrofit. The $237,000 cost of drill press X12 is a *sunk cost* because it represents an earlier cash outlay. It *would not be included* as a cash outflow when determining the cash flows relevant to the retrofit decision. Although Jankow owns the obsolete piece of equipment, the proposed use of its computerized control system represents an *opportunity cost* of $42,000—the highest price at which it could be sold today. This opportunity cost *would be included* as a cash outflow associated with using the computerized control system.

International Capital Budgeting and Long-Term Investments

Although the same basic capital budgeting principles are used for domestic and international projects, several additional factors must be addressed in evaluating foreign investment opportunities. International capital budgeting differs from the domestic version because (1) cash outflows and inflows occur in a foreign currency, and (2) foreign investments entail potentially significant political risk. Both of these risks can be minimized through careful planning.

Companies face both long-term and short-term *currency risks* related to both the invested capital and the cash flows resulting from it. Long-term currency risk can be minimized by financing the foreign investment at least partly in the local capital markets. This step ensures that the project's revenues, operating costs, and financing costs will be in the local currency. Likewise, the dollar value of short-term, local-currency cash flows can be protected by using special securities and strategies such as futures, forwards, and options market instruments.

Political risks can be minimized by using both operating and financial strategies. For example, by structuring the investment as a joint venture and selecting a well-connected local partner, the U.S. company can minimize the risk of its operations being seized or harassed. Companies also can protect themselves from having their investment returns blocked by local governments by structuring the financing of such investments as debt rather than as equity. Debt-service payments are legally enforceable claims, whereas equity returns (such as dividends) are not. Even if local courts do not support the claims of the U.S. company, the company can threaten to pursue its case in U.S. courts.

In spite of the preceding difficulties, **foreign direct investment**, which involves the transfer of capital, managerial, and technical assets to a foreign country, has surged in recent years. This is evident in the growing market values of foreign assets owned by U.S.-based companies and of foreign direct investment in the United States, particularly by British, Canadian, Dutch, German, and Japanese companies. Furthermore, foreign direct investment by U.S. companies seems to be accelerating. See the *Global Focus* box on page 388 for a discussion of recent foreign direct investment in China.

REVIEW QUESTIONS

8–5   Why is it important to evaluate capital budgeting projects on the basis of *incremental cash flows?*

8–6   What three components of cash flow may exist for a given project? How can expansion decisions be treated as replacement decisions? Explain.

Hint Sunk costs and opportunity costs are concepts you must fully understand. Funds already spent are irrelevant to future decisions, but the returns given up so that an existing asset can be used in a given project *are* considered a relevant cost.

foreign direct investment
The transfer of capital, managerial, and technical assets to a foreign country.

Global Focus   Changes May Influence Future Investments in China

Foreign direct investment in China soared in 2006. Not including banks, insurance, and securities, foreign direct investment amounted to $63.02 billion. China's economy has surged more than tenfold since 1980, the first year it allowed foreign investments and money began pouring into factories on China's east coast.

As its exports surged, China's trade surplus swelled 74 percent in 2006 to a record $177.5 billion. With a strong foreign exchange surplus, China is no longer desperate for capital from overseas, but is now primarily interested in foreign skills and technologies. Prime Minister Wen Jiabao wants to steer investments toward the manufacturing of higher-value products and toward less-developed regions. Wen is giving tax breaks and promising speedy approvals for investments away from areas in the east, such as Shanghai and the Pearl River Delta.

Typical of foreign investors in China is Intel Capital, a subsidiary of **Intel Corporation.** In late 2005, it invested $200 million into three Chinese companies: Chipsbrand Microelectronics Co., Ltd., a semiconductor design company; Onewave Technologies, Inc., a broadband entertainment-technology solutions provider; and Versilicon Holdings Co., Ltd., an integrated-circuit design foundry. Intel Capital is no beginner at foreign investment; it has invested more than $4 billion in more than 1,000 companies around the world.

China allows three types of foreign investments: a *wholly foreign-owned enterprise* (WFOE) in which the firm is entirely funded with foreign capital; a *joint venture* in which the foreign partner must provide at least 25 percent of initial capital; and a *representative office* (RO), the most common and easily established entity, which cannot perform business activities that directly result in profits. Generally an RO is the first step in establishing a China presence and includes mechanisms for upgrading to a WFOE or joint venture.

Like any foreign investment, investing in China is not without risk. One potential risk facing foreign investors in China is the likelihood of a future tax increase. Currently, domestic (Chinese) enterprises have heavy tax burdens, while foreign investment enterprises enjoy a lower tax rate. The difference is about 13 percent and it is one reason why foreign investors favor China. A new "unified tax" proposal is expected to be enacted in 2008, and this will result in a higher tax rate for foreign investors. In addition, higher production costs due to stricter requirements on environmental protection and higher salaries for Chinese employees will also pressure foreign investors.

■ *The Chinese government has encouraged foreign investments through favorable tax treatment. Can you think of similar situations in your own country?*

8–7   What effect do *sunk costs* and *opportunity costs* have on a project's incremental cash flows?

8–8   How can *currency risk* and *political risk* be minimized when one is making *foreign direct investment?*

8.3 | Finding the Initial Investment

The term *initial investment* as used here refers to the relevant cash outflows to be considered when evaluating a prospective capital expenditure. Because our discussion of capital budgeting is concerned only with investments that exhibit conventional cash flows, the initial investment occurs at *time zero*—the time at which the expenditure is made. The initial investment is calculated by subtracting all cash inflows occurring at time zero from all cash outflows occurring at time zero.

TABLE 8.2	The Basic Format for Determining Initial Investment

Installed cost of new asset =
   Cost of new asset
  + Installation costs
− After-tax proceeds from sale of old asset =
   Proceeds from sale of old asset
  ∓ Tax on sale of old asset
± Change in net working capital
Initial investment

The basic format for determining the initial investment is given in Table 8.2. The cash flows that must be considered when determining the initial investment associated with a capital expenditure are the installed cost of the new asset, the after-tax proceeds (if any) from the sale of an old asset, and the change (if any) in net working capital. Note that if there are no installation costs and the firm is not replacing an existing asset, then the cost (purchase price) of the new asset, adjusted for any change in net working capital, is equal to the initial investment.

Installed Cost of New Asset

cost of new asset
The net outflow necessary to acquire a new asset.

installation costs
Any added costs that are necessary to place an asset into operation.

installed cost of new asset
The *cost of new asset* plus its *installation costs;* equals the asset's depreciable value.

As shown in Table 8.2, the installed cost of the new asset is found by adding the cost of the new asset to its installation costs. The **cost of new asset** is the net outflow that its acquisition requires. Usually, we are concerned with the acquisition of a fixed asset for which a definite purchase price is paid. **Installation costs** are any added costs that are necessary to place an asset into operation. The Internal Revenue Service (IRS) requires the firm to add installation costs to the purchase price of an asset to determine its depreciable value, which is expensed over a period of years. The **installed cost of new asset,** calculated by adding the *cost of new asset* to its *installation costs,* equals its depreciable value.

After-Tax Proceeds from Sale of Old Asset

after-tax proceeds from sale of old asset
The difference between the old asset's sale proceeds and any applicable taxes or tax refunds related to its sale.

proceeds from sale of old asset
The cash inflows, net of any *removal* or *cleanup costs,* resulting from the sale of an existing asset.

tax on sale of old asset
Tax that depends on the relationship between the old asset's sale price and *book value,* and on existing government tax rules.

Table 8.2 shows that the **after-tax proceeds from sale of old asset** decrease the firm's initial investment in the new asset. These proceeds are the difference between the old asset's sale proceeds and any applicable taxes or tax refunds related to its sale. The **proceeds from sale of old asset** are the net cash inflows it provides. This amount is net of any costs incurred in the process of removing the asset. Included in these *removal costs* are *cleanup costs,* such as those related to removal and disposal of chemical and nuclear wastes. These costs may not be trivial.

    The proceeds from the sale of an old asset are normally subject to some type of tax.[3] This **tax on sale of old asset** depends on the relationship between its sale price and *book value,* and on existing government tax rules.

---

3. A brief discussion of the tax treatment of ordinary and capital gains income was presented in Chapter 1. Because corporate capital gains and ordinary income are taxed at the same rate, for convenience, we do not differ between them in the following discussions.

book value
The strict accounting value of an asset, calculated by subtracting its accumulated depreciation from its installed cost.

Book Value

The **book value** of an asset is its strict accounting value. It can be calculated by using the following equation:

$$\text{Book value} = \text{Installed cost of asset} - \text{Accumulated depreciation} \qquad (8.1)$$

Example

Hudson Industries, a small electronics company, 2 years ago acquired a machine tool with an installed cost of $100,000. The asset was being depreciated under MACRS using a 5-year recovery period.[4] Table 3.2 (on page 108) shows that under MACRS for a 5-year recovery period, 20% and 32% of the installed cost would be depreciated in years 1 and 2, respectively. In other words, 52% (20% + 32%) of the $100,000 cost, or $52,000 (0.52 × $100,000), would represent the accumulated depreciation at the end of year 2. Substituting into Equation 8.1, we get

$$\text{Book value} = \$100,000 - \$52,000 = \underline{\underline{\$48,000}}$$

The book value of Hudson's asset at the end of year 2 is therefore $48,000.

Basic Tax Rules

Three potential tax situations can occur when a firm sells an asset. These situations depend on the relationship between the asset's sale price and its book value. The two key forms of taxable income and their associated tax treatments are defined and summarized in Table 8.3. The assumed tax rates used throughout this text are noted in the final column. There are three possible tax situations. The asset may be sold (1) for more than its book value, (2) for its book value, or (3) for less than its book value. An example will illustrate.

Example

The old asset purchased 2 years ago for $100,000 by Hudson Industries has a current book value of $48,000. What will happen if the firm now decides to sell the asset and replace it? The tax consequences depend on the sale price. Figure 8.5

TABLE 8.3   Tax Treatment on Sales of Assets

Form of taxable income	Definition	Tax treatment	Assumed tax rate
Gain on sale of asset	Portion of the sale price that is *greater than* book value.	All gains above book value are taxed as ordinary income.	40%
Loss on sale of asset	Amount by which sale price is *less than* book value.	If the asset is depreciable and used in business, loss is deducted from ordinary income.	40% of loss is a tax savings
		If the asset is *not* depreciable or is *not* used in business, loss is deductible only against capital gains.	40% of loss is a tax savings

---

4. For a review of MACRS, see Chapter 3. Under current tax law, most manufacturing equipment has a 7-year recovery period, as noted in Table 3.1 (on page 107). Using this recovery period results in 8 years of depreciation, which unnecessarily complicates examples and problems. To simplify, *manufacturing equipment is treated as a 5-year asset in this and the following chapters.*

FIGURE 8.5   **Taxable Income from Sale of Asset**

Taxable income from sale of asset at various sale prices for Hudson Industries

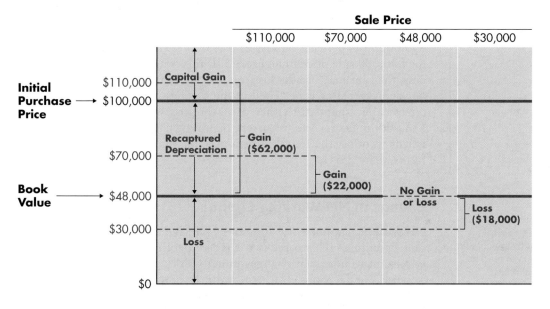

depicts the taxable income resulting from four possible sale prices in light of the asset's initial purchase price of $100,000 and its current book value of $48,000. The taxable consequences of each of these sale prices are described below.

The sale of the asset for more than its book value   If Hudson sells the old asset for $110,000, it realizes a gain of $62,000 ($110,000 − $48,000). Technically this gain is made up of two parts—a capital gain and **recaptured depreciation**, which is the portion of the sale price that is above book value and below the initial purchase price. For Hudson, the capital gain is $10,000 ($110,000 sale price − $100,000 initial purchase price); recaptured depreciation is $52,000 (the $100,000 initial purchase price − $48,000 book value).[5]

Both the $10,000 capital gain and the $52,000 recaptured depreciation are shown under the $110,000 sale price in Figure 8.5. The total gain above book value of $62,000 is taxed as ordinary income at the 40% rate, resulting in taxes of $24,800 (0.40 × $62,000). These taxes should be used in calculating the initial investment in the new asset, using the format in Table 8.2. In effect, the taxes raise the amount of the firm's initial investment in the new asset by reducing the proceeds from the sale of the old asset.

If Hudson instead sells the old asset for $70,000, it experiences a gain above book value (in the form of *recaptured depreciation*) of $22,000 ($70,000 − $48,000), as shown under the $70,000 sale price in Figure 8.5. This gain is taxed as ordinary income. Because the firm is assumed to be in the 40% tax bracket, the taxes on the $22,000 gain are $8,800 (0.40 × $22,000). This amount in taxes should be used in calculating the initial investment in the new asset.

recaptured depreciation
The portion of an asset's sale price that is above its book value and below its initial purchase price.

---

5. Although the current tax law requires corporate capital gains to be treated as ordinary income, the structure for corporate capital gains is retained under the law to facilitate a rate differential in the likely event of future tax revisions. For clarity and convenience, this distinction is *not* made throughout the text discussions.

The sale of the asset for its book value   If the asset is sold for $48,000, its book value, the firm breaks even. There is no gain or loss, as shown under the $48,000 sale price in Figure 8.5. Because *no tax results from selling an asset for its book value*, there is no tax effect on the initial investment in the new asset.

The sale of the asset for less than its book value   If Hudson sells the asset for $30,000, it experiences a loss of $18,000 ($48,000 − $30,000), as shown under the $30,000 sale price in Figure 8.5. If this is a depreciable asset used in the business, the firm may use the loss to offset ordinary operating income. If the asset is *not* depreciable or is *not* used in the business, the firm can use the loss only to offset capital gains. In either case, the loss will save the firm $7,200 (0.40 × $18,000) in taxes. And, if current operating earnings or capital gains are not sufficient to offset the loss, the firm may be able to apply these losses to prior or future years' taxes.[6]

Change in Net Working Capital

net working capital
The amount by which a firm's current assets exceed its current liabilities.

Net working capital is the amount by which a firm's current assets exceed its current liabilities.[7] This topic is treated in depth in Chapter 14; at this point it is important to note that changes in net working capital often accompany capital expenditure decisions. If a firm acquires new machinery to expand its level of operations, it will experience an increase in levels of cash, accounts receivable, inventories, accounts payable, and accruals. These increases result from the need for more cash to support expanded operations, more accounts receivable and inventories to support increased sales, and more accounts payable and accruals to support increased outlays made to meet expanded product demand. As noted in Chapter 3, increases in cash, accounts receivable, and inventories are *outflows of cash*, whereas increases in accounts payable and accruals are *inflows of cash*.

change in net working capital
The difference between a change in current assets and a change in current liabilities.

The difference between the change in current assets and the change in current liabilities is the **change in net working capital**. Generally, current assets increase by more than current liabilities, resulting in an increased investment in net working capital. This increased investment is treated as an initial outflow.[8] If the change in net working capital were negative, it would be shown as an initial inflow. The change in net working capital—regardless of whether it is an increase or a decrease—*is not taxable* because it merely involves a net buildup or net reduction of current accounts.

Example

Danson Company, a metal products manufacturer, is contemplating expanding its operations. Financial analysts expect that the changes in current accounts summarized in Table 8.4 will occur and will be maintained over the life of the

---

6. The tax law provides detailed procedures for using *tax loss carrybacks/carryforwards*. Application of such procedures to capital budgeting is beyond the scope of this text, and they are therefore ignored in subsequent discussions.

7. Occasionally, this cash outflow is intentionally ignored to enhance the attractiveness of a proposed investment and thereby improve its likelihood of acceptance. Similar intentional omissions and/or overly optimistic estimates are sometimes made to enhance project acceptance. The presence of formal review and analysis procedures should help the firm to ensure that capital budgeting cash flow estimates are realistic and unbiased and that the "best" projects—those that make the maximum contribution to owner wealth—are accepted.

8. When changes in net working capital apply to the initial investment associated with a proposed capital expenditure, they are for convenience assumed to be instantaneous and thereby occurring at time zero. In practice, the change in net working capital will frequently occur over a period of months as the capital expenditure is implemented.

TABLE 8.4	Calculation of Change in Net Working Capital for Danson Company	
Current account		Change in balance
Cash		+ $ 4,000
Accounts receivable		+ 10,000
Inventories		+ 8,000
(1) Current assets		+$22,000
Accounts payable	+$ 7,000	
Accruals	+ 2,000	
(2) Current liabilities		+ 9,000
Change in net working capital [(1) − (2)]		+$13,000

expansion. Current assets are expected to increase by $22,000, and current liabilities are expected to increase by $9,000, resulting in a $13,000 increase in net working capital. In this case, the change will represent an increased net working capital investment and will be treated as a cash outflow in calculating the initial investment.

Calculating the Initial Investment

A variety of tax and other considerations enter into the initial investment calculation. The following example illustrates calculation of the initial investment according to the format in Table 8.2.[9]

Example

Powell Corporation, a large, diversified manufacturer of aircraft components, is trying to determine the initial investment required to replace an old machine with a new, more sophisticated model. The proposed machine's purchase price is $380,000, and an additional $20,000 will be necessary to install it. It will be depreciated under MACRS using a 5-year recovery period. The present (old) machine was purchased 3 years ago at a cost of $240,000 and was being depreciated under MACRS using a 5-year recovery period. The firm has found a buyer willing to pay $280,000 for the present machine and to remove it at the buyer's expense. The firm expects that a $35,000 increase in current assets and an $18,000 increase in current liabilities will accompany the replacement; these changes will result in a $17,000 ($35,000 − $18,000) *increase* in net working capital. The firm pays taxes at a rate of 40%.

The only component of the initial investment calculation that is difficult to obtain is taxes. The book value of the present machine can be found by using the depreciation percentages from Table 3.2 (on page 108) of 20%, 32%, and 19% for years 1, 2, and 3, respectively. The resulting *book value is $69,600 ($240,000 − [(0.20 + 0.32 + 0.19) × $240,000]). A gain of $210,400 ($280,000 − $69,600)*

9. Throughout the discussions of capital budgeting, all assets evaluated as candidates for replacement are assumed to be depreciable assets that are directly used in the business, so any losses on the sale of these assets can be applied against ordinary operating income. The decisions are also structured to ensure that the usable life remaining on the old asset is just equal to the life of the new asset; this assumption enables us to avoid the problem of unequal lives, which is discussed in Chapter 10.

is realized on the sale. The total taxes on the gain are $84,160 (0.40 × $210,400). These taxes must be subtracted from the $280,000 sale price of the present machine to calculate the after-tax proceeds from its sale.

Substituting the relevant amounts into the format in Table 8.2 results in an initial investment of $221,160, which represents the net cash outflow required at time zero.

Installed cost of proposed machine		
Cost of proposed machine	$380,000	
+ Installation costs	20,000	
Total installed cost—proposed (depreciable value)		$400,000
− **After-tax proceeds from sale of present machine**		
Proceeds from sale of present machine	$280,000	
− Tax on sale of present machine	84,160	
Total after-tax proceeds—present		195,840
+ **Change in net working capital**		17,000
Initial investment		$221,160

REVIEW QUESTIONS

8–9 Explain how each of the following inputs is used to calculate the *initial investment*: (**a**) cost of new asset, (**b**) installation costs, (**c**) proceeds from sale of old asset, (**d**) tax on sale of old asset, and (**e**) change in net working capital.

8–10 How is the *book value* of an asset calculated? What are the two key forms of taxable income?

8–11 What three tax situations may result from the sale of an asset that is being replaced?

8–12 Referring to the basic format for calculating initial investment, explain how a firm would determine the *depreciable value* of the new asset.

 8.4 | Finding the Operating Cash Inflows

The benefits expected from a capital expenditure or "project" are embodied in its *operating cash inflows,* which are *incremental after-tax cash inflows.* In this section we use the income statement format to develop clear definitions of the terms *after-tax, cash inflows,* and *incremental.*

Interpreting the Term After-Tax

Benefits expected to result from proposed capital expenditures must be measured on an *after-tax basis,* because the firm will not have the use of any benefits until it has satisfied the government's tax claims. These claims depend on the firm's taxable income, so deducting taxes *before* making comparisons between proposed investments is necessary for consistency when evaluating capital expenditure alternatives.

Interpreting the Term Cash Inflows

All benefits expected from a proposed project must be measured on a *cash flow basis*. Cash inflows represent dollars that can be spent, not merely "accounting profits." A simple accounting technique for converting after-tax net profits into operating cash inflows was given in Equation 3.1 on page 111. The basic calculation requires adding depreciation and any other *noncash charges* (amortization and depletion) deducted as expenses on the firm's income statement back to net profits after taxes. Because depreciation is commonly found on income statements, it is the only noncash charge we consider.

<table>
<tr><td>*Example*</td><td>

Powell Corporation's estimates of its revenue and expenses (excluding depreciation and interest), with and without the proposed new machine described in the preceding example, are given in Table 8.5. Note that both the expected usable life of the proposed machine and the remaining usable life of the present machine are 5 years. The amount to be depreciated with the proposed machine is calculated by summing the purchase price of $380,000 and the installation costs of $20,000. The proposed machine is to be depreciated under MACRS using a 5-year recovery period.[10] The resulting depreciation on this machine for each of the 6 years, as well as the remaining 3 years of depreciation (years 4, 5, and 6) on the present machine, are calculated in Table 8.6 (see page 396).[11]

The *operating cash inflows* each year can be calculated by using the income statement format shown in Table 8.7 (see page 397). Note that we exclude interest because we are focusing purely on the "investment decision." The interest is relevant to the "financing decision," which is separately considered. Because we exclude interest expense, "earnings before interest and taxes (EBIT)" is equivalent to "net profits before taxes," and the calculation of "operating cash inflow" in Table 8.7 is equivalent to "operating cash flow (OCF)" (defined in Equation 3.4, on page 114). Simply stated, the income statement format calculates OCF.

</td></tr>
</table>

TABLE 8.5	Powell Corporation's Revenue and Expenses (Excluding Depreciation and Interest) for Proposed and Present Machines

	With proposed machine			With present machine	
Year	Revenue (1)	Expenses (excl. depr. and int.) (2)	Year	Revenue (1)	Expenses (excl. depr. and int.) (2)
1	$2,520,000	$2,300,000	1	$2,200,000	$1,990,000
2	2,520,000	2,300,000	2	2,300,000	2,110,000
3	2,520,000	2,300,000	3	2,400,000	2,230,000
4	2,520,000	2,300,000	4	2,400,000	2,250,000
5	2,520,000	2,300,000	5	2,250,000	2,120,000

---

10. As noted in Chapter 3, it takes $n + 1$ years to depreciate an n-year class asset under current tax law. Therefore, MACRS percentages are given for each of 6 years for use in depreciating an asset with a 5-year recovery period.

11. It is important to recognize that although both machines will provide 5 years of use, the proposed new machine will be depreciated over the 6-year period, whereas the present machine, as noted in the preceding example, has been depreciated over 3 years and therefore has remaining only its final 3 years (years 4, 5, and 6) of depreciation (12%, 12%, and 5%, respectively, under MACRS).

TABLE 8.6	Depreciation Expense for Proposed and Present Machines for Powell Corporation

Year	Cost (1)	Applicable MACRS depreciation percentages (from Table 3.2) (2)	Depreciation [(1) × (2)] (3)
With proposed machine			
1	$400,000	20%	$ 80,000
2	400,000	32	128,000
3	400,000	19	76,000
4	400,000	12	48,000
5	400,000	12	48,000
6	400,000	5	20,000
Totals		100%	$400,000
With present machine			
1	$240,000	12% (year-4 depreciation)	$28,800
2	240,000	12 (year-5 depreciation)	28,800
3	240,000	5 (year-6 depreciation)	12,000
4		Because the present machine is at the end of the third year of its cost	0
5		recovery at the time the analysis is performed, it has only the final 3	0
6		years of depreciation (as noted above) still applicable.	0
Total			$69,600[a]

[a]The total $69,600 represents the book value of the present machine at the end of the third year, as calculated in the preceding example.

Substituting the data from Tables 8.5 and 8.6 into this format and assuming a 40% tax rate, we get Table 8.8. It demonstrates the calculation of operating cash inflows for each year for both the proposed and the present machine. Because the proposed machine is depreciated over 6 years, the analysis must be performed over the 6-year period to capture fully the tax effect of its year-6 depreciation. The resulting operating cash inflows are shown in the final row of Table 8.8 for each machine. The $8,000 year-6 operating cash inflow for the proposed machine results solely from the tax benefit of its year-6 depreciation deduction.[12]

Interpreting the Term Incremental

The final step in estimating the operating cash inflows for a proposed replacement project is to calculate the *incremental (relevant)* cash inflows. Incremental operating cash inflows are needed, because our concern is *only* with the change in operating cash inflows that result from the proposed project. Clearly, if this were an expansion project, the project's cash flows would be the incremental cash flows.

12. Although here we have calculated the year-6 operating cash inflow for the proposed machine, this cash flow will later be eliminated as a result of the assumed sale of the machine at the end of year 5.

TABLE 8.7	Calculation of Operating Cash Inflows Using the Income Statement Format

Revenue
− Expenses (excluding depreciation and interest)
Earnings before depreciation, interest, and taxes (EBDIT)
− Depreciation
Earnings before interest and taxes (EBIT)
− Taxes (rate = T)
Net operating profit after taxes [NOPAT = EBIT × (1 − T)]
+ Depreciation
Operating cash inflows (same as OCF in Equation 3.4)

TABLE 8.8	Calculation of Operating Cash Inflows for Powell Corporation's Proposed and Present Machines

	Year 1	Year 2	Year 3	Year 4	Year 5	Year 6
With proposed machine						
Revenue[a]	$2,520,000	$2,520,000	$2,520,000	$2,520,000	$2,520,000	$ 0
− Expenses (excl. depr. and int.)[b]	2,300,000	2,300,000	2,300,000	2,300,000	2,300,000	0
Earnings before depr., int., and taxes	$ 220,000	$ 220,000	$ 220,000	$ 220,000	$ 220,000	$ 0
− Depreciation[c]	80,000	128,000	76,000	48,000	48,000	20,000
Earnings before interest and taxes	$ 140,000	$ 92,000	$ 144,000	$ 172,000	$ 172,000	−$20,000
− Taxes (rate, T = 40%)	56,000	36,800	57,600	68,800	68,800	− 8,000
Net operating profit after taxes	$ 84,000	$ 55,200	$ 86,400	$ 103,200	$ 103,200	−$12,000
+ Depreciation[c]	80,000	128,000	76,000	48,000	48,000	20,000
Operating cash inflows	$ 164,000	$ 183,200	$ 162,400	$ 151,200	$ 151,200	$ 8,000
With present machine						
Revenue[a]	$2,200,000	$2,300,000	$2,400,000	$2,400,000	$2,250,000	$ 0
− Expenses (excl. depr. and int.)[b]	1,990,000	2,110,000	2,230,000	2,250,000	2,120,000	0
Earnings before depr., int., and taxes	$ 210,000	$ 190,000	$ 170,000	$ 150,000	$ 130,000	$ 0
− Depreciation[c]	28,800	28,800	12,000	0	0	0
Earnings before interest and taxes	$ 181,200	$ 161,200	$ 158,000	$ 150,000	$ 130,000	$ 0
− Taxes (rate, T = 40%)	72,480	64,480	63,200	60,000	52,000	0
Net operating profit after taxes	$ 108,720	$ 96,720	$ 94,800	$ 90,000	$ 78,000	$ 0
+ Depreciation[c]	28,800	28,800	12,000	0	0	0
Operating cash inflows	$ 137,520	$ 125,520	$ 106,800	$ 90,000	$ 78,000	$ 0

[a]From column 1 of Table 8.5.
[b]From column 2 of Table 8.5.
[c]From column 3 of Table 8.6.

Example

Table 8.9 demonstrates the calculation of Powell Corporation's *incremental (relevant) operating cash inflows* for each year. The estimates of operating cash inflows developed in Table 8.8 appear in columns 1 and 2. Column 2 values represent the amount of operating cash inflows that Powell Corporation will receive if it does not replace the present machine. If the proposed machine replaces the present machine, the firm's operating cash inflows for each year will be those shown in column 1. Subtracting the present machine's operating cash inflows from the proposed machine's operating cash inflows, we get the incremental operating cash inflows for each year, shown in column 3. These cash flows represent the amounts by which each respective year's cash inflows will increase as a result of the replacement. For example, in year 1, Powell Corporation's cash inflows would increase by $26,480 if the proposed project were undertaken. Clearly, these are the relevant inflows to be considered when evaluating the benefits of making a capital expenditure for the proposed machine.[13]

	Operating cash inflows		
	Proposed machine[a]	Present machine[a]	Incremental (relevant) [(1) − (2)]
Year	(1)	(2)	(3)
1	$164,000	$137,520	$26,480
2	183,200	125,520	57,680
3	162,400	106,800	55,600
4	151,200	90,000	61,200
5	151,200	78,000	73,200
6	8,000	0	8,000

TABLE 8.9   Incremental (Relevant) Operating Cash Inflows for Powell Corporation

[a]From final row for respective machine in Table 8.8.

---

13. The following equation can be used to calculate more directly the incremental cash inflow in year t, ICI_t.

$$ICI_t = [\Delta EBDIT_t \times (1-T)] + (\Delta D_t \times T)$$

where

$\Delta EBDIT_t =$ change in earnings before depreciation, interest, and taxes [revenues − expenses (excl. depr. and int.)] in year t

$\Delta D_t =$ change in depreciation expense in year t

$T =$ firm's marginal tax rate

Applying this formula to the Powell Corporation data given in Tables 8.5 and 8.6 for year 3, we get the following values of variables:

$$\Delta EBDIT_3 = (\$2,520,000 - \$2,300,000) - (\$2,400,000 - \$2,230,000)$$
$$= \$220,000 - \$170,000 = \$50,000$$
$$\Delta D_3 = \$76,000 - \$12,000 = \$64,000$$
$$T = 0.40$$

Substituting into the equation yields

$$ICI_3 = [\$50,000 \times (1 - 0.40)] + (\$64,000 \times 0.40)$$
$$= \$30,000 + \$25,600 = \underline{\$55,600}$$

The $55,600 of incremental cash inflow for year 3 is the same value as that calculated for year 3 in column 3 of Table 8.9.

REVIEW QUESTIONS

8–13 How does depreciation enter into the calculation of operating cash inflows? How does the income statement format in Table 8.7 relate to Equation 3.4 (on page 114) for finding operating cash flow (OCF)?

8–14 How are the *incremental (relevant) operating cash inflows* that are associated with a replacement decision calculated?

8.5 | Finding the Terminal Cash Flow

Terminal cash flow is the cash flow resulting from termination and liquidation of a project at the end of its economic life. It represents the after-tax cash flow, exclusive of operating cash inflows, that occurs in the final year of the project. When it applies, this flow can significantly affect the capital expenditure decision. Terminal cash flow can be calculated for replacement projects by using the basic format presented in Table 8.10.

Proceeds from Sale of Assets

The proceeds from sale of the new and the old asset, often called "salvage value," represent the amount *net of any removal or cleanup costs* expected upon termination of the project. For replacement projects, proceeds from both the new asset and the old asset must be considered. For expansion and renewal types of capital expenditures, the proceeds from the old asset are zero. Of course, it is not unusual for the value of an asset to be zero at the termination of a project.

Taxes on Sale of Assets

Earlier we calculated the tax on sale of old asset (as part of finding the initial investment). Similarly, taxes must be considered on the terminal sale of both the new and the old asset for replacement projects and on only the new asset in other cases. The tax calculations apply whenever an asset is sold for a value different from its book value. If the net proceeds from the sale are expected to exceed book value, a tax payment shown as an *outflow* (deduction from sale proceeds) will

TABLE 8.10	**The Basic Format for Determining Terminal Cash Flow**

	After-tax proceeds from sale of new asset =
	Proceeds from sale of new asset
	∓ Tax on sale of new asset
−	After-tax proceeds from sale of old asset =
	Proceeds from sale of old asset
	∓ Tax on sale of old asset
±	**Change in net working capital**
	Terminal cash flow

occur. When the net proceeds from the sale are less than book value, a tax rebate shown as a cash *inflow* (addition to sale proceeds) will result. For assets sold to net exactly book value, no taxes will be due.

Change in Net Working Capital

When we calculated the initial investment, we took into account any change in net working capital that is attributable to the new asset. Now, when we calculate the terminal cash flow, the change in net working capital represents the reversion of any initial net working capital investment. Most often, this will show up as a cash inflow due to the reduction in net working capital; with termination of the project, the need for the increased net working capital investment is assumed to end.[14] Because the net working capital investment is in no way consumed, the amount recovered at termination will equal the amount shown in the calculation of the initial investment.[15] Tax considerations are not involved.

Calculating the terminal cash flow involves the same procedures as those used to find the initial investment. In the following example, the terminal cash flow is calculated for a replacement decision.

Example

Continuing with the Powell Corporation example, assume that the firm expects to be able to liquidate the new machine at the end of its 5-year usable life to net $50,000 after paying removal and cleanup costs. The old machine can be liquidated at the end of the 5 years to net $10,000. The firm expects to recover its $17,000 net working capital investment upon termination of the project. The firm pays taxes at a rate of 40%.

From the analysis of the operating cash inflows presented earlier, we can see that the proposed (new) machine will have a book value of $20,000 (equal to the year-6 depreciation) at the end of 5 years. The present (old) machine will be fully depreciated and therefore have a book value of zero at the end of the 5 years. Because the sale price of $50,000 for the proposed (new) machine is below its initial installed cost of $400,000 but greater than its book value of $20,000, taxes will have to be paid only on the recaptured depreciation of $30,000 ($50,000 sale proceeds − $20,000 book value). Applying the ordinary tax rate of 40% to this $30,000 results in a tax of $12,000 (0.40 × $30,000) on the sale of the proposed machine. Its after-tax sale proceeds would therefore equal $38,000 ($50,000 sale proceeds − $12,000 taxes). Because the present machine would net $10,000 at termination, which is less than its original purchase price of $240,000 and above its book value of zero, it would experience a taxable gain of $10,000 ($10,000 sale price − $0 book value). Applying the 40% tax rate to the $10,000 gain, the firm will have to pay a tax of $4,000 (0.40 × $10,000) on the sale of the present machine at the end of year 5. Its after-tax sale proceeds from the present machine would therefore equal $6,000 ($10,000 sale price − $4,000 taxes). Substituting

---

14. As noted earlier, the change in net working capital is for convenience assumed to occur instantaneously—in this case, on termination of the project. In actuality, it may take a number of months for the original increase in net working capital to be worked down to zero.

15. In practice, the full net working capital investment may not be recovered. This occurs because some accounts receivable may not be collectible and some inventory will probably be obsolete, so their book values cannot be fully realized.

the appropriate values into the format in Table 8.10 results in the terminal cash inflow of $49,000.

After-tax proceeds from sale of proposed machine		
Proceeds from sale of proposed machine	$50,000	
− Tax on sale of proposed machine	12,000	
Total after-tax proceeds—proposed		$38,000
− After-tax proceeds from sale of present machine		
Proceeds from sale of present machine	$10,000	
− Tax on sale of present machine	4,000	
Total after-tax proceeds—present		6,000
+ Change in net working capital		17,000
Terminal cash flow		$49,000

REVIEW QUESTION

8–15 Explain how the *terminal cash flow* is calculated for replacement projects.

 8.6 | Summarizing the Relevant Cash Flows

Hint Capital expenditures are critical to a firm's success, and these funds are usually limited. Because of this, the process of determining cash flows should be finely tuned so that it is both objective and realistic.

The initial investment, operating cash inflows, and terminal cash flow together represent a project's *relevant cash flows*. These cash flows can be viewed as the incremental after-tax cash flows attributable to the proposed project. They represent, in a cash flow sense, how much better or worse off the firm will be if it chooses to implement the proposal.

Example

The relevant cash flows for Powell Corporation's proposed replacement expenditure can be shown graphically, on a time line. *Note that because the new asset is assumed to be sold at the end of its 5-year usable life, the year-6 incremental operating cash inflow calculated in Table 8.9 has no relevance; the terminal cash flow effectively replaces this value in the analysis.* As the following time line shows, the relevant cash flows follow a *conventional cash flow pattern*.

Time line for Powell Corporation's relevant cash flows with the proposed machine

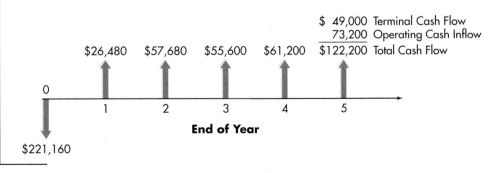

Techniques for analyzing conventional cash flow patterns to determine whether to undertake a proposed capital investment are discussed in Chapter 9.

Personal Finance Example   After receiving a sizable bonus from her employer, Tina Talor is contemplating the purchase of a new car. She feels that by estimating and analyzing its cash flows she could make a more rational decision about whether to make this large purchase. Tina's cash flow estimates for the car purchase are as follows.

Negotiated price of new car	$23,500
Taxes and fees on new car purchase	$1,650
Proceeds from trade-in of old car	$9,750
Estimated value of new car in 3 years	$10,500
Estimated value of old car in 3 years	$5,700
Estimated annual repair costs on new car	0 (in warranty)
Estimated annual repair costs on old car	$400

Using the cash flow estimates, Tina calculates the initial investment, operating cash inflows, terminal cash flow, and a summary of all cash flows for the car purchase.

Initial Investment

Total cost of new car		
Cost of car	$23,500	
+ Taxes and fees	1,650	$25,150
− Proceeds from sale of old car		9,750
Initial investment		$15,400

Operating Cash Inflows	**Year 1**	**Year 2**	**Year 3**
Cost of repairs on new car	$ 0	$ 0	$ 0
− Cost of repairs on old car	400	400	400
Operating cash inflows (savings)	$400	$400	$400

Terminal Cash Flow—End of Year 3

Proceeds from sale of new car	$10,500
− Proceeds from sale of old car	5,700
Terminal cash flow	$ 4,800

Summary of Cash Flows

End of Year	Cash Flow	
0	−$15,400	
1	+ 400	
2	+ 400	
3	+ 5,200	($400 + $4,800)

The cash flows associated with Tina's car purchase decision reflect her net costs of the new car over the assumed 3-year ownership period, but they ignore the many intangible benefits of owning a car. Whereas the fuel cost and basic transportation service provided are assumed to be the same with the new car as with the old car, Tina will have to decide if the cost of moving up to a new car can be justified in terms of intangibles, such as luxury and prestige.

REVIEW QUESTION

8–16 Diagram and describe the three components of the relevant cash flows for a capital budgeting project.

Summary

Focus on Value

A key responsibility of financial managers is to review and analyze proposed investment decisions to make sure that the firm undertakes only those that contribute positively to the value of the firm. Utilizing a variety of tools and techniques, financial managers estimate the cash flows that a proposed investment will generate and then apply decision techniques to assess the investment's impact on the firm's value. The most difficult and important aspect of this capital budgeting process is developing good estimates of the relevant cash flows.

The relevant cash flows are the incremental after-tax cash flows resulting from a proposed investment. These estimates represent the cash flow benefits that are likely to accrue to the firm as a result of implementing the investment. By applying to the cash flows decision techniques that capture the time value of money and risk factors, the financial manager can estimate how the investment will affect the firm's share price. Consistent application of capital budgeting procedures to proposed long-term investments should therefore allow the firm to **maximize its stock price**.

Review of Learning Goals

LG 1 **Understand the key motives for capital expenditure and the steps in the capital budgeting process.** Capital budgeting is the process used to evaluate and select capital expenditures. Capital expenditures are long-term investments made to expand operations, replace or renew fixed assets, or to obtain some other, less tangible benefit over a long period. The capital budgeting process includes five distinct but interrelated steps: proposal generation, review and analysis, decision making, implementation, and follow-up.

LG 2 **Define basic capital budgeting terminology.** Capital expenditure proposals may be independent or mutually exclusive. Typically, firms have only limited funds for capital investments and must ration them among projects. Two basic capital budgeting approaches are the accept–reject approach and the ranking approach. Conventional cash flow patterns consist of an initial outflow followed by a series of inflows; any other pattern is nonconventional.

LG 3 **Discuss relevant cash flows, expansion versus replacement decisions, sunk costs and opportunity costs, and international capital budgeting.** The relevant cash flows for capital budgeting decisions are the initial investment, the operating cash inflows, and the terminal cash flow. For replacement decisions, these flows are the difference between the cash flows of the new asset and the old asset. Expansion decisions are viewed as replacement decisions in which all cash flows from the old asset are zero. When estimating relevant cash flows, ignore sunk costs and include opportunity costs as cash outflows. In international capital budgeting, currency risks and political risks can be minimized through careful planning.

LG 4 **Calculate the initial investment associated with a proposed capital expenditure.** The initial investment is the initial outflow required, taking into account the installed cost of the new asset, the after-tax proceeds from the sale of the old asset, and any change in net working capital. The initial investment is reduced by finding the after-tax proceeds from sale of the old asset. The book value of an asset is used to determine the taxes owed as a result of its sale. Either of two forms of taxable income—a gain or a loss—can result from sale of an asset, depending on whether the asset is sold for (1) more than book value, (2) book value, or (3) less than book value. The change in net working capital is the difference between the change in current assets and the change in current liabilities expected to accompany a given capital expenditure.

LG 5 **Find the relevant operating cash inflows associated with a proposed capital expenditure.** The operating cash inflows are the incremental after-tax cash inflows expected to result from a project. The income statement format involves adding depreciation back to net operating profit after taxes and gives the operating cash inflows, which are the same as operating cash flows (OCF), associated with the proposed and present projects. The relevant (incremental) cash inflows for a replacement project are the difference between the operating cash inflows of the proposed project and those of the present project.

LG 6 **Determine the terminal cash flow associated with a proposed capital expenditure.** The terminal cash flow represents the after-tax cash flow (exclusive of operating cash inflows) that is expected from liquidation of a project. It is calculated for replacement projects by finding the difference between the after-tax proceeds from sale of the new and the old asset at termination and then adjusting this difference for any change in net working capital. Sale price and depreciation data are used to find the taxes and the after-tax sale proceeds on the new and old assets. The change in net working capital typically represents the reversion of any initial net working capital investment.

Self-Test Problems (Solutions in Appendix B)

ST8–1 **Book value, taxes, and initial investment** Irvin Enterprises is considering the purchase of a new piece of equipment to replace the current equipment. The new equipment costs $75,000 and requires $5,000 in installation costs. It will be depreciated under MACRS using a 5-year recovery period. The old piece of equipment was purchased 4 years ago for an installed cost of $50,000; it was being depreciated under MACRS using a 5-year recovery period. The old equipment can be sold today for $55,000 net of any removal or cleanup costs. As a result of the proposed replacement,

the firm's investment in net working capital is expected to increase by $15,000. The firm pays taxes at a rate of 40%. (Table 3.2 on page 108 contains the applicable MACRS depreciation percentages.)

a. Calculate the book value of the old piece of equipment.

b. Determine the taxes, if any, attributable to the sale of the old equipment.

c. Find the *initial investment* associated with the proposed equipment replacement.

   ST8–2 **Determining relevant cash flows**   A machine currently in use was originally purchased 2 years ago for $40,000. The machine is being depreciated under MACRS using a 5-year recovery period; it has 3 years of usable life remaining. The current machine can be sold today to net $42,000 after removal and cleanup costs. A new machine, using a 3-year MACRS recovery period, can be purchased at a price of $140,000. It requires $10,000 to install and has a 3-year usable life. If the new machine is acquired, the investment in accounts receivable will be expected to rise by $10,000, the inventory investment will increase by $25,000, and accounts payable will increase by $15,000. *Earnings before depreciation, interest, and taxes* are expected to be $70,000 for each of the next 3 years with the old machine and to be $120,000 in the first year and $130,000 in the second and third years with the new machine. At the end of 3 years, the market value of the old machine will equal zero, but the new machine could be sold to net $35,000 before taxes. The firm is subject to a 40% tax rate. (Table 3.2 on page 108 contains the applicable MACRS depreciation percentages.)

a. Determine the *initial investment* associated with the proposed replacement decision.

b. Calculate the *incremental operating cash inflows* for years 1 to 4 associated with the proposed replacement. (*Note:* Only depreciation cash flows must be considered in year 4.)

c. Calculate the *terminal cash flow* associated with the proposed replacement decision. (*Note:* This is at the end of year 3.)

d. Depict on a time line the relevant cash flows found in parts **a, b,** and **c** that are associated with the proposed replacement decision, assuming that it is terminated at the end of year 3.

Warm-Up Exercises   A blue box (■) indicates exercises available in .

 E8–1 If Halley Industries reimburses employees who earn master's degrees and who agree to remain with the firm for an additional 3 years, should the expense of the tuition reimbursement be categorized as a *capital expenditure* or an *operating expenditure?*

 E8–2 Canvas Reproductions, Inc., is considering two mutually exclusive investments. Project A requires an initial outlay of $20,000 and has expected cash inflows of $5,000 for each of the next 5 years. Project B requires an initial outlay of $25,000 and has expected cash inflows of $6,500 for each of the following 5 years. Use a simple rate of return measure to determine which project the company should choose.

E8–3 Iridium Corp. has spent $3.5 billion over the past decade developing a satellite-based telecommunication system. It is currently trying to decide whether to spend an additional $350 million on the project. The firm expects that this outlay will finish the project and will generate cash flow of $15 million per year over the next 5 years. A competitor has offered $450 million for the satellites already in orbit. Classify the firm's outlays as *sunk costs* or *opportunity costs,* and specify the *relevant cash flows.*

E8–4 A few years ago, Largo Industries implemented an inventory auditing system at an installed cost of $175,000. Since then, it has taken depreciation deductions totalling $124,250. What is the system's current *book value*? If Largo sold the system for $110,000, how much *recaptured depreciation* would result?

E8–5 Bryson Sciences is planning to purchase a high-powered microscopy machine for $55,000 and incur an additional $7,500 in installation expenses. It is replacing similar microscopy equipment that can be sold to net $35,000, resulting in taxes from a gain on the sale of $11,250. Because of this transaction, current assets will increase by $6,000 and current liabilities will increase by $4,000. Calculate the *initial investment* in the high-powered microscopy machine.

Problems

A blue box (■) indicates problems available in [myfinancelab].

P8–1 **Classification of expenditures**   Given the following list of outlays, indicate whether each is normally considered a *capital expenditure* or an *operating expenditure.* Explain your answers.
a. An initial lease payment of $5,000 for electronic point-of-sale cash register systems.
b. An outlay of $20,000 to purchase patent rights from an inventor.
c. An outlay of $80,000 for a major research and development program.
d. An $80,000 investment in a portfolio of marketable securities.
e. A $300 outlay for an office machine.
f. An outlay of $2,000 for a new machine tool.
g. An outlay of $240,000 for a new building.
h. An outlay of $1,000 for a marketing research report.

P8–2 **Basic terminology**   A firm is considering the following three separate situations.

Situation A   Build either a small office building or a convenience store on a parcel of land located in a high-traffic area. Adequate funding is available, and both projects are known to be acceptable. The office building requires an initial investment of $620,000 and is expected to provide operating cash inflows of $40,000 per year for 20 years. The convenience store is expected to cost $500,000 and to provide a growing stream of operating cash inflows over its 20-year life. The initial operating cash inflow is $20,000, and it will increase by 5% each year.

Situation B   Replace a machine with a new one that requires a $60,000 initial investment and will provide operating cash inflows of $10,000 per year for the first 5 years. At the end of year 5, a machine overhaul costing $20,000 will be required.

After it is completed, expected operating cash inflows will be $10,000 in year 6; $7,000 in year 7; $4,000 in year 8; and $1,000 in year 9, at the end of which the machine will be scrapped.

Situation C   Invest in any or all of the four machines whose relevant cash flows are given in the following table. The firm has $500,000 budgeted to fund these machines, all of which are known to be acceptable. The initial investment for each machine is $250,000.

	Operating cash inflows			
Year	Machine 1	Machine 2	Machine 3	Machine 4
1	$ 50,000	$70,000	$65,000	$90,000
2	70,000	70,000	65,000	80,000
3	90,000	70,000	80,000	70,000
4	− 30,000	70,000	80,000	60,000
5	100,000	70,000	− 20,000	50,000

For each situation, indicate:
a. Whether the projects involved are independent or mutually exclusive.
b. Whether the availability of funds is unlimited or capital rationing exists.
c. Whether accept–reject or ranking decisions are required.
d. Whether each project's cash flows are conventional or nonconventional.

P8–3   Relevant cash flow pattern fundamentals   For each of the following projects, determine the *relevant cash flows*, classify the cash flow pattern, and depict the cash flows on a time line.
a. A project that requires an initial investment of $120,000 and will generate annual operating cash inflows of $25,000 for the next 18 years. In each of the 18 years, maintenance of the project will require a $5,000 cash outflow.
b. A new machine with an installed cost of $85,000. Sale of the old machine will yield $30,000 after taxes. Operating cash inflows generated by the replacement will exceed the operating cash inflows of the old machine by $20,000 in each year of a 6-year period. At the end of year 6, liquidation of the new machine will yield $20,000 after taxes, which is $10,000 greater than the after-tax proceeds expected from the old machine had it been retained and liquidated at the end of year 6.
c. An asset that requires an initial investment of $2 million and will yield annual operating cash inflows of $300,000 for each of the next 10 years. Operating cash outlays will be $20,000 for each year except year 6, when an overhaul requiring an additional cash outlay of $500,000 will be required. The asset's liquidation value at the end of year 10 is expected to be zero.

P8–4   Expansion versus replacement cash flows   Edison Systems has estimated the cash flows over the 5-year lives for two projects, A and B. These cash flows are summarized in the table on page 408.
a. If project A were actually a *replacement* for project B and if the $12,000 initial investment shown for project B were the after-tax cash inflow expected from liquidating it, what would be the *relevant cash flows* for this replacement decision?

b. How can an *expansion decision* such as project A be viewed as a special form of a replacement decision? Explain.

	Project A	Project B
Initial investment	$40,000	$12,000[a]
Year	Operating cash inflows	
1	$10,000	$ 6,000
2	12,000	6,000
3	14,000	6,000
4	16,000	6,000
5	10,000	6,000

[a]After-tax cash inflow expected from liquidation.

P8-5 **Sunk costs and opportunity costs**   Masters Golf Products, Inc., spent 3 years and $1,000,000 to develop its new line of club heads to replace a line that is becoming obsolete. To begin manufacturing them, the company will have to invest $1,800,000 in new equipment. The new clubs are expected to generate an increase in operating cash inflows of $750,000 per year for the next 10 years. The company has determined that the existing line could be sold to a competitor for $250,000.
a. How should the $1,000,000 in development costs be classified?
b. How should the $250,000 sale price for the existing line be classified?
c. Depict all of the known relevant cash flows on a time line.

P8-6 **Sunk costs and opportunity costs**   Covol Industries is developing the relevant cash flows associated with the proposed replacement of an existing machine tool with a new, technologically advanced one. Given the following costs related to the proposed project, explain whether each would be treated as a *sunk cost* or an *opportunity cost* in developing the relevant cash flows associated with the proposed replacement decision.
a. Covol would be able to use the same tooling, which had a book value of $40,000, on the new machine tool as it had used on the old one.
b. Covol would be able to use its existing computer system to develop programs for operating the new machine tool. The old machine tool did not require these programs. Although the firm's computer has excess capacity available, the capacity could be leased to another firm for an annual fee of $17,000.
c. Covol would have to obtain additional floor space to accommodate the larger new machine tool. The space that would be used is currently being leased to another company for $10,000 per year.
d. Covol would use a small storage facility to store the increased output of the new machine tool. The storage facility was built by Covol 3 years earlier at a cost of $120,000. Because of its unique configuration and location, it is currently of no use to either Covol or any other firm.
e. Covol would retain an existing overhead crane, which it had planned to sell for its $180,000 market value. Although the crane was not needed with the old machine tool, it would be used to position raw materials on the new machine tool.

PERSONAL FINANCE PROBLEM

P8–7 **Sunk and opportunity cash flows**   Dave and Ann Stone have been living at their present home for the past 6 years. During that time, they have replaced the water heater for $375, replaced the dishwasher for $599, and have had to make miscellaneous repair and maintenance expenditures of approximately $1,500. They have decided to move out and rent the house for $975 per month. Newspaper advertising will cost $75. Dave and Ann intend to paint the interior of the home and power-wash the exterior. They estimate that that will run about $900.

   The house should be ready to rent after that. In reviewing the financial situation, Dave views all the expenditures as being relevant, and so he plans to net out the estimated expenditures discussed above from the rental income.

   a. Do Dave and Ann understand the difference between *sunk costs* and *opportunity costs?* Explain the two concepts to them.

   b. Which of the expenditures should be classified as sunk cash flows and which should be viewed as opportunity cash flows?

P8–8 **Book value**   Find the book value for each of the assets shown in the following table, assuming that MACRS depreciation is being used. (*Note:* See Table 3.2 on page 108 for the applicable depreciation percentages.)

Asset	Installed cost	Recovery period (years)	Elapsed time since purchase (years)
A	$ 950,000	5	3
B	40,000	3	1
C	96,000	5	4
D	350,000	5	1
E	1,500,000	7	5

P8–9 **Book value and taxes on sale of assets**   Troy Industries purchased a new machine 3 years ago for $80,000. It is being depreciated under MACRS with a 5-year recovery period using the percentages given in Table 3.2 on page 108. Assume a 40% tax rate.

   a. What is the *book value* of the machine?

   b. Calculate the firm's tax liability if it sold the machine for each of the following amounts: $100,000; $56,000; $23,200; and $15,000.

P8–10 **Tax calculations**   For each of the following cases, determine the total taxes resulting from the transaction. Assume a 40% tax rate. The asset was purchased 2 years ago for $200,000 and is being depreciated under MACRS using a 5-year recovery period. (See Table 3.2 on page 108 for the applicable depreciation percentages.)

   a. The asset is sold for $220,000.

   b. The asset is sold for $150,000.

   c. The asset is sold for $96,000.

   d. The asset is sold for $80,000.

P8–11 **Change in net working capital calculation**   Samuels Manufacturing is considering the purchase of a new machine to replace one it believes is obsolete. The firm has total current assets of $920,000 and total current liabilities of $640,000. As a result of the proposed replacement, the following *changes* are anticipated in the levels of the current asset and current liability accounts noted.

Account	Change
Accruals	+ $ 40,000
Marketable securities	0
Inventories	− 10,000
Accounts payable	+ 90,000
Notes payable	0
Accounts receivable	+ 150,000
Cash	+ 15,000

a. Using the information given, calculate any *change in net working capital* that is expected to result from the proposed replacement action.

b. Explain why a change in these current accounts would be relevant in determining the *initial investment* for the proposed capital expenditure.

c. Would the change in net working capital enter into any of the other cash flow components that make up the relevant cash flows? Explain.

P8–12 **Calculating initial investment**   Vastine Medical, Inc., is considering replacing its existing computer system, which was purchased 2 years ago at a cost of $325,000. The system can be sold today for $200,000. It is being depreciated using MACRS and a 5-year recovery period (see Table 3.2, page 108). A new computer system will cost $500,000 to purchase and install. Replacement of the computer system would not involve any change in net working capital. Assume a 40% tax rate.

a. Calculate the *book value* of the existing computer system.

b. Calculate the after-tax proceeds of its sale for $200,000.

c. Calculate the *initial investment* associated with the replacement project.

P8–13 **Initial investment—Basic calculation**   Cushing Corporation is considering the purchase of a new grading machine to replace the existing one. The existing machine was purchased 3 years ago at an installed cost of $20,000; it was being depreciated under MACRS using a 5-year recovery period. (See Table 3.2 on page 108 for the applicable depreciation percentages.) The existing machine is expected to have a usable life of at least 5 more years. The new machine costs $35,000 and requires $5,000 in installation costs; it will be depreciated using a 5-year recovery period under MACRS. The existing machine can currently be sold for $25,000 without incurring any removal or cleanup costs. The firm is subject to a 40% tax rate. Calculate the *initial investment* associated with the proposed purchase of a new grading machine.

P8–14 **Initial investment at various sale prices**   Edwards Manufacturing Company (EMC) is considering replacing one machine with another. The old machine was purchased 3 years ago for an installed cost of $10,000. The firm is depreciating the machine under MACRS, using a 5-year recovery period. (See Table 3.2 on page 108 for the applicable depreciation percentages.) The new machine costs $24,000 and requires $2,000 in installation costs. The firm is subject to a 40% tax rate. In each of the following cases, calculate the *initial investment* for the replacement.

a. EMC sells the old machine for $11,000.
b. EMC sells the old machine for $7,000.
c. EMC sells the old machine for $2,900.
d. EMC sells the old machine for $1,500.

P8–15 **Calculating initial investment**   DuPree Coffee Roasters, Inc., wishes to expand and modernize its facilities. The installed cost of a proposed computer-controlled automatic-feed roaster will be $130,000. The firm has a chance to sell its 4-year-old roaster for $35,000. The existing roaster originally cost $60,000 and was being depreciated using MACRS and a 7-year recovery period (see Table 3.2 on page 108). DuPree is subject to a 40% tax rate.

a. What is the *book value* of the existing roaster?
b. Calculate the after-tax proceeds of the sale of the existing roaster.
c. Calculate the *change in net working capital* using the following figures:

Anticipated Changes in Current Assets and Current Liabilities	
Accruals	−$20,000
Inventory	+ 50,000
Accounts payable	+ 40,000
Accounts receivable	+ 70,000
Cash	0
Notes payable	+ 15,000

d. Calculate the *initial investment* associated with the proposed new roaster.

P8–16 **Depreciation**   A firm is evaluating the acquisition of an asset that costs $64,000 and requires $4,000 in installation costs. If the firm depreciates the asset under MACRS, using a 5-year recovery period (see Table 3.2 on page 108 for the applicable depreciation percentages), determine the depreciation charge for each year.

P8–17 **Incremental operating cash inflows**   A firm is considering renewing its equipment to meet increased demand for its product. The cost of equipment modifications is $1.9 million plus $100,000 in installation costs. The firm will depreciate the equipment modifications under MACRS, using a 5-year recovery period. (See Table 3.2 on page 108 for the applicable depreciation percentages.) Additional sales revenue from the renewal should amount to $1.2 million per year, and additional operating expenses and other costs (excluding depreciation and interest) will amount to 40% of the additional sales. The firm is subject to a tax rate of 40%. (*Note:* Answer the following questions for each of the next 6 *years*.)

a. What incremental earnings before depreciation, interest, and taxes will result from the renewal?
b. What incremental net operating profits after taxes will result from the renewal?
c. What *incremental operating cash inflows* will result from the renewal?

PERSONAL FINANCE PROBLEM

P8–18 **Incremental operating cash flows**   Richard and Linda Thomson operate a local lawn maintenance service for commercial and residential property. They have been using a John Deere riding mower for the past several years and feel it is time to buy a new one. They would like to know the incremental (relevant) cash flows associated with the replacement of the old riding mower. The following data are available.

There are 5 years of remaining useful life on the old mower.

The old mower has a zero book value.

The new mower is expected to last 5 years.

The Thomsons will follow a 5-year MACRS recovery period for the new mower.

Depreciable value of the new law mower is $1,800.

They are subject to a 40% tax rate.

The new mower is expected to be more fuel-efficient, maneuverable, and durable than previous models and can result in reduced operating expenses of $500 per year.

The Thomsons will buy a maintenance contract that calls for annual payments of $120.

Create and *incremental operating cash flow* statement for the replacement of Richard and Linda's John Deere riding mower. Show the incremental operating cash flow for the next 6 years.

P8–19 **Incremental operating cash inflows—Expense reduction**   Miller Corporation is considering replacing a machine. The replacement will reduce operating expenses (that is, increase earnings before depreciation, interest, and taxes) by $16,000 per year for each of the 5 years the new machine is expected to last. Although the old machine has zero book value, it can be used for 5 more years. The depreciable value of the new machine is $48,000. The firm will depreciate the machine under MACRS using a 5-year recovery period (see Table 3.2 on page 108 for the applicable depreciation percentages) and is subject to a 40% tax rate. Estimate the *incremental operating cash inflows* generated by the replacement. (*Note:* Be sure to consider the depreciation in year 6.)

P8–20 **Incremental operating cash inflows**   Strong Tool Company has been considering purchasing a new lathe to replace a fully depreciated lathe that will last 5 more years. The new lathe is expected to have a 5-year life and depreciation charges of $2,000 in year 1; $3,200 in year 2; $1,900 in year 3; $1,200 in both year 4 and year 5; and $500 in year 6. The firm estimates the revenues and expenses (excluding depreciation and interest) for the new and the old lathes to be as shown in the following table. The firm is subject to a 40% tax rate.

	New lathe		Old lathe	
Year	Revenue	Expenses (excl. depr. and int.)	Revenue	Expenses (excl. depr. and int.)
1	$40,000	$30,000	$35,000	$25,000
2	41,000	30,000	35,000	25,000
3	42,000	30,000	35,000	25,000
4	43,000	30,000	35,000	25,000
5	44,000	30,000	35,000	25,000

a. Calculate the *operating cash inflows* associated with each lathe. (*Note:* Be sure to consider the depreciation in year 6.)

b. Calculate the *incremental (relevant) operating cash inflows* resulting from the proposed lathe replacement.

c. Depict on a time line the incremental operating cash inflows calculated in part **b.**

P8–21   **Determining incremental operating cash inflows**   Scenic Tours, Inc., is a provider of bus tours throughout the New England area. The corporation is considering the replacement of 10 of its older buses. The existing buses were purchased 4 years ago at a total cost of $2,700,000 and are being depreciated using MACRS and a 5-year recovery period (see Table 3.2, page 108). The new buses would have larger passenger capacity and better fuel efficiency as well as lower maintenance costs. The total cost for 10 new buses is $3,000,000. Like the older buses, the new ones would be depreciated using MACRS and a 5-year recovery period. Scenic is subject to a tax rate of 40%. The following table presents revenues and cash expenses (excluding depreciation and interest) for the proposed purchase as well as the present fleet. Use all of the information given to calculate *incremental (relevant) operating cash inflows* for the proposed bus replacement.

	Year					
	1	2	3	4	5	6
With the proposed new buses						
Revenue	$1,850,000	$1,850,000	$1,830,000	$1,825,000	$1,815,000	$1,800,000
Expenses (excl. depr. and int.)	460,000	460,000	468,000	472,000	485,000	500,000
With the present buses						
Revenue	$1,800,000	$1,800,000	$1,790,000	$1,785,000	$1,775,000	$1,750,000
Expenses (excl. depr. and int.)	500,000	510,000	520,000	520,000	530,000	535,000

P8–22   **Terminal cash flow—Various lives and sale prices**   Looner Industries is currently analyzing the purchase of a new machine that costs $160,000 and requires $20,000 in installation costs. Purchase of this machine is expected to result in an increase in net working capital of $30,000 to support the expanded level of operations. The firm plans to depreciate the machine under MACRS using a 5-year recovery period (see Table 3.2 on page 108 for the applicable depreciation percentages) and expects to sell the machine to net $10,000 before taxes at the end of its usable life. The firm is subject to a 40% tax rate.

a. Calculate the *terminal cash flow* for a usable life of (1) 3 years, (2) 5 years, and (3) 7 years.

b. Discuss the effect of usable life on terminal cash flows using your findings in part **a.**

c. Assuming a 5-year usable life, calculate the terminal cash flow if the machine were sold to net (1) $9,000 or (2) $170,000 (before taxes) at the end of 5 years.

d. Discuss the effect of sale price on terminal cash flow using your findings in part **c.**

P8–23   **Terminal cash flow—Replacement decision**   Russell Industries is considering replacing a fully depreciated machine that has a remaining useful life of 10 years with a newer, more sophisticated machine. The new machine will cost $200,000

and will require $30,000 in installation costs. It will be depreciated under MACRS using a 5-year recovery period (see Table 3.2 on page 108 for the applicable depreciation percentages). A $25,000 increase in net working capital will be required to support the new machine. The firm's managers plan to evaluate the potential replacement over a 4-year period. They estimate that the old machine could be sold at the end of 4 years to net $15,000 before taxes; the new machine at the end of 4 years will be worth $75,000 before taxes. Calculate the *terminal cash flow* at the end of year 4 that is relevant to the proposed purchase of the new machine. The firm is subject to a 40% tax rate.

   P8–24 **Relevant cash flows for a marketing campaign**   Marcus Tube, a manufacturer of high-quality aluminum tubing, has maintained stable sales and profits over the past 10 years. Although the market for aluminum tubing has been expanding by 3% per year, Marcus has been unsuccessful in sharing this growth. To increase its sales, the firm is considering an aggressive marketing campaign that centers on regularly running ads in all relevant trade journals and exhibiting products at all major regional and national trade shows. The campaign is expected to require an *annual* tax-deductible expenditure of $150,000 over the next 5 years. Sales revenue, as shown in the income statement for 2009 below, totaled $20,000,000. If the proposed marketing campaign is not initiated, sales are expected to remain at this level in each of the next 5 years, 2010–2014. With the marketing campaign, sales are expected to rise to the levels shown in the accompanying table for each of the next 5 years; cost of goods sold is expected to remain at 80% of sales; general and administrative expense (exclusive of any marketing campaign outlays) is expected to remain at 10% of sales; and annual depreciation expense is expected to remain at $500,000. Assuming a 40% tax rate, find the *relevant cash flows* over the next 5 years associated with the proposed marketing campaign.

Marcus Tube Income Statement for the Year Ended December 31, 2009		
Sales revenue		$20,000,000
Less: Cost of goods sold (80%)		16,000,000
Gross profits		$ 4,000,000
Less: Operating expenses		
General and administrative expense (10%)	$2,000,000	
Depreciation expense	500,000	
Total operating expense		2,500,000
Earnings before interest and taxes		$ 1,500,000
Less: Taxes (rate = 40%)		600,000
Net operating profit after taxes		$ 900,000

Marcus Tube Sales Forecast	
Year	Sales revenue
2010	$20,500,000
2011	21,000,000
2012	21,500,000
2013	22,500,000
2014	23,500,000

  P8–25 **Relevant cash flows—No terminal value**   Central Laundry and Cleaners is considering replacing an existing piece of machinery with a more sophisticated machine. The old machine was purchased 3 years ago at a cost of $50,000, and this amount was being depreciated under MACRS using a 5-year recovery period. The machine has 5 years of usable life remaining. The new machine that is being considered costs $76,000 and requires $4,000 in installation costs. The new machine would be depreciated under MACRS using a 5-year recovery period. The firm can currently sell the old machine for $55,000 without incurring any removal or cleanup costs. The firm is subject to a tax rate of 40%. The revenues and expenses (excluding depreciation and interest) associated with the new and the old machines for the next 5 years are given in the table below. (Table 3.2 on page 108 contains the applicable MACRS depreciation percentages.)

	New machine		Old machine	
Year	Revenue	Expenses (excl. depr. and int.)	Revenue	Expenses (excl. depr. and int.)
1	$750,000	$720,000	$674,000	$660,000
2	750,000	720,000	676,000	660,000
3	750,000	720,000	680,000	660,000
4	750,000	720,000	678,000	660,000
5	750,000	720,000	674,000	660,000

a. Calculate the *initial investment* associated with replacement of the old machine by the new one.
b. Determine the *incremental operating cash inflows* associated with the proposed replacement. (*Note:* Be sure to consider the depreciation in year 6.)
c. Depict on a time line the *relevant cash flows* found in parts **a** and **b** associated with the proposed replacement decision.

P8–26 **Integrative—Determining relevant cash flows** Lombard Company is contemplating the purchase of a new high-speed widget grinder to replace the existing grinder. The existing grinder was purchased 2 years ago at an installed cost of $60,000; it was being depreciated under MACRS using a 5-year recovery period. The existing grinder is expected to have a usable life of 5 more years. The new grinder costs $105,000 and requires $5,000 in installation costs; it has a 5-year usable life and would be depreciated under MACRS using a 5-year recovery period. Lombard can currently sell the existing grinder for $70,000 without incurring any removal or cleanup costs. To support the increased business resulting from purchase of the new grinder, accounts receivable would increase by $40,000, inventories by $30,000, and accounts payable by $58,000. At the end of 5 years, the existing grinder is expected to have a market value of zero; the new grinder would be sold to net $29,000 after removal and cleanup costs and before taxes. The firm is subject a 40% tax rate. The estimated *earnings before depreciation, interest, and taxes* over the 5 years for both the new and the existing grinder are shown in the following table. (Table 3.2 on page 108 contains the applicable MACRS depreciation percentages.)

	Earnings before depreciation, interest, and taxes	
Year	New grinder	Existing grinder
1	$43,000	$26,000
2	43,000	24,000
3	43,000	22,000
4	43,000	20,000
5	43,000	18,000

a. Calculate the *initial investment* associated with the replacement of the existing grinder by the new one.

b. Determine the *incremental operating cash inflows* associated with the proposed grinder replacement. (*Note:* Be sure to consider the depreciation in year 6.)

c. Determine the *terminal cash flow* expected at the end of year 5 from the proposed grinder replacement.

d. Depict on a time line the *relevant cash flows* associated with the proposed grinder replacement decision.

PERSONAL FINANCE PROBLEM

P8–27 **Determining relevant cash flows for a new boat**   Jan and Deana have been dreaming about owning a boat for some time and have decided that estimating its cash flows will help them in their decision process. They expect to have a disposable annual income of $24,000. Their cash flow estimates for the boat purchase are as follows:

Negotiated price of the new boat	$70,000
Sales tax rate (applicable to purchase price)	6.5%
Boat trade-in	0
Estimated value of new boat in 4 years	$40,000
Estimated monthly repair and maintenance	$800
Estimated monthly docking fee	$500

Using these cash flow estimates, calculate the following:

a. The initial investment

b. Operating cash flow

c. Terminal cash flow

d. Summary of annual cash flow

e. Based on their disposable annual income, what advice would you give Jan and Deana regarding the proposed boat purchase?

P8–28 **Integrative—Determining relevant cash flows**   Atlantic Drydock is considering replacing an existing hoist with one of two newer, more efficient pieces of equipment. The existing hoist is 3 years old, cost $32,000, and is being depreciated under MACRS using a 5-year recovery period. Although the existing hoist has only 3 years (years 4, 5, and 6) of depreciation remaining under MACRS, it has a remaining usable life of 5 years. Hoist A, one of the two possible replacement hoists, costs $40,000 to purchase and $8,000 to install. It has a 5-year usable life and will be depreciated under MACRS using a 5-year recovery period. Hoist B costs $54,000 to purchase and $6,000 to install. It also has a 5-year usable life and will be depreciated under MACRS using a 5-year recovery period.

Increased investments in net working capital will accompany the decision to acquire hoist A or hoist B. Purchase of hoist A would result in a $4,000 increase in net working capital; hoist B would result in a $6,000 increase in net working capital. The projected *earnings before depreciation, interest, and taxes* with each alternative hoist and the existing hoist are given in the following table.

| Year | Earnings before depreciation, interest, and taxes | | |
	With hoist A	With hoist B	With existing hoist
1	$21,000	$22,000	$14,000
2	21,000	24,000	14,000
3	21,000	26,000	14,000
4	21,000	26,000	14,000
5	21,000	26,000	14,000

The existing hoist can currently be sold for $18,000 and will not incur any removal or cleanup costs. At the end of 5 years, the existing hoist can be sold to net $1,000 before taxes. Hoists A and B can be sold to net $12,000 and $20,000 before taxes, respectively, at the end of the 5-year period. The firm is subject to a 40% tax rate. (Table 3.2 on page 108 contains the applicable MACRS depreciation percentages.)

a. Calculate the *initial investment* associated with each alternative.
b. Calculate the *incremental operating cash inflows* associated with each alternative. (*Note:* Be sure to consider the depreciation in year 6.)
c. Calculate the *terminal cash flow* at the end of year 5 associated with each alternative.
d. Depict on a time line the *relevant cash flows* associated with each alternative.

 P8–29 **ETHICS PROBLEM**   According to academic research, capital budgeting cash flow projections are used rarely in practice by small firms, which often use accounting projections instead. What is the most likely explanation of this behavior?

Chapter 8 Case

Developing Relevant Cash Flows for Clark Upholstery Company's Machine Renewal or Replacement Decision

Bo Humphries, chief financial officer of Clark Upholstery Company, expects the firm's *net operating profit after taxes* for the next 5 years to be as shown in the following table.

Year	Net operating profit after taxes
1	$100,000
2	150,000
3	200,000
4	250,000
5	320,000

Bo is beginning to develop the relevant cash flows needed to analyze whether to renew or replace Clark's *only* depreciable asset, a machine that originally cost $30,000, has a current book value of zero, and can now be sold for $20,000. (*Note:* Because the firm's only depreciable asset is fully depreciated—its book value is zero—its expected operating cash inflows equal its net operating profit after taxes.) He estimates that at the end of 5 years, the existing machine can be sold to net $2,000 before taxes. Bo plans to use the following information to develop the relevant cash flows for each of the alternatives.

Alternative 1   Renew the existing machine at a total depreciable cost of $90,000. The renewed machine would have a 5-year usable life and would be depreciated under MACRS using a 5-year recovery period. Renewing the machine would result in the following projected revenues and expenses (excluding depreciation and interest):

Year	Revenue	Expenses (excl. depr. and int.)
1	$1,000,000	$801,500
2	1,175,000	884,200
3	1,300,000	918,100
4	1,425,000	943,100
5	1,550,000	968,100

The renewed machine would result in an increased investment in net working capital of $15,000. At the end of 5 years, the machine could be sold to net $8,000 before taxes.

Alternative 2   Replace the existing machine with a new machine that costs $100,000 and requires installation costs of $10,000. The new machine would have a 5-year usable life and would be depreciated under MACRS using a 5-year recovery period. The firm's projected revenues and expenses (excluding depreciation and interest), if it acquires the machine, would be as follows:

Year	Revenue	Expenses (excl. depr. and int.)
1	$1,000,000	$764,500
2	1,175,000	839,800
3	1,300,000	914,900
4	1,425,000	989,900
5	1,550,000	998,900

The new machine would result in an increased investment in net working capital of $22,000. At the end of 5 years, the new machine could be sold to net $25,000 before taxes.

The firm is subject to a 40% tax rate. As noted, the company uses MACRS depreciation. (See Table 3.2 on page 108 for the applicable depreciation percentages.)

To Do

a. Calculate the *initial investment* associated with each of Clark Upholstery's alternatives.

b. Calculate the *incremental operating cash inflows* associated with each of Clark's alternatives. (*Note:* Be sure to consider the depreciation in year 6.)

c. Calculate the *terminal cash flow* at the end of year 5 associated with each of Clark's alternatives.

d. Use your findings in parts **a, b,** and **c** to depict on a time line the *relevant cash flows* associated with each of Clark Upholstery's alternatives.

e. Solely on the basis of your comparison of their relevant cash flows, which alternative appears to be better? Why?

Spreadsheet Exercise

Damon Corporation, a sports equipment manufacturer, has a machine currently in use that was originally purchased 3 years ago for $120,000. The firm depreciates the machine under MACRS using a 5-year recovery period. Once removal and cleanup costs are taken into consideration, the expected net selling price for the present machine will be $70,000.

Damon can buy a new machine for a net price of $160,000 (including installation costs of $15,000). The proposed machine will be depreciated under MACRS using a 5-year recovery period. If the firm acquires the new machine, its working capital needs will change—accounts receivable will increase $15,000, inventory will increase $19,000, and accounts payable will increase $16,000.

Earnings before depreciation, interest, and taxes (EBDIT) for the present machine are expected to be $95,000 for each of the successive 5 years. For the proposed machine, the expected EBDIT for each of the next 5 years are $105,000, $110,000, $120,000, $120,000, and $120,000, respectively. The corporate tax rate (T) for the firm is 40%. (Table 3.2 on page 108 contains the applicable MACRS depreciation percentages.)

Damon expects to be able to liquidate the proposed machine at the end of its 5-year usable life for $24,000 (after paying removal and cleanup costs). The present machine is expected to net $8,000 upon liquidation at the end of the same period. Damon expects to recover its net working capital investment upon termination of the project. The firm is subject to a tax rate of 40%.

To Do

Create a spreadsheet similar to Tables 8.2, 8.6, 8.8, and 8.10 (or the spreadsheets that can be viewed at www.prenhall.com/gitman) to answer the following:

a. Create a spreadsheet to calculate the *initial investment*.

b. Create a spreadsheet to prepare a *depreciation schedule* for both the proposed and the present machine. Both machines are depreciated under MACRS using a 5-year recovery period. Remember, the present machine has only 3 years of depreciation remaining.

c. Create a spreadsheet to calculate the *operating cash inflows* for Damon Corporation for both the proposed and the present machine.

d. Create a spreadsheet to calculate the *terminal cash flow* associated with the project.

Group Exercise

This chapter is the first of a three-chapter section on long-term investment decisions. In this group exercise, your firm will begin analyzing a capital investment decision that you will refine in Chapters 9 and 10. Keep this in mind as you develop a potential investment for your firm. This assignment may appear to be shorter than previous exercises, but spending time to adequately design possible capital investment projects will make the next chapters' work much easier.

To Do

a. Your firm, like most firms, is constantly evaluating potential capital investments. For your first task, you are to design two mutually exclusive capital investment proposals. As part of the design process, you should spend a good deal of time developing the motivation for these projects. You need to fully answer the question of *why* your firm should consider these projects.

b. The next step is to begin reviewing and analyzing these two proposals. This activity will include estimating the relevant cash flows for each of the proposals. Begin with the *initial investment* and then flesh out the *operating cash inflows* and any *terminal cash flow*. As in the text, these cash flows should be organized on an annual basis. Each project should have a minimum useful life of 5 years.

c. To complete the assignment for this chapter, summarize all relevant cash flows on a time line as done in the text.

Web Exercise

Go to the book's companion website at **www.prenhall.com/gitman** to find the Web Exercise for this chapter.

Remember to check the book's website at **www.prenhall.com/gitman** to find additional resources, including Web Exercises and a Web Case.

9 | Capital Budgeting Techniques

WHY THIS CHAPTER MATTERS TO YOU

In Your Professional Life

Accounting: You need to understand capital budgeting techniques to help determine the relevant cash flows associated with proposed capital expenditures.

Information systems: You need to understand capital budgeting techniques to design decision modules that help reduce the amount of work required to analyze proposed capital expenditures.

Management: You need to understand capital budgeting techniques to correctly analyze the relevant cash flows of proposed projects and decide whether to accept or reject them.

Marketing: You need to understand capital budgeting techniques to grasp how proposals for new marketing programs, for new products, and for the expansion of existing product lines will be evaluated by the firm's decision makers.

Operations: You need to understand capital budgeting techniques to know how proposals for the acquisition of new equipment and plants will be evaluated by the firm's decision makers.

In Your Personal Life

You can use some of the capital budgeting techniques used by financial managers to measure either the value of a given asset purchase or its compound rate of return. The IRR technique is widely applied in personal finance to measure both actual and forecast returns on investments in securities, real estate, the true cost of credit card debt, consumer loans, and leases.

LEARNING GOALS

LG 1 Understand the role of capital budgeting techniques in the capital budgeting process.

LG 2 Calculate, interpret, and evaluate the payback period.

LG 3 Calculate, interpret, and evaluate the net present value (NPV).

LG 4 Calculate, interpret, and evaluate the internal rate of return (IRR).

LG 5 Use net present value profiles to compare NPV and IRR techniques.

LG 6 Discuss NPV and IRR in terms of conflicting rankings and the theoretical and practical strengths of each approach.

Apple, Inc.

The iPhone Is Revealed

On January 17, 2007, **Apple, Inc.** introduced the iPhone, which combines a mobile phone, an iPod, and an Internet communications device. The phone's Internet connection allows users to surf the Web over Wi-Fi, access email, watch TV shows and videos, and use Google maps. A new interface allows the user to communicate by touching the screen with a finger. Another feature is that the screen will shift from portrait to landscape view when you simply rotate the device in your hand.

Apple managed to keep the details of the project secret both from the public and its partner **Cingular Wireless,** now the wireless unit of **AT&T.** Several small teams within Cingular worked on the project, but each handled its own specific task without knowing what the other teams were up to. Cingular technical personnel tested the device to make sure that it would work on the carrier's network, but were not allowed to handle or see the actual phone. When it hit the market in mid-2007, the iPhone was sold exclusively by Apple and by AT&T.

Before developing the new phone, Apple had to ensure the project's economic viablility. This involved estimating the cost of developing, manufacturing, and marketing the iPhone, as well as estimating the potential revenue. Apple expects to sell 10 million iPhones through 2008, with price tags of $499 and $599 for two different models. This estimate gives the firm's finance personnel some dollar figures, but there is no guarantee that the sales estimates are accurate.

Estimating development and marketing expenses is more difficult. There is virtually no way to precisely predict the worker-hours that will be sunk into the project. The iPhone development team mushroomed into hundreds of people and involved all levels of the company. One method of estimating development costs is to make reasonable estimates based on similar past projects. In Apple's case, it most likely used information from its development of the iPod several years earlier.

However it develops its estimates of a project's future revenues and expenses, once it has those estimates, a company can use one of several techniques to determine whether a project is acceptable. These capital budgeting techniques are the subject of Chapter 9.

> In addition to the revenues directly provided by the sale of the new iPhone, what other benefits to Apple might be relevant to evaluating the iPhone project?

9.1 | Overview of Capital Budgeting Techniques

When firms have developed relevant cash flows, as demonstrated in Chapter 8, they analyze them to assess whether a project is acceptable or to rank projects. A number of techniques are available for performing such analyses. The preferred approaches integrate time value procedures, risk and return considerations, and valuation concepts to select capital expenditures that are consistent with the firm's goal of maximizing owners' wealth. This chapter focuses on the use of these techniques in an environment of certainty. Chapter 10 covers risk and other refinements in capital budgeting.

Bennett Company's Relevant Cash Flows

We will use one basic problem to illustrate all the techniques described in this chapter. The problem concerns Bennett Company, a medium-sized metal fabricator that is currently contemplating two projects: Project A requires an initial investment of $42,000; project B requires an initial investment of $45,000. The projected relevant cash flows for the two projects are presented in Table 9.1 and depicted on the time lines in Figure 9.1.[1] The projects exhibit *conventional cash flow patterns,* which are assumed throughout the text. In addition, we initially assume that all projects' cash flows have the same level of risk, that projects being compared have equal usable lives, and that the firm has unlimited funds. (The risk assumption will be relaxed in Chapter 10.) We begin with a look at the three most popular capital budgeting techniques: payback period, net present value, and internal rate of return.[2]

Hint Remember that the initial investment is an *outflow* occurring at time zero.

TABLE 9.1	Capital Expenditure Data for Bennett Company	
	Project A	Project B
Initial investment	$42,000	$45,000
Year	Operating cash inflows	
1	$14,000	$28,000
2	14,000	12,000
3	14,000	10,000
4	14,000	10,000
5	14,000	10,000

---

1. For simplification, these 5-year-lived projects with 5 years of cash inflows are used throughout this chapter. Projects with usable lives equal to the number of years of cash inflows are also included in the end-of-chapter problems. Recall from Chapter 8 that under current tax law, MACRS depreciation results in $n + 1$ years of depreciation for an n-year class asset. This means that projects will commonly have at least 1 year of cash flow beyond their recovery period. In actual practice, the usable lives of projects (and the associated cash inflows) may differ significantly from their depreciable lives. Generally, under MACRS, usable lives are longer than depreciable lives.

2. Two other, closely related techniques that are sometimes used to evaluate capital budgeting projects are the *average (or accounting) rate of return (ARR)* and the *profitability index (PI).* The ARR is an unsophisticated technique that is calculated by dividing a project's average profits after taxes by its average investment. Because it fails to consider cash flows and the time value of money, it is ignored here. The PI, sometimes called the *benefit–cost ratio,* is calculated by dividing the present value of cash inflows by the initial investment. This technique, which does consider the time value of money, is sometimes used as a starting point in the selection of projects under *capital rationing;* the more popular NPV and IRR methods are discussed here.

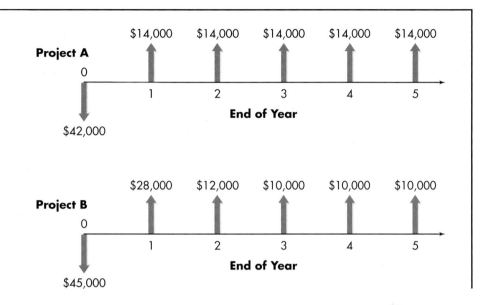

FIGURE 9.1

Bennett Company's Projects A and B
Time lines depicting the conventional cash flows of projects A and B

REVIEW QUESTION

9–1   Once the firm has determined its projects' relevant cash flows, what must it do next? What is its goal in selecting projects?

9.2 | Payback Period

payback period
The amount of time required for a firm to recover its initial investment in a project, as calculated from *cash inflows.*

Payback periods are commonly used to evaluate proposed investments. The **payback period** is the amount of time required for the firm to recover its initial investment in a project, as calculated from *cash inflows.* In the case of an *annuity,* the payback period can be found by dividing the initial investment by the annual cash inflow. For a *mixed stream* of cash inflows, the yearly cash inflows must be accumulated until the initial investment is recovered. Although popular, the payback period is generally viewed as an *unsophisticated capital budgeting technique,* because it does not *explicitly* consider the time value of money.

Decision Criteria

When the payback period is used to make accept–reject decisions, the following decision criteria apply.

- If the payback period is *less than* the maximum acceptable payback period, *accept* the project.
- If the payback period is *greater than* the maximum acceptable payback period, *reject* the project.

The length of the maximum acceptable payback period is determined by management. This value is set *subjectively* on the basis of a number of factors, including the type of project (expansion, replacement or renewal, other), the perceived risk of the project, and the perceived relationship between the payback period and the share value. It is simply a value that management feels, on average, will result in value-creating investment decisions.

Example

We can calculate the payback period for Bennett Company's projects A and B using the data in Table 9.1. *For project A, which is an annuity, the payback period is 3.0 years ($42,000 initial investment ÷ $14,000 annual cash inflow).* Because project B generates a mixed stream of cash inflows, the calculation of its payback period is not as clear-cut. In year 1, the firm will recover $28,000 of its $45,000 initial investment. By the end of year 2, $40,000 ($28,000 from year 1 + $12,000 from year 2) will have been recovered. At the end of year 3, $50,000 will have been recovered. Only 50% of the year-3 cash inflow of $10,000 is needed to complete the payback of the initial $45,000. *The payback period for project B is therefore 2.5 years (2 years + 50% of year 3).*

If Bennett's maximum acceptable payback period were 2.75 years, project A would be rejected and project B would be accepted. If the maximum payback were 2.25 years, both projects would be rejected. If the projects were being ranked, B would be preferred over A, because it has a shorter payback period.

Pros and Cons of Payback Periods

Hint In *all three* of the decision methods presented in this text, the relevant data are *after-tax cash flows.* Accounting profit is used only to help determine the after-tax cash flow.

Hint The payback period indicates to firms taking on projects of high risk how quickly they can recover their investment. In addition, it tells firms with limited sources of capital how quickly the funds invested in a given project will become available for future projects.

Large firms usually use the payback period to evaluate small projects, and small firms use it to evaluate most projects. Its popularity results from its computational simplicity and intuitive appeal. It is also appealing in that it considers cash flows rather than accounting profits. By measuring how quickly the firm recovers its initial investment, the payback period also gives *implicit* consideration to the timing of cash flows and therefore to the time value of money. Because it can be viewed as a measure of *risk exposure,* many firms use the payback period as a decision criterion or as a supplement to other decision techniques. The longer the firm must wait to recover its invested funds, the greater the possibility of a calamity. Therefore, the shorter the payback period, the lower the firm's exposure to such risk.

The major weakness of the payback period is that the appropriate payback period is merely a subjectively determined number. It cannot be specified in light of the wealth maximization goal because it is not based on discounting cash flows to determine whether they add to the firm's value. Instead, the appropriate payback period is simply the maximum acceptable period of time over which management decides that a project's cash flows must break even (that is, just equal the initial investment). The nearby *Focus on Practice* box offers more information about these time limits in actual practice.

Personal Finance Example

Seema Mehdi is considering investing $20,000 in a 5% interest in a rental property. Her good friend and real estate agent, Akbar Ahmed, put the deal together, and he conservatively estimates that Seema should receive between $4,000 and $6,000 per year in cash from her 5% interest in the property. The deal is structured in a way that forces all investors to maintain their investment in the property for at least 10 years. Seema expects to remain in the 25% income-tax bracket for quite a while. In order to be acceptable, Seema requires the investment to pay itself back in terms of after-tax cash flows in less than 7 years.

Focus on Practice   Limits on Payback Analysis

IN PRACTICE

In tough economic times, the standard for a payback period is often reduced. Chief information officers (CIOs) are apt to reject projects with payback periods of more than 2 years. "We start with payback period," says Ron Fijalkowski, CIO at **Strategic Distribution, Inc.** in Bensalem, Pennsylvania. "For sure, if the payback period is over 36 months, it's not going to get approved. But our rule of thumb is we'd like to see 24 months. And if it's close to 12, it's probably a no-brainer."

While payback period is easy to compute and easy to understand, its simplicity brings with it some drawbacks. "Payback gives you an answer that tells you a bit about the beginning stage of a project, but it doesn't tell you much about the full lifetime of the project," says Chris Gardner, a cofounder of **iValue LLC,** an IT valuation consultancy in Barrington, Illinois. "The simplicity

of computing payback may encourage sloppiness, especially the failure to include all costs associated with an investment, such as training, maintenance, and hardware upgrade costs," says Douglas Emond, senior vice president and chief technology officer at **Eastern Bank** in Lynn, Massachusetts. For example, he says, "you may be bringing in a hot new technology, but uh-oh, after implementation you realize that you need a .Net guru in-house, and you don't have one."

But payback period's emphasis on the short term has a special appeal for IT managers. "That's because the history of IT projects that take longer than 3 years is disastrous," says Gardner. Indeed, Ian Campbell, chief research officer at **Nucleus Research, Inc.** in Wellesley, Massachusetts, says payback period is an absolutely essential metric for evaluating IT projects—even more important than dis-

counted cash flow (NPV and IRR)—because it spotlights the risks inherent in lengthy IT projects. "It should be a hard and fast rule to never take an IT project with a payback period greater than 3 years, unless it's an infrastructure project you can't do without," Campbell says.

Whatever the weaknesses of the payback period method of evaluating capital projects, the simplicity of the method does allow it to be used in conjunction with other, more sophisticated measures. It can be used to screen potential projects and winnow them down to the few that merit more careful scrutiny with, for example, net present value (NPV).

■ *In your view, if the payback period method is used in conjunction with the NPV method, should it be used before or after the NPV evaluation?*

Seema's calculation of the payback period on this deal begins with calculation of the range of annual after-tax cash flow:

$$\text{After-tax cash flow} = (1 - \text{tax rate}) \times \text{Pre-tax cash flow}$$
$$= (1 - 0.25) \times \$4,000 = \$3,000$$
$$= (1 - 0.25) \times \$6,000 = \$4,500$$

The after-tax cash flow ranges from $3,000 to $4,500. Dividing the $20,000 initial investment by each of the estimated after-tax cash flows, we get the payback period:

$$\text{Payback period} = \text{Initial investment} \div \text{After-tax cash flow}$$
$$= \$20,000 \div \$3,000 = 6.67 \text{ years}$$
$$= \$20,000 \div \$4,500 = 4.44 \text{ years}$$

Because Seema's proposed rental property investment will pay itself back between 4.44 and 6.67 years, which is a range below her maximum payback of 7 years, the investment is acceptable.

TABLE 9.2	Relevant Cash Flows and Payback Periods for DeYarman Enterprises' Projects	
	Project Gold	Project Silver
Initial investment	$50,000	$50,000
Year	Operating cash inflows	
1	$ 5,000	$40,000
2	5,000	2,000
3	40,000	8,000
4	10,000	10,000
5	10,000	10,000
Payback period	3 years	3 years

A second weakness is that this approach fails to take *fully* into account the time factor in the value of money.[3] This weakness can be illustrated by an example.

Example

DeYarman Enterprises, a small medical appliance manufacturer, is considering two mutually exclusive projects, which it has named projects Gold and Silver. The firm uses only the payback period to choose projects. The relevant cash flows and payback period for each project are given in Table 9.2. Both projects have 3-year payback periods, which would suggest that they are equally desirable. But comparison of the pattern of cash inflows over the first 3 years shows that more of the $50,000 initial investment in project Silver is recovered sooner than is recovered for project Gold. For example, in year 1, $40,000 of the $50,000 invested in project Silver is recovered, whereas only $5,000 of the $50,000 investment in project Gold is recovered. Given the time value of money, project Silver would clearly be preferred over project Gold, in spite of the fact that both have identical 3-year payback periods. The payback approach does not fully account for the time value of money, which, if recognized, would cause project Silver to be preferred over project Gold.

A third weakness of payback is its failure to recognize cash flows that occur *after* the payback period.

Example

Rashid Company, a software developer, has two investment opportunities, X and Y. Data for X and Y are given in Table 9.3. The payback period for project X is 2 years; for project Y it is 3 years. Strict adherence to the payback approach suggests that project X is preferable to project Y. However, if we look beyond the payback period, we see that project X returns only an additional $1,200 ($1,000 in year 3 + $100 in year 4 + $100 in year 5), whereas project Y returns an additional $7,000 ($4,000 in year 4 + $3,000 in year 5). On the basis of this informa-

---

3. To consider differences in timing explicitly in applying the payback method, the *discounted payback period* is sometimes used. It is found by first calculating the present value of the cash inflows at the appropriate discount rate and then finding the payback period by using the present value of the cash inflows.

TABLE 9.3	Calculation of the Payback Period for Rashid Company's Two Alternative Investment Projects	
	Project X	Project Y
Initial investment	$10,000	$10,000
Year	Operating cash inflows	
1	$5,000	$3,000
2	5,000	4,000
3	1,000	3,000
4	100	4,000
5	100	3,000
Payback period	2 years	3 years

tion, project Y appears preferable to X. The payback approach ignored the cash inflows occurring after the end of the payback period.[4]

REVIEW QUESTIONS

9–2 What is the *payback period?* How is it calculated?

9–3 What weaknesses are commonly associated with the use of the payback period to evaluate a proposed investment?

9.3 | Net Present Value (NPV)

Because *net present value (NPV)* gives explicit consideration to the time value of money, it is considered a *sophisticated capital budgeting technique.* All such techniques in one way or another discount the firm's cash flows at a specified rate. This rate—often called the *discount rate, required return, cost of capital,* or *opportunity cost*—is the minimum return that must be earned on a project to leave the firm's market value unchanged. In this chapter, we take this rate as a "given." In Chapter 11 we will explore how it is determined.

net present value (NPV)
A sophisticated capital budgeting technique; found by subtracting a project's initial investment from the present value of its cash inflows discounted at a rate equal to the firm's cost of capital.

The **net present value (NPV)** is found by subtracting a project's initial investment (CF_0) from the present value of its cash inflows (CF_t) discounted at a rate equal to the firm's cost of capital (r).

$$\text{NPV} = \text{Present value of cash inflows} - \text{Initial investment}$$

$$\text{NPV} = \sum_{t=1}^{n} \frac{CF_t}{(1+r)^t} - CF_0 \tag{9.1}$$

$$= \sum_{t=1}^{n} (CF_t \times PVIF_{r,t}) - CF_0 \tag{9.1a}$$

---

4. To get around this weakness, some analysts add a desired dollar return to the initial investment and then calculate the payback period for the increased amount. For example, if the analyst wished to pay back the initial investment plus 20% for projects X and Y in Table 9.3, the amount to be recovered would be $12,000 [$10,000 + (0.20 × $10,000)]. For project X, the payback period would be infinite because the $12,000 would never be recovered; for project Y, the payback period would be 3.5 years [3 years + ($2,000 ÷ $4,000) years]. Clearly, project Y would be preferred.

When NPV is used, both inflows and outflows are measured in terms of present dollars. Because we are dealing only with investments that have *conventional cash flow patterns*, the initial investment is automatically stated in terms of today's dollars. If it were not, the present value of a project would be found by subtracting the present value of outflows from the present value of inflows.

Decision Criteria

When NPV is used to make accept–reject decisions, the decision criteria are as follows:

- If the NPV is *greater than* $0, *accept* the project.
- If the NPV is *less than* $0, *reject* the project.

If the NPV is greater than $0, the firm will earn a return greater than its cost of capital. Such action should increase the market value of the firm, and therefore the wealth of its owners by an amount equal to the NPV.

Example   We can illustrate the net present value (NPV) approach by using the Bennett Company data presented in Table 9.1. If the firm has a 10% cost of capital, the net present values for projects A (an annuity) and B (a mixed stream) can be calculated as shown on the time lines in Figure 9.2. These calculations result in net present values for projects A and B of $11,071 and $10,924, respectively. Both projects are acceptable, because the net present value of each is greater than $0. If

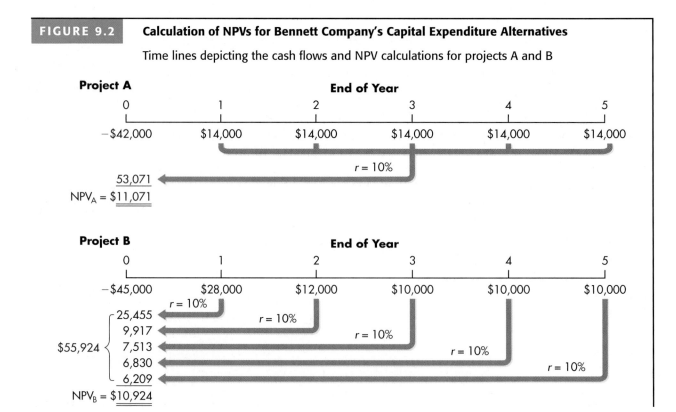

FIGURE 9.2   **Calculation of NPVs for Bennett Company's Capital Expenditure Alternatives**

Time lines depicting the cash flows and NPV calculations for projects A and B

Project A

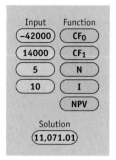

Project B

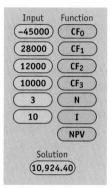

the projects were being ranked, however, project A would be considered superior to B, because it has a higher net present value than that of B ($11,071 versus $10,924).

Calculator Use   The preprogrammed NPV function in a financial calculator can be used to simplify the NPV calculation. The keystrokes for project A—the annuity—typically are as shown at left. Note that because project A is an annuity, only its first cash inflow, $CF_1 = 14000$, is input, followed by its frequency, $N = 5$.

The keystrokes for project B—the mixed stream—are as shown at left. Because the last three cash inflows for project B are the same ($CF_3 = CF_4 = CF_5 = 10000$), after inputting the first of these cash inflows, CF_3, we merely input its frequency, $N = 3$.

The calculated NPVs for projects A and B of $11,071 and $10,924, respectively, agree with the NPVs cited above.

Spreadsheet Use   The NPVs can be calculated as shown on the following Excel spreadsheet.

	A	B	C
1	DETERMINING THE NET PRESENT VALUE		
2	Firm's cost of capital		10%
3		Year-End Cash Flow	
4	Year	Project A	Project B
5	0	$ (42,000)	$ (45,000)
6	1	$ 14,000	$ 28,000
7	2	$ 14,000	$ 12,000
8	3	$ 14,000	$ 10,000
9	4	$ 14,000	$ 10,000
10	5	$ 14,000	$ 10,000
11	NPV	$ 11,071	$ 10,924
12	Choice of project		Project A

Entry in Cell B11 is
=NPV(C2,B6:B10)+B5
Copy the entry in Cell B11 to Cell C11.
Entry in Cell C12 is =IF(B11>C11,B4,C4).

REVIEW QUESTIONS

9–4   How is the *net present value (NPV)* calculated for a project with a *conventional cash flow pattern?*

9–5   What are the acceptance criteria for NPV? How are they related to the firm's market value?

---

internal rate of return (IRR)
A sophisticated capital budgeting technique; the discount rate that equates the NPV of an investment opportunity with $0 (because the present value of cash inflows equals the initial investment); it is the compound annual rate of return that the firm will earn if it invests in the project and receives the given cash inflows.

LG 4

9.4 | Internal Rate of Return (IRR)

The *internal rate of return (IRR)* is probably the most widely used *sophisticated capital budgeting technique.* However, it is considerably more difficult than NPV to calculate by hand. The **internal rate of return (IRR)** is the discount rate that equates the NPV of an investment opportunity with $0 (because the present value of cash inflows equals the initial investment). It is the compound annual rate of return that the firm will earn if it invests in the project and receives the given cash inflows. Mathematically, the IRR is the value of *r* in Equation 9.1 that causes NPV to equal $0.

$$\$0 = \sum_{t=1}^{n} \frac{CF_t}{(1 + IRR)^t} - CF_0 \tag{9.2}$$

$$\sum_{t=1}^{n} \frac{CF_t}{(1 + IRR)^t} = CF_0 \tag{9.2a}$$

Decision Criteria

When IRR is used to make accept–reject decisions, the decision criteria are as follows:

- If the IRR is *greater than* the cost of capital, *accept* the project.
- If the IRR is *less than* the cost of capital, *reject* the project.

These criteria guarantee that the firm will earn at least its required return. Such an outcome should increase the market value of the firm and therefore the wealth of its owners.

Calculating the IRR

The actual calculation by hand of the IRR from Equation 9.2a is no easy chore. It involves a complex trial-and-error search technique that logically tries different discount rates until one is found that causes the project's present value of cash inflows to just equal its initial investment (or NPV to equal $0). Details of this technique are described and demonstrated on this text's website: www.prenhall .com/gitman. Fortunately, many financial calculators have a preprogrammed IRR function that can be used to simplify the IRR calculation. With these calculators, you merely punch in all cash flows just as if to calculate NPV and then depress IRR to find the internal rate of return. Computer software, including spreadsheets, is also available for simplifying these calculations. All NPV and IRR values presented in this and subsequent chapters are obtained by using these functions on a popular financial calculator.

Example

We can demonstrate the internal rate of return (IRR) approach by using the Bennett Company data presented in Table 9.1. Figure 9.3 uses time lines to depict the framework for finding the IRRs for Bennett's projects A and B, both of which have conventional cash flow patterns. We can see in the figure that the IRR is the unknown discount rate that causes the NPV just to equal $0.

Calculator Use To find the IRR using the preprogrammed function in a financial calculator, the keystrokes for each project are the same as those shown on page 431 for the NPV calculation, except that the last two NPV keystrokes (punching **I** and then **NPV**) are replaced by a single **IRR** keystroke.

Comparing the IRRs of projects A and B given in Figure 9.3 to Bennett Company's 10% cost of capital, we can see that both projects are acceptable because

$$\text{IRR}_A = 19.9\% > 10.0\% \text{ cost of capital}$$
$$\text{IRR}_B = 21.7\% > 10.0\% \text{ cost of capital}$$

Comparing the two projects' IRRs, we would prefer project B over project A because $\text{IRR}_B = 21.7\% > \text{IRR}_A = 19.9\%$. If these projects are mutually exclusive, the IRR decision technique would recommend project B.

Spreadsheet Use   The internal rate of return also can be calculated as shown on the following Excel spreadsheet.

	A	B	C
1	DETERMINING THE INTERNAL RATE OF RETURN		
2		Year-End Cash Flow	
3	Year	Project A	Project B
4	0	$ (42,000)	$ (45,000)
5	1	$ 14,000	$ 28,000
6	2	$ 14,000	$ 12,000
7	3	$ 14,000	$ 10,000
8	4	$ 14,000	$ 10,000
9	5	$ 14,000	$ 10,000
10	IRR	19.9%	21.7%
11	Choice of project		Project B

Entry in Cell B10 is =IRR(B4:B9).
Copy the entry in Cell B10 to Cell C10.
Entry in Cell C11 is =IF(B10>C10,B3,C3).

FIGURE 9.3   **Calculation of IRRs for Bennett Company's Capital Expenditure Alternatives**

Time lines depicting the cash flows and IRR calculations for projects A and B

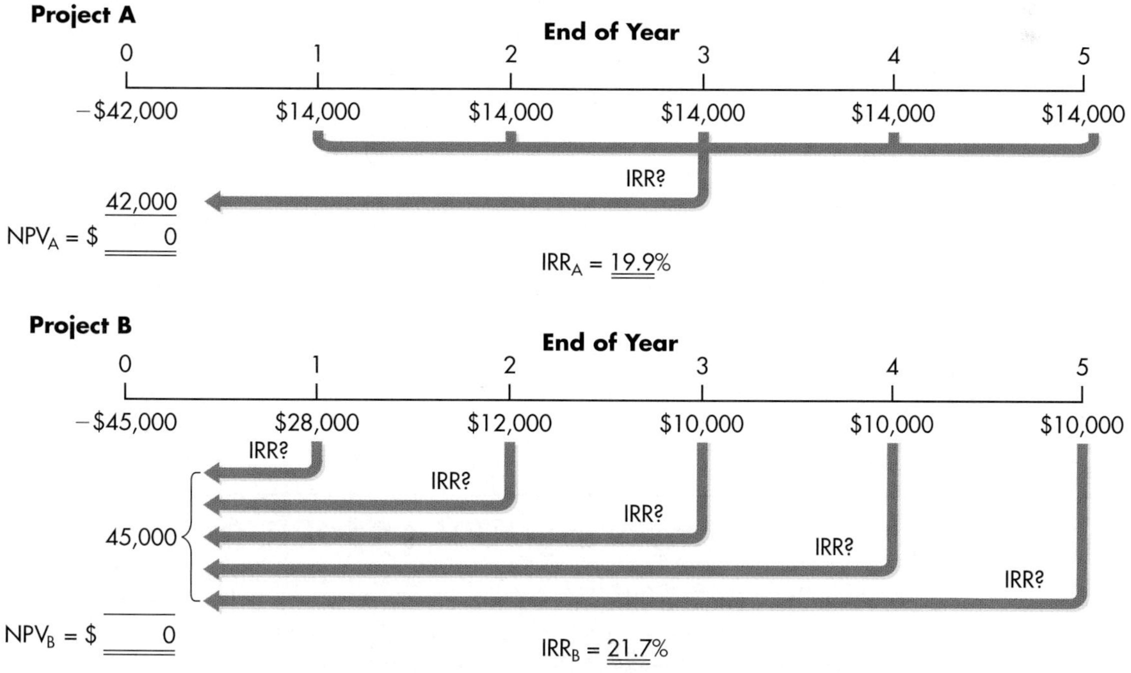

It is interesting to note in the preceding example that the IRR suggests that project B, which has an IRR of 21.7%, is preferable to project A, which has an IRR of 19.9%. This conflicts with the NPV rankings obtained in an earlier example. Such conflicts are not unusual. *There is no guarantee that NPV and IRR will rank projects in the same order. However, both methods should reach the same conclusion about the acceptability or nonacceptability of projects.*

Personal Finance Example   Tony DiLorenzo is evaluating an investment opportunity. He is comfortable with the investment's level of risk. Based on competing investment opportunities, he feels that this investment must earn a minimum compound annual after-tax return of 9% in order to be acceptable. Tony's initial investment would be $7,500, and he expects to receive annual after-tax cash flows of $500 per year in each of the first 4 years, followed by $700 per year at the end of years 5 through 8. He plans to sell the investment at the end of year 8 and net $9,000, after taxes.

To calculate the investment's IRR (compound annual return), Tony first summarizes the after-tax cash flows as shown below:

Year	Cash flow (− or +)
0	− $7,500 (Initial investment)
1	+ 500
2	+ 500
3	+ 500
4	+ 500
5	+ 700
6	+ 700
7	+ 700
8	+ 9,700 ($700 + $9,000)

Substituting the after-tax cash flows for years 0 through 8 into a financial calculator or spreadsheet, he finds the investment's IRR of 9.54%. Given that the expected IRR of 9.54% exceeds Tony's required minimum IRR of 9%, the investment is acceptable.

REVIEW QUESTIONS

9–6   What is the *internal rate of return (IRR)* on an investment? How is it determined?

9–7   What are the acceptance criteria for IRR? How are they related to the firm's market value?

9–8   Do the net present value (NPV) and internal rate of return (IRR) always agree with respect to accept–reject decisions? With respect to ranking decisions? Explain.

9.5 | Comparing NPV and IRR Techniques

To understand the differences between the NPV and IRR techniques and decision makers' preferences in their use, we need to look at net present value profiles, conflicting rankings, and the question of which approach is better.

Net Present Value Profiles

net present value profile
Graph that depicts a project's NPVs for various discount rates.

Projects can be compared graphically by constructing **net present value profiles** that depict the project's NPVs for various discount rates. These profiles are useful in evaluating and comparing projects, especially when conflicting rankings exist. They are best demonstrated via an example.

Example

To prepare net present value profiles for Bennett Company's two projects, A and B, the first step is to develop a number of "discount rate–net present value" coordinates. Three coordinates can be easily obtained for each project; they are at discount rates of 0%, 10% (the cost of capital, r), and the IRR. The net present value at a 0% discount rate is found by merely adding all the cash inflows and subtracting the initial investment. Using the data in Table 9.1 and Figure 9.1, we get

For project A:

$$(\$14{,}000 + \$14{,}000 + \$14{,}000 + \$14{,}000 + \$14{,}000) - \$42{,}000 = \$28{,}000$$

For project B:

$$(\$28{,}000 + \$12{,}000 + \$10{,}000 + \$10{,}000 + \$10{,}000) - \$45{,}000 = \$25{,}000$$

The net present values for projects A and B at the 10% cost of capital are $11,071 and $10,924, respectively (from Figure 9.2). Because the IRR is the discount rate for which net present value equals zero, the IRRs (from Figure 9.3) of 19.9% for project A and 21.7% for project B result in $0 NPVs. The three sets of coordinates for each of the projects are summarized in Table 9.4.

Plotting the data from Table 9.4 results in the net present value profiles for projects A and B shown in Figure 9.4 (on page 436). The figure indicates that for any discount rate less than approximately 10.7%, the NPV for project A is greater than the NPV for project B. Beyond this point, the NPV for project B is greater. Because the net present value profiles for projects A and B cross at a positive NPV that occurs at a discount rate (10.7%), which is higher than the firm's cost of capital (10.0%), the IRRs for the projects result in conflicting rankings with their NPVs.

Conflicting Rankings

Ranking is an important consideration when projects are mutually exclusive or when capital rationing is necessary. When projects are mutually exclusive, ranking enables the firm to determine which project is best from a financial

TABLE 9.4	**Discount Rate–NPV Coordinates for Projects A and B**	
	Net present value	
Discount rate	Project A	Project B
0 %	$28,000	$25,000
10	11,071	10,924
19.9	0	—
21.7	—	0

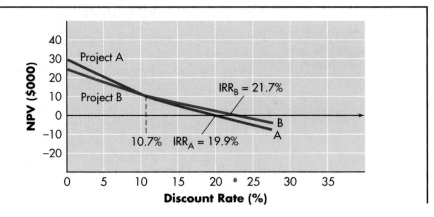

FIGURE 9.4

NPV Profiles
Net present value profiles for Bennett Company's projects A and B

standpoint. When capital rationing is necessary, ranking projects will provide a logical starting point for determining which group of projects to accept. As we'll see, **conflicting rankings** using NPV and IRR result from *differences in the magnitude and timing of cash flows.*

conflicting rankings
Conflicts in the ranking given a project by NPV and IRR, resulting from *differences in the magnitude and timing of cash flows.*

intermediate cash inflows
Cash inflows received prior to the termination of a project.

The underlying cause of conflicting rankings is different implicit assumptions about the *reinvestment* of **intermediate cash inflows**—cash inflows received prior to the termination of a project. NPV assumes that intermediate cash inflows are reinvested at the cost of capital, whereas IRR assumes that intermediate cash inflows are reinvested at a rate equal to the project's IRR.[5] These differing assumptions can be demonstrated with an example.

Example

A project requiring a $170,000 initial investment is expected to provide operating cash inflows of $52,000, $78,000, and $100,000 at the end of each of the next 3 years. The NPV of the project (at the firm's 10% cost of capital) is $16,867 and its IRR is 15%. Clearly, the project is acceptable (NPV = $16,867 > $0 and IRR = 15% > 10% cost of capital). Table 9.5 demonstrates calculation of the project's future value at the end of its 3-year life, assuming both a 10% (its cost of capital) and a 15% (its IRR) rate of return. A future value of $248,720 results from reinvestment at the 10% cost of capital (total in column 5), and a future value of $258,496 results from reinvestment at the 15% IRR (total in column 7).

If the future value in each case in Table 9.5 were viewed as the return received 3 years from today from the $170,000 initial investment, the cash flows would be those given in Table 9.6. The NPVs and IRRs in each case are shown below the cash flows in Table 9.6. You can see that at the 10% reinvestment rate,

---

5. To eliminate the reinvestment rate assumption of the IRR, some practitioners calculate the *modified internal rate of return (MIRR)*. The MIRR is found by converting each operating cash inflow to its future value measured at the end of the project's life and then summing the future values of all inflows to get the project's *terminal value.* Each future value is found by using the cost of capital, thereby eliminating the reinvestment rate criticism of the traditional IRR. The MIRR represents the discount rate that causes the terminal value just to equal the initial investment. Because it uses the cost of capital as the reinvestment rate, the MIRR is generally viewed as a better measure of a project's true profitability than the IRR. Although this technique is frequently used in commercial real estate valuation and is a preprogrammed function on some financial calculators, its failure to resolve the issue of conflicting rankings and its theoretical inferiority to NPV have resulted in the MIRR receiving only limited attention and acceptance in the financial literature. For a thorough analysis of the arguments surrounding IRR and MIRR, see D. Anthony Plath and William F. Kennedy, "Teaching Return-Based Measures of Project Evaluation," *Financial Practice and Education* (Spring/Summer 1994), pp. 77–86.

TABLE 9.5		Reinvestment Rate Comparisons for a Project[a]					

			Reinvestment rate				
			10%		15%		
Year (1)	Operating cash inflows (2)	Number of years earnings interest (t) [3 − (1)] (3)	$FVIF_{10\%,t}$ (4)	Future value [(2) × (4)] (5)	$FVIF_{15\%,t}$ (6)	Future value [(2) × (6)] (7)	
1	$ 52,000	2	1.210	$ 62,920	1.323	$ 68,796	
2	78,000	1	1.100	85,800	1.150	89,700	
3	100,000	0	1.000	100,000	1.000	100,000	
		Future value end of year 3		$248,720		$258,496	

NPV @ 10% = $16,867

IRR = 15%

[a]Initial investment in this project is $170,000.

TABLE 9.6	Project Cash Flows After Reinvestment	

	Reinvestment rate	
	10%	15%
Initial investment	$170,000	
Year	Operating cash inflows	
1	$ 0	$ 0
2	0	0
3	248,720	258,496
NPV @ 10%	$ 16,867	$ 24,213
IRR	13.5%	15.0%

the NPV remains at $16,867; reinvestment at the 15% IRR produces an NPV of $24,213.

From this result, it should be clear that the NPV technique assumes reinvestment at the cost of capital (10% in this example). (Note that with reinvestment at 10%, the IRR would be 13.5%.) On the other hand, the IRR technique assumes an ability to reinvest intermediate cash inflows at the IRR. If reinvestment does not occur at this rate, the IRR will differ from 15%. Reinvestment at a rate lower than the IRR would result in an IRR lower than that calculated (at 13.5%, for example, if the reinvestment rate were only 10%). Reinvestment at a rate higher than the IRR would result in an IRR higher than that calculated.

In general, projects with similar-size investments and lower cash inflows in the early years tend to be preferred at lower discount rates.[6] Projects that have

---

6. Because differences in the relative sizes of initial investments can also affect conflicts in rankings, the initial investments are assumed to be similar. This permits isolation of the effect of differences in the magnitude and timing of cash inflows on project rankings.

TABLE 9.7	Preferences Associated with Extreme Discount Rates and Dissimilar Cash Inflow Patterns	
	Cash inflow pattern	
Discount rate	Lower early-year cash inflows	Higher early-year cash inflows
Low	Preferred, because higher late-year cash inflows are not greatly reduced and therefore dominate in terms of present value.	Not preferred
High	Not preferred	Preferred, because the higher early-year cash inflows are not greatly reduced and therefore dominate in terms of present value.

higher cash inflows in the early years tend to be preferred at higher discount rates. Why? Because at high discount rates, later-year cash inflows tend to be severely penalized in present value terms. For example, at a high discount rate, say 20 percent, the present value of $1 received at the end of 5 years is about 40 cents, whereas for $1 received at the end of 15 years it is less than 7 cents. Clearly, at high discount rates a project's early-year cash inflows count most in terms of its NPV. Table 9.7 summarizes the preferences associated with extreme discount rates and dissimilar cash inflow patterns.

Example Bennett Company's projects A and B were found to have conflicting rankings at the firm's 10% cost of capital (as depicted in Figure 9.4). If we review each project's cash inflow pattern as presented in Table 9.1 and Figure 9.1, we see that although the projects require similar initial investments, they have dissimilar cash inflow patterns. Table 9.7 indicates that project B, which has higher early-year cash inflows than project A, would be preferred over project A at higher discount rates. Figure 9.4 shows that this is in fact the case. At any discount rate in excess of 10.7%, project B's NPV surpasses that of project A. Clearly, the magnitude and timing of the projects' cash inflows do affect their rankings.

Although the classification of cash inflow patterns in Table 9.7 is useful in explaining conflicting rankings, differences in the magnitude and timing of cash inflows do not guarantee conflicts in ranking. In general, the greater the difference between the magnitude and timing of cash inflows, the greater the likelihood of conflicting rankings. Conflicts based on NPV and IRR can be reconciled computationally; to do so, one creates and analyzes an incremental project reflecting the difference in cash flows between the two mutually exclusive projects. Because a detailed description of this procedure is beyond the scope of an introductory text, suffice it to say that IRR techniques can be used to generate consistently the same project rankings as those obtained by using NPV.

Which Approach Is Better?

Many companies use both the NPV and IRR techniques because current technology makes them easy to calculate. But it is difficult to choose one approach over the other, because the theoretical and practical strengths of the approaches differ. Clearly, it is wise to evaluate NPV and IRR techniques from both theoretical and practical points of view.

Theoretical View

On a purely theoretical basis, NPV is the better approach to capital budgeting as a result of several factors. Most important, the use of NPV implicitly assumes that any intermediate cash inflows generated by an investment are *reinvested at the firm's cost of capital.* The use of IRR assumes *reinvestment at the often high rate specified by the IRR.* Because the cost of capital tends to be a reasonable estimate of the rate at which the firm could *actually reinvest* intermediate cash inflows, the use of NPV, with its more conservative and realistic reinvestment rate, is in theory preferable.

multiple IRRs
More than one IRR resulting from a capital budgeting project with a *nonconventional cash flow pattern;* the maximum number of IRRs for a project is equal to the number of sign changes in its cash flows.

In addition, certain mathematical properties may cause a project with a *nonconventional cash flow pattern* to have **multiple IRRs**—more than one IRR. Mathematically, the maximum number of *real* roots to an equation is equal to its number of sign changes. Take an equation like $x^2 - 5x + 6 = 0$, which has two sign changes in its coefficients—from positive $(+x^2)$ to negative $(-5x)$ and then from negative $(-5x)$ to positive $(+6)$. If we factor the equation (remember factoring from high school math?), we get $(x - 2) \times (x - 3)$, which means that x can equal either 2 or 3—there are two correct values for x. Substitute them back into the equation, and you'll see that both values work.

This same outcome can occur when finding the IRR for projects with nonconventional cash flows, because they have more than one sign change. Clearly, when multiple IRRs occur for nonconventional cash flows, the analyst faces the time-consuming need to interpret their meanings so as to evaluate the project. The fact that such a challenge does not exist when using NPV enhances its theoretical superiority.

Practical View

Evidence suggests that in spite of the theoretical superiority of NPV, *financial managers prefer to use IRR.*[7] The preference for IRR is due to the general disposition of businesspeople toward *rates of return* rather than actual *dollar returns.* Because interest rates, profitability, and so on are most often expressed as annual rates of return, the use of IRR makes sense to financial decision makers. They tend to find NPV less intuitive because it does not measure benefits *relative to the amount invested.* Because a variety of techniques are available for avoiding the pitfalls of the IRR, its widespread use does not imply a lack of sophistication on the part of financial decision makers. Clearly, corporate financial analysts are responsible for identifying and resolving problems with the IRR before the decision makers use it as a decision technique.

---

7. For example, see John R. Graham and Campbell R. Harvey, "The Theory and Practice of Corporate Finance: Evidence from the Field," *Journal of Financial Economics* (May/June 2001,) pp. 187–243; Harold Bierman, Jr., "Capital Budgeting in 1992: A Survey," *Financial Management* (Autumn 1993), p. 24; and Lawrence J. Gitman and Charles E. Maxwell, "A Longitudinal Comparison of Capital Budgeting Techniques Used by Major U.S. Firms: 1986 versus 1976," *Journal of Applied Business Research* (Fall 1987), pp. 41–50, for discussions of evidence with respect to capital budgeting decision-making practices in major U.S. firms.

Focus on Ethics   Nonfinancial Considerations in Project Selection

Corporate ethics codes are often faulted for being "window dressing"—that is, for having little or no effect on actual behavior. Financial ethics expert John Dobson says day-to-day behavior in the workplace "acculturates" employees—teaches them that the behavior they see is rational and acceptable in that environment. Dobson takes issue with the notion of "neoclassical economic theory," which states that people are "material opportunists who will readily jettison honesty and integrity in favor of guile and deceit whenever the latter are more likely to maximize some payoff function."

The good news is that professional ethics codes, such as those developed for chartered financial analysts, corporate treasury professionals, and certified financial planners, actually provide sound guidelines for behavior. These codes, notes Dobson, are based on economically rational concepts such as integrity and trustworthiness, which guide the decision maker in attempting to increase shareholder wealth. Financial executives insist that there should be no separation between an individual's personal ethics and his or her business ethics. "It's a jungle out there" and "Business is business" should not be excuses for engaging in unethical behavior.

How do ethics codes apply to project selection and capital budgeting? For most companies ethical considerations are primarily concerned with the reduction of potential risks associated with a project. For example, **Gateway Computers** clearly outlines in its corporate code of ethics the increased regulatory and procurement laws with which an employee must be familiar in order to sell to the government. The company points out that knowingly submitting a false claim or statement to a governmental agency could subject Gateway and its employees to significant monetary civil damages, penalties, and even criminal sanctions.

Another way to incorporate nonfinancial considerations into capital project evaluation is to take into account the likely effect of decisions on nonshareholder parties or stakeholders—employees, customers, the local community, and suppliers. A study by Omran, Atrill, and Pointon found that U.K. companies that had a stakeholder focus (explicit mention of stakeholders in the mission statement) fared no worse in various success measures than those with a narrowly defined shareholder focus. Even risk-adjusted common stock returns were no worse for these more broadly focused firms.

■ *What are the potential risks to a company of unethical behaviors by employees? What are potential risks to the public and to stakeholders?*

In addition, decision makers should keep in mind that nonfinancial considerations may be important elements in project selection, as discussed in the *Focus on Ethics* box above.

REVIEW QUESTIONS

9–9   How is a *net present value profile* used to compare projects? What causes conflicts in the ranking of projects via net present value and internal rate of return?

9–10   Does the assumption concerning the reinvestment of intermediate cash inflow tend to favor NPV or IRR? In practice, which technique is preferred and why?

Summary

Focus on Value

After estimating the relevant cash flows, the financial manager must apply appropriate decision techniques to assess whether the project creates value. Net present value (NPV) and internal rate of return (IRR) are the generally preferred capital budgeting techniques. Both use the cost of capital as the required return. The appeal of NPV and IRR stems from the fact that both indicate whether a proposed investment creates or destroys shareholder value.

NPV clearly indicates the expected dollar amount of wealth creation from a proposed project, whereas IRR provides the same accept-or-reject decision as NPV. As a consequence of some fundamental differences, NPV and IRR do not necessarily rank projects in the same way. NPV is the theoretically preferred approach. In practice, however, IRR is preferred because of its intuitive appeal. Regardless, the application of NPV and IRR to good estimates of relevant cash flows should enable the financial manager to recommend projects that are consistent with the firm's goal of **maximizing stock price.**

Review of Learning Goals

Key formulas and decision criteria for this chapter are summarized in Table 9.8 on page 442.

LG 1 **Understand the role of capital budgeting techniques in the capital budgeting process.** Capital budgeting techniques are the tools used to assess project acceptability and ranking. Applied to each project's relevant cash flows, they indicate which capital expenditures are consistent with the firm's goal of maximizing owners' wealth.

LG 2 **Calculate, interpret, and evaluate the payback period.** The payback period is the amount of time required for the firm to recover its initial investment, as calculated from cash inflows. Shorter payback periods are preferred. The payback period is relatively easy to calculate, has simple intuitive appeal, considers cash flows, and measures risk exposure. Its weaknesses include lack of linkage to the wealth maximization goal, failure to consider time value explicitly, and the fact that it ignores cash flows that occur after the payback period.

LG 3 **Calculate, interpret, and evaluate the net present value (NPV).** Because it gives explicit consideration to the time value of money, NPV is considered a sophisticated capital budgeting technique. NPV measures the amount of value created by a given project; only positive NPV projects are acceptable. The rate at which cash flows are discounted in calculating NPV is called the discount rate, required return, cost of capital, or opportunity cost. By whatever name, this rate represents the minimum return that must be earned on a project to leave the firm's market value unchanged.

TABLE 9.8	Summary of Key Formulas/Definitions and Decision Criteria for Capital Budgeting Techniques	
Technique	Formula/definition	Decision criteria
Payback period[a]	*For annuity:* $$\frac{\text{Initial investment}}{\text{Annual cash inflow}}$$ *For mixed stream:* Calculate cumulative cash inflows on year-to-year basis until the initial investment is recovered.	*Accept* if < maximum acceptable payback period. *Reject* if > maximum acceptable payback period.
Net present value (NPV)[b]	Present value of cash inflows − Initial investment.	*Accept* if > \$0. *Reject* if < \$0.
Internal rate of return (IRR)[b]	The discount rate that causes $NPV = \$0$ (present value of cash inflows equals the initial investment).	*Accept* if > the cost of capital. *Reject* if < the cost of capital.

[a]Unsophisticated technique, because it does not give explicit consideration to the time value of money.
[b]Sophisticated technique, because it gives explicit consideration to the time value of money.

Calculate, interpret, and evaluate the internal rate of return (IRR). Like NPV, IRR is a sophisticated capital budgeting technique. IRR is the compound annual rate of return that the firm will earn by investing in a project and receiving the given cash inflows. By accepting only those projects with IRRs in excess of the firm's cost of capital, the firm should enhance its market value and the wealth of its owners. Both NPV and IRR yield the same accept–reject decisions, but they often provide conflicting rankings.

Use net present value profiles to compare NPV and IRR techniques. A net present value profile is a graph that depicts projects' NPVs for various discount rates. The NPV profile is prepared by developing a number of "discount rate–net present value" coordinates (including discount rates of 0 percent, the cost of capital, and the IRR for each project) and then plotting them on the same set of discount rate–NPV axes.

Discuss NPV and IRR in terms of conflicting rankings and the theoretical and practical strengths of each approach. Conflicting rankings of projects frequently emerge from NPV and IRR as a result of differences in the magnitude and timing of cash flows. The underlying cause is the differing implicit assumptions with regard to the reinvestment of intermediate cash inflows. NPV assumes reinvestment of intermediate cash inflows at the more conservative cost of capital; IRR assumes reinvestment at the project's IRR. On a purely theoretical basis, NPV is preferred over IRR because NPV assumes the more conservative reinvestment rate and does not exhibit the mathematical problem of multiple IRRs that often occurs when IRRs are calculated for nonconventional cash flows. In practice, the IRR is more commonly used because it is consistent with the general preference of businesspeople for rates of return, and corporate financial analysts can identify and resolve problems with the IRR before decision makers use it.

Self-Test Problem (Solution in Appendix B)

ST9–1 **All techniques with NPV profile—Mutually exclusive projects**   Fitch Industries is in the process of choosing the better of two equal-risk, mutually exclusive capital expenditure projects—M and N. The relevant cash flows for each project are shown in the following table. The firm's cost of capital is 14%.

	Project M	Project N
Initial investment (CF_0)	$28,500	$27,000
Year (*t*)	Cash inflows (CF_t)	
1	$10,000	$11,000
2	10,000	10,000
3	10,000	9,000
4	10,000	8,000

a. Calculate each project's *payback period*.
b. Calculate the *net present value (NPV)* for each project.
c. Calculate the *internal rate of return (IRR)* for each project.
d. Summarize the preferences dictated by each measure you calculated, and indicate which project you would recommend. Explain why.
e. Draw the *net present value profiles* for these projects on the same set of axes, and explain the circumstances under which a conflict in rankings might exist.

Warm-Up Exercises   A blue box (■) indicates exercises available in .

E9–1   Elysian Fields, Inc., uses a maximum payback period of 6 years, and currently must choose between two mutually exclusive projects. Project Hydrogen requires an initial outlay of $25,000; project Helium requires an initial outlay of $35,000. Using the expected cash inflows given for each project in the following table, calculate each project's *payback period*. Which project meets Elysian's standards?

	Expected cash inflows	
Year	Hydrogen	Helium
1	$6,000	$7,000
2	6,000	7,000
3	8,000	8,000
4	4,000	5,000
5	3,500	5,000
6	2,000	4,000

E9–2 Herky Foods is considering acquisition of a new wrapping machine. The initial investment is estimated at $1.25 million, and the machine will have a 5-year life with no salvage value. Using a 6% discount rate, determine the *net present value (NPV)* of the machine given its expected operating cash inflows shown in the table at the right. Based on the project's NPV, should Herky make this investment?

Year	Cash inflow
1	$400,000
2	375,000
3	300,000
4	350,000
5	200,000

 E9–3 Axis Corp. is considering investment in the best of two mutually exclusive projects. Project Kelvin involves an overhaul of the existing system; it will cost $45,000 and generate cash inflows of $20,000 per year for the next 3 years. Project Thompson involves replacement of the existing system; it will cost $275,000 and generate cash inflows of $60,000 per year for 6 years. Using an 8% cost of capital, calculate each project's NPV and make a recommendation based on your findings.

 E9–4 Billabong Tech uses the *internal rate of return (IRR)* to select projects. Calculate the IRR for each of the following projects and recommend the best project based on this measure. Project T-Shirt requires an initial investment of $15,000 and generates cash inflows of $8,000 per year for 4 years. Project Board Shorts requires an initial investment of $25,000 and produces cash inflows of $12,000 per year for 5 years.

  E9–5 Cooper Electronics uses *NPV profiles* to visually evaluate competing projects. Key data for the two projects under consideration is given in the following table. Using these data, graph, on the same set of axes, the NPV profiles for each project using discount rates of 0%, 8%, and the IRR.

	Terra	Firma
Initial investment	$30,000	$25,000
Year	Operating cash inflows	
1	$ 7,000	$ 6,000
2	10,000	9,000
3	12,000	9,000
4	10,000	8,000

Problems

A blue box (■) indicates problems available in .

 P9–1 **Payback period**   Jordan Enterprises is considering a capital expenditure that requires an initial investment of $42,000 and returns after-tax cash inflows of $7,000 per year for 10 years. The firm has a maximum acceptable payback period of 8 years.
  a. Determine the *payback period* for this project.
  b. Should the company accept the project? Why or why not?

P9–2 Payback comparisons Nova Products has a 5-year maximum acceptable payback period. The firm is considering the purchase of a new machine and must choose between two alternative ones. The first machine requires an initial investment of $14,000 and generates annual after-tax cash inflows of $3,000 for each of the next 7 years. The second machine requires an initial investment of $21,000 and provides an annual cash inflow after taxes of $4,000 for 20 years.

a. Determine the *payback period* for each machine.

b. Comment on the acceptability of the machines, assuming that they are independent projects.

c. Which machine should the firm accept? Why?

d. Do the machines in this problem illustrate any of the weaknesses of using payback? Discuss.

P9–3 Choosing between two projects with acceptable payback periods Shell Camping Gear, Inc., is considering two mutually exclusive projects. Each requires an initial investment of $100,000. John Shell, president of the company, has set a maximum payback period of 4 years. The after-tax cash inflows associated with each project are as follows:

Year	Cash inflows (CF_t)	
	Project A	Project B
1	$10,000	$40,000
2	20,000	30,000
3	30,000	20,000
4	40,000	10,000
5	20,000	20,000

a. Determine the *payback period* of each project.

b. Because they are mutually exclusive, Shell must choose one. Which should the company invest in?

c. Explain why one of the projects is a better choice than the other.

PERSONAL FINANCE PROBLEM

P9–4 Long-term investment decision, payback method Bill Williams has the opportunity to invest in project A that costs $9,000 today and promises to pay annual end-of-year payments of $2,200, $2,500, $2,500, $2,000, and $1,800 over the next 5 years. Or, Bill can invest $9,000 in project B that promises to pay annual end-of-year payments of $1,500, $1,500, $1,500, $3,500, and $4, 000 over the next 5 years.

a. How long will it take for Bill to recoup his initial investment in project A?

b. How long will it take for Bill to recoup his initial investment in project B?

c. Using the *payback period*, which project should Bill choose?

d. Do you see any problems with his choice?

P9–5 NPV Calculate the *net present value (NPV)* for the following 20-year projects. Comment on the acceptability of each. Assume that the firm has an opportunity cost of 14%.

a. Initial investment is $10,000; cash inflows are $2,000 per year.

b. Initial investment is $25,000; cash inflows are $3,000 per year.

c. Initial investment is $30,000; cash inflows are $5,000 per year.

P9–6 **NPV for varying costs of capital** Dane Cosmetics is evaluating a new fragrance-mixing machine. The machine requires an initial investment of $24,000 and will generate after-tax cash inflows of $5,000 per year for 8 years. For each of the costs of capital listed, (1) calculate the *net present value (NPV)*, (2) indicate whether to accept or reject the machine, and (3) explain your decision.
a. The cost of capital is 10%.
b. The cost of capital is 12%.
c. The cost of capital is 14%.

 P9–7 **Net present value—Independent projects** Using a 14% cost of capital, calculate the *net present value* for each of the independent projects shown in the following table, and indicate whether each is acceptable.

	Project A	Project B	Project C	Project D	Project E
Initial investment (CF_0)	$26,000	$500,000	$170,000	$950,000	$80,000
Year (t)	Cash inflows (CF_t)				
1	$4,000	$100,000	$20,000	$230,000	$ 0
2	4,000	120,000	19,000	230,000	0
3	4,000	140,000	18,000	230,000	0
4	4,000	160,000	17,000	230,000	20,000
5	4,000	180,000	16,000	230,000	30,000
6	4,000	200,000	15,000	230,000	0
7	4,000		14,000	230,000	50,000
8	4,000		13,000	230,000	60,000
9	4,000		12,000		70,000
10	4,000		11,000		

 P9–8 **NPV** Simes Innovations, Inc., is negotiating to purchase exclusive rights to manufacture and market a solar-powered toy car. The car's inventor has offered Simes the choice of either a one-time payment of $1,500,000 today or a series of 5 year-end payments of $385,000.
a. If Simes has a cost of capital of 9%, which form of payment should it choose?
b. What yearly payment would make the two offers identical in value at a cost of capital of 9%?
c. Would your answer to part a of this problem be different if the yearly payments were made at the beginning of each year? Show what difference, if any, that change in timing would make to the present value calculation.
d. The after-tax cash inflows associated with this purchase are projected to amount to $250,000 per year for 15 years. Will this factor change the firm's decision about how to fund the initial investment?

 P9–9 **NPV and maximum return** A firm can purchase a fixed asset for a $13,000 initial investment. The asset generates an annual after-tax cash inflow of $4,000 for 4 years.
a. Determine the *net present value (NPV)* of the asset, assuming that the firm has a 10% cost of capital. Is the project acceptable?
b. Determine the maximum required rate of return (closest whole-percentage rate) that the firm can have and still accept the asset. Discuss this finding in light of your response in part a.

P9–10   **NPV—Mutually exclusive projects**   Hook Industries is considering the replacement of one of its old drill presses. Three alternative replacement presses are under consideration. The relevant cash flows associated with each are shown in the following table. The firm's cost of capital is 15%.

	Press A	Press B	Press C
Initial investment (CF_0)	$85,000	$60,000	$130,000
Year (t)	Cash inflows (CF_t)		
1	$18,000	$12,000	$50,000
2	18,000	14,000	30,000
3	18,000	16,000	20,000
4	18,000	18,000	20,000
5	18,000	20,000	20,000
6	18,000	25,000	30,000
7	18,000	—	40,000
8	18,000	—	50,000

a. Calculate the *net present value (NPV)* of each press.
b. Using NPV, evaluate the acceptability of each press.
c. Rank the presses from best to worst using NPV.

PERSONAL FINANCE PROBLEM

P9–11   **Long-term investment decision, NPV method**   Jenny Jenks has researched the financial pros and cons of entering into an elite MBA program at her state university. The tuition and needed books for a master's program will have an upfront cost of $100,000. On average, a person with an MBA degree earns an extra $20,000 per year over a business career of 40 years. Jenny feels that her opportunity cost of capital is 6%. Given her estimates, find the *net present value (NPV)* of entering this MBA program. Are the benefits of further education worth the associated costs?

P9–12   **Payback and NPV**   Neil Corporation has three projects under consideration. The cash flows for each project are shown in the following table. The firm has a 16% cost of capital.

	Project A	Project B	Project C
Initial investment (CF_0)	$40,000	$40,000	$40,000
Year (t)	Cash inflows (CF_t)		
1	$13,000	$ 7,000	$19,000
2	13,000	10,000	16,000
3	13,000	13,000	13,000
4	13,000	16,000	10,000
5	13,000	19,000	7,000

a. Calculate each project's *payback period*. Which project is preferred according to this method?

b. Calculate each project's *net present value (NPV)*. Which project is preferred according to this method?

c. Comment on your findings in parts **a** and **b**, and recommend the best project. Explain your recommendation.

P9–13 **Internal rate of return**   For each of the projects shown in the following table, calculate the *internal rate of return (IRR)*. Then indicate, for each project, the maximum cost of capital that the firm could have and still find the IRR acceptable.

	Project A	Project B	Project C	Project D
Initial investment (CF_0)	$90,000	$490,000	$20,000	$240,000
Year (*t*)	\multicolumn{4}{c}{Cash inflows (CF_t)}
1	$20,000	$150,000	$7,500	$120,000
2	25,000	150,000	7,500	100,000
3	30,000	150,000	7,500	80,000
4	35,000	150,000	7,500	60,000
5	40,000	—	7,500	—

P9–14 **IRR—Mutually exclusive projects**   Bell Manufacturing is attempting to choose the better of two mutually exclusive projects for expanding the firm's warehouse capacity. The relevant cash flows for the projects are shown in the following table. The firm's cost of capital is 15%.

	Project X	Project Y
Initial investment (CF_0)	$500,000	$325,000
Year (*t*)	\multicolumn{2}{c}{Cash inflows (CF_t)}
1	$100,000	$140,000
2	120,000	120,000
3	150,000	95,000
4	190,000	70,000
5	250,000	50,000

a. Calculate the *IRR* to the nearest whole percent for each of the projects.

b. Assess the acceptability of each project on the basis of the IRRs found in part **a.**

c. Which project, on this basis, is preferred?

PERSONAL FINANCE PROBLEM

P9–15 **Long-term investment decision, IRR method**   Billy and Mandy Jones have $25,000 to invest. On average, they do not make any investment that will not return at least 7.5% per year. They have been approached with an investment opportunity that requires $25,000 upfront and has a payout of $6,000 at the end of each of the next 5 years. Using the *internal rate of return (IRR)* method and their requirements, determine whether Billy and Mandy should undertake the investment.

P9–16   IRR, investment life, and cash inflows   Oak Enterprises accepts projects earning more than the firm's 15% cost of capital. Oak is currently considering a 10-year project that provides annual cash inflows of $10,000 and requires an initial investment of $61,450. (*Note:* All amounts are after taxes.)

a. Determine the *IRR* of this project. Is it acceptable?

b. Assuming that the cash inflows continue to be $10,000 per year, how many *additional years* would the flows have to continue to make the project acceptable (that is, to make it have an IRR of 15%)?

c. With the given life, initial investment, and cost of capital, what is the minimum annual cash inflow that the firm should accept?

  P9–17   NPV and IRR   Benson Designs has prepared the following estimates for a long-term project it is considering. The initial investment is $18,250, and the project is expected to yield after-tax cash inflows of $4,000 per year for 7 years. The firm has a 10% cost of capital.

a. Determine the *net present value (NPV)* for the project.

b. Determine the *internal rate of return (IRR)* for the project.

c. Would you recommend that the firm accept or reject the project? Explain your answer.

  P9–18   NPV, with rankings   Botany Bay, Inc., a maker of casual clothing, is considering four projects. Because of past financial difficulties, the company has a high cost of capital at 15%. Which of these projects would be acceptable under those cost circumstances?

	Project A	Project B	Project C	Project D
Initial investment (CF₀)	$50,000	$100,000	$80,000	$180,000
Year (t)	Cash inflows (CFₜ)			
1	$20,000	$35,000	$20,000	$100,000
2	20,000	50,000	40,000	80,000
3	20,000	50,000	60,000	60,000

a. Calculate the *NPV* of each project, using a cost of capital of 15%.

b. Rank acceptable projects by NPV.

c. Calculate the *IRR* of each project and use it to determine the highest cost of capital at which all of the projects would be acceptable.

    P9–19   All techniques, conflicting rankings   Nicholson Roofing Materials, Inc., is considering two mutually exclusive projects, each with an initial investment of $150,000. The company's board of directors has set a maximum 4-year payback requirement and has set its cost of capital at 9%. The cash inflows associated with the two projects are shown in the table on page 450.

a. Calculate the *payback period* for each project.

b. Calculate the *NPV* of each project at 0%.

c. Calculate the *NPV* of each project at 9%.

d. Derive the *IRR* of each project.

e. Rank the projects by each of the techniques used. Make and justify a recommendation.

| | Cash inflows (CF_t) | |
Year	Project A	Project B
1	$45,000	$75,000
2	45,000	60,000
3	45,000	30,000
4	45,000	30,000
5	45,000	30,000
6	45,000	30,000

   P9–20 Payback, NPV, and IRR   Rieger International is attempting to evaluate the feasibility of investing $95,000 in a piece of equipment that has a 5-year life. The firm has estimated the *cash inflows* associated with the proposal as shown in the table at the right. The firm has a 12% cost of capital.

a. Calculate the *payback period* for the proposed investment.
b. Calculate the *net present value (NPV)* for the proposed investment.
c. Calculate the *internal rate of return (IRR)*, rounded to the nearest whole percent, for the proposed investment.
d. Evaluate the acceptability of the proposed investment using NPV and IRR. What recommendation would you make relative to implementation of the project? Why?

Year (t)	Cash inflows (CF_t)
1	$20,000
2	25,000
3	30,000
4	35,000
5	40,000

    P9–21 NPV, IRR, and NPV profiles   Thomas Company is considering two mutually exclusive projects. The firm, which has a 12% cost of capital, has estimated its cash flows as shown in the following table.

	Project A	Project B
Initial investment (CF_0)	$130,000	$85,000
Year (t)	Cash inflows (CF_t)	
1	$25,000	$40,000
2	35,000	35,000
3	45,000	30,000
4	50,000	10,000
5	55,000	5,000

a. Calculate the *NPV* of each project, and assess its acceptability.
b. Calculate the *IRR* for each project, and assess its acceptability.
c. Draw the *NPV profiles* for both projects on the same set of axes.
d. Evaluate and discuss the rankings of the two projects on the basis of your findings in parts **a, b,** and **c.**
e. Explain your findings in part **d** in light of the pattern of cash inflows associated with each project.

P9–22   All techniques—Decision among mutually exclusive investments   Pound Industries is attempting to select the best of three mutually exclusive projects. The initial investment and after-tax cash inflows associated with these projects are shown in the following table.

Cash flows	Project A	Project B	Project C
Initial investment (CF_0)	$60,000	$100,000	$110,000
Cash inflows (CF_t), $t = 1$ to 5	$20,000	$ 31,500	$ 32,500

a. Calculate the *payback period* for each project.
b. Calculate the *net present value (NPV)* of each project, assuming that the firm has a cost of capital equal to 13%.
c. Calculate the *internal rate of return (IRR)* for each project.
d. Draw the *net present value profiles* for both projects on the same set of axes, and discuss any conflict in ranking that may exist between NPV and IRR.
e. Summarize the preferences dictated by each measure, and indicate which project you would recommend. Explain why.

P9–23   All techniques with NPV profile—Mutually exclusive projects   Projects A and B, of equal risk, are alternatives for expanding Rosa Company's capacity. The firm's cost of capital is 13%. The cash flows for each project are shown in the following table.

	Project A	Project B
Initial investment (CF_0)	$80,000	$50,000
Year (t)	Cash inflows (CF_t)	
1	$15,000	$15,000
2	20,000	15,000
3	25,000	15,000
4	30,000	15,000
5	35,000	15,000

a. Calculate each project's *payback period*.
b. Calculate the *net present value (NPV)* for each project.
c. Calculate the *internal rate of return (IRR)* for each project.
d. Draw the *net present value profiles* for both projects on the same set of axes, and discuss any conflict in ranking that may exist between NPV and IRR.
e. Summarize the preferences dictated by each measure, and indicate which project you would recommend. Explain why.

P9–24   Integrative—Complete investment decision   Wells Printing is considering the purchase of a new printing press. The total installed cost of the press is $2.2 million. This outlay would be partially offset by the sale of an existing press. The old press has zero book value, cost $1 million 10 years ago, and can be sold currently for $1.2 million before taxes. As a result of acquisition of the new press, sales in each of the next 5 years are expected to be $1.6 million higher than with the existing press, but product costs (excluding depreciation) will represent 50% of sales. The new press will not affect the firm's net working capital requirements. The new press will be depreciated under MACRS using a 5-year recovery period (see Table 3.2 on page 108). The firm is subject to a 40% tax rate. Wells Printing's cost of capital is 11%. (*Note:* Assume that both the old and the new press will have terminal values of $0 at the end of year 6.)

a. Determine the *initial investment* required by the new press.
b. Determine the *operating cash inflows* attributable to the new press. (*Note:* Be sure to consider the depreciation in year 6.)
c. Determine the *payback period*.
d. Determine the *net present value (NPV)* and the *internal rate of return (IRR)* related to the proposed new press.
e. Make a recommendation to accept or reject the new press, and justify your answer.

P9–25   **Integrative—Investment decision**   Holliday Manufacturing is considering the replacement of an existing machine. The new machine costs $1.2 million and requires installation costs of $150,000. The existing machine can be sold currently for $185,000 before taxes. It is 2 years old, cost $800,000 new, and has a $384,000 book value and a remaining useful life of 5 years. It was being depreciated under MACRS using a 5-year recovery period (see Table 3.2 on page 108) and therefore has the final 4 years of depreciation remaining. If it is held for 5 more years, the machine's market value at the end of year 5 will be $0. Over its 5-year life, the new machine should reduce operating costs by $350,000 per year. The new machine will be depreciated under MACRS using a 5-year recovery period (see Table 3.2 on page 108). The new machine can be sold for $200,000 net of removal and cleanup costs at the end of 5 years. An increased investment in net working capital of $25,000 will be needed to support operations if the new machine is acquired. Assume that the firm has adequate operating income against which to deduct any loss experienced on the sale of the existing machine. The firm has a 9% cost of capital and is subject to a 40% tax rate.

a. Develop the *relevant cash flows* needed to analyze the proposed replacement.
b. Determine the *net present value (NPV)* of the proposal.
c. Determine the *internal rate of return (IRR)* of the proposal.
d. Make a recommendation to accept or reject the replacement proposal, and justify your answer.
e. What is the highest cost of capital that the firm could have and still accept the proposal? Explain.

P9–26   **ETHICS PROBLEM**   Gap, Inc., is trying to incorporate human resource and supplier considerations into its management decision making. Here is Gap's report of findings from a recent Social Responsibility Report:

> Because factory owners sometimes try to hide violations, Gap emphasizes training for factory managers. However, due to regional differences, the training varies from one site to another. The report notes that 10 to 25 percent of workers in China, Taiwan, and Saipan have been harassed and humiliated. Less than half of the factories in sub-Saharan Africa have adequate worker safety regulations and infrastructure. In Mexico, Latin America, and the Caribbean, 25 to 50 percent of the suppliers fail to pay even the minimum wage.

Calvert Group, Ltd., a mutual fund family that focuses on "socially responsible investing," had this to say about the impact of Gap's report:

> With revenues of $15.9 billion and over 300,000 employees worldwide, Gap leads the U.S. apparel sector and has contracts with over 3,000 factories globally. Calvert has been in dialogue with Gap for about five years, the last two as part of the Working Group.
>
> Gap's supplier monitoring program focuses on remediation, because its suppliers produce for multiple apparel companies and would likely move their capacity to different clients rather than adopt conditions deemed too demanding. About one-third of the factories Gap examined comfortably met Gap's criteria, another third had barely acceptable conditions, and the final third missed the minimum standards. Gap terminated contracts with 136 factories where it found conditions to be beyond remediation.
>
> Increased transparency and disclosure are crucial in measuring a company's commitment to raising human rights standards and improving the lives of workers. Gap's report is an important first step in the direction of a model format that other companies can adapt.
>
> *Source:* www.calvert.com/news_newsArticle.asp?article=4612&image=cn .gif&keepleftnav= Calvert+News

If Gap were to aggressively pursue renegotiations with suppliers, based on this report, what is the likely effect on Gap's expenses in the next 5 years? In your opinion, what would be the impact on its stock price in the immediate future? After 10 years?

Chapter 9 Case

Making Norwich Tool's Lathe Investment Decision

Norwich Tool, a large machine shop, is considering replacing one of its lathes with either of two new lathes—lathe A or lathe B. Lathe A is a highly automated, computer-controlled lathe; lathe B is a less expensive lathe that uses standard technology. To analyze these alternatives, Mario Jackson, a financial analyst, prepared estimates of the initial investment and incremental (relevant) cash inflows associated with each lathe. These are shown in the following table.

	Lathe A	Lathe B
Initial investment (CF_0)	$660,000	$360,000
Year (t)	Cash inflows (CF_t)	
1	$128,000	$ 88,000
2	182,000	120,000
3	166,000	96,000
4	168,000	86,000
5	450,000	207,000

Note that Mario plans to analyze both lathes over a 5-year period. At the end of that time, the lathes would be sold, thus accounting for the large fifth-year cash inflows.

Mario believes that the two lathes are equally risky and that the acceptance of either of them will not change the firm's overall risk. He therefore decides to apply the firm's 13% cost of capital when analyzing the lathes. Norwich Tool requires all projects to have a maximum payback period of 4.0 years.

To Do

a. Use the *payback period* to assess the acceptability and relative ranking of each lathe.

b. Assuming equal risk, use the following sophisticated capital budgeting techniques to assess the acceptability and relative ranking of each lathe:
   (1) *Net present value (NPV)*.
   (2) *Internal rate of return (IRR)*.

c. Summarize the preferences indicated by the techniques used in parts **a** and **b**. Do the projects have conflicting rankings?

d. Draw the *net present value profiles* for both projects on the same set of axes, and discuss any conflict in rankings that may exist between NPV and IRR. Explain any observed conflict in terms of the relative differences in the magnitude and timing of each project's cash flows.

e. Use your findings in parts **a** through **d** to indicate, on both (1) a theoretical basis and (2) a practical basis, which lathe would be preferred. Explain any difference in recommendations.

Spreadsheet Exercise

The Drillago Company is involved in searching for locations in which to drill for oil. The firm's current project requires an initial investment of $15 million and has an estimated life of 10 years. The expected future cash inflows for the project are as follows:

Year	Cash inflows
1	$ 600,000
2	1,000,000
3	1,000,000
4	2,000,000
5	3,000,000
6	3,500,000
7	4,000,000
8	6,000,000
9	8,000,000
10	12,000,000

The firm's current cost of capital is 13%.

To Do

Create a spreadsheet to answer the following:

a. Calculate the project's *net present value (NPV)*. Is the project acceptable under the NPV technique? Explain.
b. Calculate the project's *internal rate of return (IRR)*. Is the project acceptable under the IRR technique? Explain.
c. In this case, did the two methods produce the same results? Generally, is there a preference between the NPV and IRR techniques? Explain.
d. Calculate the *payback period* for the project. If the firm usually accepts projects that have payback periods between 1 and 7 years, is this project acceptable?

Group Exercise

This assignment continues the work begun in Chapter 8 by taking a closer look at the numbers initially estimated for capital projects. Your work for this exercise will follow a similar pattern. You will take the two projects you designed in the previous chapter and begin to choose which will be implemented according to several criteria. Some of the cash flow numbers you developed in Chapter 8 may have to be modified to allow for adequate analysis. This alteration is permitted, but your group should try to retain the flavor of the examples you designed previously.

To Do

a. Begin the analysis of the competing projects by calculating the *payback period* for each project. (You must have two projects that both have positive payback periods, so a slight adjustment of the cash flows may be required here.)
b. Calculate the *NPV* for both projects. (Again, both projects should have a NPV that is greater than zero.) The crucial step in this part of the exercise is to apply an accurate discount rate. Your group should choose this rate (typically, the cost of capital) and, more important, defend its use. In other words, explain why you used the given discount rate to calculate the NPVs of the projects and why it makes sense given the current interest rate environment. Completion of this task must include a simple *NPV profile*.
c. Calculate the *IRR* for both projects.
d. Choose the project to be implemented based on all three techniques from parts **a**, **b**, and **c**. Your analysis must include an interpretation and evaluation of all three techniques. (This choice will be revisited in Chapter 10, which will provide more complete information.)

Web Exercise

Go to the book's companion website at **www.prenhall.com/gitman** to find the Web Exercise for this chapter.

> Remember to check the book's website at **www.prenhall.com/gitman** to find additional resources, including Web Exercises and a Web Case.

10

Risk and Refinements in Capital Budgeting

WHY THIS CHAPTER MATTERS TO YOU

Accounting: You need to understand the risk caused by the variability of cash flows, how to compare projects with unequal lives, and how to measure project returns when capital is being rationed.

Information systems: You need to understand how risk is incorporated into capital budgeting techniques, and how those techniques may be refined in the face of special circumstances, so as to design decision modules for use in analyzing proposed capital projects.

Management: You need to understand behavioral approaches for dealing with risk, including international risk, in capital budgeting decisions; how to risk adjust discount rates; how to refine capital budgeting techniques when projects have unequal lives or when capital must be rationed; and how to recognize real options embedded in capital projects.

Marketing: You need to understand how the risk of proposed projects is measured in capital budgeting, how projects with unequal lives will be evaluated, how to recognize and treat real options embedded in proposed projects, and how projects will be evaluated when capital must be rationed.

Operations: You need to understand how proposals for the acquisition of new equipment and plants will be evaluated by the firm's decision makers, especially projects that are risky, have unequal lives, or may need to be abandoned or slowed, or when capital is limited.

In Your Personal Life

Risk is present in all long-term decisions. When making personal financial decisions, you should consider risk in the decision-making process. Simply put, you should demand higher returns for greater risk. Failure to incorporate risk into your financial decision-making process will likely result in poor decisions and reduced wealth.

LEARNING GOALS

LG 1 Understand the importance of recognizing risk in the analysis of capital budgeting projects.

LG 2 Discuss risk and cash inflows, scenario analysis, and simulation as behavioral approaches for dealing with risk.

LG 3 Review the unique risks that multinational companies face.

LG 4 Describe the determination and use of risk-adjusted discount rates (RADRs), portfolio effects, and the practical aspects of RADRs.

LG 5 Select the best of a group of unequal-lived, mutually exclusive projects using annualized net present values (ANPVs).

LG 6 Explain the role of real options and the objective and procedures for selecting projects under capital rationing.

State Farm Insurance

Flooded with Claims

In the wake of Hurricane Katrina, which struck the Gulf Coast in 2005, claims flooded into **State Farm Insurance.** More than 295,000 homeowner and commercial claims and 99,000 auto claims were reported as a result of Katrina; State Farm handled more than 600,000 claims arising from the four hurricanes that made landfall on the Gulf Coast that year. The company paid more than $6 billion in claims for damage done by those hurricanes.

Not everyone was satisfied with the claims process, though: State Farm and its policyholders disputed whether some of the damage was caused by wind, which is covered under the homeowner's policy, or flooding, which is not covered under the policy. About 2 percent of the State Farm claims associated with Hurricane Katrina had not been settled as of early 2007, and a number of lawsuits were filed to try to force State Farm to pay more than State Farm adjusters deemed appropriate.

As a result of the ongoing litigation, on February 14, 2007, State Farm announced that it would suspend writing new homeowners and commercial property insurance in Mississippi. "We will continue to serve our existing policyholders, write new auto insurance policies, and market our financial services products as long as market conditions allow, but the current legal and business environments with regard to homeowner and commercial insurance are becoming untenable," said State Farm Senior Vice President Bob Trippel. State Farm's primary concern is that provisions in its insurance policies are being reinterpreted after the fact—through lawsuits—to provide for coverages that were not contemplated when the policies were written. As of early 2007, State Farm continued to insure more than 30 percent of the homeowners in Mississippi.

State Farm Insurance is in the business of risk management, but all companies face a variety of risks as they conduct their daily business. Like State Farm, each company must assess the risks of conducting its current business and the risks associated with new projects. Some projects are more risky than others, and some companies must choose between projects when there is insufficient capital to invest in all prospective projects. In this chapter, you will learn about risk in capital budgeting and decision making when capital has to be rationed.

> The state of Mississippi has considered legislation that would require State Farm to continue to issue new policies. How might that affect the premiums of current policyholders?

10.1 | Introduction to Risk in Capital Budgeting

The capital budgeting techniques introduced in Chapter 9 were applied in an environment we assumed to be certain. All of the projects' relevant cash flows, developed using techniques presented in Chapter 8, were assumed to have the same level of risk as the firm. In other words, all mutually exclusive projects were equally risky, and the acceptance of any project would not change the firm's overall risk. In actuality, these situations are rare—project cash flows typically have different levels of risk, and the acceptance of a project generally does affect the firm's overall risk, though often in a minor way. We begin this chapter by relaxing the assumptions of a certain environment and equal-risk projects, so as to focus on the incorporation of risk into the capital budgeting decision process. We, of course, will utilize many of the risk concepts developed in Chapter 5.

For convenience, in this chapter, we continue the Bennett Company example that was used in Chapter 9. The relevant cash flows and NPVs for Bennett Company's two mutually exclusive projects—A and B—are summarized in Table 10.1.

In the following three sections, we use the basic risk concepts presented in Chapter 5 to demonstrate behavioral approaches for dealing with risk, international risk considerations, and the use of risk-adjusted discount rates to explicitly recognize risk in the analysis of capital budgeting projects.

REVIEW QUESTION

10–1 Are most mutually exclusive capital budgeting projects equally risky? How can the acceptance of a project change a firm's overall risk?

TABLE 10.1	Relevant Cash Flows and NPVs for Bennett Company's Projects	
	Project A	Project B
A. Relevant cash flows		
Initial investment	$42,000	$45,000
Year	Operating cash inflows	
1	$14,000	$28,000
2	14,000	12,000
3	14,000	10,000
4	14,000	10,000
5	14,000	10,000
B. Decision technique		
NPV @ 10% cost of capital[a]	$11,071	$10,924

[a]From Figure 9.2 on page 430; calculated using a financial calculator.

10.2 | Behavioral Approaches for Dealing with Risk

Behavioral approaches can be used to get a "feel" for the level of project risk, whereas other approaches explicitly recognize project risk. Here we present a few behavioral approaches for dealing with risk in capital budgeting: risk and cash inflows, scenario analysis, and simulation. In a later section, we consider a popular approach that explicitly recognizes risk.

Risk and Cash Inflows

risk (in capital budgeting)
The chance that a project will prove unacceptable or, more formally, the degree of variability of cash flows.

In the context of capital budgeting, the term **risk** refers to the chance that a project will prove unacceptable—that is, NPV < \$0 or IRR < cost of capital. More formally, risk in capital budgeting is the degree of variability of cash flows. Projects with a small chance of acceptability and a broad range of expected cash flows are more risky than projects that have a high chance of acceptability and a narrow range of expected cash flows.

In the conventional capital budgeting projects assumed here, risk stems almost entirely from *cash inflows,* because the initial investment is generally known with relative certainty. These inflows, of course, derive from a number of variables related to revenues, expenditures, and taxes. Examples include the level of sales, the cost of raw materials, labor rates, utility costs, and tax rates. We will concentrate on the risk in the cash inflows, but remember that this risk actually results from the interaction of these underlying variables. Therefore, to assess the risk of a proposed capital expenditure, the analyst needs to evaluate the probability that the cash inflows will be large enough to provide for project acceptance.

Example

breakeven cash inflow
The minimum level of cash inflow necessary for a project to be acceptable, that is, NPV > \$0.

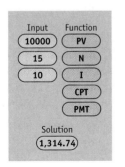

Treadwell Tire Company, a tire retailer with a 10% cost of capital, is considering investing in either of two mutually exclusive projects, A and B. Each requires a \$10,000 initial investment, and both are expected to provide equal annual cash inflows over their 15-year lives. For either project to be acceptable according to the net present value technique, its NPV must be greater than zero. If we let *CF* equal the annual cash inflow and let CF_0 equal the initial investment, the following condition must be met for projects with annuity cash inflows, such as A and B, to be acceptable.

$$NPV = [CF \times (PVIFA_{r,n})] - CF_0 > \$0 \qquad \text{(10.1)}$$

By substituting $r = 10\%$, $n = 15$ years, and $CF_0 = \$10,000$, we can find the **breakeven cash inflow**—the minimum level of cash inflow necessary for Treadwell's projects to be acceptable.

Calculator Use   Recognizing that the initial investment (CF_0) is the present value (*PV*), we can use the calculator inputs shown at the left to find the breakeven cash inflow (*CF*), which is an ordinary annuity (*PMT*).

Spreadsheet Use   The breakeven cash inflow also can be calculated as shown on the following Excel spreadsheet.

	A	B
1	BREAKEVEN CASH INFLOW	
2	Cost of capital	10%
3	Number of years	15
4	Initial investment	$10,000
5	Breakeven cash inflow	$1,314.74

Entry in Cell B5 is =PMT(B2,B3,−B4).
The minus sign appears before B4 because
the initial investment is a cash outflow.

Table Use   The present value interest factor for an ordinary annuity at 10% for 15 years ($PVIFA_{10\%,15yrs}$) found in Table A–4 is 7.606. Substituting this value and the initial investment (CF_0) of $10,000 into Equation 10.1 and solving for the breakeven cash inflow (CF), we get

$$[CF \times (PVIFA_{10\%,15yrs})] - \$10,000 > \$0$$

$$CF \times (7.606) > \$10,000$$

$$CF > \frac{\$10,000}{7.606} = \underline{\underline{\$1,314.75}}$$

The calculator, spreadsheet, and table values indicate that for the projects to be acceptable, they must have annual cash inflows of at least $1,315. Given this breakeven level of cash inflows, the risk of each project could be assessed by determining the probability that the project's cash inflows will equal or exceed this breakeven level. The various statistical techniques that would determine that probability are covered in more advanced courses.[1] For now, we can simply assume that such a statistical analysis results in the following:

Probability of $CF_A > \$1,315 \rightarrow 100\%$

Probability of $CF_B > \$1,315 \rightarrow 65\%$

Because project A is certain (100% probability) to have a positive net present value, whereas there is only a 65% chance that project B will have a positive NPV, project A is less risky than project B. Of course, the expected level of annual cash inflow and NPV associated with each project must be evaluated in view of the firm's risk preference before the preferred project is selected.

The example clearly identifies risk as it is related to the chance that a project is acceptable, but it does not address the issue of cash flow variability. Even though project B has a greater chance of loss than project A, it might result in higher potential NPVs. Recall from Chapters 5 through 7 that it is the *combination* of risk and return that determines value. Similarly, the worth of a capital expenditure and its impact on the firm's value must be viewed in light of both risk and return. The analyst must therefore consider the *variability* of cash inflows and NPVs to assess project risk and return fully.

---

1. Normal distributions are commonly used to develop the concept of the *probability of success*—that is, of a project having a positive NPV. The reader interested in learning more about this technique should see any second- or MBA-level managerial finance text.

Scenario Analysis

Scenario analysis can be used to deal with project risk to capture the variability of cash inflows and NPVs. As noted in Chapter 5, *scenario analysis* is a behavioral approach that uses several possible alternative outcomes (scenarios), such as cash inflows, to obtain a sense of the variability among returns, measured here by NPV. This technique is often useful in getting a feel for the variability of return in response to changes in a key outcome. In capital budgeting, one of the most common scenario approaches is to estimate the NPVs associated with pessimistic (worst), most likely (expected), and optimistic (best) estimates of cash inflow. The *range* can be determined by subtracting the pessimistic-outcome NPV from the optimistic-outcome NPV.

Example ▸ Continuing with Treadwell Tire Company, assume that the financial manager created three cash inflow outcome scenarios for each project: pessimistic, most likely, and optimistic. The cash inflow outcomes and resulting NPVs in each case are summarized in Table 10.2. Comparing the ranges of cash inflows ($1,000 for project A and $4,000 for B) and, more important, the ranges of NPVs ($7,606 for project A and $30,424 for B) makes it clear that project A is less risky than project B. Given that both projects have the same most likely NPV of $5,212, the assumed risk-averse decision maker will take project A because it has less risk (smaller NPV range) and no possibility of loss (all NPVs > $0).

The widespread availability of computers and spreadsheets has greatly enhanced the use of scenario analysis.

TABLE 10.2	Scenario Analysis of Treadwell's Projects A and B	
	Project A	Project B
Initial investment	$10,000	$10,000
	Annual cash inflows	
Outcome		
Pessimistic	$1,500	$ 0
Most likely	2,000	2,000
Optimistic	2,500	4,000
Range	$1,000	$ 4,000
	Net present values[a]	
Outcome		
Pessimistic	$1,409	−$10,000
Most likely	5,212	5,212
Optimistic	9,015	20,424
Range	$7,606	$30,424

[a]These values were calculated by using the corresponding annual cash inflows. A 10% cost of capital and a 15-year life for the annual cash inflows were used.

Simulation

Simulation is a statistics-based behavioral approach that applies predetermined probability distributions and random numbers to estimate risky outcomes. By tying the various cash flow components together in a mathematical model and repeating the process numerous times, the financial manager can develop a probability distribution of project returns.

Figure 10.1 presents a flowchart of the simulation of the net present value of a project. The process of generating random numbers and using the probability distributions for cash inflows and cash outflows enables the financial manager to determine values for each of these variables. Substituting these values into the mathematical model results in an NPV. By repeating this process perhaps a thousand times, managers can create a probability distribution of net present values.

Although Figure 10.1 simulates only gross cash inflows and cash outflows, more sophisticated simulations using individual inflow and outflow components, such as sales volume, sale price, raw material cost, labor cost, or maintenance expense, are quite common. From the distribution of returns, the decision maker can determine not only the expected value of the return but also the probability of achieving or surpassing a given return. The use of computers has made the

Hint These behavioral approaches may seem a bit imprecise to one who has not used them. But repeated use and an "after-the-fact" review of previous analyses improve the accuracy of the users.

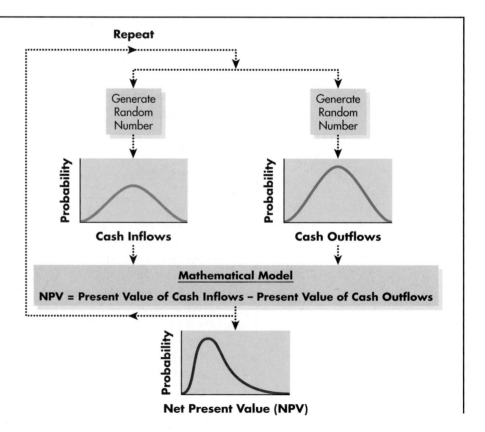

FIGURE 10.1

NPV Simulation
Flowchart of a net present value simulation

Focus on Practice

The Monte Carlo Method:
The Forecast Is for Less Uncertainty

Most capital budgeting decisions involve some degree of uncertainty. For example, a company faces some degree of uncertainty associated with the demand for a new product. One method of accounting for this uncertainty is to average the highest and the lowest prediction of sales. However, such a method is flawed. Producing the average of the expected possible demand can lead to gross overproduction or gross underproduction, neither of which is as profitable as having the right volume of production.

To combat uncertainty in the decision-making process, some companies use a Monte Carlo simulation program to model possible outcomes. Developed by mathematicians in World War II while working on the atomic bomb, the *Monte Carlo method* was not widely used until the advent of the personal computer. A Monte Carlo simu-

lation program randomly generates values for uncertain variables over and over to simulate a model. The simulation then requires project practitioners to develop low, high, and most likely cost estimates along with correlation coefficients. Once these inputs are derived, the Monte Carlo program can be run through just a few simulations, or thousands, in just a few seconds.

A Monte Carlo program usually builds a histogram of the results, referred to as a *frequency chart,* for each forecast or output cell that the user wants to analyze. The program then delivers a percentage *certainty* that a particular forecast will fall within a specified range, much like a weather forecast. The program also has an optimization feature that allows a project manager with budget constraints to figure out which combination of possible projects will result in the highest profit.

One of the problems with using a Monte Carlo program is the difficulty of establishing the correct input ranges for the variables and determining the correlation coefficients for those variables. However, the work put into developing the input for the program can often clarify some uncertainty in a proposed project. Although Monte Carlo simulation is not the perfect answer to capital budgeting problems, it is another tool that corporations, including **ALCOA, Motorola, RJR Nabisco,** and **Walt Disney,** use to manage risk and make more informed business and strategic decisions.

■ *A Monte Carlo simulation program requires the user to first build an Excel spreadsheet model that captures the input variables for the proposed project. What issues and what benefits can the user derive from this process?*

simulation approach feasible. Monte Carlo simulation programs, made popular by widespread use of personal computers, are described in the above *Focus on Practice* box.

The output of simulation provides an excellent basis for decision making, because it enables the decision maker to view a continuum of risk–return trade-offs rather than a single-point estimate.

REVIEW QUESTIONS

10–2 Define *risk* in terms of the cash inflows from a capital budgeting project. How can determination of the *breakeven cash inflow* be used to gauge project risk?

10–3 Describe how each of the following behavioral approaches can be used to deal with project risk: (**a**) scenario analysis and (**b**) simulation.

10.3 | International Risk Considerations

exchange rate risk
The danger that an unexpected change in the exchange rate between the dollar and the currency in which a project's cash flows are denominated will reduce the market value of that project's cash flow.

Although the basic techniques of capital budgeting are the same for multinational companies (MNCs) as for purely domestic firms, firms that operate in several countries face risks that are unique to the international arena. Two types of risk are particularly important: exchange rate risk and political risk.

Exchange rate risk reflects the danger that an unexpected change in the exchange rate between the dollar and the currency in which a project's cash flows are denominated will reduce the market value of that project's cash flow. The dollar value of future cash inflows can be dramatically altered if the local currency depreciates against the dollar. In the short term, specific cash flows can be hedged by using financial instruments such as currency futures and options. Long-term exchange rate risk can best be minimized by financing the project, in whole or in part, in local currency.

Political risk is much harder to protect against. Once a foreign project is accepted, the foreign government can block the return of profits, seize the firm's assets, or otherwise interfere with a project's operation. The inability to manage political risk after the fact makes it even more important that managers account for political risks *before* making an investment. They can do so either by adjusting a project's expected cash inflows to account for the probability of political interference or by using *risk-adjusted discount rates* (discussed later in this chapter) in capital budgeting formulas. In general, it is much better to adjust individual project cash flows for political risk subjectively than to use a blanket adjustment for all projects.

In addition to unique risks that MNCs must face, several other special issues are relevant only for international capital budgeting. One of these special issues is *taxes*. Because only after-tax cash flows are relevant for capital budgeting, financial managers must carefully account for taxes paid to foreign governments on profits earned within their borders. They must also assess the impact of these tax payments on the parent company's U.S. tax liability.

Another special issue in international capital budgeting is *transfer pricing*. Much of the international trade involving MNCs is, in reality, simply the shipment of goods and services from one of a parent company's subsidiaries to another subsidiary located abroad. The parent company therefore has great discretion in setting **transfer prices,** the prices that subsidiaries charge each other for the goods and services traded between them. The widespread use of transfer pricing in international trade makes capital budgeting in MNCs very difficult unless the transfer prices that are used accurately reflect actual costs and incremental cash flows.

transfer prices
Prices that subsidiaries charge each other for the goods and services traded between them.

Finally, MNCs often must approach international capital projects from a *strategic point of view*, rather than from a strictly financial perspective. For example, an MNC may feel compelled to invest in a country to ensure continued access, even if the project itself may not have a positive net present value. This motivation was important for Japanese automakers that set up assembly plants in the United States in the early 1980s. For much the same reason, U.S. investment in Europe surged during the years before the market integration of the European Community in 1992. MNCs often invest in production facilities in the home country of major rivals to deny these competitors an uncontested home market. MNCs also may feel compelled to invest in certain industries or countries to achieve a broad corporate objective such as completing a product line or diversifying raw material sources, even when the project's cash flows may not be sufficiently profitable.

REVIEW QUESTION

10–4 Briefly explain how the following items affect the capital budgeting decisions of multinational companies: **(a)** exchange rate risk; **(b)** political risk; **(c)** tax law differences; **(d)** transfer pricing; and **(e)** a strategic rather than a strict financial viewpoint.

 ## 10.4 | Risk-Adjusted Discount Rates

The approaches for dealing with risk that have been presented so far enable the financial manager to get a "feel" for project risk. Unfortunately, they do not explicitly recognize project risk. We will now illustrate the most popular risk-adjustment technique that employs the net present value (NPV) decision method.[2] The NPV decision rule of accepting only those projects with NPVs > $0 will continue to hold. Close examination of the basic equation for NPV, Equation 9.1, should make it clear that because the initial investment (CF_0) is known with certainty, a project's risk is embodied in the present value of its cash inflows:

$$\sum_{t=1}^{n} \frac{CF_t}{(1 + r)^t}$$

Two opportunities to adjust the present value of cash inflows for risk exist: (1) The cash inflows (CF_t) can be adjusted, or (2) the discount rate (r) can be adjusted. Adjusting the cash inflows is highly subjective, so here we describe the more popular process of adjusting the discount rate. In addition, we consider the portfolio effects of project analysis as well as the practical aspects of the risk-adjusted discount rate.

Determining Risk-Adjusted Discount Rates (RADRs)

A popular approach for risk adjustment involves the use of risk-adjusted discount rates (RADRs). This approach uses Equation 9.1 but employs a risk-adjusted discount rate, as noted in the following expression:[3]

risk-adjusted discount rate (RADR)
The rate of return that must be earned on a given project to compensate the firm's owners adequately—that is, to maintain or improve the firm's share price.

$$NPV = \sum_{t=1}^{n} \frac{CF_t}{(1 + RADR)^t} - CF_0 \qquad (10.2)$$

The **risk-adjusted discount rate (RADR)** is the rate of return that must be earned on a given project to compensate the firm's owners adequately—that is, to maintain or improve the firm's share price. The higher the risk of a project, the

---

2. The IRR could just as well have been used, but because NPV is theoretically preferable, it is used instead.

3. The risk-adjusted discount rate approach can be applied in using the internal rate of return as well as the net present value. When the IRR is used, the risk-adjusted discount rate becomes the cutoff rate that must be exceeded by the IRR for the project to be accepted. When NPV is used, the projected cash inflows are merely discounted at the risk-adjusted discount rate.

higher the RADR, and therefore the lower the net present value for a given stream of cash inflows.

Personal Finance Example   Talor Namtig is considering investing $1,000 in either of two stocks—A or B. She plans to hold the stock for exactly 5 years and expects both stocks to pay $80 in annual end-of-year cash dividends. At the end of the year 5 she estimates that stock A can be sold to net $1,200 and stock B can be sold to net $1,500. Talor has carefully researched the two stocks and feels that although stock A has average risk, stock B is considerably riskier. Her research indicates that she should earn an annual return on an average risk stock of 11%. Because stock B is considerably riskier, she will require a 14% return from it. Talor makes the following calculations to find the risk-adjusted net present values (NPVs) for the two stocks:

$$\text{NPV}_A = [\$80 \times (PVIFA_{11\%,5yrs})] + [\$1,200 \times (PVIF_{11\%,5yrs})] - \$1,000$$

Using a financial calculator, she gets:
$$\text{NPV}_A = \$1,007.81 - \$1,000 = \underline{\underline{\$7.81}}$$

$$\text{NPV}_B = [\$80 \times (PVIFA_{14\%,5yrs})] + [\$1,500 \times (PVIF_{14\%,5yrs})] - \$1,000$$

Using a financial calculator, she gets:
$$\text{NPV}_B = \$1,053.70 - \$1,000 = \underline{\underline{\$53.70}}$$

Although Talor's calculations indicate that both stock investments are acceptable (NPVs > $0), on a risk-adjusted basis, she should invest in Stock B because it has a higher NPV.

Because the logic underlying the use of RADRs is closely linked to the capital asset pricing model (CAPM) developed in Chapter 5, here we review CAPM and discuss its use in finding RADRs.

Review of CAPM

In Chapter 5, we used the *capital asset pricing model (CAPM)* to link the *relevant* risk and return for all assets traded in *efficient markets*. In the development of the CAPM, the *total risk* of an asset was defined as

$$\text{Total risk} = \text{Nondiversifiable risk} + \text{Diversifiable risk} \qquad (10.3)$$

For assets traded in an efficient market, the *diversifiable risk*, which results from uncontrollable or random events, can be eliminated through diversification. The relevant risk is therefore the *nondiversifiable risk*—the risk for which owners of these assets are rewarded. Nondiversifiable risk for securities is commonly measured by using *beta*, which is an index of the degree of movement of an asset's return in response to a change in the market return.

Using beta, b_j, to measure the relevant risk of any asset j, the CAPM is

$$r_j = R_F + [b_j \times (r_m - R_F)] \qquad (10.4)$$

where

r_j = required return on asset j

R_F = risk-free rate of return

b_j = beta coefficient for asset j

r_m = return on the market portfolio of assets

In Chapter 5, we demonstrated that the required return on any asset could be determined by substituting values of R_F, b_j, and r_m into the CAPM—Equation 10.4. Any security that is expected to earn in excess of its required return would be acceptable, and those that are expected to earn an inferior return would be rejected.

Using CAPM to Find RADRs

If we assume for a moment that real corporate assets such as computers, machine tools, and special-purpose machinery are traded in efficient markets, the CAPM can be redefined as noted in Equation 10.5:

$$r_{\text{project } j} = R_F + [b_{\text{project } j} \times (r_m - R_F)] \tag{10.5}$$

The *security market line* (SML)—the graphical depiction of the CAPM—is shown for Equation 10.5 in Figure 10.2. Any project having an IRR above the SML would be acceptable, because its IRR would exceed the required return, r_{project}; any project with an IRR below r_{project} would be rejected. In terms of NPV, any project falling above the SML would have a positive NPV, and any project falling below the SML would have a negative NPV.[4]

> Example
>
> Figure 10.2 shows two projects, L and R. Project L has a beta, b_L, and generates an internal rate of return, IRR_L. The required return for a project with risk b_L is r_L. Because project L generates a return greater than that required ($IRR_L > r_L$), project L is acceptable. Project L will have a positive NPV when its cash inflows are discounted at its required return, r_L. Project R, on the other hand, generates an IRR below that required for its risk, b_R ($IRR_R < r_R$). This project will have a negative NPV when its cash inflows are discounted at its required return, r_R. Project R should be rejected.

FIGURE 10.2

CAPM and SML
CAPM and SML in capital budgeting decision making

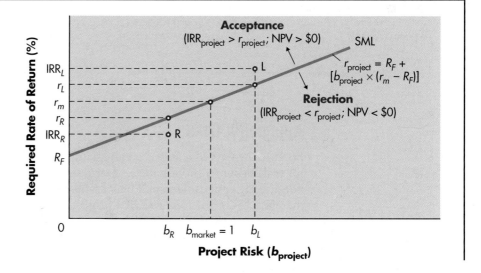

4. As noted earlier, whenever the IRR is above the cost of capital or required return (IRR > r), the NPV is positive, and whenever the IRR is below the cost of capital or required return (IRR < r), the NPV is negative. Because by definition the IRR is the discount rate that causes NPV to equal zero and the IRR and NPV always agree on accept–reject decisions, the relationship noted in Figure 10.2 logically follows.

Focus on Ethics   Environmental Compliance: Honesty Is the Best Policy

It doesn't matter whether you manufacture specialty chemicals or household cleansers, operate a paint shop, sell turf products, or dispose of complex products such as aircraft engines, regulators want you to account for the effect your operations have on the environment, consumer health, and employee safety.

Not only do today's firms need to find a way to track the product as well as the environmental and exposure specifications associated with environmental regulations, they also have to manage their manufacturing processes to ensure that their storage and distribution facilities, equipment, personnel, processes, and products conform. This goes well beyond finished-product quality testing against regulated specifications. Firms have to manage the level of emissions and waste created throughout the entire lifecycle of their products and facilities, from R&D through transportation to customers—and increasingly to disposal.

The Environmental Protection Agency (EPA) has the authority to levy significant fines on companies that violate environmental regulations. In May 2007, the EPA announced that a settlement had been reached with **Kerr-McGee** after the EPA discovered violations of the Clean Air Act at several of Kerr-McGee's natural gas compressor stations near Vernal, Utah. The agreement requires Kerr-McGee to pay a $200,000 penalty and spend $250,000 on environmental projects to benefit the area in which the violations occurred. In addition, Kerr-McGee announced that it would spend $18 million on pollution controls that will reduce harmful emissions and conserve natural gas at its production facilities. The EPA also announced a $2.9 million penalty assessed against **Total Petrochemical USA Inc.** for alleged violations of the Clean Air Act. According to Granta Nakayama, EPA's assistant administrator for Enforcement and Compliance Assurance, "With today's settlement,

86 refineries in 25 states across the nation have agreed to address environmental problems and invest more than $4.5 billion in new pollution control technologies."

Companies that self-disclose violations of federal environmental regulations are fined, but they face a smaller penalty than they otherwise would if the EPA discovered the violations first. On May 9, 2007, the EPA announced that **Kmart** would pay a $102,422 fine to settle self-disclosed violations of clean water, hazardous waste, and emergency planning and preparedness regulations. If the EPA had discovered Kmart's violations through an inspection, the company would have faced a fine of more than $1.6 million. Although still economically painful, when it comes to reporting environmental violations, honesty is the best policy.

■ *What are some factors to consider when prioritizing and budgeting environmental compliance initiatives?*

Applying RADRs

Because the CAPM is based on an assumed efficient market, which does *not* exist for real corporate (nonfinancial) assets such as plant and equipment, the CAPM is not directly applicable in making capital budgeting decisions. Financial managers therefore assess the *total risk* of a project and use it to determine the risk-adjusted discount rate (RADR), which can be used in Equation 10.2 to find the NPV.

To avoid damaging its market value, the firm must use the correct discount rate to evaluate a project. The *Focus on Ethics* box above describes real examples of companies that failed to recognize (or that ignored) certain risks associated with their business operations. As a result, their firms experienced monetary sanctions. If a firm fails to incorporate all relevant risks in its decision-making process, it may discount a risky project's cash inflows at too low a rate and accept the project. The firm's market price may drop later as investors recognize that the firm itself has become more risky. Conversely, if the firm discounts a project's cash inflows at too high a rate, it will reject acceptable projects. Eventually the firm's market price may drop, because investors who believe that the firm is being overly conservative will sell their stock, putting downward pressure on the firm's market value.

Unfortunately, there is no formal mechanism for linking *total project risk* to the level of required return. As a result, most firms subjectively determine the RADR by adjusting their existing required return. They adjust it up or down depending on whether the proposed project is more or less risky, respectively, than the average risk of the firm. This CAPM-type of approach provides a "rough estimate" of the project risk and required return because both the project risk measure and the linkage between risk and required return are estimates.

Example

Bennett Company wishes to use the risk-adjusted discount rate approach to determine, according to NPV, whether to implement project A or project B. In addition to the data presented in part A of Table 10.1, Bennett's management after much analysis subjectively assigned "risk indexes" of 1.6 to project A and 1.0 to project B. The risk index is merely a numerical scale used to classify project risk: Higher index values are assigned to higher-risk projects, and vice versa. The CAPM-type relationship used by the firm to link risk (measured by the risk index) and the required return (RADR) is shown in the following table. Management developed this relationship after analyzing CAPM and the risk–return relationships of the projects that they considered and implemented during the past few years.

	Risk index	Required return (RADR)
	0.0	6% (risk-free rate, R_F)
	0.2	7
	0.4	8
	0.6	9
	0.8	10
Project B →	1.0	11
	1.2	12
	1.4	13
Project A →	1.6	14
	1.8	16
	2.0	18

Because project A is riskier than project B, its RADR of 14% is greater than project B's 11%. The net present value of each project, calculated using its RADR, is found as shown on the time lines in Figure 10.3 (on page 471). The results clearly show that project B is preferable, because its risk-adjusted NPV of $9,798 is greater than the $6,063 risk-adjusted NPV for project A. As reflected by the NPVs in part B of Table 10.1, if the discount rates were not adjusted for risk, project A would be preferred to project B.

Project A

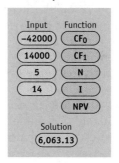

Input   Function
(−42000) (CF₀)
(14000) (CF₁)
(5) (N)
(14) (I)
  (NPV)

Solution
(6,063.13)

Project B

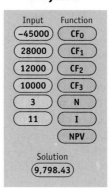

Input   Function
(−45000) (CF₀)
(28000) (CF₁)
(12000) (CF₂)
(10000) (CF₃)
(3) (N)
(11) (I)
  (NPV)

Solution
(9,798.43)

Calculator Use   We can again use the preprogrammed NPV function in a financial calculator to simplify the NPV calculation. The keystrokes for project A—the annuity—typically are as shown at the left. The keystrokes for project B—the mixed stream—are also shown at the left. The calculated NPVs for projects A and B of $6,063 and $9,798, respectively, agree with those shown in Figure 10.3.

Spreadsheet Use   Analysis of projects using risk-adjusted discount rates (RADRs) also can be performed as shown on the following Excel spreadsheet.

	A	B	C	D
1	ANALYSIS OF PROJECTS USING RISK-ADJUSTED DISCOUNT RATES			
2	Year	Cash Inflow	Present Value	Formulas for Calculated Values in Column C
3		Project A		
4	1-5	$ 14,000	$48,063	−PV(C7,5,B4,0)
5	Initial Investment		$42,000	
6	Net Present Value		$ 6,063	C4–C5
7	Required Return (RADAR)		14%	
8		Project B		
9	1	$ 28,000	$25,225	−PV(C17,A9,0,B9,0)
10	2	12,000	9,739	−PV(C17,A10,0,B10,0)
11	3	10,000	7,312	−PV(C17,A11,0,B11,0)
12	4	10,000	6,587	−PV(C17,A12,0,B12,0)
13	5	10,000	5,935	−PV(C17,A13,0,B13,0)
14	Present value		$54,798	SUM(C9:C13) or NPV(C17,B9:B13)
15	Initial Investment		$45,000	
16	Net Present Value		$ 9,798	C14–C15
17	Required Return (RADAR)		11%	
18	Choice of project	B		IF(C6>=C16,"A","B")

The minus signs appear before the entries in Cells D4 and D9:D13 to convert the results to positive values.

The usefulness of risk-adjusted discount rates should now be clear. The real difficulty lies in estimating project risk and linking it to the required return (RADR).

Portfolio Effects

As noted in Chapter 5, because investors are not rewarded for taking diversifiable risk, they should hold a diversified portfolio of securities. Because a business firm can be viewed as a portfolio of assets, is it similarly important that the firm maintain a diversified portfolio of assets?

It seems logical that by holding a diversified portfolio the firm could reduce the variability of its cash flows. By combining two projects with negatively correlated cash inflows, the firm could reduce the combined cash inflow variability—and therefore the risk.

Are firms rewarded for diversifying risk in this fashion? If they are, the value of the firm could be enhanced through diversification into other lines of business. Surprisingly, the value of the stock of firms whose shares are traded publicly in an efficient marketplace is generally *not* affected by diversification. In other words, diversification is not normally rewarded and therefore is generally not necessary.

| FIGURE 10.3 | **Calculation of NPVs for Bennett Company's Capital Expenditure Alternatives Using RADRs** |

Time lines depicting the cash flows and NPV calculations using RADRs for projects A and B

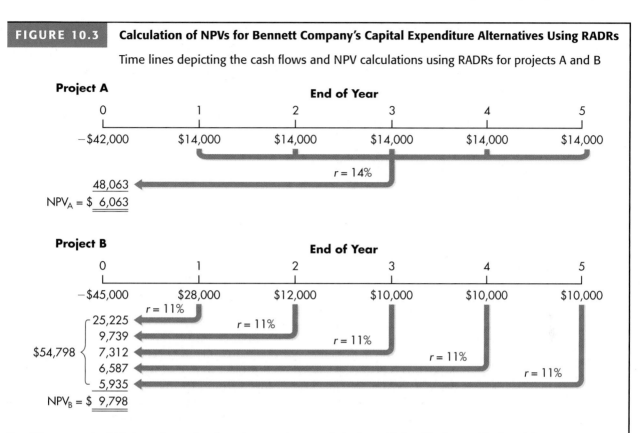

Note: When we use the risk indexes of 1.6 and 1.0 for projects A and B, respectively, along with the table above, a risk-adjusted discount rate (RADR) of 14% results for project A and a RADR of 11% results for project B.

Why are firms not rewarded for diversification? Because investors themselves can diversify by holding securities in a variety of firms; they do not need the firm to do it for them. And investors can diversify more readily—they can make transactions more easily and at a lower cost because of the greater availability of information and trading mechanisms.

Of course, if a firm acquires a new line of business and its cash flows tend to respond more to changing economic conditions (that is, greater nondiversifiable risk), greater returns would be expected. If, for the additional risk, the firm earned a return in excess of that required (IRR > r), the value of the firm could be enhanced. Also, other benefits, such as increased cash, greater borrowing capacity, guaranteed availability of raw materials, and so forth, could result from and therefore justify diversification, in spite of any immediate impact on cash flow.

Although a strict theoretical view supports the use of a technique that relies on the CAPM framework, the presence of market imperfections causes the market for real corporate assets to be inefficient. The relative inefficiency of this market, coupled with difficulties associated with measurement of nondiversifiable project risk and its relationship to return, tend to favor the use of total risk to evaluate capital budgeting projects. Therefore, the use of *total risk* as an approximation for the relevant risk does tend to have widespread practical appeal.

RADRs in Practice

In spite of the appeal of total risk, *RADRs are often used in practice.* Their popularity stems from two facts: (1) They are consistent with the general disposition of financial decision makers toward rates of return,[5] and (2) they are easily estimated and applied. The first reason is clearly a matter of personal preference, but the second is based on the computational convenience and well-developed procedures involved in the use of RADRs.

In practice, firms often establish a number of *risk classes,* with an RADR assigned to each. Like the CAPM-type risk–return relationship described earlier, management develops the risk classes and RADRs based on both CAPM and the risk–return behaviors of past projects. Each new project is then subjectively placed in the appropriate risk class, and the corresponding RADR is used to evaluate it. This is sometimes done on a division-by-division basis, in which case each division has its own set of risk classes and associated RADRs, similar to those for Bennett Company in Table 10.3. The use of *divisional costs of capital* and associated risk classes enables a large multidivisional firm to incorporate differing levels of divisional risk into the capital budgeting process and still recognize differences in the levels of individual project risk.

Hint The use of risk classes is consistent with the concept that risk-averse investors require a greater return for greater risks. To increase shareholders' wealth—and hence warrant acceptance—risky projects must earn greater returns.

Example

Assume that the management of Bennett Company decided to use risk classes to analyze projects and so placed each project in one of four risk classes according to its perceived risk. The classes ranged from I for the lowest-risk projects to IV for the highest-risk projects. Associated with each class was an RADR appropriate to the level of risk of projects in the class, as given in Table 10.3. Bennett

TABLE 10.3   Bennett Company's Risk Classes and RADRs

Risk class	Description	Risk-adjusted discount rate, RADR
I	*Below-average risk:* Projects with low risk. Typically involve routine replacement without renewal of existing activities.	8%
II	*Average risk:* Projects similar to those currently implemented. Typically involve replacement or renewal of existing activities.	10%[a]
III	*Above-average risk:* Projects with higher than normal, but not excessive, risk. Typically involve expansion of existing or similar activities.	14%
IV	*Highest risk:* Projects with very high risk. Typically involve expansion into new or unfamiliar activities.	20%

[a]This RADR is actually the firm's cost of capital, which is discussed in detail in Chapter 11. It represents the firm's required return on its existing portfolio of projects, which is assumed to be unchanged with acceptance of the "average risk" project.

5. Recall that although NPV is the theoretically preferred evaluation technique, IRR is more popular in actual business practice because of the general preference of businesspeople for rates of return rather than pure dollar returns. The popularity of RADRs is therefore consistent with the preference for IRR over NPV.

classified as lower-risk those projects that tend to involve routine replacement or renewal activities; higher-risk projects involve expansion, often into new or unfamiliar activities.

The financial manager of Bennett has assigned project A to class III and project B to class II. The cash flows for project A would be evaluated using a 14% RADR, and project B's would be evaluated using a 10% RADR.[6] The NPV of project A at 14% was calculated in Figure 10.3 to be $6,063, and the NPV for project B at a 10% RADR was shown in Table 10.1 to be $10,924. Clearly, with RADRs based on the use of risk classes, project B is preferred over project A. As noted earlier, this result is contrary to the preferences shown in Table 10.1, where differing risks of projects A and B were not taken into account.

REVIEW QUESTIONS

10–5 Describe the basic procedures involved in using *risk-adjusted discount rates (RADRs)*. How is this approach related to the *capital asset pricing model (CAPM)?*

10–6 Explain why a firm whose stock is actively traded in the securities markets need not concern itself with diversification. In spite of this, how is the risk of capital budgeting projects frequently measured? Why?

10–7 How are *risk classes* often used to apply RADRs?

10.5 | Capital Budgeting Refinements

Refinements must often be made in the analysis of capital budgeting projects to accommodate special circumstances. These adjustments permit the relaxation of certain simplifying assumptions presented earlier. Three areas in which special forms of analysis are frequently needed are (1) comparison of mutually exclusive projects having unequal lives, (2) recognition of real options, and (3) capital rationing caused by a binding budget constraint.

Comparing Projects with Unequal Lives

The financial manager must often select the best of a group of unequal-lived projects. If the projects are independent, the length of the project lives is not critical. But when unequal-lived projects are mutually exclusive, the impact of differing lives must be considered because the projects do not provide service over comparable time periods. This is especially important when continuing service is needed from the project under consideration. The discussions that follow assume that the unequal-lived, mutually exclusive projects being compared *are ongoing*. If they were not, the project with the highest NPV would be selected.

---

6. Note that the 10% RADR for project B using the risk classes in Table 10.3 differs from the 11% RADR used in the preceding example for project B. This difference is attributable to the less precise nature of the use of risk classes.

The Problem

A simple example will demonstrate the basic problem of noncomparability caused by the need to select the best of a group of mutually exclusive projects with differing usable lives.

Example

The AT Company, a regional cable television company, is evaluating two projects, X and Y. The relevant cash flows for each project are given in the following table. The applicable cost of capital for use in evaluating these equally risky projects is 10%.

	Project X	Project Y
Initial investment	$70,000	$85,000
Year	Annual cash inflows	
1	$28,000	$35,000
2	33,000	30,000
3	38,000	25,000
4	—	20,000
5	—	15,000
6	—	10,000

Project X

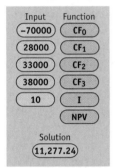

Project Y

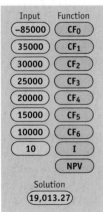

Calculator Use   Employing the preprogrammed NPV function in a financial calculator, we use the keystrokes shown at the left for project X and for project Y to find their respective NPVs of $11,277.24 and $19,013.27.

Spreadsheet Use   The net present values of two projects with unequal lives also can be compared as shown on the following Excel spreadsheet.

	A	B	C
1	COMPARISON OF NET PRESENT VALUES OF TWO PROJECTS WITH UNEQUAL LIVES		
2		Cost of Capital	10%
3		Year-End Cash Flows	
4	Year	Project X	Project Y
5	0	$ (70,000)	$ (85,000)
6	1	$ 28,000	$ 35,000
7	2	$ 33,000	$ 30,000
8	3	$ 38,000	$ 25,000
9	4		$ 20,000
10	5		$ 15,000
11	6		$ 10,000
12	NPV	$ 11,277.24	$ 19,013.27
13	Choice of project		Project Y

Entry in Cell B12 is
=NPV(C2,B6:B11)+B5.
Copy the entry in Cell B12 to Cell C12.
Entry in Cell C13 is =IF(B12>=C12,B4,C4).

Table Use   The net present value of each project at the 10% cost of capital is calculated by finding the present value of each cash inflow, summing these values, and subtracting the initial investment from the sum of the present values.

$$NPV_X = [\$28,000 \times (0.909)] + [\$33,000 \times (0.826)] + [\$38,000 \times (0.751)] - \$70,000$$
$$= (\$25,452 + \$27,258 + \$28,538) - \$70,000$$
$$= \$81,248 - \$70,000$$
$$= \underline{\$11,248}$$

$$NPV_Y = [\$35,000 \times (0.909)] + [\$30,000 \times (0.826)] + [\$25,000 \times (0.751)]$$
$$+ [\$20,000 \times (0.683)] + [\$15,000 \times (0.621)] + [\$10,000 \times (0.564)] - \$85,000$$
$$= (\$31,815 + \$24,780 + \$18,775 + \$13,660 + \$9,315 + \$5,640) - \$85,000$$
$$= \$103,985 - \$85,000$$
$$= \underline{\$18,985}$$

The NPV for project X is $11,248; that for project Y is $18,985.

Ignoring the differences in project lives, we can see that both projects are acceptable (both NPVs are greater than zero) and that project Y is preferred over project X. If the projects were independent and only one could be accepted, project Y—with the larger NPV—would be preferred. If the projects were mutually exclusive, their differing lives would have to be considered. Project Y provides 3 more years of service than project X.

The analysis in the above example is incomplete if the projects are mutually exclusive (which will be our assumption throughout the remaining discussions). To compare these unequal-lived, mutually exclusive projects correctly, we must consider the differing lives in the analysis; an incorrect decision could result from simply using NPV to select the better project. Although a number of approaches are available for dealing with unequal lives, here we present the most efficient technique—the *annualized net present value (ANPV) approach*.

Annualized Net Present Value (ANPV) Approach

annualized net present value (ANPV) approach
An approach to evaluating unequal-lived projects that converts the net present value of unequal-lived, mutually exclusive projects into an equivalent annual amount (in NPV terms).

The **annualized net present value (ANPV) approach**[7] converts the net present value of unequal-lived, mutually exclusive projects into an equivalent annual amount (in NPV terms) that can be used to select the best project.[8] This net present value based approach can be applied to unequal-lived, mutually exclusive projects by using the following steps:

Step 1   Calculate the net present value of each project j, NPV_j, over its life, n_j, using the appropriate cost of capital, r.

7. This approach is also called the "equivalent annual annuity (EAA)" or the "equivalent annual cost." The term "annualized net present value (ANPV)" is used here due to its descriptive clarity.

8. The theory underlying this as well as other approaches for comparing projects with unequal lives assumes that each project can be replaced in the future for the same initial investment and that each will provide the same expected future cash inflows. Although changing technology and inflation will affect the initial investment and expected cash inflows, the lack of specific attention to them does not detract from the usefulness of this technique.

Step 2   Divide the net present value of each project having a positive NPV by the present value interest factor for an annuity at the given cost of capital and the project's life to get the annualized net present value for each project j, $ANPV_j$, as shown below:

$$ANPV_j = \frac{NPV_j}{PVIFA_{r,n_j}}$$

(10.6)

Step 3   Select the project that has the highest ANPV.

Example

By using the AT Company data presented earlier for projects X and Y, we can apply the three-step ANPV approach as follows:

Step 1   The net present values of projects X and Y discounted at 10%—as calculated in the preceding example for a single purchase of each asset—are

$$NPV_X = \$11,277.24 \text{ (table value} = \$11,248)$$
$$NPV_Y = \$19,013.27 \text{ (table value} = \$18,985)$$

Step 2   **Calculator Use**   The keystrokes required to find the ANPV on a financial calculator are identical to those demonstrated in Chapter 4 for finding the annual payments on an installment loan. These keystrokes are shown at the left for project X and for project Y. The resulting ANPVs for projects X and Y are $4,534.74 and $4,365.59, respectively.

Spreadsheet Use   The annualized net present values of two projects with unequal lives also can be compared as shown on the following Excel spreadsheet.

Project X

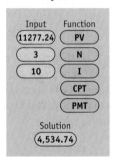

Project Y

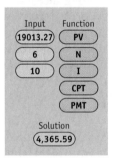

	A	B	C
1		COMPARISON OF ANNUALIZED NET PRESENT VALUES OF TWO PROJECTS WITH UNEQUAL LIVES	
2		Cost of Capital	10%
3		Year-End Cash Flows	
4	Year	Project X	Project Y
5	0	$ (70,000)	$ (85,000)
6	1	$ 28,000	$ 35,000
7	2	$ 33,000	$ 30,000
8	3	$ 38,000	$ 25,000
9	4		$ 20,000
10	5		$ 15,000
11	6		$ 10,000
12	NPV	$ 11,277.24	$ 19,013.27
13	ANPV	$ 4,534.74	$ 4,365.59
14	Choice of project		Project X

Entry in Cell B12 is
=NPV(C2,B6:B11)+B5.
Copy the entry in Cell B12 to Cell C12.
Entry in Cell B13 is =B12/PV(C2,3,–1).
Entry in Cell C13 is =C12/PV(C2,6,–1).
Entry in Cell C14 is =IF(B13>=C13,B4,C4).

Table Use   Calculate the annualized net present value for each project by applying Equation 10.6 to the NPVs.

$$\text{ANPV}_X = \frac{\$11,248}{PVIFA_{10\%,3\,\text{yrs}}} = \frac{\$11,248}{2.487} = \underline{\underline{\$4,523}}$$

$$\text{ANPV}_Y = \frac{\$18,985}{PVIFA_{10\%,6\,\text{yrs}}} = \frac{\$18,985}{4.355} = \underline{\underline{\$4,359}}$$

Step 3   Reviewing the ANPVs calculated in Step 2, we can see that project X would be preferred over project Y. Given that projects X and Y are mutually exclusive, project X would be the recommended project because it provides the higher annualized net present value.

Personal Finance Example   Wayne Stone is trying to choose between two new cars—car X and car Y. The net cost of car X is $53,000, and the net cost of car Y is $31,000. Because of its higher cost, if Wayne buys car X, he will keep it for 5 years; if he buys car Y, he will keep it for 3 years. At the end of these ownership periods, Wayne estimates that he could sell car X for $22,000 or car Y for $15,000. Wayne estimates that the end-of-year net monetary value of the annual benefit from car X to be $16,000 and for car Y to be $12,000. Wayne views the two cars as equally risky and of average risk, so he requires an annual return of 10% from them. Using these estimates, Wayne wishes to choose the car that is superior in pure financial terms. To do this, he calculates each car's annualized net present value (ANPV) as shown below:

$$NPV_X = [\$16,000 \times (PVIFA_{10\%,5\text{yrs}})] + [\$22,000 \times (PVIF_{10\%,5\text{yrs}})] - \$53,000$$

Using a financial calculator, he gets:
$$NPV_X = \$74,313 - \$53,000 = \$21,313$$

$$ANPV_X = NPV_X/PVIFA_{10\%,5\text{yrs}} = \$21,313/PVIFA_{10\%,5\text{yrs}}$$

Using a financial calculator, he gets: $\text{ANPV}_X = \underline{\underline{\$5,622}}$

$$NPV_Y = [\$12,000 \times (PVIFA_{10\%,3\text{yrs}})] + [\$15,000 \times (PVIF_{10\%,3\text{yrs}})] - \$36,000$$

Using a financial calculator, he gets:
$$NPV_Y = \$41,112 - \$31,000 = \$10,112$$

$$ANPV_Y = NPV_Y/PVIFA_{10\%,3\text{yrs}} = \$10,112/PVIFA_{10\%,3\text{yrs}}$$

Using a financial calculator, he gets: $\text{ANPV}_Y = \underline{\underline{\$4,066}}$

Because the ANPV for car X of $5,622 is greater than the ANPV for car Y of $4,066, Wayne will choose car X, the more expensive car, which he plans to hold for 5 years.

Recognizing Real Options

The procedures described in Chapters 8 and 9 and thus far in this chapter suggest that to make capital budgeting decisions, we must (1) estimate relevant cash flows, (2) apply an appropriate decision technique such as NPV or IRR to those cash flows, and (3) recognize and adjust the decision technique for project risk.

TABLE 10.4	Major Types of Real Options
Option type	Description
Abandonment option	The option to abandon or terminate a project prior to the end of its planned life. This option allows management to avoid or minimize losses on projects that turn bad. Explicitly recognizing the abandonment option when evaluating a project often increases its NPV.
Flexibility option	The option to incorporate flexibility into the firm's operations, particularly production. It generally includes the opportunity to design the production process to accept multiple inputs, use flexible production technology to create a variety of outputs by reconfiguring the same plant and equipment, and purchase and retain excess capacity in capital-intensive industries subject to wide swings in output demand and long lead time in building new capacity from scratch. Recognition of this option embedded in a capital expenditure should increase the NPV of the project.
Growth option	The option to develop follow-on projects, expand markets, expand or retool plants, and so on, that would not be possible without implementation of the project that is being evaluated. If a project being considered has the measurable potential to open new doors if successful, then recognition of the cash flows from such opportunities should be included in the initial decision process. Growth opportunities embedded in a project often increase the NPV of the project in which they are embedded.
Timing option	The option to determine when various actions with respect to a given project are taken. This option recognizes the firm's opportunity to delay acceptance of a project for one or more periods, to accelerate or slow the process of implementing a project in response to new information, or to shut down a project temporarily in response to changing product market conditions or competition. As in the case of the other types of options, the explicit recognition of timing opportunities can improve the NPV of a project that fails to recognize this option in an investment decision.

Although this traditional procedure is believed to yield good decisions, a more *strategic approach* to these decisions has emerged in recent years. This more modern view considers any **real options**—opportunities that are embedded in capital projects ("real," rather than financial, asset investments) that enable managers to alter their cash flows and risk in a way that affects project acceptability (NPV). Because these opportunities are more likely to exist in, and be more important to, large "strategic" capital budgeting projects, they are sometimes called *strategic options*.

real options
Opportunities that are embedded in capital projects that enable managers to alter their cash flows and risk in a way that affects project acceptability (NPV). Also called *strategic options*.

Table 10.4 briefly describes some of the more common types of real options—abandonment, flexibility, growth, and timing. It should be clear from their descriptions that each of these types of options could be embedded in a capital budgeting decision and that explicit recognition of them would probably alter the cash flow and risk of a project and change its NPV.

By explicitly recognizing these options when making capital budgeting decisions, managers can make improved, more strategic decisions that consider in advance the economic impact of certain contingent actions on project cash flow and risk. The explicit recognition of real options embedded in capital budgeting projects will cause the project's *strategic NPV* to differ from its *traditional NPV* as indicated by Equation 10.7.

$$NPV_{strategic} = NPV_{traditional} + \text{Value of real options} \qquad (10.7)$$

Application of this relationship is illustrated in the following example.

Example   Assume that a strategic analysis of Bennett Company's projects A and B (see cash flows and NPVs in Table 10.1) finds no real options embedded in project A and two real options embedded in project B. The two real options in project B are as follows: (1) The project would have, during the first 2 years, some downtime that would result in unused production capacity that could be used to perform contract manufacturing for another firm, and (2) the project's computerized control system could, with some modification, control two other machines, thereby reducing labor cost, without affecting operation of the new project.

Bennett's management estimated the NPV of the contract manufacturing over the 2 years following implementation of project B to be $1,500 and the NPV of the computer control sharing to be $2,000. Management felt there was a 60% chance that the contract manufacturing option would be exercised and only a 30% chance that the computer control sharing option would be exercised. The combined value of these two real options would be the sum of their expected values.

$$\text{Value of real options for project B} = (0.60 \times \$1,500) + (0.30 \times \$2,000)$$
$$= \$900 + \$600 = \$1,500$$

Substituting the $1,500 real options value along with the traditional NPV of $10,924 for project B (from Table 10.1) into Equation 10.7, we get the strategic NPV for project B.

$$\text{NPV}_{\text{strategic}} = \$10,924 + \$1,500 = \underline{\underline{\$12,424}}$$

Bennett Company's project B therefore has a strategic NPV of $12,424, which is above its traditional NPV and now exceeds project A's NPV of $11,071. Clearly, recognition of project B's real options improved its NPV (from $10,924 to $12,424) and causes it to be preferred over project A (NPV of $12,424 for B > NPV of $11,071 for A), which has no real options embedded in it.

It is important to realize that the recognition of attractive real options when determining NPV could cause an otherwise unacceptable project (NPV$_{\text{traditional}}$ < $0) to become acceptable (NPV$_{\text{strategic}}$ > $0). The failure to recognize the value of real options could therefore cause management to reject projects that are acceptable. Although doing so requires more strategic thinking and analysis, it is important for the financial manager to identify and incorporate real options in the NPV process. The procedures for doing this efficiently are emerging, and the use of the strategic NPV that incorporates real options is expected to become more commonplace in the future.

Capital Rationing

Hint Because everyone in the firm knows that long-term funds are rationed and they want a portion of them, there is *intense competition* for those funds. This competition increases the need for the firm to be objective and proficient in its analysis. Knowing how to use the techniques discussed in this chapter to justify your needs will help you get your share of the available long-term funds.

Firms commonly operate under *capital rationing*—they have more acceptable independent projects than they can fund. In theory, capital rationing should not exist. Firms should accept all projects that have positive NPVs (or IRRs > the cost of capital). However, in practice, most firms operate under capital rationing. Generally, firms attempt to isolate and select the best acceptable projects subject to a capital expenditure budget set by management. Research has found that management internally imposes capital expenditure constraints to avoid what it deems to be "excessive" levels of new financing, particularly debt. Although failing to fund all acceptable independent projects is theoretically inconsistent with the goal of maximizing owner wealth, here we will discuss capital rationing procedures because they are widely used in practice.

internal rate of return approach
An approach to capital rationing that involves graphing project IRRs in descending order against the total dollar investment to determine the group of acceptable projects.

investment opportunities schedule (IOS)
The graph that plots project IRRs in descending order against the total dollar investment.

The objective of *capital rationing* is to select the group of projects that provides the *highest overall net present value* and does not require more dollars than are budgeted. As a prerequisite to capital rationing, the best of any mutually exclusive projects must be chosen and placed in the group of independent projects. Two basic approaches to project selection under capital rationing are discussed here.

Internal Rate of Return Approach

The **internal rate of return approach** involves graphing project IRRs in descending order against the total dollar investment. This graph, which is discussed in more detail in Chapter 11, is called the **investment opportunities schedule (IOS)**. By drawing the cost-of-capital line and then imposing a budget constraint, the financial manager can determine the group of acceptable projects. The problem with this technique is that it does not guarantee the maximum dollar return to the firm. It merely provides a satisfactory solution to capital-rationing problems.

Example

Tate Company, a fast-growing plastics company, is confronted with six projects competing for its fixed budget of $250,000. The initial investment and IRR for each project are as follows:

Project	Initial investment	IRR
A	$ 80,000	12%
B	70,000	20
C	100,000	16
D	40,000	8
E	60,000	15
F	110,000	11

The firm has a cost of capital of 10%. Figure 10.4 presents the IOS that results from ranking the six projects in descending order on the basis of their IRRs. According to the schedule, only projects B, C, and E should be accepted. Together they will absorb $230,000 of the $250,000 budget. Projects A and F are acceptable but cannot be chosen because of the budget constraint. Project D is not worthy of consideration; its IRR is less than the firm's 10% cost of capital.

The drawback of this approach is that there is no guarantee that the acceptance of projects B, C, and E will maximize *total dollar returns* and therefore owners' wealth.

Net Present Value Approach

net present value approach
An approach to capital rationing that is based on the use of present values to determine the group of projects that will maximize owners' wealth.

The **net present value approach** is based on the use of present values to determine the group of projects that will maximize owners' wealth. It is implemented by ranking projects on the basis of IRRs and then evaluating the present value of the benefits from each potential project to determine *the combination of projects with the highest overall present value*. This is the same as maximizing net present value, because the entire budget is viewed as the total initial investment. Any portion of the firm's budget that is not used does not increase the firm's value. At

FIGURE 10.4

Investment Opportunities Schedule
Investment opportunities schedule (IOS) for Tate Company projects

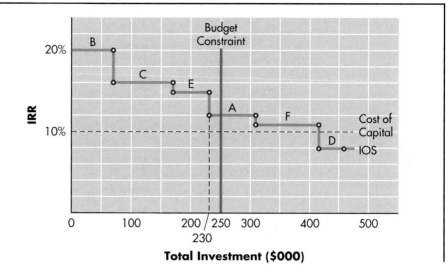

best, the unused money can be invested in marketable securities or returned to the owners in the form of cash dividends. In either case, the wealth of the owners is not likely to be enhanced.

Example

The projects described in the preceding example are ranked in Table 10.5 on the basis of IRRs. The present value of the cash inflows associated with the projects is also included in the table. Projects B, C, and E, which together require $230,000, yield a present value of $336,000. However, if projects B, C, and A were implemented, the total budget of $250,000 would be used, and the present value of the cash inflows would be $357,000. This is greater than the return expected from selecting the projects on the basis of the highest IRRs. Implementing B, C, and A is preferable, because they maximize the present value for the given budget. *The firm's objective is to use its budget to generate the highest present value of inflows.* Assuming that any unused portion of the budget does not gain or lose money, the total NPV for projects B, C, and E would be $106,000 ($336,000 − $230,000), whereas the total NPV for projects B, C, and A would be $107,000 ($357,000 − $250,000). Selection of projects B, C, and A will therefore maximize NPV.

TABLE 10.5   Rankings for Tate Company Projects

Project	Initial investment	IRR	Present value of inflows at 10%	
B	$ 70,000	20%	$112,000	
C	100,000	16	145,000	
E	60,000	15	79,000	
A	80,000	12	100,000	
F	110,000	11	126,500	Cutoff point
D	40,000	8	36,000	(IRR < 10%)

REVIEW QUESTIONS

10–8 Explain why a mere comparison of the NPVs of unequal-lived, ongoing, mutually exclusive projects is inappropriate. Describe the *annualized net present value (ANPV) approach* for comparing unequal-lived, mutually exclusive projects.

10–9 What are *real options?* What are some major types of real options?

10–10 What is the difference between the *strategic NPV* and the *traditional NPV?* Do they always result in the same accept–reject decisions?

10–11 What is *capital rationing?* In theory, should capital rationing exist? Why does it frequently occur in practice?

10–12 Compare and contrast the *internal rate of return approach* and the *net present value approach* to capital rationing. Which is better? Why?

Summary

Focus on Value

Not all capital budgeting projects have the same level of risk as the firm's existing portfolio of projects. The financial manager must adjust projects for differences in risk when evaluating their acceptability. Without such adjustment, management could mistakenly accept projects that destroy shareholder value or could reject projects that create shareholder value. To ensure that neither of these outcomes occurs, the financial manager must make sure that only those projects that create shareholder value are recommended.

Risk-adjusted discount rates (RADRs) provide a mechanism for adjusting the discount rate so that it is consistent with the risk–return preferences of market participants. Procedures for comparing projects with unequal lives, for explicitly recognizing real options embedded in capital projects, and for selecting projects under capital rationing enable the financial manager to refine the capital budgeting process further. These procedures, along with risk-adjustment techniques, should enable the financial manager to make capital budgeting decisions that are consistent with the firm's goal of **maximizing stock price.**

Review of Learning Goals

LG 1 **Understand the importance of recognizing risk in the analysis of capital budgeting projects.** The cash flows associated with capital budgeting projects typically have different levels of risk, and the acceptance of a project generally affects the firm's overall risk. Thus it is important to incorporate risk considerations in capital budgeting. Various behavioral approaches can be used to get a "feel" for the level of project risk. Other approaches explicitly recognize project risk in the analysis of capital budgeting projects.

LG 2 **Discuss risk and cash inflows, scenario analysis, and simulation as behavioral approaches for dealing with risk.** Risk in capital budgeting is the degree of variability of cash flows, which for conventional capital budgeting projects stems almost entirely from *cash inflows.* Finding the breakeven cash inflow and estimating the probability that it will be realized make up one behavioral approach for assessing capital budgeting risk. Scenario analysis is another behavioral approach for capturing the variability of cash inflows and NPVs. Simulation is a statistically based approach that results in a probability distribution of project returns.

LG 3 **Review the unique risks that multinational companies face.** Although the basic capital budgeting techniques are the same for multinational and purely domestic companies, firms that operate in several countries must also deal with exchange rate and political risks, tax law differences, transfer pricing, and strategic issues.

LG 4 **Describe the determination and use of risk-adjusted discount rates (RADRs), portfolio effects, and the practical aspects of RADRs.** The risk of a project whose initial investment is known with certainty is embodied in the present value of its cash inflows, using NPV. Two opportunities to adjust the present value of cash inflows for risk exist—adjust the cash inflows or adjust the discount rate. Because adjusting the cash inflows is highly subjective, adjusting discount rates is more popular. RADRs use a market-based adjustment of the discount rate to calculate NPV. The RADR is closely linked to CAPM, but because real corporate assets are generally not traded in an efficient market, the CAPM cannot be applied directly to capital budgeting. Instead, firms develop some CAPM-type relationship to link a project's risk to its required return, which is used as the discount rate. Often, for convenience, firms will rely on total risk as an approximation for relevant risk when estimating required project returns. RADRs are commonly used in practice, because decision makers find rates of return easy to estimate and apply.

LG 5 **Select the best of a group of unequal-lived, mutually exclusive projects using annualized net present values (ANPVs).** The ANPV approach is the most efficient method of comparing ongoing, mutually exclusive projects that have unequal usable lives. It converts the NPV of each unequal-lived project into an equivalent annual amount—its ANPV. The ANPV can be calculated using a financial calculator, a spreadsheet, or financial tables. The project with the highest ANPV is best.

LG 6 **Explain the role of real options and the objective and procedures for selecting projects under capital rationing.** Real options are opportunities that are embedded in capital projects and that allow managers to alter their cash flow and risk in a way that affects project acceptability (NPV). By explicitly recognizing real options, the financial manager can find a project's strategic NPV. Some of the more common types of real options are abandonment, flexibility, growth, and timing options. The strategic NPV improves the quality of the capital budgeting decision.

Capital rationing exists when firms have more acceptable independent projects than they can fund. Capital rationing commonly occurs in practice. Its objective is to select from all acceptable projects the group that provides the highest overall net present value and does not require more dollars than are budgeted. The two basic approaches for choosing projects under capital rationing are the internal rate of return approach and the net present value approach. The NPV approach better achieves the objective of using the budget to generate the highest present value of inflows.

Self-Test Problem (Solution in Appendix B)

ST10–1   Risk-adjusted discount rates   CBA Company is considering two mutually exclusive projects, A and B. The following table shows the CAPM-type relationship between a risk index and the required return (RADR) applicable to CBA Company.

Risk index	Required return (RADR)
0.0	7.0% (risk-free rate, R_F)
0.2	8.0
0.4	9.0
0.6	10.0
0.8	11.0
1.0	12.0
1.2	13.0
1.4	14.0
1.6	15.0
1.8	16.0
2.0	17.0

Project data are shown as follows:

	Project A	Project B
Initial investment (CF_0)	$15,000	$20,000
Project life	3 years	3 years
Annual cash inflow (CF)	$7,000	$10,000
Risk index	0.4	1.8

a. Ignoring any differences in risk and assuming that the firm's cost of capital is 10%, calculate the *net present value (NPV)* of each project.
b. Use NPV to evaluate the projects, using *risk-adjusted discount rates (RADRs)* to account for risk.
c. Compare, contrast, and explain your findings in parts **a** and **b**.

Warm-Up Exercises   A blue box (■) indicates exercises available in .

E10–1   Birkenstock's is considering an investment in a nylon-knitting machine. The machine requires an initial investment of $25,000, has a 5-year life, and has no residual value at the end of the 5 years. The company's cost of capital is 12%. Known with less certainty are the actual after-tax cash inflows for each of the 5 years. The company has estimated expected cash inflows for three scenarios: pessimistic, most likely, and optimistic. These expected cash inflows are listed below. Calculate the range for the NPV given each scenario.

| | Expected cash inflows | | |
Year	Pessimistic	Most likely	Optimistic
1	$5,500	$ 8,000	$10,500
2	6,000	9,000	12,000
3	7,500	10,500	14,500
4	6,500	9,500	11,500
5	4,500	6,500	7,500

 E10–2 You wish to evaluate a project requiring an initial investment of $45,000 and having a useful life of 5 years. What minimum amount of annual cash inflow do you need if your firm has an 8% cost of capital? If the project is forecast to earn $12,500 per year over the 5 years, what is its IRR? Is the project acceptable?

 E10–3 Like most firms in its industry, Yeastime Bakeries uses a subjective risk assessment tool of its own design. The tool is a simple index by which projects are ranked by level of perceived risk on a scale of 0–10. The scale is recreated below.

Risk	Required Return
0	4.0% (current risk-free rate)
1	4.5
2	5.0
3	5.5
4	6.0
5	6.5 (current IRR)
6	7.0
7	7.5
8	8.0
9	8.5
10	9.0

The firm is analyzing two projects based on their RADRs. Project Sourdough requires an initial investment of $12,500 and is assigned a risk index of 6. Project Greek Salad requires an initial investment of $7,500 and is assigned a risk index of 8. The two projects have 7-year lives. Sourdough is projected to generate cash inflows of $5,500 per year. Greek Salad is projected to generate cash inflows of $4,000 per year. Use each project's RADR to select the better project.

 E10–4 Outcast, Inc., has hired you to advise the firm on a capital budgeting issue involving two unequal-lived, mutually exclusive projects, M and N. The cash flows for each project are presented in the table at the top of page 486. Calculate the NPV and the *annualized net present value (ANPV)* for each project using the firm's cost of capital of 8%. Which project would you recommend?

	Project M	Project N
Initial investment	$35,000	$55,000
Year	Cash inflows	
1	$12,000	$18,000
2	25,000	15,000
3	30,000	25,000
4	—	10,000
5	—	8,000
6	—	5,000
7	—	5,000

E10–5 Longchamps Electric is faced with a capital budget of $150,000 for the coming year. It is considering six investment projects and has a cost of capital of 7%. The six projects are listed below, along with their initial investments and their IRRs. Using the data given, prepare an *investment opportunities schedule (IOS)*. Which projects does the IOS suggest should be funded? Does this group of projects maximize NPV? Explain.

Project	Initial investment	IRR
1	$75,000	8%
2	40,000	10
3	35,000	7
4	50,000	11
5	45,000	9
6	20,000	6

Problems

A blue box (■) indicates problems available in ⟨myfinancelab⟩.

P10–1 **Recognizing risk** Caradine Corp., a media services firm with net earnings of $3,200,000 in the last year, is considering several projects.

Project	Initial investment	Details
A	$ 35,000	Replace existing office furnishings.
B	500,000	Purchase digital film-editing equipment for use with several existing accounts.
C	450,000	Develop proposal to bid for a $2,000,000 per year 10-year contract with the U.S. Navy, not now an account.
D	685,000	Purchase the exclusive rights to market a quality educational television program in syndication to local markets in the European Union, a part of the firm's existing business activities.

The media services business is cyclical and highly competitive. The board of directors has asked you, as chief financial officer, to do the following:

a. Evaluate the risk of each proposed project and rank it "low," "medium," or "high."

b. Comment on why you chose each ranking.

 P10–2 **Breakeven cash inflows**   Etsitty Arts, Inc., a leading producer of fine cast silver jewelry, is considering the purchase of new casting equipment that will allow it to expand the product line into award plaques. The proposed initial investment is $35,000. The company expects that the equipment will produce steady income throughout its 12-year life.

a. If Etsitty requires a 14% return on its investment, what minimum yearly cash inflow will be necessary for the company to go forward with this project?

b. How would the minimum yearly cash inflow change if the company required a 10% return on its investment?

 P10–3 **Breakeven cash inflows and risk**   Pueblo Enterprises is considering investing in either of two mutually exclusive projects, X and Y. Project X requires an initial investment of $30,000; project Y requires $40,000. Each project's cash inflows are 5-year annuities: Project X's inflows are $10,000 per year; project Y's are $15,000. The firm has unlimited funds and, in the absence of risk differences, accepts the project with the highest NPV. The cost of capital is 15%.

a. Find the NPV for each project. Are the projects acceptable?

b. Find the *breakeven cash inflow* for each project.

c. The firm has estimated the probabilities of achieving various ranges of cash inflows for the two projects, as shown in the following table. What is the probability that each project will achieve the breakeven cash inflow found in part **b**?

| | Probability of achieving cash inflow in given range | |
Range of cash inflow	Project X	Project Y
$0 to $5,000	0%	5%
$5,000 to $7,500	10	10
$7,500 to $10,000	60	15
$10,000 to $12,500	25	25
$12,500 to $15,000	5	20
$15,000 to $20,000	0	15
Above $20,000	0	10

d. Which project is more risky? Which project has the potentially higher NPV? Discuss the risk–return tradeoffs of the two projects.

e. If the firm wished to minimize losses (that is, NPV < $0), which project would you recommend? Which would you recommend if the goal was achieving a higher NPV?

 P10–4 **Basic scenario analysis**   Murdock Paints is in the process of evaluating two mutually exclusive additions to its processing capacity. The firm's financial analysts have developed pessimistic, most likely, and optimistic estimates of the annual cash inflows associated with each project. These estimates are shown in the table on page 488.

	Project A	Project B
Initial investment (CF_0)	$8,000	$8,000
Outcome	Annual cash inflows (CF)	
Pessimistic	$ 200	$ 900
Most likely	1,000	1,000
Optimistic	1,800	1,100

a. Determine the *range* of annual cash inflows for each of the two projects.
b. Assume that the firm's cost of capital is 10% and that both projects have 20-year lives. Construct a table similar to this for the NPVs for each project. Include the *range* of NPVs for each project.
c. Do parts **a** and **b** provide consistent views of the two projects? Explain.
d. Which project do you recommend? Why?

P10–5 **Scenario analysis**   James Secretarial Services is considering the purchase of one of two new personal computers, P and Q. The company expects both to provide benefits over a 10-year period, and each has a required investment of $3,000. The firm uses a 10% cost of capital. Management has constructed the following table of estimates of annual cash inflows for pessimistic, most likely, and optimistic results.

	Computer P	Computer Q
Initial investment (CF_0)	$3,000	$3,000
Outcome	Annual cash inflows (CF)	
Pessimistic	$ 500	$ 400
Most likely	750	750
Optimistic	1,000	1,200

a. Determine the *range* of annual cash inflows for each of the two computers.
b. Construct a table similar to this for the NPVs associated with each outcome for both computers.
c. Find the *range* of NPVs, and subjectively compare the risks associated with purchasing these computers.

PERSONAL FINANCE PROBLEM

P10–6 **Impact of inflation on investments**   You are interested in an investment project that costs $7,500 initially. The investment has a 5-year horizon and promises future end-of-year cash inflows of $2,000, $2,000, $2,000, $1,500, and $1,500, respectively. Your current opportunity cost is 6.5% per year. However, the Fed has stated that inflation may rise by 1% or may fall by the same amount.

Assume a direct positive impact of inflation on the prevailing rates (Fisher effect) and answer the following questions.
a. What is the *net present value (NPV)* of the investment under the current required rate of return?
b. What is the *net present value (NPV)* of the investment under a period of rising inflation?

c. What is the *net present value (NPV)* of the investment under a period of falling inflation?

d. From your answers in **a, b,** and **c,** what relationship do you see emerge between changes in inflation and asset valuation?

P10–7 Simulation   Ogden Corporation has compiled the following information on a capital expenditure proposal:

(1) The projected cash *inflows* are normally distributed with a mean of $36,000 and a standard deviation of $9,000.

(2) The projected cash *outflows* are normally distributed with a mean of $30,000 and a standard deviation of $6,000.

(3) The firm has an 11% cost of capital.

(4) The probability distributions of cash inflows and cash outflows are not expected to change over the project's 10-year life.

a. Describe how the foregoing data can be used to develop a simulation model for finding the net present value of the project.

b. Discuss the advantages of using a simulation to evaluate the proposed project.

P10–8 Risk-adjusted discount rates—Basic   Country Wallpapers is considering investing in one of three mutually exclusive projects, E, F, and G. The firm's cost of capital, *r*, is 15%, and the risk-free rate, R_F, is 10%. The firm has gathered the following basic cash flow and risk index data for each project.

	Project (*j*)		
	E	F	G
Initial investment (CF_0)	$15,000	$11,000	$19,000
Year (*t*)	Cash inflows (CF_t)		
1	$ 6,000	$ 6,000	$ 4,000
2	6,000	4,000	6,000
3	6,000	5,000	8,000
4	6,000	2,000	12,000
Risk index (RI_j)	1.80	1.00	0.60

a. Find the *net present value (NPV)* of each project using the firm's cost of capital. Which project is preferred in this situation?

b. The firm uses the following equation to determine the risk-adjusted discount rate, $RADR_j$, for each project *j*:

$$RADR_j = R_F + [RI_j \times (r - R_F)]$$

where

R_F = risk-free rate of return

RI_j = risk index for project *j*

r = cost of capital

Substitute each project's risk index into this equation to determine its RADR.

c. Use the RADR for each project to determine its *risk-adjusted NPV*. Which project is preferable in this situation?

d. Compare and discuss your findings in parts **a** and **c.** Which project do you recommend that the firm accept?

P10–9 **Risk-adjusted discount rates—Tabular**   After a careful evaluation of investment alternatives and opportunities, Masters School Supplies has developed a CAPM-type relationship linking a risk index to the required return (RADR), as shown in the following table.

Risk index	Required return (RADR)
0.0	7.0% (risk-free rate, R_F)
0.2	8.0
0.4	9.0
0.6	10.0
0.8	11.0
1.0	12.0
1.2	13.0
1.4	14.0
1.6	15.0
1.8	16.0
2.0	17.0

The firm is considering two mutually exclusive projects, A and B. Following are the data the firm has been able to gather about the projects.

	Project A	Project B
Initial investment (CF_0)	$20,000	$30,000
Project life	5 years	5 years
Annual cash inflow (CF)	$7,000	$10,000
Risk index	0.2	1.4

All the firm's cash inflows have already been adjusted for taxes.
a. Evaluate the projects using *risk-adjusted discount rates*.
b. Discuss your findings in part **a**, and recommend the preferred project.

PERSONAL FINANCE PROBLEM

P10–10 **Mutually exclusive investments and risk**   Lara Fredericks is interested in two mutually exclusive investments. Both investments cover the same time horizon of 6 years. The cost of the first investment is $10,000, and Lara expects equal and consecutive year-end payments of $3,000. The second investment promises equal and consecutive payments of $3,800 with an initial outlay of $12,000 required. The current required return on the first investment is 8.5%, and the second carries a required return of 10.5%.
a. What is the *net present value* of the first investment?
b. What is the *net present value* of the second investment?
c. Being mutually exclusive, which investment should Lara choose? Explain.
d. Which investment was relatively more risky? Explain.

P10–11 **Risk-adjusted rates of return using CAPM**   Centennial Catering, Inc., is considering two mutually exclusive investments. The company wishes to use a risk-adjusted discount rate (RADR) in its analysis. Centennial's cost of capital (similar to the market return in CAPM) is 12%, and the current risk-free rate of return is 7%. Cash flows associated with the two projects are shown in the following table.

	Project X	Project Y
Initial investment (CF_0)	$70,000	$78,000
Year (t)	**Cash inflows (CF_t)**	
1	$30,000	$22,000
2	30,000	32,000
3	30,000	38,000
4	30,000	46,000

a. Use a *risk-adjusted discount rate* approach to calculate the net present value of each project, given that project X has a RADR factor of 1.20 and project Y has a RADR factor of 1.40. The RADR factors are similar to project betas. (Use Equation 10.5 to calculate the required project return for each.)
b. Discuss your findings in part **a,** and recommend the preferred project.

 P10–12 **Risk classes and RADR**   Moses Manufacturing is attempting to select the best of three mutually exclusive projects, X, Y, and Z. Although all the projects have 5-year lives, they possess differing degrees of risk. Project X is in class V, the highest-risk class; project Y is in class II, the below-average-risk class; and project Z is in class III, the average-risk class. The basic cash flow data for each project and the risk classes and risk-adjusted discount rates (RADRs) used by the firm are shown in the following tables.

	Project X	Project Y	Project Z
Initial investment (CF_0)	$180,000	$235,000	$310,000
Year (t)	**Cash inflows (CF_t)**		
1	$80,000	$50,000	$90,000
2	70,000	60,000	90,000
3	60,000	70,000	90,000
4	60,000	80,000	90,000
5	60,000	90,000	90,000

Risk Classes and RADRs		
Risk Class	**Description**	**Risk-adjusted discount rate (RADR)**
I	Lowest risk	10%
II	Below-average risk	13
III	Average risk	15
IV	Above-average risk	19
V	Highest risk	22

a. Find the *risk-adjusted NPV* for each project.
b. Which project, if any, would you recommend that the firm undertake?

P10–13 **Unequal lives—ANPV approach**   Evans Industries wishes to select the best of three possible machines, each of which is expected to satisfy the firm's ongoing need for additional aluminum-extrusion capacity. The three machines—A, B, and C—are equally risky. The firm plans to use a 12% cost of capital to evaluate each of them. The initial investment and annual cash inflows over the life of each machine are shown in the following table.

	Machine A	Machine B	Machine C
Initial investment (CF_0)	$92,000	$65,000	$100,500
Year (t)	Cash inflows (CF_t)		
1	$12,000	$10,000	$30,000
2	12,000	20,000	30,000
3	12,000	30,000	30,000
4	12,000	40,000	30,000
5	12,000	—	30,000
6	12,000	—	—

a. Calculate the *NPV* for each machine over its life. Rank the machines in descending order on the basis of NPV.

b. Use the *annualized net present value (ANPV)* approach to evaluate and rank the machines in descending order on the basis of ANPV.

c. Compare and contrast your findings in parts **a** and **b**. Which machine would you recommend that the firm acquire? Why?

 P10–14 **Unequal lives—ANPV approach**   Portland Products is considering the purchase of one of three mutually exclusive projects for increasing production efficiency. The firm plans to use a 14% cost of capital to evaluate these equal-risk projects. The initial investment and annual cash inflows over the life of each project are shown in the following table.

	Project X	Project Y	Project Z
Initial investment (CF_0)	$78,000	$52,000	$66,000
Year (t)	Cash inflows (CF_t)		
1	$17,000	$28,000	$15,000
2	25,000	38,000	15,000
3	33,000	—	15,000
4	41,000	—	15,000
5	—	—	15,000
6	—	—	15,000
7	—	—	15,000
8	—	—	15,000

a. Calculate the *NPV* for each project over its life. Rank the projects in descending order on the basis of NPV.

  b. Use the *annualized net present value (ANPV)* approach to evaluate and rank the projects in descending order on the basis of ANPV.

  c. Compare and contrast your findings in parts **a** and **b.** Which project would you recommend that the firm purchase? Why?

 P10–15 **Unequal lives—ANPV approach**   JBL Co. has designed a new conveyor system. Management must choose among three alternative courses of action: (1) The firm can sell the design outright to another corporation with payment over 2 years. (2) It can license the design to another manufacturer for a period of 5 years, its likely product life. (3) It can manufacture and market the system itself; this alternative will result in 6 years of cash inflows. The company has a cost of capital of 12%. Cash flows associated with each alternative are as follows:

Alternative	Sell	License	Manufacture
Initial investment (CF_0)	$200,000	$200,000	$450,000
Year (t)		Cash inflows (CF_t)	
1	$200,000	$250,000	$200,000
2	250,000	100,000	250,000
3	—	80,000	200,000
4	—	60,000	200,000
5	—	40,000	200,000
6	—	—	200,000

  a. Calculate the *net present value* of each alternative and rank the alternatives on the basis of NPV.

  b. Calculate the *annualized net present value (ANPV)* of each alternative and rank them accordingly.

  c. Why is ANPV preferred over NPV when ranking projects with unequal lives?

PERSONAL FINANCE PROBLEM

 P10–16 **NPV and ANPV decisions**   Richard and Linda Butler decide that it is time to purchase a high-definition (HD) television because the technology has improved and prices have fallen over the past 3 years. From their research, they narrow their choices to two sets, the Samsung 42-inch LCD with 1080p capability and the Sony 42-inch LCD with 1080p features. The price of the Samsung is $2,350 and the Sony will cost $2,700. They expect to keep the Samsung for 3 years; if they buy the more expensive Sony unit, they will keep the Sony for 4 years. They expect to be able to sell the Samsung for $400 by the end of 3 years; they expect they could sell the Sony for $350 at the end of the year 4. Richard and Linda estimate that the end-of-year entertainment benefits (i.e., not going to movies or events and watching at home) from the Samsung to be $900 and for the Sony to be $1,000. Both sets can be viewed as quality units and are equally risky purchases. They estimate their opportunity cost to be 9%.

  The Butlers wish to choose the better alternative from a purely financial perspective. To perform this analysis they wish to do the following:

  a. Determine the *NPV* of the Samsung HD LCD.

  b. Determine the *ANPV* of the Samsung HD LCD.

  c. Determine the *NPV* of the Sony HD LCD.

d. Determine the *ANPV* of the Sony HD LCD.

e. Which set should the Butlers purchase and why?

P10–17   **Real options and the strategic NPV**   Jenny Rene, the CFO of Asor Products, Inc., has just completed an evaluation of a proposed capital expenditure for equipment that would expand the firm's manufacturing capacity. Using the traditional NPV methodology, she found the project unacceptable because

$$\text{NPV}_{\text{traditional}} = -\$1,700 < \$0$$

Before recommending rejection of the proposed project, she has decided to assess whether there might be real options embedded in the firm's cash flows. Her evaluation uncovered three options:

Option 1: Abandonment—The project could be abandoned at the end of 3 years, resulting in an addition to NPV of $1,200.

Option 2: Growth—If the projected outcomes occurred, an opportunity to expand the firm's product offerings further would become available at the end of 4 years. Exercise of this option is estimated to add $3,000 to the project's NPV.

Option 3: Timing—Certain phases of the proposed project could be delayed if market and competitive conditions caused the firm's forecast revenues to develop more slowly than planned. Such a delay in implementation at that point has a NPV of $10,000.

Jenny estimated that there was a 25% chance that the abandonment option would need to be exercised, a 30% chance that the growth option would be exercised, and only a 10% chance that the implementation of certain phases of the project would affect timing.

a. Use the information provided to calculate the *strategic NPV*, NPV$_{\text{strategic}}$, for Asor Products' proposed equipment expenditure.

b. Judging on the basis of your findings in part **a,** what action should Jenny recommend to management with regard to the proposed equipment expenditure?

c. In general, how does this problem demonstrate the importance of considering real options when making capital budgeting decisions?

P10–18   **Capital rationing—IRR and NPV approaches**   Valley Corporation is attempting to select the best of a group of independent projects competing for the firm's fixed capital budget of $4.5 million. The firm recognizes that any unused portion of this budget will earn less than its 15% cost of capital, thereby resulting in a present value of inflows that is less than the initial investment. The firm has summarized, in the following table, the key data to be used in selecting the best group of projects.

Project	Initial investment	IRR	Present value of inflows at 15%
A	$5,000,000	17%	$5,400,000
B	800,000	18	1,100,000
C	2,000,000	19	2,300,000
D	1,500,000	16	1,600,000
E	800,000	22	900,000
F	2,500,000	23	3,000,000
G	1,200,000	20	1,300,000

a. Use the *internal rate of return (IRR) approach* to select the best group of projects.
b. Use the *net present value (NPV) approach* to select the best group of projects.
c. Compare, contrast, and discuss your findings in parts **a** and **b**.
d. Which projects should the firm implement? Why?

 P10–19 **Capital rationing—NPV approach**   A firm with a 13% cost of capital must select the optimal group of projects from those shown in the following table, given its capital budget of $1 million.

Project	Initial investment	NPV at 13% cost of capital
A	$300,000	$ 84,000
B	200,000	10,000
C	100,000	25,000
D	900,000	90,000
E	500,000	70,000
F	100,000	50,000
G	800,000	160,000

a. Calculate the *present value of cash inflows* associated with each project.
b. Select the optimal group of projects, keeping in mind that unused funds are costly.

 P10–20 **ETHICS PROBLEM**   One way to avoid the EPA penalties (see *Focus on Ethics* on page 468) for excessive air pollution is to use carbon credits. Carbon credits are a tradable permit scheme that allows businesses that cannot meet their greenhouse-gas-emissions limits to purchase carbon credits from businesses that are below their quota. By allowing credits to be bought and sold, a business for which reducing its emissions would be expensive or prohibitive can pay another business to make the reduction for it. Do you agree with this arrangement? How would you feel as an investor in a company that utilizes carbon credits to legally exceed its pollution limits?

Chapter 10 Case

Evaluating Cherone Equipment's Risky Plans for Increasing Its Production Capacity

Cherone Equipment, a manufacturer of electronic fitness equipment, wishes to evaluate two alternative plans for increasing its production capacity to meet the rapidly growing demand for its key product—the Cardiocycle. After months of investigation and analysis, the firm has pruned the list of alternatives down to the following two plans, either of which would allow it to meet its forecast product demand.

Plan X Use current proven technology to expand the existing plant and semiautomated production line. This plan is viewed as only slightly more risky than the firm's current average level of risk.

Plan Y   Install new, just-developed automatic production equipment in the existing plant to replace the current semiautomated production line. Because this plan eliminates the need to expand the plant, it is less expensive than Plan X, but it is believed to be far more risky because of the unproven nature of the technology.

Cherone, which routinely uses NPV to evaluate capital budgeting projects, has a cost of capital of 12%. Currently the risk-free rate of interest, R_F, is 9%. The firm has decided to evaluate the two plans over a 5-year time period, at the end of which each plan would be liquidated. The relevant cash flows associated with each plan are summarized in the following table.

	Plan X	Plan Y
Initial investment (CF_0)	$2,700,000	$2,100,000
Year (t)	Cash inflows (CF_t)	
1	$ 470,000	$ 380,000
2	610,000	700,000
3	950,000	800,000
4	970,000	600,000
5	1,500,000	1,200,000

The firm has determined the risk-adjusted discount rate (RADR) applicable to each plan as shown in the following table.

Plan	Risk-adjusted discount rate (RADR)
X	13%
Y	15%

Further analysis of the two plans has disclosed that each has a real option embedded within its cash flows.

Plan X Real Option—At the end of 3 years the firm could abandon this plan and install the automatic equipment, which by then would have a proven track record. This *abandonment option* is expected to add $100,000 of NPV and has a 25% chance of being exercised.

Plan Y Real Option—Because plan Y does not require current expansion of the plant, it creates an improved opportunity for future plant expansion. This option allows the firm to grow its business into related areas more easily if business and economic conditions continue to improve. This *growth option* is estimated to be worth $500,000 of NPV and has a 20% chance of being exercised.

To Do

a. Assuming that the two plans have the same risk as the firm, use the following capital budgeting techniques and the firm's cost of capital to evaluate their acceptability and relative ranking.

      (1) Net present value (NPV).

      (2) Internal rate of return (IRR).

  b. Recognizing the differences in plan risk, use the NPV method, the *risk-adjusted discount rates (RADRs)*, and the data given earlier to evaluate the acceptability and relative ranking of the two plans.

  c. Compare and contrast your finding in parts **a** and **b.** Which plan would you recommend? Did explicit recognition of the risk differences of the plans affect this recommendation?

  d. Use the real-options data given above for each plan to find the *strategic NPV,* $NPV_{strategic}$, for each plan.

  e. Compare and contrast your findings in part **d** with those in part **b.** Did explicit recognition of the real options in each plan affect your recommendation?

  f. Would your recommendations in parts **a, b,** and **d** change if the firm were operating under *capital rationing?* Explain.

Spreadsheet Exercise

Isis Corporation has two projects that it would like to undertake. However, due to capital restraints, the two projects—Alpha and Beta—must be treated as mutually exclusive. Both projects are equally risky, and the firm plans to use a 10% cost of capital to evaluate each. Project Alpha has an estimated life of 12 years, and project Beta has an estimated life of 9 years. The following cash flow data have been prepared.

	Cash flows	
	Project Alpha	Project Beta
CF_0	−$5,500,000	−$6,500,000
CF_1	300,000	400,000
CF_2	500,000	600,000
CF_3	500,000	800,000
CF_4	550,000	1,100,000
CF_5	700,000	1,400,000
CF_6	800,000	2,000,000
CF_7	950,000	2,500,000
CF_8	1,000,000	2,000,000
CF_9	1,250,000	1,000,000
CF_{10}	1,500,000	
CF_{11}	2,000,000	
CF_{12}	2,500,000	

To Do

Create a spreadsheet to answer the following questions.

  a. Calculate the *NPV* for each project over its respective life. Rank the projects in descending order on the basis of NPV. Which one would you choose?

b. Use the *annualized net present value (ANPV) approach* to evaluate and rank the projects in descending order on the basis of ANPV. Which one would you choose?

c. Compare and contrast your findings in parts **a** and **b.** Which project would you recommend that the firm choose? Explain.

Group Exercise

This chapter refined the capital budgeting techniques of previous chapters to include the concept of risk in the analysis of capital investment proposals. Your firm will now revisit the work done in Chapters 8 and 9 and apply a measurement of risk to the previously computed cash flows.

To Do

a. Create a variable or set of variables that will introduce risk—and therefore a lack of certainty regarding the estimated cash flows—for each of the two investment projects.

b. Using the variable(s) selected in part **a,** take each annual cash flow and assign three possible dollar amounts given three scenarios: pessimistic, most likely, and optimistic. Let the dollar value you originally chose be the most likely amount, the pessimistic value be less than this amount, and the optimistic value be greater than this amount.

c. Calculate the *ranges* of the NPVs between the pessimistic and optimistic outcomes, and determine which of the two projects is riskier.

d. Develop a simplified RADR by adjusting the discount rate originally chosen for the different levels of risk calculated in part **c,** and calculate the *risk-adjusted NPV* for each project.

e. Using all of the analysis from Chapters 8, 9, and 10, and concentrating on the new risk-based information, choose which project your firm will implement and explain why. Be mindful that the reasons for the decision are as important as the choice of investment made by your group. View your final decision as an opportunity to defend your choice to a broader audience, perhaps the firm's board of directors.

Web Exercise

Go to the book's companion website at www.prenhall.com/gitman to find the Web Exercise for this chapter.

Remember to check the book's website at www.prenhall.com/gitman to find additional resources, including Web Exercises and a Web Case.

Integrative Case 3

Lasting Impressions Company

Lasting Impressions (LI) Company is a medium-sized commercial printer of promotional advertising brochures, booklets, and other direct-mail pieces. The firm's major clients are ad agencies based in New York and Chicago. The typical job is characterized by high quality and production runs of more than 50,000 units. LI has not been able to compete effectively with larger printers because of its existing older, inefficient presses. The firm is currently having problems cost-effectively meeting run length requirements as well as meeting quality standards.

The general manager has proposed the purchase of one of two large, six-color presses designed for long, high-quality runs. The purchase of a new press would enable LI to reduce its cost of labor and therefore the price to the client, putting the firm in a more competitive position. The key financial characteristics of the old press and of the two proposed presses are summarized in what follows.

Old press Originally purchased 3 years ago at an installed cost of $400,000, it is being depreciated under MACRS using a 5-year recovery period. The old press has a remaining economic life of 5 years. It can be sold today to net $420,000 before taxes; if it is retained, it can be sold to net $150,000 before taxes at the end of 5 years.

Press A This highly automated press can be purchased for $830,000 and will require $40,000 in installation costs. It will be depreciated under MACRS using a 5-year recovery period. At the end of the 5 years, the machine could be sold to net $400,000 before taxes. If this machine is acquired, it is anticipated that the following current account changes would result:

Cash	+ $ 25,400
Accounts receivable	+ 120,000
Inventories	− 20,000
Accounts payable	+ 35,000

Press B This press is not as sophisticated as press A. It costs $640,000 and requires $20,000 in installation costs. It will be depreciated under MACRS using a 5-year recovery period. At the end of 5 years, it can be sold to net $330,000 before taxes. Acquisition of this press will have no effect on the firm's net working capital investment.

The firm estimates that its earnings before depreciation, interest, and taxes with the old press and with press A or press B for each of the 5 years would be as shown in Table 1 (see page 500). The firm is subject to a 40% tax rate. The firm's cost of capital, r, applicable to the proposed replacement is 14%.

TABLE 1

Year	Old press	Press A	Press B
1	$120,000	$250,000	$210,000
2	120,000	270,000	210,000
3	120,000	300,000	210,000
4	120,000	330,000	210,000
5	120,000	370,000	210,000

Earnings Before Depreciation, Interest, and Taxes for Lasting Impressions Company's Presses

To Do

a. For each of the two proposed replacement presses, determine:
   (1) Initial investment.
   (2) Operating cash inflows. (*Note:* Be sure to consider the depreciation in year 6.)
   (3) Terminal cash flow. (*Note:* This is at the end of year 5.)

b. Using the data developed in part **a,** find and depict on a time line the relevant cash flow stream associated with each of the two proposed replacement presses, assuming that each is terminated at the end of 5 years.

c. Using the data developed in part **b,** apply each of the following decision techniques:
   (1) Payback period. (*Note:* For year 5, use only the operating cash inflows—that is, exclude terminal cash flow—when making this calculation.)
   (2) Net present value (NPV).
   (3) Internal rate of return (IRR).

d. Draw *net present value profiles* for the two replacement presses on the same set of axes, and discuss conflicting rankings of the two presses, if any, resulting from use of NPV and IRR decision techniques.

e. Recommend which, if either, of the presses the firm should acquire if the firm has (1) unlimited funds or (2) capital rationing.

f. What is the impact on your recommendation of the fact that the operating cash inflows associated with press A are characterized as very risky in contrast to the low-risk operating cash inflows of press B?

Part Four
Long-Term Financial Decisions

Chapters in This Part

11 | The Cost of Capital

WHY THIS CHAPTER MATTERS TO YOU

In Your Professional Life

Accounting: You need to understand the various sources of capital and how their costs are calculated to provide the data necessary to determine the firm's overall cost of capital.

Information systems: You need to understand the various sources of capital and how their costs are calculated to develop systems that will estimate the costs of those sources of capital, as well as the overall cost of capital.

Management: You need to understand the cost of capital to select long-term investments after assessing their acceptability and relative rankings.

Marketing: You need to understand the firm's cost of capital because proposed projects must earn returns in excess of it to be acceptable.

Operations: You need to understand the firm's cost of capital to assess the economic viability of investments in plant and equipment needed to improve or grow the firm's capacity.

In Your Personal Life

You need to know, on average, how much you are paying for financing. You do not sell equity in your personal financial life, but you do borrow money and can therefore realize financial benefits by understanding cost of capital concepts. By knowing your *personal cost of capital,* you can make better long-term investment decisions and maximize the worth from each dollar of long-term investment.

LEARNING GOALS

LG 1 Understand the key assumptions, the basic concept, and the specific sources of capital associated with the cost of capital.

LG 2 Determine the cost of long-term debt and the cost of preferred stock.

LG 3 Calculate the cost of common stock equity and convert it into the cost of retained earnings and the cost of new issues of common stock.

LG 4 Calculate the weighted average cost of capital (WACC) and discuss alternative weighting schemes.

LG 5 Describe the procedures used to determine break points and the weighted marginal cost of capital (WMCC).

LG 6 Explain the weighted marginal cost of capital (WMCC) and its use with the investment opportunities schedule (IOS) to make financing/investment decisions.

502

United Airlines

Taking Off Again

In the wake of the terrorist attacks in September 2001, airlines saw costs rise and passenger volume decline. Despite huge federal subsidies, some airlines headed straight into Chapter 11 bankruptcy. **United Airlines Corporation,** for example, in 2002 sought protection from creditors while attempting to reorganize. After 3 years of complex restructuring, the airline finally emerged from bankruptcy on February 1, 2006. The extensive restructuring measures—$7 billion in yearly cost reductions from renegotiated airplane leases, new labor contracts, 20,000 job cuts, and the elimination of pension obligations—gave it the needed financial edge to fly on its own again.

As part of its restructuring, United Airlines required a $3 billion financing package, provided through a syndicate led by JPMorganChase and Citigroup Global Markets. UAL received offers of subscription for more than twice the capital necessary to support the $3 billion it sought. As a result, it was able to reduce its financing costs by 75 basis points (0.75%). The financing consisted of a $2.8 billion term loan and a $200 million revolving credit line.

In 2007, a year after emerging from bankruptcy, UAL was able to restructure its $3 billion debt. Using cash, it paid down $972 million of the original $3 billion loan and refinanced the remaining $2 billion. Once again, it was able to lower its financing costs because of oversubscription of the refinancing. The new loan was set at 200 basis points (2.00%) over LIBOR, a reduction of 175 basis points (1.75%) from the original financing cost. The lower pricing is expected to result in net pre-tax savings of approximately $70 million per year.

Although United Airlines was able to meet its capital needs primarily from operating activities and the issuance of debt, other corporations rely more heavily on issuance of common stock. Each method of raising capital has its unique costs and benefits. Often companies will strive to meet some desired mix of debt and equity capital financing. In this chapter, we will demonstrate how to calculate the cost of specific sources of capital and combine them to arrive at a weighted average cost of capital that firms can use to evaluate investment opportunities.

As part of the 2007 refinancing, UAL was able to withdraw approximately $2.5 billion in assets from a collateral pool. What does this allow the company to do in the future?

11.1 | Overview of the Cost of Capital

cost of capital
The rate of return that a firm must earn on the projects in which it invests to maintain its market value and attract funds.

The **cost of capital** is the rate of return that a firm must earn on the projects in which it invests to maintain the market value of its stock. It can also be thought of as the rate of return required by the market suppliers of capital to attract their funds to the firm. If risk is held constant, projects with a rate of return above the cost of capital will increase the value of the firm, and projects with a rate of return below the cost of capital will decrease the value of the firm.

The cost of capital is an extremely important financial concept. It acts as a major link between the firm's long-term investment decisions (discussed in Part Three) and the wealth of the owners as determined by investors in the marketplace. It is, in effect, the "magic number" that is used to decide whether a proposed corporate investment will increase or decrease the firm's stock price. Clearly, only those investments that are expected to increase stock price (NPV > $0, or IRR > cost of capital) would be recommended. Because of its key role in financial decision making, the importance of the cost of capital cannot be overemphasized.

Some Key Assumptions

The cost of capital is a dynamic concept affected by a variety of economic and firm-specific factors. To isolate the basic structure of the cost of capital, we make some key assumptions relative to risk and taxes:

business risk
The risk to the firm of being unable to cover operating costs.

financial risk
The risk to the firm of being unable to cover required financial obligations (interest, lease payments, preferred stock dividends).

1. **Business risk**—the risk to the firm of being unable to cover operating costs—*is assumed to be unchanged*. This assumption means that the firm's acceptance of a given project does not affect its ability to meet operating costs.
2. **Financial risk**—the risk to the firm of being unable to cover required financial obligations (interest, lease payments, preferred stock dividends)—*is assumed to be unchanged*. This assumption means that projects are financed in such a way that the firm's ability to meet required financing costs is unchanged. For an example of the effect that unexpected legal liabilities can have on the cost of capital, see the nearby *Focus on Ethics* box.
3. After-tax costs are considered relevant. In other words, *the cost of capital is measured on an after-tax basis*. This assumption is consistent with the after-tax framework used to make capital budgeting decisions.

Hint Because of the positive relationship between risk and return, a firm's financing cost (cost of capital) will change if the acceptance of a project changes the firm's business or financial risk. The cost of capital can therefore be more easily measured by assuming that new projects do not change these risks.

The Basic Concept

target capital structure
The desired optimal mix of debt and equity financing that most firms attempt to maintain.

The cost of capital is estimated at a given point in time. It reflects the *expected average future cost of funds over the long run*. Although firms typically raise money in lumps, the cost of capital should reflect the interrelatedness of financing activities. For example, if a firm raises funds with debt (borrowing) today, it is likely that some form of equity, such as common stock, will have to be used the next time it needs funds. Most firms attempt to maintain a desired optimal mix of debt and equity financing. In practice, this mix is commonly a range, such as 40 percent to 50 percent debt, rather than a point, such as 55 percent debt. It is called a **target capital structure**—a topic that will be addressed in Chapter 12. Here, it is sufficient to say that although firms raise money in lumps, they tend toward some desired *mix of financing*.

Focus on Ethics   The Asbestos Penalty

IN PRACTICE

Asbestos, once widely used in manufacturing and construction for its strength, durability, and resistance to heat and fire, remains the subject of lawsuits. Following the first asbestos-related lawsuit in 1966, hundreds of thousands of claims have been filed, forcing 73 companies into bankruptcy by mid-2004. Asbestos liability looks to be one of the largest liabilities ever faced by U.S. businesses. For the U.S. insurance industry, asbestos-related losses could eventually reach as much as $65 billion. By the late 1990s, claims appeared to have stabilized, but then surged again.

One reason for the new wave of claims was the realization on the part of claimants, their attorneys, and trade unions that many asbestos manufacturers had already been driven to bankruptcy and settlement funds were drying up. Up to 90 per-

cent of current claimants have no signs of serious illness, but are filing claims while there is still hope for compensation. Some asbestos-related illnesses have a latency period of up to 40 years. Also fueling litigation was the expansion of defendants to include firms that have a less direct connection with asbestos, such as contractors or current owners of companies that formerly produced products containing asbestos.

The new wave of litigation forced some states to institute tort reform beginning in 2005. Courts are now scrutinizing asbestos-related claims for fraud, and judges have been issuing more opinions limiting fraud in lawsuits brought before their courts.

A report released in March 2007 by A.M. Best suggests that, thanks to reforms on the state level, the worst of the asbestos-

liability crisis may be behind the insurance industry now, although individual companies will continue to incur charges for years. In addition to the direct costs of asbestos litigation, which includes legal fees and claims settlements, businesses subject to asbestos-related lawsuits face indirect costs, including an increased cost of capital. A study prepared in October 2003 by William O. Kerr, Ph.D., for the Financial Institute for Asbestos Reform suggests that the cost of capital increased by 4 percent to 14 percent for firms facing significant asbestos claims liabilities. The asbestos penalty, in the form of increased cost of capital, is expected to persist as long as asbestos litigation continues.

■ *What effect would an increased cost of capital have on a firm's future investments?*

To capture the interrelatedness of financing assuming the presence of a target capital structure, we need to look at the *overall cost of capital* rather than the cost of the specific source of funds used to finance a given expenditure.

Example

A firm is *currently* faced with an investment opportunity. Assume the following:

Best project available today

$$Cost = \$100,000$$
$$Life = 20 \text{ years}$$
$$IRR = 7\%$$

Cost of least-cost financing source available

$$Debt = 6\%$$

Because it can earn 7% on the investment of funds costing only 6%, the firm undertakes the opportunity. Imagine that *1 week later* a new investment opportunity is available:

Best project available 1 week later

$$\text{Cost} = \$100,000$$
$$\text{Life} = 20 \text{ years}$$
$$\text{IRR} = 12\%$$

Cost of least-cost financing source available

$$\text{Equity} = 14\%$$

In this instance, the firm rejects the opportunity, because the 14% financing cost is greater than the 12% expected return.

Were the firm's actions in the best interests of its owners? No; it accepted a project yielding a 7% return and rejected one with a 12% return. Clearly, there should be a better way, and there is: The firm can use a *combined* cost, which over the long run will yield better decisions. By weighting the cost of each source of financing by its *target proportion* in the firm's capital structure, the firm can obtain a *weighted average cost* that reflects the interrelationship of financing decisions. Assuming that a 50–50 mix of debt and equity is targeted, the weighted average cost here would be 10% [(0.50 × 6% debt) + (0.50 × 14% equity)]. With this cost, the first opportunity would have been rejected (7% IRR < 10% weighted average cost), and the second would have been accepted (12% IRR > 10% weighted average cost). Such an outcome would clearly be more desirable.

Specific Sources of Capital

This chapter focuses on finding the costs of specific sources of capital and combining them to determine the weighted average cost of capital. Our concern is only with the *long-term* sources of funds available to a business firm, because these sources supply the permanent financing. Long-term financing supports the firm's fixed-asset investments.[1] We assume throughout the chapter that such investments are selected by using appropriate capital budgeting techniques.

There are four basic sources of long-term funds for the business firm: long-term debt, preferred stock, common stock, and retained earnings. All entries on the right-hand side of the balance sheet, other than current liabilities, represent these sources:

Balance Sheet	
	Current liabilities
	Long-term debt
Assets	Stockholders' equity
	Preferred stock
	Common stock equity
	Common stock
	Retained earnings

Sources of long-term funds

---

1. The role of both long-term and short-term financing in supporting both fixed- and current-asset investments is addressed in Chapter 14. Suffice it to say that long-term funds are at minimum used to finance fixed assets.

Although not every firm will use all of these methods of financing, each firm is expected to have funds from some of these sources in its capital structure.

The *specific cost* of each source of financing is the *after-tax* cost of obtaining the financing *today*, not the historically based cost reflected by the existing financing on the firm's books. Techniques for determining the specific cost of each source of long-term funds are presented on the following pages. Although these techniques tend to develop precisely calculated values, the resulting values are at best *rough approximations* because of the numerous assumptions and forecasts that underlie them. Although we round calculated costs to the nearest 0.1 percent throughout this chapter, it is not unusual for practicing financial managers to use costs rounded to the nearest 1 percent because these values are merely estimates.

REVIEW QUESTIONS

11–1 What is the *cost of capital?* What role does it play in long-term investment decisions?

11–2 Why do we assume that *business risk* and *financial risk* are unchanged when evaluating the cost of capital? Discuss the implications of these assumptions on the acceptance and financing of new projects.

11–3 Why is the cost of capital measured on an *after-tax basis?* Why is use of a weighted average cost of capital rather than the cost of the specific source of funds recommended?

11–4 You have just been told, "Because we are going to finance this project with debt, its required rate of return must exceed the cost of debt." Do you agree or disagree? Explain.

 11.2 | Cost of Long-Term Debt

cost of long-term debt, r_i
The after-tax cost today of raising long-term funds through borrowing.

The **cost of long-term debt,** r_i, is the after-tax cost today of raising long-term funds through borrowing. For convenience, we typically assume that the funds are raised through the sale of bonds. In addition, as we did in Chapter 6, we assume that the bonds pay *annual* (rather than *semiannual*) interest.

Net Proceeds

net proceeds
Funds actually received from the sale of a security.

flotation costs
The total costs of issuing and selling a security.

Most corporate long-term debts are incurred through the sale of bonds. The **net proceeds** from the sale of a bond, or any security, are the funds that are actually received from the sale. **Flotation costs**—the total costs of issuing and selling a security—reduce the net proceeds from the sale. These costs apply to all public offerings of securities—debt, preferred stock, and common stock. They include two components: (1) *underwriting costs*—compensation earned by investment bankers for selling the security, and (2) *administrative costs*—issuer expenses such as legal, accounting, printing, and other expenses.

Example   Duchess Corporation, a major hardware manufacturer, is contemplating selling $10 million worth of 20-year, 9% coupon (stated *annual* interest rate) bonds, each with a par value of $1,000. Because similar-risk bonds earn returns greater than 9%, the firm must sell the bonds for $980 to compensate for the lower coupon interest rate. The flotation costs are 2% of the par value of the bond ($0.02 \times \$1,000$), or \$20. The *net proceeds* to the firm from the sale of each bond are therefore \$960 (\$980 − \$20).

Before-Tax Cost of Debt

The before-tax cost of debt, r_d, for a bond can be obtained in any of three ways: quotation, calculation, or approximation.

Using Cost Quotations

Hint From the issuer's
perspective, the IRR on a
bond's cash flows is its *cost to
maturity;* from the investor's
perspective, the IRR on a
bond's cash flows is its *yield to
maturity* (YTM), as explained
in Chapter 6. These two
measures are conceptually
similar, although their point
of view is different.

When the net proceeds from sale of a bond equal its par value, the before-tax cost just equals the coupon interest rate. For example, a bond with a 10 percent coupon interest rate that nets proceeds equal to the bond's \$1,000 par value would have a before-tax cost, r_d, of 10 percent.

A second quotation that is sometimes used is the *yield to maturity* (YTM) on a similar-risk bond[2] (see Chapter 6). For example, if a similar-risk bond has a YTM of 9.7 percent, this value can be used as the before-tax cost of debt, r_d.

Calculating the Cost

This approach finds the before-tax cost of debt by calculating the *internal rate of return (IRR)* on the bond cash flows. From the issuer's point of view, this value is the *cost to maturity* of the cash flows associated with the debt. The cost to maturity can be calculated by using a financial calculator, an electronic spreadsheet, or a trial-and-error technique.[3] It represents the annual before-tax percentage cost of the debt.

Example

In the preceding example, the net proceeds of a \$1,000, 9% coupon interest rate, 20-year bond were found to be \$960. The calculation of the annual cost is quite simple. The cash flow pattern is exactly the opposite of a conventional pattern; it consists of an initial inflow (the net proceeds) followed by a series of annual outlays (the interest payments). In the final year, when the debt is retired, an outlay representing the repayment of the principal also occurs. The cash flows associated with Duchess Corporation's bond issue are as follows:

End of year(s)	Cash flow
0	\$ 960
1–20	−\$ 90
20	−\$1,000

---

2. Generally, the yield to maturity of bonds with a similar "rating" is used. Bond ratings, which are published by independent agencies, were discussed in Chapter 6.

3. The trial-and-error technique is presented at the book's website www.prenhall.com/gitman.

The initial $960 inflow is followed by annual interest outflows of $90 (9% coupon interest rate $\times$ $1,000 par value) over the 20-year life of the bond. In year 20, an outflow of $1,000 (the repayment of the principal) occurs. We can determine the cost of debt by finding the IRR, which is the discount rate that equates the present value of the outflows to the initial inflow.

Input   Function
20   N
960   PV
−90   PMT
−1000   FV
CPT
I

Solution
9.452

Calculator Use   [*Note:* Most calculators require either the present (net proceeds) or the future (annual interest payments and repayment of principal) values to be input as negative numbers when we calculate cost to maturity. That approach is used here.] Using the calculator and the inputs shown at the left, you should find the before-tax cost (cost to maturity) to be 9.452%.

Spreadsheet Use   The before-tax cost of debt on the Duchess Corporation bond also can be calculated as shown in the following Excel spreadsheet.

	A	B	C	D	E	F
1	FINDING THE IRR ON A 20-YEAR BOND					
2	Net proceeds from sale of bond	$ 960				
3	Coupon payment	$ 90				
4	Years to maturity	20				
5	Par value (principal)	$ 1,000				
6						
7	Use the Trial and Error Method to determine the before-tax cost of debt.					
8	The model:	Value of the bond = Coupon payment(PVIFA) + Par(PVIF)				
9	There is a before-tax rate that will discount the future cash flows back to the $960 value.					
10						
11		Before-tax cost of debt = 9.452%				
12						
13		Payment	PVIFA	Par	PVIF	= Value
14		$ 90	8.8420	$1,000	0.1643	960.03
15						

Approximating the Cost

The before-tax cost of debt, r_d, for a bond with a $1,000 par value can be approximated by using the following equation:

$$r_d = \frac{I + \frac{\$1,000 - N_d}{n}}{\frac{N_d + \$1,000}{2}} \tag{11.1}$$

where

I = annual interest in dollars

N_d = net proceeds from the sale of debt (bond)

n = number of years to the bond's maturity

Example

Substituting the appropriate values from the Duchess Corporation example into the approximation formula given in Equation 11.1, we get

$$r_d = \frac{\$90 + \dfrac{\$1,000 - \$960}{20}}{\dfrac{\$960 + \$1,000}{2}} = \frac{\$90 + \$2}{\$980}$$

$$= \frac{\$92}{\$980} = \underline{\underline{9.4\%}}$$

This approximate before-tax cost of debt is close to the 9.452% value calculated precisely in the preceding example.

After-Tax Cost of Debt

As indicated earlier, the *specific cost* of financing must be stated on an after-tax basis. Because interest on debt is tax deductible, it reduces the firm's taxable income. The after-tax cost of debt, r_i, can be found by multiplying the before-tax cost, r_d, by 1 minus the tax rate, T, as stated in the following equation:

$$r_i = r_d \times (1 - T) \tag{11.2}$$

Example

Duchess Corporation has a 40% tax rate. Using the 9.4% before-tax debt cost calculated above, and applying Equation 11.2, we find an after-tax cost of debt of 5.6% [9.4% × (1 − 0.40)]. Typically, the cost of long-term debt is less than a given firm's cost of any of the alternative forms of long-term financing, primarily because of the tax deductibility of interest.

Personal Finance Example   Kait and Kasim Sullivan, a married couple in the 28% federal income-tax bracket, wish to borrow $60,000 to fully pay for the purchase of a new luxury car. To finance the purchase, they can either borrow the $60,000 through the auto dealer at an annual interest rate of 6.0%, or they can take a $60,000 second mortgage on their home. The best annual rate they can get on the second mortgage is 7.2%. They already have qualified for both of the loans being considered.

If they borrow from the auto dealer, the interest on this "consumer loan" will not be deductible for federal tax purposes. Because their home, which is worth $400,000 today, currently has a mortgage balance of $240,000, the second mortgage of $60,000 would result in total mortgages against the property of $300,000. This amount is well below the $1.1 million maximum mortgage against which a homeowner can deduct interest for federal tax purposes. Therefore, the interest on the second mortgage would be tax-deductible.

To choose the least-cost financing, the Sullivans calculated the after-tax cost of both sources of long-term debt. Because interest on the auto loan is *not* tax-deductible, its after-tax cost equals its stated cost of 6.0%. Because the interest on the second mortgage *is* tax-deductible, its after-tax cost can be found using Equation 11.2:

$$\text{After-tax cost of debt} = \text{Before-tax cost of debt} \times (1 - \text{Tax rate})$$
$$7.2\% \times (1 - 0.28) = 7.2\% \times 0.72 = \underline{\underline{5.2\%}}$$

Because the 5.2% after-tax cost of the second mortgage is less than the 6.0% cost of the auto loan, the Sullivans should use the second mortgage to finance the auto purchase.

REVIEW QUESTIONS

11–5 What are the *net proceeds* from the sale of a bond? What are *flotation costs* and how do they affect a bond's net proceeds?

11–6 What three methods can be used to find the before-tax cost of debt?

11–7 How is the before-tax cost of debt converted into the after-tax cost?

11.3 | Cost of Preferred Stock

Preferred stock represents a special type of ownership interest in the firm. It gives preferred stockholders the right to receive their *stated* dividends before the firm can distribute any earnings to common stockholders. Because preferred stock is a form of ownership, the proceeds from its sale are expected to be held for an infinite period of time. The key characteristics of preferred stock were described in Chapter 7. However, the one aspect of preferred stock that requires review is dividends.

Preferred Stock Dividends

Most preferred stock dividends are stated as a *dollar amount:* "*x* dollars per year." When dividends are stated this way, the stock is often referred to as "*x*-dollar preferred stock." Thus a "$4 preferred stock" is expected to pay preferred stockholders $4 in dividends each year on each share of preferred stock owned.

Sometimes preferred stock dividends are stated as an *annual percentage rate.* This rate represents the percentage of the stock's par, or face, value that equals the annual dividend. For instance, an 8 percent preferred stock with a $50 par value would be expected to pay an annual dividend of $4 per share ($0.08 \times 50 par = 4). Before the cost of preferred stock is calculated, any dividends stated as percentages should be converted to annual dollar dividends.

Calculating the Cost of Preferred Stock

cost of preferred stock, r_p
The ratio of the preferred stock dividend to the firm's net proceeds from the sale of preferred stock; calculated by dividing the annual dividend, D_p, by the net proceeds from the sale of the preferred stock, N_p.

The **cost of preferred stock,** r_p, is the ratio of the preferred stock dividend to the firm's net proceeds from the sale of the preferred stock. The net proceeds represents the amount of money to be received minus any flotation costs. Equation 11.3 gives the cost of preferred stock, r_p, in terms of the annual dollar dividend, D_p, and the net proceeds from the sale of the stock, N_p:

$$r_p = \frac{D_p}{N_p} \tag{11.3}$$

Because preferred stock dividends are paid out of the firm's *after-tax* cash flows, a tax adjustment is not required.

Example ▶ Duchess Corporation is contemplating issuance of a 10% preferred stock that is expected to sell for its $87-per-share par value.[4] The cost of issuing and selling the stock is expected to be $5 per share. The first step in finding the cost of the stock is to calculate the dollar amount of the annual preferred dividend, which is $8.70 ($0.10 \times \$87$). The net proceeds per share from the proposed sale of stock equals the sale price minus the flotation costs ($87 - \$5 = \$82$). Substituting the annual dividend, D_p, of $8.70 and the net proceeds, N_p, of $82 into Equation 11.3 gives the cost of preferred stock, 10.6% ($8.70 \div \$82$).

The cost of Duchess's preferred stock (10.6%) is much greater than the cost of its long-term debt (5.6%). This difference exists both because the cost of long-term debt (the interest) is tax deductible and because preferred stock is riskier than long-term debt.

REVIEW QUESTION

11–8 How would you calculate the cost of preferred stock?

11.4 | Cost of Common Stock

The *cost of common stock* is the return required on the stock by investors in the marketplace. There are two forms of common stock financing: (1) retained earnings and (2) new issues of common stock. As a first step in finding each of these costs, we must estimate the cost of common stock equity.

Finding the Cost of Common Stock Equity

cost of common stock equity, r_s
The rate at which investors discount the expected dividends of the firm to determine its share value.

The **cost of common stock equity,** r_s, is the rate at which investors discount the expected dividends of the firm to determine its share value. Two techniques are used to measure the cost of common stock equity.[5] One relies on the constant-growth valuation model, the other on the capital asset pricing model (CAPM).

Using the Constant-Growth Valuation (Gordon) Model

In Chapter 7 we found the value of a share of stock to be equal to the present value of all future dividends, which in one model were assumed to grow at a constant annual rate over an infinite time horizon. This is the **constant-growth**

---

4. For simplicity, the preferred stock in this example is assumed to be sold for its par value. In practice, particularly for subsequent issues of already outstanding preferred stock, it is typically sold at a price that differs from its par value.

5. Other, more subjective techniques are available for estimating the cost of common stock equity. One popular technique is the *bond yield plus a premium;* it estimates the cost of common stock equity by adding a premium, typically between 3% and 5%, to the firm's current cost of long-term debt. Another, even more subjective technique uses the firm's *expected return on equity (ROE)* as a measure of its cost of common stock equity. Here we focus only on the more theoretically based techniques.

constant-growth valuation (Gordon) model
Assumes that the value of a share of stock equals the present value of all future dividends (assumed to grow at a constant rate) that it is expected to provide over an infinite time horizon.

valuation model, also known as the **Gordon model.** The key expression derived for this model was presented as Equation 7.5 and is restated here:

$$P_0 = \frac{D_1}{r_s - g} \tag{11.4}$$

where

P_0 = value of common stock

D_1 = per-share dividend *expected* at the end of year 1

r_s = required return on common stock

g = constant rate of growth in dividends

Solving Equation 11.4 for r_s results in the following expression for the *cost of common stock equity:*

$$r_s = \frac{D_1}{P_0} + g \tag{11.5}$$

Equation 11.5 indicates that the cost of common stock equity can be found by dividing the dividend expected at the end of year 1 by the current price of the stock (the "dividend yield") and adding the expected growth rate (the "capital gains yield"). Because common stock dividends are paid from *after-tax* income, no tax adjustment is required.

Example

Duchess Corporation wishes to determine its cost of common stock equity, r_s. The market price, P_0, of its common stock is $50 per share. The firm expects to pay a dividend, D_1, of $4 at the end of the coming year, 2010. The dividends paid on the outstanding stock over the past 6 years (2004–2009) were as follows:

Year	Dividend
2009	$3.80
2008	3.62
2007	3.47
2006	3.33
2005	3.12
2004	2.97

Using a financial calculator, electronic spreadsheet, or the table for the present value interest factors, *PVIF* (Table A–2), in conjunction with the technique described for finding growth rates in Chapter 4, we can calculate the annual growth rate of dividends, g. It turns out to be approximately 5% (more precisely, it is 5.05%). Substituting $D_1 = \$4$, $P_0 = \$50$, and $g = 5\%$ into Equation 11.5 yields the cost of common stock equity:

$$r_s = \frac{\$4}{\$50} + 0.05 = 0.08 + 0.05 = 0.130, \text{ or } \underline{\underline{13.0\%}}$$

The 13.0% cost of common stock equity represents the return required by *existing* shareholders on their investment. If the actual return is less than that, shareholders are likely to begin selling their stock.

Using the Capital Asset Pricing Model (CAPM)

capital asset pricing model (CAPM)
Describes the relationship between the required return, r_s, and the nondiversifiable risk of the firm as measured by the beta coefficient, *b.*

Recall from Chapter 5 that the **capital asset pricing model (CAPM)** describes the relationship between the required return, r_s, and the nondiversifiable risk of the firm as measured by the beta coefficient, *b.* The basic CAPM is

$$r_s = R_F + [b \times (r_m - R_F)] \tag{11.6}$$

where

R_F = risk-free rate of return

r_m = market return; return on the market portfolio of assets

Using CAPM indicates that the cost of common stock equity is the return required by investors as compensation for the firm's nondiversifiable risk, measured by beta.

Example

Duchess Corporation now wishes to calculate its cost of common stock equity, r_s, by using the capital asset pricing model. The firm's investment advisors and its own analyses indicate that the risk-free rate, R_F, equals 7%; the firm's beta, *b*, equals 1.5; and the market return, r_m, equals 11%. Substituting these values into Equation 11.6, the company estimates the cost of common stock equity, r_s, to be

$$r_s = 7.0\% + [1.5 \times (11.0\% - 7.0\%)] = 7.0\% + 6.0\% = \underline{\underline{13.0\%}}$$

The 13.0% cost of common stock equity represents the required return of investors in Duchess Corporation common stock. It is the same as that found by using the constant-growth valuation model.

Comparing Constant-Growth and CAPM Techniques

The CAPM technique differs from the constant-growth valuation model in that it directly considers the firm's risk, as reflected by beta, in determining the *required* return or cost of common stock equity. The constant-growth model does not look at risk; it uses the market price, P_0, as a reflection of the *expected* risk–return preference of investors in the marketplace. The constant-growth valuation and CAPM techniques for finding r_s are theoretically equivalent. It is difficult to demonstrate that equivalency, however, because of measurement problems associated with growth, beta, the risk-free rate (what maturity of government security to use), and the market return. Firms often prefer to use the constant-growth valuation model because the data required are more readily available.

Another difference is that when the constant-growth valuation model is used to find the cost of common stock equity, it can easily be adjusted for flotation costs to find the cost of new common stock; the CAPM does not provide a simple adjustment mechanism. The difficulty in adjusting the cost of common stock equity calculated by using CAPM occurs because in its common form the model does not include the market price, P_0, a variable needed to make such an adjustment. Although CAPM has a stronger theoretical foundation, the computational appeal of the traditional constant-growth valuation model justifies its use throughout this text to measure common stock costs.

Cost of Retained Earnings

As you know, dividends are paid out of a firm's earnings. Their payment, made in cash to common stockholders, reduces the firm's retained earnings. Suppose a firm needs common stock equity financing of a certain amount. It has two choices relative to retained earnings: It can issue additional common stock in that amount and still pay dividends to stockholders out of retained earnings, or it can increase common stock equity by retaining the earnings (not paying the cash dividends) in the needed amount. In a strict accounting sense, the retention of earnings increases common stock equity in the same way that the sale of additional shares of common stock does. Thus the **cost of retained earnings, r_r,** to the firm is the same as the cost of an *equivalent fully subscribed issue of additional common stock.* Stockholders find the firm's retention of earnings acceptable only if they expect that it will earn at least their required return on the reinvested funds.

Viewing retained earnings as a fully subscribed issue of additional common stock, we can set the firm's cost of retained earnings, r_r, equal to the cost of common stock equity as given by Equations 11.5 and 11.6.[6]

$$r_r = r_s \qquad (11.7)$$

It is not necessary to adjust the cost of retained earnings for flotation costs, because by retaining earnings, the firm "raises" equity capital without incurring these costs.

cost of retained earnings, r_r
The same as the cost of an *equivalent fully subscribed issue of additional common stock,* which is equal to the cost of common stock equity, r_s.

Hint Using retained earnings as a major source of financing for capital expenditures does not give away control of the firm and does not dilute present earnings per share, as would occur if new common stock were issued. However, the firm must effectively manage retained earnings to produce profits that increase future retained earnings.

Example

The cost of retained earnings for Duchess Corporation was actually calculated in the preceding examples: It is equal to the cost of common stock equity. Thus r_r equals 13.0%. As we will show in the next section, the cost of retained earnings is always lower than the cost of a new issue of common stock, because it entails no flotation costs.

Cost of New Issues of Common Stock

Our purpose in finding the firm's overall cost of capital is to determine the after-tax cost of *new* funds required for financing projects. The **cost of a new issue of common stock, r_n,** is determined by calculating the cost of common stock, net of underpricing and associated flotation costs. Normally, for a new issue to sell, it has to be **underpriced**—sold at a price below its current market price, P_0.

Firms underprice new issues for a variety of reasons. First, when the market is in equilibrium (that is, the demand for shares equals the supply of shares), additional demand for shares can be achieved only at a lower price. Second, when additional shares are issued, each share's percentage of ownership in the firm is

cost of a new issue of common stock, r_n
The cost of common stock, net of underpricing and associated flotation costs.

underpriced
Stock sold at a price below its current market price, P_0.

6. Technically, if a stockholder received dividends and wished to invest them in additional shares of the firm's stock, he or she would first have to pay personal taxes at capital gains rates on the dividends and then pay brokerage fees before acquiring additional shares. By using pt as the average stockholder's capital gains tax rate and bf as the average brokerage fees stated as a percentage, we can specify the cost of retained earnings, r_r, as $r_r = r_s \times (1 - pt) \times (1 - bf)$. Because of the difficulty in estimating pt and bf, only the simpler definition of r_r given in Equation 11.7 is used here.

diluted, thereby justifying a lower share value. Finally, many investors view the issuance of additional shares as a signal that management is using common stock equity financing because it believes that the shares are currently overpriced. Recognizing this information, they will buy shares only at a price below the current market price. Clearly, these and other factors necessitate underpricing of new offerings of common stock. Flotation costs paid for issuing and selling the new issue will further reduce proceeds.

We can use the constant-growth valuation model expression for the cost of existing common stock, r_s, as a starting point. If we let N_n represent the net proceeds from the sale of new common stock after subtracting underpricing and flotation costs, the cost of the new issue, r_n, can be expressed as follows:[7]

$$r_n = \frac{D_1}{N_n} + g \tag{11.8}$$

The net proceeds from sale of new common stock, N_n, will be less than the current market price, P_0. Therefore, the cost of new issues, r_n, will always be greater than the cost of existing issues, r_s, which is equal to the cost of retained earnings, r_r. *The cost of new common stock is normally greater than any other long-term financing cost.* Because common stock dividends are paid from after-tax cash flows, no tax adjustment is required.

Example

In the constant-growth valuation example, we found Duchess Corporation's cost of common stock equity, r_s, to be 13%, using the following values: an expected dividend, D_1, of $4; a current market price, P_0, of $50; and an expected growth rate of dividends, g, of 5%.

To determine its cost of *new* common stock, r_n, Duchess Corporation has estimated that on the average, new shares can be sold for $47. The $3-per-share underpricing is due to the competitive nature of the market. A second cost associated with a new issue is flotation costs of $2.50 per share that would be paid to issue and sell the new shares. The total underpricing and flotation costs per share are therefore expected to be $5.50.

Subtracting the $5.50-per-share underpricing and flotation cost from the current $50 share price results in expected net proceeds of $44.50 per share ($50.00 − $5.50). Substituting $D_1 = \$4$, $N_n = \$44.50$, and $g = 5\%$ into Equation 11.8 results in a cost of new common stock, r_n, as follows:

$$r_n = \frac{\$4.00}{\$44.50} + 0.05 = 0.09 + 0.05 = 0.140, \text{ or } \underline{\underline{14.0\%}}$$

Duchess Corporation's cost of new common stock is therefore 14.0%. This is the value to be used in subsequent calculations of the firm's overall cost of capital.

---

7. An alternative, but computationally less straightforward, form of this equation is

$$r_n = \frac{D_1}{P_0 \times (1 - f)} + g \tag{11.8a}$$

where f represents the *percentage* reduction in current market price expected as a result of underpricing and flotation costs. Simply stated, N_n in Equation 11.8 is equivalent to $P_0 \times (1 - f)$ in Equation 11.8a. For convenience, Equation 11.8 is used to define the cost of a new issue of common stock, r_n.

REVIEW QUESTIONS

11–9 What premise about share value underlies the constant-growth valuation (Gordon) model that is used to measure the cost of common stock equity, r_s?

11–10 Why is the cost of financing a project with retained earnings less than the cost of financing it with a new issue of common stock?

11.5 | Weighted Average Cost of Capital

weighted average cost of capital (WACC), r_a
Reflects the expected average future cost of funds over the long run; found by weighting the cost of each specific type of capital by its proportion in the firm's capital structure.

Now that we have calculated the cost of specific sources of financing, we can determine the overall cost of capital. As noted earlier, the **weighted average cost of capital (WACC)**, r_a, reflects the expected average future cost of funds over the long run. It is found by weighting the cost of each specific type of capital by its proportion in the firm's capital structure.

Calculating Weighted Average Cost of Capital (WACC)

Calculating the weighted average cost of capital (WACC) is straightforward: Multiply the specific cost of each form of financing by its proportion in the firm's capital structure and sum the weighted values. As an equation, the weighted average cost of capital, r_a, can be specified as follows:

$$r_a = (w_i \times r_i) + (w_p \times r_p) + (w_s \times r_{r \ or \ n}) \tag{11.9}$$

where

$\quad w_i =$ proportion of long-term debt in capital structure

$\quad w_p =$ proportion of preferred stock in capital structure

$\quad w_s =$ proportion of common stock equity in capital structure

$\quad w_i + w_p + w_s = 1.0$

Three important points should be noted in Equation 11.9:

1. For computational convenience, it is best to convert the weights into decimal form and leave the specific costs in percentage terms.
2. *The sum of the weights must equal 1.0.* Simply stated, all capital structure components must be accounted for.
3. The firm's common stock equity weight, w_s, is multiplied by either the cost of retained earnings, r_r, or the cost of new common stock, r_n. Which cost is used depends on whether the firm's common stock equity will be financed using retained earnings, r_r, or new common stock, r_n.

Example   In earlier examples, we found the costs of the various types of capital for Duchess Corporation to be as follows:

$$\text{Cost of debt, } r_i = \ 5.6\%$$
$$\text{Cost of preferred stock, } r_p = 10.6\%$$
$$\text{Cost of retained earnings, } r_r = 13.0\%$$
$$\text{Cost of new common stock, } r_n = 14.0\%$$

The company uses the following weights in calculating its weighted average cost of capital:

Source of capital	Weight
Long-term debt	40%
Preferred stock	10
Common stock equity	50
Total	100%

Because the firm expects to have a sizable amount of retained earnings available ($300,000), it plans to use its cost of retained earnings, r_r, as the cost of common stock equity. Duchess Corporation's weighted average cost of capital is calculated in Table 11.1. The resulting weighted average cost of capital for Duchess is 9.8%. Assuming an unchanged risk level, the firm should accept all projects that will earn a return greater than 9.8%.

Weighting Schemes

Firms can calculate weights on the basis of either *book value* or *market value* and using either *historical* or *target* proportions.

Book Value versus Market Value

book value weights
Weights that use accounting values to measure the proportion of each type of capital in the firm's financial structure.

market value weights
Weights that use market values to measure the proportion of each type of capital in the firm's financial structure.

Book value weights use accounting values to measure the proportion of each type of capital in the firm's financial structure. **Market value weights** measure the proportion of each type of capital at its market value. Market value weights are appealing, because the market values of securities closely approximate the actual dollars to be received from their sale. Moreover, because firms calculate the costs of the various types of capital by using prevailing market prices, it seems reasonable to use market value weights. In addition, the long-term investment cash flows to which the cost of capital is applied are estimated in terms of current as well as future market values. *Market value weights are clearly preferred over book value weights.*

Hint For computational convenience, the financing proportion weights are listed in decimal form in column 1 and the specific costs are shown in percentage terms in column 2.

TABLE 11.1   Calculation of the Weighted Average Cost of Capital for Duchess Corporation

Source of capital	Weight (1)	Cost (2)	Weighted cost [(1) × (2)] (3)
Long-term debt	0.40	5.6%	2.2%
Preferred stock	0.10	10.6	1.1
Common stock equity	0.50	13.0	6.5
Totals	1.00		9.8%

Weighted average cost of capital = 9.8%

Historical versus Target

historical weights
Either book or market value weights based on *actual* capital structure proportions.

Historical weights can be either book or market value weights based on *actual* capital structure proportions. For example, past or current book value proportions would constitute a form of historical weighting, as would past or current market value proportions. Such a weighting scheme would therefore be based on real—rather than desired—proportions.

target weights
Either book or market value weights based on *desired* capital structure proportions.

Target weights, which can also be based on either book or market values, reflect the firm's *desired* capital structure proportions. Firms using target weights establish such proportions on the basis of the "optimal" capital structure they wish to achieve. (The development of these proportions and the optimal structure are discussed in detail in Chapter 12.)

When one considers the somewhat approximate nature of the calculation of weighted average cost of capital, the choice of weights may not be critical. However, from a strictly theoretical point of view, the *preferred weighting scheme is target market value proportions*, and we assume these throughout this chapter.

Personal Finance Example   Chuck Solis currently has three loans outstanding, all of which mature in exactly 6 years and can be repaid without penalty any time prior to maturity. The outstanding balances and annual interest rates on these loans are noted below.

Loan	Outstanding Balance	Annual Interest Rate
1	$26,000	9.6%
2	9,000	10.6
3	45,000	7.4

After a thorough search, Chuck found a lender who would loan him $80,000 for 6 years at an annual interest rate 9.2% on the condition that the loan proceeds be used to fully repay the three outstanding loans, which combined have an outstanding balance of $80,000 ($26,000 + $9,000 + $45,000).

Chuck wishes to choose the less costly alternative: (1) do nothing or (2) borrow the $80,000 and pay off all three loans. He calculates the weighted average cost of his current debt by weighting each debt's annual interest cost by the proportion of the $80,000 total it represents and then summing the three weighted values as follows:

$$\text{Weighted average cost of current debt} = [(\$26,000/\$80,000) \times 9.6\%] + [(\$9,000/\$80,000) \times 10.6\%]$$
$$+ [(\$45,000/\$80,000) \times 7.4\%]$$
$$= (.3250 \times 9.6\%) + (.1125 \times 10.6\%) + (.5625 \times 7.4\%)$$
$$= 3.12\% + 1.19\% + 4.16\% = 8.47\% \approx \underline{8.5\%}$$

Given that the weighted average cost of the $80,000 of current debt of 8.5% is below the 9.2% cost of the new $80,000 loan, Chuck should do nothing, and just continue to pay off the three loans as originally scheduled.

REVIEW QUESTIONS

11–11 What is the *weighted average cost of capital (WACC)*, and how is it calculated?

11–12 Describe the logic underlying the use of *target weights* to calculate the WACC, and compare and contrast this approach with the use of *historical weights*. What is the preferred weighting scheme?

11.6 | Marginal Cost and Investment Decisions

The firm's weighted average cost of capital is a key input to the investment decision-making process. As demonstrated earlier in the chapter, the firm should make only those investments for which the expected return is greater than the weighted average cost of capital. A somewhat static approach to this decision is **economic value added (EVA®)**, which is a popular measure that firms can use to determine whether an investment—proposed or existing—contributes positively to the owners' wealth.[8] The application of EVA® requires the use of the weighted average cost of capital (WACC). Despite the operational simplicity of EVA®-type models, here we continue to focus on the theoretically more sound NPV approach introduced in Chapter 9. The *Focus on Practice* box on page 521 further discusses value creation as measured by EVA®.

The use of NPV provides a more dynamic approach to investment decisions. It recognizes that at any given time, the firm's financing costs and investment returns will be affected by the volume of financing and investment undertaken. The *weighted marginal cost of capital* and the *investment opportunities schedule* are mechanisms whereby financing and investment decisions can be made simultaneously.

economic value added (EVA®)
A popular, but static, approach to investment decisions used by many firms to determine whether an investment contributes positively to the owners' wealth.

Weighted Marginal Cost of Capital (WMCC)

The weighted average cost of capital may vary over time, depending on the volume of financing that the firm plans to raise. *As the volume of financing increases, the costs of the various types of financing will increase, raising the firm's weighted average cost of capital.* Therefore, it is useful to calculate the **weighted marginal cost of capital (WMCC)**, which is simply the firm's weighted average cost of capital (WACC) associated with its *next dollar* of total new financing. This marginal cost is relevant to current decisions.

The costs of the financing components (debt, preferred stock, and common stock) rise as larger amounts are raised. Suppliers of funds require greater returns in the form of interest, dividends, or growth as compensation for the increased risk introduced by larger volumes of *new* financing. The WMCC is therefore an increasing function of the level of total new financing.

weighted marginal cost of capital (WMCC)
The firm's weighted average cost of capital (WACC) associated with its *next dollar* of total new financing.

---

8. For a good analysis of economic value added (EVA®), see Ray D. Dillon and James E. Owers, "EVA® as a Financial Metric: Attributes, Utilization, and Relationship to NPV," *Financial Practice and Education* (Spring/Summer 1997), pp. 32–40.

Focus on Practice   EVAlue Creation

Answering the question, "Does the company use investors' money wisely?" is one of the financial manager's chief responsibilities and greatest challenges. At many firms—from Fortune 500 companies and investment firms to community hospitals—economic value added (EVA®) is the measurement tool of choice for making investment decisions, measuring overall financial performance, and motivating management.

Developed in 1983 by financial consultants **Stern Stewart & Co.** and protected by trademark, EVA is the difference between an investment's net operating profits after taxes and the cost of funds used to finance the investment (the amount of capital times the company's cost of capital). The EVA calculation is similar to calculating internal rate of return (IRR), except that the result is stated *in dollars* rather than percentages. It can be applied to the company as a whole as well as to specific

long-term investments such as new facilities and acquisitions.

According to its proponents, EVA represents "real" profits and provides a more accurate measure than accounting profits. Over time, it also has better correlation with stock prices than does earnings per share. Income calculations include only the cost of debt (interest expense), whereas EVA uses the total cost of capital, both debt and equity (an expensive form of capital). In addition, EVA treats research and development outlays as investments in future products or processes and capitalizes rather than expenses them. A growing EVA can signal future increases in stock prices.

Companies that use EVA believe doing so leads to better overall performance. Managers who apply it focus on allocating assets, not just accounting profits. They will accelerate the development of a hot new product even if it reduces earnings in the near

term. Companies write off R&D each year in line with generally accepted accounting practices, so speeding up new product development will reduce earnings in the near-term. Although earnings *may* drop for a few quarters, so will taxes—and cash flow eventually increases. One benefit of the EVA (non-GAAP) treatment of R&D expenses as a capitalized expense is that managers are less tempted to reduce valuable R&D expenditures just to improve current earnings because only a fraction of the reduction in R&D would impact current earnings.

EVA is not a panacea, however. Its critics say it may not be the right measure for many companies. They claim that because it favors big projects in big companies, EVA doesn't always do a good job on capital allocation.

■ *Why might a company use EVA as a measure of its performance in addition to the standard accounting measures?*

Another factor that causes the weighted average cost of capital to increase is the use of common stock equity financing. New financing provided by common stock equity will be provided by retaining earnings until this supply is exhausted, and then it will be obtained through new common stock financing. Because retained earnings are a less expensive form of common stock equity financing than the sale of new common stock, the weighted average cost of capital will rise with the addition of new common stock.

Finding Break Points

break point
The level of *total* new financing at which the cost of one of the financing components rises, thereby causing an upward shift in the *weighted marginal cost of capital (WMCC)*.

To calculate the WMCC, we must calculate **break points,** which reflect the level of *total* new financing at which the cost of one of the financing components rises. The following general equation can be used to find break points:

$$BP_j = \frac{AF_j}{w_j}$$

(11.10)

where

BP_j = break point for financing source j

AF_j = amount of funds available from financing source j at a given cost

w_j = capital structure weight (stated in decimal form) for financing source j

---

Example

When Duchess Corporation exhausts its $300,000 of available retained earnings (at $r_r = 13.0\%$), it must use the more expensive new common stock financing (at $r_n = 14.0\%$) to meet its common stock equity needs. In addition, the firm expects that it can borrow only $400,000 of debt at the 5.6% cost; additional debt will have an after-tax cost (r_i) of 8.4%. Two break points therefore exist: (1) when the $300,000 of retained earnings costing 13.0% is exhausted, and (2) when the $400,000 of long-term debt costing 5.6% is exhausted.

The break points can be found by substituting these values and the corresponding capital structure weights given earlier into Equation 11.10. We get the dollar amounts of *total* new financing at which the costs of the given financing sources rise:

$$BP_{\text{common equity}} = \frac{\$300,000}{0.50} = \$600,000$$

$$BP_{\text{long-term debt}} = \frac{\$400,000}{0.40} = \$1,000,000$$

Calculating the WMCC

Once we have determined the break points, the next step is to calculate the weighted average cost of capital over each range of total new financing between break points. First, we find the WACC for a level of total new financing between zero and the first break point. Next, we find the WACC for a level of total new financing between the first and second break points, and so on. By definition, for each of the ranges of total new financing between break points, certain component capital costs (such as common equity or debt) will increase. This will cause the weighted average cost of capital to increase to a higher level than that over the preceding range.

weighted marginal cost of capital (WMCC) schedule Graph that relates the firm's weighted average cost of capital to the level of total new financing.

Together, these data can be used to prepare a **weighted marginal cost of capital (WMCC) schedule**. This graph relates the firm's weighted average cost of capital to the level of total new financing.

Example

Table 11.2 summarizes the calculation of the WACC for Duchess Corporation over the three ranges of total new financing created by the two break points—$600,000 and $1,000,000. Comparing the costs in column 3 of the table for each of the three ranges, we can see that the costs in the first range ($0 to $600,000) are those calculated in earlier examples and used in Table 11.1. The second range ($600,000 to $1,000,000) reflects the increase in the common stock equity cost to 14.0%. In the final range, the increase in the long-term debt cost to 8.4% is introduced.

The weighted average costs of capital (WACC) for the three ranges are summarized in the table shown at the bottom of Figure 11.1. These data describe the weighted marginal cost of capital (WMCC), which increases as levels of total new financing increase. Figure 11.1 presents the WMCC schedule. Again, it is clear that the WMCC is an increasing function of the amount of total new financing raised.

TABLE 11.2	**Weighted Average Cost of Capital for Ranges of Total New Financing for Duchess Corporation**			
Range of total new financing	Source of capital (1)	Weight (2)	Cost (3)	Weighted cost [(2) × (3)] (4)
$0 to $600,000	Debt	.40	5.6%	2.2%
	Preferred	.10	10.6	1.1
	Common	.50	13.0	6.5
			Weighted average cost of capital	9.8%
$600,000 to $1,000,000	Debt	.40	5.6%	2.2%
	Preferred	.10	10.6	1.1
	Common	.50	14.0	7.0
			Weighted average cost of capital	10.3%
$1,000,000 and above	Debt	.40	8.4%	3.4%
	Preferred	.10	10.6	1.1
	Common	.50	14.0	7.0
			Weighted average cost of capital	11.5%

FIGURE 11.1

WMCC Schedule
Weighted marginal cost of capital (WMCC) schedule for Duchess Corporation

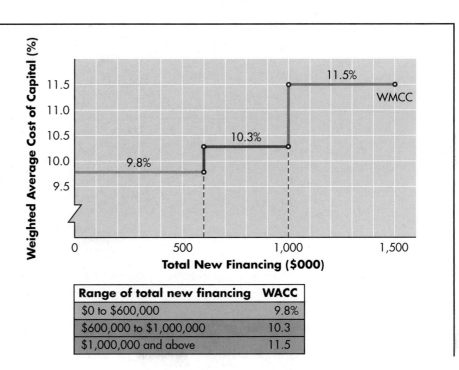

Range of total new financing	WACC
$0 to $600,000	9.8%
$600,000 to $1,000,000	10.3
$1,000,000 and above	11.5

Investment Opportunities Schedule (IOS)

investment opportunities
schedule (IOS)
A ranking of investment
possibilities from best
(highest return) to worst
(lowest return).

At any given time, a firm has certain investment opportunities available to it. These opportunities differ with respect to the size of investment, risk, and return.[9] The firm's **investment opportunities schedule (IOS)** is a ranking of investment possibilities from best (highest return) to worst (lowest return). Generally, the first project selected will have the highest return, the next project the second highest, and so on. The return on investments will *decrease* as the firm accepts additional projects.

Example   Column 1 of Table 11.3 shows Duchess Corporation's current investment opportunities schedule (IOS) listing the investment possibilities from best (highest return) to worst (lowest return). Column 2 of the table shows the initial investment required by each project. Column 3 shows the cumulative total invested funds necessary to finance all projects better than and including the corresponding investment opportunity. Plotting the project returns against the cumulative investment (column 1 against column 3) results in the firm's investment opportunities schedule (IOS). Figure 11.2 shows a graph of the IOS for Duchess Corporation.

Using the WMCC and IOS to Make Financing/Investment Decisions

As long as a project's internal rate of return is greater than the weighted marginal cost of new financing, the firm should accept the project.[10] The return will decrease with the acceptance of more projects, and the weighted marginal cost of capital will increase because greater amounts of financing will be required. The

TABLE 11.3   **Investment Opportunities Schedule (IOS) for Duchess Corporation**

Investment opportunity	Internal rate of return (IRR) (1)	Initial investment (2)	Cumulative investment[a] (3)
A	15.0%	$100,000	$ 100,000
B	14.5	200,000	300,000
C	14.0	400,000	700,000
D	13.0	100,000	800,000
E	12.0	300,000	1,100,000
F	11.0	200,000	1,300,000
G	10.0	100,000	1,400,000

[a]The cumulative investment represents the total amount invested in projects with higher returns plus the investment required for the corresponding investment opportunity.

9. Because the calculated weighted average cost of capital does not apply to risk-changing investments, we assume that all opportunities have equal risk similar to the firm's risk.

10. Although net present value could be used to make these decisions, the internal rate of return is used here because of the ease of comparison it offers.

FIGURE 11.2

IOS and WMCC Schedules
Using the IOS and WMCC
to select projects for
Duchess Corporation

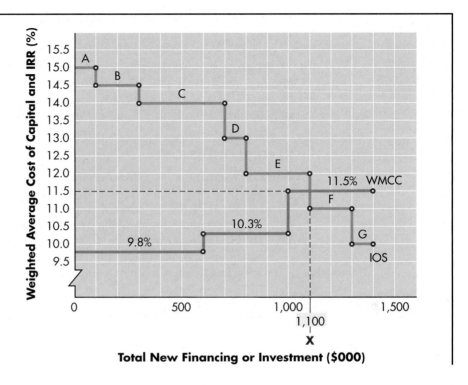

decision rule therefore would be: *Accept projects up to the point at which the marginal return on an investment equals its weighted marginal cost of capital. Beyond that point, its investment return will be less than its capital cost.*[11]

This approach is consistent with the maximization of net present value (NPV) for conventional projects for two reasons: (1) The NPV is positive as long as the IRR exceeds the weighted average cost of capital, r_a. (2) The larger the difference between the IRR and r_a, the larger the resulting NPV. Therefore, the acceptance of projects beginning with those that have the greatest positive difference between IRR and r_a, down to the point at which IRR just equals r_a, should result in the maximum total NPV for all independent projects accepted. Such an outcome is completely consistent with the firm's goal of maximizing owner wealth.

Example   Figure 11.2 shows Duchess Corporation's WMCC schedule and IOS on the same set of axes. By raising $1,100,000 of new financing and investing these funds in projects A, B, C, D, and E, the firm should maximize the wealth of its owners, because these projects result in the maximum total net present value. Note that the 12.0% return on the last dollar invested (in project E) *exceeds* its 11.5% weighted average cost. Investment in project F is not feasible, because its 11.0% return is *less than* the 11.5% cost of funds available for investment.

The firm's optimal capital budget of $1,100,000 is marked with an **X** in Figure 11.2. At that point, the IRR equals the weighted average cost of capital,

11. So as not to confuse the discussion presented here, the fact that using the IRR for selecting projects may not yield optimal decisions is ignored. The problems associated with the use of IRR in capital rationing were discussed in greater detail in Chapter 10.

and the firm's size as well as its shareholder value will be optimized. In a sense, the size of the firm is determined by the market—the availability of and returns on investment opportunities, and the availability and cost of financing.

In practice, most firms operate under *capital rationing*. That is, management imposes constraints that keep the capital expenditure budget below optimal (where IRR = r_a). Because of this, a gap frequently exists between the theoretically optimal capital budget and the firm's actual level of financing/investment.

REVIEW QUESTIONS

11–13 What is the *weighted marginal cost of capital (WMCC)*? What does the WMCC *schedule* represent? Why does this schedule increase?

11–14 What is the *investment opportunities schedule (IOS)*? Is it typically depicted as an increasing or a decreasing function? Why?

11–15 How can a firm use the WMCC schedule and the IOS to find the level of financing/investment that maximizes owner wealth? Why do many firms finance/invest at a level below this optimum?

Summary

Focus on Value

The cost of capital is an extremely important rate of return, particularly in capital budgeting decisions. It is the expected average future cost to the firm of funds over the long run. Because the cost of capital is the pivotal rate of return used in the investment decision process, its accuracy can significantly affect the quality of these decisions.

Even with good estimates of project cash flows, the application of NPV and IRR decision techniques, and adequate consideration of project risk, a poorly estimated cost of capital can result in the destruction of shareholder value. Underestimation of the cost of capital can result in the mistaken acceptance of poor projects; overestimation can cause good projects to be rejected. By applying the techniques presented in this chapter to estimate the firm's cost of capital, the financial manager will improve the likelihood that the firm's long-term decisions will be consistent with the firm's overall goal of **maximizing stock price (owner wealth)**.

Review of Learning Goals

Key definitions and formulas for this chapter are summarized in Table 11.4.

LG 1 **Understand the key assumptions, the basic concept, and the specific sources of capital associated with the cost of capital.** The cost of capital is the rate of return that a firm must earn on its investments to maintain its market value and attract needed funds. It is affected by business and financial risks, and is measured on an after-tax basis. A weighted average cost of capital should be used to find the expected average future cost of funds over the long run. The specific costs of the basic sources of capital (long-term debt, preferred stock, retained earnings, and common stock) can be calculated individually.

TABLE 11.4	**Summary of Key Definitions and Formulas for Cost of Capital**

Definitions of variables

AF_j = amount of funds available from financing source j at a given cost

b = beta coefficient or measure of nondiversifiable risk

BP_j = break point for financing source j

D_1 = per-share dividend *expected* at the end of year 1

D_p = annual preferred stock dividend (in dollars)

g = constant rate of growth in dividends

I = annual interest in dollars

r_a = weighted average cost of capital

r_d = before-tax cost of debt

r_i = after-tax cost of debt

r_m = required return on the market portfolio

r_n = cost of a new issue of common stock

r_p = cost of preferred stock

r_r = cost of retained earnings

r_s = required return on common stock

n = number of years to the bond's maturity

N_d = net proceeds from the sale of debt (bond)

N_n = net proceeds from the sale of new common stock

N_p = net proceeds from the sale of preferred stock

P_0 = value of common stock

R_F = risk-free rate of return

T = firm's tax rate

w_i = proportion of long-term debt in capital structure

w_j = capital structure proportion (historical or target, stated in decimal form) for financing source j

w_p = proportion of preferred stock in capital structure

w_s = proportion of common stock equity in capital structure

Cost of capital formulas

Before-tax cost of debt (approximation):

$$r_d = \frac{I + \frac{\$1,000 - N_d}{n}}{\frac{N_d + \$1,000}{2}}$$ [Equation 11.1]

After-tax cost of debt: $r_i = r_d \times (1 - T)$ [Equation 11.2]

Cost of preferred stock: $r_p = \frac{D_p}{N_p}$ [Equation 11.3]

Cost of common stock equity:

Using constant-growth valuation model: $r_s = \frac{D_1}{P_0} + g$ [Equation 11.5]

Using CAPM: $r_s = R_F + [b \times (r_m - R_F)]$ [Equation 11.6]

Cost of retained earnings: $r_r = r_s$ [Equation 11.7]

Cost of new issues of common stock: $r_n = \frac{D_1}{N_n} + g$ [Equation 11.8]

Weighted average cost of capital (WACC): $r_a = (w_i \times r_i) + (w_p \times r_p) + (w_s \times r_{r \text{ or } n})$ [Equation 11.9]

Break point: $BP_j = \frac{AF_j}{w_j}$ [Equation 11.10]

LG 2 Determine the cost of long-term debt and the cost of preferred stock. The cost of long-term debt is the after-tax cost today of raising long-term funds through borrowing. Cost quotations, calculation, or an approximation can be used to find the before-tax cost of debt, which must then be tax-adjusted. The cost of preferred stock is the ratio of the preferred stock dividend to the firm's net proceeds from the sale of preferred stock.

LG 3 Calculate the cost of common stock equity and convert it into the cost of retained earnings and the cost of new issues of common stock. The cost of common stock equity can be calculated by using the constant-growth valuation (Gordon) model or the CAPM. The cost of retained earnings is equal to the cost of common stock equity. An adjustment in the cost of common stock equity to reflect underpricing and flotation costs is necessary to find the cost of new issues of common stock.

LG 4 Calculate the weighted average cost of capital (WACC) and discuss alternative weighting schemes. The firm's WACC reflects the expected average future cost of funds over the long run. It combines the costs of specific types of capital after weighting each of them by its proportion. The theoretically preferred approach uses target weights based on market values.

LG 5 Describe the procedures used to determine break points and the weighted marginal cost of capital (WMCC). As total new financing increases, the costs of the various types of financing will increase, raising the firm's WACC. The WMCC is the firm's WACC associated with its next dollar of total new financing. Break points represent the level of total new financing at which the cost of one of the financing components rises, causing an upward shift in the WMCC. The WMCC schedule relates the WACC to each level of total new financing.

LG 6 Explain the weighted marginal cost of capital (WMCC) and its use with the investment opportunities schedule (IOS) to make financing/investment decisions. The IOS ranks currently available investments from best to worst. It is used with the WMCC to find the level of financing/investment that maximizes owner wealth. The firm accepts projects up to the point at which the marginal return on its investment equals its weighted marginal cost of capital.

Self-Test Problem (Solution in Appendix B)

ST11–1 **Specific costs, WACC, WMCC, and IOS**   Humble Manufacturing is interested in measuring its overall cost of capital. The firm is in the 40% tax bracket. Current investigation has gathered the following data:

Debt   The firm can raise an unlimited amount of debt by selling $1,000-par-value, 10% coupon interest rate, 10-year bonds on which *annual interest* payments will be made. To sell the issue, an average discount of $30 per bond must be given. The firm must also pay flotation costs of $20 per bond.

Preferred stock   The firm can sell 11% (annual dividend) preferred stock at its $100-per-share par value. The cost of issuing and selling the preferred stock is expected to be $4 per share. An unlimited amount of preferred stock can be sold under these terms.

Common stock   The firm's common stock is currently selling for $80 per share. The firm expects to pay cash dividends of $6 per share next year. The firm's dividends have been growing at an annual rate of 6%, and this rate is expected to continue in the future. The stock will have to be underpriced by $4 per share, and flotation costs are expected to amount to $4 per share. The firm can sell an unlimited amount of new common stock under these terms.

Retained earnings   The firm expects to have $225,000 of retained earnings available in the coming year. Once these retained earnings are exhausted, the firm will use new common stock as the form of common stock equity financing.

a. Calculate the specific cost of each source of financing. (Round to the nearest 0.1%.)
b. The firm uses the weights shown in the following table, which are based on target capital structure proportions, to calculate its weighted average cost of capital. (Round to the nearest 0.1%.)

Source of capital	Weight
Long-term debt	40%
Preferred stock	15
Common stock equity	45
Total	100%

   (1) Calculate the single *break point* associated with the firm's financial situation. *(Hint:* This point results from the exhaustion of the firm's retained earnings.)
   (2) Calculate the weighted average cost of capital associated with total new financing *below* the break point calculated in part (1).
   (3) Calculate the weighted average cost of capital associated with total new financing *above* the break point calculated in part (1).
c. Using the results of part **b** along with the information shown in the following table on the available investment opportunities, draw the firm's weighted marginal cost of capital (WMCC) schedule and investment opportunities schedule (IOS) on the same set of axes (total new financing or investment on the *x* axis and weighted average cost of capital and IRR on the *y* axis).

Investment opportunity	Internal rate of return (IRR)	Initial investment
A	11.2%	$100,000
B	9.7	500,000
C	12.9	150,000
D	16.5	200,000
E	11.8	450,000
F	10.1	600,000
G	10.5	300,000

d. Which, if any, of the available investments do you recommend that the firm accept? Explain your answer. How much total new financing is required?

Warm-Up Exercises

A blue box (■) indicates exercises available in myfinancelab.

LG 4

E11–1 Weekend Warriors, Inc., has 35% debt and 65% equity in its capital structure. The firm's estimated after-tax cost of debt is 8% and its estimated cost of equity is 13%. Determine the firm's *weighted average cost of capital (WACC)*.

LG 2

E11–2 A firm raises capital by selling $20,000 worth of debt with flotation costs equal to 2% of its par value. If the debt matures in 10 years and has a coupon interest rate of 8%, what is the bond's IRR?

LG 2

E11–3 Your firm, People's Consulting Group, has been asked to consult on a potential preferred stock offering by Brave New World. This 15% preferred stock issue would be sold at its par value of $35 per share. Flotation costs would total $3 per share. Calculate the cost of this preferred stock.

LG 3

E11–4 Duke Energy has been paying dividends steadily for 20 years. During that time, dividends have grown at a compound annual rate of 7%. If Duke Energy's current stock price is $78 and the firm plans to pay a dividend of $6.50 next year, what is Duke's *cost of common stock equity*?

LG 4

E11–5 Oxy Corporation uses debt, preferred stock, and common stock to raise capital. The firm's capital structure targets the following proportions: debt, 55%; preferred stock, 10%; and common stock, 35%. If the cost of debt is 6.7%, preferred stock costs 9.2%, and common stock costs 10.6%, what is Oxy's *weighted average cost of capital (WACC)*?

Problems

A blue box (■) indicates problems available in myfinancelab.

LG 1

P11–1 **Concept of cost of capital** Wren Manufacturing is in the process of analyzing its investment decision-making procedures. The two projects evaluated by the firm during the past month were projects 263 and 264. The basic variables surrounding each project analysis, using the IRR decision technique, and the resulting decision actions are summarized in the following table.

Basic variables	Project 263	Project 264
Cost	$64,000	$58,000
Life	15 years	15 years
IRR	8%	15%
Least-cost financing		
Source	Debt	Equity
Cost (after-tax)	7%	16%
Decision		
Action	Accept	Reject
Reason	8% IRR > 7% cost	15% IRR < 16% cost

a. Evaluate the firm's decision-making procedures, and explain why the acceptance of project 263 and rejection of project 264 may not be in the owners' best interest.

b. If the firm maintains a capital structure containing 40% debt and 60% equity, find its *weighted average cost* using the data in the table.

c. If the firm had used the weighted average cost calculated in part **b,** what actions would have been indicated relative to projects 263 and 264?

d. Compare and contrast the firm's actions with your findings in part **c.** Which decision method seems more appropriate? Explain why.

P11–2 **Cost of debt using both methods** Currently, Warren Industries can sell 15-year, $1,000-par-value bonds paying *annual interest* at a 12% coupon rate. As a result of current interest rates, the bonds can be sold for $1,010 each; flotation costs of $30 per bond will be incurred in this process. The firm is in the 40% tax bracket.

a. Find the net proceeds from sale of the bond, N_d.

b. Show the cash flows from the firm's point of view over the maturity of the bond.

c. Use the *IRR approach* to calculate the before-tax and after-tax costs of debt.

d. Use the *approximation formula* to estimate the before-tax and after-tax costs of debt.

e. Compare and contrast the costs of debt calculated in parts **c** and **d.** Which approach do you prefer? Why?

PERSONAL FINANCE PROBLEM

P11–3 **Before-tax cost of debt and after-tax cost of debt** David Abbot is interested in purchasing a bond issued by Sony. He has obtained the following information on the security:

Sony Bond					
Par value	$1,000	Coupon interest rate	6%	Tax bracket	20%
Cost	$ 930	Years to maturity	10		

Answer the following questions.

a. Calculate the *before-tax cost* of the Sony bond using the IRR method.

b. Calculate the *after-tax cost* of the Sony bond given David's tax bracket.

P11–4 **Cost of debt using the approximation formula** For each of the following $1,000-par-value bonds, assuming *annual interest* payment and a 40% tax rate, calculate the *after-tax* cost to maturity using the *approximation formula.*

Bond	Life	Underwriting fee	Discount (−) or premium (+)	Coupon interest rate
A	20 years	$25	−$20	9%
B	16	40	+ 10	10
C	15	30	− 15	12
D	25	15	Par	9
E	22	20	− 60	11

P11-5 **The cost of debt** Gronseth Drywall Systems, Inc., is in discussions with its investment bankers regarding the issuance of new bonds. The investment banker has informed the firm that different maturities will carry different coupon rates and sell at different prices. The firm must choose among several alternatives. In each case, the bonds will have a $1,000 par value and flotation costs will be $30 per bond. The company is taxed at a rate of 40%. Calculate the *after-tax cost of financing* with each of the following alternatives.

Alternative	Coupon rate	Time to maturity	Premium or discount
A	9%	16 years	$250
B	7	5	50
C	6	7	par
D	5	10	− 75

PERSONAL FINANCE PROBLEM

 P11-6 **After-tax cost of debt** Rick and Stacy Stark, a married couple, are interested in purchasing their first boat. They have decided to borrow the boat's purchase price of $100,000. The family is in the 28% federal income tax bracket. There are two choices for the Stark family: They can borrow the money from the boat dealer at an annual interest rate of 8%, or they could take out a $100,000 second mortgage on their home. Currently, home equity loans are at rates of 9.2%. There is no problem securing either of these two alternative financing choices.

Rick and Stacy learn that if they borrow from the boat dealership, the interest will not be tax-deductible. However, the interest on the second mortgage will qualify as being tax-deductible on their federal income tax return.

a. Calculate the *after-tax cost* of borrowing from the boat dealership.
b. Calculate the *after-tax cost* of borrowing through a second mortgage on their home.
c. Which source of borrowing is less costly for the Stark family?

 P11-7 **Cost of preferred stock** Taylor Systems has just issued preferred stock. The stock has a 12% annual dividend and a $100 par value and was sold at $97.50 per share. In addition, flotation costs of $2.50 per share must be paid.

a. Calculate the *cost of the preferred stock*.
b. If the firm sells the preferred stock with a 10% annual dividend and nets $90.00 after flotation costs, what is its cost?

 P11-8 **Cost of preferred stock** Determine the cost for each of the following preferred stocks.

Preferred stock	Par value	Sale price	Flotation cost	Annual dividend
A	$100	$101	$9.00	11%
B	40	38	$3.50	8%
C	35	37	$4.00	$5.00
D	30	26	5% of par	$3.00
E	20	20	$2.50	9%

P11–9 **Cost of common stock equity—CAPM**   J&M Corporation common stock has a beta, b, of 1.2. The risk-free rate is 6%, and the market return is 11%.
  a. Determine the risk premium on J&M common stock.
  b. Determine the required return that J&M common stock should provide.
  c. Determine J&M's *cost of common stock equity* using the CAPM.

P11–10 **Cost of common stock equity**   Ross Textiles wishes to measure its cost of common stock equity. The firm's stock is currently selling for $57.50. The firm expects to pay a $3.40 dividend at the end of the year (2010). The dividends for the past 5 years are shown in the following table.

Year	Dividend
2009	$3.10
2008	2.92
2007	2.60
2006	2.30
2005	2.12

After underpricing and flotation costs, the firm expects to net $52 per share on a new issue.
  a. Determine the growth rate of dividends.
  b. Determine the net proceeds, N_n, that the firm will actually receive.
  c. Using the constant-growth valuation model, determine the *cost of retained earnings, r_r*.
  d. Using the constant-growth valuation model, determine the *cost of new common stock, r_n*.

P11–11 **Retained earnings versus new common stock**   Using the data for each firm shown in the following table, calculate the *cost of retained earnings* and the *cost of new common stock* using the constant-growth valuation model.

Firm	Current market price per share	Dividend growth rate	Projected dividend per share next year	Underpricing per share	Flotation cost per share
A	$50.00	8%	$2.25	$2.00	$1.00
B	20.00	4	1.00	0.50	1.50
C	42.50	6	2.00	1.00	2.00
D	19.00	2	2.10	1.30	1.70

P11–12 **The effect of tax rate on WACC**   Equity Lighting Corp. wishes to explore the effect on its cost of capital of the rate at which the company pays taxes. The firm wishes to maintain a capital structure of 30% debt, 10% preferred stock, and 60% common stock. The cost of financing with retained earnings is 14%, the cost of preferred stock financing is 9%, and the before-tax cost of debt financing is 11%. Calculate the weighted average cost of capital (WACC) given the tax rate assumptions in parts a to c.
  a. Tax rate = 40%
  b. Tax rate = 35%

c. Tax rate = 25%
d. Describe the relationship between changes in the rate of taxation and the
weighted average cost of capital.

 P11–13 **WACC—Book weights**   Ridge Tool has on its books the amounts and specific
(after-tax) costs shown in the following table for each source of capital.

Source of capital	Book value	Specific cost
Long-term debt	$700,000	5.3%
Preferred stock	50,000	12.0
Common stock equity	650,000	16.0

a. Calculate the firm's *weighted average cost of capital using book value weights.*
b. Explain how the firm can use this cost in the investment decision-making
process.

 P11–14 **WACC—Book weights and market weights**   Webster Company has compiled the
information shown in the following table.

Source of capital	Book value	Market value	After-tax cost
Long-term debt	$4,000,000	$3,840,000	6.0%
Preferred stock	40,000	60,000	13.0
Common stock equity	1,060,000	3,000,000	17.0
Totals	$5,100,000	$6,900,000	

a. Calculate the weighted average cost of capital using *book value weights.*
b. Calculate the weighted average cost of capital using *market value weights.*
c. Compare the answers obtained in parts **a** and **b.** Explain the differences.

 P11–15 **WACC and target weights**   After careful analysis, Dexter Brothers has determined
that its optimal capital structure is composed of the sources and target market value
weights shown in the following table.

Source of capital	Target market value weight
Long-term debt	30%
Preferred stock	15
Common stock equity	55
Total	100%

The cost of debt is estimated to be 7.2%; the cost of preferred stock is estimated
to be 13.5%; the cost of retained earnings is estimated to be 16.0%; and the cost
of new common stock is estimated to be 18.0%. All of these are after-tax rates.
The company's debt represents 25%, the preferred stock represents 10%, and the
common stock equity represents 65% of total capital on the basis of the market

values of the three components. The company expects to have a significant amount of retained earnings available and does not expect to sell any new common stock.

a. Calculate the weighted average cost of capital on the basis of *historical market value weights*.

b. Calculate the weighted average cost of capital on the basis of *target market value weights*.

c. Compare the answers obtained in parts **a** and **b**. Explain the differences.

P11–16   **Cost of capital and break point**   Edna Recording Studios, Inc., reported earnings available to common stock of $4,200,000 last year. From those earnings, the company paid a dividend of $1.26 on each of its 1,000,000 common shares outstanding. The capital structure of the company includes 40% debt, 10% preferred stock, and 50% common stock. It is taxed at a rate of 40%.

a. If the market price of the common stock is $40 and dividends are expected to grow at a rate of 6% per year for the foreseeable future, what is the company's *cost of retained earnings* financing?

b. If underpricing and flotation costs on new shares of common stock amount to $7.00 per share, what is the company's *cost of new common stock* financing?

c. The company can issue $2.00 dividend preferred stock for a market price of $25.00 per share. Flotation costs would amount to $3.00 per share. What is the *cost of preferred stock* financing?

d. The company can issue $1,000-par-value, 10% coupon, 5-year bonds that can be sold for $1,200 each. Flotation costs would amount to $25.00 per bond. Use the estimation formula to figure the approximate *cost of debt* financing.

e. What is the maximum investment that Edna Recording Studios can make in new projects before it must issue new common stock?

f. What is the *WACC* for projects with a cost at or below the amount calculated in part **e**?

g. What is the *WACC* for projects with a cost above the amount calculated in part **e** (assuming that debt across all ranges remains at the percentage cost calculated in part **d**)?

P11–17   **Calculation of specific costs, WACC, and WMCC**   Dillon Labs has asked its financial manager to measure the cost of each specific type of capital as well as the weighted average cost of capital. The weighted average cost is to be measured by using the following weights: 40% long-term debt, 10% preferred stock, and 50% common stock equity (retained earnings, new common stock, or both). The firm's tax rate is 40%.

Debt   The firm can sell for $980 a 10-year, $1,000-par-value bond paying *annual interest* at a 10% coupon rate. A flotation cost of 3% of the par value is required in addition to the discount of $20 per bond.

Preferred stock   Eight percent (annual dividend) preferred stock having a par value of $100 can be sold for $65. An additional fee of $2 per share must be paid to the underwriters.

Common stock   The firm's common stock is currently selling for $50 per share. The dividend expected to be paid at the end of the coming year (2010) is $4. Its dividend payments, which have been approximately 60% of earnings per share in each of the past 5 years, were as shown in the table at the top of page 536.

Year	Dividend
2009	$3.75
2008	3.50
2007	3.30
2006	3.15
2005	2.85

It is expected that to attract buyers, new common stock must be underpriced $5 per share, and the firm must also pay $3 per share in flotation costs. Dividend payments are expected to continue at 60% of earnings.

a. Calculate the specific cost of each source of financing. (Assume that $r_r = r_s$.)

b. If earnings available to common shareholders are expected to be $7 million, what is the *break point* associated with the exhaustion of retained earnings?

c. Determine the *weighted average cost of capital* between zero and the break point calculated in part **b**.

d. Determine the *weighted average cost of capital* just beyond the break point calculated in part **b**.

PERSONAL FINANCE PROBLEM

  P11-18 **Weighted average cost of capital**   John Dough has just been awarded his degree in business. He has three education loans outstanding. They all mature in 5 years and can be repaid without penalty any time before maturity. The amounts owed on each loan and the annual interest rate associated with each loan are given in the following table.

Loan	Balance due	Annual interest rate
1	$20,000	6%
2	12,000	9
3	32,000	5

John can also combine the total of his three debts (i.e., $64,000) and create a consolidated loan from his bank. His bank will charge a 7.2% annual interest rate for a period of 5 years.

Should John do nothing (leave the three individual loans as is) or create a consolidated loan (the $64,000 question)?

   P11-19 **Calculation of specific costs, WACC, and WMCC**   Lang Enterprises is interested in measuring its overall cost of capital. Current investigation has gathered the following data. The firm is in the 40% tax bracket.

Debt   The firm can raise an unlimited amount of debt by selling $1,000-par-value, 8% coupon interest rate, 20-year bonds on which *annual interest* payments will be made. To sell the issue, an average discount of $30 per bond would have to be given. The firm also must pay flotation costs of $30 per bond.

Preferred stock   The firm can sell 8% preferred stock at its $95-per-share par value. The cost of issuing and selling the preferred stock is expected to be $5 per share. An unlimited amount of preferred stock can be sold under these terms.

Common stock   The firm's common stock is currently selling for $90 per share. The firm expects to pay cash dividends of $7 per share next year. The firm's dividends have been growing at an annual rate of 6%, and this growth is expected to continue into the future. The stock must be underpriced by $7 per share, and flotation costs are expected to amount to $5 per share. The firm can sell an unlimited amount of new common stock under these terms.

Retained earnings   When measuring this cost, the firm does not concern itself with the tax bracket or brokerage fees of owners. It expects to have available $100,000 of retained earnings in the coming year; once these retained earnings are exhausted, the firm will use new common stock as the form of common stock equity financing.

a. Calculate the specific cost of each source of financing. (Round answers to the nearest 0.1%.)

b. The firm's capital structure weights used in calculating its weighted average cost of capital are shown in the following table. (Round answer to the nearest 0.1%.)

Source of capital	Weight
Long-term debt	30%
Preferred stock	20
Common stock equity	50
Total	100%

(1) Calculate the single *break point* associated with the firm's financial situation. (*Hint:* This point results from exhaustion of the firm's retained earnings.)

(2) Calculate the *weighted average cost of capital* associated with total new financing below the break point calculated in part (1).

(3) Calculate the *weighted average cost of capital* associated with total new financing above the break point calculated in part (1).

P11–20   **Integrative—WACC, WMCC, and IOS**   Cartwell Products has compiled the data shown in the following table for the current costs of its three basic sources of capital—long-term debt, preferred stock, and common stock equity—for various ranges of new financing.

Source of capital	Range of new financing	After-tax cost
Long-term debt	$0 to $320,000	6%
	$320,000 and above	8
Preferred stock	$0 and above	17%
Common stock equity	$0 to $200,000	20%
	$200,000 and above	24

The company's capital structure weights used in calculating its weighted average cost of capital are shown in the following table.

Source of capital	Weight
Long-term debt	40%
Preferred stock	20
Common stock equity	40
Total	100%

a. Determine the *break points* and ranges of *total* new financing associated with each source of capital.

b. Using the data developed in part **a,** determine the break points (levels of *total* new financing) at which the firm's weighted average cost of capital will change.

c. Calculate the *weighted average cost of capital* for each range of total new financing found in part **b.** (*Hint:* There are three ranges.)

d. Using the results of part **c,** along with the following information on the available investment opportunities, draw the firm's *weighted marginal cost of capital (WMCC) schedule* and *investment opportunities schedule (IOS)* on the same set of axes (total new financing or investment on the x axis and weighted average cost of capital and IRR on the y axis).

Investment opportunity	Internal rate of return (IRR)	Initial investment
A	19%	$200,000
B	15	300,000
C	22	100,000
D	14	600,000
E	23	200,000
F	13	100,000
G	21	300,000
H	17	100,000
I	16	400,000

e. Which, if any, of the available investments do you recommend that the firm accept? Explain your answer.

   P11–21 **Integrative—WACC, WMCC, and IOS**   Grainger Corp., a supplier of fitness equipment, is trying to decide whether to undertake any or all of the proposed projects in its investment opportunities schedule (IOS). The firm's cost-of-capital schedule and investment opportunities schedules follow below and on page 539.

Cost-of-Capital Schedule			
Range of total new financing	Source	Weight	After-tax cost
0–$600,000	Debt	.50	6.3%
	Preferred stock	.10	12.5
	Common stock	.40	15.3
$600,000–$1,000,000	Debt	.50	6.3%
	Preferred stock	.10	12.5
	Common stock	.40	16.4
$1,000,000 and above	Debt	.50	7.8%
	Preferred stock	.10	12.5
	Common stock	.40	16.4

Investment Opportunities Schedule		
Investment opportunity	Internal rate of return	Cost
Project H	14.5%	$200,000
Project G	13.0	700,000
Project K	12.8	500,000
Project M	11.4	600,000

a. Complete the cost-of-capital schedule by calculating the WACC and the WMCC schedule for the various ranges of total new financing.
b. Identify those projects that you recommend that Grainger Corp. undertake in the next year.
c. Illustrate your recommendations by drawing a graph of Grainger's weighted average costs and investment opportunities similar to Figure 11.2.
d. Explain why certain projects are recommended and other(s) are not.

 P11–22   ETHICS PROBLEM   Because the latency period for asbestos-related illnesses can be as long as 40 years, some claimants are filing for damages based on their previous work around the dangerous material even though they currently have no symptoms or impairments from their exposure to asbestos. If you were a company faced with such a claim, how would you refute the claim? If you were the claimant, how would you support your claim?

Chapter 11 Case

Making Star Products' Financing/Investment Decision

Star Products Company is a growing manufacturer of automobile accessories whose stock is actively traded on the over-the-counter (OTC) market. During 2009, the Dallas-based company experienced sharp increases in both sales and earnings. Because of this recent growth, Melissa Jen, the company's treasurer, wants to make sure that available funds are being used to their fullest. Management policy is to maintain the current capital structure proportions of 30% long-term debt, 10% preferred stock, and 60% common stock equity for at least the next 3 years. The firm is in the 40% tax bracket.

Star's division and product managers have presented several competing investment opportunities to Jen. However, because funds are limited, choices of which projects to accept must be made. The investment opportunities schedule (IOS) is shown in the table on page 540.

Investment Opportunities Schedule (IOS) for Star Products Company		
Investment opportunity	Internal rate of return (IRR)	Initial investment
A	15%	$400,000
B	22	200,000
C	25	700,000
D	23	400,000
E	17	500,000
F	19	600,000
G	14	500,000

To estimate the firm's weighted average cost of capital (WACC), Jen contacted a leading investment banking firm, which provided the financing cost data shown in the following table.

Financing Cost Data
Star Products Company

Long-term debt: The firm can raise $450,000 of additional debt by selling 15-year, $1,000-par-value, 9% coupon interest rate bonds that pay *annual interest*. It expects to net $960 per bond after flotation costs. Any debt in excess of $450,000 will have a before-tax cost, r_d, of 13%.

Preferred stock: Preferred stock, regardless of the amount sold, can be issued with a $70 par value and a 14% annual dividend rate and will net $65 per share after flotation costs.

Common stock equity: The firm expects dividends and earnings per share to be $0.96 and $3.20, respectively, in 2010 and to continue to grow at a constant rate of 11% per year. The firm's stock currently sells for $12 per share. Star expects to have $1,500,000 of retained earnings available in the coming year. Once the retained earnings have been exhausted, the firm can raise additional funds by selling new common stock, netting $9 per share after underpricing and flotation costs.

To Do

a. Calculate the cost of each source of financing, as specified:
   (1) Long-term debt, first $450,000.
   (2) Long-term debt, greater than $450,000.
   (3) Preferred stock, all amounts.
   (4) Common stock equity, first $1,500,000.
   (5) Common stock equity, greater than $1,500,000.
b. Find the *break points* associated with each source of capital, and use them to specify each of the ranges of total new financing over which the firm's weighted average cost of capital (WACC) remains constant.
c. Calculate the *weighted average cost of capital (WACC)* over each of the ranges of total new financing specified in part **b.**

d. Using your findings in part **c** along with the investment opportunities schedule (IOS), draw the firm's *weighted marginal cost of capital (WMCC)* and IOS on the same set of axes (total new financing or investment on the x axis and weighted average cost of capital and IRR on the y axis).

e. Which, if any, of the available investments would you recommend that the firm accept? Explain your answer.

Spreadsheet Exercise

Nova Corporation is interested in measuring the cost of each specific type of capital as well as the weighted average cost of capital. Historically, the firm has raised capital in the following manner:

Source of capital	Weight
Long-term debt	35%
Preferred stock	12
Common stock equity	53

The tax rate of the firm is currently 40%. The needed financial information and data are as follows:

Debt   Nova can raise an unlimited amount of debt by selling $1,000-par-value, 6.5% coupon interest rate, 10-year bonds on which *annual interest payments* will be made. To sell the issue, an average discount of $20 per bond needs to be given. There is an associated flotation cost of 2% of par value.

Preferred stock   An unlimited amount of preferred stock can be sold under the following terms: The security has a par value of $100 per share, the annual dividend rate is 6% of the par value, and the flotation cost is expected to be $4 per share. The preferred stock is expected to sell for $102 before cost considerations.

Common stock   The current price of Nova's common stock is $35 per share. The cash dividend is expected to be $3.25 per share next year. The firm's dividends have grown at an annual rate of 5%, and it is expected that the dividend will continue at this rate for the foreseeable future. The flotation costs are expected to be approximately $2 per share. Nova can sell an unlimited amount of new common stock under these terms.

Retained earnings   The firm expects to have available $100,000 of retained earnings in the coming year. Once these retained earnings are exhausted, the firm will use new common stock as the form of common stock equity financing. (*Note:* When measuring this cost, the firm does not concern itself with the tax bracket or brokerage fees of owners.)

To Do

Create a spreadsheet to answer the following questions:

a. Calculate the specific cost of *each source of financing*. (Round answers to the nearest 0.1%.)
b. Calculate the single *break point* associated with the firm's financial situation. This point results from exhaustion of the firm's retained earnings.
c. Calculate the *weighted average cost of capital (WACC)* associated with total financing *below* the break point calculated in part **b**.
d. Calculate the *weighted average cost of capital (WACC)* associated with total financing *above* the break point calculated in part **b**.

Group Exercise

By this time, you should be well aware of the linkages between theory and practice as shown throughout the text and previous exercises. The topic covered in this chapter is a good example of practice catching up with theory. U.S. corporations increasingly are using the tools discussed in the text to more accurately measure the cost of capital and therefore make better capital budgeting decisions. This exercise likewise attempts to bridge the gap between textbook theory and actual management practice.

To Do

a. By looking at the balance sheet of your shadow firm, investigate how the firm has raised capital for investment opportunities. Begin by describing the mix of debt and equity, and calculate the proportions for each source of long-term funds.
b. Return to your group's fictitious firm. Design a balance sheet that approximates the sources and uses of financing of your shadow firm.
c. Assign rough cost estimates, rounding where necessary, and calculate the weighted average cost of capital for your fictitious firm.
d. Design a new investment opportunity and calculate its IRR. Use the cost estimates from part **c** and make a decision with regard to the investment opportunity.

Web Exercise

Go to the book's companion website at www.prenhall.com/gitman to find the Web Exercise for this chapter.

Remember to check the book's website at www.prenhall.com/gitman to find additional resources, including Web Exercises and a Web Case.

12 | Leverage and Capital Structure

WHY THIS CHAPTER MATTERS TO YOU

In Your Professional Life

Accounting: You need to understand how to calculate and analyze operating and financial leverage and to be familiar with the tax and earnings effects of various capital structures.

Information systems: You need to understand the types of capital and what capital structure is, because you will provide much of the information needed in management's determination of the best capital structure for the firm.

Management: You need to understand leverage so that you can control risk and magnify returns for the firm's owners and to understand capital structure theory so that you can make decisions about the firm's optimal capital structure.

Marketing: You need to understand breakeven analysis, which you will use in pricing and product feasibility decisions.

Operations: You need to understand the impact of fixed and variable operating costs on the firm's breakeven point and its operating leverage, because these costs will have a major impact on the firm's risk and return.

In Your Personal Life

Like corporations, you routinely incur debt, using both credit cards for short-term needs and negotiated long-term loans. When you borrow long-term, you experience the benefits and consequences of leverage. Also, the level of your outstanding debt relative to net worth is conceptually the same as a firm's capital structure. It reflects your financial risk and affects the availability and cost of borrowing.

LEARNING GOALS

LG 1 Discuss leverage, capital structure, breakeven analysis, the operating breakeven point, and the effect of changing costs on it.

LG 2 Understand operating, financial, and total leverage and the relationships among them.

LG 3 Describe the types of capital, external assessment of capital structure, the capital structure of non-U.S. firms, and capital structure theory.

LG 4 Explain the optimal capital structure using a graphical view of the firm's cost-of-capital functions and a zero-growth valuation model.

LG 5 Discuss the EBIT–EPS approach to capital structure.

LG 6 Review the return and risk of alternative capital structures, their linkage to market value, and other important considerations related to capital structure.

CVS/Caremark Corporation

Optimizing Its Capital Structure

On March 22, 2007, drugstore giant **CVS Pharmacy** merged with pharmacy-benefits manager **Caremark Rx** to form **CVS/Caremark Corporation**. The $26.5 billion merger created the nation's largest combined mail-order and retail provider of medicine. Caremark shareholders would receive 1.67 shares of CVS/Caremark shares for each share of Caremark stock. In addition, each shareholder would receive a special cash dividend of $7.50.

The newly combined company is expected to offer stronger competition to Wal-Mart's pharmacies. In addition, CVS will have more clout when negotiating prices with drug makers and will be positioned to slow the defection of pharmacy customers who have been filling prescriptions through other channels—for example, by mail, through companies like Caremark.

Following the merger, the company set about modifying its capital structure. On May 9, 2007, CVS/Caremark's board of directors approved a share repurchase for up to $5 billion of its outstanding stock. By May 15, the company had completed half of the repurchase program. On May 22, the company offered a $5.5 billion investment-grade debt offering. Part of the offering was to be used to complete the share buyback, with the rest used to pay down a bridge loan and for general corporate purposes The new loan will raise CVC/Caremark's debt ratio, increasing its financial leverage; it is expected to enable the company to significantly increase its return on equity in 2008.

Is a capital structure consisting of increased debt better than one with a lower percentage of debt? Not necessarily. Capital structure varies among companies in the same industry and across industry groups. A company's choice of debt versus equity depends on many factors. Conditions in the equity markets may be unfavorable when a company needs to raise funds. When interest rates are low, the debt markets become attractive.

> Before the merger, CVS's debt ratio was about 22.4%. After the merger, CVS/Caremark's debt ratio was about 7.8%. What does that tell you about Caremark's debt ratio prior to the merger?

Each type of long-term capital has its advantages. As we learned in Chapter 11, debt costs less than equity. Adding debt, with its fixed rate, to the capital structure creates *financial leverage*, the use of fixed financial costs to magnify returns. Leverage also increases risk. This chapter will show that financial leverage and capital structure are closely related concepts that can minimize the cost of capital and maximize owners' wealth.

12.1 | Leverage

leverage
Results from the use of fixed-cost assets or funds to magnify returns to the firm's owners.

capital structure
The mix of long-term debt and equity maintained by the firm.

Leverage results from the use of fixed-cost assets or funds to magnify returns to the firm's owners. Generally, increases in leverage result in increased return and risk, whereas decreases in leverage result in decreased return and risk. The amount of leverage in the firm's **capital structure**—the mix of long-term debt and equity maintained by the firm—can significantly affect its value by affecting return and risk. Unlike some causes of risk, management has almost complete control over the risk introduced through the use of leverage. Because of its effect on value, the financial manager must understand how to measure and evaluate leverage, particularly when making capital structure decisions.

The three basic types of leverage can best be defined with reference to the firm's income statement, as shown in the general income statement format in Table 12.1.

- *Operating leverage* is concerned with the relationship between the firm's sales revenue and its earnings before interest and taxes, or EBIT. (EBIT is a descriptive label for *operating profits*.)
- *Financial leverage* is concerned with the relationship between the firm's EBIT and its common stock earnings per share (EPS).
- *Total leverage* is concerned with the relationship between the firm's sales revenue and EPS.

We will examine the three types of leverage concepts in detail. First, though, we will look at breakeven analysis, which lays the foundation for leverage concepts by demonstrating the effects of fixed costs on the firm's operations.

TABLE 12.1   General Income Statement Format and Types of Leverage

Operating leverage {	Sales revenue
	Less: Cost of goods sold
	Gross profits
	Less: Operating expenses
Financial leverage {	Earnings before interest and taxes (EBIT)
	Less: Interest
	Net profits before taxes
	Less: Taxes
	Net profits after taxes
	Less: Preferred stock dividends
	Earnings available for common stockholders
	Earnings per share (EPS)

Total leverage

Breakeven Analysis

Firms use **breakeven analysis,** also called *cost-volume-profit analysis*, (1) to determine the level of operations necessary to cover all costs and (2) to evaluate the profitability associated with various levels of sales. The firm's **operating breakeven point** is the level of sales necessary to cover all *operating costs*. At that point, earnings before interest and taxes (EBIT) equals $0.[1]

The first step in finding the operating breakeven point is to divide the cost of goods sold and operating expenses into fixed and variable operating costs. *Fixed costs* are a function of time (dollars per period), not sales volume, and are typically contractual; rent, for example, is a fixed cost. *Variable costs* vary directly with sales and are a function of volume (dollars per unit), not time; shipping costs, for example, are a variable cost.[2]

Algebraic Approach

Using the following variables, we can recast the operating portion of the firm's income statement given in Table 12.1 into the algebraic representation shown in Table 12.2.

$$P = \text{sale price per unit}$$
$$Q = \text{sales quantity in units}$$
$$FC = \text{fixed } operating \text{ cost per period}$$
$$VC = \text{variable } operating \text{ cost per unit}$$

Rewriting the algebraic calculations in Table 12.2 as a formula for earnings before interest and taxes yields Equation 12.1:

$$EBIT = (P \times Q) - FC - (VC \times Q) \qquad \text{(12.1)}$$

Simplifying Equation 12.1 yields

$$EBIT = Q \times (P - VC) - FC \qquad \text{(12.2)}$$

TABLE 12.2   Operating Leverage, Costs, and Breakeven Analysis

	Item	Algebraic representation
Operating leverage	Sales revenue	$(P \times Q)$
	Less: Fixed operating costs	$- \quad FC$
	Less: Variable operating costs	$-(VC \times Q)$
	Earnings before interest and taxes	EBIT

1. Quite often, the breakeven point is calculated so that it represents the point at which *all costs—both operating and financial*—are covered. Our concern in this chapter is not with this overall breakeven point.

2. Some costs, commonly called *semifixed* or *semivariable,* are partly fixed and partly variable. An example is sales commissions that are fixed for a certain volume of sales and then increase to higher levels for higher volumes. For convenience and clarity, we assume that all costs can be classified as either fixed or variable.

As noted above, the operating breakeven point is the level of sales at which all fixed and variable *operating costs* are covered—the level at which EBIT equals $0. Setting EBIT equal to $0 and solving Equation 12.2 for Q yield

$$Q = \frac{FC}{P - VC}$$

(12.3)

Q is the firm's operating breakeven point.[3]

Example

Assume that Cheryl's Posters, a small poster retailer, has fixed operating costs of $2,500, its sale price per unit (poster) is $10, and its variable operating cost per unit is $5. Applying Equation 12.3 to these data yields

$$Q = \frac{\$2,500}{\$10 - \$5} = \frac{\$2,500}{\$5} = 500 \text{ units}$$

At sales of 500 units, the firm's EBIT should just equal $0. The firm will have positive EBIT for sales greater than 500 units and negative EBIT, or a loss, for sales less than 500 units. We can confirm this by substituting values above and below 500 units, along with the other values given, into Equation 12.1.

Graphical Approach

Figure 12.1 presents in graphical form the breakeven analysis of the data in the preceding example. The firm's operating breakeven point is the point at which its *total operating cost*—the sum of its fixed and variable operating costs—equals sales revenue. At this point, EBIT equals $0. The figure shows that for sales *below* 500 units, total operating cost exceeds sales revenue, and EBIT is less than $0 (a loss). For sales *above* the breakeven point of 500 units, sales revenue exceeds total operating cost, and EBIT is greater than $0.

Changing Costs and the Operating Breakeven Point

A firm's operating breakeven point is sensitive to a number of variables: fixed operating cost (FC), the sale price per unit (P), and the variable operating cost per unit (VC). The effects of increases or decreases in these variables can be readily seen by referring to Equation 12.3. The sensitivity of the breakeven sales volume (Q) to an *increase* in each of these variables is summarized in Table 12.3. As might be expected, an increase in cost (FC or VC) tends to increase the operating breakeven point, whereas an increase in the sale price per unit (P) decreases the operating breakeven point.

Example

Assume that Cheryl's Posters wishes to evaluate the impact of several options: (1) increasing fixed operating costs to $3,000, (2) increasing the sale price per unit to $12.50, (3) increasing the variable operating cost per unit to $7.50, and

---

3. Because the firm is assumed to be a single-product firm, its operating breakeven point is found in terms of unit sales, Q. For multiproduct firms, the operating breakeven point is generally found in terms of dollar sales, S. This is done by substituting the contribution margin, which is 100% minus total variable operating costs as a percentage of total sales, denoted $VC\%$, into the denominator of Equation 12.3. The result is Equation 12.3a:

$$S = \frac{FC}{1 - VC\%}$$

(12.3a)

This multiproduct-firm breakeven point assumes that the firm's product mix remains the same at all levels of sales.

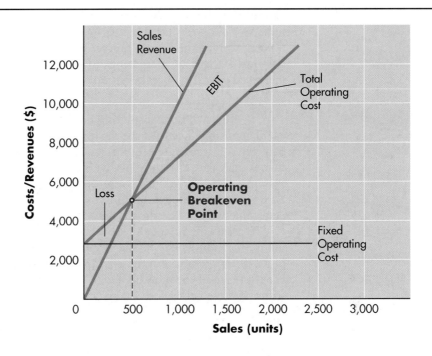

FIGURE 12.1

Breakeven Analysis
Graphical operating
breakeven analysis

(4) simultaneously implementing all three of these changes. Substituting the appropriate data into Equation 12.3 yields the following results:

$$(1)\ \text{Operating breakeven point} = \frac{\$3,000}{\$10 - \$5} = 600\ \text{units}$$

$$(2)\ \text{Operating breakeven point} = \frac{\$2,500}{\$12.50 - \$5} = 333\tfrac{1}{3}\ \text{units}$$

$$(3)\ \text{Operating breakeven point} = \frac{\$2,500}{\$10 - \$7.50} = 1,000\ \text{units}$$

$$(4)\ \text{Operating breakeven point} = \frac{\$3,000}{\$12.50 - \$7.50} = 600\ \text{units}$$

TABLE 12.3   Sensitivity of Operating Breakeven Point to Increases in Key Breakeven Variables

Increase in variable	Effect on operating breakeven point
Fixed operating cost (FC)	Increase
Sale price per unit (P)	Decrease
Variable operating cost per unit (VC)	Increase

Note: Decreases in each of the variables shown would have the opposite effect on the operating breakeven point.

Comparing the resulting operating breakeven points to the initial value of 500 units, we can see that the cost increases (actions 1 and 3) raise the breakeven point, whereas the revenue increase (action 2) lowers the breakeven point. The combined effect of increasing all three variables (action 4) also results in an increased operating breakeven point.

Personal Finance Example   Rick Polo is considering having a new fuel-saving device installed in his car. The installed cost of the device is $240 paid up-front, plus a monthly fee of $15. He can terminate use of the device any time without penalty. Rick estimates that the device will reduce his average monthly gas consumption by 20%, which, assuming no change in his monthly mileage, translates into a savings of about $28 per month. He is planning to keep the car for 2 more years and wishes to determine whether he should have the device installed in his car.

To assess the financial feasibility of purchasing the device, Rick calculates the number of months it will take for him to break even on it. Letting the installed cost of $240 represent the fixed cost (*FC*), the monthly savings of $28 represent the benefit (*P*), and the monthly fee of $15 represent the variable cost (*VC*), and substituting these values into the breakeven point equation, Equation 12.3, we get:

Breakeven point (in months) = $240/($28 − $15) = $240/$13 = 18.5 months

Because the fuel-saving device pays itself back in 18.5 months, which is less than the 24 months that Rick is planning to continue owning the car, he should have the fuel-saving device installed in his car.

We now turn our attention to the three types of leverage. It is important to recognize that the demonstrations of leverage that follow are conceptual in nature and that the measures presented are *not* routinely used by financial managers for decision-making purposes.

operating leverage
The potential use of *fixed operating costs* to magnify the effects of changes in sales on the firm's earnings before interest and taxes.

Operating Leverage

Operating leverage results from the existence of *fixed operating costs* in the firm's income stream. Using the structure presented in Table 12.2, we can define **operating leverage** as the potential use of *fixed operating costs* to magnify the effects of changes in sales on the firm's earnings before interest and taxes.

Example   Using the data for Cheryl's Posters (sale price, *P* = $10 per unit; variable operating cost, *VC* = $5 per unit; fixed operating cost, *FC* = $2,500), Figure 12.2 presents the operating breakeven graph originally shown in Figure 12.1. The additional notations on the graph indicate that as the firm's sales increase from 1,000 to 1,500 units (Q_1 to Q_2), its EBIT increases from $2,500 to $5,000 ($EBIT_1$ to $EBIT_2$). In other words, a 50% increase in sales (1,000 to 1,500 units) results in a 100% increase in EBIT ($2,500 to $5,000). Table 12.4 includes the data for Figure 12.2 as well as relevant data for a 500-unit sales level. We can illustrate two cases using the 1,000-unit sales level as a reference point.

> **Case 1**   A 50% *increase* in sales (from 1,000 to 1,500 units) results in a 100% *increase* in earnings before interest and taxes (from $2,500 to $5,000).

FIGURE 12.2

Operating Leverage
Breakeven analysis and
operating leverage

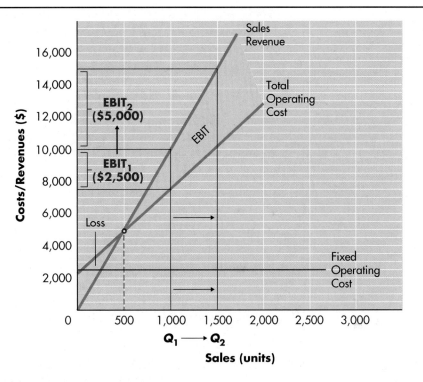

TABLE 12.4	The EBIT for Various Sales Levels		
		Case 2		Case 1

	Case 2		Case 1
	−50%		+50%
Sales (in units)	500	1,000	1,500
Sales revenue[a]	$5,000	$10,000	$15,000
Less: Variable operating costs[b]	2,500	5,000	7,500
Less: Fixed operating costs	2,500	2,500	2,500
Earnings before interest and taxes (EBIT)	$ 0	$ 2,500	$ 5,000
	−100%		+100%

[a]Sales revenue = $10/unit × sales in units.
[b]Variable operating costs = $5/unit × sales in units.

Case 2   A 50% *decrease* in sales (from 1,000 to 500 units) results in a
100% *decrease* in earnings before interest and taxes (from $2,500
to $0).

From the preceding example, we see that operating leverage works in *both
directions*. When a firm has fixed operating costs, operating leverage is present.
An increase in sales results in a more-than-proportional increase in EBIT; a
decrease in sales results in a more-than-proportional decrease in EBIT.

Measuring the Degree of Operating Leverage (DOL)

degree of operating leverage (DOL)
The numerical measure of the firm's operating leverage.

The **degree of operating leverage (DOL)** is the numerical measure of the firm's operating leverage. It can be derived using the following equation:[4]

$$DOL = \frac{\text{Percentage change in EBIT}}{\text{Percentage change in sales}} \qquad (12.4)$$

Whenever the percentage change in EBIT resulting from a given percentage change in sales is greater than the percentage change in sales, operating leverage exists. This means that as long as DOL is greater than 1, there is operating leverage.

Example

Applying Equation 12.4 to cases 1 and 2 in Table 12.4 yields the following results:[5]

Case 1: $\dfrac{+100\%}{+50\%} = 2.0$

Case 2: $\dfrac{-100\%}{-50\%} = 2.0$

Because the result is greater than 1, operating leverage exists. For a given base level of sales, the higher the value resulting from applying Equation 12.4, the greater the degree of operating leverage.

A more direct formula for calculating the degree of operating leverage at a base sales level, Q, is shown in Equation 12.5.[6]

$$\text{DOL at base sales level } Q = \frac{Q \times (P - VC)}{Q \times (P - VC) - FC} \qquad (12.5)$$

Example

Substituting $Q = 1,000$, $P = \$10$, $VC = \$5$, and $FC = \$2,500$ into Equation 12.5 yields the following result:

$$\text{DOL at 1,000 units} = \frac{1,000 \times (\$10 - \$5)}{1,000 \times (\$10 - \$5) - \$2,500} = \frac{\$5,000}{\$2,500} = 2.0$$

The use of the formula results in the same value for DOL (2.0) as that found by using Table 12.4 and Equation 12.4.[7]

---

4. The degree of operating leverage also depends on the base level of sales used as a point of reference. The closer the base sales level used is to the operating breakeven point, the greater the operating leverage. *Comparison of the degree of operating leverage of two firms is valid only when the same base level of sales is used for both firms.*

5. Because the concept of leverage is *linear,* positive and negative changes of equal magnitude will always result in equal degrees of leverage when the same base sales level is used as a point of reference. This relationship holds for all types of leverage discussed in this chapter.

6. Technically, the formula for DOL given in Equation 12.5 should include absolute value signs because it is possible to get a negative DOL when the EBIT for the base sales level is negative. Because we assume that the EBIT for the base level of sales is positive, we do not use the absolute value signs.

7. When total revenue in dollars from sales—instead of unit sales—is available, the following equation, in which TR = total revenue in dollars at a base level of sales and TVC = total variable operating costs in dollars, can be used:

$$\text{DOL at base dollar sales } TR = \frac{TR - TVC}{TR - TVC - FC}$$

This formula is especially useful for finding the DOL for multiproduct firms. It should be clear that because in the case of a single-product firm, $TR = Q \times P$ and $TVC = Q \times VC$, substitution of these values into Equation 12.5 results in the equation given here.

Focus on Practice   Adobe's Leverage

IN PRACTICE

Adobe Systems, the second largest PC software company in the United States, dominates the graphic design, imaging, dynamic media, and authoring-tool software markets. Website designers favor its Photoshop and Illustrator software applications, and Adobe's Acrobat software has become a standard for sharing documents online.

Adobe's ability to manage discretionary expenses helps keep its bottom line strong. Adobe has an additional advantage: *operating leverage,* the use of fixed operating costs to magnify the effect of changes in sales on earnings before interest and taxes (EBIT). Adobe and its peers in the software industry incur the bulk of their costs early in a product's life cycle, in the research and development and initial marketing stages. The up-front development costs are fixed, and subsequent production costs are practically zero. The economies of scale are

huge: Once a company sells enough copies to cover its fixed costs, incremental dollars go primarily to profit. Because the company has no long-term debt in its capital structure, its total leverage is derived only from fixed operating costs.

As demonstrated in the table below, operating leverage magnified Adobe's *decrease* in EBIT in 2002 while magnifying the increase in EBIT from 2003 to 2005. A 5.3 percent drop in 2002 sales resulted in an EBIT reduction of 24.6 percent. In 2003, a modest increase in sales—just over 11 percent— became a 33 percent increase

in EBIT. In 2006, Adobe, for the first time in 5 years, appeared to have lost its operating leverage. This can be attributed to its acquisition of Macromedia for approximately $3.5 billion in December 2005 and related restructuring charges during fiscal 2006. Once it has digested this purchase, Adobe should see its operating leverage rebound.

The table below demonstrates the impact of operating leverage on Adobe Systems in fiscal years (FYs) 2002–2006.

■ *What might cause the gradual decrease in operating leverage for Adobe?*

Item	FY2002	FY2003	FY2004	FY2005	FY2006
Sales revenue (millions)	$1,165	$1,295	$1,666	$1,966	$2,575
EBIT (millions)	$285	$380	$608	$766	$678
(1) Percent change in sales	−5.3%	11.2%	28.6%	18.0%	31.0%
(2) Percent change in EBIT	−24.6%	33.3%	60.0%	26.0%	−11.5%
DOL [(2) ÷ (1)]	4.6	3.0	2.1	1.4	−0.4

See the above *Focus on Practice* box for discussion of operating leverage at software maker Adobe.

Fixed Costs and Operating Leverage

Changes in fixed operating costs affect operating leverage significantly. Firms sometimes can incur fixed operating costs rather than variable operating costs and at other times may be able to substitute one type of cost for the other. For example, a firm could make fixed-dollar lease payments rather than payments equal to a specified percentage of sales. Or it could compensate sales representatives with a fixed salary and bonus rather than on a pure percent-of-sales commission basis. The effects of changes in fixed operating costs on operating leverage can best be illustrated by continuing our example.

Example

Assume that Cheryl's Posters exchanges a portion of its variable operating costs for fixed operating costs by eliminating sales commissions and increasing sales salaries. This exchange results in a reduction in the variable operating cost per

TABLE 12.5	Operating Leverage and Increased Fixed Costs		
		Case 2	Case 1
		−50%	+50%
Sales (in units)	500	1,000	1,500
Sales revenue[a]	$5,000	$10,000	$15,000
Less: Variable operating costs[b]	2,250	4,500	6,750
Less: Fixed operating costs	3,000	3,000	3,000
Earnings before interest and taxes (EBIT)	−$ 250	$ 2,500	$ 5,250
		−110%	+110%

[a]Sales revenue was calculated as indicated in Table 12.4.
[b]Variable operating costs = $4.50/unit × sales in units.

unit from $5 to $4.50 and an increase in the fixed operating costs from $2,500 to $3,000. Table 12.5 presents an analysis like that in Table 12.4, but using the new costs. Although the EBIT of $2,500 at the 1,000-unit sales level is the same as before the shift in operating cost structure, Table 12.5 shows that the firm has increased its operating leverage by shifting to greater fixed operating costs.

With the substitution of the appropriate values into Equation 12.5, the degree of operating leverage at the 1,000-unit base level of sales becomes

$$\text{DOL at 1,000 units} = \frac{1,000 \times (\$10 - \$4.50)}{1,000 \times (\$10 - \$4.50) - \$3,000} = \frac{\$5,500}{\$2,500} = 2.2$$

Comparing this value to the DOL of 2.0 before the shift to more fixed costs makes it clear that the higher the firm's fixed operating costs relative to variable operating costs, the greater the degree of operating leverage.

Financial Leverage

financial leverage
The potential use of *fixed financial costs* to magnify the effects of changes in earnings before interest and taxes on the firm's earnings per share.

Financial leverage results from the presence of *fixed financial costs* in the firm's income stream. Using the framework in Table 12.1, we can define **financial leverage** as the potential use of *fixed financial costs* to magnify the effects of changes in earnings before interest and taxes on the firm's earnings per share. The two fixed financial costs that may be found on the firm's income statement are (1) interest on debt and (2) preferred stock dividends. These charges must be paid regardless of the amount of EBIT available to pay them.[8]

8. As noted in Chapter 7, although preferred stock dividends can be "passed" (not paid) at the option of the firm's directors, it is generally believed that payment of such dividends is necessary. *This text treats the preferred stock dividend as a contractual obligation, not only to be paid as a fixed amount, but also to be paid as scheduled.* Although failure to pay preferred dividends cannot force the firm into bankruptcy, it increases the common stockholders' risk because they cannot be paid dividends until the claims of preferred stockholders are satisfied.

TABLE 12.6	The EPS for Various EBIT Levels[a]		
		Case 2	Case 1
		−40%	+40%
EBIT	$6,000	$10,000	$14,000
Less: Interest (I)	2,000	2,000	2,000
Net profits before taxes	$4,000	$ 8,000	$12,000
Less: Taxes ($T = 0.40$)	1,600	3,200	4,800
Net profits after taxes	$2,400	$ 4,800	$ 7,200
Less: Preferred stock dividends (PD)	2,400	2,400	2,400
Earnings available for common (EAC)	$ 0	$ 2,400	$ 4,800
Earnings per share (EPS)	$\frac{\$0}{1,000}=\$0$	$\frac{\$2,400}{1,000}=\$2.40$	$\frac{\$4,800}{1,000}=\$4.80$
		−100%	+100%

[a]As noted in Chapter 1, for accounting and tax purposes, interest is a *tax-deductible expense*, whereas dividends must be paid from after-tax cash flows.

Example

Chen Foods, a small Asian food company, expects EBIT of $10,000 in the current year. It has a $20,000 bond with a 10% (annual) coupon rate of interest and an issue of 600 shares of $4 (annual dividend per share) preferred stock outstanding. It also has 1,000 shares of common stock outstanding. The annual interest on the bond issue is $2,000 ($0.10 \times \$20,000$). The annual dividends on the preferred stock are $2,400 ($4.00/share $\times$ 600 shares). Table 12.6 presents the EPS corresponding to levels of EBIT of $6,000, $10,000, and $14,000, assuming that the firm is in the 40% tax bracket. Two situations are shown:

Case 1 A 40% *increase* in EBIT (from $10,000 to $14,000) results in a 100% *increase* in earnings per share (from $2.40 to $4.80).

Case 2 A 40% *decrease* in EBIT (from $10,000 to $6,000) results in a 100% *decrease* in earnings per share (from $2.40 to $0).

The effect of financial leverage is such that an increase in the firm's EBIT results in a more-than-proportional increase in the firm's earnings per share, whereas a decrease in the firm's EBIT results in a more-than-proportional decrease in EPS.

Measuring the Degree of Financial Leverage (DFL)

degree of financial leverage (DFL)
The numerical measure of the firm's financial leverage.

The **degree of financial leverage (DFL)** is the numerical measure of the firm's financial leverage. Computing it is much like computing the degree of operating leverage. The following equation presents one approach for obtaining the DFL.[9]

9. This approach is valid only when the same base level of EBIT is used to calculate and compare these values. In other words, *the base level of EBIT must be held constant to compare the financial leverage associated with different levels of fixed financial costs.*

$$DFL = \frac{\text{Percentage change in EPS}}{\text{Percentage change in EBIT}} \tag{12.6}$$

Whenever the percentage change in EPS resulting from a given percentage change in EBIT is greater than the percentage change in EBIT, financial leverage exists. This means that whenever DFL is greater than 1, there is financial leverage.

Example   Applying Equation 12.6 to cases 1 and 2 in Table 12.6 yields

Case 1: $\dfrac{+100\%}{+40\%} = 2.5$

Case 2: $\dfrac{-100\%}{-40\%} = 2.5$

In both cases, the quotient is greater than 1, so financial leverage exists. The higher this value, the greater the degree of financial leverage.

Personal Finance Example   Shanta and Ravi Shandra, a married couple with no children, wish to assess the impact of additional long-term borrowing on their degree of financial leverage (DFL). The Shandras currently have $4,200 available after meeting all of their monthly living (operating) expenses, *before* making monthly loan payments. They currently have monthly loan payment obligations of $1,700 and are considering the purchase of a new car, which would result in a $500 per month increase (to $2,200) in their total monthly loan payments. Because a large portion of Ravi's monthly income represents commissions, the Shandras feel that the $4,200 per month currently available for making loan payments could vary by 20% above or below that amount.

In order to assess the potential impact of the additional borrowing on their financial leverage, the Shandras calculate their DFL for both their current ($1,700) and proposed ($2,200) loan payments as follows, using the currently available $4,200 as a base and a 20% change.

	Current DFL			**Proposed DFL**		
Available for making loan payments	$4,200	(+20%)	$5,040	$4,200	(+20%)	$5,040
Less: Loan payments	1,700		1,700	2,200		2,200
Available after loan payments	$2,500	(+33.6%)	$3,340	$2,000	(+42%)	$2,840
	DFL = +33.6%/+20% = 1.68			DFL = +42%/+20% = 2.10		

Based on their calculations, the amount the Shandras will have available after loan payments with their current debt changes by 1.68% for every 1% change in the amount they will have available for making the loan payments. This is considerably less responsive—and therefore less risky—than the 2.10% change in the amount available after loan payments for each 1% change in the amount available for making loan payments with the proposed additional $500 in monthly debt payments. Although it appears that the Shandras can afford the additional loan payments, they must decide if, given the variability of Ravi's income, they feel comfortable with the increased financial leverage and risk.

A more direct formula for calculating the degree of financial leverage at a base level of EBIT is given by Equation 12.7, where the notation from Table 12.6 is used.[10] Note that in the denominator, the term $1/(1 - T)$ converts the after-tax preferred stock dividend to a before-tax amount for consistency with the other terms in the equation.

$$\text{DFL at base level EBIT} = \frac{\text{EBIT}}{\text{EBIT} - I - \left(PD \times \dfrac{1}{1 - T}\right)} \tag{12.7}$$

Example

Substituting EBIT = $10,000, I = $2,000, PD = $2,400, and the tax rate (T = 0.40) into Equation 12.7 yields the following result:

$$\text{DFL at \$10,000 EBIT} = \frac{\$10,000}{\$10,000 - \$2,000 - \left(\$2,400 \times \dfrac{1}{1 - 0.40}\right)}$$

$$= \frac{\$10,000}{\$4,000} = 2.5$$

Note that the formula given in Equation 12.7 provides a more direct method for calculating the degree of financial leverage than the approach illustrated using Table 12.6 and Equation 12.6.

Total Leverage

total leverage
The potential use of *fixed costs, both operating and financial,* to magnify the effects of changes in sales on the firm's earnings per share.

We also can assess the combined effect of operating and financial leverage on the firm's risk by using a framework similar to that used to develop the individual concepts of leverage. This combined effect, or **total leverage,** can be defined as the potential use of *fixed costs, both operating and financial,* to magnify the effects of changes in sales on the firm's earnings per share. Total leverage can therefore be viewed as the *total impact of the fixed costs* in the firm's operating and financial structure.

Example

Cables Inc., a computer cable manufacturer, expects sales of 20,000 units at $5 per unit in the coming year and must meet the following obligations: variable operating costs of $2 per unit, fixed operating costs of $10,000, interest of $20,000, and preferred stock dividends of $12,000. The firm is in the 40% tax bracket and has 5,000 shares of common stock outstanding. Table 12.7 on page 558 presents the levels of earnings per share associated with the expected sales of 20,000 units and with sales of 30,000 units.

---

10. By using the formula for DFL in Equation 12.7, it is possible to get a negative value for the DFL if the EPS for the base level of EBIT is negative. Rather than show absolute value signs in the equation, we instead assume that the base-level EPS is positive.

TABLE 12.7	The Total Leverage Effect

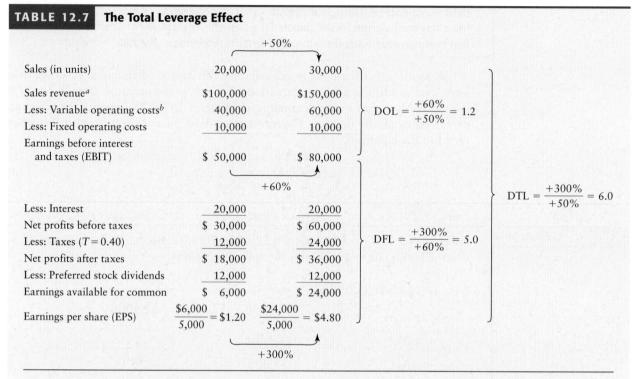

aSales revenue = $5/unit × sales in units.

bVariable operating costs = $2/unit × sales in units.

The table illustrates that as a result of a 50% increase in sales (from 20,000 to 30,000 units), the firm would experience a 300% increase in earnings per share (from $1.20 to $4.80). Although it is not shown in the table, a 50% decrease in sales would, conversely, result in a 300% decrease in earnings per share. The linear nature of the leverage relationship accounts for the fact that sales changes of equal magnitude in opposite directions result in EPS changes of equal magnitude in the corresponding direction. At this point, it should be clear that whenever a firm has fixed costs—operating or financial—in its structure, total leverage will exist.

Measuring the Degree of Total Leverage (DTL)

degree of total leverage (DTL)
The numerical measure of the firm's total leverage.

The **degree of total leverage (DTL)** is the numerical measure of the firm's total leverage. It can be computed much as operating and financial leverage are computed. The following equation presents one approach for measuring DTL:[11]

$$DTL = \frac{\text{Percentage change in EPS}}{\text{Percentage change in sales}} \qquad (12.8)$$

11. This approach is valid only when the same base level of sales is used to calculate and compare these values. In other words, *the base level of sales must be held constant if we are to compare the total leverage associated with different levels of fixed costs.*

Whenever the percentage change in EPS resulting from a given percentage change in sales is greater than the percentage change in sales, total leverage exists. This means that as long as the DTL is greater than 1, there is total leverage.

Example

Applying Equation 12.8 to the data in Table 12.7 yields

$$\text{DTL} = \frac{+300\%}{+50\%} = 6.0$$

Because this result is greater than 1, total leverage exists. The higher the value, the greater the degree of total leverage.

A more direct formula for calculating the degree of total leverage at a given base level of sales, Q, is given by Equation 12.9,[12] which uses the same notation that was presented earlier:

$$\text{DTL at base sales level } Q = \frac{Q \times (P - VC)}{Q \times (P - VC) - FC - I - \left(PD \times \dfrac{1}{1 - T}\right)} \tag{12.9}$$

Example

Substituting $Q = 20{,}000$, $P = \$5$, $VC = \$2$, $FC = \$10{,}000$, $I = \$20{,}000$, $PD = \$12{,}000$, and the tax rate ($T = 0.40$) into Equation 12.9 yields

DTL at 20,000 units

$$= \frac{20{,}000 \times (\$5 - \$2)}{20{,}000 \times (\$5 - \$2) - \$10{,}000 - \$20{,}000 - \left(\$12{,}000 \times \dfrac{1}{1 - 0.40}\right)}$$

$$= \frac{\$60{,}000}{\$10{,}000} = 6.0$$

Clearly, the formula used in Equation 12.9 provides a more direct method for calculating the degree of total leverage than the approach illustrated using Table 12.7 and Equation 12.8.

Relationship of Operating, Financial, and Total Leverage

Total leverage reflects the *combined impact* of operating and financial leverage on the firm. High operating leverage and high financial leverage will cause total leverage to be high. The opposite will also be true. The relationship between operating leverage and financial leverage is *multiplicative* rather than *additive*. The relationship between the degree of total leverage (DTL) and the degrees of operating leverage (DOL) and financial leverage (DFL) is given by Equation 12.10.

$$\text{DTL} = \text{DOL} \times \text{DFL} \tag{12.10}$$

---

12. By using the formula for DTL in Equation 12.9, it is possible to get a negative value for the DTL if the EPS for the base-level of sales is negative. For our purposes, rather than show absolute value signs in the equation, we instead assume that the base-level EPS is positive.

Focus on Ethics The Buyout Binge

The 1980s were the decade of *leveraging,* or adding debt to capital structure. A *Harvard Business Review* article warned managers that if they didn't "lever up" with debt, a hostile takeover would do it for them. Much of the debt binge had to be reversed in the 1990s—the decade of de-levering.

In 2007, the deals were heating up again. The acquirers this time were *private-equity* firms. Renewed concern arose that companies might be adding debt to the balance sheet as a defensive measure. **Health Management Associates** did so, announcing in January 2007 that it would take on $2.4 billion in new debt to finance a one-time $10-per-share dividend. While the move would lower HMA's credit rating from investment grade to junk levels, CFO Robert Farnham noted in a conference call that it would drop the company's cost of capital from the

low teens to 7.5 percent to 8 percent. The move makes a private-equity buyout nearly impossible. **Anheuser-Busch** signaled that it was pursuing a similar strategy when it announced in December 2006 that it was moving to an "aggressive leverage target."

Following the special dividend announcement, Health Management Associate's stock value fell approximately 8 percent. Although both the stock price and bond prices might fall due to overleveraging, stockholders were content because the cash they received more than offset the drop in the stock price. Moving to a highly leveraged position may help shareholders, but it is generally harmful to the interests of bondholders and other lenders.

As private-equity funds have consistently beaten market returns, money has poured in by the billions. By some estimates,

U.S. private-equity firms collectively were sitting on a $400 billion war chest. Combine that cash with leverage, and private-equity's buying power increases fourfold or fivefold.

The danger, of course, is that with that much money available, deals will be made that should not be made, and some deals will simply be so expensive that making them pay off could be difficult. Witness the Chrysler buyout by Germany's Daimler Corporation: The initial deal in 1998 was for $36 bil-lion. In 2007, **Cerebus Capital Management LP,** a private-equity firm, bought 80 percent of Chrysler Group from **DaimlerChrysler AG** for a mere $7.4 billion.

■ *What effect would a decreased cost of capital have on a firm's future investments?*

Example

Substituting the values calculated for DOL and DFL, shown on the right-hand side of Table 12.7, into Equation 12.10 yields

$$DTL = 1.2 \times 5.0 = 6.0$$

The resulting degree of total leverage is the same value that we calculated directly in the preceding examples.

The *Focus on Ethics* box above considers some ethical issues relating to the topic of leverage.

REVIEW QUESTIONS

12–1 What is meant by the term *leverage?* How are operating leverage, financial leverage, and total leverage related to the income statement?

12–2 What is the *operating breakeven point?* How do changes in fixed operating costs, the sale price per unit, and the variable operating cost per unit affect it?

12–3 What is *operating leverage?* What causes it? How is the *degree of operating leverage (DOL)* measured?

12–4 What is *financial leverage?* What causes it? How is the *degree of financial leverage (DFL)* measured?

12–5 What is the general relationship among operating leverage, financial leverage, and the total leverage of the firm? Do these types of leverage complement one another? Why or why not?

12.2 | The Firm's Capital Structure

Capital structure is one of the most complex areas of financial decision making because of its interrelationship with other financial decision variables.[13] Poor capital structure decisions can result in a high cost of capital, thereby lowering the NPVs of projects and making more of them unacceptable. Effective capital structure decisions can lower the cost of capital, resulting in higher NPVs and more acceptable projects—and thereby increasing the value of the firm. This section links together many of the concepts presented in Chapters 4, 5, 6, 7, and 11 and the discussion of leverage in this chapter.

Types of Capital

All of the items on the right-hand side of the firm's balance sheet, excluding current liabilities, are sources of capital. The following simplified balance sheet illustrates the basic breakdown of total capital into its two components, *debt capital* and *equity capital.*

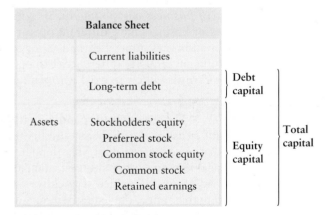

Hint The various types and characterisitcs of *corporate bonds,* a major source of *debt capital,* were discussed in detail in Chapter 6.

The cost of debt is lower than the cost of other forms of financing. Lenders demand relatively lower returns because they take the least risk of any long-term contributors of capital: (1) They have a higher priority of claim against any earnings or assets available for payment. (2) They can exert far greater legal pressure against the company to make payment than can owners of preferred or common

---

13. Of course, although capital structure is financially important, it—like many business decisions—is generally not so important as the firm's products or services. In a practical sense, a firm can probably more readily increase its value by improving quality and reducing costs than by fine-tuning its capital structure.

stock. (3) The tax deductibility of interest payments lowers the debt cost to the firm substantially.

Unlike debt capital, which must be repaid at some future date, *equity capital* is expected to remain in the firm for an indefinite period of time. The two basic sources of equity capital are (1) preferred stock and (2) common stock equity, which includes common stock and retained earnings. Common stock is typically the most expensive form of equity, followed by retained earnings and then preferred stock. Our concern here is the relationship between debt and equity capital. Because of equity's secondary position relative to debt, suppliers of equity capital take greater risk than suppliers of debt capital and therefore must be compensated with higher expected returns.

Hint Key differences between these two types of capital, relative to voice in management, claims on income and assets, maturity, and tax treatment, were summarized in Chapter 7, Table 7.1.

External Assessment of Capital Structure

We saw earlier that *financial leverage* results from the use of fixed-cost financing, such as debt and preferred stock, to magnify return and risk. The amount of leverage in the firm's capital structure can affect its value by affecting return and risk. Those outside the firm can make a rough assessment of capital structure by using measures found in the firm's financial statements. Some of these important debt ratios were presented in Chapter 2. For example, a direct measure of the degree of indebtedness is the *debt ratio*. The higher this ratio, the greater the relative amount of debt (or financial leverage) in the firm's capital structure. Measures of the firm's ability to meet contractual payments associated with debt include the *times interest earned ratio* and the *fixed-payment coverage ratio*. These ratios provide indirect information on financial leverage. Generally, the smaller these ratios, the greater the firm's financial leverage and the less able it is to meet payments as they come due.

The level of debt (financial leverage) that is acceptable for one industry or line of business can be highly risky in another, because different industries and lines of business have different operating characteristics. Table 12.8 presents the debt and times interest earned ratios for selected industries and lines of business. Significant industry differences can be seen in these data. Differences in debt positions are also likely to exist *within* an industry or line of business.

Personal Finance Example   Those who lend to individuals, like lenders to corporations, typically use ratios to assess the applicant's ability to meet the contractual payments associated with the requested debt. The lender, after obtaining information from a loan application and other sources, calculates ratios and compares them to predetermined allowable values. Typically, if the applicant's ratio values are within the acceptable range, the lender will make the requested loan.

The best example of this process is a real estate mortgage loan application. The mortgage lender usually invokes the following two requirements:

1. Monthly mortgage payments < 25% to 30% of monthly gross (before-tax) income
2. Total monthly installment payments (including the mortgage payment) < 33% to 38% of monthly gross (before-tax) income

Assume that the Loo family is applying for a mortgage loan. The family's monthly gross (before-tax) income is $5,380, and they currently have monthly

TABLE 12.8	Debt Ratios for Selected Industries and Lines of Business (Fiscal Years Ended 4/1/05 through 3/31/06)					
Industry or line of business	Debt ratio	Times interest earned ratio	Industry or line of business	Debt ratio	Times interest earned ratio
Manufacturing industries			**Retailing industries**		
Books printing	70.4%	2.9	Department stores	65.0%	3.0
Dairy products	70.3	3.1	New car dealers	82.2	1.8
Electronic computers	71.1	4.7	Supermarkets and grocery stores	72.9	3.4
Iron and steel forgings	59.9	4.9			
Machine tools, metal cutting types	64.1	4.3	**Service industries**		
			Advertising agencies	81.2	8.8
Wines and distilled alcoholic beverages	66.9	5.0	General automotive repair	85.3	2.8
Women's and girls' dresses	64.1	2.7	Insurance agencies and brokerages	80.4	7.3
Wholesaling industries			Offices of Certified Public Accountants	71.3	10.2
Furniture	69.3	4.0			
General groceries	70.5	3.0			
Men's and boys' clothing	66.9	3.7			

Source: RMA Annual Statement Studies, 2006–2007 (fiscal years ended 4/1/05 through 3/31/06) (Philadelphia: Risk Management Association, 2006). Copyright © 2006 by Risk Management Association.

Note: The Risk Management Association recommends that these ratios be regarded only as general guidelines and not as absolute industry norms. No claim is made as to the representativeness of these figures.

installment loan obligations that total $560. The $200,000 mortgage loan they are applying for will require monthly payments of $1,400. The lender requires (1) the monthly mortgage payment to be less than 28% of monthly gross income and (2) total monthly installment payments (including the mortgage payment) to be less than 37% of monthly gross income. The lender calculates and evaluates these ratios for the Loos, as shown below.

1. Mort. pay./Gross income = $1,400/$5,380 = 26% < 28% maximum, therefore **OK**
2. Tot. instal. pay./Gross income = ($560 + $1,400)/$5,380 = $1,960/$5,380
   = 36.4% < 37% maximum, therefore **OK**

Because the Loos' ratios meet the lender's standards, assuming they have adequate funds for the down payment and meet other lender requirements, the Loos will be granted the loan.

 ## *Capital Structure of Non-U.S. Firms*

In general, non-U.S. companies have much higher degrees of indebtedness than their U.S. counterparts. Most of the reasons relate to the fact that U.S. capital markets are more developed than those elsewhere and have played a greater role in corporate financing than has been the case in other countries. In most European countries and especially in Japan and other Pacific Rim nations, large commercial banks are more actively involved in the financing of corporate activity than has been true in the United States. Furthermore, in many of these countries, banks are allowed to make large equity investments in nonfinancial corporations—a practice prohibited for U.S. banks. Finally, share ownership tends to be more tightly controlled among founding-family, institutional, and even public investors in Europe and Asia than it is for most large U.S. corporations. Tight ownership enables owners to understand the firm's financial condition better, resulting in their willingness to tolerate a higher degree of indebtedness.

On the other hand, similarities do exist between U.S. corporations and corporations in other countries. First, the same industry patterns of capital structure tend to be found all around the world. For example, in nearly all countries, pharmaceutical and other high-growth industrial firms tend to have lower debt ratios than do steel companies, airlines, and electric utility companies. Second, the capital structures of the largest U.S.-based multinational companies, which have access to capital markets around the world, typically resemble the capital structures of multinational companies from other countries more than they resemble those of smaller U.S. companies. Finally, the worldwide trend is away from reliance on banks for financing and toward greater reliance on security issuance. Over time, the differences in the capital structures of U.S. and non-U.S. firms will probably lessen.

Capital Structure Theory

Research suggests that there is an optimal capital structure range. *It is not yet possible to provide financial managers with a specified methodology for use in determining a firm's optimal capital structure.* Nevertheless, financial theory does offer help in understanding how a firm's chosen financing mix affects the firm's value.

In 1958, Franco Modigliani and Merton H. Miller[14] (commonly known as "M and M"),[15] the capital structure that a firm chooses does not affect its value. Many researchers, including M and M, have examined the effects of less restrictive assumptions on the relationship between capital structure and the firm's value. The result is a theoretical *optimal* capital structure based on balancing the benefits and costs of debt financing. The major benefit of debt financing is the *tax shield,* which allows interest payments to be deducted in calculating taxable income. The cost of debt financing results from (1) the increased probability of bankruptcy caused by debt obligations, (2) the *agency costs* of the lender's constraining the firm's actions, and (3) the costs associated with managers having more information about the firm's prospects than do investors.

Tax Benefits

Allowing firms to deduct interest payments on debt when calculating taxable income reduces the amount of the firm's earnings paid in taxes, thereby making more earnings available for bondholders and stockholders. The deductibility of

---

14. Franco Modigliani and Merton H. Miller, "The Cost of Capital, Corporation Finance, and the Theory of Investment," *American Economic Review* (June 1958), pp. 261–297.

15. Perfect-market assumptions include (1) no taxes, (2) no brokerage or flotation costs for securities, (3) symmetrical information—investors and managers have the same information about the firm's investment prospects, and (4) investor ability to borrow at the same rate as corporations.

interest means the cost of debt, r_i, to the firm is subsidized by the government. Letting r_d equal the before-tax cost of debt and letting T equal the tax rate, from Chapter 11 (Equation 11.2), we have $r_i = r_d \times (1 - T)$.

Probability of Bankruptcy

The chance that a firm will become bankrupt because of an inability to meet its obligations as they come due depends largely on its level of both business risk and financial risk.

Business Risk   In Chapter 11, we defined *business risk* as the risk to the firm of being unable to cover its operating costs. In general, the greater the firm's *operating leverage*—the use of fixed operating costs—the higher its business risk. Although operating leverage is an important factor affecting business risk, two other factors—revenue stability and cost stability—also affect it. *Revenue stability* reflects the relative variability of the firm's sales revenues. Firms with reasonably stable levels of demand and with products that have stable prices have stable revenues. The result is low levels of business risk. Firms with highly volatile product demand and prices have unstable revenues that result in high levels of business risk. *Cost stability* reflects the relative predictability of input prices such as those for labor and materials. The more predictable and stable these input prices are, the lower the business risk; the less predictable and stable they are, the higher the business risk.

Business risk varies among firms, regardless of their lines of business, and is not affected by capital structure decisions. The level of business risk must be taken as a "given." The higher a firm's business risk, the more cautious the firm must be in establishing its capital structure. Firms with high business risk therefore tend toward less highly leveraged capital structures, and firms with low business risk tend toward more highly leveraged capital structures. We will hold business risk constant throughout the discussions that follow.

Example

Cooke Company, a soft drink manufacturer, is preparing to make a capital structure decision. It has obtained estimates of sales and the associated levels of earnings before interest and taxes (EBIT) from its forecasting group: There is a 25% chance that sales will total $400,000, a 50% chance that sales will total $600,000, and a 25% chance that sales will total $800,000. Fixed operating costs total $200,000, and variable operating costs equal 50% of sales. These data are summarized, and the resulting EBIT calculated, in Table 12.9.

TABLE 12.9	Sales and Associated EBIT Calculations for Cooke Company ($000)		
Probability of sales	.25	.50	.25
Sales revenue	$400	$600	$800
Less: Fixed operating costs	200	200	200
Less: Variable operating costs (50% of sales)	200	300	400
Earnings before interest and taxes (EBIT)	$ 0	$100	$200

The table shows that there is a 25% chance that the EBIT will be $0, a 50% chance that it will be $100,000, and a 25% chance that it will be $200,000. When developing the firm's capital structure, the financial manager must accept as given these levels of EBIT and their associated probabilities. These EBIT data effectively reflect a certain level of business risk that captures the firm's operating leverage, sales revenue variability, and cost predictability.

Financial Risk   The firm's capital structure directly affects its *financial risk*, which is the risk to the firm of being unable to cover required financial obligations. The penalty for not meeting financial obligations is bankruptcy. The more fixed-cost financing—debt (including financial leases) and preferred stock—a firm has in its capital structure, the greater its financial leverage and risk. Financial risk depends on the capital structure decision made by the management, and that decision is affected by the business risk the firm faces.

Total Risk   The *total risk* of a firm—business and financial risk combined—determines its probability of bankruptcy. Financial risk, its relationship to business risk, and their combined impact can be demonstrated by continuing the Cooke Company example.

Hint The cash flows to investors from bonds are less risky than the dividends from preferred stock, which are ess risky than dividends from common stock. Only with bonds is the issuer contractually obligated to pay the scheduled interest, and the amounts due to bondholders and preferred stockholders are usually fixed. Therefore, the required return for bonds is generally lower than that for preferred stock, which is lower than that for common stock.

Example

Cooke Company's current capital structure is as follows:

Current capital structure	
Long-term debt	$ 0
Common stock equity (25,000 shares at $20)	500,000
Total capital (assets)	$500,000

Hint As you learned in Chapter 2, the *debt ratio* is equal to the amount of total debt divided by the total assets. The higher this ratio, the more financial leverage a firm is using.

Let us assume that the firm is considering seven alternative capital structures. If we measure these structures using the debt ratio, they are associated with ratios of 0%, 10%, 20%, 30%, 40%, 50%, and 60%. Assuming that (1) the firm has no current liabilities, (2) its capital structure currently contains all equity as shown, and (3) the total amount of capital remains constant[16] at $500,000, the mix of debt and equity associated with the seven debt ratios would be as shown in Table 12.10. Also shown in the table is the number of shares of common stock outstanding under each alternative.

Associated with each of the debt levels in column 3 of Table 12.10 would be an interest rate that would be expected to increase with increases in financial leverage. The level of debt, the associated interest rate (assumed to apply to *all* debt), and the dollar amount of annual interest associated with each of the alternative capital structures are summarized in Table 12.11. Because both the level of debt and the interest rate increase with increasing financial leverage (debt ratios), the annual interest increases as well.

---

16. This assumption is needed so that we can assess alternative capital structures without having to consider the returns associated with the investment of additional funds raised. Attention here is given only to the *mix* of capital, not to its investment.

TABLE 12.10	Capital Structures Associated with Alternative Debt Ratios for Cooke Company

| | Capital structure ($000) | | | Shares of common |
Debt ratio (1)	Total assets[a] (2)	Debt [(1) × (2)] (3)	Equity [(2) − (3)] (4)	stock outstanding (000) [(4) ÷ $20][b] (5)
0%	$500	$ 0	$500	25.00
10	500	50	450	22.50
20	500	100	400	20.00
30	500	150	350	17.50
40	500	200	300	15.00
50	500	250	250	12.50
60	500	300	200	10.00

[a]Because the firm, for convenience, is assumed to have no current liabilities, its total assets equal its total capital of $500,000.

[b]The $20 value represents the book value per share of common stock equity noted earlier.

TABLE 12.11	Level of Debt, Interest Rate, and Dollar Amount of Annual Interest Associated with Cooke Company's Alternative Capital Structures

Capital structure debt ratio	Debt ($000) (1)	Interest rate on *all* debt (2)	Interest ($000) [(1) × (2)] (3)
0%	$ 0	0.0%	$ 0.00
10	50	9.0	4.50
20	100	9.5	9.50
30	150	10.0	15.00
40	200	11.0	22.00
50	250	13.5	33.75
60	300	16.5	49.50

Table 12.12 on page 568 uses the levels of EBIT and associated probabilities developed in Table 12.9, the number of shares of common stock found in column 5 of Table 12.10, and the annual interest values calculated in column 3 of Table 12.11 to calculate the earnings per share (EPS) for debt ratios of 0%, 30%, and 60%. A 40% tax rate is assumed. Also shown are the resulting expected EPS, the standard deviation of EPS, and the coefficient of variation of EPS associated with each debt ratio.[17]

17. For explanatory convenience, the *coefficient of variation of EPS*, which measures total (nondiversifiable and diversifiable) risk, is used throughout this chapter as a proxy for beta, which measures the relevant nondiversifiable risk.

TABLE 12.12 **Calculation of EPS for Selected Debt Ratios ($000) for Cooke Company**

Probability of EBIT	.25	.50	.25
Debt ratio = 0%			
EBIT (Table 12.9)	$ 0.00	$100.00	$200.00
Less: Interest (Table 12.11)	0.00	0.00	0.00
Net profits before taxes	$ 0.00	$100.00	$200.00
Less: Taxes ($T = 0.40$)	0.00	40.00	80.00
Net profits after taxes	$ 0.00	$ 60.00	$120.00
EPS (25.0 shares, Table 12.10)	$ 0.00	$ 2.40	$ 4.80
Expected EPS[a]		$ 2.40	
Standard deviation of EPS[a]		$ 1.70	
Coefficient of variation of EPS[a]		0.71	
Debt ratio = 30%			
EBIT (Table 12.9)	$ 0.00	$100.00	$200.00
Less: Interest (Table 12.11)	15.00	15.00	15.00
Net profits before taxes	($15.00)	$ 85.00	$185.00
Less: Taxes ($T = 0.40$)	(6.00)[b]	34.00	74.00
Net profits after taxes	($ 9.00)	$ 51.00	$111.00
EPS (17.50 shares, Table 12.10)	($ 0.51)	$ 2.91	$ 6.34
Expected EPS[a]		$ 2.91	
Standard deviation of EPS[a]		$ 2.42	
Coefficient of variation of EPS[a]		0.83	
Debt ratio = 60%			
EBIT (Table 12.9)	$ 0.00	$100.00	$200.00
Less: Interest (Table 12.11)	49.50	49.50	49.50
Net profits before taxes	($49.50)	$ 50.50	$150.50
Less: Taxes ($T = 0.40$)	(19.80)[b]	20.20	60.20
Net profits after taxes	($29.70)	$ 30.30	$ 90.30
EPS (10.00 shares, Table 12.10)	($ 2.97)	$ 3.03	$ 9.03
Expected EPS[a]		$ 3.03	
Standard deviation of EPS[a]		$ 4.24	
Coefficient of variation of EPS[a]		1.40	

[a]The procedures used to calculate the expected value, standard deviation, and coefficient of variation were presented in Equations 5.2, 5.3, and 5.4, respectively, in Chapter 5.

[b]It is assumed that the firm receives the tax benefit from its loss in the current period as a result of applying the *tax loss carryback* procedures specified in the tax law but not discussed in this text.

TABLE 12.13	Expected EPS, Standard Deviation, and Coefficient of Variation for Alternative Capital Structures for Cooke Company		
Capital structure debt ratio	Expected EPS (1)	Standard deviation of EPS (2)	Coefficient of variation of EPS [(2) ÷ (1)] (3)
0%	$2.40	$1.70	0.71
10	2.55	1.88	0.74
20	2.72	2.13	0.78
30	2.91	2.42	0.83
40	3.12	2.83	0.91
50	3.18	3.39	1.07
60	3.03	4.24	1.40

Table 12.13 summarizes the pertinent data for the seven alternative capital structures. The values shown for 0%, 30%, and 60% debt ratios were developed in Table 12.12, whereas calculations of similar values for the other debt ratios (10%, 20%, 40%, and 50%) are not shown. Because the coefficient of variation measures the risk relative to the expected EPS, it is the preferred risk measure for use in comparing capital structures. As the firm's financial leverage increases, so does its coefficient of variation of EPS. As expected, an increasing level of risk is associated with increased levels of financial leverage.

The relative risks of the two extremes of the capital structures evaluated in Table 12.12 (debt ratios = 0% and 60%) can be illustrated by showing the probability distribution of EPS associated with each of them. Figure 12.3 shows these two distributions. The expected level of EPS increases with increasing financial

FIGURE 12.3

Probability Distributions
Probability distributions of EPS for debt ratios of 0% and 60% for Cooke Company

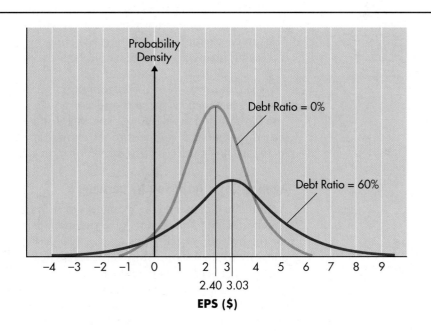

FIGURE 12.4

Expected EPS and Coefficient of Variation of EPS
Expected EPS and coefficient of variation of EPS for alternative capital structures for Cooke Company

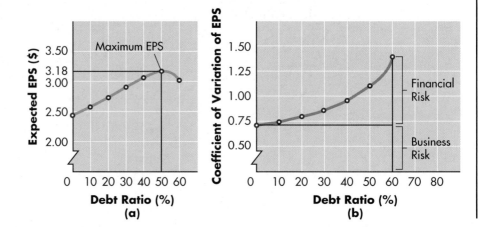

leverage, and so does risk, as reflected in the relative dispersion of each of the distributions. Clearly, the uncertainty of the expected EPS, as well as the chance of experiencing negative EPS, is greater when higher degrees of financial leverage are employed.

Further, the nature of the risk–return tradeoff associated with the seven capital structures under consideration can be clearly observed by plotting the expected EPS and coefficient of variation relative to the debt ratio. Plotting the data from Table 12.13 results in Figure 12.4. The figure shows that as debt is substituted for equity (as the debt ratio increases), the level of EPS rises and then begins to fall (graph **a**). The graph demonstrates that the peak earnings per share occurs at a debt ratio of 50%. The decline in earnings per share beyond that ratio results from the fact that the significant increases in interest are not fully offset by the reduction in the number of shares of common stock outstanding.

If we look at the risk behavior as measured by the coefficient of variation (graph **b**), we can see that risk increases with increasing leverage. A portion of the risk can be attributed to business risk, but the portion that changes in response to increasing financial leverage would be attributed to financial risk.

Clearly, a risk–return tradeoff exists relative to the use of financial leverage. Later in the chapter we will address how to combine these risk–return factors into a valuation framework. The key point to recognize here is that as a firm introduces more leverage into its capital structure, it will typically experience increases in both the expected level of return and the associated risk.

Agency Costs Imposed by Lenders

As noted in Chapter 1, the managers of firms typically act as *agents* of the owners (stockholders). The owners give the managers the authority to manage the firm for the owners' benefit. The *agency problem* created by this relationship extends not only to the relationship between owners and managers but also to the relationship between owners and lenders.

When a lender provides funds to a firm, the interest rate charged is based on the lender's assessment of the firm's risk. The lender–borrower relationship, therefore, depends on the lender's expectations for the firm's subsequent behavior.

The borrowing rates are, in effect, locked in when the loans are negotiated. After obtaining a loan at a certain rate, the firm could increase its risk by investing in risky projects or by incurring additional debt. Such action could weaken the lender's position in terms of its claim on the cash flow of the firm. From another point of view, if these risky investment strategies paid off, the stockholders would benefit. Because payment obligations to the lender remain unchanged, the excess cash flows generated by a positive outcome from the riskier action would enhance the value of the firm to its owners. In other words, if the risky investments pay off, the owners receive all the benefits; if the risky investments do not pay off, the lenders share in the costs.

Clearly, an incentive exists for the managers acting on behalf of the stockholders to "take advantage" of lenders. To avoid this situation, lenders impose certain monitoring techniques on borrowers, who as a result incur *agency costs*. The most obvious strategy is to deny subsequent loan requests or to increase the cost of future loans to the firm. But this strategy is an after-the-fact approach. Therefore, lenders typically protect themselves by including in the loan agreement provisions that limit the firm's ability to alter significantly its business and financial risk. These loan provisions tend to center on issues such as the minimum level of liquidity, asset acquisitions, executive salaries, and dividend payments.

By including appropriate provisions in the loan agreement, the lender can control the firm's risk and thus protect itself against the adverse consequences of this agency problem. Of course, in exchange for incurring agency costs by agreeing to the operating and financial constraints placed on it by the loan provisions, the firm should benefit by obtaining funds at a lower cost.

Hint Typical loan provisions included in corporate bonds are discussed in Chapter 6.

Asymmetric Information

Two surveys examined capital structure decisions.[18] Financial executives were asked which of two major criteria determined their financing decisions: (1) maintaining a *target capital structure* or (2) following a hierarchy of financing. This hierarchy, called a **pecking order,** begins with retained earnings, which is followed by debt financing and finally external equity financing. Respondents from 31 percent of *Fortune* 500 firms and from 11 percent of the (smaller) 500 largest over-the-counter firms answered target capital structure. Respondents from 69 percent of the *Fortune* 500 firms and 89 percent of the 500 largest OTC firms chose the pecking order.

At first glance, on the basis of financial theory, this choice appears to be inconsistent with wealth maximization goals, but Stewart Myers has explained how "asymmetric information" could account for the pecking order financing preferences of financial managers.[19] **Asymmetric information** results when managers of a firm have more information about operations and future prospects than do investors. Assuming that managers make decisions with the goal of maximizing the wealth of existing stockholders, then asymmetric information can affect the capital structure decisions that managers make.

pecking order
A hierarchy of financing that begins with retained earnings, which is followed by debt financing and finally external equity financing.

asymmetric information
The situation in which managers of a firm have more information about operations and future prospects than do investors.

18. The results of the survey of *Fortune* 500 firms are reported in J. Michael Pinegar and Lisa Wilbricht, "What Managers Think of Capital Structure Theory: A Survey," *Financial Management* (Winter 1989), pp. 82–91, and the results of a similar survey of the 500 largest OTC firms are reported in Linda C. Hittle, Kamal Haddad, and Lawrence J. Gitman, "Over-the-Counter Firms, Asymmetric Information, and Financing Preferences," *Review of Financial Economics* (Fall 1992), pp. 81–92.
19. Stewart C. Myers, "The Capital Structure Puzzle," *Journal of Finance* (July 1984), pp. 575–592.

Suppose, for example, that management has found a valuable investment that will require additional financing. Management believes that the prospects for the firm's future are very good and that the market, as indicated by the firm's current stock price, does not fully appreciate the firm's value. In this case, it would be advantageous to current stockholders if management raised the required funds using debt rather than issuing new stock. Using debt to raise funds is frequently viewed as a **signal** that reflects management's view of the firm's stock value. Debt financing is a *positive signal* suggesting that management believes that the stock is "undervalued" and therefore a bargain. When the firm's positive future outlook becomes known to the market, the increased value will be fully captured by existing owners, rather than having to be shared with new stockholders.

If, however, the outlook for the firm is poor, management may believe that the firm's stock is "overvalued." In that case, it would be in the best interest of existing stockholders for the firm to issue new stock. Therefore, investors often interpret the announcement of a stock issue as a *negative signal*—bad news concerning the firm's prospects—and the stock price declines. This decrease in stock value, along with high underwriting costs for stock issues (compared to debt issues), make new stock financing very expensive. When the negative future outlook becomes known to the market, the decreased value is shared with new stockholders, rather than being fully captured by existing owners.

Because conditions of asymmetric information exist from time to time, firms should maintain some reserve borrowing capacity by keeping debt levels low. This reserve allows the firm to take advantage of good investment opportunities without having to sell stock at a low value and thus send signals that unduly influence the stock price.

signal
A financing action by management that is believed to reflect its view of the firm's stock value; generally, debt financing is viewed as a *positive signal* that management believes the stock is "undervalued," and a stock issue is viewed as a *negative signal* that management believes the stock is "overvalued."

Optimal Capital Structure

What, then, *is* the optimal capital structure, even if it exists (so far) only in theory? To provide some insight into an answer, we will examine some basic financial relationships. It is generally believed that *the value of the firm is maximized when the cost of capital is minimized*. By using a modification of the simple zero-growth valuation model (see Equation 7.3 in Chapter 7), we can define the value of the firm, V, by Equation 12.11.

$$V = \frac{\text{EBIT} \times (1 - T)}{r_a} = \frac{\text{NOPAT}}{r_a} \tag{12.11}$$

where

$\quad\quad$ EBIT = earnings before interest and taxes

$\quad\quad\quad\quad$ T = tax rate

$\quad$ NOPAT = net operating profits after taxes, which (as noted in Chapters 3 and 8) is the after-tax operating earnings available to the debt and equity holders, EBIT $\times (1 - T)$

$\quad\quad\quad\quad$ r_a = weighted average cost of capital

Clearly, if we assume that NOPAT (and therefore EBIT) is constant, the value of the firm, V, is maximized by minimizing the weighted average cost of capital, r_a.

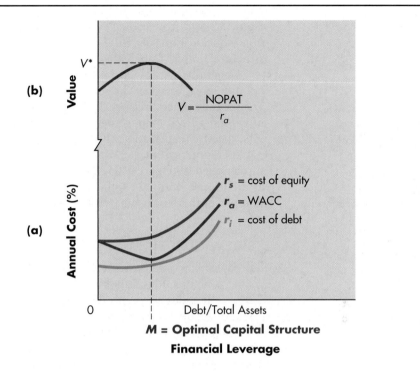

FIGURE 12.5

Cost Functions and Value
Capital costs and the
optimal capital structure

Cost Functions

Figure 12.5(*a*) plots three cost functions—the cost of debt, the cost of equity, and the weighted average cost of capital (WACC)—as a function of financial leverage measured by the debt ratio (debt to total assets). The *cost of debt*, r_i, remains low because of the tax shield, but it slowly increases as leverage increases, to compensate lenders for increasing risk. The *cost of equity*, r_s, is above the cost of debt. It increases as financial leverage increases, but it generally increases more rapidly than the cost of debt. The cost of equity rises because the stockholders require a higher return as leverage increases, to compensate for the higher degree of financial risk.

The *weighted average cost of capital*, r_a (*WACC*) results from a weighted average of the firm's debt and equity capital costs. At a debt ratio of zero, the firm is 100 percent equity-financed. As debt is substituted for equity and as the debt ratio increases, the WACC declines because the debt cost is less than the equity cost ($r_i < r_s$). As the debt ratio continues to increase, the increased debt and equity costs eventually cause the WACC to rise (after point *M* in Figure 12.5(*a*)). This behavior results in a U-shaped, or saucer-shaped, weighted average cost-of-capital function, r_a.

Graphical View of Optimal Structure

optimal capital structure
The capital structure at which the weighted average cost of capital is minimized, thereby maximizing the firm's value.

Because the maximization of value, *V*, is achieved when the overall cost of capital, r_a, is at a minimum (see Equation 12.11), the **optimal capital structure** is that at which the weighted average cost of capital, r_a, is minimized. In Figure 12.5(*a*), point *M* represents the *minimum weighted average cost of capital*—the point of optimal financial leverage and hence of optimal capital structure for the firm.

Figure 12.5(b) plots the value of the firm that results from substitution of r_a in Figure 12.5(a) for various levels of financial leverage into the zero-growth valuation model in Equation 12.11. As shown in Figure 12.5(b), at the optimal capital structure, point M, the value of the firm is maximized at V^*.

Generally, the lower the firm's weighted average cost of capital, the greater the difference between the return on a project and the WACC, and therefore the greater the owners' return. Simply stated, minimizing the weighted average cost of capital allows management to undertake a larger number of profitable projects, thereby further increasing the value of the firm.

As a practical matter, there is no way to calculate the optimal capital structure implied by Figure 12.5. Because it is impossible either to know or to remain at the precise optimal capital structure, firms generally try to operate in a *range* that places them near what they believe to be the optimal capital structure.

REVIEW QUESTIONS

12–6 What is a firm's *capital structure?* What ratios assess the degree of financial leverage in a firm's capital structure?

12–7 In what ways are the capital structures of U.S. and non-U.S. firms different? How are they similar?

12–8 What is the major benefit of debt financing? How does it affect the firm's cost of debt?

12–9 What are *business risk* and *financial risk?* How does each of them influence the firm's capital structure decisions?

12–10 Briefly describe the *agency problem* that exists between owners and lenders. How do lenders cause firms to incur *agency costs* to resolve this problem?

12–11 How does *asymmetric information* affect the firm's capital structure decisions? How do the firm's financing actions give investors *signals* that reflect management's view of stock value?

12–12 How do the cost of debt, the cost of equity, and the weighted average cost of capital (WACC) behave as the firm's financial leverage increases from zero? Where is the *optimal capital structure?* What is its relationship to the firm's value at that point?

12.3 | EBIT–EPS Approach to Capital Structure

EBIT–EPS approach
An approach for selecting the capital structure that maximizes earnings per share (EPS) over the expected range of earnings before interest and taxes (EBIT).

It should be clear from earlier chapters that the goal of the financial manager is to maximize owner wealth—that is, the firm's stock price. One of the widely followed variables affecting the firm's stock price is its earnings, which represents the returns earned on behalf of owners. In spite of the fact that focusing on earnings ignores risk (the other key variable affecting the firm's stock price), earnings per share (EPS) can be conveniently used to analyze alternative capital structures. The **EBIT–EPS approach** to capital structure involves selecting the capital structure that maximizes EPS over the expected range of earnings before interest and taxes (EBIT).

Presenting a Financing Plan Graphically

To analyze the effects of a firm's capital structure on the owners' returns, we consider the relationship between earnings before interest and taxes (EBIT) and earnings per share (EPS). A constant level of EBIT—constant *business risk*—is assumed, to isolate the effect on returns of the financing costs associated with alternative capital structures. EPS is used to measure the owners' returns, which are expected to be closely related to share price.[20]

Data Required

To graph a financing plan, we need to know at least two EBIT–EPS coordinates. The following example illustrates the approach for obtaining coordinates.

Example

EBIT–EPS coordinates can be found by assuming specific EBIT values and calculating the EPS associated with them.[21] Such calculations for three capital structures—debt ratios of 0%, 30%, and 60%—for Cooke Company were presented in Table 12.12. For EBIT values of $100,000 and $200,000, the associated EPS values calculated there are summarized in the table below the graph in Figure 12.6 on page 576.

Plotting the Data

financial breakeven point
The level of EBIT necessary to just cover all *fixed financial costs;* the level of EBIT for which EPS = $0.

The Cooke Company data can be plotted on a set of EBIT–EPS axes, as shown in Figure 12.6. The figure shows the level of EPS expected for each level of EBIT. For levels of EBIT below the *x*-axis intercept, a loss (negative EPS) results. Each of the *x*-axis intercepts is a **financial breakeven point**, the level of EBIT necessary to just cover all *fixed financial costs* (EPS = $0).

Comparing Alternative Capital Structures

We can compare alternative capital structures by graphing financing plans as shown in Figure 12.6.

Example

Cooke Company's capital structure alternatives were plotted on the EBIT–EPS axes in Figure 12.6. This figure shows that each capital structure is superior to the others in terms of maximizing EPS over certain ranges of EBIT. The zero-leverage capital structure (debt ratio = 0%) is superior to either of the other

---

20. The relationship that is expected to exist between EPS and owner wealth is not one of cause and effect. As indicated in Chapter 1, the maximization of profits does not necessarily ensure that owners' wealth is also maximized. Nevertheless, it is expected that the movement of earnings per share will have some effect on owners' wealth, because EPS data constitute one of the few pieces of information investors receive, and they often bid the firm's share price up or down in response to the level of these earnings.

21. A convenient method for finding one EBIT–EPS coordinate is to calculate the *financial breakeven point,* the level of EBIT for which the firm's EPS just equals $0. It is the level of EBIT needed just to cover all fixed financial costs—annual interest (*I*) and preferred stock dividends (*PD*). The equation for the financial breakeven point is

$$\text{Financial breakeven point} = I + \frac{PD}{1 - T}$$

where *T* is the tax rate. It can be seen that when *PD* = $0, the financial breakeven point is equal to *I*, the annual interest payment.

FIGURE 12.6

EBIT–EPS Approach
A comparison of selected capital structures for Cooke Company (data from Table 12.12)

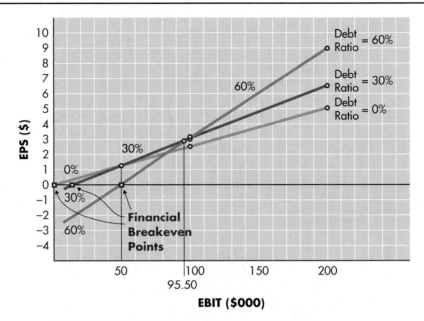

| Capital structure | EBIT | |
| debt ratio | $100,000 | $200,000 |
	Earnings per share (EPS)	
0%	$2.40	$4.80
30	2.91	6.34
60	3.03	9.03

capital structures for levels of EBIT between $0 and $50,000. Between $50,000 and $95,500 of EBIT, the capital structure associated with a debt ratio of 30% is preferred. And at a level of EBIT above $95,500, the 60% debt ratio capital structure provides the highest earnings per share.[22]

---

22. An algebraic technique can be used to find the *indifference points* between the capital structure alternatives. This technique involves expressing each capital structure as an equation stated in terms of earnings per share, setting the equations for two capital structures equal to each other, and solving for the level of EBIT that causes the equations to be equal. When we use the notation from footnote 21 and let n equal the number of shares of common stock outstanding, the general equation for the earnings per share from a financing plan is

$$\text{EPS} = \frac{(1 - T) \times (\text{EBIT} - I) - PD}{n}$$

Comparing Cooke Company's 0% and 30% capital structures, we get

$$\frac{(1 - 0.40) \times (\text{EBIT} - \$0) - \$0}{25.00} = \frac{(1 - 0.40) \times (\text{EBIT} - \$15.00) - \$0}{17.50}$$

$$\frac{0.60 \times \text{EBIT}}{25.00} = \frac{0.60 \times \text{EBIT} - \$9.00}{17.50}$$

$$10.50 \times \text{EBIT} = 15.00 \times \text{EBIT} - \$225.00$$

$$\$225.00 = 4.50 \times \text{EBIT}$$

$$\text{EBIT} = \$50$$

The calculated value of the indifference point between the 0% and 30% capital structures is therefore $50,000, as can be seen in Figure 12.6.

Considering Risk in EBIT–EPS Analysis

When interpreting EBIT–EPS analysis, it is important to consider the risk of each capital structure alternative. Graphically, the risk of each capital structure can be viewed in light of two measures: (1) the *financial breakeven point* (EBIT-axis intercept) and (2) the *degree of financial leverage* reflected in the slope of the capital structure line: *The higher the financial breakeven point and the steeper the slope of the capital structure line, the greater the financial risk.*[23]

Further assessment of risk can be performed by using ratios. As financial leverage (measured by the debt ratio) increases, we expect a corresponding decline in the firm's ability to make scheduled interest payments (measured by the times interest earned ratio).

Example ▸

Reviewing the three capital structures plotted for Cooke Company in Figure 12.6, we can see that as the debt ratio increases, so does the financial risk of each alternative. Both the financial breakeven point and the slope of the capital structure lines increase with increasing debt ratios. If we use the $100,000 EBIT value, for example, the times interest earned ratio (EBIT ÷ interest) for the zero-leverage capital structure is infinity ($100,000 ÷ $0); for the 30% debt case, it is 6.67 ($100,000 ÷ $15,000); and for the 60% debt case, it is 2.02 ($100,000 ÷ $49,500). Because lower times interest earned ratios reflect higher risk, these ratios support the conclusion that the risk of the capital structures increases with increasing financial leverage. The capital structure for a debt ratio of 60% is riskier than that for a debt ratio of 30%, which in turn is riskier than the capital structure for a debt ratio of 0%.

Basic Shortcoming of EBIT–EPS Analysis

The most important point to recognize when using EBIT–EPS analysis is that this technique tends to concentrate on *maximizing earnings* rather than maximizing owner wealth as reflected in the firm's stock price. The use of an EPS-maximizing approach generally ignores risk. If investors did not require risk premiums (additional returns) as the firm increased the proportion of debt in its capital structure, a strategy involving maximizing EPS would also maximize stock price. But because risk premiums increase with increases in financial leverage, the maximization of EPS *does not* ensure owner wealth maximization. To select the best capital structure, firms must integrate both return (EPS) and risk (via the required return, r_s) into a valuation framework consistent with the capital structure theory presented earlier.

REVIEW QUESTION

12–13 Explain the *EBIT–EPS approach* to capital structure. Include in your explanation a graph indicating the *financial breakeven point;* label the axes. Is this approach consistent with maximization of the owners' wealth?

---

23. The degree of financial leverage (DFL) is reflected in the slope of the EBIT–EPS function. The steeper the slope, the greater the degree of financial leverage, because the change in EPS (y axis) that results from a given change in EBIT (x axis) increases with increasing slope and decreases with decreasing slope.

12.4 | Choosing the Optimal Capital Structure

A wealth maximization framework for use in making capital structure decisions should include the two key factors of return and risk. This section describes the procedures for linking to market value the return and risk associated with alternative capital structures.

Linkage

To determine the firm's value under alternative capital structures, the firm must find the level of return that it must earn to compensate owners for the risk being incurred. This approach is consistent with the overall valuation framework developed in Chapters 6 and 7 and applied to capital budgeting decisions in Chapters 9 and 10.

The required return associated with a given level of financial risk can be estimated in a number of ways. Theoretically, the preferred approach would be first to estimate the beta associated with each alternative capital structure and then to use the CAPM framework presented in Equation 5.8 to calculate the required return, r_s. A more operational approach involves linking the financial risk associated with each capital structure alternative directly to the required return. Such an approach is similar to the CAPM-type approach demonstrated in Chapter 10 for linking project risk and required return (RADR). Here it involves estimating the required return associated with each level of financial risk, as measured by a statistic such as the coefficient of variation of EPS. Regardless of the approach used, one would expect the required return to increase as the financial risk increases.

Example Cooke Company, using as risk measures the coefficients of variation of EPS associated with each of the seven alternative capital structures, estimated the associated required returns. These are shown in Table 12.14. As expected, the estimated required return of owners, r_s, increases with increasing risk, as measured by the coefficient of variation of EPS.

Estimating Value

The value of the firm associated with alternative capital structures can be estimated by using one of the standard valuation models. If, for simplicity, we assume that all earnings are paid out as dividends, we can use a zero-growth valuation model such as that developed in Chapter 7. The model, originally stated in Equation 7.3, is restated here with EPS substituted for dividends (because in each year the dividends would equal EPS):

$$P_0 = \frac{EPS}{r_s} \tag{12.12}$$

By substituting the expected level of EPS and the associated required return, r_s, into Equation 12.12, we can estimate the per-share value of the firm, P_0.

TABLE 12.14	Required Returns for Cooke Company's Alternative Capital Structures	
Capital structure debt ratio	Coefficient of variation of EPS (from column 3 of Table 12.13) (1)	Estimated required return, r_s (2)
0%	0.71	11.5%
10	0.74	11.7
20	0.78	12.1
30	0.83	12.5
40	0.91	14.0
50	1.07	16.5
60	1.40	19.0

Example

We can now estimate the value of Cooke Company's stock under each of the alternative capital structures. Substituting the expected EPS (column 1 of Table 12.13) and the required returns, r_s (column 2 of Table 12.14 in decimal form), into Equation 12.12 for each of the capital structures, we obtain the share values given in column 3 of Table 12.15. Plotting the resulting share values against the associated debt ratios, as shown in Figure 12.7 on page 580, clearly illustrates that the maximum share value occurs at the capital structure associated with a debt ratio of 30%.

Maximizing Value versus Maximizing EPS

Throughout this text, we have specified the goal of the financial manager as maximizing owner wealth, not profit. Although some relationship exists between expected profit and value, there is no reason to believe that profit-maximizing

TABLE 12.15	Calculation of Share Value Estimates Associated with Alternative Capital Structures for Cooke Company		
Capital structure debt ratio	Expected EPS (from column 1 of Table 12.13) (1)	Estimated required return, r_s (from column 2 of Table 12.14) (2)	Estimated share value [(1) ÷ (2)] (3)
0%	$2.40	.115	$20.87
10	2.55	.117	21.79
20	2.72	.121	22.48
30	2.91	.125	23.28
40	3.12	.140	22.29
50	3.18	.165	19.27
60	3.03	.190	15.95

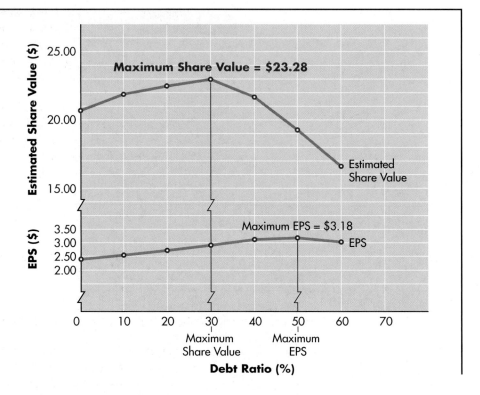

FIGURE 12.7

Estimating Value
Estimated share value and EPS for alternative capital structures for Cooke Company

strategies necessarily result in wealth maximization. It is therefore the wealth of the owners as reflected in the estimated share value that should serve as the criterion for selecting the best capital structure. A final look at Cooke Company will highlight this point.

Example

Further analysis of Figure 12.7 clearly shows that although the firm's profits (EPS) are maximized at a debt ratio of 50%, share value is maximized at a 30% debt ratio. Therefore, the preferred capital structure would be the 30% debt ratio. The two approaches provide different conclusions because EPS maximization does not consider risk.

Some Other Important Considerations

Because there is really no practical way to calculate the optimal capital structure, any quantitative analysis of capital structure must be tempered with other important considerations. Table 12.16 on page 581 summarizes some of the more important additional factors involved in capital structure decisions.

REVIEW QUESTIONS

12–14 Why do *maximizing EPS* and *maximizing value* not necessarily lead to the same conclusion about the optimal capital structure?

12–15 What important factors in addition to quantitative factors should a firm consider when it is making a capital structure decision?

TABLE 12.16	**Important Factors to Consider in Making Capital Structure Decisions**	
Concern	Factor	Description
Business risk	Revenue stability	Firms that have stable and predictable revenues can more safely undertake highly leveraged capital structures than can firms with volatile patterns of sales revenue. Firms with growing sales tend to benefit from added debt; they can reap the positive benefits of financial leverage, which magnifies the effect of these increases.
	Cash flow	When considering a new capital structure, the firm must focus on its ability to generate the cash flows necessary to meet obligations. Cash forecasts reflecting an ability to service debts (and preferred stock) must support any shift in capital structure.
Agency costs	Contractual obligations	A firm may be contractually constrained with respect to the type of funds that it can raise. For example, a firm might be prohibited from selling additional debt except when the claims of holders of such debt are made subordinate to the existing debt. Contractual constraints on the sale of additional stock, as well as on the ability to distribute dividends on stock, might also exist.
	Management preferences	Occasionally, a firm will impose an internal constraint on the use of debt to limit its risk exposure to a level deemed acceptable to management. In other words, because of risk aversion, the firm's management constrains the firm's capital structure at a level that may or may not be the true optimum.
	Control	A management group concerned about control may prefer to issue debt rather than (voting) common stock. Under favorable market conditions, a firm that wanted to sell equity could make a *preemptive offering* or issue *nonvoting shares*, allowing each shareholder to maintain proportionate ownership. Generally, only in closely held firms or firms threatened by takeover does control become a major concern in the capital structure decision.
Asymmetric information	External risk assessment	The firm's ability to raise funds quickly and at favorable rates depends on the external risk assessments of lenders and bond raters. The firm must consider the impact of capital structure decisions both on share value and on published financial statements from which lenders and raters assess the firm's risk.
	Timing	At times when interest rates are low, debt financing might be more attractive; when interest rates are high, the sale of stock may be more appealing. Sometimes both debt and equity capital become unavailable at reasonable terms. General economic conditions—especially those of the capital market—can thus significantly affect capital structure decisions.

Summary

Focus on Value

The amount of leverage (fixed-cost assets or funds) employed by a firm directly affects its risk, return, and share value. Generally, higher leverage raises risk and return, and lower leverage reduces risk and return. Operating leverage concerns the level of fixed operating costs; financial leverage focuses on fixed financial costs, particularly interest on debt and any preferred stock dividends. The firm's capital structure determines its financial leverage. Because of its fixed interest payments, the more debt a firm employs relative to its equity, the greater its financial leverage.

The value of the firm is clearly affected by its degree of operating leverage and by the composition of its capital structure. The financial manager must therefore carefully consider the types of operating and financial costs it incurs, recognizing that with greater fixed costs comes higher risk. Major decisions with regard to both operating cost structure and capital structure must therefore focus on their impact on the firm's value. The firm should implement only those leverage and capital structure decisions that are consistent with its goal of **maximizing its stock price**.

Review of Learning Goals

LG 1 **Discuss leverage, capital structure, breakeven analysis, the operating breakeven point, and the effect of changing costs on it.** Leverage results from the use of fixed costs to magnify returns to a firm's owners. Capital structure, the firm's mix of long-term debt and equity, affects leverage and therefore the firm's value. Breakeven analysis measures the level of sales necessary to cover total operating costs. The operating breakeven point may be calculated algebraically, by dividing fixed operating costs by the difference between the sale price per unit and variable operating cost per unit, or it may be determined graphically. The operating breakeven point increases with increased fixed and variable operating costs and decreases with an increase in sale price, and vice versa.

LG 2 **Understand operating, financial, and total leverage and the relationships among them.** Operating leverage is the use of fixed operating costs by the firm to magnify the effects of changes in sales on EBIT. The higher the fixed operating costs, the greater the operating leverage. Financial leverage is the use of fixed financial costs by the firm to magnify the effects of changes in EBIT on EPS. The higher the fixed financial costs, the greater the financial leverage. The total leverage of the firm is the use of fixed costs—both operating and financial—to magnify the effects of changes in sales on EPS.

LG 3 **Describe the types of capital, external assessment of capital structure, the capital structure of non-U.S. firms, and capital structure theory.** Debt capital and equity capital make up a firm's capital structure. Capital structure can be externally assessed by using financial ratios—debt ratio, times interest earned ratio, and fixed-payment coverage ratio. Non-U.S. companies tend to have much higher degrees of indebtedness than do their U.S. counterparts, primarily because U.S. capital markets are more developed.

Research suggests that there is an optimal capital structure that balances the firm's benefits and costs of debt financing. The major benefit of debt financing is the tax shield. The costs of debt financing include the probability of bankruptcy; agency costs imposed by lenders; and asymmetric information, which typically causes firms to raise funds in a pecking order so as to send positive signals to the market and thereby enhance shareholder wealth.

LG 4 **Explain the optimal capital structure using a graphical view of the firm's cost-of-capital functions and a zero-growth valuation model.** The zero-growth valuation model defines the firm's value as its net operating profits after taxes (NOPAT), or after-tax EBIT, divided by its weighted average cost of capital. Assuming that NOPAT is constant, the value of the firm is maximized by minimizing its weighted average cost of capital (WACC). The optimal capital structure minimizes the WACC. Graphically, the firm's WACC exhibits a U-shape, whose minimum value defines the optimal capital structure that maximizes owner wealth.

LG 5 **Discuss the EBIT–EPS approach to capital structure.** The EBIT–EPS approach evaluates capital structures in light of the returns they provide the firm's owners and their degree of financial risk. Under the EBIT–EPS approach, the preferred capital structure is the one that is expected to provide maximum EPS over the firm's expected range of EBIT. Graphically, this approach reflects risk in terms of the financial breakeven point and the slope of the capital structure line. The major shortcoming of EBIT–EPS analysis is that it concentrates on maximizing earnings (returns) rather than owners' wealth, which considers risk as well as return.

LG 6 **Review the return and risk of alternative capital structures, their linkage to market value, and other important considerations related to capital structure.** The best capital structure can be selected by using a valuation model to link return and risk factors. The preferred capital structure is the one that results in the highest estimated share value, not the highest EPS. Other important nonquantitative factors must also be considered when making capital structure decisions.

Self-Test Problems (Solutions in Appendix B)

  ST12–1 Breakeven point and all forms of leverage   TOR most recently sold 100,000 units at $7.50 each; its variable operating costs are $3.00 per unit, and its fixed operating costs are $250,000. Annual interest charges total $80,000, and the firm has 8,000 shares of $5 (annual dividend) preferred stock outstanding. It currently has 20,000 shares of common stock outstanding. Assume that the firm is subject to a 40% tax rate.

a. At what level of sales (in units) would the firm break even on operations (that is, EBIT = $0)?

b. Calculate the firm's *earnings per share (EPS)* in tabular form at (1) the current level of sales and (2) a 120,000-unit sales level.

c. Using the current *$750,000 level of sales as a base,* calculate the firm's degree of operating leverage (DOL).

d. Using the EBIT *associated with the $750,000 level of sales as a base,* calculate the firm's degree of financial leverage (DFL).

e. Use the degree of total leverage (DTL) concept to determine the effect (in percentage terms) of a 50% increase in TOR's sales *from the $750,000 base level* on its earnings per share.

ST12–2 **EBIT–EPS analysis** Newlin Electronics is considering additional financing of $10,000. It currently has $50,000 of 12% (annual interest) bonds and 10,000 shares of common stock outstanding. The firm can obtain the financing through a 12% (annual interest) bond issue or through the sale of 1,000 shares of common stock. The firm has a 40% tax rate.

a. Calculate two EBIT–EPS coordinates for each plan by selecting any two EBIT values and finding their associated EPS values.

b. Plot the two financing plans on a set of EBIT–EPS axes.

c. On the basis of your graph in part **b,** at what level of EBIT does the bond plan become superior to the stock plan?

ST12–3 **Optimal capital structure** Hawaiian Macadamia Nut Company has collected the following data with respect to its capital structure, expected earnings per share, and required return.

Capital structure debt ratio	Expected earnings per share	Required return, r_s
0%	$3.12	13%
10	3.90	15
20	4.80	16
30	5.44	17
40	5.51	19
50	5.00	20
60	4.40	22

a. Compute the *estimated share value* associated with each of the capital structures, using the simplified method described in this chapter (see Equation 12.12).

b. Determine the optimal capital structure on the basis of (1) maximization of expected earnings per share and (2) maximization of share value.

c. Which capital structure do you recommend? Why?

Warm-Up Exercises   A blue box (■) indicates exercises available in .

E12–1 Canvas Reproductions has fixed operating costs of $12,500, variable operating costs of $10 per unit, and sells its paintings for $25 each. At what level of unit sales will the company breakeven in terms of EBIT?

E12–2 The Great Fish Taco Corporation currently has fixed operating costs of $15,000, sells its pre-made tacos for $6 per box, and incurs variable operating costs of $2.50 per box. If the firm has a potential investment that would simultaneously raise its fixed costs to $16,500 and allow it to charge a per-box sale price of $6.50 due to better-textured tacos, what will the impact be on its operating breakeven point in boxes?

E12–3 Chico's has sales of 15,000 units at a price of $20 per unit. The firm incurs fixed operating costs of $30,000 and variable operating costs of $12 per unit. What is Chico's *degree of operating leverage (DOL)* at a base level of sales of 15,000 units?

E12–4 Parker Investments has EBIT of $20,000, interest expense of $3,000, and preferred dividends of $4,000. If it pays taxes at a rate of 38%, what is Parker's *degree of financial leverage (DFL)* at a base level of EBIT of $20,000?

E12–5 Cobalt Industries had sales of 150,000 units at a price of $10 per unit. It faced fixed operating costs of $250,000 and variable operating costs of $5 per unit. The company is subject to a tax rate of 38% and has a weighted average cost of capital of 8.5%. Calculate Cobalt's *net operating profits after taxes (NOPAT)*, and use it to estimate the value of the firm.

Problems

A blue box (■) indicates problems available in myfinancelab.

P12–1 **Breakeven point—Algebraic**   Kate Rowland wishes to estimate the number of flower arrangements she must sell at $24.95 to break even. She has estimated fixed operating costs of $12,350 per year and variable operating costs of $15.45 per arrangement. How many flower arrangements must Kate sell to break even on operating costs?

P12–2 **Breakeven comparisons—Algebraic**   Given the price and cost data shown in the accompanying table for each of the three firms, F, G, and H, answer the following questions.

Firm	F	G	H
Sale price per unit	$ 18.00	$ 21.00	$ 30.00
Variable operating cost per unit	6.75	13.50	12.00
Fixed operating cost	45,000	30,000	90,000

a. What is the *operating breakeven point* in units for each firm?
b. How would you rank these firms in terms of their risk?

P12–3 **Breakeven point—Algebraic and graphical**   Fine Leather Enterprises sells its single product for $129.00 per unit. The firm's fixed operating costs are $473,000 annually, and its variable operating costs are $86.00 per unit.
a. Find the firm's *operating breakeven point* in units.
b. Label the *x* axis "Sales (units)" and the *y* axis "Costs/Revenues ($)," and then graph the firm's sales revenue, total operating cost, and fixed operating cost functions on these axes. In addition, label the operating breakeven point and the areas of loss and profit (EBIT).

P12–4 **Breakeven analysis**   Barry Carter is considering opening a music store. He wants to estimate the number of CDs he must sell to break even. The CDs will be sold for $13.98 each, variable operating costs are $10.48 per CD, and annual fixed operating costs are $73,500.
a. Find the *operating breakeven point* in number of CDs.
b. Calculate the total operating costs at the breakeven volume found in part a.

c. If Barry estimates that at a minimum he can sell 2,000 CDs *per month*, should he go into the music business?

d. How much EBIT will Barry realize if he sells the minimum 2,000 CDs per month noted in part **c?**

PERSONAL FINANCE PROBLEM

 P12–5 **Breakeven analysis**   Paul Scott has a 2008 Cadillac that he wants to update with a geo-tracker device so he will have access to road maps and directions. After-market equipment can be fitted for a flat fee of $500, and the service provider requires monthly charges of $20. In his line of work as a traveling salesman, he estimates that this device can save him time and money—about $35 per month (as the price of gas keeps increasing).

In order to determine the financial feasibility of purchasing the geo-tracker, Paul wants to determine the number of months it will take to break even. He plans to keep the car for another 3 years.

a. Calculate the *breakeven point* for the device in months.

b. Based on **a**, should Paul have the tracker installed in his car?

 P12–6 **Breakeven point—Changing costs/revenues**   JWG Company publishes *Creative Crosswords*. Last year the book of puzzles sold for $10 with variable operating cost per book of $8 and fixed operating costs of $40,000. How many books must JWG sell this year to achieve the *breakeven point* for the stated operating costs, given the following different circumstances?

a. All figures remain the same as for last year.

b. Fixed operating costs increase to $44,000; all other figures remain the same.

c. The selling price increases to $10.50; all costs remain the same as for last year.

d. Variable operating cost per book increases to $8.50; all other figures remain the same.

e. What conclusions about the operating breakeven point can be drawn from your answers?

 P12–7 **Breakeven analysis**   Molly Jasper and her sister, Caitlin Peters, got into the novelties business almost by accident. Molly, a talented sculptor, often made little figurines as gifts for friends. Occasionally, she and Caitlin would set up a booth at a crafts fair and sell a few of the figurines along with jewelry that Caitlin made. Little by little, demand for the figurines, now called Mollycaits, grew, and the sisters began to reproduce some of the favorites in resin, using molds of the originals. The day came when a buyer for a major department store offered them a contract to produce 1,500 figurines of various designs for $10,000. Molly and Caitlin realized that it was time to get down to business. To make bookkeeping simpler, Molly had priced all of the figurines at $8.00. Variable operating costs amounted to an average of $6.00 per unit. To produce the order, Molly and Caitlin would have to rent industrial facilities for a month, which would cost them $4,000.

a. Calculate Mollycaits' *operating breakeven point*.

b. Calculate Mollycaits' EBIT on the department store order.

c. If Molly renegotiates the contract at a price of $10.00 per figurine, what will the EBIT be?

d. If the store refuses to pay more than $8.00 per unit but is willing to negotiate quantity, what quantity of figurines will result in an EBIT of $4,000?

e. At this time, Mollycaits come in 15 different varieties. Whereas the average variable cost per unit is $6.00, the actual cost varies from unit to unit. What recommendation would you have for Molly and Caitlin with regard to pricing and/or the numbers and types of units that they offer for sale?

 P12–8 **EBIT sensitivity**   Stewart Industries sells its finished product for $9 per unit. Its fixed operating costs are $20,000, and the variable operating cost per unit is $5.
a. Calculate the firm's earnings before interest and taxes (EBIT) for sales of 10,000 units.
b. Calculate the firm's EBIT for sales of 8,000 and 12,000 units, respectively.
c. Calculate the percentage changes in sales (from the 10,000-unit base level) and associated percentage changes in EBIT for the shifts in sales indicated in part **b.**
d. On the basis of your findings in part **c,** comment on the sensitivity of changes in EBIT in response to changes in sales.

 P12–9 **Degree of operating leverage**   Grey Products has fixed operating costs of $380,000, variable operating costs of $16 per unit, and a selling price of $63.50 per unit.
a. Calculate the *operating breakeven point* in units.
b. Calculate the firm's EBIT at 9,000, 10,000, and 11,000 units, respectively.
c. With 10,000 units as a base, what are the percentage changes in units sold and EBIT as sales move from the base to the other sales levels used in part **b?**
d. Use the percentages computed in part **c** to determine the *degree of operating leverage (DOL).*
e. Use the formula for degree of operating leverage to determine the DOL at 10,000 units.

 P12–10 **Degree of operating leverage—Graphical**   Levin Corporation has fixed operating costs of $72,000, variable operating costs of $6.75 per unit, and a selling price of $9.75 per unit.
a. Calculate the *operating breakeven point* in units.
b. Compute the *degree of operating leverage (DOL)* using the following unit sales levels as a base: 25,000, 30,000, 40,000. Use the formula given in the chapter.
c. Graph the DOL figures that you computed in part **b** (on the *y* axis) against base sales levels (on the *x* axis).
d. Compute the degree of operating leverage at 24,000 units; add this point to your graph.
e. What principle do your graph and figures illustrate?

 P12–11 **EPS calculations**   Southland Industries has $60,000 of 16% (annual interest) bonds outstanding, 1,500 shares of preferred stock paying an annual dividend of $5 per share, and 4,000 shares of common stock outstanding. Assuming that the firm has a 40% tax rate, compute *earnings per share (EPS)* for the following levels of EBIT:
a. $24,600
b. $30,600
c. $35,000

 P12–12 **Degree of financial leverage**   Northwestern Savings and Loan has a current capital structure consisting of $250,000 of 16% (annual interest) debt and 2,000 shares of common stock. The firm pays taxes at the rate of 40%.

a. Using EBIT values of $80,000 and $120,000, determine the associated *earnings per share (EPS)*.

b. Using $80,000 of EBIT as a base, calculate the *degree of financial leverage (DFL)*.

c. Rework parts **a** and **b** assuming that the firm has $100,000 of 16% (annual interest) debt and 3,000 shares of common stock.

PERSONAL FINANCE PROBLEM

 P12–13 **Financial leverage**   Max Small has outstanding school loans that require a monthly payment of $1,000. He needs to purchase a new car for work and estimates that this will add $350 per month to his existing monthly obligations. Max will have $3,000 available after meeting all of his monthly living (operating) expenses. This amount could vary by plus or minus 10%.

a. In order to assess the potential impact of the additional borrowing on his financial leverage, calculate the *DFL* in tabular form for both the current and proposed loan payments using Max's available $3,000 as a base and a 10% change.

b. Can Max afford the additional loan payment?

c. Should Max take on the additional loan payment?

  P12–14 **DFL and graphical display of financing plans**   Wells and Associates has EBIT of $67,500. Interest costs are $22,500, and the firm has 15,000 shares of common stock outstanding. Assume a 40% tax rate.

a. Use the degree of financial leverage (DFL) formula to calculate the *DFL* for the firm.

b. Using a set of EBIT–EPS axes, plot Wells and Associates' financing plan.

c. If the firm also has 1,000 shares of preferred stock paying a $6.00 annual dividend per share, what is the DFL?

d. Plot the financing plan, including the 1,000 shares of $6.00 preferred stock, on the axes used in part **b**.

e. Briefly discuss the graph of the two financing plans.

 P12–15 **Integrative—Multiple leverage measures**   Play-More Toys produces inflatable beach balls, selling 400,000 balls per year. Each ball produced has a variable operating cost of $0.84 and sells for $1.00. Fixed operating costs are $28,000. The firm has annual interest charges of $6,000, preferred dividends of $2,000, and a 40% tax rate.

a. Calculate the *operating breakeven point* in units.

b. Use the degree of operating leverage (DOL) formula to calculate *DOL*.

c. Use the degree of financial leverage (DFL) formula to calculate *DFL*.

d. Use the degree of total leverage (DTL) formula to calculate *DTL*. Compare this to the product of DOL and DFL calculated in parts **b** and **c**.

 P12–16 **Integrative—Leverage and risk**   Firm R has sales of 100,000 units at $2.00 per unit, variable operating costs of $1.70 per unit, and fixed operating costs of $6,000. Interest is $10,000 per year. Firm W has sales of 100,000 units at $2.50 per unit, variable operating costs of $1.00 per unit, and fixed operating costs of $62,500. Interest is $17,500 per year. Assume that both firms are in the 40% tax bracket.

a. Compute the degree of operating, financial, and total leverage for firm R.

b. Compute the degree of operating, financial, and total leverage for firm W.

c. Compare the relative risks of the two firms.

d. Discuss the principles of leverage that your answers illustrate.

  P12–17 Integrative—Multiple leverage measures and prediction   Carolina Fastener, Inc., makes a patented marine bulkhead latch that wholesales for $6.00. Each latch has variable operating costs of $3.50. Fixed operating costs are $50,000 per year. The firm pays $13,000 interest and preferred dividends of $7,000 per year. At this point, the firm is selling 30,000 latches per year and is taxed at a rate of 40%.

a. Calculate Carolina Fastener's *operating breakeven point*.

b. On the basis of the firm's current sales of 30,000 units per year and its interest and preferred dividend costs, calculate its EBIT and earnings available for common.

c. Calculate the firm's *degree of operating leverage (DOL)*.

d. Calculate the firm's *degree of financial leverage (DFL)*.

e. Calculate the firm's *degree of total leverage (DTL)*.

f. Carolina Fastener has entered into a contract to produce and sell an additional 15,000 latches in the coming year. Use the DOL, DFL, and DTL to predict and calculate the changes in EBIT and earnings available for common. Check your work by a simple calculation of Carolina Fastener's EBIT and earnings available for common, using the basic information given.

PERSONAL FINANCE PROBLEM

 P12–18 Capital structure   Kirsten Neal is interested in purchasing a new house given that mortgage rates are at a historical low. Her bank has specific rules regarding an applicant's ability to meet the contractual payments associated with the requested debt. Kirsten must submit personal financial data for her income, expenses, and existing installment loan payments. The bank then calculates and compares certain ratios to predetermined allowable values to determine if it will make the requested loan. The requirements are as follows:

(1) Monthly mortgage payments < 28% of monthly gross (before-tax) income.

(2) Total monthly installment payments (including the mortgage payments) < 37% of monthly gross (before-tax) income.

Kirsten submits the following personal financial data:

Monthly gross (before-tax) income	$4,500
Monthly installment loan obligations	$375
Requested mortgage	$150,000
Monthly mortgage payments	$1,100

a. Calculate the ratio for requirement 1.

b. Calculate the ratio for requirement 2.

c. Assuming that Kirsten has adequate funds for the down payment and meets other lender requirements, will Kirsten be granted the loan?

  Various capital structures   Charter Enterprises currently has $1 million in total assets and is totally equity-financed. It is contemplating a change in its capital structure. Compute the amount of debt and equity that would be outstanding if the firm were to shift to each of the following debt ratios: 10%, 20%, 30%, 40%, 50%, 60%, and 90%. (*Note:* The amount of total assets would not change.) Is there a limit to the debt ratio's value?

P12–20 Debt and financial risk Tower Interiors has made the forecast of sales shown in the following table. Also given is the probability of each level of sales.

Sales	Probability
$200,000	.20
300,000	.60
400,000	.20

The firm has fixed operating costs of $75,000 and variable operating costs equal to 70% of the sales level. The company pays $12,000 in interest per period. The tax rate is 40%.

a. Compute the earnings before interest and taxes (EBIT) for each level of sales.
b. Compute the earnings per share (EPS) for each level of sales, the expected EPS, the standard deviation of the EPS, and the coefficient of variation of EPS, assuming that there are 10,000 shares of common stock outstanding.
c. Tower has the opportunity to reduce its leverage to zero and pay no interest. This will require that the number of shares outstanding be increased to 15,000. Repeat part **b** under this assumption.
d. Compare your findings in parts **b** and **c**, and comment on the effect of the reduction of debt to zero on the firm's financial risk.

P12–21 EPS and optimal debt ratio Williams Glassware has estimated, at various debt ratios, the expected earnings per share and the standard deviation of the earnings per share as shown in the following table.

Debt ratio	Earnings per share (EPS)	Standard deviation of EPS
0%	$2.30	$1.15
20	3.00	1.80
40	3.50	2.80
60	3.95	3.95
80	3.80	5.53

a. Estimate the *optimal debt ratio* on the basis of the relationship between earnings per share and the debt ratio. You will probably find it helpful to graph the relationship.
b. Graph the relationship between the *coefficient of variation* and the debt ratio. Label the areas associated with business risk and financial risk.

P12–22 EBIT–EPS and capital structure Data-Check is considering two capital structures. The key information is shown in the following table. Assume a 40% tax rate.

Source of capital	Structure A	Structure B
Long-term debt	$100,000 at 16% coupon rate	$200,000 at 17% coupon rate
Common stock	4,000 shares	2,000 shares

a. Calculate two *EBIT–EPS coordinates* for each of the structures by selecting any two EBIT values and finding their associated EPS values.
b. Plot the two capital structures on a set of EBIT–EPS axes.
c. Indicate over what EBIT range, if any, each structure is preferred.
d. Discuss the leverage and risk aspects of each structure.
e. If the firm is fairly certain that its EBIT will exceed $75,000, which structure would you recommend? Why?

 P12–23 EBIT–EPS and preferred stock   Litho-Print is considering two possible capital structures, A and B, shown in the following table. Assume a 40% tax rate.

Source of capital	Structure A	Structure B
Long-term debt	$75,000 at 16% coupon rate	$50,000 at 15% coupon rate
Preferred stock	$10,000 with an 18% annual dividend	$15,000 with an 18% annual dividend
Common stock	8,000 shares	10,000 shares

a. Calculate two *EBIT–EPS coordinates* for each of the structures by selecting any two EBIT values and finding their associated EPS values.
b. Graph the two capital structures on the same set of EBIT–EPS axes.
c. Discuss the leverage and risk associated with each of the structures.
d. Over what range of EBIT is each structure preferred?
e. Which structure do you recommend if the firm expects its EBIT to be $35,000? Explain.

   P12–24 Integrative—Optimal capital structure   Medallion Cooling Systems, Inc., has total assets of $10,000,000, EBIT of $2,000,000, and preferred dividends of $200,000 and is taxed at a rate of 40%. In an effort to determine the optimal capital structure, the firm has assembled data on the cost of debt, the number of shares of common stock for various levels of indebtedness, and the overall required return on investment:

Capital structure debt ratio	Cost of debt, r_d	No. of common stock shares	Required return, r_s
0%	0%	200,000	12%
15	8	170,000	13
30	9	140,000	14
45	12	110,000	16
60	15	80,000	20

a. Calculate *earnings per share* for each level of indebtedness.
b. Use Equation 12.12 and the earnings per share calculated in part **a** to calculate a *price per share* for each level of indebtedness.
c. Choose the optimal capital structure. Justify your choice.

P12–25 **Integrative—Optimal capital structure**   Nelson Corporation has made the following forecast of sales, with the associated probabilities of occurrence noted.

Sales	Probability
$200,000	.20
300,000	.60
400,000	.20

The company has fixed operating costs of $100,000 per year, and variable operating costs represent 40% of sales. The existing capital structure consists of 25,000 shares of common stock that have a $10 per share book value. No other capital items are outstanding. The marketplace has assigned the following required returns to risky earnings per share.

Coefficient of variation of EPS	Estimated required return, r_s
0.43	15%
0.47	16
0.51	17
0.56	18
0.60	22
0.64	24

The company is contemplating *shifting its capital structure* by substituting debt in the capital structure for common stock. The three different debt ratios under consideration are shown in the following table, along with an estimate, for each ratio, of the corresponding required interest rate on *all* debt.

Debt ratio	Interest rate on *all* debt
20%	10%
40	12
60	14

The tax rate is 40%. The market value of the equity for a leveraged firm can be found by using the simplified method (see Equation 12.12).
a. Calculate the expected earnings per share (EPS), the standard deviation of EPS, and the coefficient of variation of EPS for the three proposed capital structures.
b. Determine the *optimal capital structure*, assuming (1) maximization of earnings per share and (2) maximization of share value.
c. Construct a graph (similar to Figure 12.7) showing the relationships in part **b**. (*Note:* You will probably have to sketch the lines, because you have only three data points.)

   P12–26 **Integrative—Optimal capital structure**   The board of directors of Morales Publishing, Inc., has commissioned a capital structure study. The company has total assets of $40,000,000. It has earnings before interest and taxes of $8,000,000 and is taxed at a rate of 40%.

a. Create a spreadsheet like the one in Table 12.10 showing values of debt and equity as well as the total number of shares, assuming a book value of $25 per share.

% Debt	Total assets	$ Debt	$ Equity	No. of shares @ $25
0%	$40,000,000	$_____	$_____	_____
10	40,000,000	_____	_____	_____
20	40,000,000	_____	_____	_____
30	40,000,000	_____	_____	_____
40	40,000,000	_____	_____	_____
50	40,000,000	_____	_____	_____
60	40,000,000	_____	_____	_____

b. Given the before-tax cost of debt at various levels of indebtedness, calculate the yearly interest expenses.

% Debt	$ Total debt	Before-tax cost of debt, r_d	$ Interest expense
0%	$_____	0.0%	$_____
10	_____	7.5	_____
20	_____	8.0	_____
30	_____	9.0	_____
40	_____	11.0	_____
50	_____	12.5	_____
60	_____	15.5	_____

c. Using EBIT of $8,000,000, a 40% tax rate, and the information developed in parts **a** and **b,** calculate the most likely earnings per share for the firm at various levels of indebtedness. Mark the level of indebtedness that maximizes EPS.

% Debt	EBIT	Interest expense	EBT	Taxes	Net income	No. of shares	EPS
0%	$8,000,000	_____	_____	_____	_____	_____	_____
10	8,000,000	_____	_____	_____	_____	_____	_____
20	8,000,000	_____	_____	_____	_____	_____	_____
30	8,000,000	_____	_____	_____	_____	_____	_____
40	8,000,000	_____	_____	_____	_____	_____	_____
50	8,000,000	_____	_____	_____	_____	_____	_____
60	8,000,000	_____	_____	_____	_____	_____	_____

d. Using the EPS developed in part **c,** the estimates of required return, r_s, and Equation 12.12, estimate the value per share at various levels of indebtedness. Mark the level of indebtedness in the table on page 594 that results in the maximum price per share, P_0.

Debt	EPS	r_s	P_0
0%	_____	10.0%	_____
10	_____	10.3	_____
20	_____	10.9	_____
30	_____	11.4	_____
40	_____	12.6	_____
50	_____	14.8	_____
60	_____	17.5	_____

e. Prepare a recommendation to the board of directors of Morales Publishing that specifies the degree of indebtedness that will accomplish the firm's goal of optimizing shareholder wealth. Use your findings in parts **a** through **d** to justify your recommendation.

P12–27 **Integrative—Optimal capital structure** Country Textiles, which has fixed operating costs of $300,000 and variable operating costs equal to 40% of sales, has made the following three sales estimates, with their probabilities noted.

Sales	Probability
$ 600,000	.30
900,000	.40
1,200,000	.30

The firm wishes to analyze five possible capital structures—0%, 15%, 30%, 45%, and 60% debt ratios. The firm's total assets of $1 million are assumed to be constant. Its common stock has a book value of $25 per share, and the firm is in the 40% tax bracket. The following additional data have been gathered for use in analyzing the five capital structures under consideration.

Capital structure debt ratio	Before-tax cost of debt, r_d	Required return, r_s
0%	0.0%	10.0%
15	8.0	10.5
30	10.0	11.6
45	13.0	14.0
60	17.0	20.0

a. Calculate the level of EBIT associated with each of the three levels of sales.
b. Calculate the amount of debt, the amount of equity, and the number of shares of common stock outstanding for each of the five capital structures being considered.
c. Calculate the annual interest on the debt under each of the five capital structures being considered. (*Note:* The before-tax cost of debt, r_d, is the interest rate applicable to *all* debt associated with the corresponding debt ratio.)
d. Calculate the EPS associated with each of the three levels of EBIT calculated in part **a** for each of the five capital structures being considered.
e. Calculate (1) the expected EPS, (2) the standard deviation of EPS, and (3) the coefficient of variation of EPS for each of the five capital structures, using your findings in part **d**.

f. Plot the expected EPS and coefficient of variation of EPS against the capital structures (*x* axis) on separate sets of axes, and comment on the return and risk relative to capital structure.

g. Using the EBIT–EPS data developed in part **d,** plot the 0%, 30%, and 60% capital structures on the same set of EBIT–EPS axes, and discuss the ranges over which each is preferred. What is the major problem with the use of this approach?

h. Using the valuation model given in Equation 12.12 and your findings in part **e,** estimate the share value for each of the capital structures being considered.

i. Compare and contrast your findings in parts **f** and **h.** Which structure is preferred if the goal is to *maximize EPS?* Which structure is preferred if the goal is to *maximize share value?* Which capital structure do you recommend? Explain.

 P12–28 **ETHICS PROBLEM**   "Information asymmetry lies at the heart of the ethical dilemma that managers, stockholders, and bondholders confront when companies initiate management buyouts or swap debt for equity." Comment on this statement. What steps might a board of directors take to ensure that the company's actions are ethical to all parties?

Chapter 12 Case

Evaluating Tampa Manufacturing's Capital Structure

Tampa Manufacturing, an established producer of printing equipment, expects its sales to remain flat for the next 3 to 5 years because of both a weak economic outlook and an expectation of little new printing technology development over that period. On the basis of this scenario, the firm's board has instructed its management to institute programs that will allow it to operate more efficiently, earn higher profits, and, most important, maximize share value. In this regard, the firm's chief financial officer (CFO), Jon Lawson, has been charged with evaluating the firm's capital structure. Lawson believes that the current capital structure, which contains 10% debt and 90% equity, may lack adequate financial leverage. To evaluate the firm's capital structure, Lawson has gathered the data summarized in the following table on the current capital structure (10% debt ratio) and two alternative capital structures—A (30% debt ratio) and B (50% debt ratio)—that he would like to consider.

| | Capital structure[a] | | |
| | Current (10% debt) | A (30% debt) | B (50% debt) |
Source of capital			
Long-term debt	$1,000,000	$3,000,000	$5,000,000
Coupon interest rate[b]	9%	10%	12%
Common stock	100,000 shares	70,000 shares	40,000 shares
Required return on equity, r_s[c]	12%	13%	18%

[a]These structures are based on maintaining the firm's current level of $10,000,000 of total financing.
[b]Interest rate applicable to *all* debt.
[c]Market-based return for the given level of risk.

Lawson expects the firm's earnings before interest and taxes (EBIT) to remain at its current level of $1,200,000. The firm has a 40% tax rate.

To Do

a. Use the current level of EBIT to calculate the times interest earned ratio for each capital structure. Evaluate the current and two alternative capital structures using the times interest earned and debt ratios.

b. Prepare a single EBIT–EPS graph showing the current and two alternative capital structures.

c. On the basis of the graph in part **b,** which capital structure will maximize Tampa's earnings per share (EPS) at its expected level of EBIT of $1,200,000? Why might this *not* be the best capital structure?

d. Using the zero-growth valuation model given in Equation 12.12, find the market value of Tampa's equity under each of the three capital structures at the $1,200,000 level of expected EBIT.

e. On the basis of your findings in parts **c** and **d,** which capital structure would you recommend? Why?

Spreadsheet Exercise

Starstruck Company would like to determine its optimal capital structure. Several of its managers believe that the best method is to rely on the estimated earnings per share (EPS) of the firm, because they feel that profits and stock price are closely related. The financial managers have suggested another method that uses estimated required returns to estimate the share value of the firm. The following financial data are available.

Capital structure debt ratio	Estimated EPS	Estimated required return
0%	$1.75	11.40%
10	1.90	11.80
20	2.25	12.50
30	2.55	13.25
40	3.18	18.00
50	3.06	19.00
60	3.10	25.00

To Do

a. Based upon the given financial data, create a spreadsheet to calculate the estimated share values associated with the seven alternative capital structures. Refer to Table 12.15 in the text (or view it at **www.prenhall.com/gitman**).

b. Use Excel to graph the relationship between capital structure and the estimated EPS of the firm. What is the optimal debt ratio? Refer to Figure 12.7 in the text (or view it at **www.prenhall.com/gitman**).

    c. Use Excel to graph the relationship between capital structure and the estimated share value of the firm. What is the optimal debt ratio? Refer to Figure 12.7 in the text (or view it at **www.prenhall.com/gitman**).

    d. Do both methods lead to the same *optimal capital structure?* Which method do you favor? Explain.

    e. What is the major difference between the EPS and share value methods?

Group Exercise

This chapter continues the valuation process of the firm by investigating different types of leverage in conjunction with the capital structure. Here the analysis begins by bringing in the income statement to broaden the methodology introduced in Chapter 11. Your group will continue to combine data for your shadow and fictitious firm.

To Do

    a. Return to your shadow firm and view its most recent income statement. Identify the important measures used in reporting leverage including EBIT and fixed and variable operating costs.

    b. Use your shadow firm's information to design a similar set of numbers for your fictitious firm. Assign a simple per-unit price for your product.

    c. Calculate the *operating breakeven point* for your firm. Create a simple graph for sales revenue and total operating costs, highlighting the breakeven sales level in units.

    d. Calculate the *degree of operating leverage* for your fictitious firm at a base sales level.

    e. Return to your shadow firm and calculate its *degree of financial leverage* at its current levels of EBIT and EPS. Likewise, calculate your shadow firm's *degree of total leverage* at current sales and EPS levels.

    f. Use Equation 12.11 to value your shadow firm. Use estimates for your firm's weighted average cost of capital. Do the same for your fictitious firm, using the numbers you assigned in Chapter 11's exercise.

Web Exercise

Go to the book's companion website at **www.prenhall.com/gitman** to find the Web Exercise for this chapter.

> Remember to check the book's website at **www.prenhall.com/gitman** to find additional resources, including Web Exercises and a Web Case.

13 | Dividend Policy

WHY THIS CHAPTER MATTERS TO YOU

In Your Professional Life

Accounting: You need to understand the types of dividends and payment procedures for them because you will need to record and report the declaration and payment of dividends; you also will provide the financial data that management must have to make dividend decisions.

Information systems: You need to understand types of dividends, payment procedures, and the financial data that the firm must have to make and implement dividend decisions.

Management: To make appropriate dividend decisions for the firm, you need to understand types of dividends, arguments about the relevance of dividends, the factors that affect dividend policy, and types of dividend policies.

Marketing: You need to understand factors affecting dividend policy because you may want to argue that the firm would be better off retaining funds for use in new marketing programs or products, rather than paying them out as dividends.

Operations: You need to understand factors affecting dividend policy because you may find that the firm's dividend policy imposes limitations on planned expansion, replacement, or renewal projects.

In Your Personal Life

Many individual investors buy common stock for the anticipated cash dividends. From a personal finance perspective, you should understand why and how firms pay dividends and the informational and financial implications of receiving them. Such understanding will help you select common stocks that have dividend-paying patterns consistent with your long-term financial goals.

LEARNING GOALS

LG 1 Understand cash dividend payment procedures, the tax treatment of dividends, and the role of dividend reinvestment plans.

LG 2 Describe the residual theory of dividends and the key arguments with regard to dividend irrelevance and relevance.

LG 3 Discuss the key factors involved in establishing a dividend policy.

LG 4 Review and evaluate the three basic types of dividend policies.

LG 5 Evaluate stock dividends from accounting, shareholder, and company points of view.

LG 6 Explain stock splits and stock repurchases and the firm's motivation for undertaking each of them.

Microsoft Corporation

Giving Back to the Shareholders

Can a company have too much cash? For years since its founding in 1975 **Microsoft Corporation** had paid no dividends. With assets in cash and short-term investments of over $49 billion, the company was faced with a decision of how to deploy that capital. Finally, in 2003, recognizing that it was no longer a young, fast-growing company that needed every penny for growth, the company dipped its toe into the dividend waters, issuing an annual dividend of $0.08 per share, which it increased to $0.16 per share for 2004.

As profits and cash continued to pile up, Microsoft began to encounter investor frustration. On July 20, 2004, Microsoft's board of directors approved an $0.08 per share quarterly dividend, a 4-year $30 billion stock buyback, and a one-time special dividend of $3 per share. Under the plan, the company would change its $0.16 per share annual dividend to a quarterly dividend of $0.08 per share, essentially doubling the annual dividend payout to $3.5 billion. The cost of the $3 special dividend would be about $32 billion, given the nearly 10.8 billion shares outstanding in mid-2004.

In 2005, Microsoft changed its regular dividend payout to the more typical quarterly payout structure. The company's current dividend policy is that "the Board will continue to evaluate whether to pay a dividend on a quarterly basis and will base its decisions on the Company's potential future long-term capital requirements relating to research and development, investments and acquisitions, dilution management, and legal and business risks faced by the company."

Maintaining its dividend policy is not the only way that Microsoft has returned money to its shareholders. In 2006, the company embarked on another stock repurchase program that could total $40 billion by 2010.

Microsoft has spent cash for regular dividends, a special dividend, and stock buybacks. As you read this chapter ponder this question: From the shareholders' viewpoint, what value have they received from each of the three cash disbursements (regular, special dividends, stock repurchases)?

Some stockholders want and expect to receive dividends, whereas others would rather see those funds invested in the company to increase its stock price. This chapter addresses the issue of whether dividends matter to stockholders. We'll also describe the key factors involved in setting a firm's dividend policy, the different types of dividend policies (constant-payout-ratio, regular, and low-regular-and-extra), and other decisions regarding stock dividends and stock repurchases.

599

13.1 | Dividend Fundamentals

Expected cash dividends are the key return variable from which owners and investors determine share value. They represent a source of cash flow to stockholders and provide information about the firm's current and future performance. Because **retained earnings,** earnings not distributed to owners as dividends, are a form of *internal* financing, the dividend decision can significantly affect the firm's *external* financing requirements. In other words, if the firm needs financing, the larger the cash dividend paid, the greater the amount of financing it must raise externally through borrowing or through the sale of common or preferred stock. (Remember that although dividends are charged to retained earnings, they are actually paid out of cash.) The first thing to know about cash dividends is the procedures for paying them.

retained earnings
Earnings not distributed to owners as dividends; a form of *internal* financing.

Cash Dividend Payment Procedures

At quarterly or semiannual meetings, a firm's board of directors decides whether and in what amount to pay cash dividends to corporate stockholders. The past period's financial performance and future outlook, as well as recent dividends paid, are key inputs to the dividend decision. The payment date of the cash dividend, if one is declared, must also be established.

Amount of Dividends

Whether dividends should be paid, and if so, in what amount, are important decisions that depend primarily on the firm's dividend policy. Most firms have a set policy with respect to the periodic dividend, but the firm's directors can change this amount, largely on the basis of significant increases or decreases in earnings.

Relevant Dates

If the directors of the firm declare a dividend, they also typically issue a statement indicating the dividend decision, the record date, and the payment date. This statement is generally quoted in the *Wall Street Journal* and other financial news media.

date of record (dividends)
Set by the firm's directors, the date on which all persons whose names are recorded as stockholders receive a declared dividend at a specified future time.

Record Date   All persons whose names are recorded as stockholders on the **date of record** set by the directors receive a declared dividend at a specified future time. These stockholders are often referred to as *holders of record.*

Because of the time needed to make bookkeeping entries when a stock is traded, the stock begins selling **ex dividend** 2 *business days* prior to the date of record. Purchasers of a stock selling ex dividend do not receive the current dividend. A simple way to determine the first day on which the stock sells ex dividend is to subtract 2 days from the date of record; if a weekend intervenes, subtract 4 days. Ignoring general market fluctuations, the stock's price is expected to drop by the amount of the declared dividend on the ex dividend date.

ex dividend
Period, beginning 2 *business days* prior to the date of record, during which a stock is sold without the right to receive the current dividend.

payment date
Set by the firm's directors, the actual date on which the firm mails the dividend payment to the holders of record.

Payment Date   The **payment date,** also set by the directors, is the actual date on which the firm mails the dividend payment to the holders of record. It is generally a few weeks after the record date. An example will clarify the various dates and the accounting effects.

Example

At the quarterly dividend meeting of Rudolf Company, a distributor of office products, held on June 10, the directors declared an $0.80-per-share cash dividend for holders of record on Friday, July 2. The firm had 100,000 shares of common stock outstanding. The payment date for the dividend was Monday, August 2. Figure 13.1 shows a time line depicting the key dates relative to the Rudolf Company's dividend. Before the dividend was declared, the key accounts of the firm were as follows:

Cash	$200,000	Dividends payable	$ 0
		Retained earnings	1,000,000

When the dividend was announced by the directors, $80,000 of the retained earnings ($0.80 per share × 100,000 shares) was transferred to the dividends payable account. The key accounts thus became

Cash	$200,000	Dividends payable	$ 80,000
		Retained earnings	920,000

Rudolf Company's stock began selling ex dividend 2 *business days* prior to the date of record, which was Wednesday, June 30. This date was found by subtracting 2 days from the July 2 date of record. Purchasers of Rudolf's stock on Tuesday, June 29 or earlier received the rights to the dividends; those who purchased the stock on or after June 30 did not. Assuming a stable market, Rudolf's stock price was expected to drop by approximately $0.80 per share when it began selling ex dividend on June 30. On August 2 the firm mailed dividend checks to the holders of record as of July 2. This produced the following balances in the key accounts of the firm:

Cash	$120,000	Dividends payable	$ 0
		Retained earnings	920,000

The net effect of declaring and paying the dividend was to reduce the firm's total assets (and stockholders' equity) by $80,000.

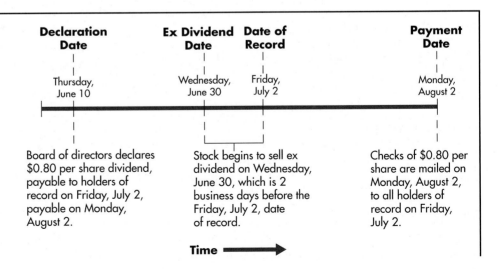

FIGURE 13.1

Dividend Payment Time Line
Time line for the announcement and payment of a cash dividend for Rudolf Company

Tax Treatment of Dividends

The *Jobs and Growth Tax Relief Reconciliation Act of 2003* significantly changed the tax treatment of corporate dividends for most taxpayers. Prior to passage of the 2003 law, dividends received by investors were taxed as ordinary income at rates as high as 35 percent. The 2003 act reduced the tax rate on corporate dividends for most taxpayers to the tax rate applicable to capital gains, which is a maximum rate of 5 percent to 15 percent, depending on the taxpayer's tax bracket. This change significantly diminishes the degree of "double taxation" of dividends, which results when the corporation is first taxed on its income and then when the investor who receives the dividend is also taxed on it. After-tax cash flow to dividend recipients is much greater at the lower applicable tax rate; the result is noticeably higher dividend payouts by corporations today than prior to passage of the 2003 legislation. (For more details on the impact of the 2003 act, see the *Focus on Practice* box below.)

(**Focus on Practice**)   **Capital Gains and Dividend Tax Treatment Extended to 2010**

IN PRACTICE

In 1980, the percentage of firms paying monthly, quarterly, semi-annual, or annual dividends stood at 60 percent. By the end of 2002, this percentage had declined to 20 percent. In May 2003, President George W. Bush signed into law the *Jobs and Growth Tax Relief Reconciliation Act of 2003* (JGTRRA). Prior to that new law, dividends were taxed once as part of corporate earnings, and again as the personal income of the investor, in both cases with a potential top rate of 35 percent. The result was an effective tax rate of 57.75 percent on some dividends. Though the 2003 tax law did not completely eliminate the double taxation of dividends, it reduced the maximum possible effect of the double taxation of dividends to 44.75 percent. For taxpayers in the lower tax brackets, the combined effect was a maximum of 38.25 percent.

Both the number of companies paying dividends and the amount of dividends spiked following the lowering of tax rates on dividends. S&P 500 dividends rose at an 11 percent compound annual rate from 2002 to 2005, a major increase over the prior 10 years when dividends grew at only a 2 percent annual pace, according to Goldman Sachs.

The tax rates under JGTRRA were originally programmed to expire at the end of 2008. However, in May 2006, Congress passed the *Tax Increase Prevention and Reconciliation Act of 2005* (TIPRA), extending the beneficial tax rates for 2 more years. Taxpayers in tax brackets above 15 percent pay a 15 percent rate on dividends paid before December 31, 2008. For taxpayers with a marginal tax rate of 15 percent or lower, the dividend tax rate is 5 percent until December 31, 2007, and 0 percent from 2008 to 2010. Long-term capital gains tax rates were reduced to the same rates as the new dividend tax rates through 2010. Pre-JGTRRA taxation of dividends reappears in 2011, unless further legislation makes the law permanent.

The reduction of the tax burden on dividends has two potential benefits. First, the equalization of the tax treatment of dividends and capital gains allows corporations to base their payout policies on the economic value of a decision, not the tax consequences. And second, if corporations increase their dividend payouts, lower cash reserves will force managers to undertake only the most productive internal investments. In addition, the regular payment of quarterly dividends can be paid only out of earnings or cash reserves that actually exist, which promotes honest accounting practices.

■ *How might the expected future reappearance of higher tax rates on individuals receiving dividends affect corporate dividend payout policies?*

Personal Finance Example   The board of directors of Espinoza Industries, Inc., on October 4 of the current year, declared a quarterly dividend of $0.46 per share payable to all holders of record on Friday, October 30. They set a payment date of November 19. Rob and Kate Heckman, who purchased 500 shares of Espinoza's common stock on Thursday, October 15, wish to determine whether they will receive the recently declared dividend and, if so, when and how much they would net after taxes from the dividend given that the dividends would be subject to a 15% federal income tax.

Given the Friday, October 30, date of record, the stock would begin selling *ex dividend* 2 business days earlier on Wednesday, October 28. Purchasers of the stock on or before Tuesday, October 27, would receive the right to the dividend. Because the Heckmans purchased the stock on October 15, they would be eligible to receive the dividend of $0.46 per share. Thus, the Heckmans will receive $230 in dividends ($0.46 per share × 500 shares), which will be mailed to them on the November 19 payment date. Because they are subject to a 15% federal income tax on the dividends, the Heckmans will net $195.50 [(1 − 0.15) × $230] after taxes from the Espinoza Industries dividend.

Dividend Reinvestment Plans

dividend reinvestment plans (DRIPs)
Plans that enable stockholders to use dividends received on the firm's stock to acquire additional shares—even fractional shares—at little or no transaction cost.

Today many firms offer **dividend reinvestment plans (DRIPs),** which enable stockholders to use dividends received on the firm's stock to acquire additional shares—even fractional shares—at little or no transaction cost. Some companies even allow investors to make their *initial purchases* of the firm's stock directly from the company without going through a broker. With DRIPs, plan participants typically can acquire shares at about 5 percent below the prevailing market price. From its point of view, the firm can issue new shares to participants more economically, avoiding the underpricing and flotation costs that would accompany the public sale of new shares. Clearly, the existence of a DRIP may enhance the market appeal of a firm's shares.

REVIEW QUESTIONS

13–1 Who are *holders of record?* When does a stock sell *ex dividend?*

13–2 What effect did the *Jobs and Growth Tax Relief Reconciliation Act of 2003* have on the taxation of corporate dividends? On corporate dividend payouts?

13–3 What benefit is available to participants in a *dividend reinvestment plan?* How might the firm benefit?

13.2 | Relevance of Dividend Policy

The financial literature has reported numerous theories and empirical findings concerning dividend policy. Although this research provides some interesting insights about dividend policy, capital budgeting and capital structure decisions are generally considered far more important than dividend decisions. In other words, firms should not sacrifice good investment and financing decisions for a dividend policy of questionable importance.

A number of key questions have yet to be resolved: Does dividend policy matter? What effect does dividend policy have on share price? Is there a model that can be used to evaluate alternative dividend policies in view of share value? Here we begin by describing the residual theory of dividends, which is used as a backdrop for discussion of the key arguments in support of dividend irrelevance and then those in support of dividend relevance.

Residual Theory of Dividends

residual theory of dividends
A school of thought that suggests that the dividend paid by a firm should be viewed as a *residual*—the amount left over after all acceptable investment opportunities have been undertaken.

The **residual theory of dividends** is a school of thought that suggests that the dividend paid by a firm should be viewed as a *residual*—the amount left over after all acceptable investment opportunities have been undertaken. Using this approach, the firm would treat the dividend decision in three steps, as follows:

Step 1   Determine its optimal level of capital expenditures, which would be the level generated by the point of intersection of the investment opportunities schedule (IOS) and weighted marginal cost of capital (WMCC) schedule (see Chapter 11).

Step 2   Using the optimal capital structure proportions (see Chapter 12), estimate the total amount of equity financing needed to support the expenditures generated in Step 1.

Step 3   Because the cost of retained earnings, r_r, is less than the cost of new common stock, r_n, use retained earnings to meet the equity requirement determined in Step 2. If retained earnings are inadequate to meet this need, sell new common stock. If the available retained earnings are in excess of this need, distribute the surplus amount—the residual—as dividends.

According to this approach, as long as the firm's equity need exceeds the amount of retained earnings, no cash dividend is paid. The argument for this approach is that it is sound management to be certain that the company has the money it needs to compete effectively. This view of dividends suggests that the required return of investors, r_s, is *not* influenced by the firm's dividend policy—a premise that in turn implies that dividend policy is irrelevant.

Example   Overbrook Industries, a manufacturer of canoes and other small watercraft, has available from the current period's operations $1.8 million that can be retained or paid out in dividends. The firm's optimal capital structure is at a debt ratio of 30%, which represents 30% debt and 70% equity. Figure 13.2 depicts the firm's weighted marginal cost of capital (WMCC) schedule along with three investment opportunities schedules. For each IOS, the level of total new financing or investment determined by the point of intersection of the IOS and the WMCC has been noted. For IOS_1, it is $1.5 million, for IOS_2 $2.4 million, and for IOS_3 $3.2 million. Although only one IOS will exist in practice, it is useful to look at the possible dividend decisions generated by applying the residual theory in each of the three cases. Table 13.1 summarizes this analysis.

FIGURE 13.2

WMCC and IOSs
WMCC and IOSs for
Overbrook Industries

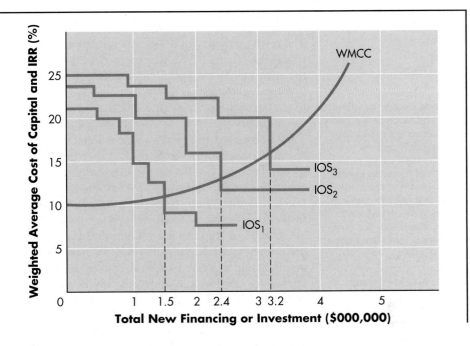

TABLE 13.1 **Applying the Residual Theory of Dividends to Overbrook Industries for Each of Three IOSs (Shown in Figure 13.2)**

	Investment opportunities schedules		
Item	IOS_1	IOS_2	IOS_3
(1) New financing or investment (Fig. 13.2)	$1,500,000	$2,400,000	$3,200,000
(2) Retained earnings available (given)	$1,800,000	$1,800,000	$1,800,000
(3) Equity needed [70% × (1)]	1,050,000	1,680,000	2,240,000
(4) Dividends [(2) − (3)]	$ 750,000	$ 120,000	$ 0[a]
(5) Dividend payout ratio [(4) ÷ (2)]	41.7%	6.7%	0%

[a]In this case, additional new common stock in the amount of $440,000 ($2,240,000 needed − $1,800,000 available) would have to be sold; no dividends would be paid.

Table 13.1 shows that if IOS_1 exists, the firm will pay out $750,000 in dividends, because only $1,050,000 of the $1,800,000 of available earnings is needed. A 41.7% payout ratio results. For IOS_2, dividends of $120,000 (a payout ratio of 6.7%) result. Should IOS_3 exist, the firm would pay no dividends (a 0% payout ratio), because its retained earnings of $1,800,000 would be less than the $2,240,000 of equity needed. In this case, the firm would have to obtain additional new common stock financing to meet the new requirements generated by the intersection of the IOS_3 and WMCC. Depending on which IOS exists, the firm's dividend would in effect be the residual, if any, remaining after all acceptable investments had been financed.

Arguments for Dividend Irrelevance

The residual theory of dividends implies that if the firm cannot invest its earnings to earn a return (IRR) that is in excess of cost (WMCC), it should distribute the earnings by paying dividends to stockholders. This approach suggests that dividends represent an earnings residual rather than an active decision variable that affects the firm's value. Such a view is consistent with the **dividend irrelevance theory** put forth by Merton H. Miller and Franco Modigliani (M and M).[1] They argue that the firm's value is determined solely by the earning power and risk of its assets (investments) and that the manner in which it splits its earnings stream between dividends and internally retained (and reinvested) funds does not affect this value. M and M's theory suggests that in a perfect world (certainty, no taxes, no transactions costs, and no other market imperfections), the value of the firm is unaffected by the distribution of dividends.

However, studies have shown that large changes in dividends do affect share price. Increases in dividends result in increased share price, and decreases in dividends result in decreased share price. In response, M and M argue that these effects are attributable not to the dividend itself but rather to the **informational content** of dividends with respect to future earnings. In other words, say M and M, it is not the preference of shareholders for current dividends (rather than future capital gains) that is responsible for this behavior. Instead, investors view a change in dividends, up or down, as a *signal* that management expects future earnings to change in the same direction. Investors view an increase in dividends as a *positive signal,* and they bid up the share price. They view a decrease in dividends as a *negative signal* that causes a decrease in share price as investors sell their shares.

M and M further argue that a **clientele effect** exists: A firm attracts shareholders whose preferences for the payment and stability of dividends correspond to the firm's actual payment pattern and stability of dividends. Investors who desire stable dividends as a source of income hold the stock of firms that pay about the same dividend amount each period. Investors who prefer to earn capital gains are more attracted to growing firms that reinvest a large portion of their earnings, favoring growth over a stable pattern of dividends. Because the shareholders get what they expect, M and M argue, the value of their firm's stock is unaffected by dividend policy.

In summary, M and M and other proponents of dividend irrelevance argue that, all else being equal, an investor's required return—and therefore the value of the firm—is unaffected by dividend policy for three reasons:

1. The firm's value is determined solely by the earning power and risk of its assets (investments).
2. If dividends do affect value, they do so solely because of their *informational content,* which signals management's earnings expectations.
3. A *clientele effect* exists that causes a firm's shareholders to receive the dividends they expect.

These views of M and M with respect to dividend irrelevance are consistent with the residual theory, which focuses on making the best investment decisions to maximize share value. The proponents of dividend irrelevance conclude that because dividends are irrelevant to a firm's value, the firm does not need to have

---

1. Merton H. Miller and Franco Modigliani, "Dividend Policy, Growth and the Valuation of Shares," *Journal of Business* 34 (October 1961), pp. 411–433.

a dividend policy. Although many research studies have been performed to validate or refute the dividend irrelevance theory, none has been successful in providing irrefutable evidence.

Arguments for Dividend Relevance

dividend relevance theory
The theory, advanced by Gordon and Lintner, that there is a direct relationship between a firm's dividend policy and its market value.

bird-in-the-hand argument
The belief, in support of *dividend relevance theory*, that investors see current dividends as less risky than future dividends or capital gains.

The key argument in support of **dividend relevance theory** is attributed to Myron J. Gordon and John Lintner,[2] who suggest that there is, in fact, a direct relationship between the firm's dividend policy and its market value. Fundamental to this proposition is their **bird-in-the-hand argument**, which suggests that investors see current dividends as less risky than future dividends or capital gains. "A bird in the hand is worth two in the bush." Gordon and Lintner argue that current dividend payments reduce investor uncertainty, causing investors to discount the firm's earnings at a lower rate and, all else being equal, to place a higher value on the firm's stock. Conversely, if dividends are reduced or are not paid, investor uncertainty will increase, raising the required return and lowering the stock's value.

Although many other arguments related to dividend relevance have been put forward, *empirical studies fail to provide conclusive evidence in support of the intuitively appealing dividend relevance argument.* In practice, however, the actions of both financial managers and stockholders tend to support the belief that dividend policy does affect stock value.[3] Because we focus on the day-to-day behavior of firms, the remainder of this chapter is consistent with the belief that *dividends are relevant*—that each firm must develop a dividend policy that fulfills the goals of its owners and maximizes their wealth as reflected in the firm's share price.

REVIEW QUESTIONS

13–4 Does following the *residual theory of dividends* lead to a stable dividend? Is this approach consistent with dividend relevance?

13–5 Contrast the basic arguments about dividend policy advanced by Miller and Modigliani (M and M) and by Gordon and Lintner.

13.3 | Factors Affecting Dividend Policy

dividend policy
The firm's plan of action to be followed whenever it makes a dividend decision.

The firm's **dividend policy** represents a plan of action to be followed whenever it makes a dividend decision. Firms develop policies consistent with their goals. Before we review some of the popular types of dividend policies, we discuss six factors that firms consider in establishing a dividend policy. They are legal constraints, contractual constraints, internal constraints, the firm's growth prospects, owner considerations, and market considerations.

2. Myron J. Gordon, "Optimal Investment and Financing Policy," *Journal of Finance* 18 (May 1963), pp. 264–272, and John Lintner, "Dividends, Earnings, Leverage, Stock Prices, and the Supply of Capital to Corporations," *Review of Economics and Statistics* 44 (August 1962), pp. 243–269.

3. A common exception is small firms, because they frequently treat dividends as a residual remaining after all acceptable investments have been initiated. Small firms follow this course of action because they usually do not have ready access to capital markets. The use of retained earnings therefore is a key source of financing for growth, which is generally an important goal of a small firm.

Legal Constraints

Most states prohibit corporations from paying out as cash dividends any portion of the firm's "legal capital," which is typically measured by the par value of common stock. Other states define legal capital to include not only the par value of the common stock, but also any paid-in capital in excess of par. These *capital impairment restrictions* are generally established to provide a sufficient equity base to protect creditors' claims. An example will clarify the differing definitions of capital.

Example

The stockholders' equity account of Miller Flour Company, a large grain processor, is presented in the following table.

Miller Flour Company Stockholders' Equity	
Common stock at par	$100,000
Paid-in capital in excess of par	200,000
Retained earnings	140,000
Total stockholders' equity	$440,000

In states where the firm's legal capital is defined as the par value of its common stock, the firm could pay out $340,000 ($200,000 + $140,000) in cash dividends without impairing its capital. In states where the firm's legal capital includes all paid-in capital, the firm could pay out only $140,000 in cash dividends.

Firms sometimes impose an earnings requirement limiting the amount of dividends. With this restriction, the firm cannot pay more in cash dividends than the sum of its most recent and past retained earnings. However, *the firm is not prohibited from paying more in dividends than its current earnings.*[4]

Example

excess earnings accumulation tax
The tax the IRS levies on retained earnings above $250,000 for most businesses when it determines that the firm has accumulated an excess of earnings to allow owners to delay paying ordinary income taxes on dividends received.

Assume that Miller Flour Company, from the preceding example, in the year just ended has $30,000 in earnings available for common stock dividends. As the preceding table indicates, the firm has past retained earnings of $140,000. Thus it can legally pay dividends of up to $170,000.

If a firm has overdue liabilities or is legally insolvent or bankrupt, most states prohibit its payment of cash dividends. In addition, the Internal Revenue Service prohibits firms from accumulating earnings to reduce the owners' taxes. If the IRS can determine that a firm has accumulated an excess of earnings to allow owners to delay paying ordinary income taxes on dividends received, it may levy an **excess earnings accumulation tax** on any retained earnings above $250,000 for most businesses.

---

4. A firm that has an operating loss in the current period can still pay cash dividends as long as sufficient retained earnings against which to charge the dividend are available and, of course, as long as it has the cash with which to make the payments.

Contractual Constraints

Often the firm's ability to pay cash dividends is constrained by restrictive provisions in a loan agreement. Generally, these constraints prohibit the payment of cash dividends until the firm achieves a certain level of earnings, or they may limit dividends to a certain dollar amount or percentage of earnings. Constraints on dividends help to protect creditors from losses due to the firm's insolvency.

Internal Constraints

The firm's ability to pay cash dividends is generally constrained by the amount of liquid assets (cash and marketable securities) available. Although it is possible for a firm to borrow funds to pay dividends, lenders are generally reluctant to make such loans because they produce no tangible or operating benefits that will help the firm repay the loan.

Example

Miller Flour Company's stockholders' equity account, presented earlier, indicates that if the firm's legal capital is defined as all paid-in capital, the firm can pay $140,000 in dividends. If the firm has total liquid assets of $50,000 ($20,000 in cash plus marketable securities worth $30,000) and it needs $35,000 of this for operations, the maximum cash dividend the firm can pay is $15,000 ($50,000 − $35,000).

Growth Prospects

Hint Firms that grow very rapidly, such as high-tech firms, cannot afford to pay dividends. Their stockholders are influenced by the possibility of exceptionally higher share price and dividend levels in the future.

The firm's financial requirements are directly related to how much it expects to grow and what assets it will need to acquire. It must evaluate its profitability and risk to develop insight into its ability to raise capital externally. In addition, the firm must determine the cost and speed with which it can obtain financing. Generally, a large, mature firm has adequate access to new capital, whereas a rapidly growing firm may not have sufficient funds available to support its acceptable projects. A growth firm is likely to have to depend heavily on internal financing through retained earnings, so it is likely to pay out only a very small percentage of its earnings as dividends. A more established firm is in a better position to pay out a large proportion of its earnings, particularly if it has ready sources of financing.

Owner Considerations[5]

The firm must establish a policy that has a favorable effect on the wealth of the *majority* of owners. One consideration is the *tax status of a firm's owners*. If a firm has a large percentage of wealthy stockholders who have sizable incomes, it

---

5. Theoretically, in an *efficient market,* owner considerations are automatically handled by the pricing mechanism. The logic is as follows. A firm that pays a dividend that is smaller than required by a large number of owners will experience a decline in price because the dissatisfied shareholders will sell their shares. The resulting drop in share price will (as explained in Chapter 7) raise the expected return to investors, which will cause the firm's WMCC to rise. As a result—all else being equal—the firm's optimal capital budget will become smaller, and the demand for retained earnings will fall. This decrease should allow the firm to satisfy shareholders by paying the larger dividends that they demand. In spite of this logic, it is helpful to understand some of the important considerations underlying owner behavior.

may decide to pay out a *lower* percentage of its earnings to allow the owners to delay the payment of taxes until they sell the stock.[6] Because cash dividends are taxed at the same rate as capital gains (as a result of the 2003 Tax Act), this strategy benefits owners through the tax deferral rather than as a result of a lower tax rate. Lower-income shareholders, however, who need dividend income, will prefer a *higher* payout of earnings.

A second consideration is the *owners' investment opportunities*. A firm should not retain funds for investment in projects yielding lower returns than the owners could obtain from external investments of equal risk. If it appears that the owners have better opportunities externally, the firm should pay out a higher percentage of its earnings. If the firm's investment opportunities are at least as good as similar-risk external investments, a lower payout is justifiable.

A final consideration is the *potential dilution of ownership*. If a firm pays out a high percentage of earnings, new equity capital will have to be raised with common stock. The result of a new stock issue may be dilution of both control and earnings for the existing owners. By paying out a low percentage of its earnings, the firm can minimize the possibility of such dilution.

Market Considerations

Hint The risk–return concept also applies to the firm's dividend policy. A firm that lets its dividends fluctuate from period to period will be viewed as risky, and investors will require a higher rate of return, which will increase the firm's cost of capital.

An awareness of the market's probable response to certain types of policies is also helpful in formulating dividend policy. Stockholders are believed to value a *fixed or increasing level of dividends* as opposed to a fluctuating pattern of dividends. This belief is supported by the research of John Lintner, who found that corporate managers are averse to changing the dollar amount of dividends in response to changes in earnings, particularly when earnings decline.[7] In addition, stockholders are believed to value a policy of *continuous dividend payment*. Because regularly paying a fixed or increasing dividend eliminates uncertainty about the frequency and magnitude of dividends, the returns of the firm are likely to be discounted at a lower rate. This should result in an increase in the market value of the stock and therefore an increase in the owners' wealth.

A final market consideration is *informational content*. As noted earlier, shareholders often view a dividend payment as a *signal* of the firm's future success. A stable and continuous dividend is a *positive signal*, conveying the firm's good financial health. Shareholders are likely to interpret a passed dividend payment due to a loss or to very low earnings as a *negative signal*. The nonpayment of the dividend creates uncertainty about the future, which is likely to result in lower stock value. Owners and investors generally construe a dividend payment during a period of losses as an indication that the loss is merely temporary.

REVIEW QUESTION

13–6 What six factors do firms consider in establishing *dividend policy?* Briefly describe each of them.

---

6. It is illegal to consider the owners' tax status in making dividend policy decisions, although it is difficult for the IRS to enforce this law. Rather, the IRS will look for high retained earnings and high liquidity. Firms in this situation are penalized through the *excess earnings accumulation tax*. It is quite difficult, if not impossible, to determine the extent to which the tax status of a firm's owners affects dividend policy decisions.

7. John Lintner, "Distribution of Income of Corporations Among Dividends, Retained Earnings, and Taxes," *American Economic Review* 46 (May 1956), pp. 97–113.

13.4 | Types of Dividend Policies

The firm's dividend policy must be formulated with two basic objectives in mind: providing for sufficient financing and maximizing the wealth of the firm's owners. Three commonly used dividend policies are described in the following sections. A particular firm's cash dividend policy may incorporate elements of each.

dividend payout ratio
Indicates the percentage of each dollar earned that a firm distributes to the owners in the form of cash. It is calculated by dividing the firm's cash dividend per share by its earnings per share.

constant-payout-ratio dividend policy
A dividend policy based on the payment of a certain percentage of earnings to owners in each dividend period.

Constant-Payout-Ratio Dividend Policy

One type of dividend policy involves use of a constant payout ratio. The **dividend payout ratio** indicates the percentage of each dollar earned that the firm distributes to the owners in the form of cash. It is calculated by dividing the firm's cash dividend per share by its earnings per share. With a **constant-payout-ratio dividend policy,** the firm establishes that a certain percentage of earnings is paid to owners in each dividend period.

The problem with this policy is that if the firm's earnings drop or if a loss occurs in a given period, the dividends may be low or even nonexistent. Because dividends are often considered an indicator of the firm's future condition and status, the firm's stock price may be adversely affected.

Example

Peachtree Industries, a miner of potassium, has a policy of paying out 40% of earnings in cash dividends. In periods when a loss occurs, the firm's policy is to pay no cash dividends. Data on Peachtree's earnings, dividends, and average stock prices for the past 6 years follow.

Year	Earnings/share	Dividends/share	Average price/share
2009	−$0.50	$0.00	$42.00
2008	3.00	1.20	52.00
2007	1.75	0.70	48.00
2006	− 1.50	0.00	38.00
2005	2.00	0.80	46.00
2004	4.50	1.80	50.00

Dividends increased in 2007 and in 2008 but decreased in the other years. In years of decreasing dividends, the firm's stock price dropped; when dividends increased, the price of the stock increased. Peachtree's sporadic dividend payments appear to make its owners uncertain about the returns they can expect.

Hint Regulated utilities in low-growth areas can use a constant-payout-ratio dividend policy. Their capital requirements are usually low and their earnings are more stable than those of most firms.

Although some firms use a constant-payout-ratio dividend policy, it is *not* recommended.

regular dividend policy
A dividend policy based on the payment of a fixed-dollar dividend in each period.

Regular Dividend Policy

The **regular dividend policy** is based on the payment of a fixed-dollar dividend in each period. This policy provides the owners with generally positive information, thereby minimizing their uncertainty. Often, firms that use this policy increase the regular dividend once a *proven* increase in earnings has occurred. Under this policy, dividends are almost never decreased.

Example

The dividend policy of Woodward Laboratories, a producer of a popular artificial sweetener, is to pay annual dividends of $1.00 per share until per-share earnings have exceeded $4.00 for 3 consecutive years. At that point, the annual dividend is raised to $1.50 per share, and a new earnings plateau is established. The firm does not anticipate decreasing its dividend unless its liquidity is in jeopardy. Data for Woodward's earnings, dividends, and average stock prices for the past 12 years follow.

Year	Earnings/share	Dividends/share	Average price/share
2009	$4.50	$1.50	$47.50
2008	3.90	1.50	46.50
2007	4.60	1.50	45.00
2006	4.20	1.00	43.00
2005	5.00	1.00	42.00
2004	2.00	1.00	38.50
2003	6.00	1.00	38.00
2002	3.00	1.00	36.00
2001	0.75	1.00	33.00
2000	0.50	1.00	33.00
1999	2.70	1.00	33.50
1998	2.85	1.00	35.00

Whatever the level of earnings, Woodward Laboratories paid dividends of $1.00 per share through 2006. In 2007, the dividend increased to $1.50 per share because earnings in excess of $4.00 per share had been achieved for 3 years. In 2007, the firm also had to establish a new earnings plateau for further dividend increases. Woodward Laboratories' average price per share exhibited a stable, increasing behavior in spite of a somewhat volatile pattern of earnings.

---

target dividend-payout ratio
A dividend policy under which the firm attempts to pay out a certain *percentage* of earnings as a stated dollar dividend and adjusts that dividend toward a target payout as proven earnings increases occur.

Often a regular dividend policy is built around a **target dividend-payout ratio.** Under this policy, the firm attempts to pay out a certain *percentage* of earnings, but rather than let dividends fluctuate, it pays a stated dollar dividend and adjusts that dividend toward the target payout as proven earnings increases occur. For instance, Woodward Laboratories appears to have a target payout ratio of around 35 percent. The payout was about 35 percent ($1.00 ÷ $2.85) when the dividend policy was set in 1998, and when the dividend was raised to $1.50 in 2007, the payout ratio was about 33 percent ($1.50 ÷ $4.60).

low-regular-and-extra dividend policy
A dividend policy based on paying a low regular dividend, supplemented by an additional ("extra") dividend when earnings are higher than normal in a given period.

Low-Regular-and-Extra Dividend Policy

Some firms establish a **low-regular-and-extra dividend policy,** paying a low regular dividend, supplemented by an additional ("extra") dividend when earnings are higher than normal in a given period. By calling the additional dividend an

extra dividend
An additional dividend optionally paid by the firm when earnings are higher than normal in a given period.

extra dividend, the firm avoids giving shareholders false hopes. This policy is especially common among companies that experience cyclical shifts in earnings.

By establishing a low regular dividend that is paid each period, the firm gives investors the stable income necessary to build confidence in the firm, and the extra dividend permits them to share in the earnings from an especially good period. Firms using this policy must raise the level of the regular dividend once proven increases in earnings have been achieved. The extra dividend should not be a regular event; otherwise, it becomes meaningless. The use of a target dividend-payout ratio in establishing the regular dividend level is advisable.

REVIEW QUESTION

13–7 Describe a constant-payout-ratio dividend policy, a regular dividend policy, and a low-regular-and-extra dividend policy. What are the effects of these policies?

13.5 | Other Forms of Dividends

Dividends can be paid in forms other than cash. Here we discuss two other methods of paying dividends—stock dividends and stock repurchases—as well as a closely related topic, stock splits.

Stock Dividends

stock dividend
The payment, to existing owners, of a dividend in the form of stock.

A **stock dividend** is the payment, to existing owners, of a dividend in the form of stock. Often firms pay stock dividends as a replacement for or a supplement to cash dividends. Although stock dividends do not have a real value, stockholders may perceive them to represent something they did not have before.

Accounting Aspects

small (ordinary) stock dividend
A stock dividend representing less than 20 percent to 25 percent of the common stock outstanding when the dividend is declared.

In an accounting sense, the payment of a stock dividend is a shifting of funds between stockholders' equity accounts rather than an outflow of funds. When a firm declares a stock dividend, the procedures for announcement and distribution are the same as those described earlier for a cash dividend. The accounting entries associated with the payment of a stock dividend vary depending on its size. A **small (ordinary) stock dividend** is a stock dividend that represents less than 20 percent to 25 percent of the common stock outstanding when the dividend is declared. Small stock dividends are most common.

Example

The current stockholders' equity on the balance sheet of Garrison Corporation, a distributor of prefabricated cabinets, is as shown in the following accounts.

Preferred stock	$ 300,000
Common stock (100,000 shares at $4 par)	400,000
Paid-in capital in excess of par	600,000
Retained earnings	700,000
Total stockholders' equity	$2,000,000

Garrison, which has 100,000 shares of common stock outstanding, declares a 10% stock dividend when the market price of its stock is $15 per share. Because 10,000 new shares (10% of 100,000) are issued at the prevailing market price of $15 per share, $150,000 ($15 per share × 10,000 shares) is shifted from retained earnings to the common stock and paid-in capital accounts. A total of $40,000 ($4 par × 10,000 shares) is added to common stock, and the remaining $110,000 [($15 − $4) × 10,000 shares] is added to the paid-in capital in excess of par. The resulting account balances are as follows:

Preferred stock	$ 300,000
Common stock (110,000 shares at $4 par)	440,000
Paid-in capital in excess of par	710,000
Retained earnings	550,000
Total stockholders' equity	$2,000,000

The firm's total stockholders' equity has not changed; funds have merely been *shifted* among stockholders' equity accounts.

Shareholder's Viewpoint

The shareholder receiving a stock dividend typically receives nothing of value. After the dividend is paid, the per-share value of the shareholder's stock decreases in proportion to the dividend in such a way that the market value of his or her total holdings in the firm remains unchanged. Therefore stock dividends are usually nontaxable. The shareholder's proportion of ownership in the firm also remains the same, and *as long as the firm's earnings remain unchanged,* so does his or her share of total earnings. (However, if the firm's earnings and cash dividends increase when the stock dividend is issued, an increase in share value is likely to result.)

Example

Ms. X owned 10,000 shares of Garrison Corporation's stock. The company's most recent earnings were $220,000, and earnings are not expected to change in the near future. Before the stock dividend, Ms. X owned 10% (10,000 shares ÷ 100,000 shares) of the firm's stock, which was selling for $15 per share. Earnings per share were $2.20 ($220,000 ÷ 100,000 shares). Because Ms. X owned 10,000 shares, her earnings were $22,000 ($2.20 per share × 10,000 shares). After receiving the 10% stock dividend, Ms. X has 11,000 shares, which again is 10% of the ownership (11,000 shares ÷ 110,000 shares). The market price of the stock can be expected to drop to $13.64 per share [$15 × (1.00 ÷ 1.10)], which means that the market value of Ms. X's holdings is $150,000 (11,000 shares × $13.64 per share). This is the same as the initial value of her holdings (10,000 shares × $15 per share). The future earnings per share drops to $2 ($220,000 ÷ 110,000 shares) because the same $220,000 in earnings must now be divided among 110,000 shares. Because Ms. X still owns 10% of the stock, her share of total earnings is still $22,000 ($2 per share × 11,000 shares).

In summary, if the firm's earnings remain constant and total cash dividends do not increase, a stock dividend results in a lower per-share market value for the firm's stock.

The Company's Viewpoint

Stock dividends are more costly to issue than cash dividends, but certain advantages may outweigh these costs. Firms find the stock dividend to be a way to give owners something without having to use cash. Generally, when a firm needs to preserve cash to finance rapid growth, it uses a stock dividend. When the stockholders recognize that the firm is reinvesting the cash flow so as to maximize future earnings, the market value of the firm should at least remain unchanged. However, if the stock dividend is paid so as to retain cash to satisfy past-due bills, a decline in market value may result.

Stock Splits

stock split
A method commonly used to lower the market price of a firm's stock by increasing the number of shares belonging to each shareholder.

Although not a type of dividend, *stock splits* have an effect on a firm's share price similar to that of stock dividends. A **stock split** is a method commonly used to lower the market price of a firm's stock by increasing the number of shares belonging to each shareholder. In a 2-for-1 split, for example, two new shares are exchanged for each old share, with each new share being worth half the value of each old share. A stock split has no effect on the firm's capital structure and is usually nontaxable.

Quite often, a firm believes that its stock is priced too high and that lowering the market price will enhance trading activity. Stock splits are often made prior to issuing additional stock to enhance that stock's marketability and stimulate market activity. It is not unusual for a stock split to cause a slight increase in the market value of the stock, attributable to its informational content and to the fact that *total* dividends paid commonly increase slightly after a split.[8]

Example

Delphi Company, a forest products concern, had 200,000 shares of $2-par-value common stock and no preferred stock outstanding. Because the stock is selling at a high market price, the firm has declared a 2-for-1 stock split. The total before- and after-split stockholders' equity is shown in the following table.

Before split		After 2-for-1 split	
Common stock (200,000 shares at $2 par)	$ 400,000	Common stock (400,000 shares at $1 part)	$ 400,000
Paid-in capital in excess of par	4,000,000	Paid-in-capital in excess of part	4,000,000
Retained earnings	2,000,000	Retained earnings	2,000,000
Total stockholders' equity	$6,400,000	Total stockholders' equity	$6,400,000

The insignificant effect of the stock split on the firm's books is obvious.

---

8. Eugene F. Fama, Lawrence Fisher, Michael C. Jensen, and Richard Roll, "The Adjustment of Stock Prices to New Information," *International Economic Review* 10 (February 1969), pp. 1–21, found that the stock price increases before the split announcement and that the increase in stock price is maintained if dividends per share are increased, but is lost if dividends per share are *not* increased, following the split.

reverse stock split
A method used to raise the market price of a firm's stock by exchanging a certain number of outstanding shares for one new share.

Stock can be split in any way desired. Sometimes a **reverse stock split** is made: The firm exchanges a certain number of outstanding shares for one new share. For example, in a 1-for-3 split, one new share is exchanged for three old shares. Reverse stock splits are initiated to raise the market price of a firm's stock when it is selling at too low a price to appear respectable.[9]

Personal Finance Example   Shakira Washington, a single investor in the 25% federal income tax bracket, owns 260 shares of Advanced Technology, Inc., common stock. She originally bought the stock 2 years ago at its initial public offering (IPO) price of $9 per share. The stock of this fast-growing technology company is currently trading for $60 per share, so the current value of her Advanced Technology stock is $15,600 (260 shares x $60 per share). Because the firm's board believes that the stock would trade more actively in the $20 to $30 price range, it just announced a 3-for-1 stock split. Shakira wishes to determine the impact of the stock split on her holdings and taxes.

Because the stock will split 3 for 1, after the split Shakira will own 780 shares (3×260 shares). She should expect the market price of the stock to drop to $20 ($1/3 \times \$60$) immediately after the split; the value of her after-split holding will be $15,600 (780 shares $\times$ $20 per share). Because the $15,600 value of her after-split holdings in Advanced Technology stock exactly equals the before-split value of $15,600, Shakira has experienced neither a gain nor a loss on the stock as a result of the 3-for-1 split. Even if there were a gain or loss attributable to the split, Shakira would not have any tax liability unless she actually sold the stock and realized that (or any other) gain or loss.

Stock Repurchases

stock repurchase
The repurchase by the firm of outstanding common stock in the marketplace; their popularity and importance is due to the fact that they either enhance shareholder value or help to discourage an unfriendly takeover.

In recent years, firms have increased their repurchasing of outstanding common stock in the marketplace. The practical motives for **stock repurchases** include obtaining shares to be used in acquisitions, having shares available for employee stock option plans, and retiring shares. The popularity and importance of stock repurchases is due to the fact that they either enhance shareholder value or help to discourage an unfriendly takeover. Stock repurchases enhance shareholder value by (1) reducing the number of shares outstanding and thereby raising earnings per share, (2) sending a *positive signal* to investors in the marketplace that management believes that the stock is undervalued, and (3) providing a temporary floor for the stock price, which may have been declining. The use of repurchases to discourage unfriendly takeovers is predicated on the belief that a corporate raider is less likely to gain control of the firm if there are fewer publicly traded shares available. Here we focus on retiring shares through repurchase, because this motive for repurchase is similar to the payment of cash dividends.

---

9. If a firm's stock is selling at a low price—possibly less than a few dollars—many investors are hesitant to purchase it because they believe it is "cheap." These somewhat unsophisticated investors correlate cheapness and quality, and they feel that a low-priced stock is a low-quality investment. A reverse stock split raises the stock price and increases per-share earnings.

Stock Repurchases Viewed as a Cash Dividend

When firms repurchase common stock for retirement, the underlying motive is to distribute excess cash to the owners. Generally, as long as earnings remain constant, the repurchase reduces the number of outstanding shares, raising the earnings per share and therefore the market price per share. In addition, an owner tax-deferral benefit may result. The repurchase of common stock results in a type of *reverse dilution*, because the EPS and the market price of stock are increased by reducing the number of shares outstanding. The net effect of the repurchase is similar to the payment of a cash dividend.

Example

Benton Company, a national sportswear chain, has released the following financial data:

Earnings available for common stockholders	$1,000,000
Number of shares of common stock outstanding	400,000
Earnings per share ($1,000,000 ÷ 400,000)	$2.50
Market price per share	$50
Price/earnings (P/E) ratio ($50 ÷ $2.50)	20

The firm wants to use $800,000 of its earnings either to pay cash dividends or to repurchase shares. If the firm paid cash dividends, the amount of the dividend would be $2 per share ($800,000 ÷ 400,000 shares). If the firm paid $52 per share to repurchase stock, it could repurchase approximately 15,385 shares ($800,000 ÷ $52 per share). As a result of this repurchase, 384,615 shares (400,000 shares − 15,385 shares) of common stock would remain outstanding. Earnings per share (EPS) would rise to $2.60 ($1,000,000 ÷ 384,615). If the stock still sold at 20 times earnings (P/E = 20), its market price could be estimated by multiplying the new EPS by this P/E ratio (the *price/earnings multiple approach* presented in Chapter 7). The price would therefore rise to $52 per share ($2.60 × 20). In both cases, the stockholders would receive $2 per share: a $2 cash dividend in the dividend case or a $2 increase in share price ($50 per share to $52 per share) in the repurchase case.

Besides the advantage of an increase in per-share earnings, an owner tax-deferral benefit results. Although the owners would have to pay capital gains taxes in either case (the $2 dividend or the $2 increase in market value), the dividend tax would be paid in the current year. In contrast, the tax on the gain from the repurchase would effectively be deferred until the stock is sold. Clearly, the repurchase provides the stockholder with the opportunity to defer taxes. The IRS is alleged to monitor firms that regularly repurchase stock and levies a penalty when it believes repurchases have been deliberately made to delay the payment of taxes by stockholders.

Accounting Entries

The accounting entries that result when firms repurchase common stock are a reduction in cash and the establishment of a contra capital account called "treasury stock," which is shown as a deduction from stockholders' equity. The label *treasury stock* is used on the balance sheet to indicate the presence of repurchased shares.

Repurchase Process

When a company intends to repurchase a block of outstanding shares, it should make shareholders aware of its intentions. Specifically, it should advise them of the purpose of the repurchase (acquisition, stock options, retirement) and the disposition (if any) planned for the repurchased shares (traded for shares of another firm, distribution to executives, or held in the treasury).

Three basic methods of repurchase are common. One is to purchase shares on the *open market*. This places upward pressure on the price of shares if the number of shares being repurchased is reasonably large in comparison with the total number outstanding. The second method is through tender offers. A **tender offer** is a formal offer to purchase a given number of shares of a firm's stock at a specified price. The price at which a tender offer is made is set above the current market price to attract sellers. If the number of shares desired cannot be repurchased through the tender offer, firms can obtain the additional shares on the open market. Tender offers are preferred when large numbers of shares are repurchased, because the company's intentions are clearly stated and each stockholder has an opportunity to sell shares at the tendered price. A third method involves

tender offer
A formal offer to purchase a given number of shares of a firm's stock at a specified price.

Focus on Ethics   Are Buybacks Really a Bargain?

IN PRACTICE

When **CBS** announced in March 2007 that it would buy back $1.4 billion worth of stock, its sagging share price saw the biggest spike since the media giant parted ways with **Viacom** in 2005. The 4.5 percent jump may be an omen of good fortune—at the very least it shows how much shareholders like buybacks.

Companies have been gobbling up their own shares faster than ever in a world of inexpensive capital and swollen balance sheets. Since 2003, the market for buybacks has boomed, with repurchases nearly on a par with capital expenditures. In 2006, $437 billion of stock was repurchased, according to Howard Silverblatt, an analyst at Standard & Poor's. Some, however, have questioned the moves and motives that lead to a big buyback.

In addition to simply returning cash to shareholders, companies also typically say they do so because they believe their stock is undervalued. Yet new research shows that companies often use creative financial reporting to push earnings downward before buybacks, making the stock seem undervalued and causing its price to bounce higher after the buyback. That pleases investors who then amplify the effect by pushing the price even higher.

"Managers who are acting opportunistically can use their reporting discretion to reduce the repurchase price by temporarily deflating earnings," argue Guojin Gong, Henock Louis, and Amy Sun at Penn State University's Smeal College of Business. Observing data from 1,720 companies, the authors say companies can easily create an apparent slump by speeding

up or slowing down expense recognition, changing inventory accounting, or revising estimates of bad debt—all classic methods of making the numbers look worse without actually breaking accounting rules.

The penalty for being caught deliberately managing earnings in advance of a buyback could be severe. With the backdating scandals that popped up regularly in the early 2000s, executives would no doubt be wary of deflating earnings just to get a boost from a buyback. Still, that's what Louis believes some are doing. "I don't think what they're doing is illegal," he says. "But it's misleading their investors."

■ *Do you agree that corporate managers would manipulate their stock's value prior to a buyback, or do you believe that corporations are more likely to initiate a buyback to enhance shareholder value?*

the purchase, on a *negotiated basis,* of a large block of shares from one or more major stockholders. Again, in this case, the firm has to state its intentions and make certain that the purchase price is fair and equitable in view of the interests and opportunities of the remaining shareholders.

For discussion of some less-than-worthy motives behind some stock buy-backs, see the *Focus on Ethics* box on page 618.

REVIEW QUESTIONS

13–8   Why do firms issue *stock dividends?* Comment on the following statement: "I have a stock that promises to pay a 20 percent stock dividend every year, and therefore it guarantees that I will break even in 5 years."

13–9   Compare a *stock split* with a *stock dividend.*

13–10 What is the logic behind *repurchasing shares* of common stock to distribute excess cash to the firm's owners?

Summary

Focus on Value

Cash dividends are the cash flows that a firm distributes to its common stockholders. A share of common stock gives its owner the right to receive all future dividends. The present value of all those future dividends expected over a firm's assumed infinite life determines the firm's stock value.

Dividends not only represent cash flows to shareholders but also contain useful information about the firm's current and future performance. Such information affects the shareholders' perception of the firm's risk. A firm can also pay stock dividends, initiate stock splits, or repurchase stock. All of these dividend-related actions can affect the firm's risk, return, and value as a result of their cash flows and informational content.

Although the theory of relevance of dividends is still evolving, the behavior of most firms and stockholders suggests that dividend policy affects share prices. Therefore financial managers try to develop and implement dividend policy that is consistent with the firm's goal of **maximizing stock price.**

Review of Learning Goals

LG 1   **Understand cash dividend payment procedures, the tax treatment of dividends, and the role of dividend reinvestment plans.** The board of directors makes the cash dividend decision and establishes the record and payment dates. Generally, the larger the dividend charged to retained earnings and paid in cash, the greater the amount of financing that must be raised externally. As a result of a tax-law change in 2003, most taxpayers pay taxes on corporate dividends at a maximum rate of 5 percent to 15 percent, depending on the taxpayer's tax bracket. Some firms offer dividend reinvestment plans that allow stockholders to acquire shares in lieu of cash dividends.

LG 2 **Describe the residual theory of dividends and the key arguments with regard to dividend irrelevance and relevance.** The residual theory suggests that dividends should be viewed as the earnings left after all acceptable investment opportunities have been undertaken.

Miller and Modigliani argue in favor of dividend irrelevance, using a perfect world wherein information content and clientele effects exist. Gordon and Lintner advance the theory of dividend relevance, basing their argument on the uncertainty-reducing effect of dividends, supported by their bird-in-the-hand argument. Empirical studies fail to provide clear support of dividend relevance. Even so, the actions of financial managers and stockholders tend to support the belief that dividend policy does affect stock value.

LG 3 **Discuss the key factors involved in establishing a dividend policy.** A firm's dividend policy should provide for sufficient financing and maximize stockholders' wealth. Dividend policy is affected by legal, contractual, and internal constraints, by growth prospects, and by owner and market considerations. Legal constraints prohibit corporations from paying out as cash dividends any portion of the firm's "legal capital." Nor can firms with overdue liabilities and legally insolvent or bankrupt firms pay cash dividends. Contractual constraints result from restrictive provisions in the firm's loan agreements. Internal constraints result from a firm's limited availability of excess cash. Growth prospects affect the relative importance of retaining earnings rather than paying them out in dividends. The tax status of owners, the owners' investment opportunities, and the potential dilution of ownership are important owner considerations. Finally, market considerations are related to the stockholders' preference for the continuous payment of fixed or increasing streams of dividends and the perceived informational content of dividends.

LG 4 **Review and evaluate the three basic types of dividend policies.** With a constant-payout-ratio dividend policy, the firm pays a fixed percentage of earnings to the owners each period; dividends move up and down with earnings, and no dividend is paid when a loss occurs. Under a regular dividend policy, the firm pays a fixed-dollar dividend each period; it increases the amount of dividends only after a proven increase in earnings. The low-regular-and-extra dividend policy is similar to the regular dividend policy, except that it pays an extra dividend when the firm's earnings are higher than normal. The regular and the low-regular-and-extra dividend policies are generally preferred because they reduce uncertainty.

LG 5 **Evaluate stock dividends from accounting, shareholder, and company points of view.** Firms may pay stock dividends as a replacement for or supplement to cash dividends. The payment of stock dividends involves a shifting of funds between capital accounts rather than an outflow of funds. Stock dividends do not change the market value of stockholders' holdings, proportion of ownership, or share of total earnings. Therefore stock dividends are usually nontaxable. However, stock dividends may satisfy owners and enable the firm to preserve its market value without having to use cash.

LG 6 **Explain stock splits and stock repurchases and the firm's motivation for undertaking each of them.** Stock splits are used to enhance trading activity of a firm's shares by lowering or raising their market price. A stock split merely involves accounting adjustments; it has no effect on the firm's cash or on its capital structure and is usually nontaxable.

Firms can repurchase stock in lieu of paying a cash dividend, to retire outstanding shares. Reducing the number of outstanding shares increases earnings per share and the market price per share. Stock repurchases also defer the tax payments of stockholders.

Self-Test Problem (Solution in Appendix B)

ST13–1 **Stock repurchase**   The Off-Shore Steel Company has earnings available for common stockholders of $2 million and has 500,000 shares of common stock outstanding at $60 per share. The firm is currently contemplating the payment of $2 per share in cash dividends.

    a. Calculate the firm's current *earnings per share (EPS)* and *price/earnings (P/E) ratio*.

    b. If the firm can repurchase stock at $62 per share, how many shares can be purchased in lieu of making the proposed cash dividend payment?

    c. How much will the EPS be after the proposed repurchase? Why?

    d. If the stock sells at the old P/E ratio, what will the market price be after repurchase?

    e. Compare and contrast the earnings per share before and after the proposed repurchase.

    f. Compare and contrast the stockholders' position under the dividend and repurchase alternatives.

Warm-Up Exercises   A blue box (■) indicates exercises available in .

E13–1 Stephanie's Cafes, Inc. has declared a dividend of $1.30 per share for shareholders of record on Tuesday, May 2. The firm has 200,000 shares outstanding and will pay the dividend on May 24. How much cash will be needed to pay the dividend? When will the stock begin selling *ex dividend?*

E13–2 Chancellor Industries has retained earnings available of $1.2 million. The firm plans to make two investments that require financing of $950,000 and $1.75 million, respectively. Chancellor uses a target capital structure with 60% debt and 40% equity. Apply the *residual theory* to determine what dividends, if any, can be paid out, and calculate the resulting *dividend payout ratio*.

E13–3 Ashkenazi Companies has the following stockholders' equity account:

Common stock (350,000 shares at $3 par)	$1,050,000
Paid-in capital in excess of par	2,500,000
Retained earnings	750,000
Total stockholders' equity	$4,300,000

Assuming that state laws define legal capital solely as the par value of common stock, how much of a *per-share dividend* can Ashkenazi pay? If legal capital were more broadly defined to include all paid-in capital, how much of a *per-share dividend* can Ashkenazi pay?

E13–4 The board of Kopi Industries is considering a new dividend policy that would set dividends at 60% of earnings. The recent past has witnessed earnings per share (EPS) and dividends paid per share as follows:

Year	EPS	Dividend/share
2006	$1.75	$0.95
2007	1.95	1.20
2008	2.05	1.25
2009	2.25	1.30

Based on Kopi's historical dividend payout ratio, discuss whether a *constant payout ratio* of 60% would benefit shareholders.

E13–5 The current stockholders' equity account for Hilo Farms is as follows:

Common stock (50,000 shares at $3 par)	$150,000
Paid-in capital in excess of par	250,000
Retained earnings	450,000
Total stockholders' equity	$850,000

Hilo has announced plans to issue an additional 5,000 shares of common stock as part of its stock dividend plan. The current market price of Hilo's common stock is $20 per share. Show how the proposed *stock dividend* would affect the stockholder's equity account.

Problems

A blue box (■) indicates problems available in .

P13–1 **Dividend payment procedures**   At the quarterly dividend meeting, Wood Shoes declared a cash dividend of $1.10 per share for holders of record on Monday, July 10. The firm has 300,000 shares of common stock outstanding and has set a payment date of July 31. Prior to the dividend declaration, the firm's key accounts were as follows:

Cash	$500,000	Dividends payable	$	0
		Retained earnings		2,500,000

  a. Show the entries after the meeting adjourned.
  b. When is the *ex dividend* date?
  c. What values would the key accounts have after the July 31 payment date?
  d. What effect, if any, will the dividend have on the firm's total assets?
  e. Ignoring general market fluctuations, what effect, if any, will the dividend have on the firm's stock price on the ex dividend date?

PERSONAL FINANCE PROBLEM

P13–2 **Dividend payment** Kathy Snow wishes to purchase shares of Countdown Computing, Inc. The company's board of directors has declared a cash dividend of $0.80 to be paid to holders of record on Wednesday, May 12.

a. What is the last day that Kathy can purchase the stock (trade date) and still receive the dividend?

b. What day does this stock begin trading "ex dividend"?

c. What change, if any, would you expect in the price per share when the stock begins trading on the ex dividend day?

d. If Kathy held the stock for less than one quarter and then sold it for $39 per share, would she achieve a higher investment return by (1) buying the stock *prior to* the ex dividend date at $35 per share and collecting the $0.80 dividend, or (2) buying it *on* the ex dividend date at $34.20 per share but not receiving the dividend?

P13–3 **Residual dividend policy** As president of Young's of California, a large clothing chain, you have just received a letter from a major stockholder. The stockholder asks about the company's dividend policy. In fact, the stockholder has asked you to esti-mate the amount of the dividend that you are likely to pay next year. You have not yet collected all the information about the expected dividend payment, but you do know the following:

(1) The company follows a residual dividend policy.

(2) The total capital budget for next year is likely to be one of three amounts, depending on the results of capital budgeting studies that are currently under way. The capital expenditure amounts are $2 million, $3 million, and $4 million.

(3) The forecasted level of potential retained earnings next year is $2 million.

(4) The target or optimal capital structure is a debt ratio of 40%.

You have decided to respond by sending the stockholder the best information avail-able to you.

a. Describe a *residual dividend policy.*

b. Compute the amount of the dividend (or the amount of new common stock needed) and the dividend payout ratio for each of the three capital expenditure amounts.

c. Compare, contrast, and discuss the amount of dividends (calculated in part **b**) associated with each of the three capital expenditure amounts.

P13–4 **Dividend constraints** The Howe Company's stockholders' equity account follows:

Common stock (400,000 shares at $4 par)	$1,600,000
Paid-in capital in excess of par	1,000,000
Retained earnings	1,900,000
Total stockholders' equity	$4,500,000

The earnings available for common stockholders from this period's operations are $100,000, which have been included as part of the $1.9 million retained earnings.

a. What is the *maximum dividend per share* that the firm can pay? (Assume that legal capital includes *all* paid-in capital.)

b. If the firm has $160,000 in cash, what is the largest per-share dividend it can pay without borrowing?

c. Indicate the accounts and changes, if any, that will result if the firm pays the divi-dends indicated in parts **a** and **b**.

d. Indicate the effects of an $80,000 cash dividend on stockholders' equity.

P13–5 **Dividend constraints**   A firm has $800,000 in paid-in capital, retained earnings of $40,000 (including the current year's earnings), and 25,000 shares of common stock outstanding. In the current year, it has $29,000 of earnings available for the common stockholders.

a. What is the most the firm can pay in cash dividends to each common stockholder? (Assume that legal capital includes *all* paid-in capital.)

b. What effect would a cash dividend of $0.80 per share have on the firm's balance sheet entries?

c. If the firm cannot raise any new funds from external sources, what do you consider the key constraint with respect to the magnitude of the firm's dividend payments? Why?

P13–6 **Low-regular-and-extra dividend policy**   Bennett Farm Equipment Sales, Inc., is in a highly cyclic business. Although the firm has a target payout ratio of 25%, its board realizes that strict adherence to that ratio would result in a fluctuating dividend and create uncertainty for the firm's stockholders. Therefore, the firm has declared a regular dividend of $0.50 per share per year with extra cash dividends to be paid when earnings justify them. Earnings per share for the last several years are as follows:

Year	EPS	Year	EPS
2009	$3.00	2006	$2.80
2008	2.40	2005	2.15
2007	2.20	2004	1.97

a. Calculate the *payout ratio* for each year on the basis of the regular $0.50 dividend and the cited EPS.

b. Calculate the difference between the regular $0.50 dividend and a 25% payout for each year.

c. Bennett has established a policy of paying an extra dividend of $0.25 only when the difference between the regular dividend and a 25% payout amounts to $1.00 or more. Show the regular and extra dividends in those years when an extra dividend would be paid. What would be done with the "extra" earnings that are not paid out?

d. The firm expects that future earnings per share will continue to cycle but will remain above $2.20 per share in most years. What factors should be considered in making a revision to the amount paid as a regular dividend? If the firm revises the regular dividend, what new amount should it pay?

P13–7 **Alternative dividend policies**   Over the last 10 years, a firm has had the earnings per share shown in the following table.

Year	Earnings per share	Year	Earnings per share
2009	$4.00	2004	$2.40
2008	3.80	2003	1.20
2007	3.20	2002	1.80
2006	2.80	2001	− 0.50
2005	3.20	2000	0.25

a. If the firm's dividend policy were based on a *constant payout ratio* of 40% for all years with positive earnings and 0% otherwise, what would be the annual dividend for each year?

b. If the firm had a dividend payout of $1.00 per share, increasing by $0.10 per share whenever the dividend payout fell below 50% for two consecutive years, what annual dividend would the firm pay each year?

c. If the firm's policy were to pay $0.50 per share each period except when earnings per share exceed $3.00, when an extra dividend equal to 80% of earnings beyond $3.00 would be paid, what annual dividend would the firm pay each year?

d. Discuss the pros and cons of each dividend policy described in parts **a** through **c**.

P13–8 **Alternative dividend policies**   Given the earnings per share over the period 2002–2009 shown in the following table, determine the annual dividend per share under each of the policies set forth in parts **a** through **d**.

Year	Earnings per share
2009	$1.40
2008	1.56
2007	1.20
2006	− 0.85
2005	1.05
2004	0.60
2003	1.00
2002	0.44

a. Pay out 50% of earnings in all years with positive earnings.

b. Pay $0.50 per share and increase to $0.60 per share whenever earnings per share rise above $0.90 per share for two consecutive years.

c. Pay $0.50 per share except when earnings exceed $1.00 per share, in which case pay an extra dividend of 60% of earnings above $1.00 per share.

d. Combine the policies described in parts **b** and **c**. When the dividend is raised (in part **b**), raise the excess dividend base (in part **c**) from $1.00 to $1.10 per share.

e. Compare and contrast each of the dividend policies described in parts **a** through **d**.

P13–9 **Stock dividend—Firm**   Columbia Paper has the following stockholders' equity account. The firm's common stock has a current market price of $30 per share.

Preferred stock	$100,000
Common stock (10,000 shares at $2 par)	20,000
Paid-in capital in excess of par	280,000
Retained earnings	100,000
Total stockholders' equity	$500,000

a. Show the effects on Columbia of a 5% stock dividend.

b. Show the effects of (1) a 10% and (2) a 20% stock dividend.

c. In light of your answers to parts **a** and **b**, discuss the effects of stock dividends on stockholders' equity.

P13–10 **Cash versus stock dividend**   Milwaukee Tool has the following stockholders' equity account. The firm's common stock currently sells for $4 per share.

Preferred stock	$ 100,000
Common stock (400,000 shares at $1 par)	400,000
Paid-in capital in excess of par	200,000
Retained earnings	320,000
Total stockholders' equity	$1,020,000

a. Show the effects on the firm of a *cash* dividend of $0.01, $0.05, $0.10, and $0.20 per share.
b. Show the effects on the firm of a 1%, 5%, 10%, and 20% *stock* dividend.
c. Compare the effects in parts **a** and **b**. What are the significant differences between the two methods of paying dividends?

P13–11 **Stock dividend—Investor**   Sarah Warren currently holds 400 shares of Nutri-Foods. The firm has 40,000 shares outstanding. The firm most recently had earnings available for common stockholders of $80,000, and its stock has been selling for $22 per share. The firm intends to retain its earnings and pay a 10% stock dividend.
a. How much does the firm currently earn per share?
b. What proportion of the firm does Warren currently own?
c. What proportion of the firm will Warren own after the stock dividend? Explain your answer.
d. At what market price would you expect the stock to sell after the stock dividend?
e. Discuss what effect, if any, the payment of stock dividends will have on Warren's share of the ownership and earnings of Nutri-Foods.

P13–12 **Stock dividend—Investor**   Security Data Company has outstanding 50,000 shares of common stock currently selling at $40 per share. The firm most recently had earnings available for common stockholders of $120,000, but it has decided to retain these funds and is considering either a 5% or a 10% stock dividend in lieu of a cash dividend.
a. Determine the firm's current *earnings per share*.
b. If Sam Waller currently owns 500 shares of the firm's stock, determine his proportion of ownership currently and under each of the proposed stock dividend plans. Explain your findings.
c. Calculate and explain the market price per share under each of the stock dividend plans.
d. For each of the proposed stock dividends, calculate the earnings per share after payment of the stock dividend.
e. What is the value of Waller's holdings under each of the plans? Explain.
f. Should Waller have any preference with respect to the proposed stock dividends? Why or why not?

P13–13 **Stock split—Firm**   Growth Industries' current stockholders' equity account is as follows at the top of page 627:

Preferred stock	$ 400,000
Common stock (600,000 shares at $3 par)	1,800,000
Paid-in capital in excess of par	200,000
Retained earnings	800,000
Total stockholders' equity	$3,200,000

a. Indicate the change, if any, expected if the firm declares a 2-for-1 stock split.
b. Indicate the change, if any, expected if the firm declares a 1-for-1¹/₂ *reverse* stock split.
c. Indicate the change, if any, expected if the firm declares a 3-for-1 stock split.
d. Indicate the change, if any, expected if the firm declares a 6-for-1 stock split.
e. Indicate the change, if any, expected if the firm declares a 1-for-4 *reverse* stock split.

PERSONAL FINANCE PROBLEM

P13–14 **Stock splits**   Nathan Detroit owns 400 shares of Apple Inc., which he purchased in September 2006 for $18 per share. Apple is regarded as a high-tech computer stock and has introduced new innovations in the electronics field over the past 3 years. As of May 2009, the price of the stock was at $121 per share. Nathan read in the *Wall Street Journal* that Apple's board of directors believed that the stock may be priced too high and would trade more actively in a lower price range. The board announced a 4-for-1 stock split.

Answer the following questions about the impact of the stock split on his holdings and taxes. Nathan is in the 28% federal income tax bracket.
a. How many shares of Apple will Nathan own after the stock split?
b. Immediately after the split, what do you expect the value of Apple to be?
c. Compare the total value of Nathan's stock holdings before and after the split. What do you find?
d. Does Nathan experience a gain or loss on the stock as a result of the 4-for-1 split?
e. What is Nathan's tax liability from the event?

P13–15 **Stock split versus stock dividend—Firm**   Mammoth Corporation is considering a 3-for-2 stock split. It currently has the stockholders' equity position shown. The current stock price is $120 per share. The most recent period's earnings available for common stock is included in retained earnings.

Preferred stock	$ 1,000,000
Common stock (100,000 shares at $3 par)	300,000
Paid-in capital in excess of par	1,700,000
Retained earnings	10,000,000
Total stockholders' equity	$13,000,000

a. What effects on Mammoth would result from the *stock split?*
b. What change in stock price would you expect to result from the stock split?
c. What is the maximum cash dividend per share that the firm could pay on common stock before and after the stock split? (Assume that legal capital includes *all* paid-in capital.)
d. Contrast your answers to parts **a** through **c** with the circumstances surrounding a 50% *stock dividend.*
e. Explain the differences between stock splits and stock dividends.

P13–16 **Stock dividend versus stock split—Firm**   The board of Wicker Home Health Care, Inc., is exploring ways to expand the number of shares outstanding in an effort to reduce the market price per share to a level that the firm considers more appealing to investors. The options under consideration are a 20% stock dividend and, alternatively, a 5-for-4 stock split. At the present time, the firm's equity account and other per-share information are as follows:

Preferred stock	$ 0
Common stock (100,000 shares at $1 par)	100,000
Paid-in capital in excess of par	900,000
Retained earnings	700,000
Total stockholders' equity	$1,700,000
Price per share	$30.00
Earnings per share	$3.60
Dividend per share	$1.08

a. Show the effect on the equity accounts and per-share data of a 20% *stock dividend*.
b. Show the effect on the equity accounts and per-share data of a 5-for-4 *stock split*.
c. Which option will accomplish Wicker's goal of reducing the current stock price while maintaining a stable level of retained earnings?
d. What legal constraints might encourage the firm to choose a stock split over a stock dividend?

P13–17 **Stock repurchase**   The following financial data on the Bond Recording Company are available:

Earnings available for common stockholders	$800,000
Number of shares of common stock outstanding	400,000
Earnings per share ($800,000 ÷ 400,000)	$2
Market price per share	$20
Price/earnings (P/E) ratio ($20 ÷ $2)	10

The firm is currently considering whether it should use $400,000 of its earnings to pay cash dividends of $1 per share or to repurchase stock at $21 per share.
a. Approximately how many shares of stock can the firm repurchase at the $21-per-share price, using the funds that would have gone to pay the cash dividend?
b. Calculate the *EPS* after the repurchase. Explain your calculations.
c. If the stock still sells at 10 times earnings, what will the *market price* be after the repurchase?
d. Compare the pre- and post-repurchase earnings per share.
e. Compare and contrast the stockholders' positions under the dividend and repurchase alternatives. What are the tax implications under each alternative?

P13–18 **Stock repurchase**   Harte Textiles, Inc., a maker of custom upholstery fabrics, is concerned about preserving the wealth of its stockholders during a cyclic downturn in the home furnishings business. The company has maintained a constant dividend payout of $2.00 tied to a target payout ratio of 40%. Management is preparing a share repurchase recommendation to present to the firm's board of directors. The following data have been gathered from the last two years:

	2008	2009
Earnings available for common stockholders	$1,260,000	$1,200,000
Number of shares outstanding	300,000	300,000
Earnings per share	$4.20	$4.00
Market price per share	$23.50	$20.00
Price/earnings ratio	5.6	5.0

    a. How many shares should the company have outstanding in 2009 if its earnings available for common stockholders in that year is $1,200,000 and it pays a dividend of $2.00, given that its desired payout ratio is 40%?

    b. How many shares would Harte have to repurchase to have the level of shares outstanding calculated in part **a**?

P13–19   **ETHICS PROBLEM**   Assume that you are the CFO of a company contemplating a stock repurchase next quarter. You know that there are several methods of reducing the current quarterly earnings, which may cause the stock price to fall prior to the announcement of the proposed stock repurchase. What course of action would you recommend to your CEO? If your CEO came to you first and recommended reducing the current quarter's earnings, what would be your response?

Chapter 13 Case

Establishing General Access Company's Dividend Policy and Initial Dividend

General Access Company (GAC) is a fast-growing Internet access provider that initially went public in early 2003. Its revenue growth and profitability have steadily risen since the firm's inception in late 2001. GAC's growth has been financed through the initial common stock offering, the sale of bonds in 2006, and the retention of all earnings. Because of its rapid growth in revenue and profits, with only short-term earnings declines, GAC's common stockholders have been content to let the firm reinvest earnings as part of its plan to expand capacity to meet the growing demand for its services. This strategy has benefited most stockholders in terms of stock splits and capital gains. Since the company's initial public offering in 2003, GAC's stock twice has been split 2-for-1. In terms of total growth, the market price of GAC's stock, after adjustment for stock splits, has increased by 800% during the 7-year period 2003–2009.

    Because GAC's rapid growth is beginning to slow, the firm's CEO, Marilyn McNeely, believes that its shares are becoming less attractive to investors. McNeely has had discussions with her CFO, Bobby Joe Rook, who believes that the firm must begin to pay cash dividends. He argues that many investors value regular dividends and that by beginning to pay them, GAC would increase the demand—and therefore the price—for its shares. McNeely decided that at the next board meeting she would propose that the firm begin to pay dividends on a regular basis.

    McNeely realized that if the board approved her recommendation, it would have to (1) establish a dividend policy and (2) set the amount of the initial annual dividend.

She had Rook prepare a summary of the firm's annual EPS. It is given in the following table.

Year	EPS
2009	$3.70
2008	4.10
2007	3.90
2006	3.30
2005	2.20
2004	0.83
2003	0.55

Rook indicated that he expects EPS to remain within 10% (plus or minus) of the most recent (2009) value during the next 3 years. His most likely estimate is an annual increase of about 3%.

After much discussion, McNeely and Rook agreed that she would recommend to the board one of the following types of dividend policies:

1. Constant-payout-ratio dividend policy
2. Regular dividend policy
3. Low-regular-and-extra dividend policy

McNeely realizes that her dividend proposal would significantly affect future financing opportunities and costs and the firm's share price. She also knows that she must be sure that her proposal is complete and that it fully educates the board with regard to the long-term implications of each policy.

To Do

a. Analyze each of the three dividend policies in light of GAC's financial position.
b. Which dividend policy would you recommend? Justify your recommendation.
c. What are the key factors to consider when setting the amount of a firm's initial annual dividend?
d. How should Ms. McNeely go about deciding what initial annual dividend she will recommend to the board?
e. In view of your dividend policy recommendation in part **b**, how large an initial dividend would you recommend? Justify your recommendation.

Spreadsheet Exercise

One way to lower the market price of a firm's stock is via a stock split. Rock-O Corporation finds itself in a different situation: Its stock has been selling at relatively low prices. To increase the market price of the stock, the company chooses to use a *reverse stock split* of 2-for-3.

The company currently has 700,000 common shares outstanding and no preferred stock. The common stock carries a par value of $1. At this time, the paid-in capital in excess of par is $7,000,000, and the firm's retained earnings is $3,500,000.

To Do

Create a spreadsheet to determine the following:

a. The stockholders' equity section of the balance sheet *before* the reverse stock split.

b. The stockholders' equity section of the balance sheet *after* the reverse stock split.

Group Exercise

Dividends have been drawn into the spotlight of late because of scandal and "fictitious" earnings. Dividends have also attained greater prominence as a result of tax law changes and increased shareholder activism. This chapter looked at dividend policy in the context of a firm's long-term financing decisions. This exercise continues to combine data for your shadow firm and your group's fictitious firm in considering some dividend issues.

To Do

a. Return to your shadow firm's financials. Describe the extent to which dividends are used by your shadow firm, both currently and in the recent past. Compare this information to the EPS for each of the recent years.

b. Apply similar numbers for your fictitious firm. (If your shadow firm doesn't currently pay dividends, simulate numbers that make sense in the context of your previous work.)

c. Describe a change in dividends that has been approved by your fictitious firm's board. You must specify the amount of the dividend, its frequency, and the relevant dates for payment. Explain and defend the change.

d. Return to your shadow firm and describe its stockholders' equity account.

e. Use similar numbers in designing your fictitious firm's equity account.

f. Describe any recent events related to your shadow firm's equity financing, including dividend changes and stock repurchases or splits.

Web Exercise

Go to the book's companion website at **www.prenhall.com/gitman** to find the Web Exercise for this chapter.

Remember to check the book's website at **www.prenhall.com/gitman** to find additional resources, including Web Exercises and a Web Case.

Integrative Case 4

O'Grady Apparel Company

O'Grady Apparel Company was founded nearly 160 years ago when an Irish merchant named Garrett O'Grady landed in Los Angeles with an inventory of heavy canvas, which he hoped to sell for tents and wagon covers to miners headed for the California goldfields. Instead, he turned to the sale of harder-wearing clothing.

Today, O'Grady Apparel Company is a small manufacturer of fabrics and clothing whose stock is traded in the OTC market. In 2009, the Los Angeles–based company experienced sharp increases in both domestic and European markets resulting in record earnings. Sales rose from $15.9 million in 2008 to $18.3 million in 2009 with earnings per share of $3.28 and $3.84, respectively.

European sales represented 29% of total sales in 2009, up from 24% the year before and only 3% in 2004, 1 year after foreign operations were launched. Although foreign sales represent nearly one-third of total sales, the growth in the domestic market is expected to affect the company most markedly. Management expects sales to surpass $21 million in 2010, and earnings per share are expected to rise to $4.40. (Selected income statement items are presented in Table 1.)

Because of the recent growth, Margaret Jennings, the corporate treasurer, is concerned that available funds are not being used to their fullest potential. The projected $1,300,000 of internally generated 2010 funds is expected to be insufficient to meet the company's expansion needs. Management has set a policy of maintaining the current capital structure proportions of 25% long-term debt, 10% preferred stock, and 65% common stock equity for at least the next 3 years. In addition, it plans to continue paying out 40% of its earnings as dividends. Total capital expenditures are yet to be determined.

Jennings has been presented with several competing investment opportunities by division and product managers. However, because funds are limited, choices of which projects to accept must be made. The investment opportunities schedule (IOS) is shown in Table 2. To analyze the effect of the increased financing requirements on the weighted average cost of capital (WACC), Jennings contacted a leading investment banking firm that provided the financing cost data given in Table 3. O'Grady is in the 40% tax bracket.

TABLE 1

				Projected
Selected Income Statement Items				
	2007	2008	2009	2010
Net sales	$13,860,000	$15,940,000	$18,330,000	$21,080,000
Net profits after taxes	1,520,000	1,750,000	2,020,000	2,323,000
Earnings per share (EPS)	2.88	3.28	3.84	4.40
Dividends per share	1.15	1.31	1.54	1.76

TABLE 2

	Investment Opportunities Schedule (IOS)	
Investment opportunity	Internal rate of return (IRR)	Initial investment
A	21%	$400,000
B	19	200,000
C	24	700,000
D	27	500,000
E	18	300,000
F	22	600,000
G	17	500,000

TABLE 3

Financing Cost Data

Long-term debt: The firm can raise $700,000 of additional debt by selling 10-year, $1,000, 12% annual interest rate bonds to net $970 after flotation costs. Any debt in excess of $700,000 will have a before-tax cost, r_d, of 18%.

Preferred stock: Preferred stock, regardless of the amount sold, can be issued with a $60 par value and a 17% annual dividend rate. It will net $57 per share after flotation costs.

Common stock equity: The firm expects its dividends and earnings to continue to grow at a constant rate of 15% per year. The firm's stock is currently selling for $20 per share. The firm expects to have $1,300,000 of available retained earnings. Once the retained earnings has been exhausted, the firm can raise additional funds by selling new common stock, netting $16 per share after underpricing and flotation costs.

To Do

a. Over the relevant ranges noted in the following table, calculate the after-tax cost of each source of financing needed to complete the table.

Source of capital	Range of new financing	After-tax cost (%)
Long-term debt	$0–$700,000	_____
	$700,000 and above	_____
Preferred stock	$0 and above	_____
Common stock equity	$0–$1,300,000	_____
	$1,300,000 and above	_____

b. (1) Determine the *break points* associated with each source of capital.

    (2) Using the break points developed in part (1), determine each of the ranges of *total* new financing over which the firm's weighted average cost of capital (WACC) remains constant.

    (3) Calculate the weighted average cost of capital for each range of total new financing.

c. (1) Using your findings in part **b**(3) with the investment opportunities schedule (IOS), draw the firm's weighted marginal cost of capital (WMCC) schedule and the IOS on the same set of axes, with total new financing or investment on the *x* axis and weighted average cost of capital and IRR on the *y* axis.

    (2) Which, if any, of the available investments would you recommend that the firm accept? Explain your answer.

d. (1) Assuming that the specific financing costs do not change, what effect would a shift to a more highly leveraged *capital structure* consisting of 50% long-term debt, 10% preferred stock, and 40% common stock have on your previous findings? (*Note:* Rework parts **b** and **c** using these capital structure weights.)

    (2) Which capital structure—the original one or this one—seems better? Why?

e. (1) What type of *dividend policy* does the firm appear to employ? Does it seem appropriate given the firm's recent growth in sales and profits and given its current investment opportunities?

    (2) Would you recommend an alternative dividend policy? Explain. How would this policy affect the investments recommended in part **c**(2)?

Part Five
Short-Term Financial Decisions

Chapters in This Part

14 **Working Capital and Current Assets Management**

15 **Current Liabilities Management**

INTEGRATIVE CASE 5: **Casa de Diseño**

14 Working Capital and Current Assets Management

WHY THIS CHAPTER MATTERS TO YOU

In Your Professional Life

Accounting: You need to understand the cash conversion cycle and the management of inventory, accounts receivable, and receipts and disbursements of cash.

Information systems: You need to understand the cash conversion cycle, inventory, accounts receivable, and receipts and disbursements of cash to design financial information systems that facilitate effective short-term financial management.

Management: You need to understand the management of working capital so that you can efficiently manage current assets and decide whether to finance the firm's funds requirements aggressively or conservatively.

Marketing: You need to understand credit selection and monitoring because sales will be affected by the availability of credit to purchasers; sales will also be affected by inventory management.

Operations: You need to understand the cash conversion cycle because you will be responsible for reducing the cycle through the efficient management of production, inventory, and costs.

In Your Personal Life

You often will be faced with short-term purchasing decisions, which tend to focus on consumable items. Many involve tradeoffs between quantity and price: Should you buy large quantities in order to pay a lower unit price, hold the items, and use them over time? Or should you buy smaller quantities more frequently and pay a slightly higher unit price? Analyzing these types of short-term purchasing decisions will help you make the most of your money.

LEARNING GOALS

LG 1 Understand short-term financial management, net working capital, and the related tradeoff between profitability and risk.

LG 2 Describe the cash conversion cycle, its funding requirements, and the key strategies for managing it.

LG 3 Discuss inventory management: differing views, common techniques, and international concerns.

LG 4 Explain the credit selection process and the quantitative procedure for evaluating changes in credit standards.

LG 5 Review the procedures for quantitatively considering cash discount changes, other aspects of credit terms, and credit monitoring.

LG 6 Understand the management of receipts and disbursements, including float, speeding up collections, slowing down payments, cash concentration, zero-balance accounts, and investing in marketable securities.

AT&T

Outsourcing Is in the Cards

AT&T is among the world's premiere voice, video, and data communications companies, serving consumers, businesses, and government. Backed by the research and development capabilities of AT&T Labs, the company runs the world's largest, most sophisticated communications network.

One of AT&T's services to its customers is prepaid phone cards. The company, which is highly skilled at delivering telecommunications services, had minimal experience in the supply chain management processes needed to bring tangible, packaged goods to channels such as convenience stores and mass merchants. AT&T made a strategic business decision to outsource its PrePaid Card end-to-end supply chain management functions. AT&T chose **Accenture,** a global management-consulting, technology services company, to solve its problem.

Accenture teamed with AT&T to develop a customer-focused supply chain that integrated all of the needed business processes—sourcing, production, scheduling, account service, warehousing, fulfillment, inventory, billing, and systems management. Using its supply chain management expertise, Accenture transformed purchasing and inventory decision-making processes. Together, AT&T and Accenture reduced PrePaid Card production costs by 15 percent, improved warehouse productivity by 25 percent, and reduced raw materials inventory by 25 percent.

Reducing raw materials inventory through outsourcing or by converting to just-in-time manufacturing can lower net working capital requirements, the difference between a firm's current assets including inventory and a firm's current liabilities. Because long-term assets provide a better return than short-term assets, reducing short-term assets can free up capital, which can then be better employed by the company.

Pleased with its partnership with Accenture, AT&T turned to the company again to develop and bring to market a unique new offering called PrePaid WebCentsSM Service, a secure alternative to credit cards for purchasing online content.

In this chapter, we look at techniques and strategies for managing working capital and current assets. We first discuss the fundamentals of net working capital and then demonstrate the cash conversion cycle. The balance of the chapter considers the management of inventory, accounts receivable, and receipts and disbursements in the context of the cash conversion cycle.

> **What are the possible benefits of outsourcing finance and accounting activities?**

LG 1   14.1 | Net Working Capital Fundamentals

The firm's balance sheet provides information about the structure of the firm's investments on the one hand and the structure of its financing sources on the other hand. The structures chosen should consistently lead to the maximization of the value of the owners' investment in the firm.

Short-Term Financial Management

short-term financial management
Management of current assets and current liabilities.

Important components of the firm's financial structure include the level of investment in current assets and the extent of current liability financing. In U.S. manufacturing firms, current assets account for about 40 percent of total assets; current liabilities represent about 26 percent of total financing. Therefore, it should not be surprising to learn that **short-term financial management**—managing current assets and current liabilities—is one of the financial manager's most important and time-consuming activities. A study of *Fortune* 1000 firms found that more than one-third of financial management time is spent managing current assets and about one-fourth of financial management time is spent managing current liabilities.[1]

The goal of short-term financial management is to manage each of the firm's current assets (inventory, accounts receivable, cash, and marketable securities) and current liabilities (accounts payable, accruals, and notes payable) to achieve a balance between profitability and risk that contributes positively to the firm's value. This chapter does not discuss the optimal level of current assets and current liabilities that a firm should have. That issue is unresolved in the financial literature. Here, we first use *net working capital* to consider the basic relationship between current assets and current liabilities and then use the *cash conversion cycle* to consider the key aspects of current asset management. In the following chapter, we consider current liability management.

Net Working Capital

working capital
Current assets, which represent the portion of investment that circulates from one form to another in the ordinary conduct of business.

Current assets, commonly called **working capital,** represent the portion of investment that circulates from one form to another in the ordinary conduct of business. This idea embraces the recurring transition from cash to inventories to receivables and back to cash. As cash substitutes, *marketable securities* are considered part of working capital.

Current liabilities represent the firm's short-term financing, because they include all debts of the firm that come due (must be paid) in 1 year or less. These debts usually include amounts owed to suppliers (accounts payable), employees and governments (accruals), and banks (notes payable), among others.

net working capital
The difference between the firm's current assets and its current liabilities; can be *positive* or *negative.*

As noted in Chapter 8, **net working capital** is commonly defined as the difference between the firm's current assets and its current liabilities. When the current assets exceed the current liabilities, the firm has *positive net working capital.*

---

1. Lawrence J. Gitman and Charles E. Maxwell, "Financial Activities of Major U.S. Firms: Survey and Analysis of Fortune's 1000," *Financial Management* (Winter 1985), pp. 57–65.

When current assets are less than current liabilities, the firm has *negative net working capital.*

The conversion of current assets from inventory to receivables to cash provides the cash used to pay the current liabilities. The cash outlays for current liabilities are relatively predictable. When an obligation is incurred, the firm generally knows when the corresponding payment will be due. What is difficult to predict are the cash inflows—the conversion of the current assets to more liquid forms. The more predictable its cash inflows, the less net working capital a firm needs. Because most firms are unable to match cash inflows to cash outflows with certainty, they usually need current assets that more than cover outflows for current liabilities. In general, the greater the margin by which a firm's current assets cover its current liabilities, the better able it will be to pay its bills as they come due.

Hint Stated differently, some portion of current assets is usually held to provide liquidity in case it is unexpectedly needed.

Tradeoff between Profitability and Risk

A tradeoff exists between a firm's profitability and its risk. **Profitability,** in this context, is the relationship between revenues and costs generated by using the firm's assets—both current and fixed—in productive activities. A firm can increase its profits by (1) increasing revenues or (2) decreasing costs. **Risk,** in the context of short-term financial management, is the probability that a firm will be unable to pay its bills as they come due. A firm that cannot pay its bills as they come due is said to be **technically insolvent.** It is generally assumed that the greater the firm's net working capital, the lower its risk. In other words, the more net working capital, the more liquid the firm and therefore the lower its risk of becoming technically insolvent. Using these definitions of profitability and risk, we can demonstrate the tradeoff between them by considering changes in current assets and current liabilities separately.

profitability
The relationship between revenues and costs generated by using the firm's assets—both current and fixed—in productive activities.

risk (of technical insolvency)
The probability that a firm will be unable to pay its bills as they come due.

technically insolvent
Describes a firm that is unable to pay its bills as they come due.

Changes in Current Assets

We can demonstrate how changing the level of the firm's current assets affects its profitability–risk tradeoff by using the ratio of current assets to total assets. This ratio indicates the *percentage of total assets* that is current. For purposes of illustration, we will assume that the level of total assets remains unchanged.[2] The effects on both profitability and risk of an increase or decrease in this ratio are summarized in the upper portion of Table 14.1 (on page 640). When the ratio increases—that is, when current assets increase—profitability decreases. Why? Because current assets are less profitable than fixed assets. Fixed assets are more profitable because they add more value to the product than that provided by current assets. Without fixed assets, the firm could not produce the product.

The risk effect, however, decreases as the ratio of current assets to total assets increases. The increase in current assets increases net working capital, thereby reducing the risk of technical insolvency. In addition, as you go down the asset side of the balance sheet, the risk associated with the assets increases: Investment in cash and marketable securities is less risky than investment in accounts receivable,

Hint It is generally easier to turn receivables into the more liquid asset cash than it is to turn inventory into cash. As we will learn in Chapter 15, the firm can sell its receivables for cash. Often inventory is sold on credit and is therefore converted to a receivable before it becomes cash.

---

2. To isolate the effect of changing asset and financing mixes on the firm's profitability and risk, we assume the level of total assets to be *constant* in this and the following discussion.

	TABLE 14.1	Effects of Changing Ratios on Profits and Risk		
Ratio	Change in ratio	Effect on profit	Effect on risk
Current assets / Total assets	Increase	Decrease	Decrease
	Decrease	Increase	Increase
Current liabilities / Total assets	Increase	Increase	Increase
	Decrease	Decrease	Decrease

inventories, and fixed assets. Accounts receivable investment is less risky than investment in inventories and fixed assets. Investment in inventories is less risky than investment in fixed assets. The nearer an asset is to cash, the less risky it is. The opposite effects on profit and risk result from a decrease in the ratio of current assets to total assets.

Changes in Current Liabilities

We also can demonstrate how changing the level of the firm's current liabilities affects its profitability–risk tradeoff by using the ratio of current liabilities to total assets. This ratio indicates the percentage of total assets that has been financed with current liabilities. Again, assuming that total assets remain unchanged, the effects on both profitability and risk of an increase or decrease in the ratio are summarized in the lower portion of Table 14.1. When the ratio increases, profitability increases. Why? Because the firm uses more of the less expensive current liabilities financing and less long-term financing. Current liabilities are less expensive because only notes payable, which represent about 20 percent of the typical manufacturer's current liabilities, have a cost. The other current liabilities are basically debts on which the firm pays no charge or interest. However, when the ratio of current liabilities to total assets increases, the risk of technical insolvency also increases, because the increase in current liabilities in turn decreases net working capital. The opposite effects on profit and risk result from a decrease in the ratio of current liabilities to total assets.

REVIEW QUESTIONS

14–1 Why is *short-term financial management* one of the most important and time-consuming activities of the financial manager? What is *net working capital?*

14–2 What is the relationship between the predictability of a firm's cash inflows and its required level of net working capital? How are net working capital, liquidity, and *risk of technical insolvency* related?

14–3 Why does an increase in the ratio of current assets to total assets decrease both profits and risk as measured by net working capital? How do changes in the ratio of current liabilities to total assets affect profitability and risk?

14.2 | Cash Conversion Cycle

Central to short-term financial management is an understanding of the firm's *cash conversion cycle.*[3] This cycle frames discussion of the management of the firm's current assets in this chapter and that of the management of current liabilities in Chapter 15. Here, we begin by demonstrating the calculation and application of the cash conversion cycle.

Calculating the Cash Conversion Cycle

operating cycle (OC)
The time from the beginning of the production process to collection of cash from the sale of the finished product.

A firm's **operating cycle (OC)** is the time from the beginning of the production process to collection of cash from the sale of the finished product. The operating cycle encompasses two major short-term asset categories: inventory and accounts receivable. It is measured in elapsed time by summing the *average age of inventory (AAI)* and the *average collection period (ACP)*.

$$OC = AAI + ACP \qquad \text{(14.1)}$$

Hint A firm can lower its working capital if it can speed up its operating cycle. For example, if a firm accepts bank credit (like a Visa card), it will receive cash sooner after the sale is transacted than if it has to wait until the customer pays its accounts receivable.

However, the process of producing and selling a product also includes the purchase of production inputs (raw materials) on account, which results in accounts payable. Accounts payable reduce the number of days a firm's resources are tied up in the operating cycle. The time it takes to pay the accounts payable, measured in days, is the *average payment period (APP)*. The operating cycle less the average payment period is referred to as the **cash conversion cycle (CCC)**. It represents the amount of time the firm's resources are tied up. The formula for the cash conversion cycle is

cash conversion cycle (CCC)
The amount of time a firm's resources are tied up; calculated by subtracting the average payment period from the *operating cycle.*

$$CCC = OC - APP \qquad \text{(14.2)}$$

Substituting the relationship in Equation 14.1 into Equation 14.2, we can see that the cash conversion cycle has three main components, as shown in Equation 14.3: (1) average age of the inventory, (2) average collection period, and (3) average payment period.

$$CCC = AAI + ACP - APP \qquad \text{(14.3)}$$

Clearly, if a firm changes any of these time periods, it changes the amount of resources tied up in the day-to-day operation of the firm.

Example

MAX Company, a producer of paper dinnerware, has annual sales of $10 million, a cost of goods sold of 75% of sales, and purchases that are 65% of cost of goods sold. MAX has an average age of inventory (AAI) of 60 days, an average collection period (ACP) of 40 days, and an average payment period (APP) of 35 days. Thus the cash conversion cycle for MAX is 65 days (60 + 40 − 35). Figure 14.1 (on page 642) presents MAX Company's cash conversion cycle as a time line.

---

3. The conceptual model that is used in this section to demonstrate basic short-term financial management strategies was developed by Lawrence J. Gitman in "Estimating Corporate Liquidity Requirements: A Simplified Approach," *The Financial Review* (1974), pp. 79–88, and refined and operationalized by Lawrence J. Gitman and Kanwal S. Sachdeva in "A Framework for Estimating and Analyzing the Required Working Capital Investment," *Review of Business and Economic Research* (Spring 1982), pp. 35–44.

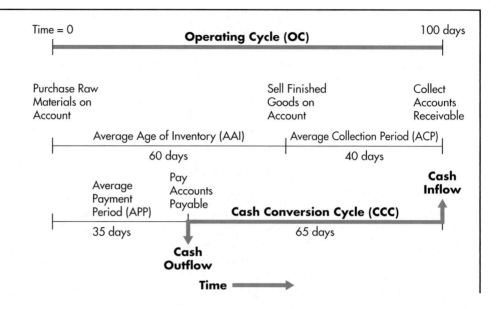

FIGURE 14.1

Time Line for MAX Company's Cash Conversion Cycle
MAX Company's operating cycle is 100 days, and its cash conversion cycle is 65 days.

The resources MAX has invested in this cash conversion cycle (assuming a 365-day year) are

Inventory	$= (\$10,000,000 \times 0.75) \times (60/365)$	$= \$1,232,877$
+ Accounts receivable	$= (\ 10,000,000 \times 40/365)$	$= 1,095,890$
− Accounts payable	$= (\ 10,000,000 \times 0.75 \times 0.65) \times (35/365) =$	$467,466$
	= Resources invested	$= \$1,861,301$

Changes in any of the time periods will change the resources tied up in operations. For example, if MAX could reduce the average collection period on its accounts receivable by 5 days, it would shorten the cash conversion time line and thus reduce the amount of resources MAX has invested in operations. For MAX, a 5-day reduction in the average collection period would reduce the resources invested in the cash conversion cycle by $136,986 [$10,000,000 \times (5/365)]$.

Funding Requirements of the Cash Conversion Cycle

We can use the cash conversion cycle as a basis for discussing how the firm funds its required investment in operating assets. We first differentiate between permanent and seasonal funding needs and then describe aggressive and conservative seasonal funding strategies.

permanent funding requirement
A constant investment in operating assets resulting from constant sales over time.

Permanent versus Seasonal Funding Needs

If the firm's sales are constant, then its investment in operating assets should also be constant, and the firm will have only a **permanent funding requirement**. If the firm's sales are cyclic, then its investment in operating assets will vary over time

seasonal funding requirement
An investment in operating assets that varies over time as a result of cyclic sales.

with its sales cycles, and the firm will have **seasonal funding requirements** in addition to the permanent funding required for its minimum investment in operating assets.

Example

Nicholson Company holds, on average, $50,000 in cash and marketable securities, $1,250,000 in inventory, and $750,000 in accounts receivable. Nicholson's business is very stable over time, so its operating assets can be viewed as permanent. In addition, Nicholson's accounts payable of $425,000 are stable over time. Thus Nicholson has a permanent investment in operating assets of $1,625,000 ($50,000 + $1,250,0000 + $750,000 − $425,000). That amount would also equal its permanent funding requirement.

In contrast, Semper Pump Company, which produces bicycle pumps, has seasonal funding needs. Semper has seasonal sales, with its peak sales being driven by the summertime purchases of bicycle pumps. Semper holds, at minimum, $25,000 in cash and marketable securities, $100,000 in inventory, and $60,000 in accounts receivable. At peak times, Semper's inventory increases to $750,000, and its accounts receivable increase to $400,000. To capture production efficiencies, Semper produces pumps at a constant rate throughout the year. Thus accounts payable remain at $50,000 throughout the year. Accordingly, Semper has a permanent funding requirement for its minimum level of operating assets of $135,000 ($25,000 + $100,000 + $60,000 − $50,000) and peak seasonal funding requirements (in excess of its permanent need) of $990,000 [($25,000 + $750,000 + $400,000 − $50,000) − $135,000]. Semper's total funding requirements for operating assets vary from a minimum of $135,000 (permanent) to a seasonal peak of $1,125,000 ($135,000 + $990,000). Figure 14.2 depicts these needs over time.

FIGURE 14.2	**Semper Pump Company's Total Funding Requirements**

Semper Pump Company's peak funds need is $1,125,000, and its minimum need is $135,000.

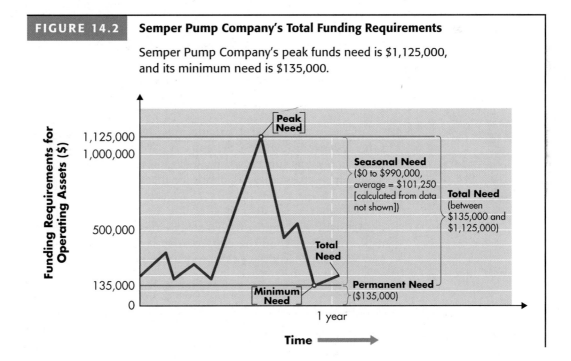

Aggressive versus Conservative Seasonal Funding Strategies

Short-term funds are typically less expensive than long-term funds. (The yield curve is typically upward-sloping.) However, long-term funds allow the firm to lock in its cost of funds over a period of time and thus avoid the risk of increases in short-term interest rates. Also, long-term funding ensures that the required funds are available to the firm when needed. Short-term funding exposes the firm to the risk that it may not be able to obtain the funds needed to cover its seasonal peaks. Under an **aggressive funding strategy,** the firm funds its seasonal requirements with short-term debt and its permanent requirements with long-term debt. Under a **conservative funding strategy,** the firm funds both its seasonal and its permanent requirements with long-term debt.

Example

Semper Pump Company has a permanent funding requirement of $135,000 in operating assets and seasonal funding requirements that vary between $0 and $990,000 and average $101,250 (calculated from data not shown). If Semper can borrow short-term funds at 6.25% and long-term funds at 8%, and if it can earn 5% on the investment of any surplus balances, then the annual cost of an aggressive strategy for seasonal funding will be

Cost of short-term financing	$= 0.0625 \times$	$101,250 =$	$ 6,328.13
+ Cost of long-term financing	$= 0.0800 \times$	$135,000 =$	10,800.00
− Earnings on surplus balances[4]	$= 0.0500 \times$	$0 =$	0
Total cost of aggressive strategy			$17,128.13

Alternatively, Semper can choose a conservative strategy, under which surplus cash balances are fully invested. (In Figure 14.2, this surplus will be the difference between the peak need of $1,125,000 and the total need, which varies between $135,000 and $1,125,000 during the year.) The cost of the conservative strategy will be

Cost of short-term financing	$= 0.0625 \times$	$ 0 =$	$ 0
+ Cost of long-term financing	$= 0.0800 \times$	1,125,000 $=$	90,000.00
− Earnings on surplus balances[5]	$= 0.0500 \times$	888,750 $=$	44,437.50
Total cost of conservative strategy			$45,562.50

It is clear from these calculations that for Semper, the aggressive strategy is far less expensive than the conservative strategy. However, it is equally clear that Semper has substantial peak-season operating-asset needs and that it must have adequate funding available to meet the peak needs and ensure ongoing operations.

Clearly, the aggressive strategy's heavy reliance on short-term financing makes it riskier than the conservative strategy because of interest rate swings and possible difficulties in obtaining needed short-term financing quickly when

---

4. Because under this strategy the amount of financing exactly equals the estimated funding need, no surplus balances exist.

5. The average surplus balance would be calculated by subtracting the sum of the permanent need ($135,000) and the average seasonal need ($101,250) from the seasonal peak need ($1,125,000) to get $888,750 ($1,125,000 − $135,000 − $101,250). This represents the surplus amount of financing that on average could be invested in short-term vehicles that earn a 5% annual return.

seasonal peaks occur. The conservative strategy avoids these risks through the locked-in interest rate and long-term financing, but it is more costly because of the negative spread between the earnings rate on surplus funds (5% in the example) and the cost of the long-term funds that create the surplus (8% in the example). Where the firm operates, between the extremes of the aggressive and conservative seasonal funding strategies, depends on management's disposition toward risk and the strength of its banking relationships.

Strategies for Managing the Cash Conversion Cycle

Some firms establish a *target* cash conversion cycle and then monitor and manage the *actual* cash conversion cycle toward the targeted value. A positive cash conversion cycle, as we saw for MAX Company in the earlier example, means the firm must use negotiated liabilities (such as bank loans) to support its operating assets. Negotiated liabilities carry an explicit cost, so the firm benefits by minimizing their use in supporting operating assets. Simply stated, the goal is to *minimize the length of the cash conversion cycle,* which minimizes negotiated liabilities. This goal can be realized through use of the following strategies:

1. *Turn over inventory as quickly as possible* without stockouts that result in lost sales.
2. *Collect accounts receivable as quickly as possible* without losing sales from high-pressure collection techniques.
3. *Manage mail, processing, and clearing time* to reduce them when collecting from customers and to increase them when paying suppliers.
4. *Pay accounts payable as slowly as possible* without damaging the firm's credit rating.

Techniques for implementing these four strategies are the focus of the remainder of this chapter and the following chapter.

REVIEW QUESTIONS

14–4 What is the difference between the firm's *operating cycle* and its *cash conversion cycle?*

14–5 Why is it helpful to divide the funding needs of a seasonal business into its permanent and seasonal funding requirements when developing a funding strategy?

14–6 What are the benefits, costs, and risks of an *aggressive funding strategy* and of a *conservative funding strategy?* Under which strategy is the borrowing often in excess of the actual need?

14–7 Why is it important for a firm to minimize the length of its cash conversion cycle?

14.3 | Inventory Management

The first component of the cash conversion cycle is the average age of inventory. The objective for managing inventory, as noted earlier, is to turn over inventory as quickly as possible without losing sales from stockouts. The financial manager tends to act as an advisor or "watchdog" in matters concerning inventory; he or she does not have direct control over inventory but does provide input to the inventory management process.

Differing Viewpoints about Inventory Level

Differing viewpoints about appropriate inventory levels commonly exist among a firm's finance, marketing, manufacturing, and purchasing managers. Each views inventory levels in light of his or her own objectives. The *financial manager's* general disposition toward inventory levels is to keep them low, to ensure that the firm's money is not being unwisely invested in excess resources. The *marketing manager*, on the other hand, would like to have large inventories of the firm's finished products. This would ensure that all orders could be filled quickly, eliminating the need for backorders due to stockouts.

The *manufacturing manager's* major responsibility is to implement the production plan so that it results in the desired amount of finished goods of acceptable quality available on time at a low cost. In fulfilling this role, the manufacturing manager would keep raw materials inventories high to avoid production delays. He or she also would favor large production runs for the sake of lower unit production costs, which would result in high finished goods inventories.

The *purchasing manager* is concerned solely with the raw materials inventories. He or she must have on hand, in the correct quantities at the desired times and at a favorable price, whatever raw materials are required by production. Without proper control, in an effort to get quantity discounts or in anticipation of rising prices or a shortage of certain materials, the purchasing manager may purchase larger quantities of resources than are actually needed at the time.

Common Techniques for Managing Inventory

Numerous techniques are available for effectively managing the firm's inventory. Here we briefly consider four commonly used techniques.

ABC System

ABC inventory system
Inventory management technique that divides inventory into three groups—A, B, and C, in descending order of importance and level of monitoring, on the basis of the dollar investment in each.

A firm using the **ABC inventory system** divides its inventory into three groups: A, B, and C. The A group includes those items with the largest dollar investment. Typically, this group consists of 20 percent of the firm's inventory items but 80 percent of its investment in inventory. The B group consists of items that account for the next largest investment in inventory. The C group consists of a large number of items that require a relatively small investment.

The inventory group of each item determines the item's level of monitoring. The A group items receive the most intense monitoring because of the high dollar investment. Typically, A group items are tracked on a perpetual inventory system that allows daily verification of each item's inventory level. B group items are frequently controlled through periodic, perhaps weekly, checking of their levels. C group items are monitored with unsophisticated techniques, such as the two-bin method. With the **two-bin method,** the item is stored in two bins. As an item is needed, inventory is removed from the first bin. When that bin is empty, an order is placed to refill the first bin while inventory is drawn from the second bin. The second bin is used until empty, and so on.

two-bin method
Unsophisticated inventory-monitoring technique that is typically applied to C group items and involves reordering inventory when one of two bins is empty.

The large dollar investment in A and B group items suggests the need for a better method of inventory management than the ABC system. The EOQ model, discussed next, is an appropriate model for the management of A and B group items.

Economic Order Quantity (EOQ) Model

One of the most common techniques for determining the optimal order size for inventory items is the **economic order quantity (EOQ) model.** The EOQ model considers various costs of inventory and then determines what order size minimizes total inventory cost.

EOQ assumes that the relevant costs of inventory can be divided into *order costs* and *carrying costs.* (The model excludes the actual cost of the inventory item.) Each of them has certain key components and characteristics. **Order costs** include the fixed clerical costs of placing and receiving orders: the cost of writing a purchase order, of processing the resulting paperwork, and of receiving an order and checking it against the invoice. Order costs are stated in dollars per order. **Carrying costs** are the variable costs per unit of holding an item of inventory for a specific period of time. Carrying costs include storage costs, insurance costs, the costs of deterioration and obsolescence, and the opportunity or financial cost of having funds invested in inventory. These costs are stated in dollars per unit per period.

Order costs decrease as the size of the order increases. Carrying costs, however, increase with increases in the order size. The EOQ model analyzes the tradeoff between order costs and carrying costs to determine the *order quantity that minimizes the total inventory cost.*

Mathematical Development of EOQ   A formula can be developed for determining the firm's EOQ for a given inventory item, where

S = usage in units per period

O = order cost per order

C = carrying cost per unit per period

Q = order quantity in units

The first step is to derive the cost functions for order cost and carrying cost. The order cost can be expressed as the product of the cost per order and the number of orders. Because the number of orders equals the usage during the period divided by the order quantity (S/Q), the order cost can be expressed as follows:

$$\text{Order cost} = O \times S/Q \quad \text{(14.4)}$$

The carrying cost is defined as the cost of carrying a unit of inventory per period multiplied by the firm's average inventory. The average inventory is the order quantity divided by 2 ($Q/2$), because inventory is assumed to be depleted at a constant rate. Thus carrying cost can be expressed as follows:

$$\text{Carrying cost} = C \times Q/2 \quad \text{(14.5)}$$

The firm's **total cost of inventory** is found by summing the order cost and the carrying cost. Thus the total cost function is

$$\text{Total cost} = (O \times S/Q) + (C \times Q/2) \quad \text{(14.6)}$$

economic order quantity (EOQ) model
Inventory management technique for determining an item's optimal order size, which is the size that minimizes the total of its *order costs* and *carrying costs.*

order costs
The fixed clerical costs of placing and receiving an inventory order.

carrying costs
The variable costs per unit of holding an item in inventory for a specific period of time.

total cost of inventory
The sum of order costs and carrying costs of inventory.

Hint The EOQ calculation helps management minimize the total cost of inventory. Lowering order costs will cause an increase in carrying costs and may increase total cost. Likewise, a decrease in total cost may result from reduced carrying costs. The goal, facilitated by using the EOQ calculation, is to lower total cost.

Because the EOQ is defined as the order quantity that minimizes the total cost function, we must solve the total cost function for the EOQ.[6] The resulting equation is

$$EOQ = \sqrt{\frac{2 \times S \times O}{C}} \tag{14.7}$$

Although the EOQ model has weaknesses, it is certainly better than subjective decision making. Despite the fact that the use of the EOQ model is outside the control of the financial manager, the financial manager must be aware of its utility and must provide certain inputs, specifically with respect to inventory carrying costs.

Personal Finance Example Individuals sometimes are confronted with personal finance decisions involving cost tradeoffs similar to the tradeoff between the fixed order costs and variable carrying costs of inventory that corporations face. Take the case of the von Dammes, who are trying to decide whether a conventional car (uses gas) or a hybrid car (uses gas and electric battery) would be more cost-effective.

The von Dammes plan to keep whichever car they choose for 3 years and expect to drive it 12,000 miles in each of those years. They will use the same dollar amount of financing repaid under the same terms for either car and they expect the cars to have identical repair costs over the 3-year ownership period. They also assume that the trade-in value of the two cars at the end of 3 years will be identical. Both cars use regular unleaded gas, which they estimate will cost, on average, $3.20 per gallon over the 3 years. The key data for each car follows:

	Conventional	Hybrid
Total cost	$24,500	$27,300
Average miles per gallon	27	42

We can begin by calculating the total fuel cost for each car over the 3-year ownership period:

Conventional: [(3 years × 12,000 miles per year)/27 miles per gallon]
×$3.20 per gallon

= 1,333.33 gallons × $3.20 per gallon = $4,267

Hybrid: [(3 years × 12,000 miles per year)/42 miles per gallon]
× $3.20 per gallon

= 857.14 gallons × $3.20 per gallon = $2,743

---

6. In this simple model the EOQ occurs at the point where the order cost $(O \times S/Q)$ just equals the carrying cost $(C \times Q/2)$. To demonstrate, we set the two costs equal and solve for Q:

$$OS/Q = CQ/2$$

Then cross-multiplying, we get:

$$2OS = CQ^2$$

Dividing both sides by C, we get:

$$Q^2 = 2OS/C, \text{ so } Q = \sqrt{2SO/C}$$

In order to buy the hybrid car, the von Dammes will have to pay $2,800 more ($27,300 − $24,500) than the cost of the conventional car, but they will save about $1,524 ($4,267 − $2,743) in fuel costs over the 3-year ownership period. Ignoring differences in timing, on a strict economic basis *they should buy the conventional car because the $2,800 marginal cost of the hybrid results in a marginal fuel cost savings of only $1,524.* Clearly, other factors such as environmental concerns and the reasonableness of the assumptions could affect their decision.

Reorder Point   Once the firm has determined its economic order quantity, it must determine when to place an order. The **reorder point** reflects the number of days of lead time the firm needs to place and receive an order and the firm's daily usage of the inventory item. Assuming that inventory is used at a constant rate, the formula for the reorder point is

reorder point
The point at which to reorder inventory, expressed as days of lead time × daily usage.

$$\text{Reorder point} = \text{Days of lead time} \times \text{Daily usage} \qquad (14.8)$$

For example, if a firm knows it takes 3 days to place and receive an order, and if it uses 15 units per day of the inventory item, then the reorder point is 45 units of inventory (3 days × 15 units/day). Thus, as soon as the item's inventory level falls to the reorder point (45 units, in this case) an order will be placed at the item's EOQ. If the estimates of lead time and usage are correct, then the order will arrive exactly as the inventory level reaches zero. However, lead times and usage rates are not precise, so most firms hold **safety stock** (extra inventory) to prevent stockouts of important items.

safety stock
Extra inventory that is held to prevent stockouts of important items.

Example

MAX Company has an A group inventory item that is vital to the production process. This item costs $1,500, and MAX uses 1,100 units of the item per year. MAX wants to determine its optimal order strategy for the item. To calculate the EOQ, we need the following inputs:

$$\text{Order cost per order} = \$150$$
$$\text{Carrying cost per unit per year} = \$200$$

Substituting into Equation 14.7, we get

$$\text{EOQ} = \sqrt{\frac{2 \times 1,100 \times \$150}{\$200}} \approx \underline{\underline{41}} \text{ units}$$

The reorder point for MAX depends on the number of days MAX operates per year. Assuming that MAX operates 250 days per year and uses 1,100 units of this item, its daily usage is 4.4 units (1,100 ÷ 250). If its lead time is 2 days and MAX wants to maintain a safety stock of 4 units, the reorder point for this item is 12.8 units [(2 × 4.4) + 4]. However, orders are made only in whole units, so the order is placed when the inventory falls to 13 units.

The firm's goal for inventory is to turn it over as quickly as possible without stockouts. Inventory turnover is best calculated by dividing cost of goods sold by average inventory. The EOQ model determines the optimal order size and, indirectly, through the assumption of constant usage, the average inventory. Thus the EOQ model determines the firm's optimal inventory turnover rate, given the firm's specific costs of inventory.

Just-in-Time (JIT) System

just-in-time (JIT) system
Inventory management technique that minimizes inventory investment by having materials arrive at exactly the time they are needed for production.

The **just-in-time (JIT) system** is used to minimize inventory investment. The philosophy is that materials should arrive at exactly the time they are needed for production. Ideally, the firm would have only work-in-process inventory. Because its objective is to minimize inventory investment, a JIT system uses no (or very little) safety stock. Extensive coordination among the firm's employees, its suppliers, and shipping companies must exist to ensure that material inputs arrive on time. Failure of materials to arrive on time results in a shutdown of the production line until the materials arrive. Likewise, a JIT system requires high-quality parts from suppliers. When quality problems arise, production must be stopped until the problems are resolved.

The goal of the JIT system is manufacturing efficiency. It uses inventory as a tool for attaining efficiency by emphasizing quality of the materials used and their timely delivery. When JIT is working properly, it forces process inefficiencies to surface.

Knowing the level of inventory is, of course, an important part of any inventory management system. As described in the nearby *Focus on Practice* box, radio frequency identification technology may be the "next new thing" in improving inventory and supply chain management.

Computerized Systems for Resource Control

materials requirement planning (MRP) system
Inventory management technique that applies EOQ concepts and a computer to compare production needs to available inventory balances and determine when orders should be placed for various items on a product's *bill of materials*.

manufacturing resource planning II (MRP II)
A sophisticated computerized system that integrates data from numerous areas such as finance, accounting, marketing, engineering, and manufacturing and generates production plans as well as numerous financial and management reports.

enterprise resource planning (ERP)
A computerized system that electronically integrates external information about the firm's suppliers and customers with the firm's departmental data so that information on all available resources—human and material—can be instantly obtained in a fashion that eliminates production delays and controls costs.

Today a number of systems are available for controlling inventory and other resources. One of the most basic is the **materials requirement planning (MRP) system.** It is used to determine what materials to order and when to order them. MRP applies EOQ concepts to determine how much to order. Using a computer, MRP simulates each product's bill of materials, inventory status, and manufacturing process. The *bill of materials* is simply a list of all parts and materials that go into making the finished product. For a given production plan, the computer simulates material requirements by comparing production needs to available inventory balances. On the basis of the time it takes for a product that is in process to move through the various production stages and the lead time to get materials, the MRP system determines when orders should be placed for various items on the bill of materials. The objective of this system is to lower the firm's inventory investment without impairing production. If the firm's opportunity cost of capital for investments of equal risk is 15 percent, every dollar of investment released from inventory will increase before-tax profits by $0.15.

A popular extension of MRP is **manufacturing resource planning II (MRP II),** which integrates data from numerous areas such as finance, accounting, marketing, engineering, and manufacturing using a sophisticated computer system. This system generates production plans as well as numerous financial and management reports. In essence, it models the firm's processes so that the effects of changes in one area of operations on other areas can be assessed and monitored. For example, the MRP II system would allow the firm to assess the effect of an increase in labor costs on sales and profits.

Whereas MRP and MRP II tend to focus on internal operations, **enterprise resource planning (ERP)** systems expand the focus to the external environment by including information about suppliers and customers. ERP electronically integrates all of a firm's departments so that, for example, production can call up sales information and immediately know how much must be produced to fill cus-

Focus on Practice   RFID: The Wave of the Future

IN PRACTICE

Wal-Mart Stores, Inc., the world's number 1 retailer, has more than 6,700 stores, including discount stores, Supercenters, Sam's Clubs, Neighborhood Markets, and nearly 2,800 international units. With fiscal 2007 sales of $345 billion, Wal-Mart is able to exert tremendous pressure on its suppliers. So when Wal-Mart announced in April 2004 that it was beginning a pilot program to test *radio frequency identification* (RFID) technology to improve its inventory and supply chain management, suppliers and competitors alike sat up and took notice.

One of the first companies to introduce bar codes in the early 1980s, Wal-Mart planned to require its top 100 suppliers to put RFID tags on shipping crates and pallets by January 2005, with the next 200 largest suppliers using the technology by January 2006. As of February 2007, Wal-Mart officials said that

600 of its suppliers were RFID-enabled. The ultimate Wal-Mart goal is to have all of its 86,000-plus suppliers on board using electronic product codes (EPC) with RFID technology.

The major issue with RFID tags is per-chip cost. In 2004, when Wal-Mart announced its intent to use RFID tags, they sold for 30 to 50 cents each. Wal-Mart requested a price of 5 cents per tag, expecting increased demand and economies of scale to push the price down to make them more competitive with inexpensive barcodes. Increased demand has brought the price of current-generation RFID tags to about 15 cents apiece, but barcodes only cost a fraction of a cent. Barcodes help track inventory and can match a product to a price, but they lack the electronic tags' ability to store more detailed information, such as the serial number of a product, the location of the factory that made

it, when it was made, and when it was sold.

In their inventory-control capacity, passive RFID chips with small antennae are attached to cases and pallets. A reader activates the chip and its unique product identifier code is transmitted back to an inventory control system. Wal-Mart expects the RFID technology to improve its inventory management. One of the company's measures of efficiency is inventory growth at a rate of less than half of sales growth. For 2003, Wal-Mart's inventories grew at 9.1 percent while sales increased 11.6 percent; for fiscal 2007, inventories were up 5.6 percent over fiscal 2006 inventory levels while sales rose 11.7 percent for the year.

■ *What problem might occur with the full implementation of RFID technology in retail industries? Specifically, consider the amount of data that might be collected.*

tomer orders. Because all available resources—human and material—are known, the system can eliminate production delays and control costs. ERP systems automatically note changes, such as a supplier's inability to meet a scheduled delivery date, so that necessary adjustments can be made.

International Inventory Management

International inventory management is typically much more complicated for exporters in general, and for multinational companies in particular, than for purely domestic firms. The production and manufacturing economies of scale that might be expected from selling products globally may prove elusive if products must be tailored for individual local markets, as frequently happens, or if actual production takes place in factories around the world. When raw materials, intermediate goods, or finished products must be transported over long distances—particularly by ocean shipping—there will be more delays, confusion, damage, and theft than occur in a one-country operation. The international inventory manager, therefore, puts a premium on flexibility. He or she is usually less concerned about ordering the economically optimal quantity of inventory than about making sure that sufficient quantities of inventory are delivered where they are needed, when they are needed, and in a condition to be used as planned.

REVIEW QUESTIONS

14–8 What are likely to be the viewpoints of each of the following managers about the levels of the various types of inventory: finance, marketing, manufacturing, and purchasing? Why is inventory an investment?

14–9 Briefly describe the following techniques for managing inventory: ABC system, economic order quantity (EOQ) model, just-in-time (JIT) system, and computerized systems for resource control—MRP, MRP II, and ERP.

14–10 What factors make managing inventory more difficult for exporters and multinational companies?

14.4 | Accounts Receivable Management

The second component of the cash conversion cycle is the average collection period. This period is the average length of time from a sale on credit until the payment becomes usable funds for the firm. The average collection period has two parts. The first part is the time from the sale until the customer mails the payment. The second part is the time from when the payment is mailed until the firm has the collected funds in its bank account. The first part of the average collection period involves managing the credit available to the firm's customers, and the second part involves collecting and processing payments. This section of the chapter discusses the firm's accounts receivable credit management.

The objective for managing accounts receivable is to collect accounts receivable as quickly as possible without losing sales from high-pressure collection techniques. Accomplishing this goal encompasses three topics: (1) credit selection and standards, (2) credit terms, and (3) credit monitoring.

> **Hint** Some small businesses resolve these problems by selling their accounts receivable to a third party at a discount. Though expensive, this strategy overcomes the problem of not having adequate personnel. It also creates a buffer between the small business and those customers who need a little prodding to stay current.

Credit Selection and Standards

Credit selection involves application of techniques for determining which customers should receive credit. This process involves evaluating the customer's creditworthiness and comparing it to the firm's **credit standards,** its minimum requirements for extending credit to a customer.

> **credit standards**
> The firm's minimum requirements for extending credit to a customer.

Five C's of Credit

One popular credit selection technique is the **five C's of credit,** which provides a framework for in-depth credit analysis. Because of the time and expense involved, this credit selection method is used for large-dollar credit requests. The five C's are

> **five C's of credit**
> The five key dimensions—character, capacity, capital, collateral, and conditions—used by credit analysts to provide a framework for in-depth credit analysis.

1. *Character:* The applicant's record of meeting past obligations.
2. *Capacity:* The applicant's ability to repay the requested credit, as judged in terms of financial statement analysis focused on cash flows available to repay debt obligations.
3. *Capital:* The applicant's debt relative to equity.

4. *Collateral:* The amount of assets the applicant has available for use in securing the credit. The larger the amount of available assets, the greater the chance that a firm will recover funds if the applicant defaults.
5. *Conditions:* Current general and industry-specific economic conditions, and any unique conditions surrounding a specific transaction.

Analysis via the five C's of credit does not yield a specific accept/reject decision, so its use requires an analyst experienced in reviewing and granting credit requests. Application of this framework tends to ensure that the firm's credit customers will pay, without being pressured, within the stated credit terms.

Credit Scoring

Credit scoring is a method of credit selection that firms commonly use with high-volume/small-dollar credit requests. **Credit scoring** applies statistically derived weights to a credit applicant's scores on key financial and credit characteristics to predict whether he or she will pay the requested credit in a timely fashion. Simply stated, the procedure results in a score that measures the applicant's overall credit strength, and the score is used to make the accept/reject decision for granting the applicant credit. Credit scoring is most commonly used by large credit card operations, such as those of banks, oil companies, and department stores. The purpose of credit scoring is to make a relatively informed credit decision quickly and inexpensively, recognizing that the cost of a single bad scoring decision is small. However, if bad debts from scoring decisions increase, then the scoring system must be reevaluated. For a demonstration of credit scoring, including use of a spreadsheet for that purpose, see the book's website at www.prenhall.com/gitman.

credit scoring
A credit selection method commonly used with high-volume/small-dollar credit requests; relies on a credit score determined by applying statistically derived weights to a credit applicant's scores on key financial and credit characteristics.

Changing Credit Standards

Hint Relaxing the credit standards and/or credit terms will increase the risk of the firm, but it may also increase the return to the firm. The average collection period and bad debts will both increase with more lenient credit standards and/or credit terms, but the increased revenue may produce profits that exceed these costs.

The firm sometimes will contemplate changing its credit standards in an effort to improve its returns and create greater value for its owners. To demonstrate, consider the following changes and effects on profits expected to result from the *relaxation* of credit standards.

Effects of Relaxation of Credit Standards		
Variable	Direction of change	Effect on profits
Sales volume	Increase	Positive
Investment in accounts receivable	Increase	Negative
Bad-debt expenses	Increase	Negative

If credit standards were tightened, the opposite effects would be expected.

Example

Dodd Tool, a manufacturer of lathe tools, is currently selling a product for $10 per unit. Sales (all on credit) for last year were 60,000 units. The variable cost per unit is $6. The firm's total fixed costs are $120,000.

The firm is currently contemplating a *relaxation of credit standards* that is expected to result in the following: a 5% increase in unit sales to 63,000 units; an increase in the average collection period from 30 days (the current level) to 45 days; an increase in bad-debt expenses from 1% of sales (the current level) to 2%. The firm's required return on equal-risk investments, which is the opportunity cost of tying up funds in accounts receivable, is 15%.

To determine whether to relax its credit standards, Dodd Tool must calculate its effect on the firm's additional profit contribution from sales, the cost of the marginal investment in accounts receivable, and the cost of marginal bad debts.

Additional Profit Contribution from Sales Because fixed costs are "sunk" and therefore are unaffected by a change in the sales level, the only cost relevant to a change in sales is variable costs. Sales are expected to increase by 5%, or 3,000 units. The profit contribution per unit will equal the difference between the sale price per unit ($10) and the variable cost per unit ($6). The profit contribution per unit therefore will be $4. The total additional profit contribution from sales will be $12,000 (3,000 units $\times$ $4 per unit).

Cost of the Marginal Investment in Accounts Receivable To determine the cost of the marginal investment in accounts receivable, Dodd must find the difference between the cost of carrying receivables under the two credit standards. Because its concern is only with the out-of-pocket costs, *the relevant cost is the variable cost*. The average investment in accounts receivable can be calculated by using the following formula:

$$\frac{\text{Average investment}}{\text{in accounts receivable}} = \frac{\text{Total variable cost of annual sales}}{\text{Turnover of accounts receivable}} \qquad (14.9)$$

where

$$\text{Turnover of accounts receivable} = \frac{365}{\text{Average collection period}}$$

The total variable cost of annual sales under the present and proposed plans can be found as follows, using the variable cost per unit of $6.

Total variable cost of annual sales

Under present plan: ($6 $\times$ 60,000 units) = $360,000
Under proposed plan: ($6 $\times$ 63,000 units) = $378,000

The turnover of accounts receivable is the number of times each year that the firm's accounts receivable are actually turned into cash. It is found by dividing the average collection period into 365 (the number of days assumed in a year).

Turnover of accounts receivable

Under present plan: $\dfrac{365}{30} = 12.2$

Under proposed plan: $\dfrac{365}{45} = 8.1$

By substituting the cost and turnover data just calculated into Equation 14.9 for each case, we get the following average investments in accounts receivable:

Average investment in accounts receivable

Under present plan: $\dfrac{\$360,000}{12.2} = \$29,508$

Under proposed plan: $\dfrac{\$378,000}{8.1} = \$46,667$

We calculate the marginal investment in accounts receivable and its cost as follows:

Cost of marginal investment in accounts receivable

Average investment under proposed plan	$46,667
− Average investment under present plan	29,508
Marginal investment in accounts receivable	$17,159
× Required return on investment	0.15
Cost of marginal investment in A/R	$ 2,574

The resulting value of $2,574 is considered a cost because it represents the maximum amount that could have been earned on the $17,159 had it been placed in the best equal-risk investment alternative available at the firm's required return on investment of 15%.

Cost of Marginal Bad Debts   We find the cost of marginal bad debts by taking the difference between the levels of bad debts before and after the proposed relaxation of credit standards.

Cost of marginal bad debts

Under proposed plan: $(0.02 \times \$10/\text{unit} \times 63,000 \text{ units})$	=	$12,600
Under present plan: $(0.01 \times \$10/\text{unit} \times 60,000 \text{ units})$	=	6,000
Cost of marginal bad debts		$ 6,600

Note that the bad-debt costs are calculated by using the sale price per unit ($10) to deduct not just the true loss of variable cost ($6) that results when a customer fails to pay its account, but also the profit contribution per unit (in this case $4) that is included in the "additional profit contribution from sales." Thus the resulting cost of marginal bad debts is $6,600.

Making the Credit Standard Decision   To decide whether to relax its credit standards, the firm must compare the additional profit contribution from sales to the added costs of the marginal investment in accounts receivable and marginal bad debts. If the additional profit contribution is greater than marginal costs, credit standards should be relaxed.

Example   The results and key calculations related to Dodd Tool's decision whether to relax its credit standards are summarized in Table 14.2 on page 656. The net addition to total profits resulting from such an action will be $2,826 per year. Therefore, the firm *should* relax its credit standards as proposed.

The procedure described here for evaluating a proposed change in credit standards is also commonly used to evaluate other changes in the management of accounts receivable. If Dodd Tool had been contemplating tightening its credit standards, for example, the cost would have been a reduction in the profit contribution from sales, and the return would have been from reductions in the cost of the investment in accounts receivable and in the cost of bad debts. Another application of this procedure is demonstrated later in the chapter.

TABLE 14.2   Effects on Dodd Tool of a Relaxation of Credit Standards

Additional profit contribution from sales		
[3,000 units × ($10 − $6)]		$12,000
Cost of marginal investment in A/R[a]		
Average investment under proposed plan:		
$\dfrac{\$6 \times 63{,}000}{8.1} = \dfrac{\$378{,}000}{8.1}$	$46,667	
Average investment under present plan:		
$\dfrac{\$6 \times 60{,}000}{12.2} = \dfrac{\$360{,}000}{12.2}$	29,508	
Marginal investment in A/R	$17,159	
Cost of marginal investment in A/R (0.15 × $17,159)		($ 2,574)
Cost of marginal bad debts		
Bad debts under proposed plan (0.02 × $10 × 63,000)	$12,600	
Bad debts under present plan (0.01 × $10 × 60,000)	6,000	
Cost of marginal bad debts		($ 6,600)
Net profit from implementation of proposed plan		$ 2,826

[a]The denominators 8.1 and 12.2 in the calculation of the average investment in accounts receivable under the proposed and present plans are the accounts receivable turnovers for each of these plans (365/45 = 8.1 and 365/30 = 12.2).

Managing International Credit

Credit management is difficult enough for managers of purely domestic companies, and these tasks become much more complex for companies that operate internationally. This is partly because (as we have seen before) international operations typically expose a firm to *exchange rate risk*. It is also due to the dangers and delays involved in shipping goods long distances and in having to cross at least two international borders.

Exports of finished goods are usually priced in the currency of the importer's local market; most commodities, on the other hand, are priced in dollars. Therefore, a U.S. company that sells a product in Japan, for example, would have to price that product in Japanese yen and extend credit to a Japanese wholesaler in the local currency (yen). If the yen *depreciates* against the dollar before the U.S. exporter collects on its account receivable, the U.S. company experiences an exchange rate loss; the yen collected are worth fewer dollars than expected at the time the sale was made. Of course, the dollar could just as easily depreciate against the yen, yielding an exchange rate gain to the U.S. exporter. Most companies fear the loss more than they welcome the gain.

For a major currency such as the Japanese yen, the exporter can *hedge* against this risk by using the currency futures, forward, or options markets, but it is costly to do so, particularly for relatively small amounts. If the exporter is selling to a customer in a developing country—where 40 percent of U.S. exports are now sold—there will probably be no effective instrument available for protecting against exchange rate risk at any price. This risk may be further magnified because credit standards may be much lower (and acceptable collection techniques much different) in developing countries than in the United States. Although it may seem tempting just "not to bother" with exporting, U.S. companies no longer can concede foreign markets to international rivals. These export sales, if carefully monitored and (where possible) effectively hedged against exchange rate risk, often prove to be very profitable.

Credit Terms

Credit terms are the terms of sale for customers who have been extended credit by the firm. Terms of *net 30* mean the customer has 30 days from the beginning of the credit period (typically *end of month* or *date of invoice*) to pay the full invoice amount. Some firms offer **cash discounts,** percentage deductions from the purchase price for paying within a specified time. For example, terms of *2/10 net 30* mean the customer can take a 2 percent discount from the invoice amount if the payment is made within 10 days of the beginning of the credit period or can pay the full amount of the invoice within 30 days.

A firm's business strongly influences its regular credit terms. For example, a firm selling perishable items will have very short credit terms, because its items have little long-term collateral value; a firm in a seasonal business may tailor its terms to fit the industry cycles. A firm wants its regular credit terms to conform to its industry's standards. If its terms are more restrictive than its competitors', it will lose business; if its terms are less restrictive than its competitors', it will attract poor-quality customers that probably could not pay under the standard industry terms. The bottom line is that a firm should compete on the basis of quality and price of its product and service offerings, not its credit terms. Accordingly, the firm's regular credit terms should match the industry standards, but individual customer terms should reflect the riskiness of the customer.

Cash Discount

Including a cash discount in the credit terms is a popular way to speed up collections without putting pressure on customers. The cash discount provides an incentive for customers to pay sooner. By speeding collections, the discount decreases the firm's investment in accounts receivable, but it also decreases the per-unit profit. Additionally, initiating a cash discount should reduce bad debts because customers will pay sooner, and it should increase sales volume because customers who take the discount pay a lower price for the product. Accordingly, firms that consider offering a cash discount must perform a benefit–cost analysis to determine whether extending a cash discount is profitable.

Example
MAX Company has an average collection period of 40 days (turnover = 365/40 = 9.1). In accordance with the firm's credit terms of net 30, this period is divided into 32 days until the customers place their payments in the mail (not everyone pays within 30 days) and 8 days to receive, process, and collect payments once they are mailed. MAX is considering initiating a cash discount by changing its credit terms from net 30 to 2/10 net 30. The firm expects this change to reduce the amount of time until the payments are placed in the mail, resulting in an average collection period of 25 days (turnover = 365/25 = 14.6).

As noted earlier in the EOQ example (on page 649), MAX has a raw material with current annual usage of 1,100 units. Each finished product produced

TABLE 14.3   Analysis of Initiating a Cash Discount for MAX Company

Additional profit contribution from sales		
[50 units × ($3,000 − $2,300)]		$35,000
Cost of marginal investment in A/R[a]		
Average investment presently (without discount):		
$\dfrac{\$2,300 \times 1,100 \text{ units}}{9.1} = \dfrac{\$2,530,000}{9.1}$	$278,022	
Average investment with proposed cash discount:[b]		
$\dfrac{\$2,300 \times 1,150 \text{ units}}{14.6} = \dfrac{\$2,645,000}{14.6}$	181,164	
Reduction in accounts receivable investment	$ 96,858	
Cost savings from reduced investments in accounts receivable (0.14 × $96,858)[c]		$13,560
Cost of cash discount (0.02 × 0.80 × 1,150 × $3,000)		($55,200)
Net profit from initiation of proposed cash discount		($ 6,640)

[a]In analyzing the investment in accounts receivable, we use the variable cost of the product sold ($1,500 raw materials cost + $800 production cost = $2,300 per unit variable cost) instead of the sale price, because the variable cost is a better indicator of the firm's investment.

[b]The average investment in accounts receivable with the proposed cash discount is estimated to be tied up for an average of 25 days instead of the 40 days under the original terms.

[c]MAX's opportunity cost of funds is 14%.

requires 1 unit of this raw material at a variable cost of $1,500 per unit, incurs another $800 of variable cost in the production process, and sells for $3,000 on terms of net 30. Variable costs therefore total $2,300 ($1,500 + $800). MAX estimates that 80% of its customers will take the 2% discount and that offering the discount will increase sales of the finished product by 50 units (from 1,100 to 1,150) per year but will not alter its bad-debt percentage. MAX's opportunity cost of funds invested in accounts receivable is 14%. Should MAX offer the proposed cash discount? An analysis similar to that demonstrated earlier for the credit standard decision, presented in Table 14.3, shows a net loss from the cash discount of $6,640. Thus *MAX should not initiate the proposed cash discount.* However, other discounts may be advantageous.

Cash Discount Period

cash discount period
The number of days after the beginning of the credit period during which the cash discount is available.

The financial manager can change the **cash discount period,** the number of days after the beginning of the credit period during which the cash discount is available. The net effect of changes in this period is difficult to analyze because of the nature of the forces involved. For example, if a firm were to increase its cash discount period by 10 days (for example, changing its credit terms from 2/10 net 30 to 2/20 net 30), the following changes would be expected to occur: (1) Sales would increase, positively affecting profit. (2) Bad-debt expenses would decrease, positively affecting profit. (3) The profit per unit would decrease as a result of more people taking the discount, negatively affecting profit.

The difficulty for the financial manager lies in assessing what impact an increase in the cash discount period would have on the firm's investment in accounts receivable. This investment will decrease because of non–discount takers now paying earlier. However, the investment in accounts receivable will increase for two reasons: (1) Discount takers will still get the discount but will pay later, and (2) new customers attracted by the new policy will result in new accounts receivable. If the firm were to decrease the cash discount period, the effects would be the opposite of those just described.

Credit Period

credit period
The number of days after the beginning of the credit period until full payment of the account is due.

Changes in the **credit period,** the number of days after the beginning of the credit period until full payment of the account is due, also affect a firm's profitability. For example, increasing a firm's credit period from net 30 days to net 45 days should increase sales, positively affecting profit. But both the investment in accounts receivable and bad-debt expenses would also increase, negatively affecting profit. The increased investment in accounts receivable would result from both more sales and generally slower pay, on average, as a result of the longer credit period. The increase in bad-debt expenses results from the fact that the longer the credit period, the more time available for a firm to fail, making it unable to pay its accounts payable. A decrease in the length of the credit period is likely to have the opposite effects. Note that the variables affected by an increase in the credit period behave in the same way they would have if the credit standards had been relaxed, as demonstrated earlier in Table 14.2.

Credit Monitoring

credit monitoring
The ongoing review of a firm's accounts receivable to determine whether customers are paying according to the stated credit terms.

The final issue a firm should consider in its accounts receivable management is credit monitoring. **Credit monitoring** is an ongoing review of the firm's accounts receivable to determine whether customers are paying according to the stated credit terms. If they are not paying in a timely manner, credit monitoring will alert the firm to the problem. Slow payments are costly to a firm because they lengthen the average collection period and thus increase the firm's investment in accounts receivable. Two frequently used techniques for credit monitoring are average collection period and aging of accounts receivable. In addition, a number of popular collection techniques are used by firms.

Average Collection Period

The *average collection period* is the second component of the cash conversion cycle. As noted in Chapter 2, it is the average number of days that credit sales are outstanding. The average collection period has two components: (1) the time from sale until the customer places the payment in the mail and (2) the time to receive, process, and collect the payment once it has been mailed by the customer. The formula for finding the average collection period is

$$\text{Average collection period} = \frac{\text{Accounts receivable}}{\text{Average sales per day}} \qquad \text{(14.10)}$$

Assuming receipt, processing, and collection time is constant, the average collection period tells the firm, on average, when its customers pay their accounts.

Knowing its average collection period enables the firm to determine whether there is a general problem with accounts receivable. For example, a firm that has credit terms of net 30 would expect its average collection period (minus receipt, processing, and collection time) to equal about 30 days. If the actual collection period is significantly greater than 30 days, the firm has reason to review its credit operations. If the firm's average collection period is increasing over time, it has cause for concern about its accounts receivable management. A first step in analyzing an accounts receivable problem is to "age" the accounts receivable. By this process the firm can determine whether the problem exists in its accounts receivable in general or is attributable to a few specific accounts.

aging schedule
A credit-monitoring technique that breaks down accounts receivable into groups on the basis of their time of origin; it indicates the percentages of the total accounts receivable balance that have been outstanding for specified periods of time.

Aging of Accounts Receivable

An **aging schedule** breaks down accounts receivable into groups on the basis of their time of origin. The breakdown is typically made on a month-by-month basis, going back 3 or 4 months. The resulting schedule indicates the percentages of the total accounts receivable balance that have been outstanding for specified periods of time. The purpose of the aging schedule is to enable the firm to pinpoint problems. A simple example will illustrate the form and evaluation of an aging schedule.

Example

The accounts receivable balance on the books of Dodd Tool on December 31, 2009, was $200,000. The firm extends net 30-day credit terms to its customers. To gain insight into the firm's relatively lengthy—51.3-day—average collection period, Dodd prepared the following aging schedule.

Age of account	Balance outstanding	Percentage of total balance outstanding
0–30 days	$ 80,000	40%
31–60 days	36,000	18
61–90 days	52,000	26
91–120 days	26,000	13
Over 120 days	6,000	3
Totals at 12/31/09	$200,000	100%

Because Dodd extends 30-day credit terms to its customers, they have 30 days after the end of the month of sale to remit payment. Therefore, the 40% of the balance outstanding with an age of 0–30 days is *current*. The balances outstanding for 31–60 days, 61–90 days, 91–120 days, and over 120 days are *overdue*.

Reviewing the aging schedule, we see that 40% of the accounts are current (age < 30 days) and the remaining 60% are overdue (age > 30 days). Eighteen percent of the balance outstanding is 1–30 days overdue, 26% is 31–60 days overdue, 13% is 61–90 days overdue, and 3% is more than 90 days overdue. Although the collections seem generally slow, a noticeable irregularity in these data is the high percentage of the balance outstanding that is 31–60 days overdue (ages of 61–90 days). Clearly, a problem must have occurred 61–90 days ago. Investigation may find that the problem can be attributed to the hiring of a new credit manager, the acceptance of a new account that made a large credit purchase but has not yet paid for it, or ineffective collection policy. When these types of discrepancies are found in the aging schedule, the analyst should determine, evaluate, and remedy its cause.

TABLE 14.4	Popular Collection Techniques
Technique[a]	Brief description
Letters	After a certain number of days, the firm sends a polite letter reminding the customer of the overdue account. If the account is not paid within a certain period after this letter has been sent, a second, more demanding letter is sent.
Telephone calls	If letters prove unsuccessful, a telephone call may be made to the customer to request immediate payment. If the customer has a reasonable excuse, arrangements may be made to extend the payment period. A call from the seller's attorney may be used.
Personal visits	This technique is much more common at the consumer credit level, but it may also be effectively employed by industrial suppliers. Sending a local salesperson or a collection person to confront the customer can be very effective. Payment may be made on the spot.
Collection agencies	A firm can turn uncollectible accounts over to a collection agency or an attorney for collection. The fees for this service are typically quite high; the firm may receive less than 50 cents on the dollar from accounts collected in this way.
Legal action	Legal action is the most stringent step, an alternative to the use of a collection agency. Not only is direct legal action expensive, but it may force the debtor into bankruptcy without guaranteeing the ultimate receipt of the overdue amount.

[a]The techniques are listed in the order in which they are typically followed in the collection process.

Popular Collection Techniques

A number of collection techniques, ranging from letters to legal action, are employed. As an account becomes more and more overdue, the collection effort becomes more personal and more intense. In Table 14.4 the popular collection techniques are listed, and briefly described, in the order typically followed in the collection process.

REVIEW QUESTIONS

14–11 What is the role of the *five C's of credit* in the credit selection activity?

14–12 Explain why *credit scoring* is typically applied to consumer credit decisions rather than to mercantile credit decisions.

14–13 What are the basic tradeoffs in a *tightening* of credit standards?

14–14 Why are the risks involved in international credit management more complex than those associated with purely domestic credit sales?

14–15 Why do a firm's regular credit terms typically conform to those of its industry?

14–16 Why should a firm actively monitor the accounts receivable of its credit customers? How are the *average collection period* and an *aging schedule* used for credit monitoring?

14.5 | Management of Receipts and Disbursements

As discussed in the previous section, the average collection period (the second component of the cash conversion cycle) has two parts: (1) the time from sale until the customer mails the payment and (2) the receipt, processing, and collection

float
Funds that have been sent by the payer but are not yet usable funds to the payee.

mail float
The time delay between when payment is placed in the mail and when it is received.

processing float
The time between receipt of a payment and its deposit into the firm's account.

clearing float
The time between deposit of a payment and when spendable funds become available to the firm.

lockbox system
A collection procedure in which customers mail payments to a post office box that is emptied regularly by the firm's bank, which processes the payments and deposits them in the firm's account. This system speeds up collection time by reducing processing time as well as mail and clearing time.

time. The third component of the cash conversion cycle, the average payment period, also has two parts: (1) the time from purchase of goods on account until the firm mails its payment and (2) the receipt, processing, and collection time required by the firm's suppliers. The receipt, processing, and collection time for the firm, both from its customers and to its suppliers, is the focus of receipts and disbursements management.

Float

Float refers to funds that have been sent by the payer but are not yet usable funds to the payee. Float is important in the cash conversion cycle because its presence lengthens both the firm's average collection period and its average payment period. However, the goal of the firm should be to shorten its average collection period and lengthen its average payment period. Both can be accomplished by managing float.

Float has three component parts:

1. **Mail float** is the time delay between when payment is placed in the mail and when it is received.
2. **Processing float** is the time between receipt of the payment and its deposit into the firm's account.
3. **Clearing float** is the time between deposit of the payment and when spendable funds become available to the firm. This component of float is attributable to the time required for a check to clear the banking system.

Some popular techniques for managing the component parts of float to speed up collections and slow down payments are described here.

Speeding Up Collections

Speeding up collections reduces customer *collection float* time and thus reduces the firm's average collection period, which reduces the investment the firm must make in its cash conversion cycle. In our earlier examples, MAX Company had annual sales of $10 million and 8 days of total collection float (receipt, processing, and collection time). If MAX can reduce its float time by 3 days, it will reduce its investment in the cash conversion cycle by $82,192 [$10,000,000 × (3/365)].

A popular technique for speeding up collections is a lockbox system. A **lockbox system** works as follows: Instead of mailing payments to the company, customers mail payments to a post office box. The firm's bank empties the post office box regularly, processes each payment, and deposits the payments in the firm's account. Deposit slips, along with payment enclosures, are sent (or transmitted electronically) to the firm by the bank so that the firm can properly credit customers' accounts. Lockboxes are geographically dispersed to match the locations of the firm's customers. A lockbox system affects all three components of float. Lockboxes reduce mail time and often clearing time by being near the firm's customers. Lockboxes reduce processing time to nearly zero because the bank deposits payments before the firm processes them. Obviously a lockbox system reduces collection float time, but not without a cost; therefore, a firm must perform an economic analysis to determine whether to implement a lockbox system.

Lockbox systems are commonly used by large firms whose customers are geographically dispersed. However, a firm does not have to be large to benefit from a lockbox. Smaller firms can also benefit from a lockbox system. The benefit to small firms often comes primarily from transferring the processing of payments to the bank.

Slowing Down Payments

Float is also a component of the firm's average payment period. In this case, the float is in the favor of the firm. The firm may benefit by increasing all three of the components of its *payment float*. One popular technique for increasing payment float is **controlled disbursing,** which involves the strategic use of mailing points and bank accounts to lengthen mail float and clearing float, respectively. Firms must use this approach carefully, though, because longer payment periods may strain supplier relations.

The *Focus on Ethics* box on page 664 takes a closer look at the ethical issues involved in slowing down payments through controlled disbursing and other methods—a technique known collectively as *stretching accounts payable*. This is a topic we will come back to in Chapter 15.

In summary, a reasonable overall policy for float management is (1) to collect payments as quickly as possible, because once the payment is in the mail, the funds belong to the firm, and (2) to delay making payment to suppliers, because once the payment is mailed, the funds belong to the supplier.

Cash Concentration

Cash concentration is the process used by the firm to bring lockbox and other deposits together into one bank, often called the *concentration bank*. Cash concentration has three main advantages. First, it creates a large pool of funds for use in making short-term cash investments. Because there is a fixed-cost component in the transaction cost associated with such investments, investing a single pool of funds reduces the firm's transaction costs. The larger investment pool also allows the firm to choose from a greater variety of short-term investment vehicles. Second, concentrating the firm's cash in one account improves the tracking and internal control of the firm's cash. Third, having one concentration bank enables the firm to implement payment strategies that reduce idle cash balances.

There are a variety of mechanisms for transferring cash from the lockbox bank and other collecting banks to the concentration bank. One mechanism is a **depository transfer check (DTC),** which is an unsigned check drawn on one of the firm's bank accounts and deposited in another. For cash concentration, a DTC is drawn on each lockbox or other collecting bank account and deposited in the concentration bank account. Once the DTC has cleared the bank on which it is drawn (which may take several days), the transfer of funds is completed. Most firms currently provide deposit information by telephone to the concentration bank, which then prepares and deposits into its account the DTC drawn on the lockbox or other collecting bank account.

A second mechanism is an **ACH (automated clearinghouse) transfer,** which is a preauthorized electronic withdrawal from the payer's account. A computerized

Margin notes

controlled disbursing
The strategic use of mailing points and bank accounts to lengthen mail float and clearing float, respectively.

Hint Data on clearing times among banks located in various cities can be developed by the firm itself. They also can be obtained from a major bank's cash management service department or purchased from a firm that sells such information.

cash concentration
The process used by the firm to bring lockbox and other deposits together into one bank, often called the *concentration bank*.

depository transfer check (DTC)
An unsigned check drawn on one of a firm's bank accounts and deposited in another.

ACH (automated clearinghouse) transfer
Preauthorized electronic withdrawal from the payer's account and deposit into the payee's account via a settlement among banks by the *automated clearinghouse*, or *ACH*.

Focus on Ethics

Stretching Accounts Payable—Is It a Good Policy?

Stretching payables has often been considered good cash management. By delaying bill payments as long as possible without damaging the firm's credit, companies get interest-free loans from suppliers. Other businesses deliberately increase their accounts payable lag to cover temporary cash shortages.

There are two negative ramifications of stretching accounts payables (A/P). First, the stretching out of payables can be pushed too far, and a business can get tagged as a slow-payer. Vendors will eventually put increasing pressure on the company to make more timely payments.

Stretching accounts payables also raises ethical issues. First, it may cause the firm to violate the agreement it entered with its supplier when it purchased the merchandise. More important to investors, the firm may stretch A/P to artificially boost reported operating cash flow during a reporting period. In other words, firms can improve reported operating cash flows due solely to a decision to slow the payment

rate to vendors. Unfortunately for investors, the improvement in operating cash flows may be unsustainable if vendors force the company to improve its payment record; at a minimum, any year-over-year improvement in operating cash flow may be unsustainable.

The extension of payables can be identified by monitoring *days sales payables* (DSP), calculated as the end-of-period accounts payable balance divided by the cost of goods sold and multiplied by the number of days in the period. As DSP grows, operating cash flows are boosted.

A more complicated version of stretching payables is the financing of payables. This occurs when a company uses a third-party financial institution to pay the vendor in the current period and pays back the bank in a subsequent period. This approach reclassifies the amount from accounts payable to short-term loans. The reclassification results in a decrease to operating cash flow in that quarter and an increase in financing cash flow. Normally, cash expenditures for

accounts payable are included in operating activities. Because the timing and extent of vendor financing is at the discretion of company management, the temptation to manipulate operating cash flows may prove too great for some.

Setting aside the ethical ramifications of stretching accounts payable, there may be financial incentives for avoiding the practice. Companies that can move to an automated A/P system may be able to take advantage of beneficial early payment discounts that provide a far better risk-free rate of return than stretching out accounts payable. For example, a 2/10 net 30 discount equates to about a 36 percent annualized return. Viewed this way, an A/P balance may be the most expensive debt on the balance sheet.

■ *While vendor discounts for early payment are very rewarding, what are some of the difficulties that may arise to keep a firm from taking advantage of those discounts?*

clearing facility (called the *automated clearinghouse,* or *ACH*) makes a paperless transfer of funds between the payer and payee banks. An ACH settles accounts among participating banks. Individual accounts are settled by respective bank balance adjustments. ACH transfers clear in one day. For cash concentration, an ACH transfer is made from each lockbox bank or other collecting bank to the concentration bank. An ACH transfer can be thought of as an electronic DTC, but because the ACH transfer clears in one day, it provides benefits over a DTC; however, both banks in the ACH transfer must be members of the clearinghouse.

A third cash concentration mechanism is a **wire transfer.** A wire transfer is an electronic communication that, via bookkeeping entries, removes funds from the

wire transfer
An electronic communication that, via bookkeeping entries, removes funds from the payer's bank and deposits them in the payee's bank.

payer's bank and deposits them in the payee's bank. Wire transfers can eliminate mail and clearing float and may reduce processing float as well. For cash concentration, the firm moves funds using a wire transfer from each lockbox or other collecting account to its concentration account. Wire transfers are a substitute for DTC and ACH transfers, but they are more expensive.

It is clear that the firm must balance the costs and benefits of concentrating cash to determine the type and timing of transfers from its lockbox and other collecting accounts to its concentration account. The transfer mechanism selected should be the one that is most profitable. (The profit per period of any transfer mechanism equals earnings on the increased availability of funds minus the cost of the transfer system.)

Zero-Balance Accounts

zero-balance account (ZBA)
A disbursement account that always has an end-of-day balance of zero because the firm deposits money to cover checks drawn on the account only as they are presented for payment each day.

Zero-balance accounts (**ZBAs**) are disbursement accounts that always have an end-of-day balance of zero. The purpose is to eliminate nonearning cash balances in corporate checking accounts. A ZBA works well as a disbursement account under a cash concentration system.

ZBAs work as follows: Once all of a given day's checks are presented for payment from the firm's ZBA, the bank notifies the firm of the total amount of checks, and the firm transfers funds into the account to cover the amount of that day's checks. This leaves an end-of-day balance of $0 (zero dollars). The ZBA enables the firm to keep all of its operating cash in an interest-earning account, thereby eliminating idle cash balances. Thus a firm that used a ZBA in conjunction with a cash concentration system would need two accounts. The firm would concentrate its cash from the lockboxes and other collecting banks into an interest-earning account and would write checks against its ZBA. The firm would cover the exact dollar amount of checks presented against the ZBA with transfers from the interest-earning account, leaving the end-of-day balance in the ZBA at $0.

A ZBA is a disbursement-management tool. As we discussed earlier, the firm would prefer to maximize its payment float. However, some cash managers feel that actively attempting to increase float time on payments is unethical. A ZBA enables the firm to maximize the use of float on each check without altering the float time of payments to its suppliers. Keeping all the firm's cash in an interest-earning account enables the firm to maximize earnings on its cash balances by capturing the full float time on each check it writes.

Personal Finance Example   Megan Laurie, a 25-year-old nurse, works at a hospital that pays her every 2 weeks by direct deposit into her checking account, which pays no interest and has no minimum balance requirement. She takes home about $1,800 every 2 weeks—or about $3,600 per month. She maintains a checking account balance of around $1,500. Whenever it exceeds that amount she transfers the excess into her savings account, which currently pays 1.5% annual interest. She currently has a savings account balance of $17,000 and estimates that she transfers about $600 per month from her checking account into her savings account.

Megan pays her bills immediately when she receives them. Her monthly bills average about $1,900, and her monthly cash outlays for food and gas total about

$900. An analysis of Megan's bill payments indicates that on average she pays her bills 8 days early. Most marketable securities are currently yielding about 4.2% annual interest. Megan is interested in learning how she might better manage her cash balances.

Megan talks with her sister, who has had a finance course, and they come up with three ways for Megan to better manage her cash balance:

1. **Invest current balances.** Megan can transfer her current savings account balances into a liquid marketable security, thereby increasing the rate of interest earned from 1.5% to about 4.2%. On her current $17,000 balance, she will immediately increase her annual interest earnings by about $460 [(0.042 − 0.015) × $17,000].
2. **Invest monthly surpluses.** Megan can transfer monthly the $600 from her checking account to the liquid marketable security, thereby increasing the annual earnings on each monthly transfer by about $16 [(0.042 − 0.015) × $600], which for the 12 transfers would generate additional annual earnings of about $192 (12 months × $16).
3. **Slow down payments.** Rather than paying her bills immediately upon receipt, Megan can pay her bills nearer their due date. By doing this she can gain 8 days of disbursement float each month, or 96 days per year (8 days per month × 12 months), on an average of $1,900 of bills. Assuming she can earn 4.2% annual interest on the $1,900, slowing down her payments would save about $21 annually [(96/365) × 0.042 × $1,900].

Based on these three recommendations, Megan would increase her annual earnings by a total of about $673 ($460 + $192 + $21). Clearly, Megan can grow her earnings by better managing her cash balances.

Investing in Marketable Securities

Marketable securities are short-term, interest-earning, money market instruments that can easily be converted into cash.[7] Marketable securities are classified as part of the firm's liquid assets. The firm uses them to earn a return on temporarily idle funds. To be truly marketable, a security must have (1) a ready market so as to minimize the amount of time required to convert it into cash, and (2) safety of principal, which means that it experiences little or no loss in value over time.

The securities that are most commonly held as part of the firm's marketable-securities portfolio are divided into two groups: (1) government issues, which have relatively low yields as a consequence of their low risk, and (2) nongovernment issues, which have slightly higher yields than government issues with similar maturities because of the slightly higher risk associated with them. Table 14.5 summarizes the key features and recent (July 23, 2007) yields for popular marketable securities.

---

7. As explained in Chapter 1, the *money market* results from a financial relationship between the suppliers and demanders of short-term funds, that is, marketable securities.

TABLE 14.5	Features and Recent Yields on Popular Marketable Securities[a]

Security	Issuer	Description	Initial maturity	Risk and return	Yield on July 23, 2007[b]
Government Issues					
Treasury bills	U.S. Treasury	Issued weekly at auction; sold at a discount; strong secondary market	4, 13, and 26 weeks	Lowest, virtually risk-free	4.97%
Treasury notes	U.S. Treasury	Stated interest rate; interest paid semiannually; strong secondary market	1 to 10 years	Low, but slightly higher than U.S. Treasury bills	5.03%
Federal agency issues	Agencies of federal goverment	Not an obligation of U.S. Treasury; strong secondary market	9 months to 30 years	Slightly higher than U.S. Treasury issues	5.17%[c]
Nongovernment Issues					
Negotiable certificates of deposit (CDs)	Commercial banks	Represent specific cash deposits in commercial banks; amounts and maturities tailored to investor needs; large denominations; good secondary market	1 month to 3 years	Higher than U.S. Treasury issues and comparable to commercial paper	4.95%
Commercial paper	Corporation with a high credit standing	Unsecured note of issuer; large denominations	3 to 270 days	Higher than U.S. Treasury issues and comparable to negotiable CDs	5.23%
Banker's acceptances	Banks	Results from a bank guarantee of a business transaction; sold at discount from maturity value	30 to 180 days	About the same as negotiable CDs and commercial paper but higher than U.S. Treasury issues	5.31%
Eurodollar deposits	Foreign banks	Deposits of currency not native to the country in which the bank is located; large denominations; active secondary market	1 day to 3 years	High, due to less regulation of despository banks and some foreign exchange risk	5.36%
Money market mutual funds	Professional portfolio management companies	Professionally managed portfolios of marketable securities; provide instant liquidity	None—depends on wishes of investor	Vary, but generally higher than U.S. Treasury issues and comparable to negotiable CDs and commercial paper	4.98%[d]
Repurchase agreements	Bank or security dealer	Bank or security dealer sells specific securities to firm and agrees to repurchase them at a specific price and time	Customized to purchaser's needs	Generally slightly below that associated with the outright purchase of the security	5.13%

[a]The prime rate of interest at this time was 8.25%.

[b]Yields obtained for 3-month maturities of each security.

[c]Federal National Mortgage Association (Fannie Mae) issue with 3 months to maturity is used here.

[d]Fidelity Cash Reserves Fund with an average maturity of 51 days is used here in the absence of any average-yield data.

Source: Wall Street Journal, July 24, 2007, p. C6.

REVIEW QUESTIONS

14–17   What is *float* and what are its three components?

14–18   What are the firm's objectives with regard to *collection float* and to *payment float*?

14–19   What are the three main advantages of *cash concentration*?

14–20   What are three mechanisms of cash concentration? What is the objective of using a *zero-balance account (ZBA)* in a cash concentration system?

14–21   What two characteristics make a security marketable? Why are the yields on nongovernment marketable securities generally higher than the yields on government issues with similar maturities?

Summary

Focus on Value

It is important for a firm to maintain a reasonable level of net working capital. To do so, it must balance the high profit and high risk associated with low levels of current assets and high levels of current liabilities against the low profit and low risk that result from high levels of current assets and low levels of current liabilities. A strategy that achieves a reasonable balance between profits and risk should positively contribute to the firm's value.

Similarly, the firm should manage its cash conversion cycle by turning inventory quickly; collecting accounts receivable quickly; managing mail, processing, and clearing time; and paying accounts payable slowly. These strategies should enable the firm to manage its current accounts efficiently and to minimize the amount of resources invested in operating assets.

The financial manager can manage inventory, accounts receivable, and cash receipts to minimize the firm's operating cycle investment, thereby reducing the amount of resources needed to support its business. Employing these strategies, and managing accounts payable and cash disbursements so as to shorten the cash conversion cycle, should minimize the negotiated liabilities needed to support the firm's resource requirements. Active management of the firm's net working capital and current assets should positively contribute to the firm's goal of **maximizing its stock price.**

Review of Learning Goals

LG 1   **Understand short-term financial management, net working capital, and the related tradeoff between profitability and risk.** Short-term financial management focuses on managing each of the firm's current assets (inventory, accounts receivable, cash, and marketable securities) and current liabilities (accounts payable, accruals, and notes payable) in a manner that positively contributes to the firm's value. Net working capital is the difference between current assets and current liabilities. Risk, in the context of short-term financial decisions, is the probability that a firm will be unable to pay its bills as they come due. Assuming a constant level of total assets, the higher a firm's ratio of current assets to total assets, the less profitable the firm, and the less risky it is. The converse is also true. With constant total assets, the higher a firm's ratio of current liabilities to total assets, the more profitable and the more risky the firm is. The converse of this statement is also true.

LG 2 **Describe the cash conversion cycle, its funding requirements, and the key strategies for managing it.** The cash conversion cycle has three components: (1) average age of inventory, (2) average collection period, and (3) average payment period. The length of the cash conversion cycle determines the amount of time resources are tied up in the firm's day-to-day operations. The firm's investment in short-term assets often consists of both permanent and seasonal funding requirements. The seasonal requirements can be financed using either an aggressive (low-cost, high-risk) financing strategy or a conservative (high-cost, low-risk) financing strategy. The firm's funding decision for its cash conversion cycle ultimately depends on management's disposition toward risk and the strength of the firm's banking relationships. To minimize its reliance on negotiated liabilities, the financial manager seeks to (1) turn over inventory as quickly as possible, (2) collect accounts receivable as quickly as possible, (3) manage mail, processing, and clearing time, and (4) pay accounts payable as slowly as possible. Use of these strategies should minimize the length of the cash conversion cycle.

LG 3 **Discuss inventory management: differing views, common techniques, and international concerns.** The viewpoints of marketing, manufacturing, and purchasing managers about the appropriate levels of inventory tend to cause higher inventories than those deemed appropriate by the financial manager. Four commonly used techniques for effectively managing inventory to keep its level low are (1) the ABC system, (2) the economic order quantity (EOQ) model, (3) the just-in-time (JIT) system, and (4) computerized systems for resource control—MRP, MRP II, and ERP. International inventory managers place greater emphasis on making sure that sufficient quantities of inventory are delivered where and when needed, and in the right condition, than on ordering the economically optimal quantities.

LG 4 **Explain the credit selection process and the quantitative procedure for evaluating changes in credit standards.** Credit selection techniques determine which customers' creditworthiness is consistent with the firm's credit standards. Two popular credit selection techniques are the five C's of credit and credit scoring. Changes in credit standards can be evaluated mathematically by assessing the effects of a proposed change on profits from sales, the cost of accounts receivable investment, and bad-debt costs.

LG 5 **Review the procedures for quantitatively considering cash discount changes, other aspects of credit terms, and credit monitoring.** Changes in credit terms—the cash discount, the cash discount period, and the credit period—can be quantified similarly to changes in credit standards. Credit monitoring, the ongoing review of accounts receivable, frequently involves use of the average collection period and an aging schedule. Firms use a number of popular collection techniques.

Understand the management of receipts and disbursements, including float, speeding up collections, slowing down payments, cash concentration, zero-balance accounts, and investing in marketable securities. Float refers to funds that have been sent by the payer but are not yet usable funds to the payee. The components of float are mail time, processing time, and clearing time. Float occurs in both the average collection period and the average payment period. One technique for speeding up collections is a lockbox system. A popular technique for slowing payments is controlled disbursing.

The goal for managing operating cash is to balance the opportunity cost of nonearning balances against the transaction cost of temporary investments. Firms commonly use depository transfer checks (DTCs), ACH transfers, and wire transfers to transfer lockbox receipts to their concentration banks quickly. Zero-balance accounts (ZBAs) can be used to eliminate nonearning cash balances in corporate checking accounts. Marketable securities are short-term, interest-earning, money market instruments used by the firm to earn a return on temporarily idle funds. They may be government or nongovernment issues.

Self-Test Problems (Solutions in Appendix B)

ST14–1 **Cash conversion cycle** Hurkin Manufacturing Company pays accounts payable on the tenth day after purchase. The average collection period is 30 days, and the average age of inventory is 40 days. The firm currently has annual sales of about $18 million. The firm is considering a plan that would stretch its accounts payable by 20 days. If the firm pays 12% per year for its resource investment, what annual savings can it realize by this plan? Assume no difference in the investment per dollar of sales in inventory, receivables, and payables; no discount for early payment of accounts payable; and a 365-day year.

ST14–2 **EOQ analysis** Thompson Paint Company uses 60,000 gallons of pigment per year. The cost of ordering pigment is $200 per order, and the cost of carrying the pigment in inventory is $1 per gallon per year. The firm uses pigment at a constant rate every day throughout the year.
a. Calculate the EOQ.
b. Assuming that it takes 20 days to receive an order once it has been placed, determine the reorder point in terms of gallons of pigment. (*Note:* Use a 365-day year.)

ST14–3 **Relaxing credit standards** Regency Rug Repair Company is trying to decide whether it should relax its credit standards. The firm repairs 72,000 rugs per year at an average price of $32 each. Bad-debt expenses are 1% of sales, the average collection period is 40 days, and the variable cost per unit is $28. Regency expects that if it does relax its credit standards, the average collection period will increase to 48 days and that bad debts will increase to 1½% of sales. Sales will increase by 4,000 repairs per year. If the firm has a required rate of return on equal-risk investments of 14%, what recommendation would you give the firm? Use your analysis to justify your answer. (*Note:* Use a 365-day year.)

Warm-Up Exercises

A blue box (■) indicates exercises available in .

 E14–1   Sharam Industries has a 120-day *operating cycle*. If its average age of inventory is 50 days, how long is its average collection period? If its average payment period is 30 days, what is its *cash conversion cycle*? Place all of this information on a time line similar to Figure 14.1 on page 642.

 E14–2   Icy Treats, Inc., is a seasonal business that sells frozen desserts. At the peak of its summer selling season the firm has $35,000 in cash, $125,000 in inventory, $70,000 in accounts receivable, and $65,000 in accounts payable. During the slow winter period the firm holds $10,000 in cash, $55,000 in inventory, $40,000 in accounts receivable, and $35,000 in accounts payable. Calculate Icy Treats' minimum and peak funding requirements.

 E14–3   Mama Leone's Frozen Pizzas uses 50,000 units of cheese per year. Each unit costs $2.50. The ordering cost for the cheese is $250 per order, and its carrying cost is $0.50 per unit per year. Calculate the firm's *economic order quantity (EOQ)* for the cheese. Mama Leone's operates 250 days per year and maintains a minimum inventory level of 2 days' worth of cheese as a safety stock. If the lead time to receive orders of cheese is 3 days, calculate the *reorder point*.

 E14–4   Forrester Fashions has annual credit sales of 250,000 units with an average collection period of 70 days. The company has a per-unit variable cost of $20 and a per-unit sale price of $30. Bad debts currently are 5% of sales. The firm estimates that a proposed relaxation of credit standards would not affect its 70-day average collection period, but would increase bad debts to 7.5% of sales, which would increase to 300,000 units per year. Forrester requires a 12% return on investments. Show all necessary calculations required to evaluate Forrester's proposed relaxation of credit standards.

 E14–5   Klein's Tools is considering offering a cash discount to speed up the collection of accounts receivable. Currently the firm has an average collection period of 65 days, annual sales are 35,000 units, the per-unit price is $40, and the per-unit variable cost is $29. A 2% cash discount is being considered. Klein's Tools estimates that 80% of its customers will take the 2% discount. If sales are expected to rise to 37,000 units per year and the firm has a 15% required rate of return, what minimum average collection period is required to approve the cash discount plan?

Problems

A blue box (■) indicates problems available in .

 P14–1   **Cash conversion cycle**   American Products is concerned about managing cash efficiently. On the average, inventories have an age of 90 days, and accounts receivable are collected in 60 days. Accounts payable are paid approximately 30 days after they arise. The firm has annual sales of about $30 million. Assume there is no difference in the investment per dollar of sales in inventory, receivables, and payables; and a 365-day year.

a. Calculate the firm's *operating cycle*.
b. Calculate the firm's *cash conversion cycle*.
c. Calculate the amount of resources needed to support the firm's cash conversion cycle.
d. Discuss how management might be able to reduce the cash conversion cycle.

P14–2 **Changing cash conversion cycle**   Camp Manufacturing turns over its inventory 8 times each year, has an average payment period of 35 days, and has an average collection period of 60 days. The firm's annual sales are $3.5 million. Assume there is no difference in the investment per dollar of sales in inventory, receivables, and payables; and a 365-day year.

a. Calculate the firm's *operating cycle* and *cash conversion cycle*.
b. Calculate the firm's daily cash operating expenditure. How much in resources must be invested to support its cash conversion cycle?
c. If the firm pays 14% for these resources, by how much would it increase its annual profits by *favorably* changing its current cash conversion cycle by 20 days?

P14–3 **Multiple changes in cash conversion cycle**   Garrett Industries turns over its inventory 6 times each year; it has an average collection period of 45 days and an average payment period of 30 days. The firm's annual sales are $3 million. Assume there is no difference in the investment per dollar of sales in inventory, receivables, and payables; and a 365-day year.

a. Calculate the firm's *cash conversion cycle*, its daily cash operating expenditure, and the amount of resources needed to support its cash conversion cycle.
b. Find the firm's cash conversion cycle and resource investment requirement if it makes the following changes simultaneously.
   (1) Shortens the average age of inventory by 5 days.
   (2) Speeds the collection of accounts receivable by an average of 10 days.
   (3) Extends the average payment period by 10 days.
c. If the firm pays 13% for its resource investment, by how much, if anything, could it increase its annual profit as a result of the changes in part **b**?
d. If the annual cost of achieving the profit in part **c** is $35,000, what action would you recommend to the firm? Why?

P14–4 **Aggressive versus conservative seasonal funding strategy**   Dynabase Tool has forecast its total funds requirements for the coming year as shown in the following table.

Month	Amount	Month	Amount
January	$2,000,000	July	$12,000,000
February	2,000,000	August	14,000,000
March	2,000,000	September	9,000,000
April	4,000,000	October	5,000,000
May	6,000,000	November	4,000,000
June	9,000,000	December	3,000,000

a. Divide the firm's monthly funds requirement into (1) a *permanent* component and (2) a *seasonal* component, and find the monthly average for each of these components.

b. Describe the amount of long-term and short-term financing used to meet the total funds requirement under (1) an *aggressive funding strategy* and (2) a *conservative funding strategy.* Assume that under the aggressive strategy, long-term funds finance permanent needs and short-term funds are used to finance seasonal needs.

c. Assuming that short-term funds cost 12% annually and that the cost of long-term funds is 17% annually, use the averages found in part **a** to calculate the total cost of each of the strategies described in part **b.**

d. Discuss the profitability–risk tradeoffs associated with the aggressive strategy and those associated with the conservative strategy.

 P14–5 **EOQ analysis** Tiger Corporation purchases 1,200,000 units per year of one component. The fixed cost per order is $25. The annual carrying cost of the item is 27% of its $2 cost.

a. Determine the EOQ under each of the following conditions: (1) no changes, (2) order cost of zero, and (3) carrying cost of zero.

b. What do your answers illustrate about the EOQ model? Explain.

 P14–6 **EOQ, reorder point, and safety stock** Alexis Company uses 800 units of a product per year on a continuous basis. The product has a fixed cost of $50 per order, and its carrying cost is $2 per unit per year. It takes 5 days to receive a shipment after an order is placed, and the firm wishes to hold 10 days' usage in inventory as a safety stock.

a. Calculate the EOQ.

b. Determine the average level of inventory. *(Note:* Use a 365-day year to calculate daily usage.)

c. Determine the *reorder point.*

d. Indicate which of the following variables change if the firm does not hold the safety stock: (1) order cost, (2) carrying cost, (3) total inventory cost, (4) reorder point, (5) economic order quantity. Explain.

PERSONAL FINANCE PROBLEM

 P14–7 **Marginal costs** Jimmy Johnson is interested in buying a new Jeep SUV. There are two options available, a V-6 model and a V-8 model. Whichever model he chooses, he plans to drive it for a period of 5 years and then sell it. Assume that the trade-in value of the two vehicles at the end of the 5-year ownership period will be identical.

There are definite differences between the two models and Jimmy needs to make a financial comparison. The manufacturer's suggested retail price (MSRP) of the V-6 and V-8 are $30,260 and $44,320, respectively. Jimmy believes the difference of $14,060 to be the marginal cost difference between the two vehicles. However, there is much more data available, and you suggest to Jimmy that his analysis may be too simple and will lead him to a poor financial decision. Assume that the prevailing discount rate for both vehicles is 5.5% annually. Other pertinent information on this purchase is shown in the table on page 674:

	V-6	V-8
MSRP	$30,260	$44,320
Engine (liters)	3.7	5.7
Cylinders	6	8
Depreciation over 5 years	$17,337	$25,531
Finance charges* over entire 5-year period	$5,171	$7,573
Insurance over 5 years	$7,546	$8,081
Taxes and fees over 5 years	$2,179	$2,937
Maintenance/repairs over 5 years	$5,600	$5,600
Average miles per gallon	19	14
Ownership period in years	5	5
Miles driven per year over 5 years	15,000	15,000
Cost per gallon of gas over 5 year ownership	$3.15	$3.15

*The finance charges are the difference between the total principal and interest paid over the entire 5-year period less the actual cost of the SUV. Assuming an annual 5.5% discount rate over each of the 5 years of $30,260 for the V-6 and $44,320 for the V-8, the annual annuity payments are $7,086.20 and $10,379.70, respectively. [V-6: (5 × $7,086.20) − $30,260 = $5,171, and V-8: (5 × $10,379.70) − $44,320 = $7,573]

a. Calculate the total "true" cost for each vehicle over the 5-year ownership period.
b. Calculate the total fuel cost for each vehicle over the 5-year ownership period.
c. What is the marginal fuel cost from purchasing the larger V-8 SUV?
d. What is the marginal cost of purchasing the larger and more expensive V-8 SUV?
e. What is the total marginal cost associated with purchasing the V-8 SUV? How does this figure compare with the $14,060 that Jimmy calculated?

P14–8   Accounts receivable changes without bad debts   Tara's Textiles currently has credit sales of $360 million per year and an average collection period of 60 days. Assume that the price of Tara's products is $60 per unit and that the variable costs are $55 per unit. The firm is considering an accounts receivable change that will result in a 20% increase in sales and a 20% increase in the average collection period. No change in bad debts is expected. The firm's equal-risk opportunity cost on its investment in accounts receivable is 14%. (*Note:* Use a 365-day year.)

a. Calculate the *additional profit contribution from sales* that the firm will realize if it makes the proposed change.
b. What *marginal investment in accounts receivable* will result?
c. Calculate the *cost of the marginal investment in accounts receivable*.
d. Should the firm implement the proposed change? What other information would be helpful in your analysis?

P14–9   Accounts receivable changes with bad debts   A firm is evaluating an accounts receivable change that would increase bad debts from 2% to 4% of sales. Sales are currently 50,000 units, the selling price is $20 per unit, and the variable cost per unit is $15. As a result of the proposed change, sales are forecast to increase to 60,000 units.

a. What are bad debts in dollars currently and under the proposed change?
b. Calculate the *cost of the marginal bad debts* to the firm.
c. Ignoring the additional profit contribution from increased sales, if the proposed change saves $3,500 and causes no change in the average investment in accounts receivable, would you recommend it? Explain.

d. Considering *all* changes in costs and benefits, would you recommend the proposed change? Explain.

e. Compare and discuss your answers in parts **c** and **d**.

P14–10 **Relaxation of credit standards**   Lewis Enterprises is considering relaxing its credit standards to increase its currently sagging sales. As a result of the proposed relaxation, sales are expected to increase by 10% from 10,000 to 11,000 units during the coming year; the average collection period is expected to increase from 45 to 60 days; and bad debts are expected to increase from 1% to 3% of sales. The sale price per unit is $40, and the variable cost per unit is $31. The firm's required return on equal-risk investments is 25%. Evaluate the proposed relaxation, and make a recommendation to the firm. (*Note:* Assume a 365-day year.)

P14–11 **Initiating a cash discount**   Gardner Company currently makes all sales on credit and offers no cash discount. The firm is considering offering a 2% cash discount for payment within 15 days. The firm's current average collection period is 60 days, sales are 40,000 units, selling price is $45 per unit, and variable cost per unit is $36. The firm expects that the change in credit terms will result in an increase in sales to 42,000 units, that 70% of the sales will take the discount, and that the average collection period will fall to 30 days. If the firm's required rate of return on equal-risk investments is 25%, should the proposed discount be offered? (*Note:* Assume a 365-day year.)

P14–12 **Shortening the credit period**   A firm is contemplating *shortening* its credit period from 40 to 30 days and believes that as a result of this change, its average collection period will decline from 45 to 36 days. Bad-debt expenses are expected to decrease from 1.5% to 1% of sales. The firm is currently selling 12,000 units but believes that as a result of the proposed change, sales will decline to 10,000 units. The sale price per unit is $56, and the variable cost per unit is $45. The firm has a required return on equal-risk investments of 25%. Evaluate this decision, and make a recommendation to the firm. (*Note:* Assume a 365-day year.)

P14–13 **Lengthening the credit period**   Parker Tool is considering lengthening its credit period from 30 to 60 days. All customers will continue to pay on the net date. The firm currently bills $450,000 for sales and has $345,000 in variable costs. The change in credit terms is expected to increase sales to $510,000. Bad-debt expenses will increase from 1% to 1.5% of sales. The firm has a required rate of return on equal-risk investments of 20%. (*Note:* Assume a 365-day year.)

a. What *additional profit contribution from sales* will be realized from the proposed change?

b. What is the *cost of the marginal investment in accounts receivable?*

c. What is the *cost of the marginal bad debts?*

d. Do you recommend this change in credit terms? Why or why not?

P14–14 **Float**   Simon Corporation has daily cash receipts of $65,000. A recent analysis of its collections indicated that customers' payments were in the mail an average of 2.5 days. Once received, the payments are processed in 1.5 days. After payments are deposited, it takes an average of 3 days for these receipts to clear the banking system.

a. How much *collection float (in days)* does the firm currently have?

b. If the firm's opportunity cost is 11%, would it be economically advisable for the firm to pay an annual fee of $16,500 to reduce collection float by 3 days? Explain why or why not.

 P14–15 **Lockbox system**   Eagle Industries feels that a lockbox system can shorten its accounts receivable collection period by 3 days. Credit sales are $3,240,000 per year, billed on a continuous basis. The firm has other equally risky investments that earn a return of 15%. The cost of the lockbox system is $9,000 per year. (*Note:* Assume a 365-day year.)

a. What amount of cash will be made available for other uses under the lockbox system?

b. What net benefit (cost) will the firm realize if it adopts the lockbox system? Should it adopt the proposed lockbox system?

 P14–16 **Zero-balance account**   Union Company is considering establishment of a zero-balance account. The firm currently maintains an average balance of $420,000 in its disbursement account. As compensation to the bank for maintaining the zero-balance account, the firm will have to pay a monthly fee of $1,000 and maintain a $300,000 non–interest-earning deposit in the bank. The firm currently has no other deposits in the bank. Evaluate the proposed zero-balance account, and make a recommendation to the firm, assuming that it has a 12% opportunity cost.

PERSONAL FINANCE PROBLEM

 P14–17 **Management of cash balance**   Alexis Morris, an assistant manager at a local department store, gets paid every 2 weeks by direct deposit into her checking account. This account pays no interest and has no minimum balance requirement. Her monthly income is $4,200. Alexis has a "target" cash balance of around $1,200, and whenever it exceeds that amount she transfers the excess into her savings account, which currently pays 2.0% annual interest. Her current savings balance is $15,000, and Alexis estimates she transfers about $500 per month from her checking account into her savings account. Alexis doesn't waste any time in paying her bills, and her monthly bills average about $2,000. Her monthly cash outlay for food, gas, and other sundry items totals about $850. Reviewing her payment habits indicates that on average she pays her bills 9 days early. At this time, most marketable securities are yielding about 4.75% annual interest.

   Show how Alexis can better manage her cash balance:

a. What can Alexis do regarding the handling of her current balances?

b. What do you suggest that she do with her monthly surpluses?

c. What do you suggest Alexis do about the manner in which she pays her bills?

d. Can Alexis grow her earnings by better managing her cash balances? Show your work.

P14–18 **ETHICS PROBLEM**   A group of angry shareholders has placed a corporate resolution before all shareholders at a company's annual stockholders' meeting. The resolution demands that the company *stretch its accounts payable,* because these shareholders have determined that all of the company's competitors do so, and the firm operates in a highly competitive industry. How could management at the annual stockholders' meeting defend the firm's practice of paying suppliers on time?

Chapter 14 Case

Assessing Roche Publishing Company's Cash Management Efficiency

Lisa Pinto, vice president of finance at Roche Publishing Company, a rapidly growing publisher of college texts, is concerned about the firm's high level of short-term resource investment. She believes that the firm can improve the management of its cash and, as a result, reduce this investment. In this regard, she charged Arlene Bessenoff, the treasurer, with assessing the firm's cash management efficiency. Arlene decided to begin her investigation by studying the firm's operating and cash conversion cycles.

Arlene found that Roche's average payment period was 25 days. She consulted industry data, which showed that the average payment period for the industry was 40 days. Investigation of three similar publishing companies revealed that their average payment period was also 40 days. She estimated the annual cost of achieving a 40-day payment period to be $53,000.

Next, Arlene studied the production cycle and inventory policies. The average age of inventory was 120 days. She determined that the industry standard as reported in a survey done by *Publishing World*, the trade association journal, was 85 days. She estimated the annual cost of achieving an 85-day average age of inventory to be $150,000.

Further analysis showed Arlene that the firm's average collection period was 60 days. The industry average, derived from the trade association data and information on three similar publishing companies, was found to be 42 days—30% lower than Roche's. Arlene estimated that if Roche initiated a 2% cash discount for payment within 10 days of the beginning of the credit period, the firm's average collection period would drop from 60 days to the 42-day industry average. She also expected the following to occur as a result of the discount: Annual sales would increase from $13,750,000 to $15,000,000; bad debts would remain unchanged; and the 2% cash discount would be applied to 75% of the firm's sales. The firm's variable costs equal 80% of sales.

Roche Publishing Company is currently spending $12,000,000 per year on its operating-cycle investment, but it expects that initiating a cash discount will increase its operating-cycle investment to $13,100,000 per year. (*Note:* The operating-cycle investment per dollar of inventory, receivables, and payables is assumed to be the same.) Arlene's concern was whether the firm's cash management was as efficient as it could be. Arlene knew that the company paid 12% annual interest for its resource investment and therefore viewed this value as the firm's required return. For this reason, she was concerned about the resource investment cost resulting from any inefficiencies in the management of Roche's cash conversion cycle. (*Note:* Assume a 365-day year.)

To Do

a. Assuming a constant rate for purchases, production, and sales throughout the year, what are Roche's existing *operating cycle (OC)*, *cash conversion cycle (CCC)*, and *resource investment* need?

b. If Roche can optimize operations according to industry standards, what would its *operating cycle (OC)*, *cash conversion cycle (CCC)*, and *resource investment* need be under these more efficient conditions?

c. In terms of resource investment requirements, what is the annual cost of Roche's operational inefficiency?

d. Evaluate whether Roche's strategy for speeding its collection of accounts receivable would be acceptable. What annual net profit or loss would result from implementation of the cash discount?

e. Use your finding in part **d,** along with the payables and inventory costs given, to determine the total annual cost the firm would incur to achieve the industry level of operational efficiency.

f. Judging on the basis of your findings in parts **c** and **e,** should the firm incur the annual cost to achieve the industry level of operational efficiency? Explain why or why not.

Spreadsheet Exercise

The current balance in accounts receivable for Eboy Corporation is $443,000. This level was achieved with annual (365 days) credit sales of $3,544,000. The firm offers its customers credit terms of *net 30*. However, in an effort to help its cash flow position and to follow the actions of its rivals, the firm is considering changing its credit terms from net 30 to *2/10 net 30*. The objective is to speed up the receivable collections and thereby improve the firm's cash flows. Eboy would like to increase its accounts receivable turnover to 12.0.

The firm works with a raw material whose current annual usage is 1,450 units. Each finished product requires 1 unit of this raw material at a variable cost of $2,600 per unit and sells for $4,200 on terms of net 30. It is estimated that 70% of the firm's customers will take the 2% cash discount and that with the discount, sales of the finished product will increase by 50 units per year. The firm's opportunity cost of funds invested in accounts receivable is 12.5%

In analyzing the investment in accounts receivable, use the variable cost of the product sold instead of the sale price, because the variable cost is a better indicator of the firm's investment.

To Do

Create a spreadsheet similar to Table 14.3 to analyze whether the firm should initiate the proposed cash discount. What is your advice? Make sure you calculate the following:

a. Additional profit contribution from sales.

b. Average investment in accounts receivable at present (without cash discount).

c. Average investment in accounts receivable with the proposed cash discount.

d. Reduction in investment in accounts receivable.

e. Cost savings from reduced investment in accounts receivable.

f. Cost of the cash discount.

g. Net profit (loss) from initiation of proposed cash discount.

Group Exercise

This chapter covers several short-term financial management topics that are vital to any business's success. These topics are often overlooked by the inexperienced manager/owner. Many businesses fail not because of a lack of sales but because of an inability to adequately manage current assets and current liabilities. With this point in mind, your group will "get its hands dirty" as it establishes proper controls meant to better manage short-term finances.

To Do

Your group's fictitious firm, like all firms, needs to develop proper controls to ensure that short-term needs are met and that the firm gets the most out of its limited funds. To that end your group should do the following:

a. Establish your firm's operating cycle by determining its AAI and ACP as well as its CCC based on its OC and its APP.
b. Discuss the funding requirements, and state whether there is any seasonality to your required resource investment.
c. Choose a method for managing inventory, and discuss how this method applies to your business.
d. Establish the specific credit terms by which you will be selling your firm's good/service.

Web Exercise

Go to the book's companion website at **www.prenhall.com/gitman** to find the Web Exercise for this chapter.

> Remember to check the book's website at **www.prenhall.com/gitman** to find additional resources, including Web Exercises and a Web Case.

15 | Current Liabilities Management

Why This Chapter Matters to You

In Your Professional Life

Accounting: You need to understand how to analyze supplier credit terms to decide whether the firm should take or give up cash discounts; you also need to understand the various types of short-term loans, both unsecured and secured, that you will be required to record and report.

Information systems: You need to understand what data the firm will need to process accounts payable, track accruals, and meet bank loans and other short-term debt obligations in a timely manner.

Management: You need to know the sources of short-term loans so that if short-term financing is needed, you will understand its availability and cost.

Marketing: You need to understand how accounts receivable and inventory can be used as loan collateral; the procedures used by the firm to secure short-term loans with such collateral could affect customer relationships.

Operations: You need to understand the use of accounts payable as a form of short-term financing and the effect on one's suppliers of stretching payables; you also need to understand the process by which a firm uses inventory as collateral.

In Your Personal Life

Management of current liabilities is an important part of your financial strategy. It takes discipline to avoid viewing cash and credit purchases equally. You need to borrow for a purpose, not convenience. You need to repay credit purchases in a timely fashion. Excessive use of short-term credit, particularly with credit cards, can create personal liquidity problems and, at the extreme, personal bankruptcy.

Learning Goals

LG 1 Review accounts payable, the key components of credit terms, and the procedures for analyzing those terms.

LG 2 Understand the effects of stretching accounts payable on their cost, and the use of accruals.

LG 3 Describe interest rates and the basic types of unsecured bank sources of short-term loans.

LG 4 Discuss the basic features of commercial paper and the key aspects of international short-term loans.

LG 5 Explain the characteristics of secured short-term loans and the use of accounts receivable as short-term-loan collateral.

LG 6 Describe the various ways in which inventory can be used as short-term-loan collateral.

Memorial Sloan-Kettering Cancer Center

Reducing Accounts Payable Expenses

Automating accounts payables can save both time and expense. Much of the savings comes from eliminating the processing of paper invoices—a time-consuming process of matching purchase orders with invoices, checking that shipments or services were received, and then writing and mailing a check. For decades, nearly every large company employed staffs of dozens of accounts payable clerks to do the work.

Memorial Sloan-Kettering Cancer Center, the New York–based nonprofit medical research and health care institution, was looking for a better way to process the nearly half-million invoices it receives annually from suppliers. It turned to **Xign Corporation,** a California-based online payments service. Launched in June 2001, Xign provides a network that enables companies to issue purchase orders, receive invoices, and make electronic payments to suppliers.

Sloan-Kettering's goal was to speed up the payment process while eliminating paper invoicing and most of the labor-intensive work of matching invoices and purchase orders. In 2003, the task of prodding hundreds of major suppliers to change the way they billed Sloan-Kettering for some $413 million worth of goods and services was anything but a sure thing. "In 2003, we were not really sure that the suppliers would be willing to give up their banking information in an online environment," admits Barbara Cassera, manager of financial systems at Sloan-Kettering.

By moving to Xign (which was purchased in 2007 by JPMorgan Chase), Sloan-Kettering boosted the percentage of invoices it processed electronically from roughly 60 percent in 2003 to about 85 percent in 2006. As a result, the organization is receiving $500,000 annually in supplier discounts. In addition, Sloan-Kettering has found that the time saved on the sheer volume of invoices processed electronically has enabled the accounts payable department to reduce its full-time staff from six to four, saving about $120,000 annually.

As firms grow, so do their needs for capital to fund the buildup of inventory and accounts receivable. Controlling accounts payable expenses and improving its management of other current liabilities allow a company to reduce them. In this chapter, you will learn how some companies use current liabilities, including accounts payable, accruals, lines of credit, commercial paper, and short-term loans, to finance current assets.

> As you read this chapter, consider: Of the techniques used to finance current assets, which method is a small business more likely to use?

15.1 | Spontaneous Liabilities

spontaneous liabilities
Financing that arises from the normal course of business; the two major short-term sources of such liabilities are accounts payable and accruals.

unsecured short-term financing
Short-term financing obtained without pledging specific assets as collateral.

Spontaneous liabilities arise from the normal course of business. The two major spontaneous sources of short-term financing are accounts payable and accruals. As the firm's sales increase, accounts payable increase in response to the increased purchases necessary to produce at higher levels. Also in response to increasing sales, the firm's accruals increase as wages and taxes rise because of greater labor requirements and the increased taxes on the firm's increased earnings. There is normally no explicit cost attached to either of these current liabilities, although they do have certain implicit costs. In addition, both are forms of **unsecured short-term financing**—short-term financing obtained without pledging specific assets as collateral. The firm should take advantage of these "interest-free" sources of unsecured short-term financing whenever possible.

Accounts Payable Management

Hint An account payable of a purchaser is an account receivable on the supplier's books. Chapter 14 highlighted the key strategies and considerations involved in extending credit to customers.

Accounts payable are the major source of unsecured short-term financing for business firms. They result from transactions in which merchandise is purchased but no formal note is signed to show the purchaser's liability to the seller. The purchaser in effect agrees to pay the supplier the amount required in accordance with credit terms normally stated on the supplier's invoice. The discussion of accounts payable here is presented from the viewpoint of the purchaser.

Role in the Cash Conversion Cycle

The average payment period is the final component of the *cash conversion cycle* introduced in Chapter 14. The average payment period has two parts: (1) the time from the purchase of raw materials until the firm mails the payment and (2) payment float time (the time it takes after the firm mails its payment until the supplier has withdrawn spendable funds from the firm's account). In the preceding chapter, we discussed issues related to payment float time. Here we discuss the firm's management of the time that elapses between its purchase of raw materials and its mailing payment to the supplier. This activity is **accounts payable management**.

accounts payable management
Management by the firm of the time that elapses between its purchase of raw materials and its mailing payment to the supplier.

The firm's goal is to pay as slowly as possible without damaging its credit rating. This means that accounts should be paid on the last day possible, given the supplier's stated credit terms. For example, if the terms are net 30, then the account should be paid 30 days from the *beginning of the credit period*, which is typically either the *date of invoice* or the *end of the month* (EOM) in which the purchase was made. This allows for the maximum use of an interest-free loan from the supplier and will not damage the firm's credit rating (because the account is paid within the stated credit terms).

Example

In the demonstration of the cash conversion cycle in Chapter 14 (see pages 641–642), MAX Company had an average payment period of 35 days (consisting of 30 days until payment was mailed and 5 days of payment float), which resulted in average accounts payable of $467,466. Thus the daily accounts payable generated by MAX totaled $13,356 ($467,466/35). If MAX were to mail its payments in 35 days instead of 30 days, its accounts payable would increase by $66,780 (5 × $13,356). As a result, MAX's cash conversion cycle would decrease by 5 days, and the firm would reduce its investment in operations by $66,780. Clearly, if this action did not damage MAX's credit rating, it would be in the company's best interest.

Analyzing Credit Terms

The credit terms that a firm is offered by its suppliers enable it to delay payments for its purchases. Because the supplier's cost of having its money tied up in merchandise after it is sold is probably reflected in the purchase price, the purchaser is already indirectly paying for this benefit. The purchaser should therefore carefully analyze credit terms to determine the best trade credit strategy. If a firm is extended credit terms that include a cash discount, it has two options—to take the cash discount or to give it up.

Taking the Cash Discount   If a firm intends to take a cash discount, it should pay on the last day of the discount period. There is no cost associated with taking a cash discount.

Example   Lawrence Industries, operator of a small chain of video stores, purchased $1,000 worth of merchandise on February 27 from a supplier extending terms of 2/10 net 30 EOM. If the firm takes the cash discount, it must pay $980 [$1,000 − (0.02 × $1,000)] by March 10, thereby saving $20.

---

cost of giving up a cash discount
The implied rate of interest paid to delay payment of an account payable for an additional number of days.

Giving Up the Cash Discount   If the firm chooses to give up the cash discount, it should pay on the final day of the credit period. There is an implicit cost associated with giving up a cash discount. The **cost of giving up a cash discount** is the implied rate of interest paid to delay payment of an account payable for an additional number of days. In other words, it is the interest being paid by the firm to keep its money for a number of days. This cost can be illustrated by a simple example. The example assumes that payment will be made on the last possible day (either the final day of the cash discount period or the final day of the credit period).

Example   In the prior example, we saw that Lawrence Industries could take the cash discount on its February 27 purchase by paying $980 on March 10. If Lawrence gives up the cash discount, it can pay on March 30. To keep its money for an extra 20 days, the firm must give up an opportunity to pay $980 for its $1,000 purchase. In other words, it will cost the firm $20 to delay payment for 20 days. Figure 15.1 (on page 684) shows the payment options that are open to the company.

To calculate the cost of giving up the cash discount, the *true purchase price* must be viewed as the *discounted cost of the merchandise,* which is $980 for Lawrence Industries. The annual percentage cost of giving up the cash discount can be calculated using Equation 15.1:[1]

$$\text{Cost of giving up cash discount} = \frac{CD}{100\% - CD} \times \frac{365}{N} \qquad \textbf{(15.1)}$$

---

1. Equation 15.1 and the related discussions are based on the assumption that only one discount is offered. In the event that multiple discounts are offered, calculation of the cost of giving up the discount must be made for each alternative.

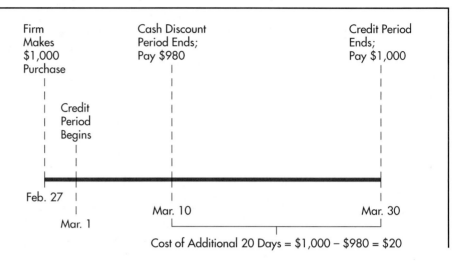

FIGURE 15.1

Payment Options
Payment options for
Lawrence Industries

where

CD = stated cash discount in percentage terms

N = number of days that payment can be delayed by giving up the cash
discount

Substituting the values for CD (2%) and N (20 days) into Equation 15.1 results
in an annualized cost of giving up the cash discount of 37.24% [(2% ÷ 98%) ×
(365 ÷ 20)]. A 365-day year is assumed.[2]

A simple way to *approximate* the cost of giving up a cash discount is to
use the stated cash discount percentage, CD, in place of the first term of Equation 15.1:

$$\text{Approximate cost of giving up cash discount} = CD \times \frac{365}{N} \qquad \textbf{(15.2)}$$

The smaller the cash discount, the closer the approximation to the actual cost of
giving it up. Using this approximation, the cost of giving up the cash discount for
Lawrence Industries is 36.5% [2% × (365 ÷ 20)].

Using the Cost of Giving Up a Cash Discount in Decision Making   The
financial manager must determine whether it is advisable to take a cash discount.
Financial managers must remember that taking cash discounts may represent an
important source of additional profitability.

---

2. This example assumes that Lawrence Industries gives up only one discount during the year, which costs it 2.04%
for 20 days (that is, 2% ÷ 98%) or 37.24% when annualized. However, if Lawrence Industries *continually* gives up
the 2% cash discounts, the effect of compounding will cause the annualized cost to rise to 44.59%:

$$\begin{aligned}\text{Annualized cost when discounts}\atop\text{are \textit{continually} given up} &= \left(1 + \frac{CD}{100\% - CD}\right)^{365/N} - 1 \qquad \textbf{(15.1a)}\\[6pt] &= \left(1 + \frac{2\%}{100\% - 2\%}\right)^{365/20} - 1 = \underline{44.59\%}\end{aligned}$$

TABLE 15.1	Cash Discounts and Associated Costs for Mason Products	
Supplier	Credit terms	Approximate cost of giving up a cash discount
A	2/10 net 30 EOM	36.5%
B	1/10 net 55 EOM	8.1
C	3/20 net 70 EOM	21.9
D	4/10 net 60 EOM	29.2

Example

Mason Products, a large building-supply company, has four possible suppliers, each offering different credit terms. Otherwise, their products and services are identical. Table 15.1 presents the credit terms offered by suppliers A, B, C, and D and the cost of giving up the cash discounts in each transaction. The approximation method of calculating the cost of giving up a cash discount (Equation 15.2) has been used. The cost of giving up the cash discount from supplier A is 36.5%; from supplier B, 8.1%; from supplier C, 21.9%; and from supplier D, 29.2%.

If the firm needs short-term funds, which it can borrow from its bank at an interest rate of 13%, and if each of the suppliers is viewed *separately*, which (if any) of the suppliers' cash discounts will the firm give up? In dealing with supplier A, the firm takes the cash discount, because the cost of giving it up is 36.5%, and then borrows the funds it requires from its bank at 13% interest. With supplier B, the firm would do better to give up the cash discount, because the cost of this action is less than the cost of borrowing money from the bank (8.1% versus 13%). With either supplier C or supplier D, the firm should take the cash discount, because in both cases the cost of giving up the discount is greater than the 13% cost of borrowing from the bank.

The example shows that the cost of giving up a cash discount is relevant when one is evaluating a single supplier's credit terms in light of certain *bank borrowing costs*. However, other factors relative to payment strategies may also need to be considered. For example, some firms, particularly small firms and poorly managed firms, routinely give up *all* discounts because they either lack alternative sources of unsecured short-term financing or fail to recognize the implicit costs of their actions.

Effects of Stretching Accounts Payable

stretching accounts payable
Paying bills as late as possible without damaging the firm's credit rating.

A strategy that is often employed by a firm is **stretching accounts payable**—that is, paying bills as late as possible without damaging its credit rating. Such a strategy can reduce the cost of giving up a cash discount.

Example

Lawrence Industries was extended credit terms of 2/10 net 30 EOM. The cost of giving up the cash discount, assuming payment on the last day of the credit period, was approximately 36.5% [$2\% \times (365 \div 20)$]. If the firm were able to stretch its account payable to 70 days without damaging its credit rating, the cost of giving up the cash discount would be only 12.2% [$2\% \times (365 \div 60)$]. Stretching accounts payable reduces the implicit cost of giving up a cash discount.

Although stretching accounts payable may be financially attractive, it raises an important ethical issue: It may cause the firm to violate the agreement it entered into with its supplier when it purchased merchandise. Clearly, a supplier would not look kindly on a customer who regularly and purposely postponed paying for purchases.

Personal Finance Example   Jack and Mary Nobel, a young married couple, are in the process of purchasing a 42-inch HD TV at a cost of $1,900. The electronics dealer currently has a special financing plan that would allow them to either (1) put $200 down and finance the balance of $1,700 at 3% annual interest over 24 months, resulting in payments of $73 per month, or (2) receive an immediate $150 cash rebate, thereby paying only $1,750 cash. The Nobels, who have saved enough to pay cash for the TV, can currently earn 5% annual interest on their savings. They wish to determine whether to borrow or to pay cash to purchase the TV.

The upfront outlay for the financing alternative is the $200 down payment, whereas the Nobels will pay out $1,750 upfront under the cash purchase alternative. So the cash purchase will require an initial outlay that is $1,550 ($1,750 − $200) greater than under the financing alternative. Given that they can earn 5% on savings, the cash purchase will cause the Nobels to give up an opportunity to earn $155 (2 years × 0.05 × $1,550) over the 2 years.

If they choose the financing alternative, the $1,550 would grow to $1,705 ($1,550 + $155) at the end of 2 years. But under the financing alternative, the Nobels will pay out a total of $1,752 (24 months × $73 per month) over the 2-year loan term. Ignoring the time value of money, the cost of the financing alternative can be viewed as $1,752 and the cost of the cash payment (including forgone interest earnings) would be $1,705. Because it is less expensive, *the Nobels should pay cash for the TV*. The lower cost of the cash alternative is largely the result of the $150 cash rebate.

Accruals

accruals
Liabilities for services received for which payment has yet to be made.

The second spontaneous source of short-term business financing is accruals. **Accruals** are liabilities for services received for which payment has yet to be made. The most common items accrued by a firm are wages and taxes. Because taxes are payments to the government, their accrual cannot be manipulated by the firm. However, the accrual of wages can be manipulated to some extent. This is accomplished by delaying payment of wages, thereby receiving an interest-free loan from employees who are paid sometime after they have performed the work. The pay period for employees who earn an hourly rate is often governed by union regulations or by state or federal law. However, in other cases, the frequency of payment is at the discretion of the company's management.

Example   Tenney Company, a large janitorial service company, currently pays its employees at the end of each work week. The weekly payroll totals $400,000. If the firm were to extend the pay period so as to pay its employees 1 week later throughout an entire year, the employees would in effect be lending the firm $400,000 for a year. If the firm could earn 10% annually on invested funds, such a strategy would be worth $40,000 per year (0.10 × $400,000).

REVIEW QUESTIONS

15–1 What are the two major sources of spontaneous short-term financing for a firm? How do their balances behave relative to the firm's sales?

15–2 Is there a cost associated with *taking a cash discount?* Is there any cost associated with *giving up a cash discount?* How do short-term borrowing costs affect the cash discount decision?

15–3 What is "stretching accounts payable"? What effect does this action have on the cost of giving up a cash discount?

15.2 | Unsecured Sources of Short-Term Loans

Businesses obtain unsecured short-term loans from two major sources, banks and sales of commercial paper. Unlike the spontaneous sources of unsecured short-term financing, bank loans and commercial paper are negotiated and result from actions taken by the firm's financial manager. Bank loans are more popular, because they are available to firms of all sizes; commercial paper tends to be available only to large firms. In addition, firms can use international loans to finance international transactions.

Bank Loans

short-term, self-liquidating loan
An unsecured short-term loan in which the use to which the borrowed money is put provides the mechanism through which the loan is repaid.

Banks are a major source of unsecured short-term loans to businesses. The major type of loan made by banks to businesses is the **short-term, self-liquidating loan.** These loans are intended merely to carry the firm through seasonal peaks in financing needs that are due primarily to buildups of inventory and accounts receivable. As the firm converts inventories and receivables into cash, the funds needed to retire these loans are generated. In other words, the use to which the borrowed money is put provides the mechanism through which the loan is repaid—hence the term *self-liquidating.* Though most business borrowers take out loans honestly and repay them as agreed, a few do not. The *Focus on Ethics* box on page 688 discusses the issue of loan fraud.

Banks lend unsecured, short-term funds in three basic ways: through single-payment notes, lines of credit, and revolving credit agreements. Before we look at these types of loans, we consider loan interest rates.

Loan Interest Rates

prime rate of interest (prime rate)
The lowest rate of interest charged by leading banks on business loans to their most important business borrowers.

The interest rate on a bank loan can be a fixed or a floating rate, typically based on the prime rate of interest. The **prime rate of interest (prime rate)** is the lowest rate of interest charged by leading banks on business loans to their most important business borrowers.[3] The prime rate fluctuates with changing supply-and-

---

3. A trend away from using the prime rate as a benchmark has begun in the United States in response to various borrower lawsuits against banks. Some banks now use the term *base rate* or *reference rate* rather than *prime rate* for pricing corporate and other loans. In fact, the use of the *London Interbank Offered Rate (LIBOR)* is gaining momentum as a base lending rate in the United States.

Focus on Ethics   Loan Fraud

IN PRACTICE

In June 2007, the creator of the Backstreet Boys and 'N Sync was indicted by a federal grand jury on charges that he defrauded a bank out of $20 million. He was accused of fraudulently securing millions in bank loans with documents from a fake accounting firm.

What constitutes *loan fraud*? A loan fraud is a scheme or artifice or making false statements orally or in writing in order to receive a loan. Loan frauds may sometimes be committed with the assistance of outside agents such as appraisers who inflate appraisals that support loans or, as in the case just cited, a fake or disreputable accounting firm.

Loan fraud is covered under a variety of federal statutes, and the perpetrator can be fined up to $1 million and imprisoned for up to 30 years. More extensive loan frauds, in which criminal enterprises commit a series of specified crimes against financial institutions, are covered by the

"S&L Kingpin" statute. This law provides for fines of up to $20 million for organizational defendants and up to $10 million and life imprisonment for individuals.

Common types of loan fraud include making false application, loans to nonexistent borrowers, nominee loans, double pledging of collateral, and misapplication of loan funds. *False applications* can include false information about persons, understated or missing debts, and/or overstated asset valuations. They also may include false income tax documents or false financial statements. *Loans to nonexistent borrowers* are loan frauds perpetrated by individuals or businesses who supply false names and addresses. *Nominee loans* are loans taken out by one party for the benefit of a second party whose identity is concealed from the financial institution. Some borrowers fraudulently secure two loans by *pledging the same collateral with different lenders* before the liens are recorded

and without telling the lenders. *Misapplication of loan funds* involves using the money for a purpose other than that stated in the loan.

How does a bank or lending institution protect itself from loan fraud? Deterioration in a borrower's finances can be a red flag. Lenders can calculate horizontal analyses by comparing financial ratios over several periods. Lenders can also perform vertical analysis in which they compare ratios to total assets or total sales and to benchmark ratios for similar companies.

Second, strong internal controls such as independent reviews, internal auditors, committee and officer lending limits, and sound underwriting can help prevent loan fraud. Physical inspections of collateral can also help detect a potential fraud.

■ *How might lenders use sales tax information to verify portions of the financial statements?*

---

demand relationships for short-term funds.[4] Banks generally determine the rate to be charged to various borrowers by adding a premium to the prime rate to adjust it for the borrower's "riskiness." The premium may amount to 4 percent or more, although most unsecured short-term loans carry premiums of less than 2 percent.[5]

fixed-rate loan
A loan with a rate of interest that is determined at a set increment above the prime rate and remains unvarying until maturity.

Fixed- and Floating-Rate Loans   Loans can have either fixed or floating interest rates. On a **fixed-rate loan,** the rate of interest is determined at a set increment above the prime rate on the date of the loan and remains unvarying at that

---

4. During the past 25 years, the prime rate has varied from a record high of 21.5% (December 1980) to a low of 4.00% (July 2003 through June 2004). Since January 2001, it has fluctuated in the range from a high of 9.50% to a low of 4.00%.

5. Some, generally very large, firms can borrow from their banks at an interest rate slightly below the prime rate. This typically occurs when the borrowing firm either maintains high deposit balances at the bank over time or agrees to pay an upfront fee to "buy down" the interest rate. Below-prime-rate loans are clearly the exception rather than the rule.

floating-rate loan
A loan with a rate of interest initially set at an increment above the prime rate and allowed to "float," or vary, above prime *as the prime rate varies* until maturity.

fixed rate until maturity. On a **floating-rate loan,** the increment above the prime rate is initially established, and the rate of interest is allowed to "float," or vary, above prime *as the prime rate varies* until maturity. Generally, the increment above the prime rate will be *lower* on a floating-rate loan than on a fixed-rate loan of equivalent risk, because the lender bears less risk with a floating-rate loan. As a result of the volatile nature of the prime rate during recent years, today *most short-term business loans are floating-rate loans.*

Method of Computing Interest   Once the *nominal (or stated) annual rate* is established, the method of computing interest is determined. Interest can be paid either when a loan matures or in advance. If interest is paid *at maturity,* the *effective (or true) annual rate*—the actual rate of interest paid—for an assumed 1-year period[6] is equal to

$$\frac{\text{Interest}}{\text{Amount borrowed}} \tag{15.3}$$

Most bank loans to businesses require the interest payment at maturity.

discount loans
Loans on which interest is paid in advance by being deducted from the amount borrowed.

When interest is paid *in advance,* it is deducted from the loan so that the borrower actually receives less money than is requested. Loans on which interest is paid in advance are called **discount loans.** The *effective annual rate for a discount loan,* assuming a 1-year period, is calculated as

$$\frac{\text{Interest}}{\text{Amount borrowed} - \text{Interest}} \tag{15.4}$$

Paying interest in advance raises the effective annual rate above the stated annual rate.

Example

Wooster Company, a manufacturer of athletic apparel, wants to borrow $10,000 at a stated annual rate of 10% interest for 1 year. If the interest on the loan is paid at maturity, the firm will pay $1,000 ($0.10 \times $10,000$) for the use of the $10,000 for the year. Substituting into Equation 15.3 reveals that the effective annual rate is therefore

$$\frac{\$1,000}{\$10,000} = 10.0\%$$

If the money is borrowed at the same *stated* annual rate for 1 year but interest is paid in advance, the firm still pays $1,000 in interest, but it receives only $9,000 ($10,000 − $1,000). The effective annual rate in this case is

$$\frac{\$1,000}{\$10,000 - \$1,000} = \frac{\$1,000}{\$9,000} = 11.1\%$$

Paying interest in advance thus makes the effective annual rate (11.1%) greater than the stated annual rate (10.0%).

---

6. Effective annual rates (EARs) for loans with maturities of less than 1 year can be found by using the technique presented in Chapter 4 for finding EARs when interest is compounded more frequently than annually. See Equation 4.24.

Single-Payment Notes

single-payment note
A short-term, one-time loan made to a borrower who needs funds for a specific purpose for a short period.

A **single-payment note** can be obtained from a commercial bank by a creditworthy business borrower. This type of loan is usually a one-time loan made to a borrower who needs funds for a specific purpose for a short period. The resulting instrument is a *note*, signed by the borrower, that states the terms of the loan, including the length of the loan and the interest rate. This type of short-term note generally has a maturity of 30 days to 9 months or more. The interest charged is usually tied in some way to the prime rate of interest.

Example ┐

Gordon Manufacturing, a producer of rotary mower blades, recently borrowed $100,000 from each of two banks—bank A and bank B. The loans were incurred on the same day, when the prime rate of interest was 6%. Each loan involved a 90-day note with interest to be paid at the end of 90 days. The interest rate was set at 1½% above the prime rate on bank A's *fixed-rate note*. Over the 90-day period, the rate of interest on this note will remain at 7½% (6% prime rate + 1½% increment) regardless of fluctuations in the prime rate. The total interest cost on this loan is $1,849 [$100,000 × (7½% × 90/365)]. The effective 90-day rate on this loan is 1.85% ($1,849/$100,000).

Assuming that the loan from bank A is rolled over each 90 days throughout the year under the same terms and circumstances, we can find its effective *annual* interest rate by using Equation 4.24. Because the loan costs 1.85% for 90 days, it is necessary to compound $(1 + 0.0185)$ for 4.06 periods in the year (that is, 365/90) and then subtract 1:

$$\text{Effective annual rate} = (1 + 0.0185)^{4.06} - 1$$
$$= 1.0773 - 1 = 0.0773 = \underline{7.73\%}$$

The effective annual rate of interest on the fixed-rate, 90-day note is 7.73%.

Bank B set the interest rate at 1% above the prime rate on its *floating-rate note*. The rate charged over the 90 days will vary directly with the prime rate. Initially, the rate will be 7% (6% + 1%), but when the prime rate changes, so will the rate of interest on the note. For instance, if after 30 days the prime rate rises to 6.5%, and after another 30 days it drops to 6.25%, the firm will be paying 0.575% for the first 30 days (7% × 30/365), 0.616% for the next 30 days (7.5% × 30/365), and 0.596% for the last 30 days (7.25% × 30/365). Its total interest cost will be $1,787 [$100,000 × (0.575% + 0.616% + 0.596%)], resulting in an effective 90-day rate of 1.79% ($1,787/$100,000).

Again, assuming the loan is rolled over each 90 days throughout the year under the same terms and circumstances, its effective *annual* rate is 7.46%:

$$\text{Effective annual rate} = (1 + 0.01787)^{4.06} - 1$$
$$= 1.0746 - 1 = 0.0746 = \underline{7.46\%}$$

Clearly, in this case the floating-rate loan would have been less expensive than the fixed-rate loan because of its generally lower effective annual rate.

Personal Finance Example ┐

Megan Schwartz has been approved by Clinton National Bank for a 180-day loan of $30,000 that will allow her to make the down payment and close the loan on her new condo. She needs the funds to bridge the time until the sale of her current condo closes and she receives the $42,000 in proceeds from it.

Clinton National offered Megan the following two financing options for the $30,000 loan: (1) a *fixed-rate loan* at 2% above the prime rate, or (2) a *variable-rate loan* at 1% above the prime rate. Currently, the prime rate of interest is 8% and the consensus forecast of a group of mortgage economists for changes in the prime rate over the next 180 days are as follows:

> 60 days from today the prime rate will rise by 1%
>
> 90 days from today the prime rate will rise another ½%
>
> 150 days from today the prime rate will drop by 1%

Using the forecast prime rate changes, Megan wishes to determine the lowest interest-cost loan for the next 6 months.

Fixed-rate loan: Total interest cost over 180 days
$$= \$30,000 \times (0.08 + 0.02) \times (180/365)$$
$$= \$30,000 \times 0.04932 \approx \underline{\underline{\$1,480}}$$

Variable-rate loan: The applicable interest rate would begin at 9% (8% + 1%) and remain there for 60 days. Then the applicable rate would rise to 10% (9% + 1%) for the next 30 days, and then to 10.50% (10% + 0.50%) for the next 60 days. Finally the applicable rate would drop to 9.50% (10.50% − 1%) for the final 30 days.

Total interest cost over 180 days
$$= \$30,000 \times [(0.09 \times 60/365) + (0.10 \times 30/365)$$
$$+ (0.105 \times 60/365) + (0.095 \times 30/365)]$$
$$= \$30,000 \times (0.01479 + 0.00822 + 0.01726 + 0.00781)$$
$$= \$30,000 \times 0.04808 \approx \underline{\underline{\$1,442}}$$

Because the estimated total interest cost on the variable-rate loan of $1,442 is less than the total interest cost of $1,480 on the fixed-rate loan, *Megan should take the variable-rate loan.* By doing this she will save about $38 ($1,480 − $1,442) in interest cost over the 180 days.

Lines of Credit

line of credit
An agreement between a commercial bank and a business specifying the amount of unsecured short-term borrowing the bank will make available to the firm over a given period of time.

A **line of credit** is an agreement between a commercial bank and a business, specifying the amount of unsecured short-term borrowing the bank will make available to the firm over a given period of time. It is similar to the agreement under which issuers of bank credit cards, such as MasterCard, Visa, and Discover, extend preapproved credit to cardholders. A line-of-credit agreement is typically made for a period of 1 year and often places certain constraints on the borrower. It is *not a guaranteed loan* but indicates that if the bank has sufficient funds available, it will allow the borrower to owe it *up to* a certain amount of money. The amount of a line of credit is the *maximum amount the firm can owe the bank* at any point in time.

When applying for a line of credit, the borrower may be required to submit such documents as its cash budget, pro forma income statement, pro forma balance sheet, and recent financial statements. If the bank finds the customer acceptable, the line of credit will be extended. The major attraction of a line of credit from the bank's point of view is that it eliminates the need to examine the creditworthiness of a customer each time it borrows money within the year.

Interest Rates The interest rate on a line of credit is normally stated as a floating rate—the *prime rate plus a premium.* If the prime rate changes, the interest rate charged on new *as well as outstanding* borrowing automatically changes. The amount a borrower is charged in excess of the prime rate depends on its creditworthiness. The more creditworthy the borrower, the lower the premium (interest increment) above prime, and vice versa.

Operating-Change Restrictions In a line-of-credit agreement, a bank may impose **operating-change restrictions,** which give it the right to revoke the line if any major changes occur in the firm's financial condition or operations. The firm is usually required to submit up-to-date, and preferably audited, financial statements for periodic review. In addition, the bank typically needs to be informed of shifts in key managerial personnel or in the firm's operations before changes take place. Such changes may affect the future success and debt-paying ability of the firm and thus could alter its credit status. If the bank does not agree with the proposed changes and the firm makes them anyway, the bank has the right to revoke the line of credit.

operating-change restrictions
Contractual restrictions that a bank may impose on a firm's financial condition or operations as part of a line-of-credit agreement.

Compensating Balances To ensure that the borrower will be a "good customer," many short-term unsecured bank loans—single-payment notes and lines of credit—require the borrower to maintain, in a checking account, a **compensating balance** equal to a certain percentage of the amount borrowed. Banks frequently require compensating balances of 10 to 20 percent. A compensating balance not only forces the borrower to be a good customer of the bank but may also raise the interest cost to the borrower.

compensating balance
A required checking account balance equal to a certain percentage of the amount borrowed from a bank under a line-of-credit or revolving credit agreement.

Example

Hint Sometimes the compensating balance is stated as a percentage of the amount of the line of credit. In other cases, it is linked to both the amount borrowed and the amount of the line of credit.

Estrada Graphics, a graphic design firm, has borrowed $1 million under a line-of-credit agreement. It must pay a stated interest rate of 10% and maintain, in its checking account, a compensating balance equal to 20% of the amount borrowed, or $200,000. Thus it actually receives the use of only $800,000. To use that amount for a year, the firm pays interest of $100,000 ($0.10 \times \$1,000,000$). The effective annual rate on the funds is therefore 12.5% ($100,000 \div \$800,000$), 2.5% more than the stated rate of 10%.

If the firm normally maintains a balance of $200,000 or more in its checking account, the effective annual rate equals the stated annual rate of 10% because none of the $1 million borrowed is needed to satisfy the compensating-balance requirement. If the firm normally maintains a $100,000 balance in its checking account, only an additional $100,000 will have to be tied up, leaving it with $900,000 of usable funds. The effective annual rate in this case would be 11.1% ($100,000 \div \$900,000$). Thus a compensating balance raises the cost of borrowing *only if* it is larger than the firm's normal cash balance.

annual cleanup
The requirement that for a certain number of days during the year borrowers under a line of credit carry a zero loan balance (that is, owe the bank nothing).

Annual Cleanups To ensure that money lent under a line-of-credit agreement is actually being used to finance seasonal needs, many banks require an **annual cleanup.** This means that the borrower must have a loan balance of zero—that is, owe the bank nothing—for a certain number of days during the year. Insisting that the borrower carry a zero loan balance for a certain period ensures that short-term loans do not turn into long-term loans.

All the characteristics of a line-of-credit agreement are negotiable to some extent. Today, banks bid competitively to attract large, well-known firms. A prospective borrower should attempt to negotiate a line of credit with the most favorable interest rate, for an optimal amount of funds, and with a minimum of restrictions. Borrowers today frequently pay fees to lenders instead of maintaining deposit balances as compensation for loans and other services. The lender attempts to get a good return with maximum safety. Negotiations should produce a line of credit that is suitable to both borrower and lender.

Revolving Credit Agreements

revolving credit agreement
A line of credit *guaranteed* to a borrower by a commercial bank regardless of the scarcity of money.

commitment fee
The fee that is normally charged on a *revolving credit agreement;* it often applies to the *average unused portion* of the borrower's credit line.

A **revolving credit agreement** is nothing more than a *guaranteed line of credit*. It is guaranteed in the sense that the commercial bank assures the borrower that a specified amount of funds will be made available regardless of the scarcity of money. The interest rate and other requirements are similar to those for a line of credit. It is not uncommon for a revolving credit agreement to be for a period greater than 1 year.[7] Because the bank guarantees the availability of funds, a **commitment fee** is normally charged on a revolving credit agreement.[8] This fee often applies to the average unused balance of the borrower's credit line. It is normally about 0.5 percent of the *average unused portion* of the line.

Example ▸ REH Company, a major real estate developer, has a $2 million revolving credit agreement with its bank. Its average borrowing under the agreement for the past year was $1.5 million. The bank charges a commitment fee of 0.5% on the average unused balance. Because the average unused portion of the committed funds was $500,000 ($2 million − $1.5 million), the commitment fee for the year was $2,500 (0.005 × $500,000). Of course, REH also had to pay interest on the actual $1.5 million borrowed under the agreement. Assuming that $112,500 interest was paid on the $1.5 million borrowed, the effective cost of the agreement was 7.67% [($112,500 + $2,500)/$1,500,000]. Although more expensive than a line of credit, a revolving credit agreement can be less risky from the borrower's viewpoint, because the availability of funds is guaranteed. ◂

Commercial Paper

commercial paper
A form of financing consisting of short-term, unsecured promissory notes issued by firms with a high credit standing.

Commercial paper is a form of financing that consists of short-term, unsecured promissory notes issued by firms with a high credit standing. Generally, only large firms of unquestionable financial soundness are able to issue commercial paper. Most commercial paper issues have maturities ranging from 3 to 270 days. Although there is no set denomination, such financing is generally issued in multiples of $100,000 or more. A large portion of the commercial paper today is issued

---

7. Many authors classify the revolving credit agreement as a form of *intermediate-term financing,* defined as having a maturity of 1 to 7 years. In this text, we do not use the intermediate-term financing classification; only short-term and long-term classifications are made. Because many revolving credit agreements are for more than 1 year, they can be classified as a form of long-term financing; however, they are discussed here because of their similarity to line-of-credit agreements.

8. Some banks not only require payment of the commitment fee but also require the borrower to maintain, in addition to a compensating balance against actual borrowings, a compensating balance of 10% or so against the unused portion of the commitment.

Focus on Practice

Commercial Paper Boom to Continue after Depressed Start to the Decade

The difficult economic and credit environment in the post–September 11 era, combined with historically low interest rates and a deep desire by corporate issuers to reduce exposure to refinancing risk, had a depressing effect on commercial paper volumes from 2001 through 2003. According to the Federal Reserve, U.S. nonfinancial commercial paper, for example, declined 68 percent over the 3-year period, from $315.8 billion outstanding at the beginning of 2001 to $101.4 billion by December 2003. In addition to lower volume, credit quality of commercial paper declined over the same period, with the ratio of downgrades outpacing upgrades 17 to 1 in 2002.

In 2004, signs emerged that the volume and rating contraction in commercial paper was finally coming to an end. The most encouraging of these was

the pickup in economic growth, which spurs the need for short-term debt to finance corporate working capital. Although commercial paper is typically used to fund working capital, it is often boosted by a sudden surge of borrowing activity for other strategic activities—mergers and acquisitions and long-term capital investments, among others. According to Federal Reserve Board data, at the end of July 2004, total U.S. commercial paper outstanding was $1.33 trillion.

By 2006, commercial paper surged to $1.98 trillion—an increase of 21.5 percent over 2005 levels. Total commercial paper outstanding was expected to rise 15.8 percent in 2007, to $2.29 trillion, according to Standard & Poor's. S&P observed two major factors behind the boom: First, the then recent inverted yield curve had pulled

in many investors from the long end of the market. Second, a hectic pace for mergers and acquisitions was requiring many companies to put bridge financing into place.

As for credit quality, 2006 was mixed, according to Standard & Poor's. Upgrades nearly doubled to 34, from 19 in 2005; downgrades rose to 39 from 37. Although the ratings agency saw little need for immediate concern, it did warn that nonfinancial commercial paper ratings "were a shade more negative in 2006." A total of 25 commercial paper programs are on negative CreditWatch, concentrated in the utility and media/entertainment sectors.

■ *What factors would contribute to the continuation of the boom in commercial paper? What factors would cause a contraction in the commercial paper market?*

by finance companies; manufacturing firms account for a smaller portion of this type of financing. Businesses often purchase commercial paper, which they hold as marketable securities, to provide an interest-earning reserve of liquidity. For further information on recent use of commercial paper, see the *Focus on Practice* box above.

Interest on Commercial Paper

Commercial paper is sold at a discount from its *par*, or *face*, *value*. The size of the discount and the length of time to maturity determines the interest paid by the issuer of commercial paper. The actual interest earned by the purchaser is determined by certain calculations, illustrated by the following example.

Example

Bertram Corporation, a large shipbuilder, has just issued $1 million worth of commercial paper that has a 90-day maturity and sells for $990,000. At the end of 90 days, the purchaser of this paper will receive $1 million for its $990,000 investment. The interest paid on the financing is therefore $10,000 on a principal of $990,000. The effective 90-day rate on the paper is 1.01% ($10,000/$990,000). Assuming that the paper is rolled over each 90 days throughout the year (that is, $365/90 = 4.06$ times per year), the effective annual rate for Bertram's commercial paper, found by using Equation 4.24, is 4.16% $[(1 + 0.0101)^{4.06} - 1]$.

An interesting characteristic of commercial paper is that its interest cost is *normally* 2 percent to 4 percent below the prime rate. In other words, firms are able to raise funds more cheaply by selling commercial paper than by borrowing from a commercial bank. The reason is that many suppliers of short-term funds do not have the option, as banks do, of making low-risk business loans at the prime rate.[9] They can invest safely only in marketable securities such as Treasury bills and commercial paper. The yields on these marketable securities on July 23, 2007, when the prime rate of interest was 8.25 percent, were about 4.97 percent for 3-month Treasury bills and about 5.23 percent for 3-month commercial paper.

Although the stated interest cost of borrowing through the sale of commercial paper is normally lower than the prime rate, the *overall cost* of commercial paper may not be less than that of a bank loan. Additional costs include various fees and flotation costs. In addition, even if it is slightly more expensive to borrow from a commercial bank, it may at times be advisable to do so to establish a good working relationship with a bank. This strategy ensures that when money is tight, funds can be obtained promptly and at a reasonable interest rate.

Hint Commercial paper is directly placed with investors by the issuer or is sold by dealers in commercial paper. Most of it is purchased by other businesses and financial institutions.

International Loans

In some ways, arranging short-term financing for international trade is no different from financing purely domestic operations. In both cases, producers must finance production and inventory and then continue to finance accounts receivable before collecting any cash payments from sales. In other ways, however, the short-term financing of international sales and purchases is fundamentally different from that of strictly domestic trade.

International Transactions

The important difference between international and domestic transactions is that payments are often made or received in a foreign currency. Not only must a U.S. company pay the costs of doing business in the foreign exchange market, but it also is exposed to *exchange rate risk*. A U.S.-based company that exports goods and has accounts receivable denominated in a foreign currency faces the risk that the U.S. dollar will appreciate in value relative to the foreign currency. The risk to a U.S. importer with foreign-currency-denominated accounts payable is that the dollar will depreciate. Although *exchange rate risk* can often be *hedged* by using currency forward, futures, or options markets, doing so is costly and is not possible for all foreign currencies.

---

9. Commercial banks are legally prohibited from lending amounts in excess of 15% (plus an additional 10% for loans secured by readily marketable collateral) of the bank's unimpaired capital and surplus to any one borrower. This restriction is intended to protect depositors by forcing the commercial bank to spread its risk across a number of borrowers. In addition, smaller commercial banks do not have many opportunities to lend to large, high-quality business borrowers.

Typical international transactions are large in size and have long maturity dates. Therefore, companies that are involved in international trade generally have to finance larger dollar amounts for longer time periods than companies that operate domestically. Furthermore, because foreign companies are rarely well known in the United States, some financial institutions are reluctant to lend to U.S. exporters or importers, particularly smaller firms.

Financing International Trade

Several specialized techniques have evolved for financing international trade. Perhaps the most important financing vehicle is the **letter of credit,** a letter written by a company's bank to the company's foreign supplier, stating that the bank guarantees payment of an invoiced amount if all the underlying agreements are met. The letter of credit essentially substitutes the bank's reputation and creditworthiness for that of its commercial customer. A U.S. exporter is more willing to sell goods to a foreign buyer if the transaction is covered by a letter of credit issued by a well-known bank in the buyer's home country.

Firms that do business in foreign countries on an ongoing basis often finance their operations, at least in part, in the local market. A company that has an assembly plant in Mexico, for example, might choose to finance its purchases of Mexican goods and services with peso funds borrowed from a Mexican bank. This not only minimizes exchange rate risk but also improves the company's business ties to the host community. Multinational companies, however, sometimes finance their international transactions through dollar-denominated loans from international banks. The *Eurocurrency loan markets* allow creditworthy borrowers to obtain financing on attractive terms.

Transactions between Subsidiaries

Much international trade involves transactions between corporate subsidiaries. A U.S. company might, for example, manufacture one part in an Asian plant and another part in the United States, assemble the product in Brazil, and sell it in Europe. The shipment of goods back and forth between subsidiaries creates accounts receivable and accounts payable, but the parent company has considerable discretion about how and when payments are made. In particular, the parent can minimize foreign exchange fees and other transaction costs by "netting" what affiliates owe each other and paying only the net amount due, rather than having both subsidiaries pay each other the gross amounts due.

REVIEW QUESTIONS

15–4 How is the *prime rate of interest* relevant to the cost of short-term bank borrowing? What is a *floating-rate loan?*

15–5 How does the *effective annual rate* differ between a loan requiring interest payments *at maturity* and another, similar loan requiring interest *in advance?*

15–6 What are the basic terms and characteristics of a *single-payment note?* How is the *effective annual rate* on such a note found?

15–7 What is a *line of credit?* Describe each of the following features that are often included in these agreements: (**a**) operating-change restrictions; (**b**) compensating balance; and (**c**) annual cleanup.

---

letter of credit
A letter written by a company's bank to the company's foreign supplier, stating that the bank guarantees payment of an invoiced amount if all the underlying agreements are met.

15–8   What is a *revolving credit agreement?* How does this arrangement differ from the line-of-credit agreement? What is a *commitment fee?*

15–9   How do firms use *commercial paper* to raise short-term funds? Who can issue commercial paper? Who buys commercial paper?

15–10 What is the important difference between international and domestic transactions? How is a *letter of credit* used in financing international trade transactions? How is "netting" used in transactions between subsidiaries?

15.3 | Secured Sources of Short-Term Loans

secured short-term financing
Short-term financing (loan) that has specific assets pledged as collateral.

security agreement
The agreement between the borrower and the lender that specifies the collateral held against a secured loan.

When a firm has exhausted its sources of unsecured short-term financing, it may be able to obtain additional short-term loans on a secured basis. **Secured short-term financing** has specific assets pledged as collateral. The *collateral* commonly takes the form of an asset, such as accounts receivable or inventory. The lender obtains a security interest in the collateral through the execution of a **security agreement** with the borrower that specifies the collateral held against the loan. In addition, the terms of the loan against which the security is held form part of the security agreement. A copy of the security agreement is filed in a public office within the state—typically, a county or state court. Filing provides subsequent lenders with information about which assets of a prospective borrower are unavailable for use as collateral. The filing requirement protects the lender by legally establishing the lender's security interest.

Characteristics of Secured Short-Term Loans

Although many people believe that holding collateral as security reduces the risk of a loan, lenders do not usually view loans in this way. Lenders recognize that holding collateral can reduce losses if the borrower defaults, but *the presence of collateral has no impact on the risk of default.* A lender requires collateral to ensure recovery of some portion of the loan in the event of default. What the lender wants above all, however, is to be repaid as scheduled. In general, lenders prefer to make less risky loans at lower rates of interest than to be in a position in which they must liquidate collateral.

Collateral and Terms

Lenders of secured short-term funds prefer collateral that has a duration closely matched to the term of the loan. Current assets are the most desirable short-term-loan collateral, because they can normally be converted into cash much sooner than fixed assets. Thus, the short-term lender of secured funds generally accepts only liquid current assets as collateral.

percentage advance
The percentage of the book value of the collateral that constitutes the principal of a secured loan.

Typically, the lender determines the desirable **percentage advance** to make against the collateral. This percentage advance constitutes the principal of the secured loan and is normally between 30 and 100 percent of the book value of the collateral. It varies according to the type and liquidity of collateral.

The interest rate that is charged on secured short-term loans is typically *higher* than the rate on unsecured short-term loans. Lenders do not normally consider secured loans less risky than unsecured loans. In addition, negotiating and administering secured loans is more troublesome for the lender than negotiating and administering unsecured loans. The lender therefore normally requires added compensation in the form of a service charge, a higher interest rate, or both.

Institutions Extending Secured Short-Term Loans

The primary sources of secured short-term loans to businesses are commercial banks and commercial finance companies. Both institutions deal in short-term loans secured primarily by accounts receivable and inventory. We have already described the operations of commercial banks. **Commercial finance companies** are lending institutions that make *only* secured loans—both short-term and long-term—to businesses. Unlike banks, finance companies are not permitted to hold deposits.

Only when its unsecured and secured short-term borrowing power from the commercial bank is exhausted will a borrower turn to the commercial finance company for additional secured borrowing. Because the finance company generally ends up with higher-risk borrowers, its interest charges on secured short-term loans are usually higher than those of commercial banks. The leading U.S. commercial finance companies include The CIT Group and GE Corporate Financial Services.

Use of Accounts Receivable as Collateral

Two commonly used means of obtaining short-term financing with accounts receivable are *pledging accounts receivable* and *factoring accounts receivable*. Actually, only a pledge of accounts receivable creates a secured short-term loan; factoring really entails the *sale* of accounts receivable at a discount. Although factoring is not actually a form of secured short-term borrowing, it does involve the use of accounts receivable to obtain needed short-term funds.

Pledging Accounts Receivable

A **pledge of accounts receivable** is often used to secure a short-term loan. Because accounts receivable are normally quite liquid, they are an attractive form of short-term-loan collateral.

The Pledging Process   When a firm requests a loan against accounts receivable, the lender first evaluates the firm's accounts receivable to determine their desirability as collateral. The lender makes a list of the acceptable accounts, along with the billing dates and amounts. If the borrowing firm requests a loan for a fixed amount, the lender needs to select only enough accounts to secure the funds requested. If the borrower wants the maximum loan available, the lender evaluates all the accounts to select the maximum amount of acceptable collateral.

After selecting the acceptable accounts, the lender normally adjusts the dollar value of these accounts for expected returns on sales and other allowances. If a customer whose account has been pledged returns merchandise or receives some type of allowance, such as a cash discount for early payment, the amount of the collat-

Hint Remember that firms typically borrow on a secured basis only after exhausting less costly, unsecured sources of short-term funds.

commercial finance companies
Lending institutions that make *only* secured loans—both short-term and long-term—to businesses.

pledge of accounts receivable
The use of a firm's accounts receivable as security, or collateral, to obtain a short-term loan.

eral is automatically reduced. For protection from such occurrences, the lender normally reduces the value of the acceptable collateral by a fixed percentage.

Next, the percentage to be advanced against the collateral must be determined. The lender evaluates the quality of the acceptable receivables and the expected cost of their liquidation. This percentage represents the principal of the loan and typically ranges between 50 and 90 percent of the face value of acceptable accounts receivable. To protect its interest in the collateral, the lender files a **lien,** which is a publicly disclosed legal claim on the collateral. For an example of the complete pledging process, see the book's website at **www.prenhall.com/gitman.**

Notification   Pledges of accounts receivable are normally made on a **nonnotification basis,** meaning that a customer whose account has been pledged as collateral is not notified. Under the nonnotification arrangement, the borrower still collects the pledged account receivable, and the lender trusts the borrower to remit these payments as they are received. If a pledge of accounts receivable is made on a **notification basis,** the customer is notified to remit payment directly to the lender.

Pledging Cost   The stated cost of a pledge of accounts receivable is normally 2 to 5 percent above the prime rate. In addition to the stated interest rate, a service charge of up to 3 percent may be levied by the lender to cover its administrative costs. Clearly, pledges of accounts receivable are a high-cost source of short-term financing.

Factoring Accounts Receivable

Factoring accounts receivable involves selling them outright, at a discount, to a financial institution. A **factor** is a financial institution that specializes in purchasing accounts receivable from businesses. Although it is not the same as obtaining a short-term loan, factoring accounts receivable is similar to borrowing with accounts receivable as collateral.

Factoring Agreement   A factoring agreement normally states the exact conditions and procedures for the purchase of an account. The factor, like a lender against a pledge of accounts receivable, chooses accounts for purchase, selecting only those that appear to be acceptable credit risks. Where factoring is to be on a continuing basis, the factor will actually make the firm's credit decisions, because this will guarantee the acceptability of accounts.[10] Factoring is normally done on a *notification basis,* and the factor receives payment of the account directly from the customer. In addition, most sales of accounts receivable to a factor are made on a **nonrecourse basis,** meaning that the factor agrees to accept all credit risks. Thus, if a purchased account turns out to be uncollectible, the factor must absorb the loss.

lien
A publicly disclosed legal claim on loan collateral.

nonnotification basis
The basis on which a borrower, having pledged an account receivable, continues to collect the account payments without notifying the account customer.

notification basis
The basis on which an account customer whose account has been pledged (or factored) is notified to remit payment directly to the lender (or factor).

factoring accounts receivable
The outright sale of accounts receivable at a discount to a *factor* or other financial institution.

factor
A financial institution that specializes in purchasing accounts receivable from businesses.

nonrecourse basis
The basis on which accounts receivable are sold to a factor with the understanding that the factor accepts all credit risks on the purchased accounts.

---

10. The use of credit cards such as MasterCard, Visa, and Discover by consumers has some similarity to factoring, because the vendor that accepts the card is reimbursed at a discount for purchases made with the card. The difference between factoring and credit cards is that cards are nothing more than a line of credit extended by the issuer, which charges the vendors a fee for accepting the cards. In factoring, the factor does not analyze credit until after the sale has been made; in many cases (except when factoring is done on a continuing basis), the initial credit decision is the responsibility of the vendor, not the factor that purchases the account.

Typically, the factor is not required to pay the firm until the account is collected or until the last day of the credit period, whichever occurs first. The factor sets up an account similar to a bank deposit account for each customer. As payment is received or as due dates arrive, the factor deposits money into the seller's account, from which the seller is free to make withdrawals as needed.

In many cases, if the firm leaves the money in the account, a *surplus* will exist on which the factor will pay interest. In other instances, the factor may make *advances* to the firm against uncollected accounts that are not yet due. These advances represent a negative balance in the firm's account, on which interest is charged.

Factoring Cost   Factoring costs include commissions, interest levied on advances, and interest earned on surpluses. The factor deposits in the firm's account the book value of the collected or due accounts purchased by the factor, less the commissions. The commissions are typically stated as a 1 to 3 percent discount from the book value of factored accounts receivable. The *interest levied on advances* is generally 2 to 4 percent above the prime rate. It is levied on the actual amount advanced. The *interest paid on surpluses* is generally between 0.2 percent and 0.5 percent per month. An example of the factoring process is included on the book's website at **www.prenhall.com/gitman**.

Although its costs may seem high, factoring has certain advantages that make it attractive to many firms. One is the ability it gives the firm to *turn accounts receivable immediately into cash* without having to worry about repayment. Another advantage is that it ensures a *known pattern of cash flows*. In addition, if factoring is undertaken on a continuing basis, the firm *can eliminate its credit and collection departments*.

Use of Inventory as Collateral

Inventory is generally second to accounts receivable in desirability as short-term loan collateral. Inventory normally has a market value that is greater than its book value, which is used to establish its value as collateral. A lender whose loan is secured with inventory will probably be able to sell that inventory for at least book value if the borrower defaults on its obligations.

The most important characteristic of inventory being evaluated as loan collateral is *marketability*. A warehouse of *perishable* items, such as fresh peaches, may be quite marketable, but if the cost of storing and selling the peaches is high, they may not be desirable collateral. *Specialized items*, such as moon-roving vehicles, are not desirable collateral either, because finding a buyer for them could be difficult. When evaluating inventory as possible loan collateral, the lender looks for items with very stable market prices that have ready markets and that lack undesirable physical properties.

Floating Inventory Liens

floating inventory lien
A secured short-term loan against inventory under which the lender's claim is on the borrower's inventory in general.

A lender may be willing to secure a loan under a **floating inventory lien,** which is a claim on inventory in general. This arrangement is most attractive when the firm has a stable level of inventory that consists of a diversified group of relatively inexpensive merchandise. Inventories of items such as auto tires, screws and bolts, and shoes are candidates for floating-lien loans. Because it is difficult for a lender to verify the presence of the inventory, the lender generally advances less than 50 percent of the book value of the average inventory. The interest charge on a floating lien is 3 to 5 percent above the prime rate. Commercial banks often require floating liens as extra security on what would otherwise be an unsecured loan. Floating-lien inventory loans may also be available from commercial finance companies. An example of a floating inventory lien is included on the book's website at **www.prenhall.com/gitman**.

Trust Receipt Inventory Loans

trust receipt inventory loan
A secured short-term loan against inventory under which the lender advances 80 to 100 percent of the cost of the borrower's relatively expensive inventory items in exchange for the borrower's promise to repay the lender, with accrued interest, immediately after the sale of each item of collateral.

A **trust receipt inventory loan** often can be made against relatively expensive automotive, consumer durable, and industrial goods that can be identified by serial number. Under this agreement, the borrower keeps the inventory, and the lender may advance 80 to 100 percent of its cost. The lender files a *lien* on all the items financed. The borrower is free to sell the merchandise but is *trusted* to remit the amount lent, along with accrued interest, to the lender immediately after the sale. The lender then releases the lien on the item. The lender makes periodic checks of the borrower's inventory to make sure that the required collateral remains in the hands of the borrower. The interest charge to the borrower is normally 2 percent or more above the prime rate.

Trust receipt loans are often made by manufacturers' wholly owned financing subsidiaries, known as *captive finance companies,* to their customers. Captive finance companies are especially popular in industries that manufacture consumer durable goods, because they provide the manufacturer with a useful sales tool. For example, General Motors Acceptance Corporation (GMAC), the financing subsidiary of General Motors, grants these types of loans to its dealers. Trust receipt loans are also available through commercial banks and commercial finance companies.

Warehouse Receipt Loans

warehouse receipt loan
A secured short-term loan against inventory under which the lender receives control of the pledged inventory collateral, which is stored by a designated warehousing company on the lender's behalf.

A **warehouse receipt loan** is an arrangement whereby the lender, which may be a commercial bank or finance company, receives control of the pledged inventory collateral, which is stored by a designated agent on the lender's behalf. After selecting acceptable collateral, the lender hires a warehousing company to act as its agent and take possession of the inventory.

Two types of warehousing arrangements are possible. A *terminal warehouse* is a central warehouse that is used to store the merchandise of various customers. The lender normally uses such a warehouse when the inventory is easily transported and can be delivered to the warehouse relatively inexpensively. Under a *field warehouse* arrangement, the lender hires a field-warehousing company to set up a warehouse on the borrower's premises or to lease part of the borrower's warehouse to store the pledged collateral. Regardless of the type of warehouse, the warehousing company places a guard over the inventory. Only on written approval of the lender can any portion of the secured inventory be released by the warehousing company.

The actual lending agreement specifically states the requirements for the release of inventory. As in the case of other secured loans, the lender accepts only collateral that is believed to be readily marketable and advances only a portion—generally 75 to 90 percent—of the collateral's value. The specific costs of warehouse receipt loans are generally higher than those of any other secured lending arrangements because of the need to hire and pay a warehousing company to guard and supervise the collateral. The basic interest charged on warehouse receipt loans is higher than that charged on unsecured loans, generally ranging from 3 to 5 percent above the prime rate. In addition to the interest charge, the borrower must absorb the costs of warehousing by paying the warehouse fee, which is generally between 1 and 3 percent of the amount of the loan. The borrower is normally also required to pay the insurance costs on the warehoused merchandise. An example of the procedures and costs of a warehouse receipt loan is included on the book's website at www.prenhall.com/gitman.

REVIEW QUESTIONS

15–11 Are secured short-term loans viewed as more risky or less risky than unsecured short-term loans? Why?

15–12 In general, what interest rates and fees are levied on secured short-term loans? Why are these rates generally *higher* than the rates on unsecured short-term loans?

15–13 Describe and compare the basic features of the following methods of using *accounts receivable* to obtain short-term financing: (a) pledging accounts receivable, and (b) factoring accounts receivable. Be sure to mention the institutions that offer each of them.

15–14 For the following methods of using *inventory* as short-term loan collateral, describe the basic features of each, and compare their use: (a) floating lien, (b) trust receipt loan, and (c) warehouse receipt loan.

Summary

Focus on Value

Current liabilities represent an important and generally inexpensive source of financing for a firm. The level of short-term (current liabilities) financing employed by a firm affects its profitability and risk. Accounts payable and accruals are spontaneous liabilities that should be carefully managed because they represent free financing. Notes payable, which represent negotiated short-term financing, should be obtained at the lowest cost under the best possible terms. Large, well-known firms can obtain unsecured short-term financing through the sale of commercial paper. On a secured basis, the firm can obtain loans from banks or commercial finance companies, using either accounts receivable or inventory as collateral.

The financial manager must obtain the right quantity and form of current liabilities financing to provide the lowest-cost funds with the least risk. Such a strategy should positively contribute to the firm's goal of **maximizing the stock price.**

Review of Learning Goals

Key features of the common sources of short-term financing are summarized in Table 15.2 on pages 704–705.

LG 1 **Review accounts payable, the key components of credit terms, and the procedures for analyzing those terms.** The major spontaneous source of short-term financing is accounts payable. They are the primary source of short-term funds. Credit terms may differ with respect to the credit period, cash discount, cash discount period, and beginning of the credit period. Cash discounts should be given up only when a firm in need of short-term funds must pay an interest rate on borrowing that is greater than the cost of giving up the cash discount.

LG 2 **Understand the effects of stretching accounts payable on their cost, and the use of accruals.** Stretching accounts payable can lower the cost of giving up a cash discount. Accruals, which result primarily from wage and tax obligations, are virtually free.

LG 3 **Describe interest rates and the basic types of unsecured bank sources of short-term loans.** Banks are the major source of unsecured short-term loans to businesses. The interest rate on these loans is tied to the prime rate of interest by a risk premium and may be fixed or floating. It should be evaluated by using the effective annual rate. Whether interest is paid when the loan matures or in advance affects the rate. Bank loans may take the form of a single-payment note, a line of credit, or a revolving credit agreement.

LG 4 **Discuss the basic features of commercial paper and the key aspects of international short-term loans.** Commercial paper is an unsecured IOU issued by firms with a high credit standing. International sales and purchases expose firms to exchange rate risk. Such transactions are larger and of longer maturity than domestic transactions, and they can be financed by using a letter of credit, by borrowing in the local market, or through dollar-denominated loans from international banks. On transactions between subsidiaries, "netting" can be used to minimize foreign exchange fees and other transaction costs.

LG 5 **Explain the characteristics of secured short-term loans and the use of accounts receivable as short-term-loan collateral.** Secured short-term loans are those for which the lender requires collateral—typically, current assets such as accounts receivable or inventory. Only a percentage of the book value of acceptable collateral is advanced by the lender. These loans are more expensive than unsecured loans. Commercial banks and commercial finance companies make secured short-term loans. Both pledging and factoring involve the use of accounts receivable to obtain needed short-term funds.

LG 6 **Describe the various ways in which inventory can be used as short-term-loan collateral.** Inventory can be used as short-term-loan collateral under a floating lien, a trust receipt arrangement, or a warehouse receipt loan.

TABLE 15.2 Summary of Key Features of Common Sources of Short-Term Financing

Type of short-term financing	Source	Cost or conditions	Characteristics
I. Spontaneous liabilities			
Accounts payable	Suppliers of merchandise	No stated cost except when a cash discount is offered for early payment.	Credit extended on open account for a specified number of days. The largest source of short-term financing.
Accruals	Employees and government	Free.	Result because wages (employees) and taxes (government) are paid at discrete points in time after the service has been rendered. Hard to manipulate this source of financing.
II. Unsecured sources of short-term loans			
Bank sources			
(1) Single-payment notes	Commercial banks	Prime plus 0% to 4% risk premium—fixed or floating rate.	A single-payment loan used to meet a funds shortage expected to last only a short period of time.
(2) Lines of credit	Commercial banks	Prime plus 0% to 4% risk premium—fixed or floating rate. Often must maintain 10% to 20% compensating balance and clean up the line annually.	A prearranged borrowing limit under which funds, if available, will be lent to allow the borrower to meet seasonal needs.
(3) Revolving credit agreements	Commercial banks	Prime plus 0% to 4% risk premium—fixed or floating rate. Often must maintain 10% to 20% compensating balance and pay a commitment fee of approximately 0.5% of the average unused balance.	A line-of-credit agreement under which the availability of funds is guaranteed. Often for a period greater than 1 year.
Commercial paper	Business firms—both nonfinancial and financial	Generally 2% to 4% below the prime rate of interest.	A short-term, unsecured promissory note issued by the most financially sound firms.

(continued)

Type of short-term financing	Source	Cost or conditions	Characteristics
III. Secured sources of short-term loans			
Accounts receivable collateral			
(1) Pledging	Commercial banks and commercial finance companies	2% to 5% above prime plus up to 3% in fees. Advance 50% to 90% of collateral value.	Selected accounts receivable are used as collateral. The borrower is trusted to remit to the lender on collection of pledged accounts. Done on a nonnotification basis.
(2) Factoring	Factors, commercial banks, and commercial finance companies	1% to 3% discount from face value of factored accounts. Interest of 2% to 4% above prime levied on advances. Interest between 0.2% and 0.5% per month earned on surplus balances left with factor.	Selected accounts are sold—generally without recourse—at a discount. All credit risks go with the accounts. Factor will lend (make advances) against uncollected accounts that are not yet due. Factor will also pay interest on surplus balances. Typically done on a notification basis.
Inventory collateral			
(1) Floating liens	Commercial banks and commercial finance companies	3% to 5% above prime. Advance less than 50% of collateral value.	A loan against inventory in general. Made when firm has stable inventory of a variety of inexpensive items.
(2) Trust receipts	Manufacturers' captive financing subsidiaries, commercial banks, and commercial finance companies	2% or more above prime. Advance 80% to 100% of cost of collateral.	Loan against relatively expensive automotive, consumer durable, and industrial goods that can be identified by serial number. Collateral remains in possession of the borrower, who is trusted to remit proceeds to the lender upon its sale.
(3) Warehouse receipts	Commercial banks and commercial finance companies	3% to 5% above prime plus a 1% to 3% warehouse fee. Advance 75% to 90% of collateral value.	Inventory used as collateral is placed under control of the lender either through a terminal warehouse or through a field warehouse. A third party—a warehousing company—guards the inventory for the lender. Inventory is released only on written approval of the lender.

Self-Test Problem (Solution in Appendix B)

ST15–1   **Cash discount decisions**   The credit terms for each of three suppliers are shown in the following table. (*Note:* Assume a 365-day year.)

Supplier	Credit terms
X	1/10 net 55 EOM
Y	2/10 net 30 EOM
Z	2/20 net 60 EOM

a. Determine the *approximate* cost of giving up the cash discount from each supplier.

b. Assuming that the firm needs short-term financing, indicate whether it would be better to give up the cash discount or take the discount and borrow from a bank at 15% annual interest. Evaluate each supplier *separately* using your findings in part **a.**

c. What impact, if any, would the fact that the firm could stretch its accounts payable (net period only) by 20 days from supplier Z have on your answer in part **b** relative to this supplier?

Warm-Up Exercises   A blue box (■) indicates exercises available in .

E15–1   Lyman Nurseries purchased seeds costing $25,000 with terms of 3/15 net 30 EOM on January 12. How much will the firm pay if it takes the cash discount? What is the *approximate cost of giving up the cash discount,* using the simplified formula?

E15–2   Cleaner's, Inc., is switching to paying employees every 2 weeks rather than weekly and will therefore "skip" 1 week's pay. The firm has 25 employees who work a 60-hour week and earn an average wage of $12.50 per hour. Using a 10% rate of interest, how much will this change save the firm annually?

E15–3   Jasmine Scents has been given two competing offers for short-term financing. Both offers are for borrowing $15,000 for 1 year. The first offer is a *discount loan* at 8%; the second offer is for interest to be paid *at maturity* at a stated interest rate of 9%. Calculate the *effective annual rates* for each loan and indicate which loan offers the better terms.

E15–4   Jackson Industries has borrowed $125,000 under a line-of-credit agreement. While the company normally maintains a checking account balance of $15,000 in the lending bank, this credit line requires a 20% compensating balance. The stated interest rate on the borrowed funds is 10%. What is the *effective annual rate of interest* on the line of credit?

E15–5   Horizon Telecom sold $300,000 worth of 120-day commercial paper for $298,000. What is the dollar amount of interest paid on the commercial paper? What is the *effective 120-day rate* on the paper?

Problems   A blue box (■) indicates problems available in myfinancelab.

P15–1 **Payment dates**   Determine when a firm must pay for purchases made and invoices dated on November 25 under each of the following credit terms.
a. net 30 date of invoice
b. net 30 EOM
c. net 45 date of invoice
d. net 60 EOM

P15–2 **Cost of giving up cash discounts**   Determine the *cost of giving up cash discounts* under each of the following terms of sale. (*Note:* Assume a 365-day year.)
a. 2/10 net 30
b. 1/10 net 30
c. 2/10 net 45
d. 3/10 net 45
e. 1/10 net 60
f. 3/10 net 30
g. 4/10 net 180

P15–3 **Credit terms**   Purchases made on credit are due in full by the end of the billing period. Many firms extend a discount for payment made in the first part of the billing period. The original invoice contains a type of "short-hand" notation that explains the credit terms that apply. (*Note:* Assume a 365-day year.)
a. Write the short-hand expression of credit terms for each of the following.

Cash discount	Cash discount period	Credit period	Beginning of credit period
1%	15 days	45 days	date of invoice
2	10	30	end of month
2	7	28	date of invoice
1	10	60	end of month

b. For each of the sets of credit terms in part **a**, calculate the number of days until full payment is due for invoices dated March 12.
c. For each of the sets of credit terms, calculate the *cost of giving up the cash discount.*
d. If the firm's cost of short-term financing is 8%, what would you recommend in regard to taking the discount or giving it up in each case?

P15–4 **Cash discount versus loan**   Erica Stone works in an accounts payable department. She has attempted to convince her boss to take the discount on the 3/10 net 45 credit terms most suppliers offer, but her boss argues that giving up the 3% discount is less costly than a short-term loan at 14%. Prove to whoever is wrong that the other is correct. (*Note:* Assume a 365-day year.)

PERSONAL FINANCE PROBLEM

P15–5 **Borrow or pay cash for an asset**   Bob and Carol Gibbs are set to move into their first apartment. They visited Furniture R'Us, looking for a dining room table and buffet. Dining room sets are typically one of the more expensive home furnishing items, and the store offers financing arrangements to customers. Bob and Carol have the cash to pay for the furniture, but it would definitely deplete their savings so they want to look at all their options.

The dining room set costs $3,000 and Furniture R'Us offers a financing plan that would allow them to either (1) put 10% down and finance the balance at 4% annual interest over 24 months or (2) receive an immediate $200 cash rebate, thereby paying only $2,800 cash to buy the furniture.

Bob and Carol currently earn 5.2% annual interest on their savings.

a. Calculate the cash down payment for the loan.
b. Calculate the monthly payment on the available loan. (*Hint:* Treat the current loan as an annuity and solve for the monthly payment.)
c. Calculate the initial cash outlay under the cash purchase option. Do not forget to reduce this figure by the cash down payment forgone on the loan.
d. Given that they can earn 5.2% on savings, what will Bob and Carol give up (opportunity cost) over the 2 years if they pay cash?
e. What is the cost of the cash alternative at the end of 2 years?
f. Should Bob and Carol choose the financing or the cash alternative?

  P15–6 Cash discount decisions   Prairie Manufacturing has four possible suppliers, all of which offer different credit terms. Except for the differences in credit terms, their products and services are virtually identical. The credit terms offered by these suppliers are shown in the following table. (*Note:* Assume a 365-day year.)

Supplier	Credit terms
J	1/10 net 30 EOM
K	2/20 net 80 EOM
L	1/20 net 60 EOM
M	3/10 net 55 EOM

a. Calculate the *approximate cost of giving up the cash discount* from each supplier.
b. If the firm needs short-term funds, which are currently available from its commercial bank at 16%, and if each of the suppliers is viewed *separately*, which, if any, of the suppliers' cash discounts should the firm give up? Explain why.
c. What impact, if any, would the fact that the firm could stretch by 30 days its accounts payable (net period only) from supplier M have on your answer in part **b** relative to this supplier?

 P15–7 Changing payment cycle   Upon accepting the position of chief executive officer and chairman of Reeves Machinery, Frank Cheney changed the firm's weekly payday from Monday afternoon to the following Friday afternoon. The firm's weekly payroll was $10 million, and the cost of short-term funds was 13%. If the effect of this change was to delay check clearing by 1 week, what *annual* savings, if any, were realized?

 P15–8 Spontaneous sources of funds, accruals   When Tallman Haberdashery, Inc., merged with Meyers Men's Suits, Inc., Tallman's employees were switched from a weekly to a biweekly pay period. Tallman's weekly payroll amounted to $750,000. The cost of funds for the combined firms is 11%. What annual savings, if any, are realized by this change of pay period?

P15–9   **Cost of bank loan**   Data Back-Up Systems has obtained a $10,000, 90-day bank loan at an annual interest rate of 15%, payable at maturity. (*Note:* Assume a 365-day year.)

a. How much interest (in dollars) will the firm pay on the 90-day loan?

b. Find the *effective 90-day rate* on the loan.

c. Annualize your result in part **b** to find the *effective annual rate* for this loan, assuming that it is rolled over every 90 days throughout the year under the same terms and circumstances.

PERSONAL FINANCE PROBLEM

P15–10   **Unsecured sources of short-term loans**   John Savage has obtained a short-term loan from First Carolina Bank. The loan matures in 180 days and is in the amount of $45,000. John needs the money to cover start-up costs in a new business. He hopes to have sufficient backing from other investors by the end of the next 6 months. First Carolina Bank offers John two financing options for the $45,000 loan: a *fixed-rate loan* at 2.5% above prime rate, or a *variable-rate loan* at 1.5% above prime.

Currently, the prime rate of interest is 6.5%, and the consensus forecasts of a group of mortgage economists for changes in the prime rate over the next 180 days are as follows: 60 days from today the prime rate will rise by 0.5%; 90 days from today the prime rate will rise another 1%; 180 days from today the prime rate will drop by 0.5%.

Using the forecast prime rate changes, answer the following questions.

a. Calculate the total interest cost over 180 days for a *fixed-rate loan*.

b. Calculate the total interest cost over 180 days for a *variable-rate loan*.

c. Which is the lower-interest-cost loan for the next 180 days?

P15–11   **Effective annual rate**   A financial institution made a $10,000, 1-year discount loan at 10% interest, requiring a compensating balance equal to 20% of the face value of the loan. Determine the *effective annual rate* associated with this loan. (*Note:* Assume that the firm currently maintains $0 on deposit in the financial institution.)

P15–12   **Compensating balances and effective annual rates**   Lincoln Industries has a line of credit at Bank Two that requires it to pay 11% interest on its borrowing and to maintain a compensating balance equal to 15% of the amount borrowed. The firm has borrowed $800,000 during the year under the agreement. Calculate the *effective annual rate* on the firm's borrowing in each of the following circumstances:

a. The firm normally maintains no deposit balances at Bank Two.

b. The firm normally maintains $70,000 in deposit balances at Bank Two.

c. The firm normally maintains $150,000 in deposit balances at Bank Two.

d. Compare, contrast, and discuss your findings in parts **a, b,** and **c.**

P15–13   **Compensating balance versus discount loan**   Weathers Catering Supply, Inc., needs to borrow $150,000 for 6 months. State Bank has offered to lend the funds at a 9% annual rate subject to a 10% compensating balance. (*Note:* Weathers currently maintains $0 on deposit in State Bank.) Frost Finance Co. has offered to lend the funds at a 9% annual rate with discount-loan terms. The principal of both loans would be payable at maturity as a single sum.

a. Calculate the *effective annual rate of interest* on each loan.

b. What could Weathers do that would reduce the effective annual rate on the State Bank loan?

P15–14 **Integrative—Comparison of loan terms**   Cumberland Furniture wishes to establish a prearranged borrowing agreement with a local commercial bank. The bank's terms for a line of credit are 3.30% over the prime rate, and each year the borrowing must be reduced to zero for a 30-day period. For an equivalent revolving credit agreement, the rate is 2.80% over prime with a commitment fee of 0.50% on the average unused balance. With both loans, the required compensating balance is equal to 20% of the amount borrowed. (*Note:* Cumberland currently maintains $0 on deposit at the bank.) The prime rate is currently 8%. Both agreements have $4 million borrowing limits. The firm expects on average to borrow $2 million during the year no matter which loan agreement it decides to use.

a. What is the *effective annual rate* under the line of credit?

b. What is the *effective annual rate* under the revolving credit agreement? (*Hint:* Compute the ratio of the dollars that the firm will pay in interest and commitment fees to the dollars that the firm will effectively have use of.)

c. If the firm does expect to borrow an average of half the amount available, which arrangement would you recommend for the borrower? Explain why.

 P15–15 **Cost of commercial paper**   Commercial paper is usually sold at a discount. Fan Corporation has just sold an issue of 90-day commercial paper with a face value of $1 million. The firm has received initial proceeds of $978,000. (*Note:* Assume a 365-day year.)

a. What *effective annual rate* will the firm pay for financing with commercial paper, assuming that it is rolled over every 90 days throughout the year?

b. If a brokerage fee of $9,612 was paid from the initial proceeds to an investment banker for selling the issue, what *effective annual rate* will the firm pay, assuming that the paper is rolled over every 90 days throughout the year?

 P15–16 **Accounts receivable as collateral**   Kansas City Castings (KCC) is attempting to obtain the maximum loan possible using accounts receivable as collateral. The firm extends net-30-day credit. The amounts that are owed KCC by its 12 credit customers, the average age of each account, and the customer's average payment period are as shown in the following table.

Customer	Account receivable	Average age of account	Average payment period of customer
A	$37,000	40 days	30 days
B	42,000	25	50
C	15,000	40	60
D	8,000	30	35
E	50,000	31	40
F	12,000	28	30
G	24,000	30	70
H	46,000	29	40
I	3,000	30	65
J	22,000	25	35
K	62,000	35	40
L	80,000	60	70

a. If the bank will accept all accounts that can be collected in 45 days or less as long as the customer has a history of paying within 45 days, which accounts will be acceptable? What is the total dollar amount of accounts receivable collateral? (*Note:* Accounts receivable that have an average age greater than the customer's average payment period are also excluded.)

b. In addition to the conditions in part **a,** the bank recognizes that 5% of credit sales will be lost to returns and allowances. Also, the bank will lend only 80% of the acceptable collateral (after adjusting for returns and allowances). What level of funds would be made available through this lending source?

P15–17 **Accounts receivable as collateral** Springer Products wishes to borrow $80,000 from a local bank using its accounts receivable to secure the loan. The bank's policy is to accept as collateral any accounts that are normally paid within 30 days of the end of the credit period, as long as the average age of the account is not greater than the customer's average payment period. Springer's accounts receivable, their average ages, and the average payment period for each customer are shown in the following table. The company extends terms of net 30 days.

Customer	Account receivable	Average age of account	Average payment period of customer
A	$20,000	10 days	40 days
B	6,000	40	35
C	22,000	62	50
D	11,000	68	65
E	2,000	14	30
F	12,000	38	50
G	27,000	55	60
H	19,000	20	35

a. Calculate the dollar amount of acceptable accounts receivable collateral held by Springer Products.

b. The bank reduces collateral by 10% for returns and allowances. What is the level of acceptable collateral under this condition?

c. The bank will advance 75% against the firm's acceptable collateral (after adjusting for returns and allowances). What amount can Springer borrow against these accounts?

  P15–18 **Accounts receivable as collateral, cost of borrowing** Maximum Bank has analyzed the accounts receivable of Scientific Software, Inc. The bank has chosen eight accounts totaling $134,000 that it will accept as collateral. The bank's terms include a lending rate set at prime + 3% and a 2% commission charge. The prime rate currently is 8.5%.

a. The bank will adjust the accounts by 10% for returns and allowances. It then will lend up to 85% of the adjusted acceptable collateral. What is the maximum amount that the bank will lend to Scientific Software?

b. What is Scientific Software's *effective annual rate of interest* if it borrows $100,000 for 12 months? For 6 months? For 3 months? (*Note:* Assume a 365-day year and a prime rate that remains at 8.5% during the life of the loan.)

P15–19 **Factoring** Blair Finance factors the accounts of the Holder Company. All eight factored accounts are shown in the following table, with the amount factored, the date due, and the status on May 30. Indicate the amounts that Blair should have remitted to Holder as of May 30 and the dates of those remittances. Assume that the factor's commission of 2% is deducted as part of determining the amount of the remittance.

Account	Amount	Date due	Status on May 30
A	$200,000	May 30	Collected May 15
B	90,000	May 30	Uncollected
C	110,000	May 30	Uncollected
D	85,000	June 15	Collected May 30
E	120,000	May 30	Collected May 27
F	180,000	June 15	Collected May 30
G	90,000	May 15	Uncollected
H	30,000	June 30	Collected May 30

  P15–20 **Inventory financing** Raymond Manufacturing faces a liquidity crisis—it needs a loan of $100,000 for 1 month. Having no source of additional unsecured borrowing, the firm must find a secured short-term lender. The firm's accounts receivable are quite low, but its inventory is considered liquid and reasonably good collateral. The book value of the inventory is $300,000, of which $120,000 is finished goods. (*Note:* Assume a 365-day year.)

(1) City-Wide Bank will make a $100,000 *trust receipt* loan against the finished goods inventory. The annual interest rate on the loan is 12% on the outstanding loan balance plus a 0.25% administration fee levied against the $100,000 initial loan amount. Because it will be liquidated as inventory is sold, the average amount owed over the month is expected to be $75,000.

(2) Sun State Bank will lend $100,000 against a *floating lien* on the book value of inventory for the 1-month period at an annual interest rate of 13%.

(3) Citizens' Bank and Trust will lend $100,000 against a *warehouse receipt* on the finished goods inventory and charge 15% annual interest on the outstanding loan balance. A 0.5% warehousing fee will be levied against the average amount borrowed. Because the loan will be liquidated as inventory is sold, the average loan balance is expected to be $60,000.

a. Calculate the dollar cost of each of the proposed plans for obtaining an initial loan amount of $100,000.
b. Which plan do you recommend? Why?
c. If the firm had made a purchase of $100,000 for which it had been given terms of 2/10 net 30, would it increase the firm's profitability to give up the discount and not borrow as recommended in part b? Why or why not?

 P15–21 **ETHICS PROBLEM** Rancco Inc. reported total sales of $73 million last year including $13 million in revenue (labor, sales to tax-exempt entities) exempt from sales tax. The company collects sales tax at a rate of 5%. In reviewing its information as part of its loan application, you notice that Rancco's sales tax payments show a total of $2 million in payments over the same time period. What are your conclusions regarding the financial statements that you are reviewing? How might you verify any discrepancies?

Chapter 15 Case

Selecting Kanton Company's Financing Strategy and Unsecured Short-Term Borrowing Arrangement

Morton Mercado, the CFO of Kanton Company, carefully developed the estimates of the firm's total funds requirements for the coming year. These are shown in the following table.

Month	Total funds	Month	Total funds
January	$1,000,000	July	$6,000,000
February	1,000,000	August	5,000,000
March	2,000,000	September	5,000,000
April	3,000,000	October	4,000,000
May	5,000,000	November	2,000,000
June	7,000,000	December	1,000,000

In addition, Morton expects short-term financing costs of about 10% and long-term financing costs of about 14% during that period. He developed the three possible financing strategies that follow:

Strategy 1—Aggressive: Finance seasonal needs with short-term funds and permanent needs with long-term funds.

Strategy 2—Conservative: Finance an amount equal to the peak need with long-term funds and use short-term funds only in an emergency.

Strategy 3—Tradeoff: Finance $3,000,000 with long-term funds and finance the remaining funds requirements with short-term funds.

Using the data on the firm's total funds requirements, Morton estimated the average annual short-term and long-term financing requirements for each strategy in the coming year, as shown in the following table.

| Type of financing | Average annual financing | | |
	Strategy 1 (aggressive)	Strategy 2 (conservative)	Strategy 3 (tradeoff)
Short-term	$2,500,000	$ 0	$1,666,667
Long-term	1,000,000	7,000,000	3,000,000

To ensure that, along with spontaneous financing from accounts payable and accruals, adequate short-term financing will be available, Morton plans to establish an unsecured short-term borrowing arrangement with its local bank, Third National. The bank has offered either a line-of-credit agreement or a revolving credit agreement. Third National's terms for a line of credit are an interest rate of 2.50% above the prime rate, and the borrowing must be reduced to zero for a 30-day period during the year. On an equivalent revolving credit agreement, the interest rate would be 3%

above prime with a commitment fee of 0.50% on the average unused balance. Under both loans, a compensating balance equal to 20% of the amount borrowed would be required. The prime rate is currently 7%. Both the line-of-credit agreement and the revolving credit agreement would have borrowing limits of $1,000,000. For purposes of his analysis, Morton estimates that Kanton will borrow $600,000 on the average during the year, regardless of which financing strategy and loan arrangement it chooses. (*Note:* Assume a 365-day year.)

To Do

a. Determine the total annual cost of each of the three possible financing strategies.
b. Assuming that the firm expects its current assets to total $4 million throughout the year, determine the average amount of net working capital under each financing strategy. (*Hint:* Current liabilities equal average short-term financing.)
c. Using the net working capital found in part **b** as a measure of risk, discuss the profitability–risk tradeoff associated with each financing strategy. Which strategy would you recommend to Morton Mercado for Kanton Company? Why?
d. Find the *effective annual rate* under:
   (1) The line-of-credit agreement.
   (2) The revolving credit agreement. (*Hint:* Find the ratio of the dollars that the firm will pay in interest and commitment fees to the dollars that the firm will effectively have use of.)
e. If the firm does expect to borrow an average of $600,000, which borrowing arrangement would you recommend to Kanton? Explain why.

Spreadsheet Exercise

Your company is considering manufacturing carrying cases for the portable video game machines that are currently popular. Management decides to borrow $200,000 from each of two banks—First American and First Citizen. On the day that you visit both banks, the quoted prime interest rate is 7%. Each loan is similar in that each involves a 60-day note, with interest to be paid at the end of 60 days.

The interest rate was set at 2% above the prime rate on First American's *fixed-rate note*. Over the 60-day period, the rate of interest on this note will remain at the 2% premium over the prime rate regardless of fluctuations in the prime rate.

First Citizen sets its interest rate at 1.5% above the prime rate on its *floating-rate note*. The rate charged over the 60 days will vary directly with the prime rate.

To Do

First, create a spreadsheet to calculate the following for the First American loan:

a. Calculate the total dollar interest cost on the loan. Assume a 365-day year.
b. Calculate the *effective 60-day rate* on the loan.
c. Assume that the loan is rolled over each 60 days throughout the year under identical conditions and terms. Calculate the *effective annual rate of interest* on the fixed-rate, 60-day First American note.

Next, create a spreadsheet to calculate the following for the First Citizen loan:

d. Calculate the initial interest rate.

e. If the prime rate immediately jumps to 7.5%, and after 30 days it drops to 7.25%, calculate the interest rate for the first 30 days and the second 30 days of the loan.

f. Calculate the total dollar interest cost.

g. Calculate the *effective 60-day rate of interest.*

h. Assume the loan is rolled over each 60 days throughout the year under the same conditions and terms. Calculate the *effective annual rate of interest.*

i. Which loan would you choose, and why?

Group Exercise

This chapter continues the discussion of short-term financial management decision making, now concentrating on the current liabilities side. As in previous chapters, you will be developing numbers and systems for managing the current liabilities of your fictitious firm.

To Do

As in Chapter 14, your assignment is to flesh out the details of your firm's short-term financial decisions. Here the focus is on current liabilities and how they are, in essence, sources of short-term financing. You will be developing accounts payable, accrual, and notes payable procedures that should allow your firm to maintain and maximize profitability. For this chapter your group is required to do the following:

a. Identify a specific type of merchandise your firm would purchase as part of its ordinary course of business. Set possible scenarios for the terms that could apply to the purchase of this merchandise.

b. Elaborate on the wage structure of your firm, including the frequency with which employees are paid. Discuss the accruals that your firm encounters.

c. Determine a need for short-term financing, and discuss the terms your firm faces in securing these funds.

d. Decide on one other source of short-term financing from the options listed in the text. These measures include pledging or factoring accounts receivable, and using inventory through a floating lien, trust receipt, or warehouse receipt loan.

Web Exercise

Go to the book's companion website at **www.prenhall.com/gitman** to find the Web Exercise for this chapter.

Remember to check the book's website at **www.prenhall.com/gitman** to find additional resources, including Web Exercises and a Web Case.

Integrative Case 5

Casa de Diseño

In January 2010, Teresa Leal was named treasurer of Casa de Diseño. She decided that she could best orient herself by systematically examining each area of the company's financial operations. She began by studying the firm's short-term financial activities.

Casa de Diseño is located in southern California and specializes in a furniture line called "Ligne Moderna." Of high quality and contemporary design, the furniture appeals to the customer who wants something unique for his or her home or apartment. Most Ligne Moderna furniture is built by special order, because a wide variety of upholstery, accent trimming, and colors are available. The product line is distributed through exclusive dealership arrangements with well-established retail stores. Casa de Diseño's manufacturing process virtually eliminates the use of wood. Plastic and metal provide the basic framework, and wood is used only for decorative purposes.

Casa de Diseño entered the plastic-furniture market in late 2004. The company markets its plastic-furniture products as indoor–outdoor items under the brand name "Futuro." Futuro plastic furniture emphasizes comfort, durability, and practicality and is distributed through wholesalers. The Futuro line has been very successful, accounting for nearly 40 percent of the firm's sales and profits in 2009. Casa de Diseño anticipates some additions to the Futuro line and also some limited change of direction in its promotion in an effort to expand the applications of the plastic furniture.

Leal has decided to study the firm's cash management practices. To determine the effects of these practices, she must first determine the current operating and cash conversion cycles. In her investigations, she found that Casa de Diseño purchases all of its raw materials and production supplies on open account. The company is operating at production levels that preclude volume discounts. Most suppliers do not offer cash discounts, and Casa de Diseño usually receives credit terms of net 30. An analysis of Casa de Diseño's accounts payable showed that its average payment period is 30 days. Leal consulted industry data and found that the industry average payment period was 39 days. Investigation of six California furniture manufacturers revealed that their average payment period was also 39 days.

Next, Leal studied the production cycle and inventory policies. Casa de Diseño tries not to hold any more inventory than necessary in either raw materials or finished goods. The average inventory age was 110 days. Leal determined that the industry standard, as reported in a survey done by *Furniture Age*, the trade association journal, was 83 days.

Casa de Diseño sells to all of its customers on a net-60 basis, in line with the industry trend to grant such credit terms on specialty furniture. Leal discovered, by aging the accounts receivable, that the average collection period for the firm was 75 days. Investigation of the trade association's and California manufacturers' averages showed that the same collection period existed where net-60 credit terms were given. Where cash discounts were offered, the collection period was significantly shortened. Leal believed that if Casa de Diseño were to offer credit terms of 3/10 net 60, the average collection period could be reduced by 40 percent.

Casa de Diseño was spending an estimated $26,500,000 per year on operating-cycle investments. Leal considered this expenditure level to be the minimum she could expect the firm to disburse during 2010. Her concern was whether the firm's cash management was as efficient as it could be. She knew that the company paid 15 percent annual interest for its resource investment. For this reason, she was concerned about the financing cost resulting from any inefficiencies in the management of Casa de Diseño's cash conversion cycle. (*Note:* Assume a 365-day year and that the operating-cycle investment per dollar of payables, inventory, and receivables is the same.)

To Do

a. Assuming a constant rate for purchases, production, and sales throughout the year, what are Casa de Diseño's existing operating cycle (OC), cash conversion cycle (CCC), and resource investment need?

b. If Leal can optimize Casa de Diseño's operations according to industry standards, what will Casa de Diseño's operating cycle (OC), cash conversion cycle (CCC), and resource investment need to be under these more efficient conditions?

c. In terms of resource investment requirements, what is the cost of Casa de Diseño's operational inefficiency?

d. (1) If in addition to achieving industry standards for payables and inventory, the firm can reduce the average collection period by offering credit terms of 3/10 net 60, what additional savings in resource investment costs will result from the shortened cash conversion cycle, assuming that the level of sales remains constant?

   (2) If the firm's sales (all on credit) are $40,000,000 and 45% of the customers are expected to take the cash discount, by how much will the firm's annual revenues be reduced as a result of the discount?

   (3) If the firm's variable cost of the $40,000,000 in sales is 80%, determine the reduction in the average investment in accounts receivable and the annual savings that will result from this reduced investment, assuming that sales remain constant.

   (4) If the firm's bad-debts expenses decline from 2% to 1.5% of sales, what annual savings will result, assuming that sales remain constant?

   (5) Use your findings in parts (2) through (4) to assess whether offering the cash discount can be justified financially. Explain why or why not.

e. On the basis of your analysis in parts **a** through **d**, what recommendations would you offer Teresa Leal?

f. Review for Teresa Leal the key sources of short-term financing, other than accounts payable, that she may consider to finance Casa de Diseño's resource investment need calculated in part **b**. Be sure to mention both unsecured and secured sources.

Part Six
Special Topics in Managerial Finance

Chapters in This Part

16 | Hybrid and Derivative Securities

Why This Chapter Matters to You

(In Your Professional Life)

Accounting: You need to understand the types of leasing arrangements and the general features of convertible securities, stock purchase warrants, and options, which you will be required to record and report.

Information systems: You need to understand types of leasing arrangements and of convertible securities to design systems that will track data used to make lease-or-purchase and conversion decisions.

Management: You need to understand when and why it may make better sense to lease assets rather than to purchase them. You need to understand how convertible securities and stock purchase warrants work to decide when the firm would benefit from their use. You also need to understand the impact of call and put options on the firm.

Marketing: You need to understand leasing as a way to finance a new project proposal. You also should understand how hybrid securities can be used to raise funds for new projects.

Operations: You need to understand the role of leasing in financing new equipment. You also need to understand the maintenance obligations associated with leased equipment.

(In Your Personal Life)

Understanding hybrid and derivative securities will benefit you in your investment activities. Even more useful is an understanding of leasing, which you may use to finance certain long-lived assets such as housing or cars. Knowing how to analyze and compare leasing to the alternative of purchasing should help you to better manage your personal finances.

Learning Goals

LG 1 Differentiate between hybrid and derivative securities and their roles in the corporation.

LG 2 Review the types of leases, leasing arrangements, the lease-versus-purchase decision, the effects of leasing on future financing, and the advantages and disadvantages of leasing.

LG 3 Describe the types of convertible securities, their general features, and financing with convertibles.

LG 4 Demonstrate the procedures for determining the straight bond value, the conversion (or stock) value, and the market value of a convertible bond.

LG 5 Explain the key characteristics of stock purchase warrants, the implied price of an attached warrant, and the values of warrants.

LG 6 Define options and discuss calls and puts, options markets, options trading, the role of call and put options in fund raising, and hedging foreign-currency exposures with options.

Boeing

"We Will Build the Dreamliner; Others Will Lease It"

In 2008, **Boeing**'s new 787 Dreamliner will enter service for the first time. Using 20 percent less fuel per passenger than similarly sized airplanes, the 787 is designed to help the environment with its lower emissions and quieter takeoffs and landings. Inside the airplane, passengers will find a new interior environment with cleaner air, larger windows, more stowage space, improved lighting, and other passenger-preferred conveniences.

By mid-2007, the 787 Dreamliner became the fastest-selling commercial aircraft in history—47 customers had announced 677 orders since the Dreamliner was launched in April 2004. Overall, the 787 Dreamliner order book is valued at more than $110 billion at list prices.

Although many of the Dreamliners are sold directly to airlines around the world, many are not. By mid-2007, the largest order, for 74 Dreamliners, had been booked by the International Lease Finance Corp (ILFC). Another leasing company, Aviation Lease and Finance Company (ALAFCO) of Kuwait, had ordered 22 of the new planes, and CIT Group Inc. had 10 of the aircraft on order. Leasing firms such as these are financial intermediaries that purchase large pieces of equipment and subsequently lease them to a variety of end-users, including airlines.

Aircraft are just one example of equipment that is leased. Other commonly leased equipment includes computers, oil-drilling equipment, railway cars, cable television, medical equipment, pollution-control devices, and solar energy devices. Most leased equipment is expensive and would require large cash outlays if purchased outright. Leasing provides an easier method of obtaining an up-to-date piece of equipment with a much smaller cash outlay.

Leasing is a tool that 80 percent of U.S. businesses have used at some time to acquire equipment. By leasing a large piece of equipment, the lessee can improve cash flow, keep pace with technology by leasing the latest models, and sometimes improve the company's financial ratios by excluding some leased assets (operating leases) from the balance sheet.

(What other types of equipment can you think of which might be leased?)

In this chapter, we'll demonstrate how to analyze lease financing, a hybrid financing technique that incorporates elements of debt and equity. You will also learn about other hybrids including convertible securities, stock purchase warrants, and derivative securities such as stock options.

16.1 | Overview of Hybrids and Derivatives

hybrid security
A form of debt or equity financing that possesses characteristics of *both* debt and equity financing.

derivative security
A security that is neither debt nor equity but derives its value from an underlying asset that is often another security; called "derivatives," for short.

Chapters 6 and 7 described the characteristics of the key securities—corporate bonds, common stock, and preferred stock—used by corporations to raise long-term funds. In their simplest form, bonds are pure debt and common stock is pure equity. Preferred stock, on the other hand, is a form of equity that promises to pay fixed periodic dividends that are similar to the fixed contractual interest payments on bonds. Because it blends the characteristics of *both* debt (a fixed dividend payment) and equity (ownership), preferred stock is considered a **hybrid security.** Other popular hybrid securities include financial leases, convertible securities, and stock purchase warrants. Each of these hybrid securities is described in the following pages.

The final section of this chapter focuses on *options,* a popular **derivative security**—a security that is neither debt nor equity but derives its value from an underlying asset that is often another security. As you'll learn, *derivatives* are not used by corporations to raise funds, but rather serve as a useful tool for managing certain aspects of the firm's risk.

REVIEW QUESTION

16–1 Differentiate between a *hybrid security* and a *derivative security.* How do their uses by the corporation differ?

16.2 | Leasing

leasing
The process by which a firm can obtain the use of certain fixed assets for which it must make a series of contractual, periodic, tax-deductible payments.

lessee
The receiver of the services of the assets under a lease contract.

lessor
The owner of assets that are being leased.

operating lease
A *cancelable* contractual arrangement whereby the lessee agrees to make periodic payments to the lessor, often for 5 or fewer years, to obtain an asset's services; generally, the total payments over the term of the lease are *less* than the lessor's initial cost of the leased asset.

Leasing enables the firm to obtain the use of certain fixed assets for which it must make a series of contractual, periodic, tax-deductible payments. The **lessee** is the receiver of the services of the assets under the lease contract; the **lessor** is the owner of the assets. Leasing can take a number of forms.

Types of Leases

The two basic types of leases that are available to a business are *operating leases* and *financial leases* (often called *capital leases* by accountants).

Operating Leases

An **operating lease** is normally a contractual arrangement whereby the lessee agrees to make periodic payments to the lessor, often for 5 or fewer years, to obtain an asset's services. Such leases are generally *cancelable* at the option of the lessee, who may be required to pay a penalty for cancellation. Assets that are leased under operating leases have a usable life that is *longer* than the term of the lease. Usually, however, they would become less efficient and technologically obsolete if leased for a longer period. Computer systems are prime examples of assets whose relative efficiency is expected to diminish as the technology changes. The operating lease is therefore a common arrangement for obtaining such systems, as well as for other relatively short-lived assets such as automobiles.

If an operating lease is held to maturity, the lessee at that time returns the leased asset to the lessor, who may lease it again or sell the asset. Normally, the asset still has a positive market value at the termination of the lease. In some instances, the lease contract gives the lessee the opportunity to purchase the leased asset. Generally, the total payments made by the lessee to the lessor are *less* than the lessor's initial cost of the leased asset.

Financial (or Capital) Leases

A **financial (or capital) lease** is a *longer-term* lease than an operating lease. Financial leases are *noncancelable* and obligate the lessee to make payments for the use of an asset over a predefined period of time. Financial leases are commonly used for leasing land, buildings, and large pieces of equipment. The noncancelable feature of the financial lease makes it similar to certain types of long-term debt. The lease payment becomes a fixed, tax-deductible expenditure that must be paid at predefined dates. As with debt, failure to make the contractual lease payments can result in bankruptcy for the lessee.

With a financial lease, the total payments over the term of the lease are *greater* than the lessor's initial cost of the leased asset. In other words, the lessor must receive more than the asset's purchase price to earn its required return on the investment. Technically, under *FASB* (Financial Accounting Standards Board) *Statement No. 13,* "Accounting for Leases," a financial (or capital) lease is defined as one that has *any* of the following elements:

1. The lease transfers ownership of the property to the lessee by the end of the lease term.
2. The lease contains an option to purchase the property at a "bargain price." Such an option must be exercisable at a "fair market value."
3. The lease term is equal to 75 percent or more of the estimated economic life of the property (exceptions exist for property leased toward the end of its usable economic life).
4. At the beginning of the lease, the present value of the lease payments is equal to 90 percent or more of the fair market value of the leased property.

The emphasis in this chapter is on financial leases, because they result in inescapable long-term financial commitments by the firm.

The *Focus on Practice* box on page 725 discusses leasing by Disney that did not have a happy ending.

Leasing Arrangements

Lessors use three primary techniques for obtaining assets to be leased. The method depends largely on the desires of the prospective lessee.

1. A **direct lease** results when a lessor owns or acquires the assets that are leased to a given lessee. In other words, the lessee did not previously own the assets that it is leasing.
2. In a **sale–leaseback arrangement,** lessors acquire leased assets by purchasing assets already owned by the lessee and leasing them back. This technique is normally initiated by a firm that needs funds for operations. By selling an existing asset to a lessor and then *leasing it back,* the lessee receives cash for the asset immediately, while obligating itself to make fixed periodic payments for use of the leased asset.

financial (or capital) lease A *longer-term* lease than an operating lease that is *noncancelable* and obligates the lessee to make payments for the use of an asset over a predefined period of time; the total payments over the term of the lease are *greater* than the lessor's initial cost of the leased asset.

direct lease A lease under which a lessor owns or acquires the assets that are leased to a given lessee.

sale–leaseback arrangement A lease under which the lessee sells an asset to a prospective lessor and then *leases back* the same asset, making fixed periodic payments for its use.

leveraged lease
A lease under which the lessor acts as an equity participant, supplying only about 20 percent of the cost of the asset, while a lender supplies the balance.

maintenance clauses
Provisions normally included in an operating lease that require the lessor to maintain the assets and to make insurance and tax payments.

renewal options
Provisions especially common in operating leases that grant the lessee the right to re-lease assets at the expiration of the lease.

purchase options
Provisions frequently included in both operating and financial leases that allow the lessee to purchase the leased asset at maturity, typically for a prespecified price.

lease-versus-purchase (or lease-versus-buy) decision
The decision facing firms needing to acquire new fixed assets: whether to lease the assets or to purchase them, using borrowed funds or available liquid resources.

Hint Although, for clarity, the approach demonstrated here compares the present values of the cash flows for the lease and the purchase, a more direct approach would calculate the NPV of the *incremental* cash flows.

3. Leasing arrangements that include one or more third-party lenders are **leveraged leases.** Under a leveraged lease, the lessor acts as an equity participant, supplying only about 20 percent of the cost of the asset, and a lender supplies the balance. Leveraged leases are especially popular in structuring leases of very expensive assets.

A lease agreement typically specifies whether the lessee is responsible for maintenance of the leased assets. Operating leases normally include **maintenance clauses** requiring the lessor to maintain the assets and to make insurance and tax payments. Financial leases nearly always require the lessee to pay maintenance and other costs.

The lessee is usually given the option to renew a lease at its expiration. **Renewal options,** which grant lessees the right to re-lease assets at expiration, are especially common in operating leases, because their term is generally shorter than the usable life of the leased assets. **Purchase options** allowing the lessee to purchase the leased asset at maturity, typically for a prespecified price, are frequently included in both operating and financial leases.

The lessor can be one of a number of parties. In operating leases, the lessor is likely to be the manufacturer's leasing subsidiary or an independent leasing company. Financial leases are frequently handled by independent leasing companies or by the leasing subsidiaries of large financial institutions such as commercial banks and life insurance companies. Life insurance companies are especially active in real estate leasing. Pension funds, like commercial banks, have also been increasing their leasing activities.

Lease-versus-Purchase Decision

Firms that are contemplating the acquisition of new fixed assets commonly confront the **lease-versus-purchase (or lease-versus-buy) decision.** The alternatives available are (1) lease the assets, (2) borrow funds to purchase the assets, or (3) purchase the assets using available liquid resources. Alternatives 2 and 3, although they differ, are analyzed in a similar fashion; even if the firm has the liquid resources with which to purchase the assets, the use of these funds is viewed as equivalent to borrowing. Therefore, we need to compare only the leasing and purchasing alternatives.

The lease-versus-purchase decision involves application of the capital budgeting methods presented in Chapters 8 through 10. First, we determine the relevant cash flows and then apply present value techniques. The following steps are involved in the analysis:

Step 1 Find the *after-tax cash outflows for each year under the lease alternative.* This step generally involves a fairly simple tax adjustment of the annual lease payments. In addition, the cost of exercising a purchase option in the final year of the lease term must frequently be included.[1]

---

1. Including the cost of exercising a purchase option in the cash flows for the lease alternative ensures that under both lease and purchase alternatives the firm owns the asset at the end of the relevant time horizon. The other approach would be to include the cash flows from sale of the asset in the cash flows for the purchase alternative at the end of the lease term. These strategies guarantee avoidance of unequal lives, which were discussed in Chapter 10. In addition, they make any subsequent cash flows irrelevant because these would be either identical or nonexistent, respectively, under each alternative.

Focus on Practice   Leases to Airlines End on a Sour Note

Walt Disney Co. is in the business of providing entertainment experiences based on its rich legacy of creative content and exceptional storytelling. From theme parks and resorts to motion pictures and cartoons, the Walt Disney Company presents tales in which many Disney characters live happily ever after. However, one Disney tale that did not have a happy ending was Disney's investment in leveraged aircraft leases.

Using a structure known as a *leveraged lease*, cash-rich Disney purchased airplanes in the early 1990s and leased them out to air carriers. The deals, with iron-clad terms, were seen as safe and offered tax advantages. Since the 1980s, large corporations have been leasing out planes to take advantage of tax rules that allow for accelerated depreciation of large equipment. Under a typical leveraged lease, Disney put up 20 percent of

the purchase price. The rest was borrowed under a loan using the plane as collateral. None of Disney's other assets were put at risk.

During the 1990s, leveraged leases were attractive investments that boosted a company's return on investment. However, the destruction of the World Trade Center on September 11, 2001, and the ensuing reaction to potential terrorist threats crippled air travel and put U.S. air carriers under tremendous financial pressure. The result for **United Airlines** was bankruptcy. Under bankruptcy protection, United was able to break any lease it didn't want, giving the airline powerful leverage to renegotiate lower lease payments, at lower market rates. When no deal was reached, United Airlines was able to walk away from the leases. Disney had to write off entirely the $114 million book value assigned to its investment

in two Boeing 747s and two 767s leased to United. Pursuing the matter in the courts, Disney was able to recoup $50 million from United for its lost tax benefits.

With additional aircraft leased out to **Delta Air Lines** (five aircraft, $119 million), the Disney tale of leveraged leases had not reached its final reel. Delta Air Lines announced 7,000 jobs cut in September 2004 as part of a $5 billion cost-saving program and entered bankruptcy in late 2005. At that time Disney was forced to declare a write-off of $68 million for its Delta leases, and the company eventually left the aircraft-leasing business entirely.

■ *Were the Disney leases of aircraft to United Airlines operating leases or financial leases?*

Step 2 Find the *after-tax cash outflows for each year under the purchase alternative.* This step involves adjusting the sum of the scheduled loan payment and maintenance cost outlay for the tax shields resulting from the tax deductions attributable to maintenance, depreciation, and interest.

Step 3 Calculate the *present value of the cash outflows* associated with the lease (from Step 1) and purchase (from Step 2) alternatives using the *after-tax cost of debt* as the discount rate. The after-tax cost of debt is used to evaluate the lease-versus-purchase decision because the decision itself involves the choice between two *financing* techniques—leasing and borrowing—that have very low risk.

Step 4 Choose the alternative with the *lower present value* of cash outflows from Step 3. It will be the *least-cost* financing alternative.

The application of each of these steps is demonstrated in the following example.

Example

Roberts Company, a small machine shop, is contemplating acquiring a new machine that costs $24,000. Arrangements can be made to lease or purchase the machine. The firm is in the 40% tax bracket.

Lease   The firm would obtain a 5-year lease requiring annual end-of-year lease payments of $6,000.[2] All maintenance costs would be paid by the lessor, and insurance and other costs would be borne by the lessee. The lessee would exercise its option to purchase the machine for $4,000 at termination of the lease.

Purchase   The firm would finance the purchase of the machine with a 9%, 5-year loan requiring end-of-year installment payments of $6,170.[3] The machine would be depreciated under MACRS using a 5-year recovery period. The firm would pay $1,500 per year for a service contract that covers all maintenance costs; insurance and other costs would be borne by the firm. The firm plans to keep the machine and use it beyond its 5-year recovery period.

Using these data, we can apply the steps presented earlier.

Step 1   The after-tax cash outflow from the lease payments can be found by multiplying the before-tax payment of $6,000 by 1 minus the tax rate, T, of 40%.

$$\text{After-tax cash outflow from lease} = \$6,000 \times (1 - T)$$
$$= \$6,000 \times (1 - 0.40) = \$3,600$$

Therefore, the lease alternative results in annual cash outflows over the 5-year lease of $3,600. In the final year, the $4,000 cost of the purchase option would be added to the $3,600 lease outflow to get a total cash outflow in year 5 of $7,600 ($3,600 + $4,000).

Step 2   The after-tax cash outflow from the purchase alternative is a bit more difficult to find. First, the interest component of each annual loan payment must be determined, because the Internal Revenue Service allows the deduction of interest only—not principal—from income for tax purposes.[4] Table 16.1 presents the calculations necessary to split the loan payments into their interest and principal components. Columns 3 and 4 show the annual interest and principal paid.

In Table 16.2, the annual loan payment is shown in column 1, and the annual maintenance cost, which is a tax-deductible expense, is shown in column 2. Next, we find the annual depreciation write-off resulting

---

2. Lease payments are generally made at the beginning of the year. To simplify the following discussions, *end-of-year lease payments are assumed.*

3. The annual loan payment on the 9%, 5-year loan of $24,000 is calculated by using the loan amortization technique described in Chapter 4. Dividing the present value interest factor for an annuity, *PVIFA*, from Table A–4 at 9% for 5 years (3.890) into the loan principal of $24,000 results in the annual loan payment of $6,170. (*Note:* If a financial calculator were used, the annual loan payment would be $6,170.22.) For a more detailed discussion of loan amortization, see Chapter 4.

4. When the rate of interest on the loan used to finance the purchase just equals the cost of debt, the present value of the after-tax loan payments (annual loan payments − interest tax shields) discounted at the after-tax cost of debt just equals the initial loan principal. In such a case, it is unnecessary to amortize the loan to determine the payment amount and the amounts of interest when finding after-tax cash outflows. The loan payments and interest payments (columns 1 and 4 in Table 16.2) can be ignored, and in their place, the initial loan principal ($24,000) is shown as an outflow occurring at time zero. To allow for a loan interest rate that is different from the firm's cost of debt and for easier understanding, here we isolate the loan payments and interest payments rather than use this computationally more efficient approach.

TABLE 16.1	**Determining the Interest and Principal Components of the Roberts Company Loan Payments**

| End of year | Loan payments (1) | Beginning-of-year principal (2) | Payments | | End-of-year principal $[(2) - (4)]$ (5) |
			Interest $[0.09 \times (2)]$ (3)	Principal $[(1) - (3)]$ (4)	
1	$6,170	$24,000	$2,160	$4,010	$19,990
2	6,170	19,990	1,799	4,371	15,619
3	6,170	15,619	1,406	4,764	10,855
4	6,170	10,855	977	5,193	5,662
5	6,170	5,662	510	5,660	—[a]

[a]The values in this table have been rounded to the nearest dollar, which results in a slight difference ($2) between the beginning-of-year-5 principal (in column 2) and the year-5 principal payment (in column 4).

from the $24,000 machine. Using the applicable MACRS 5-year recovery period depreciation percentages—20% in year 1, 32% in year 2, 19% in year 3, and 12% in years 4 and 5—given in Table 3.2 on page 108 results in the annual depreciation for years 1 through 5 given in column 3 of Table 16.2.[5]

Table 16.2 presents the calculations required to determine the cash outflows[6] associated with borrowing to purchase the new machine. Column 7 of the table presents the after-tax cash outflows associated with the purchase alternative. A few points should be clarified with

TABLE 16.2	**After-Tax Cash Outflows Associated with Purchasing for Roberts Company**

End of year	Loan payments (1)	Maintenance costs (2)	Depreciation (3)	Interest[a] (4)	Total deductions $[(2) + (3) + (4)]$ (5)	Tax shields $[(0.40 \times (5)]$ (6)	After-tax cash outflows $[(1) + (2) - (6)]$ (7)
1	$6,170	$1,500	$4,800	$2,160	$ 8,460	$3,384	$4,286
2	6,170	1,500	7,680	1,799	10,979	4,392	3,278
3	6,170	1,500	4,560	1,406	7,466	2,986	4,684
4	6,170	1,500	2,880	977	5,357	2,143	5,527
5	6,170	1,500	2,880	510	4,890	1,956	5,714

[a]From Table 16.1, column 3.

5. The year-6 depreciation is ignored, because we are considering the cash flows solely over a 5-year time horizon. Similarly, depreciation on the leased asset, when it is purchased at the end of the lease for $4,000, is ignored. The tax benefits resulting from this depreciation would make the lease alternative even more attractive. Clearly, the analysis would become both more precise and more complex if we chose to look beyond the 5-year time horizon.

6. Although other cash outflows such as insurance and operating expenses may be relevant here, they would be the same under the lease and purchase alternatives and therefore would cancel out in the final analysis.

| TABLE 16.3 | Comparison of Cash Outflows Associated with Leasing versus Purchasing for Roberts Company | | | | | |

| | Leasing | | | Purchasing | | |
End of Year	After-tax cash outflows (1)	Present value factors[a] (2)	Present value of outflows [(1) × (2)] (3)	After-tax cash outflows[b] (4)	Present value factors[a] (5)	Present value of outflows [(4) × (5)] (6)
1	$3,600	0.943	$ 3,395	$4,286	0.943	$ 4,042
2	3,600	0.890	3,204	3,278	0.890	2,917
3	3,600	0.840	3,024	4,684	0.840	3,935
4	3,600	0.792	2,851	5,527	0.792	4,377
5	7,600[c]	0.747	5,677	5,714	0.747	4,268
		PV of cash outflows	$18,151		PV of cash outflows	$19,539

[a]From Table A–2, *PVIF*, for 6% and the corresponding year.
[b]From column 7 of Table 16.2.
[c]After-tax lease payment outflow of $3,600 plus the $4,000 cost of exercising the purchase option.

respect to the calculations in Table 16.2. The major cash outflows are the total loan payment for each year given in column 1 and the annual maintenance cost in column 2. The sum of these two outflows is reduced by the tax savings from writing off the maintenance, depreciation, and interest expenses associated with the new machine and its financing. The resulting cash outflows are the after-tax cash outflows associated with the purchase alternative.

Step 3 The present values of the cash outflows associated with the lease (from Step 1) and purchase (from Step 2) alternatives are calculated in Table 16.3 using the firm's 6% after-tax cost of debt.[7] Applying the appropriate present value interest factors given in columns 2 and 5 to the after-tax cash outflows in columns 1 and 4 results in the present values of lease and purchase cash outflows in columns 3 and 6, respectively. The sum of the present values of the cash outflows for the leasing alternative is given in column 3 of Table 16.3, and the sum of those for the purchasing alternative is given in column 6.

Step 4 Because the present value of cash outflows for leasing ($18,151) is lower than that for purchasing ($19,539), *the leasing alternative is preferred.* Leasing results in an incremental savings of $1,388 ($19,539 − $18,151) and is therefore the less costly alternative.[8]

The techniques described here for comparing lease and purchase alternatives may be applied in different ways. The approach illustrated by the Roberts Com-

---

7. If we ignore any flotation costs, the firm's after-tax cost of debt would be 5.4% [9% debt cost × (1 − 0.40 tax rate)]. To reflect both the flotation costs associated with selling new debt and the possible need to sell the debt at a discount, we use an after-tax debt cost of 6% as the applicable discount rate. A more detailed discussion of techniques for calculating the after-tax cost of debt is found in Chapter 11.

8. Using a financial calculator would reveal the present value of the cash outflows for the lease to be $18,154, and that for the purchase to be $19,541, resulting in an incremental savings of $1,387.

pany data is one of the most straightforward. It is important to recognize that the lower cost of one alternative over the other results from factors such as the differing tax brackets of the lessor and lessee, different tax treatments of leases versus purchases, and differing risks and borrowing costs for lessor and lessee. Therefore, when making a lease-versus-purchase decision, the firm will find that inexpensive borrowing opportunities, high required lessor returns, and a low risk of obsolescence increase the attractiveness of purchasing. Subjective factors must also be included in the decision-making process. Like most financial decisions, the lease-versus-purchase decision requires some judgment or intuition.

Personal Finance Example   Jake Jiminez is considering either leasing or purchasing a new Honda Fit that will cost $15,000 out the door. The 3-year lease requires an initial payment of $1,800 ($1,500 down payment and $300 security deposit) and monthly payments of $300. Purchasing requires a $2,500 down payment, sales tax of 5% ($750), and 36 monthly payments of $392. He estimates the trade-in value of the new car will be $8,000 at the end of 3 years. Assuming Jake can earn 4% annual interest on his savings and is subject to a 5% sales tax on purchases, we can make a reasonable recommendation to Jake using the following analysis (for simplicity, ignoring the time value of money).

Lease Cost

Down payment	$ 1,500
Total lease payments (36 months × $300/month)	10,800
Opportunity cost of initial payment (3 years × 0.04 × $1,800)	216
Total cost of leasing	$12,516

Purchase Cost

Down payment	$ 2,500
Sales tax (0.05 × $15,000)	750
Total loan payments (36 months × $392/month)	14,112
Opportunity cost of down payment (3 years × 0.04 × $2,500)	300
Less: Estimated trade-in value of car at end of loan	(8,000)
Total cost of purchasing	$ 9,662

Because the total cost of leasing of $12,516 is greater than the $9,662 total cost of purchasing, Jake should purchase rather than lease the car.

Effects of Leasing on Future Financing

capitalized lease
A *financial (capital) lease* that has the present value of all its payments included as an asset and corresponding liability on the firm's balance sheet, as required by the Financial Accounting Standards Board (FASB) in *FASB Statement No. 13*.

Because leasing is considered a type of financing, it affects the firm's future financing. Lease payments are shown as a tax-deductible expense on the firm's income statement. Anyone analyzing the firm's income statement would probably recognize that an asset is being leased, although the amount and term of the lease would be unclear.

The Financial Accounting Standards Board (FASB), in *FASB Statement No. 13*, "Accounting for Leases," requires explicit disclosure of *financial (capital) lease* obligations on the firm's balance sheet. Such a lease must be shown as a **capitalized lease**, meaning that the present value of all its payments is included as an asset and corresponding liability on the firm's balance sheet. An *operating lease,* on the other hand, need not be capitalized, but its basic features must be disclosed in a footnote to the financial statements. *FASB Statement No. 13*, of course, establishes detailed guidelines to be used in capitalizing leases. Subsequent standards have further refined lease capitalization and disclosure procedures.

Example ⏐ Jeffrey Company, a manufacturer of water purifiers, is leasing an asset under a 10-year lease requiring annual end-of-year payments of $15,000. The lease can be capitalized merely by calculating the present value of the lease payments over the life of the lease. However, the rate at which the payments should be discounted is difficult to determine.[9] If 10% were used, the present, or capitalized, value of the lease would be $92,175 ($15,000 × 6.145). (The value calculated by using a financial calculator is $92,169.) This value would be shown as an asset and corresponding liability on the firm's balance sheet, which should result in an accurate reflection of the firm's true financial position.

Because the consequences of missing a financial lease payment are the same as those of missing an interest or principal payment on debt, a financial analyst must view the lease as a long-term financial commitment of the lessee. With FASB *Statement No. 13*, the inclusion of each financial (capital) lease as an asset and corresponding liability (i.e., long-term debt) provides for a balance sheet that more accurately reflects the firm's financial status. It thereby permits various types of financial ratio analyses to be performed directly on the statement by any interested party.

Advantages and Disadvantages of Leasing

Leasing has a number of commonly cited advantages and disadvantages that managers should consider when making a lease-versus-purchase decision. It is not unusual for a number of them to apply in a given situation. Table 16.4 describes the commonly cited advantages and disadvantages of leasing.

REVIEW QUESTIONS

16–2 What is *leasing?* Define, compare, and contrast *operating leases* and *financial (or capital) leases.* How does the Financial Accounting Standards Board's *Statement No. 13* define a financial (or capital) lease? Describe three methods used by lessors to acquire assets to be leased.

16–3 Describe the four basic steps involved in the *lease-versus-purchase decision* process. How are capital budgeting methods applied in this process?

16–4 What type of lease must be treated as a *capitalized lease* on the balance sheet? How does the financial manager capitalize a lease?

16–5 List and discuss the commonly cited advantages and disadvantages that should be considered when deciding whether to lease or purchase.

---

9. The Financial Accounting Standards Board in *Statement No. 13* established certain guidelines for the appropriate discount rate to use when capitalizing leases. Most commonly, the rate that the lessee would have incurred to borrow the funds to buy the asset with a secured loan under terms similar to the lease repayment schedule is used. This simply represents the *before-tax cost of a secured debt.*

TABLE 16.4	**Advantages and Disadvantages of Leasing**

Advantages

- The firm may *avoid the cost of obsolescence.* This is especially true in the case of operating leases, which generally have relatively short lives.
- A lessee *avoids many of the restrictive covenants* (e.g., minimum liquidity, subsequent borrowing, and cash dividend payments) that are normally included as part of a long-term loan, but are *not* normally found in a lease agreement.
- In the case of low-cost assets that are infrequently acquired, leasing—especially operating leases—may provide the firm with needed *financing flexibility.* The firm does not have to arrange other financing for these assets.
- Sale–leaseback arrangements may permit the firm to *increase its liquidity* by converting an *existing* asset into cash. This can benefit a firm that is short of working capital or in a liquidity bind.
- Leasing allows the lessee, in effect, to *depreciate land,* which is prohibited if the land were purchased. Because the lessee who leases land is permitted to deduct the *total lease pay-*

ment as an expense for tax purposes, the effect is the same as if the firm had purchased the land and then depreciated it.
- Because leasing does not increase the assets or liabilities on the firm's balance sheet, leasing may result in misleading *financial ratios.* Understating assets and liabilities can cause certain ratios, such as the total asset turnover, to look better than they might be. With the adoption of *FASB Statement No. 13,* this advantage no longer applies to financial leases, although it remains a potential advantage for operating leases.
- Leasing provides *100 percent financing.* Most loan agreements for the purchase of fixed assets require a down payment; thus the borrower is able to borrow only 90 to 95 percent of the purchase price of the asset.
- In the case of *bankruptcy* or *reorganization,* the maximum claim of lessors against the corporation is 3 years of lease payments. If debt is used to purchase an asset, the creditors have a claim that is equal to the total outstanding loan balance.

Disadvantages

- In many leases the *return to the lessor is quite high;* the firm might be better off borrowing to purchase the asset.
- The *terminal value* of an asset, if any, is realized by the lessor. If the lessee had purchased the asset, it could have claimed its terminal value. Of course, an expected terminal value when recognized by the lessor results in lower lease payments.

- The lessee is generally *prohibited from making improvements* on the leased property or asset without the lessor's approval. However, lessors generally encourage leasehold improvements when these are expected to enhance the asset's salvage value.
- If a lessee leases an *asset that subsequently becomes obsolete,* it still must make lease payments over the remaining term of the lease. This is true even if the asset is unusable.

  ## 16.3 | Convertible Securities

conversion feature
An option that is included as part of a bond or a preferred stock issue and allows its holder to change the security into a stated number of shares of common stock.

A **conversion feature** is an option that is included as part of a bond or a preferred stock issue and allows its holder to change the security into a stated number of shares of common stock. The conversion feature typically enhances the marketability of an issue.

Types of Convertible Securities

Corporate bonds and preferred stocks may be convertible into common stock. The most common type of convertible security is the bond. Convertibles normally have an accompanying *call feature,* which permits the issuer to retire or encourage conversion of outstanding convertibles when appropriate.

Convertible Bonds

convertible bond
A bond that can be changed into a specified number of shares of common stock.

A **convertible bond** can be changed into a specified number of shares of common stock. It is nearly always a *debenture*—an unsecured bond—with a call feature. Because the conversion feature provides the purchaser with the possibility of becoming a stockholder on favorable terms, convertible bonds are generally a less

straight bond
A bond that is nonconvertible, having no conversion feature.

expensive form of financing than similar-risk nonconvertible or **straight bonds.** The conversion feature adds a degree of speculation to a bond issue, although the issue still maintains its value as a bond.

Convertible Preferred Stock

convertible preferred stock
Preferred stock that can be changed into a specified number of shares of common stock.

straight preferred stock
Preferred stock that is nonconvertible, having no conversion feature.

Convertible preferred stock is preferred stock that can be changed into a specified number of shares of common stock. It can normally be sold with a lower stated dividend than a similar-risk nonconvertible or **straight preferred stock.** The reason is that the convertible preferred holder is assured of the fixed dividend payment associated with a preferred stock and also may receive the appreciation resulting from increases in the market price of the underlying common stock. Convertible preferred stock behaves much like convertible bonds. The following discussions will concentrate on the more popular convertible bonds.

General Features of Convertibles

Convertible securities are nearly always convertible at any time during the life of the security. Occasionally, conversion is permitted only for a limited number of years—say, for 5 or 10 years after issuance of the convertible.

conversion ratio
The ratio at which a convertible security can be exchanged for common stock.

conversion price
The per-share price that is effectively paid for common stock as the result of conversion of a convertible security.

Conversion Ratio

The **conversion ratio** is the ratio at which a convertible security can be exchanged for common stock. The conversion ratio can be stated in two ways.

1. Sometimes the conversion ratio is stated in terms of a given number of shares of common stock. To find the **conversion price,** which is the per-share price that is effectively paid for common stock as the result of conversion, divide the *par value* (not the market value) of the convertible security by the conversion ratio.

> **Example**   Western Wear Company, a manufacturer of denim products, has outstanding a bond that has a $1,000 par value and is convertible into 25 shares of common stock. The bond's conversion ratio is 25. The conversion price for the bond is $40 per share ($1,000 ÷ 25).

2. Sometimes, instead of the conversion ratio, the conversion price is given. The conversion ratio can be obtained by dividing the *par value* of the convertible by the conversion price.

> **Example**   Mosher Company, a franchiser of seafood restaurants, has outstanding a convertible 20-year bond with a par value of $1,000. The bond is convertible at $50 per share into common stock. The conversion ratio is 20 ($1,000 ÷ $50).

The issuer of a convertible security normally establishes a conversion ratio or conversion price that *sets the conversion price per share at the time of issuance above the current market price of the firm's stock.* If the prospective purchasers do not expect conversion ever to be feasible, they will purchase a straight security or some other convertible issue.

conversion (or stock) value
The value of a convertible security measured in terms of the market price of the common stock into which it can be converted.

Conversion (or Stock) Value

The **conversion (or stock) value** is the value of the convertible measured in terms of the market price of the common stock into which it can be converted. The conversion value can be found simply by multiplying the conversion ratio by the current market price of the firm's common stock.

Example

McNamara Industries, a petroleum processor, has outstanding a $1,000 bond that is convertible into common stock at $62.50 per share. The conversion ratio is therefore 16 ($1,000 ÷ $62.50). Because the current market price of the common stock is $65 per share, the conversion value is $1,040 (16 × $65). Because the conversion value is above the bond value of $1,000, conversion is a viable option for the owner of the convertible security.

Effect on Earnings

contingent securities
Convertibles, warrants, and stock options. Their presence affects the reporting of a firm's earnings per share (EPS).

The presence of **contingent securities,** which include convertibles as well as warrants (described later in this chapter) and stock options (described in Chapter 1 and later in this chapter), affects the reporting of the firm's earnings per share (EPS). Firms with contingent securities that if converted or exercised would dilute (that is, lower) earnings per share are required to report earnings in two ways—*basic EPS* and *diluted EPS.*

basic EPS
Earnings per share (EPS) calculated without regard to any contingent securities.

Basic EPS are calculated without regard to any contingent securities. They are found by dividing earnings available for common stockholders by the number of shares of common stock outstanding. We use this standard method of calculating EPS throughout this textbook.

diluted EPS
Earnings per share (EPS) calculated under the assumption that *all* contingent securities that would have dilutive effects are converted and exercised and are therefore common stock.

Diluted EPS are calculated under the assumption that *all* contingent securities that would have dilutive effects are converted and exercised and are therefore common stock. They are found by adjusting basic EPS for the impact of converting all convertibles and exercising all warrants and options that would have dilutive effects on the firm's earnings. This approach treats as common stock *all* contingent securities. It is calculated by dividing earnings available for common stockholders (adjusted for interest and preferred stock dividends that would *not* be paid, given assumed conversion of *all* outstanding contingent securities that would have dilutive effects) by the number of shares of common stock that would be outstanding if *all* contingent securities that would have dilutive effects were converted and exercised. Rather than demonstrate these accounting calculations,[10] suffice it to say that firms with outstanding convertibles, warrants, and/or stock options must report basic and diluted EPS on their income statements.

Financing with Convertibles

Using convertible securities to raise long-term funds can help the firm achieve its cost-of-capital and capital structure goals. There also are a number of more specific motives and considerations involved in evaluating convertible financing.

---

10. For excellent discussions and demonstrations of the two methods of reporting EPS, see Donald A. Kieso, Jerry J. Weygandt, and Terry D. Warfield, *Intermediate Accounting,* 12th ed. (New York: John Wiley, 2007), pp. 792–805, 812–816.

Motives for Convertible Financing

Convertibles can be used for a variety of reasons. One popular motive is their use as a form of *deferred common stock financing*. When a convertible security is issued, both issuer and purchaser expect the security to be converted into common stock at some future point. Because the security is first sold with a conversion price above the current market price of the firm's stock, conversion is initially not attractive. The issuer of a convertible could alternatively sell common stock, but only at or below its current market price. By selling the convertible, the issuer in effect makes a *deferred sale* of common stock. As the market price of the firm's common stock rises to a higher level, conversion may occur. Deferring the issuance of new common stock until the market price of the stock has increased means that fewer shares will have to be issued, thereby decreasing the dilution of both ownership and earnings.

Another motive for convertible financing is its *use as a "sweetener" for financing*. Because the purchaser of the convertible is given the opportunity to become a common stockholder and share in the firm's future success, *convertibles can be normally sold with lower interest rates than nonconvertibles*. Therefore, from the firm's viewpoint, including a conversion feature reduces the interest cost of debt. The purchaser of the issue sacrifices a portion of interest return for the potential opportunity to become a common stockholder. Another important motive for issuing convertibles is that, generally speaking, *convertible securities can be issued with far fewer restrictive covenants than nonconvertibles*. Because many investors view convertibles as equity, the covenant issue is not important to them.

A final motive for using convertibles is to *raise cheap funds temporarily*. By using convertible bonds, the firm can temporarily raise debt, which is typically less expensive than common stock, to finance projects. Once such projects are under way, the firm may wish to shift its capital structure to a less highly levered position. A conversion feature gives the issuer the opportunity, through actions of convertible holders, to shift its capital structure at a future time.

Hint Convertible securities are advantageous to both the issuer and the holder. The issuer does not have to give up immediate control as it would have to if it were issuing common stock. The holder of a convertible security has the possibility of a future speculative gain.

Other Considerations

When the price of the firm's common stock rises above the conversion price, the market price of the convertible security will normally rise to a level close to its conversion value. When this happens, many convertible holders will not convert, because they already have the market price benefit obtainable from conversion and can still receive fixed periodic interest payments. Because of this behavior, virtually all convertible securities have a *call feature* that enables the issuer to encourage or *"force" conversion*. The call price of the security generally exceeds the security's par value by an amount equal to 1 year's stated interest on the security. Although the issuer must pay a premium for calling a security, the call privilege is generally not exercised until the conversion value of the security is 10 to 15 percent *above the call price*. This type of premium above the call price helps to assure the issuer that the holders of the convertible will convert it when the call is made, instead of accepting the call price.

Unfortunately, there are instances when the market price of a security does not reach a level sufficient to stimulate the conversion of associated convertibles. A convertible security that cannot be forced into conversion by using the call feature is called an **overhanging issue**. An overhanging issue can be quite detrimental

overhanging issue
A convertible security that cannot be forced into conversion by using the call feature.

to a firm. If the firm were to call the issue, the bondholders would accept the call price rather than convert the bonds. In this case, the firm not only would have to pay the call premium but would also require additional financing to pay off the bonds at their par value. If the firm raised these funds through the sale of equity, a large number of shares would have to be issued because of their low market price. This, in turn, could result in the dilution of existing ownership. Another means of financing the call would be the use of debt or preferred stock, but this use would leave the firm's capital structure no less levered than before the call.

Determining the Value of a Convertible Bond

The key characteristic of convertible securities that enhances their marketability is their ability to minimize the possibility of a loss while providing a possibility of capital gains. Here we discuss the three values of a convertible bond: (1) the straight bond value, (2) the conversion value, and (3) the market value.

Straight Bond Value

straight bond value
The price at which a convertible bond would sell in the market without the conversion feature.

The **straight bond value** of a convertible bond is the price at which it would sell in the market without the conversion feature. This value is found by determining the value of a nonconvertible bond with similar payments issued by a firm with the same risk. The straight bond value is typically the *floor*, or minimum, price at which the convertible bond would be traded. The straight bond value equals the present value of the bond's interest and principal payments discounted at the interest rate the firm would have to pay on a nonconvertible bond.

Example

Duncan Company, a Southeastern discount store chain, has just sold a $1,000-par-value, 20-year convertible bond with a 12% coupon interest rate. The bond interest will be paid at the end of each year, and the principal will be repaid at maturity.[11] A straight bond could have been sold with a 14% coupon interest rate, but the conversion feature compensates for the lower rate on the convertible. The straight bond value of the convertible is calculated as shown:

Year(s)	Payments (1)	Present value interest factor at 14% (2)	Present value [(1) × (2)] (3)
1–20	$ 120[a]	6.623[b]	$794.76
20	1,000	0.073[c]	73.00
		Straight bond value	$867.76

[a]$1,000 at 12% = $120 interest per year.
[b]Present value interest factor for an annuity, *PVIFA*, discounted at 14% for 20 years, from Table A–4.
[c]Present value interest factor for $1, *PVIF*, discounted at 14% for year 20, from Table A–2.

---

11. Just as we did in Chapter 6, we continue to assume the payment of annual rather than semiannual bond interest. This assumption simplifies the calculations involved, while maintaining the conceptual accuracy of the procedures presented.

This value, $867.76, is the minimum price at which the convertible bond is expected to sell. (The value calculated using a financial calculator is $867.54.) Generally, only in certain instances in which the stock's market price is below the conversion price will the bond be expected to sell at this level.

Conversion (or Stock) Value

Recall that the *conversion (or stock) value* of a convertible security is the value of the convertible measured in terms of the market price of the common stock into which the security can be converted. When the market price of the common stock exceeds the conversion price, the conversion (or stock) value exceeds the par value. An example will clarify the point.

Example ▸

Duncan Company's convertible bond described earlier is convertible at $50 per share. Each bond can be converted into 20 shares, because each bond has a $1,000 par value. The conversion values of the bond when the stock is selling at $30, $40, $50, $60, $70, and $80 per share are shown in the following table.

Market price of stock	Conversion value
$30	$ 600
40	800
50 (conversion price)	1,000 (par value)
60	1,200
70	1,400
80	1,600

When the market price of the common stock exceeds the $50 conversion price, the conversion value exceeds the $1,000 par value. Because the straight bond value (calculated in the preceding example) is $867.76, the bond will, in a stable environment, never sell for less than this amount, regardless of how low its conversion value is. If the market price per share were $30, the bond would still sell for $867.76—not $600—because its value as a bond would dominate.

Market Value

market premium
The amount by which the market value exceeds the straight or conversion value of a convertible security.

The market value of a convertible is likely to be greater than its straight value or its conversion value. The amount by which the market value exceeds its straight or conversion value is called the **market premium.** The general relationships among the straight bond value, conversion value, market value, and market premium for Duncan Company's convertible bond are shown in Figure 16.1. The straight bond value acts as a floor for the security's value up to the point X, where the stock price is high enough to cause the conversion value to exceed the straight bond value. The market premium is attributed to the fact that the convertible gives investors a chance to experience attractive capital gains from increases in the stock price, while taking less risk. The floor (straight bond value) provides protection against losses resulting from a decline in the stock price caused by falling profits or other factors. The market premium tends to be greatest when the straight bond value and conversion (or stock) value are nearly

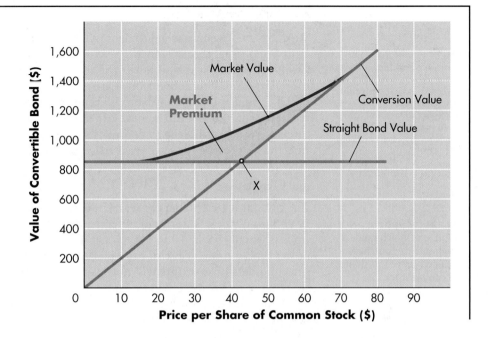

FIGURE 16.1

Values and Market Premium

The values and market premium for Duncan Company's convertible bond

equal. Investors perceive the benefits of these two sources of value to be greatest at this point.

REVIEW QUESTIONS

16–6   What is the *conversion feature?* What is a *conversion ratio?* How do convertibles and other *contingent securities* affect EPS? Briefly describe the motives for convertible financing.

16–7   When the market price of the stock rises above the conversion price, why may a convertible security *not* be converted? How can the *call feature* be used to force conversion in this situation? What is an *overhanging issue?*

16–8   Define the *straight bond value, conversion (or stock) value, market value,* and *market premium* associated with a convertible bond, and describe the general relationships among them.

 16.4 | Stock Purchase Warrants

stock purchase warrant
An instrument that gives its holder the right to purchase a certain number of shares of common stock at a specified price over a certain period of time.

Stock purchase warrants are similar to stock *rights,* which were briefly described in Chapter 7. A **stock purchase warrant** gives the holder the right to purchase a certain number of shares of common stock at a specified price over a certain period of time. (Of course, holders of warrants earn no income from them until the warrants are exercised or sold.) Warrants also bear some similarity to convertibles in that they provide for the injection of additional equity capital into the firm at some future date.

Key Characteristics

Warrants are often attached to debt issues as "sweeteners." When a firm makes a large bond issue, the attachment of stock purchase warrants may add to the marketability of the issue and lower the required interest rate. As sweeteners, warrants are similar to conversion features. Often, when a new firm is raising its initial capital, suppliers of debt will require warrants to permit them to share in whatever success the firm achieves. In addition, established companies sometimes offer warrants with debt to compensate for risk and thereby lower the interest rate and/or provide for fewer *restrictive covenants*.

Exercise Prices

exercise (or option) price
The price at which holders of warrants can purchase a specified number of shares of common stock.

The price at which holders of warrants can purchase a specified number of shares of common stock is normally referred to as the **exercise (or option) price**. This price is usually set at 10 to 20 percent above the market price of the firm's stock at the time of issuance. Until the market price of the stock exceeds the exercise price, holders of warrants will not exercise them, because they can purchase the stock more inexpensively in the marketplace.

Warrants normally have a life of no more than 10 years, although some have infinite lives. Although, unlike convertible securities, warrants cannot be called, their limited life stimulates holders to exercise them when the exercise price is below the market price of the firm's stock.

Warrant Trading

A warrant is usually *detachable*, which means that the bondholder may sell the warrant without selling the security to which it is attached. Many detachable warrants are actively traded in both broker and dealer markets. Many actively traded warrants are listed on the American Stock Exchange. Warrants often provide investors with better opportunities for gain (with increased risk) than the underlying common stock.

Comparison of Warrants to Rights and Convertibles

The similarity between a warrant and a right should be clear. Both result in new equity capital, although the warrant provides for *deferred* equity financing. The life of a right is typically not more than a few months; a warrant is generally exercisable for a period of years. Rights are issued at a subscription price *below* the prevailing market price of the stock; warrants are generally issued at an exercise price 10 to 20 percent *above* the prevailing market price.

Warrants and convertibles also have similarities. The exercise of a warrant shifts the firm's capital structure to a less highly levered position because new common stock is issued without any change in debt. If a convertible bond were converted, the reduction in leverage would be even more pronounced, because common stock would be issued in exchange for a reduction in debt. In addition, the exercise of a warrant provides an influx of new capital; with convertibles, the new capital is raised when the securities are originally issued rather than when they are converted. The influx of new equity capital resulting from the exercise of a warrant does not occur until the firm has achieved a certain degree of success that is reflected in an increased price for its stock. In this case, the firm conveniently obtains needed funds.

Implied Price of an Attached Warrant

implied price of a warrant
The price effectively paid for each warrant attached to a bond.

When warrants are attached to a bond, the **implied price of a warrant**—the price that is effectively paid for each attached warrant—can be found by first using Equation 16.1:

$$\frac{\text{Implied price of}}{\text{all warrants}} = \frac{\text{Price of bond with}}{\text{warrants attached}} - \text{Straight bond value} \quad (16.1)$$

The straight bond value is found in a fashion similar to that used in valuing convertible bonds. Dividing the implied price of *all* warrants by the number of warrants attached to each bond results in the implied price of *each* warrant.

Example

Martin Marine Products, a manufacturer of marine drive shafts and propellers, just issued a 10.5%-coupon-interest-rate, $1,000-par, 20-year bond paying annual interest and having 20 warrants attached for the purchase of the firm's stock. The bonds were initially sold for their $1,000 par value. When issued, similar-risk straight bonds were selling to yield a 12% rate of return. The straight value of the bond would be the present value of its payments discounted at the 12% yield on similar-risk straight bonds.

Year(s)	Payments (1)	Present value interest factor at 12% (2)	Present value[a] [(1) × (2)] (3)
1–20	$ 105[b]	7.469[c]	$784
20	1,000	0.104[d]	104
		Straight bond value[e]	$888

[a]For convenience, these values have been rounded to the nearest $1.
[b]$1,000 at 10.5% = $105 interest per year.
[c]Present value interest factor for an annuity, *PVIFA*, discounted at 12% for 20 years, from Table A–4.
[d]Present value interest factor for $1, *PVIF*, discounted at 12% for year 20, from Table A–2.
[e]The value calculated by using a financial calculator and rounding to the nearest $1 is also $888.

Substituting the $1,000 price of the bond with warrants attached and the $888 straight bond value into Equation 16.1, we get an implied price of *all* warrants of $112:

$$\text{Implied price of } all \text{ warrants} = \$1,000 - \$888 = \underline{\$112}$$

Dividing the implied price of *all* warrants by the number of warrants attached to each bond—20 in this case—we find the implied price of *each* warrant:

$$\text{Implied price of } each \text{ warrant} = \frac{\$112}{20} = \underline{\$5.60}$$

Therefore, by purchasing Martin Marine Products' bond with warrants attached for $1,000, one is effectively paying $5.60 for each warrant.

The implied price of each warrant is meaningful only when compared to the specific features of the warrant—the number of shares that can be purchased and the specified exercise price. These features can be analyzed in light of the prevailing common stock price to estimate the true *market value* of each warrant. Clearly, if the implied price is above the estimated market value, the price of the bond with warrants attached may be too high. If the implied price is below the estimated market value, the bond may be quite attractive. Firms must therefore price their bonds with warrants attached in a way that causes the implied price of its warrants to fall slightly below their estimated market value. Such an approach allows the firm to sell the bonds more easily at a lower coupon interest rate than would apply to straight debt, thereby reducing its debt service costs.

Values of Warrants

warrant premium
The difference between the market value and the theoretical value of a warrant.

Like a convertible security, a warrant has both a market value and a theoretical value. The difference between these values, or the **warrant premium**, depends largely on investor expectations and on the ability of investors to get more leverage from the warrants than from the underlying stock.

Theoretical Value of a Warrant

The *theoretical value* of a stock purchase warrant is the amount one would expect the warrant to sell for in the marketplace. Equation 16.2 gives the theoretical value of a warrant:

$$TVW = (P_0 - E) \times N \tag{16.2}$$

where

TVW = theoretical value of a warrant
P_0 = current market price of a share of common stock
E = exercise price of the warrant
N = number of shares of common stock obtainable with one warrant

The use of Equation 16.2 can be illustrated by the following example.

Example

Dustin Electronics, a major producer of transistors, has outstanding warrants that are exercisable at $40 per share and entitle holders to purchase three shares of common stock. The warrants were initially attached to a bond issue to sweeten the bond. The common stock of the firm is currently selling for $45 per share. Substituting $P_0 = \$45$, $E = \$40$, and $N = 3$ into Equation 16.2 yields a theoretical warrant value of $15 [(\$45 - \$40) \times 3]$. Therefore, Dustin's warrants should sell for $15 in the marketplace.

Market Value of a Warrant

The market value of a stock purchase warrant is generally above the theoretical value of the warrant. Only when the theoretical value of the warrant is very high or the warrant is near its expiration date are the market and theoretical values close. The general relationship between the theoretical and market values of Dustin Electronics' warrants is presented graphically in Figure 16.2. The market value of warrants generally exceeds the theoretical value by the greatest amount when the stock's market price is close to the warrant exercise price per share. The

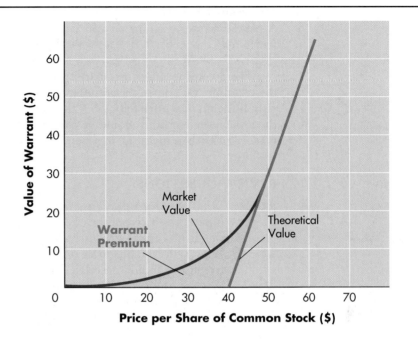

FIGURE 16.2

Values and Warrant Premium

The values and warrant premium for Dustin Electronics' stock purchase warrants

amount of time until expiration also affects the market value of the warrant. Generally speaking, the closer the warrant is to its expiration date, the more likely that its market value will equal its theoretical value.

Warrant Premium

The *warrant premium,* or the amount by which the market value of Dustin Electronics' warrants exceeds the theoretical value of these warrants, is also shown in Figure 16.2. This premium results from a combination of positive investor expectations and the ability of the investor with a fixed sum to invest to obtain much larger potential returns (and risk) by trading in warrants rather than the underlying stock.

Personal Finance Example   Stan Buyer has $2,430, which he is interested in investing in Dustin Electronics. The firm's stock is currently selling for $45 per share, and its warrants are selling for $18 per warrant. Each warrant entitles the holder to purchase three shares of Dustin's common stock at $40 per share. Because the stock is selling for $45 per share, the theoretical warrant value, calculated in the preceding example, is $15 [($45 − $40) × 3].

The warrant premium results from positive investor expectations and leverage opportunities. Stan Buyer could spend his $2,430 in either of two ways: He could purchase 54 shares of common stock at $45 per share, or 135 warrants at $18 per warrant, ignoring brokerage fees. If Mr. Buyer purchases the stock and its price rises to $48, he will gain $162 ($3 per share × 54 shares) by selling the stock. If instead he purchases the 135 warrants and the stock price increases by $3 per share, Mr. Buyer will gain approximately $1,215. Because the price of a share of stock rises by $3, the price of each warrant can be expected to rise by

$9 (because each warrant can be used to purchase three shares of common stock). A gain of $9 per warrant on 135 warrants means a total gain of $1,215 on the warrants.

The greater leverage associated with trading warrants should be clear from the example. Of course, because leverage works both ways, it results in greater risk. If the market price fell by $3, the loss on the stock would be $162, whereas the loss on the warrants would be close to $1,215. Clearly, investing in warrants is more risky than investing in the underlying stock.

REVIEW QUESTIONS

16–9   What are *stock purchase warrants?* What are the similarities and key differences between the effects of warrants and those of convertibles on the firm's capital structure and its ability to raise new capital?

16–10   What is the *implied price of a warrant?* How is it estimated? To be effective, how should it be related to the estimated *market value* of a warrant?

16–11   What is the general relationship between the theoretical and market values of a warrant? In what circumstances are these values quite close? What is a *warrant premium?*

16.5 | Options

option
An instrument that provides its holder with an opportunity to purchase or sell a specified asset at a stated price on or before a set *expiration date.*

In the most general sense, an **option** can be viewed as an instrument that provides its holder with an opportunity to purchase or sell a specified asset at a stated price on or before a set *expiration date.* Options are probably the most popular type of *derivative security.* Today, the interest in options centers on options on common stock.[12] The development of organized options exchanges has created markets in which to trade these options, which themselves are securities. Three basic forms of options are rights, warrants, and calls and puts. Rights are discussed in Chapter 7, and warrants were described in the preceding section.

Calls and Puts

call option
An option to *purchase* a specified number of shares of a stock (typically 100) on or before a specified future date at a stated price.

striking price
The price at which the holder of a call option can buy (or the holder of a put option can sell) a specified amount of stock at any time prior to the option's expiration date.

The two most common types of options are calls and puts. A **call option** is an option to *purchase* a specified number of shares of a stock (typically 100) on or before a specified future date at a stated price. Call options usually have initial lives of 1 to 9 months, occasionally 1 year. The **striking price** is the price at which the holder of the option can buy a specified amount of stock at any time prior to the option's expiration date; it is generally set at or near the prevailing market price of the stock at the time the option is issued. For example, if a firm's stock is

---

12. *Real* options—opportunities embedded in capital projects that enable management to alter their cash flows and risk—were discussed in Chapter 10. The *options* described here differ from real options; they are a type of derivative security that derives its value from an underlying financial asset, typically common stock. Although some of the analytical tools used to value both types of options are similar, the focus here is merely on the definitional aspects of options. The models used to value these options are typically discussed in more advanced financial management textbooks.

currently selling for $50 per share, a call option on the stock initiated today will probably have a striking price set at $50 per share. One must pay a specified price (normally a few hundred dollars) to purchase a call option.

put option
An option to *sell* a specified number of shares of a stock (typically 100) on or before a specified future date at a stated price.

A **put option** is an option to *sell* a specified number of shares of a stock (typically 100) on or before a specified future date at a stated striking price. Like the call option, the striking price of the put is set close to the market price of the underlying stock at the time of issuance. The lives and costs of puts are similar to those of calls.

Options Markets

There are two ways of making options transactions. The first involves making a transaction through one of 20 or so call and put options dealers with the help of a stockbroker. The other, more popular mechanism is the organized options exchanges. The dominant exchange is the *Chicago Board Options Exchange (CBOE),* which was established in 1973. Other exchanges on which options are traded include the International Securities Exchange (ISE), the American Stock Exchange, and the Philadelphia Stock Exchange. The options traded on these exchanges are standardized and thus are considered registered securities. Each option is for 100 shares of the underlying stock. The price at which options transactions can be made is determined by the forces of supply and demand.

Options Trading

The most common motive for purchasing call options is the expectation that the market price of the underlying stock will *rise* by more than enough to cover the cost of the option, thereby allowing the purchaser of the call to profit.

Personal Finance Example   Assume that Cindy Peters pays $250 for a 3-month *call option* on Wing Enterprises, a maker of aircraft components, at a striking price of $50. This means that by paying $250, Cindy is guaranteed that she can purchase 100 shares of Wing at $50 per share at any time during the next 3 months. The stock price must climb $2.50 per share ($250 ÷ 100 shares) to $52.50 per share to cover the cost of the option (ignoring any brokerage fees or dividends). If the stock price were to rise to $60 per share during the period, Cindy's net profit would be $750 [(100 shares × $60/share) − (100 shares × $50/share) − $250].

Because this return would be earned on a $250 investment, it illustrates the high potential return on investment that options offer. Of course, had the stock price not risen above $50 per share, Cindy would have lost the $250 she invested, because there would have been no reason to exercise the option. Had the stock price risen to between $50 and $52.50 per share, Cindy probably would have exercised the option to reduce her loss to an amount less than $250.

Hint Put and call options are created by individuals and other firms. The firm itself has nothing to do with the creation of these options. Convertibles and warrants, by contrast, are created by the issuing firm.

Put options are purchased in the expectation that the share price of a given security will *decline* over the life of the option. Purchasers of puts commonly own the shares and wish to protect a gain they have realized since their initial purchase. Buying a put locks in the gain because it enables them to sell their shares at a known price during the life of the option. Investors gain from put options when the price of the underlying stock declines by more than the per-share cost of the option. The logic underlying the purchase of a put is exactly the opposite of that underlying the use of call options.

Personal Finance Example   Assume that Don Kelly pays $325 for a 6-month *put option* on Dante United, a baked goods manufacturer, at a striking price of $40. Don purchased the put option in expectation that the stock price would drop because of the introduction of a new product line by Dante's chief competitor. By paying $325, Don is assured that he can sell 100 shares of Dante at $40 per share at any time during the next 6 months. The stock price must drop by $3.25 per share ($325 ÷ 100 shares) to $36.75 per share to cover the cost of the option (ignoring any brokerage fees or dividends). If the stock price were to drop to $30 per share during the period, Don's net profit would be $675 [(100 shares × $40/share) − (100 shares × $30/share) − $325].

Because the return would be earned on a $325 investment, it again illustrates the high potential return on investment that options offer. Of course, had the stock price risen above $40 per share, Don would have lost the $325 he invested, because there would have been no reason to exercise the option. Had the stock price fallen to between $36.75 and $40.00 per share, Don probably would have exercised the option to reduce his loss to an amount less than $325.

Role of Call and Put Options in Fund Raising

Although call and put options are extremely popular investment vehicles, they play *no* direct role in the fund-raising activities of the financial manager. These options are issued by investors, not businesses. *They are not a source of financing to the firm.* Corporate pension managers, whose job it is to invest and manage corporate pension funds, may use call and put options as part of their investment activities to earn a return or to protect or lock in returns already earned on securities. The presence of options trading in the firm's stock could—by increasing trading activity—stabilize the firm's share price in the marketplace, but the financial manager has no direct control over this. Buyers of options have neither any say in the firm's management nor any voting rights; only stockholders are given these privileges. Despite the popularity of call and put options as an investment vehicle, the financial manager has very little need to deal with them, especially as part of fund-raising activities.

Employee stock options are a form of call options. As the *Focus on Ethics* box on page 745 discusses, a number of companies and company executives have skated close to, or over, the ethical edge with regard to backdating of options.

 ## Hedging Foreign-Currency Exposures with Options

The Chicago Mercantile Exchange (CME) and the Philadelphia Stock Exchange (PHLX) offer exchange-traded options contracts on the Canadian dollar, the euro, the Japanese yen, the Swiss franc, and several other important currencies. *Currency options* are used by a wide range of traders, from the largest multinational companies to small exporters and importers, as well as by individual investors and speculators. Unlike futures and forward contracts, options offer the

Focus on Ethics   Options Backdating

IN PRACTICE

Granting stock options to key employees was a popular practice in the dot-com heyday. Start-up companies could offer stock options to employees in the expectation that the options would be worth a great deal if the company took off. Indeed, that proved true for many people in high-tech fields. However, the SEC recognized that stock options were liable to misuse, and in 1992 it imposed a rule requiring companies to report executive stock options in detail.

One possible abuse of stock options involves *backdating—* granting an employee stock option that is dated *prior* to the date the company actually granted the option. By backdating an option, a company assigns a lower value to the option, which gives the holder of the option more money when he or she exercises the option. Many stockholders view this as essentially unfair; after all, stockholders cannot reprice their shares to improve their returns.

In 2004, finance professor Erik Lie of the University of Iowa conducted a study in which he noted that many options grants were timed to exploit market-wide price depressions that nobody, including insiders, could predict. His conclusion was that at least some of the grants must have been backdated. The SEC subsequently conducted a year-long investigation and began to crack down on companies with questionable policies governing stock-option grants. By late 2006, at least 135 companies, according to the *Washington Post,* were being probed by the SEC for backdating irregularities. As a result of the increased scrutiny, a number of top-level executives at a variety of companies either resigned or were fired. A number of companies announced that they would have to issue a restatement of prior results to record charges against earnings that should have been recorded when the options were granted.

While backdating of options is not necessarily illegal, the issues relating to backdating of options involve failure to provide full disclosure to shareholders, failure to pay extra applicable taxes, and earnings statements that should have reflected the modified grant dates. Any of these three issues could yield civil (and perhaps criminal) legal action.

Fortunately, accelerated reporting requirements have made unreported backdating more difficult. Section 403 of the Sarbanes-Oxley Act of 2002 now requires that directors and officers report options grants to the SEC within 2 business days, instead of within weeks and months as allowed under the prior law.

■ *Despite the negatives of the options backdating scandal, stock options have beneficial uses. List several appropriate uses of stock options.*

hedging
Offsetting or protecting against the risk of adverse price movements.

key benefit of **hedging,** which involves offsetting or protecting against the risk of adverse price movements, while simultaneously preserving the possibility of profiting from favorable price movements. The key drawback to using options to hedge foreign-currency exposures is their high cost relative to using more traditional futures or forward contracts.

Example

Assume that a U.S. exporter just booked a sale denominated in Swiss francs with payment due upon delivery in 3 months. The company could hedge the risk of depreciation in the dollar by purchasing a Swiss franc put option. This would give the company the right to sell Swiss francs at a fixed price (say, $0.83/Sf). This option would become valuable if the Swiss franc were to depreciate from today's $0.86/Sf to, say, $0.78/Sf before the exporter receives payment in Swiss francs. On the other hand, if the Swiss franc were to appreciate from $0.86/Sf to, say,

$0.93/Sf, the U.S. exporter would allow the put option to expire unexercised and would instead convert the Swiss francs received in payment into dollars at the new, higher dollar price. The exporter would be protected from adverse price risk but would still be able to profit from favorable price movements.

REVIEW QUESTIONS

16–12 What is an *option?* Define *calls* and *puts.* What role, if any, do call and put options play in the fund-raising activities of the financial manager?

16–13 How can the firm use currency options to *hedge* foreign-currency exposures resulting from international transactions? Describe the key benefit and the key drawback of using currency options rather than futures and forward contracts.

Summary

Focus on Value

In addition to the basic corporate securities, the firm can use various types of hybrid securities to improve its fund-raising activities. These securities, which possess characteristics of both debt and equity, enable the firm to raise funds at less cost or to provide for desired future changes in the firm's capital structure.

Leasing, particularly financial (capital) leases, may enable the firm to use the lease as a substitute for the debt-financed purchase of a given asset, with more attractive risk–return tradeoffs. Similarly, by issuing convertible rather than straight debt or by attaching stock purchase warrants to a bond issue or debt financing, the firm may provide lenders with the potential to benefit from stock price movements in exchange for a lower interest rate or less restrictive covenants in the bond or debt agreement. Although options are not a source of financing to the firm, this derivative security can help stabilize the firm's share price. Currency options can be used to hedge adverse currency movements in international transactions.

Clearly, the financial manager should use hybrid and derivative securities to increase return (often by lowering financing costs) and reduce risk. By taking only those actions believed to result in attractive risk–return tradeoffs, the financial manager can positively contribute to the firm's goal of **maximizing the stock price.**

Review of Learning Goals

LG 1 **Differentiate between hybrid and derivative securities and their roles in the corporation.** Hybrid securities are forms of debt or equity financing that possess characteristics of both debt and equity financing. Popular hybrid securities include preferred stock, financial leases, convertible securities, and stock purchase warrants. Derivative securities are neither debt nor equity and derive their value from an underlying asset that is often another security. Options are a popular derivative security.

LG 2 **Review the types of leases, leasing arrangements, the lease-versus-purchase decision, the effects of leasing on future financing, and the advantages and disadvantages of leasing.** A lease enables the firm to make contractual, tax-deductible payments to obtain the use of fixed assets. Operating leases are generally 5 or fewer years in term, cancelable, and renewable, and they provide for maintenance by the lessor. Financial leases are longer-term, noncancelable, and not renewable, and they nearly always require the lessee to maintain the asset. *FASB Statement No. 13* provides specific guidelines for defining a financial (capital) lease. A lessor can obtain assets to be leased through a direct lease, a sale–leaseback arrangement, or a leveraged lease. The lease-versus-purchase decision can be evaluated by calculating the after-tax cash outflows associated with the leasing and purchasing alternatives. The more desirable alternative is the one that has the lower present value of after-tax cash outflows. *FASB Statement No. 13* requires firms to show financial leases as assets and corresponding liabilities on their balance sheets; operating leases must be shown in footnotes to the financial statements. Advantages and disadvantages should be considered when making lease-versus-purchase decisions.

LG 3 **Describe the types of convertible securities, their general features, and financing with convertibles.** Corporate bonds and preferred stock may both be convertible into common stock. The conversion ratio indicates the number of shares for which a convertible can be exchanged and determines the conversion price. A conversion privilege is nearly always available at any time in the life of the security. The conversion (or stock) value is the value of the convertible measured in terms of the market price of the common stock into which it can be converted. The presence of convertibles and other contingent securities (warrants and stock options) often requires the firm to report both basic and diluted earnings per share (EPS). Convertibles are used to obtain deferred common stock financing, to "sweeten" bond issues, to minimize restrictive covenants, and to raise cheap funds temporarily. The call feature is sometimes used to encourage or "force" conversion; occasionally, an overhanging issue results.

LG 4 **Demonstrate the procedures for determining the straight bond value, the conversion (or stock) value, and the market value of a convertible bond.** The straight bond value of a convertible is the price at which it would sell in the market without the conversion feature. It typically represents the minimum value at which a convertible bond trades. The conversion value is found by multiplying the conversion ratio by the current market price of the underlying common stock. The market value of a convertible generally exceeds both its straight and conversion values, resulting in a market premium. The premium is largest when the straight and conversion values are nearly equal.

LG 5 **Explain the key characteristics of stock purchase warrants, the implied price of an attached warrant, and the values of warrants.** Stock purchase warrants enable their holders to purchase a certain number of shares of common stock at the specified exercise price. Warrants are often attached to debt issues as "sweeteners," generally have limited lives, are detachable, and may be traded in broker and dealer markets. Warrants are similar to stock rights, except that the exercise price of a warrant is initially set above the underlying stock's current market price. Warrants are similar to convertibles, but exercising them has a less pronounced effect on the firm's leverage and brings in new funds. The implied price of an attached warrant can be found by dividing the difference between the bond price with warrants attached and the straight bond value by the number of warrants attached to each bond. The market value of a warrant usually exceeds its theoretical value, creating a warrant premium. Investors generally get more leverage from trading warrants than from trading the underlying stock.

LG 6   **Define options and discuss calls and puts, options markets, options trading, the role of call and put options in fund raising, and hedging foreign-currency exposures with options.** An option provides its holder with an opportunity to purchase or sell a specified asset at a stated price on or before a set expiration date. Rights, warrants, and calls and puts are all options. Calls are options to purchase common stock, and puts are options to sell common stock. Options exchanges provide organized marketplaces in which purchases and sales of call and put options can be made. The options traded on the exchanges are standardized, and the prices at which they trade are determined by the forces of supply and demand. Call and put options do not play a direct role in the fund-raising activities of the financial manager. Currency options can be used to hedge the firm's foreign-currency exposures resulting from international transactions.

Self-Test Problems (Solutions in Appendix B)

ST16–1   Lease versus purchase   The Hot Bagel Shop wishes to evaluate two plans for financing an oven: leasing and borrowing to purchase. The firm is in the 40% tax bracket.

Lease   The shop can lease the oven under a 5-year lease requiring annual end-of-year payments of $5,000. All maintenance costs will be paid by the lessor, and insurance and other costs will be borne by the lessee. The lessee will exercise its option to purchase the asset for $4,000 at termination of the lease.

Purchase   The oven costs $20,000 and will have a 5-year life. It will be depreciated under MACRS using a 5-year recovery period. (See Table 3.2 on page 108 for the applicable depreciation percentages.) The total purchase price will be financed by a 5-year, 15% loan requiring equal annual end-of-year payments of $5,967. The firm will pay $1,000 per year for a service contract that covers all maintenance costs; insurance and other costs will be borne by the firm. The firm plans to keep the equipment and use it beyond its 5-year recovery period.

a. For the leasing plan, calculate the following:
   (1) The after-tax cash outflow each year.
   (2) The present value of the cash outflows, using a 9% *discount rate*.
b. For the purchasing plan, calculate the following:
   (1) The annual interest expense deductible for tax purposes for each of the 5 years.
   (2) The after-tax cash outflow resulting from the purchase for each of the 5 years.
   (3) The present value of the cash outflows, using a 9% *discount rate*.

c. Compare the present values of the cash outflow streams for these two plans, and determine which plan would be preferable. Explain your answer.

 ST16–2 **Finding convertible bond values** Mountain Mining Company has an outstanding issue of convertible bonds with a $1,000 par value. These bonds are convertible into 40 shares of common stock. They have an 11% annual coupon interest rate and a 25-year maturity. The interest rate on a straight bond of similar risk is currently 13%.

a. Calculate the *straight bond value* of the bond.
b. Calculate the *conversion (or stock) value* of the bond when the market price of the common stock is $20, $25, $28, $35, and $50 per share.
c. For each of the stock prices given in part **b**, at what price would you expect the bond to sell? Why?
d. What is the least you would expect the bond to sell for, regardless of the common stock price behavior?

Warm-Up Exercises   A blue box (■) indicates exercises available in .

 E16–1 N and M Corp. is considering leasing a new machine for $25,000 per year. The lease arrangement calls for a 5-year lease with an option to purchase the machine at the end of the lease for $3,500. The firm is in the 34% tax bracket. What is the present value of the lease outflows, including the purchase option, if lease payments are made at the end of each year and if the after-tax cost of debt is 7%?

 E16–2 During the past 2 years Meacham Industries issued three separate convertible bonds. For each of them, calculate the *conversion price.*

a. A $1,000-par-value bond that is convertible into 10 shares of common stock.
b. A $2,000-par-value bond that is convertible into 20 shares of common stock.
c. A $1,500-par-value bond that is convertible into 30 shares of common stock.

 E16–3 Newcomb Company has a bond outstanding with a $1,500 par value and convertible at $30 per share. What is the bond's *conversion ratio?* If the underlying stock currently trades at $25 per share, what is the bond's *conversion value?* Would it be advisable for a bondholder to exercise the conversion option?

 E16–4 Crystal Cafes recently sold a $2,000-par-value, 10-year convertible bond with an 8% coupon interest rate. The interest payments will be paid annually at the end of each year and the principal will be repaid at maturity. A similar bond without a conversion feature would have sold with a 9% coupon interest rate. What is the minimum price that the Crystal Cafes' convertible bond should sell for?

 E16–5 A 6-month call option on 100 shares of SRS Corp. stock is selling for $300. The striking price for the option is $40. The stock is currently selling at $38 per share. Ignoring brokerage fees, what price must the stock achieve to just cover the expense of the option? If the stock price rises to $45, what will the net profit on the option contract be?

Problems

A blue box (■) indicates problems available in ⟨⟩myfinancelab.

P16–1   Lease cash flows   Given the lease payments and terms shown in the following table, determine the *yearly after-tax cash outflows* for each firm, assuming that lease payments are made at the end of each year and that the firm is in the 40% tax bracket. Assume that no purchase option exists.

Firm	Annual lease payment	Term of lease
A	$100,000	4 years
B	80,000	14
C	150,000	8
D	60,000	25
E	20,000	10

P16–2   Loan interest   For each of the loan amounts, interest rates, annual payments, and loan terms shown in the following table, calculate the *annual interest paid* each year over the term of the loan, assuming that the payments are made at the end of each year.

Loan	Amount	Interest rate	Annual payment	Term
A	$14,000	10%	$ 4,416	4 years
B	17,500	12	10,355	2
C	2,400	13	1,017	3
D	49,000	14	14,273	5
E	26,500	16	7,191	6

P16–3   Loan payments and interest   Schuyler Company wishes to purchase an asset costing $117,000. The full amount needed to finance the asset can be borrowed at 14% interest. The terms of the loan require equal end-of-year payments for the next 6 years. Determine the total annual loan payment, and break it into the amount of interest and the amount of principal paid for each year. (*Hint:* Use the techniques presented in Chapter 4 to find the loan payment.)

P16–4   Lease versus purchase   JLB Corporation is attempting to determine whether to lease or purchase research equipment. The firm is in the 40% tax bracket, and its after-tax cost of debt is currently 8%. The terms of the lease and of the purchase are as follows:

Lease   Annual end-of-year lease payments of $25,200 are required over the 3-year life of the lease. All maintenance costs will be paid by the lessor; insurance and other costs will be borne by the lessee. The lessee will exercise its option to purchase the asset for $5,000 at termination of the lease.

Purchase   The research equipment, costing $60,000, can be financed entirely with a 14% loan requiring annual end-of-year payments of $25,844 for 3 years. The firm in this case will depreciate the equipment under MACRS using a 3-year recovery period. (See Table 3.2 on page 108 for the applicable depreciation percentages.) The firm will pay $1,800 per year for a service contract that covers all maintenance costs; insurance and other costs will be borne by the firm. The firm plans to keep the equipment and use it beyond its 3-year recovery period.

a. Calculate the *after-tax cash outflows* associated with each alternative.
b. Calculate the present value of each cash outflow stream, using the after-tax cost of debt.
c. Which alternative—lease or purchase—would you recommend? Why?

 P16–5   **Lease versus purchase**   Northwest Lumber Company needs to expand its facilities. To do so, the firm must acquire a machine costing $80,000. The machine can be leased or purchased. The firm is in the 40% tax bracket, and its after-tax cost of debt is 9%. The terms of the lease and purchase plans are as follows:

Lease   The leasing arrangement requires end-of-year payments of $19,800 over 5 years. All maintenance costs will be paid by the lessor; insurance and other costs will be borne by the lessee. The lessee will exercise its option to purchase the asset for $24,000 at termination of the lease.

Purchase   If the firm purchases the machine, its cost of $80,000 will be financed with a 5-year, 14% loan requiring equal end-of-year payments of $23,302. The machine will be depreciated under MACRS using a 5-year recovery period. (See Table 3.2 on page 108 for the applicable depreciation percentages.) The firm will pay $2,000 per year for a service contract that covers all maintenance costs; insurance and other costs will be borne by the firm. The firm plans to keep the equipment and use it beyond its 5-year recovery period.

a. Determine the *after-tax cash outflows* of Northwest Lumber under each alternative.
b. Find the present value of each after-tax cash outflow stream, using the after-tax cost of debt.
c. Which alternative—lease or purchase—would you recommend? Why?

PERSONAL FINANCE PROBLEM

 Lease-versus-purchase decision   Joanna Browne is considering either leasing or purchasing a new Chrysler Sebring convertible that has a manufacturer's suggested retail price (MSRP) of $33,000. The dealership offers a 3-year lease that requires a capital payment of $3,300 ($3,000 down payment + $300 security deposit) and monthly payments of $494. Purchasing requires a $2,640 down payment, sales tax of 6.5% ($2,145), and 36 monthly payments of $784. Joanna estimates the value of the car will be $17,000 at the end of 3 years. She can earn 5% annual interest on her savings and is subject to a 6.5% sales tax on purchases.

Make a reasonable recommendation to Joanna using a lease-versus-purchase analysis that, for simplicity, ignores the time value of money.

a. Calculate the total cost of leasing.
b. Calculate the total cost of purchasing.
c. Which should Joanna do?

P16–7 **Capitalized lease values** Given the lease payments, terms remaining until the leases expire, and discount rates shown in the following table, calculate the *capitalized value* of each lease, assuming that lease payments are made annually at the end of each year.

Lease	Lease payment	Remaining term	Discount rate
A	$ 40,000	12 years	10%
B	120,000	8	12
C	9,000	18	14
D	16,000	3	9
E	47,000	20	11

 P16–8 **Conversion price** Calculate the *conversion price* for each of the following convertible bonds:
a. A $1,000-par-value bond that is convertible into 20 shares of common stock.
b. A $500-par-value bond that is convertible into 25 shares of common stock.
c. A $1,000-par-value bond that is convertible into 50 shares of common stock.

 P16–9 **Conversion ratio** What is the *conversion ratio* for each of the following bonds?
a. A $1,000-par-value bond that is convertible into common stock at $43.75 per share.
b. A $1,000-par-value bond that is convertible into common stock at $25 per share.
c. A $600-par-value bond that is convertible into common stock at $30 per share.

 P16–10 **Conversion (or stock) value** What is the *conversion (or stock) value* of each of the following convertible bonds?
a. A $1,000-par-value bond that is convertible into 25 shares of common stock. The common stock is currently selling for $50 per share.
b. A $1,000-par-value bond that is convertible into 12.5 shares of common stock. The common stock is currently selling for $42 per share.
c. A $1,000-par-value bond that is convertible into 100 shares of common stock. The common stock is currently selling for $10.50 per share.

 P16–11 **Conversion (or stock) value** Find the *conversion (or stock) value* for each of the $1,000-par-value convertible bonds described in the following table.

Convertible	Conversion ratio	Current market price of stock
A	25	$42.25
B	16	50.00
C	20	44.00
D	5	19.50

 P16–12 **Straight bond value** Calculate the *straight bond value* for each of the bonds shown in the table on page 753.

Bond	Par value	Coupon interest rate (paid annually)	Interest rate on equal-risk straight bond	Years to maturity
A	$1,000	10%	14%	20
B	800	12	15	14
C	1,000	13	16	30
D	1,000	14	17	25

P16–13 **Determining values—Convertible bond** Eastern Clock Company has an outstanding issue of convertible bonds with a $1,000 par value. These bonds are convertible into 50 shares of common stock. They have a 10% annual coupon interest rate and a 20-year maturity. The interest rate on a straight bond of similar risk is currently 12%.
  a. Calculate the *straight bond value* of the bond.
  b. Calculate the *conversion (or stock) value* of the bond when the market price of the common stock is $15, $20, $23, $30, and $45 per share.
  c. For each of the stock prices given in part **b,** at what price would you expect the bond to sell? Why?
  d. What is the least you would expect the bond to sell for, regardless of the common stock price behavior?

P16–14 **Determining values—Convertible bond** Craig's Cake Company has an outstanding issue of 15-year convertible bonds with a $1,000 par value. These bonds are convertible into 80 shares of common stock. They have a 13% annual coupon interest rate, whereas the interest rate on straight bonds of similar risk is 16%.
  a. Calculate the *straight bond value* of this bond.
  b. Calculate the *conversion (or stock) value* of the bond when the market price is $9, $12, $13, $15, and $20 per share of common stock.
  c. For each of the common stock prices given in part **b,** at what price would you expect the bond to sell? Why?
  d. Graph the straight value and conversion value of the bond for each common stock price given. Plot the per-share common stock prices on the *x* axis and the bond values on the *y* axis. Use this graph to indicate the minimum market value of the bond associated with each common stock price.

P16–15 **Implied prices of attached warrants** Calculate the implied price of *each* warrant for each of the bonds shown in the following table.

Bond	Price of bond with warrants attached	Par value	Coupon interest rate (paid annually)	Interest rate on equal-risk straight bond	Years to maturity	Number of warrants attached to bond
A	$1,000	$1,000	12 %	13%	15	10
B	1,100	1,000	9.5	12	10	30
C	500	500	10	11	20	5
D	1,000	1,000	11	12	20	20

P16–16 **Evaluation of the implied price of an attached warrant**   Dinoo Mathur wishes to determine whether the $1,000 price asked for Stanco Manufacturing's bond is fair in light of the theoretical value of the attached warrants. The $1,000-par-value, 30-year, 11.5%-coupon-interest-rate bond pays annual interest and has 10 warrants attached for purchase of common stock. The theoretical value of each warrant is $12.50. The interest rate on an equal-risk straight bond is currently 13%.

   a. Find the *straight value* of Stanco Manufacturing's bond.

   b. Calculate the implied price of *all* warrants attached to Stanco's bond.

   c. Calculate the implied price of *each* warrant attached to Stanco's bond.

   d. Compare the implied price for each warrant calculated in part **c** to its theoretical value. On the basis of this comparison, what assessment would you give Dinoo with respect to the fairness of Stanco's bond price? Explain.

P16–17 **Warrant values**   Kent Hotels has warrants that allow the purchase of three shares of its outstanding common stock at $50 per share. The common stock price per share and the market value of the warrant associated with that stock price are shown in the table.

Common stock price per share	Market value of warrant
$42	$ 2
46	8
48	9
54	18
58	28
62	38
66	48

   a. For each of the common stock prices given, calculate the *theoretical warrant value*.

   b. Graph the theoretical and market values of the warrant on a set of axes with per-share common stock price on the x axis and warrant value on the y axis.

   c. If the warrant value is $12 when the market price of common stock is $50, does this contradict or support the graph you have constructed? Explain.

   d. Specify the area of *warrant premium*. Why does this premium exist?

   e. If the expiration date of the warrants is quite close, would you expect your graph to look different? Explain.

PERSONAL FINANCE PROBLEM

P16–18 **Common stock versus warrant investment**   Susan Michaels is evaluating the Burton Tool Company's common stock and warrants to choose the better investment. The firm's stock is currently selling for $50 per share; its warrants to purchase three shares of common stock at $45 per share are selling for $20. Ignoring transactions costs, Ms. Michaels has $8,000 to invest. She is quite optimistic with respect to Burton because she has certain "inside information" about the firm's prospects with respect to a large government contract.

   a. How many shares of stock and how many warrants can Ms. Michaels purchase?

b. Suppose Ms. Michaels purchased the stock, held it 1 year, and then sold it for $60 per share. What total gain would she realize, ignoring brokerage fees and taxes?

c. Suppose Ms. Michaels purchased warrants and held them for 1 year and the market price of the stock increased to $60 per share. Ignoring brokerage fees and taxes, what would be her total gain if the market value of the warrants increased to $45 and she sold out?

d. What benefit, if any, would the warrants provide? Are there any differences in the risk of these two alternative investments? Explain.

PERSONAL FINANCE PROBLEM

 P16–19 **Common stock versus warrant investment**   Tom Baldwin can invest $6,300 in the common stock or the warrants of Lexington Life Insurance. The common stock is currently selling for $30 per share. Its warrants, which provide for the purchase of two shares of common stock at $28 per share, are currently selling for $7. The stock is expected to rise to a market price of $32 within the next year, so the expected theoretical value of a warrant over the next year is $8. The expiration date of the warrant is 1 year from the present.

a. If Mr. Baldwin purchases the stock, holds it for 1 year, and then sells it for $32, what is his total gain? (Ignore brokerage fees and taxes.)

b. If Mr. Baldwin purchases the warrants and converts them to common stock in 1 year, what is his total gain if the market price of common shares is actually $32? (Ignore brokerage fees and taxes.)

c. Repeat parts **a** and **b**, assuming that the market price of the stock in 1 year is (1) $30 and (2) $28.

d. Discuss the two alternatives and the tradeoffs associated with them.

 P16–20 **Options profits and losses**   For each of the *100-share options* shown in the following table, use the underlying stock price at expiration and other information to determine the amount of profit or loss an investor would have had, ignoring brokerage fees.

Option	Type of option	Cost of option	Striking price per share	Underlying stock price per share at expiration
A	Call	$200	$50	$55
B	Call	350	42	45
C	Put	500	60	50
D	Put	300	35	40
E	Call	450	28	26

PERSONAL FINANCE PROBLEM

 P16–21 **Call option**   Carol Krebs is considering buying 100 shares of Sooner Products, Inc., at $62 per share. Because she has read that the firm will probably soon receive certain large orders from abroad, she expects the price of Sooner to increase to $70 per share. As an alternative, Carol is considering purchase of a call option for 100 shares of Sooner at a striking price of $60. The 90-day option will cost $600. Ignore any brokerage fees or dividends.

a. What will Carol's profit be on the stock transaction if its price does rise to $70 and she sells?

    b. How much will Carol earn on the option transaction if the underlying stock price rises to $70?

    c. How high must the stock price rise for Carol to break even on the option transaction?

    d. Compare, contrast, and discuss the relative profit and risk associated with the stock and the option transactions.

PERSONAL FINANCE PROBLEM

 P16–22 **Put option**   Ed Martin, the pension fund manager for Stark Corporation, is considering purchase of a put option in anticipation of a price decline in the stock of Carlisle, Inc. The option to sell 100 shares of Carlisle, Inc., at any time during the next 90 days at a striking price of $45 can be purchased for $380. The stock of Carlisle is currently selling for $46 per share.

    a. Ignoring any brokerage fees or dividends, what profit or loss will Ed make if he buys the option and the lowest price of Carlisle stock during the 90 days is $46, $44, $40, and $35?

    b. What effect would the fact that the price of Carlisle's stock slowly rose from its initial $46 level to $55 at the end of 90 days have on Ed's purchase?

    c. In light of your findings, discuss the potential risks and returns from using put options to attempt to profit from an anticipated decline in share price.

 P16–23 **ETHICS PROBLEM**   Many economists and accountants argue that expensing of options is not necessary because the dilutive impact of options is accounted for by the increased number of shares. Do you agree with them?

Chapter 16 Case

Financing L. Rashid Company's Chemical Waste Disposal System

L. Rashid Company, a rapidly growing chemical processor, needs to raise $3 million in external funds to finance the acquisition of a new chemical waste disposal system. After carefully analyzing alternative financing sources, Denise McMahon, the firm's vice president of finance, reduced the financing possibilities to three alternatives: (1) debt, (2) debt with warrants, and (3) a financial lease. The key terms of each of these financing alternatives follow.

Debt   The firm can borrow the full $3 million from First Shreveport Bank. The bank will charge 12% annual interest and require annual end-of-year payments of $1,249,050 over the next 3 years. The disposal system will be depreciated under MACRS using a 3-year recovery period. (See Table 3.2 on page 108 for the applicable depreciation percentages.) The firm will pay $45,000 at the end of each year for a service contract that covers all maintenance costs; insurance and other costs will be borne by the firm. The firm plans to keep the equipment and use it beyond its 3-year recovery period.

Debt with Warrants   The firm can borrow the full $3 million from Southern National Bank. The bank will charge 10% annual interest and will, in addition, require a grant of 50,000 warrants, each allowing the purchase of two shares of the firm's stock for $30 per share at any time during the next 10 years. The stock is currently selling for $28 per share, and the warrants are estimated to have a market value of $1 each. The price (market value) of the debt with the warrants attached is estimated to equal the $3 million initial loan principal. The annual end-of-year payments on this loan will be $1,206,345 over the next 3 years. Depreciation, maintenance, insurance, and other costs will have the same costs and treatments under this alternative as those described before for the straight debt financing alternative.

Financial Lease   The waste disposal system can be leased from First International Capital. The lease will require annual end-of-year payments of $1,200,000 over the next 3 years. All maintenance costs will be paid by the lessor; insurance and other costs will be borne by the lessee. The lessee will exercise its option to purchase the system for $220,000 at termination of the lease at the end of 3 years.

Denise decided first to determine which of the debt financing alternatives—debt or debt with warrants—would least burden the firm's cash flows over the next 3 years. In this regard, she felt that very few, if any, warrants would be exercised during this period. Once the better debt financing alternative was found, Denise planned to use lease-versus-purchase analysis to evaluate it in light of the lease alternative. Assume the firm is in the 40% tax bracket, and its after-tax cost of debt is 7% under the debt alternative and 6% under the debt with warrants alternative.

To Do

a. Under the debt with warrants, find the following:
  (1) Straight debt value.
  (2) Implied price of *all* warrants.
  (3) Implied price of *each* warrant.
  (4) Theoretical value of a warrant.
b. On the basis of your findings in part **a**, do you think the price of the debt with warrants is too high or too low? Explain.
c. Assuming that the firm can raise the needed funds under the specified terms, which debt financing alternative—debt or debt with warrants—would you recommend in view of your findings above? Explain.
d. For the purchase alternative, financed as recommended in part **c**, calculate the following:
  (1) The annual interest expense deductible for tax purposes for each of the next 3 years.
  (2) The after-tax cash outflow for each of the next 3 years.
  (3) The present value of the cash outflows using the appropriate discount rate.
e. For the lease alternative, calculate the following:
  (1) The after-tax cash outflow for each of the next 3 years.
  (2) The present value of the cash outflows using the appropriate discount rate applied in part **d**(3).
f. Compare the present values of the cash outflow streams for the purchase [in part **d**(3)] and lease [in part **e**(2)] alternatives, and determine which would be preferable. Explain and discuss your recommendation.

Spreadsheet Exercise

Morris Company, a small manufacturing firm, wants to acquire a new machine that costs $30,000. Arrangements can be made to lease or purchase the machine. The firm is in the 40% tax bracket. The firm has gathered the following information about the two alternatives.

Lease   Morris would obtain a 5-year lease requiring annual end-of-year lease payments of $10,000. The lessor would pay all maintenance costs; insurance and other costs would be borne by the lessee. Morris would be given the right to exercise its option to purchase the machine for $3,000 at the end of the lease term.

Purchase   Morris can finance the purchase of the machine with an 8.5%, 5-year loan requiring annual end-of-year installment payments. The machine would be depreciated under MACRS using a 5-year recovery period. The exact depreciation rates over the next six periods would be 20%, 32%, 19%, 12%, 12%, and 5%, respectively. Morris would pay $1,200 per year for a service contract that covers all maintenance costs. The firm plans to keep the machine and use it beyond its 5-year recovery period.

To Do

Create a spreadsheet similar to Tables 16.1, 16.2, and 16.3 to answer the following:

a. Calculate the after-tax cash outflow from the lease for Morris Company.
b. Calculate the annual loan payment.
c. Determine the interest and principal components of the loan payments.
d. Calculate the after-tax cash outflows associated with the purchasing option.
e. Calculate and compare the present values of the cash outflows associated with both the leasing and purchasing options.
f. Which alternative is preferable? Explain.

Group Exercise

This chapter is the first of three chapters focusing on special topics in managerial finance. The hybrid and derivative securities covered in Chapter 16 (leases, convertible securities, warrants, and options) show creative solutions to financing needs. In that vein, this assignment will require your group to be creative as we near the end of your fictitious firm's story.

To Do

For many weeks your group has been creating all of the financials necessary to tell the story of your fictitious firm. At this point you can almost see the firm as a real entity. Given your familiarity with the specifics of your firm's financials, you will now add your own touches to the story. To complete this assignment your group will use several types of the hybrid and derivative securities described in this chapter. Specifically, you are to do the following:

a. Design a leasing arrangement for your firm.
b. Describe the issuance of a convertible security, either a bond or preferred stock, by your firm.
c. Choose a third type of creative financing—for example, warrants or options—that your firm could use to meet its needs.

Web Exercise

Go to the book's companion website at www.prenhall.com/gitman to find the Web Exercise for this chapter.

Remember to check the book's website at www.prenhall.com/gitman to find additional resources, including Web Exercises and a Web Case.

17 | Mergers, LBOs, Divestitures, and Business Failure

WHY THIS CHAPTER MATTERS TO YOU

In Your Professional Life

Accounting: You need to understand mergers, leveraged buyouts, and divestitures of assets to record and report these organizational changes; you also need to understand bankruptcy procedures because you will play a large part in any reorganization or liquidation.

Information systems: You need to understand what data need to be tracked in the case of mergers, leveraged buyouts, divestitures of assets, or bankruptcy, to devise the systems needed to effect these organizational changes.

Management: You need to understand the motives for mergers so that you will know when and why a merger is a good idea. Also, you may need to know how to fend off an unwelcome takeover attempt, when to divest the firm of assets for strategic reasons, and what options are available in the case of business failure.

Marketing: You need to understand mergers and divestitures, which may enable the firm to grow, diversify, or achieve synergy and therefore require changes in the firm's marketing organization, plans, and goals.

Operations: You need to understand mergers and divestitures because ongoing operations will be significantly affected by these organizational changes. Also, you should know that business failure may result in reorganization of the firm to provide adequate financing for ongoing operations.

In Your Personal Life

As an investor, you should understand corporate mergers, leveraged buyouts, and divestitures. More important, though, is an understanding of the causes and remedies associated with corporate bankruptcy. Clearly, an unstated personal financial goal is to avoid bankruptcy, an outcome that those who develop and implement reasonable personal financial plans are not likely to experience.

LEARNING GOALS

LG 1 Understand merger fundamentals, including terminology, motives for merging, and types of mergers.

LG 2 Describe the objectives and procedures used in leveraged buyouts (LBOs) and divestitures.

LG 3 Demonstrate the procedures used to value the target company, and discuss the effect of stock swap transactions on earnings per share.

LG 4 Discuss the merger negotiation process, holding companies, and international mergers.

LG 5 Understand the types and major causes of business failure and the use of voluntary settlements to sustain or liquidate the failed firm.

LG 6 Explain bankruptcy legislation and the procedures involved in reorganizing or liquidating a bankrupt firm.

Sprint Nextel

Growing by Merging

On August 12, 2005, **Sprint Nextel Corporation** completed the merger of Nextel Communications, Inc. with Sprint Corporation. Founded in 1899 as the Brown Telephone Co., Sprint by the 1970s was the nation's largest independent local telephone provider. When long-distance was opened to competition in the 1980s, Sprint established the first nationwide, 100% digital, fiber optic network. It was also a pioneer in data communications. In 1993, Sprint merged with Centel to become a unique provider of local, wireless, and long-distance services.

Nextel Communications began in 1987 as a company called Fleet Net. Renamed Nextel in 1993, it rapidly established itself in wireless communications. In less than a year, Nextel merged with Dial Call and OneComm, acquired all of Motorola's specialized mobile radio licenses, and received a $1 billion investment from wireless pioneer Craig McCaw. In 1996, Nextel introduced digital-cellular, two-way radio and text/numeric paging in one phone—the famed Nextel phone. Since then, Nextel has aggressively expanded its reach and product capabilities to include its signature Nationwide Direct Connect walkie-talkie service, IP broadband access, and a steady stream of feature-rich, Internet-ready phones and smart devices.

The $35 billion combination of the No. 3 and No. 5 U.S. wireless carriers forms a wireless giant with about 40 million customers. The merger was beneficial to both: Sprint was eager to sign up Nextel's higher-paying business customers and Nextel needed to build a new advanced wireless network, which would have cost $2 to $3 billion; in a merger, Nextel could share the network that Sprint was already building at a similar cost.

The merger got off to a rocky start. The two companies used incompatible technologies, and they also had very different business models. Gary Forsee, chairman and CEO of Sprint Nextel Corp., expected it to take about 3 years to complete the major pieces of the merger. The company decided to keep its executive headquarters in Reston, Virginia, where Nextel was based, and to retain Sprint's Overland Park, Kansas, operational headquarters.

As you read this chapter, compile a list of the most likely reasons for corporate mergers.

Most large companies have at one time or another purchased or merged with another company. This chapter looks at several types of corporate restructuring—mergers, leveraged buyouts, and divestitures—as well as restructuring due to business failure. Whether growing or shrinking, organizational changes are a way of life for many corporations.

17.1 | Merger Fundamentals

Firms sometimes use mergers to expand externally by acquiring control of another firm. Whereas the overriding objective for a merger should be to improve the firm's share value, a number of more immediate motivations such as diversification, tax considerations, and increasing owner liquidity frequently exist. Sometimes mergers are pursued to acquire needed assets rather than the going concern. Here we discuss merger fundamentals—terminology, motives, and types. In the following sections, we will describe the related topics of leveraged buyouts (LBOs) and divestitures and will review the procedures used to analyze and negotiate mergers.

Terminology

corporate restructuring
The activities involving expansion or contraction of a firm's operations or changes in its asset or financial (ownership) structure.

In the broadest sense, activities involving expansion or contraction of a firm's operations or changes in its asset or financial (ownership) structure are called **corporate restructuring**. The topics addressed in this chapter—mergers, LBOs, and divestitures—are some of the most common forms of corporate restructuring; there are many others, which are beyond the scope of this text.[1] Here, we define some basic merger terminology; other terms are introduced and defined as needed in subsequent discussions.

Mergers, Consolidations, and Holding Companies

merger
The combination of two or more firms, in which the resulting firm maintains the identity of one of the firms, usually the larger.

consolidation
The combination of two or more firms to form a completely new corporation.

holding company
A corporation that has voting control of one or more other corporations.

subsidiaries
The companies controlled by a holding company.

A **merger** occurs when two or more firms are combined and the resulting firm maintains the identity of one of the firms. Usually, the assets and liabilities of the smaller firm are merged into those of the larger firm. **Consolidation,** by contrast, involves the combination of two or more firms to form a completely new corporation. The new corporation normally absorbs the assets and liabilities of the companies from which it is formed. Because of the similarity of mergers and consolidations, we use the term *merger* throughout this chapter to refer to both.

A **holding company** is a corporation that has voting control of one or more other corporations. Having control in large, widely held companies generally requires ownership of between 10 and 20 percent of the outstanding stock. The companies controlled by a holding company are normally referred to as its **subsidiaries.** Control of a subsidiary is typically obtained by purchasing a sufficient number of shares of its stock.

Acquiring versus Target Companies

acquiring company
The firm in a merger transaction that attempts to acquire another firm.

target company
The firm in a merger transaction that the acquiring company is pursuing.

The firm in a merger transaction that attempts to acquire another firm is commonly called the **acquiring company.** The firm that the acquiring company is pursuing is referred to as the **target company.** Generally, the acquiring company identifies, evaluates, and negotiates with the management and/or shareholders of the target company. Occasionally, the management of a target company initiates its acquisition by seeking to be acquired.

---

1. For comprehensive coverage of the many aspects of corporate restructuring, see J. Fred Weston, Mark L. Mitchell, and J. Harold Mulherin, *Takeovers, Restructuring, and Corporate Governance,* 4th ed. (Upper Saddle River, NJ: Prentice-Hall, 2004).

Friendly versus Hostile Takeovers

friendly merger
A merger transaction endorsed by the target firm's management, approved by its stockholders, and easily consummated.

Mergers can occur on either a friendly or a hostile basis. Typically, after identifying the target company, the acquirer initiates discussions. If the target management is receptive to the acquirer's proposal, it may endorse the merger and recommend shareholder approval. If the stockholders approve the merger, the transaction is typically consummated either through a cash purchase of shares by the acquirer or through an exchange of the acquirer's stock, bonds, or some combination for the target firm's shares. This type of negotiated transaction is known as a **friendly merger.**

hostile merger
A merger transaction that the target firm's management does not support, forcing the acquiring company to try to gain control of the firm by buying shares in the marketplace.

If the takeover target's management does not support the proposed takeover, it can fight the acquirer's actions. In this case, the acquirer can attempt to gain control of the firm by buying sufficient shares of the target firm in the marketplace. This is typically accomplished by using a *tender offer,* which, as noted in Chapter 13, is a formal offer to purchase a given number of shares at a specified price. This type of unfriendly transaction is commonly referred to as a **hostile merger.** Clearly, hostile mergers are more difficult to consummate because the target firm's management acts to deter rather than facilitate the acquisition. Regardless, hostile takeovers are sometimes successful.

Strategic versus Financial Mergers

strategic merger
A merger transaction undertaken to achieve economies of scale.

Mergers are undertaken for either strategic or financial reasons. **Strategic mergers** seek to achieve various economies of scale by eliminating redundant functions, increasing market share, improving raw material sourcing and finished product distribution, and so on.[2] In these mergers, the operations of the acquiring and target firms are somehow combined to achieve economies, thereby causing the performance of the merged firm to exceed that of the premerged firms. The mergers of Daimler-Benz and Chrysler (both auto manufacturers) and Norwest and Wells Fargo (both banks) are examples of strategic mergers. An interesting variation of the strategic merger involves the purchase of specific product lines (rather than the whole company) for strategic reasons. The acquisition of HarperCollins' college publishing division by Addison-Wesley is an example of such a merger.

financial merger
A merger transaction undertaken with the goal of restructuring the acquired company to improve its cash flow and unlock its hidden value.

Financial mergers are based on the acquisition of companies that can be restructured to improve their cash flow. These mergers involve the acquisition of the target firm by an acquirer, which may be another company or a group of investors—often the firm's existing management. The objective of the acquirer is to cut costs drastically and sell off certain unproductive or noncompatible assets in an effort to increase the firm's cash flow. The increased cash flow is used to service the sizable debt that is typically incurred to finance these transactions. Financial mergers are based not on the firm's ability to achieve economies of scale, but rather on the acquirer's belief that through restructuring, the firm's hidden value can be unlocked.

The ready availability of *junk bond* financing throughout the 1980s fueled the financial merger mania during that period. With the collapse of the junk bond

---

2. A somewhat similar nonmerger arrangement is the *strategic alliance,* an agreement typically between a large company with established products and channels of distribution and an emerging technology company with a promising research and development program in areas of interest to the larger company. In exchange for its financial support, the larger, established company obtains a stake in the technology being developed by the emerging company. Today, strategic alliances are commonplace in the biotechnology, information technology, and software industries.

market in the early 1990s, the bankruptcy filings of a number of prominent financial mergers of the 1980s, and the rising stock market of the later 1990s, financial mergers lost their luster. As a result, the strategic merger, which does not rely so heavily on debt, continues to dominate today.

Motives for Merging

Firms merge to fulfill certain objectives. The overriding goal for merging is maximization of the owners' wealth as reflected in the acquirer's share price. More specific motives include growth or diversification, synergy, fund raising, increased managerial skill or technology, tax considerations, increased ownership liquidity, and defense against takeover. These motives should be pursued when they are believed to be consistent with owner wealth maximization.

Growth or Diversification

Companies that desire rapid growth in *size* or *market share* or diversification in *the range of their products* may find that a merger can be used to fulfill this objective. Instead of going through the time-consuming process of internal growth or diversification, the firm may achieve the same objective in a short period of time by merging with an existing firm. Such a strategy is often less costly than the alternative of developing the necessary production capacity. If a firm that wants to expand operations can find a suitable going concern, it may avoid many of the risks associated with the design, manufacture, and sale of additional or new products. Moreover, when a firm expands or extends its product line by acquiring another firm, it removes a potential competitor.[3]

Synergy

Hint Synergy is said to be present when a whole is greater than the sum of its parts—when "1 + 1 = 3."

The *synergy* of mergers is the economies of scale resulting from the merged firms' lower overhead. These economies of scale from lowering the combined overhead increase earnings to a level greater than the sum of the earnings of each of the independent firms. Synergy is most obvious when firms merge with other firms in the same line of business, because many redundant functions and employees can be eliminated. Staff functions, such as purchasing and sales, are probably most greatly affected by this type of combination.

Fund Raising

Often, firms combine to enhance their fund-raising ability. A firm may be unable to obtain funds for its own internal expansion but able to obtain funds for external business combinations. Quite often, one firm may combine with another that has high liquid assets and low levels of liabilities. The acquisition of this type of "cash-rich" company immediately increases the firm's borrowing power by decreasing its financial leverage. This should allow funds to be raised externally at lower cost.

---

3. Certain legal constraints on growth exist—especially when the elimination of competition is expected. The various antitrust laws, which are strictly enforced by the Federal Trade Commission (FTC) and the Justice Department, prohibit business combinations that eliminate competition, particularly when the resulting enterprise would be a monopoly.

Increased Managerial Skill or Technology

Occasionally, a firm will have good potential that it finds itself unable to develop fully because of deficiencies in certain areas of management or an absence of needed product or production technology. If the firm cannot hire the management or develop the technology it needs, it might combine with a compatible firm that has the needed managerial personnel or technical expertise. Of course, any merger should contribute to maximizing the owners' wealth.

Tax Considerations

tax loss carryforward
In a merger, the tax loss of one of the firms that can be applied against a limited amount of future income of the merged firm over 20 years or until the total tax loss has been fully recovered, whichever comes first.

Quite often, tax considerations are a key motive for merging. In such a case, the tax benefit generally stems from the fact that one of the firms has a **tax loss carryforward.** This means that the company's tax loss can be applied against a limited amount of future income of the merged firm over 20 years or until the total tax loss has been fully recovered, whichever comes first.[4] Two situations could actually exist. A company with a tax loss could acquire a profitable company to utilize the tax loss. In this case, the acquiring firm would boost the combination's after-tax earnings by reducing the taxable income of the acquired firm. A tax loss may also be useful when a profitable firm acquires a firm that has such a loss. In either situation, however, the merger must be justified not only on the basis of the tax benefits but also on grounds consistent with the goal of owner wealth maximization. Moreover, the tax benefits described can be used only in mergers—not in the formation of holding companies—because only in the case of mergers are operating results reported on a consolidated basis. An example will clarify the use of the tax loss carryforward.

Example

Bergen Company, a wheel bearing manufacturer, has a total of $450,000 in tax loss carryforwards resulting from operating tax losses of $150,000 per year in each of the past 3 years. To use these losses and to diversify its operations, Hudson Company, a molder of plastics, has acquired Bergen through a merger. Hudson expects to have *earnings before taxes* of $300,000 per year. We assume that these earnings are realized, that they fall within the annual limit that is legally allowed for application of the tax loss carryforward resulting from the merger (see footnote 4), that the Bergen portion of the merged firm just breaks even, and that Hudson is in the 40% tax bracket. The total taxes paid by the two firms and their after-tax earnings without and with the merger are as shown in Table 17.1 on page 766.

With the merger the total tax payments are less—$180,000 (total of line 7) versus $360,000 (total of line 2). With the merger the total after-tax earnings are more—$720,000 (total of line 8) versus $540,000 (total of line 3). The merged firm is able to deduct the tax loss over 20 years or until the total tax loss is fully recovered, whichever comes first. In this example, the total tax loss is fully deducted by the end of year 2.

---

4. To deter firms from combining solely to take advantage of tax loss carryforwards, the *Tax Reform Act of 1986* imposed an annual limit on the amount of taxable income against which such losses can be applied. The annual limit is determined by formula and is tied to the value of the loss corporation before the combination. Although not fully eliminating this motive for combination, the act makes it more difficult for firms to justify combinations solely on the basis of tax loss carryforwards.

| TABLE 17.1 | Total Taxes and After-Tax Earnings for Hudson Company without and with Merger | | | |

| | Year | | | Total for |
	1	2	3	3 years
Total taxes and after-tax earnings without merger				
(1) Earnings before taxes	$300,000	$300,000	$300,000	$900,000
(2) Taxes [0.40 × (1)]	120,000	120,000	120,000	360,000
(3) Earnings after taxes [(1) − (2)]	$180,000	$180,000	$180,000	$540,000
Total taxes and after-tax earnings with merger				
(4) Earnings before losses	$300,000	$300,000	$300,000	$900,000
(5) Tax loss carryforward	300,000	150,000	0	450,000
(6) Earnings before taxes [(4) − (5)]	$ 0	$150,000	$300,000	$450,000
(7) Taxes [0.40 × (6)]	0	60,000	120,000	180,000
(8) Earnings after taxes [(4) − (7)]	$300,000	$240,000	$180,000	$720,000

Increased Ownership Liquidity

The merger of two small firms or of a small and a larger firm may provide the owners of the small firm(s) with greater liquidity. This is due to the higher marketability associated with the shares of larger firms. Instead of holding shares in a small firm that has a very "thin" market, the owners will receive shares that are traded in a broader market and can thus be liquidated more readily. Also, owning shares for which market price quotations are readily available provides owners with a better sense of the value of their holdings. Especially in the case of small, closely held firms, the improved liquidity of ownership obtainable through merger with an acceptable firm may have considerable appeal.

Defense against Takeover

Hint In an unfriendly takeover, top management and/or the major stockholders do not want to become a part of another firm. In some cases, not all of the stockholders feel the same way about the impending takeover.

Occasionally, when a firm becomes the target of an unfriendly takeover, it will as a defense acquire another company. Such a strategy typically works like this: The original target firm takes on additional debt to finance its defensive acquisition; because of the debt load, the target firm becomes too highly levered financially to be of any further interest to its suitor. To be effective, a defensive takeover must create greater value for shareholders than they would have realized had the firm been merged with its suitor.

Types of Mergers

horizontal merger
A merger of two firms *in the same line of business.*

The four types of mergers are the (1) horizontal merger, (2) vertical merger, (3) congeneric merger, and (4) conglomerate merger. A **horizontal merger** results when two firms *in the same line of business* are merged. An example is the merger of two machine tool manufacturers. This form of merger results in the expansion of a firm's operations in a given product line and at the same time eliminates a

vertical merger
A merger in which a firm acquires *a supplier or a customer.*

Hint A merger undertaken to obtain the synergy benefit is usually a horizontal merger. Diversification can be either a vertical or a conglomerate merger. The other benefits of merging can be achieved by any one of the four types of mergers.

congeneric merger
A merger in which one firm acquires another firm that is *in the same general industry* but is neither in the same line of business nor a supplier or customer.

conglomerate merger
A merger combining firms in *unrelated businesses.*

competitor. A **vertical merger** occurs when a firm acquires *a supplier or a customer.* For example, the merger of a machine tool manufacturer with its supplier of castings is a vertical merger. The economic benefit of a vertical merger stems from the firm's increased control over the acquisition of raw materials or the distribution of finished goods.

A **congeneric merger** is achieved by acquiring a firm that is *in the same general industry* but is neither in the same line of business nor a supplier or customer. An example is the merger of a machine tool manufacturer with the manufacturer of industrial conveyor systems. The benefit of a congeneric merger is the resulting ability to use the same sales and distribution channels to reach customers of both businesses. A **conglomerate merger** involves the combination of firms in *unrelated businesses.* The merger of a machine tool manufacturer with a chain of fast-food restaurants is an example of this kind of merger. The key benefit of the conglomerate merger is its ability to *reduce risk* by merging firms that have different seasonal or cyclic patterns of sales and earnings.[5]

REVIEW QUESTIONS

17-1 Define and differentiate among the members of each of the following sets of terms: (**a**) mergers, consolidations, and holding companies; (**b**) acquiring company and target company; (**c**) friendly merger and hostile merger; and (**d**) strategic merger and financial merger.

17-2 Briefly describe each of the following motives for merging: (**a**) growth or diversification, (**b**) synergy, (**c**) fund raising, (**d**) increased managerial skill or technology, (**e**) tax considerations, (**f**) increased ownership liquidity, and (**g**) defense against takeover.

17-3 Briefly describe each of the following types of mergers: (**a**) horizontal, (**b**) vertical, (**c**) congeneric, and (**d**) conglomerate.

17.2 | LBOs and Divestitures

Before we address the mechanics of merger analysis and negotiation, you need to understand two topics that are closely related to mergers—leveraged buyouts (LBOs) and divestitures. An LBO is a method of structuring an acquisition, and divestitures involve the sale of a firm's assets.

Leveraged Buyouts (LBOs)

leveraged buyout (LBO)
An acquisition technique involving the use of a large amount of debt to purchase a firm; an example of a *financial merger.*

A popular technique that was widely used during the 1980s to make acquisitions is the **leveraged buyout (LBO)**, which involves the use of a large amount of debt to purchase a firm. LBOs are a clear-cut example of a *financial merger* undertaken to create a high-debt private corporation with improved cash flow and

---

5. A discussion of the key concepts underlying the portfolio approach to the diversification of risk was presented in Chapter 5. In the theoretical literature, some questions exist about whether diversification by the firm is a proper motive consistent with shareholder wealth maximization. Many scholars argue that by buying shares in different firms, investors can obtain the same benefits as they would realize from owning stock in the merged firm. It appears that other benefits need to be available to justify mergers.

Hint The acquirers in LBOs are other firms or groups of investors that frequently include key members of the firm's existing management.

value. Typically, in an LBO, 90 percent or more of the purchase price is financed with debt. A large part of the borrowing is secured by the acquired firm's assets, and the lenders, because of the high risk, take a portion of the firm's equity. *Junk bonds* have been routinely used to raise the large amounts of debt needed to finance LBO transactions. Of course, the purchasers in an LBO expect to use the improved cash flow to service the large amount of junk bond and other debt incurred in the buyout.

An attractive candidate for acquisition via a leveraged buyout should possess three key attributes:

1. It must have a good position in its industry, with a solid profit history and reasonable expectations of growth.
2. The firm should have a relatively low level of debt and a high level of "bank-able" assets that can be used as loan collateral.
3. It must have stable and predictable cash flows that are adequate to meet interest and principal payments on the debt and provide adequate working capital.

Of course, a willingness on the part of existing ownership and management to sell the company on a leveraged basis is also needed.

Many LBOs did not live up to original expectations. One of the largest ever was the late 1988, $24.5 billion buyout of RJR Nabisco by KKR. RJR was taken public in 1991, and the firm continued to struggle under the heavy debt of the LBO for a few years before improving its debt position and credit rating. Campeau Corporation's buyouts of Allied Stores and Federated Department Stores resulted in its later filing for bankruptcy protection, from which reorganized companies later emerged. In earlier years, other highly publicized LBOs have defaulted on the high-yield debt incurred to finance the buyout. Although the LBO remains a viable financing technique under the right circumstances, its use is greatly diminished from the frenzied pace of the 1980s. Whereas the LBOs of the 1980s were used, often indiscriminately, for hostile takeovers, today LBOs are most often used to finance management buyouts.

Divestitures

operating unit
A part of a business, such as a plant, division, product line, or subsidiary, that contributes to the actual operations of the firm.

divestiture
The selling of some of a firm's assets for various strategic reasons.

Companies often achieve external expansion by acquiring an **operating unit**—plant, division, product line, subsidiary, and so on—of another company. In such a case, the seller generally believes that the value of the firm will be enhanced by converting the unit into cash or some other more productive asset. The selling of some of a firm's assets is called **divestiture**. Unlike business failure, divestiture is often undertaken for positive motives: to generate cash for expansion of other product lines, to get rid of a poorly performing operation, to streamline the corporation, or to restructure the corporation's business in a manner consistent with its strategic goals.

Personal Finance Example   A personal finance decision that young families with children frequently face is whether a stay-at-home parent should "divest" their child-care duties, hire child care, and return to work. Whereas the emotional aspects of such a decision are nonquantifiable, the economics of such a decision are measurable.

Take the case of Elena and Gino Deluca, who have two children, ages 2 and 4. They are in the process of analyzing if it makes economic sense to hire child care and have Elena return to work as a credit analyst. They estimate that Elena will earn $5,800 per month gross, including her employer's 401(k) contributions. In addition, she expects to receive monthly employer-paid benefits that include health insurance, life insurance, and pension contributions totaling $1,800. She expects her federal and state income taxes to total about $1,900 per month. The Delucas estimate total additional expenses (child care, clothing and personal expenses, meals away from home, and transportation) related to Elana's job to total $1,500 per month. They summarized these monthly estimates as follows:

Additional gross income	$5,800	
+ Employer-paid benefits	1,800	
(1) Additional income and benefits		$7,600
Additional taxes	1,900	
+ Additional expenses	1,500	
(2) Additional taxes and expenses		3,400
Net income (loss) [(1) − (2)]		$4,200

Because the Delucas will increase their net income by $4,200 per month, having Elena divest her child-care responsibilities and hire child care is economically justifiable.

Firms divest themselves of operating units by a variety of methods. One involves the *sale of a product line to another firm.* An example is Paramount's sale of Simon and Schuster to Pearson PLC to free up cash and allow Paramount to focus its business better on global mass consumer markets. Outright sales of operating units can be accomplished on a cash or stock swap basis via the procedures described later in this chapter. A second method that has become popular involves the *sale of the unit to existing management.* This sale is often achieved through the use of a *leveraged buyout (LBO).*

spin-off
A form of divestiture in which an operating unit becomes an independent company through the issuance of shares in it, on a pro rata basis, to the parent company's shareholders.

Sometimes divestiture is achieved through a **spin-off,** which results in an operating unit becoming an independent company. A spin-off is accomplished by issuing shares in the divested operating unit on a pro rata basis to the parent company's shareholders. Such an action allows the unit to be separated from the corporation and to trade as a separate entity. An example was the decision by AT&T to spin off its Global Information Solutions unit (formerly and now NCR, which produces electronic terminals and computers), to allow AT&T to focus better on its core communications business. Like outright sale, this approach achieves the divestiture objective, although it does not bring additional cash or stock to the parent company. The final and least popular approach to divestiture involves *liquidation of the operating unit's individual assets.*

Regardless of the method used to divest a firm of an unwanted operating unit, the goal typically is to create a more lean and focused operation that will enhance the efficiency as well as the profitability of the enterprise and create maximum value for shareholders. Recent divestitures seem to suggest that many operating units are worth much more to others than to the firm itself. Comparisons of postdivestiture and predivestiture market values have shown that the

breakup value
The value of a firm measured as the sum of the values of its operating units if each were sold separately.

breakup value—the sum of the values of a firm's operating units if each were sold separately—of many firms is significantly greater than their combined value. As a result of market valuations, divestiture often creates value in excess of the cash or stock received in the transaction. Although these outcomes frequently occur, financial theory has been unable to explain them fully and satisfactorily.[6]

REVIEW QUESTIONS

17–4 What is a *leveraged buyout (LBO)?* What are the three key attributes of an attractive candidate for acquisition via an LBO?

17–5 What is an *operating unit?* What is a *divestiture?* What are four common methods used by firms to divest themselves of operating units? What is *breakup value?*

17.3 | Analyzing and Negotiating Mergers

We now turn to the procedures that are used to analyze and negotiate mergers. Initially, we will consider how to value the target company and how to use stock swap transactions to acquire companies. Next, we will look at the merger negotiation process. We will then review the major advantages and disadvantages of holding companies. Finally, we will discuss international mergers.

Valuing the Target Company

Once the acquiring company isolates a target company that it wishes to acquire, it must estimate the target's value. The value is then used, along with a proposed financing scheme, to negotiate the transaction—on a friendly or hostile basis. The value of the target is estimated by using the valuation techniques presented in Chapter 7 and applied to long-term investment decisions in Chapters 8, 9, and 10. Similar capital budgeting techniques are applied whether the target firm is being acquired for its assets or as a going concern.

Acquisitions of Assets

Occasionally, a firm is acquired not for its income-earning potential but as a collection of assets (generally fixed assets) that the acquiring company needs. The price paid for this type of acquisition depends largely on which assets are being acquired; consideration must also be given to the value of any tax losses. To determine whether the purchase of assets is financially justified, the acquirer must estimate both the costs and the benefits of the target assets. This is a capital budgeting problem (see Chapters 8, 9, and 10), because an initial cash outlay is made to acquire assets, and as a result, future cash inflows are expected.

---

6. For an excellent discussion and theoretical explanation of *breakup value,* see Edward M. Miller, "Why the Breakup of Conglomerate Business Enterprises Often Increases Value," *Journal of Social, Political & Economic Studies* (Fall 1995), pp. 317–341.

Example

Clark Company, a major manufacturer of electrical transformers, is interested in acquiring certain fixed assets of Noble Company, an industrial electronics company. Noble, which has tax loss carryforwards from losses over the past 5 years, is interested in selling out, but it wishes to sell out entirely, not just to get rid of certain fixed assets. A condensed balance sheet for Noble Company follows.

Noble Company
Balance Sheet

Assets		Liabilities and Stockholders' Equity	
Cash	$ 2,000	Total liabilities	$ 80,000
Marketable securities	0	Stockholders' equity	120,000
Accounts receivable	8,000	Total liabilities and	
Inventories	10,000	stockholders' equity	$200,000
Machine A	10,000		
Machine B	30,000		
Machine C	25,000		
Land and buildings	115,000		
Total assets	$200,000		

Clark Company needs only machines B and C and the land and buildings. However, it has made some inquiries and has arranged to sell the accounts receivable, inventories, and machine A for $23,000. Because there is also $2,000 in cash, Clark will get $25,000 for the excess assets. Noble wants $100,000 for the entire company, which means that Clark will have to pay the firm's creditors $80,000 and its owners $20,000. The actual outlay required of Clark after liquidating the unneeded assets will be $75,000 [($80,000 + $20,000) − $25,000]. In other words, to obtain the use of the desired assets (machines B and C and the land and buildings) and the benefits of Noble's tax losses, Clark must pay $75,000. The *after-tax cash inflows* that are expected to result from the new assets and applicable tax losses are $14,000 per year for the next 5 years and $12,000 per year for the following 5 years. The desirability of this asset acquisition can be determined by calculating the net present value of this outlay using Clark Company's 11% cost of capital, as shown in Table 17.2 on page 772. *Because the net present value of $3,072 is greater than zero, Clark's value should be increased by acquiring Noble Company's assets.*

Acquisitions of Going Concerns

Acquisitions of target companies that are going concerns are best analyzed by using capital budgeting techniques similar to those described for asset acquisitions. The methods of estimating expected cash flows from an acquisition are similar to those used in estimating capital budgeting cash flows. Typically, *pro forma income statements* reflecting the postmerger revenues and costs attributable to the target company are prepared (see Chapter 3). They are then adjusted to reflect the expected cash flows over the relevant time period. Whenever a firm considers acquiring a target company that has different risk behaviors, it should risk-adjust the cost of capital before applying the appropriate capital budgeting techniques (see Chapter 10).

TABLE 17.2	Net Present Value of Noble Company's Assets		
Year(s)	Cash inflows (1)	Present value factor at 11% (2)	Present value [(1) × (2)] (3)
1–5	$14,000	3.696[a]	$51,744
6	12,000	0.535[b]	6,420
7	12,000	0.482[b]	5,784
8	12,000	0.434[b]	5,208
9	12,000	0.391[b]	4,692
10	12,000	0.352[b]	4,224
		Present value of inflows	$78,072
		Less: Cash outlay required	75,000
		Net present value[c]	$ 3,072

[a]The present value interest factor for an annuity, *PVIFA*, with a 5-year life discounted at 11% obtained from Table A–4.

[b]The present value interest factor, *PVIF*, for $1 discounted at 11% percent for the corresponding year obtained from Table A–2.

[c]When we use a financial calculator, we get a net present value of $3,063.

Example

Square Company, a major media company, is contemplating the acquisition of Circle Company, a small independent film producer that can be purchased for $60,000. Square currently has a high degree of financial leverage, which is reflected in its 13% cost of capital. Because of the low financial leverage of Circle Company, Square estimates that its overall cost of capital will drop to 10% after the acquisition. Because the effect of the less risky capital structure cannot be reflected in the expected cash flows, the postmerger cost of capital (10%) must be used to evaluate the cash flows that are expected from the acquisition. The post-merger cash flows attributable to the target company are forecast over a 30-year time horizon. These estimated cash flows (all inflows) and the resulting net present value of the target company, Circle Company, are shown in Table 17.3.

Because the $2,357 net present value of the target company is greater than zero, the merger is acceptable. Note that if the effect of the changed capital structure on the cost of capital had not been considered, the acquisition would have been found unacceptable, because the net present value *at a 13% cost of capital* is negative $11,864 (or −$11,868 using a financial calculator).

Stock Swap Transactions

Once the value of the target company is determined, the acquirer must develop a proposed financing package. The simplest (but probably the least common) case is a pure cash purchase. Beyond this extreme case, there are virtually an infinite number of financing packages that use various combinations of cash, debt, preferred stock, and common stock.

Here we look at the other extreme—**stock swap transactions,** in which the acquisition is paid for using an exchange of common stock. The acquiring firm exchanges its shares for shares of the target company according to a predeter-

stock swap transaction
An acquisition method in which the acquiring firm exchanges its shares for shares of the target company according to a predetermined ratio.

TABLE 17.3   Net Present Value of the Circle Company Acquisition

Year(s)	Cash inflows (1)	Present value factor at 10%[a] (2)	Present value [(1) × (2)] (3)
1–10	$ 5,000	6.145	$30,725
11–18	13,000	(8.201 − 6.145)[b]	26,728
19–30	4,000	(9.427 − 8.201)[b]	4,904
		Present value of inflows	$62,357
		Less: Cash purchase price	60,000
		Net present value[c]	$ 2,357

[a]Present value interest factors for annuities, *PVIFA*, obtained from Table A–4.

[b]These factors are found by using a shortcut technique that can be applied to annuities for periods of years beginning at some point in the future. By finding the appropriate interest factor for the present value of an annuity given for the last year of the annuity and subtracting the present value interest factor of an annuity for the year immediately preceding the beginning of the annuity, the appropriate interest factor for the present value of an annuity beginning sometime in the future can be obtained. You can check this shortcut by using the long approach and comparing the results.

[c]When we use a financial calculator, we get a net present value of $2,364.

mined ratio. The *ratio of exchange* of shares is determined in the merger negotiations. This ratio affects the various financial yardsticks that are used by existing and prospective shareholders to value the merged firm's shares. The use of stock swaps to finance mergers is a popular approach.

Ratio of Exchange

When one firm swaps its stock for the shares of another firm, the firms must determine the number of shares of the acquiring firm to be exchanged for each share of the target firm. The first requirement, of course, is that the acquiring company have sufficient shares available to complete the transaction. Often, a firm's repurchase of shares (discussed in Chapter 13) is necessary to obtain sufficient shares for such a transaction. The acquiring firm generally offers more for each share of the target company than the current market price of its publicly traded shares. The actual **ratio of exchange** is merely the ratio of the amount *paid* per share of the target company to the market price per share of the acquiring firm. It is calculated in this manner because the acquiring firm pays the target firm in stock, which has a value equal to its market price.

ratio of exchange
The ratio of the amount *paid* per share of the target company to the market price per share of the acquiring firm.

Example ▸ Grand Company, a leather products concern, whose stock is currently selling for $80 per share, is interested in acquiring Small Company, a producer of belts. To prepare for the acquisition, Grand has been repurchasing its own shares over the past 3 years. Small's stock is currently selling for $75 per share, but in the merger negotiations, Grand has found it necessary to offer Small $110 per share. Because Grand does not have sufficient financial resources to purchase the firm for cash and does not wish to raise these funds, Small has agreed to accept Grand's stock in exchange for its shares. As stated, Grand's stock currently sells for $80 per share, and it must pay $110 per share for Small's stock. Therefore, the ratio of exchange is 1.375 ($110 ÷ $80). This means that Grand Company must exchange 1.375 shares of its stock for each share of Small's stock.

Effect on Earnings per Share

Although cash flows and value are the primary focus, it is useful to consider the effects of a proposed merger on earnings per share—the accounting returns that are related to cash flows and value (see Chapter 7). Ordinarily, the resulting earnings per share differ from the premerger earnings per share for both the acquiring firm and the target firm. They depend largely on the ratio of exchange and the premerger earnings per share of each firm. It is best to view the initial and long-run effects of the ratio of exchange on earnings per share separately.

Initial Effect   When the ratio of exchange is equal to 1 and both the acquiring firm and the target firm have the *same* premerger earnings per share, the merged firm's earnings per share will initially remain constant. In this rare instance, both the acquiring firm and the target firm would also have equal price/earnings (P/E) ratios. In actuality, the earnings per share of the merged firm are generally above the premerger earnings per share of one firm and below the premerger earnings per share of the other, after the necessary adjustment has been made for the ratio of exchange.

Example   As we saw in the preceding example, Grand Company is contemplating acquiring Small Company by swapping 1.375 shares of its stock for each share of Small's stock. The current financial data related to the earnings and market price for each of these companies are given in Table 17.4.

To complete the merger and retire the 20,000 shares of Small Company stock outstanding, Grand will have to issue and (or) use treasury stock totaling 27,500 shares (1.375 × 20,000 shares). Once the merger is completed, Grand will have 152,500 shares of common stock (125,000 + 27,500) outstanding. If the earnings of each of the firms remain constant, the merged company will be expected to have earnings available for the common stockholders of $600,000 ($500,000 + $100,000). The earnings per share of the merged company therefore should equal approximately $3.93 ($600,000 ÷ 152,500 shares).

It would appear at first that Small Company's shareholders have sustained a decrease in per-share earnings from $5 to $3.93, but because each share of Small Company's original stock is equivalent to 1.375 shares of the merged company's stock, the equivalent earnings per share are actually $5.40 ($3.93 × 1.375). In

TABLE 17.4   Grand Company's and Small Company's Financial Data

Item	Grand Company	Small Company
(1) Earnings available for common stock	$500,000	$100,000
(2) Number of shares of common stock outstanding	125,000	20,000
(3) Earnings per share [(1) ÷ (2)]	$4	$5
(4) Market price per share	$80	$75
(5) Price/earnings (P/E) ratio [(4) ÷ (3)]	20	15

TABLE 17.5	Summary of the Effects on Earnings per Share of a Merger between Grand Company and Small Company at $110 per Share	

| | Earnings per share | |
Stockholders	Before merger	After merger
Grand Company	$4.00	$3.93[a]
Small Company	5.00	5.40[b]

[a] $\frac{\$500,000 + \$100,000}{125,000 + (1.375 \times 20,000)} = \$3.93$

[b] $\$3.93 \times 1.375 = \$5.40$

other words, as a result of the merger, Grand Company's original shareholders experience a decrease in earnings per share from $4 to $3.93 to the benefit of Small Company's shareholders, whose earnings per share increase from $5 to $5.40. These results are summarized in Table 17.5.

The postmerger earnings per share for owners of the acquiring and target companies can be explained by comparing the price/earnings ratio paid by the acquiring company with its initial P/E ratio. Table 17.6 summarizes this relationship. By paying more than its current value per dollar of earnings to acquire each dollar of earnings (P/E paid > P/E of acquiring company), the acquiring firm transfers the claim on a portion of its premerger earnings to the owners of the target firm. Therefore, on a postmerger basis *the target firm's EPS increases, and the acquiring firm's EPS decreases.* Note that this outcome is *nearly always* the case, because the acquirer typically pays, on average, a 50 percent premium above the target firm's market price, which results in the P/E paid being much above its own P/E. The P/E ratios associated with the Grand–Small merger demonstrate the effect of the merger on EPS.

Hint If the acquiring company were to pay less than its current value per dollar of earnings to acquire each dollar of earnings (P/E paid < P/E of acquiring company), the opposite effects would result.

Example Grand Company's P/E ratio is 20, and the P/E ratio paid for Small Company's earnings was 22 ($110 ÷ $5). Because the P/E paid for Small Company was greater than the P/E for Grand Company (22 versus 20), the effect of the merger was to decrease the EPS for original holders of shares in Grand Company (from $4.00 to $3.93) and to increase the effective EPS of original holders of shares in Small Company (from $5.00 to $5.40).

TABLE 17.6	Effect of Price/Earnings (P/E) Ratios on Earnings per Share (EPS)	

| | Effect on EPS | |
Relationship between P/E paid and P/E of acquiring company	Acquiring company	Target company
P/E paid > P/E of acquiring company	Decrease	Increase
P/E paid = P/E of acquiring company	Constant	Constant
P/E paid < P/E of acquiring company	Increase	Decrease

Long-Run Effect   The long-run effect of a merger on the earnings per share of the merged company depends largely on whether the earnings of the merged firm grow. Often, although an initial decrease in the per-share earnings of the stock held by the original owners of the acquiring firm is expected, the long-run effects of the merger on earnings per share are quite favorable. Because firms generally expect growth in earnings, the key factor enabling the acquiring company to experience higher future EPS than it would have without the merger is that the earnings attributable to the target company's assets grow more rapidly than those resulting from the acquiring company's premerger assets. An example will clarify this point.

Example

In 2009, Grand Company acquired Small Company by swapping 1.375 shares of its common stock for each share of Small Company. Other key financial data and the effects of this exchange ratio were discussed in preceding examples. The total earnings of Grand Company were expected to grow at an annual rate of 3% without the merger; Small Company's earnings were expected to grow at a 7% annual rate without the merger. The same growth rates are expected to apply to the component earnings streams with the merger.[7] The table in Figure 17.1 shows the future effects on EPS for Grand Company without and with the proposed Small Company merger, on the basis of these growth rates.

The table indicates that the earnings per share without the merger will be greater than the EPS with the merger for the years 2009 through 2011. After 2011, however, the EPS will be higher than they would have been without the merger as a result of the faster earnings growth rate of Small Company (7% versus 3%). Although a few years are required for this difference in the growth rate of earnings to pay off, in the future Grand Company will receive an earnings benefit as a result of merging with Small Company at a 1.375 ratio of exchange. The long-run earnings advantage of the merger is clearly depicted in Figure 17.1.[8]

Effect on Market Price per Share

ratio of exchange in market price
Indicates the market price per share of the acquiring firm *paid* for each dollar of market price per share of the target firm.

The market price per share does not necessarily remain constant after the acquisition of one firm by another. Adjustments occur in the marketplace in response to changes in expected earnings, the dilution of ownership, changes in risk, and certain other operating and financial changes. By using the ratio of exchange, we can calculate a **ratio of exchange in market price**. It indicates the market price per share of the acquiring firm *paid* for each dollar of market price per share of the target firm. This ratio, the *MPR*, is defined by Equation 17.1:

$$MPR = \frac{MP_{\text{acquiring}} \times RE}{MP_{\text{target}}}$$

(17.1)

---

7. Frequently, because of synergy, the combined earnings stream is greater than the sum of the individual earnings streams. This possibility is ignored here.

8. To discover properly whether the merger is beneficial, the earnings estimates under each alternative would have to be made over a long period of time—say, 50 years—and then converted to cash flows and discounted at the appropriate rate. The alternative with the higher present value would be preferred. For simplicity, only the basic intuitive view of the long-run effect is presented here.

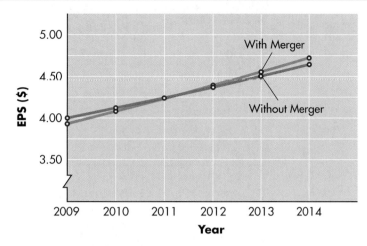

FIGURE 17.1

Future EPS
Future EPS without and with the Grand–Small merger

	Without Merger		With Merger	
Year	**Total earnings**[a]	**Earnings per share**[b]	**Total earnings**[c]	**Earnings per share**[d]
2009	$500,000	$4.00	$600,000	$3.93
2010	515,000	4.12	622,000	4.08
2011	530,450	4.24	644,940	4.23
2012	546,364	4.37	668,868	4.39
2013	562,755	4.50	693,835	4.55
2014	579,638	4.64	719,893	4.72

[a]Based on a 3% annual growth rate.
[b]Based on 125,000 shares outstanding.
[c]Based on a 3% annual growth in the Grand Company's earnings and a 7% annual growth in the Small Company's earnings.
[d]Based on 152,500 shares outstanding [125,000 shares + (1.375 × 20,000 shares)].

where

$$MPR = \text{market price ratio of exchange}$$
$$MP_{acquiring} = \text{market price per share of the acquiring firm}$$
$$MP_{target} = \text{market price per share of the target firm}$$
$$RE = \text{ratio of exchange}$$

Example

The market price of Grand Company's stock was $80, and that of Small Company's was $75. The ratio of exchange was 1.375. Substituting these values into Equation 17.1 yields a ratio of exchange in market price of 1.47 [($80 × 1.375) ÷ $75]. This means that $1.47 of the market price of Grand Company is given in exchange for every $1.00 of the market price of Small Company.

The ratio of exchange in market price is normally greater than 1, which indicates that to acquire a firm, the acquirer must pay a premium above its market price. Even so, the original owners of the acquiring firm may still gain, because

TABLE 17.7	Postmerger Market Price of Grand Company Using a P/E Ratio of 21

Item	Merged company
(1) Earnings available for common stock	$600,000
(2) Number of shares of common stock outstanding	152,500
(3) Earnings per share [(1) ÷ (2)]	$3.93
(4) Price/earnings (P/E) ratio	21
(5) Expected market price per share [(3) × (4)]	$82.53

the merged firm's stock may sell at a price/earnings ratio above the individual premerger ratios. This results from the improved risk and return relationship perceived by shareholders and other investors.

Example

The financial data developed earlier for the Grand–Small merger can be used to explain the market price effects of a merger. If the earnings of the merged company remain at the premerger levels, and if the stock of the merged company sells at an assumed multiple of 21 times earnings, the values in Table 17.7 can be expected. Although Grand Company's earnings per share decline from $4.00 to $3.93 (see Table 17.5), the market price of its shares will increase from $80.00 to $82.53 as a result of the merger.

Although the behavior exhibited in the preceding example is not unusual, the financial manager must recognize that only with proper management of the merged enterprise can its market value be improved. If the merged firm cannot achieve sufficiently high earnings in view of its risk, there is no guarantee that its market price will reach the forecast value. Nevertheless, a policy of acquiring firms with low P/Es can produce favorable results for the owners of the acquiring firm. Acquisitions are especially attractive when the acquiring firm's stock price is high, because fewer shares must be exchanged to acquire a given firm.

Merger Negotiation Process

investment bankers
Financial intermediaries who, in addition to their role in selling new security issues, can be hired by acquirers in mergers to find suitable target companies and assist in negotiations.

Mergers are often handled by **investment bankers**—financial intermediaries who, in addition to their role in selling new security issues (described in Chapter 7), can be hired by acquirers to find suitable target companies and assist in negotiations. Once a target company is selected, the investment banker negotiates with its management or investment banker. Likewise, when management wishes to sell the firm or an operating unit of the firm, it will hire an investment banker to seek out potential buyers.

If attempts to negotiate with the management of the target company break down, the acquiring firm, often with the aid of its investment banker, can make a direct appeal to shareholders by using *tender offers* (as explained below). The investment banker is typically compensated with a fixed fee, a commission tied to the transaction price, or a combination of fees and commissions.

Management Negotiations

To initiate negotiations, the acquiring firm must make an offer either in cash or based on a stock swap with a specified ratio of exchange. The target company then reviews the offer and, in light of alternative offers, accepts or rejects the terms presented. A desirable merger candidate usually receives more than a single offer. Normally, it is necessary to resolve certain nonfinancial issues related to the existing management, product line policies, financing policies, and the independence of the target firm. The key factor, of course, is the per-share price offered in cash or reflected in the ratio of exchange. Sometimes negotiations break down.

Tender Offers

When negotiations for an acquisition break down, tender offers may be used to negotiate a "hostile merger" directly with the firm's stockholders. As noted in Chapter 13, a *tender offer* is a formal offer to purchase a given number of shares of a firm's stock at a specified price. The offer is made to all the stockholders at a premium above the market price. Occasionally, the acquirer will make a **two-tier offer,** in which the terms offered are more attractive to those who tender shares early. For example, the acquirer offers to pay $25 per share for the first 60 percent of the outstanding shares tendered and only $23 per share for the remaining shares. The stockholders are advised of a tender offer through announcements in financial newspapers or through direct communications from the offering firm. Sometimes a tender offer is made to add pressure to existing merger negotiations. In other cases, the tender offer may be made without warning as an attempt at an abrupt corporate takeover.

two-tier offer
A *tender offer* in which the terms offered are more attractive to those who tender shares early.

Fighting Hostile Takeovers

If the management of a target firm does not favor a merger or considers the price offered in a proposed merger too low, it is likely to take defensive actions to ward off the *hostile takeover.* Such actions are generally taken with the assistance of investment bankers and lawyers who help the firm develop and employ effective **takeover defenses.** There are obvious strategies, such as informing stockholders of the alleged damaging effects of a takeover, acquiring another company (discussed earlier in the chapter), or attempting to sue the acquiring firm on antitrust or other grounds. In addition, many other defenses exist (some with colorful names)—white knight, poison pills, greenmail, leveraged recapitalization, golden parachutes, and shark repellents.

The **white knight** strategy involves the target firm finding a more suitable acquirer (the "white knight") and prompting it to compete with the initial hostile acquirer to take over the firm. If being taken over is nearly certain, the target firm attempts to be taken over by a firm deemed most acceptable to its management. **Poison pills** typically involve the creation of securities that give their holders certain rights that become effective when a takeover is attempted. The "pill" allows the shareholders to receive special voting rights or securities that make the firm less desirable to the hostile acquirer. **Greenmail** is a strategy by which the firm repurchases, through private negotiation, a large block of stock at a premium from one or more shareholders to end a hostile takeover attempt by those shareholders. Clearly, greenmail is a form of corporate blackmail by the holders of a large block of shares.

takeover defenses
Strategies for fighting hostile takeovers.

white knight
A takeover defense in which the target firm finds an acquirer more to its liking than the initial hostile acquirer and prompts the two to compete to take over the firm.

poison pill
A takeover defense in which a firm issues securities that give their holders certain rights that become effective when a takeover is attempted; these rights make the target firm less desirable to a hostile acquirer.

greenmail
A takeover defense under which a target firm repurchases, through private negotiation, a large block of stock at a premium from one or more shareholders to end a hostile takeover attempt by those shareholders.

leveraged recapitalization
A takeover defense in which the target firm pays a large debt-financed cash dividend, increasing the firm's financial leverage and thereby deterring the takeover attempt.

golden parachutes
Provisions in the employment contracts of key executives that provide them with sizable compensation if the firm is taken over; deters hostile takeovers to the extent that the cash outflows required are large enough to make the takeover unattractive.

shark repellents
Antitakeover amendments to a corporate charter that constrain the firm's ability to transfer managerial control of the firm as a result of a merger.

Another defense against hostile takeover involves the use of a **leveraged recapitalization,** which is a strategy involving the payment of a large debt-financed cash dividend. This strategy significantly increases the firm's financial leverage, thereby deterring the takeover attempt. In addition, as a further deterrent, the recapitalization is often structured to increase the equity and control of the existing management. **Golden parachutes** are provisions in the employment contracts of key executives that provide them with sizable compensation if the firm is taken over. Golden parachutes deter hostile takeovers to the extent that the cash outflows required by these contracts are large enough to make the takeover unattractive to the acquirer. Another defense is use of **shark repellents,** which are antitakeover amendments to the corporate charter that constrain the firm's ability to transfer managerial control of the firm as a result of a merger. Although this defense could entrench existing management, many firms have had these amendments ratified by shareholders.

Because takeover defenses tend to insulate management from shareholders, the potential for litigation is great when these strategies are employed. Lawsuits are sometimes filed against management by dissident shareholders. In addition, federal and state governments frequently intervene when a proposed takeover is deemed to be in violation of federal or state law. A number of states have legislation on their books limiting or restricting hostile takeovers of companies domiciled within their boundaries.

Holding Companies

A *holding company* is a corporation that has voting control of one or more other corporations. The holding company may need to own only a small percentage of the outstanding shares to have this voting control. In the case of companies with a relatively small number of shareholders, as much as 30 to 40 percent of the stock may be required. In the case of firms with a widely dispersed ownership, 10 to 20 percent of the shares may be sufficient to gain voting control. A holding company that wants to obtain voting control of a firm may use direct market purchases or tender offers to acquire needed shares. Although there are relatively few holding companies and they are far less important than mergers, it is helpful to understand their key advantages and disadvantages.

Advantages of Holding Companies

The primary advantage of holding companies is the *leverage effect* that permits the firm to control a large amount of assets with a relatively small dollar investment. In other words, the owners of a holding company can *control* significantly larger amounts of assets than they could *acquire* through mergers.

Example   Carr Company, a holding company, currently holds voting control of two subsidiaries—company X and company Y. Table 17.8 presents the balance sheets for Carr and its two subsidiaries. Carr owns approximately 17% ($10 ÷ $60) of company X and 20% ($14 ÷ $70) of company Y. These holdings are sufficient for voting control.

TABLE 17.8	Balance Sheets for Carr Company and Its Subsidiaries	

Assets		Liabilities and Stockholders' Equity	
Carr Company			
Common stock holdings		Long-term debt	$ 6
Company X	$10	Preferred stock	6
Company Y	14	Common stock equity	12
Total	$24	Total	$24
Company X			
Current assets	$ 30	Current liabilities	$ 15
Fixed assets	70	Long-term debt	25
Total	$100	Common stock equity	60
		Total	$100
Company Y			
Current assets	$ 20	Current liabilities	$ 10
Fixed assets	140	Long-term debt	60
Total	$160	Preferred stock	20
		Common stock equity	70
		Total	$160

The owners of Carr Company's $12 worth of equity have control over $260 worth of assets (company X's $100 worth and company Y's $160 worth). Thus the owners' equity represents only about 4.6% ($12 ÷ $260) of the total assets controlled. From the discussions of ratio analysis, leverage, and capital structure in Chapters 2 and 12, you should recognize that this is quite a high degree of leverage. If an individual stockholder or even another holding company owns $3 of Carr Company's stock, which is assumed to be sufficient for its control, it will in actuality control the whole $260 of assets. The investment itself in this case would represent only 1.15% ($3 ÷ $260) of the assets controlled.

The high leverage obtained through a holding company arrangement greatly magnifies earnings and losses for the holding company. Quite often, a **pyramiding** of holding companies occurs when one holding company controls other holding companies, thereby causing an even greater magnification of earnings and losses. The greater the leverage, the greater the risk involved. The risk–return tradeoff is a key consideration in the holding company decision.

Another commonly cited advantage of holding companies is the *risk protection* resulting from the fact that the failure of one of the companies (such as Y in the preceding example) does not result in the failure of the entire holding company. Because each subsidiary is a separate corporation, the failure of one company should cost the holding company, at maximum, no more than its investment in that subsidiary. Other advantages include the following: (1) Certain state *tax benefits* may be realized by each subsidiary in its state of incorporation. (2) *Lawsuits*

pyramiding
An arrangement among holding companies wherein one holding company controls other holding companies, thereby causing an even greater magnification of earnings and losses.

or legal actions against a subsidiary do not threaten the remaining companies. (3) It is *generally easy to gain control* of a firm, because stockholder or management approval is not generally necessary.

Disadvantages of Holding Companies

A major disadvantage of holding companies is the *increased risk* resulting from the leverage effect. When general economic conditions are unfavorable, a loss by one subsidiary may be magnified. For example, if subsidiary company X in Table 17.8 experiences a loss, its inability to pay dividends to Carr Company could result in Carr Company's inability to meet its scheduled payments.

Another disadvantage is *double taxation*. Before paying dividends, a subsidiary must pay federal and state taxes on its earnings. Although a 70 percent tax exclusion is allowed on dividends received by one corporation from another, the remaining 30 percent received is taxable. (In the event that the holding company owns between 20 and 80 percent of the stock in a subsidiary, the exclusion is 80 percent; if it owns more than 80 percent of the stock in the subsidiary, 100 percent of the dividends are excluded.) If a subsidiary were part of a merged company, double taxation would *not* exist.

The fact that holding companies are *difficult to analyze* is another disadvantage. Security analysts and investors typically have difficulty understanding holding companies because of their complexity. As a result, these firms tend to sell at low multiples of earnings (P/Es), and the shareholder value of holding companies may suffer.

A final disadvantage of holding companies is the generally *high cost of administration* that results from maintaining each subsidiary company as a separate entity. A merger, on the other hand, is likely to result in certain administrative economies of scale. The need for coordination and communication between the holding company and its subsidiaries may further elevate these costs.

 ## International Mergers

Perhaps in no other area does U.S. financial practice differ more fundamentally from practices in other countries than in the field of mergers. Outside of the United States (and, to a lesser degree, Great Britain), hostile takeovers are virtually nonexistent, and in some countries (such as Japan), takeovers of any kind are uncommon. The emphasis in the United States and Great Britain on shareholder value and reliance on public capital markets for financing has generally been inapplicable in continental Europe. This occurs because companies there are generally smaller and because other stakeholders, such as employees, bankers, and governments, are accorded greater consideration. The U.S. approach is also a poor fit for business in Japan and other Asian nations.

Changes in Western Europe

Today, it is clear that Western Europe is moving toward a U.S.-style approach to shareholder value and public capital market financing. Since the European Union's (EU's) economic and monetary union (EMU) integration involving the introduction of a single European currency, the euro, on January 1, 2002, the number, size, and importance of cross-border European mergers has continued to grow rapidly. Nationally focused companies want to achieve economies of scale in manufacturing, encourage international product development strategies, and develop distribution networks across the continent. They are also driven by the need to compete with U.S. companies, which have been operating on a continentwide basis in Europe for decades.

These larger European-based companies are expected to become even more formidable competitors as more national barriers are fully removed. Although the vast majority of these cross-border mergers are friendly in nature, a few have been actively resisted by target firm managements. It seems clear that as European companies come to rely more on public capital markets for financing, and as the market for common stock becomes more truly European in character, rather than French or British or German, active markets for European corporate equity will continue to evolve.

Foreign Takeovers of U.S. Companies

Both European and Japanese companies have been active as acquirers of U.S. companies in recent years. Foreign companies purchased U.S. firms for two major reasons: to gain access to the world's single largest, richest, and least regulated market and to acquire world-class technology at a bargain price. British companies have been historically the most active acquirers of U.S. firms. In the late 1980s, Japanese corporations surged to prominence with a series of very large acquisitions, including two in the entertainment industry: Sony's purchase of Columbia Pictures and Matsushita's acquisition of MCA. More recently, German firms have become especially active acquirers of U.S. companies as producing export goods in Germany has become prohibitively expensive. (German workers have some of the world's highest wages and one of the shortest workweeks.) The *Global Focus* box on page 784 describes recent mergers by Australian media giant News Corp. It seems inevitable that in the years ahead, foreign companies will continue to acquire U.S. firms even as U.S. companies continue to seek attractive acquisitions abroad.

REVIEW QUESTIONS

17–6   Describe the procedures that are typically used by an acquirer to value a target company, whether it is being acquired for its assets or as a going concern.

17–7   What is the *ratio of exchange?* Is it based on the current market prices of the shares of the acquiring and target firms? Why may a long-run view of the merged firm's earnings per share change a merger decision?

17–8   What role do *investment bankers* often play in the merger negotiation process? What is a *tender offer?* When and how is it used?

17–9   Briefly describe each of the following *takeover defenses* against a hostile merger: (**a**) white knight, (**b**) poison pill, (**c**) greenmail, (**d**) leveraged recapitalization, (**e**) golden parachutes, and (**f**) shark repellents.

17–10 What key advantages and disadvantages are associated with holding companies? What is *pyramiding* and what are its consequences?

17–11 Discuss the differences in merger practices between U.S. companies and companies in other countries. What changes are occurring in international merger activity, particularly in Western Europe and Japan?

Global Focus   International Mergers

In July 2005, Australian-based media giant **News Corp** launched a series of acquisitions involving U.S. assets. The first was a $580 million buyout of **Intermix Media,** owner of Myspace.com, the fifth most viewed Internet domain in the United States at the time. Rupert Murdoch, the media mogul running News Corp, calculated that the Myspace networking site would drive traffic to his Fox TV sites.

Murdoch's next purchase came in September 2006, when News Corp acquired, from **Verisign,** a majority stake in **Jamba,** which runs Jamster, a download service for such commodities as ring tones and screen "wallpapers." News Corp's intent was to hardwire Fox's presence in the entire content lifecycle, from creation, through production, to delivery on your cell phone screen. It already had a mobile content provider, **Mobizzo,** launched in June 2005 under the Fox Mobile Entertainment division. Among the things Mobizzo was designed

to offer were 1-minute episodes derived from Fox properties such as its *American Idol* franchise.

In May 2007, News Corp set its sight on a new target, **Dow Jones,** publisher of *The Wall Street Journal* and *Barron's* and the owner of other financial news and content assets including the Dow Jones Newswires, the financial website MarketWatch, and several stock market indicators (e.g., the Dow Jones Industrial Average). Murdoch's News Corp bid $5 billion for Dow Jones but faced resistance from members of the Bancroft family—descendents of Clarence Barron, the "father of financial journalism"—which controls more than 50 percent of the voting power in the company. The News Corp bid was remarkable for its premium, which would value Dow Jones at more than double its trading value prior to the bid.

International mergers, such as the ones pursued by News Corp, are not as easy to execute as in-country mergers. Complicating matters are multiple legal and regulatory regimes, cultural

differences, and complex timing requirements involving simultaneously closing the deal in multiple jurisdictions. Further complications may arise from a potential distrust of employees or owners from another country. In the Dow Jones case, the Dow Jones board and the Bancroft family sought to negotiate some level of independence for the *Journal* so that it may remain free of corporate interference.

Not all international mergers end well. In May 2007, 9 years after purchasing **Chrysler Group** for $36 billion, **DaimlerChrysler AG** sold 80.1% of Chrysler Holdings to the **Cerebus Capital Management LP** private-equity operation for a mere $7.9 billion. Of that amount, Daimler will get very little, as it will pay almost $6 billion of the $7.9 billion directly into Chrysler Corp and Chrysler Financial Services LLC.

■ *Why might the potential News Corp acquisition of Dow Jones be a better fit than the Daimler-Benz AG purchase of Chrysler?*

17.4 | Business Failure Fundamentals

A business failure is an unfortunate circumstance. Although the majority of firms that fail do so within the first year or two of life, other firms grow, mature, and fail much later. The failure of a business can be viewed in a number of ways and can result from one or more causes.

Types of Business Failure

A firm may fail because its *returns are negative or low.* A firm that consistently reports operating losses will probably experience a decline in market value. If the firm fails to earn a return that is greater than its cost of capital, it can be viewed as having failed. Negative or low returns, unless remedied, are likely to result eventually in one of the following more serious types of failure.

A second type of failure, **technical insolvency,** occurs when a firm is unable to pay its liabilities as they come due. When a firm is technically insolvent, its assets are still greater than its liabilities, but it is confronted with a *liquidity crisis*. If some of its assets can be converted into cash within a reasonable period, the company may be able to escape complete failure. If not, the result is the third and most serious type of failure, bankruptcy.

Bankruptcy occurs when the stated value of a firm's liabilities exceeds the fair market value of its assets. A bankrupt firm has a *negative* stockholders' equity.[9] This means that the claims of creditors cannot be satisfied unless the firm's assets can be liquidated for more than their book value. Although bankruptcy is an obvious form of failure, *the courts treat technical insolvency and bankruptcy in the same way*. They are both considered to indicate the financial failure of the firm.

technical insolvency
Business failure that occurs when a firm is unable to pay its liabilities as they come due.

bankruptcy
Business failure that occurs when the stated value of a firm's liabilities exceeds the fair market value of its assets.

Major Causes of Business Failure

The primary cause of business failure is *mismanagement,* which accounts for more than 50 percent of all cases. Numerous specific managerial faults can cause the firm to fail. Overexpansion, poor financial actions, an ineffective sales force, and high production costs can all singly or in combination cause failure. For example, *poor financial actions* include bad capital budgeting decisions (based on unrealistic sales and cost forecasts, failure to identify all relevant cash flows, or failure to assess risk properly), poor financial evaluation of the firm's strategic plans prior to making financial commitments, inadequate or nonexistent cash flow planning, and failure to control receivables and inventories. Because all major corporate decisions are eventually measured in terms of dollars, the financial manager may play a key role in avoiding or causing a business failure. It is his or her duty to monitor the firm's financial pulse. For example, the largest bankruptcy ever, Enron Corporation's early 2002 bankruptcy, was largely attributed to questionable partnerships set up by Enron's CFO, Andrew Fastow. Those partnerships were intended to hide Enron's debt, inflate its profits, and enrich its top management. In late 2001, these transactions blew up, causing the corporation to file bankruptcy and resulting in criminal charges against Enron's key executives as well as its auditor, Arthur Andersen, which failed to accurately disclose Enron's financial condition.

Economic activity—especially economic downturns—can contribute to the failure of a firm.[10] If the economy goes into a recession, sales may decrease abruptly, leaving the firm with high fixed costs and insufficient revenues to cover them. Rapid rises in interest rates just prior to a recession can further contribute to cash flow problems and make it more difficult for the firm to obtain and maintain needed financing.

9. Because on a balance sheet the firm's assets equal the sum of its liabilities and stockholders' equity, the only way a firm that has more liabilities than assets can balance its balance sheet is to have a *negative* stockholders' equity.

10. The success of some firms runs countercyclical to economic activity, and other firms are unaffected by economic activity. For example, the auto repair business is likely to grow during a recession, because people are less likely to buy new cars and therefore need more repairs on their unwarrantied older cars. The sales of boats and other luxury items may decline during a recession, whereas sales of staple items such as electricity are likely to be unaffected. In terms of beta—the measure of nondiversifiable risk developed in Chapter 5—a negative-beta stock would be associated with a firm whose behavior is generally countercyclical to economic activity.

A final cause of business failure is *corporate maturity*. Firms, like individuals, do not have infinite lives. Like a product, a firm goes through the stages of birth, growth, maturity, and eventual decline. The firm's management should attempt to prolong the growth stage through research, new products, and mergers. Once the firm has matured and has begun to decline, it should seek to be acquired by another firm or liquidate before it fails. Effective management planning should help the firm to postpone decline and ultimate failure.

Voluntary Settlements

voluntary settlement
An arrangement between a technically insolvent or bankrupt firm and its creditors enabling it to bypass many of the costs involved in legal bankruptcy proceedings.

When a firm becomes technically insolvent or bankrupt, it may arrange with its creditors a **voluntary settlement**, which enables it to bypass many of the costs involved in legal bankruptcy proceedings. The settlement is normally initiated by the debtor firm, because such an arrangement may enable it to continue to exist or to be liquidated in a manner that gives the owners the greatest chance of recovering part of their investment. The debtor arranges a meeting between itself and all its creditors. At the meeting, a committee of creditors is selected to analyze the debtor's situation and recommend a plan of action. The recommendations of the committee are discussed with both the debtor and the creditors, and a plan for sustaining or liquidating the firm is drawn up.

Voluntary Settlement to Sustain the Firm

extension
An arrangement whereby the firm's creditors receive payment in full, although not immediately.

composition
A pro rata cash settlement of creditor claims by the debtor firm; a uniform percentage of each dollar owed is paid.

creditor control
An arrangement in which the creditor committee replaces the firm's operating management and operates the firm until all claims have been settled.

Normally, the rationale for sustaining a firm depends on whether the firm's recovery is feasible. By sustaining the firm, the creditor can continue to receive business from it. A number of strategies are commonly used. An **extension** is an arrangement whereby the firm's creditors receive payment in full, although not immediately. Normally, when creditors grant an extension, they require the firm to make cash payments for purchases until all past debts have been paid. A second arrangement, called **composition**, is a pro rata cash settlement of creditor claims. Instead of receiving full payment of their claims, creditors receive only a partial payment. A uniform percentage of each dollar owed is paid in satisfaction of each creditor's claim.

A third arrangement is **creditor control**. In this case, the creditor committee may decide that maintaining the firm is feasible only if the operating management is replaced. The committee may then take control of the firm and operate it until all claims have been settled. Sometimes, a plan involving some combination of extension, composition, and creditor control will result. An example of this is a settlement whereby the debtor agrees to pay a total of 75 cents on the dollar in three annual installments of 25 cents on the dollar, and the creditors agree to sell additional merchandise to the firm on 30-day terms if the existing management is replaced by new management that is acceptable to them.

Voluntary Settlement Resulting in Liquidation

After the situation of the firm has been investigated by the creditor committee, the only acceptable course of action may be liquidation of the firm. Liquidation can be carried out in two ways—privately or through the legal procedures provided by bankruptcy law. If the debtor firm is willing to accept liquidation, legal procedures may not be required. Generally, the avoidance of litigation enables the creditors to obtain *quicker* and *higher* settlements. However, all the creditors must agree to a private liquidation for it to be feasible.

The objective of the voluntary liquidation process is to recover as much per dollar owed as possible. Under voluntary liquidation, common stockholders (the firm's true owners) cannot receive any funds until the claims of all other parties have been satisfied. A common procedure is to have a meeting of the creditors at which they make an **assignment** by passing the power to liquidate the firm's assets to an adjustment bureau, a trade association, or a third party, which is designated the *assignee*. The assignee's job is to liquidate the assets, obtaining the best price possible. The assignee is sometimes referred to as the *trustee*, because it is entrusted with the title to the company's assets and the responsibility to liquidate them efficiently. Once the trustee has liquidated the assets, it distributes the recovered funds to the creditors and owners (if any funds remain for the owners). The final action in a private liquidation is for the creditors to sign a release attesting to the satisfactory settlement of their claims.

assignment
A voluntary liquidation procedure by which a firm's creditors pass the power to liquidate the firm's assets to an adjustment bureau, a trade association, or a third party, which is designated the *assignee.*

REVIEW QUESTIONS

17–12 What are the three types of business failure? What is the difference between *technical insolvency* and *bankruptcy*? What are the major causes of business failure?

17–13 Define an *extension* and a *composition*, and explain how they might be combined to form a voluntary settlement plan to sustain the firm. How is a voluntary settlement resulting in liquidation handled?

17.5 | Reorganization and Liquidation in Bankruptcy

If a voluntary settlement for a failed firm cannot be agreed upon, the firm can be forced into bankruptcy by its creditors. As a result of bankruptcy proceedings, the firm may be either reorganized or liquidated. The *Focus on Ethics* box on page 788 examines some ethical issues related to bankruptcy.

Bankruptcy Legislation

Bankruptcy in the legal sense occurs when the firm cannot pay its bills or when its liabilities exceed the fair market value of its assets. In either case, a firm may be declared legally bankrupt. However, creditors generally attempt to avoid forcing a firm into bankruptcy if it appears to have opportunities for future success.

The governing bankruptcy legislation in the United States today is the **Bankruptcy Reform Act of 1978,** which significantly modified earlier bankruptcy legislation. This law contains eight odd-numbered chapters (1 through 15) and one even-numbered chapter (12). A number of these chapters would apply in the instance of failure; the two key ones are Chapters 7 and 11. **Chapter 7** of the Bankruptcy Reform Act of 1978 details the procedures to be followed when liquidating a failed firm. Chapter 7 typically comes into play once it has been determined that a fair, equitable, and feasible basis for the reorganization of a failed firm does not exist (although a firm may of its own accord choose not to reorganize and may instead go directly into liquidation). **Chapter 11** outlines the procedures for reorganizing a failed (or failing) firm, whether its petition is filed

Bankruptcy Reform Act of 1978
The governing bankruptcy legislation in the United States today.

Chapter 7
The portion of the *Bankruptcy Reform Act of 1978* that details the procedures to be followed when liquidating a failed firm.

Chapter 11
The portion of the *Bankruptcy Reform Act of 1978* that outlines the procedures for reorganizing a failed (or failing) firm, whether its petition is filed voluntarily or involuntarily.

Focus on Ethics   Is It Unethical to Declare Bankruptcy?

IN PRACTICE

Businesses that declare bankruptcy are committing crimes if they knowingly and fraudulently file a false proof of claim, if managers lie about a bankruptcy schedule, or if they fraudulently conceal assets. More intriguing is the possibility of acting *unethically* when declaring bankruptcy while following the letter of the law.

Bankruptcy has increasingly been viewed as a morally neutral event, used to give a struggling company a fresh start. Some corporate executives may view bankruptcy declarations as one among many strategic alternatives—leading some observers to coin the phrase "strategic bankruptcy." Such bankruptcies may be unethical for at least three reasons.

First, although bankruptcy may enable a company to survive by giving it time to rebuild liquidity, *the company never has to "make whole" those to whom moneys were owed*, including employees, creditors, or plaintiffs who have won a lawsuit against the company. In the **United Airlines** bankruptcy case, United was allowed to settle $5.1 billion in creditor claims for a mere $150 million.

Second, bankruptcy proceedings *take from others amounts that were agreed upon in good-faith contracts and bargaining.* For example, **Delphi Corporation** was required to pay GM-level wages to its 24,000 UAW-represented employees when it was spun off from GM. In 2005, Delphi proposed cutting those wages from $27 per hour to $10 to $12 per hour. When the union objected, Delphi entered bankruptcy, where it could proceed with the cuts in wages, benefits, and jobs without the UAW's approval. The "no fault" bankruptcy world downplays the moral obligations arising from signing a contract.

Third, when a company declares Chapter 11 bankruptcy, *nonbankrupt competitors are harmed.* Competitors are no longer playing on a level field during the reorganization period. In industries where profit margins are already very tight, shareholders of nonbankrupt firms may suffer significant losses as bankrupt firms hold clearance sales and keep prices artificially low while they are freed from some of their prebankruptcy payables, wages, and loan interest and principal. This possibility is an especially tricky issue in the airline industry, where companies are able to declare bankruptcy more than once and stay in bankruptcy for extended periods of time.

■ *Some analysts favor easy bankruptcy declarations because they allow management teams to recover from uncontrollable outside economic events and correctable management decision mistakes. How might you counter this argument, both on practical and ethical grounds?*

---

voluntary reorganization
A petition filed by a failed firm on its own behalf for reorganizing its structure and paying its creditors.

involuntary reorganization
A petition initiated by an outside party, usually a creditor, for the reorganization and payment of creditors of a failed firm.

voluntarily or involuntarily. If a workable plan for reorganization cannot be developed, the firm will be liquidated under Chapter 7.

Reorganization in Bankruptcy (Chapter 11)

There are two basic types of reorganization petitions—voluntary and involuntary. Any firm that is not a municipal or financial institution can file a petition for **voluntary reorganization** on its own behalf.[11] **Involuntary reorganization** is initiated by an outside party, usually a creditor. An involuntary petition against a firm can be filed if one of three conditions is met:

---

11. Firms sometimes file a voluntary petition to obtain temporary legal protection from creditors or from prolonged litigation. Once they have straightened out their financial or legal affairs—prior to further reorganization or liquidation actions—they will have the petition dismissed. Although such actions are not the intent of the bankruptcy law, difficulty in enforcing the law has allowed this abuse to occur.

1. The firm has past-due debts of $5,000 or more.
2. Three or more creditors can prove that they have aggregate unpaid claims of $5,000 against the firm. If the firm has fewer than 12 creditors, any creditor that is owed more than $5,000 can file the petition.
3. The firm is *insolvent*, which means that (a) it is not paying its debts as they come due, (b) within the preceding 120 days a custodian (a third party) was appointed or took possession of the debtor's property, or (c) the fair market value of the firm's assets is less than the stated value of its liabilities.

Procedures

debtor in possession (DIP) The term for a firm that files a reorganization petition under Chapter 11 and then develops, if feasible, a reorganization plan.

A reorganization petition under Chapter 11 must be filed in a federal bankruptcy court. Upon the filing of this petition, the filing firm becomes the **debtor in possession (DIP)** of the assets. If creditors object to the filing firm being the debtor in possession, they can ask the judge to appoint a trustee. After reviewing the firm's situation, the debtor in possession submits a plan of reorganization and a disclosure statement summarizing the plan to the court. A hearing is held to determine whether the plan is *fair, equitable,* and *feasible* and whether the disclosure statement contains adequate information. The court's approval or disapproval is based on its evaluation of the plan in light of these standards. A plan is considered *fair and equitable* if it *maintains the priorities* of the contractual claims of the creditors, preferred stockholders, and common stockholders. The court must also find the reorganization plan *feasible,* which means that it must be *workable.* The reorganized corporation must have sufficient working capital, sufficient funds to cover fixed charges, sufficient credit prospects, and sufficient ability to retire or refund debts as proposed by the plan.

Hint Some firms, particularly those in the airline industry, have used the bankruptcy laws to prevent technical insolvency. The courts have allowed them to nullify labor contracts on the basis that to force the firm to continue to conform to the contract would cause the firm eventually to become insolvent.

Once approved, the plan and the disclosure statement are given to the firm's creditors and shareholders for their acceptance. Under the Bankruptcy Reform Act, creditors and owners are separated into groups with similar types of claims. In the case of creditor groups, approval of the plan is required by holders of at least two-thirds of the dollar amount of claims, as well as by a numerical majority of creditors. In the case of ownership groups (preferred and common stockholders), two-thirds of the shares in each group must approve the reorganization plan for it to be accepted. Once accepted and confirmed by the court, the plan is put into effect as soon as possible.

Personal Finance Example   Individuals, like corporations, sometimes fail financially. Typically, a lack of financial planning, a heavy debt load, or an economic recession are factors that cause debtors to start missing payments and experiencing deterioration in their credit ratings. Unless they take corrective action, repossession of debt-financed property and eventually personal bankruptcy will follow. Individuals in dire financial straits have two legal options: a wage earner plan or straight bankruptcy.

A *wage earner plan,* defined under *Chapter 13* of the U.S. Bankruptcy Code, is a "work-out" procedure that involves some type of debt restructuring—typically establishing a debt-repayment schedule that is workable in light of the individual's personal income. This is similar to *reorganization* in a corporate bankruptcy. A majority of creditors must agree to this plan, under which interest payments and late fees are waived during the repayment period. If approved, the individual, who retains the use of and title to all assets, makes payments to the court, which then pays off all creditors.

Straight bankruptcy is allowed under *Chapter 7* of the bankruptcy code. It is a legal procedure, similar to *liquidation* in corporate bankruptcy, that effectively allows the debtor to "wipe the slate clean and start anew." However straight bankruptcy does not eliminate all of a debtor's obligations, nor does the debtor lose all of his or her assets. For example, the debtor must make certain tax payments and keep up alimony and child-support payments but can retain certain payments from Social Security, retirement, and disability benefits. Depending on state law, the debtor can retain a certain amount of equity in a home, a car, and other assets.

Role of the Debtor in Possession (DIP)

Because reorganization activities are largely in the hands of the debtor in possession (DIP), it is useful to understand the DIP's responsibilities. The DIP's first responsibility is the valuation of the firm to determine whether reorganization is appropriate. To do this, the DIP must estimate both the *liquidation value* of the business and its value as a *going concern*. If the firm's value as a going concern is less than its liquidation value, the DIP will recommend liquidation. If the opposite is found to be true, the DIP will recommend reorganization, and a plan of reorganization must be drawn up.

recapitalization
The reorganization procedure under which a failed firm's debts are generally exchanged for equity or the maturities of existing debts are extended.

The key portion of the reorganization plan generally concerns the firm's capital structure. Because most firms' financial difficulties result from high fixed charges, the company's capital structure is generally *recapitalized* to reduce these charges. Under **recapitalization,** debts are generally exchanged for equity or the maturities of existing debts are extended. When recapitalizing the firm, the DIP seeks to build a mix of debt and equity that will allow the firm to meet its debts and provide a reasonable level of earnings for its owners.

Once the revised capital structure has been determined, the DIP must establish a plan for exchanging outstanding obligations for new securities. The guiding principle is to observe priorities. Senior claims (those with higher legal priority) must be satisfied before junior claims (those with lower legal priority). To comply with this principle, senior suppliers of capital must receive a claim on new capital equal to their previous claim. The common stockholders are the last to receive any new securities. (It is not unusual for them to receive nothing.) Security holders do not necessarily have to receive the same type of security they held before; often they receive a combination of securities. Once the debtor in possession has determined the new capital structure and distribution of capital, it will submit the reorganization plan and disclosure statement to the court as described.

Liquidation in Bankruptcy (Chapter 7)

The liquidation of a bankrupt firm usually occurs once the bankruptcy court has determined that reorganization is not feasible. A petition for reorganization must normally be filed by the managers or creditors of the bankrupt firm. If no petition is filed, if a petition is filed and denied, or if the reorganization plan is denied, the firm must be liquidated.

Procedures

When a firm is adjudged bankrupt, the judge may appoint a *trustee* to perform the many routine duties required in administering the bankruptcy. The trustee takes charge of the property of the bankrupt firm and protects the interest of its creditors. A meeting of creditors must be held between 20 and 40 days after the bankruptcy judgment. At this meeting, the creditors are made aware of the prospects for the liquidation. The trustee is given the responsibility to liquidate the firm, keep records, examine creditors' claims, disburse money, furnish information as required, and make final reports on the liquidation. In essence, the trustee is responsible for the liquidation of the firm. Occasionally, the court will call subsequent creditor meetings, but only a final meeting for closing the bankruptcy is required.

Priority of Claims

It is the trustee's responsibility to liquidate all the firm's assets and to distribute the proceeds to the holders of *provable claims*. The courts have established certain procedures for determining the provability of claims. The priority of claims, which is specified in Chapter 7 of the Bankruptcy Reform Act, must be maintained by the trustee when distributing the funds from liquidation. Any **secured creditors** have specific assets pledged as collateral and, in liquidation, receive proceeds from the sale of those assets. If these proceeds are inadequate to fully satisfy their claims, the secured creditors become **unsecured, or general, creditors** for the unrecovered amount, because specific collateral no longer exists. These and all other unsecured creditors will divide up, on a pro rata basis, any funds remaining after all prior claims have been satisfied. If the proceeds from the sale of secured assets are in excess of the claims against them, the excess funds become available to meet claims of unsecured creditors.

The complete order of priority of claims is given in Table 17.9. In spite of the priorities listed in items 1 through 7, secured creditors have first claim on proceeds from the sale of their collateral. The claims of unsecured creditors, including

secured creditors
Creditors who have specific assets pledged as collateral and, in liquidation of the failed firm, receive proceeds from the sale of those assets.

unsecured, or general, creditors
Creditors who have a general claim against all the firm's assets other than those specifically pledged as collateral.

TABLE 17.9   Order of Priority of Claims in Liquidation of a Failed Firm

1. The expenses of administering the bankruptcy proceedings.
2. Any unpaid interim expenses incurred in the ordinary course of business between filing the bankruptcy petition and formal action by the court in an involuntary proceeding. (This step is *not* applicable in a voluntary bankruptcy.)
3. Wages of not more than $4,650 per worker that have been earned by workers in the 90-day period immediately preceding the commencement of bankruptcy proceedings.
4. Unpaid employee benefit plan contributions that were to be paid in the 180-day period preceding the filing of bankruptcy or the termination of business, whichever occurred first. For any employee, the sum of this claim plus eligible unpaid wages (item 3) cannot exceed $4,650.
5. Claims of farmers or fishermen in a grain-storage or fish-storage facility, not to exceed $4,650 for each producer.
6. Unsecured customer deposits, not to exceed $2,100 each, resulting from purchasing or leasing a good or service from the failed firm.
7. Taxes legally due and owed by the bankrupt firm to the federal government, state government, or any other governmental subdivision.
8. Claims of secured creditors, who receive the proceeds from the sale of collateral held, regardless of the preceding priorities. If the proceeds from the liquidation of the collateral are insufficient to satisfy the secured creditors' claims, the secured creditors become unsecured creditors for the unpaid amount.
9. Claims of unsecured creditors. The claims of unsecured, or general, creditors and unsatisfied portions of secured creditors' claims (item 8) are all treated equally.
10. Preferred stockholders, who receive an amount up to the par, or stated, value of their preferred stock.
11. Common stockholders, who receive any remaining funds, which are distributed on an equal per-share basis. If different classes of common stock are outstanding, priorities may exist.

the unpaid claims of secured creditors, are satisfied next, and then, finally, the claims of preferred and common stockholders. An example of the application of these priorities is included on the text's website at **www.prenhall.com/gitman**.

Final Accounting

After the trustee has liquidated all the bankrupt firm's assets and distributed the proceeds to satisfy all provable claims in the appropriate order of priority, he or she makes a final accounting to the bankruptcy court and creditors. Once the court approves the final accounting, the liquidation is complete.

REVIEW QUESTIONS

17–14 What is the concern of Chapter 11 of the Bankruptcy Reform Act of 1978? How is the *debtor in possession (DIP)* involved in (1) the valuation of the firm, (2) the recapitalization of the firm, and (3) the exchange of obligations using the priority rule?

17–15 What is the concern of Chapter 7 of the Bankruptcy Reform Act of 1978? Under which conditions is a firm liquidated in bankruptcy? Describe the procedures (including the role of the *trustee*) involved in liquidating the bankrupt firm.

17–16 Indicate in which order the following claims would be settled when distributing the proceeds from liquidating a bankrupt firm: (**a**) claims of preferred stockholders; (**b**) claims of secured creditors; (**c**) expenses of administering the bankruptcy; (**d**) claims of common stockholders; (**e**) claims of unsecured, or general, creditors; (**f**) taxes legally due; (**g**) unsecured deposits of customers; (**h**) certain eligible wages; (**i**) unpaid employee benefit plan contributions; (**j**) unpaid interim expenses incurred between the time of filing and formal action by the court; and (**k**) claims of farmers or fishermen in a grain-storage or fish-storage facility.

Summary

Focus on Value

The financial manager is sometimes involved in corporate restructuring activities, which involve the expansion and contraction of the firm's operations or changes in its asset or ownership structure. A variety of motives could drive a firm toward a merger, but the overriding goal should be maximization of the owners' wealth. Occasionally, merger transactions are heavily debt-financed leveraged buyouts (LBOs). In other cases, firms attempt to improve value by divesting themselves of certain operating units that they believe constrain the firm's value, particularly when the breakup value is believed to be greater than the firm's current value.

Whether the firm makes a cash purchase or uses a stock swap to acquire another firm, the risk-adjusted net present value of the transaction should be positive. In stock swap transactions, the long-run impact on the firm's earnings and risk can be evaluated to estimate the acquiring firm's post-acquisition value. Only in cases where additional value is created should the transaction be undertaken.

Business failure, though unpleasant, must be treated similarly; a failing firm should be reorganized only when such an act will maximize the owners' wealth. Otherwise, liquidation should be pursued in a fashion that allows the owners the greatest amount of recovery. Regardless of whether the firm is growing, contracting, or being reorganized or liquidated in bankruptcy, the firm should take action only when that action is believed to result in a positive contribution to the **maximization of the owners' wealth.**

Review of Learning Goals

LG 1 **Understand merger fundamentals, including terminology, motives for merging, and types of mergers.** Mergers result from the combining of firms. Typically, the acquiring company pursues and attempts to merge with the target company, on either a friendly or a hostile basis. Mergers are undertaken either for strategic reasons to achieve economies of scale or for financial reasons to restructure the firm to improve its cash flow. The overriding goal of merging is maximization of share price. Other specific merger motives include growth or diversification, synergy, fund raising, increased managerial skill or technology, tax considerations, increased ownership liquidity, and defense against takeover. The four basic types of mergers are horizontal, vertical, congeneric, and conglomerate.

LG 2 **Describe the objectives and procedures used in leveraged buyouts (LBOs) and divestitures.** LBOs involve use of a large amount of debt to purchase a firm. Divestiture involves the sale of a firm's assets, typically an operating unit; the spin-off of assets into an independent company; or the liquidation of assets. Motives for divestiture include cash generation and corporate restructuring.

LG 3 **Demonstrate the procedures used to value the target company, and discuss the effect of stock swap transactions on earnings per share.** The value of a target company can be estimated by applying capital budgeting techniques to the relevant cash flows. All proposed mergers with positive net present values are considered acceptable. In a stock swap transaction, a ratio of exchange must be established to measure the amount paid per share of the target company relative to the per-share market price of the acquiring firm. The resulting relationship between the price/earnings (P/E) ratio paid by the acquiring firm and its initial P/E affects the merged firm's earnings per share (EPS) and market price. If the P/E paid is greater than the P/E of the acquiring company, the EPS of the acquiring company decrease and the EPS of the target company increase.

LG 4 **Discuss the merger negotiation process, holding companies, and international mergers.** Acquirers commonly hire investment bankers to find a suitable target company and assist in negotiations. A merger can be negotiated with the target firm's management or, in the case of a hostile merger, directly with the firm's shareholders by using tender offers. Management of the target firm can employ various takeover defenses—a white knight, poison pill, greenmail, leveraged recapitalization, golden parachutes, and shark repellents. A holding company can be created by one firm gaining control of other companies, often by owning as little as 10 to 20 percent of their stock. The chief advantages of holding companies are the leverage effect, risk protection, tax benefits, protection against lawsuits, and the ease of gaining control of a subsidiary. Disadvantages include increased risk due to the magnification of losses, double taxation, difficulty of analysis, and the high cost of administration. Today, mergers of companies in Western Europe have moved toward the U.S.-style approach to shareholder value and public capital market financing. Both European and Japanese companies have become active acquirers of U.S. firms.

LG 5 **Understand the types and major causes of business failure and the use of voluntary settlements to sustain or liquidate the failed firm.** A firm may fail because it has negative or low returns, is technically insolvent, or is bankrupt. The major causes of business failure are mismanagement, downturns in economic activity, and corporate maturity. Voluntary settlements are initiated by the debtor and can result in sustaining the firm via an extension, a composition, creditor control of the firm, or a combination of these strategies. If creditors do not agree to a plan to sustain a firm, they may recommend voluntary liquidation, which bypasses many of the legal requirements and costs of bankruptcy proceedings.

LG 6 **Explain bankruptcy legislation and the procedures involved in reorganizing or liquidating a bankrupt firm.** A failed firm can voluntarily or involuntarily file in federal bankruptcy court for reorganization under Chapter 11 or for liquidation under Chapter 7 of the Bankruptcy Reform Act of 1978. Under Chapter 11, the judge will appoint the debtor in possession, which develops a reorganization plan. A firm that cannot be reorganized under Chapter 11 or does not petition for reorganization is liquidated under Chapter 7. The responsibility for liquidation is placed in the hands of a court-appointed trustee, whose duties include liquidating assets, distributing the proceeds, and making a final accounting. Liquidation procedures follow a priority of claims for distribution of the proceeds from the sale of assets.

Self-Test Problems (Solutions in Appendix B)

 ST17–1 **Cash acquisition decision** Luxe Foods is contemplating acquisition of Valley Canning Company for a cash price of $180,000. Luxe currently has high financial leverage and therefore has a cost of capital of 14%. As a result of acquiring Valley Canning, which is financed entirely with equity, the firm expects its financial leverage to be reduced and its cost of capital to drop to 11%. The acquisition of Valley Canning is expected to increase Luxe's cash inflows by $20,000 per year for the first 3 years and by $30,000 per year for the following 12 years.

a. Determine whether the proposed cash acquisition is desirable. Explain your answer.

b. If the firm's financial leverage would actually remain unchanged as a result of the proposed acquisition, would this alter your recommendation in part **a**? Support your answer with numerical data.

ST17–2 **Expected EPS—Merger decision**   At the end of 2009, Lake Industries had 80,000 shares of common stock outstanding and had earnings available for common of $160,000. Butler Company, at the end of 2009, had 10,000 shares of common stock outstanding and had earned $20,000 for common shareholders. Lake's earnings are expected to grow at an annual rate of 5%, and Butler's growth rate in earnings should be 10% per year.

    a. Calculate *earnings per share (EPS)* for Lake Industries for each of the next 5 years (2010–2014), assuming that there is no merger.

    b. Calculate the next 5 years' (2010–2014) *earnings per share (EPS)* for Lake if it acquires Butler at a *ratio of exchange* of 1.1.

    c. Compare your findings in parts **a** and **b,** and explain why the merger looks attractive when viewed over the long run.

Warm-Up Exercises

A blue box (■) indicates exercises available in .

E17–1 Toni's Typesetters is analyzing a possible merger with Pete's Print Shop. Toni's has a tax loss carryforward of $200,000, which it could apply to Pete's expected earnings before taxes of $100,000 per year for the next 5 years. Using a 34% tax rate, compare the *earnings after taxes* for Pete's over the next 5 years both *without* and *with* the merger.

E17–2 Cautionary Tales, Inc., is considering the acquisition of Danger Corp. at its asking price of $150,000. Cautionary would immediately sell some of Danger's assets for $15,000 if it makes the acquisition. Danger has a cash balance of $1,500 at the time of the acquisition. If Cautionary believes it can generate after-tax cash inflows of $25,000 per year for the next 7 years from the Danger acquisition, should the firm make the acquisition? Base your recommendation on the net present value of the outlay using Cautionary's 10% cost of capital.

E17–3 Willow Enterprises is considering the acquisition of Steadfast Corp. in a stock swap transaction. Currently, Willow's stock is selling for $45 per share. Although Steadfast's shares are currently trading at $30 per share, the firm's asking price is $60 per share.

    a. If Willow accepts Steadfast's terms, what is the *ratio of exchange?*

    b. If Steadfast has 15,000 shares outstanding, how many new shares must Willow issue to consummate the transaction?

    c. If Willow has 110,000 shares outstanding before the acquisition, and earnings for the merged company are estimated to be $450,000, what is the *EPS* for the merged company?

E17–4 Phylum Plants' stock is currently trading at a price of $55 per share. The company is considering the acquisition of Taxonomy Central, whose stock is currently trading at $20 per share. The transaction would require Phylum to swap its shares for those of Taxonomy, which would be paid $60 per share. Calculate the *ratio of exchange* and the *ratio of exchange in market price* for this transaction.

E17–5   All-Stores, Inc., is a holding company that has voting control over both General Stores and Star Stores. All-Stores owns General Stores and Star Stores common stock valued at $15,000 and $12,000, respectively. General's balance sheet lists $130,000 of total assets; Star has total assets of $110,000. All-Stores has total common stock equity of $20,000.

    a. What *percentage of the total assets controlled* by All-Stores does its common stock equity represent?

    b. If a stockholder holds $5,000 worth of All-Stores common stock equity, and this amount gives this stockholder voting control, what *percentage of the total assets controlled* does this stockholder's equity investment represent?

Problems

A blue box (■) indicates problems available in .

P17–1   **Tax effects of acquisition**   Connors Shoe Company is contemplating the acquisition of Salinas Boots, a firm that has shown large operating tax losses over the past few years. As a result of the acquisition, Connors believes that the total pretax profits of the merger will not change from their present level for 15 years. The tax loss carryforward of Salinas is $800,000, and Connors projects that its annual earnings before taxes will be $280,000 per year for each of the next 15 years. These earnings are assumed to fall within the annual limit legally allowed for application of the tax loss carryforward resulting from the proposed merger (see footnote 4 on page 765). The firm is in the 40% tax bracket.

    a. If Connors does not make the acquisition, what will be the company's tax liability and earnings after taxes each year over the next 15 years?

    b. If the acquisition is made, what will be the company's tax liability and earnings after taxes each year over the next 15 years?

    c. If Salinas can be acquired for $350,000 in cash, should Connors make the acquisition, judging on the basis of tax considerations? (Ignore present value.)

 Tax effects of acquisition   Trapani Tool Company is evaluating the acquisition of Sussman Casting. Sussman has a tax loss carryforward of $1.8 million. Trapani can purchase Sussman for $2.1 million. It can sell the assets for $1.6 million—their book value. Trapani expects its earnings before taxes in the 5 years after the merger to be as shown in the following table.

Year	Earnings before taxes
1	$150,000
2	400,000
3	450,000
4	600,000
5	600,000

The expected earnings given are assumed to fall within the annual limit that is legally allowed for application of the tax loss carryforward resulting from the proposed merger (see footnote 4 on page 765). Trapani is in the 40% tax bracket.

a. Calculate the firm's tax payments and earnings after taxes for each of the next 5 years *without* the merger.

b. Calculate the firm's tax payments and earnings after taxes for each of the next 5 years *with* the merger.

c. What are the total benefits associated with the tax losses from the merger? (Ignore present value.)

d. Discuss whether you would recommend the proposed merger. Support your decision with figures.

   P17–3   **Tax benefits and price**   Hahn Textiles has a tax loss carryforward of $800,000. Two firms are interested in acquiring Hahn for the tax loss advantage. Reilly Investment Group has expected earnings before taxes of $200,000 per year for each of the next 7 years and a cost of capital of 15%. Webster Industries has expected earnings before taxes for the next 7 years as shown in the following table.

	Webster Industries
Year	Earnings before taxes
1	$ 80,000
2	120,000
3	200,000
4	300,000
5	400,000
6	400,000
7	500,000

Both Reilly's and Webster's expected earnings are assumed to fall within the annual limit legally allowed for application of the tax loss carryforward resulting from the proposed merger (see footnote 4 on page 765). Webster has a cost of capital of 15%. Both firms are subject to a 40% tax rate on ordinary income.

a. What is the tax advantage of the merger each year for Reilly?

b. What is the tax advantage of the merger each year for Webster?

c. What is the maximum cash price each interested firm would be willing to pay for Hahn Textiles? (*Hint:* Calculate the present value of the tax advantages.)

d. Use your answers in parts **a** through **c** to explain why a target company can have different values to different potential acquiring firms.

 P17–4   **Asset acquisition decision**   Zarin Printing Company is considering the acquisition of Freiman Press at a cash price of $60,000. Freiman Press has liabilities of $90,000. Freiman has a large press that Zarin needs; the remaining assets would be sold to net $65,000. As a result of acquiring the press, Zarin would experience an increase in cash inflow of $20,000 per year over the next 10 years. The firm has a 14% cost of capital.

a. What is the *effective or net cost* of the large press?

b. If this is the only way Zarin can obtain the large press, should the firm go ahead with the merger? Explain your answer.

c. If the firm could purchase a press that would provide slightly better quality and $26,000 annual cash inflow for 10 years for a price of $120,000, which alternative would you recommend? Explain your answer.

P17–5 **Cash acquisition decision**   Benson Oil is being considered for acquisition by Dodd Oil. The combination, Dodd believes, would increase its cash inflows by $25,000 for each of the next 5 years and by $50,000 for each of the following 5 years. Benson has high financial leverage, and Dodd can expect its cost of capital to increase from 12% to 15% if the merger is undertaken. The cash price of Benson is $125,000.

   a. Would you recommend the merger?

   b. Would you recommend the merger if Dodd could use the $125,000 to purchase equipment that will return cash inflows of $40,000 per year for each of the next 10 years?

   c. If the cost of capital did not change with the merger, would your decision in part **b** be different? Explain.

PERSONAL FINANCE PROBLEM

 P17–6 **Divestitures**   In corporate settings, it is not unusual for firms to assess the financial viability of a business unit and decide whether to retain it within the corporation or divest it. The selling of units that do not seem to "fit" should bring about greater synergy for the firm. This same logic can be applied in a personal finance situation as well. An important question that comes up for families with two working parents and young children is whether one of the working adults should stay at home or whether the family should use day-care services.

   Assume that Ted and Maggie Smith have two young children who need child-care services. Currently, Maggie is a stay-at-home mother but could go back to her former job as a marketing analyst. She estimates that she could earn $3,800 per month gross, including her employer's 401(k) contributions. She will receive monthly employer-paid benefits that include health insurance, life insurance, and pension contributions totaling $1,200.

   Maggie expects her federal and state income taxes to total about $1,300 per month. The Smiths have calculated that total additional expenses such as child care, clothing, personal expenses, meals away from home, and transportation related to Maggie's job could total $1,400 per month.

   Does it make economic sense for the Smiths to hire child care and have Maggie return to work? To answer this question, calculate the net income or loss from her possible return to work.

 P17–7 **Ratio of exchange and EPS**   Marla's Cafe is attempting to acquire the Victory Club. Certain financial data on these corporations are summarized in the following table.

Item	Marla's Cafe	Victory Club
Earnings available for common stock	$20,000	$8,000
Number of shares of common stock outstanding	20,000	4,000
Market price per share	$12	$24

Marla's Cafe has sufficient authorized but unissued shares to carry out the proposed merger.

   a. If the *ratio of exchange* is 1.8, what will be the earnings per share (EPS) based on the original shares of each firm?

   b. Repeat part **a** if the *ratio of exchange* is 2.0.

   c. Repeat part **a** if the *ratio of exchange* is 2.2.

   d. Discuss the principle illustrated by your answers to parts **a** through **c**.

P17–8   **EPS and merger terms**   Cleveland Corporation is interested in acquiring Lewis Tool Company by swapping 0.4 share of its stock for each share of Lewis stock. Certain financial data on these companies are given in the following table.

Item	Cleveland Corporation	Lewis Tool
Earnings available for common stock	$200,000	$50,000
Number of shares of common stock outstanding	50,000	20,000
Earnings per share (EPS)	$4.00	$2.50
Market price per share	$50.00	$15.00
Price/earnings (P/E) ratio	12.5	6

Cleveland has sufficient authorized but unissued shares to carry out the proposed merger.

a. How many new shares of stock will Cleveland have to issue to make the proposed merger?

b. If the earnings for each firm remain unchanged, what will the *postmerger earnings per share* be?

c. How much, effectively, has been earned on behalf of each of the original shares of Lewis stock?

d. How much, effectively, has been earned on behalf of each of the original shares of Cleveland Corporation's stock?

P17–9   **Ratio of exchange**   Calculate the *ratio of exchange* (1) of shares and (2) in market price for each of the cases shown in the following table. What does each ratio signify? Explain.

	Current market price per share		
Case	Acquiring company	Target company	Price per share offered
A	$50	$25	$ 30.00
B	80	80	100.00
C	40	60	70.00
D	50	10	12.50
E	25	20	25.00

P17–10   **Expected EPS—Merger decision**   Graham & Sons wishes to evaluate a proposed merger into the RCN Group. Graham had 2009 earnings of $200,000, has 100,000 shares of common stock outstanding, and expects earnings to grow at an annual rate of 7%. RCN had 2009 earnings of $800,000, has 200,000 shares of common stock outstanding, and expects its earnings to grow at 3% per year.

a. Calculate the *expected earnings per share (EPS)* for Graham & Sons for each of the next 5 years (2010–2014) *without* the merger.

b. What would Graham's stockholders earn in each of the next 5 years (2010–2014) on each of their Graham shares swapped for RCN shares at a ratio of (1) 0.6 and (2) 0.8 share of RCN for 1 share of Graham?

    c. Graph the premerger and postmerger EPS figures developed in parts **a** and **b** with the year on the x axis and the EPS on the y axis.

    d. If you were the financial manager for Graham & Sons, which would you recommend from part **b**, (1) or (2)? Explain your answer.

 P17–11 **EPS and postmerger price**   Data for Henry Company and Mayer Services are given in the following table. Henry Company is considering merging with Mayer by swapping 1.25 shares of its stock for each share of Mayer stock. Henry Company expects its stock to sell at the same price/earnings (P/E) multiple after the merger as before merging.

Item	Henry Company	Mayer Services
Earnings available for common stock	$225,000	$50,000
Number of shares of common stock outstanding	90,000	15,000
Market price per share	$45	$50

    a. Calculate the *ratio of exchange* in market price.

    b. Calculate the earnings per share (EPS) and price/earnings (P/E) ratio for each company.

    c. Calculate the price/earnings (P/E) ratio used to purchase Mayer Services.

    d. Calculate the *postmerger earnings per share (EPS)* for Henry Company.

    e. Calculate the expected market price per share of the merged firm. Discuss this result in light of your findings in part **a**.

 P17–12 **Holding company**   Scully Corporation holds enough stock in company A and company B to give it voting control of both firms. Consider the accompanying simplified balance sheets for these companies.

Assets		Liabilities and Stockholders' Equity	
Scully Corporation			
Common stock holdings		Long-term debt	$ 40,000
Company A	$ 40,000	Preferred stock	25,000
Company B	60,000	Common stock equity	35,000
Total	$100,000	Total	$100,000
Company A			
Current assets	$100,000	Current liabilities	$100,000
Fixed assets	400,000	Long-term debt	200,000
Total	$500,000	Common stock equity	200,000
		Total	$500,000
Company B			
Current assets	$180,000	Current liabilities	$100,000
Fixed assets	720,000	Long-term debt	500,000
Total	$900,000	Common stock equity	300,000
		Total	$900,000

    a. What *percentage of the total assets controlled* by Scully Corporation does its common stock equity represent?

b. If another company owns 15% of the common stock of Scully Corporation and, by virtue of this fact, has voting control, what *percentage of the total assets controlled* does the outside company's equity represent?

c. How does a holding company effectively provide a great deal of control for a small dollar investment?

d. Answer parts **a** and **b** in light of the following additional facts.

   (1) Company A's fixed assets consist of $20,000 of common stock in Company C. This level of ownership provides voting control.

   (2) Company C's total assets of $400,000 include $15,000 of stock in Company D, which gives Company C voting control over Company D's $50,000 of total assets.

   (3) Company B's fixed assets consist of $60,000 of stock in both Company E and Company F. In both cases, this level of ownership gives it voting control. Companies E and F have total assets of $300,000 and $400,000, respectively.

P17–13 Voluntary settlements   Classify each of the following voluntary settlements as an extension, a composition, or a combination of the two.

a. Paying all creditors 30 cents on the dollar in exchange for complete discharge of the debt.

b. Paying all creditors in full in three periodic installments.

c. Paying a group of creditors with claims of $10,000 in full over 2 years and immediately paying the remaining creditors 75 cents on the dollar.

P17–14 Voluntary settlements   For a firm with outstanding debt of $125,000, classify each of the following voluntary settlements as an extension, a composition, or a combination of the two.

a. Paying a group of creditors in full in four periodic installments and paying the remaining creditors in full immediately.

b. Paying a group of creditors 90 cents on the dollar immediately and paying the remaining creditors 80 cents on the dollar in two periodic installments.

c. Paying all creditors 15 cents on the dollar.

d. Paying all creditors in full in 180 days.

P17–15 Voluntary settlements—Payments   Jacobi Supply Company recently ran into certain financial difficulties that have resulted in the initiation of voluntary settlement procedures. The firm currently has $150,000 in outstanding debts and approximately $75,000 in liquidatable short-term assets. Indicate, for each of the following plans, whether the plan is an extension, a composition, or a combination of the two. Also indicate the cash payments and timing of the payments required of the firm under each plan.

a. Each creditor will be paid 50 cents on the dollar immediately, and the debts will be considered fully satisfied.

b. Each creditor will be paid 80 cents on the dollar in two quarterly installments of 50 cents and 30 cents. The first installment is to be paid in 90 days.

c. Each creditor will be paid the full amount of its claims in three installments of 50 cents, 25 cents, and 25 cents on the dollar. The installments will be made in 60-day intervals, beginning in 60 days.

d. A group of creditors with claims of $50,000 will be immediately paid in full; the rest will be paid 85 cents on the dollar, payable in 90 days.

PERSONAL FINANCE PROBLEM

P17–16 **Bankruptcy legislation—wage-earner plan** Jon Morgan is in a financial position where he owes more than he earns each month. Due to his lack of financial planning and a heavy debt load, Jon started missing payments and saw his credit rating plunge. Unless corrective action is taken, personal bankruptcy will follow.

Jon recently contacted his lawyer in order to set up a *wage earner plan* with his creditors and establish a debt repayment schedule that is workable in light of his personal income. His creditors have all agreed to a plan under which interest payments and late fees will be waived during the repayment period. The process would have Jon make payments to the court, which then will pay off his creditors.

Jon has outstanding debt of $28,000. His creditors have set a repayment period of 4 years during which monthly principal payments are required. They have waived all interest charges and late fees. Jon's yearly take-home income is $30,600.

a. Calculate the monthly debt repayment amount.

b. Determine how much excess income Jon will have each month after making these payments.

P17–17 **ETHICS PROBLEM** Why might employees and suppliers support management in a Chapter 11 bankruptcy declaration if they will have to wait to be paid, and may never get paid? How can a CEO act ethically toward these two groups of stakeholders in the time before, during, and after the bankruptcy period?

Chapter 17 Case

Deciding Whether to Acquire or Liquidate Procras Corporation

Sharon Scotia, CFO of Rome Industries, must decide what to do about Procras Corporation, a major customer that is bankrupt. Rome Industries is a large plastic-injection-molding firm that produces plastic products to customer order. Procras Corporation is a major customer of Rome Industries that designs and markets a variety of plastic toys. As a result of mismanagement and inventory problems, Procras has become bankrupt. Among its unsecured debts are total past-due accounts of $1.9 million owed to Rome Industries.

Recognizing that it probably cannot recover the full $1.9 million that Procras Corporation owes it, the management of Rome Industries has isolated two mutually exclusive alternative actions: (1) acquire Procras through an exchange of stock or (2) let Procras be liquidated and recover Rome Industries' proportionate claim against any funds available for unsecured creditors. Rome's management feels that acquisition of Procras would have appeal in that it would allow Rome to integrate vertically and expand its business from strictly industrial manufacturing to include product development and marketing. Of course, the firm wants to select the alternative that will create the most value for its shareholders. Charged with making a recommendation as to whether Rome should acquire Procras Corporation or allow it to be liquidated, Ms. Scotia gathered the following data.

Acquire Procras Corporation   Negotiations with Procras management have resulted in a planned ratio of exchange of 0.6 share of Rome Industries for each share of Procras Corporation common stock. The following table reflects current data for Rome Industries and Rome's expectations of the data values for Procras Corporation with proper management in place.

Item	Rome Industries	Procras Corporation
Earnings available for common stock	$640,000	$180,000
Number of shares of common stock outstanding	400,000	60,000
Market price per share	$32	$30

Rome Industries estimates that after the proposed acquisition of Procras Corporation, its price/earnings (P/E) ratio will be 18.5.

Liquidation of Procras Corporation   Procras Corporation was denied its petition for reorganization, and the court-appointed trustee was expected to charge $150,000 for his services in liquidating the firm. In addition, $100,000 in unpaid bills were expected to be incurred between the time of filing the bankruptcy petition and formal action by the court. The firm's preliquidation balance sheet is shown below. Use the liquidation example ("Order of Priority of Claims in Liquidation") on the text's website at **www.prenhall.com/gitman** as a guide in analyzing this alternative.

Procras Corporation Balance Sheet			
Assets		**Liabilities and Stockholders' Equity**	
Cash	$ 20,000	Accounts payable	$2,700,000
Marketable securities	1,000	Notes payable—bank	1,300,000
Accounts receivable	1,800,000	Accrued wages[a]	120,000
Inventories	3,000,000	Unsecured customer deposits[b]	60,000
Prepaid expenses	14,000	Taxes payable	70,000
Total current assets	$4,835,000	Total current liabilities	$4,250,000
Land	$ 415,000	First mortgage[c]	$ 300,000
Net plant	200,000	Second mortgage[c]	200,000
Net equipment	350,000	Unsecured bonds	400,000
Total fixed assets	$ 965,000	Total long-term debt	$ 900,000
Total	$5,800,000	Common stock (60,000 shares)	$ 120,000
		Paid-in capital in excess of par	480,000
		Retained earnings	50,000
		Total stockholders' equity	$ 650,000
		Total	$5,800,000

[a]Represents wages of $600 per employee earned within 90 days of filing bankruptcy for 200 of the firm's employees.
[b]Unsecured customer deposits not exceeding $2,100 each.
[c]The first and second mortgages are on the firm's total fixed assets.

The trustee expects to liquidate the assets for $3.2 million—$2.5 million from current assets and $700,000 from fixed assets.

To Do

a. Calculate (1) the *ratio of exchange in market price* and (2) the *earnings per share (EPS)* and *price/earnings (P/E) ratio* for each company on the basis of the data given in the table that accompanies discussion of the acquisition alternative.

b. Find the *postmerger earnings per share (EPS)* for Rome Industries, assuming that it acquires Procras Corporation under the terms given.

c. Use the estimated postmerger price/earnings (P/E) ratio and your finding in part **b** to find the postmerger share price.

d. Use your finding in part **c** to determine how much, if any, the *total market value* of Rome Industries will change as a result of acquiring Procras Corporation.

e. Determine how much each claimant will receive if Procras Corporation is liquidated under the terms given.

f. How much, if any, of its $1.9 million balance due from Procras Corporation will Rome Industries recover as a result of liquidation of Procras?

g. Compare your findings in parts **d** and **f**, and make a recommendation for Rome Industries with regard to its best action—acquisition of Procras or the liquidation of Procras.

h. Which alternative would the shareholders of Procras Corporation prefer? Why?

Spreadsheet Exercise

Ram Electric Company is being considered for acquisition by Cavalier Electric. Cavalier expects the combination to increase its cash flows by $100,000 for each of the next 5 years and by $125,000 for each of the following 5 years. Ram Electric has relatively high financial leverage; Cavalier expects its cost of capital to be 12% for the first 5 years and estimates that it will increase to 16% for the following 5 years if the merger is undertaken. The cash price of Ram Electric is $325,000.

To Do

Create a spreadsheet similar to Table 17.3 to answer the following questions.

a. Determine the *present value of the expected future cash inflows* over the next 10 years.

b. Calculate the *net present value (NPV)* for the Ram Electric acquisition.

c. All else being equal, would you recommend the acquisition of Ram Electric by Cavalier Electric? Explain.

Group Exercise

This chapter described several types of corporate restructurings, including expansions, contractions, and changes in financial structures. As pointed out in the text, firms undergo such changes for a variety of reasons. The ultimate goal, however, should always be to increase the value of the firm. Keep this simple fact in mind as your group experiences restructurings of your own design.

To Do

Your fictitious firm is looking to acquire a competitor in hopes of improving its own value. This acquisition will be financed with a stock swap. Your assignment is to do following:

a. Establish the basics of the target firm, including its current stock price.
b. Defend your firm's motive(s) for making this acquisition.
c. Use the stock prices of the target and of your own firm to calculate the *ratio of exchange* and the *ratio of exchange in market price*.
d. Develop simple numbers that show how the *postmerger firm's earnings per share* are enhanced.

Web Exercise

Go to the book's companion website at **www.prenhall.com/gitman** to find the Web Exercise for this chapter.

Remember to check the book's website at **www.prenhall.com/gitman** to find additional resources, including Web Exercises and a Web Case.

18 International Managerial Finance

WHY THIS CHAPTER MATTERS TO YOU

In Your Professional Life

Accounting: You need to understand the tax rules for multinational companies, how to prepare consolidated financial statements for subsidiary companies, and how to account for international items in financial statements.

Information systems: You need to understand that if the firm undertakes foreign operations, it will need systems that track investments and operations in another currency and their fluctuations against the domestic currency.

Management: You need to understand both the opportunities and the risks involved in international operations; the possible role of international financial markets in raising capital; and the basic hedging strategies that multinational companies can use to protect themselves against exchange rate risk.

Marketing: You need to understand the potential for expanding into international markets and the ways of doing so (exports, foreign direct investment, mergers, and joint ventures); also, you should know how investment cash flows in foreign projects will be measured.

Operations: You need to understand the costs and benefits of moving operations offshore and/or buying equipment, parts, and inventory in foreign markets. Such an understanding will allow you to participate in the firm's decisions with regard to international operations.

In Your Personal Life

Your direct involvement in the global marketplace is most likely to result from expenditures made during foreign travel. In addition, you may invest directly or indirectly (via mutual funds) in the stocks of foreign companies. Probably the greatest personal benefit gained from this chapter is an understanding of exchange rates, which can significantly impact foreign expenditures, purchases, and investment returns.

LEARNING GOALS

LG 1 Understand the major factors that influence the financial operations of multinational companies (MNCs).

LG 2 Describe the key differences between purely domestic and international financial statements—consolidation, translation of individual accounts, and international profits.

LG 3 Discuss exchange rate risk and political risk, and explain how MNCs manage them.

LG 4 Describe foreign direct investment, investment cash flows and decisions, the MNCs' capital structure, and the international debt and equity instruments available to MNCs.

LG 5 Discuss the role of the Eurocurrency market in short-term borrowing and investing (lending) and the basics of international cash, credit, and inventory management.

LG 6 Review recent trends in international mergers and joint ventures.

General Electric Co.

Establishing a Presence in China

General Electric Co., the world's second largest firm, considers globalization one of its core competencies. A third of its leadership team is global. In 2006, GE had global revenues of $87.4 billion, almost 49 percent of total revenues. GE believes that global growth requires more than simply shipping products. A global company must be equally committed to developing capabilities and relationships in the markets where it wants to succeed.

One of GE's markets is China, where its revenues totaled $5 billion in 2006. China will invest $400 billion for infrastructure in this decade. The 2008 Olympics in Beijing will be one of its massive infrastructure projects, and GE expects to be a major player in helping China prepare for the games. To support its Chinese customers, GE has more than 1,700 sales and service people on the ground. It built a Global Research Center in Shanghai to develop the capabilities of its Chinese suppliers. GE is also training Chinese business leaders in GE management techniques.

GE paid nearly $200 million to become an Olympic sponsor. The hefty sponsorship fee covers four Olympic Games through 2012, but GE is particularly interested in playing a role in Beijing. It is targeting about $1 billion in Olympics-related contracts to provide everything from lighting and security at stadiums to electrical equipment at subway stations, treatment systems at wastewater facilities, and ultrasound equipment for diagnosing athletes' ailments. GE's goal is to double its revenue in China to $10 billion by 2010.

GE created a team of 100 engineers and sales people in Beijing to work on Olympics-related projects. It then broke them up into smaller groups focusing on the Beijing Olympic Committee, Chinese companies developing the stadiums, and the government agencies in charge of transportation. As an Olympic sponsor in several categories, GE will provide specific services during the games. Company officials say the company is now bidding on 25 to 30 contracts a month.

Like GE, many companies are looking beyond their home country's borders for new market opportunities. Although globalization can bring controversy, companies like GE believe that future growth requires U.S. companies to view the world as their market. This chapter will explain the additional considerations they must take into account as they apply the principles of managerial finance in the international setting.

> As you read this chapter, focus on this question: What might make an international market attractive to a U.S. company?

18.1 | The Multinational Company and Its Environment

multinational companies (MNCs)
Firms that have international assets and operations in foreign markets and draw part of their total revenue and profits from such markets.

Hint One of the reasons why firms have operations in foreign markets is the portfolio concept discussed in Chapter 5. Just as it is not wise for you to put all of your investment into the stock of one firm, it is not wise for a firm to invest in only one market. By having operations in many markets, firms can smooth out some of the cyclic changes that occur in each market.

North American Free Trade Agreement (NAFTA)
The treaty establishing free trade and open markets between Canada, Mexico, and the United States.

In recent years, as world markets have become more interdependent, international finance has become an increasingly important element in the management of **multinational companies (MNCs)**. Since World War II, an increasing number of firms, including many based in emerging or developing countries, have become MNCs (also referred to as *global firms* or *transnational corporations*) by developing targeted overseas markets, mainly through foreign direct investment (FDI)—that is, by establishing foreign subsidiaries or affiliates—and via mergers and acquisitions. The principles of managerial finance in this text apply to the management of MNCs as well as to purely domestic firms. However, certain factors unique to the international setting tend to complicate the financial management of multinational companies. A simple comparison between a domestic U.S. firm (firm A) and a U.S.-based MNC (firm B), as illustrated in Table 18.1, indicates the influence of some of the international factors on MNCs' operations.

Multinationals face a variety of laws and restrictions when operating in different nation-states. The legal and economic complexities existing in this environment are significantly different from those a domestic firm would face. Here we take a brief look at that environment, starting with key trading blocs.

Key Trading Blocs

In late 1992, the presidents of the United States and Mexico and the prime minister of Canada signed the **North American Free Trade Agreement (NAFTA)**. The U.S. Congress ratified NAFTA in November 1993. This trade pact simply mirrors underlying economic reality—Canada and Mexico are among the United States' largest trading partners. In 2003–2004, the United States signed a bilateral trade

TABLE 18.1	**International Factors and Their Influence on MNCs' Operations**	
Factor	Firm A (Domestic)	Firm B (MNC)
Foreign ownership	All assets owned by domestic entities	Portions of equity of foreign investments owned by foreign partners, thus affecting foreign decision making and profits
Multinational capital markets	All debt and equity structures based on the domestic capital market	Opportunities and challenges arise from the different capital markets in which firms can issue debt and equity
Multinational accounting	All consolidation of financial statements based on one currency	Different currencies and specific translation rules influence the consolidation of financial statements into one currency
Foreign exchange risks	All operations in one currency	Fluctuations in foreign exchange markets can affect foreign revenues and profits as well as the overall value of the firm

Central American Free Trade Agreement (CAFTA)
A trade agreement signed in 2003–2004 by the United States, the Dominican Republic, and five Central American countries (Costa Rica, El Salvador, Guatemala, Honduras, and Nicaragua).

European Union (EU)
A significant economic force currently made up of 27 nations that permit free trade within the union.

European Open Market
The transformation of the European Union into a *single* market at year-end 1992.

euro
A single currency adopted on January 1, 1999, by 12 EU nations, which switched to a single set of euro bills and coins on January 1, 2002.

monetary union
The official melding of the national currencies of the EU nations into one currency, the *euro,* on January 1, 2002.

Mercosur
A major South American trading bloc that includes countries that account for more than half of total Latin American GDP.

ASEAN
A large trading bloc that comprises 10 member nations, all in Southeast Asia. China is expected to join this bloc in 2010. Also called the *Association of Southeast Asian Nations.*

deal with Chile and also a regional pact, known as the **Central American Free Trade Agreement (CAFTA)**, with the Dominican Republic and five Central American countries (Costa Rica, El Salvador, Guatemala, Honduras, and Nicaragua). Since 1985, the U.S. has signed bilateral and regional trade agreements with more than 62 other nations.

The **European Union,** or **EU,** has been in existence since 1957. It has a current membership of 27 nations. With a total population estimated at more than 470 million (compared to the U.S. population of about 300 million) and an overall gross national income paralleling that of the United States, the EU is a significant global economic force. The countries of Western Europe opened a new era of free trade within the union when intraregional tariff barriers fell at the end of 1992. This transformation is commonly called the **European Open Market.** Although the EU has managed to reach agreement on most economic, monetary, financial, and legal provisions, debates continue on certain other aspects (some key), including those related to automobile production and imports, monetary union, taxes, and workers' rights.

As a result of the Maastricht Treaty of 1991, 12 EU nations adopted a single currency, the **euro,** as a continent-wide medium of exchange. And beginning January 1, 2002, those 12 EU nations switched to a single set of euro bills and coins, causing the national currencies of all 12 countries participating in **monetary union** to slowly disappear in the following months. As of 2007, 13 members were using the euro as their national currency.

At the same time that the European Union implemented monetary union, (which also involved creating a new European Central Bank), the EU experienced a wave of new applicants, resulting in the May 1, 2004, admission of 10 and in the January 1, 2007, admission of two new members from eastern Europe and the Mediterranean region. The rapidly emerging new community of Europe offers both challenges and opportunities to a variety of players, including multinational firms. MNCs today face heightened levels of competition when operating inside the EU. As more of the existing restrictions and regulations are eliminated, for instance, U.S. multinationals will have to face other MNCs, some from within the EU itself.

In addition to NAFTA and the EU, a number of other bilateral or regional trading blocs have emerged. The EU itself has entered into trade accords involving at least 35 countries. Latin America has several such blocs, including its largest, **Mercosur,** which is composed of Argentina, Brazil, Paraguay, Uruguay, and Venezuela. It has a population of more than 250 million and a combined economic size of about US$1.1 trillion. An even larger bloc exists in the form of **ASEAN** (Association of Southeast Asian Nations), with 10 members. China has signed a trade deal with ASEAN, to be phased in by 2010. This will create a regional free market encompassing more than 1.8 billion people by 2015. Other trading agreements involving Japan, India, South Korea, Singapore, Australia, New Zealand, and various nations in Africa either have been completed or are under negotiation.

These deals will result in an increasing share of world trade being covered by regional accords. Meanwhile, an unintended consequence is the emergence of contradictions and incompatibilities vis-á-vis the multilateral-based system embedded in WTO (discussed below). All of this will force the multinationals to navigate through a rising number of trade agreements worldwide. Despite the challenges, though, U.S. companies can benefit from the formation of regional and bilateral trade pacts, but only if they are prepared to exploit them. They must offer a desirable mix of products to a collection of varied consumers and be ready to take advantage of a variety of currencies and of financial markets and instruments (such as the Euroequities discussed later in this chapter). They must staff their operations with the appropriate combination of local and foreign personnel and, when necessary, enter into joint ventures and strategic alliances.

GATT and the WTO

General Agreement on Tariffs and Trade (GATT)
A treaty that has governed world trade throughout most of the postwar era; it extends free-trading rules to broad areas of economic activity and is policed by the *World Trade Organization (WTO)*.

Although it may seem that the world is splitting into a handful of trading blocs, this is less of a danger than it may appear to be, because many international treaties are in force that guarantee relatively open access to at least the largest economies. The most important such treaty is the **General Agreement on Tariffs and Trade (GATT)**. In 1994, Congress ratified the most recent version of this treaty, which has governed world trade throughout most of the postwar era. The current agreement extends free-trading rules to broad areas of economic activity—such as agriculture, financial services, and intellectual property rights—that had not previously been covered by international treaty and were thus effectively off-limits to foreign competition.

World Trade Organization (WTO)
International body that polices world trading practices and mediates disputes between member countries.

The 1994 GATT treaty also established a new international body, the **World Trade Organization (WTO)**, to police world trading practices and to mediate disputes between member countries. The WTO began operating in January 1995. In 2004, preliminary approvals were granted for an eventual membership of the Russian Federation in the WTO. In December 2001, the People's Republic of China was, after years of controversy, granted membership. As of 2007, the WTO had 151 members. Given the emergence of more bilateral and regional trade accords, however, its long-term prospects and effectiveness are becoming increasingly clouded. Key evidence was the organization's lack of achieving final agreement by 2007 on the global round of trade negotiations, the Doha Round, which began in 2001.

Legal Forms of Business Organization

In many countries outside the United States, operating a foreign business as a subsidiary or affiliate can take two forms, both similar to the U.S. corporation. In German-speaking nations the two forms are the *Aktiengesellschaft* (A.G.) or the *Gesellschaft mit beschrankter Haftung* (GmbH). In many other countries the similar forms are a *Société Anonyme* (S.A.) or a *Société à Responsibilité Limitée* (S.A.R.L.). The A.G. and the S.A. are the most common forms, but the GmbH and the S.A.R.L. require fewer formalities for formation and operation.

joint venture
A partnership under which the participants have contractually agreed to contribute specified amounts of money and expertise in exchange for stated proportions of ownership and profit.

Establishing a business in a form such as the S.A. can involve most of the provisions that govern a U.S.-based corporation. In addition, to operate in many foreign countries, it is often essential to enter into joint-venture business agreements with private investors or with government-based agencies of the host country. A **joint venture** is a partnership under which the participants have contractually agreed to contribute specified amounts of money and expertise in exchange for stated proportions of ownership and profit. Joint ventures are common in many emerging and developing nations.

Emerging and developing countries have varying laws and regulations regarding MNCs' subsidiary and joint-venture operations. Whereas many host countries (including Mexico, Brazil, South Korea, and Taiwan) have either completely removed or significantly liberalized their local-ownership requirements, other major economies (including China and India) are just beginning to relax these restrictions. China, for instance, has gradually opened up new economic sectors and industries to partial (and, in a few cases, full) foreign participation. India continues to insist on majority local ownership in wide-ranging segments of its economy. MNCs, especially those based in the United States, the EU, and Japan, will face new challenges and opportunities in the future in terms of ownership requirements, mergers, and acquisitions.

The existence of joint-venture laws and restrictions has implications for the operation of foreign-based subsidiaries. First, majority foreign ownership may result in a substantial degree of management and control by host country participants. This, in turn, can influence day-to-day operations to the detriment of the managerial policies and procedures MNCs normally pursue. Next, foreign ownership may result in disagreements among the partners as to the exact distribution of profits and the portion to be allocated for reinvestment. Moreover, operating in foreign countries, especially on a joint-venture basis, can involve problems regarding the remittance of profits. In the past, the governments of Argentina, Brazil, Venezuela, and Thailand, among others, have imposed ceilings not only on the repatriation (return) of capital by MNCs but also on profit remittances by these firms to the parent companies. These governments usually cite the shortage of foreign exchange as the motivating factor. Finally, from a "positive" point of view, it can be argued that MNCs operating in many of the less developed countries benefit from joint-venture agreements, given the potential risks stemming from political instability in the host countries. This issue will be addressed in detail in subsequent discussions.

Taxes

Multinational companies, unlike domestic firms, have financial obligations in foreign countries. One of their basic responsibilities is international taxation—a complex issue because national governments follow a variety of tax policies. In general, U.S.-based MNCs must take into account several factors.

Tax Rates and Taxable Income

First, MNCs need to examine the *level* of foreign taxes. Among the major industrial countries, corporate tax rates do vary. While the average rates in the United States, Germany, and Japan are close to 40 percent, those in the United Kingdom and Australia are near 30 percent. Ireland has a rate of about 12 percent. Many less industrialized nations maintain relatively moderate rates, partly as an incentive for attracting foreign capital. Certain countries—in particular, the Bahamas, Switzerland, Liechtenstein, the Cayman Islands, and Bermuda—are known for their "low" tax levels. As discussed in the *Global Focus* box in Chapter 8, China has had a low rate for foreign investors, to encourage investment. These nations typically have no withholding taxes on *intra-MNC dividends*.

Next, there is a question as to the definition of *taxable income*. Some countries tax profits as received on a *cash basis,* whereas others tax profits earned on an *accrual basis*. Differences can also exist in treatments of noncash charges, such as depreciation, amortization, and depletion. Finally, the existence of tax agreements between the United States and other governments can influence not only the total tax bill of the parent MNC but also its international operations and financial activities.

Tax Rules

Different home countries apply varying tax rates and rules to the global earnings of their own multinationals. Moreover, tax rules are subject to frequent modifications. In the United States, for instance, the Tax Reform Act of 1986 resulted in certain changes affecting the taxation of U.S.-based MNCs. Special provisions apply to tax deferrals by MNCs on foreign income; operations set up in U.S. possessions, such as the U.S. Virgin Islands, Guam, and American Samoa; capital gains from the sale of stock in a foreign corporation; and withholding taxes. Furthermore, MNCs (both U.S. and foreign) can be subject to national as well as local taxes. Obviously, these laws can make a big difference in a multinational's tax bill.[1]

As a general practice, the U.S. government claims jurisdiction over *all* the income of an MNC, wherever earned. (Special rules apply to foreign corporations conducting business in the United States.) However, it may be possible for a multinational company to take foreign income taxes as a direct credit against its U.S. tax liabilities. The following example illustrates one way of accomplishing this objective.

Example

American Enterprises, a U.S.-based MNC that manufactures heavy machinery, has a foreign subsidiary that earns $100,000 before local taxes. All of the after-tax funds are available to the parent in the form of dividends. The applicable taxes consist of a 35% foreign income tax rate, a foreign dividend withholding tax rate of 10%, and a U.S. tax rate of 34%.

Subsidiary income before local taxes	$100,000
Foreign income tax at 35%	−35,000
Dividend available to be declared	$ 65,000
Foreign dividend withholding tax at 10%	−6,500
MNC's receipt of dividends	$ 58,500

Using the so-called *grossing up procedure,* the MNC will add the full before-tax subsidiary income to its total taxable income. Next, the company calculates the U.S. tax liability on the grossed-up income. Finally, the related taxes paid in the foreign country are applied as a credit against the additional U.S. tax liability:

Additional MNC income		$100,000
U.S. tax liability at 34%	$ 34,000	
Total foreign taxes paid, to be used as a credit ($35,000 + $6,500)	−41,500	−41,500
U.S. taxes due		0
Net funds available to the parent MNC		$ 58,500

---

1. For updated details on various countries' tax laws, consult relevant publications of international accounting firms.

Because the U.S. tax liability is less than the total taxes paid to the foreign government, *no additional U.S. taxes are due* on the income from the foreign subsidiary. In our example, if tax credits had not been allowed, then "double taxation" by the two authorities, as shown in what follows, would have resulted in a substantial drop in the overall net funds available to the parent MNC:

Subsidiary income before local taxes	$100,000
Foreign income tax at 35%	− 35,000
Dividend available to be declared	$ 65,000
Foreign dividend withholding tax at 10%	− 6,500
MNC's receipt of dividends	$ 58,500
U.S. tax liability at 34%	− 19,890
Net funds available to the parent MNC	$ 38,610

The preceding example clearly demonstrates that the existence of bilateral tax treaties and the subsequent application of tax credits can significantly enhance the overall net funds available to MNCs from their worldwide earnings. Consequently, in an increasingly complex and competitive international financial environment, international taxation is one of the variables that multinational corporations should fully utilize to their advantage.

The *Focus on Ethics* box on page 814 discusses the ethical issues of gift-giving and bribery when doing business in foreign countries, which some consider a form of additional "taxation."

Financial Markets

Euromarket
The international financial market that provides for borrowing and lending currencies outside their country of origin.

During the last two decades the **Euromarket**—which provides for borrowing and lending currencies outside their country of origin—has grown rapidly. The Euromarket provides multinational companies with an "external" opportunity to borrow or lend funds, and to do so with less government regulation.

Growth of the Euromarket

The Euromarket has grown large for several reasons. First, beginning in the early 1960s, the Russians wanted to maintain their dollar earnings outside the legal jurisdiction of the United States, mainly because of the Cold War. Second, the consistently large U.S. balance-of-payments deficits helped to "scatter" dollars around the world. Third, the existence of specific regulations and controls on dollar deposits in the United States, including interest rate ceilings imposed by the government, helped to send such deposits to places outside the United States.

These and other factors have combined and contributed to the creation of an "external" capital market. Its size cannot be accurately determined, mainly because of its lack of regulation and control. Several sources that periodically estimate its size are the Bank for International Settlements (BIS), Morgan Guaranty Trust, the World Bank, and the Organization for Economic Cooperation and Development (OECD). By 2007, the overall size of the Euromarket was well above $4.0 trillion *net* international lending.

Focus on Ethics   Cracking Down on Bribery for Business

IN PRACTICE

On January 19, 2007, the managers of seven multinational corporations operating in China received some bad news: The Shanghai police had announced the arrest of 22 businesspeople on suspicion of bribery. Shady deals are nothing new in China—the country's complex antibribery laws are not often enforced rigorously—but the arrests came as a shock to the multinational corporations.

In many respects, China's laws resemble the U.S. antibribery law, the Foreign Corrupt Practices Act (FCPA) of 1977. The FCPA prohibits payments to foreign officials for the purpose of obtaining or keeping business. However, the FCPA alone was insufficient because of considerable concern that U.S. companies would be operating at a disadvantage against foreign companies who routinely paid bribes. In some countries, companies even were permitted to deduct the cost of such bribes as business expenses on their taxes. In 1997, the United States was among the Organization for Economic Co-operation and Development (OECD) members who signed the OECD Convention on Combating Bribery of Foreign Public Officials in International Business Transactions. Today, nearly 40 countries pledge compliance with the OECD agreement that prohibits corporate bribery to obtain business.

Not all competitors uphold the same standards in international trade. In a survey published in October 2006 by Control Risks and the law firm Simmons & Simmons, more than 40 percent of the 350 respondents said that they had lost new business at some point during the prior 5 years because a rival had paid a bribe. What is more, most respondents had little or no understanding of their own country's anticorruption laws. This could explain why many companies wrongly assume that they can circumvent the laws by hiring local intermediaries, who may then pay local officials and business contacts on their behalf. Unknown to these companies, both direct and indirect payments are illegal in many jurisdictions.

Criminal sanctions against bribing foreign officials can result in a fine of up to $2 million for corporations. Officers, directors, stockholders, employees, and agents are subject to a fine of up to $100,000 and imprisonment for up to 5 years. This seems like a very stiff penalty for running afoul of a law that prohibits payments to Chinese officials of more than 200 renminbi ($25.80)—less than the cost of dinner at many restaurants in Shanghai.

■ *What are some steps multinational corporations can take to make sure that their employees are in compliance with local antibribery laws?*

---

offshore centers
Certain cities or states (including London, Singapore, Bahrain, Nassau, Hong Kong, and Luxembourg) that have achieved prominence as major centers for Euromarket business.

One aspect of the Euromarket is the so-called **offshore centers.** Certain cities or states around the world—including London, Singapore, Bahrain, Nassau, Hong Kong, and Luxembourg—are considered major offshore centers for Euromarket business. The availability of communication and transportation facilities, along with language, costs, time zones, taxes, and local banking regulations, are among the main reasons for the prominence of these centers.

In recent decades, various new financial instruments have appeared in the international financial markets. One is interest rate and currency swaps. Another is various combinations of forward and options contracts on different currencies. A third is new types of bonds and notes—along with an international version of U.S. commercial paper—with flexible characteristics in terms of currency, maturity, and interest rate. More details will be provided in subsequent discussions.

Major Participants

The U.S. dollar continues to dominate various segments of the global financial markets. For example, central banks worldwide maintain the major portion of their reserves in the dollar. Yet, in other activities—including currency in circulation and the international bond market—the euro has surpassed the dollar, with more challenges coming from other, potential contenders such as the Chinese yuan. Similarly, although U.S. banks and other financial institutions continue to play a significant role in the global markets, financial giants from Japan and Europe have become major participants in the Euromarket.

In the three decades leading up to the new millennium, many countries in Latin America, Asia, and Africa borrowed in the global financial markets. They accumulated huge international debts, resulting in many financial and currency crises. Clearly, as the 1997 financial/currency crises of Asia, the 1998 currency collapse of Russia, and the 2001–2002 default of Argentina showed, too much international debt, along with unstable economies and currencies, can cause massive financial losses and problems for the world's MNCs. The latest IMF data, however, confirm that beginning in 2000, nonindustrialized countries' external debt (as a percentage of exports of goods and services) has been declining and is expected to continue to do so. Many of these nations have replaced their foreign-currency debts with local-currency instruments. Also, they have further liberalized their respective economies by allowing long-term capital inflows of foreign direct investments, thus reducing their exposure to foreign exchange risk.

Although nation-states may have slowed down their official borrowings in this decade, private enterprises, including multinational companies, continue to obtain funds (and invest) in international markets. Both Eurocurrency and Eurobond markets are extensively used by MNCs.

REVIEW QUESTIONS

18–1 What are the important international trading blocs? What is the *European Union* and what is its single unit of currency? What is *GATT*? What is the *WTO*?

18–2 What is a *joint venture*? Why is it often essential to use this arrangement? What effect do joint-venture laws and restrictions have on the operation of foreign-based subsidiaries?

18–3 From the point of view of a U.S.-based MNC, what key tax factors need to be considered?

18–4 Discuss the major reasons for the growth of the *Euromarket*. What is an *offshore center*? Name the major participants in the Euromarket.

18.2 | Financial Statements

Several features differentiate internationally based reports from domestically oriented financial statements. Among these are the issues of foreign subsidiary characterization, the functional currency approach of U.S. MNCs, and the translation of individual accounts.

Subsidiary Characterization and Functional Currency

For a multinational company based outside the United States, its foreign subsidiaries' type of operations will determine the translation method the firm will use. For U.S.-based MNCs, the determining factor is the functional currency of each subsidiary. Table 18.2 on page 816 provides further details on these points.

TABLE 18.2	Subsidiary/Currency Operations and Translation Method
Type of operation	**Translation method**
Integrated foreign entity (international practice)	Operates as an extension of the parent MNC; temporal method is the primary translation tool
Self-sustaining foreign entity (international practice)	Operates independent of the parent multinational; the current-rate method is the primary approach
Functional currency approach (used by U.S. MNCs)	The dominant currency in which the foreign subsidiary conducts its activities; it may be the same as the parent's (in which case, the temporal method is applied), the subsidiary's (the current-rate method), or a third currency (temporal, then current)

Source: David K. Eiteman, Arthur I. Stonehill, and Michael H. Moffett, *Multinational Business Finance,* 11th ed. (Boston, MA: Addison-Wesley, 2007), pp. 336–342.

Translation of Individual Accounts

FASB No. 52
Statement issued by the FASB requiring U.S. multinationals first to convert the financial statement accounts of foreign subsidiaries into the *functional currency* and then to translate the accounts into the parent firm's currency using the *all-current-rate method.*

Unlike domestic items in financial statements, international items require translation back into U.S. dollars. Since December 1982, all financial statements of U.S. multinationals (with the exceptions noted below) have had to conform to *Statement No. 52* issued by the Financial Accounting Standards Board (FASB). The basic rules of *FASB No. 52* are given in Figure 18.1.

FASB No. 52

Under *FASB No. 52,* the *current-rate method* is implemented in a two-step process. First, each subsidiary's balance sheet and income statement are *measured*

FIGURE 18.1

Procedure Flow Chart for U.S. Translation Practices
Purpose: Foreign currency financial statements must be translated into U.S. dollars

Source: David K. Eiteman, Arthur I. Stonehill, and Michael H. Moffett, *Multinational Business Finance,* 11th ed. (Boston, MA: Addison-Wesley, 2007), p. 341.

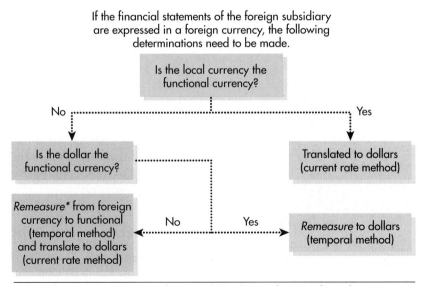

If the financial statements of the foreign subsidiary are expressed in a foreign currency, the following determinations need to be made.

* The term "remeasure" means to translate, as to change the unit of measure, from a foreign currency to the functional currency.

in terms of the functional currency by using generally accepted accounting principles (GAAP). That is, each subsidiary translates foreign-currency elements into the **functional currency**—the currency in which a subsidiary primarily generates and expends cash and in which its accounts are maintained before financial statements are submitted to the parent for consolidation.

functional currency
The currency in which a subsidiary primarily generates and expends cash and in which its accounts are maintained.

In the second step, the functional-currency-denominated financial statements of the foreign subsidiary are translated into the parent's currency. This is done using the **all-current-rate method,** which requires the translation of all balance sheet items at the closing rate and all income statement items at average rates.

all-current-rate method
The method by which the *functional-currency-denominated* financial statements of an MNC's subsidiary are translated into the parent company's currency.

Each of these steps can result in certain gains or losses. The first step can lead to transaction (cash) gains or losses. Whether realized or not, these gains or losses are charged directly to current income. The completion of the second step can result in translation (accounting) adjustments, which are excluded from current income. Instead, the MNC discloses and charges these amounts to a separate component of stockholders' equity.

Temporal Method

temporal method
A method that requires specific assets and liabilities to be translated at so-called historical exchange rates, and that foreign-exchange translation gains or losses be reflected in the current year's income.

The temporal method, along with a variation called *monetary/non-monetary method,* is an alternative translation approach used throughout the world. For U.S.-based multinationals, as highlighted in both Table 18.2 and Figure 18.1, when the functional currency is the U.S. dollar or a third currency, the **temporal method** is used. This method requires that specific assets and liabilities be translated at so-called historical exchange rates, and that foreign-exchange translation gains or losses be reflected in current year's income. Also, if a U.S. MNC has a subsidiary in a *hyperinflation* country—defined as a host nation experiencing a cumulative inflation of more than 100 percent over a 3-year period—then the temporal method is used. (In some countries, the inflation rates can be significantly higher. In Zimbabwe, for example, in early 2007 the *monthly* inflation rate exceeded 1,500 percent.)

REVIEW QUESTION

18–5   Under *FASB No. 52,* what are the translation rules for financial statement accounts? How does the *temporal method* differ from these rules?

18.3 | Risk

The concept of risk clearly applies to international investments as well as to purely domestic ones. However, MNCs must take into account additional factors, including both exchange rate and political risks.

Exchange Rate Risks

exchange rate risk
The risk caused by varying exchange rates between two currencies.

Because multinational companies operate in many different foreign markets, portions of these firms' revenues and costs are based on foreign currencies. To understand the **exchange rate risk** caused by varying exchange rates between two currencies, we examine the relationships that exist among various currencies, the causes of exchange rate changes, and the impact of currency fluctuations.

Relationships among Currencies

Since the mid-1970s, the major currencies of the world have had a *floating*—as opposed to a *fixed*—relationship with respect to the U.S. dollar and to one another. Among the currencies regarded as being major (or "hard") currencies are the British pound sterling (£), the European Union euro (€), the Japanese yen (¥), the Canadian dollar (C$), and, of course, the U.S. dollar (US$). As previously pointed out, by 2007, 13 members of the EU had adopted the euro, in circulation since 2002. It has gained wide acceptance and usage in international transactions—particularly debt securities issues.

foreign exchange rate
The value of two currencies with respect to each other.

The value of two currencies with respect to each other, or their **foreign exchange rate,** is expressed as follows:

$$US\$1.00 = ¥119.77$$
$$¥1.00 = US\$0.008349$$

Because the U.S. dollar has served as the principal currency of international finance for more than 60 years, the usual exchange rate quotation in international markets is given as ¥119.77/US$, where the unit of account is the Japanese yen and the unit of currency being priced is one U.S. dollar. In this case, the dollar is the currency that is actually being priced. Expressing the exchange rate as US$0.008349/¥ would indicate a dollar price for the Japanese yen.

floating relationship
The fluctuating relationship of the values of two currencies with respect to each other.

fixed (or semifixed) relationship
The constant (or relatively constant) relationship of a currency to one of the major currencies, a combination (basket) of major currencies, or some type of international foreign exchange standard.

For the major currencies, the existence of a **floating relationship** means that the value of any two currencies with respect to each other is allowed to fluctuate on a daily basis. Conversely, some of the nonmajor currencies of the world try to maintain a **fixed (or semifixed) relationship** with respect to one of the major currencies, a combination (basket) of major currencies, or some type of international foreign exchange standard.

On any given day, the relationship between any two of the major currencies will contain two sets of figures. One reflects the **spot exchange rate**—the rate on that day. The other indicates the **forward exchange rate**—the rate at some specified future date. The foreign exchange rates given in Figure 18.2 illustrate these concepts. For instance, the figure shows that on Tuesday, May 1, 2007, the spot rate for the Japanese yen was US$0.008349 (or ¥119.77/US$, as usually stated), and the forward (future) rate was US$0.008382/¥ (or ¥119.30/US$) for 1-month delivery. In other words, on May 1, 2007, one could execute a contract to take delivery of Japanese yen in 1 month at a dollar price of US$0.008382/¥. Forward rates are also quoted for 3-month and 6-month contracts (with other, tailor-made contracts of desired maturities available to clients through the inter-bank market). For all such contracts, the agreements and signatures are completed on, say, May 1, 2007, but the actual exchange of dollars and Japanese yen between buyers and sellers will take place on the future date (say, 1 month later).

spot exchange rate
The rate of exchange between two currencies on any given day.

forward exchange rate
The rate of exchange between two currencies at some specified future date.

Figure 18.2 also illustrates the differences between floating currencies and those that are either fixed or exhibit less movement over time. The third data column in Figure 18.2 shows the year-to-date percentage change in each currency's movement vis-à-vis the U.S. dollar. All the major currencies previously mentioned, along with minor (or "soft") currencies such as the Indian rupee and the Thai baht, have experienced some changes since the beginning of the year. On the other hand, the Kuwaiti dinar and the Saudi Arabian riyal have undergone no change over this period.

FIGURE 18.2

Exchange Rates (Tuesday, May 1, 2007)
Spot and forward exchange rate quotations

Source: The Wall Street Journal, http://online.wsj.com/mdc/public/page/2_3021-forex.html, May 2, 2007, p. C12.

Currencies

May 1, 2007

U.S.-dollar foreign-exchange rates in late New York trading

Country/currency	Tues in US$	per US$	US$ vs, YTD chg (%)
Americas			
Argentina peso*	.3238	3.0883	1.0
Brazil real	.4916	2.0342	–4.8
Canada dollar	.9005	1.1105	–4.8
1-mos forward	.9014	1.1094	–4.8
3-mos forward	.9030	1.1074	–4.8
6-mos forward	.9050	1.1050	–4.7
Chile peso	.001904	525.21	–1.3
Colombia peso	.0004746	2107.04	–5.9
Ecuador US dollar	1	1	unch
Mexico peso*	.0915	10.9349	1.2
Peru new sol	.3152	3.173	–0.7
Uruguay peso†	.04180	23.92	–1.9
Venezuela bolivar	.000466	2145.92	unch
Asia-Pacific			
Australian dollar	.8282	1.2074	–4.7
China yuan	.1298	7.7055	–1.3
Hong Kong dollar	.1278	7.8221	0.6
India rupee	.02438	41.017	–7.0
Indonesia rupiah	.0001102	9074	0.9
Japan yen	.008349	119.77	0.6
1-mos forward	.008382	119.30	0.7
3-mos forward	.008448	118.37	0.7
6-mos forward	.008544	117.04	0.7
Malaysia ringgit§	.2922	3.4223	–3.0
New Zealand dollar	.7417	1.3483	–5.0
Pakistan rupee	.01648	60.680	–0.2
Philippines peso	.0210	47.574	–3.0
Singapore dollar	.6577	1.5205	–0.8
South Korea won	.0010742	930.93	0.1
Taiwan dollar	.03002	33.311	2.2
Thailand baht	.03037	32.927	–7.1

Country/currency	Tues in US$	per US$	US$ vs, YTD chg (%)
Europe			
Czech Rep. koruna**	.04835	20.683	–0.7
Denmark krone	.1827	5.4735	–3.1
Euro area euro	1.3612	.7346	–3.0
Hungary forint	.005484	182.35	–4.2
Malta lira	3.1709	.3154	–3.0
Norway krone	.1675	5.9701	–4.2
Poland zloty	.3601	2.7770	–4.4
Russia ruble‡	.03887	25.727	–2.3
Slovak Rep koruna	.04046	24.716	–5.3
Sweden krona	.1488	6.7204	–1.8
Switzerland franc	.8236	1.2142	–0.4
1-mos forward	.8259	1.2108	–0.4
3-mos forward	.8299	1.2050	–0.3
6-mos forward	.8356	1.1967	–0.3
Turkey lira**	.7373	1.3563	–4.2
UK pound	1.9990	.5003	–2.0
1-mos forward	1.9987	.5003	–2.0
3-mos forward	1.9976	.5006	–2.0
6-mos forward	1.9949	.5013	–1.8
Middle East/Africa			
Bahrain dollar	2.6525	.3770	unch
Egypt pound*	.1761	5.6786	–0.6
Israel shekel	.2475	4.0404	–4.2
Jordan dinar	1.4104	.7090	unch
Kuwait dinar	3.4584	.2892	unch
Lebanon pound	.0006616	1511.49	unch
Saudi Arabia riyal	.2666	3.7509	unch
South Africa rand	.1421	7.0373	0.6
UAE dirham	.2723	3.6724	unch
SDR††	1.5262	.6552	–1.4

*Floating rate †Financial §Government rate ‡Russian Central Bank rate **Rebased as of Jan 1, 2005
††Special Drawing Rights (SDR); from the International Monetary Fund; based on exchange rates for U.S., British and Japanese currencies.
Note: Based on trading among banks of $1 million and more, as quoted at 4 p.m. ET by Reuters.

For the floating currencies, changes in the value of foreign exchange rates are called appreciation or depreciation. For any currency that is fixed in value (with respect to the U.S. dollar or another major currency), changes in values are called official *revaluation* or *devaluation*, but these terms have the same meanings as *appreciation* and *depreciation*, respectively.

Personal Finance Example   Floyd Armstrong, an avid cyclist, is considering a bicycling tour that for 1 week during the Tour de France will ride ahead of the actual race. The cost of the tour, which includes ground transportation, hotels, and route support in France, is 3,675 euros (€). He estimates that his round-trip airfare (including shipment of his bike) from his home in Iowa will be $1,160; in addition he will incur another $100 in incidental U.S. travel expenses. Floyd estimates the cost of meals in France to be about €400, and he plans to take an additional $1,000 to buy gifts and other merchandise while in France. The current exchange rate is US$1.3605/€1.00 (or €0.7350/US$1.00). Given this information, Floyd wishes to determine (1) the total dollar cost of the trip and (2) the amount in euros he will need to cover the cost of meals, gifts, and other merchandise while in France.

(1) Total cost of trip in U.S. dollars

Cost of tour (€3,675 × US$1.3605/€)	$5,000
Round-trip airfare	1,100
Incidental U.S. travel expenses	100
Cost of meals in France (€400 × US$1.3605/€)	544
Gifts and other merchandise	1,000
Total cost of trip in $	$7,744

(2) Amount of euros needed in France

Cost of meals in France	€ 400
Gifts and other merchandice ($US1,000 × €0.7350)	735
Amount of €s needed in France	€1,135

The total cost of Floyd's trip would be $7,744, and he would need 1,135 euros to cover his cost of meals, gifts, and other merchandise while in France.

What Causes Exchange Rates to Change?

Although several economic and political factors influence foreign exchange rate movements, by far the most important explanation for long-term changes in exchange rates is a differing inflation rate between two countries. Countries that experience high inflation rates will see their currencies decline in value (depreciate) relative to the currencies of countries with lower inflation rates.

Example ▶ Assume that the current exchange rate between the United States and the new nation of Farland is 2 Farland guineas (FG) per U.S. dollar, FG 2.00/US$, which is also equal to $0.50/FG. This exchange rate means that a basket of goods worth $100 in the United States sells for $100 × FG 2/US$ = FG 200 in Farland, and vice versa (goods worth FG 200 in Farland sell for $100 in the United States).

Now assume that inflation is running at a 25% annual rate in Farland but at only a 2% annual rate in the United States. In one year, the same basket of goods will sell for 1.25 × FG 200 = FG 250 in Farland, and for 1.02 × $100 = $102 in the United States. These relative prices imply that in 1 year, FG 250 will be worth $102, so the exchange rate in 1 year should change to FG 250/$102 = FG 2.45/US$, or $0.41/FG. In other words, the Farland guinea will depreciate from FG 2/US$ to FG 2.45/US$, while the dollar will appreciate from $0.50/FG to $0.41/FG.

Hint A firm that borrows money in a developing nation faces the possibility of a double penalty due to inflation. Because many of the loans have floating interest rates, inflation will increase the interest rate on the loan as well as affect the exchange rate of the currencies.

This simple example can also predict the level of interest rates in the two countries. To be enticed to save money, an investor must be offered a return that exceeds the country's inflation rate—otherwise, there would be no reason to forgo the pleasure of spending money (consuming) today because inflation would make that money less valuable 1 year from now. Let's assume that this *real rate of interest* is 3 percent per year in both Farland and the United States. Using Equation 6.1 (page 283), we can now reason that the *nominal rate of interest*—

the quoted market rate, not adjusted for risk—will be approximately equal to the real rate plus the inflation rate in each country, or $3 + 25 = 28$ percent in Farland and $3 + 2 = 5$ percent in the United States.[2]

Impact of Currency Fluctuations

Multinational companies face exchange rate risks under both floating and fixed arrangements. Floating currencies can be used to illustrate these risks. Consider the U.S. dollar–U.K. British pound relationship; note that the forces of international supply and demand, as well as economic and political elements, help to shape both the spot and the forward rates between these two currencies. Because the MNC cannot control much (or most) of these "outside" elements, the company faces potential changes in exchange rates. These changes can, in turn, affect the MNC's revenues, costs, and profits as measured in U.S. dollars. For fixed-rate currencies, official revaluation or devaluation, like the changes brought about by the market in the case of floating currencies, can affect the MNC's operations and its dollar-based financial position.

Example

MNC, Inc., a multinational manufacturer of dental drills, has a subsidiary in Great Britain that at the end of 2009 had the financial statements shown in Table 18.3 on page 822. The figures for the balance sheet and income statement are given in the local currency, British pounds (£). Using an assumed foreign exchange rate of £0.70/US$ for December 31, 2009, MNC has translated the statements into U.S. dollars. For simplicity, it is assumed that all the local figures are expected to remain the same during 2110. As a result, as of January 1, 2010, the subsidiary expects to show the same British pound figures on 12/31/10 as on 12/31/09. However, because of the *appreciation* in the assumed value of the British pound relative to the dollar, from £0.70/US$ to £0.60/US$, the translated dollar values of the items on the balance sheet, along with the dollar profit value on 12/31/10, are higher than those of the previous year. The changes are due only to fluctuations in the foreign exchange rate. In this case, the British pound *appreciated* relative to the U.S. dollar, which means that the U.S. dollar *depreciated* relative to the British pound.

accounting exposure
The risk resulting from the effects of changes in foreign exchange rates on the translated value of a firm's financial statement accounts denominated in a given foreign currency.

economic exposure
The risk resulting from the effects of changes in foreign exchange rates on the firm's value.

There are additional complexities attached to each individual account in the financial statements. For instance, it is important whether a subsidiary's debt is all in the local currency, all in U.S. dollars, or in several currencies. Moreover, it is important which currency (or currencies) the revenues and costs are denominated in. The risks shown so far relate to what is called the **accounting exposure.** In other words, foreign exchange rate fluctuations affect individual accounts in the financial statements.

A different, and perhaps more important, risk element concerns **economic exposure,** which is the potential impact of foreign exchange rate fluctuations on the firm's value. Given that all future revenues and thus net profits can be subject

---

2. This is an approximation of the true relationship, which is actually multiplicative. The correct formula says that 1 plus the nominal rate of interest, r, is equal to the product of 1 plus the real rate of interest, r^*, and 1 plus the inflation rate, IP; that is, $(1 + r) = (1 + r^*) \times (1 + IP)$. This means that the nominal interest rates for Farland and the United States should be 28.75% and 5.06%, respectively.

TABLE 18.3	**Financial Statements for MNC, Inc.'s British Subsidiary**		

Translation of Balance Sheet

	12/31/09		12/31/10
Assets	£	US$[a]	US$[b]
Cash	8.00	11.43	13.33
Inventory	60.00	85.72	100.00
Plant and equipment (net)	32.00	45.71	53.34
Total	100.00	142.86	166.67

Liabilities and Stockholders' Equity

Debt	48.00	68.57	80.00
Paid-in capital	40.00	57.15	66.67
Retained earnings	12.00	17.14	20.00
Total	100.00	142.86	166.67

Translation of Income Statement

Sales	600.00	857.14	1,000.00
Cost of goods sold	550.00	785.71	916.67
Operating profits	50.00	71.43	83.33

[a]Foreign exchange rate assumed: US$1.00 = £0.70

[b]Foreign exchange rate assumed: US$1.00 = £0.60

Note: This example is simplified to show how the balance sheet and income statement are subject to foreign exchange rate fluctuations. For the applicable rules on the translation of foreign accounts, review Section 18.2 on international financial statements.

to foreign exchange rate changes, it is obvious that the *present value* of the net profits derived from foreign operations will have, as a part of its total diversifiable risk, an element reflecting appreciation (revaluation) or depreciation (devaluation) of various currencies with respect to the U.S. dollar.

What can the management of MNCs do about these risks? The actions will depend on the attitude of the management toward risk. This attitude, in turn, translates into how aggressively management wants to hedge (that is, protect against) the company's undesirable positions and exposures. The firm can use the money markets, the forward (futures) markets, and the foreign-currency options markets—either individually or in combination—to hedge foreign exchange exposures. Further details on certain hedging strategies are described later.

Political Risks

political risk
The potential discontinuity or seizure of an MNC's operations in a host country via the host's implementation of specific rules and regulations.

Another important risk facing MNCs is political risk. **Political risk** refers to a host government's implementation of specific rules and regulations that can result in the discontinuity or seizure of the operations of a foreign company. Political risk is usually manifested in the form of nationalization, expropriation, or confiscation. In general, the host government takes over the assets and operations of a foreign firm, usually without proper (or any) compensation.

macro political risk
The subjection of *all* foreign firms to *political risk* (takeover) by a host country because of political change, revolution, or the adoption of new policies.

micro political risk
The subjection of an individual firm, a specific industry, or companies from a particular foreign country to *political risk* (takeover) by a host country.

Political risk has two basic paths: *macro* and *micro*. **Macro political risk** refers to political change, revolution, or the adoption of new policies by a host government, which subject *all* foreign firms in the country to political risk. In other words, no individual country or firm is treated differently; all assets and operations of foreign firms are taken over wholesale. An example of macro political risk occurred after communist regimes came to power in China in 1949 and Cuba in 1959–1960. **Micro political risk,** on the other hand, refers to the case in which an individual firm, a specific industry, or companies from a particular foreign country are subjected to takeover. In the first decade of the twenty-first century—especially in the second half—Russia, Venezuela, and Bolivia were among those countries that had either nationalized the operations or suspended the long-term contractual agreements held by foreign multinationals in their respective nations. Recent years have also seen the emergence of a *third* path to political risk that encompasses "global" events such as terrorism, antiglobalization movements and protests, Internet-based risks, and concerns over poverty, AIDS, and the environment, all of which affect various MNCs' operations worldwide.

Although political risk can take place in any country—even in the United States—the political instability of many developing nations generally makes the positions of multinational companies most vulnerable there. At the same time, some of these countries have the most promising markets for the goods and services MNCs offer. The main question, therefore, is how to engage in operations and foreign investment in such countries and yet avoid or minimize the potential political risk.

Table 18.4 shows some of the approaches that MNCs may be able to adopt to cope with political risk. The *negative approaches* are generally used by firms in

---

TABLE 18.4   Approaches for Coping with Political Risks

Positive approaches		Negative approaches
Prior negotiation of controls and operating contracts		License or patent restrictions under international agreements
Prior agreement for sale	Direct	Control of external raw materials
Joint venture with government or local private sector		Control of transportation to (external) markets
Use of locals in management		Control of downstream processing
Joint venture with local banks		Control of external markets
Equity participation by middle class	Indirect	
Local sourcing		
Local retail outlets		

External approaches to minimize loss

International insurance or investment guarantees

Thinly capitalized firms:
  Local financing
  External financing secured only by the local operation

Source: Rita M. Rodriguez and E. Eugene Carter, *International Financial Management,* 3rd ed. (Englewood Cliffs, NJ: Prentice-Hall, 1984), p. 512.

extractive industries such as oil and gas and mining. The *external approaches* are also of limited use. The best policies MNCs can follow are the *positive approaches,* which have both economic and political aspects.

In recent years, MNCs have been relying on a variety of complex forecasting techniques whereby international experts, using available historical data, predict the chances for political instability in a host country and the potential effects on MNC operations. Events in Afghanistan, Pakistan, India, and Russia, among others, however, point to the limited use of such techniques and tend to reinforce the usefulness of the positive approaches.

A final point relates to the introduction by most host governments in the last two decades of comprehensive sets of rules, regulations, and incentives. Known as **national entry control systems,** they are aimed at regulating inflows of *foreign direct investments* involving MNCs. They are designed to extract more benefits from MNCs' presence by regulating flows of a variety of factors—local ownership, level of exportation, use of local inputs, number of local managers, internal geographic location, level of local borrowing, and the percentages of profits to be remitted and of capital to be repatriated to parent firms. Host countries expect that as MNCs comply with these regulations, the potential for acts of political risk will decline, thus benefiting the MNCs as well.

national entry control systems
Comprehensive rules, regulations, and incentives introduced by host governments to regulate inflows of *foreign direct investments* from MNCs and at the same time extract more benefits from their presence.

REVIEW QUESTIONS

18–6 Define *spot exchange rate* and *forward exchange rate.* Define and compare *accounting exposures* and *economic exposures* to exchange rate fluctuations.

18–7 Explain how differing inflation rates between two countries affect their exchange rate over the long term.

18–8 Discuss *macro* and *micro political risk.* What is the emerging *third* path to political risk? Describe some techniques for dealing with political risk.

18.4 | Long-Term Investment and Financing Decisions

Important long-term aspects of international managerial finance include foreign direct investment, investment cash flows and decisions, capital structure, long-term debt, and equity capital. Here we consider the international dimensions of these topics.

Foreign Direct Investment

foreign direct investment (FDI)
The transfer by a multinational firm of capital, managerial, and technical assets from its home country to a host country.

Foreign direct investment (FDI) is the transfer by a multinational firm of capital, managerial, and technical assets from its home country to a host country. FDI can be explained on the basis of two main approaches: the *OLI paradigm* and *strategic motives* by MNCs. The first encompasses "O" (owner-specific) advantages in an MNC's home market, "L" (location-specific) characteristics abroad, and "I" (internalization) through which the multinational controls the value chain in its industry. The second refers to companies that invest abroad as they seek markets, raw materials, production efficiency, knowledge, and/or political safety.

The equity participation on the part of an MNC can be 100 percent (resulting in a wholly owned foreign subsidiary) or less (leading to a joint-venture project with foreign participants). In contrast to short-term, foreign portfolio investments undertaken by individuals and companies (such as internationally diversified mutual funds), FDI involves equity participation, managerial control, and day-to-day operational activities on the part of MNCs. Therefore, FDI projects will be subjected not only to business, financial, inflation, and exchange rate risks (as would foreign portfolio investments) but also to the additional element of political risk.

For several decades, U.S.-based MNCs dominated the international scene in terms of both the *flow* and the *stock* of FDI. The total FDI stock of U.S.-based MNCs, for instance, increased from $7.7 billion in 1929 to more than $2,050 billion at the end of 2005. Since the 1970s, though, their global presence is being challenged by MNCs based in Western Europe, Japan, and other developed and developing nations. In fact, even the "home" market of U.S. multinationals is being challenged by foreign firms. For instance, in 1960, FDI *into* the United States amounted to only 11.5 percent of U.S. investment overseas. According to figures released by the U.S. Department of Commerce's Bureau of Economic Analysis, at the end of 2005, the U.S. direct investment position abroad on a historical-cost basis was about $2,070 billion, while foreign direct investment position in the United States on a historical-cost basis stood at about $1,635 billion. The latter figure is close to 80 percent of the former.

Investment Cash Flows and Decisions

Measuring the amount invested in a foreign project, its resulting cash flows, and the associated risk is difficult. The returns and NPVs of such investments can significantly vary from the subsidiary's and parent's points of view. Therefore, several factors that are unique to the international setting need to be examined when one is making long-term investment decisions.

First, firms need to consider elements related to a parent company's *investment* in a subsidiary and the concept of taxes. For example, in the case of manufacturing investments, questions may arise as to the value of the equipment a parent may contribute to the subsidiary. Is the value based on market conditions in the parent country or in the local host economy? In general, the market value in the host country is the relevant "price."

The existence of different taxes—as pointed out earlier—can complicate measurement of the *cash flows* to be received by the parent because different definitions of taxable income can arise. There are still other complications when it comes to measuring the actual cash flows. From a parent firm's viewpoint, the cash flows are those that are repatriated from the subsidiary. In some countries, however, such cash flows may be totally or partially blocked. Obviously, depending on the life of the project in the host country, the returns and NPVs associated with such projects can vary significantly from the subsidiary's and the parent's points of view. For instance, for a project of only 5 years' duration, if all yearly cash flows are blocked by the host government, the subsidiary may show a "normal" or even superior return and NPV, although the parent may show no return at all. For a project of longer life, even if cash flows are blocked for the first few years, the remaining years' cash flows can contribute to the parent's returns and NPV.

Hint The discount rates used by the parent and subsidiary to calculate the NPV will also be different. The parent company has to add in a risk premium based on the possibility of exchange rates changing and the risk of not being able to get the cash out of the foreign country.

Finally, there is the issue of *risk* attached to international cash flows. The three basic types of risks are (1) business and financial risks, (2) inflation and exchange rate risks, and (3) political risks. The first category reflects the type of industry the subsidiary is in as well as its financial structure. We will present more details on financial risks later. As for the other two categories, we have already discussed the risks of having investments, profits, and assets/liabilities in different currencies and the potential impacts of political risks.

The presence of the three types of risks will influence the discount rate to be used when evaluating international cash flows. The basic rule is this: The local cost of equity capital (applicable to the local business and financial environments within which a subsidiary operates) is the starting discount rate. To this rate, the MNC would add the risks stemming from exchange rate and political factors, and from it, would subtract the benefits reflecting the parent's lower capital costs.

Capital Structure

Both theory and empirical evidence indicate that the capital structures of multinational companies differ from those of purely domestic firms. Furthermore, differences are observed among the capital structures of MNCs domiciled in various countries. Several factors tend to influence the capital structures of MNCs.

International Capital Markets

MNCs, unlike smaller, domestic firms, have access to the Euromarket (discussed earlier) and the variety of financial instruments available there. Because of their access to the international bond and equity markets, MNCs may have lower long-term financing costs, which result in differences between the capital structures of MNCs and those of purely domestic companies. Similarly, MNCs based in different countries and regions may have access to different currencies and markets, resulting in variances in capital structures for these multinationals.

International Diversification

It is well established that MNCs, in contrast to domestic firms, can achieve further risk reduction in their cash flows by diversifying internationally. International diversification may lead to varying degrees of debt versus equity. Empirically, the evidence on debt ratios is mixed. Some studies have found MNCs' debt proportions to be higher than those of domestic firms. Other studies have concluded the opposite, citing imperfections in certain foreign markets, political risk factors, and complexities in the international financial environment that cause higher agency costs of debt for MNCs.

Personal Finance Example   An important aspect of personal financial planning involves channeling savings into investments that can grow and fund long-term financial goals. Investors can invest in both domestic and foreign-based companies. Investing internationally offers greater diversification than investing only domestically. A number of academic studies overwhelmingly support the argument that well-structured international diversification does indeed reduce the risk of a portfolio and increase the return of portfolios of comparable risk. One study found that over the 10 years ended in 1994, a diversified portfolio consisting of 70% domestic and 30% foreign stocks reduced risk by about 5% and increased return by about 7%.

To capture these higher returns and lower risks, most individual investors buy *international mutual funds*. These funds take advantage of international economic developments by (1) capitalizing on changing foreign market conditions and (2) positioning their investments to benefit from devaluation of the dollar. Clearly, individuals should consider including some international investments— probably international mutual funds—in their investment portfolios.

Country Factors

A number of studies conclude that certain factors unique to each host country can cause differences in capital structures. These factors include legal, tax, political, social, and financial aspects, as well as the overall relationship between the public and private sectors. Owing to these factors, differences have been found not only among MNCs based in various countries but also among the foreign subsidiaries of an MNC. However, because no one capital structure is ideal for all MNCs, each multinational has to consider a set of global and domestic factors when deciding on the appropriate capital structure for both the overall corporation and its subsidiaries. Understanding country factors can help financial managers make better-informed decisions. As the *Global Focus* box on page 828 discusses, one way to improve one's ability to understand how business is conducted in other countries is to take an overseas assignment.

Long-Term Debt

As noted earlier, multinational companies have access to a variety of international financial instruments. Here we will discuss international bonds, the role of international financial institutions in underwriting such instruments, and the use of various techniques by MNCs to change the structure of their long-term debt.

International Bonds

international bond
A bond that is initially sold outside the country of the borrower and is often distributed in several countries.

foreign bond
An *international bond* that is sold primarily in the country of the currency in which the issue is denominated.

Eurobond
An *international bond* that is sold primarily in countries other than the country of the currency in which the issue is denominated.

In general, an **international bond** is one that is initially sold outside the country of the borrower and is often distributed in several countries. When a bond is sold primarily in the country of the currency in which the issue is denominated, it is called a **foreign bond**. For example, an MNC based in Germany might float a foreign bond issue in the British capital market underwritten by a British syndicate and denominated in British pounds. When an international bond is sold primarily in countries other than the country of the currency in which the issue is denominated, it is called a **Eurobond**. Thus, an MNC based in the United States might float a Eurobond in several European capital markets, underwritten by an international syndicate and denominated in U.S. dollars.

The U.S. dollar and the euro are the most frequently used currencies for Eurobond issues, with the euro rapidly increasing in popularity relative to the U.S. dollar. In the foreign bond category, the U.S. dollar and the euro are major choices. Low interest rates, the general stability of the currency, and the overall efficiency of the European Union's capital markets are among the primary reasons for the growing popularity of the euro.

Global Focus

Take an Overseas Assignment to Take a Step Up the Corporate Ladder

There is nothing like an extended stay in a foreign country to get a different perspective on world events, and there are sound career-enhancing reasons to work abroad. International experience can give you a competitive edge and may be vital to career advancement. Such experience goes far beyond mastering country-specific tax and accounting codes.

The demand for employees interested in an overseas assignment appears to be on an upward trend. Driven by a booming global economy, more than two-thirds of multinational corporations reported an increase in the number of international assignments in 2006, according to the Global Relocation Trends Survey, published annually by GMAC Global Relocation Services. A similar percentage of employers intended to send even more employees on overseas assignments in 2007 as compared to 2006.

Two years seems to be the bare minimum to gain experience. Staying away more than 5 years can weaken one's con-tacts with key personnel in the home office. Apart from that career risk, there are real security risks involved with an international posting to some parts of the world. The security risks can easily reduce the fun of living abroad and the opportunities to immerse oneself in the local populace.

Upon arrival in a foreign city, the tendency for expatriates is to live in a section of the city favored by other visitors from home. For security reasons, some executives also travel everywhere by chauffeured limo with an English-speaking driver. It is possible for U.S. executives to live abroad for an extended period of time without soaking up much of the local culture. Doing so may increase one's comfort level but at the loss of some of the valuable lessons to be learned from living abroad.

Oversees assignments do not come without some sacrifices. Long overseas postings can put stress on a family. The most common reason for turning down an international assignment involved family concerns such as chil-dren's education, family adjust-ment, partner resistance, and language. The second most common reason for refusing an assignment was concern for a spouse's career, not unlike the same concern some employees have about a job that requires a cross-country transfer.

Yet as globalization has pushed companies across more borders, CFOs with international experience have found themselves in greater demand. Some chief executives value international experience in their CFOs more highly than either mergers and acquisitions or capital-raising experience. If you have the chance to go abroad, you should avail yourself of the opportunity. Your life may be forever changed by the experience, and it just may give you a boost up the corporate ladder.

■ *If going abroad for a full-immersion assignment is not possible, what are some substitutes for a global assignment that may provide some—albeit limited—global experience?*

Eurobonds are much more popular than foreign bonds. These instruments are heavily used, especially in relation to Eurocurrency loans in recent years, by major market participants, including U.S. corporations. The so-called *equity-linked Eurobonds* (that is, Eurobonds convertible to equity), especially those offered by a number of U.S. firms, have found strong demand among Euromarket participants. It is expected that more of these innovative types of instruments will emerge on the international scene in the coming years.

A final point concerns the levels of interest rates in international markets. In the case of foreign bonds, interest rates are usually directly correlated with the domestic rates prevailing in the respective countries. For Eurobonds, several interest rates may be influential. For instance, for a Eurodollar bond, the interest rate will reflect several different rates, most notably the U.S. long-term rate, the Eurodollar rate, and long-term rates in other countries.

The Role of International Financial Institutions

For *foreign bonds,* the underwriting institutions are those that handle bond issues in the respective countries in which such bonds are issued. For *Eurobonds,* a number of financial institutions in the United States, Western Europe, and Japan form international underwriting syndicates. The underwriting costs for Eurobonds are comparable to those for bond flotation in the U.S. domestic market. Although U.S. institutions once dominated the Eurobond scene, economic and financial strengths exhibited by some Western European (especially German) financial firms have led to an erosion in that dominance. Since 1986, a number of European firms have shared with U.S. firms the top positions in terms of acting as lead underwriters of Eurobond issues. However, U.S. investment banks continue to dominate most other international security issuance markets—such as international equity, medium-term note, syndicated loan, and commercial paper markets. U.S. corporations account for well over half of the worldwide securities issues made each year.

To raise funds through international bond issues, many MNCs establish their own financial subsidiaries. Many U.S.-based MNCs, for example, have created subsidiaries in the United States and Western Europe, especially in Luxembourg. Such subsidiaries can be used to raise large amounts of funds in "one move," the funds being redistributed wherever MNCs need them. (Special tax rules applicable to such subsidiaries also make them desirable to MNCs.)

Changing the Structure of Debt

As will be more fully explained later, MNCs can use *hedging strategies* to change the structure/characteristics of their long-term assets and liabilities. For instance, multinationals can utilize *interest rate swaps* to obtain a desired stream of interest payments (for example, fixed rate) in exchange for another (for example, floating rate). With *currency swaps,* they can exchange an asset/liability denominated in one currency (for example, the U.S. dollar) for another (for example, the British pound). The use of these tools allows MNCs to gain access to a broader set of markets, currencies, and maturities, thus leading to both cost savings and a means of restructuring the existing assets/liabilities. There has been significant growth in such use during the last few years, and this trend is expected to continue.

Equity Capital

Here we look at how multinational companies can raise equity capital abroad. They can sell their shares in international capital markets, or they can use joint ventures, which the host country sometimes requires.

Equity Issues and Markets

One means of raising equity funds for MNCs is to have the parent's stock distributed internationally and owned by stockholders of different nationalities. Despite some advancements made in recent years that have allowed numerous

international stock market
A market with uniform rules and regulations governing major stock exchanges. MNCs would benefit greatly from such a market, which has yet to evolve.

MNCs to simultaneously list their respective stocks on a number of exchanges, the world's equity markets continue to be dominated by distinct *national* stock exchanges (such as the New York, London, and Tokyo exchanges). At the end of 2006, for example, a rather small portion of each of the world's major stock exchanges consisted of "foreign company" listings. Many commentators agree that most MNCs would benefit enormously from an **international stock market** that had uniform rules and regulations governing the major stock exchanges. Unfortunately, it will likely be many years before such a market becomes a reality.

Even with the full financial integration of the European Union, some European stock exchanges continue to compete with each other. Others have called for more cooperation in forming a single market capable of competing with the New York and Tokyo exchanges. As noted above, from the multinationals' perspective, the most desirable outcome would be to have uniform international rules and regulations with respect to all the major national stock exchanges. Such uniformity would allow MNCs unrestricted access to an international equity market paralleling the international currency and bond markets.

Joint Ventures

Earlier, we discussed the basic aspects of foreign ownership of international operations. Worth emphasizing here is that certain laws and regulations enacted by a number of host countries require MNCs to maintain less than 50 percent ownership in their subsidiaries in those countries. For a U.S.-based MNC, for example, establishing foreign subsidiaries in the form of joint ventures means that a certain portion of the firm's total international equity stock is (indirectly) held by foreign owners.

In establishing a foreign subsidiary, an MNC may wish to use as little equity and as much debt as possible, with the debt coming from local sources in the host country or the MNC itself. Each of these actions can be supported: The use of local debt can be a good protective measure to lessen the potential impacts of political risk. Because local sources are involved in the capital structure of a subsidiary, there may be fewer threats from local authorities in the event of changes in government or the imposing of new regulations on foreign business.

In support of the other action—having *more MNC-based debt* in a subsidiary's capital structure—many host governments are less restrictive toward intra-MNC interest payments than toward intra-MNC dividend remittances. The parent firm, therefore, may be in a better position if it has more MNC-based debt than equity in the capital structure of its subsidiaries.

REVIEW QUESTIONS

18–9 Indicate how NPV can differ depending on whether it is measured from the parent MNC's point of view or from that of the foreign subsidiary, when cash flows may be blocked by local authorities.

18–10 Briefly discuss some of the international factors that cause the capital structures of MNCs to differ from those of purely domestic firms.

18–11 Describe the difference between *foreign bonds* and *Eurobonds*. Explain how each is sold, and discuss the determinant(s) of their interest rates.

18–12 What are the long-run advantages of having more *local* debt and less MNC-based equity in the capital structure of a foreign subsidiary?

18.5 | Short-Term Financial Decisions

In international operations, the usual domestic sources of short-term financing, along with other sources, are available to MNCs. Included are accounts payable, accruals, bank and nonbank sources in each subsidiary's local environment, and the Euromarket. Our emphasis here is on the "foreign" sources.

The local economic market is a basic source of both short- and long-term financing for a subsidiary of a multinational company. Moreover, the subsidiary's borrowing and lending status, relative to a local firm in the same economy, can be superior, because the subsidiary can rely on the potential backing and guarantee of its parent MNC. One drawback, however, is that most local markets and local currencies are regulated by local authorities. A subsidiary may ultimately choose to turn to the Euromarket and take advantage of borrowing and investing in an unregulated financial forum.

Eurocurrency markets
The portion of the Euromarket that provides short-term, foreign-currency financing to subsidiaries of MNCs.

The Euromarket offers nondomestic long-term financing opportunities through Eurobonds, which were discussed in Chapter 6. Short-term financing opportunities are available in **Eurocurrency markets**. The forces of supply and demand are among the main factors determining exchange rates in Eurocurrency markets. Each currency's normal interest rate is influenced by economic policies pursued by the respective "home" government. For example, the interest rates offered in the Euromarket on the U.S. dollar are greatly affected by the prime rate inside the United States, and the dollar's exchange rates with other major currencies are influenced by the supply and demand forces in such markets (and in response to interest rates).

nominal interest rate
In the international context, the stated interest rate charged on financing when only the MNC parent's currency is involved.

effective interest rate
In the international context, the rate equal to the nominal rate plus (or minus) any forecast appreciation (or depreciation) of a foreign currency relative to the currency of the MNC parent.

Unlike borrowing in the domestic markets, where only one currency and a **nominal interest rate** are involved, financing activities in the Euromarket can involve several currencies and both nominal and effective interest rates. **Effective interest rates** are equal to nominal rates plus (or minus) any forecast appreciation (or depreciation) of a foreign currency relative to the currency of the MNC parent. Stated differently, the figures for effective rates are derived by adjusting the nominal interest rates for the impact of foreign-currency movements on both the principal and interest amounts. Equation 18.1 can be used to calculate the effective interest rate for a specific currency (E), given the nominal interest rate for the currency (N) and its forecast percentage change (F).

$$E = N + F + (N \times F) \qquad (18.1)$$

An example will illustrate the application and interpretation of this relationship.

Example

A multinational plastics company, International Molding, has subsidiaries in Switzerland (local currency, Swiss franc, Sf) and Japan (local currency, Japanese yen, ¥). On the basis of each subsidiary's forecast operations, the short-term financial needs (in equivalent U.S. dollars) are as follows:

Switzerland: $80 million excess cash to be invested (lent)

Japan: $60 million funds to be raised (borrowed)

On the basis of all the available information, the parent firm has provided each subsidiary with the figures given in the table on page 832 for exchange rates and interest rates. (The figures for the effective rates shown are derived using Equation 18.1.)

	Currency		
Item	US$	Sf	¥
Spot exchange rates		Sf 1.27/US$	¥108.37/US$
Forecast percent change		−2.0%	+1.0%
Interest rates			
Nominal			
Euromarket	3.30%	4.10%	1.50%
Domestic	3.00%	3.80%	1.70%
Effective			
Euromarket	3.30%	2.01%	2.51%
Domestic	3.00%	1.72%	2.71%

From the MNC's point of view, the effective rates of interest, which take into account each currency's forecast percentage change (appreciation or depreciation) relative to the U.S. dollar, are the main considerations in investment and borrowing decisions. (It is assumed here that because of local regulations, a subsidiary is *not* permitted to use the domestic market of *any other* subsidiary.) The relevant question is where funds should be invested and borrowed.

For investment purposes, the highest available effective rate of interest is 3.30% in the US$ Euromarket. Therefore, the Swiss subsidiary should invest the $80 million in Swiss francs in U.S. dollars. To raise funds, the cheapest source *open* to the Japanese subsidiary is the 2.01% effective rate for the Swiss franc in the Euromarket. The subsidiary should therefore raise the $60 million in Swiss francs in the Euromarket. These two transactions will result in the most revenues and least costs, respectively.

Several points should be made with respect to the preceding example. First, this is a simplified case of the actual workings of the Eurocurrency markets. The example ignores taxes, intersubsidiary investing and borrowing, and periods longer or shorter than a year. Nevertheless, it shows how the existence of many currencies can provide both challenges and opportunities for MNCs. Next, the focus has been solely on accounting values; of greater importance would be the impact of these actions on market value. Finally, it is important to note the following details about the figures presented. The forecast percentage change data are those normally supplied by the MNC's international financial managers. Management may instead want a *range of forecasts,* from the most likely to the least likely. In addition, the company's management is likely to take a specific position in terms of its response to any remaining exchange rate exposures. If any action is to be taken, certain amounts of one or more currencies will be borrowed and then invested in other currencies in the hope of realizing potential gains to offset potential losses associated with the exposures.

Cash Management

In its international cash management, a multinational firm can respond to exchange rate risks by protecting (hedging) its undesirable cash and marketable securities exposures or by making certain adjustments in its operations. The former approach is more applicable in responding to *accounting exposures*, the latter to *economic exposures*. Here, we examine each of these two approaches.

Hedging Strategies

hedging strategies
Techniques used to offset or protect against risk; in the international context, these include borrowing or lending in different currencies; undertaking contracts in the forward, futures, and/or options markets; and swapping assets/liabilities with other parties.

Hedging strategies are techniques used to offset or protect against risk. In international cash management, these strategies include actions such as borrowing or lending in different currencies; undertaking contracts in the forward, futures, and/or options markets; and swapping assets/liabilities with other parties. Table 18.5 briefly outlines some of the major hedging tools available to MNCs. By far, the most commonly used technique is hedging with a forward contract.

To demonstrate how you can use a forward contract to hedge exchange rate risk, assume you are a financial manager for Boeing Company, which has just booked a sale of three airplanes worth $360 million to Japan's All Nippon Airways. The sale is denominated in Japanese yen, and the current spot exchange

TABLE 18.5	Exchange Rate Risk Hedging Tools	
Tool	**Description**	**Impact on risk**
Borrowing or lending	Borrowing or lending in different currencies to take advantage of interest rate differentials and foreign exchange appreciation/depreciation; can be either on a certainty basis with "up-front" costs or speculative.	Can be used to offset exposures in existing assets/liabilities and in expected revenues/expenses.
Forward contract	"Tailor-made" contracts representing an *obligation* to buy/sell, with the amount, rate, and maturity agreed upon between the two parties; has little up-front cost.	Can eliminate downside risk but locks out any upside potential.
Futures contract	Standardized contracts offered on organized exchanges; same basic tool as a forward contract but less flexible because of standardization; more flexibility because of secondary-market access; has some up-front cost.	Can eliminate downside risk, plus position can be nullified, creating possible upside potential.
Options	Tailor-made or standardized contracts providing the *right* to buy or to sell an amount of the currency, at a particular price, during a specified time period; has up-front cost (premium).	Can eliminate downside risk and retain unlimited upside potential.
Interest rate swap	Allows the trading of one interest rate stream (e.g., on a fixed-rate U.S. dollar instrument) for another (e.g., on a floating-rate U.S. dollar instrument); fee to be paid to the intermediary.	Permits firms to change the interest rate structure of their assets/liabilities and achieves cost savings via broader market access.
Currency swap	Two parties exchange principal amounts of two different currencies initially; they pay each other's interest payments and then reverse principal amounts at a preagreed exchange rate at maturity; more complex than interest rate swaps.	Has all the features of interest rate swaps, plus allows firms to change the currency structure of their assets/liabilities.
Hybrids	A variety of combinations of some of the preceding tools; may be quite costly and/or speculative.	Can create, with the right combination, a perfect hedge against certain exchange rate exposures.

Note: The participants in these activities include MNCs, financial institutions, and brokers. The organized exchanges include Amsterdam, Chicago, London, New York, Philadelphia, and Zurich, among others. Although most of these tools can be utilized for short-term exposure management, some, such as swaps, are more appropriate for long-term hedging strategies.

rate is ¥108.37/US$. Therefore, you have priced this airplane sale at ¥39.0132 billion. If delivery were to occur today, there would be no foreign exchange risk. However, delivery and payment will not occur for 90 days. If this transaction is not hedged, Boeing will be exposed to a significant risk of loss if the Japanese yen depreciates over the next 3 months.

Suppose that between now and the delivery date, the dollar appreciates against the yen from ¥108.37/US$ to ¥110.25/US$. Upon delivery of the airplanes, the agreed-upon ¥39.0132 billion will then be worth only US$353.861 million [(¥39.0132 billion) ÷ (¥110.25/US$)], rather than the US$360 million you originally planned for—a foreign exchange *loss* of more than US$6.1 million. If, instead of remaining unhedged, you had sold the ¥39.0132 billion forward 3 months earlier at the 90-day forward rate of ¥107.92/US$ offered by your bank, you could have locked in a net dollar sale price of US$361.501 million [(¥39.0132 billion/US$) ÷ (¥107.92/US$)], realizing a foreign exchange *gain* of more than $1.5 million. Clearly, this is a better alternative. Of course, if you had remained unhedged, and the Japanese yen had appreciated beyond ¥107.92/US$, your firm would have experienced an even larger foreign exchange profit—but most MNCs prefer to make profits through sales of goods and services rather than by speculating on the direction of exchange rates.

Adjustments in Operations

In responding to exchange rate fluctuations, MNCs can give their international cash flows some protection through appropriate adjustments in assets and liabilities. Two routes are available to a multinational company. The first centers on the operating relationships that a subsidiary of an MNC maintains with *other* firms—*third parties.* Depending on management's expectation of a local currency's position, adjustments in operations would involve the reduction of liabilities if the currency is appreciating or the reduction of financial assets if it is depreciating. For example, if a U.S.-based MNC with a subsidiary in Mexico expects the peso to *appreciate* in value relative to the U.S. dollar, local customers' accounts receivable would be *increased* and accounts payable would be reduced if at all possible. Because the dollar is the currency in which the MNC parent will have to prepare consolidated financial statements, the net result in this case would be favorably to increase the Mexican subsidiary's resources in local currency. If the peso were instead expected to *depreciate,* the local customers' accounts receivable would be *reduced* and accounts payable would be increased, thereby reducing the Mexican subsidiary's resources in the local currency.

The second route focuses on the operating relationship a subsidiary has with its parent or with other subsidiaries within the same MNC. In dealing with exchange rate risks, a subsidiary can rely on *intra-MNC accounts.* Specifically, undesirable exchange rate exposures can be corrected to the extent that the subsidiary can take the following steps:

1. In appreciation-prone countries, collect intra-MNC accounts receivable as soon as possible, and delay payment of intra-MNC accounts payable as long as possible.
2. In depreciation-prone countries, collect intra-MNC accounts receivable as late as possible, and pay intra-MNC accounts payable as soon as possible.

This technique is known as "leading and lagging" or simply as "leads and lags."

Example

Assume that a U.S.-based parent company, American Computer Corporation (ACC), both buys parts from and sells parts to its wholly owned Mexican subsidiary, Tijuana Computer Company (TCC). Assume further that ACC has accounts payable of $10,000,000 that it is scheduled to pay TCC in 30 days and, in turn, has accounts receivable of (Mexican peso) MP 115.00 million due from TCC within 30 days. Because today's exchange rate is MP 11.50/US$, the accounts receivable are also worth $10,000,000. Therefore, parent and subsidiary owe each other equal amounts (though in different currencies), and both are payable in 30 days, but because TCC is a wholly owned subsidiary of ACC, the parent has complete discretion over the timing of these payments.

If ACC believes that the Mexican peso will depreciate from MP 11.50/US$ to, say, MP 12.75/US$ during the next 30 days, the combined companies can profit by collecting the weak currency (MP) debt immediately but delaying payment of the strong currency (US$) debt for the full 30 days allowed. If parent and subsidiary do this, and the peso depreciates as predicted, the net result is that the MP 115.00 million payment from TCC to ACC is made immediately and is safely converted into $10,000,000 at today's exchange rate. In comparison, the delayed $10,000,000 payment from ACC to TCC will be worth MP 127.50 million [($10 million) × (MP 12.75/US$)]. Thus the Mexican subsidiary will experience a foreign exchange trading profit of MP 12.50 million (MP 127.50 million − MP 115.00 million), whereas the U.S. parent receives the full amount ($10 million) due from TCC and therefore is unharmed.

As this example suggests, the manipulation of an MNC's consolidated intracompany accounts by one subsidiary generally benefits one subsidiary (or the parent) while leaving the other subsidiary (or the parent) unharmed. The exact degree and direction of the actual manipulations, however, may depend on the tax status of each country. The MNC obviously would want to have the exchange rate losses in the country with the higher tax rate. Finally, changes in intra-MNC accounts can also be subject to restrictions and regulations put forward by the respective host countries of various subsidiaries.

Credit and Inventory Management

Multinational firms based in different countries compete for the same global export markets. Therefore, it is essential that they offer attractive credit terms to potential customers. Increasingly, however, the maturity of developed markets is forcing MNCs to maintain and increase revenues by exporting and selling a higher percentage of their output to developing countries. Given the risks associated with these buyers, as partly evidenced by their lack of a major (hard) currency, the MNC must use a variety of tools to protect such revenues. In addition to the use of hedging and various asset and liability adjustments (described earlier), MNCs should seek the backing of their respective governments in both identifying target markets and extending credit. Multinationals based in a number of Western European nations and those based in Japan benefit from extensive involvement of government agencies that provide them with the needed service and financial support. For U.S.-based MNCs, government agencies such as the Export-Import Bank do not provide a comparable level of support.

In terms of inventory management, MNCs must consider a number of factors related to both economics and politics. In addition to maintaining the appropriate level of inventory in various locations around the world, a multinational firm must deal with exchange rate fluctuations, tariffs, nontariff barriers, integration schemes such as the EU, and other rules and regulations. Politically, inventories could be subjected to wars, expropriations, blockages, and other forms of government intervention.

REVIEW QUESTIONS

18–13 What is the *Eurocurrency market?* What are the main factors determining foreign exchange rates in that market? Differentiate between the *nominal interest rate* and the *effective interest rate* in this market.

18–14 Discuss the steps to be followed in adjusting a subsidiary's accounts relative to *third parties* when that subsidiary's local currency is expected to *appreciate* in value in relation to the currency of the parent MNC.

18–15 Outline the changes to be undertaken in *intra-MNC accounts* if a subsidiary's currency is expected to *depreciate* in value relative to the currency of the parent MNC.

18.6 | Mergers and Joint Ventures

The motives for domestic mergers—growth or diversification, synergy, fund raising, increased managerial skill or technology, tax considerations, increased ownership liquidity, and defense against takeover—are all applicable to MNCs' international mergers and joint ventures. And we should consider several additional points.

First, international mergers and joint ventures, especially those involving European firms acquiring assets in the United States, increased significantly beginning in the 1980s. MNCs based in Western Europe, Japan, and North America are numerous. Moreover, a fast-growing group of MNCs has emerged in the past two decades, some based in the so-called newly industrialized countries (including Singapore, South Korea, Taiwan, and China's Hong Kong), and others operating from emerging nations (such as Brazil, Argentina, Mexico, Israel, China, Malaysia, Thailand, and India). Even though many of these companies were hit hard by economic and currency crises (Asia in 1997, Russia in 1998, and Latin America in 2001–2003), top firms from these and other countries have been able to survive and even prosper. Additionally, many Western companies have taken advantage of these economies' weakness to buy into companies that were previously off-limits to foreign investors. This has added further to the number and value of international mergers.

The U.S. economy is among the largest recipients of FDI inflows. Most of the foreign direct investors in the United States come from seven countries: the United Kingdom, Canada, France, the Netherlands, Japan, Switzerland, and Germany. The available data indicate that in terms of the method of entry—

namely mergers and acquisitions (M&A) versus "establishments"—an over-whelming share of outlays committed by foreign multinationals in the United States between 1980 and 2006 has consisted of M&A. These firms prefer M&A through which they can target U.S. companies for their advanced technology (e.g., biotechnology firms), worldwide brands (restaurant chains and food products), entertainment/media (theme parks), and financial institutions (investment banks). In contrast, in most emerging/developing nations (including China), FDI inflows take place primarily via establishments.

Although the United States remains one of the most "open" countries to FDI inflows, some of its actions in recent years have been viewed as less than welcoming. In 2005, for example, the U.S. governnment opposed a bid by a Chinese state-owned oil company (CNOOC) to purchase an American one (UNOCAL), which led to the ultimate withdrawal of the offer. Then, in 2005 and 2006, similar opposition, along with an identical outcome, took place in relation to a bid by a firm owned by the government of Dubai (in the United Arab Emirates) to acquire port operations in the United States.

Another trend is the current increase in the number of joint ventures between companies based in Japan and firms domiciled elsewhere in the industrialized world, especially U.S.-based MNCs. In the eyes of some U.S. corporate executives, such business ventures are viewed as a "ticket into the Japanese market" as well as a way to curb a potentially tough competitor.

Developing countries, too, have been attracting foreign direct investments in many industries. Meanwhile, during the last two decades, a number of these nations have adopted specific policies and regulations aimed at controlling the inflows of foreign investments, a major provision being the 49 percent ownership limitation applied to MNCs. Of course, international competition among MNCs has benefited some developing countries in their attempts to extract concessions from the multinationals. However, an increasing number of such nations have shown greater flexibility in their recent dealings with MNCs, as MNCs have become more reluctant to form joint ventures under the stated conditions. Furthermore, it is likely that as more developing countries recognize the need for foreign capital and technology, they will show even greater flexibility in their agreements with MNCs.

A final point relates to the existence of international holding companies. Places such as Liechtenstein and Panama have long been considered promising spots for forming holding companies because of their favorable legal, corporate, and tax environments. International holding companies control many business entities in the form of subsidiaries, branches, joint ventures, and other agreements. For international legal (especially tax-related) reasons, as well as anonymity, such holding companies have become increasingly popular in recent years.

REVIEW QUESTION

18–16 What are some of the major reasons for the rapid expansion in international mergers and joint ventures of firms?

Summary

Focus on Value

The growing interdependence of world markets has increased the importance of international finance in managing the multinational company (MNC). As a result, the financial manager must deal with international issues related to taxes, financial markets, accounting and profit measurement and repatriation, exchange rate risks caused by doing business in more than one currency, political risks, financing (both debt and equity) and capital structure, short-term financing, cash management issues related to hedging and adjustments in operations, and merger and joint-venture opportunities.

The complexity of each of these issues is significantly greater for the multinational firm than for a purely domestic firm. Consequently, the financial manager must approach actions and decisions in the multinational firm using both standard financial tools and techniques and additional procedures that recognize the legal, institutional, and operating differences that exist in the multinational environment. Just as in a purely domestic firm, action should be undertaken only after the financial manager has determined that it will contribute to the parent company's overall goal of **maximizing the owners' wealth** as reflected in its share price.

Review of Learning Goals

 Understand the major factors that influence the financial operations of multinational companies (MNCs). Important international trading blocs emerged in the 1990s: one in the Americas as a result of NAFTA; the European Union (EU); and Mercosur in South America. The EU is becoming even more competitive as it achieves monetary union and many of its members use the euro as a single currency. Free trade among the largest economic powers is governed by the General Agreement on Tariffs and Trade (GATT) and is policed by the World Trade Organization (WTO).

Setting up operations in foreign countries can entail special problems related to the legal form of business organization chosen, the degree of ownership allowed by the host country, and possible restrictions and regulations on the return of capital and profits. Taxation of multinational companies is a complex issue because of the existence of varying tax rates, differing definitions of taxable income, measurement differences, and tax treaties.

The existence and expansion of dollars held outside the United States have contributed to the development of a major international financial market, the Euromarket. The large international banks, developing and industrialized nations, and multinational companies participate as borrowers and lenders in this market.

LG 2 Describe the key differences between purely domestic and international financial statements—consolidation, translation of individual accounts, and international profits. Regulations that apply to international operations complicate the preparation of foreign-based financial statements. Rulings in the United States require the determination for translation purposes of the functional currency used in the operations of a foreign subsidiary. Individual accounts of subsidiaries must be translated back into U.S. dollars using the procedures outlined in *FASB No. 52* and/or the temporal method. This standard also requires that only certain transactional gains or losses from international operations be included in the U.S. parent's income statement.

LG 3 **Discuss exchange rate risk and political risk, and explain how MNCs manage them.** Economic exposure from exchange rate risk results from the existence of different currencies and their impact on the value of foreign operations. Long-term changes in foreign exchange rates result primarily from differing inflation rates in the two countries. The money markets, the forward (futures) markets, and the foreign-currency options markets can be used to hedge foreign exchange exposure. Political risks stem mainly from the implications of political instability for the assets and operations of MNCs. MNCs can employ negative, external, and positive approaches to cope with political risk.

LG 4 **Describe foreign direct investment, investment cash flows and decisions, the MNCs' capital structure, and the international debt and equity instruments available to MNCs.** Foreign direct investment (FDI) involves an MNC's transfer of capital, managerial, and technical assets from its home country to the host country. The investment cash flows of FDIs are subject to a variety of factors, including taxes in host countries, regulations that may block the repatriation of MNCs' cash flow, various business and financial risks, and the application of a local cost of capital.

The capital structures of MNCs differ from those of purely domestic firms because of the MNCs' access to the Euromarket and the financial instruments it offers; their ability to reduce risk in their cash flows through international diversification; and the impact of factors unique to each host country. MNCs can raise long-term debt by issuing international bonds in various currencies. Foreign bonds are sold primarily in the country of the currency of issue; Eurobonds are sold primarily in countries other than the country of the issue's currency. MNCs can raise equity through sale of shares in international capital markets or through joint ventures. In establishing foreign subsidiaries, it may be more advantageous to issue debt than MNC-owned equity.

LG 5 **Discuss the role of the Eurocurrency market in short-term borrowing and investing (lending) and the basics of international cash, credit, and inventory management.** Eurocurrency markets allow multinationals to invest (lend) and raise (borrow) short-term funds in a variety of currencies and to protect themselves against exchange rate risk. MNCs consider effective interest rates, which take into account currency fluctuations, in making investment and borrowing decisions. MNCs invest in the currency with the highest effective rate and borrow in the currency with the lowest effective rate. MNCs must offer competitive credit terms and maintain adequate inventories to provide timely delivery to foreign buyers. Obtaining the backing of foreign governments is helpful to MNCs in effectively managing credit and inventory.

Review recent trends in international mergers and joint ventures. International mergers and joint ventures, including international holding companies, increased significantly beginning in the 1980s. Special factors affecting these mergers include economic and trade conditions and various regulations imposed on MNCs by host countries.

Self-Test Problem (Solution in Appendix B)

ST18–1 **Tax credits** A U.S.-based MNC has a foreign subsidiary that earns $150,000 before local taxes, with all the after-tax funds to be available to the parent in the form of dividends. The applicable taxes consist of a 32% foreign income tax rate, a foreign dividend withholding tax rate of 8%, and a U.S. tax rate of 34%. Calculate the net funds available to the parent MNC if:
a. Foreign taxes can be applied as a credit against the MNC's U.S. tax liability.
b. No tax credits are allowed.

Warm-Up Exercises   A blue box (■) indicates exercises available in .

E18–1 Santana Music is a U.S.-based MNC whose foreign subsidiary had pretax income of $55,000; all after-tax income is available in the form of dividends to the parent company. The local tax rate is 40%, the foreign dividend withholding tax rate is 5%, and the U.S. tax rate is 34%. Compare the net funds available to the parent corporation (a) if foreign taxes can be applied against the U.S. tax liability and (b) if they cannot.

E18–2 Assume that the Mexican peso currently trades at 12 pesos to the U.S. dollar. During the year U.S. inflation is expected to average 3%, while Mexican inflation is expected to average 5%. What is the current value of one peso in terms of U.S. dollars? Given the relative inflation rates, what will the exchange rates be 1 year from now? Which currency is expected to *appreciate* and which currency is expected to *depreciate* over the next year?

E18–3 If Like A Lot Corp. borrows yen at a nominal annual interest rate of 2% and during the year the yen appreciates by 10%, what will the *effective annual interest rate* be for the loan?

E18–4 Carry Trade, Inc., borrows yen when the yen is trading at ¥110/US$. If the nominal annual interest rate of the loan is 3% and at the end of the year the yen trades at ¥120/US$, what is the *effective annual interest rate* of the loan?

E18–5 Denim Industries can borrow its needed financing for expansion using one of two foreign lending facilities. It can borrow at a nominal annual interest rate of 8% in Mexican pesos or at 3% in Canadian dollars. If the peso is expected to depreciate by 10% and the Canadian dollar is expected to appreciate by 3%, which loan has the lower *effective annual interest rate*?

Problems

A blue box (■) indicates problems available in myfinancelab.

P18–1 Tax credits   A U.S.-based MNC has a foreign subsidiary that earns $250,000 before local taxes, with all the after-tax funds to be available to the parent in the form of dividends. The applicable taxes consist of a 33% foreign income tax rate, a foreign dividend withholding tax rate of 9%, and a U.S. tax rate of 34%. Calculate the net funds available to the parent MNC if:

a. Foreign taxes can be applied as a credit against the MNC's U.S. tax liability.
b. No tax credits are allowed.

P18–2 Translation of financial statements   A U.S.-based MNC has a subsidiary in France (local currency, euro, €). The balance sheet and income statement of the subsidiary follow. On 12/31/09, the exchange rate is US$1.20/€. Assume that the local (euro) figures for the statements remain the same on 12/31/10. Calculate the U.S. dollar-translated figures for the two ending time periods, assuming that between 12/31/09 and 12/31/10 the euro has appreciated against the U.S. dollar by 6%.

Translation of Income Statement			
	12/31/09		**12/31/10**
	Euro	US$	US$
Sales	30,000.00		
Cost of goods sold	29,750.00		
Operating profits	250.00		

Translation of Balance Sheet			
	12/31/09		**12/31/10**
Assets	Euro	US$	US$
Cash	40.00		
Inventory	300.00		
Plant and equipment (net)	160.00		
Total	500.00		
Liabilities and Stockholders' Equity			
Debt	240.00		
Paid-in capital	200.00		
Retained earnings	60.00		
Total	500.00		

PERSONAL FINANCE PROBLEM

P18–3 Exchange rates   Fred Nappa is planning to take a wine-tasting tour through Italy this summer. The tour will cost 2,750 euros (€) and includes transportation, hotels, and a guide. Fred estimates that round-trip airfare from his home in North Carolina to Rome, Italy, will be $1,490; he also will incur another $300 (U.S.) in incidental travel expenses. Fred estimates the cost of meals in Italy to be about €500, and he will take an additional $1,000 to cover miscellaneous expenditures. Currently the exchange rate is US$1.3411/€1.00 (or €.7456/US$1.00).

a. Determine the total dollar cost of the trip to Italy.

b. Determine the amount of euros (€) Fred will need to cover meals and miscellaneous expenditures.

PERSONAL FINANCE PROBLEM

P18–4 **International investment diversification**   The economies of the world tend to rise and fall in cycles that offset each other. International stocks can provide possible diversification for a portfolio heavy on U.S. equities. Because research on foreign companies is usually difficult for individual investors to track on their own, a foreign equity mutual fund offers the investor the expertise of a global fund manager.

Foreign-stock funds provide exposure to overseas markets at varying levels of risk. Economic and currency risk can swing in a positive or negative direction. Hence, diversification is the key to managing risk. Funds that invest overseas fall into four basic categories: global, international, emerging-market, and country-specific. The wider the reach of the fund, the less risky it is likely to be.

a. Go to www.yahoo.com. Click on the "Investing" tab and then click on "Mutual Funds." On the left, find "Education" and click on "Types of Mutual Funds." In the middle of the page, click on "Foreign Stock Funds Explained."

b. Briefly explain the differences between the following funds:

(1) Global fund.

(2) International fund.

(3) Emerging-market fund.

(4) Country-specific fund.

P18–5 **Euromarket investment and fund raising**   A U.S.-based multinational company has two subsidiaries, one in Mexico (local currency, Mexican peso, MP) and one in Japan (local currency, yen, ¥). Forecasts of business operations indicate the following short-term financing position for each subsidiary (in equivalent U.S. dollars):

Mexico: $80 million excess cash to be invested (lent)

Japan: $60 million funds to be raised (borrowed)

The management gathered the following data:

Item	US$	MP	¥
		Currency	
Spot exchange rates		MP 11.60/US$	¥108.25/US$
Forecast percent change		−3.0%	+1.5%
Interest rates			
Nominal			
Euromarket	4.00%	6.20%	2.00%
Domestic	3.75%	5.90%	2.15%
Effective			
Euromarket	_____	_____	_____
Domestic	_____	_____	_____

Determine the *effective interest rates* for all three currencies in both the Euromarket and the domestic market; then indicate where the funds should be invested and raised. (*Note:* Assume that because of local regulations, a subsidiary is *not* permitted to use the domestic market of *any other* subsidiary.)

P18–6   **ETHICS PROBLEM**   Is there a conflict between maximizing shareholder wealth and never paying bribes when doing business abroad? If so, how might you explain the firm's position to shareholders asking why the company does not pay bribes when its foreign competitors in various nations clearly do so?

Chapter 18 Case

Assessing a Direct Investment in Chile by U.S. Computer Corporation

David Smith is chief financial officer for U.S. Computer Corporation (USCC), a successful and rapidly growing manufacturer of personal computers. He has been asked to evaluate an investment project calling for USCC to build a factory in Chile to assemble the company's most popular computer for sale in the Chilean market. David knows that Chile has been a real business success story in recent years—having achieved real economic growth rates averaging over 5% per year from 1990 through 2006, even as it made the transition from military dictatorship to democracy—and USCC is eager to invest in this developing economy if an attractive opportunity arises. David's job is to use the information below to see whether this particular proposal meets the company's investment standards.

On the basis of the current Chilean peso (Ps)-to-dollar exchange rate of Ps 700/US$ (assumed value), David calculates that the factory would cost Ps 7 billion ($10 million) to build (including working capital) and would generate sales of Ps 14 billion ($20 million) per year for the first several years. Initially, the factory would import key components from the United States and assemble the computers in Chile using local labor. Smith estimates that half the company's costs will be dollar-denominated components and half will be local currency (peso) costs, but all USCC's revenues will be in pesos. As long as the peso/dollar exchange rate is stable, the company's operating cash flow is expected to equal 20% of sales. If, however, the peso were to depreciate relative to the dollar, the company's peso cost of acquiring dollar-denominated components would increase, and its profit margin would shrink because the peso sale prices of its computers would not change.

If USCC made this investment, it would set up a subsidiary in Chile and structure the factory investment so that the subsidiary's capital structure was 60% debt and 40% equity. Therefore, to finance the Ps 7 billion factory cost, USCC must obtain Ps 4.2 billion ($6 million) in debt and Ps 2.8 billion ($4 million) in equity. The debt can be obtained either by issuing $6 million of dollar-denominated bonds in the Eurobond market at a 6% annual rate and then converting the proceeds into pesos or by borrowing the Ps 4.2 billion in the Chilean market at a 14% annual interest rate. If borrowing is done in dollars, however, the parent company must also service and repay the debt in dollars, even though all project revenues will be in pesos.

For simplicity, assume the parent company decides to contribute the equity capital for the project itself. USCC would do this by contributing $4 million to the subsidiary from its existing resources or from the proceeds of newly issued stock. This equity financing would then be converted to pesos. (Alternatively, the subsidiary could sell Ps 2.8 billion of stock to Chilean investors by listing shares on the Santiago Stock Exchange.) USCC has a 12% required return on equity on its dollar-denominated investments.

To Do

a. Compute the *weighted average cost of capital* for this project, assuming that the long-term debt financing is in dollars and ignoring any taxes.

b. Assuming that the peso/dollar exchange rate remains unchanged, compute the present value of the first 5 years of the project's cash flows, using the weighted average cost of capital computed in part **a**. (*Note:* Round off your answer in part **a** to the nearest 1% prior to making this calculation.) What happens to the present value if the dollar appreciates against the peso?

c. Identify the exchange rate risks involved in this project. Given that no forward, futures, or options market exists for the Chilean peso, how might USCC minimize the exchange rate risk of this project via changes in production, sourcing, and sales? (*Hint:* Exchange rate risk can be minimized by decreasing dollar-denominated costs, by increasing dollar-denominated revenue, or by doing both.)

d. What are the risks involved in financing this project as much as possible with local funds (pesos)? Which financing strategy—dollar versus peso—would minimize the project's exchange rate risk? Would your answer change if Chile began to experience political instability? What would happen to the attractiveness of the project if Chile signed a bilateral trade pact with the United States?

Spreadsheet Exercise

As the financial manager for a large multinational corporation (MNC), you have been asked to assess the firm's *economic exposure*. The two major currencies, other than the U.S. dollar, that affect the company are the Mexican peso (MP) and the British pound (£). You have been given the projected future cash flows for next year:

Currency	Total inflow	Total outflow
British pounds	£17,000,000	£11,000,000
Mexican pesos	MP 100,000,000	MP 25,000,000

The current expected exchange rate in U.S. dollars with respect to the two currencies is as follows:

Currency	Exchange rate
British pounds	$1.66
Mexican pesos	$0.10

To Do

Assume that the movements in the Mexican peso and the British pound are highly correlated. Create a spreadsheet to answer the following questions.

a. Determine the net cash flows for both the Mexican peso and the British pound.
b. Determine the net cash flow as measured in U.S. dollars. It will represent the value of the *economic exposure*.
c. Provide your assessment as to the company's degree of economic exposure. In other words, is it high or low based on your findings in part **b**?

Group Exercise

This is the final chapter in this text and the final group assignment for your fictitious firm. In this chapter we have "gone international" and your firm has now developed to a point where it is time to look for opportunities abroad.

To Do

The first objective for your firm is to decide whether you are looking abroad for a new supplier or to expand your sales. You will then have to choose which country to investigate. Once you have made and defended these choices, you must address exchange rate risk. Up until now we have assumed that all costs and revenues were in dollars and therefore we avoided this issue. Accordingly, you have to find the recent exchange rate for this country in relation to the dollar and also look at the recent exchange rate history, say the last 5 years, to get a sense of its volatility. Now look up this country's inflation rate and compare it to the US CPI. If we expect the current inflation rates to continue over the following year, this information can be used to form expectations of changing exchange rates during the year. Compare your analysis of exchange rates using the respective inflation rates to the recent historical pattern of the exchange rate for your country. Lastly, explain what your firm perceives as the risk–reward tradeoff of going international.

Web Exercise

Go to the book's companion website at **www.prenhall.com/gitman** to find the Web Exercise for this chapter.

> Remember to check the book's website at **www.prenhall.com/gitman** to find additional resources, including Web Exercises and a Web Case.

Integrative Case 6

Organic Solutions

Organic Solutions (OS), one of the nation's largest plant wholesalers in the southeastern United States, was poised for expansion. Through strong profitability, a conservative dividend policy, and some recent realized gains in real estate, OS had a strong cash position and was searching for a target company to acquire. The executive members on the acquisition search committee had agreed that they preferred to find a firm in a similar line of business rather than one that would provide broad diversification. This would be their first acquisition, and they preferred to stay in a familiar line of business. Jennifer Morgan, director of marketing, had identified the targeted lines of business through exhaustive market research.

Ms. Morgan had determined that the servicing of plants in large commercial offices, hotels, zoos, and theme parks would complement the existing wholesale distribution business. Frequently, OS was requested by its large clients to bid on a service contract. However, the company was neither staffed nor equipped to enter this market. Ms. Morgan was familiar with the major plant service companies in the Southeast and had suggested Green Thumbs, Inc. (GTI), as an acquisition target because of its significant market share and excellent reputation.

GTI had successfully commercialized a market that had been dominated by small local contractors and in-house landscaping departments. Beginning with a contract from one of the largest theme parks in the United States, GTI's growth in sales had compounded remarkably over its 8-year history.

GTI had also been selected because of its large portfolio of long-term service contracts with several major *Fortune* 500 companies. These contracted clients would provide a captive customer base for the wholesale distribution of OS's plant products.

At the National Horticultural meeting in Los Angeles this past March, Ms. Morgan and OS's chief financial officer, Jack Levine, had approached the owner of GTI (a closely held corporation) to determine whether a merger offer would be welcomed. GTI's majority owner and president, Herb Merrell, had reacted favorably and subsequently provided financial data, including GTI's earnings record and current balance sheet. This data is presented in Tables 1 (below) and 2 (on the next page).

TABLE 1

Green Thumbs, Inc. Earning Record			
Year	EPS	Year	EPS
2002	$2.20	2006	$2.85
2003	2.35	2007	3.00
2004	2.45	2008	3.10
2005	2.60	2009	3.30

TABLE 2

<table>
<tr><td colspan="4" align="center">Green Thumbs, Inc.
Balance Sheet (December 31, 2009)</td></tr>
<tr><td>Assets</td><td></td><td>Liabilities and Equity</td><td></td></tr>
<tr><td>Cash</td><td>$ 2,500,000</td><td>Current liabilities</td><td>$ 5,250,000</td></tr>
<tr><td>Accounts receivable</td><td>1,500,000</td><td>Mortgage payable</td><td>3,125,000</td></tr>
<tr><td>Inventories</td><td>7,625,000</td><td>Common stock</td><td>15,625,000</td></tr>
<tr><td>Land</td><td>7,475,000</td><td>Retained earnings</td><td>9,000,000</td></tr>
<tr><td>Fixed assets (net)</td><td>13,900,000</td><td>Total liabilities and equity</td><td>$33,000,000</td></tr>
<tr><td>Total assets</td><td>$33,000,000</td><td></td><td></td></tr>
</table>

TABLE 3

OS and GTI Financial Data (December 31, 2009)		
Item	OS	GTI
Earnings available for common stock	$35,000,000	$15,246,000
Number of shares of common stock	10,000,000	4,620,000
Market price per share	$50	$30[a]

[a]Estimated by Organic Solutions.

Jack Levine had estimated that the incremental cash inflow after taxes from the acquisition would be $18,750,000 for years 1 and 2; $20,500,000 for year 3; $21,750,000 for year 4; $24,000,000 for year 5; and $25,000,000 for years 6 through 30. He also estimated that the company should earn a rate of return of at least 16% on an investment of this type. Additional financial data for 2009 are given in Table 3.

To Do

a. What is the maximum price that Organic Solutions should offer GTI for a cash acquisition? (*Note:* Assume the relevant time horizon for analysis is 30 years.)
b. If OS planned to sell bonds to finance 80% of the cash acquisition price found in part **a**, how might issuance of each of the following bonds affect the firm? Describe the characteristics and pros and cons of each bond.
   (1) Straight bonds.
   (2) Convertible bonds.
   (3) Bonds with stock purchase warrants attached.

c. (1) What is the *ratio of exchange* in a stock swap acquisition if OS pays $30 per share for GTI? Explain why.

(2) What effect will this swap of stock have on the EPS of the original shareholders of (i) Organic Solutions and (ii) Green Thumbs, Inc.? Explain why.

(3) If the earnings attributed to GTI's assets grow at a much slower rate than those attributed to OS's premerger assets, what effect might this have on the EPS of the merged firm over the long run?

d. What other merger proposals could OS make to GTI's owners?

e. What impact would the fact that GTI is actually a foreign-based company have on the foregoing analysis? Describe the added regulations, costs, benefits, and risks that are likely to be associated with such an international merger.

Appendix A

Financial Tables

TABLE A–1 Future Value Interest Factors for One Dollar Compounded at i Percent for n Periods:

$$FVIF_{i,n} = (1 + i)^n$$

TABLE A–2 Present Value Interest Factors for One Dollar Discounted at i Percent for n Periods:

$$PVIF_{i,n} = \frac{1}{(1 + i)^n}$$

TABLE A–3 Future Value Interest Factors for a One-Dollar Ordinary Annuity Compounded at i Percent for n Periods:

$$FVIFA_{i,n} = \sum_{t=1}^{n} (1 + i)^{t-1}$$

TABLE A–4 Present Value Interest Factors for a One-Dollar Annuity Discounted at i Percent for n Periods:

$$PVIFA_{i,n} = \sum_{t=1}^{n} \frac{1}{(1 + i)^t}$$

TABLE A–1 — Future Value Interest Factors for One Dollar Compounded at i Percent for n Periods: $FVIF_{i,n} = (1 + i)^n$

Period	1%	2%	3%	4%	5%	6%	7%	8%	9%	10%	11%	12%	13%	14%	15%	16%	17%	18%	19%	20%
1	1.010	1.020	1.030	1.040	1.050	1.060	1.070	1.080	1.090	1.100	1.110	1.120	1.130	1.140	1.150	1.160	1.170	1.180	1.190	1.200
2	1.020	1.040	1.061	1.082	1.102	1.124	1.145	1.166	1.188	1.210	1.232	1.254	1.277	1.300	1.322	1.346	1.369	1.392	1.416	1.440
3	1.030	1.061	1.093	1.125	1.158	1.191	1.225	1.260	1.295	1.331	1.368	1.405	1.443	1.482	1.521	1.561	1.602	1.643	1.685	1.728
4	1.041	1.082	1.126	1.170	1.216	1.262	1.311	1.360	1.412	1.464	1.518	1.574	1.630	1.689	1.749	1.811	1.874	1.939	2.005	2.074
5	1.051	1.104	1.159	1.217	1.276	1.338	1.403	1.469	1.539	1.611	1.685	1.762	1.842	1.925	2.011	2.100	2.192	2.288	2.386	2.488
6	1.062	1.126	1.194	1.265	1.340	1.419	1.501	1.587	1.677	1.772	1.870	1.974	2.082	2.195	2.313	2.436	2.565	2.700	2.840	2.986
7	1.072	1.149	1.230	1.316	1.407	1.504	1.606	1.714	1.828	1.949	2.076	2.211	2.353	2.502	2.660	2.826	3.001	3.185	3.379	3.583
8	1.083	1.172	1.267	1.369	1.477	1.594	1.718	1.851	1.993	2.144	2.305	2.476	2.658	2.853	3.059	3.278	3.511	3.759	4.021	4.300
9	1.094	1.195	1.305	1.423	1.551	1.689	1.838	1.999	2.172	2.358	2.558	2.773	3.004	3.252	3.518	3.803	4.108	4.435	4.785	5.160
10	1.105	1.219	1.344	1.480	1.629	1.791	1.967	2.159	2.367	2.594	2.839	3.106	3.395	3.707	4.046	4.411	4.807	5.234	5.695	6.192
11	1.116	1.243	1.384	1.539	1.710	1.898	2.105	2.332	2.580	2.853	3.152	3.479	3.836	4.226	4.652	5.117	5.624	6.176	6.777	7.430
12	1.127	1.268	1.426	1.601	1.796	2.012	2.252	2.518	2.813	3.138	3.498	3.896	4.334	4.818	5.350	5.936	6.580	7.288	8.064	8.916
13	1.138	1.294	1.469	1.665	1.886	2.133	2.410	2.720	3.066	3.452	3.883	4.363	4.898	5.492	6.153	6.886	7.699	8.599	9.596	10.699
14	1.149	1.319	1.513	1.732	1.980	2.261	2.579	2.937	3.342	3.797	4.310	4.887	5.535	6.261	7.076	7.987	9.007	10.147	11.420	12.839
15	1.161	1.346	1.558	1.801	2.079	2.397	2.759	3.172	3.642	4.177	4.785	5.474	6.254	7.138	8.137	9.265	10.539	11.974	13.589	15.407
16	1.173	1.373	1.605	1.873	2.183	2.540	2.952	3.426	3.970	4.595	5.311	6.130	7.067	8.137	9.358	10.748	12.330	14.129	16.171	18.488
17	1.184	1.400	1.653	1.948	2.292	2.693	3.159	3.700	4.328	5.054	5.895	6.866	7.986	9.276	10.761	12.468	14.426	16.672	19.244	22.186
18	1.196	1.428	1.702	2.026	2.407	2.854	3.380	3.996	4.717	5.560	6.543	7.690	9.024	10.575	12.375	14.462	16.879	19.673	22.900	26.623
19	1.208	1.457	1.753	2.107	2.527	3.026	3.616	4.316	5.142	6.116	7.263	8.613	10.197	12.055	14.232	16.776	19.748	23.214	27.251	31.948
20	1.220	1.486	1.806	2.191	2.653	3.207	3.870	4.661	5.604	6.727	8.062	9.646	11.523	13.743	16.366	19.461	23.105	27.393	32.429	38.337
21	1.232	1.516	1.860	2.279	2.786	3.399	4.140	5.034	6.109	7.400	8.949	10.804	13.021	15.667	18.821	22.574	27.033	32.323	38.591	46.005
22	1.245	1.546	1.916	2.370	2.925	3.603	4.430	5.436	6.658	8.140	9.933	12.100	14.713	17.861	21.644	26.186	31.629	38.141	45.923	55.205
23	1.257	1.577	1.974	2.465	3.071	3.820	4.740	5.871	7.258	8.954	11.026	13.552	16.626	20.361	24.891	30.376	37.005	45.007	54.648	66.247
24	1.270	1.608	2.033	2.563	3.225	4.049	5.072	6.341	7.911	9.850	12.239	15.178	18.788	23.212	28.625	35.236	43.296	53.108	65.031	79.496
25	1.282	1.641	2.094	2.666	3.386	4.292	5.427	6.848	8.623	10.834	13.585	17.000	21.230	26.461	32.918	40.874	50.656	62.667	77.387	95.395
30	1.348	1.811	2.427	3.243	4.322	5.743	7.612	10.062	13.267	17.449	22.892	29.960	39.115	50.949	66.210	85.849	111.061	143.367	184.672	237.373
35	1.417	2.000	2.814	3.946	5.516	7.686	10.676	14.785	20.413	28.102	38.574	52.799	72.066	98.097	133.172	180.311	243.495	327.988	440.691	590.657
40	1.489	2.208	3.262	4.801	7.040	10.285	14.974	21.724	31.408	45.258	64.999	93.049	132.776	188.876	267.856	378.715	533.846	750.353	1051.642	1469.740
45	1.565	2.438	3.781	5.841	8.985	13.764	21.002	31.920	48.325	72.888	109.527	163.985	244.629	363.662	538.752	795.429	1170.425	1716.619	2509.583	3657.176
50	1.645	2.691	4.384	7.106	11.467	18.419	29.456	46.900	74.354	117.386	184.559	288.996	450.711	700.197	1083.619	1670.669	2566.080	3927.189	5988.730	9100.191

Using the Calculator to Compute the Future Value of a Single Amount

Before you begin, make sure to clear the memory, ensure that you are in the *end mode* and that your calculator is set for *one payment per year*, and set the number of decimal places that you want (usually two for dollar-related accuracy).

Sample Problem

You place $800 in a savings account at 6% compounded annually. What is your account balance at the end of 5 years?

Hewlett-Packard HP 12C, 17 BII, and 19 BII[a]

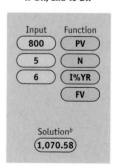

Input	Function
800	PV
5	N
6	I%YR
	FV

Solution[b]
1,070.58

---

[a]For the 12C, you would use the (n) key instead of the (N) key and use the (i) key instead of the (I%YR) key.
[b]The minus sign that precedes the solution should be ignored.

TABLE A-1 (Continued)

Period	21%	22%	23%	24%	25%	26%	27%	28%	29%	30%	31%	32%	33%	34%	35%	40%	45%	50%
1	1.210	1.220	1.230	1.240	1.250	1.260	1.270	1.280	1.290	1.300	1.310	1.320	1.330	1.340	1.350	1.400	1.450	1.500
2	1.464	1.488	1.513	1.538	1.562	1.588	1.613	1.638	1.664	1.690	1.716	1.742	1.769	1.796	1.822	1.960	2.102	2.250
3	1.772	1.816	1.861	1.907	1.953	2.000	2.048	2.097	2.147	2.197	2.248	2.300	2.353	2.406	2.460	2.744	3.049	3.375
4	2.144	2.215	2.289	2.364	2.441	2.520	2.601	2.684	2.769	2.856	2.945	3.036	3.129	3.224	3.321	3.842	4.421	5.063
5	2.594	2.703	2.815	2.932	3.052	3.176	3.304	3.436	3.572	3.713	3.858	4.007	4.162	4.320	4.484	5.378	6.410	7.594
6	3.138	3.297	3.463	3.635	3.815	4.001	4.196	4.398	4.608	4.827	5.054	5.290	5.535	5.789	6.053	7.530	9.294	11.391
7	3.797	4.023	4.259	4.508	4.768	5.042	5.329	5.629	5.945	6.275	6.621	6.983	7.361	7.758	8.172	10.541	13.476	17.086
8	4.595	4.908	5.239	5.589	5.960	6.353	6.767	7.206	7.669	8.157	8.673	9.217	9.791	10.395	11.032	14.758	19.541	25.629
9	5.560	5.987	6.444	6.931	7.451	8.004	8.595	9.223	9.893	10.604	11.362	12.166	13.022	13.930	14.894	20.661	28.334	38.443
10	6.727	7.305	7.926	8.594	9.313	10.086	10.915	11.806	12.761	13.786	14.884	16.060	17.319	18.666	20.106	28.925	41.085	57.665
11	8.140	8.912	9.749	10.657	11.642	12.708	13.862	15.112	16.462	17.921	19.498	21.199	23.034	25.012	27.144	40.495	59.573	86.498
12	9.850	10.872	11.991	13.215	14.552	16.012	17.605	19.343	21.236	23.298	25.542	27.982	30.635	33.516	36.644	56.694	86.380	129.746
13	11.918	13.264	14.749	16.386	18.190	20.175	22.359	24.759	27.395	30.287	33.460	36.937	40.745	44.912	49.469	79.371	125.251	194.620
14	14.421	16.182	18.141	20.319	22.737	25.420	28.395	31.691	35.339	39.373	43.832	48.756	54.190	60.181	66.784	111.119	181.614	291.929
15	17.449	19.742	22.314	25.195	28.422	32.030	36.062	40.565	45.587	51.185	57.420	64.358	72.073	80.643	90.158	155.567	263.341	437.894
16	21.113	24.085	27.446	31.242	35.527	40.357	45.799	51.923	58.808	66.541	75.220	84.953	95.857	108.061	121.713	217.793	381.844	656.841
17	25.547	29.384	33.758	38.740	44.409	50.850	58.165	66.461	75.862	86.503	98.539	112.138	127.490	144.802	164.312	304.911	553.674	985.261
18	30.912	35.848	41.523	48.038	55.511	64.071	73.869	85.070	97.862	112.454	129.086	148.022	169.561	194.035	221.822	426.875	802.826	1477.892
19	37.404	43.735	51.073	59.567	69.389	80.730	93.813	108.890	126.242	146.190	169.102	195.389	225.517	260.006	299.459	597.625	1164.098	2216.838
20	45.258	53.357	62.820	73.863	86.736	101.720	119.143	139.379	162.852	190.047	221.523	257.913	299.937	348.408	404.270	836.674	1687.942	3325.257
21	54.762	65.095	77.268	91.591	108.420	128.167	151.312	178.405	210.079	247.061	290.196	340.446	398.916	466.867	545.764	1171.343	2447.515	4987.883
22	66.262	79.416	95.040	113.572	135.525	161.490	192.165	228.358	271.002	321.178	380.156	449.388	530.558	625.601	736.781	1639.878	3548.896	7481.824
23	80.178	96.887	116.899	140.829	169.407	203.477	244.050	292.298	349.592	417.531	498.004	593.192	705.642	838.305	994.653	2295.829	5145.898	11222.738
24	97.015	118.203	143.786	174.628	211.758	256.381	309.943	374.141	450.974	542.791	652.385	783.013	938.504	1123.328	1342.781	3214.158	7461.547	16834.109
25	117.388	144.207	176.857	216.539	264.698	323.040	393.628	478.901	581.756	705.627	854.623	1033.577	1248.210	1505.258	1812.754	4499.816	10819.242	25251.164
30	304.471	389.748	497.904	634.810	807.793	1025.904	1300.477	1645.488	2078.208	2619.936	3297.081	4142.008	5194.516	6503.285	8128.426	24201.043	69348.375	191751.000
35	789.716	1053.370	1401.749	1861.020	2465.189	3258.053	4296.547	5653.840	7423.988	9727.598	12719.918	16598.906	21617.363	28096.695	36448.051	130158.687	*	*
40	2048.309	2846.941	3946.340	5455.797	7523.156	10346.879	14195.051	19426.418	26520.723	36117.754	49072.621	66519.313	89962.188	121388.437	163433.875	700022.688	*	*
45	5312.758	7694.418	11110.121	15994.316	22958.844	32859.457	46897.973	66748.500	94739.937	134102.187	*	*	*	*	*	*	*	*
50	13779.844	20795.680	31278.301	46889.207	70064.812	104354.562	154942.687	229345.875	338440.000	497910.125	*	*	*	*	*	*	*	*

*Not shown because of space limitations.

Texas Instruments, BA-35, BAII, and BAII Plus[c]

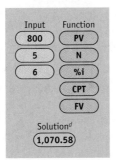

Input	Function
800	PV
5	N
6	%i
	CPT
	FV
Solution[d]	
1,070.58	

[c]For the Texas Instruments BAII, you would use the [2nd] key instead of the [CPT] key; for the Texas Instruments BAII Plus, you would use the [I/Y] key instead of the [%i] key.

[d]If a minus sign precedes the solution, it should be ignored.

TABLE A-2 — Present Value Interest Factors for One Dollar Discounted at *i* Percent

for *n* Periods: $PVIF_{i,n} = \dfrac{1}{(1 + i)^n}$

Period	1%	2%	3%	4%	5%	6%	7%	8%	9%	10%	11%	12%	13%	14%	15%	16%	17%	18%	19%	20%
1	.990	.980	.971	.962	.952	.943	.935	.926	.917	.909	.901	.893	.885	.877	.870	.862	.855	.847	.840	.833
2	.980	.961	.943	.925	.907	.890	.873	.857	.842	.826	.812	.797	.783	.769	.756	.743	.731	.718	.706	.694
3	.971	.942	.915	.889	.864	.840	.816	.794	.772	.751	.731	.712	.693	.675	.658	.641	.624	.609	.593	.579
4	.961	.924	.888	.855	.823	.792	.763	.735	.708	.683	.659	.636	.613	.592	.572	.552	.534	.516	.499	.482
5	.951	.906	.863	.822	.784	.747	.713	.681	.650	.621	.593	.567	.543	.519	.497	.476	.456	.437	.419	.402
6	.942	.888	.837	.790	.746	.705	.666	.630	.596	.564	.535	.507	.480	.456	.432	.410	.390	.370	.352	.335
7	.933	.871	.813	.760	.711	.665	.623	.583	.547	.513	.482	.452	.425	.400	.376	.354	.333	.314	.296	.279
8	.923	.853	.789	.731	.677	.627	.582	.540	.502	.467	.434	.404	.376	.351	.327	.305	.285	.266	.249	.233
9	.914	.837	.766	.703	.645	.592	.544	.500	.460	.424	.391	.361	.333	.308	.284	.263	.243	.225	.209	.194
10	.905	.820	.744	.676	.614	.558	.508	.463	.422	.386	.352	.322	.295	.270	.247	.227	.208	.191	.176	.162
11	.896	.804	.722	.650	.585	.527	.475	.429	.388	.350	.317	.287	.261	.237	.215	.195	.178	.162	.148	.135
12	.887	.789	.701	.625	.557	.497	.444	.397	.356	.319	.286	.257	.231	.208	.187	.168	.152	.137	.124	.112
13	.879	.773	.681	.601	.530	.469	.415	.368	.326	.290	.258	.229	.204	.182	.163	.145	.130	.116	.104	.093
14	.870	.758	.661	.577	.505	.442	.388	.340	.299	.263	.232	.205	.181	.160	.141	.125	.111	.099	.088	.078
15	.861	.743	.642	.555	.481	.417	.362	.315	.275	.239	.209	.183	.160	.140	.123	.108	.095	.084	.074	.065
16	.853	.728	.623	.534	.458	.394	.339	.292	.252	.218	.188	.163	.141	.123	.107	.093	.081	.071	.062	.054
17	.844	.714	.605	.513	.436	.371	.317	.270	.231	.198	.170	.146	.125	.108	.093	.080	.069	.060	.052	.045
18	.836	.700	.587	.494	.416	.350	.296	.250	.212	.180	.153	.130	.111	.095	.081	.069	.059	.051	.044	.038
19	.828	.686	.570	.475	.396	.331	.277	.232	.194	.164	.138	.116	.098	.083	.070	.060	.051	.043	.037	.031
20	.820	.673	.554	.456	.377	.312	.258	.215	.178	.149	.124	.104	.087	.073	.061	.051	.043	.037	.031	.026
21	.811	.660	.538	.439	.359	.294	.242	.199	.164	.135	.112	.093	.077	.064	.053	.044	.037	.031	.026	.022
22	.803	.647	.522	.422	.342	.278	.226	.184	.150	.123	.101	.083	.068	.056	.046	.038	.032	.026	.022	.018
23	.795	.634	.507	.406	.326	.262	.211	.170	.138	.112	.091	.074	.060	.049	.040	.033	.027	.022	.018	.015
24	.788	.622	.492	.390	.310	.247	.197	.158	.126	.102	.082	.066	.053	.043	.035	.028	.023	.019	.015	.013
25	.780	.610	.478	.375	.295	.233	.184	.146	.116	.092	.074	.059	.047	.038	.030	.024	.020	.016	.013	.010
30	.742	.552	.412	.308	.231	.174	.131	.099	.075	.057	.044	.033	.026	.020	.015	.012	.009	.007	.005	.004
35	.706	.500	.355	.253	.181	.130	.094	.068	.049	.036	.026	.019	.014	.010	.008	.006	.004	.003	.002	.002
40	.672	.453	.307	.208	.142	.097	.067	.046	.032	.022	.015	.011	.008	.005	.004	.003	.002	.001	.001	.001
45	.639	.410	.264	.171	.111	.073	.048	.031	.021	.014	.009	.006	.004	.003	.002	.001	.001	.001	*	*
50	.608	.372	.228	.141	.087	.054	.034	.021	.013	.009	.005	.003	.002	.001	.001	.001	*	*	*	*

*PVIF is zero to three decimal places.

Using the Calculator to Compute the Present Value of a Single Amount

Hewlett-Packard HP 12C, 17 BII, and 19 BII[a]

Before you begin, make sure to clear the memory, ensure that you are in the *end mode* and that your calculator is set for *one payment per year*, and set the number of decimal places that you want (usually two for dollar-related accuracy).

Sample Problem

You want to know the present value of $1,700 to be received at the end of 8 years, assuming an 8% discount rate.

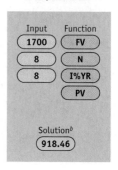

Input	Function
1700	FV
8	N
8	I%YR
	PV

Solution[b]
918.46

---

[a]For the 12C, you would use the **n** key instead of the **N** key and use the **i** key instead of the **I%YR** key.
[b]The minus sign that precedes the solution should be ignored.

TABLE A–2 (Continued)

Period	21%	22%	23%	24%	25%	26%	27%	28%	29%	30%	31%	32%	33%	34%	35%	40%	45%	50%
1	.826	.820	.813	.806	.800	.794	.787	.781	.775	.769	.763	.758	.752	.746	.741	.714	.690	.667
2	.683	.672	.661	.650	.640	.630	.620	.610	.601	.592	.583	.574	.565	.557	.549	.510	.476	.444
3	.564	.551	.537	.524	.512	.500	.488	.477	.466	.455	.445	.435	.425	.416	.406	.364	.328	.296
4	.467	.451	.437	.423	.410	.397	.384	.373	.361	.350	.340	.329	.320	.310	.301	.260	.226	.198
5	.386	.370	.355	.341	.328	.315	.303	.291	.280	.269	.259	.250	.240	.231	.223	.186	.156	.132
6	.319	.303	.289	.275	.262	.250	.238	.227	.217	.207	.198	.189	.181	.173	.165	.133	.108	.088
7	.263	.249	.235	.222	.210	.198	.188	.178	.168	.159	.151	.143	.136	.129	.122	.095	.074	.059
8	.218	.204	.191	.179	.168	.157	.148	.139	.130	.123	.115	.108	.102	.096	.091	.068	.051	.039
9	.180	.167	.155	.144	.134	.125	.116	.108	.101	.094	.088	.082	.077	.072	.067	.048	.035	.026
10	.149	.137	.126	.116	.107	.099	.092	.085	.078	.073	.067	.062	.058	.054	.050	.035	.024	.017
11	.123	.112	.103	.094	.086	.079	.072	.066	.061	.056	.051	.047	.043	.040	.037	.025	.017	.012
12	.102	.092	.083	.076	.069	.062	.057	.052	.047	.043	.039	.036	.033	.030	.027	.018	.012	.008
13	.084	.075	.068	.061	.055	.050	.045	.040	.037	.033	.030	.027	.025	.022	.020	.013	.008	.005
14	.069	.062	.055	.049	.044	.039	.035	.032	.028	.025	.023	.021	.018	.017	.015	.009	.006	.003
15	.057	.051	.045	.040	.035	.031	.028	.025	.022	.020	.017	.016	.014	.012	.011	.006	.004	.002
16	.047	.042	.036	.032	.028	.025	.022	.019	.017	.015	.013	.012	.010	.009	.008	.005	.003	.002
17	.039	.034	.030	.026	.023	.020	.017	.015	.013	.012	.010	.009	.008	.007	.006	.003	.002	.001
18	.032	.028	.024	.021	.018	.016	.014	.012	.010	.009	.008	.007	.006	.005	.005	.002	.001	.001
19	.027	.023	.020	.017	.014	.012	.011	.009	.008	.007	.006	.005	.004	.003	.003	.002	.001	*
20	.022	.019	.016	.014	.012	.010	.008	.007	.006	.005	.005	.004	.003	.003	.002	.001	.001	*
21	.018	.015	.013	.011	.009	.008	.007	.006	.005	.004	.003	.003	.003	.002	.002	.001	*	*
22	.015	.013	.011	.009	.007	.006	.005	.004	.004	.003	.003	.002	.002	.002	.001	.001	*	*
23	.012	.010	.009	.007	.006	.005	.004	.003	.003	.002	.002	.002	.001	.001	.001	*	*	*
24	.010	.008	.007	.006	.005	.004	.003	.003	.002	.002	.002	.001	.001	.001	.001	*	*	*
25	.009	.007	.006	.005	.004	.003	.003	.002	.002	.001	.001	.001	.001	.001	.001	*	*	*
30	.003	.003	.002	.002	.001	.001	.001	.001	*	*	*	*	*	*	*	*	*	*
35	.001	.001	.001	.001	*	*	*	*	*	*	*	*	*	*	*	*	*	*
40	*	*	*	*	*	*	*	*	*	*	*	*	*	*	*	*	*	*
45	*	*	*	*	*	*	*	*	*	*	*	*	*	*	*	*	*	*
50	*	*	*	*	*	*	*	*	*	*	*	*	*	*	*	*	*	*

*$PVIF$ is zero to three decimal places.

**Texas Instruments,
BA-35, BAII,
and BAII Plus[c]**

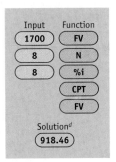

Input	Function
1700	FV
8	N
8	%i
	CPT
	FV

Solution[d]
918.46

[c]For the Texas Instruments BAII, you would use the `2nd` key instead of the `CPT` key; for the Texas Instruments BAII Plus, you would use the `I/Y` key instead of the `%i` key.

[d]If a minus sign precedes the solution, it should be ignored.

TABLE A–3   Future Value Interest Factors for a One-Dollar Ordinary Annuity

Compounded at i Percent for n Periods: $FVIFA_{i,n} = \sum_{t=1}^{n} (1 + i)^{t-1}$

Period	1%	2%	3%	4%	5%	6%	7%	8%	9%	10%	11%	12%	13%	14%	15%	16%	17%	18%	19%	20%
1	1.000	1.000	1.000	1.000	1.000	1.000	1.000	1.000	1.000	1.000	1.000	1.000	1.000	1.000	1.000	1.000	1.000	1.000	1.000	1.000
2	2.010	2.020	2.030	2.040	2.050	2.060	2.070	2.080	2.090	2.100	2.110	2.120	2.130	2.140	2.150	2.160	2.170	2.180	2.190	2.200
3	3.030	3.060	3.091	3.122	3.152	3.184	3.215	3.246	3.278	3.310	3.342	3.374	3.407	3.440	3.472	3.506	3.539	3.572	3.606	3.640
4	4.060	4.122	4.184	4.246	4.310	4.375	4.440	4.506	4.573	4.641	4.710	4.779	4.850	4.921	4.993	5.066	5.141	5.215	5.291	5.368
5	5.101	5.204	5.309	5.416	5.526	5.637	5.751	5.867	5.985	6.105	6.228	6.353	6.480	6.610	6.742	6.877	7.014	7.154	7.297	7.442
6	6.152	6.308	6.468	6.633	6.802	6.975	7.153	7.336	7.523	7.716	7.913	8.115	8.323	8.535	8.754	8.977	9.207	9.442	9.683	9.930
7	7.214	7.434	7.662	7.898	8.142	8.394	8.654	8.923	9.200	9.487	9.783	10.089	10.405	10.730	11.067	11.414	11.772	12.141	12.523	12.916
8	8.286	8.583	8.892	9.214	9.549	9.897	10.260	10.637	11.028	11.436	11.859	12.300	12.757	13.233	13.727	14.240	14.773	15.327	15.902	16.499
9	9.368	9.755	10.159	10.583	11.027	11.491	11.978	12.488	13.021	13.579	14.164	14.776	15.416	16.085	16.786	17.518	18.285	19.086	19.923	20.799
10	10.462	10.950	11.464	12.006	12.578	13.181	13.816	14.487	15.193	15.937	16.722	17.549	18.420	19.337	20.304	21.321	22.393	23.521	24.709	25.959
11	11.567	12.169	12.808	13.486	14.207	14.972	15.784	16.645	17.560	18.531	19.561	20.655	21.814	23.044	24.349	25.733	27.200	28.755	30.403	32.150
12	12.682	13.412	14.192	15.026	15.917	16.870	17.888	18.977	20.141	21.384	22.713	24.133	25.650	27.271	29.001	30.850	32.824	34.931	37.180	39.580
13	13.809	14.680	15.618	16.627	17.713	18.882	20.141	21.495	22.953	24.523	26.211	28.029	29.984	32.088	34.352	36.786	39.404	42.218	45.244	48.496
14	14.947	15.974	17.086	18.292	19.598	21.015	22.550	24.215	26.019	27.975	30.095	32.392	34.882	37.581	40.504	43.672	47.102	50.818	54.841	59.196
15	16.097	17.293	18.599	20.023	21.578	23.276	25.129	27.152	29.361	31.772	34.405	37.280	40.417	43.842	47.580	51.659	56.109	60.965	66.260	72.035
16	17.258	18.639	20.157	21.824	23.657	25.672	27.888	30.324	33.003	35.949	39.190	42.753	46.671	50.980	55.717	60.925	66.648	72.938	79.850	87.442
17	18.430	20.012	21.761	23.697	25.840	28.213	30.840	33.750	36.973	40.544	44.500	48.883	53.738	59.117	65.075	71.673	78.978	87.067	96.021	105.930
18	19.614	21.412	23.414	25.645	28.132	30.905	33.999	37.450	41.301	45.599	50.396	55.749	61.724	68.393	75.836	84.140	93.404	103.739	115.265	128.116
19	20.811	22.840	25.117	27.671	30.539	33.760	37.379	41.446	46.018	51.158	56.939	63.439	70.748	78.968	88.211	98.603	110.283	123.412	138.165	154.739
20	22.019	24.297	26.870	29.778	33.066	36.785	40.995	45.762	51.159	57.274	64.202	72.052	80.946	91.024	102.443	115.379	130.031	146.626	165.417	186.687
21	23.239	25.783	28.676	31.969	35.719	39.992	44.865	50.422	56.764	64.002	72.264	81.698	92.468	104.767	118.809	134.840	153.136	174.019	197.846	225.024
22	24.471	27.299	30.536	34.248	38.505	43.392	49.005	55.456	62.872	71.402	81.213	92.502	105.489	120.434	137.630	157.414	180.169	206.342	236.436	271.028
23	25.716	28.845	32.452	36.618	41.430	46.995	53.435	60.893	69.531	79.542	91.147	104.602	120.203	138.295	159.274	183.600	211.798	244.483	282.359	326.234
24	26.973	30.421	34.426	39.082	44.501	50.815	58.176	66.764	76.789	88.496	102.173	118.154	136.829	158.656	184.166	213.976	248.803	289.490	337.007	392.480
25	28.243	32.030	36.459	41.645	47.726	54.864	63.248	73.105	84.699	98.346	114.412	133.333	155.616	181.867	212.790	249.212	292.099	342.598	402.038	471.976
30	34.784	40.567	47.575	56.084	66.438	79.057	94.459	113.282	136.305	164.491	199.018	241.330	293.192	356.778	434.738	530.306	647.423	790.932	966.698	1181.865
35	41.659	49.994	60.461	73.651	90.318	111.432	138.234	172.314	215.705	271.018	341.583	431.658	546.663	693.552	881.152	1120.699	1426.448	1816.607	2314.173	2948.294
40	48.885	60.401	75.400	95.024	120.797	154.758	199.630	259.052	337.872	442.580	581.812	767.080	1013.667	1341.979	1779.048	2360.724	3134.412	4163.094	5529.711	7343.715
45	56.479	71.891	92.718	121.027	159.695	212.737	285.741	386.497	525.840	718.881	986.613	1358.208	1874.086	2590.464	3585.031	4965.191	6879.008	9531.258	13203.105	18280.914
50	64.461	84.577	112.794	152.664	209.341	290.325	406.516	573.756	815.051	1163.865	1668.723	2399.975	3459.344	4994.301	7217.488	10435.449	15088.805	21812.273	31514.492	45496.094

Using the Calculator to Compute the Future Value of an Ordinary Annuity

Before you begin, make sure to clear the memory, ensure that you are in the *end mode* and that your calculator is set for *one payment per year,* and set the number of decimal places that you want (usually two for dollar-related accuracy).

Sample Problem

You want to know what the future value will be at the end of 5 years if you place five end-of-year deposits of $1,000 in an account paying 7% annually. What is your account balance at the end of 5 years?

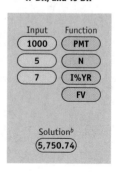

Hewlett-Packard HP 12C, 17 BII, and 19 BII[a]

Input	Function
1000	PMT
5	N
7	I%YR
	FV

Solution[b]
5,750.74

---

[a]For the 12C, you would use the **n** key instead of the **N** key and use the **i** key instead of the **I%YR** key.
[b]The minus sign that precedes the solution should be ignored.

TABLE A-3   (Continued)

Period	21%	22%	23%	24%	25%	26%	27%	28%	29%	30%	31%	32%	33%	34%	35%	40%	45%	50%
1	1.000	1.000	1.000	1.000	1.000	1.000	1.000	1.000	1.000	1.000	1.000	1.000	1.000	1.000	1.000	1.000	1.000	1.000
2	2.210	2.220	2.230	2.240	2.250	2.260	2.270	2.280	2.290	2.300	2.310	2.320	2.330	2.340	2.350	2.400	2.450	2.500
3	3.674	3.708	3.743	3.778	3.813	3.848	3.883	3.918	3.954	3.990	4.026	4.062	4.099	4.136	4.172	4.360	4.552	4.750
4	5.446	5.524	5.604	5.684	5.766	5.848	5.931	6.016	6.101	6.187	6.274	6.362	6.452	6.542	6.633	7.104	7.601	8.125
5	7.589	7.740	7.893	8.048	8.207	8.368	8.533	8.700	8.870	9.043	9.219	9.398	9.581	9.766	9.954	10.946	12.022	13.188
6	10.183	10.442	10.708	10.980	11.259	11.544	11.837	12.136	12.442	12.756	13.077	13.406	13.742	14.086	14.438	16.324	18.431	20.781
7	13.321	13.740	14.171	14.615	15.073	15.546	16.032	16.534	17.051	17.583	18.131	18.696	19.277	19.876	20.492	23.853	27.725	32.172
8	17.119	17.762	18.430	19.123	19.842	20.588	21.361	22.163	22.995	23.858	24.752	25.678	26.638	27.633	28.664	34.395	41.202	49.258
9	21.714	22.670	23.669	24.712	25.802	26.940	28.129	29.369	30.664	32.015	33.425	34.895	36.429	38.028	39.696	49.152	60.743	74.887
10	27.274	28.657	30.113	31.643	33.253	34.945	36.723	38.592	40.556	42.619	44.786	47.062	49.451	51.958	54.590	69.813	89.077	113.330
11	34.001	35.962	38.039	40.238	42.566	45.030	47.639	50.398	53.318	56.405	59.670	63.121	66.769	70.624	74.696	98.739	130.161	170.995
12	42.141	44.873	47.787	50.895	54.208	57.738	61.501	65.510	69.780	74.326	79.167	84.320	89.803	95.636	101.840	139.234	189.734	257.493
13	51.991	55.745	59.778	64.109	68.760	73.750	79.106	84.853	91.016	97.624	104.709	112.302	120.438	129.152	138.484	195.928	276.114	387.239
14	63.909	69.009	74.528	80.496	86.949	93.925	101.465	109.611	118.411	127.912	138.169	149.239	161.183	174.063	187.953	275.299	401.365	581.858
15	78.330	85.191	92.669	100.815	109.687	119.346	129.860	141.302	153.750	167.285	182.001	197.996	215.373	234.245	254.737	386.418	582.980	873.788
16	95.779	104.933	114.983	126.010	138.109	151.375	165.922	181.867	199.337	218.470	239.421	262.354	287.446	314.888	344.895	541.985	846.321	1311.681
17	116.892	129.019	142.428	157.252	173.636	191.733	211.721	233.790	258.145	285.011	314.642	347.307	383.303	422.949	466.608	759.778	1228.165	1968.522
18	142.439	158.403	176.187	195.993	218.045	242.583	269.885	300.250	334.006	371.514	413.180	459.445	510.792	567.751	630.920	1064.689	1781.838	2953.783
19	173.351	194.251	217.710	244.031	273.556	306.654	343.754	385.321	431.868	483.968	542.266	607.467	680.354	761.786	852.741	1491.563	2584.665	4431.672
20	210.755	237.986	268.783	303.598	342.945	387.384	437.568	494.210	558.110	630.157	711.368	802.856	905.870	1021.792	1152.200	2089.188	3748.763	6648.508
21	256.013	291.343	331.603	377.461	429.681	489.104	556.710	633.589	720.962	820.204	932.891	1060.769	1205.807	1370.201	1556.470	2925.862	5436.703	9973.762
22	310.775	356.438	408.871	469.052	538.101	617.270	708.022	811.993	931.040	1067.265	1223.087	1401.215	1604.724	1837.068	2102.234	4097.203	7884.215	14961.645
23	377.038	435.854	503.911	582.624	673.626	778.760	900.187	1040.351	1202.042	1388.443	1603.243	1850.603	2135.282	2462.669	2839.014	5737.078	11433.109	22443.469
24	457.215	532.741	620.810	723.453	843.032	982.237	1144.237	1332.649	1551.634	1805.975	2101.247	2443.795	2840.924	3300.974	3833.667	8032.906	16579.008	33666.207
25	554.230	650.944	764.596	898.082	1054.791	1238.617	1454.180	1706.790	2002.608	2348.765	2753.631	3226.808	3779.428	4424.301	5176.445	11247.062	24040.555	50500.316
30	1445.111	1767.044	2160.459	2640.881	3227.172	3941.953	4812.891	5873.172	7162.785	8729.805	10632.543	12940.672	15737.945	19124.434	23221.258	60500.207	154105.313	383500.000
35	3755.814	4783.520	6090.227	7750.094	9856.746	12527.160	15909.480	20188.742	25596.512	32422.090	41028.887	51868.563	65504.199	82634.625	104134.500	325394.688	*	*
40	9749.141	12936.141	17153.691	22728.367	30088.621	39791.957	52570.707	69376.562	91447.375	120389.375	*	*	*	*	*	*	*	*
45	25294.223	34970.230	48300.660	66638.937	91831.312	126378.937	173692.875	238384.312	326686.375	447005.062	*	*	*	*	*	*	*	*

*Not shown because of space limitations.

**Texas Instruments,
BA-35, BAII,
and BAII Plus[c]**

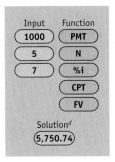

Input	Function
1000	PMT
5	N
7	%i
	CPT
	FV

Solution[d]
5,750.74

[c]For the Texas Instruments BAII, you would use the **2nd** key instead of the **CPT** key; for the Texas Instruments BAII Plus, you would use the **I/Y** key instead of the **%i** key.
[d]If a minus sign precedes the solution, it should be ignored.

TABLE A–4 — Present Value Interest Factors for a One-Dollar Annuity Discounted at *i* Percent for *n* Periods: $PVIFA_{i,n} = \sum_{t=1}^{n} \dfrac{1}{(1 + i)^t}$

Period	1%	2%	3%	4%	5%	6%	7%	8%	9%	10%	11%	12%	13%	14%	15%	16%	17%	18%	19%	20%
1	.990	.980	.971	.962	.952	.943	.935	.926	.917	.909	.901	.893	.885	.877	.870	.862	.855	.847	.840	.833
2	1.970	1.942	1.913	1.886	1.859	1.833	1.808	1.783	1.759	1.736	1.713	1.690	1.668	1.647	1.626	1.605	1.585	1.566	1.547	1.528
3	2.941	2.884	2.829	2.775	2.723	2.673	2.624	2.577	2.531	2.487	2.444	2.402	2.361	2.322	2.283	2.246	2.210	2.174	2.140	2.106
4	3.902	3.808	3.717	3.630	3.546	3.465	3.387	3.312	3.240	3.170	3.102	3.037	2.974	2.914	2.855	2.798	2.743	2.690	2.639	2.589
5	4.853	4.713	4.580	4.452	4.329	4.212	4.100	3.993	3.890	3.791	3.696	3.605	3.517	3.433	3.352	3.274	3.199	3.127	3.058	2.991
6	5.795	5.601	5.417	5.242	5.076	4.917	4.767	4.623	4.486	4.355	4.231	4.111	3.998	3.889	3.784	3.685	3.589	3.498	3.410	3.326
7	6.728	6.472	6.230	6.002	5.786	5.582	5.389	5.206	5.033	4.868	4.712	4.564	4.423	4.288	4.160	4.039	3.922	3.812	3.706	3.605
8	7.652	7.326	7.020	6.733	6.463	6.210	5.971	5.747	5.535	5.335	5.146	4.968	4.799	4.639	4.487	4.344	4.207	4.078	3.954	3.837
9	8.566	8.162	7.786	7.435	7.108	6.802	6.515	6.247	5.995	5.759	5.537	5.328	5.132	4.946	4.772	4.607	4.451	4.303	4.163	4.031
10	9.471	8.983	8.530	8.111	7.722	7.360	7.024	6.710	6.418	6.145	5.889	5.650	5.426	5.216	5.019	4.833	4.659	4.494	4.339	4.192
11	10.368	9.787	9.253	8.760	8.306	7.887	7.499	7.139	6.805	6.495	6.207	5.938	5.687	5.453	5.234	5.029	4.836	4.656	4.486	4.327
12	11.255	10.575	9.954	9.385	8.863	8.384	7.943	7.536	7.161	6.814	6.492	6.194	5.918	5.660	5.421	5.197	4.988	4.793	4.611	4.439
13	12.134	11.348	10.635	9.986	9.394	8.853	8.358	7.904	7.487	7.013	6.750	6.424	6.122	5.842	5.583	5.342	5.118	4.910	4.715	4.533
14	13.004	12.106	11.296	10.563	9.899	9.295	8.745	8.244	7.786	7.367	6.982	6.628	6.302	6.002	5.724	5.468	5.229	5.008	4.802	4.611
15	13.865	12.849	11.938	11.118	10.380	9.712	9.108	8.560	8.061	7.606	7.191	6.811	6.462	6.142	5.847	5.575	5.324	5.092	4.876	4.675
16	14.718	13.578	12.561	11.652	10.838	10.106	9.447	8.851	8.313	7.824	7.379	6.974	6.604	6.265	5.954	5.668	5.405	5.162	4.938	4.730
17	15.562	14.292	13.166	12.166	11.274	10.477	9.763	9.122	8.544	8.022	7.549	7.120	6.729	6.373	6.047	5.749	5.475	5.222	4.990	4.775
18	16.398	14.992	13.754	12.659	11.690	10.828	10.059	9.372	8.756	8.201	7.702	7.250	6.840	6.467	6.128	5.818	5.534	5.273	5.033	4.812
19	17.226	15.679	14.324	13.134	12.085	11.158	10.336	9.604	8.950	8.365	7.839	7.366	6.938	6.550	6.198	5.877	5.584	5.316	5.070	4.843
20	18.046	16.352	14.878	13.590	12.462	11.470	10.594	9.818	9.129	8.514	7.963	7.469	7.025	6.623	6.259	5.929	5.628	5.353	5.101	4.870
21	18.857	17.011	15.415	14.029	12.821	11.764	10.836	10.017	9.292	8.649	8.075	7.562	7.102	6.687	6.312	5.973	5.665	5.384	5.127	4.891
22	19.661	17.658	15.937	14.451	13.163	12.042	11.061	10.201	9.442	8.772	8.176	7.645	7.170	6.743	6.359	6.011	5.696	5.410	5.149	4.909
23	20.456	18.292	16.444	14.857	13.489	12.303	11.272	10.371	9.580	8.883	8.266	7.718	7.230	6.792	6.399	6.044	5.723	5.432	5.167	4.925
24	21.244	18.914	16.936	15.247	13.799	12.550	11.469	10.529	9.707	8.985	8.348	7.784	7.283	6.835	6.434	6.073	5.746	5.451	5.182	4.937
25	22.023	19.524	17.413	15.622	14.094	12.783	11.654	10.675	9.823	9.077	8.422	7.843	7.330	6.873	6.464	6.097	5.766	5.467	5.195	4.948
30	25.808	22.396	19.601	17.292	15.373	13.765	12.409	11.258	10.274	9.427	8.694	8.055	7.496	7.003	6.566	6.177	5.829	5.517	5.235	4.979
35	29.409	24.999	21.487	18.665	16.374	14.498	12.948	11.655	10.567	9.644	8.855	8.176	7.586	7.070	6.617	6.215	5.858	5.539	5.251	4.992
40	32.835	27.356	23.115	19.793	17.159	15.046	13.332	11.925	10.757	9.779	8.951	8.244	7.634	7.105	6.642	6.233	5.871	5.548	5.258	4.997
45	36.095	29.490	24.519	20.720	17.774	15.456	13.606	12.108	10.881	9.863	9.008	8.283	7.661	7.123	6.654	6.242	5.877	5.552	5.261	4.999
50	39.196	31.424	25.730	21.482	18.256	15.762	13.801	12.233	10.962	9.915	9.042	8.304	7.675	7.133	6.661	6.246	5.880	5.554	5.262	4.999

Using the Calculator to Compute the Present Value of an Annuity

Before you begin, make sure to clear the memory, ensure that you are in the *end mode* and that your calculator is set for *one payment per year,* and set the number of decimal places that you want (usually two for dollar-related accuracy).

Sample Problem

You want to know what the present value of an annuity of $700 received at the end of each year for 5 years, given a discount rate of 8%.

Hewlett-Packard HP 12C, 17 BII, and 19 BII[a]

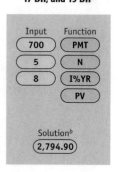

Input	Function
700	PMT
5	N
8	I%YR
	PV

Solution[b]
2,794.90

---

[a]For the 12C, you would use the ⟨ n ⟩ key instead of the ⟨ N ⟩ key and use the ⟨ i ⟩ key instead of the ⟨ I%YR ⟩ key.
[b]The minus sign that precedes the solution should be ignored.

TABLE A–4   (Continued)

Period	21%	22%	23%	24%	25%	26%	27%	28%	29%	30%	31%	32%	33%	34%	35%	40%	45%	50%
1	.826	.820	.813	.806	.800	.794	.787	.781	.775	.769	.763	.758	.752	.746	.741	.714	.690	.667
2	1.509	1.492	1.474	1.457	1.440	1.424	1.407	1.392	1.376	1.361	1.346	1.331	1.317	1.303	1.289	1.224	1.165	1.111
3	2.074	2.042	2.011	1.981	1.952	1.923	1.896	1.868	1.842	1.816	1.791	1.766	1.742	1.719	1.696	1.589	1.493	1.407
4	2.540	2.494	2.448	2.404	2.362	2.320	2.280	2.241	2.203	2.166	2.130	2.096	2.062	2.029	1.997	1.849	1.720	1.605
5	2.926	2.864	2.803	2.745	2.689	2.635	2.583	2.532	2.483	2.436	2.390	2.345	2.302	2.260	2.220	2.035	1.876	1.737
6	3.245	3.167	3.092	3.020	2.951	2.885	2.821	2.759	2.700	2.643	2.588	2.534	2.483	2.433	2.385	2.168	1.983	1.824
7	3.508	3.416	3.327	3.242	3.161	3.083	3.009	2.937	2.868	2.802	2.739	2.677	2.619	2.562	2.508	2.263	2.057	1.883
8	3.726	3.619	3.518	3.421	3.329	3.241	3.156	3.076	2.999	2.925	2.854	2.786	2.721	2.658	2.598	2.331	2.109	1.922
9	3.905	3.786	3.673	3.566	3.463	3.366	3.273	3.184	3.100	3.019	2.942	2.868	2.798	2.730	2.665	2.379	2.144	1.948
10	4.054	3.923	3.799	3.682	3.570	3.465	3.364	3.269	3.178	3.092	3.009	2.930	2.855	2.784	2.715	2.414	2.168	1.965
11	4.177	4.035	3.902	3.776	3.656	3.544	3.437	3.335	3.239	3.147	3.060	2.978	2.899	2.824	2.752	2.438	2.185	1.977
12	4.278	4.127	3.985	3.851	3.725	3.606	3.493	3.387	3.286	3.190	3.100	3.013	2.931	2.853	2.779	2.456	2.196	1.985
13	4.362	4.203	4.053	3.912	3.780	3.656	3.538	3.427	3.322	3.223	3.129	3.040	2.956	2.876	2.799	2.469	2.204	1.990
14	4.432	4.265	4.108	3.962	3.824	3.695	3.573	3.459	3.351	3.249	3.152	3.061	2.974	2.892	2.814	2.478	2.210	1.993
15	4.489	4.315	4.153	4.001	3.859	3.726	3.601	3.483	3.373	3.268	3.170	3.076	2.988	2.905	2.825	2.484	2.214	1.995
16	4.536	4.357	4.189	4.033	3.887	3.751	3.623	3.503	3.390	3.283	3.183	3.088	2.999	2.914	2.834	2.489	2.216	1.997
17	4.576	4.391	4.219	4.059	3.910	3.771	3.640	3.518	3.403	3.295	3.193	3.097	3.007	2.921	2.840	2.492	2.218	1.998
18	4.608	4.419	4.243	4.080	3.928	3.786	3.654	3.529	3.413	3.304	3.201	3.104	3.012	2.926	2.844	2.494	2.219	1.999
19	4.635	4.442	4.263	4.097	3.942	3.799	3.664	3.539	3.421	3.311	3.207	3.109	3.017	2.930	2.848	2.496	2.220	1.999
20	4.657	4.460	4.279	4.110	3.954	3.808	3.673	3.546	3.427	3.316	3.211	3.113	3.020	2.933	2.850	2.497	2.221	1.999
21	4.675	4.476	4.292	4.121	3.963	3.816	3.679	3.551	3.432	3.320	3.215	3.116	3.023	2.935	2.852	2.498	2.221	2.000
22	4.690	4.488	4.302	4.130	3.970	3.822	3.684	3.556	3.436	3.323	3.217	3.118	3.025	2.936	2.853	2.498	2.222	2.000
23	4.703	4.499	4.311	4.137	3.976	3.827	3.689	3.559	3.438	3.325	3.219	3.120	3.026	2.938	2.854	2.499	2.222	2.000
24	4.713	4.507	4.318	4.143	3.981	3.831	3.692	3.562	3.441	3.327	3.221	3.121	3.027	2.939	2.855	2.499	2.222	2.000
25	4.721	4.514	4.323	4.147	3.985	3.834	3.694	3.564	3.442	3.329	3.222	3.122	3.028	2.939	2.856	2.499	2.222	2.000
30	4.746	4.534	4.339	4.160	3.995	3.842	3.701	3.569	3.447	3.332	3.225	3.124	3.030	2.941	2.857	2.500	2.222	2.000
35	4.756	4.541	4.345	4.164	3.998	3.845	3.703	3.571	3.448	3.333	3.226	3.125	3.030	2.941	2.857	2.500	2.222	2.000
40	4.760	4.544	4.347	4.166	3.999	3.846	3.703	3.571	3.448	3.333	3.226	3.125	3.030	2.941	2.857	2.500	2.222	2.000
45	4.761	4.545	4.347	4.166	4.000	3.846	3.704	3.571	3.448	3.333	3.226	3.125	3.030	2.941	2.857	2.500	2.222	2.000
50	4.762	4.545	4.348	4.167	4.000	3.846	3.704	3.571	3.448	3.333	3.226	3.125	3.030	2.941	2.857	2.500	2.222	2.000

Texas Instruments, BA-35, BAII, and BAII Plus[c]

Input	Function
700	PMT
5	N
8	%i
	CPT
	FV

Solution[d]
2,794.90

[c]For the Texas Instruments BAII, you would use the [2nd] key instead of the [CPT] key; for the Texas Instruments BAII Plus, you would use the [I/Y] key instead of the [%i] key.

[d]If a minus sign precedes the solution, it should be ignored.

Appendix B

Solutions to Self-Test Problems

Chapter 1

ST1–1 **a.** Capital gains = $180,000 sale price − $150,000 original purchase price = $30,000

b. Total taxable income = $280,000 operating earnings + $30,000 capital gain = $310,000

c. Firm's tax liability:

Using Table 1.5:

$$\text{Total taxes due} = \$22{,}250 + [0.39 \times (\$310{,}000 - \$100{,}000)]$$
$$= \$22{,}250 + (0.39 \times \$210{,}000) = \$22{,}250 + \$81{,}900$$
$$= \underline{\underline{\$104{,}150}}$$

d. Average tax rate $= \dfrac{\$104{,}150}{\$310{,}000} = \underline{\underline{33.6\%}}$

Marginal tax rate = $\underline{\underline{39\%}}$

Chapter 2

ST2–1

Ratio	Too high	Too low
Current ratio = current assets/ current liabilities	May indicate that the firm is holding excessive cash, accounts receivable, or inventory.	May indicate poor ability to satisfy short-term obligations.
Inventory turnover = CGS/inventory	May indicate lower level of inventory, which may cause stockouts and lost sales.	May indicate poor inventory management, excessive inventory, or obsolete inventory.
Times interest earned = earnings before interest and taxes/interest	✕	May indicate poor ability to pay contractual interest payments.
Gross profit margin = gross profits/sales	Indicates the low cost of merchandise sold relative to the sales price; may indicate noncompetitive pricing and potential lost sales.	Indicates the high cost of the merchandise sold relative to the sales price; may indicate either a low sales price or a high cost of goods sold.
Return on total assets = net profits after taxes/total assets	✕	Indicates ineffective management in generating profits with the available assets.
Price/earnings (P/E) ratio = market price per share of common stock/earnings per share	Investors may have an excessive degree of confidence in the firm's future and underestimate its risk.	Investors lack confidence in the firm's future outcomes and feel that the firm has an excessive level of risk.

ST2–2

O'Keefe Industries
Balance Sheet
December 31, 2009

Assets		Liabilities and Stockholders' Equity	
Cash	$ 32,720	Accounts payable	$ 120,000
Marketable securities	25,000	Notes payable	160,000^e
Accounts receivable	197,280^a	Accruals	20,000
Inventories	225,000^b	Total current liabilities	$ 300,000^d
Total current assets	$ 480,000	Long-term debt	$ 600,000^f
Net fixed assets	$1,020,000^c	Stockholders' equity	$ 600,000
Total assets	$1,500,000	Total liabilities and stockholders' equity	$1,500,000

^{a}Average collection period (ACP) = 40 days
ACP = Accounts receivable/Average sales per day
40 = Accounts receivable/($1,800,000/365)
40 = Accounts receivable/$4,932
$197,280 = Accounts receivable

^{b}Inventory turnover = 6.0
Inventory turnover = Cost of goods sold/Inventory
6.0 = [Sales × (1 = Gross profit margin)]/Inventory
6.0 = [$1,800,000 × (1 = 0.25)]/Inventory
$225,000 = Inventory

^{c}Total asset turnover = 1.20
Total asset turnover = Sales/Total assets
1.20 = $1,800,000/Total assets
$1,500,000 = Total assets
Total assets = Current assets + Net fixed assets
$1,500,000 = $480,000 + Net fixed assets
$1,020,000 = Net fixed assets

^{d}Current ratio = 1.60
Current ratio = Current assets/Current liabilities
1.60 = $480,000/Current liabilities
$300,000 = Current liabilities

^{e}Notes payable = Total current liabilities − Accounts payable − Accruals
= $300,000 − $120,000 − $20,000
= $160,000

^{f}Debt ratio = 0.60
Debt ratio = Total liabilities/Total assets
0.60 = Total liabilities/$1,500,000
$900,000 = Total liabilities

Total liabilities = Current liabilities + Long-term debt
$900,000 = $300,000 + Long-term debt
$600,000 = Long-term debt

Chapter 3

ST3–1 **a.** Depreciation Schedule

Year	Cost[a] (1)	Percentages (from Table 3.2) (2)	Depreciation [(1) × (2)] (3)
1	$150,000	20%	$ 30,000
2	150,000	32	48,000
3	150,000	19	28,500
4	150,000	12	18,000
5	150,000	12	18,000
6	150,000	5	7,500
	Totals	100%	$150,000

[a]$140,000 asset cost + $10,000 installation cost.

b. Accounting definition:

Year	EBIT (1)	Interest (2)	Net profits before taxes [(1) − (2)] (3)	Taxes [0.40 × (3)] (4)	Net profits after taxes [(3) − (4)] (5)	Depreciation (from part a, col. 3) (6)	Cash flows from operations [(5) + (6)] (7)
1	$160,000	$15,000	$145,000	$58,000	$87,000	$30,000	$117,000
2	160,000	15,000	145,000	58,000	87,000	48,000	135,000
3	160,000	15,000	145,500	58,000	87,000	28,500	115,500
4	160,000	15,000	145,000	58,000	87,000	18,000	105,000
5	160,000	15,000	145,000	58,000	87,000	18,000	105,000
6	160,000	15,000	145,500	58,000	87,000	7,500	94,500

Financial definition:

Year	EBIT (1)	NOPAT [(1) × (1 − 0.40)] (2)	Depreciation (3)	Operating cash flows [(2) + (3)] (4)
1	$160,000	$96,000	$30,000	$126,000
2	160,000	96,000	48,000	144,000
3	160,000	96,000	28,500	124,500
4	160,000	96,000	18,000	114,000
5	160,000	96,000	18,000	114,000
6	160,000	96,000	7,500	103,500

c. Change in net fixed assets in year 6 = $0 − $7,500 = −$7,500

NFAI in year 6 = −$7,500 + $7,500 = $0

Change in current assets in year 6 = $110,000 − $90,000 = $20,000

Change in (Accounts payable + Accruals) in year 6 = ($45,000 + $7,000) − ($40,000 + $8,000) = $52,000 − $48,000 = $4,000

NCAI in year 6 = $20,000 − $4,000 = $16,000

For year 6

FCF = OCF − NFAI − NCAI

$\quad$ = $103,500* − $0 − $16,000 = $87,500

*From part **b** financial definition, column 4 value for year 6.

d. In part **b** we can see that in each of the six years, the operating cash flow is greater when viewed from a financial perspective than when viewed from a strict accounting point of view. This difference results from the fact that the accounting definition includes interest as an operating flow, whereas the financial definition excludes it. This causes (in this case) each year's accounting flow to be $9,000 below the financial flow; $9,000 is equal to the after-tax cost of the $15,000 annual interest, $15,000 × (1 − 0.40). The free cash flow (FCF) calculated in part **c** for year 6 represents the cash flow available to investors—providers of debt and equity—after covering all operating needs and paying for net fixed asset investment (NFAI) and net current asset investment (NCAI) that occurred during the year.

ST3–2 a.

	Caroll Company Cash Budget April–June					Accounts receivable at end of June	
	February	March	April	May	June	July	August
Forecast sales	$500	$600	$400	$200	$200		
Cash sales (0.30)	$150	$180	$120	$ 60	$ 60		
Collections of A/R							
$\quad$ Lagged 1 month [(0.7 × 0.7) = 0.49]		245	294	196	98	$ 98	
$\quad$ Lagged 2 months [(0.3 × 0.7) = 0.21]			105	126	84	42	$42
						$140 + $42 = $182	
Total cash receipts			$519	$382	$242		
Less: Total cash disbursements			600	500	200		
Net cash flow			($ 81)	($118)	$ 42		
Add: Beginning cash			115	34	(84)		
Ending cash			$ 34	($ 84)	($ 42)		
Less: Minimum cash balance			25	25	25		
Required total financing (notes payable)			—	$109	$ 67		
Excess cash balance (marketable securities)			$ 9	—	—		

b. Caroll Company would need a maximum of $109 in financing over the 3-month period.

c.

Account	Amount	Source of amount
Cash	$ 25	Minimum cash balance—June
Notes payable	67	Required total financing—June
Marketable securities	0	Excess cash balance—June
Accounts receivable	182	Calculation at right of cash budget statement

ST3–3 a.

Euro Designs, Inc., Pro Forma Income Statement for the Year Ended December 31, 2010	
Sales revenue (given)	$3,900,000
Less: Cost of goods sold (0.55)[a]	2,145,000
Gross profits	$1,755,000
Less: Operating expenses (0.12)[b]	468,000
Operating profits	$1,287,000
Less: Interest expense (given)	325,000
Net profits before taxes	$ 962,000
Less: Taxes (0.40 × $962,000)	384,800
Net profits after taxes	$ 577,200
Less: Cash dividends (given)	320,000
To retained earnings	$ 257,200

[a]From 2009: CGS/Sales = $1,925,000/$3,500,000 = 0.55.
[b]From 2009: Oper. Exp./Sales = $420,000/$3,500,000 = 0.12.

b. The percent-of-sales method may underestimate actual 2010 pro forma income by assuming that all costs are variable. If the firm has fixed costs, which by definition would not increase with increasing sales, the 2010 pro forma income would probably be underestimated.

Chapter 4

ST4–1 a. *Bank A:*

$FV_3 = \$10,000 \times FVIF_{4\%/3yrs} = \$10,000 \times 1.125 = \underline{\$11,250}$

(Calculator solution = $11,248.64)

Bank B:

$FV_3 = \$10,000 \times FVIF_{4\%/2, 2 \times 3yrs} = \$10,000 \times FVIF_{2\%,6yrs}$
$= \$10,000 \times 1.126 = \underline{\$11,260}$

(Calculator solution = $11,261.62)

Bank C:

$FV_3 = \$10,000 \times FVIF_{4\%/4, 4 \times 3yrs} = \$10,000 \times FVIF_{1\%,12yrs}$
$= \$10,000 \times 1.127 = \underline{\$11,270}$

(Calculator solution = $11,268.25)

b. *Bank A:*

$EAR = (1 + 4\%/1)^1 - 1 = (1 + 0.04)^1 - 1 = 1.04 - 1 = 0.04 = \underline{4\%}$

Bank B:

$EAR = (1 + 4\%/2)^2 - 1 = (1 + 0.02)^2 - 1 = 1.0404 - 1 = 0.0404 = \underline{4.04\%}$

Bank C:

$EAR = (1 + 4\%/4)^4 - 1 = (1 + 0.01)^4 - 1 = 1.0406 - 1 = 0.0406 = \underline{4.06\%}$

c. Ms. Martin should deal with Bank C: The quarterly compounding of interest at the given 4% rate results in the highest future value as a result of the corresponding highest effective annual rate.

d. *Bank D:*

$FV_3 = \$10,000 \times FVIF_{4\%,3yrs}$ (continuous compounding)

$\qquad = \$10,000 \times e^{0.04 \times 3} = \$10,000 \times e^{0.12}$

$\qquad = \$10,000 \times 1.127497$

$\qquad = \underline{\underline{\$11,274.97}}$

This alternative is better than Bank C; it results in a higher future value because of the use of continuous compounding, which with otherwise identical cash flows always results in the highest future value of any compounding period.

ST4–2 a. On a purely subjective basis, annuity Y looks more attractive than annuity X because it provides $1,000 more each year than does annuity X. Of course, the fact that X is an annuity due means that the $9,000 would be received at the beginning of the first year, unlike the $10,000 at the end of the year, and this makes annuity X awfully tempting.

b. *Annuity X:*

$FVA_6 = \$9,000 \times FVIFA_{15\%,6yrs} \times (1 + 0.15)$

$\qquad = \$9,000 \times 8.754 \times 1.15 = \underline{\underline{\$90,603.90}}$

(Calculator solution = $90,601.19)

Annuity Y:

$FVA_6 = \$10,000 \times FVIFA_{15\%,6yrs}$

$\qquad = \$10,000 \times 8.754 = \underline{\underline{\$87,540.00}}$

(Calculator solution = $87,537.38)

c. Annuity X is more attractive, because its future value at the end of year 6, FVA_6, of $90,603.90 is greater than annuity Y's end-of-year-6 future value, FVA_6, of $87,540.00. The subjective assessment in part **a** was incorrect. The benefit of receiving annuity X's cash inflows at the beginning of each year appears to have outweighed the fact that annuity Y's annual cash inflow, which occurs at the end of each year, is $1,000 larger ($10,000 vs. $9,000) than annuity X's.

ST4–3 *Alternative A:*

Cash flow stream:

$PVA_5 = \$700 \times PVIFA_{9\%,5yrs}$

$\qquad = \$700 \times 3.890 = \underline{\underline{\$2,723}}$

(Calculator solution = $2,722.76)

Single amount: $\underline{\$2,825}$

Alternative B:

Cash flow stream:

Year (n)	Cash flow (1)	$PVIF_{9\%,n}$ (2)	Present value [(1) × (2)] (3)
1	$1,100	0.917	$1,008.70
2	900	0.842	757.80
3	700	0.772	540.40
4	500	0.708	354.00
5	300	0.650	195.00
		Present value	$2,855.90

(Calculator solution = $2,856.41)

Single amount: $2,800

Conclusion: Alternative B in the form of a cash flow stream is preferred because its present value of $2,855.90 is greater than the other three values.

ST4–4 $FVA_5 = \$8,000$; $FVIFA_{7\%,5yrs} = 5.751$; $PMT = ?$

$FVA_n = PMT \times (FVIFA_{i,n})$ [Equation 4.14 or 4.24]

$\$8,000 = PMT \times 5.751$

$PMT = \$8,000/5.751 = \$1,391.06$

(Calculator solution = $1,391.13)

Judi should deposit $1,391.06 at the end of each of the 5 years to meet her goal of accumulating $8,000 at the end of the fifth year.

Chapter 5

ST5–1 **a.** Expected return, $\bar{r} = \dfrac{\Sigma\text{Returns}}{3}$ (*Equation 5.2a in footnote 9*)

$$\bar{r}_A = \frac{12\% + 14\% + 16\%}{3} = \frac{42\%}{3} = 14\%$$

$$\bar{r}_B = \frac{16\% + 14\% + 12\%}{3} = \frac{42\%}{3} = 14\%$$

$$\bar{r}_C = \frac{12\% + 14\% + 16\%}{3} = \frac{42\%}{3} = 14\%$$

b. Standard deviation, $\sigma_r = \sqrt{\dfrac{\sum\limits_{j=1}^{n}(r_i - \bar{r})^2}{n - 1}}$ (*Equation 5.3a in footnote 10*)

$$\sigma_{r_A} = \sqrt{\frac{(12\% - 14\%)^2 + (14\% - 14\%)^2 + (16\% - 14\%)^2}{3 - 1}}$$

$$= \sqrt{\frac{4\% + 0\% + 4\%}{2}} = \sqrt{\frac{8\%}{2}} = 2\%$$

$$\sigma_{r_B} = \sqrt{\frac{(16\% - 14\%)^2 + (14\% - 14\%)^2 + (12\% - 14\%)^2}{3 - 1}}$$

$$= \sqrt{\frac{4\% + 0\% + 4\%}{2}} = \sqrt{\frac{8\%}{2}} = \underline{2\%}$$

$$\sigma_{r_C} = \sqrt{\frac{(12\% - 14\%)^2 + (14\% - 14\%)^2 + (16\% - 14\%)^2}{3 - 1}}$$

$$= \sqrt{\frac{4\% + 0\% + 4\%}{2}} = \sqrt{\frac{8\%}{2}} = \underline{\underline{2\%}}$$

c.

		Annual expected returns	
Year	Portfolio AB		Portfolio AC
2010	$(0.50 \times 12\%) + (0.50 \times 16\%) = 14\%$		$(0.50 \times 12\%) + (0.50 \times 12\%) = 12\%$
2011	$(0.50 \times 14\%) + (0.50 \times 14\%) = 14\%$		$(0.50 \times 14\%) + (0.50 \times 14\%) = 14\%$
2012	$(0.50 \times 16\%) + (0.50 \times 12\%) = 14\%$		$(0.50 \times 16\%) + (0.50 \times 16\%) = 16\%$

Over the 3-year period:

$$\bar{r}_{AB} = \frac{14\% + 14\% + 14\%}{3} = \frac{42\%}{3} = \underline{\underline{14\%}}$$

$$\bar{r}_{AC} = \frac{12\% + 14\% + 16\%}{3} = \frac{42\%}{3} = \underline{\underline{14\%}}$$

d. AB is perfectly negatively correlated.

AC is perfectly positively correlated.

e. Standard deviation of the portfolios

$$\sigma_{r_{AB}} = \sqrt{\frac{(14\% - 14\%)^2 + (14\% - 14\%)^2 + (14\% - 14\%)^2}{3 - 1}}$$

$$= \sqrt{\frac{(0\% + 0\% + 0\%)}{2}} = \sqrt{\frac{0\%}{2}} = \underline{\underline{0\%}}$$

$$\sigma_{r_{AC}} = \sqrt{\frac{(12\% - 14\%)^2 + (14\% - 14\%)^2 + (16\% - 14\%)^2}{3 - 1}}$$

$$= \sqrt{\frac{4\% + 0\% + 4\%}{2}} = \sqrt{\frac{8\%}{2}} = \underline{\underline{2\%}}$$

f. Portfolio AB is preferred, because it provides the same return (14%) as AC but with less risk $[(\sigma_{r_{AB}} = 0\%) < (\sigma_{r_{AC}} = 2\%)]$.

ST5–2 a. When the market return increases by 10%, the project's required return would be expected to increase by 15% $(1.50 \times 10\%)$. When the market return decreases by 10%, the project's required return would be expected to decrease by 15% $[1.50 \times (-10\%)]$.

b. $r_j = R_F + [b_j \times (r_m - R_F)]$

$= 7\% + [1.50 \times (10\% - 7\%)]$

$= 7\% + 4.5\% = \underline{\underline{11.5\%}}$

c. No, the project should be rejected, because its *expected* return of 11% is less than the 11.5% return *required* from the project.

d. $r_j = 7\% + [1.50 \times (9\% - 7\%)]$
   $= 7\% + 3\% = \underline{\underline{10\%}}$

The project would now be acceptable, because its *expected* return of 11% is now in excess of the *required* return, which has declined to 10% as a result of investors in the marketplace becoming less risk-averse.

Chapter 6

ST6–1   a. $B_0 = I \times (PVIFA_{r_d,n}) + M \times (PVIF_{r_d,n})$

$I = 0.08 \times \$1,000 = \$80$

$M = \$1,000$

$n = 12$ yrs

(1) $r_d = 7\%$

$B_0 = \$80 \times (PVIFA_{7\%,12yrs}) + \$1,000 \times (PVIF_{7\%,12yrs})$
$= (\$80 \times 7.943) + (\$1,000 \times 0.444)$
$= \$635.44 + \$444.00 = \underline{\$1,079.44}$

(Calculator solution = \$1,079.43)

(2) $r_d = 8\%$

$B_0 = \$80 \times (PVIFA_{8\%,12yrs}) + \$1,000 \times (PVIF_{8\%,12yrs})$
$= (\$80 \times 7.536) + (\$1,000 \times 0.397)$
$= \$602.88 + \$397.00 = \underline{\$999.88}$

(Calculator solution = \$1,000)

(3) $r_d = 10\%$

$B_0 = \$80 \times (PVIFA_{10\%,12yrs}) + \$1,000 \times (PVIF_{10\%,12yrs})$
$= (\$80 \times 6.814) + (\$1,000 \times 0.319)$
$= \$545.12 + \$319.00 = \underline{\$864.12}$

(Calculator solution = \$863.73)

b. (1) $r_d = 7\%$, $B_0 = \$1,079.44$; sells at a *premium*
   (2) $r_d = 8\%$, $B_0 = \$999.88 \approx \$1,000.00$; sells at its *par value*
   (3) $r_d = 10\%$, $B_0 = \$864.12$; sells at a *discount*

c. $B_0 = \dfrac{I}{2} \times (PVIFA_{r_d/2,2n}) + M \times (PVIF_{r_d/2,2n})$

$= \dfrac{\$80}{2} \times (PVIFA_{10\%/2,2\times12periods}) + \$1,000 \times (PVIF_{10\%/2,2\times12periods})$

$= \$40 \times (PVIFA_{5\%,24periods}) + \$1,000 \times (PVIF_{5\%,24periods})$
$= (\$40 \times 13.799) + (\$1,000 \times 0.310)$
$= \$551.96 + \$310.00 = \underline{\$861.96}$

(Calculator solution = \$862.01)

ST6–2 **a.** $B_0 = \$1,150$

$I = 0.11 \times \$1,000 = \$110$

$M = \$1,000$

$n = 18$ yrs

$$\text{Current yield} = \frac{\text{annual interest}}{\text{current price}}$$

$$= \frac{\$110}{\$1,150} = 9.57\%$$

b. $\$1,150 = \$110 \times (PVIFA_{r_d, 18\text{yrs}}) + \$1,000 \times (PVIF_{r_d, 18\text{yrs}})$

Because if $r_d = 11\%$, $B_0 = \$1,000 = M$, try $r_d = 10\%$.

$B_0 = \$110 \times (PVIFA_{10\%, 18\text{yrs}}) + \$1,000 \times (PVIF_{10\%, 18\text{yrs}})$

    $= (\$110 \times 8.201) + (\$1,000 \times 0.180)$

    $= \$902.11 + \$180.00 = \$1,082.11$

Because $\$1,082.11 < \$1,150$, try $r_d = 9\%$.

$B_0 = \$110 \times (PVIFA_{9\%, 18\text{yrs}}) + \$1,000 \times (PVIF_{9\%, 18\text{yrs}})$

    $= (\$110 \times 8.756) + (\$1,000 \times 0.212)$

    $= \$963.16 + \$212.00 = \$1,175.16$

Because the $1,175.16 value at 9% is higher than $1,150, and the $1,082.11 value at 10% rate is lower than $1,150, the bond's yield to maturity must be between 9% and 10%. Because the $1,175.16 value is closer to $1,150, rounding to the nearest whole percent, the YTM is 9%. (By using interpolation, the more precise YTM value is 9.27%.)

(Calculator solution = 9.26%)

c. The calculated YTM of 9.26% is below both the bond's 11% coupon interest rate and its current yield of 9.57% calculated in part **a**, because the bond's market value of $1,150 is above its $1,000 par value. Whenever a bond's market value is above its par value (it sells at a *premium*), its YTM and current yield will be below its coupon interest rate; when a bond sells at *par*, the YTM and current yield will equal its coupon interest rate; and when the bond sells for less than par (at a *discount*), its YTM and current yield will be greater than its coupon interest rate.

Chapter 7

ST7–1 $D_0 = \$1.80$/share

$r_s = 12\%$

a. *Zero growth:*

$$P_0 = \frac{D_1}{r_s} = \frac{D_1 = D_0 = \$1.80}{0.12} = \underline{\underline{\$15\text{/share}}}$$

b. *Constant growth, $g = 5\%$:*

$D_1 = D_0 \times (1 + g) = \$1.80 = (1 + 0.05) = \$1.89$/share

$$P_0 = \frac{D_1}{r_s - g} = \frac{\$1.89}{0.12 - 0.05} = \frac{\$1.89}{0.07} = \underline{\underline{\$27\text{/share}}}$$

c. *Variable growth, $N = 3$, $g_1 = 5\%$ for years 1 to 3 and $g_2 = 4\%$ for years 4 to ∞:*

$D_1 = D_0 \times (1 + g_1)^1 = \$1.80 \times (1 + 0.05)^1 = \$1.89$/share

$D_2 = D_0 \times (1 + g_1)^2 = \$1.80 \times (1 + 0.05)^2 = \$1.98$/share

$D_3 = D_0 \times (1 + g_1)^3 = \$1.80 \times (1 + 0.05)^3 = \$2.08$/share

$D_4 = D_3 \times (1 + g_2) = \$2.08 \times (1 + 0.04) = \$2.16$/share

$$P_0 = \sum_{t=1}^{N} \frac{D_0 \times (1 + g_1)^t}{(1 + r_s)^t} + \left(\frac{1}{(1 + r_s)^N} \times \frac{D_{N+1}}{r_s - g_2} \right)$$

$$\sum_{t=1}^{N} \frac{D_0 \times (1 + g_1)^t}{(1 + r_s)^t} = \frac{1.89}{(1 + 0.12)^1} + \frac{1.98}{(1 + 0.12)^2} + \frac{2.08}{(1 + 0.12)^3}$$

$$= [\$1.89 \times (PVIF_{12\%,1yr})] + [\$1.98 \times (PVIF_{12\%,2yrs})]$$
$$+ [\$2.08 \times (PVIF_{12\%,3yrs})]$$

$$= (\$1.89 \times 0.893) + (\$1.98 \times 0.797) + (\$2.08 \times 0.712)$$

$$= \$1.69 + \$1.58 + \$1.48 = \$4.75$$

$$\left[\frac{1}{(1 + r_s)^N} \times \frac{D_{N+1}}{r_s - g_2} \right] = \frac{1}{(1 + 0.12)^3} \times \frac{D_4 = \$2.16}{0.12 - 0.04}$$

$$= (PVIF_{12\%,3yrs}) \times \frac{\$2.16}{0.08}$$

$$= 0.712 \times \$27.00 = \$19.22$$

$$P_0 = \sum_{t=1}^{N} \frac{D_0 \times (1 + g_1)^t}{(1 + r_s)^t} + \left[\frac{1}{(1 + r_s)^N} \times \frac{D_{N+1}}{r_s - g_2} \right] = \$4.75 + \$19.22$$

$$= \$23.97/\text{share}$$

ST7–2 **a.** **Step 1:** Present value of free cash flow from end of 2011 to infinity measured at the end of 2010.

$$FCF_{2014} = \$1,500,000 \times (1 + 0.04) = \$1,560,000$$

$$\text{Value of } FCF_{2014 \to \infty} = \frac{\$1,560,000}{0.10 - 0.04} = \frac{\$1,560,000}{0.06} = \$26,000,000$$

Step 2: Add the value found in Step 1 to the 2013 FCF.

Total $FCF_{2013} = \$1,500,000 + \$26,000,000 = \$27,500,000$

Step 3: Find the sum of the present values of the FCFs for 2010 through 2013 to determine company value, V_C.

Year (t)	FCF_t (1)	$PVIF_{10\%,t}$ (2)	Present value of FCF_t [(1) × (2)] (3)
2010	$ 800,000	0.909	$ 727,200
2011	1,200,000	0.826	991,200
2012	1,400,000	0.751	1,051,400
2013	27,500,000	0.683	18,782,500
		Value of entire company, V_C =	$21,552,300

(Calculator solution = $21,553,719)

b. Common Stock value, $V_S = V_C - V_D - V_P$

$V_C = \$21,552,300$ (calculated in part **a**)

$V_D = \$12,500,000$ (given)

$V_P = \$0$ (given)

$V_S = \$21,552,300 - \$12,500,000 - \$0 = \$9,052,300$

(Calculator solution = $9,053,719)

c. Price per share $= \dfrac{\$9,052,300}{500,000} = \underline{\$18.10/\text{share}}$

(Calculator solution = $18.11/share)

Chapter 8

ST8–1 a. Book value = Installed cost − Accumulated depreciation
Installed cost = $50,000
Accumulated depreciation $= \$50,000 \times (0.20 + 0.32 + 0.19 + 0.12)$
$$= \$50,000 \times 0.83 = \$41,500$$
Book value $= \$50,000 - \$41,500 = \underline{\$8,500}$

b. Taxes on sale of old equipment:
Gain on sale = Sale price − Book value
$$= \$55,000 - \$8,500 = \$46,500$$
Taxes $= 0.40 \times \$46,500 = \underline{\$18,600}$

c. Initial investment:

Installed cost of new equipment		
Cost of new equipment	$75,000	
+ Installation costs	5,000	
Total installed cost—new		$80,000
− After-tax proceeds from sale of old equipment		
Proceeds from sale of old equipment	$55,000	
− Taxes on sale of old equipment	18,600	
Total after-tax proceeds—old		36,400
+ Change in net working capital		15,000
Initial investment		$58,600

ST8–2 a. Initial investment:

Installed cost of new machine		
Cost of new machine	$140,000	
+ Installation costs	10,000	
Total installed cost—new (depreciable value)		$150,000
− After-tax proceeds from sale of old machine		
Proceeds from sale of old machine	$ 42,000	
− Taxes on sale of old machine[1]	9,120	
Total after-tax proceeds—old		32,880
+ Change in net working capital[2]		20,000
Initial investment		$137,120

[1]Book value of old machine $= \$40,000 - [(0.20 + 0.32) \times \$40,000]$
$$= \$40,000 - (0.52 \times \$40,000)$$
$$= \$40,000 - \$20,800 = \$19,200$$
Gain on sale $= \$42,000 - \$19,200 = \$22,800$
Taxes $= .40 \times \$22,800 = \underline{\$9,120}$

[2]Change in net working capital $= +\$10,000 + \$25,000 - \$15,000$
$$= \$35,000 - \$15,000 = \underline{\$20,000}$$

b. Incremental operating cash inflows:

Calculation of Depreciation Expense

Year	Cost (1)	Applicable MACRS depreciation percentages (from Table 3.2) (2)	Depreciation [(1) × (2)] (3)
With new machine			
1	$150,000	33%	$ 49,500
2	150,000	45	67,500
3	150,000	15	22,500
4	150,000	7	10,500
		Totals 100%	$150,000
With old machine			
2	$ 40,000	19% (year-3 depreciation)	$ 7,600
2	40,000	12 (year-4 depreciation)	4,800
3	40,000	12 (year-5 depreciation)	4,800
4	40,000	5 (year-6 depreciation)	2,000
		Total	$19,200[a]

[a]The total of $19,200 represents the book value of the old machine at the end of the second year, which was calculated in part **a**.

Calculation of Operating Cash Inflows

	Year 1	Year 2	Year 3	Year 4
With new machine				
Earnings before depr., int., and taxes[a]	$120,000	$130,000	$130,000	$ 0
− Depreciation[b]	49,500	67,500	22,500	10,500
Earnings before int. and taxes	$ 70,500	$ 62,500	$107,500	−$10,500
− Taxes (rate, $T = 40\%$)	28,200	25,000	43,000	− 4,200
Net operating profit after taxes	$ 42,300	$ 37,500	$ 64,500	−$ 6,300
+ Depreciation[b]	49,500	67,500	22,500	10,500
Operating cash inflows	$ 91,800	$105,000	$ 87,000	$ 4,200
With old machine				
Earnings before depr., int., and taxes[a]	$ 70,000	$ 70,000	$ 70,000	$ 0
− Depreciation[c]	7,600	4,800	4,800	2,000
Earnings before int. and taxes	$ 62,400	$ 65,200	$ 65,200	−$ 2,000
− Taxes (rate, $T = 40\%$)	24,960	26,080	26,080	− 800
Net operating profit after taxes	$ 37,440	$ 39,120	$ 39,120	−$ 1,200
+ Depreciation	7,600	4,800	4,800	2,000
Operating cash inflows	$ 45,040	$ 43,920	$ 43,920	$ 800

[a]Given in the problem.
[b]From column 3 of the preceding table, top.
[c]From column 3 of the preceding table, bottom.

Calculation of Incremental Operating Cash Inflows

Operating cash inflows

Year	New machine[a] (1)	Old machine[a] (2)	Incremental (relevant) [(1) − (2)] (3)
1	$ 91,800	$45,040	$46,760
2	105,000	43,920	61,080
3	87,000	43,920	43,080
4	4,200	800	3,400

[a]From the final row for the respective machine in the preceding table.

c. Terminal cash flow (end of year 3):

After-tax proceeds from sale of new machine			
Proceeds from sale of new machine	$35,000		
Total after-tax proceeds—new[1]	9,800		
Total after-tax proceeds—new			$25,200
− After-tax proceeds from sale of old machine			
Proceeds from sale of old machine	$ 0		
− Tax on sale of old machine[2]	− 800		
Total after-tax proceeds—old			800
+ Change in net working capital			20,000
Terminal cash flow			$44,400

_____

[1]Book value of new machine at end of year 3
$$= \$150,000 - [(0.33 + 0.45 + 0.15) \times \$150,000] = \$150,000 - (0.93 \times \$150,000)$$
$$= \$15,000 - \$139,500 = \$10,500$$
Tax on sale $= 0.40 \times (\$35,000 \text{ sale price} - \$10,500 \text{ book value})$
$$= 0.40 \times \$24,500 = \underline{\$9,800}$$

[2]Book value of old machine at end of year 3
$$= \$40,000 - [(0.20 + 0.32 + 0.19 + 0.12 + 0.12) \times \$40,000] = \$40,000 - (0.95 \times \$40,000)$$
$$= \$40,000 - \$38,000 = \$2,000$$
Tax on sale $= 0.40 \times (\$0 \text{ sale price} - \$2,000 \text{ book value})$
$$= 0.40 \times (-\$2,500 = -\underline{\$800} \text{ (i.e., \$800 tax saving)}$$

d.

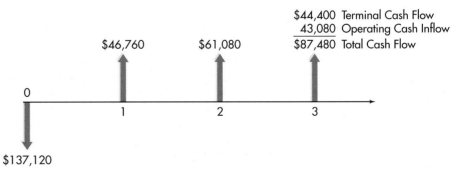

End of Year

Note: The year-4 incremental operating cash inflow of $3,400 is not directly included; it is instead reflected in the book values used to calculate the taxes on sale of the machines at the end of year 3 and is therefore part of the terminal cash flow.

Chapter 9

ST9–1   a. Payback period:

Project M: $\dfrac{\$28,500}{\$10,000} = \underline{\underline{2.85}}$ years

Project N:

Year (t)	Cash inflows (CF_t)	Cumulative cash inflows
1	$11,000	$11,000
2	10,000	21,000 ←
3	9,000	30,000
4	8,000	38,000

$$2 + \dfrac{\$27,000 - \$21,000}{\$9,000} \text{ years}$$

$$2 + \dfrac{\$6,000}{\$9,000} \text{ years} = \underline{\underline{2.67}} \text{ years}$$

b. Net present value (NPV):

Project M: $NPV = (\$10,000 \times PVIFA_{14\%,4\text{yrs}}) - \$28,500$
$= (\$10,000 \times 2.914) - \$28,500$
$= \$29,140 - \$28,500 = \underline{\underline{\$640}}$

(Calculator solution = $637.12)

Project N:

Year (t)	Cash inflows (CF_t) (1)	$PVIF_{14\%,t}$ (2)	Present value at 14% [(1) ÷ (2)] (3)
1	$11,000	0.877	$ 9,647
2	10,000	0.769	7,690
3	9,000	0.675	6,075
4	8,000	0.592	4,736
		Present value of cash inflows	$28,148
		− Initial investment	27,000
		Net present value (NPV)	$ 1,148

(Calculator solution = $1,155.18)

c. Internal rate of return (IRR):

Project M: $\dfrac{\$28,500}{\$10,000} = 2.850$

$PVIFA_{IRR,4yrs} = 2.850$

From Table A–4:

$PVIFA_{15\%,4yrs} = 2.855$

$PVIFA_{16\%,4yrs} = 2.798$

IRR = $\underline{\underline{15\%}}$ (2.850 is closest to 2.855)

(Calculator solution = 15.09%)

Project N:

Average annual cash inflow $= \dfrac{\$11,000 + \$10,000 + \$9,000 + \$8,000}{4}$

$$= \dfrac{\$38,000}{4} = \$9,500$$

$PVIFA_{r,4yrs} = \dfrac{\$27,000}{\$9,500} = 2.842$

$r \approx 15\%$

Try 16%, because there are more cash inflows in early years.

Year (t)	CF_t (1)	$PVIF_{16\%,t}$ (2)	Present value at 16% [(1) × (2)] (3)	$PVIF_{17\%,t}$ (4)	Present value at 17% [(1) × (4)] (5)
1	$11,000	0.862	$ 9,482	0.855	$ 9,405
2	10,000	0.743	7,430	0.731	7,310
3	9,000	0.641	5,769	0.624	5,616
4	8,000	0.552	4,416	0.534	4,272
	Present value of cash inflows		$27,097		$26,603
	− Initial investment		27,000		27,000
	NPV		$ 97		−$ 397

IRR = $\underline{\underline{16\%}}$ (rounding to nearest whole percent)

(Calculator solution = 16.19%)

d.

	Project	
	M	N
Payback period	2.85 years	2.67 years[a]
NPV	$640	$1,148[a]
IRR	15%	16%[a]

[a]Preferred project.

Project N is recommended, because it has the shorter payback period and the higher NPV, which is greater than zero, and the larger IRR, which is greater than the 14% cost of capital.

e. Net present value profiles:

	Data	
		NPV
Discount rate	Project M	Project N
0%	$11,500^a	$11,000^b
14	640	1,148
15	0	—
16	—	0

^{a}($10,000 + $10,000 + $10,000 + $10,000) − $28,500
  = $40,000 − $28,500
  = $11,500

^{b}($11,000 + $10,000 + $9,000 + $8,000) − $27,000
  = $38,000 − $27,000
  = $11,000

From the NPV profile that follows, it can be seen that if the firm has a cost of capital below approximately 6% (exact value is 5.75%), conflicting rankings of the projects would exist using the NPV and IRR decision techniques. Because the firm's cost of capital is 14%, it can be seen in part **d** that no conflict exists.

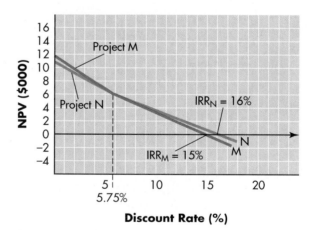

Chapter 10

ST10–1 **a.** $NPV_A = ($7,000 \times PVIFA_{10\%, 3yrs}) − $15,000$
$= ($7,000 \times 2.487) − $15,000$
$= $17,409 − $15,000 = \underline{\underline{$2,409}}$

(Calculator solution = $2,407.96)

$$NPV_B = (\$10,000 \times PVIFA_{10\%,3yrs}) - \$20,000$$
$$= (\$10,000 - 2.487) - \$20,000$$
$$= \$24,870 - \$20,000 = \underline{\$4,870}^*$$

(Calculator solution = $4,868.52)

*Preferred project, because higher NPV.

b. From the CAPM-type relationship, the risk-adjusted discount rate ($RADR$) for project A, which has a risk index of 0.4, is 9%; for project B, with a risk index of 1.8, the $RADR$ is 16%.

$$NPV_A = (\$7,000 \times PVIFA_{9\%,3yrs}) - \$15,000$$
$$= (\$7,000 \times 2.531) - \$15,000$$
$$= \$17,717 - \$15,000 = \underline{\$2,717}^*$$

(Calculator solution = $2,719.06)

$$NPV_B = (\$10,000 \times PVIFA_{16\%,3yrs}) - \$20,000$$
$$= (\$10,000 \times 2.246) - \$20,000$$
$$= \$22,460 - \$20,000 = \underline{\$2,460}$$

(Calculator solution = $2,458.90)

*Preferred project, because higher NPV.

c. When the differences in risk were ignored in part **a**, project B was preferred over project A; but when the higher risk of project B is incorporated into the analysis using risk-adjusted discount rates in part **b**, *project A is preferred over project B.* Clearly, project A should be implemented.

Chapter 11

ST11–1 a. Cost of debt, r_i (using approximation formula)

$$r_d = \frac{I + \dfrac{\$1,000 - N_d}{n}}{\dfrac{N_d + \$1,000}{2}}$$

$$I = 0.10 \times \$1,000 = \$100$$
$$N_d = \$1,000 - \$30 \text{ discount} - \$20 \text{ flotation cost} = \$950$$
$$n = 10 \text{ years}$$

$$r_d = \frac{\$100 + \dfrac{\$1,000 - \$950}{10}}{\dfrac{\$950 + \$1,000}{2}} = \frac{\$100 + \$5}{\$975} = 10.8\%$$

(Calculator solution = 10.8%)

$$r_i = r_d \times (1 - T)$$
$$T = 0.40$$
$$r_i = 10.8\% \times (1 - 0.40) = \underline{\underline{6.5\%}}$$

Cost of preferred stock, r_p

$$r_p = \frac{D_p}{N_p}$$

$D_p = 0.11 \times \$100 = \$11$

$N_p = \$100 - \$4 \text{ flotation cost} = \$96$

$$r_p = \frac{\$11}{\$96} = \underline{\underline{11.5\%}}$$

Cost of retained earnings, r_r

$$r_r = r_s = \frac{D_1}{P_0} + g$$

$$= \frac{\$6}{\$80} + 6.0\% = 7.5\% + 6.0\% = \underline{\underline{13.5\%}}$$

Cost of new common stock, r_n

$$r_n = \frac{D_1}{N_n} + g$$

$D_1 = \$6$

$N_n = \$80 - \$4 \text{ underpricing} - \$4 \text{ flotation cost} = \$72$

$g = 6.0\%$

$$r_n = \frac{\$6}{\$72} + 6.0\% = 8.3\% + 6.0\% = \underline{\underline{14.3\%}}$$

b. (1) Break point, BP

$$BP_{\text{common equity}} = \frac{AF_{\text{common equity}}}{w_{\text{common equity}}}$$

$AF_{\text{common equity}} = \$225,000$

$w_{\text{common equity}} = 45\%$

$$BP_{\text{common equity}} = \frac{\$225,000}{0.45} = \$500,000$$

(2) WACC for total new financing $< \$500,000$

Source of capital	Weight (1)	Cost (2)	Weighted cost [(1) × (2)] (3)
Long-term debt	.40	6.5%	2.6%
Preferred stock	.15	11.5	1.7
Common stock equity	.45	13.5	6.1
Totals	1.00		10.4%
Weighted average cost of capital = 10.4%			

(3) WACC for total new financing > $500,000

Source of capital	Weight (1)	Cost (2)	Weighted cost [(1) × (2)] (3)
Long-term debt	.40	6.5%	2.6%
Preferred stock	.15	11.5	1.7
Common stock equity	.45	14.3	6.4
Totals	1.00		10.7%

Weighted average cost of capital = 10.7%

c. IOS data for graph

Investment opportunity	Internal rate of return (IRR)	Initial investment	Cumulative investment
D	16.5%	$200,000	$ 200,000
C	12.9	150,000	350,000
E	11.8	450,000	800,000
A	11.2	100,000	900,000
G	10.5	300,000	1,200,000
F	10.1	600,000	1,800,000
B	9.7	500,000	2,300,000

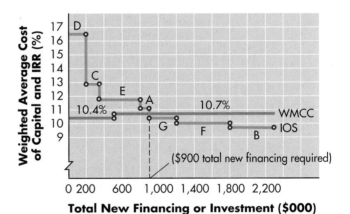

d. Projects D, C, E, and A should be accepted because their respective IRRs exceed the WMCC. They will require $900,000 of total new financing.

Chapter 12

ST12–1 a. $Q = \dfrac{FC}{P - VC}$

$= \dfrac{\$250,000}{\$7.50 - \$3.00} = \dfrac{\$250,000}{\$4.50} = \underline{55,556}$ units

b.

		+20%	
Sales (in units)		100,000	120,000
Sales revenue (units × $7.50/unit)		$750,000	$900,000
Less: Variable operating costs (units × $3.00/unit)		300,000	360,000
Less: Fixed operating costs		250,000	250,000
Earnings before interest and taxes (EBIT)		$200,000	$290,000

+45%

Less: Interest		80,000	80,000
Net profits before taxes		$120,000	$210,000
Less: Taxes ($T = 0.40$)		48,000	84,000
Net profits after taxes		$ 72,000	$126,000
Less: Preferred dividends (8,000 shares × $5.00/share)		40,000	40,000
Earnings available for common		$132,000	$ 86,000
Earnings per share (EPS)	$32,000/20,000 = $1.60/share		$86,000/20,000 = $4.30/share

+169%

c. $\text{DOL} = \dfrac{\% \text{ change in EBIT}}{\% \text{ change in sales}} = \dfrac{+45\%}{+20\%} = \underline{\underline{2.25}}$

d. $\text{DFL} = \dfrac{\% \text{ change in EPS}}{\% \text{ change in EBIT}} = \dfrac{+169\%}{+45} = \underline{\underline{3.76}}$

e. $\text{DTL} = \text{DOL} \times \text{DFL}$

$\quad = 2.25 \times 3.76 = \underline{\underline{8.46}}$

Using the other DTL formula:

$\text{DTL} = \dfrac{\% \text{ change in EPS}}{\% \text{ change in sales}}$

$8.46 = \dfrac{\% \text{ change in EPS}}{+50\%}$

$\% \text{ change in EPS} = 8.46 \times 0.50 = 4.23 = \underline{\underline{+423}}\%$

ST12–2

Data summary for alternative plans		
Source of capital	Plan A (bond)	Plan B (stock)
Long-term debt	$60,000 at 12% annual interest	$50,000 at 12% annual interest
Annual interest =	0.12 = $60,000 = $7,200	0.12 × $50,000 = $6,000
Common stock	10,000 shares	11,000 shares

a.

	Plan A (bond)		Plan B (stock)	
EBIT[a]	$30,000	$40,000	$30,000	$40,000
Less: Interest	7,200	7,200	6,000	6,000
Net profits before taxes	$22,800	$32,800	$24,000	$34,000
Less: Taxes ($T = 0.40$)	9,120	13,120	9,600	13,600
Net profits after taxes	$13,680	$19,680	$14,400	$20,400
EPS (10,000 shares)	$1.37	$1.97		
(11,000 shares)			$1.31	$1.85

[a]Values were arbitrarily selected; other values could have been used.

	Coordinates	
	EBIT	
	$30,000	$40,000
Financing plan	Earnings per share (EPS)	
A (Bond)	$1.37	$1.97
B (Stock)	1.31	1.85

b.

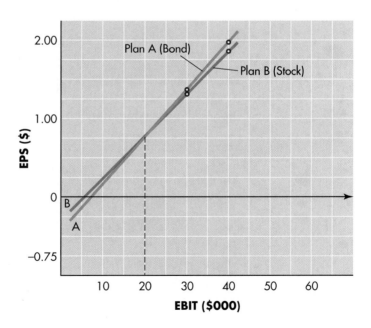

c. The bond plan (Plan A) becomes superior to the stock plan (Plan B) at *around $20,000* of EBIT, as represented by the dashed vertical line in the figure in part **b.** (*Note:* The actual point is $19,200, which was determined algebraically by using the technique described in footnote 22.)

ST12–3 a.

Capital structure debt ratio	Expected EPS (1)	Required return, r_s (2)	Estimated share value [(1) ÷ (2)] (3)
0%	$3.12	.13	$24.00
10	3.90	.15	26.00
20	4.80	.16	30.00
30	5.44	.17	32.00
40	5.51	.19	29.00
50	5.00	.20	25.00
60	4.40	.22	20.00

b. Using the table in part **a:**
  (1) Maximization of EPS: *40% debt ratio*, EPS = $5.51/share (see column 1).
  (2) Maximization of share value: *30% debt ratio*, share value = $32.00 (see column 3).

c. Recommend *30% debt ratio*, because it results in the maximum share value and is therefore consistent with the firm's goal of owner wealth maximization.

Chapter 13

ST13–1 a. Earnings per share (EPS) = $\dfrac{\$2{,}000{,}000 \text{ earnings available}}{500{,}000 \text{ shares of common outstanding}}$

= $4.00/share

Price/earnings (P/E) ratio = $\dfrac{\$60 \text{ market price}}{\$4.00 \text{ EPS}} = 15$

b. Proposed dividends = 500,000 shares × $2 per share = $1,000,000

Shares that can be repurchased = $\dfrac{\$1{,}000{,}000}{\$62} = 16{,}129$ shares

c. *After proposed repurchase:*
Shares outstanding = 500,000 − 16,129 = 483,871

EPS = $\dfrac{\$2{,}000{,}000}{483{,}871} = \$4.13$/share

d. Market price = $4.13/share × 15 = $61.95/share

e. The earnings per share (EPS) are higher after the repurchase, because there are fewer shares of stock outstanding (483,871 shares versus 500,000 shares) to divide up the firm's $2,000,000 of available earnings.

f. In both cases, the stockholders would receive $2 per share—a $2 cash dividend in the dividend case or an approximately $2 increase in share price ($60.00 per share to $61.95 per share) in the repurchase case. [*Note:* The difference of $0.05 per share ($2.00 − $1.95) difference is due to rounding.]

Chapter 14

ST14–1

	Basic data	
Time component	Current	Proposed
Average payment period (APP)	10 days	30 days
Average collection period (ACP)	30 days	30 days
Average age of inventory (AAI)	40 days	40 days

$$\text{Cash conversion cycle (CCC)} = \text{AAI} + \text{ACP} - \text{APP}$$
$$\text{CCC}_{current} = 40 \text{ days} + 30 \text{ days} - 10 \text{ days} = 60 \text{ days}$$
$$\text{CCC}_{proposed} = 40 \text{ days} + 30 \text{ days} - 30 \text{ days} = \underline{40} \text{ days}$$
$$\text{Reduction in CCC} \quad \underline{\underline{20}} \text{ days}$$

Annual operating cycle investment = $18,000,000

Daily expenditure = $18,000,000 ÷ 365 = $49,315

Reduction in resource investment = $49,315 × 20 days = $986,300

Annual profit increase = 0.12 × $986,300 = $\underline{\underline{\$118,356}}$

ST14–2 **a.** *Data:*

$S = 60,000$ gallons

$O = \$200$ per order

$C = \$1$ per gallon per year

Calculation:

$$EOQ = \sqrt{\frac{2 \times S \times O}{C}}$$

$$= \sqrt{\frac{2 \times 60{,}000 \times \$200}{\$1}}$$

$$= \sqrt{24{,}000{,}000}$$

$$= \underline{\underline{4{,}899}} \text{ gallons}$$

b. *Data:*

Lead time = 20 days

Daily usage = 60,000 gallons/365 days

= 164.38 gallons/day

Calculation:

Reorder point = lead time in days × daily usage

= 20 days × 164.38 gallons/day

= $\underline{\underline{3{,}287.6}}$ gallons

ST14–3 Tabular Calculation of the Effects of Relaxing Credit Standards on Regency Rug Repair Company:

Additional profit contribution from sales
  [4,000 rugs × ($32 avg. sale price − $28 var. cost)] $16,000

Cost of marginal investment in accounts receivable
  Average investment under proposed plan:

$$\frac{(\$28 \times 76{,}000 \text{ rugs})}{365/48} = \frac{\$2{,}128{,}000}{7.6} \qquad \$280{,}000$$

  Average investment under present plan:

$$\frac{(\$28 \times 72{,}000 \text{ rugs})}{365/40} = \frac{\$2{,}016{,}000}{9.1} \qquad \underline{221{,}538}$$

    Marginal investment in A/R $ 58,462
      Cost of marginal investment in
        A/R (0.14 × $58,462)   ($ 8,185)

Cost of marginal bad debts
  Bad debts under proposed plan
    (0.015 × $32 × 76,000 rugs) $ 36,480
  Bad debts under present plan
    (0.010 × $32 × 72,000 rugs)   23,040
    Cost of marginal bad debts   ($13,440)
Net loss from implementation of proposed plan   ($ 5,625)

Recommendation: Because a net loss of $5,625 is expected to result from relaxing credit standards, *the proposed plan should not be implemented.*

Chapter 15

ST15–1 a.

Supplier	Approximate cost of giving up cash discount
X	1% × [365/(55 − 10)] = 1% × 365/45 = 1% × 8 = 8.1%
Y	2% × [365/(30 − 10)] = 2% × 365/20 = 2% × 18 = 36.5%
Z	2% × [365/(60 − 20)] = 2% × 365/40 = 2% × 9 = 18.3%

b.

Supplier	Recommendation
X	8.1% cost of giving up discount < 15% interest cost from bank; therefore, *give up discount.*
Y	36.5% cost of giving up discount > 15% interest cost from bank; therefore, *take discount and borrow from bank.*
Z	18.3% cost of giving up discount > 15% interest cost from bank; therefore, *take discount and borrow from bank.*

c. Stretching accounts payable for supplier Z would change the cost of giving up the cash discount to

$$2\% \times [365/[(60 + 20) - 20]] = 2\% \times 365/60 = 2\% \times 6.1 = \underline{12.2\%}$$

In this case, in light of the 15% interest cost from the bank, the recommended strategy in part **b** would be to *give up the discount,* because the 12.2% cost of giving up the discount would be less than the 15% interest cost from the bank.

Chapter 16

ST16–1 **a.** (1) and (2). In tabular form—after-tax cash outflows in column 3 and present value of the cash outflows in column 5.

End of year	Lease payment (1)	Tax adjustment $[(1-0.40)=0.60]$ (2)	After-tax cash outflows $[(1)\times(2)]$ (3)	Present value factors[a] (4)	Present value of outflows $[(3)\times(4)]$ (5)
1	$5,000	0.60	$3,000	0.917	$ 2,751
2	5,000	0.60	3,000	0.842	2,526
3	5,000	0.60	3,000	0.772	2,316
4	5,000	0.60	3,000	0.708	2,124
5	5,000	0.60	7,000[b]	0.650	4,550
				Present value of cash outflows	$14,267

[a]From Table A–2, *PVIF*, for 9% and the corresponding year.
[b]After-tax lease payment outflow of $3,000 plus the $4,000 cost of exercising the purchase option.

(Calculator solution = $14,269)

b. (1) In tabular form—annual interest expense in column 3.

End of year	Loan payments (1)	Beginning of-year principal (2)	Payments Interest $[0.15\times(2)]$ (3)	Payments Principal $[(1)-(3)]$ (4)	End-of-year principal $[(2)-(4)]$ (5)
1	$5,967	$20,000	$3,000	$2,967	$17,033
2	5,967	17,033	2,555	3,412	13,621
3	5,967	13,621	2,043	3,924	9,697
4	5,967	9,697	1,455	4,512	5,185
5	5,967	5,185	778	5,189	—[a]

[a]The values in this table have been rounded to the nearest dollar, which results in a slight difference ($4) between the beginning-of-year-5 principal (in column 2) and the year-5 principal payment (in column 4).

(2) In tabular form—after-tax cash outflows in column 9.

End of year	Loan payments (1)	Maintenance costs (2)	Cost of oven (3)	Depreciation percentages[a] (4)	Depreciation $[(3)\times(4)]$ (5)	Interest[b] (6)	Total deductions $[(2)+(5)+(6)]$ (7)	Tax shields $[0.40\times(7)]$ (8)	After-tax cash outflows $[(1)+(2)-(8)]$ (9)
1	$5,967	$1,000	$20,000	.20	$4,000	$3,000	$8,000	$3,200	$3,767
2	5,967	1,000	20,000	.32	6,400	2,555	9,955	3,982	2,985
3	5,967	1,000	20,000	.19	3,800	2,043	6,843	2,737	4,230
4	5,967	1,000	20,000	.12	2,400	1,455	4,855	1,942	5,025
5	5,967	1,000	20,000	.12	2,400	778	4,178	1,671	5,296

[a]From Table 3.2 on page 108.
[b]From column 3 of table in part **b**(1).

(3) In tabular form—present value of the cash outflows in column 3.

End of year	After-tax cash outflows[a] (1)	Present value factors[b] (2)	Present value of outflows [(1) × (2)] (3)
1	$3,767	0.917	$ 3,454
2	2,985	0.842	2,513
3	4,230	0.772	3,266
4	5,025	0.708	3,558
5	5,296	0.650	3,442
		Present value of cash outflows	$16,233

[a]From column 9 of table in part **b**(2).
[b]From Table A–2, *PVIF*, for 9% and the corresponding year.

(Calculator solution = $16,237)

c. Because the present value of the lease outflows of $14,267 is well below the present value of the purchase outflows of $16,233, *the lease is preferred.* Leasing rather than purchasing the oven should result in an incremental savings of $1,966 ($16,233 purchase cost − $14,267 lease cost).

ST16–2   a. In tabular form:

Year(s)	Payments (1)	Present value interest factor at 13 percent (2)	Present value [(1) × (2)] (3)
1–25	$ 110[a]	7.330[b]	$806.30
25	1,000	0.047[c]	47.00
		Straight bond value	$853.30

[a]$1,000 at 11% = $110 interest per year.
[b]Present value interest factor for an annuity, *PVIFA*, discounted at 13% for 25 years, from Table A–4.
[c]Present value interest factor for $1, *PVIF*, discounted at 13% for year 25, from Table A–2.

(Calculator solution = $853.40)

b. In tabular form:

Market price of stock (1)	Conversion ratio (2)	Conversion value [(1) × (2)] (3)
$20	40	$ 800
25 (conversion price)	40	1,000 (par value)
28	40	1,120
35	40	1,400
50	40	2,000

   c. The bond would be expected to sell at the higher of the conversion value and the straight value. In no case would it be expected to sell for less than the straight value of $853.30. Therefore, at a price of $20, the bond would sell for its straight value of $853.30, and at prices of $25, $28, $35, and $50, the bond would be expected to sell at the associated conversion values (calculated in part **b**) of $1,000, $1,120, $1,400, and $2,000, respectively.

   d. The straight bond value of $853.30.

Chapter 17

ST17–1   **a.** Net present value at 11%:

Year(s)	Cash inflow (1)	Present value factor at 11%[a] (2)	Present value [(1) × (2)] (3)
1–3	$20,000	2.444	$ 48,880
4–15	30,000	(7.191 − 2.444)	142,410
		Present value of inflows	$191,290
		Less: Cash purchase price	180,000
		Net present value (NPV)	$ 11,290

[a]Present value interest factors for annuities, *PVIFA*, from Table A–4.

   (Calculator solution = 11,289)

   Because the NPV of $11,290 is greater than zero, *Luxe Foods should acquire Valley Canning*.

   b. In this case, the 14% cost of capital must be used. Net present value at 14%:

Year(s)	Cash inflow (1)	Present value factor at 14%[a] (2)	Present value [(1) × (2)] (3)
1–3	$20,000	2.322	$ 46,440
4–15	30,000	(6.142 − 2.322)	114,600
		Present value of inflows	$161,040
		Less: Cash purchase price	180,000
		Net present value (NPV)	($ 18,960)

[a]Present value interest factors for annuities, *PVIFA*, from Table A–4.

   (Calculator solution = $18,951)

   At the higher cost of capital, the *acquisition of Valley by Luxe cannot be justified*.

ST17–2   a. Lake Industries' EPS without merger:

| | Earnings available for common | | | | |
Year	Initial value (1)	Future value factor at 5%[a] (2)	End-of-year value [(1) × (2)] (3)	Number of shares outstanding (4)	EPS [(3) ÷ (4)] (5)
2009	$160,000	1.000	$160,000	80,000	$2.00
2010	160,000	1.050	168,000	80,000	2.10
2011	160,000	1.102	176,320	80,000	2.20
2012	160,000	1.158	185,280	80,000	2.32
2013	160,000	1.216	194,560	80,000	2.43
2014	160,000	1.276	204,160	80,000	2.55

[a]Future value interest factors, *FVIF*, from Table A–1.

b. Number of postmerger shares outstanding for Lake Industries:

$$\frac{\text{Number of new}}{\text{shares issued}} = \frac{\text{Initial number of}}{\text{Butler Company shares}} \times \text{Ratio of exchange}$$

$$= \quad 10,000 \times 1.1 \quad = \quad 11,000 \text{ shares}$$

Plus: Lake's premerger shares   80,000

Lake's postmerger shares   91,000 shares

	Earnings available for common					
	Butler Company			Lake Industries			
				Without merger	With merger		
Year	Initial value (1)	Future value factor at 10%[a] (2)	End-of-year value [(1) × (2)] (3)	End-of-year value[b] (4)	End-of-year value [(3) + (4)] (5)	Number of shares outstanding[c] (6)	EPS [(5) ÷ (6)] (7)
2009	$20,000	1.000	$20,000	$160,000	$180,000	91,000	$1.98
2010	20,000	1.100	22,000	168,000	190,000	91,000	2.09
2011	20,000	1.210	24,200	176,320	200,520	91,000	2.20
2012	20,000	1.331	26,620	185,280	211,900	91,000	2.33
2013	20,000	1.464	29,280	194,560	223,840	91,000	2.46
2014	20,000	1.611	32,220	204,160	236,380	91,000	2.60

[a]Future value interest factors, *FVIF*, from Table A–1.
[b]From column 3 of table in part **a.**
[c]Calculated at beginning of this part.

c. Comparing the EPS without the proposed merger calculated in part **a** (see column 5 of table in part **a**) with the EPS with the proposed merger calculated in part **b** (see column 7 of table in part **b**), we can see that after 2011, the EPS *with* the merger rises above the EPS *without* the merger. Clearly, over the long run, the EPS with the merger will exceed those without the merger. This outcome is attributed to the higher rate of growth associated with Butler's earnings (10% versus 5% for Lake).

Chapter 18

ST18–1 MNC's receipt of dividends can be calculated as follows:

Subsidiary income before local taxes	$150,000
Foreign income tax at 32%	48,000
Dividend available to be declared	$102,000
Foreign dividend withholding tax at 8%	− 8,160
MNC's receipt of dividends	$ 93,840

a. If tax credits are allowed, then the so-called grossing up procedure will be applicable:

Additional MNC income		$150,000
U.S. tax liability at 34%	$51,000	
Total foreign taxes paid to be used as a credit ($48,000 + $8,160)	− 56,160	− 56,160
U.S. taxes due		− 0
Net funds available to the MNC		$ 93,840

b. If no tax credits are permitted, then:

MNC's receipt of dividends	$93,840
U.S. tax liability at 34%	− 31,906
Net funds available to the parent MNC	$61,934

Appendix C

Answers to Selected End-of-Chapter Problems

The following list of answers to selected problems and portions of problems is included to provide "check figures" for use in preparing detailed solutions to end-of-chapter problems requiring calculations. For problems that are relatively straightforward, the key answer is given; for more complex problems, answers to a number of parts of the problem are included. Detailed calculations are not shown—only the final and, in some cases, intermediate answers, which should help to confirm whether the correct solution is being developed. Answers to problems involving present and future value were solved by using the appropriate tables; calculator solutions are not given. For problems containing a variety of cases for which similar calculations are required, the answers for only one or two cases have been included. The only verbal answers included are simple yes-or-no or "choice of best alternative" responses; answers to problems requiring detailed explanations or discussions are not given

The problems and portions of problems for which answers have been included were selected randomly; therefore, there is no discernible pattern to the choice of problem answers given. The answers given are based on what are believed to be the most obvious and reasonable assumptions related to the given problem; in some cases, other reasonable assumptions could result in equally correct answers.

1–1	a.	Ms. Harper has unlimited liability: $60,000
	c.	Ms. Harper has limited liability
1–2	a.	$160,000
	b.	$150,000
1–4	a.	Cash inflows: $4,950
1–6	a.	$19,700
	b.	$72,800
	c.	21.3%
1–9	e.	Total tax liability: $206,400
1–10	a.	Earnings after tax: $18,000
1–11	b.	Asset X: $100
		Asset Y: $2,000
2–3	a.	Net profit after tax: $38,500
2–5	a.	Earnings per share: $1.162
2–7	a.	Total liquid assets: $5,700
		Total current liabilities: $2,400
2–9		Initial sales price: $9.50
2–10	b.	Earnings per share: $2.36
	c.	Cash dividend per share: $1.50

2–13 a.

Current ratio	2006: 1.88	2008: 1.79
Quick ratio	2006: 1.22	2008: 1.24

2–16 a. 45.62 days

2–18

	Creek	Industry
Debt ratio	0.73	0.51
Times interest earned	3.00	7.30

2–20 a.

	Pelican	Timberland
(1) Debt ratio	10%	50%
(2) Times interest earned	62.5	12.5

b.

	Pelican	Timberland
(1) Operating margin	25%	25%
(2) Net profit margin	14.8%	13.8%
(3) ROA	36.9%	34.5%
(4) ROE	41.0%	69.0%

2–23 a.

	Actual 2009
Current ratio:	1.04
Average collection period:	57 days
Debt ratio:	61.3%
Net profit margin:	4.1%
Return on equity:	11.3%

2–25 a. 2006 Johnson ROE = 21.21%
Industry ROE = 14.46%

2–26 a.

	Actual 2009
Quick ratio:	2.20
Total asset turnover	2.00
Times interest earned	3.85
Operating profit margin	16.0%
Price earnings ratio	9.8

3–3	a.	$16,000
	c.	$289,240
3–6	b.	$1,620
	c.	$13,367

3–8

	April	May
	($000)	
Cash 1 month delay	168	183
Cash 2 months delay	120	134.4
Total disbursements	465.3	413.1

3–10	c.	Cumulative cash surplus at end of October 2010: $907
3–15	a.	To retained earnings: $146,600
	b.	To retained earnings: $157,400
3–17	a.	Total assets: $1,383,000
		Total current liabilities: $510,000
		External funds required: $53,000
3–19	a.	To retained earnings: $32,500
	c.	$11,250
4–3		C: 3 years $< n <$ 4 years
4–4		A: $530.60
		D: $78.450
4–6	a.	(1) $15,456
4–8	a.	8% $< i <$ 9%
4–11		B: $6,020
		D $80,250
4–18	a.	(1) A: $36,217.50
		(2) A: $39,114.90
4–19	a.	(1) C: $2,821.70
		(2) C: $3,386.04
4–23	b.	$30,950.64
4–25	b.	B: $1,000,000
		D: $1,200,000
4–27	a.	A: $3,862.50
4–29	b.	B: $26,039
4–32	a.	$22,215
4–33	b.	B: 12.6%
		D: 17.0%

4–34 a.

(1) Annual:	$8,810
Semiannual:	$8,955
Quarterly:	$9,030

4–40		B: $2,439.32
4–43	a.	$60,000
	b.	$3,764.82
4–45		A: $4,656.58
		B: $10,619.47
		C: $7,955.87
4–49	a.	A: 12% $< i <$ 13%
		Calculator solution 12.47%
		C: 2% $< i <$ 3%
		Calculator solution 2.50%
4–51	a.	B: 8% $< i <$ 9%
		Calculator solution 8.02%
		D: 10% $< i <$ 11%
		Calculator solution 10.03%
4–56		A: 17 $< n <$ 18
		Calculator solution 17.79
		D: 18 $< n <$ 19
		Calculator solution 18.68

5–1	a.	X: 12.50%
		Y: 12.36%
5–2	A: 25%	
5–4	a.	A: 8%
		B: 20%
5–5	a.	R: 10%
		S: 20%
	b.	R: 25%
		S: 25.5%
5–9	a.	2008 return (hypothetical): 11.73%
5–10	a.	(4) Project 257 CV: .368
		Project 432 CV: .354
5–11	a.	F: 4%
	b.	F: 13.38%
	c.	F: 3.345
5–13	b.	Portfolio return: 15.5%
	c.	Standard deviation: 1.511%
5–16	a.	20.73%
	c.	12.89%
5–19	a.	18% increase
	b.	9.6% decrease
	c.	No change
5–23	A: 8.9%	
	D: 15%	
5–25	b.	10%
5–28	b.	12.4%
	c.	10.4%
6–1	3.5%	
6–5	a.	20 year bond = 11.5%
		5 year bond = 10.5%
6–8	a.	A: 9%
		B: 12%
6–10	b.	$175,000
	c.	$113,750
6–12	b.	$8,789.40
6–13	C: $16,660.00	
	D: $9,717.00	
6–15	a.	$1,156.88
6–19	a.	(1) $1,120.23
		(2) $1,000.00
		(3) $896.63
6–22	a.	A: approximate: 12.36%
		Calculator solution: 12.71%
		C: approximate: 10.38%
		Calculator solution: 10.22%
		E: approximate: 8.77%
		Calculator solution: 8.95%
6–25	A: $1,152.35	
	C: $464.72	
	E: $76.11	
7–1	b.	800,000 shares
7–3	A: $15.00	
	C: $11.00	
	D: $25.50	

7–6	a.	$20
	b.	$12
7–8	a.	$68.82
	b.	$60.95
7–9	A: $24.00	
	B: $40.00	
	E: $18.75	
7–10	a.	$37.75
	b.	$60.40
7–12	$81.19	
7–14	a.	$34.12
	b.	$20.21
	c.	$187.87
7–16	a.	(1) $5,021,250
		(2) $5,411,250
		(3) $4,049,331
	b.	$2,191,331
	c.	$10.96
7–18	a.	Book value: $36.00
	b.	Liquidation value: $30.20
7–19	a.	9.5%
	b.	14.7%
8–1	a.	Operating expenditure
	d.	Operating expenditure
	f.	Capital expenditure
8–4	*Year Relevant cash flow*	
	1 $4,000	
	2 $6,000	
	4 $10,000	
8–8	A: $275,500	
	B: $26,800	
8–9	a.	$23,200
	b.	@$100,000: $30,720
		@$56,000: $13,120
8–10	a.	Total tax: $49,600
	d.	Total tax: ($6,400)
8–13	Initial investment $22,680	
8–14	a.	Initial investment: $18,240
	c.	Initial investment: $23,100
8–17	c.	Cash inflow, Year 3: $584,000
8–18	Incremental operating cash flow, Year 2: $458	
8–20	b.	Incremental cash flow, Year 3: $1,960
8–23	Terminal cash flow: $76,640	
8–27	b.	Operating cash flow, Year 1: ($15,600)
8–28	a.	Initial investment, Asset B: $51,488
	b.	Incremental cash flow, Year 2, Hoist A: $8,808
	c.	Terminal cash flow, Hoist B: $18,600
9–2	a.	Machine 1: 4 years, 8 months
		Machine 2: 5 years, 3 months
9–4	a.	Project A payback: 3.9 years
9–5	a.	$3,246 Accept
	b.	−$5,131 Reject

9–6   a. $2,675 Accept
      c. −$805 Reject
9–8   a. $1,497,650
      b. $385,604
      c. $1,632,400
9–12 a. Project A: 3.08 years
         Project C: 2.38 years
      b. Project C: NPV $5,451
9–13 a. Project A: 17%
         Project D: 21%
9–17 a. NPV = $1,222
      b. IRR = 12%
      c. Accept
9–19 a. Project A: payback
         3 years 4 months
      b. A: $120,000; B: $105,000
      c. Project B: NPV $51,137
      d. Project A: IRR 19.91%
9–24 a. Initial Investment: $1,480,000
      b. *Year   Cash Flow*
            1     $656,000
            2   761,600
            3   647,200
            4   585,600
            5   585,600
            6   44,000
      c. 2.1 years
      d. NPV = $959,289
         IRR = 35%
10–2 a. $6,183.75
10–4 a. Range A: $1,600
         Range B: $200
10–5 b. Project A:
         Pessimistic: $73
         Most likely: $1,609
         Optimistic: $3,145
10–8 a. Project E: $2,130; Project F: $1,678
      c. Project E: $834; Project F: $1,678
10–10 b. $2,223
10–12 a. Project X: NPV = $14,960
         Project Y: NPV = $2,650
10–14 a. Project X: NPV = $2,681
         Project Y: NPV = $1,778
      b. Project X: ANPV = $920.04
         Project Y: ANPV = $1,079.54
10–16 a. $237
      d. $243
10–17 a. Value of real options: $2,200
         NPV$_{strategic}$: $500
11–2 a. $980
      d. 7.36% after tax
11–3 a. $930
11–5 a. A: 4.12% after tax
         D: 3.83% after tax

11–9 a. 6%
      b. 12%
11–10 d. 16.54%
11–12 a. 11.28%
      b. 11.45%
11–15 a. 13.55%
      b. 12.985%
11–16 e. Breakpoint common stock: $5,880,000
      f. 7.02%
      g. 7.07%
11–21 a. WACC 0 to $600,000: 10.52%
         WACC $600,001 to $1,000,000: 10.96%
12–1 1,300
12–4 a. 21,000 CDs
      b. $293,580
      d. $10,500
12–5 a. 36 months
12–7 a. 2,000 figurines
      b. −$3,000
      c. $2,000
12–9 a. 8,000 units
      b. @ 10,000 units: $95,000
12–12 b. 2
      c. 1.25
12–13 a. DFL, current: 1.50
12–17 a. 20,000 latches
      b. $7,200
      e. 225.24
12–23 a. Structure A:
         EBIT $30,000: EPS $1.125
         Structure B:
         EBIT $50,000: EPS 2.28
12–26 a., b., c.

% Debt	# shs. @$25	$ Interest expense	EPS
0	1,600,000	0	$3.00
10	1,440,000	300,000	$3.21
40	960,000	1,760,000	$3.90
60	640,000	3,720,000	$4.01

13–4 a. $4.75 per share
      b. $0.40 per share
13–7 a. *Year $ Dividend*
         2000   0.10
         2004   0.96
         2007   1.28
         2009   1.60
      c. *Year $ Dividend*
         2000   0.50
         2004   0.50
         2007   0.66
         2009   1.30
13–9 a. Common stock: $21,000
         Paid in capital: $294,000
         Retained earnings: $85,000

13–11 **a.** $2.00
         d. $20.00 per share
13–13 **a.** 1,200,000 shares @ $1.50 par
         d. 3,600,000 shares @ $0.50 par
13–14 **a.** 1,600 shares
13–17 **a.** 19,047 shares
         b. $2.10
14–1   **a.** OC = 150 days
         b. CCC = 120 days
         c. $9,863,013.70
14–2   **b.** CCC = 70 days
         c. $26,849
14–4   **a.** Average season requirement: $4,000,000
14–6   **a.** 200 units
         b. 121.92 units
         c. 32.88 units
14–7   **d.** $4,441
14–10 Loss from implementation: $4,659
14–12 Loss from implementation: $11,972
14–14 **a.** 7 days
         b. $21,450
15–2   **a.** 37.21%
         b. 18.43%
         c. 7.37%
15–5   **b.** $119/month
         e. $2,429
15–7 $1,300,000
15–8 $82,500
15–11 14.29%
15–12 **a.** Effective rate: 12.94%
         b. Effective rate: 11.73%
15–15 **a.** Effective 90-day rate: 2.25%
         b. Effective annual rate: 13.89%
15–19   *Amount remitted*
         A: $196,000
         C: $107,800
         F: $176,400
         G: $ 88,200
16–2   *Loan*   *Year*   *Interest amount*
          A   1 $1,400
          A   4 $ 402
          D   2 $5,822
          D   4 $3,290

16–4   **b.** Lease: PV of outflows: $42,934
                Purchase: PV of outflows: $43,896
16–11 A: $1,056.25
16–14 **a.** $832.75
         c. @$9 price: $832.75
                @$13 price: $1,040.00
16–18 **a.** 160 shares; 400 warrants
         b. $1,600 profit; 20% return
         c. $10,000 profit; 125% return
16–20 A: $300
         B: −$50
         C: $500
16–21 **b.** $400 profit
         c. $66 to break even
16–22 **a.** @$46: −$100
                @$40: $120
17–2   **a.** Tax liability: $1,680,000
         b. Total tax savings: $320,000
17–4   **a.** NPV: $19,320
         c. NPV: $15,616
17–7   **a.** EPS Marla's: $1.029
                EPS Victory: $1.852
         d. (a) 10.8
                (b) 12.0
                (c) 13.2
17–9   A: (1) 0.60 (2) 1.20
         B: (1) 1.25 (2) 1.25
         D: (1) 0.25 (2) 1.25
17–11 **a.** 1.125
         c. P/E: 16.89
         d. EPS: $2.529
17–13 **a.** Composition
         b. Extension
         c. Combination
17–16 **a.** $583
18–1   **a.** $152,425
         b. $100,600
18–3   **b.** €1,246
18–5   Effective rates   *U.S.$*   *MP*   *¥*
         Euromarket   4.00%   3.20%   3.50%
         Domestic   3.75%   2.90%   3.65%

Glossary

ABC inventory system Inventory management technique that divides inventory into three groups—A, B, and C, in descending order of importance and level of monitoring, on the basis of the dollar investment in each. (Chapter 14)

ability to service debts The ability of a firm to make the payments required on a scheduled basis over the life of a debt. (Chapter 2)

accept–reject approach The evaluation of capital expenditure proposals to determine whether they meet the firm's minimum acceptance criterion. (Chapter 8)

accounting exposure The risk resulting from the effects of changes in foreign exchange rates on the translated value of a firm's financial statement accounts denominated in a given foreign currency. (Chapter 18)

accounts payable management Management by the firm of the time that elapses between its purchase of raw materials and its mailing payment to the supplier. (Chapter 15)

accrual basis In preparation of financial statements, recognizes revenue at the time of sale and recognizes expenses when they are incurred. (Chapter 1)

accruals Liabilities for services received for which payment has yet to be made. (Chapter 15)

ACH (automated clearinghouse) transfer Preauthorized electronic withdrawal from the payer's account and deposit into the payee's account via a settlement among banks by the *automated clearinghouse,* or *ACH.* (Chapter 14)

acquiring company The firm in a merger transaction that attempts to acquire another firm. (Chapter 17)

activity ratios Measure the speed with which various accounts are converted into sales or cash—inflows or outflows. (Chapter 2)

after-tax proceeds from sale of old asset The difference between the old asset's sale proceeds and any applicable taxes or tax refunds related to its sale. (Chapter 8)

agency costs The costs borne by stockholders to maintain a *governance structure* that minimizes agency problems and contributes to the maximization of owner wealth. (Chapter 1)

agency problem The likelihood that managers may place personal goals ahead of corporate goals. (Chapter 1)

aggressive funding strategy A funding strategy under which the firm funds its seasonal requirements with short-term debt and its permanent requirements with long-term debt. (Chapter 14)

aging schedule A credit-monitoring technique that breaks down accounts receivable into groups on the basis of their time of origin; it shows the percentages of the total accounts receivable balance that have been outstanding for specified periods of time. (Chapter 14)

all-current-rate method The method by which the *functional-currency-denominated* financial statements of an MNC's subsidiary are translated into the parent company's currency. (Chapter 18)

American depositary receipts (ADRs) Claims issued by U.S. banks representing ownership of shares of a foreign company's stock held on deposit by the U.S. bank in the foreign market and issued in dollars to U.S. investors. (Chapter 7)

American depositary shares (ADSs) Securities backed by *American depositary receipts (ADRs)* that permit U.S. investors to hold shares of non-U.S. companies and trade them in U.S. markets. (Chapter 7)

angel capitalists (angels) Wealthy individual investors who do not operate as a business but invest in promising early-stage companies in exchange for a portion of the firm's equity. (Chapter 7)

annual cleanup The requirement that for a certain number of days during the year borrowers under a line of credit carry a zero loan balance (that is, owe the bank nothing). (Chapter 15)

annual percentage rate (APR) The *nominal annual rate* of interest, found by multiplying the periodic rate by the number of periods in 1 year, that must be disclosed to consumers on credit cards and loans as a result of "truth-in-lending laws." (Chapter 4)

annual percentage yield (APY) The *effective annual rate* of interest that must be disclosed to consumers by banks on their savings products as a result of "truth-in-savings laws." (Chapter 4)

annualized net present value (ANPV) approach   An approach to evaluating unequal-lived projects that converts the net present value of unequal-lived, mutually exclusive projects into an equivalent annual amount (in NPV terms). (Chapter 10)

annuity   A stream of equal periodic cash flows, over a specified time period. These cash flows can be *inflows* of returns earned on investments or *outflows* of funds invested to earn future returns. (Chapter 4)

annuity due   An annuity for which the cash flow occurs at the *beginning* of each period. (Chapter 4)

articles of partnership   The written contract used to formally establish a business partnership. (Chapter 1)

ASEAN   A large trading bloc with 10 member nations, all in Southeast Asia. China is expected to join this bloc in 2010. Also called the *Association of Southeast Asian Nations.* (Chapter 18)

ask price   The lowest price at which a security is offered for sale. (Chapter 1)

assignment   A voluntary liquidation procedure by which a firm's creditors pass the power to liquidate the firm's assets to an adjustment bureau, a trade association, or a third party, which is designated the *assignee.* (Chapter 17)

asymmetric information   The situation in which managers of a firm have more information about operations and future prospects than do investors. (Chapter 12)

authorized shares   The number of shares of common stock that a firm's corporate charter allows it to issue. (Chapter 7)

average age of inventory   Average number of days' sales in inventory. (Chapter 2)

average collection period   The average amount of time needed to collect accounts receivable. (Chapter 2)

average payment period   The average amount of time needed to pay accounts payable. (Chapter 2)

average tax rate   A firm's taxes divided by its taxable income. (Chapter 1)

balance sheet   Summary statement of the firm's financial position at a given point in time. (Chapter 2)

bankruptcy   Business failure that occurs when the stated value of a firm's liabilities exceeds the fair market value of its assets. (Chapter 17)

Bankruptcy Reform Act of 1978   The governing bankruptcy legislation in the United States today. (Chapter 17)

bar chart   The simplest type of probability distribution; shows only a limited number of outcomes and associated probabilities for a given event. (Chapter 5)

basic EPS   Earnings per share (EPS) calculated without regard to any contingent securities. (Chapter 16)

behavioral finance   A growing body of research that focuses on investor behavior and its impact on investment decisions and stock prices. Advocates are commonly referred to as "behaviorists." (Chapter 7)

benchmarking   A type of *cross-sectional analysis* in which the firm's ratio values are compared to those of a key competitor or group of competitors that it wishes to emulate. (Chapter 2)

beta coefficient (b)   A relative measure of nondiversifiable risk. An *index* of the degree of movement of an asset's return in response to a change in the *market return.* (Chapter 5)

bid price   The highest price offered to purchase a security. (Chapter 1)

bird-in-the-hand argument   The belief, in support of *dividend relevance theory,* that investors see current dividends as less risky than future dividends or capital gains. (Chapter 13)

board of directors   Group elected by the firm's stockholders and typically responsible for developing strategic goals and plans, setting general policy, guiding corporate affairs, approving major expenditures, and hiring/firing, compensating, and monitoring key officers and executives. (Chapter 1)

bond   Long-term debt instrument used by business and government to raise large sums of money, generally from a diverse group of lenders. (Chapter 1)

bond indenture   A legal document that specifies both the rights of the bondholders and the duties of the issuing corporation. (Chapter 6)

book value   The strict accounting value of an asset, calculated by subtracting its accumulated depreciation from its installed cost. (Chapter 8)

book value per share   The amount per share of common stock that would be received if all of the firm's assets were *sold for their exact book (accounting) value* and the proceeds remaining after paying all liabilities (including preferred stock) were divided among the common stockholders. (Chapter 7)

book value weights   Weights that use accounting values to measure the proportion of each type of capital in the firm's financial structure. (Chapter 11)

breakeven analysis   Indicates the level of operations necessary to cover all operating costs and the profitability associated with various levels of sales. (Chapter 12)

breakeven cash inflow   The minimum level of cash inflow necessary for a project to be acceptable, that is, NPV > \$0. (Chapter 10)

break point   The level of *total* new financing at which the cost of one of the financing components rises, thereby causing an upward shift in the *weighted marginal cost of capital (WMCC).* (Chapter 11)

breakup value   The value of a firm measured as the sum of the values of its operating units if each were sold separately. (Chapter 17)

broker market   The securities exchanges on which the two sides of a transaction, the buyer and seller, are brought together to trade securities. (Chapter 1)

business ethics   Standard of conduct or moral judgment that applies to persons engaged in commerce. (Chapter 1)

business risk   The risk to the firm of being unable to cover operating costs. (Chapter 11)

call feature   A feature included in nearly all corporate bond issues that gives the issuer the opportunity to repurchase bonds at a stated *call price* prior to maturity. (Chapter 6)

call option   An option to *purchase* a specified number of shares of a stock (typically 100) on or before a specified future date at a stated price. (Chapter 16)

call premium   The amount by which a bond's *call price* exceeds its par value. (Chapter 6)

call price   The stated price at which a bond may be repurchased, by use of a *call feature*, prior to maturity. (Chapter 6)

capital   The long-term funds of a firm; all items on the right-hand side of the firm's balance sheet, *excluding current liabilities*. (Chapter 7)

capital asset pricing model (CAPM)   The basic theory that links risk and return for all assets; describes the relationship between the required return, r_s, and the nondiversifiable risk of the firm as measured by the beta coefficient, b. (Chapters 5 and 11)

capital budgeting   The process of evaluating and selecting long-term investments that are consistent with the firm's goal of maximizing owner wealth. (Chapter 8)

capital budgeting process   Five distinct but interrelated steps: *proposal generation, review and analysis, decision making, implementation,* and *follow-up*. (Chapter 8)

capital expenditure   An outlay of funds by the firm that is expected to produce benefits over a period of time *greater than* 1 year. (Chapter 8)

capital gain   The amount by which the sale price of an asset exceeds the asset's initial purchase price. (Chapter 1)

capital market   A market that enables suppliers and demanders of *long-term funds* to make transactions. (Chapter 1)

capital rationing   The financial situation in which a firm has only a fixed number of dollars available for capital expenditures, and numerous projects compete for these dollars. (Chapter 8)

capital structure   The mix of long-term debt and equity maintained by the firm. (Chapter 12)

capitalized lease   A *financial (capital) lease* that has the present value of all its payments included as an asset and corresponding liability on the firm's balance sheet, as required by Financial Accounting Standards Board (FASB) Standard No. 13. (Chapter 16)

carrying costs   The variable costs per unit of holding an item in inventory for a specific period of time. (Chapter 14)

cash basis   Recognizes revenues and expenses only with respect to actual inflows and outflows of cash. (Chapter 1)

cash bonuses   Cash paid to management for achieving certain performance goals. (Chapter 1)

cash budget (cash forecast)   A statement of the firm's planned inflows and outflows of cash that is used to estimate its short-term cash requirements. (Chapter 3)

cash concentration   The process used by the firm to bring lockbox and other deposits together into one bank, often called the *concentration bank*. (Chapter 14)

cash conversion cycle (CCC)   The amount of time a firm's resources are tied up; calculated by subtracting the average payment period from the *operating cycle*. (Chapter 14)

cash disbursements   All outlays of cash by the firm during a given financial period. (Chapter 3)

cash discount   A percentage deduction from the purchase price; available to the credit customer who pays its account within a specified time. (Chapter 14)

cash discount period   The number of days after the beginning of the credit period during which the cash discount is available. (Chapter 14)

cash receipts   All of a firm's inflows of cash in a given financial period. (Chapter 3)

Central American Free Trade Agreement (CAFTA)   A trade agreement signed in 2003–2004 by the United States and five Central American countries (Costa Rica, El Salvador, Guatemala, Honduras, and Nicaragua). (Chapter 18)

change in net working capital   The difference between a change in current assets and a change in current liabilities. (Chapter 8)

Chapter 7   The portion of the *Bankruptcy Reform Act of 1978* that details the procedures to be followed when liquidating a failed firm. (Chapter 17)

Chapter 11   The portion of the *Bankruptcy Reform Act of 1978* that outlines the procedures for reorganizing a failed (or failing) firm, whether its petition is filed voluntarily or involuntarily. (Chapter 17)

clearing float The time between deposit of a payment and when spendable funds become available to the firm. (Chapter 14)

clientele effect The argument that a firm attracts shareholders whose preferences for the payment and stability of dividends correspond to the payment pattern and stability of the firm itself. (Chapter 13)

closely owned (stock) All common stock of a firm owned by a small group of investors (such as a family). (Chapter 7)

coefficient of variation (CV) A measure of relative dispersion that is useful in comparing the risks of assets with differing expected returns. (Chapter 5)

collateral trust bonds See Table 6.4. (Chapter 6)

commercial finance companies Lending institutions that make *only* secured loans—both short-term and long-term—to businesses. (Chapter 15)

commercial paper A form of financing consisting of short-term, unsecured promissory notes issued by firms with a high credit standing. (Chapter 15)

commitment fee The fee that is normally charged on a *revolving credit agreement*; it often applies to the average unused balance of the borrower's credit line. (Chapter 15)

common stock The purest and most basic form of corporate ownership. (Chapter 1)

common-size income statement An income statement in which each item is expressed as a percentage of sales. (Chapter 2)

compensating balance A required checking account balance equal to a certain percentage of the amount borrowed from a bank under a line-of-credit or revolving credit agreement. (Chapter 15)

composition A pro rata cash settlement of creditor claims by the debtor firm; a uniform percentage of each dollar owed is paid. (Chapter 17)

compound interest Interest that is earned on a given deposit and has become part of the principal at the end of a specified period. (Chapter 4)

conflicting rankings Conflicts in the ranking given a project by NPV and IRR, resulting from *differences in the magnitude and timing of cash flows*. (Chapter 9)

congeneric merger A merger in which one firm acquires another firm that is *in the same general industry* but neither in the same line of business nor a supplier or customer. (Chapter 17)

conglomerate merger A merger combining firms in *unrelated businesses*. (Chapter 17)

conservative funding strategy A funding strategy under which the firm funds both its seasonal and its permanent requirements with long-term debt. (Chapter 14)

consolidation The combination of two or more firms to form a completely new corporation. (Chapter 17)

constant-growth model A widely cited dividend valuation approach that assumes that dividends will grow at a constant rate, but a rate that is less than the required return. (Chapter 7)

constant-growth valuation (Gordon) model Assumes that the value of a share of stock equals the present value of all future dividends (assumed to grow at a constant rate) that it is expected to provide over an infinite time horizon. (Chapter 11)

constant-payout-ratio dividend policy A dividend policy based on the payment of a certain percentage of earnings to owners in each dividend period. (Chapter 13)

contingent securities Convertibles, warrants, and stock options. Their presence affects the reporting of a firm's earnings per share (EPS). (Chapter 16)

continuous compounding Compounding of interest an infinite number of times per year at intervals of microseconds. (Chapter 4)

continuous probability distribution A probability distribution showing all the possible outcomes and associated probabilities for a given event. (Chapter 5)

controlled disbursing The strategic use of mailing points and bank accounts to lengthen mail float and clearing float, respectively. (Chapter 14)

controller The firm's chief accountant, who is responsible for the firm's accounting activities, such as corporate accounting, tax management, financial accounting, and cost accounting. (Chapter 1)

conventional cash flow pattern An initial outflow followed only by a series of inflows. (Chapter 8)

conversion (or stock) value The value of a convertible security measured in terms of the market price of the common stock into which it can be converted. (Chapter 16)

conversion feature An option that is included as part of a bond or a preferred stock issue and allows its holder to change the security into a stated number of shares of common stock. (Chapters 6 and 16)

conversion feature (preferred stock) A feature of *convertible preferred stock* that allows holders to change each share into a stated number of shares of common stock. (Chapter 7)

conversion price The per-share price that is effectively paid for common stock as the result of conversion of a convertible security. (Chapter 16)

conversion ratio The ratio at which a convertible security can be exchanged for common stock. (Chapter 16)

convertible bond A bond that can be changed into a specified number of shares of common stock. (Chapter 16)

convertible preferred stock   Preferred stock that can be changed into a specified number of shares of common stock. (Chapter 16)

corporate bond   A long-term debt instrument indicating that a corporation has borrowed a certain amount of money and promises to repay it in the future under clearly defined terms. (Chapter 6)

corporate governance   The system used to direct and control a corporation. Defines the rights and responsibilities of key corporate participants, decision-making procedures, and the way in which the firm will set, achieve, and monitor objectives. (Chapter 1)

corporate restructuring   The activities involving expansion or contraction of a firm's operations or changes in its asset or financial (ownership) structure. (Chapter 17)

corporation   An artificial being created by law (often called a "legal entity"). (Chapter 1)

correlation   A statistical measure of the relationship between any two series of numbers representing data of any kind. (Chapter 5)

correlation coefficient   A measure of the degree of correlation between two series. (Chapter 5)

cost of capital   The rate of return that a firm must earn on the projects in which it invests to maintain its market value and attract funds. (Chapter 11)

cost of common stock equity, r_s   The rate at which investors discount the expected dividends of the firm to determine its share value. (Chapter 11)

cost of giving up a cash discount   The implied rate of interest paid to delay payment of an account payable for an additional number of days. (Chapter 15)

cost of long-term debt, r_i   The after-tax cost today of raising long-term funds through borrowing. (Chapter 11)

cost of new asset   The net outflow necessary to acquire a new asset. (Chapter 8)

cost of a new issue of common stock, r_n   The cost of common stock, net of underpricing and associated flotation costs. (Chapter 11)

cost of preferred stock, r_p   The ratio of the preferred stock dividend to the firm's net proceeds from the sale of preferred stock; calculated by dividing the annual dividend, D_p, by the net proceeds from the sale of the preferred stock, N_p. (Chapter 11)

cost of retained earnings, r_r   The same as the cost of an *equivalent fully subscribed issue of additional common stock,* which is equal to the cost of common stock equity, r_s. (Chapter 11)

coupon interest rate   The percentage of a bond's par value that will be paid annually, typically in two equal semiannual payments, as interest. (Chapter 6)

coverage ratios   Ratios that measure the firm's ability to pay certain fixed charges. (Chapter 2)

credit monitoring   The ongoing review of a firm's accounts receivable to determine whether customers are paying according to the stated credit terms. (Chapter 14)

credit period   The number of days after the beginning of the credit period until full payment of the account is due. (Chapter 14)

credit scoring   A credit selection method commonly used with high-volume/small-dollar credit requests; relies on a credit score determined by applying statistically derived weights to a credit applicant's scores on key financial and credit characteristics. (Chapter 14)

credit standards   The firm's minimum requirements for extending credit to a customer. (Chapter 14)

credit terms   The terms of sale for customers who have been extended credit by the firm. (Chapter 14)

creditor control   An arrangement in which the creditor committee replaces the firm's operating management and operates the firm until all claims have been settled. (Chapter 17)

cross-sectional analysis   Comparison of different firms' financial ratios at the same point in time; involves comparing the firm's ratios to those of other firms in its industry or to industry averages. (Chapter 2)

cumulative preferred stock   Preferred stock for which all passed (unpaid) dividends in arrears, along with the current dividend, must be paid before dividends can be paid to common stockholders. (Chapter 7)

current assets   Short-term assets, expected to be converted into cash within 1 year or less. (Chapter 2)

current liabilities   Short-term liabilities, expected to be paid within 1 year or less. (Chapter 2)

current rate (translation) method   Technique used by U.S.-based companies to translate their foreign-currency-denominated assets and liabilities into dollars, for consolidation with the parent company's financial statements, using the exchange rate prevailing at the fiscal year ending date (the current rate). (Chapter 2)

current ratio   A measure of liquidity calculated by dividing the firm's current assets by its current liabilities. (Chapter 2)

current yield   A measure of a bond's cash return for the year; calculated by dividing the bond's annual interest payment by its current price. (Chapter 6)

date of record (dividends)   Set by the firm's directors, the date on which all persons whose names are recorded as stockholders receive a declared dividend at a specified future time. (Chapter 13)

dealer market   The market in which the buyer and seller are not brought together directly but instead have their orders executed by securities dealers that "make markets" in the given security. (Chapter 1)

debentures   See Table 6.4. (Chapter 6)

debt capital   All long-term borrowing incurred by a firm, including bonds. (Chapter 7)

debt ratio   Measures the proportion of total assets financed by the firm's creditors. (Chapter 2)

debtor in possession (DIP)   The term for a firm that files a reorganization petition under Chapter 11 and then develops, if feasible, a reorganization plan. (Chapter 17)

degree of financial leverage (DFL)   The numerical measure of the firm's financial leverage. (Chapter 12)

degree of indebtedness   Measures the amount of debt relative to other significant balance sheet amounts. (Chapter 2)

degree of operating leverage (DOL)   The numerical measure of the firm's operating leverage. (Chapter 12)

degree of total leverage (DTL)   The numerical measure of the firm's total leverage. (Chapter 12)

depository transfer check (DTC)   An unsigned check drawn on one of a firm's bank accounts and deposited in another. (Chapter 14)

depreciable life   Time period over which an asset is depreciated. (Chapter 3)

depreciation   The systematic charging of a portion of the costs of fixed assets against annual revenues over time. (Chapter 3)

derivative security   A security that is neither debt nor equity but derives its value from an underlying asset that is often another security; called "derivatives," for short. (Chapter 16)

diluted EPS   Earnings per share (EPS) calculated under the assumption that *all* contingent securities that would have dilutive effects are converted and exercised and are therefore common stock. (Chapter 16)

dilution of ownership   Occurs when a new stock issue results in each present shareholder having a claim on a *smaller* part of the firm's earnings than previously. (Chapter 7)

direct lease   A lease under which a lessor owns or acquires the assets that are leased to a given lessee. (Chapter 16)

discount   The amount by which a bond sells at a value that is less than its par value. (Chapter 6)

discount loans   Loans on which interest is paid in advance by being deducted from the amount borrowed. (Chapter 15)

discounting cash flows   The process of finding present values; the inverse of compounding interest. (Chapter 4)

diversifiable risk   The portion of an asset's risk that is attributable to firm-specific, random causes; can be eliminated through diversification. Also called *unsystematic risk*. (Chapter 5)

divestiture   The selling of some of a firm's assets for various strategic reasons. (Chapter 17)

dividend irrelevance theory   Miller and Modigliani's theory that in a perfect world, the firm's value is determined solely by the earning power and risk of its assets (investments) and that the manner in which it splits its earnings stream between dividends and internally retained (and reinvested) funds does not affect this value. (Chapter 13)

dividend payout ratio   Indicates the percentage of each dollar earned that is distributed to the owners in the form of cash. It is calculated by dividing the firm's cash dividend per share by its earnings per share. (Chapter 13)

dividend per share (DPS)   The dollar amount of cash distributed during the period on behalf of each outstanding share of common stock. (Chapter 2)

dividend policy   The firm's plan of action to be followed whenever a dividend decision is made. (Chapter 13)

dividend reinvestment plans (DRIPs)   Plans that enable stockholders to use dividends received on the firm's stock to acquire additional shares—even fractional shares—at little or no transaction cost. (Chapter 13)

dividend relevance theory   The theory, advanced by Gordon and Lintner, that there is a direct relationship between a firm's dividend policy and its market value. (Chapter 13)

dividends   Periodic distributions of earnings to the stockholders of a firm. (Chapter 1)

double taxation   Occurs when the already once-taxed earnings of a corporation are distributed as cash dividends to stockholders, who must pay taxes of up to a maximum rate of 15 percent on them. (Chapter 1)

DuPont formula   Multiplies the firm's *net profit margin* by its *total asset turnover* to calculate the firm's *return on total assets (ROA)*. (Chapter 2)

DuPont system of analysis   System used to dissect the firm's financial statements and to assess its financial condition. (Chapter 2)

earnings per share (EPS)   The amount earned during the period on behalf of each outstanding share of common stock, calculated by dividing the period's total earnings available for the firm's common stockholders by the number of shares of common stock outstanding. (Chapter 1)

EBIT–EPS approach   An approach for selecting the capital structure that maximizes earnings per share (EPS) over the expected range of earnings before interest and taxes (EBIT). (Chapter 12)

economic exposure   The risk resulting from the effects of changes in foreign exchange rates on the firm's value. (Chapter 18)

economic order quantity (EOQ) model Inventory management technique for determining an item's optimal order size, which is the size that minimizes the total of its *order costs* and *carrying costs*. (Chapter 14)

economic value added (EVA®) A popular measure used by many firms to determine whether an investment contributes positively to the owners' wealth; calculated as the difference between an investment's *net operating profit after taxes (NOPAT)* and the cost of funds used to finance the investment which is found by multiplying the dollar amount of funds used to finance the investment by the firm's weighted average cost of capital (WACC). (Chapter 11)

effective (true) annual rate (EAR) The annual rate of interest actually paid or earned. (Chapter 4)

effective interest rate In the international context, the rate equal to the nominal rate plus (or minus) any forecast appreciation (or depreciation) of a foreign currency relative to the currency of the MNC parent. (Chapter 18)

efficient market A market that allocates funds to their most productive uses as a result of competition among wealth-maximizing investors that determines and publicizes prices that are believed to be close to their true value; a market with the following characteristics: many small investors, all having the same information and expectations with respect to securities; no restrictions on investment, no taxes, and no transaction costs; and rational investors, who view securities similarly and are risk-averse, preferring higher returns and lower risk. (Chapters 1 and 5)

efficient-market hypothesis Theory describing the behavior of an assumed "perfect" market in which (1) securities are typically in equilibrium, (2) security prices fully reflect all public information available and react swiftly to new information, and, (3) because stocks are fully and fairly priced, investors need not waste time looking for mispriced securities. (Chapter 7)

efficient portfolio A portfolio that maximizes return for a given level of risk or minimizes risk for a given level of return. (Chapter 5)

ending cash The sum of the firm's beginning cash and its net cash flow for the period. (Chapter 3)

enterprise resource planning (ERP) A computerized system that electronically integrates external information about the firm's suppliers and customers with the firm's departmental data so that information on all available resources—human and material—can be instantly obtained in a fashion that eliminates production delays and controls costs. (Chapter 14)

equipment trust certificates See Table 6.4. (Chapter 6)

equity capital The long-term funds provided by the firm's owners, the stockholders. (Chapter 7)

euro A single currency adopted on January 1, 1999, by 12 of the 15 EU nations, who switched to a single set of euro bills and coins on January 1, 2002. (Chapter 18)

Eurobond An *international bond* that is sold primarily in countries other than the country of the currency in which the issue is denominated. (Chapters 6 and 18)

Eurobond market The market in which corporations and governments typically issue bonds denominated in dollars and sell them to investors located outside the United States. (Chapter 1)

Eurocurrency market International equivalent of the domestic money market. (Chapter 1)

Eurocurrency markets The portion of the Euromarket that provides short-term, foreign-currency financing to subsidiaries of MNCs. (Chapter 18)

Euromarket The international financial market that provides for borrowing and lending currencies outside their country of origin. (Chapter 18)

European Open Market The transformation of the European Union into a *single* market at year-end 1992. (Chapter 18)

European Union (EU) A significant economic force currently made up of 15 nations that permit free trade within the union. (Chapter 18)

ex dividend Period, beginning 2 *business days* prior to the date of record, during which a stock is sold without the right to receive the current dividend. (Chapter 13)

excess cash balance The (excess) amount available for investment by the firm if the period's ending cash is greater than the desired minimum cash balance; assumed to be invested in marketable securities. (Chapter 3)

excess earnings accumulation tax The tax the IRS levies on retained earnings above $250,000 when it determines that the firm has accumulated an excess of earnings to allow owners to delay paying ordinary income taxes on dividends received. (Chapter 13)

exchange rate risk The danger that an unexpected change in the exchange rate between the dollar and the currency in which a project's cash flows are denominated will reduce the market value of that project's cash flow; the risk caused by varying exchange rates between two currencies. (Chapters 10 and 18)

exercise (or option) price The price at which holders of warrants can purchase a specified number of shares of common stock. (Chapter 16)

expectations theory The theory that the yield curve reflects investor expectations about future interest rates; an increasing inflation expectation results in an upward-sloping yield curve, and a decreasing inflation expectation results in a downward-sloping yield curve. (Chapter 6)

expected return, $\hat{r}$ The return that is expected to be earned on a given asset each period over an infinite time horizon. (Chapter 7)

expected value of a return ($\bar{r}$)   The most likely return on a given asset. (Chapter 5)

extendible notes   See Table 6.5. (Chapter 6)

extension   An arrangement whereby the firm's creditors receive payment in full, although not immediately. (Chapter 17)

external financing required ("plug" figure)   Under the judgmental approach for developing a pro forma balance sheet, the amount of external financing needed to bring the statement into balance. It can be either a positive or a negative value. (Chapter 3)

external forecast   A sales forecast based on the relationships observed between the firm's sales and certain key external economic indicators. (Chapter 3)

extra dividend   An additional dividend optionally paid by the firm if earnings are higher than normal in a given period. (Chapter 13)

factor   A financial institution that specializes in purchasing accounts receivable from businesses. (Chapter 15)

factoring accounts receivable   The outright sale of accounts receivable at a discount to a *factor* or other financial institution. (Chapter 15)

FASB No. 52   Statement issued by the FASB requiring U.S. multinationals first to convert the financial statement accounts of foreign subsidiaries into the *functional currency* and then to translate the accounts into the parent firm's currency using the *all-current-rate method.* (Chapter 18)

finance   The art and science of managing money. (Chapter 1)

financial (or capital) lease   A *longer-term* lease than an operating lease that is *noncancelable* and obligates the lessee to make payments for the use of an asset over a predefined period of time; the total payments over the term of the lease are *greater* than the lessor's initial cost of the leased asset. (Chapter 16)

Financial Accounting Standards Board (FASB) Standard No. 52   Mandates that U.S.-based companies translate their foreign-currency-denominated assets and liabilities into dollars, for consolidation with the parent company's financial statements. This is done by using the *current rate (translation method).* (Chapter 2)

Financial Accounting Standards Board (FASB)   The accounting profession's rule-setting body, which authorizes *generally accepted accounting principles (GAAP).* (Chapter 2)

financial breakeven point   The level of EBIT necessary to just cover all *fixed financial costs;* the level of EBIT for which EPS = \$0. (Chapter 12)

financial institution   An intermediary that channels the savings of individuals, businesses, and governments into loans or investments. (Chapter 1)

financial leverage multiplier (FLM)   The ratio of the firm's total assets to its common stock equity. (Chapter 2)

financial leverage   The potential use of *fixed financial costs* to magnify the effects of changes in earnings before interest and taxes on the firm's earnings per share. (Chapters 2 and 12)

financial manager   Actively manages the financial affairs of any type of business, whether financial or nonfinancial, private or public, large or small, profit-seeking or not-for-profit. (Chapter 1)

financial markets   Forums in which suppliers of funds and demanders of funds can transact business directly. (Chapter 1)

financial merger   A merger transaction undertaken with the goal of restructuring the acquired company to improve its cash flow and unlock its hidden value. (Chapter 17)

financial planning process   Planning that begins with long-term, or *strategic,* financial plans that in turn guide the formulation of short-term, or *operating,* plans and budgets. (Chapter 3)

financial risk   The risk to the firm of being unable to cover required financial obligations (interest, lease payments, preferred stock dividends). (Chapter 11)

financial services   The part of finance concerned with the design and delivery of advice and financial products to individuals, business, and government. (Chapter 1)

financing flows   Cash flows that result from debt and equity financing transactions; includes incurrence and repayment of debt, cash inflow from the sale of stock, and cash outflows to pay cash dividends or repurchase stock. (Chapter 3)

five C's of credit   The five key dimensions—character, capacity, capital, collateral, and conditions—used by credit analysts to provide a framework for in-depth credit analysis. (Chapter 14)

fixed (or semifixed) relationship   The constant (or relatively constant) relationship of a currency to one of the major currencies, a combination (basket) of major currencies, or some type of international foreign exchange standard. (Chapter 18)

fixed-payment coverage ratio   Measures the firm's ability to meet all fixed-payment obligations. (Chapter 2)

fixed-rate loan   A loan with a rate of interest that is determined at a set increment above the prime rate and at which it remains fixed until maturity. (Chapter 15)

flat yield curve A yield curve that reflects relatively similar borrowing costs for both short- and longer-term loans. (Chapter 6)

float Funds that have been sent by the payer but are not yet usable funds to the payee. (Chapter 14)

floating inventory lien A secured short-term loan against inventory under which the lender's claim is on the borrower's inventory in general. (Chapter 15)

floating relationship The fluctuating relationship of the values of two currencies with respect to each other. (Chapter 18)

floating-rate bonds See Table 6.5. (Chapter 6)

floating-rate loan A loan with a rate of interest initially set at an increment above the prime rate and allowed to "float," or vary, above prime *as the prime rate varies* until maturity. (Chapter 15)

flotation costs The total costs of issuing and selling a security. (Chapter 11)

foreign bond Bond that is issued by a foreign corporation or government and is denominated in the investor's home currency and sold in the investor's home market. (Chapters 1, 6, and 18)

foreign direct investment (FDI) The transfer by a multinational firm of capital, managerial, and technical assets from its home country to a host country. (Chapters 8 and 18)

foreign exchange manager The manager responsible for monitoring and managing the firm's exposure to loss from currency fluctuations. (Chapter 1)

foreign exchange rate The value of two currencies with respect to each other. (Chapter 18)

forward exchange rate The rate of exchange between two currencies at some specified future date. (Chapter 18)

free cash flow (FCF) The amount of cash flow available to investors (creditors and owners) after the firm has met all operating needs and paid for investments in net fixed assets and net current assets. (Chapter 3)

free cash flow valuation model A model that determines the value of an entire company as the present value of its expected free cash flows discounted at the firm's *weighted average cost of capital*, which is its expected average future cost of funds over the long run. (Chapter 7)

friendly merger A merger transaction endorsed by the target firm's management, approved by its stockholders, and easily consummated. (Chapter 17)

functional currency The currency of the host country in which a subsidiary primarily generates and expends cash and in which its accounts are maintained. (Chapter 18)

future value The value at a given future date of a present amount placed on deposit today and earning interest at a specified rate. Found by applying *compound interest* over a specified period of time. (Chapter 4)

future value interest factor The multiplier used to calculate, at a specified interest rate, the future value of a present amount as of a given time. (Chapter 4)

future value interest factor for an ordinary annuity The multiplier used to calculate the future value of an *ordinary annuity* at a specified interest rate over a given period of time. (Chapter 4)

General Agreement on Tariffs and Trade (GATT) A treaty that has governed world trade throughout most of the postwar era; it extends free-trading rules to broad areas of economic activity and is policed by the *World Trade Organization (WTO)*. (Chapter 18)

generally accepted accounting principles (GAAP) The practice and procedure guidelines used to prepare and maintain financial records and reports; authorized by the *Financial Accounting Standards Board (FASB)*. (Chapter 2)

golden parachutes Provisions in the employment contracts of key executives that provide them with sizable compensation if the firm is taken over; deters hostile takeovers to the extent that the cash outflows required are large enough to make the takeover unattractive. (Chapter 17)

Gordon model A common name for the *constant-growth model* that is widely cited in dividend valuation. (Chapter 7)

greenmail A takeover defense under which a target firm repurchases, through private negotiation, a large block of stock at a premium from one or more shareholders to end a hostile takeover attempt by those shareholders. (Chapter 17)

gross profit margin Measures the percentage of each sales dollar remaining after the firm has paid for its goods. (Chapter 2)

hedging Offsetting or protecting against the risk of adverse price movements. (Chapter 16)

hedging strategies Techniques used to offset or protect against risk; in the international context, these include borrowing or lending in different currencies; undertaking contracts in the forward, futures, and/or options markets; and swapping assets/liabilities with other parties. (Chapter 18)

historical weights Either book or market value weights based on *actual* capital structure proportions. (Chapter 11)

holding company A corporation that has voting control of one or more other corporations. (Chapter 17)

horizontal merger   A merger of two firms *in the same line of business*. (Chapter 17)

hostile merger   A merger transaction that the target firm's management does not support, forcing the acquiring company to try to gain control of the firm by buying shares in the marketplace. (Chapter 17)

hybrid security   A form of debt or equity financing that possesses characteristics of *both* debt and equity financing. (Chapter 16)

implied price of a warrant   The price effectively paid for each warrant attached to a bond. (Chapter 16)

incentive plans   Management compensation plans that tend to tie management compensation to share price; most popular incentive plan involves the grant of *stock options*. (Chapter 1)

income bonds   See Table 6.4. (Chapter 6)

income statement   Provides a financial summary of the firm's operating results during a specified period. (Chapter 2)

incremental cash flows   The *additional* cash flows—outflows or inflows—expected to result from a proposed capital expenditure. (Chapter 8)

independent projects   Projects whose cash flows are unrelated or independent of one another; the acceptance of one *does not eliminate* the others from further consideration. (Chapter 8)

individual investors   Investors who buy relatively small quantities of shares in order to meet personal investment goals. (Chapter 1)

informational content   The information provided by the dividends of a firm with respect to future earnings, which causes owners to bid up or down the price of the firm's stock. (Chapter 13)

initial investment   The relevant cash outflow for a proposed project at time zero. (Chapter 8)

initial public offering (IPO)   The first public sale of a firm's stock. (Chapter 7)

installation costs   Any added costs that are necessary to place an asset into operation. (Chapter 8)

installed cost of new asset   The cost of *a new asset* plus its *installation costs*; equals the asset's depreciable value. (Chapter 8)

institutional investors   Investment professionals, such as insurance companies, mutual funds, and pension funds, that are paid to manage other people's money and that trade large quantities of securities. (Chapter 1)

interest rate   The compensation paid by the borrower of funds to the lender; from the borrower's point of view, the cost of borrowing funds. (Chapter 6)

interest rate risk   The chance that interest rates will change and thereby change the required return and bond value. Rising rates, which result in decreasing bond values, are of greatest concern. (Chapter 6)

intermediate cash inflows   Cash inflows received prior to the termination of a project. (Chapter 9)

internal forecast   A sales forecast based on a buildup, or consensus, of sales forecasts through the firm's own sales channels. (Chapter 3)

internal rate of return (IRR)   A sophisticated capital budgeting technique; the discount rate that equates the NPV of an investment opportunity with $0 (because the present value of cash inflows equals the initial investment); it is the compound annual rate of return that the firm will earn if it invests in the project and receives the given cash inflows. (Chapter 9)

internal rate of return approach   An approach to capital rationing that involves graphing project IRRs in descending order against the total dollar investment to determine the group of acceptable projects. (Chapter 10)

international bond   A bond that is initially sold outside the country of the borrower and is often distributed in several countries. (Chapter 18)

international equity market   A market that allows corporations to sell blocks of shares to investors in a number of different countries simultaneously. (Chapter 1)

international stock market   A market with uniform rules and regulations governing major stock exchanges. MNCs would benefit greatly from such a market that is yet to evolve. (Chapter 18)

inventory turnover   Measures the activity, or liquidity, of a firm's inventory. (Chapter 2)

inverted yield curve   A *downward-sloping* yield curve that indicates generally cheaper long-term borrowing costs than short-term borrowing costs. (Chapter 6)

investment bankers   Financial intermediaries who, in addition to their role in selling new security issues, can be hired by acquirers in mergers to find suitable target companies and assist in negotiations. (Chapters 7 and 17)

investment flows   Cash flows associated with purchase and sale of both fixed assets and equity investments in other firms. (Chapter 3)

investment opportunities schedule (IOS)   A ranking of investment possibilities from best (highest return) to worst (lowest return); the graph that plots project IRRs in descending order against the total dollar investment. (Chapters 10 and 11)

involuntary reorganization   A petition initiated by an outside party, usually a creditor, for the reorganization and payment of creditors of a failed firm. (Chapter 17)

issued shares   The number of shares of common stock that have been put into circulation; the sum of outstanding shares and treasury stock. (Chapter 7)

joint venture   A partnership under which the participants have contractually agreed to contribute specified amounts of money and expertise in exchange for stated proportions of ownership and profit. (Chapter 18)

judgmental approach   A simplified approach for preparing the pro forma balance sheet under which the values of certain balance sheet accounts are estimated, some as a percentage of sales and others by management assumption, and the firm's external financing is used as a balancing, or "plug," figure. (Chapter 3)

junk bonds   See Table 6.5. (Chapter 6)

just-in-time (JIT) system   Inventory management technique that minimizes inventory investment by having materials arrive at exactly the time they are needed for production. (Chapter 14)

lease-versus-purchase (lease-versus-buy) decision   The decision facing firms needing to acquire new fixed assets: whether to lease the assets or to purchase them, using borrowed funds or available liquid resources. (Chapter 16)

leasing   The process by which a firm can obtain the use of certain fixed assets for which it must make a series of contractual, periodic, tax-deductible payments. (Chapter 16)

lessee   The receiver of the services of the assets under a lease contract. (Chapter 16)

lessor   The owner of assets that are being leased. (Chapter 16)

letter of credit   A letter written by a company's bank to the company's foreign supplier, stating that the bank guarantees payment of an invoiced amount if all the underlying agreements are met. (Chapter 15)

letter to stockholders   Typically, the first element of the annual stockholders' report and the primary communication from management. (Chapter 2)

leverage   Results from the use of fixed-cost assets or funds to magnify returns to the firm's owners. (Chapter 12)

leveraged buyout (LBO)   An acquisition technique involving the use of a large amount of debt to purchase a firm; an example of a *financial merger*. (Chapter 17)

leveraged lease   A lease under which the lessor acts as an equity participant, supplying only about 20 percent of the cost of the asset, while a lender supplies the balance. (Chapter 16)

leveraged recapitalization   A takeover defense in which the target firm pays a large debt-financed cash dividend, increasing the firm's financial leverage and thereby deterring the takeover attempt. (Chapter 17)

lien   A publicly disclosed legal claim on collateral. (Chapter 15)

limited liability corporation (LLC)   See Table 1.2. (Chapter 1)

limited liability partnership (LLP)   See Table 1.2. (Chapter 1)

limited partnership (LP)   See Table 1.2. (Chapter 1)

line of credit   An agreement between a commercial bank and a business specifying the amount of unsecured short-term borrowing the bank will make available to the firm over a given period of time. (Chapter 15)

liquidation value per share   The *actual amount* per share of common stock that would be received if all of the firm's assets were *sold for their market value*, liabilities (including preferred stock) were paid, and any remaining money were divided among the common stockholders. (Chapter 7)

liquidity   A firm's ability to satisfy its short-term obligations *as they come due.* (Chapter 2)

liquidity preferences   General preferences of investors for shorter-term securities. (Chapter 6)

liquidity preference theory   Theory suggesting that for any given issuer, long-term interest rates tend to be higher than short-term rates because (1) lower liquidity and higher responsiveness to general interest rate movements of longer-term securities exists and (2) borrower willingness to pay a higher rate for long-term financing causes the yield curve to be upward-sloping. (Chapter 6)

loan amortization   The determination of the equal periodic loan payments necessary to provide a lender with a specified interest return and to repay the loan principal over a specified period. (Chapter 4)

loan amortization schedule   A schedule of equal payments to repay a loan. It shows the allocation of each loan payment to interest and principal. (Chapter 4)

lockbox system   A collection procedure in which customers mail payments to a post office box that is emptied regularly by the firm's bank, who processes the payments and deposits them in the firm's account. This system speeds up collection time by reducing processing time as well as mail and clearing time. (Chapter 14)

long-term debt   Debts for which payment is not due in the current year. (Chapter 2)

long-term (strategic) financial plans   Lay out a company's planned financial actions and the anticipated impact of those actions over periods ranging from 2 to 10 years. (Chapter 3)

low-regular-and-extra dividend policy   A dividend policy based on paying a low regular dividend, supplemented by an additional dividend when earnings are higher than normal in a given period. (Chapter 13)

macro political risk   The subjection of *all* foreign firms to *political risk* (takeover) by a host country because of political change, revolution, or the adoption of new policies. (Chapter 18)

mail float   The time delay between when payment is placed in the mail and when it is received. (Chapter 14)

maintenance clauses   Provisions normally included in an operating lease that require the lessor to maintain the assets and to make insurance and tax payments. (Chapter 16)

managerial finance   Concerns the duties of the financial manager in the business firm. (Chapter 1)

manufacturing resource planning II (MRP II)   A sophisticated computerized system that integrates data from numerous areas such as finance, accounting, marketing, engineering, and manufacturing and generates production plans as well as numerous financial and management reports. (Chapter 14)

marginal cost-benefit analysis   Economic principle that states that financial decisions should be made and actions taken only when the added benefits exceed the added costs. (Chapter 1)

marginal tax rate   The rate at which *additional income* is taxed. (Chapter 1)

market/book (M/B) ratio   Provides an assessment of how investors view the firm's performance. Firms expected to earn high returns relative to their risk typically sell at higher M/B multiples. (Chapter 2)

market makers   Securities dealers who "make markets" by offering to buy or sell certain securities at stated prices. (Chapter 1)

market premium   The amount by which the market value exceeds the straight or conversion value of a convertible security. (Chapter 16)

market ratios   Relate a firm's market value, as measured by its current share price, to certain accounting values. (Chapter 2)

market return   The return on the market portfolio of all traded securities. (Chapter 5)

market segmentation theory   Theory suggesting that the market for loans is segmented on the basis of maturity and that the supply of and demand for loans within each segment determine its prevailing interest rate; the slope of the yield curve is determined by the general relationship between the prevailing rates in each segment. (Chapter 6)

market value weights   Weights that use market values to measure the proportion of each type of capital in the firm's financial structure. (Chapter 11)

marketable securities   Short-term debt instruments, such as U.S. Treasury bills, commercial paper, and negotiable certificates of deposit issued by government, business, and financial institutions, respectively. (Chapter 1)

materials requirement planning (MRP) system   Applies EOQ concepts to determine what materials to order and when to order them; simulates each product's bill of materials, inventory status, and manufacturing process. (Chapter 14)

Mercosur Group   A major South American trading bloc that includes countries that account for more than half of total Latin American GDP. (Chapter 18)

merger   The combination of two or more firms, in which the resulting firm maintains the identity of one of the firms, usually the larger. (Chapter 17)

micro political risk   The subjection of an individual firm, a specific industry, or companies from a particular foreign country to *political risk* (takeover) by a host country. (Chapter 18)

mixed stream   A stream of unequal periodic cash flows that reflect no particular pattern. (Chapter 4)

modified accelerated cost recovery system (MACRS)   System used to determine the depreciation of assets for tax purposes. (Chapter 3)

modified DuPont formula   Relates the firm's *return on total assets (ROA)* to its *return on common equity (ROE)* using the *financial leverage multiplier (FLM)*. (Chapter 2)

monetary union   The official melding of the national currencies of the EU nations into one currency, the *euro*, on January 1, 2002. (Chapter 18)

money market   A financial relationship created between suppliers and demanders of *short-term funds*. (Chapter 1)

mortgage bonds   See Table 6.4. (Chapter 6)

multinational companies (MNCs)   Firms that have international assets and operations in foreign markets and draw part of their total revenue and profits from such markets. (Chapter 18)

multiple IRRs   More than one IRR resulting from a capital budgeting project with a *nonconventional cash flow pattern*; the maximum number of IRRs for a project is equal to the number of sign changes in its cash flows. (Chapter 9)

mutually exclusive projects   Projects that compete with one another, so that the acceptance of one *eliminates* from further consideration all other projects that serve a similar function. (Chapter 8)

Nasdaq Market   An all-electronic trading platform used to execute securities trades. (Chapter 1)

national entry control systems   Comprehensive rules, regulations, and incentives introduced by host governments to regulate inflows of *foreign direct investments* from MNCs and at the same time extract more benefits from their presence. (Chapter 18)

negatively correlated   Describes two series that move in opposite directions. (Chapter 5)

net cash flow   The mathematical difference between the firm's cash receipts and its cash disbursements in each period. (Chapter 3)

net operating profits after taxes (NOPAT)   A firm's earnings before interest and after taxes, EBIT $\times$ $(1 - T)$. (Chapter 3)

net present value (NPV)   A sophisticated capital budgeting technique; found by subtracting a project's initial investment from the present value of its cash inflows discounted at a rate equal to the firm's cost of capital. (Chapter 9)

net present value approach   An approach to capital rationing that is based on the use of present values to determine the group of projects that will maximize owners' wealth. (Chapter 10)

net present value profile   Graph that depicts a project's NPV for various discount rates. (Chapter 9)

net proceeds   Funds actually received from the sale of a security. (Chapter 11)

net profit margin   Measures the percentage of each sales dollar remaining after all costs and expenses, *including* interest, taxes, and preferred stock dividends, have been deducted. (Chapter 2)

net working capital   The amount by which a firm's current assets exceed its current liabilities; can be *positive* or *negative*. (Chapters 8 and 14)

nominal (stated) annual rate   Contractual annual rate of interest charged by a lender or promised by a borrower. (Chapter 4)

nominal interest rate   In the international context, the stated interest rate charged on financing when only the MNC parent's currency is involved. (Chapter 18)

nominal rate of interest   The actual rate of interest charged by the supplier of funds and paid by the demander. (Chapter 6)

noncash charge   An expense that is deducted on the income statement but does not involve the actual outlay of cash during the period; includes depreciation, amortization, and depletion. (Chapter 3)

nonconventional cash flow pattern   An initial outflow followed by a series of inflows *and* outflows. (Chapter 8)

noncumulative preferred stock   Preferred stock for which passed (unpaid) dividends do not accumulate. (Chapter 7)

nondiversifiable risk   The relevant portion of an asset's risk attributable to market factors that affect all firms; cannot be eliminated through diversification. Also called *systematic risk*. (Chapter 5)

nonnotification basis   The basis on which a borrower, having pledged an account receivable, continues to collect the account payments without notifying the account customer. (Chapter 15)

nonrecourse basis   The basis on which accounts receivable are sold to a factor with the understanding that the factor accepts all credit risks on the purchased accounts. (Chapter 15)

nonvoting common stock   Common stock that carries no voting rights; issued when the firm wishes to raise capital through the sale of common stock but does not want to give up its voting control. (Chapter 7)

no-par preferred stock   Preferred stock with no stated face value but with a stated annual dollar dividend. (Chapter 7)

normal probability distribution   A symmetrical probability distribution whose shape resembles a "bell-shaped" curve. (Chapter 5)

normal yield curve   An *upward-sloping* yield curve that indicates generally cheaper short-term borrowing costs than long-term borrowing costs. (Chapter 6)

North American Free Trade Agreement (NAFTA)   The treaty establishing free trade and open markets between Canada, Mexico, and the United States. (Chapter 18)

notes to the financial statements   Footnotes detailing information on the accounting policies, procedures, calculations, and transactions underlying entries in the financial statements. (Chapter 2)

notification basis   The basis on which an account customer whose account has been pledged (or factored) is notified to remit payment directly to the lender (or factor). (Chapter 15)

offshore centers   Certain cities or states (including London, Singapore, Bahrain, Nassau, Hong Kong, and Luxembourg) that have achieved prominence as major centers for Euromarket business. (Chapter 18)

operating breakeven point   The level of sales necessary to cover all *operating costs;* the point at which EBIT = \$0. (Chapter 12)

operating cash flow (OCF)   The cash flow a firm generates from its normal operations; calculated as EBIT − taxes + depreciation. (Chapter 3)

operating cash inflows   The incremental after-tax cash inflows resulting from implementation of a project during its life. (Chapter 8)

operating cycle (OC)   The time from the beginning of the production process to the collection of cash from the sale of the finished product. (Chapter 14)

operating expenditure   An outlay of funds by the firm resulting in benefits received *within* 1 year. (Chapter 8)

operating flows   Cash flows directly related to sale and production of the firm's products and services. (Chapter 3)

operating lease   A *cancelable* contractual arrangement whereby the lessee agrees to make periodic payments to the lessor, often for 5 or fewer years, to obtain an asset's services; generally, the total payments over the term of the lease are *less* than the lessor's initial cost of the leased asset. (Chapter 16)

operating leverage   The potential use of *fixed operating costs* to magnify the effects of changes in sales on the firm's earnings before interest and taxes. (Chapter 12)

operating profit margin   Measures the percentage of each sales dollar remaining after all costs and expenses *other than* interest, taxes, and preferred stock dividends are deducted; the "pure profits" earned on each sales dollar. (Chapter 2)

operating unit   A part of a business, such as a plant, division, product line, or subsidiary, that contributes to the actual operations of the firm. (Chapter 17)

operating-change restrictions   Contractual restrictions that a bank may impose on a firm's financial condition or operations as part of a line-of-credit agreement. (Chapter 15)

opportunity costs   Cash flows that could be realized from the best alternative use of an owned asset. (Chapter 8)

optimal capital structure   The capital structure at which the weighted average cost of capital is minimized, thereby maximizing the firm's value. (Chapter 12)

option   An instrument that provides its holder with an opportunity to purchase or sell a specified asset at a stated price on or before a set *expiration date*. (Chapter 16)

order costs   The fixed clerical costs of placing and receiving an inventory order. (Chapter 14)

ordinary annuity   An annuity for which the cash flow occurs at the *end* of each period. (Chapter 4)

ordinary income   Income earned through the sale of a firm's goods or services. (Chapter 1)

outstanding shares   The number of shares of common stock held by the public. (Chapter 7)

overhanging issue   A convertible security that cannot be forced into conversion by using the call feature. (Chapter 16)

over-the-counter (OTC) market   Market where smaller, unlisted securities are traded. (Chapter 1)

paid-in capital in excess of par   The amount of proceeds in excess of the par value received from the original sale of common stock. (Chapter 2)

partnership   A business owned by two or more people and operated for profit. (Chapter 1)

par value (stock)   A relatively useless value for a stock established for legal purposes in the firm's corporate charter. (Chapter 7)

par-value preferred stock   Preferred stock with a stated face value that is used with the specified dividend percentage to determine the annual dollar dividend. (Chapter 7)

payback period   The amount of time required for a firm to recover its initial investment in a project, as calculated from *cash inflows*. (Chapter 9)

payment date   Set by the firm's directors, the actual date on which the firm mails the dividend payment to the holders of record. (Chapter 13)

pecking order   A hierarchy of financing that begins with retained earnings, which is followed by debt financing and finally external equity financing. (Chapter 12)

percentage advance   The percent of the book value of the collateral that constitutes the principal of a secured loan. (Chapter 15)

percent-of-sales method   A simple method for developing the pro forma income statement; it forecasts sales and then expresses the various income statement items as percentages of projected sales. (Chapter 3)

perfectly negatively correlated   Describes two *negatively correlated* series that have a *correlation coefficient* of −1. (Chapter 5)

perfectly positively correlated   Describes two *positively correlated* series that have a *correlation coefficient* of +1. (Chapter 5)

performance plans   Plans that tie management compensation to measures such as EPS, growth in EPS, and other ratios of return. *Performance shares* and/or *cash bonuses* are used as compensation under these plans. (Chapter 1)

performance shares   Shares of stock given to management for meeting stated performance goals. (Chapter 1)

permanent funding requirement   A constant investment in operating assets resulting from constant sales over time. (Chapter 14)

perpetuity   An annuity with an infinite life, providing continual annual cash flow. (Chapter 4)

pledge of accounts receivable   The use of a firm's accounts receivable as security, or collateral, to obtain a short-term loan. (Chapter 15)

poison pill A takeover defense in which a firm issues securities that give their holders certain rights that become effective when a takeover is attempted; these rights make the target firm less desirable to a hostile acquirer. (Chapter 17)

political risk Risk that arises from the possibility that a host government will take actions harmful to foreign investors or that political turmoil in a country will endanger investments there. (Chapters 5 and 18)

portfolio A collection, or group, of assets. (Chapter 5)

positively correlated Describes two series that move in the same direction. (Chapter 5)

preemptive right Allows common stockholders to maintain their *proportionate* ownership in the corporation when new shares are issued. (Chapter 7)

preferred stock A special form of ownership having a fixed periodic dividend that must be paid prior to payment of any common stock dividends. (Chapter 1)

premium The amount by which a bond sells at a value that is greater than its par value. (Chapter 6)

present value The current dollar value of a future amount—the amount of money that would have to be invested today at a given interest rate over a specified period to equal the future amount. (Chapter 4)

present value interest factor The multiplier used to calculate, at a specified discount rate, the present value of an amount to be received in a future period. (Chapter 4)

present value interest factor for an ordinary annuity The multiplier used to calculate the present value of an *ordinary annuity* at a specified discount rate over a given period of time. (Chapters 4 and 11)

president or chief executive officer (CEO) Corporate official responsible for managing the firm's day-to-day operations and carrying out the policies established by the board of directors. (Chapter 1)

price/earnings multiple approach A popular technique used to estimate the firm's share value; calculated by multiplying the firm's expected earnings per share (EPS) by the average price/earnings (P/E) ratio for the industry. (Chapter 7)

price/earnings (P/E) ratio Measures the amount that investors are willing to pay for each dollar of a firm's earnings; the higher the P/E ratio, the greater is investor confidence. (Chapter 2)

primary market Financial market in which securities are initially issued; the only market in which the issuer is directly involved in the transaction. (Chapter 1)

prime rate of interest (prime rate) The lowest rate of interest charged by leading banks on business loans to their most important business borrowers. (Chapter 15)

principal The amount of money on which interest is paid. (Chapter 4)

private placement The sale of a new security issue, typically bonds or preferred stock, directly to an investor or group of investors. (Chapter 1)

privately owned (stock) All common stock of a firm owned by a single individual. (Chapter 7)

pro forma statements Projected, or forecast, income statements and balance sheets. (Chapter 3)

probability The *chance* that a given outcome will occur. (Chapter 5)

probability distribution A model that relates probabilities to the associated outcomes. (Chapter 5)

proceeds from sale of old asset The cash inflows, net of any *removal* or *cleanup costs,* resulting from the sale of an existing asset. (Chapter 8)

processing float The time between receipt of a payment and its deposit into the firm's account. (Chapter 14)

profitability The relationship between revenues and costs generated by using the firm's assets—both current and fixed—in productive activities. (Chapter 14)

prospectus A portion of a security registration statement that describes the key aspects of the issue, the issuer, and its management and financial position. (Chapter 7)

proxy battle The attempt by a nonmanagement group to gain control of the management of a firm by soliciting a sufficient number of proxy votes. (Chapter 7)

proxy statement A statement giving the votes of a stockholder to another party. (Chapter 7)

Public Company Accounting Oversight Board (PCAOB) A not-for-profit corporation established by the *Sarbanes-Oxley Act of 2002* to protect the interests of investors and further the public interest in the preparation of informative, fair, and independent audit reports. (Chapter 2)

public offering The nonexclusive sale of either bonds or stocks to the general public. (Chapter 1)

publicly owned (stock) Common stock of a firm owned by a broad group of unrelated individual or institutional investors. (Chapter 7)

purchase options Provisions frequently included in both operating and financial leases that allow the lessee to purchase the leased asset at maturity, typically for a pre-specified price. (Chapter 16)

put option An option to *sell* a specified number of shares of a stock (typically 100) on or before a specified future date at a stated price. (Chapter 16)

putable bonds See Table 6.5. (Chapter 6)

pyramiding An arrangement among holding companies wherein one holding company controls other holding companies, thereby causing an even greater magnification of earnings and losses. (Chapter 17)

quarterly compounding   Compounding of interest over four periods within the year. (Chapter 4)

quick (acid-test) ratio   A measure of liquidity calculated by dividing the firm's current assets minus inventory by its current liabilities. (Chapter 2)

range   A measure of an asset's risk, which is found by subtracting the pessimistic (worst) outcome from the optimistic (best) outcome. (Chapter 5)

ranking approach   The ranking of capital expenditure projects on the basis of some predetermined measure, such as the rate of return. (Chapter 8)

ratio analysis   Involves methods of calculating and interpreting financial ratios to analyze and monitor the firm's performance. (Chapter 2)

ratio of exchange   The ratio of the amount *paid* per share of the target company to the market price per share of the acquiring firm. (Chapter 17)

ratio of exchange in market price   Indicates the market price per share of the acquiring firm *paid* for each dollar of market price per share of the target firm. (Chapter 17)

real options   Opportunities that are embedded in capital projects that enable managers to alter their cash flows and risk in a way that affects project acceptability (NPV). Also called *strategic options*. (Chapter 10)

real rate of interest   The rate that creates an equilibrium between the supply of savings and the demand for investment funds in a perfect world, without inflation, where funds suppliers and demanders are indifferent to the term of loans or investments and have no liquidity preference, and where all outcomes are certain. (Chapter 6)

recapitalization   The reorganization procedure under which a failed firm's debts are generally exchanged for equity or the maturities of existing debts are extended. (Chapter 17)

recaptured depreciation   The portion of an asset's sale price that is above its book value and below its initial purchase price. (Chapter 8)

recovery period   The appropriate depreciable life of a particular asset as determined by MACRS. (Chapter 3)

red herring   A preliminary prospectus made available to prospective investors during the waiting period between the registration statement's filing with the SEC and its approval. (Chapter 7)

regular dividend policy   A dividend policy based on the payment of a fixed-dollar dividend in each period. (Chapter 13)

relevant cash flows   The *incremental cash outflow (investment) and resulting subsequent inflows* associated with a proposed capital expenditure. (Chapter 8)

renewal options   Provisions especially common in operating leases that grant the lessee the right to re-lease assets at the expiration of the lease. (Chapter 16)

reorder point   The point at which to reorder inventory, expressed as days of lead time × daily usage. (Chapter 14)

required return   The cost of funds obtained by selling an ownership interest; it reflects the funds supplier's level of expected return. (Chapter 6)

required total financing   Amount of funds needed by the firm if the ending cash for the period is less than the desired minimum cash balance; typically represented by notes payable. (Chapter 3)

residual theory of dividends   A school of thought that suggests that the dividend paid by a firm should be viewed as a *residual*—the amount left over after all acceptable investment opportunities have been undertaken. (Chapter 13)

restrictive covenants   Provisions in a *bond indenture* that place operating and financial constraints on the borrower. (Chapter 6)

retained earnings   The cumulative total of all earnings, net of dividends, that have been retained and reinvested in the firm since its inception; earnings not distributed to owners as dividends—a form of *internal* financing. (Chapters 2 and 13)

return   The total gain or loss experienced on an investment over a given period of time; calculated by dividing the asset's cash distributions during the period, plus change in value, by its beginning-of-period investment value. (Chapter 5)

return on common equity (ROE)   Measures the return earned on the common stockholders' investment in the firm. (Chapter 2)

return on total assets (ROA)   Measures the overall effectiveness of management in generating profits with its available assets; also called the *return on investment (ROI)*. (Chapter 2)

reverse stock split   A method used to raise the market price of a firm's stock by exchanging a certain number of outstanding shares for one new share. (Chapter 13)

revolving credit agreement   A line of credit *guaranteed* to a borrower by a commercial bank regardless of the scarcity of money. (Chapter 15)

rights   Financial instruments that permit stockholders to purchase additional shares at a price below the market price, in direct proportion to their number of owned shares. (Chapter 7)

risk   The chance of financial loss or, more formally, the *variability of returns associated with a given asset*. (Chapters 1 and 5)

risk (in capital budgeting) The chance that a project will prove unacceptable or, more formally, the degree of variability of cash flows. (Chapter 10)

risk (of technical insolvency) The probability that a firm will be unable to pay its bills as they come due. (Chapter 14)

risk-adjusted discount rate (RADR) The rate of return that must be earned on a given project to compensate the firm's owners adequately—that is, to maintain or improve the firm's share price. (Chapter 10)

risk-averse The attitude toward risk in which an increased return would be required for an increase in risk. (Chapters 1 and 5)

risk-free rate of return, R_F The required return on a *risk-free asset,* typically a 3-month *U.S. Treasury bill.* (Chapter 5)

risk-indifferent The attitude toward risk in which no change in return would be required for an increase in risk. (Chapter 5)

risk-seeking The attitude toward risk in which a decreased return would be accepted for an increase in risk. (Chapter 5)

S corporation (S corp) See Table 1.2. (Chapter 1)

safety stock Extra inventory that is held to prevent stockouts of important items. (Chapter 14)

sale–leaseback arrangement A lease under which the lessee sells an asset for cash to a prospective lessor and then *leases back* the same asset, making fixed periodic payments for its use. (Chapter 16)

sales forecast The prediction of the firm's sales over a given period, based on external and/or internal data; used as the key input to the short-term financial planning process. (Chapter 3)

Sarbanes-Oxley Act of 2002 (SOX) An act aimed at eliminating corporate disclosure and conflict of interest. Contains provisions about corporate financial disclosures and the relationships among corporations, analysts, auditors, attorneys, directors, officers, and shareholders. (Chapter 1)

scenario analysis A behavioral approach that evaluates the impact on the firm's return of simultaneous changes in a number of variables. (Chapter 5)

seasonal funding requirement An investment in operating assets that varies over time as a result of cyclic sales. (Chapter 14)

secondary market Financial market in which preowned securities (those that are not new issues) are traded. (Chapter 1)

secured creditors Creditors who have specific assets pledged as collateral and, in liquidation of the failed firm, receive proceeds from the sale of those assets. (Chapter 17)

secured short-term financing Short-term financing (loan) that has specific assets pledged as collateral. (Chapter 15)

Securities and Exchange Commission (SEC) The federal regulatory body that governs the sale and listing of securities. (Chapter 2)

securities exchanges Organizations that provide the marketplace in which firms can raise funds through the sale of new securities and purchasers can resell securities. (Chapter 1)

security agreement The agreement between the borrower and the lender that specifies the collateral held against a secured loan. (Chapter 15)

security market line (SML) The depiction of the *capital asset pricing model* (*CAPM*) as a graph that reflects the required return in the marketplace for each level of nondiversifiable risk (beta). (Chapter 5)

selling group A large number of brokerage firms that join the originating investment banker(s); each accepts responsibility for selling a certain portion of a new security issue on a commission basis. (Chapter 7)

semiannual compounding Compounding of interest over two periods within the year. (Chapter 4)

shark repellents Antitakeover amendments to a corporate charter that constrain the firm's ability to transfer managerial control of the firm as a result of a merger. (Chapter 17)

short-term (operating) financial plans Specify short-term financial actions and the anticipated impact of those actions. (Chapter 3)

short-term financial management Management of current assets and current liabilities. (Chapter 14)

short-term, self-liquidating loan An unsecured short-term loan in which the use to which the borrowed money is put provides the mechanism through which the loan is repaid. (Chapter 15)

signal A financing action by management that is believed to reflect its view of the firm's stock value; generally, debt financing is viewed as a *positive signal* that management believes the stock is "undervalued," and a stock issue is viewed as a *negative signal* that management believes the stock is "overvalued." (Chapter 12)

simulation A statistics-based behavioral approach that applies predetermined probability distributions and random numbers to estimate risky outcomes. (Chapter 10)

single-payment note A short-term, one-time loan made to a borrower who needs funds for a specific purpose for a short period. (Chapter 15)

sinking-fund requirement   A restrictive provision often included in a bond indenture, providing for the systematic retirement of bonds prior to their maturity. (Chapter 6)

small (ordinary) stock dividend   A stock dividend representing less than 20 to 25 percent of the common stock outstanding when the dividend is declared. (Chapter 13)

sole proprietorship   A business owned by one person and operated for his or her own profit. (Chapter 1)

spin-off   A form of divestiture in which an operating unit becomes an independent company through the issuance of shares in it, on a pro rata basis, to the parent company's shareholders. (Chapter 17)

spontaneous liabilities   Financing that arises from the normal course of business; the two major short-term sources of such liabilities are accounts payable and accruals. (Chapter 15)

spot exchange rate   The rate of exchange between two currencies on any given day. (Chapter 18)

stakeholders   Groups such as employees, customers, suppliers, creditors, owners, and others who have a direct economic link to the firm. (Chapter 1)

standard debt provisions   Provisions in a *bond indenture* specifying certain record-keeping and general business practices that the bond issuer must follow; normally, they do not place a burden on a financially sound business. (Chapter 6)

standard deviation (σ_r)   The most common statistical indicator of an asset's risk; it measures the dispersion around the *expected value*. (Chapter 5)

statement of cash flows   Provides a summary of the firm's operating, investment, and financing cash flows and reconciles them with changes in its cash and marketable securities during the period. (Chapter 2)

statement of retained earnings   Reconciles the net income earned during a given year, and any cash dividends paid, with the change in retained earnings between the start and the end of that year. An abbreviated form of the *statement of stockholders' equity*. (Chapter 2)

statement of stockholders' equity   Shows all equity account transactions that occur during a given year. (Chapter 2)

stock dividend   The payment, to existing owners, of a dividend in the form of stock. (Chapter 13)

stock options   An incentive allowing managers to purchase stock at the market price set at the time of the grant. (Chapter 1)

stock purchase warrants   Instruments that give their holders the right to purchase a certain number of shares of the issuer's common stock at a specified price over a certain period of time. (Chapters 6 and 16)

stock repurchase   The repurchase by the firm of outstanding common stock in the marketplace; desired effects of stock repurchases are that they either enhance shareholder value or help to discourage an unfriendly takeover. (Chapter 13)

stock split   A method commonly used to lower the market price of a firm's stock by increasing the number of shares belonging to each shareholder. (Chapter 13)

stock swap transaction   An acquisition method in which the acquiring firm exchanges its shares for shares of the target company according to a predetermined ratio. (Chapter 17)

stockholders   The owners of a corporation, whose ownership, or *equity*, is evidenced by either common stock or preferred stock. (Chapter 1)

stockholders' report   Annual report that publicly owned corporations must provide to stockholders; it summarizes and documents the firm's financial activities during the past year. (Chapter 2)

straight bond   A bond that is nonconvertible, having no conversion feature. (Chapter 16)

straight bond value   The price at which a convertible bond would sell in the market without the conversion feature. (Chapter 16)

straight preferred stock   Preferred stock that is nonconvertible, having no conversion feature. (Chapter 16)

strategic merger   A merger transaction undertaken to achieve economies of scale. (Chapter 17)

stretching accounts payable   Paying bills as late as possible without damaging the firm's credit rating. (Chapter 15)

striking price   The price at which the holder of a call option can buy (or the holder of a put option can sell) a specified amount of stock at any time prior to the option's expiration date. (Chapter 16)

subordinated debentures   See Table 6.4. (Chapter 6)

subordination   In a bond indenture, the stipulation that subsequent creditors agree to wait until all claims of the *senior debt* are satisfied. (Chapter 6)

subsidiaries   The companies controlled by a holding company. (Chapter 17)

sunk costs   Cash outlays that have already been made (past outlays) and therefore have no effect on the cash flows relevant to a current decision. (Chapter 8)

supervoting shares   Stock that carries with it multiple votes per share rather than the single vote per share typically given on regular shares of common stock. (Chapter 7)

takeover defenses   Strategies for fighting hostile takeovers. (Chapter 17)

target capital structure   The desired optimal mix of debt and equity financing that most firms attempt to maintain. (Chapter 11)

target company   The firm in a merger transaction that the acquiring company is pursuing. (Chapter 17)

target dividend-payout ratio   A dividend policy under which the firm attempts to pay out a certain *percentage* of earnings as a stated dollar dividend and adjusts that dividend toward a target payout as proven earnings increases occur. (Chapter 13)

target weights   Either book or market value weights based on *desired* capital structure proportions. (Chapter 11)

tax loss carryforward   In a merger, the tax loss of one of the firms that can be applied against a limited amount of future income of the merged firm over 20 years or until the total tax loss has been fully recovered, whichever comes first. (Chapter 17)

tax on sale of old asset   Tax that depends on the relationship among the old asset's sale price, initial purchase price, and *book value*, and on existing government tax rules. (Chapter 8)

technical insolvency   Business failure that occurs when a firm is unable to pay its liabilities as they come due. (Chapter 17)

technically insolvent   Describes a firm that is unable to pay its bills as they come due. (Chapter 14)

tender offer   A formal offer to purchase a given number of shares of a firm's stock at a specified price. (Chapter 13)

temporal method   A method that requires specific assets and liabilities to be translated at so-called historical exchange rates, and that foreign-exchange translation gains or losses be reflected in current year's income. (Chapter 18)

term structure of interest rates   The relationship between the interest rate or rate of return and the time to maturity. (Chapter 6)

terminal cash flow   The after-tax nonoperating cash flow occurring in the final year of a project. It is usually attributable to liquidation of the project. (Chapter 8)

time line   A horizontal line on which time zero appears at the leftmost end and future periods are marked from left to right; can be used to depict investment cash flows. (Chapter 4)

times interest earned ratio   Measures the firm's ability to make contractual interest payments; sometimes called the *interest coverage ratio*. (Chapter 2)

time-series analysis   Evaluation of the firm's financial performance over time using financial ratio analysis. (Chapter 2)

total asset turnover   Indicates the efficiency with which the firm uses its assets to generate sales. (Chapter 2)

total cost of inventory   The sum of order costs and carrying costs of inventory. (Chapter 14)

total leverage   The potential use of *fixed costs, both operating and financial,* to magnify the effect of changes in sales on the firm's earnings per share. (Chapter 12)

total risk   The combination of a security's *nondiversifiable* and *diversifiable risk*. (Chapter 5)

transfer prices   Prices that subsidiaries charge each other for the goods and services traded between them. (Chapter 10)

treasurer   The firm's chief financial manager, who is responsible for the firm's financial activities, such as financial planning and fund raising, making capital expenditure decisions, and managing cash, credit, the pension fund, and foreign exchange. (Chapter 1)

treasury stock   The number of shares of outstanding stock that have been repurchased by the firm. (Chapter 7)

trust receipt inventory loan   A secured short-term loan against inventory under which the lender advances 80 to 100 percent of the cost of the borrower's relatively expensive inventory items in exchange for the borrower's promise to repay the lender, with accrued interest, immediately after the sale of each item of collateral. (Chapter 15)

trustee   A paid individual, corporation, or commercial bank trust department that acts as the third party to a bond indenture and can take specified actions on behalf of the bondholders if the terms of the indenture are violated. (Chapter 6)

two-bin method   Unsophisticated inventory-monitoring technique that is typically applied to C group items and involves reordering inventory when one of two bins is empty. (Chapter 14)

two-tier offer   A *tender offer* in which the terms offered are more attractive to those who tender shares early. (Chapter 17)

uncorrelated   Describes two series that lack any interaction and therefore have a correlation coefficient close to zero. (Chapter 5)

U.S. Treasury bills (T-bills)   Short-term IOUs issued by the U.S. Treasury; considered the *risk-free asset*. (Chapter 5)

underpriced   Stock sold at a price below its current market price, P_0. (Chapter 11)

underwriting   The role of the *investment banker* in bearing the risk of reselling, at a profit, the securities purchased from an issuing corporation at an agreed-on price. (Chapter 7)

underwriting syndicate   A group formed by an investment banker to share the financial risk associated with *underwriting* new securities. (Chapter 7)

unlimited funds   The financial situation in which a firm is able to accept all independent projects that provide an acceptable return. (Chapter 8)

unlimited liability   The condition of a sole proprietorship (or general partnership) allowing the owner's total wealth to be taken to satisfy creditors. (Chapter 1)

unsecured short-term financing   Short-term financing obtained without pledging specific assets as collateral. (Chapter 15)

unsecured, or general, creditors   Creditors who have a general claim against all the firm's assets other than those specifically pledged as collateral. (Chapter 17)

valuation   The process that links risk and return to determine the worth of an asset. (Chapter 6)

variable-growth model   A dividend valuation approach that allows for a change in the dividend growth rate. (Chapter 7)

venture capital   Privately raised external equity capital used to fund early-stage firms with attractive growth prospects. (Chapter 7)

venture capitalists (VCs)   Providers of venture capital; typically, formal businesses that maintain strong oversight over the firms they invest in and that have clearly defined exit strategies. (Chapter 7)

vertical merger   A merger in which a firm acquires *a supplier or a customer*. (Chapter 17)

voluntary reorganization   A petition filed by a failed firm on its own behalf for reorganizing its structure and paying its creditors. (Chapter 17)

voluntary settlement   An arrangement between a technically insolvent or bankrupt firm and its creditors enabling it to bypass many of the costs involved in legal bankruptcy proceedings. (Chapter 17)

warehouse receipt loan   A secured short-term loan against inventory under which the lender receives control of the pledged inventory collateral, which is stored by a designated warehousing company on the lender's behalf. (Chapter 15)

warrant premium   The difference between the market value and the theoretical value of a warrant. (Chapter 16)

weighted average cost of capital (WACC), r_a   Reflects the expected average future cost of funds over the long run; found by weighting the cost of each specific type of capital by its proportion in the firm's capital structure. (Chapter 11)

weighted marginal cost of capital (WMCC)   The firm's weighted average cost of capital (WACC) associated with its *next dollar* of total new financing. (Chapter 11)

weighted marginal cost of capital (WMCC) schedule   Graph that relates the firm's weighted average cost of capital to the level of total new financing. (Chapter 11)

white knight   A takeover defense in which the target firm finds an acquirer more to its liking than the initial hostile acquirer and prompts the two to compete to take over the firm. (Chapter 17)

wire transfer   An electronic communication that, via bookkeeping entries, removes funds from the payer's bank and deposits them in the payee's bank. (Chapter 14)

working capital   Current assets, which represent the portion of investment that circulates from one form to another in the ordinary conduct of business. (Chapter 14)

World Trade Organization (WTO)   International body that polices world trading practices and mediates disputes between member countries. (Chapter 18)

yield curve   A graph of the relationship between the debt's remaining time to maturity (*x* axis) and its yield to maturity (*y* axis); it shows the yield to maturity for debts of equal quality and different maturities. Graphically depicts the *term structure of interest rates*. (Chapter 6)

yield to maturity   Compound annual rate of return earned on a debt security purchased on a given day and held to maturity. (Chapter 6)

zero- (or low-) coupon bonds   See Table 6.5. (Chapter 6)

zero-balance account (ZBA)   A disbursement account that always has an end-of-day balance of zero because the firm deposits money to cover checks drawn on the account only as they are presented for payment each day. (Chapter 14)

zero-growth model   An approach to dividend valuation that assumes a constant, nongrowing dividend stream. (Chapter 7)

Index